The Palgrave Handbook of Organizational Change Thinkers

David B. Szabla • William A. Pasmore
Mary A. Barnes • Asha N. Gipson
Editors

The Palgrave Handbook of Organizational Change Thinkers

Volume 2

With 61 Figures and 14 Tables

Editors
David B. Szabla
College of Education and Human Development
Western Michigan University
Kalamazoo, MI, USA

William A. Pasmore
Teachers College
Columbia University
New York, NY, USA

Mary A. Barnes
The George Washington University
Washington, DC, USA

Asha N. Gipson
Teachers College
Columbia University
New York, NY, USA

ISBN 978-3-319-52877-9 ISBN 978-3-319-52878-6 (eBook)
ISBN 978-3-319-52879-3 (print and electronic bundle)
DOI 10.1007/978-3-319-52878-6

Library of Congress Control Number: 2017943059

Printed on acid-free paper

This Palgrave Macmillan imprint is published by Springer Nature
The registered company is Springer International Publishing AG
The registered company address is: Gewerbestrasse 11, 6330 Cham, Switzerland

Foreword to Organizational Change Thinkers Book

I really appreciate the opportunity to write a forword for this most interesting book because it allows me to reminisce a bit about the history of organization development (OD) and its focus on the management of change. I remember well in the mid-1960s my efforts with Warren Bennis and Richard Beckhard to capture the essence of OD, not by writing an integrated text but by accepting the fact that the best we could do is produce a paperback series which allowed various of us to express our own views of what OD was at this point in its youth. The Addison-Wesley Series eventually grew to over 30 volumes and reflected the many strands of thinking and practice that evolved. In many ways, this current volume is another iteration of this enormous diversity in presenting a field that we think has some common assumptions and values yet continues to evolve new directions. What better way to track this evolution than by many of us writing about many others of us.

By presenting the contributions of so many different OD practitioners and theorists, the editors have exposed us to a deeper cultural truth about our approach to knowledge and practice. The rampant individualism and pragmatism that has been the hallmark of US culture shows up very well in the variety of styles of thinking, practicing, and writing about these organizational issues and organizational change. In a way, I lament this diversity because it reflects another issue that derives from individualism, namely, that we are not very concerned about interconnecting or coordinating our various theories and practices.

Rather, even as academics, we seem to play out the marketing dream of putting our ideas out there and seeing who will buy. We have very little taste for acknowledging and critiquing each other, we have very little impulse to construct the grand theory that pulls it all together, and we have no great desire to acknowledge all versions of our own model that may have already been presented in other writings. We built our own edifice with our small team of collaborators and put our energy into improving it rather than seeing how it might connect to others. We let the market decide and compete as best as we can, but have little energy for integrating the many theories and practices that are out there. This willingness to tolerate diversity of thought, even encourage it, is well reflected in reviews of research. It will be an interesting challenge to the readers of this handbook to find the common elements, the integrative strands that have emerged from over 75 years of work in this arena.

There may be another cultural reason for this diversity. I have recently "discovered" that the English language is much more context dependent than most of us have realized or acknowledged. Words like *organization*, *management*, *leadership*, *trust*, *openness*, *relationship*, and *change* are incredibly ambiguous until they are put into concrete examples that give us the context of whether we are talking about a particular organization in a particular industry in a particular culture, at a particular stage in its growth, and so on. This linguistic ambiguity makes it very difficult to compare models, theories, and practices primarily because the authors usually do not provide enough examples to pin down what exactly is the essence of what they are talking about.

When we do talk about each other's theories or practices, it has been my experiences that my concepts such as *process consultation*, *career anchors*, *culture*, and *change* are often not understood by both critics and supporters. I don't fault them for this, nor do I fault myself for being a poor communicator. Instead, I attribute this to the inherent ambiguity in the English language. It may be inherently impossible to construct a tight theory in a high context language, which is, of course, the reason why we invent new terms such as Theory X and Theory Y or create mathematical models.

Having said that, the model that is presented in this book is particularly interesting wherein our ideas are presented by our colleagues rather than by ourselves. That mode of presentation will provide interesting experiences for each of us who are represented in this book and will provide a level of feedback we are ordinarily not privy to. The readers will get the unusual opportunity to compare how they read a particular author and how the biographer writing in this book represents that same author.

The editors are to be commended for having found a way to go beyond presenting several of us in our traditional writing or speaking mode, and to give us a new voice through the many authors writing these chapters. That will provide readers an opportunity to see how their interpretation of what each of us said matches the written presentations in this book, and for those of us who are still present, yet another opportunity to see how our own perception of what we said matches with what our biographers have said.

I look forward to an exciting read and congratulate the editors for providing us with a whole new approach to understanding the many points of view toward organization development and the management of change. The reader will get a great view of the history of this field through reading about almost three generations of thinkers and practitioners in this field.

Edgar H. Schein

Preface

Introduction to the Handbook

We, the editors, have had the great pleasure of assembling this volume. It has turned out to be more of a "labor of love" than we expected; both more labor and more love. We have been inspired by the stories of the great thinkers profiled here. We have loved learning more about them than we ever knew, even in the case of some close colleagues. And, we have thoroughly enjoyed making new friends and reconnecting with friends whom we haven't been in touch with for far too long. The "more labor" part was also the painstaking care that the contributing authors took in researching the great thinkers they profiled. It is to these authors and to all the great thinkers who created the field of Organization Development that we owe the existence of this handbook.

For readers who might not be familiar with Organization Development, it is a field pioneered by the social scientists whose stories you can read in this handbook. These individuals were concerned about social justice, organizational effectiveness, improving teamwork, understanding the role of the change agent and the effects of different styles of leadership, and much more. The focus of the field is on change, and especially change that takes place in organizations. Even more to the point, the kind of change that has been at the heart of Organization Development is change that helps organizations fulfill their purpose while at the same time offering opportunities for greater dignity and meaning to the people who live within them or are touched by their existence.

Although the roots of the field took hold even earlier, the real blossoming of thought began following the Second World War. The war was an abomination to everything that was good or worthwhile about society and human kind. It raised questions for many about what was going wrong in the world and what could be done to prevent something like it from happening again.

Early studies by Kurt Lewin, who fled to the United States from Nazi Germany, investigated how attitudes were shaped by group opinion and the effects of democratic versus autocratic leadership. Coch and French explored the power of participation in decision-making related to overcoming resistance to change. Eric Trist and his colleagues at the Tavistock Institute for Human Relations in London worked with the British Coal Board to find ways to make coal production more efficient after the war and in so doing discovered that workers held valuable insights regarding the work they did that engineers and managers had overlooked. Bion, also at Tavistock, had experimented with group therapy among traumatized soldiers during the war and from those experiences and others began to help us see previously invisible dynamics that affected the work of groups and teams. Lewin and Reginal Revans independently piloted what became known as "action research." This was work intended to bring about change that took place in a real setting as opposed to a laboratory to study what happened as a result of trying out a variety of different approaches. What made action research unique was the collaboration of the "subject" or client in conducting and interpreting the work. It was discovered, as was the case in British coal mines, that the people on the front lines of change have valuable perspectives that even scientists studying an organization would have missed. The resulting tradition of involving those affected by change in planning and executing it has remained a hallmark of OD ever since and continues to differentiate it from "expert change" in which consultants decide for others what is best for them, or "top-down" change in which leaders attempt to use their position power to force others to comply with their directives.

Kurt Lewin's concerns about racial justice also led to the "T-group" or sensitivity training phenomena, later formalized under the egis of the National Training Labs, or NTL as it became known. On the other side of the Atlantic, Bion and his colleagues invented the Group Relations Conference, which helped participants examine their relationship with authority and their interpersonal relations. Together, these powerful movements in human relations led to an age of "personal enlightenment" which became central to the field for a time. Ever since, there has been a debate about whether Organization Development belongs in a serious business environment, since some leaders seem to be of the belief that one should leave his or her emotions and identity at the door before starting work every morning.

It wasn't until the next generation of scholars that the name of the field "Organization Development" was coined, simultaneously by Dick Beckhard and Robert Blake and Jane Mouton in the 1960s. The 1960s also saw the establishment of the first doctoral programs in Organization Development, which was followed by a proliferation of institutions that offered masters degrees to people working full time.

The 1970s and early 1980s saw recessions that added to the excuse for cutting out anything "touchy-feely" and instead focus on downsizing, cost-cutting, total quality, reengineering, and Lean Six-Sigma – anything that focused squarely on the bottom line and was driven by objective data rather than feelings. None of these "advancements" fit the values and methods of organization development and for a time, there were real questions about the field's survival. However, advances in scholarship continued and the need to pay attention to people in organizations didn't simply disappear. In the 1980s and 1990s, in areas like employee engagement and innovation, there were clear needs to call on people to do things that they would only do if committed to the success of their organization. Gaining that commitment required more than a single-minded focus on the bottom line. What's more, work on high performance systems and organizational culture brought about significant gains in organizational performance that were hard to ignore. Accountants could cite the costs of change but investors appreciated the returns.

The 1980s and 1990s also brought exciting new change innovations to the forefront, based on glimmers of earlier thinking. Appreciative inquiry, large group interventions, and future search conferences gave Organization Development a new lease on life and thrust it squarely into the realm of dealing with societal as well as organizational issues. This "second age of enlightenment" has us all believing that anything was possible and that our dream of making the world a better place was finally coming true. Then, another recession and a new villain on the scene interrupted our progress once again. By the early 2000s, investment bankers and deal makers who cared only about short-term shareholder profit started breaking up organizations and selling the pieces to the highest bidder through mergers or acquisitions. Leaders who cared about their people, took a longer-term view, or sought a more socially responsible role for their organizations were swept aside by operators who had no choice but to focus on cutting costs at all costs. The 2007–2008 recession led to another round of budget slashing in many organizations, turning back the clock. Once again the field appeared to be in peril, and yet competition and change remained constants that simply couldn't be eliminated by pretending they weren't happening. By the 2010s, new forms of organizing were investigated – forms that would allow organizations to be efficient and innovative at the same time, local and global, and socially responsible while caring about the bottom line. Technology continued to present new challenges as well, and those who didn't understand its potential for disruption at first were run over by those who did.

The thinkers profiled here didn't just stand by and watch this happen. They took challenges as opportunities to rethink and reposition the field. They offered new methodologies for change, more connected to the strategic directions organizations are trying to move. They didn't forget human beings, but leveraged the growing interest in all things talent related to make change both a responsibility for able leaders and a development opportunity for others. They learned about the future and found ways to help clients see it and want to make it happen. They embraced diversity and globalism, knowing that these forces could be temporarily blunted but never overcome. Although many of the early thinkers are no longer with us, their ideas and ideals continue to live on in the youngest generation of our scholars.

So, for those who are not yet familiar with the field of Organization Development, this handbook will tell the story of its evolution, from its earliest beginnings to the current day. In the profiles here you will read about important ideas, theories, and practices that gained widespread attention as they shaped not just the field itself but our societies and even the world.

Those who are very familiar with the field will find herein much of value and we hope delight. Our experience as editors was that we individually were more familiar with the works of some of the great thinkers than others. To read the profiles of these assembled thinkers and their work was to take a high-speed tour of our shared history, filling in spots in the landscape that we had previously zoomed past, not noticing or interpreting clearly. Beyond that, the people we did know as scholars we got to know as people, through the eyes of their biographers who were often students or close friends. In this fuller and inclusive picture, we could more easily grasp where the great ideas in our field came from, which caused us to reflect on our own motivations for doing the work we do. This handbook is like a personal journal; it's as if the intellectual giants kept private diaries that they decided to throw into one collective pot with the hope that others would read them and perhaps be inspired to add their own.

We wanted to know more about the influences in these thinker's lives, both educational and collegial. We asked for insights about their mentors or heroes, and what problems they wanted to solve. We sought insights into how the times in which they lived might have directed their thinking and extrapolated this to present times and even into the future. We wanted to know why they did the research they did and how they did it. We were curious about where they applied their ideas and with what effect. We wondered about collaboration with other colleagues and especially about how ideas took hold and led to branches of the field being defined by their committed followers.

As we read on, we saw the evolution of ideas as the progression of science added finer filigree to earlier rough sketches. We also saw continued breakthroughs, intellectual leaps that could not be predicted simply by drawing a straight line between the past and present. Stepping back even further, we saw parts of the canvas that were still blank, waiting to be filled in. Other parts of the canvas were painted over many times, without a satisfactory result (One more time, how can we get those in power to share it willingly and for the benefit of all? Why, with all we know, are we still not more successful in bringing about change? How is it that with all of our research, we still allow inept leaders to rise to power and then follow them to our own destruction?). The field of Organization Development is alive, despite several inquiries into its health by undertakers arriving a little too early on the scene. Gratefully, the handbook will be continuously updated thanks to the miracle of online publishing. If new thinkers emerge or there are new ideas to report, they will be added in the years to come.

With the amazing help of our colleagues who rose to the challenge, this handbook has delivered on our intentions.

1. The handbook presents inspiring and thought provoking profiles of prominent organizational change thinkers, highlighting significant advancements in how organizational change has been conceived, theorized, researched, and practiced.
2. Each profile chapter captures the professional background of a legendary thinker and presents his or her key insights, new thinking, and major legacies to the field of organizational change.
3. The handbook includes, in one manuscript, the concepts, theories, and models of the sages who invented, built, and advanced the research and practice of change in organizations.
4. The structure of this handbook creates "relationships" with the highlighted scholars that are not obtained by simply reading a collection of their work.
5. The theories presented in the handbook are brought to life within the context of the scholar's experiences, which in turn inspires progressive thoughts for the readers of this handbook, furthering organizational change research and practice of today.

While you may choose to read only a few of the profiles, we suspect that you will be drawn in to read additional profiles as were we. The field of Organization Development has always been concerned about people and driven by a sense of what is right and just. Gaining insight into the ways in which the values and purposes of these incredible thinkers shaped their work makes for interesting drama. One might expect a handbook about scholars to be a little on the dry side, hardly something to be read like a novel on a plane or when without a date on a Friday evening. That might be true in a field like Mathematics, but after this experience, we choose to withhold our judgment. There are real people behind the great ideas in our field, and their stories are both compelling and endearing.

A Guide to the Structure of the Chapters

It won't take you long to notice that the vast majority of the profiles follow a similar structure. The first section briefly describes the influences that motivated the thinker to investigate change in organizations, for example, the theorist's scholarly mentors. The focus is on the professional, intellectual, educational, social, and real-world influences that stimulated the theorist's curiosities about change in organizations and acts as an introduction to the theorist's story.

The second section focuses on the thinker's key contributions. Four or five advancements that were central to the work of the thinker are reviewed in this section. These are theoretical, methodological, and practical contributions. This is not an exhaustive coverage, but a presentation and discussion of their most significant contributions to organizational change. Those innovations or ideas that have endured over time are emphasized.

The third section of each profile addresses new insights that the work of the thinker inspired in others. This section will underscore how the work of these scholars has spurred new developments in theory and research that have led us to view change in organizations in new and surprising ways.

The fourth section focuses on legacies and unfinished business. What are the major intellectual legacies of this thinker? Which later thinkers has he or she influenced? Which parts of the thinker's legacy are still being investigated or have yet to be fully investigated? Are there themes that have been criticized by later thinkers that have shed light on the problem that motivated the original thinker? What later thinkers have explored the issues of this thinker and carried them further?

Finally, the profile concludes with suggested further readings. This final section includes a short list of books and journal articles that enable readers to take their interests further.

How to Use This Book

Actually, we can't wait to see how people use this book. As designed, the expectation is that most people will access the book online, a profile at a time. While print copies of the book will be available on demand, the projected cost would make buying a hard-bound volume prohibitive for all but libraries and a few especially dedicated individuals. Therefore, it's probably not a candidate as a text for graduate study as an entire volume, but to assign chapters to students to read and discuss is entirely doable. We can't imagine a better use for this handbook than to introduce the next generation of scholars to the people and history that preceded them. We won't tell you how to teach the book; you'll have your own ideas about that. We can envision lots of opportunities ranging from individual research efforts to group projects, covering eras or themes or looking for overarching messages much as we found ourselves doing. When you come up with a great idea that works, please let us know.

For those beyond their educational years, reading selected chapters about friends or mentors can be enlightening. Perhaps, it will encourage you to drop a note to someone you haven't spoken to for a while, saying you read about them and were surprised at something you learned. They probably won't mind and you may gain a renewed friendship in return.

On a more serious note, if you're undertaking research and looking for some original references or trying to come up with an original idea of your own, the handbook could be a good place to start. Most of the profiles are well-referenced and the suggestions for further reading are worth pursuing. The stories of these great thinkers are inspiring and remind us that despite their stature, they were after all just people like us.

Going Forward

This journey hasn't ended; it's just beginning. That applies to the field of Organization Development and to this handbook as well. You may know of someone not included here who should be. There are several chapters in progress that didn't make it in time for the first print edition. Profiles on people like Rensis Likert, Noel Tichy, and Amy Edmonson haven't been overlooked; they are just taking longer to get done. Still, it's entirely possible that we have missed someone you think needs to be written about; please let us know, and let us know who should write about them – maybe it's you.

Over time, we'll be excited to be introduced to the new great thinkers in Organization Development. They are probably already making presentations at the Academy of Management or other conferences around the world. Let us know if you spot one before we do. We haven't established firm criteria by which we include or exclude people; we tried but found the task impossible. There were some social scientists who write about organizations with a concern about change but not from an Organization Development perspective. There are organizational theorists who help us understand how organizations work, which is something we need to understand, but don't write about change. It's hard to draw hard lines between the ins and the outs.

One criticism we are well aware of is that the volume, in the current version, includes more men than women, more whites than minorities, and more Americans than people from the rest of the world. More women are now attending graduate programs in the field than men; we hope that as a result, the gender picture will become more balanced over time. If you know someone who should be profiled who will help accelerate the shift, let us know. To a lesser extent, the same thing is happening in terms of minorities and people outside the USA. The numbers of nontraditional great thinkers are growing and your editors are on the lookout for them. All that said, we don't think that the online volume should become more like Facebook, where anyone can join. If there is no distinction between great thinkers and noncontributors, the handbook wouldn't serve a purpose.

We trust that you will enjoy reading some of the profiles as much as we have. We also hope that your reading inspires you to make your own contribution to the future of the field. There's room for you to be included in the next volume or to have your existing profile updated. More importantly, with all the great thinking represented here, we haven't seemed to solve all the world's problems. We need to keep up the effort.

Kalamazoo, MI, USA — David B. Szabla
New York, NY, USA — William A. Pasmore
Washington, DC, USA — Mary A. Barnes
New York, NY, USA — Asha N. Gipson

Acknowledgments

After an intensive period of selecting the many great thinkers of organizational change, contracting with contributing authors to craft their profiles, and working with Michael Hermann and Audrey Wong-Hillmann, our tireless editors at Palgrave Macmillan, this acknowledgment puts the finishing touch on our *Handbook of Organizational Change Thinkers*. The experience of creating this handbook, for each of us, was absorbing, enlightening, and truly enjoyable. There are several people to thank.

First, we would like to thank the many contributing authors who took the time out of their busy schedules to write the profile chapters. The handbook represents a diverse group of authors from many parts of the world: United States, Canada, Europe, South America, Asia, and Australia, many of whom are great organizational change thinkers, scholars, and practitioners themselves. Their efforts to conduct research, organize content, and determine and present the backgrounds, contributions, insights, and legacies of their thinkers are much appreciated.

Second, it's important to acknowledge a person who was instrumental in the conceptualization of this handbook. David Schwandt, thank you for the many hours we spent together in the classrooms and hallways of the George Washington University exploring the concept and content of this handbook. Your knowledge of the field of organizational change appears in many indirect ways throughout this handbook. One memorable image is three classroom whiteboard walls filled with timelines, listings of great thinkers, key change movements, and various ways to organize the book, some chronological and others conceptual.

As we developed the handbook, we realized that organizing the thinkers into our original format of early, contemporary, and emerging proved problematic as it was difficult to place many of the thinkers into a specific period. With advice from our editors at Palgrave Macmillan, we decided that an alphabetical organization of the thinkers seemed the best fit for a handbook of this magnitude. We envision many subsequent publications that explore the patterns of thought across the profiles.

Finally, for those great thinkers of organizational change who are still with us, thank you for agreeing to be profiled in this handbook. Many of you spent several hours interacting with our contributing authors to provide them with what they needed to craft your profile. We express our sincere gratitude.

March, 2017

David B. Szabla
William A. Pasmore
Mary A. Barnes
Asha N. Gipson

Contents

Volume 1

Volume 2

About the Editors

David B. Szabla College of Education and Human Development, Western Michigan University, Kalamazoo, MI, USA

David B. Szabla leads the M.A. in Organizational Change Leadership in the Department of Educational Leadership, Research, and Technology at Western Michigan University where he teaches courses in group dynamics, large-scale change, and organization design. His research and writing center on resistance to change and the relationships among the content, process, and context of organizational change. David is recognized by executive business leaders for strong diagnostic, intervention design and evaluation skills, as well as keen communication, creative problem-solving, and program management capabilities. He has been published in *Research in Organizational Change and Development*, *Human Resource Development Quarterly*, *Emergence: Complexity and Organization*, and *The International Journal of Knowledge, Culture, and Change Management*. He is a member of the Management Consulting and Organization Development and Change Divisions of the Academy of Management, the Society for Industrial and Organizational Psychology, and the International Leadership Association.

William A. Pasmore Teachers College, Columbia University, New York, NY, USA

William A. Pasmore, Ph.D., is a Professor of Practice at Teachers College, Columbia University, and Senior Vice President at the Center for Creative Leadership. As a thought leader in the field of organization development, he has published 28 books including *Leading Continuous Change*, *Designing Effective Organizations*, *Creating Strategic Change*, *Relationships That Enable Enterprise Change*, and *Sociotechnical Systems: A Sourcebook*. He served as editor of the *Journal of Applied Behavioral Science* and, along with Richard Woodman, was the founding coeditor of the annual series *Research in Organizational Change and Development*.

Mary A. Barnes George Washington University, Washington, DC, USA

Mary A. Barnes is a scholar-practitioner who leads the Workforce Transformation Division for a medium-sized Federal agency. She has over 20 years of experience managing people, programs, projects, operations, and more. Her interest and expertise are in developing organizational and talent-related solutions, including facilitating business model and organizational restructuring, planning and implementing change, business process redesign, and developing new programs and learning initiatives. She is a trusted advisor to executive leadership, helping them identify and remove barriers that get in the way of optimal levels of organizational performance and individual engagement. She has been a speaker on various organizational topics at conferences for the Academy of Human Resource Development, Academy of Management, and the Society for Human Resource Management. Her educational background includes an MBA, an M.S. in Financial Management, and a graduate certificate in Project Management. She is currently a doctoral candidate at George Washington University, studying Human and Organizational Learning, with a research focus on Change Management.

Asha N. Gipson Teachers College, Columbia University, New York, NY, USA

Asha N. Gipson is a doctoral student studying Social-Organizational Psychology at Teachers College, Columbia University. Her research explores intersectionality, leadership development, and group/team dynamics and effectiveness. In addition to her studies, she also teaches courses in leadership and group dynamics and industrial-organizational psychology. She currently serves on the executive committee of the New York Center, an affiliate of the A.K. Rice Institute and is a member of the OD Network of New York. Asha received her Bachelor of Arts in Psychology from Pomona College and a Master of Arts in Organizational Psychology from Teachers College, Columbia University.

Contributors

Paul S. Adler University of Southern California, Los Angeles, CA, USA

Franck Aggeri MINES ParisTech, PSL Research University, CGS -Centre de gestion scientifique, i3 UMR CNRS 9217, Paris, France

Beth Applegate Applegate Consulting Group, Bloomington, IN, USA

John R. Austin Three Translation Leadership, State College, PA, USA

Dick Axelrod The Axelrod Group, Inc., Wilmette, IL, USA

Elise Barho Huron Consulting, Chicago, IL, USA

Mary A. Barnes George Washington University, Washington, DC, USA

Frank J. Barrett Graduate School of Business and Public Policy, Naval Postgraduate School, Monterey, CA, USA

Michael Beyerlein Educational Administration and Human Resource Development Program, Texas A&M University, College Station, TX, USA

Monica E. Biggs The Kaleel Jamison Consulting Group Inc., Troy, NY, USA

Matthew Bird Graduate School of Business, Universidad del Pacífico, Lima, Lima, Peru

Albert B. Blixt New Campus Dynamics – Consulting Firm, Ann Arbor, MI, USA

Dannemiller Tyson Associate, Ann Arbor, MI, USA

Lee Bolman Bloch School of Management, University of Missouri-Kansas City, Kansas City, MO, USA

Sarah J. Brazaitis Department of Organization and Leadership, Teachers College, Columbia University, New York, NY, USA

David S. Bright Department of Management and International Business, Wright State University, Dayton, OH, USA

Bart Brock Concordia University, Mequon, WI, USA

Barbara Benedict Bunker Department of Psychology, The University at Buffalo, Buffalo, NY, USA

Anthony F. Buono Department of Management, Bentley University, Waltham, MA, USA

W. Warner Burke Teachers College, Columbia University, New York, NY, USA

Bernard Burnes Stirling Management School, University of Stirling, Stirling, Scotland, UK

Brett Clay Fielding Graduate University, Santa Barbara, CA, USA

Change Leadership Group, LLC, Bellevue, WA, USA

David Coghlan Trinity Business School, Trinity College Dublin, Dublin, Ireland

Bill Cooke University of York, York, UK

Hervé Corvellec Department of Service Studies, Lund University, Helsingborg, Sweden

Gothenburg Research Institute (GRI), University of Gothenburg, Gothenburg, Sweden

Thomas G. Cummings USC Marshall School of Business, University of Southern California, Los Angeles, CA, USA

Sébastien Damart CNRS, UMR 7088, DRM, M-LAB, Université Paris-Dauphine, PSL Research University, Paris, France

Albert David M-Lab, Dauphine Université, PSL Research University, Paris, France

Khalil M. Dirani Educational Administration and Human Resource Development Program, Texas A&M University, College Station, TX, USA

Mary L. Eggers Dannemiller Tyson Associates, Springfield, VA, USA

Richard Ennals Department of Working Life and Innovation, University of Agder, Grimstad, Norway

Department of Skill and Technology, Linnaeus University, Växjö, Sweden

Kingston Business School, Kingston University, London, UK

Glenda H. Eoyang Human Systems Dynamics Institute, Circle Pines, MN, USA

Ulla Eriksson-Zetterquist Gothenburg Research Institute (GRI), University of Gothenburg, Gothenburg, Sweden

Weatherhead Center for International Affairs, Harvard University, Cambridge, MA, USA

Francesca Falcone Department of Political and Social Sciences, University of Calabria, Arcavacata di Rende, Italy

Elizabeth Florent-Treacy INSEAD, Paris, France

Tobias Fredberg Chalmers University of Technology, Gothenburg, Sweden

Ronald Fry Case Western Reserve University, Cleveland, OH, USA

Sasha Galbraith Galbraith Management Consultants, Breckenridge, CO, USA

Brett A. Geier Western Michigan University, Kalamazoo, MI, USA

Martin D. Goldberg Distant Drummer LLC, Easton, MD, USA

Pepperdine University, Malibu, CA, USA

Kathryn Goldman Schuyler California School of Professional Psychology, Alliant International University and Coherent Change, San Francisco, CA, USA

Frank D. Golom Department of Psychology, Loyola University Maryland, Baltimore, MD, USA

Margaret Gorman Graduate School of Education, College of Professional Studies, Northeastern University, Boston, MA, USA

Demetris Hadjimichael Warwick Business School, University of Warwick, Coventry, UK

Aamir Hasan Western Michigan University, Kalamazoo, MI, USA

George W. Hay Business Psychology Department, The Chicago School of Professional Psychology, Chicago, IL, USA

Tonya L. Henderson Tonya Lynn Henderson, Limited, Colorado Springs, CO, USA

Søren Henning Jensen Department of Management, Politics and Philosophy, Copenhagen Business School, Copenhagen, Denmark

François Héon François Héon Consulting, Montréal, QC, Canada

Robert Hooijberg IMD Business School, Lausanne, Switzerland

Mark Hughes Brighton Business School/CROME, University of Brighton, Brighton, East Sussex, UK

Geralyn Hynes School of Nursing and Midwifery, Trinity College Dublin, Dublin, Ireland

Sylvia L. James Dannemiller Tyson Associate, Ann Arbor, MI, USA

David W. Jamieson Organization Development and Change, University of St Thomas, Minneapolis, MN, USA

Judith H. Katz The Kaleel Jamison Consulting Group Inc., Troy, New York, USA

Tom Kenward The Roffey Park Institute, Horsham, West Sussex, UK

Konstantin Korotov Center for Leadership Development Research, ESMT-Berlin, Berlin, Germany

Lindsey Kotrba Denison Consulting, LLC, Ann Arbor, MI, USA

Marc Lavine Department of Management, University of Massachusetts, Boston, MA, USA

Pascal Le Masson MINES ParisTech, PSL Research University, CGS -Centre de gestion scientifique, i3 UMR CNRS 9217, Paris, France

Paul M. Leonardi Technology Management Program, University of California, Santa Barbara, CA, USA

Michael Lewis Assumption College, Worcester, MA, USA

Roland J. Loup Dannemiller Tyson Associates, New Albany, OH, USA

Jeanne D. Maes Mitchell College of Business, University of South Alabama, Mobile, AL, USA

Gary Mangiofico Organization Theory and Management/Organization Development, Pepperdine University's Graziadio School of Business and Management, Los Angeles, CA, USA

Michael R. Manning Center for Values-Driven Leadership, Goodwin College of Business, Benedictine University, Chicago, IL, USA

Jackie M. Milbrandt Organization Development and Change, University of St Thomas, Minneapolis, MN, USA

Frederick A. Miller The Kaleel Jamison Consulting Group Inc., Troy, New York, USA

Susan Albers Mohrman Center for Effective Organizations, Marshall School of Business, University of Southern California, Los Angeles, CA, USA

Chris Mowles Hertfordshire Business School, Hatfield, UK

Rachael L. Narel Benedictine University, Chicago, IL, USA

Lisa A. T. Nelson Department of Management, Saint Joseph's University, Philadelphia, PA, USA

Jean E. Neumann The Tavistock Institute of Human Relations, London, UK

Levi R. G. Nieminen Denison Consulting, LLC, Ann Arbor, MI, USA

Walter Nord University of South Florida, Tampa, FL, USA

Debra A. Noumair Department of Organization and Leadership, Teachers College, Columbia University, New York, NY, USA

Bert Painter Consulting Social Scientist and Filmmaker, Bowen Island, BC, Canada

Angeliki Papachroni Warwick Business School, University of Warwick, Coventry, UK

William Pasmore Teachers College, Columbia University, New York, NY, USA

Mike Pedler Henley Business School, University of Reading and Centre for Action Learning Facilitation (CALF), Reading, UK

Anthony Petrella Arnold, MD, USA

Flemming Poulfelt Copenhagen Business School, Copenhagen, Denmark

Johanna Pregmark Chalmers University of Technology, Gothenburg, Sweden

Joanne C. Preston Joanne C. Preston and Associates, Colorado Springs, CO, USA

Magnus Ramage School of Computing and Communications, The Open University, Milton Keynes, UK

Caroline Rook Henley Business School, University of Reading, Reading, UK

Sonja Sackmann Department of Economics, Management and Organization Sciences, EZO Institute for Developing Viable Organizations, University Bundeswehr Munich, Neubiberg, Germany

Antonio Sama Canterbury Christ Church University, Canterbury, UK

Eric J. Sanders College of Business and Management, Cardinal Stritch University, Milwaukee, WI, USA

Dave Schwandt George Washington University, Washington, DC, USA

Blanche Segrestin MINES ParisTech, PSL Research University, CGS -Centre de gestion scientifique, i3 UMR CNRS 9217, Paris, France

Dennis R. Self Sorrell College of Business, Troy University, Troy, AL, USA

Department of Human Resource Management and Law, Sorrell College of Business at Troy University, Montgomery, AL, USA

Abraham B. (Rami) Shani Drop Faculty and Research, California Polytechnic State University, San Luis Obispo, CA, USA

Harry Sminia Department of Strategy and Organization, University of Strathclyde Business School, Glasgow, Scotland, UK

Peter F. Sorensen Organization Development Department, Benedictine University, Lisle, IL, USA

Gretchen M. Spreitzer Ross School of Business, Center for Positive Organizations, University of Michigan, Ann Arbor, MI, USA

Param Srikantia School of Business, Baldwin Wallace University, Berea, OH, USA

Doug Stace AGSM, University of New South Wales Business School, Sydney, NSW, Australia

Cass Business School, City University, London, UK

Richard W. Stackman University of San Francisco, San Francisco, CA, USA

Michael W. Stebbins Orfalea College of Business, California Polytechnic State University, San Luis Obispo, CA, USA

Christopher Sykes School of Management, Operations and Marketing, Faculty of Business, University of Wollongong, Sydney, Australia

David B. Szabla College of Education and Human Development, Western Michigan University, Kalamazoo, MI, USA

Steven S. Taylor Foisie School of Business, Worcester Polytechnic Institute, Worcester, MA, USA

Ramkrishnan V. Tenkasi The Benedictine University, Chicago, IL, USA

Tojo Thatchenkery George Mason University, Arlington, VA, USA

Linda Thorne Arnold, MD, USA

Tomas G. Thundiyil Management, Central Michigan University, Michigan, MI, USA

Paul D. Tolchinsky Performance Development Associates, Scottsdale, AZ, USA

Michael L. Tushman Harvard Business School, Boston, MA, USA

Timo O. Vuori Department of Industrial Engineering and Management, Department of Management Studies, Aalto University, Helsinki, Finland

Ruth Scogna Wagner School of Public Affairs, American University, Washington, DC, USA

Marlene Walk School of Public and Environmental Affairs, Indiana University-Purdue University Indianapolis, Indianapolis, IN, USA

Kenneth L. Wall Epic Investments, Inc., Colorado Springs, CO, USA

Patricia A. Wilson Graduate Program in Community and Regional Planning, University of Texas, Austin, TX, USA

Stu Winby SPRING Network LLC, Palo Alto, CA, USA

Christopher G. Worley Strategy and Entrepreneurship, NEOMA Business School, Reims, France

Lei Xie Educational Administration and Human Resource Development Program, Texas A&M University, College Station, TX, USA

Therese F. Yaeger Organization Development Department, Benedictine University, Lisle, IL, USA

44 Edward Emmet Lawler, III: Scholar, Change Agent, Sports Fanatic, and a Hell of a Nice Guy

Susan Albers Mohrman

Abstract

Edward Emmett Lawler, III, has been a central figure in the development of the fields of organizational behavior, management, and organization development. His early work generated and tested theoretical frameworks about motivation and performance, and he was a leader in investigating how organizational practices impact employee and organizational outcomes, including work design, compensation, performance management, and participation and involvement. The Quality of Worklife studies at the University of Michigan that he co-led with Stan Seashore provided a model and developed a methodology for studying and understanding organizations as dynamic systems and for creating knowledge about organizations by intentionally changing them. From this work, he developed his highly influential high-involvement management framework.

During a career that has spanned 50 years, he has influenced both the theory and practice of organizing for effectiveness during a period when organizations have had to change fundamentally to adapt to the emerging dynamic, digitalized, global economy. Lawler has been a scholar of how organizations are changing to be effective in their changing contexts more than he has been a scholar of change processes. His emphasis on doing useful research led to partnerships with companies to address and learn from the challenges they face and to ensuring that the knowledge created is accessible to both academia and practice. His work has helped shape the development and increasing strategic orientation of the human resource function. He founded and for almost 40 years has led the Center for Effective Organizations (CEO), a research center at the Marshall School of Business at the University of Southern California, which he designed to carry out useful research. He and his colleagues at CEO have contributed to the

S.A. Mohrman (✉)
Center for Effective Organizations, Marshall School of Business, University of Southern California, Los Angeles, CA, USA
e-mail: smohrman@marshall.usc.edu

D.B. Szabla et al. (eds.), *The Palgrave Handbook of Organizational Change Thinkers*, DOI 10.1007/978-3-319-52878-6_11

development of methodologies for doing useful research and to the debates in the Academy about the legitimacy of such approaches.

This chapter describes Lawler's evolution as a scholar, the many contributions that he has made to the understanding of how organizations can change to be more effective, and the immense impact he has had on practice and academia.

Keywords
Organizational effectiveness • High involvement management • Useful research • Strategic human resources

Contents

Introduction

Ed Lawler's career has spanned five decades during which modern organization and management sciences have coevolved with the growth and development of the complex global economy, digitalization, and the transition to the postindustrial knowledge economy. He has had enormous influence on organizational people management practices. His early work helped shape the new field of organizational behavior and contributed foundational perspectives in the fields of organizational and industrial (I-O) psychology and organization development. He has had many substantive influences on our understanding and practice of organizational change but first and foremost has been that he has provided a framework of knowledge and has been a role model for how academic research can be relevant in changing times.

Lawler has been less concerned with generating knowledge to help organizations with the process of change than with generating knowledge about the kinds of changes they could make in order to be effective. He has challenged conventional wisdom and served as his own counsel in defining a career and building methodologies and institutional settings for investigating the issues of organizational effectiveness that he believed to be important.

Ed would rather talk about sports than about his career successes and contributions. He attributes his professional accomplishments to the good fortune of having been in institutions where he has had "great people to work with" – something he attributes to "pure luck" (There may have been less luck involved in seeking out universities with great football teams). There is a long list of people, myself included, who feel fortunate to know Ed and to have collaborated with him. And many of us have even have had the chance to go to a football game with him. There the camaraderie was all about what was happening on the field, and the Scholastic All-Ivy Football Team member from Brown University was just as keenly focused, perceptive, and analytic about the behavior on the field (the action) as he is about organizational effectiveness when at work.

A very common way that his colleagues and friends refer to him is as a "hell of a nice guy." One can't capture the essence of Ed Lawler if one doesn't know that about him. This "hell of a nice guy" has put together a stellar career with a mind-boggling list of accomplishments, as will be evidenced below in my attempt to do justice to Edward Emmett Lawler, III, the scholar change agent.

Influences and Motivations: Institutions and Colleagues

Ed Lawler's influence on the field of organizational change has been deep and pervasive but first and foremost has been his ability to understand and be a role model for how academic research can be relevant in changing times. He has anticipated and rapidly sensed societal and market changes and has focused on generating and disseminating knowledge and practices to help organizations be effective in their changing contexts. He understands that practice evolves faster than academic research. In order for organizational research to be relevant, he has advocated that researchers connect more effectively to organizations and that the knowledge they generate should be useful in addressing the effectiveness challenges that they face.

Lawler's career unfolded in four chapters in four institutional settings: the University of California-Berkeley Psychology Department, Yale University's Administrative Science Department, the Institute for Social Research and the Psychology Department of the University of Michigan, and as a professor of Management and director of the Center for Effective Organizations in the Management and Organizational Behavior Department in the Marshall School of Business at the University of Southern California (USC). Lawler's contribution to the field of change is best understood through his own metamorphosis as he moved through these settings and developed an increasing commitment to doing useful research. In his own words, his development has been strongly influenced by his succession of experiences in these four institutions. Close collaborations with colleagues and the opportunities for learning and building new methodological and organizational approaches to doing research have been critical elements of his contributions to academia and to practice.

University of California-Berkeley (1960–1964)

After graduating from Brown University with a degree in psychology and experience on the football and track teams, Lawler received a PhD in psychology from the University of California-Berkeley in 1964. There he developed the habits for and value of theoretical framing and methodological rigor. Working closely with Lyman Porter, he received a solid grounding in traditional I-O psychology approaches, albeit through field studies that had him out in organizations interacting with managers and employees about how they experienced their organizations. As a doctoral student and subsequently as a young faculty member at Yale University, Lawler conducted psychology research that would help define the field of organizational behavior by extending the focus beyond the industrial worker to managerial and professional organizational members and by focusing increasingly on organizational practices that yield high performance.

Lawler's dissertation examined the relationship between managers' attitudes and performance and became the basis for his book with Lyman Porter, *Managerial Attitudes and Performance* (1968). This seminal work proposed and found empirical support for what came to be known as the value-expectancy theory of motivation. This model expanded the range of variables believed to impact performance and reversed the prevailing causality assumption that employee satisfaction leads to higher performance. It established empirically that satisfaction results from high performance that leads to outcomes that are valued and are perceived as equitable. This core principle has underpinned Lawler's subsequent work, in particular, his focus on creating work systems and practices that motivate high performance rather than trying to satisfy employees. This breakthrough perspective was an early and important example of Lawler having and testing insights that were at odds with current thinking in academia and practice.

Yale Administrative Science Department (1964–1972)

As a new faculty member in Yale's Administrative Science Department, Lawler built on and extended the theoretical constructs underpinning high performance and motivation (Lawler 1973). He continued doing fieldwork focusing on the interface between individuals and the organization. With his close colleague Richard Hackman and others, Lawler oriented himself increasingly to the practical concern of understanding how organizational contexts can be designed to foster high performance, contributing a body of work in the area of work design (Lawler 1969) and compensation.

He rapidly became one of the foremost authorities on compensation and rewards in the eyes both of academic researchers and corporate leaders (Lawler 1971, 1981, 1990). His multi-community following, and the intentional strategy of focusing on books that were aimed at a dual audience, would be a hallmark of Lawler's career and the underpinning of his undeniable influence on both academic research and organizational practice.

At Yale, Lawler also encountered and was influenced by the work of Chris Argyris, Clay Alderfer, and others who were working within a Lewinian tradition and developing an action science perspective using participatory change processes. Yale provided a fertile environment for exploring the tensions and connections between this group and those who, like himself, were pursuing more traditional quantitative methodologies. He has described his relationship with Argyris as "transformative." It laid the foundation for a fundamental change in how he positioned his work in the field of organization behavior that would be defined during his tenure at the University of Michigan's Institute for Social Research (ISR).

The University of Michigan's Institute for Social Research (1972–1980)

At ISR, Lawler saw the opportunity to do larger scale, funded, field research about effective organizational systems and to focus on research that could make a difference. ISR had been founded in the 1970s to do social science research to help address conflicts and social issues that had been manifest in the preceding decades of wars and social unrest. Scholars such as Rensis Likert, Bob Kahn, Stan Seashore, and Dan Katz found fertile ground there to test their advancing theories of organizational systems and human behavior through field studies. Lawler partnered with Stan Seashore to establish a Quality of Worklife (QWL) Program – securing funding from the US Department of Health, Education, and Welfare (HEW). HEW was seeking empirical studies to find ways to address the workplace problems of low morale and its manifestations in absenteeism, turnover, low quality, and worker-management conflict. These issues had been starkly reported in the HEW-sponsored *Work in America* report (O'Toole et al. 1973). The aim of the QWL program was to incorporate theories and research knowledge about organization structure, work design, supervision, participative approaches, compensation, and other organizational features in a coherent organizational system that could be created and empirically studied to understand how the various elements of the system can operate together to yield productive organizations with higher morale.

To achieve that purpose, Lawler and his colleagues had to investigate system level dynamics. Lawler was developing comfort with the Lewinian perspective that the best way to understand an organization is to change it – combined with the belief that there is nothing as useful as good theory. Nevertheless, focusing on organizations that were changing represented a departure from the presumed wisdom among traditional organizational psychologists that creditable knowledge comes from tightly controlled studies holding everything constant but the variables in question.

Lawler and Seashore led a multidisciplined team to study eight large system change efforts. The changes were occurring in very different organizational settings and were based on a variety of intervention models and frameworks that were formulated and implemented by experts in organization development, labor management cooperation, and sociotechnical systems (STS), i.e., by action researchers. To maintain the objectivity that Lawler had learned to value, the Michigan QWL group independently "assessed" the change process, the impact of the various elements of the changes that were being put in place, and the outcomes for the company and for the employees. The ultimate purpose was to generate knowledge that could help organizations change themselves to become more effective. Lawler wasn't particularly focused on the change process and didn't think of himself as an interventionist. Rather, he maintained his concern with (1) generating theory, (2) testing – with as much rigor as possible – the practices that lead to effectiveness, and (3) disseminating knowledge.

The QWL work represented a methodological advance in research about organization system change. The research challenge was to find ways to study the linkages of the various elements of change and of the overall system to productivity and morale, in order to assess and learn from different approaches to improve quality of work life. In order to do this, he and his colleagues had to become change agents in a different way: by "inventing" and implementing new methodological and organizational ways of doing the work of research and knowledge generation. They had to invent approaches to study complex system change and develop a social system capable of doing that. They created a matrix structure, including cross-discipline research teams for projects, and specialist sub-teams with deep knowledge of various organizational frameworks and disciplines, and an overall approach to developing and implementing common instruments to measure the phenomena of focus (Mirvis and Lawler 2010).

The interventions they were studying were multifaceted and drew on multi-level, multidisciplinary theories, and multiple methods for data gathering and analysis that included observation, qualitative approaches, surveys, and the gathering of quantitative archival information. A comprehensive survey was developed to measure the key parameters of the system that were believed to relate to motivation and performance. Archival data were collected measuring financial and productivity outcomes and behavioral outcomes such as absenteeism and turnover. In addition to an overall assessment of outcomes that was foundational to program assessment, various team members carried out focused mini-studies of particular sub-systems that were changing, using a comparison group when possible. Lawler coined the term "adaptive research" to describe a methodology for adjusting the research approaches to fit a dynamic context and to take advantage of the particulars of a site that enabled focused learning (1977). The multidisciplinarity of the research team made it possible to look at the full system while also homing in on particular facets of the system and of the change dynamics. The studies resulted in an interwoven pattern of findings that shed light both on the impact of particular practices and of the system overall.

This research required managing collaboration among multiple stakeholders – each with different interests, understandings, beliefs, values, purposes, and preferences. Among the stakeholders were executives in corporations where the interventions were occurring. Others were the HEW program sponsors, labor unions, teams of interventionists, managers and employees in the research sites, and the multidisciplinary QWL research team members themselves. An office was set up in Washington to identify research sites and assemble the group of stakeholders that would have to participate in each of the projects to agree to an overall approach. Ed had become a manager of a complex research system, one that could only work effectively if it was populated by people who were energized by the opportunity, excited by the challenges, collaborative in orientation, and able to be heavily involved in making the program a success.

As the work proceeded, the reality of studying such a complex tapestry of interests, interventions, and actors resulted in research approaches that moved farther away from a controlled experimental design. Through long hours of discussion and debate among the research team, each of whom had their own perspectives on relevance and rigor, complex interwoven approaches were generated across the eight projects. Lawler and Seashore ensured that the emerging multidisciplinary, multi-method, multi-level, and longitudinal methodology was systematically documented in articles and books aimed at introducing this systemic and adaptive approach to the field of organizational studies (Seashore et al. 1983; Lawler et al. 1980). This reflects another theme that would characterize Lawler's career – his continual emphasis on generating knowledge about and catalyzing interest in doing useful research.

During his time at ISR, Lawler developed an interest in testing knowledge through new plant startups (greenfield sites) built from scratch to embody the elements of the emerging high-performance, QWL framework (Lawler 1978). The greenfield approach was already being used successfully by companies such as Procter and Gamble and Shell Oil, following a STS approach. The elements of the plant could be developed from scratch by the participants without having to go through the hard work entailed in changing already existing sites, systems, and understandings. This approach provided a different organizational change and intervention methodology in which organizations could build, learn from, and improve prototypes of new ways of operating and disseminate them to other plants. The opportunity to consult to and learn from the start-ups moved him even closer to action science and away from a strict insistence that there should be walls between the research and the intervention.

Lawler was now squarely positioned in the nexus of the methodological tensions and schisms between advocates of qualitative and quantitative methodology and between rigorous positivistic versus action science-oriented research. His emphasis on the importance of research usefulness – albeit with as much rigor as is possible given the constraints of and realities faced by organizations – was now his primary guiding value. This perspective guided him as he moved to the University of Southern California (USC) and founded the Center for Effective Organizations (CEO) to pursue that purpose.

The Center for Effective Organizations (1978 Through Present)

Before arriving at the USC, Lawler spent time at the Battelle Memorial Institute where he led contract research programs. There he developed the belief that dependence on elaborate contracting mechanisms and large overhead costs worked against research productivity, flexibility to pursue topics of high relevance, and performance motivation. In 1978, Lawler moved to USC, where he had the opportunity to design a research center based on the knowledge he had generated about high performance. He founded CEO with the mission of partnering with organizations to conduct research that contributes to organizational effectiveness through the simultaneous advancing of theoretical understanding and practical impact. In the CEO model, sponsor companies pay a fee to join CEO, help shape its research agenda based on the issues they are facing, host and partner in the conduct of studies, and are the beneficiaries of rich learning from their own and other organizations that are inventing and adopting leading-edge approaches.

He did not want the researchers in the center to be constrained by the increasing pressure in academic departments to focus solely on A-journal articles through what he had come to perceive as methodologies, theoretical perspectives, and focuses that were increasingly distant from useful knowledge about organizational effectiveness. He designed all aspects of the center to motivate and provide a supportive context for relevant work and in so doing departed from many of the norms and assumptions underpinning traditional academic departments. He secured agreement that the center would report directly to the Dean of the Business School and that the researchers who joined it could choose to be on a track that rewarded a combination of academic and practitioner-oriented publications and research impact. This model was enabled by CEO's pledge to be largely self-supporting, which also enabled the development of a staff of skilled administrative and research services professionals so that the research teams could be maximally productive. He and his first hire and Associate Director Allan (Monty) Mohrman, rolled up their sleeves, built a team, developed a cadre of corporate partners, and went about the hard work of building several large research programs in the areas of strategic human resources practices, the design of high performance systems, and organizational change.

The attitudes and values of many in companies and academia at this time had been shaped during the societal turbulence of the 1960s and had been influenced by the visibility that Lawler's work had achieved both in academia and companies. CEO recruited a cadre of researchers who valued doing systematic research that both advanced theory and positively impacted organizations and society and who valued the opportunity to cocreate this nascent institution to carry out its mission. It was also able to attract and rapidly grow a sponsor network of more than 50 companies that wanted to be partners in this mission.

In order to be well positioned to do research useful to organizations in dealing with emerging issues, CEO recruited researchers from multiple disciplines, including psychology, organizational sociology, economics, information systems, strategy, organization design, and system dynamics. It quickly developed a model of partnering with researchers from across the USC campus, and from other universities nationally and globally, in order to expand its domains of expertise. Lawler did what he espoused. He created a high performance system fashioned to address the needs of the time and sufficiently agile to be able to change itself to address the emerging needs of the next four decades.

The corporate members of CEO came largely from the HR function. Lawler and others at CEO maintained a strong presence in studying effective human resource practices, an area where Lawler had become a globally recognized thought leader. This was a natural fit at the time, as the HR function was beginning to evolve from being a personnel function to becoming a strategic business partner. This evolution reflected the emerging knowledge economy where talent management was becoming a competitive differentiator. Lawler foresaw this trend, and he and his colleagues pursued the generation of useful research that focused on the effectiveness issues inherent in this transition. Over its four decades, CEO maintained an engaged group of sponsors by repeatedly anticipating trends and challenges that organizations were beginning to face and by applying and generating multidisciplinary knowledge to generate useful knowledge.

CEO's multidisciplinary group of scholars took CEO toward more macro and change-oriented focuses, generating knowledge useful to organizations in developing new capabilities and practices to deal with the profound changes they were experiencing, such as the digitalization of information and communication, new ways of organizing and working, and the emergence of the global economy. Challenges addressed in CEO research included dealing with multicultural workforces; coordination and work-life challenges of 24/7 work around the globe; new automated work systems; outsourcing and the associated dislocation of work, workers, and communities; the movement away from life-long employment expectations and fundamental changes in the employment contract; sea changes in the awareness, education levels, and expectations of employees; and the increasingly lateral and networked organizing approaches that called into question traditional assumptions about the role of hierarchy.

With colleague Chris Worley, Lawler expanded his interests to how organizations can become sufficiently agile to operate effectively in an ever-changing world. In another twist on conventional wisdom, they argue that instead of being built to last, organizations should be built to change (Lawler and Worley 2006, 2011; Worley et al. 2014). As societal side effects of the ballooning growth of the highly networked global economy became evident, CEO also began to look beyond shareholder value and employee outcomes as the primary metrics of organization success. One stream of research focuses on how organizations can effectively address the purposes and legitimate interests of a complex web of stakeholders that are impacting and changing the way organizations function, in order to be sustainable into the future. Lawler and colleague Sue Mohrman argue for a reframing of how academics approach and design their research to reflect this new reality (Lawler and Mohrman 2014).

Key Contributions: A Relentless Pursuit of Research Usefulness

Lawler's primary identity is not as a scholar of organizational change. Rather, he is a scholar who has made substantive research contributions that have contributed to change in organizations and introduced new research methodologies for the study of organizations. He has been a change agent with influence both on the directions taken in the field of organizational behavior and on practice. His early contributions were foundational in establishing the field of organizational behavior and provided core tenets for I/O psychologists who would work with and in companies to advance practice. His more recent contributions identify important ways in which organizational practices need to advance to fit changing demands and have influenced the fields of organizational development and organizational effectiveness.

Much of what Lawler has studied and advocated over the years has now been widely embedded in organizational practice, including greater attention to employee development, knowledge sharing, increased participation in decision-making, and a more strategic application of rewards and performance management. The widespread influence his work has had on companies, on the education of managers, and on other academics studying and working with companies to solve effectiveness problems has likely played a role in the adoption of these practices.

Through the way he has crafted his career and the strong stance he has taken with respect to the importance of usefulness, he has been a key figure in keeping alive a debate about the role and methodologies of organizational research. He has questioned assumptions and operated outside of and resisted the institutionalization of an increasingly narrow, discipline-based approach to conducting research. A number of Lawler's key contributions are discussed below.

Systemic and Multi-level Treatment of Organizational Practices Leading to Organizational Effectiveness

As described earlier, Lawler's early work conceptualizing the key link between organizational practices and the motivation of employees and his role in providing a framework clarifying the link between motivation and performance were foundational contributions. Lawler stood out in his early embrace of an integrative perspective on the organization as a system of practices that shape its performance capabilities. This perspective led to a more complex, multi-level treatment of the relationship between the individual and the organization. In the world of organizational practice, it provided the backdrop for the gradual transition of the largely transactional personnel function into a more strategic human resources function.

Related to his work in the QWL program, Lawler developed a system framework for high performance, known as high involvement management (Lawler 1986, 1992). It focuses on a set of mutually supportive practices to increase employee involvement in the success of the business by distributing four resources – knowledge, information, power, and rewards – throughout the employee population. With its simultaneous focus on employee and organizational outcomes, this framework inspired a generation of scholars who honed, extended, and tested it, both through interventional work and assessment of impact and through systematic articulation and testing of theoretical precepts.

Definitional Work on Research Usefulness

Lawler has been persistent in advocating that usefulness should be a major criterion for organizational research. He advocates empirical field research driven by a clear theoretical foundation and yielding useful, data-based knowledge about effectiveness. This value is instantiated in his own scholarly work and in the research programs and the research center he has led. He and his colleagues have edited three volumes providing frameworks, guidance, and exemplars about the conduct of useful research (Lawler et al. 1985, 1999; Mohrman et al. 2011).

Key to his capacity to achieve usefulness is staying closely connected to organizational practice. Believing that practice generally precedes academic research, Lawler has been a keen observer of trends and even of weak signals that change is underway. Over the years, he has anticipated the trajectory of the emerging and dynamic context in which organizations operate and anticipated the challenges they will face and what that means for organization practice and research. For example, under his leadership, CEO developed expertise in information technology and anticipated the fundamental changes to work and organization that would result from digitalization. CEO researchers were early contributors to cross-functional teaming and other lateral approaches to organizing that would become increasingly important in the global, digitalized economy. A strong organization design capability has been nurtured at CEO, so that it can simultaneously shed useful light on the macro-design issues that organizations are facing and on their implications for the management and human resource practices.

As Lawler and colleagues have written, knowledge is only useful if it is used, and their activities have had that intent. Continual sensing of issues companies are facing combined with research that tests ideas in practice are underpinnings for the value that companies find in his work. Usefulness is enhanced by writing, speaking, and making knowledge about effective practice accessible to multiple audiences. Providing consultative support to companies trying to put new knowledge into practice enables a real-world test of usefulness, as well as feedback to enrich and iterate what is being learned and disseminated. Company relationships provide access to research sites in which to study dynamics and practices in the changing contexts faced by organizations.

Methodology for Learning from Organizations That Are Purposefully Transforming Themselves

The rigorous methodological approach (described earlier in this chapter) developed in the QWL studies at ISR for learning about the practices that lead to organizational effectiveness provided a methodological framework for many academics whose focus was to do useful research. I include myself among those who were deeply impacted by this approach. In fact, it was this framework and the QWL research that led me to remain in academia when I left graduate school, rather than go directly to a company to try to help make it more effective for its employees.

Elements of the instruments that were developed at ISR in the 1970s have been used by researchers for decades and can be found in the surveys and assessment methodologies that have become part of the fabric of many organizations. Lawler's influence on the use of survey methodology by companies is also a key contribution to the field of organizational effectiveness and change (Lawler 1967).

Designing a Research Center to Conduct Useful Research

In setting up a purpose-driven research center that has evolved and lasted for 39 years, Lawler was both a social entrepreneur and an innovator. CEO's organizing model is described earlier in the paper. Lawler combined his knowledge of practices that lead to effectiveness, his framework for high involvement, and his experience with greenfield organizations to start up and evolve an organization designed to foster high performance in its mission of relevant research. In so doing, CEO deviated substantially from the traditional academic organization. A key decision Lawler made was to have the research scientists in the center have the choice not to be on a tenure track appointment but rather to have ongoing employment based on research performance. Lawler believed firmly that this was the best way to foster ongoing relevance and productivity. CEO might be considered an exemplar for others thinking about designing high performing organizations for knowledge work.

Lawler carefully designed a strategy to establish legitimacy in the academic world for research that is carried out in a research center by researchers with nontraditional links to the long established ivory towers of academia and mission. He took steps to ensure that CEO's work was connected to the mainstream work in the organizational sciences, while simultaneously connecting it to practitioners. In its early years, CEO convened two conferences involving CEO researchers and a number of highly productive, established organizational academics who at the time were carrying out useful research, and a group of reflective practitioners, to collaboratively produce seminal books on the topics of *Doing Useful Research* (1985) and *Managing Large-Scale Change* (1989). This was a time when scholarly work in the academic fields of management and organization was becoming increasingly distant from the actual operations and concerns of organizations. Lawler's avowed intent was to nudge the field to contribute knowledge that would be useful to practice and to accept its importance.

As a distinguished management professor, Lawler was able to transcend the pressures for research and publications that advances narrow academic disciplines. He could focus on cross-cutting issues that require new methodologies, highly collaborative approaches, and an openness to discovering knowledge for the future rather than painstakingly analyzing and chronicling what the past has generated. In short, Lawler positioned himself as a bridge between traditional discipline-based university departments and the cross-discipline, problem-oriented research that was being carried out at CEO.

Insights: Reframing Prevailing Frameworks

Lawler's astute observational powers and capacity to cut through complexity and get to the heart of the matter have allowed him to frame and investigate interesting questions and issues throughout his career. His influence on organization change has stemmed from using empirical data to reframe prevailing assumptions and change how people think about the issues they face and the problems they have to solve. For example, his and his colleagues' early work offered an alternative to the prevailing views of organizations as engineering and industrial systems supplemented by industrial relations and administrative processes. They began collecting data and investigating behavioral and attitudinal dynamics and the professional and managerial workforce and contributed to the emerging fields of management and organizational studies.

Always building on the fundamentals of motivation and performance, he has expanded and reframed the internally focused issues of individuals, teams, and the organization to take into account the impact of the global and knowledge-based economy on the nature of performance and on the employee organization relationship as it was evolving in society.

Keeping in mind that Lawler sees his contributions as resulting from collaboration with colleagues, just a few of his important insights are briefly described below.

Motivation, Satisfaction, and Performance

A significant early reframing came from his work establishing that performance leads to satisfaction – rather than causality going in the opposite direction. Lawler continues even in current times to remind academics and practitioners of the fallacy of believing that satisfying employees will lead to performance motivation – and of the futility of trying to achieve engagement by focusing on programs to make employees happy. He reminds us that the research finds that the source of employee engagement in the business is the work and performance outcomes.

Integrative Scholarship

Lawler's work while at ISR cemented his stature as an integrative scholar, one who merged the understanding of individual and organizational behavior and effectiveness in relationship to the changing market and societal contexts that were unfolding. At the time, this represented a reframing for a relatively internally focused field of study. He shifted from research on particular constructs and practices and their individual impact on performance to the investigation of high performance as stemming from a system of practices. His methodological contributions reflect this insight by suggesting ways, imperfect though they may be from a positivistic research perspective, to study, understand, and advance practice in organization systems. This insight led him to question the fragmented production of knowledge both in academia and organizations. A practical manifestation of his impact is the increasing integration of HR functional approaches to support the performance required to deliver on the organization's strategy.

Criticality of Connection to Practice

Lawler dedicated a lot of his personal attention to creating awareness of good practice and drawing attention to areas where companies are falling short in putting in place practices that would be good for the performance of the companies and the well-being of employees. He believed that useful research could not be done at arm's length as is espoused by many positivist researchers and that usefulness required going far beyond simply discovering and writing up knowledge about organizational effectiveness and implications for practice and then declaring victory and moving on to the next topic of interest. He sought ways to share knowledge with new executives and managers, emerging professional societies, young and established academics and practitioners, and professionals and managers in many fields, industry sectors, functions, and institutional settings. Through example, he redefined the mix of work required to make research useful.

Built to Change

After three decades of work studying organizations trying to increase performance in the midst of fundamentally changing market demands, Lawler was one of the first to draw the profound conclusion that organizations should be built to change, not to be stable. He partnered with colleague Chris Worley, who led a series of studies of Organizational Agility that yielded a system of organizational elements that enables an organization to be agile (Lawler and Worley 2006, 2011; Worley et al. 2014). Sustainable organizational effectiveness, in their view, depends not only on sound management practices and value-adding capabilities but also on building the ability to change into the fabric of the organization. Change isn't an episodic occurrence that calls for periodically assembling deep knowledge about change management.

Rather, effective organizations are always changing, and change is a core capability. Agility is enabled by a system of routines built into the fabric of the organization. These promote ongoing strategic thinking, sensing of how the environment is changing and what that means for how the organization should operate, testing and learning from new approaches, and effectively implementing new directions. This perspective on change is a significant reframing from many of the core change frameworks in the fields of organizational development and organizational effectiveness that focus on transformations and/or the implementation of episodic change.

Individualization

Individualization of the treatment of employees has been one of Lawler's key focuses for his entire career (Lawler 1974, 2014; Lawler and Finegold 2000). His insight is that individualization, not homogeneous human resource practices, relates to greater motivation and performance. Despite the field of psychology's concern for individual differences, I/O psychologists have had a quest for ever more sophisticated ways of measuring these and fitting individually different employees into common systems. Lawler has advocated such practices as person-based pay, eliminating job descriptions, cafeteria benefits programs, and other practices that move away from homogenous treatment of employees and that recognize individual capabilities and preferences. In advocating these approaches, he has often been swimming upstream given the legal environment and associated risk aversion of companies, the preferences of managers for commonality and the preferences of many employees and organizations for stability.

Lawler's recent work (Lawler 2017) advocates individualization as a key organizing principle for talent management. He believes this as a key to the agility organizations need to be sustainably effective in today's rapidly shifting society and economy. He points out that individualization is already underway given that lifelong employment is rapidly disappearing, and that companies are increasingly relying on contractors and freelancers rather than expanding their full-time employee base to carry out tasks that may not be needed in the future. This perspective is congruent with the pervasiveness of knowledge work that does not fall readily into well-defined jobs, job families, and grading and compensation systems.

Ed Lawler's Pervasive and Deep Legacy

My perception of Ed Lawler's legacy is no doubt biased by the fact that I share the values built into CEO, and have found it to be an ideal setting in which to pursue my interests. My own academic career has been largely based in CEO, where I have had the opportunity not only to pursue my research interests and build my research programs and networks of collaborators but also to do things that I personally believe contribute to society. I have worked, often closely, with Ed Lawler for almost 40 years.

My view that Ed's legacy is pervasive and deep is congruent with the perceptions from many in both academia and the corporate world. Ed is a highly honored academic. He is a distinguished professor at USC and has been honored for his lifetime contribution by the American Psychological Association, the Society for Industrial and Organizational Psychology, the Academy of Management, the Association for Training and Development, the Society for Human Resource Management, and others. He is a fellow in the Academy of Management, The British Academy of Management, and Divisions 8 and 14 of the American Psychological Association, and others and has served on the directing boards of many of these organizations. He has been on the editorial board of more than 15 academic journals.

Ed's expansive influence on academia has been described in some detail earlier in this chapter. Yet it is important to emphasize the continuity: for almost 50 years, he has evolved his underlying concern with motivation, behavior, and performance in organizations. He has built on core theoretical ideas and has studied and described practices that are continuously changing to adjust to the unfolding contexts in which organizations are operating. His research trajectory, though anchored, has been blown by the winds of change. His foundational frameworks have been catalytic for several generations of unfolding theoretical knowledge as well as for the translational research taking theory into organizational practices.

Ed attributes much of his impact to the longevity of his career and the opportunity to pursue his core interests through time. Just one example is CEO's work on performance management that led to the seminal book *Designing Performance Appraisal Systems* (Mohrman et al. 1989b) that squarely positioned performance appraisal as a strategic tool and one that was all about involving employees not only in the process of their own assessment but also in the success of the organization. Twenty years later, Gerry Ledford, Ben Schneider, George Benson, and Ed are revisiting the performance management practices needed in our changed, digitally enabled world of work. I use this focus not only to demonstrate the longevity, continuity, and dynamic nature of Ed's contribution but also to bring to life his belief that dynamic collaborations have been a source of his impact.

Many organizational practices have been profoundly influenced by his work, including the way people are appraised and paid, how work is designed, and how people are involved in the organization. His work has been an important enabler of the transition of human resource management to address the key talent requirements and challenges of today's global knowledge economy. The field of human resource management is substantively different because of his contributions, and the same is true for hundreds or even thousands of practitioners.

I have been struck by how often I hear managers and executives – even those who have never met Ed Lawler – talk about the influence his work has had on how they think about managing and organizing. Although teaching in USC's MBA programs has not been a large part of his responsibilities at USC, he has nevertheless penetrated that pathway for dissemination of his work. Many if not most students have encountered his work as part of their coursework. Other practitioners have become familiar through his dedication to sharing his ideas with professional associations, in practitioner outlets, and in companies. Practitioners frequently comment that his writing and speaking are clear and the implications are pragmatic and straightforward. He has generated a steady stream of highly varied publications containing a drumbeat of key empirically based principles of high performance situated in the real, constantly unfolding challenges that are being faced in practice. This approach has clearly been successful in accomplishing his major goal of generating and disseminating knowledge that is useful.

Unfinished Business

Lawler's strategy of achieving change through empirical evidence of what constitutes effective practice has had great impact. But he has also come to believe that such approaches are necessary and helpful but not sufficient. Many organizations proceed with and even escalate commitment to approaches to managing people that are ineffective. He has a very realistic appreciation that organizational leaders will not always "do the right thing" for their companies, shareholders, employees, and other stakeholders, even if they know what the right thing would be. During the last 20 years, he has been part of a team with David Finegold and Jay Conger examining Boards of Directors and helping understand how they can be organized to more effectively play their role in ensuring that companies are operating effectively for their owners, employees, and stakeholders. Lawler acknowledges that organizational changes are largely driven by the operating necessity to confront the powerful winds of market changes and competition. But he also views change as a political phenomenon. Organizations respond to powerful stakeholders who can influence the way they operate, often through the legislative and regulatory process or through the creation of reputational risks.

Lawler reflects that those who create compelling knowledge about effective practice run into societal limits and into the power structures that control decision making about how organizations are run. In commenting on his latest writing focusing on the individualization of the relationship of workers and companies, for example, he acknowledges that although inevitable given the current trends in the digitalized and global economy, the individualization of human resource practices raises many societal issues that will have to be addressed and crashes into conflicting beliefs and preferences about the responsibility of corporations. What this trend means for the character of companies and the nature of society opens up a whole new area of focus for the organization and social sciences and for economists and political scientists. This reality, one might say, makes it even more important for researchers to get out of the narrow silos of knowledge and develop a more systemic perspective on how all the pieces fit together for effective outcomes for companies, employees, society, and the earth. Those who are taking on this challenge will find in Lawler's work much learning about how to organize to carry out research to inform this transition.

References

Lawler, E. E. (1967). Attitude surveys as predictors of employee behavior: The missing link. *Personnel Administrator, 30*(5), 22–24.

Lawler, E. E. (1969). Job design and employee motivation. *Personnel Psychology, 22*, 426–434.

Lawler, E. E. (1971). *Pay and organizational effectiveness: A psychological view*. New York: McGraw-Hill.

Lawler, E. E. (1973). *Motivation in work organizations*. Monterey: Brooks/Cole.

Lawler, E. E. (1974). For a more effective organization – Match the job to the man. *Organizational Dynamics, 3*(1), 19–29.

Lawler, E. E. (1977). Adaptive experiments: An approach to organizational behavior research. *Academy of Management Review, 2*, 576–585.

Lawler, E. E. (1978). The new plant revolution. *Organizational Dynamics, 6*(3), 2–12.

Lawler, E. E. (1981). *Pay and organization development*. Reading: Addison Wesley.

Lawler, E. E. (1986). *High-involvement management*. San Francisco: Jossey-Bass.

Lawler, E. E. (1990). *Strategic pay*. San Francisco: Jossey-Bass.

Lawler, E. E. (1992). *The ultimate advantage: Creating the high-involvement organization*. San Francisco: Jossey-Bass.

Lawler, E. E. (2014). Individualizing organizations: Progress and possibilities. In E. E. Lawler & S. A. Mohrman (Eds.), *Special issue: Effective organizations in the new environment. Organizational Dynamics*, *43*(3), 157–167.

Lawler, E. E. (2017). *Reinventing talent management: Principles and practices for the new world of work*. Oakland: Berrett-Koehler.

Lawler, E. E., & Finegold, D. (2000). Individualizing the organization: Past, present, and future. *Organizational Dynamics, 29*(1), 1–15.

Lawler, E. E., & Mohrman, S. A. (2014). Designing organizations for sustainable effectiveness: A new paradigm for organizations and academic researchers. *Journal of Organizational Effectiveness: People and Performance, 1*(1), 14–34.

Lawler, E. E., & Worley, C. G. (2006). *Built to change: How to achieve sustained organizational effectiveness*. San Francisco: Jossey-Bass.

Lawler, E. E., & Worley, C. G. (2011). *Management reset: Organizing for sustainable effectiveness*. San Francisco: Jossey-Bass.

Lawler, E. E., Nadler, D., & Cammann, C. (1980). *Organizational assessment*. New York: Wiley Interscience.

Lawler, E. E., Mohrman, A. M., Mohrman, S. A., Ledford, G. E., Cummings, T. G., & Associates. (1985). *Doing research that is useful for theory and practice*. San Francisco: Jossey-Bass.

Lawler, E. E., Mohrman, A. M., Mohrman, S. A., Ledford, G. E., Cummings, T. G. (1999). *Doing research that is useful for theory and practice* (new edition). Lanham: Lexington Press.

Mirvis, P., & Lawler, E. E. (2010). Rigor and relevance in organizational research: Experience, reflection and a look ahead. In S. A. Mohrman, E. E. Lawler, & Associates (Eds.), *Useful research: Advancing theory and practice* (pp. 112–135). San Francisco: Berrett-Koehler.

Mohrman, A. M., Mohrman, S. A., Ledford, G. E., Cummings, T. G., Lawler, E. E., & Associates. (1989a). *Large-scale organizational change*. San Francisco: Jossey-Bass.

Mohrman, A. M., Resnick-West, S. M., & Lawler, E. E. (1989b). *Designing performance appraisal systems: Aligning appraisals and organizational realities*. San Francisco: Jossey-Bass Publishers.

Mohrman, S. A., Lawler, E. E., & Associates. (2011). *Useful research: Advancing theory and practice*. San Francisco: Berrett-Koehler.

O'Toole, J., et al. (1973). *Work in America: Report of a special task force to the secretary of health, education, and welfare*. Cambridge, MA: MIT Press.

Porter, L. W., & Lawler, E. E. (1968). *Managerial attitudes and performance*. Homewood: Irwin-Dorsey.

Seashore, S. E., Lawler, E. E., Mirvis, P., & Cammann, C. (1983). *Assessing organizational change*. New York: Wiley-Interscience.

Worley, C. G., Williams, T., & Lawler, E. E. (2014). *The agility factor: Building adaptable organizations for superior performance*. San Francisco: Jossey-Bass.

Further Reading

Conger, J. A., Lawler, E. E., & Finegold, D. (2001). *Corporate boards: New strategies for adding value at the top*. San Francisco: Jossey-Bass.

Lawler, E. E., & Boudreau, J. W. (2015). *Global trends in human resource management: A twenty-year analysis*. Palo Alto: Stanford University Press.

Ledford, G. E., Benson, G., & Lawler, E. E. (2016). Aligning research and the current practice of performance management. *Industrial and Organizational Psychology: Perspectives on Science and Practice*, *9*(2), 253–260.

Mohrman, S. A., O'Toole, J., & Lawler, E. E. (2015). *Corporate stewardship: Achieving sustainable effectiveness*. Sheffield, UK: Greenleaf Publishing.

O'Toole, J., & Lawler, E. E. (2006). *The new American workplace*. New York: Palgrave-Macmillan.

Shani, A. B., Mohrman, S. A., Pasmore, W. A., Stymne, B., & Adler, N. (Eds.). (2007). *Handbook of collaborative management research*. Thousand Oaks: Sage Press.

Van de Ven, A. H. (2007) *Engaged scholarship: A guide for organizaational and social research*. Oxford: Oxford University Press.

Paul R. Lawrence: A Career of Rigor, Relevance, and Passion

45

Michael L. Tushman

Abstract
Paul R. Lawrence was one of the earliest and most influential figures in the emergence of organizational behavior as a field of study. He was a pioneer in creating a body of work on organization design, leadership, and change in both the private and public sectors. Lawrence's professional work was rooted in an aspiration to do work that was rigorous, relevant to practicing managers, and of service to society. Beyond his research, Lawrence was committed to building the field of organizational behavior at HBS and more broadly in our profession. He had a lifelong passion for participant-centered learning and for the training of doctoral students.

Keywords
Organization design • Contingency theory • Public and private organizations • Leadership • Leading change • Rigor and relevance

Contents

This essay built on Anne Lawrence's remarkable interview with her father (Lawrence and Lawrence 1993). Bill Pasmore, Jay Lorsch, Jim Aisner, Marjorie Williams, Nitin Nohria, and Ranjay Gulati provided critical comments that substantially improved this essay.

M.L. Tushman (✉)
Harvard Business School, Boston, MA, USA
e-mail: mtushman@hbs.edu

D.B. Szabla et al. (eds.), *The Palgrave Handbook of Organizational Change Thinkers*,
DOI 10.1007/978-3-319-52878-6_12

Introduction

Paul R. Lawrence was one of the earliest and most influential figures in the emergence of organizational behavior as a field of study. He was a pioneer in creating a body of work on organization design, leadership, and change, in both the private and public sectors. Influenced by his early experiences with labor/management conflict, Lawrence's professional work was rooted in an aspiration to do work that was rigorous, relevant to practicing managers, and of service to society.

Lawrence spent his entire professional career at the Harvard Business School. He started at HBS before the field we now know as organizational behavior (OB) existed. Lawrence was instrumental in building Harvard's OB unit, its MBA program, as well as several of its long executive education programs. Besides Lawrence's institution building and research, he was also pivotal in building an innovative doctoral program in organizational behavior and was a mentor and role model to over 60 doctoral students. His students, in turn, helped shape the evolving field of organizational behavior in business schools worldwide and at the Academy of Management.

Even after his retirement, Lawrence's passion for his research never diminished. He never let up on his quest to understand the roles of organizations in society and of leaders in shaping organizational, community, and societal outcomes. As a scholar, teacher, mentor to doctoral students, and institution builder, Paul Lawrence set a standard to which our field should aspire.

This essay is both descriptive of Lawrence's career as well as personal. Paul was a mentor and friend. I first met him when I was a doctoral student at MIT in 1973. He was visiting the Sloan School during a sabbatical year. I was interested in determinants of productivity in R&D settings and, more generally, the management of innovation. As a rookie doctoral student, I did not then know of Paul's research. What I did realize immediately was his commitment both to his research and to doctoral education.

I also felt his enthusiasm for the work of a professor and appreciation for the unique and complex responsibilities of faculty in business schools. In contrast to many in the profession, Paul always believed that research should matter. He believed that teaching should draw on this research to help managers solve real-world problems. While Paul was quiet and listened carefully, he was opinionated and firm when it came to the choice of research topics ("work on significant, managerially important problems"), the importance of field data ("carefully collected and detailed"), and the importance of induced theory/conceptual schemes ("the importance of inducing theoretical and managerial 'walking sticks'").

Paul offered a doctoral seminar in organization theory to students at MIT and HBS. His syllabus was exciting, as it included the intellectual pioneers of our field, like Roethlisberger, Barnard, Homans, Selznick, Mayo, and Warner, as well as then-current research on organizations as social systems (e.g., March and Simon, Chandler, Katz and Kahn, Farris, Perrow, Thompson, Burns and Stalker, Trist, Woodward, and Likert). His syllabus was not bound by a single discipline but by managerial problems and the diversity of social science theory that could help managers solve those problems.

The week before our seminar was to begin, Paul hurt his back. The doctoral students were stunned by his response to this injury. Rather than canceling classes, Paul met with the group in his home. Because he had to be lying down, he managed to conduct the seminar for weeks on his back! I will never forget his passion for our field and his commitment to doctoral students, even while debilitated.

Quite apart from the process by which he managed this class, his students quickly learned the core ideas of organizational theory at the time, and, perhaps more importantly, we were infused with his own passion for problem-oriented work and the relationship between field data and induced theory. His notion of theory as a "walking stick" for managers and our role in creating these tools has always stayed with me.

Paul became an invaluable member of my doctoral committee. He pushed me to use my dissertation's data on social networks and performance in R&D settings to build an overarching midrange theory. At the time, I found his theoretical pushing painful. It did, however, lead to my early work on information processing and social networks in R&D and to my work with David Nadler on the congruence model.

Paul was always there for me during my transition from a doctoral student at MIT to faculty member at Columbia. He actively helped me and David Nadler develop our core MBA course on organizations and our congruence model. When I moved to HBS in 1998, Paul was a trusted guide, mentor, and friend to me in this transition. In 1999, I was named the Paul R. Lawrence, Class of 1942 Professor. As I told Paul on numerous occasions, the professional achievement that I'm proudest of is to hold the professorship named in his honor.

Influences and Motivations: A Life of Research, Teaching, and Institution Building

As a teenager in Grand Rapids, Michigan, Lawrence's lifelong concern with social problems was influenced by his grandfather's Methodist faith (he was a Methodist minister), his parents' commitment to their children's higher education, and their active role in community affairs. Lawrence's interest in leadership, organizations, and change was sparked as a teenager when he observed labor-management conflict and the eventual unionization of the auto industry in Michigan. Lawrence was sympathetic to both workers and management. He developed a strong sense of doing useful work – work that would help employees as well as the firm. With this interest in leadership, organizational change, and communities, Lawrence enrolled in HBS's MBA program in 1942.

After his first year at HBS, Lawrence interrupted his graduate work to enlist in the Navy. He served in the South Pacific for 3 years where he had significant managerial responsibilities. Because of his ongoing interest in the sociology of organizations (stimulated by a course he had taken at Harvard with Pitirim Sorokin), Lawrence had books by Roethlisberger and Mayo sent to him in New Guinea! After his discharge from the Navy, Lawrence took a job working on an assembly line at Chevrolet Gear and Axle, an experience that directly exposed him to union-management relations and to the evolution of informal organizations in the workplace. He observed emergent social relations such that management could not take advantage of the workers.

Interested in pursuing doctoral studies in industrial sociology, Lawrence followed the advice of Burleigh Gardner at the University of Chicago to return to HBS to work with faculty in several disciplines who were interested in organizations, communities, and industrial relations. Lawrence finished his MBA and immediately entered the doctoral program at HBS, where he studied with Fritz Roethlisberger, Elton Mayo, and George Lombard, among others.

Following his interest in industrial conflict, Lawrence's dissertation was an analysis of intensive intergroup conflict among engineers, technicians, and production managers. He was interested in conflict dynamics and what top management needed to do to integrate these groups' divergent perspectives and interests. Lawrence earned his doctorate in commercial sciences in 1950 and immediately started work as an assistant professor at HBS. After Lawrence graduated, he was involved in the creation of a doctoral program in organizational behavior. Soon after, HBS created an organization behavior area composed of cross-disciplinary faculty interested in industrial relations and organizations. This faculty was perhaps the world's first OB department.

Lawrence remained at HBS in its organizational behavior unit until his retirement in 1991 and continued to be active as an emeritus faculty member until 2002. He continued writing until his death in 2011. During his more than 50 years on the HBS faculty, Lawrence was involved in teaching MBAs and executives. He was MBA course head, faculty chair of the Advanced Management Program and Owner/President Management executive programs, and was head of the OB unit twice. For more than 50 years, Lawrence played a pivotal role at HBS in the development of OB as a research domain and as a key element in its MBA and executive education curricula.

Particularly meaningful to Lawrence was his work with doctoral students. He taught his doctoral course in what became organization theory each year for over 30 years. He sponsored and mentored more than 60 doctoral students. Many of these students went on to be leaders in the field. To further the training and development of doctoral students, in 1983, Lawrence collaborated with Freed Bales (psychology) and Harrison White (sociology) to create a cross-disciplinary joint PhD program in organizational behavior. This program remains vital to this day.

Throughout his career, Lawrence retained his interest in solving real-world problems. This orientation was reflected in Harvard's doctoral program and in Lawrence's personal mentoring of doctoral students. He took seriously Lewin's emphasis on the importance of good theory and Roethlisberger's metaphor of theory as a managerial "walking stick." Lawrence was adamant with his students. If we could induce research-based models of work and organization design, these models could help managers make more informed and integrated decisions. Since OB was in a formative state in those years, Lawrence's theoretical work on organizations as complex social systems was induced from his own and his students' careful fieldwork.

To Lawrence, field research, case writing, and theory development were entirely synergistic. His fieldwork generated his cases that furthered his teaching and his emerging theory of organizations as social systems. His research and theory, in turn, shaped his subsequent fieldwork, case, and course development. Well before Stokes' (1997) work on the synergies between rigor and relevance, Lawrence demonstrated the power of the field informing research and research informing, in turn, subsequent field research.

Key Contributions and Insights: The Emergence of Contingency Theory and Beyond

Lawrence's first three books were devoted to understanding the leadership of organizational change in private firms (Flint Electric and a large supermarket chain) and in a large governmental organization (the Pentagon). These three studies focused on coordination and intergroup conflict associated with new products, programs, or services. Lawrence's early empirical work built on Bales' (1950) careful attention to interaction patterns. His conceptual work built on Homans' (1950) conclusion that social systems outcomes were driven by the interplay among interactions, activities, and sentiments. In his first book, *Administering Changes* (with Harriet Ronken, 1952), Lawrence and Ronken's field observations led to a systems approach to organizational change. They observed that organizational outcomes were not driven solely by external constraints but rather by the complex interactions among external influences, interaction patterns, self-concepts, and work activities.

These themes were then picked up in his second book, *Changing Organizational Behavior Patterns* (1958). In this study of decentralization processes in a large supermarket chain, Lawrence observed that organizational change resulted from the interdependent interactions among the firm's structure, roles, communication patterns, group sentiments, and individual predispositions. Lawrence also observed that organizational outcomes included not just task accomplishment but also self-maintenance and growth as well as social satisfactions. Group and organizational scholars later picked up these ideas on multiple organizational outcomes (e.g., Duncan 1976; Hackman and Morris 1975). Further, Lawrence's conceptualization of organizational change as an interaction among communication patterns, decision-making practices, rewards, structure, and individual predispositions was an early version of what became known as open systems theory (e.g., Katz and Kahn 1966).

Lawrence's earliest work on what was to become contingency theory was his next book *Industrial Jobs and the Worker: An Investigation of Responses to Task Attributes* (1965) coauthored with Arthur Turner. Lawrence and Turner explored the notion that work context or task requirements would influence individual outcomes (satisfaction, turnover, absenteeism). Through their field observations, Lawrence and

Turner first induced the importance and nature of task characteristics. They found that tasks could be described by work variety, autonomy, skill requirements, and individual responsibility. These observations were later picked up by the job design literature (e.g., Hackman and Oldham 1980). Rather than finding that enriched jobs were positively associated with individual outcomes such as job satisfaction, Lawrence and Turner found that the response to enlarged jobs was contingent on individual and cultural differences. Those individuals predisposed to autonomy and control thrived under job enlargement, while those not so predisposed did not.

In the context of administrative sciences at the time, most scholars sought to discover basic, universal principles of administration. In sharp contrast to this work, Lawrence and Turner discovered contingent relationships among task characteristics, individual predispositions, and outcomes. Lawrence then took this surprise observation that individual differences moderate the relations between task characteristics and individual outcomes to a higher level of analysis. Working with one of his doctoral students, Jay Lorsch, Lawrence explored whether this contingency between task characteristics and individual differences might extend to the organizational level of analysis.

Lawrence and Lorsch reasoned that task uncertainty and environmental complexity might be important organizational contingencies. To get at this hunch, they designed a comparative analysis of high- and low-performing organizations competing in low-uncertainty (container), medium-uncertainty (food), and high-uncertainty (plastics) task environments. Based on their field observations, halfway through this research, Lawrence and Lorsch decided to use level of differentiation and level of integration as their dependent variables.

Borrowing ideas from biology and from Eric Trist's work at the Tavistock Institute, Lawrence and Lorsch observed that high-performing firms in different contexts had fundamentally different designs and that these designs also differed from low-performing firms. They observed that the most effective organizational designs were contingent on task and environmental conditions.

Lawrence and Lorsch found that in high-performing firms, the level of differentiation was systematically related to the intensity of integration devices. Further, they found that high-performing firms in uncertain contexts had high levels of differentiation, while high-performing firms in low-uncertainty contexts had low levels of differentiation. Low-performing firms either had inappropriate levels of differentiation and/or did not match the level of integration with the level of differentiation.

Organization and Environment: Managing Differentiation and Integration (1967b) and Lawrence and Lorsch's associated ASQ (1967a) article transformed how scholars thought about organizational design and the role of leaders in making design decisions. It also shaped the evolving view of organizations as social and technical systems. Beyond systems ideas and task/environmental contingencies, their comparative methodology influenced generations of subsequent scholars.

Building on these contingency ideas, Lawrence went on to do more work on organization design and leading change in both the public and private sectors. He explored urban dynamics in *Mayors in Action* with John Kotter (1974), matrix designs in *Matrix* (1977) with Stanley Davis, and the difficulties of managing academic medical centers with Marvin Weisbord and Martin Charns (JABS 1978). The research by Lawrence, Weisbord, and Charns explored the performance consequences of highly differentiated systems lacking correspondingly intensive integration mechanisms. Lawrence's research after *Organization and Environment* extended his view of organizations as social and technical systems and demonstrated how organizational design is an outcome of complex social and political dynamics.

Continuing this theme of leadership and organization design at higher levels of analysis, Lawrence and Davis Dyer (an historian) initiated a multiyear comparative analysis of organizational adaptation and industrial competiveness across seven major US industries. This research took place in a period when American firms were lagging behind their Japanese counterparts. Lawrence and Dyer in *Renewing American Industry* (1983) observed that those firms that were able to renew themselves were both efficient and innovative. They observed that the nature of adaptation was contingent on the firm's levels of resource scarcity and information complexity. This book brought Lawrence's work to the public policy level of analysis even as it made links among economics, history, and organizational behavior.

Continuing this theme of fieldwork-inspired comparative analysis, Lawrence's last major book on organizational design, *Behind Factory Walls* (1990) (with Charalambos Vlachoutsicos), was a collaboration among American and Russian scholars. Like many of his prior studies, this research used a comparative method; it matched four US factories with four Soviet factories. The advent of glasnost (openness) and perestroika (restructuring) provided Lawrence and his colleagues with an opportunity to explore how Soviet firms would respond to fundamentally altered market conditions and to explore the challenges in joint venture relations between Russian and American firms.

This research was the first time non-Soviet scholars were permitted to do research in Russian firms. This research found systematic differences between American and Soviet approaches to leadership styles, decision-making, work/life boundaries, social networks, and organizational design. Knowing these systematic differences could, in turn, help inform joint venture relations between these countries.

Lawrence became an emeritus professor in 1991. He did not, however, slow down, although he did shift his energies and intellectual ambitions. He became even more passionate about OB's need to dig deeper into how and why individuals, firms, and communities worked the way they did. His intellectual curiosity and passion for these topics convinced him that the disparate fields of evolutionary biology, history, neuroscience, and anthropology held important keys to understanding leadership and organizational behavior.

Lawrence was concerned that rather than opening up, the field of OB was closing in on itself; that important research questions were being crowded out by narrow disciplinary or methodological constraints. His last decade was dedicated to the development of a new, unified theory of human behavior. Lawrence immersed himself in Darwin's writing, especially *The Descent of Man*. This led Lawrence to more recent work in the evolutionary, biological, and social sciences, including his Harvard University colleague E.O. Wilson's work. These explorations led to *Driven:*

How Human Nature Shapes our Choices (2002), coauthored with Nitin Nohria. Lawrence and Nohria suggested that four primary innate drives direct human behavior: the drives to acquire, to bond, to comprehend, and to defend. Lawrence and Nohria explained how these four drives are kept in balance and how they interact with culture, emotion, and skills in driving outcomes.

Well into his 80s, Lawrence published his last book. *Driven to Lead: Good, Bad, and Misguided Leadership* (2010) examined human behavior and leadership and developed what Lawrence called the "renewed Darwinian theory of human behavior." This book focused on the impulse/check/balance mechanisms in leaders not addressed in *Driven*. He argued that our moral sense, or conscience, is crucial to effective leadership and that all facets of leadership, from visionary to evil, are natural to the human condition. Lawrence believed that leadership is a trait that we can apply and improve upon as effectively as we do in medicine or technology.

In *Driven to Lead*, Lawrence returned to his earliest work on leadership and change. He reinforced the importance of developing more effective leaders and observed the catastrophic consequences of ineffective leaders and flawed decision-making for organizations, communities, and societies. Lawrence's last work takes full circle his interest in building ideas, concepts, and theory that help individuals, firms, and their communities. It was also a call for OB professionals to hold their work to high standards and a challenge to the community to never take their eyes off working on societies' most pressing leadership and organizational challenges.

Legacy and Unfinished Business: The Continued Evolution of Organizational Behavior

As I look at the scope of Lawrence's career, I am struck by his enthusiasm and passion for his work, his irrepressible and enduring curiosity, his institutional building at HBS, and his commitment to collaboration with doctoral students. Lawrence never veered from his focus on problems that were critically important to managers and the firms and communities within which they operated. These problems were defined by the real world, and all had aspects of conflict in the context of interdependence.

His research was always comparative and field based. Throughout his career, Lawrence and his students built their midrange theoretical concepts inductively from their fieldwork and from interacting with managers grappling with the organizational, social, and political challenges of innovation and change. His last decade's work focused on leadership and the leader's responsibility to the firm and the broader community.

His ideas continually unfolded from his early work at the individual level to subsequent work at the firm (both public and private), urban, community, and societal levels of analysis. Prior to his work on evolutionary biology, his work on leadership, organizations, and change was rooted in organizations as complex social and technical systems. Such open systems ideas, in turn, provided leaders with more and more sophisticated tools to diagnose and take informed action.

Lawrence's final two books, written after he retired, were different from his prior work. He broadened the sources of knowledge that served as his inspiration. Frustrated with the increasingly narrow state of the OB field, Lawrence immersed himself in the broad range of social and behavioral sciences to develop a grand theory of human behavior. His focus never left the central issues that defined his professional career – the role of individuals, leaders, and organizations in creating contexts that would serve both other individuals and the communities in which they lived.

Lawrence's prolific research stream was executed even as he devoted himself to developing the OB unit at HBS and HBS more generally. He was an accomplished institutional builder. Extending his training under Roethlisberger, Homans, and Mayo, Lawrence built an OB unit that was interdisciplinary in nature. In a profession that became more and more based in narrow academic disciplines, Lawrence helped keep Harvard's OB unit broadly interdisciplinary. He took this interdisciplinary passion and helped co-create the joint OB doctoral program with faculty from psychology and sociology. His focus was always on the phenomena of organizations that were inherently understandable through interdisciplinary field-based research and teaching (Aisner 2011).

Lawrence was also an accomplished teacher and pedagogical innovator. He helped build innovative MBA and executive education courses and curriculum. His teaching was always case based and participant centered, even as he infused his courses with those "walking sticks" developed from his field research. His case fieldwork was a source of these theoretical insights. While Lawrence did a limited amount of consulting, he felt that consulting work was not an important source of ideas for him. As such, he limited his external consulting in order to focus on fieldwork associated with his research, case, and course development activities (see Lawrence and Lawrence 1993).

But perhaps his greatest professional pleasure, a pleasure I saw firsthand, was the energy he derived from working with and mentoring his doctoral students. These students helped Lawrence continue to deliver on his aspiration to do work that was both rigorous and relevant. These legions of students helped Lawrence induce conceptual models of leadership and organizations that helped managers solve complex organizational problems across sectors and countries. Lawrence trained his students to do work that was rigorous and relevant. He was a role model for doctoral students aspiring to do research that mattered, build institutions that mattered, and teach in a way that respected participant-centered learning that emerged from working on problems of practice.

There is much unfinished business for scholars interested in leadership, organizations, and change. These topics are more important than ever. While we know much about organizations in their environment, more work remains. Indeed, it is not at all clear that theory and research born in the industrial Chandlerian tradition will have traction in our post-Chandlerian web and community-dominated contexts. The very nature of organizational design and leadership may be different in this post-Chandlerian world (e.g., Gulati et al. 2012; Lakhani et al. 2013).

Important work remains to retool systems ideas such that they take into account more complex contexts, more complex interdependencies, and more complex institutional environments. Leadership and organizations in the twenty-first century may well be fundamentally different from leadership and organizations in the twentieth century. If so, Lawrence's passion for field-based research and learning from the phenomenon itself could not be more important (e.g., Benner and Tushman 2015).

Conclusion

Paul R. Lawrence's legacy reminds us to set our professional aspirations high. The topics he spent a lifetime grappling with, organizational and community design, leadership, and change in the public and private spheres, remain vitally important. While we know much about these topics, we do not understand how open and distributed logics affect these areas. If so, Lawrence's legacy of rigor and relevance must be carried forward by scholars who are not afraid of grappling with important real-world problems. We must not shy away from research that spans levels of analysis and different disciplinary traditions. Finally, Lawrence's legacy can only be carried forward in OB departments and OB doctoral programs that recognize the power of research that is informed by practice and the two-way street between rigor and relevance.

References

Aisner, James. Harvard Business School News Release, 2011. Boston.

Bales, R. F. (1950). *Interaction process analysis: A method for the study of small groups*. Cambridge, MA: Addison-Wesley Press.

Benner, M., & Tushman, M. (2015). Reflections on the 2013 decade award: "Exploitation, exploration, and process management: The productivity dilemma revisited" ten years later (with Mary Benner). *Academy of Management Review, 40*(4), 497–514.

Davis, S. M., & Lawrence, P. R. (1977). *Matrix*. Reading: Addison-Wesley Publications.

Duncan, R. (1976). The ambidextrous organization: Designing dual structures for innovation. In R. Kilman & L. Pondy (Eds.), *The management of organizational design*. New York: North Holland.

Gulati, R., Puranam, P., & Tushman, M. (2012). Meta-organization design: Rethinking design in interorganizational and community contexts. *Strategic Management Journal, 33*(6), 571–586.

Hackman, R., & Morris, C. G. (1975). Group tasks, group interaction process, and group performance strategies in determining group effectiveness. In L. Berkowitz (Ed.), *Advances in experimental social psychology*. New York: Academic.

Hackman, J. R., & Oldham, G. R. (1980). *Work redesign*. Reading: Addison-Wesley.

Homans, G. C. (1950). *The human group*. New York: Harcourt.

Katz, D., & Kahn, R. L. (1966). *The Social Psychology of Organizations*. New York: Wiley.

Kotter, J. P., & Lawrence, P. R. (1974). *Mayors in action: Five approaches to urban governance*. New York: Wiley.

Lakhani, K. R., Lifshitz-Assaf, H., & Tushman, M. L. (2013). Open innovation and organizational boundaries: Task decomposition, knowledge distribution and the locus of innovation. In A. Grandori (Ed.), *Handbook of economic organization integrating economic and organization theory* (pp. 355–382). Northampton: Edward Elgar Publishing.

Lawrence, P. R. (2010). *Driven to lead: Good, bad, and misguided leadership* (1st ed.). Jossey-Bass: San Francisco.

Lawrence, P. R., & Doriot, G. F. (1958). *The changing of organizational behavior patterns; A case study of decentralization*. Boston: Harvard University Graduate School of Business Administration Division of Research.

Lawrence, P. R., & Dyer, D. (1983). *Renewing American industry*. New York: Free Press.

Lawrence, P. R., & Lawrence, A. T. (1993). Doing problem-oriented research: A daughter's interview. In A. Bedeian (Ed.), *Management laureates: A collection of autobiographical essays* (pp. 113–148). Greenwich: JAI Press.

Lawrence, P. R., & Lorsch, J. W. (1967a). Differentiation and integration in complex organizations. *Administrative Science Quarterly, 12*(1), 1–47.

Lawrence, P. R., & Lorsch, J. W. (1967b). *Organization and environment: Managing differentiation and integration*. Boston: Harvard Business School Press.

Lawrence, P. R., & Nohria, N. (2002). *Driven: How human nature shapes our choices* (1st ed.). San Francisco: Jossey-Bass.

Lawrence, P. R., & Vlachoutsicos, C. A. (1990). *Behind the factory walls: Decision making in soviet and US enterprises* (US ed.). Boston: Harvard Business School Press.

Ronken, H. O., & Lawrence, P. R. (1952). *Administering changes: A case study of human relations in a factory*. Boston: Harvard University Division of Research Graduate School of Business Administration.

Stokes, D. E. (1997). *Pasteur's quadrant: Basic science and technological innovation*. Washington, DC: Brookings Institution Press.

Turner, A. N., & Lawrence, P. R. (1965). *Industrial jobs and the worker: An investigation of response to task attributes*. Boston: Harvard University Division of Research Graduate School of Business Administration.

Weisbord, M. R., Lawrence, P. R., & Charns, M. P. (1978). Three dilemmas of academic medical centers. *The Journal of Applied Behavioral Science, 14*(3), 284–304.

Further Reading

Battilana, J., & Lee, M. (2014). Advancing research on hybrid organizing. *The Academy of Management Annals, 8*, 397–441.

Burgelman, R., McKinney, W., & Meza. (2016). *Becoming Hewlett Packard: Why strategic leadership matters*. New York: Oxford University Press.

Henderson, R., Gulati, R., & Tushman, M. (2015). *Leading sustainable change*. New York: Oxford University Press.

O'Reilly, C., & Tushman, M. (2016). *Lead and disrupt*. Stanford: Stanford University Press.

Thornton, P., Ocasio, W., & Lounsbury, M. (2012). *The institutional logics perspective*. New York: Oxford University Press.

Kurt Lewin (1890–1947): The Practical Theorist

46

Bernard Burnes

Abstract

Few social scientists can have received the level of praise and admiration that has been heaped upon Kurt Lewin. Edward Tolman, one of the most distinguished psychologists of his day, put his contribution to psychology on a par with that of Sigmund Freud (Tolman, Psychological Review 55:1–4, 1948). The distinguished scholar Edgar Schein (Organizational psychology, 3rd edn. Prentice Hall, Englewood Cliffs, p 239, 1988) called Lewin "the intellectual father of contemporary theories of applied behavioural science." Recently, the Nobel Prize winner Daniel Kahneman (Foreword. E Shafir: The behavioral foundations of public policy. Princeton University Press, Princeton, p viii, 2013) declared that "We are all Lewinians now." Tributes such as these, from such distinguished figures, show that Lewin made an outstanding and enduring contribution to the field of psychology. He is now best known for his work in the field of organizational change, but, as this chapter will show, he had a wider agenda aimed at resolving social conflict. Among the main factors that influenced and motivated his work were his application of Gestalt psychology to child psychology and the impact of the anti-Semitism he encountered growing up and working in Germany. On moving to the USA, he gravitated from studying child psychology in the laboratory to bringing about social and organizational change in the real world. His key contributions were the creation of planned change, his work on participative management, and countering religious and racial discrimination. He was also responsible for establishing important institutions, such as the National Training Laboratories and the Research Center for Group Dynamics. Lewin's lasting legacy consists not just of his groundbreaking scholarly work but also of his example as a "practical theorist" who wanted to make the world a better place.

B. Burnes (✉)
Stirling Management School, University of Stirling, Stirling, Scotland, UK
e-mail: bernard.burnes@stir.ac.uk

D.B. Szabla et al. (eds.), *The Palgrave Handbook of Organizational Change Thinkers*,
DOI 10.1007/978-3-319-52878-6_13

Keywords
Kurt Lewin • Gestalt psychology • Field theory • Democratic participation • Resolving conflict • Planned change

Contents

Introduction

Lewin was born in Mogilno, then in Western Prussia, where he received an Orthodox Jewish education. He completed a doctoral degree in philosophy and psychology at Berlin University in 1914 on the topic of "The Psychic Activity: On Interrupting the Process of the Will and the Fundamental Laws of Association'. After serving in the military during World War I, he was appointed as a researcher at the Psychological Institute of Berlin University and then, from 1926 to 1933, served there as a professor of philosophy and psychology. With the rise of Nazism, Lewin realized that the position of Jews in Germany was becoming untenable, and he moved to the USA. He was first employed as a "refugee scholar" at Cornell University. Then, from 1935 to 1945, he worked at the University of Iowa's Child Welfare Research Station. Lewin died of a heart attack in 1947 at the age of 56 just after he had established both the Research Center for Group Dynamics (RCGD) at the Massachusetts Institute of Technology and the Commission on Community Interrelations (CCI) and laid the foundations of what was to become the National Training Laboratory (NTL).

I initially encountered Lewin's work sometime in the 1980s. The first time I had to examine his work in-depth was when I was preparing the first edition of my book *Managing Change* (Burnes 1992). It was obvious to me that a serious examination of the change field could not be undertaken without reviewing Lewin's contribution. However, the 1980s and 1990s were not good years for studying Lewin. This was a period when the received wisdom was that organizations, if they were to survive, needed to change in a rapid, large-scale, and continuous fashion. In such a context, Lewin's small-group, slow, participative, and ethical approach to change was seen as outmoded or even just plain wrong in the first place. This view was perhaps most trenchantly summed up by Kanter et al. (1992, p. 10), who referred to his change model as a "quaintly linear and static conception" which was "wildly inappropriate." It was also a period when it was very difficult to obtain Lewin's publications or even identify the extent of his published work. The Internet was in its infancy; there were no effective search engines and little academic material available in digital format, especially if that material had been published some 50 or 60 years earlier. It took me over a decade of collecting, reading, and rereading Lewin's work in order to gain a good understanding of the breath, depth, and profundity of his research. In the process, I was able to address and refute many of the criticisms levelled against him. Even now, after nearly three decades of studying Lewin, I am still finding new material and gaining new insights.

I have come to realize that there are three factors that one needs to take into account when studying Lewin. Firstly, for most of his life, Lewin's research focused on child psychology rather than social or organizational change, and it is difficult to appreciate the basis and rationale for his later work on change unless one understands his work on child psychology. Secondly, though Lewin's pioneering work on social, organizational, and behavioral change was only undertaken in the last 9 years of his life, it comprises an enormous number and variety of studies. As Table 1 shows, between 1938 and 1947, Lewin carried out an ambitious program of research which covered topics which went far beyond child psychology, including conflict in marriage, styles of leadership, worker motivation and performance, conflict in industry, group problem solving, communication and attitude change, anti-Semitism, antiracism, discrimination and prejudice, integration segregation, peace, war, and poverty. Table 1 does not encompass the full range of Lewin's work at this time. The records of his work are scattered across numerous articles published by Lewin and his collaborators, notably Alex Bavalas, John R P French, and especially his friend and biographer Alfred Marrow. Much unpublished material can also be found in the Lewin, Marrow, and French archives, which are located in the Cummings Center for the History of Psychology at the University of Akron. However, a great deal of Lewin's research was never published, such as his secret work for the US war effort, or was published in the names of his collaborators and students. For example, one of the earliest and most cited articles on resistance to change, Coch and French (1948), was based on research directed by Lewin and based on his methods and theories. It would have been just as accurate, if not more so, for it to have been attributed to Lewin, Coch, and French. Lastly, at the time of his death, his work on change was very much a work in progress. Indeed, some elements, such as his three-step model of change, were barely covered in his writings.

Therefore, in order to understand Lewin's work, the reader needs to piece it together for themselves rather having it presented as a whole by Lewin. Even Marrow's 1969 biography, *The Practical Theorist: The Life and Work of Kurt Lewin*, is a somewhat sketchy and partial account. Despite its title, as Marrow (1969: x) comments in its *Preface*, it does not attempt to provide a "complete summation and appraisal" of Lewin's life and work, but instead is based on reminiscences supplied by a number of Lewin's colleagues some 20 years after his death.

In writing this chapter, it has not been possible to draw on a rounded and agreed picture of Lewin's life and work. Instead, it is based on my own attempts to understand the nature of Lewin's work and how it was developed. The chapter begins by identifying the main influences on, and motivations for, his work. This section also shows how the focus of his work moved from studying child psychology in the laboratory to bringing about social and organizational change in the real world. The next section reviews his key contributions to the field of change and especially his contribution to the creation of organization development (OD). This is followed

Table 1 Kurt Lewin – key projects and events 1939–1947 (Adapted from Burnes 2007)

Date	Study/event	Location	Focus	Concepts
1938/1939	Autocracy-democracy	Iowa	The effects of different leadership styles on children's behavior	Participation and group decision-making
1939	Employee turnover	Harwood	Employee retention	Changing supervisory behavior
1940/1941	Group decision-making	Harwood	Democratic participation and productivity	Participation and group decision-making
1941?	Training in democratic leadership	Iowa	Improving leadership behaviors and techniques	Sensitivity training
1942	Food habits	Iowa	Changing the food-buying habits of housewives	Participation and group decision-making
1942	Self-management	Harwood	Increasing workers' control over the pace of work	Group decision-making
1944/1945	Leadership training	Harwood	Improving the interpersonal skills and effectiveness of supervisors	Role play
1944/1945	Commission on Community Interrelations (CCI)	New York	The problems and conflicts of group and community life	Action research
1945	Research Center for Group Dynamics	MIT	Understanding and changing group behavior	Action research
1946	Changing stereotypes	Harwood	Changing attitudes to older workers	Information gathering, discussion, and reflection
1946	Connecticut State Inter-Racial Commission	New Britain, Connecticut	Leadership training	Sensitivity training/role play
1947	National Training Laboratory	Bethel, Maine	Leadership training	T-groups (sensitivity training/role play)
1947	Overcoming resistance to change	Harwood	The impact of different approaches to change on productivity	Participative change/force field analysis

by a discussion of the new insights Lewin's work provided into the nature of social and organizational change. The last section of the chapter examines his enduring legacy and especially the example he set as a "practical theorist" who worked to change the world for the better.

Influence and Motivations: From Gestalt Psychology to Democratic Participation

At the Psychological Institute of Berlin University, Lewin's field of study was child psychology, an area in which he published many groundbreaking papers and where, in the 1920s and 1930s, he achieved worldwide distinction (Lindzey 1952). However, in the late 1930s, after his move to the USA, he began to change direction and use his theoretical insights to develop practical approaches to social and organizational change. He is now best known as the originator of planned change, which comprises field theory, group dynamics, action research, and the three-step model of change. In developing planned change, Lewin was influenced by four main factors.

Firstly, Gestalt psychology: At the Berlin Psychological Institute, Lewin worked with and was influenced by two of the founders of Gestalt psychology, Max Wertheimer and Wolfgang Köhler. It was the holistic nature of Gestaltism which attracted Lewin. For psychologists, a Gestalt is a perceptual pattern or configuration which is the construct of the individual mind. It is a coherent whole which has specific properties that can neither be derived from the individual elements nor be considered merely as the sum of them. Through his work with Wertheimer and Köhler, Lewin came to appreciate that the piecemeal analysis of individual stimuli and actions could not give a true or accurate picture of the reasons why a person or group behaved as they did. Instead, he felt that Gestalt psychology, by seeking to understand the totality of a person's situation, seemed much nearer to the way in which an individual actually experienced life. As such, it provided the theoretical understanding that allowed Lewin to construct much of his later work, especially field theory or topological psychology as he also referred to it.

Secondly, mathematics and physics: In developing field theory, Lewin was strongly influenced by the work of mathematicians and physicists. He argued that to be seen as a rigorous, scientific discipline, psychology had to represent behavior in mathematical terms. Lewin argued that mathematics allowed psychologists to develop an effective means of theory building, because it enabled the meaning of any concept to be derived from its relationship to other concepts, which he referred to as the "constructive method" (Lewin 1942). Like other Gestaltians, Lewin was attracted by the parallels between the psychological concept of perceptual fields and the work that physicists were doing on field theory (Köhler 1967). However, in the pursuit of scientific rigor, he sought to take this parallel further than other Gestaltians by attempting to base his field theory on the same process of "mathematization" as in the physical sciences (Lewin 1949). In this, he was strongly drawn to the writings of the philosopher Ernst Cassirer, who tried to establish physics as the "paradigm science" (Danziger 2000). In particular, Lewin (1949, p. 35) saw Cassirer's development of a "mathematical constructive procedure" as a way of determining the relationship between general psychological laws and individual behavior, which he saw as central to applying the constructive method to psychology.

Thirdly, child psychology: Lewin's experimental studies of child psychology began at the University of Berlin and continued at the University of Iowa. Lewin's studies focused on child development, especially the forces motivating children's behavior at particular developmental stages. He observed that children developed at different rates and that some children might move from one stage to the next, but then regress back to the earlier stage. As Lewin (1941, p. 87) noted, "In psychology the term regression refers to a primitivation of behavior, a "going back" to a less mature state which the individual had already outgrown." Drawing on Gestalt psychology and applying his field theory, Lewin sought to determine a child's life space, i.e., identify the environmental forces shaping the child's behavior in terms of progression and regression, which was a major break from established thinking on child development.

Of particular concern to Lewin was the behavior of children in conflict situations. He used field theory to understand how the strength and nature of positive and negative forces in a child's life space generated conflict. In this respect, he drew particular attention to group membership, which he saw as playing a significant role in terms of a child's behavior and development. He also came to recognize that the style of group "leadership" also strongly influenced a child's behavior in terms of the degree of conflict (Lewin 1946). Lewin's work on child psychology, especially in the areas of regression and conflict, has clear links with the unfreezing, moving, and [re] freezing elements of his later three-step model of organizational change.

The last influence was his experience of anti-Semitism: For a Jew growing up and living in Germany, discrimination was a fact of life. Indeed, as he commented to Marrow (1969), not only was anti-Semitism something he experienced everyday of his life in Germany, but by the time he left Germany, his own children, as Jews, were not allowed to attend the university where he taught. In 1933, Lewin decided that the situation for Jews in Germany had deteriorated to such an extent that the lives of his family were no longer safe and they must leave. Even though Lewin and his wife and children got out of Germany, others of his family did not. His mother and other relatives died in the Holocaust.

Given how well Lewin was regarded as a child psychologist, it seems strange that he should leave that behind and instead devote himself to studying and bringing about social, organizational and behavioral change in the real world. The impetus for this move arose from two main motivators.

The first motivator was combating social conflict. With his experience of anti-Semitism in Germany, the rise of Hitler, and the killing of millions of Jews in the concentration camps, it is not surprising that Lewin, like many at that time, felt passionately about the need to resolve social conflict in all its forms (Cooke 1999). Though he rarely spoke of how he had been affected by the Holocaust, he once commented to Marrow (1967, p. 146), who had warned him about overworking, that:

> When you go to sleep each night, hearing the anguished screams of your mother as the brutal Nazis tortured her to death in a concentration camp, you can't think of 'taking it easy.'

Lewin's antipathy to discrimination and persecution was reinforced and broadened by the widespread religious and racial discrimination he found in the USA. This can be seen in his role as chief architect of the CCI, which he established in 1946.

Though it was founded and funded by the American Jewish Congress, its aim was the eradication of discrimination against all minority groups. As Lewin stated:

> We Jews will have to fight for ourselves and we will do so strongly and with good conscience. We also know that the fight of the Jews is part of the fight of all minorities for democratic equality of rights and opportunities... (quoted in Marrow 1969, p. 175).

The second main motivator was promoting democracy. For Lewin, the scourge of Nazism could only be eradicated if Germany's authoritarian and racist culture was replaced with one imbued with democratic values. Indeed, he believed that it would be impossible to prevent the worst extremes of social conflict in any country unless democratic values were spread throughout all the institutions of a society, whether they are public bodies or private enterprises. This is why, as the next section will show, the pursuit of "democratic equality of rights and opportunities" for all lies at the heart of Lewin's approach to change. As his wife Gertrude wrote in the *Preface* to a volume of his collected work published after his death, Lewin was ". . . filled with the urgent desire to use his theoretical insight for the building of a better world" (Lewin 1948: xv).

Key Contributions: The Emergence of Planned Change

Lewin was a prolific researcher, writer, activist, and networker, the range of whose activities are only touched on in Table 1. Though his contributions to shaping our understanding and practice of change were many, the four described in this section help to explain why Lewin's work had such an impact in his lifetime and why it has proved so enduring. The first two contributions arose from events in 1939 and were crucial in enabling him to turn his experimental and theoretical work on child psychology into a practical approach to bringing about social, organizational, and behavioral change in the real world. These events also allowed him to demonstrate his famous dictum that "there is nothing so practical as a good theory" (Lewin 1943/1944, p. 169). The two events were the publication of the Lewin et al. (1939) autocracy-democracy studies and the invitation from his close friend Marrow to carry out experiments in his family business, the Harwood Manufacturing Corporation.

The autocracy-democracy studies: These showed that children working in groups to achieve a common task behaved very differently depending on whether they worked under autocratic, democratic, or laissez-faire leadership (Lewin et al. 1939). Lewin et al. found that leaders who promoted democratic participation obtained far better results than autocratic or laissez-faire leaders. Consequently, if autocratic leaders or laissez-faire leaders wanted to improve the performance of their followers, they first had to reflect on and change their own behavior before attempting to change that of others. The implications of this research for Lewin's future work were threefold:

- It provided the theoretical basis on which Lewin built his participative-democratic approach to social and organizational change.
- It initiated the participative management movement which grew rapidly in the 1950s and 1960s.
- Its emphasis on the need for leaders to reflect on their own behavior led to the creation of T-groups through his leadership of the 1946 New Britain workshop and the creation of the NTL (Burnes 2007; Burnes and Cooke 2012; French 1982; Marrow 1969).

The Harwood studies: 1939 marked the formal beginning of Lewin's relationship with the Harwood Manufacturing Corporation, which lasted until his death in 1947 (Marrow 1969). Its CEO, Alfred Marrow, asked Lewin to assist the company in overcoming the twin problems of low productivity and high labor turnover, which it was experiencing at its new plant. In essence, Lewin was asked to apply his theoretical insights and experimental approach to resolving the practical problems of industry. As Marrow (1969, p. 145) observed, "... experimentation at Harwood had to be subordinate to practical factory needs," but between 1939 and 1947, Lewin carried out a wide range of interventions that eventually involved all of Harwood's managers and workers. The key experiments concerned group decision-making, self-management, leadership training, changing stereotypes, and overcoming resistance to change (Marrow 1969).

Harwood was the main test bed for the elements that would comprise up Lewin's planned approach to change, especially action research. As Marrow (1972, p. 90) stated:

> We agreed that the emphasis was to be on action, but action as a function of research. Each step taken was to be studied. Continuous evaluation of all steps would be made as they followed one another. The rule would be: No research without action, no action without research.

Lewin maintained that action research was an iterative, learning process whereby those involved had to be free to analyze their current situation, identify the appropriateness of their current behavior, consider alternatives, and choose what action to take. Therefore, for Lewin (1946), change was a learning process, but to bring about change successfully, there had to be "felt need." However, felt need only arises where individuals and groups feel they have a choice in whether to change or not, which emphasizes the importance of democratic participation to the change process (Carpenter 2013; Diamond 1992; Tversky and Kahneman 1981). It also shows the continuing influence of Gestalt psychology on Lewin's work, which stresses that change can be successfully achieved only by helping individuals to reflect on and gain new insights into the totality of their situation.

Though the Harwood studies in themselves were significant (Dent 2002), it is best to see them as part of an interrelated set of research projects and events covering similar issues and adopting a similar approach that spanned both industrial and social settings (see Table 1). From these studies, Lewin developed a democratic-humanist approach to resolving social conflict and demonstrated that it could be effective in both industry and society at large. A key element in this respect was Lewin's third main contribution to the development of our understanding of change – the New Britain workshop.

The New Britain workshop: In 1946, Lewin was asked by the Connecticut Interracial Commission to organize a training workshop to equip community leaders with the skills necessary to help black and Jewish Americans counter discrimination in housing, education, and jobs (Marrow 1967). Lewin saw this as an opportunity to put his democratic-humanist values into practice to help disadvantaged groups. The resultant workshop has become famous in the annals of behavioral science and can claim to be one of the foundation stones of the OD movement. What emerged from New Britain was both an approach to change – T-groups – and an organization for promoting that approach, the NTL. The creation of T-groups, where the T stands for training, has been described as one of the most important, and contentious, social inventions of the twentieth century (Burnes and Cooke 2012). In essence, the creation of T-groups was an extension of Lewin's autocracy-democracy studies, which showed that leaders often needed to reflect on and change their behavior before they can change other people's behavior. This can be seen in Burke's (2006, p. 15) observation that in T-groups:

> Participants receive feedback from one another regarding their behavior in the group and this becomes the learning source for personal insight and development. Participants also have the opportunity to learn more about group behavior and intergroup relationships.

Most of those who became leading figures in the OD movement were involved in the NTL and shared its zealot-like commitment to the promotion of T-groups, which created the conditions for the rapid expansion of OD in the 1960s. Though the dramatic growth of T-groups overshadowed other branches of OD, these were able to grow by virtue of their relationship to the T-group movement. Consequently, when the T-group bubble burst in the early 1970s, these other branches of OD, especially planned change, could fill the gap. Thus many of those involved in running T-groups transferred their efforts into providing other OD services to their clients, which ensured that OD continued to thrive and they continued to earn a living.

An inspirational figure: From the 1920s onward, Lewin was a leading international scholar with friends, collaborators, and admirers in countries as diverse as Japan, Russia, and the USA. As Marrow (1969: xi) noted, Lewin was a charismatic individual who:

> . . . kept exchanging ideas with all sorts of men on all sorts of occasions – fellow professionals, students in his own and other fields, colleagues both sympathetic and unpersuaded by his theoretical position, research subjects, casual acquaintances.

The fact that in the last year of his life he was involved in establishing and running bodies as diverse as the RCGD, the CCI, and the NTL is a testament to his restless energy, the breadth of his interests, and circle of coworkers – not forgetting, of course, that those activities were additional to his other work, such as the Harwood studies. At the time of his death, it would have been very easy for Lewin's work to collapse in on itself in the absence of the central figure around which it all revolved. That it did not, but instead grew, is a testament to the nature of Lewin's legacy and, more importantly, to the inspirational figure that was Kurt Lewin. To quote Marrow's (1969, p. 232) biography once again:

> Lewin left his mark on the thinking of a whole generation of social scientists. He put his stamp on a whole discipline, giving it a name (group dynamics), a scope (action research), and a purpose that transcended psychology itself by setting as its goal not only the study of man but the betterment of society.

New Insights: The Nature of Change

Though there are many areas where Lewin's work can be seen to be groundbreaking and still relevant, from my own perspective, I believe that Lewin's continuing influence can be attributed to three new insights he offered into the nature of social and organizational change.

Firstly, he showed that change can be viewed as a participative, learning process. This can be seen in his planned approach to change, which laid the foundations for how the field of change was to develop. His planned approach identified that successful change involves four elements: enabling those concerned to understand their current situation and behavior (field theory); assessing how they interact with each other (group dynamics); that change is an iterative, learning process of identifying, trying, and revisiting alternatives to the current situation (action research); and that successful change proceeds through three stages (unfreezing, moving, and (re) freezing). Above all, he showed that change could not be achieved unless those concerned could understand their current situation, evaluate alternatives, and choose the most appropriate. As Lewin maintained and subsequent research has confirmed, if people are enabled to learn about their current behavior and make choices over alternatives, their commitment to making the change work will be greatly enhanced (Burnes and Cooke 2013; Oreg et al. 2011). These are insights which are still highly relevant to social and organizational change today.

Secondly, Lewin made the case for a value-based, ethical approach to change and linked this to creating a better world. He argued that attempts to trick, manipulate, or coerce people to change were doomed to failure and would result in increased conflict and resentment. Instead, his approach to change was based on a set of radical values and utopian aspirations that sought to treat all people equally and fairly regardless of their race, religion, or social standing. This viewpoint underpinned his argument that only an approach to change based on democratic values, power equalization, and participation could achieve effective change. Even today, as we see civil strife, racism, and religious intolerance accompanied by autocratic and often unethical management of organizations, many may see such an approach as utopian. Yet, much research and many people's everyday experience show that it is this lack of democracy and the lack of respect for human beings that bring about conflict (Burnes et al. 2016; Marrow 1969; Mirvis 2006).

Thirdly, Lewin did not draw a distinction between the laboratory and the real world or between theory and practice. Instead, Lewin (1943/1944, p. 169) argued, in the words of his famous dictum referred to earlier, that "there is nothing so practical as a good theory," by which he meant that theories which cannot be turned into practical solutions to society's ills are not good theories. Similarly, practices that are not based on sound theories are not good practices. Indeed, it was this characteristic which gave Marrow (1969) the title for his biography of Lewin: *The Practical Theorist*. In recent years, there has been much debate about how to achieve rigor and relevance – how to develop robust theories on which to build effective practices (Gulati 2007). Lewin addressed these issues in the 1940s and showed that not only can rigor and relevance be aligned, but that effective change cannot be achieved unless they are aligned. In so doing, he ushered in the age of the scholar practitioner, arguing that academics had a duty not just to study the world but also to help create a better world.

Legacies and Unfinished Business: The Challenge of Change

In the 70 years since Lewin's death, sufficient time has elapsed to judge not only the originality and enduring relevance of his work but also how it has developed in the ensuing period. At the time of his death, Lewin's approach to change was still a work in progress. After his death, his friends and colleagues enthusiastically carried on his work, most notably through the institutions he established, i.e., the RCGD, the CCI, and the NTL. Chief among his friends and colleagues was Marrow, who became Lewin's foremost publicist and a key figure in the institutions he established, as well as continuing his work at Harwood. Other leading figures, such as Douglas McGregor and Herbert Shepard, working as change consultants at General Mills and Esso, respectively, developed their own Lewin-based approaches to OD while at the same time working closely with the NTL. Therefore, Lewin's work, though unfinished, did not fragment or stagnate after his death. Instead, it took a number of separate forms that were linked by the close personal and professional links of the people and institutions involved.

However, there was one important area where these paths did diverge. Lewin had never drawn a distinction between work and the wider society, between resolving industrial conflict and resolving social conflict. For example, in tackling racism, he was active in combating it both in society, by promoting integrated housing, and in the workplace, through getting shops to hire and integrate black sales staff (Lippitt 1949; Marrow 1969). In contrast, those who carried on his work and their successors tended to focus either on organizational change, such as the RCGD, or social change, such as the CCI. The only real exception was Marrow, who straddled both camps with his role as CEO of Harwood and Chairman of the New York City Commission on Intergroup Relations (French 1979). Therefore, uniting the social and organizational wings of Lewin's work constitutes a major area unfinished business.

In the organizational field, Lewin's work has experienced peaks and troughs since he died. In the 1980s and 1990s, his group-based, participative, slow approach to change was seen by many as unsuitable to the nature of modern organizations. In its place, many tried to argue for rapid, large-scale, imposed change. Also, the popularity of the power-politics perspective on organizations seemed to undermine much of Lewin's argument for a participative and ethical approach to change (Burnes 2004). In addition, many of Lewin's original coworkers retired or died; Marrow died in 1978. However, over the last decade or so, interest in Lewin seems to have experienced something of a reemergence, especially among those industrial-social psychologists who focus their work on social concerns and the greater good of society (Olson-Buchahan et al. 2013), hence Kahneman's (2013: vii) assertion that "We are all Lewinians now." It should also be pointed out that in some areas, such as social work and nursing, Lewin was never out of fashion. This is possibly because these are professions which have explicit ethical codes and standards, which align more closely with Lewin's ethical values than those of many business organizations over the last few decades. Nevertheless, it is clear that there is much work left to be done to develop and utilize Lewin's approach to change fully.

In examining his life and work, we can see that Lewin set an example for other scholars to follow. As a Jew growing up in Germany and losing his mother and other relatives in the Holocaust, Lewin was no stranger to hardship and tragedy in his own life. He also saw around him that he was not unique in this respect. He saw that social conflict was endemic in the world, but he did not believe that it was inevitable. He argued that conflict should be resolved and showed that it could be resolved. Lewin's work offered many new and radical insights into understanding and changing the behavior of individuals and groups. He bequeathed us theories, tools, and techniques for doing so that are still proving effective today. However, one of his greatest legacies was the example he set as a scholar who encountered a hostile and dysfunctional world and chose to use his scholarly knowledge to achieve practical change in the real world. In so doing, not only did he inspire his friends and colleagues to do likewise but he also threw down a challenge to future generations of academics to follow suit. Today, we see that the world faces many difficult and dangerous challenges. It is just not enough for us as scholars to try to understand the nature of these challenges: like Lewin, we also have to work with others to resolve them.

So we can see that much of Lewin's work was unfinished when he died and that there are areas that are unfinished today, especially the need to develop fully his planned approach to change and unite the social and organizational wings of his work. However, in terms of Lewin's wider social agenda – his desire to resolve social conflict – we should see this not so much as unfinished business, but as challenge that Lewin has laid down to all of us to continue his work.

References

Burke, W. W. (2006). Where did OD come from? In J. V. Gallos (Ed.), *Organization development: A Jossey-Bass reader* (pp. 13–38). San Francisco: Jossey-Bass.

Burnes, B. (1992). *Managing change*. London: Pitman.

Burnes, B. (2004). Kurt Lewin and the planned approach to change: A re-appraisal. *Journal of Management Studies, 41*(6), 977–1002.

Burnes, B. (2007). Kurt Lewin and the Harwood studies: The foundations of OD. *Journal of Applied Behavioral Science, 43*(2), 213–231.

Burnes, B., & Cooke, B. (2012). The past, present and future of organization development: Taking the long view. *Human Relations, 65*(11), 1395–1429.

Burnes, B., & Cooke, B. (2013). Kurt Lewin's field theory: A review and re-evaluation. *International Journal of Management Reviews, 15*, 408–425.

Burnes, B., Hughes, M., & By, R. T. (2016). Reimagining organisational change leadership. *Leadership* . doi:10.1177/1742715016662188.Published online 9 August 2016.

Carpenter, C. J. (2013). A meta-analysis of the effectiveness of the 'but you are free' compliance-gaining technique. *Communication Studies, 64*(1), 6–17.

Coch, L., & French Jr., J. R. P. (1948). Overcoming resistance to change. *Human Relations, 1*(4), 512–532.

Cooke, B. (1999). Writing the left out of management theory: The historiography of the management of change. *Organization, 6*(1), 81–105.

Danziger, K. (2000). Making social psychology experimental: A conceptual history, 1920–1970. *Journal of the History of the Behavioral Sciences, 36*, 329–347.

Dent, E. B. (2002). The messy history of OB&D: How three strands came to be seen as one rope. *Management Decision, 40*(3), 266–280.

Diamond, G. A. (1992). Field theory and rational choice: A Lewinian approach to modelling motivation. *Journal of Social Issues, 48*(2), 79–94.

French Jr., J. R. P. (1979). Obituary: Alfred J. Marrow (1905–1978). *American Psychologist, 34*, 1109–1110.

French, W. L. (1982). The emergence and early history of organization development: With reference to influences on and interaction among some of the key actors. *Group & Organization Studies, 7*(3), 261–278.

Gulati, R. (2007). Tent poles, tribalism, and boundary spanning: The rigor–relevance debate in management research. *Academy of Management Journal, 50*(4), 775–782.

Kahneman, D. (2013). Foreword. In E. Shafir (Ed.), *The behavioral foundations of public policy* (pp. vii–vix). Princeton: Princeton University Press.

Kanter, R. M., Stein, B. A., & Jick, T. D. (1992). *The challenge of organizational change*. New York: Free Press.

Köhler, W. (1967). Gestalt psychology. *Psychological Research, 31*(1), XVIII–XVXXX.

Lewin, K. (1941). Regression, retrogression, and development. In D. Cartwright (Ed.). (1952), *Field theory in social science: Selected theoretical papers by Kurt Lewin* (pp. 87–129). London: Social Science Paperbacks.

Lewin, K. (1942). Field theory and learning. In D. Cartwright (Ed.). (1952), *Field theory in social science: Selected theoretical papers by Kurt Lewin* (pp. 60–86). London: Social Science Paperbacks.

Lewin, K. (1943/1944). Problems of research in social psychology. In D. Cartwright (Ed.). (1952), *Field theory in social science* (pp. 155–169). London: Social Science Paperbacks.
Lewin, K. (1946). Action research and minority problems. In G. W. Lewin (Ed.). (1948), *Resolving social conflict* (pp. 201–230). London: Harper & Row.
Lewin, G. W. (1948). Preface. In G. W. Lewin (Ed.). (1948), *Resolving social conflict* (pp. xv–xviii). London: Harper & Row.
Lewin, K. (1949). Cassirer's philosophy of science and the social sciences. In M. Gold (Ed.). (1999), *The complete social scientist: A Kurt Lewin reader* (pp. 23–36). Washington, DC: American Psychological Association.
Lewin, K., Lippitt, R., & White, R. (1939). Patterns of aggressive behavior in experimentally created 'social climates'. *Journal of Social Psychology, 10*, 271–299.
Lippitt, R. (1949). *Training in community relations*. New York: Harper and Bros.
Lindzey, G. (1952). Review of Lewin's field theory in social science. *Journal of Abnormal Social Psychology, 47*, 132–133.
Marrow, A. J. (1967). Events leading to the establishment of the National Training Laboratories. *The Journal of Applied Behavioral Science, 3*, 144–150.
Marrow, A. J. (1969). *The practical theorist: The life and work of Kurt Lewin*. New York: Teachers College Press.
Marrow, A. J. (1972). The effects of participation on performance. In A. J. Marrow (Ed.), *The failure of success* (pp. 90–102). New York: Amacom.
Mirvis, P. H. (2006). Revolutions in OD: The new and the new, new things. In J. V. Gallos (Ed.), *Organization development: A Jossey-Bass reader* (pp. 39–88). San Francisco: Jossey-Bass.
Olson-Buchanan, J., Bryan, L. K., & Thompson, L. F. (Eds.). (2013). *Using industrial and organizational psychology for the greater good*. New York: Routledge.
Oreg, S., Vakola, M., & Armenakis, A. (2011). Change recipients' reactions to organiza-tional change: A 60-year review of quantitative studies. *Journal of Applied Behavioral Science, 47*(4), 461–524.
Schein, E. H. (1988). *Organizational psychology* (3rd ed.). Englewood Cliffs: Prentice Hall.
Tolman, E. (1948). Kurt Lewin (1890–1947). *Psychological Review, 55*, 1–4.
Tversky, A., & Kahneman, D. (1981). The framing of decisions and the psychology of choice. *Science, 211*(4481), 453–458.

Further Reading

With any writer, a good place to start is usually their own work. However, for those unfamiliar with Lewin's background and theories, I would suggest starting with Marrow's biography of Lewin:

Marrow, A. J. (1969). *The practical theorist: The life and work of Kurt Lewin*. New York: Teachers College Press.

Though this is out of print, it can be obtained through most libraries and can be bought from second-hand book sites such as Amazon, Abe Books, or Barnes & Noble.

I would then advise moving on to some of the critiques of his work, notably the special issue of the *Journal of Social Issues*, 48 (2) (The Heritage of Kurt Lewin: Theory, Research and Practice) published in 1992 To mark (belatedly) the 100th anniversary of Lewin's birth. The following articles should also prove useful:

Burnes, B. (2004). Kurt Lewin and the planned approach to change: A re-appraisal. *Journal of Management Studies, 41*(6), 977–1002.

Burnes, B. (2007). Kurt Lewin and the Harwood studies: The foundations of OD. *Journal of Applied Behavioral Science, 43*(2), 213–231.

Burnes, B. (2009). Reflections: Ethics and organisational change – time for a return to Lewinian values. *Journal of Change Management, 9*(4), 359–381.

In terms of Lewin's own work, there are three collections of his papers that provide a good coverage of his interests and contributions, as follows:

Gold, M. (Ed.). (1999). *The complete social scientist: A Kurt Lewin reader.* Washington, DC: American Psychological Association.

Cartwright, D. (Ed.). (1952). *Field theory in social science: Selected theoretical papers by Kurt Lewin.* London: Social Science Paperbacks.

Lewin, G. W. (Ed.). (1948). *Resolving social conflict: Selected papers on group dynamics by Kurt Lewin.* London: Harper & Row.

The collections edited by Dorwin Cartwright and Gertrud Lewin are out of print, but like the Marrow's biography of Lewin, they can be obtained through most libraries and bought from second-hand book sites.

One can also use Google Scholar or other search engines to identify those of Lewin's publications that are accessible in journals, though this is not necessarily as easy as one might imagine. However, the following articles are accessible and a good place to start:

Lewin, K. (1947). Frontiers in group dynamics. *Human Relations, 1*(1), 5–41.

Lewin, K. (1947). Frontiers in group dynamics II. *Human Relations, 1*(2), 143–153.

Lewin, K. (1946). Action research and minority problems. *Journal of Social Issues, 2*, 34–46.

Lewin, K., Lippitt, R., & White, R. (1939). Patterns of aggressive behavior in experimentally created 'social climates'. *Journal of Social Psychology, 10*, 271–299.

47 Ronald Lippitt: The Master of Planned Change

David B. Szabla

Abstract

Ron Lippitt, an innovator throughout his distinguished career, was one of the founders of group dynamics and the "T-group" (sensitivity group), a cofounder of the National Training Center for Group Dynamics at the Massachusetts Institute of Technology, and again later was a cofounder of the Center on the Research for the Utilization of Scientific Knowledge at the University of Michigan. A pioneer in the development of experimental social psychology, he is renowned for his classic work on the effects of democratic, autocratic and laissez faire leadership of small groups, and for his later work on planned change. Throughout his life, he demonstrated the power of controlled research in natural settings, creating scientific foundations for small group, organizational and societal change. His hundreds of writings span articles, chapters, and books that contribute his insights and methods to resolve organizational and social problems. He leaves behind a rich legacy for researchers, consultants, organizational and societal leaders, and students.

Keywords

Planned change • Group dynamics • Change agentry • NTL • Center for Group Dynamics • Center for Research on the Utilization of Scientific Knowledge

---

D.B. Szabla (✉)
College of Education and Human Development, Western Michigan University, Kalamazoo, MI, USA
e-mail: david.szabla@wmich.edu

D.B. Szabla et al. (eds.), *The Palgrave Handbook of Organizational Change Thinkers*,
DOI 10.1007/978-3-319-52878-6_15

Contents

Introduction

It was the mid-1970s through the early 1980s that many would gather as early as seven in the morning at a home on Cambridge Road in Ann Arbor, Michigan. Upon entering the house, which was set well back from the road, guests would jot down on a newsprint flipchart why they had come. Most came to gain insights into how to change their own lives or the lives of others. Nevertheless, everyone who joined the gathering had a specific problem on their minds they wanted to unravel. School heads came with long-range planning challenges. Preachers brought problems of declining church memberships. Consultants arrived saddled with client predicaments they couldn't solve on their own. Business managers brought employee motivation enigmas and meeting effectiveness complexities. Sometimes a neighbor, who was out of a job, would walk over in the hope of learning how to make a career change. Known around town as *The Lippitt Clusters*, these informal gatherings were hosted by an emeritus professor from the nearby University of Michigan, Ron Lippitt, a gentleman who had spent the greater part of his life pursuing his longtime goal: to help make individuals, groups, and organizations more effective through carefully structured change. Once everyone had settled into the living room for the morning, the master of planned change himself would facilitate a session during which guests would sit elbow to elbow and brainstorm each other's difficulties. Pairs or trios would be directed to the kitchen or porch or one of the upstairs bedrooms to develop change plans they would paper over the windows back in the living room for reactions from Ron. Feedback from Ron combined theoretical creativity and scientific rigor, and it was always warm and showed human concern for others. Around noon every guest would leave with a take-home plan of action for addressing the problem they brought to the session. Many who were there confirmed that, "Ron never let anyone leave his house without an action plan." It was here at these unofficial get-togethers of people tasked with change challenges that Ron Lippitt, the originator of preferred futuring, innovator of planned change, coinventor of the T-Group, and cofounder of the National Training Laboratories, would share his insights to help others reach their human potential.

Influences and Motivations: From Scout Master to Change Master

Ronald Lippit was born in Jackson, Minnesota on March 21, 1914. He was the eldest of three boys, one of whom, Gordon, he collaborated with later in life. His father was a superintendent, and his mother a hard-driving authority who expected top performance of her sons. Some say that it was his mother who instilled in him tall touchstones which he pursued relentlessly throughout his life. Whatever the causes, Ron developed an exhaustive work style and became in adulthood an introverted expert of human systems who continually surpassed his previous efforts.

Ron relished his boyhood experiences in the rolling hills of western Minnesota as a leader in scouts, athletics, fishing, and camping. A young man who enjoyed leading and participating in groups, Ron chose to attend Springfield College, a small college in Western Massachusetts that specialized in group leadership and was, at the time, a training center for YM-YWCA leaders. It was during his undergraduate education at Springfield College in Massachusetts that the foundation of his thought about changing human systems and reaching one's potential began to form. At Springfield, he studied group methods under the direction of L. K. Hall, the director of the Boys' Work Studies Program and a man who became a YMCA Hall of Famer in 1992. In weekly practicum meetings, Lippitt and his fellow students who were involved in fieldwork leading small groups of 10–12-year-old boys met to share their leadership experiences which were written up in logs. Hall provided rigorous feedback to students emphasizing insights about methods for improving the leadership of the groups. Hall frequently referenced the writings of John Dewey and Edward Lindaman discussing group methods as a means to an end, the implications of democracy in the forming of group goals, and the importance of the development of self-management and discipline as contrasted with coercive leadership direction and tactics. In addition to facilitating the learning of group techniques among his students, Hall also shared his philosophy of positive thought, often urging Lippitt and his students not to be disheartened by the way things are or the way things ought to be but to be enthusiastic and hopeful about making one step of progress from week to week. Lippitt's "images of potentiality," a concept he used later in his work as an organizational change consultant, was shaped early on by Hall, a man who cultivated the extraordinary potential that lied dormant in many of the young men he taught and counseled at Springfield.

During his junior year, Ron travelled to Switzerland and spent a year abroad on a Foreign Study Scholarship studying under Jean Piaget in the Rousseau Institute at the University of Geneva, from which he received a Certificat de Pedagogie in Child Development in 1935. Ron was the first male to teach in Piaget's experimental nursery school. It was here in Geneva that Ron was introduced to Piaget's research methods, which emphasized the observation of real-life events, and, which Ron subsequently practiced throughout his career. From Piaget, Ron also discovered that learning requires active experimentation and participation, another practice Ron exercised in his ensuing teaching and consulting. Ron believed that only by keeping students and clients actively thinking, analyzing, and practicing do people absorb and use new information.

Back at Springfield for his senior year and extremely motivated by Piaget's vision of applying scientific methods to group work, Ron was recruited by Harold Seashore, the new professor of psychology, to act as his assistant. Lippitt began teaching a number of Psychology courses and organizing a variety of experimental research projects ranging from managing a population of guinea pigs to organizing field observations of preschool children. Seashore and Lippitt were particularly interested in the influence of leadership style on preschool children's behavior. Their early investigations became the basis for later studies on the relationship between leadership and group performance that were widely cited in psychology and sociology manuscripts. While assisting Harold, Ron began to develop his research, counseling, and teaching skills – all of which would be of great value in the succeeding years of his life.

After receiving his Bachelor of Science from Springfield College, Ron enrolled at the University of Iowa (Seashore's alma mater) and began working on a master's degree in Child Development. Upon admission, he was awarded a research apprenticeship in the Child Welfare Research Studies. His first research project entailed coding protocols for an experiment on the frustration of preschool children under the direction of a professor who expressed his ideas in German-accented English, Kurt Lewin. Lewin had ingenious ideas about how to interpret data on the behavior of children, and Lippitt was soon immersed in new theory and research techniques. When each of the professors in the program shared topics, they would be interested supervising for master's projects, one curiosity mentioned by Lewin was group structure. Lippitt contacted Lewin and told him that, "Groups are my bag." Lewin responded in a genial manner with "Ja, ja, ja!" The two struck up a friendship that influenced Lewin to shift from child psychology to social psychology where he and Lippitt launched the subfield of group dynamics and generated several theories that explained organizational and social change. Later Lewin confessed that the paper was supposed to be a mathematical analysis of the group structure of numbers, or sets, used in statistical research. Before meeting Lippitt, Lewin had not thought of analyzing human groups. In his many interviews, Lippitt shares this story and ends it with a smile saying, "So you see, my paper really started group dynamics." Lippitt achieved his master's degree in 1938 and immediately pursued a Ph.D. in Social Psychology under the guidance of Kurt Lewin. Lippitt completed his dissertation, "An analysis of group reactions to three types of experimentally-created social climates," in 1940.

Upon receiving his Ph.D. in 1940, Lippitt taught as an assistant professor of psychology at Southern Illinois University from 1940 to 1941. In 1941, Charles Hendry, a respected leader in the field of social work, invited Lippitt to be the Director of Field Research for the National Boy Scouts Council where he conducted national studies on the impact of leadership styles on character development climates. Here, Lippitt began to merge his training as a professional group worker with his training as a social scientist conducting research on groups and, along with Hendry, cofounded the American Association for the Study of Group Work.

A critical project at the time compared successful and unsuccessful scout troops and involved a research team comprised of Fritz Redl, L. K. Hall, Kurt Lewin, Alvin Zander, and John French. Lippitt was heavily influenced by the planning and analysis sessions of the team, which integrated Lewinian theory, the psychoanalytic insights of Redl, and the creation of many new concepts and methods that emerged during the sessions. In fact, Lippitt played a role in the development of new approaches to data collection which combined systematic qualitative inquiry with quantitative observation methods.

With the onset of World War II, he became an officer in the Commissioned Corps of the Public Health Service, conducting group therapy sessions for the navy. Lippitt then directed the Far East Psychological Warfare Training School for the Office of Strategic Services, with a multidisciplinary staff including anthropologists Margaret Mead and Ruth Benedict, media, intelligence specialists, and Japanese and Chinese psychiatrists. From Mead and Benedict, Lippitt learned cross-cultural applied anthropology which became a new aspect of his skill repertoire as he prepared for the years after the war. When the war ended, Lippitt became director of training for the Federal Security Agency. There he coled with Leland Bradford organization change initiatives in federal agencies and hospitals.

In 1946, Lippitt reengaged with Kurt Lewin. Together, they designed the Research Center for Group Dynamics at MIT where Lippitt was an associate professor of social science from 1946 to 1948. The center focused on group productivity, communication, social perception, intergroup relations, group membership, leadership, and improving the functioning of groups. In 1947, Lippitt, Lewin, Leland Bradford, and Kenneth Benne cofounded the National Training Laboratories for Applied Behavioral Science (NTL) at Bethel, Maine, the first occurrence of laboratory training for organizational development. As one of the founders of NTL, Lippitt now had the opportunity to apply his vast knowledge of group dynamics to the creation of the T-group or sensitivity training, a form of training that helps people become more sensitive to others and more aware of their own prejudices.

Upon Lewin's untimely death in 1948, Lippitt moved the Research Center for Group Dynamics to the University of Michigan's Institute of Social Research. At Michigan, Lippitt acted as the Center's director and secured an associate professor faculty position of sociology and psychology becoming a full professor in 1952. In 1964, dissatisfied with the emphasis on pure research without concern for its utility, Lippitt founded, along with Floyd Mann, the Center for Research on the Utilization of Social Knowledge (CRUSK) as a part of the Institute of Social Research. This was a laboratory of planned change which became a training and consultation organization, drawing clients from the surrounding community.

In 1974, Lippitt retired as professor emeritus of psychology and sociology from the University of Michigan to help private and public sector systems use behavioral science to improve organizational effectiveness. In the following years, he founded and participated in several organizations that offered management and planned change consultation, including Human Resource Development Associates with Ken Cowing and Della Cowing, Hilltop Associates with Eva Schindler-Rainman,

Organization Renewal Incorporated (ORI) with his brother Gordon Lippitt, Planned Change Associates (PCA), and Xicom, Inc. In conjunction with these organizations, Lippitt conducted numerous workshops and training programs in the United States and abroad and, as described at the beginning of this chapter, led Lippitt Clusters at his home in Ann Arbor until he passed away on Tuesday, October 28, 1986, at the age of 72. He was survived by his wife, Peggy Lippitt; son Larry Lippitt; daughters Martha Lippitt, Carolyn McCarthy, and Connie Cohn; and nine grandchildren.

Key Contributions: Utilizing Research to Change Groups, Organizations, and Society

Lippitt's contributions to the discipline of social science and to the field of organizational change are many, adding significantly to both research and practice. Over his lifetime, he and his colleagues published over 200 articles and books on such topics as group dynamics, futuring, the processes of learning, socialization and the growth of children and youth, leadership, planned change and change agentry, community planning, and renewal and reconstruction of the traditional educational system and practices. Covering his many contributions is beyond the scope of this profile. Therefore, only his weighty advancements are reviewed – his contributions to the development of the field of group dynamics, his many advancements to the practice of planned change, and his efforts to mobilize the utilization of social science research in practical settings to effect change in groups, organizations, and society.

Group Dynamics

Lippitt, an innovator of experimental psychology, is renowned for participating in the development of the field of group dynamics. His many contributions to the field explored and defined both the psychological and social processes that occur among members of groups. From his early research studying children to his later investigations with adults, Lippitt discovered and exposed many of the dynamic processes that lead to effective group functioning.

From 1938 to 1943, Lippitt published several papers and studies that explored the effects of various leadership behaviors on group life (Adler et al. 1939; Lewin and Lippitt 1938; Lippitt 1939, 1940a, 1943; Lippitt and Zander 1943; Lippitt and White 1943). One of the more interesting studies on the topic and one of the most noteworthy in the history of the field of group dynamics is a 1939 study conducted by Lewin, Lippitt, and Ralph White, a fellow researcher of both Lewin and Lippitt that investigated the relationship between leadership style and social climates (Lewin et al. 1939). The three researchers organized what they referred to as G-Man clubs, groups of public school middle-class 11-year-old boys led by college leaders. The research was conducted at a boy's club, an organization Lippitt knew well. Three groups of five boys each were created. The boys were given a task to complete led by a leader with a different leadership style: laissez-faire, democratic, and autocratic. The laissez-faire leader stayed out of the way; the autocratic leader provided strict directions; and the democratic leader helped the boys using participative techniques. While the boys played indoors, a group of researchers observed them. In fact, Lewin filmed the experiment with a movie camera. What Lippitt and his colleagues learned was that a laissez-faire style led to confusion and cynicism, an autocratic style led to overly obedient boys who started bullying one another and destroying toys, and the democratic style led to a situation in which the boys discussed the project and made their own decisions. What was interesting was that when the different groups changed their leadership styles, the boys changed their behaviors to match the new dynamics. Boys with a democratic leader got on much better with one another and respected their leader. Slightly less work was completed under the democratic leader than the autocratic leader, and very little work was completed under the influence of the laissez-faire leader. This stud, and much of Lippitt's early work on group life are considered classic in the field of organizational change because they demonstrate the importance of leadership style in effecting organizational change. The years after this study and throughout his career were marked by many more studies and change initiatives centered on the country's youth. For example, Lippitt initiated research on delinquency with the Flint Michigan Youth Studies (Lippitt and Withey 1961; Lippitt 1962b), investigated the social structure of elementary classrooms in Michigan (Lippitt and Jenkins 1953; Lippitt and Gold 1958, 1961; Lippitt 1960, 1961; Lippitt et al. 1963), researched delinquent gangs in collaboration with the Chicago Boys Club (Lippitt and Withey 1961), and developed a national study on the impact of leadership styles on character development climates while Director of Research for National Council of Boy Scouts (White and Lippitt 1960).

Throughout the 1940s, Lippitt continued to explore group life and to contribute to the burgeoning field of group dynamics. His early research during this decade focused on the leadership and social climates of children (Lippitt 1940a, b, 1942; Lippitt and Zander 1943; Lippitt and White 1943), with much of the research attentive to studying the dynamics of scout troops. Toward the middle of the decade, he began to integrate the study of adult work groups (Lippitt and Bradford 1945a) and prejudice (Lippitt 1945; Lippitt and Weltfish 1945; Lippitt and Radke 1946) into his research agenda. By the end of the decade, his research and practice expanded to training in community relations culminating in a research exploration titled, *Training in Community Relations*. This book (Lippitt 1949), which Lippitt wrote while at the Center for Group Dynamics at the University of Michigan, presents effective ways of teaching individual and group skills required for affable and productive living in society. A significant and interesting contribution, the book explores the functional relationships among educational technology, action methodology, and research methodology in the solution of social problems pronounced with tension and conflict.

In the book, Lippitt presents a detailed account of an experiment conducted in Connecticut to develop new group skills among various leaders across the state. The leadership of the project consisted of a "state team" and a social science team.

The state team consisted of members of two public agencies, the State Interracial Commission and the State Department of Education's Citizenship Consultant Service. One private organization also comprised the state team – the National Conference of Christians and Jews. Members of the social science team were drawn from the Research Center for Group Dynamics and included in addition to Lippitt: Kurt Lewin, Leon Festinger, Morton Deustch, Murray Horvitz, Gordon Hearn, Benjamin Willerman, David Emery, Albert Pepitone, Jeanne Frankel, and Dorothy Swirling. The heart of the experiment was a 2-week workshop that engaged workers from Connecticut communities, each of which held a strategic relationship to some type of intergroup conflict. As examples, trainees included a leader from a politically active Negro association, a leader of a community Jewish group, and a leader from a high active veteran's organization. The social science team designed activities in which trainees would learn by studying themselves, using techniques such as role playing, which the goal of building new understandings of prejudice, attitude change, and resistance. Researchers observed the different training groups and reviewed interactions with the consultants each evening. One night three trainees asked to sit in on the debriefings. Lippitt recalled, "Sometime during the meeting an observer made some remarks about the behavior of one of the three." For a while there was quite an active dialogue between the researcher, the trainer, and the trainee about the interpretation of the event, with Lippitt and Lewin both active probers, obviously enjoying the different source of data that had to be coped with and integrated" (Marrow 1969, p. 212). On the next night, half of the group of trainees attended the debriefing which lasted well into the night. Bradford recalled a "tremendous electric charge as people reacted to data about their own behavior" (Marrow 1969, p. 212). At the time, no one understood the potential of feedback, but it was this experience that led to the establishment of the first National Training Laboratory (NTL) in Group Development (held at Gould Academy in Bethel, Maine in the summer of 1947) cofounded by Lippitt, Leland Bradford, and Kenneth Benne. By this time Lewin was dead, but his thinking and practice was very much a part of the development of NTL.

Based on their learnings during the Connecticut project, Lippitt, Benne, and Bradford designed and launched NTL. Their purpose was to convert scientific knowledge of human behavior into practice – they set out to help people to use available but relatively unused knowledge to gain skills to work effectively. Some of the goals developed by Lippitt and his colleagues were to help people become more competent in solving problems, more keenly aware of the potential for changing, more skillful in how to change, more aware of race and sex issues inherent in society at the time, and more resourceful in establishing conditions under which human energy, one's own and others, could be mobilized toward reaching individual and organizational objectives.

The T (Training)-Group is a training method. A group of 10–12 individuals meet to develop their individual learnings in a group setting. The T-Group's relaxed, yet energetic atmosphere, helps participants to expose their behavior to examination by themselves and to others. Through a feedback process, participants reflect on their behaviors in group interaction – they come to recognize how others see them and the effects they have others. The T-Group is a caring, personal, rigorous, and analytical methodology. Through the training learners become personally responsible for their own learning. The programs were educational in nature and not a substitute for psychotherapy. NTL saw its value in creating environments in which participants feel free to make choices in an atmosphere which promotes freedom, thought, concern, and support. Lippitt explained the T-Group and how it was designed in a book edited by Leland Bradford, Jack Gibb, and Kenneth Benne (1964) titled, *T-Group Theory and the Laboratory Method.* Much of the concepts, tools, and techniques were based on Lippitt's wealth of knowledge researching and working with groups since his days at Springfield College.

Planned Change

In addition to his contributions to the development of the field of group dynamics, Lippitt was also a forerunner in the creation of the theory and practice of planned change. If Lewin invented the notion of planned change, Lippitt industrialized it and then mastered it. He led the development of many contributions to the practice of planned change. Two significant contributions are discussed here: the process of planned change and the conception of change agentry.

The Process of Planned Change

In his 1958 book, *The Dynamics of Planned Change*, Lippitt, along with his colleagues Jeanne Watson and Bruce Westley, developed a seven-phase model of planned change that built upon Lewin's three phase model (unfreezing, moving, and freezing): (1) development of a need for change (unfreezing), (2) establishment of a change relationship, (3) diagnosis of the problem (moving), (4) establishing goals and intentions of action (moving), (5) initiation of change efforts (moving), (6) generalization and stabilization of change (freezing), and (7) achieving a terminal relationship. For each phase, Lippitt and his colleagues developed specific change methods. As an example, helping methods for phase II (establishment of a change relationship) requires that the capacity and motivation of the system to accept and use help is assessed, in addition to the resources and motivation of the change agent. Expectations must be clarified including the kind and amount of work required. A mutuality of expectation for the change relationship must be secured, and any anticipated difficulties which may emerge in the change relationship must be discussed. The influence relationship should be defined, and the goals of the change agent must be clarified. The many meticulous helping methods prescribed by Lippitt and his associates for each of the different phases recognize the importance and responsibility of the change agent to think diagnostically about the client's problem throughout the entire change process. Lippitt's seven-phase model of planned change became the foundation upon which many others would craft their own consulting archetypes and processes. Supporting its different phases were methods and practices that are still critical today to the leadership and management of change, for example, the importance of establishing the need for change, the significance of a strong relationship between the change agent and the client system, and the consequence of transforming intentions into actual change events.

In a subsequent book, *The Consulting Process in Action*, Lippitt and his brother, Gordon, presented a more practical rendition of the aforementioned model (Lippitt and Lippitt 1978). Instead of a seven-phase model, they simplified their model to include six phases. Similar to the change methods presented in the earlier model, for each of the six phases, Ron and Gordon stipulated the "work focus" to be carried out by consultants. For example, for phase II, *formulating a contract and establishing a helpful relationship*, they suggested that the consulting work focus on identifying desired outcomes, determining who should do what, and clarifying the time perspective and accountability. During the final phase, *completing the contract,* they recommended that the consulting work emphasize designing continuity supports and establishing termination plans. In addition to suggesting the work to be completed during each phase, Ron and Gordon developed a set of critical intervention questions for each phase. As examples, for phase III, *identifying problems through diagnostic analysis,* important intervention questions for consultants include: How can I help people in the client system to be open and to question their assumptions about the causes of their problems? How can I involve them enough in the diagnostic data collection process so they feel ownership of the data and accept the validity of these data? How can I arrange for people in the appropriate parts of the client system to review the data and draw conclusions for action? In *The Consulting Process in Action*, Lippitt's original consulting model is designed for practical use by consultants: subprocesses are integrated; change agent actions for each phase are stipulated; critical questions that need to be asked are posed; and the actions that need to occur to help ensure effective change are identified.

A review of the construction of recent consulting models and processes demonstrate the potency of Lippitt's early efforts. Consider Peter Block's *Flawless Consulting.* Block provides his own rendering of the consulting process along with an abundance of tools, techniques, and activities for leading change, many of which are grounded in the labor of Lippitt and his colleagues (Block 1978). An examination of Jeanne Neumann's consulting model (presented in a chapter in this book) includes many of the phases and processes of Lippitt's model, however, she presents a nonlinear, systemic consultancy model that captures the dynamic nature of the organizational change and development process.

Later in his life, Lippitt and his brother, Gordon, revisited their development work on consulting models and created a new process model titled, The Multocular Process (Lippitt and Lippitt 1985). Like their previous models, it included a series of traditional consulting components, some of which were analysis of the problem, analysis of possible solutions, and recommendations to the leader. Multocular means having several eyes. With their revised model, Ron and Gordon integrated planning groups (the Multocular Group) and assessment groups (the Multocular Panel) into the consulting process (See Figs. 1 and 2). At the initiation of a project, a group was formed to analyze the problem. Groups would be assembled from different disciplines, professions, and industries based on the crux of the problem. Once a problem

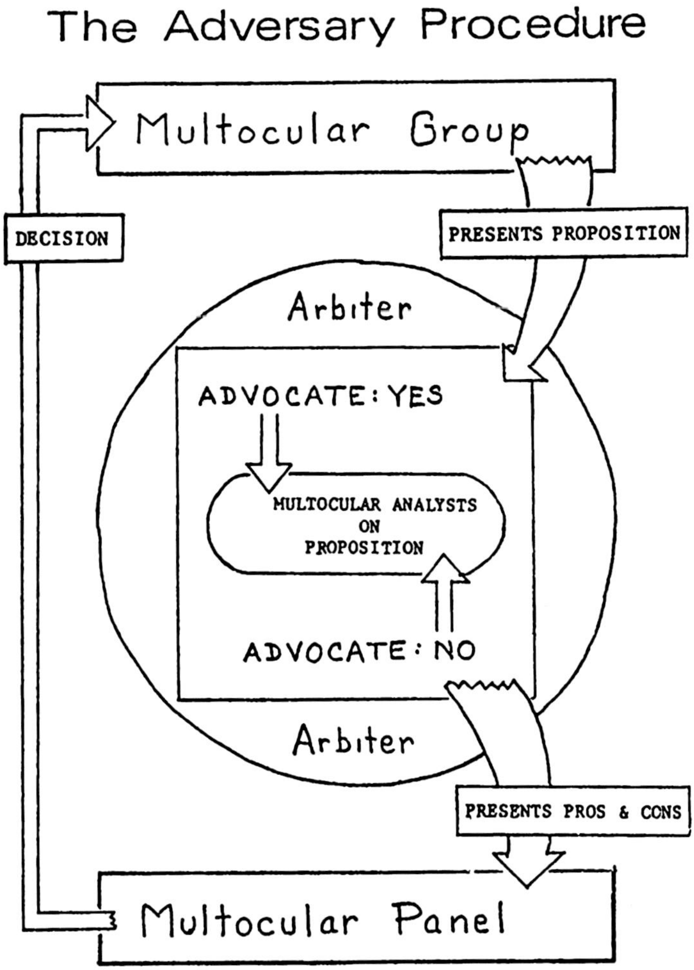

Fig. 1 With the Multocular Process carefully composed diverse groups of adversaries (i.e., the notion of many different eyes) are established to analyze propositions and make decisions

was analyzed, a proposition would be formed and analyzed, and the pros and cons would be presented to a Multocular Panel (also a diverse group) for evaluation and decision-making. Decisions made by the Multocular Panel would be evaluated by the Multocular Group. Solutions would be explored, recommendations would be presented to the leader, and action planning would begin. What was unique about the Multocular process was its emphasis on exploring the problem of the client. At the outset of a project, change agents would focus on getting the right people in the room to explore a problem and getting the right people in the room to analyze propositions. This weight given to problem-solving over planning and action was distinctive at the time, and many have been influenced by their own experiences working with varying

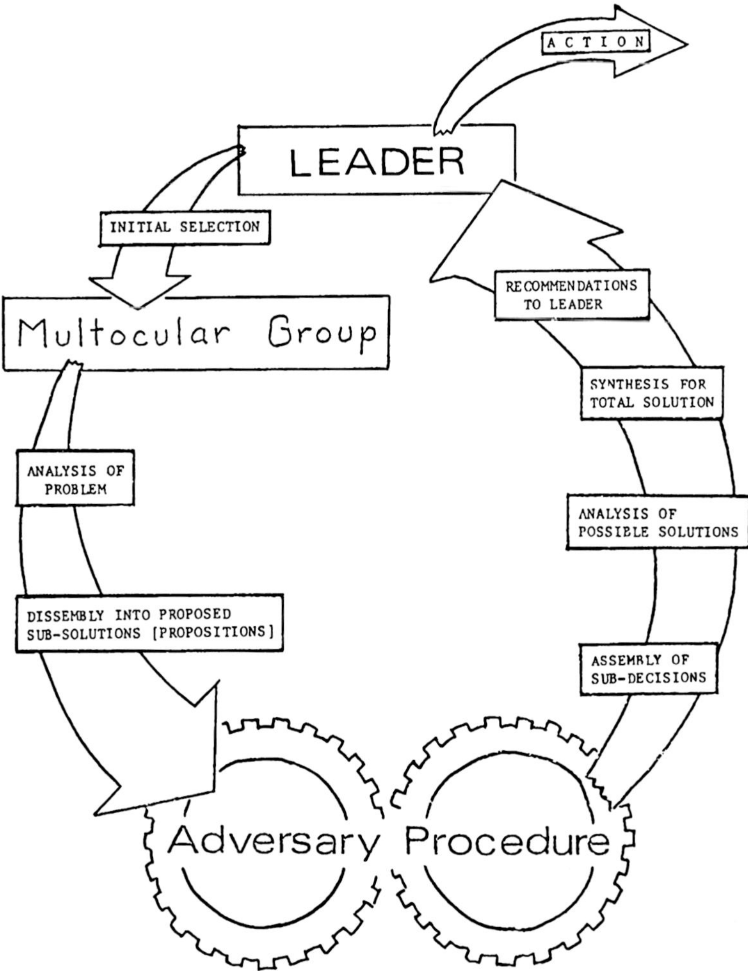

Fig. 2 As seen here, the Multocular Process follows an established consulting process of problem identification, analysis of possible solutions and recommendations to a leader. What's unique is that the model involves a wisely-selected group of people to analyze propositions and explore solutions

levels of diversity. Ron and Gordon started to write a book on the process, but because of Gordon's passing in 1985 and Ron's in 1986, the book was never completed.

The Role of the Change Agent

In addition to establishing a change model with which consultants could do their best work and upon which scholars and practitioners could enhance and strengthen, Lippitt and his colleagues also began to define and shape the role of the professional change agent. Lippitt conceived of change agents as professional helpers. He believed that their primary role was to give help and that it was up to the change agent to select the role he or she was going to play. Shall I mediate, counsel, teach, motivate, guide, or encourage? Each role emphasized helping the client, and the role change agents assumed would change based on the conditions of the system undergoing a change. A recent book relevant to this discussion is Schein's *Helping*. Like Lippitt, Schein, who is also profiled in this book, views helping as a logical extension of the consulting process, and like Lippitt, Schein defines consulting as helping and that means creating a relationship with a client in which they can both figure out what to do (Schein 2009).

In *The Dynamics of Planned Change*, Lippitt and his colleagues present a full discussion of the classification of helping roles based on their experiences as change agents consulting with organizations (Lippitt et al. 1958). Some of the main dimensions of the change agent's role include mediating and stimulating new connections, functioning as experts in matters of procedures, creating environments conducive to learning, giving emotional support during the process of change, and sometimes joining a subpart of the client system and providing strength from within. Lippitt expounded on these roles a year later in an article that explored the dimensions of a consultant's job (Lippitt 1959), providing seven self-reflective questions that actuated the role of the consultant. The different role dimensions established by Lippitt in the 1950s prevail in much of today's organizational change and development literature. In addition to performing these different roles, Lippitt believed that it was the responsibility of change agents to not only foster their own growth but to play a role in the development of the helping profession through research and conceptualization. He encouraged change agents to integrate research into their change initiatives by noting observations of the helping process and then writing and reporting on the significance of these observations.

Utilization of Research to Change Social Practice

Like many social scientists, Lippitt was frustrated by the fact that vital research on the books was gathering dust; it was not being utilized by the institutions for which it was intended. To tackle the issue, in 1964, Lippitt and a fellow researcher from the Institute for Social (ISR), Floyd Mann, started a separate unit with ISR the Center on Research for the Utilization of Scientific Knowledge (CRUSK). Staff teams of sociologists, psychologists, and others involved with social problems such as delinquency and teen pregnancy, a lack of creative teaching methods, and mental health and productivity problems or work groups in government and industry focused on the process through which scientific knowledge and personnel can help develop and validate significant improvements in education and social practice (Lippitt 1965). Along with Kenneth Benne and Ronald Havelock, their research centered on the internal conditions of the utilization unit needed if knowledge is to be utilized and the external conditions which facilitate or prevent new knowledge from reaching potential users. They modeled the social system needed to ensure a flow of knowledge to effective utilization (See Fig. 3). The model included four levels of analysis.

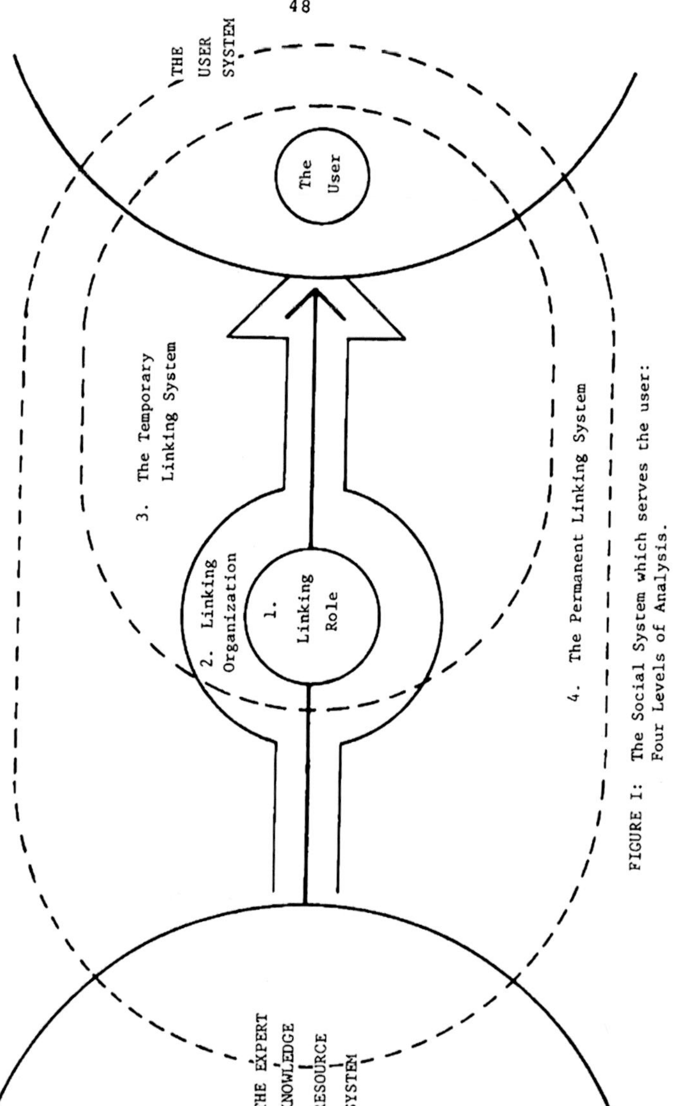

Fig. 3 Lippitt's utilization of scientific knowledge brings knowledge to users with individual roles, organizations and both temporary and permanent systems and processes

The first level, the linking role, is a defined position in the system that maintains a bridge between potential consumers and expert resources. The second level, the linking organization, is a specific group with a number of linking roles to effect knowledge utilization. The third level, temporary systems, supports situations in which a special group comes into existence to accomplish a specific task, such as a training seminar, and terminates when the action is complete. Finally, the permanent linking system comprises the entire range of activities, roles, and institutions involved in the transformation of knowledge into practice (Lippitt and Havelock 1968; Lippitt 1971). Lippitt and his colleagues emphasized the need to not only research these four levels but also to further develop and improve them (Jung and Lippitt 1966). Lippitt believed that only through research and development on "research utilization" could change in education, communities, and policy transpire (Lippitt 1965.)

New Insights: Images of Potentiality

In 1949, during his consultations with YMCA teams in Michigan, Lippitt and a small group of his students conducted a research project that involved tape recording strategic planning sessions. As the recordings were analyzed, students observed that as participants of the planning meetings identified, discussed, and prioritized problems, their voices became more soft and stressed. It was clear from the recordings that a focus on problems drained the energy of the group and depressed its members. A second finding identified by students was an increase in the frequency of statements about the causes of the problems to sources outside the control of the group. This was interpreted by the researchers as mobilizing a rationale for rejecting problem-solving responsibility. A third finding was an increase in frequency of words and phrases indicating feelings of impotence, futility, and frustration (Lippitt 1983).

These findings led Lippitt to experiment with what he called "images of potentiality" exercises. Lippitt and two of his colleagues at the time, Robert Fox and Eva Schindler-Rainman believed that, "The motivations and perspectives generated by getting away from pain are not likely to contain the creativity or to generate the energy that derives from aspirations generated by images of concrete feasible steps toward desirable goals. Images of potential are not only strong initial sources of direction and motivation, but they also provide the basis for continuous feedback, motivation, and renewal. The excitement and rationality of taking initiative toward the future must replace the anxiety associated with reactive coping with confrontation (Fox et al. 1973, p. 4)." Lippitt affirmed the validity of these arguments many times throughout his consulting years working with school boards, agency staffs, company staffs, families, and individuals.

His "images of potentiality" exercises encouraged participants to focus on the future and not problems. During one of his "images of potentiality" exercises, he would encourage participants to envision the future. "Let's say its 20 years into the future," he would say, "and you are flying over the region in a helicopter, what do you see down there?" He found that the more detailed the future descriptions of participants, the more energized they became. As participants clearly visualized the future, a variety of different perspectives emerged, and participants started to come up with solutions to problems (Lindaman and Lippitt 1979).

The discovery of the power of "images of potentiality" spawned the development of futuring as a change methodology. With assistance from Edward Lindaman, program planning director for the design and manufacture of the Apollo Space

Craft at Rockwell International and professor and futurist at Whitworth College, Lippitt began to conceptualize the method of preferred futuring. The methodology is rooted in planned change theory and democratic philosophy. It supports the argument that real answers lie both within us individually and the whole system. The method involves all stakeholders, embraces differences, mobilizes widespread support, and unleashes energy by connecting change with values, and results with core purpose. The practice requires the examination of data from the past, the present, and the events, trends, and developments going on in our world, community, organization, and personal lives. These data are used to envision images of the future preferred, a future not limited by presently perceived boundaries but one prompted by the realities of the present and emerging human situation. Based on the prioritized images of potentiality, an intentional goal-and-action plan is constructed which makes optimal use of the human and technical resources of an organization. In his early writings about the futuring process, Lippitt discussed a six-component process:

1. Creating a leadership nucleus (a group of key people who are listened to and able to get things done)
2. Designing for organization futuring (nucleus gathers date, i.e., where we have come from and what we are proud of, and trains persons to lead the futuring sessions)
3. Creating integrated scenarios of preferred futures (identify top priority images of the many images developed during future shop sessions)
4. Determine major goals and thrusts (small task teams convert images into goal statements with measurable criteria and achievement)
5. Operational goal setting and implementation designing (all staff develop involved in the futuring develop implementation designs)
6. Continuous progress measurement, scanning, and re-futuring (planning staff monitored goals, identify any new trends and generated new images of potential) (Lindaman and Lippitt 1979; Lippitt 1984)

As Lippitt and his colleagues worked with planning teams in both organizations and communities, they observed a distinction between futuring and planning. Some of the futuring versus planning distinctions they identified included right versus left brain, wide angle as opposed to zoom, open versus committed, rainbow in contrast to black, white and gray, inclusive versus selective, abstract versus concrete, and possible juxtaposed with feasible. These distinctions were used continuously to enhance their explanations of futuring to participants and to extend and strengthen its methods.

Lippitt and his colleagues conducted futuring projects in a variety of different settings, including 80 US and Canadian cities, several industrial projects, and numerous nonacademic agencies and businesses. These initiatives generated hundreds of "images of potentiality" and mobilized thousands of citizens and organizational members to envision the futures they wanted. The practice produced groups of enormous power and drive. Creating "images of potential" provided participants with a decisive direction for goal setting, planning, and skill development (Lippitt 1983). In 1998, Lippitt's son, Lawrence Lippitt, wrote *Preferred Futuring*, which provided consultants and managers with a step-by-step guide for creating and actualizing preferred futures. Additionally, we see the influence of Lippitt's "images of potentiality" and futuring practices in many redesign and transformation methods that are in use today, for example, the "dream" component of appreciative inquiry which asks participants to envision "What might be?" (Cooperrider et al. 2000) and the development of ideal future scenarios, a module of the Future Search process (Weisbord and Janoff 1995).

Legacies and Unfinished Business: To Better Human Life Through Social Science

The shy, imaginative, and people-wise social scientist, professor, and consultant leaves behind several lasting impressions. Dr. Ron Lippitt will be long remembered for his use of social science to better the lives of individuals, groups, organizations, and societies. There are many reasons why we remember a man who changed the lives of so many.

We remember Lippitt for his contributions to the field of group dynamics. He published numerous studies on the effects of authoritarian, democratic, and laissez-faire leadership on group process and productivity. His national study of the impact of leadership styles on character development climates while Director of Research for the National Council of Boy Scouts will be long remembered for laying the foundation for the study and advancement of the constructs of change leadership and organization climate.

We remember Lippitt for cofounding institutes that advanced the research and practice of organizational change. He cofounded the Center for Group Dynamics at MIT with Kurt Lewin, the NTL Institute for Applied Behavioral Science with Leland Bradford and Kenneth Benne, and the Center for Research on the Utilization of Knowledge with Rensis Likert and Floyd Mann. Through these collaborations, Lippitt brought together researchers, practitioners, educators, and students. He not only created new knowledge of how to change human systems but also developed models and processes to utilize the new understandings in practice.

We remember Lippitt for developing the systematic discipline of planned change. He originated models of planned change, developed the role of the change agent, formulated many methods for moving a group through the change process, and created toolkits of humane change agentry that comprised exercises such as the "prouds" and "sorries" brainstrorm, alternative scenarios, and internal dialog (Lippitt 1981). His continued interest in the professional development of applied behavioral scientists captured in *The Dynamics of Planned Change*, *The Consulting Process in Action*, and *Training for Community Relations* has left an enduring impression on the practice of organizational development and change.

As a side note, one of Lippitt's legacies is the invention of flip chart paper. As the story goes, flip chart paper originated during the Connecticut Workshops described earlier in this chapter. Kurt Lewin needed paper for his force-field diagrams, so Lippitt went out searching in the area. He passed a print shop and brought newsprint which was taped to the walls providing a living memory of the work of the group. The use of flip chart paper during planning meetings began and soon became a mainstay. Meeting rooms today are often a maze of paper-covered walls with arrows, diagrams, sentences, and scribbles that depict the envisioned futures and action items of planning groups.

We remember Lippitt for the numerous "images of potentiality" he helped to create to change communities across the country. The power of his futuring methodology was observed and validated by the extraordinary levels of citizen involvement his methods helped to activate and mobilize in numerous cities in the country. Throughout his career, his work showed a growing priority for the revitalization of community life and the development of interagency collaboration and management teamwork seen in such works as *Building the Collaborative Community* and *The Volunteer Community* with Eva Schindler-Rainman.

We remember Lippitt for his teaching of planned change. Lippitt leaves behind a three-semester laboratory practicum on planned change that he taught at the University of Michigan. The Planned Change Graduate Seminar was a fixture on the campus for over 15 years. It was grounded in his beliefs about learning and change that he developed throughout his years working with groups at Bethel and facilitating planned change in organizations and communities. Students designed their own personal and organizational change projects. As the leader of his classes, Lippitt created the same democratic atmospheres he observed in his early Boy's Clubs studies. He played the role of the chief organizer and empowered his students to choose books for the course, to develop and deliver mini lectures, to manage class sessions and projects, and to experiment with new approaches. It was one of the most popular courses at Michigan at the time and drew students and a large volunteer faculty from 15 departments and colleges.

Finally, we remember Lippitt for his active participation in several professional societies. Lippitt was a fellow in the International Association of Applied Social Scientists, the Society for the Psychological Study of Social Issues, the Association of Voluntary Action Scholars, the Clinical Sociology Association, and the American Psychological Association. In addition, he served on the editorial board of the Clinical Sociology Review. The many honors he received during his career include the Distinguished Career Award of the Clinical Sociology Association in 1985, a Concurrent Resolution of Tribute from the Michigan Legislature in 1984, and honorary doctorates from Springfield College, in 1962, and Leslie College, in 1965.

In conclusion, it can be safely said that today, Lippitt's many legacies exert a strong influence in all aspects of group living – from life in families to organizational life and life in communities. His years of experimental research and practiced-developed group work still touch many of the human systems in which he worked: the research labs and lecture halls of universities, the classrooms of school systems, the boardrooms of organizations, and the county seats of communities. Ronal Lippitt was a man of change. He studied it, practiced it, advanced it, and mastered it. Whether it was on a camping trip outside Springfield, in an NTL lab in Bethel, or at a cluster he hosted in his home in Ann Arbor, what energized him and urged his every action was his undying compulsion to help human systems realize their full potential.

References

Adler, D. C., Lippitt, R., & White, R. K. (1939). An experiment with young people under democratic, autocratic, and laissez-faire atmospheres. In *National Council of Social Work, Proceedings of the National Council of Social Work, Selected Papers, Sixty-Sixth Annual Conference*, Buffalo, June 18–24, 1939. New York: Columbia University Press, Vol. 66, pp. 152–299.

Bradford, L. P., Gibb, J. R., & Benne, K. D. (1964). *T-group theory and the laboratory method*. New York: Wiley.

Cooperrider, D., Sorenson, P., Whitney, D., & Yaeger, T. (2000). *Appreciative inquiry: Rethinking human organization toward a positive theory of change*. Champaign: Stipes Publishing.

Fox, R., Lippitt, R., & Schindler-Raiman, E. (1973). *The humanized future: Some new images*. La Jolla, CA: University Associates, (Out of print).

Jung, C., & Lippitt, R. (1966). The study of change as a concept in research utilization. *Theory Into Practice, 5*(1), 25–29.

Lewin, K., & Lippit, R. (1938). An experimental approach to the study of autocracy and democracy: A preliminary note. *Sociometry, 1*(3/4), 292–300.

Lindaman, E., & Lippitt, R. (1979). *Choosing the future you prefer*. Washington, DC: Development Publications.

Lippitt, R. (1939). Field theory and experiment in social psychology: Authoritarian and democratic group atmosphere. *American Journal Sociology, 4*(1), 26–49.

Lippitt, R. (1940a). An experimental study of authoritarian and democratic group atmospheres. *Studies in Topological and Vector Psychology, 16*(3), University of Iowa, Studies in Child Welfare, pp. 43–195

Lippitt, R. (1940b). *An analysis of group reaction to three types of experimentally created social climate* (Doctoral Dissertation). University of Iowa. Ann Arbor: University Microfilms. (5922204).

Lippitt, R. (1942). The morale of youth groups, chapter 7. In G. Watson (Ed.), *Civilian morale* (p. 119). Boston: Houghton Miffin Company.

Lippitt, R. (1943). From domination to leadership. *Journal of the National Association of Women Deans and Counselors, 6*, 147–152.

Lippitt, R. (1945). To be or not to be – A Jew (racial and religious prejudice in everyday living). *Journal of Social Issues, 1*(1), 18–21.

Lippitt, R. (1949). *Training in community relations*. New York: Harper and Brothers.

Lippitt, R. (1959). Dimensions of the consultant's job. *The Journal of Social Issues, 15*(2), 5–12.

Lippitt, R. (1960). *The individual pupil and the classroom group*. Paper presented at the ASCD Research Workshop, Palo Alto, May 1960. Published by NEA-ASCD.

Lippitt, R. (1961). The learner and the classroom group. Reprinted in NTL-NEA Selected Readings Series #3, *Forces in Learning*, Washington, DC, pp. 25–33.

Lippitt, R. (1962a). *Flint youth study. Flint community leaders seminar reports* (with Flint Action-Research Team). Flint-ISR, Ann Arbor, MI: University of Michigan cooperative enterprise.

Lippitt, R. (1962b). *Unplanned maintenance and planned change in the group work process*. Paper presented at Edward C. Lindaman Memorial Lecture. Published for the National Conference on Social Welfare; reprinted from Social Work Practice, 1962.

Lippitt, R. (1965). The process of utilization of social research to improve social practice. *American Journal of Orthopsychiatry, 35*(4), 663–669.

Lippitt, R. (1971). *The research utilization conference: An illustrative model*, Working paper. Ann Arbor: Center for the Utilization of Scientific Knowledge, Institute for Social Research.

Lippitt, R. (1981). Humanizing planned change. In H. Metzer (Ed.), *Making organizations humane and productive: A handbook for practitioners* (pp. 463–474). New York: Wiley.

Lippitt, R. (1983). Future before you plan. In R. A. Ritvo & A. G. Seargent (Eds.), *The NTL Manager's handbook* (pp. 374–381). Arlington: NTL Institute.
Lippitt, R. (1984). *Dreaming the possible: Futuring with its feet on the ground*. Futuring book project. Unpublished paper. Bethel: NTL Institute.
Lippitt, R., & Bradford, L. (1945a). Building a democratic work group. *Personnel, 22*(3), 1–12.
Lippitt, R., & Bradford, L. (1945b). Employee success in work groups. *Personnel Administration, 8*(4), 6–10.
Lippitt, R., & Gold, M. (1958). Classroom social structure as a mental health problem. *Journal of Social Issues, 15*(1), 40–49.
Lippitt, R., & Gold, M. (1961). Classroom social structure as a mental health problem. Reprinted in NTL-NEA Selected Readings Series #3, *Forces in Learning*, Washington, DC, pp. 61–69.
Lippitt, R., & Havelock, R. (1968). Needed research on research utilization. Research implications for educational diffusion – Major papers presented at the National Conference on the Diffusion of Educational Ideas, March 26–28, 1968, East Lansing.
Lippitt, R., & Jenkins, D. (1953). Interpersonal perceptions in the classroom. In Seidman (Ed.), *The adolescent* (pp. 583–599). New York: Dryden Press.
Lippitt, G., & Lippitt, R. (1978). *The consulting process in action*. San Francisco: Jossey-Bass.
Lippitt, R., & Lippitt, G. (1985). *The Multocular process*. Unpublished Paper, Ann Arbor.
Lippitt, R., & Radke, M. (1946). New trends in the investigation of prejudice. *Annals of the American Academy of Political and Social Science, 244*, 167–176.
Lippitt, R., & Weltfish, G. (1945). Further remarks on the re-education of racial and religious prejudice. *Journal of Social Issues, 1*(2), 49–53.
Lippitt, R., & White, R. (1943). The "social climate" of children's groups. In Barker, Kouin, & Wright (Eds.), *Child behavior and development*. New York: McGraw Hill.
Lippitt, R., & Withey, S. (1961). *The Flint youth studies. A progress report on social psychological studies on juvenile delinquency*. NINH Grant 3M-9109, January.
Lippitt, R., & Zander, A. (1943). A study of boy attitudes toward participation of the war effort. *Journal of Social Psychology, 17*(2), 309–325.
Lippitt, R., Watson, J., & Westley, B. (1958). *The dynamics of planned change*. New York, Harcourt, Brace and World, Inc.
Lippitt, R., Kaufman, M., & Schmuck, R. (1963). *Creative practices developed by teachers for improving classroom atmospheres*. Document #14 in document series of Inter-Center Program on Children, Youth and Family Life. Institute for Social Research, Ann Arbor, University of Michigan, 66 pp.
Marrow, A. F. (1969). *The practical theorist*. New York: Basic Books.
Schein, E. H. (2009). *Helping: How to offer, give and receive help*. San Francisco: Berrett Koehler Publishing.
Weisbord, M., & Janoff, S. (1995). *Future search: An action guide to finding common ground in organizations and communities*. San Francisco: Berrett-Koehler.
White, R. H., & Lippitt, R. (1960). *Autocracy and democracy*. Westport: Greenwood Press.

Further Reading

The Following Materials Were Vital to the Development of This Profile

Block, P. (1978). *Flawless consulting: A guide to getting your expertise used*. San Francisco: Jossey-Bass.
Kleiner, A. (2008). *The age of heretics: The history of the radical thinkers who reinvented corporate management*. San Francisco: Jossey-Bass.

Kolb, D. A. (1984). *Experiential learning. Experience as the source of learning and development.* Englewood Cliffs: Prentice-Hall.

Lewin, K., Lippit, R., & White, R. K. (1939). Patterns of aggressive behavior in experimentally created "social climates". *Journal Social Psychology, 10*, 271–299.

Lippitt, R. (1949). *Training in community relations*. New York: Harper and Brothers.

Lippitt, R. (1982). Retrospective reflections on group work and group dynamics. *Social Work with Groups, 4*(3/4), 9–19.

Lippitt, R., & Gould, R. (1961). *Delinquency patterns: Causes, cures*. Document Series #3 in Document Series of Inter-Center Program on Children, Youth and Family Life, Institute for Social Research, Ann Arbor, 53 pages. Symposium of American Psychological Assn. Convention, 1960.

Lippitt, G., & Lippitt, R. (1978). *The consulting process in action*. San Francisco: Jossey-Bass.

Lippitt, R., & Lippitt, G. (1985). The multocular process. Unpublished paper. Ann Arbor.

Lippitt, R., Watson, J., & Westley, B. (1958). *The dynamics of planned change.* New York: Harcourt, Brace & World, Inc.

Lippitt, R., & White, R. (1960). *Autocracy and democracy: An experimental inquiry.* New York: Harper and Brothers.

Lippitt, R., Withey, S., & Moles, O. (1959a). *A selective review of research and theories concerning the dynamics of delinquency.* Ann Arbor: Institute of Social Research, Intercenter Program of Research on Children, Youth and Family Life.

Lippitt, R., Withey, S., & Moles, O. (1959b). Toward the integration of theoretical orientations (Ch. 10). In *A selective review of research and theories concerning the dynamics of delinquency.* Ann Arbor: Institute of Social Research.

Schindler-Raiman, E., & Lippitt, R. (1980). *Building the collaborative community.* Development Publications, 5605 Lamar Road, Washington, DC: Development Publications, 20016.

The Methodological Revolutionary, The Ann Arbor Observer, 1984. http://annarborobserver.com/articles/front_page.html

Weisbord, M. (2012). *Productive workplaces, dignity, meaning and community in the 21st century.* San Francisco: Jossey-Bass.

Jay W. Lorsch: The Academic Who Changed the Corporate Board Room 48

Brett A. Geier and Aamir Hasan

Abstract
The contributions of Jay W. Lorsch, the Louis Kirstein Professor of Human Relations at the Harvard Business School to the fields of organizational change and organizational behavior, are far reaching and fundamental. He has written and edited 19 books (currently writing twentieth), and the list contains critical pieces including *Organization and Environment* (with Paul Lawrence) that won the Academy of Management's Book of the Year Award in 1969 and was reissued as a Harvard Business School Classic in 1986. The book is listed at number 6 among the 25 most influential books on management of the twentieth century, which include the works of giants like Frederick Taylor, Max Weber, Abraham Maslow, Douglas McGregor, and Peter Drucker. In addition, he has published dozens of articles and contributed scores of case studies to academia. Jay Lorsch has taught in all Harvard Business School's educational programs and chaired the doctoral program as well as countless other units and initiatives at Harvard. He has also acted as a consultant to Citicorp, Deloitte Touche, Goldman Sachs, and many others, and his research on and work with corporate boardrooms has changed the very nature in which they construct, function, and assess themselves. Lorsch was elected to the Corporate Governance Hall of Fame of the highly respected industry magazine *Directorship* in 2009. He serves on the Board of Trustees of Antioch College and is a Fellow of the American Academy of Arts & Sciences.

B.A. Geier (✉) • A. Hasan
Western Michigan University, Kalamazoo, MI, USA
e-mail: brett.geier@wmich.edu; hasan.aamir@wmich.edu

D.B. Szabla et al. (eds.), *The Palgrave Handbook of Organizational Change Thinkers*,
DOI 10.1007/978-3-319-52878-6_16

Keywords
Organizational behavior • Organizational change • Organizational climate • Board relations • Board governance

Contents

Introduction

Lorsch was born in Kansas City, Missouri, and studied at Antioch College in Yellow Springs, Ohio, at a time when Douglas McGregor, the creator of Theories X and Y of human motivation (McGregor 1960), was its President. The progressive college also has the distinction of having had Horace Mann, one of America's greatest thinkers and proponents of universal education, as its founding President (Cubberley 1919). Lorsch completed his bachelor's at Antioch in 1955 where only a few years earlier Warren Bennis, referred to by *Forbes* (1996) as the "dean of leadership gurus," had graduated and was being mentored by the college president. As luck would have it, Bennis became Lorsch's freshmen advisor and, hence, introduced him to McGregor vicariously. Lorsch also took courses in business with Fred Klien who had an MBA from Harvard and which got him later thinking about the Harvard Business School. As Lorsch puts it in an interview with the authors, "I have been very fortunate in my career to keep running into people who were giants in their fields at the time; people who eventually got into organizational behavior and organizational theory and so I too developed an interest in it" (J.W. Lorsch, personal communication, Jan 19, 2017).

From Antioch College, Lorsch went to Colombia University to earn a master's degree in business and thereafter got direct commission into the US Army Finance Corps and was stationed in Europe from January 1957 to August 1959. He ran an office with 25–30 servicemen as well as civilians and also worked as a consultant implementing accounting systems for the armed forces. Finding himself thrust into the role of a manager, Lorsch became involved, as well as fascinated, with the problems of dealing with people in trying to bring about change. Following his service in the army, Lorsch returned home and, after trying his hand at various jobs, got the opportunity to teach an evening course at the University of Missouri at Kansas City (formerly University of Kansas City), which in many ways can be called the turning point in his life. Having already taught in the military and having enjoyed it, Lorsch decided to turn it into a career and applied to various doctoral programs. He got accepted at the Harvard Business School in spring 1961 and the rest as they say is history, and where he has been since.

Influences and Motivations: Harvard and His Colleagues

At Harvard Business School, Lorsch took the doctoral seminar with the celebrated Fritz Roethlisberger who along with Elton Mayo conducted the famous, as well as the much criticized, Hawthorne experiments that were carried out at Western Electric Company in Cicero, Illinois, in the 1920s. Roethlisberger and William John Dickson later published the official account and findings of the studies (Roethlisberger and Dickson 1939), and the book is placed at number ten among the most influential writings on management (Bedeian and Wren 2001). From Roethlisberger, Lorsch acquired an understanding of the history and perspectives on organizations and organizational theory. However, it was his work, initially as a case writer, with Paul Lawrence, a young faculty member at the Harvard Business School, that shaped Lorsch's academic and intellectual trajectory. He completed his doctorate in 1964 and became part of the faculty in early 1965.

Lawrence was thinking about how to conceptualize the problems one encounters when initiating the process of organizational change and later became chairman of Lorsch's dissertation committee. He was a powerful mentor and influence on Lorsch's career, and they jointly wrote a number of books including *Organization and Environment* (1967), which was reissued as a Harvard Business School classic in 1986. The book was not explicitly about change but rather the design and functioning of large organizations as organizational change was not the primary focus of their research at the time (Lorsch studied the notion of contingency theory for his dissertation). However, the problem associated with bringing about organizational change was an area of interest to Lorsch and is a much analyzed topic in the many cases he has written. He points out that although the faculty at Harvard and elsewhere were pretty good at conceptualizing small groups, and the leadership problems associated with bringing about change within small groups, they had yet to figure out those issues as related to larger multifunctional multiunit organizations.

A few years after becoming full professor at the Harvard Business School in the early 1970s, Lorsch was approached by Citicorp Chairman John Reed, who later served as Chairman of the Massachusetts Institute of Technology (MIT) Board of Trustees and as Chairman of the New York Stock Exchange (Augier 2006), to help the group institute a much needed change process in their back office in order to take advantage of computers. It was the work with Citicorp (later Citigroup) that got Lorsch embroiled directly with thinking about change and the process of how to bring about change in organizations effectively. He points out that he was absolutely convinced that the problems Citicorp was having stemmed from the fact that, although they were going about changing and installing computer systems, they were failing to recognize the existence and nature of the huge social system, made up mostly of women, that had to adapt to the changes that the organization needed and wanted to institute. Lorsch always felt that organizations are basically social systems, and everything in them is deeply interrelated, and, accordingly, one should remain aware that any change strategy will have intended consequences, but unintended consequences as well.

To Lorsch, organizations are complex entities, and the complexity emerges as a result of their systemic qualities whereby everything is related to everything else at one level or another. This varies from organization to organization but without grasping this interrelatedness, one can neither understand nor deal with issues the organization may be facing. The fact that no two organizations are alike makes this process even more difficult. One example of such complexity is the delicate relationship that exists between directors of boards and the chief executive officer and is something he has written extensively about in recent years and has offered advice on how this relationship can and should be managed (Lorsch 2015).

Lorsch emphasizes, that given the complexity within organizations, the importance of diagnosing how a system works and the unanticipated consequences one might get in response to changes one is trying to bring about cannot be overstated. He stresses on the need to diagnose and understand a system before attempting to improve it as something that is critical and points out that these were the very issues he and Paul Lawrence were raising and discussing in the many books they wrote together. The contributions that he and Lawrence made to the theory of the workings of large organizations through their research on differentiation and integration are also of great import (Lawrence and Lorsch 1967).

In how his position that diagnosis should come before change may be opposed to Kurt Lewin's famous quote that "if you truly want to understand something, try to change it," Lorsch posits that Lewin's position may be one way, an effective way, to understand a system, but it is certainly not the only way. To Lorsch, Lewin's inference was that when one changes a system, one is able to see what is related to what and the points of resistance, and therefore one gets to understand something about the relationships among the variables that constitute the system. He further clarifies that what he thinks Lewin was saying was that the easiest way to try to understand a system is to try to change it, whereas what he and Lawrence were saying was that one does not go around necessarily changing systems just to understand them since once the system is torn apart, one may never get it back together the way it was. His final comment on the subject is that essentially both were perhaps expressing the same idea; that if you want to understand a system, understand how the parts relate to each other. That Lewin felt that the best way to do that was to change the system is something he understands (J.W. Lorsch, personal communication, Feb 28, 2017).

Key Contributions: Organization Development

Around the late 1960s, Lorsch's longtime friend Warren Bennis along with Edgar H. Schein and Richard Beckhard of MIT founded the Addison-Wesley series on the emerging field of organization development and toward what has come to be regarded as a seminal work in this field, Lorsch and Lawrence contributed a volume to the series. Lorsch considers this volume, which is called *Developing Organizations: Diagnosis and Action* (Lawrence and Lorsch 1969), as the most significant piece he wrote on organizational change, which was published as part of a collection of very significant books on the topic. The book is based on the authors' experience as collaborators in the work of developing organizations and focuses on three critical interfaces: the organization-environment, the group-group, and the individual organization. Attention is paid to the attainment both of organizational goals and of individual purpose. A sequence of intervention in which diagnosis precedes action planning and the notion that organizations can usefully be conceived of as systems is emphasized. The book is arranged to present first the authors' overview of organization development and a summary of the research on which it is based, then to examine each of the three critical interfaces, presenting brief examples of work on each.

Among the many people that Lorsch worked with at Harvard with developing ideas around change were Larry Greiner (professor emeritus at the University of Southern California) and Michael Beer (current professor emeritus at the Harvard Business School). The latter had come from industry (Corning, Inc.), and Lorsch, Greiner, and Beer were among the people who were most directly involved with focusing on organizational studies and organizational behavior related to change and change strategies and processes in the 1970s and 1980s. They were each writing on their own but had common ideas and were teaching in the same courses. Interacting around those courses and reading each other's research, the ideas around change began to connect out of those interactions. Though good friends with Greiner, as well as with Beer, Lorsch did not write anything together with either of them (J.W. Lorsch, personal communication, Feb 28, 2017).

In addition, to the classics he wrote with Lawrence, Lorsch has consistently written and edited books as well as articles and case studies. Many of the books he has written (Donaldson and Lorsch 1983) and edited (Dalton et al. 1970) have been about the notion of using structure or formal systems to redesign organizations to take advantage of the change process, as well as the notion that the organization has to be designed to fit into the environment it is trying to compete in. Change and the change process were among the important areas that Lorsch and his colleagues at the Harvard Business School were trying to teach students in the MBA program, and he was the head of the first year course related to this topic and focused on what could be taught to young managers on how to bring about change through innovation and creativity in an organization.

The course has been taught in one form or another since before World War II, but the Harvard Business School had shut down during the war in order to train executives of defense companies. Prior to the shutdown in the late 1930s, the course was called Administrative Practices which was essentially about organizational behavior and human relations and after the school reopened in 1946, it gradually went thru a number of modifications.

When Lorsch started teaching at Harvard in 1965, organizational change was a topic within the first year course and was constantly a work in progress. From the time he got involved, the business school was always teaching something about change as it was a thing people were always interested in, and gradually over time they became more sophisticated and explicit about what was involved in bringing about organizational change. Gradually as he, Larry Grienier, Mike Beer, and others began to focus on it, change increasingly became the topic of the course because they came to know more about it (J.W. Lorsch, personal communication, Feb 28, 2017).

Lorsch points out that anytime we are structuring change or redesigning the organization, we are dealing with organizational change because of the process side on the one hand and the structural side on the other. However, irrespective of how one reorganizes departments or moves groups around, the real question to him that underlies everything has always been, "how does one get people to accept the new ways in which they are being expected to do things." In other words, how does one bring about new ways of organizing and getting people motivated around the change process? He feels that the greatest obstacle to change is getting people to accept new ways of doing things whether it is a change of structure or a proposed change of strategy.

In speaking about the difference between organizational development and organizational change, a topic that Lorsch has been around for a very long time, he expresses a certain degree of skepticism and posits that people who talk about organizational development and those who talk about organizational change are essentially talking about the same thing. He feels that the work of the Academy of Management is significant, yet at the same time he is unable to clearly differentiate between the work being done at the department that deals with organizational change and the one dealing with organizational development. To him, irrespective of whatever title one wants to put on it, organizational development and organizational change are basically the same thing, which is essentially about using group dynamics to bring about change and moving an organization in a certain direction. In a lighter vein, Lorsch posits that people in organizational development act as if they had the holy grail and that everybody else is missing the point, but he is still not sure what they have other than the idea that one can use small groups to try to bring about change or to use group dynamics to try to influence people to change their points of view (J.W. Lorsch, personal communication, Jan 19, 2017).

New Insights: Boards of Directors

As a consultant, Lorsch has had clients as diverse as applied materials, Berkshire Partners, Biogen Idec, Citicorp, Cleary Gottlieb, Steen & Hamilton LLP, Deloitte Touche, DLA Piper Rudnick, Goldman Sachs, Kellwood Company, MassMutual Financial Group, Tyco International, Shire Pharmaceuticals, and Sullivan & Cromwell LLC. He has been an advocate of greater shareholder democracy (Lorsch and Holstein 2007) and is a member of the Board of Directors of New Sector Alliance and formerly served on the boards of Benckiser (now Reckitt Benckiser), Blasland Bouck & Lee Inc., Brunswick Corporation, Sandy Corporation and CA, Inc. Accordingly, his work has been more on practical implementation, advising organizations on how to institute change and guide the change process, rather than theorizing about it. And it is the work that Lorsch did with organizational behavior related to change that led him to the incisive work that he has been doing, working with and writing about boards and their functioning over the last 25 years.

Lorsch says that probably the most significant work he has been involved with in his career has been in trying to change the way boards function, particularly in the United States. His argument is that the functioning of boards can be improved once you recognize their systemic properties. However, as he points out, the problem in trying to bring about change in the board room through research is that boards are sacrosanct places and a young academic or researcher cannot walk into a boardroom and observe how it operates. In other words, many people try to study boards without ever having seen their machinations from the inside which amounts to trying to change a system without really understanding it. This reality, that observers are not going to be invited into boardrooms for legal and competitive reasons, is something that Lorsch has been trying to get people to recognize and feels that the understanding of the workings of boards is enhanced once they are viewed as systems. He puts it succinctly when he says, "It's not what you know, it's how you think." In other words, one has to take into account the complexity that surrounds the workings of boards in order to understand decisions that emanate from boardrooms.

The efforts that Lorsch has made in writing about and helping boards improve their functioning have been monumental. He is among the preeminent scholars in this area and has made it his niche and enjoys the rare vantage point and license that comes from having served on numerous boards. From this privileged position, he feels that only people who actually serve on boards understand their working or are able to recognize that boards are systems and the amount of change that can be brought about once you acknowledge those systemic properties.

From the time he wrote the book *Pawns or Potentates: The Reality of America's Corporate Boards* in 1989 to publishing his article "America's Changing Corporate Boardrooms: The Last Twenty-Five Years" in 2013, and the many books and dozens of articles on the topic in-between and since, Lorsch has emerged not only as the specialist but also the leading researcher in the field. His contributions include not just writings on how to improve the workings of boards but also how to compose effective boards, and most importantly how to carry out the assessment of boards. Needless to say, his influence on the latter has been truly fundamental.

Some of the earliest research and writing that Lorsch carried out with regards to the assessments of boardrooms with the aim of creating more vital boards highlighted the important difference that self-examination by members could make (Lorsch 1997). Many core issues were brought to light among which was the fact that evaluation of individual directors was harder to do than evaluating overall performance. Assessments of individual members as well as CEO performance were carried out either through questionnaires or appraisals made by committees made up of board members or consultants, and it emerged that members were careful not to criticize the CEO whom they were often beholden to for their own position on the board. Among issues also covered was how well was the most precious commodity that the board had – time together – was being utilized (Lorsch 1994), and he points out that time together is of little value if directors lack the information to hold critical discussion (Lorsch 1996). Other areas of assessment discuss the board's role in strategy formulation, director compensation, board size and composition, and the board's role in top-management succession and development, as well as many others.

In almost all cases, Lorsch discovered in his initial research that boards were carrying out self-assessments for the first time and as a result of his pioneering work in this area, many home truths emerged not least among which was that boards used to spend too much time on boilerplate or management issues (often placed at the top of the agenda) and not enough time discussing important strategic matters (often placed at the bottom). His recommended solution was to reverse their order on the agenda, which many did. Among other issues that came to light as a result of his designed assessments was that directors were being provided too much data instead of the carefully selected and organized information they needed (Boudett et al. 2013). Another positive realization that emerged from assessments was that instead of the traditional "half-day with lunch," board meetings could be so much more productive if they were turned into longer or full day events, which is generally the case now. Concerns about CEO successor development also surfaced from the assessments as well as skepticism about the need for the executive committees that split boards into tiers. Those who were not on the executive committee felt that its members had access to information and decisions that they did not (Lorsch 1997).

His writings about CEO compensation (Lorsch 1999) and the relationship between boards and CEOs (Lorsch 1996) have also been hugely impactful. He emphasized that new leaders must "unfreeze" the corporate change processes and understand the importance of creating new equilibriums through adaptability. In other words, anticipate and adapt to change. In addition, he has always written about the role that the board has to play as an independent auditor as well as a strategic change agent by closely monitoring company performance by asking the tough questions that management might not ask of itself. In his belief, despite constraints, like the fact that many directors are beholden to the CEO (often also the Chairman), the board can play this role successfully by balancing power between directors and CEO. He wrote on the need for directors to spend time together without the CEO as well as to have access to sources beyond, such as direct discussion with top management to assess performance and provide meaningful feedback to the leader who may have his or her own biases and blind spots. He used the incisive expression "improved balance of information" between directors and CEOs that would result from his suggestions and was correct in his prediction that in the future directors would share influence, which is what we see in the rise of the activist investor (George and Lorsch 2014).

Another area that Lorsch developed and contributed to was how to cultivate balanced board rooms and, along with Colin Carter, presented the six essential and fundamental qualities that any director must possess, namely, intellect, instinct, interest, integrity, interpersonal skills, and a commitment to contribute (Lorsch and Carter 2003). He posited that given the increasingly complex business world, the age of the classic generalist was almost over and advised leaders to think strategically about the mix of the board and the need of performance standards for members. He recommended that boards must be made up of members who bring specialized core strengths with them. He questioned unchallenged tenure and advised on the need for financial experts on the board who would, correctly, apply "pedantic intensity" to the work of audit committees. He also counseled boards to consider the trade-off between independence and knowledge as sometimes a member may compensate for potential conflict of interest by possessing in-depth experience in a core area or industry. And we see his humane side when he says that empathy with the concerns of the wider population is a good attribute in a director and advises businesses to seek social legitimacy in order to prosper (Lorsch and Carter 2003).

Unfinished Business: Organizations Are Not People

Lorsch points out that in the latter part of the twentieth century and the first part of this century, there were a lot of people for whom organizational change or organizational development was kind of a formulaic concept and presents the management grid of Blake and Mouton (Blake et al. 1964) as an example. To Lorsch formulaic ideas, whether related to structural change, leadership behavior, or strategy border on the dangerous, because creativity notwithstanding, organizations are not like people. He says that when we study the human system, we know that things we might be looking at, such as the liver or the kidneys, must function in a certain manner, and life and health requires that those organs continue functioning in that way. But in an organizational setup, systems do not always function in the same way, and it is not so clear that organizations have to have the same characteristics to function effectively. Hence, in order to bring about effective change, whether implemented through wide participation or directed from the top down, one has to diagnose the properties of the organization to figure out which approach will give the most effective result.

Lorsch feels that an important contribution he made to theories around organizational change is the idea that there is no one best way to organize, as well as the concepts around contingency theory that he and Paul Lawrence outlined in *Organization and Environment*. He adds that in order to bring about change in an organization, one has to understand how the structure of the organization and the processes of the organization relate to the strategy of the organization. Only then can one think about what one wants to change and what needs to be changed.

Lorsch is presently working on a book about how the group at Harvard, starting with Elton Mayo, L. J. Henderson, and Fritz Roethlisberger in the 1920s, which has been studying organizational behavior coalesced and why it developed in the manner it did. He explains that for this group, including himself, what has been more explicit than it has been to others is the notion that organizations are systems and the recognition of those systemic qualities. Accordingly, he and his colleagues have tried to teach students to think, as leaders and managers, as to how one manages a system that has systemic properties.

The book will essentially be about the history of the evolution of organizational behavior and human relations at the Harvard Business School starting in the early twentieth century when President Abbott Lawrence Lowell and Dean Wallace Brett Donham brought the topic into the curriculum. The fact that they thought this important was revolutionary at the time as most business schools simply equated the teaching of economics to the teaching of business. Lorsch is attempting a pretty thorough look up to the present by using the considerable amount of material and documents that are available at the business school and trying to pull them all together into a history in order to talk about the field of organizational behavior as it has evolved. He feels that there will probably be some criticism of the way it has evolved because in some ways a sense of direction and purpose has been lost (J.W. Lorsch, personal communication, Feb 28, 2017).

References

Augier, M. (2006). Making management matter: An interview with John Reed. *Academy of Management Learning & Education, 5*(1), 84–100.

Bedeian, A. G., & Wren, D. A. (2001). Most influential management books of the 20th century. *Organizational Dynamics, 29*(3), 221–225. Retrieved from http://www.bus.lsu.edu/bedeian/articles/MostInfluentialBooks-OD2001.pdf

Blake, R. R., & Mouton, J. S. (1964). *The managerial grid: The key to leadership excellence.* Houston: Gulf Publishing.

Boudett, K. P., City, E. A., & Murnane, R. J. (Eds.). (2013). *Data wise: A step by step guide to using assessment results to improve teaching and learning.* Cambridge, MA: Harvard Education Press.

Cubberley, E. P. (1919). *Public education in the United States: A study and interpretation of American educational history; an introductory textbook dealing with the larger problems of present-day education in the light of their historical development.* Boston: Houghton Mifflin.

Dalton, G. W., Lawrence, P. R., & Lorsch, J. W. (Eds.). (1970). *Organizational structure and design.* Homewood: Richard D. Irwin.

Donaldson, G., & Lorsch, J. W. (1983). *Decision making at the top: The shaping of strategic direction.* New York: Basic Books.

George, B., & Lorsch J. (2014, May). How to outsmart activist investors. *Harvard Business Review.* Retrieved from: https://hbr.org/2014/05/how-to-outsmart-activist-investors

Lawrence, P. R., & Lorsch, J. W. (1967). Differentiation and integration in complex organizations. *Administrative Science Quarterly, 12*(1), 1–47.

Lawrence, P. R., & Lorsch, J. W. (1969). *Developing organisations: Diagnosis and action.* Reading: Addision-Wesley.

Lorsch, J. W. (1994). Performance assessment in the boardroom. *Directors & Boards 18*(3). Retrieved from http://www.hbs.edu/faculty/product/4177

Lorsch, J. W. (1996). The board as a change agent. *Corporate Board.* Retrieved from http://www.hbs.edu/faculty/product/4172

Lorsch, J. W. (1997). Should directors grade themselves. *Across the Board, 34*(5), 40–44. Retrieved from http://www.hbs.edu/faculty/Pages/item.aspx?num=4168

Lorsch, J. W. (1999). CEO pay: Facts and fallacies. *Corporate Board.* Retrieved from http://www.hbs.edu/faculty/product/4165

Lorsch, J. W. (2015). Should boards mentor their CEOs? It is a complex question. Here are the significant considerations. *Directors & Boards, 39*(5), 25–27. Retrieved from http://www.directorsandboards.com/issue/third-quarter-2015

Lorsch, J. W., & Carter, C. B. (2003). A visit to board 'central casting'. *Directors & Boards, 28* (1), 25–30. Retrieved from http://www.hbs.edu/faculty/product/15687

Lorsch, J. W., & Holstein, W. J. (2007). A conversation with Jay Lorsch: Is the minority yelling too loud? *Q&A. Directorship, 33* (1). Retrieved from http://www.hbs.edu/faculty/product/23524

McGregor, D. (1960). *The human side of enterprise.* New York: McGraw Hill Education.

Roethlisberger, F. J., & Dickson, W. J. (1939). *Management and the worker: An account of a research program conducted by the Western electric company, Hawthorne works, Chicago*. Cambridge, MA: Harvard University Press.

Further Reading

Blake, R. R., & Mouton, J. S. (1966). *Managerial grid* (9th ed.). Houston: Gulf Publishing.

Lorsch, J. W. (2013). America's changing corporate boardrooms: The last twenty-five years. *Harvard Business Law Review, 3*(1), 119–134.

Lorsch J. W. (2014). How to outsmart activist investors. *Harvard Business Review, 92*(5), 88–95. Retrieved from http://hbr.org/2014/05/how-to-outsmart-activist-investors/ar/1

Lorsch, J. W., & MacIver, E. (1989). *Pawns or potentates: The reality of America's corporate boards*. Boston: Harvard Business School Press.

Robert J. Marshak: Challenging Traditional Thinking About Organizational Change 49

Ruth Scogna Wagner

Abstract
This chapter addresses the key contributions, insights, and legacies of Robert J. "Bob" Marshak to the field of organization development and change. The narrative opens with a discussion of the concepts, individuals, and institutions (US Army, American University, NTL, and US Department of Agriculture) that influenced his early career, honed his curiosity, and shaped his world view. The chapter highlights his pattern of perceiving change as a cognitive, linguistic construct and his exploration of the impact of language, symbolism, metaphors, and mindsets on how we think about change. Through his writings, Marshak poses critical questions, stimulates controversy, and challenges our beliefs and assumptions about how we think about what constitutes organizational change; for example, in an early article he contrasts our traditional Lewinian, Western perspectives on change with an unfamiliar Confucian, Eastern perspective of change. The chapter highlights his collaborations: in the 1980s and 1990s, he and cocreator Judith Katz explore the hidden dimension of change, creating the "Covert Process Model™"; in the 1990s and 2000s, he collaborates with numerous other scholars on articles and book chapters in the burgeoning field of organizational discourse studies; and in the 2000s and 2010s, he collaborates with Gervase Bushe with articles that explore the distinctions between classical OD (Diagnostic OD) and a new, emergent form of OD (Dialogic OD), culminating in a paradigm shifting book on Dialogic OD. The chapter concludes with a themed list of Marshak's most influential writings.

Keywords
Organizational change • Language • Symbolism • Metaphors • Mindsets • Covert processes • Dialogic OD

R.S. Wagner (✉)
School of Public Affairs, American University, Washington, DC, USA
e-mail: wagner@american.edu

D.B. Szabla et al. (eds.), *The Palgrave Handbook of Organizational Change Thinkers*,
DOI 10.1007/978-3-319-52878-6_84

Contents

This chapter presents Robert J. "Bob" Marshak whose contributions on language, symbolism, metaphors, and mindsets have challenged, enriched, and expanded the field of organizational change, for almost four decades through his publications for academics and practitioners. Marshak is simultaneously a wise, accomplished, acknowledged insider to the field of organization development and change and an outsider, who poses critical questions and stimulates controversy about our beliefs and assumptions about what constitutes organizational change. Leveraging his deep understanding of classical organization development (OD) theory, he most recently has brought voice and coherence to the distinction between classical OD and a new, emergent form of OD.

This chapter addresses the key contributions, insights, and legacies of Marshak to the field of organization development and change as a Distinguished Scholar in Residence at American University's School of Public Affairs, an executive in the US Government, a practicing international consultant, an award-winning author, and a recipient of the OD Network's Lifetime Achievement Award. Marshak began his contributions by helping to start an internal OD function in the US Government's Agricultural Research Service in 1974, began teaching organization theory and change leadership as an adjunct professor at American University (AU) in 1977, and established his own consulting practice in 1983. He has authored or coedited several books and is the author or coauthor of more than 85 articles or book chapters on topics related to consulting, organizational discourse, organizational change, and the theory and practice of OD. At present, he is actively teaching at American University, consulting, and writing. In this chapter, the reader is introduced to the people, events, and books that influenced Marshak's career and helped shape the thinking and character of this outstanding scholar, educator, and practitioner. This chapter highlights his major contributions to the field of OD; traces how his perspectives on symbolism, language, culture, and mindsets have influenced the field; and finally, reviews his most recent contribution – cocreating a new mindset on transformational change called Dialogic Organization Development. The chapter concludes with a short list of Marshak's most influential works.

Influences and Motivations: Diverse Experiences Nurture Intellectual Curiosity

Marshak grew up on Long Island, New York where he attended public schools and graduated from high school in 1964. Unlike most of his classmates, who went on to colleges in the northeast, he became the first person in his high school to enroll at Duke University in North Carolina where he pursued a liberal arts education, majoring in political science. When asked what kind of student he was, he shared a story where his faculty advisor suggested during his junior year that with his mediocre grade point average and the absence of career plans, he might best aspire to become a social studies teacher in middle school (R. J. Marshak, personal communication, March 31, 2016). Recall that in the mid-1960s in the United States, the environmental context included the Vietnam War and the compulsory military draft with deferments offered for those in college or graduate school. With this as an incentive to stay in school, Marshak insured he got good enough grades to be a student in good standing but found most of his courses uninteresting. The war and threat of the draft hung over the heads of all his male classmates and like them he sought options for what to do if the war did not end by the time he graduated. He even went so far as to apply for and be accepted into officer training school for the Air Force in December 1967 with induction planned for right after graduation the following June. Those plans were disrupted in the spring of 1968 when the Air Force rescinded its offer unless Marshak could be flight qualified. Given his eyeglasses he could not, and he resigned himself to being drafted sometime after graduating as the deferments for attending graduate school had just been ended and the lottery system did not come into effect until the spring of 1969. Upon graduating from Duke in June of 1968, he left Durham, NC and decided in essence to "hang out in Washington, DC until drafted" (R. J. Marshak, personal communication, March 31, 2016). He received his draft notice 2 weeks later and passed his physical in July and then began filing the three appeals he was entitled to in order to delay being drafted in the hopes that the war would wind down. While his appeals were being processed, in the fall 1968, he enrolled in a master of public administration (MPA) degree at American University (AU) in Washington, DC. His first course was in modern public management, taught by Professor Morley Segal, who exposed Marshak to classical organization theory, which he had never read before. He was surprised and delighted that he quickly understood these readings and found them highly interesting. The readings in classical organization theory amplified his natural curiosity about how things worked, built on his training to see the political dimensions of organizations, and exercised his bright, analytic mind in a way that other subjects had never done.

Military Intelligence: Special Agent Assigned to Korea

With his three appeals exhausted, he was inducted into the US Army on December 24, 1968 with a delayed entry provision so he could complete his one semester of graduate school before reporting for active duty in March 1969. Private Marshak did his 2 months of basic training at Ft. Jackson, South Carolina; during that period he found Goffman's (1961) work on total institutions helpful for understanding his experiences especially the mortification process in basic training. After basic training he completed 6 months of training in Army intelligence at Fort Holabird, Maryland, where he was trained in interviewing and data collection methods that he later applied in his work as a consultant and was promoted to corporal. Following intelligence training in 1970, he was assigned to a 47-week Korean language program at the Defense Language Institute, Monterey, California, where he was certified in the Korean language and promoted to sergeant. In January 1971, he was credentialed as a military intelligence special agent and stationed in Uijeongbu, Republic of Korea. Many of the skills acquired in his intelligence training and learning the Korean language and culture foreshadowed the data-collection and sense-making aspects of OD and eventually helped shape a significant event in Marshak's life: writing his first article for the *Journal of Applied Behavioral Sciences* (JABS) – "Lewin Meets Confucius" (Marshak 1993) – that influenced the course of his career and his contributions to OD and change theory. With the Vietnam War still underway, he was honorably discharged from the Army in October 1971.

Influences from American University and the NTL Institute

In January 1972 Marshak returned to American University to pursue his interrupted MPA degree and resumed his studies with Professor Morley Segal in organization theory and organization behavior. At this time, Segal was experimenting with a revolution in teaching styles, in which he replaced the traditional teaching podium and instead was "sitting amongst the students providing theoretical insights through more interactive methods" (Marshak 2008, p. 638). Marshak also took courses with Hal Kellner, a colleague of Professor Segal at AU and a pioneer of the group dynamics movement (Lamb 2008). Kellner introduced Segal and Marshak to the National Training Laboratory for the Applied Behavioral Sciences (NTL Institute) in 1972. The association with NTL was fateful for Segal and Marshak, as this is where they both were introduced to the T-group training method, a unique form of experiential education. It was also through Hal Kellner that Segal met Edie Seashore, who became president of NTL in 1975. Soon Segal and Seashore began thinking about how to structure a unique master's degree that would combine the contributions of NTL in the applied behavioral sciences with those of American University.

This collaboration resulted in the founding of a joint venture between AU and NTL, and in 1980 the first class of graduate students began their studies in the AU/NTL master's program with an emphasis in organization development. Although not yet a member of NTL nor on the full-time faculty of American University, Marshak, who had completed his PhD in public administration at American University in 1977 (discussed below) and immediately began teaching courses in organization theory and behavior, was asked by Professor Segal to help design and then teach a course in organization dynamics in the inaugural program. Marshak is currently the only member of the original faculty still teaching in 2016. Today this program is called the AU MSOD program and continues to be one of the top OD programs in the United States.

Pursuing Ph.D. in Public Administration. In spring 1973, Marshak graduated from American University with a MPA, having received a prestigious Presidential Management Intern Award with the expectation of starting a career in the US government. Meanwhile faculty at AU were lobbying Marshak to pursue a Ph.D. in public administration. He resisted the idea as he did not envision himself as an academic, did not want to waste his time pursuing a degree he did not think he could complete, and wanted to get on with his career and start making money as he felt he had lost 3 years because of his military service. Finally the Director of the doctoral program at the School of Government and Public Administration offered to make an exception and permit Marshak to enroll part time in the doctoral program while everyone else had to be a full-time student. This tempting offer would allow Marshak to start a career while continuing to take courses that stimulated his intellectual curiosity. After briefly investigating other universities, who all required full-time study, Marshak began his PhD studies in public administration at AU in the summer 1973. He thrived in the doctoral program and completed his Ph.D. in 1977 ahead of all his full-time doctoral classmates. During his doctoral studies, he was exposed to courses in organization theory and behavior, management theory, and organization development. These became central to his conceptual thinking and foundations for his later thinking about change and consulting to organizations. These ideas also informed and reinforced what he was dealing with as an internal organizational consultant and began his lifelong curiosity about how theory could be applied to practice and how practice could shed new or additional light on existing theory.

Membership in NTL Institute. For Marshak, the relationship with NTL was fruitful and influential. From 1976 to 1978, Marshak attended numerous week-long NTL workshops as part of their program for specialists in organization development where he learned from such influential and well-known scholar/practitioners as Ron Lippitt, Richard (Dick) Beckhard, Eva Schindler Rainman, Joe Luft, and Bob Tannenbaum (R. J. Marshak, personal communication, April 30, 2016). Overlapping this period and before becoming an NTL member in 1984, Marshak audited a course in 1977 on conflict management at AU being taught by Don Klein – a clinical psychologist, active NTL member, and community researcher and consultant. Intrigued and challenged by Don Klein's style and knowledge, Marshak offered to teach as an apprentice with Klein, who became an important mentor. Together they taught conflict management workshops through NTL and courses at American University and Johns Hopkins University from 1977 to 1986. Whereas Segal was Marshak's intellectual mentor, Klein became a role model and mentor as an educator and practitioner. For several years Marshak taught a conflict management workshop through NTL entitled "Beyond Conflict" with Klein, Darya Funches, and Edie Seashore, who as noted was one of the founders with Segal of the AU/NTL program and a past president of NTL Institute. Close in age and experience, Darya Funches became a valued colleague, collaborator, and friend and someone with whom he could compare his experiences and perceptions as a white male with her experiences and insights as an African American woman while exploring their joint interest in the edges and limits of existing OD theories and practices. Edie Seashore also became an important mentor, friend, colleague, and collaborator until her death in 2013 and someone who always pushed and supported him to explore his emerging insights and ideas about change theory and practices. Through NTL Marshak also met Judith Katz, who became one of his most important colleagues and collaborators. Together they developed and offered workshops in covert processes, which they co-led for 13 years. In the book *Covert Processes at Work* (Marshak 2006), he indicates that his and Katz's work on covert processes built on the pioneering work of Ed Schein, who had written "One of the most important functions of process consultation is to make visible that which is invisible" (1999, p. 84 as cited in Marshak 2006, p. xii).

Together Marshak and Katz created the Covert Processes Model™ for understanding and addressing the hidden dynamics of individuals, groups, and organizations. It was also an impetus to begin putting his ideas into writing, and together they published four practitioner-oriented articles about covert processes and organization development (Marshak and Katz 1990, 1991, 1997, 2001). The Covert Processes Model™ was an integration of a range of ideas about hidden dynamics in the social sciences, spoke to dynamics that both Marshak and Katz witnessed in their consulting practices, and was the foundation for a 7-day residential workshop for OD consultants offered through NTL Institute.

Early Work Experiences

Other key influences in Marshak's formative career were the connections he made while at AU. One was with fellow doctorate in public administration alumnus and student of Morley Segal, Len Covello, who was the Director of the Management Improvement Staff in the Agricultural Research Service at the US Department of Agriculture (USDA). Covello recruited Marshak to his staff in 1974 and also hired other AU alumni who had studied under Professor Segal, and collectively they were referred to as the "AU Mafia" (R. J. Marshak, personal communication, March 31, 2016). While initially hired to be a management analyst providing expert management studies, Marshak began to successfully introduce OD methods in his work and the work of the staff began to become more OD oriented, and consequently, the staff was renamed the Organization and Management Development Staff. In that capacity he found himself frequently working on reorganizations and used his understanding of organization theory or organization development to help shape his thinking and actions. He found his use of theory made up for his early lack of experience, and he quickly became a sought-after participant to work on important organizational issues including the merger of four USDA agencies into the Science and Education Administration. His ability to conceptualize, facilitate action, and work with senior leaders was duly noted, and he was rapidly promoted into higher-level positions within the career civil service, graduated from the first Senior Executive Service Development Program at USDA in 1981, and served in various senior executive positions in his last 3 years of government service. These experiences were critical to Marshak's thinking and approaches to theory and practice. He learned how to relate to government agency leaders and to develop his thinking about organizational processes and politics, the dimensions of change in large complex systems, and a style of consulting that was successful with scientists and engineers who were skeptical of most social science ideas.

In 1983, after working on successive rounds of reorganizations and downsizings that included his own job being abolished two times, Marshak was reassigned to become the Deputy Area Director for agricultural research in the states of Texas and Oklahoma based in College Station, Texas. Although he would have been the first person in a position of that importance who did not have a doctorate and research experience in an agricultural science, he tired of working on the ongoing agency downsizings and reorganizations. Consequently, he decided his future was to continue to be an organizational consultant and not an agricultural research administrator. In June 1983, he left his government career and set up his own consulting practice, which he has continued to the present.

In his more than 40 years as an internal and independent consultant, Marshak has consulted to a wide range of public and private sector organizations both in the USA and abroad. Among the organizations Marshak has worked with as a consultant or educator are AOL-Europe, BASF Southeast Asia, BAE Systems, Exxon, Freddie Mac, GlaxoSmithKline, The Inter-American Development Bank, HSBC, JP Morgan Chase, Kodak, MITRE, NPR, National Science Foundation Board, PSI Consulting-Korea, Singapore Training and Development Association, UNICEF, Unisys, The World Bank, and a wide range of US government agencies and offices.

Influence of Works in Classical Organization Theory and OD

In several of Segal's courses, Marshak was exposed to a seminal book by James Thompson (1967) titled *Organizations in Action*, in which the author focused on the behavior of complex organizations as entities, how organizations manage uncertainty, and the tension between the closed-system strategy of classical organization theory and the open-system strategy of the "newer tradition" of "bounded rationality" (Thompson 1967, p. 9). It may be from this text that Marshak began to wonder about the challenge of contemporary organizational change issues and how different premises and cultural assumptions can lead to different ways of thinking about organizations and change. For example, Thompson writes:

> . . .the two strategies reflect something fundamental about the cultures surrounding complex organization – the fact that our culture does not contain concepts for simultaneously thinking about rationality and indeterminateness. These appear to be incompatible concepts, and we have no ready way of thinking about something as half-closed, half-rational. (1967, pp. 9–10)

This theme of how our cultural perspectives limit what we can see and what we have the language to describe is a recurring theme in Marshak's work, such as "Lewin Meets Confucius" (Marshak 1993a) and "Changing the Language of Change" (Marshak 2002).

Influences from Organizational Discourse

In the early 1990s, Marshak still considered himself primarily a practitioner and had written little beyond a few articles for practitioner journals. That began to change with the publication in 1993 of his seminal articles "Lewin Meets Confucius" (Marshak 1993a) in the *Journal of Applied Behavioral Science*, discussed in more detail below, and "Managing the Metaphors of Change" (Marshak 1993b) in *Organization Dynamics*. The article on metaphors drew the attention of the organizers of an academic conference on metaphor and organization held at King's College London in 1994; they called Marshak out of the blue and asked if he would write a chapter for an edited book they were publishing on metaphor and organization. Marshak at first demurred saying he was not sure he had time to write a chapter, but in the end sent them a chapter that was published in their book *Metaphor and Organization* (Grant and Oswick 1996). This began a series of collaborations between Marshak and several of the founders and early contributors to what has become the field of organizational discourse studies. Key colleagues and coauthors of articles, book chapters, and journal special issues on organizational discourse and change include in alphabetical order: David Grant, Loizos Heracleous, Tom Keenoy, and Cliff Oswick (Grant and Marshak 2009, 2011; Heracleous and Marshak 2004a, b; Keenoy et al. 2000; Marshak and Heracleous 2005; Marshak et al. 2000; Oswick et al. 2000, 2010; Oswick and Marshak 2012).

This "discourse crowd" welcomed Marshak and accepted him as a fellow academic, whereas up until then he considered himself primarily a practitioner, not an academic. Collaboration with this international group of scholars also legitimized Marshak's thinking about language and change (R.J. Marshak, personal communication May 5, 2016). With them he found a home for his innate thinking: How someone talks about something reveals a window into what is going on in their mind. In addition to reinforcing and contributing to his thinking about language and change, these collaborations with welcoming colleagues also began to shift Marshak's identity from being primarily a consultant to someone who could and should make contributions to the conceptual and academic literatures especially related to language and change as well as the shifting contours of change theory and practice. This shift in identity continued as indicated by an increase in his academic and practitioner publications, his greater willingness to point out the limiting edges of various traditional change assumptions and concepts including even the word "change" itself as discussed in "Changing the Language of Change" (Marshak 2002), becoming the acting editor of *The Journal of Applied Behavioral Science* in 2004, and accepting for the first time a full-time academic appointment as a Distinguished Scholar in Residence at American University in 2006.

Key Contributions: Continuously Challenging Traditional OD Thinking

Before exploring the key contributions of this great thinker, it seems appropriate to ponder the following: What gifts does Marshak possess that have enabled him to contribute so significantly to the field of organizational change? The answer may lie in his own values and beliefs. First, the review of his early influences suggests someone who was energized by organization theory and learned in his early work in large bureaucratic organizations the impact of skillfully applying theory to bring about positive change. His teaching and writing continually make this linkage between theory and practice. For example, most of his writings include some specific vignettes that make the theory come alive. Although he initially saw himself as a practitioner, his successes as a scholar and academic have never diminished his belief in the importance and value of practice. Marshak's thinking and practices have been guided by the continuous interaction of theory and practice, where theories informed his actions and experiences in his practice inspired his search for new ideas and concepts.

Second, his attention to language, symbolism, and narrative has enabled him to see beyond words and actions, and he has raised our awareness of how our culture privileges actions over words. He has a gift for identifying patterns in client systems and is just as adept at seeing patterns in bodies of literature and the evolving interventions under the umbrella of organizational change. Third, he combines his gift at observation and his curiosity to fuel his exploration into a variety of literatures and fields. For example, he borrowed the term "morphogenesis" from biology to juxtapose the concept of creating a new shape within the context of OD. Fourth, his penchant to explore the edges of current theories and practices and raise questions for himself and others about the limits of prevailing assumptions has highlighted how different assumptions might lead to new ways of thinking and acting. His natural curiosity about what goes on behind the scenes and outside of conscious awareness coupled with his approach to analyzing a situation by drawing similarities and differences within the situation and with other situations comes through in his writing, which is full of tables that compare one thing with another, raising our awareness that there is not just one perspective but rather contrasting perspectives. Finally, he has developed his skills through the years to become the gifted writer that he is today. As one of his academic colleagues and coauthors said, "Marshak writes like an angel" (D. Grant, personal communication, June 7, 2016).

Marshak has applied these gifts over the last 40 years in his writings and teachings as a scholar/practitioner, resulting in at least five significant contributions to the field of organizational change.

Contrasting Lewinian, Western with Confucian, Eastern Perspectives of Change

The impetus for "Lewin Meets Confucius: A Re-View of the OD Model of Change" (Marshak 1993a) was a workshop Marshak presented in Korea in 1991 when an alumnus of the AU/NTL program invited Marshak to Korea to conduct two workshops, one on conflict and one on organizational change. During the change workshop, Marshak felt that "something was off in how the participants responded to the ideas and models he was presenting" and as a result became curious as to what might be going on with this Korean audience (R.J. Marshak, personal communication, March 31, 2016). Knowing from his Army training and experiences 20 years earlier that Korea had been deeply influenced by Confucian philosophy, Marshak decided to learn more about Confucianism and especially the assumptions or models of change in traditional Confucian thinking. He embarked on several years of reading books about Confucian thinking, the *I Ching*, traditional Chinese Medicine, and the like before realizing that Confucian philosophy envisioned change as continuous and cyclical, whereas most Western theories were based on ideas of discontinuous and linear change (e.g., Lewin's unfreeze-movement-refreeze model (1951)). These insights led him to write his first scholarly article for a refereed journal "Lewin Meets Confucius: A Re-View of the OD Model of Change" (1993a) in which he ponders:

> ...whether or not a change model that emphasizes creating change is as relevant to contemporary managers and organization facing continual change, 'permanent white water' (Vaill 1989), as it was to their counterparts of past decades when organizational life was more stable and bureaucratic. (Marshak 1993a, p. 403)

In this seminal article, Marshak compares and contrasts the assumptions about change from a Lewinian, Western perspective to assumptions from a Confucian, Eastern perspective. See Table 1 for a summary of this comparison.

This article not only attempted to identify and raise questions about the deep cultural assumptions underlying OD change theory but also was one of the first discussions of continuous change in a field that had been implicitly based on planned, episodic change. In a later and widely influential article, Weick and Quinn (1999) extensively drew on Marshak's ground breaking analysis for their comments on continuous change.

A year after the publication of "Lewin Meets Confucius," Marshak wrote an article for OD practitioners called "The Tao of Change" (Marshak 1994) in which he presented and explained his perspective on the Lewinian view of change and introduced the cyclical/Confucian view of change as captured in Table 2.

Table 1 Assumptions About Change

Lewinian/OD	Confucian/East Asian
A → B Change is:	Change is:
1. *Linear*. One moves from one state to another state in a forward direction	1. *Cyclical*. There is a constant ebb and flow to the universe and everything in it is cyclical
2. *Progressive*. One moves from a less to a more desired state	2. *Processional*. One moves constantly from one condition/form/state to the next condition/form/state in an orderly sequence through a cycle
3. *Destination Oriented*. One moves toward a specific end state	3. *Journey Oriented*. Because there is constant cyclical change, what matters is how well one follows the way
4. *Based on Creating Disequilibrium*. In order to get movement from the current state, one must alter the equilibrium of the status quo	4. *Based on Restoring/Maintaining Equilibrium*. Everything is naturally in harmony and perfect. One acts only as needed to restore balance and equilibrium
5. *Planned and Managed by People Who Exist Separate From and Act on Things to Achieve Their Goals*. One learns the principles about how to master and manipulate the forces in the world in order to achieve one's own ends	5. *Observed and Followed by People Who Are One With Everything and Must Act Correctly to Maintain Harmony in the Universe*.
6. *Unusual, Because Everything Is Normally in a Quasi-Stationary or Static State*. Unless something is done, things will stay the same because a body at rest stays at rest until force is applied	6. *Usual, Because Everything Is Normally in a Continually Changing Dynamic State*. The continual process of everything in the universe is change. The Yin-Yang law of opposites says everything contains its own negation, so nothing stays forever (Marshak 1993, p. 403)

Table 2 Two Views of Change

OD/Western	Cyclical/Confucian
Focus on the Future	Attend to the Past-Present-Future
Assume Satisfied People Hold On	Assume Wise People Let Go & Realign
Overcome Resistance	Maintain Balance & Harmony
Think in Terms of Either/Or	Think in Terms of Both/And
Plan and Manage Change	Cultivate System Self-Renewal
Think Analytically	Think Holistically
Use Reason and Logic	Use Artistry & Composition
Measure Progress	Be Values Centered

Marshak (1994, p. 24)

These two articles "marked a significant shift in [Marshak's] thinking and writing as well as a clear example of 'views from the edge' presented via contrasting ideal types" (Marshak 2009, p. 65) and introduced his cross-cultural views on organization development and change.

Creating a Framework for Analyzing the Hidden Dimensions of Change: The Covert Processes Model™

Another key contribution is his work with Judith Katz in the late 1980s and 1990s on covert processes and change. Here he and Katz explored the edge of conventional OD practices that tended to emphasize that change would result from rationally putting issues and dynamics out openly "on the table." Marshak and Katz thought this was important but insufficient to explain what they both observed in their practices. Not everything could or even should be put out on the table openly as they asserted that things were hidden for a multitude of reasons that may have included desires to manipulate a situation, but also fear of punishment or retribution, blind spots, limiting mindsets, and unconscious dynamics. After developing a conceptual model that integrated these differing dynamics, they named it "The Covert Processes Model™" drawing on the use in many of the social sciences of the term "covert" to represent hidden dynamics and of course an obvious connection to Marshak's experience in the Army as a special agent in military intelligence. (See Fig. 1.)

They later facilitated intensive residential workshops on covert processes for OD practitioners through NTL Institute, presented workshops at annual ODN conferences (Marshak and Katz 1990, 1991), and wrote a series of articles about covert processes also for practitioners (Marshak and Katz 1997, 2001). An important aspect of his work with covert processes was how symbolic representations (i.e., the four Ms of metaphors, music, movement, and media (Marshak 2006, p. 57)) could reveal unspoken and often subconscious framings and dynamics guiding actions in individuals, groups, and organizations. He and Katz summarized this way of thinking with the phrase "Explore literal messages symbolically, and symbolic messages literally" (Marshak 2006, p. 55). This furthered his interest in the power of metaphors and symbols and also contributed to his later thinking about language and discourse being "situated, symbolic action" as discussed in an article he coauthored with Loizos Heracleous (Heracleous and Marshak 2004a, p. 1285), who Marshak knew from his interactions with the academics developing the new field of organizational discourse studies in the 1990s and early 2000s.

In his book, *Covert Processes at Work* (2006a), Marshak presented the model and captured much of what he and Katz had learned. "In some ways this book can be seen as an extension of the pioneering work by organizational psychologist Ed Schein on process consultation, especially on the importance of being able to decipher hidden forces" (Marshak 2006, p. xii). Marshak and Katz's work on covert processes added an explicit focus on the unconscious and symbolic diagnosis; in

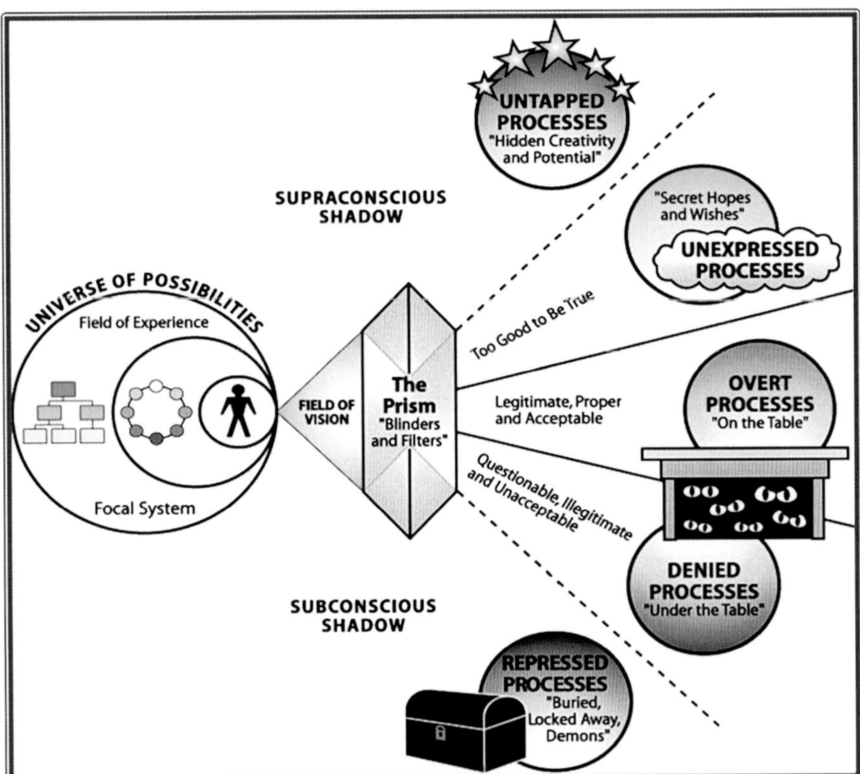

Fig. 1 The Covert Processes Model™ (Marshak and Katz 1991)

addition, it challenged the implicit OD thinking of putting everything on the table. In their workshops, they trained hundreds of OD practitioners in the basic concepts of covert processes, and through these workshops, articles, and Marshak's book, the concept and language of covert processes became more fully integrated into the OD profession. Covert processes has added to or reenforced in the practice of OD an explicit interest in a range of hidden dynamics including unspoken hopes and dreams, the importance of establishing psychological safety before things can be openly "put on the table," the importance of tacit mindsets in determining what can be openly addressed, and how symbols can be understood as representations of subconscious knowing and framings.

Focusing on Language, Symbolism, and Metaphors of Change

A large body of Marshak's work deals with how language, symbolism, and metaphors influence how we think about change and are reflected in our actions and theories of change. In the introduction to a collection of his previously published

Table 3 Metaphors of Change and Change Agents

Image of Change	Image of Change Agent
Fix and Maintain	Repair Person, Maintenance Worker
Build and Develop	Trainer, Coach, Developer
Move and Relocate	Planner, Guide, Explorer
Liberate and Recreate	Liberator, Visionary, Creator

Marshak (1993b, p. 49)

articles grouped under the heading "Metaphors, Language, and Change," Marshak provides an insight into his curiosity with language:

> Behind this curiosity originally was an untrained belief that specific words and phrases might also reveal unspoken or even unconscious beliefs and understandings. This early predilection has over the years grown into a more educated and practice-proven orientation about how metaphors and language reflect inner cognitive schemata. (2009a, p. 123)

From his earliest consulting experiences in the 1970s, Marshak had a linguistic ear and noted, for example, that people resisting changes frequently used the expression "If it's not broke don't fix it." It was years later that he realized that the phrase was likely connected to thinking about organizations as machines and that change therefore implicitly involved repairs and fixing things that had broken down. This ultimately led to his article "Managing the Metaphors of Change," (Marshak 1993b) where he described different implicit metaphors of change that potentially impacted or revealed unspoken mindsets, as indicated in Table 3.

The concept of how metaphors, and more broadly language, shaped thinking and action became a central aspect of his thinking, practice, and writings. His book chapter entitled "Metaphors, Metaphoric Fields, and Organizational Change" (Marshak 1996) was included in a book by David Grant and Cliff Oswick on metaphors and organizations. The chapter itself extended his previous discussion of the metaphors of change and further explored the relationship of language and symbolism related to organizations and change. Marshak contributed another chapter to a book on discourse and organization, "A Discourse on Discourse" (1998a), where he explained how talk was a form of action and elaborated on how discourse shaped both thinking and action. Several articles addressed concepts and practices associated with language, discourse, and change all derived from his consulting practice: "Changing the Language of Change" (Marshak 2002), "From Outer Words to Inner Worlds" (Marshak et al. 2000), "A Discursive Approach to Organization Development" (Marshak and Heracleous 2005), "Generative Conversations" (Marshak 2013a), and "Leveraging Language for Change" (Marshak 2013b). In addition to his strong theoretical contributions to the field of organizational discourse studies, other contributions were seeing discourse as a vehicle for affecting change and demonstrating how the emerging theory of organizational discourse could be applied (D. Grant, personal communication, June 7, 2016).

This work in organizational discourse besides being a major contribution in itself became a cornerstone of his thinking that led to his next major contribution to the field, which was his work with Gervase Bushe on conceptualizing Dialogic OD.

Conceptualizing and Describing a New Form of Organization Development: Dialogic OD

Another major contribution to the field of organizational change was identifying a new form of OD. In an award winning article in 2009, Marshak, with colleague and coauthor Gervase Bushe (Bushe and Marshak 2009), conceptualized and described the emergence of a form of OD that differs from the traditional, foundational form of OD. They label the old form of OD "Diagnostic OD" as it focused on diagnosis and problem solving and this new form of OD "Dialogic OD."

Dialogic OD is a recent, important, and still evolving conceptualization of organizational change that integrates a number of different developments that have emerged in OD theory and practice over the past 30 years. In a recent review of the field, two important scholars – Jean Bartunek and Richard Woodman (2015) – noted that Bushe and Marshak (2009) were responsible for a major advancement in the field of organization change theory and practices. See Table 4 for a comparison of Diagnostic and Dialogic OD.

For Marshak the path to conceptualizing a new form of OD and change started in the early 1980s. From the mid-1980s through the 1990s, Marshak had noted developments in OD theory and practice and how they differed from the classical

Table 4 Contrasting Diagnostic and Dialogic OD

	Diagnostic OD	Dialogic OD
Influenced by	Classical science, positivism, and modernist philosophy	Interpretive approaches, social constructionism, critical, and postmodern philosophy
Dominant Organizational Construct	Organizations are like living systems	Organizations are like meaning-making systems
Ontology and Epistemology	Reality is an objective fact	Reality is socially constructed
	There is a single reality	There are multiple realities
	Truth is transcendent and discoverable	Truth is immanent and emerges from the situation
	Reality can be discovered using rational and analytic processes	Reality is negotiated and may involve power and political processes
Constructs of Change	Usually teleological	Often Dialogical or Dialectical
	Collecting and applying valid data using objective problem-solving methods leads to change	Creating container and processes to produce generative ideas leads to change
	Change can be created, planned, and managed	Change can be encouraged but is mainly self-organizing
	Change is episodic, linear, and goal oriented	Change may be continuous and/or cyclical
Focus of Change	Emphasis on changing behavior and what people do	Emphasis on changing mindsets and what people think

Bushe and Marshak (2014, p. 58)

concepts of OD he had learned in textbooks and through NTL Institute. He describes the anomalies he saw in how OD was practiced in an article "My Journey into Dialogic Organization Development" (Marshak 2015). Some of these anomalies were observable shifts: from close facilitation of small groups as was found in OD teambuilding in the 1960s–1970s to the more choreographed processes found in "large group interventions" (Bunker and Alban 1997); from "diagnosis," which was labeled as problem centric, to "discovery" in appreciative inquiry (Watkins et al. 2011); the shift from episodic change to continuous change (Weick and Quinn 1999); the shift from planned, episodic change to the introduction in the 1990s of ideas of continuous and self-organizing change from the complexity sciences and some pioneers such as Meg Wheatley (1992); a shift from objective reality to constructed reality (Berger and Luckmann 1966); and many of the ideas in organizational discourse (R.J. Marshak, personal communication, May 5, 2016). By the early 2000s Marshak began to see these newer assumptions and approaches as beginning to converge in a way that suggested a newer form of OD was emerging. In 2005 he published a short article in an OD practitioner journal asking, "Is there a new OD?" (Marshak 2006). This drew the attention of Gervase Bushe who called Marshak and said he was thinking some of the same things. This led to a collaboration in working through the conceptual framework of a newer form of OD that combined influences from the interpretive sciences (e.g., social construction, discourse, and meaning making) with ideas from the complexity sciences (e.g., continuous change, self-organizing systems, and complex adaptive systems) (Bushe and Marshak 2015b).

Bushe and Marshak writing separately and together sought to conceptualize a newer form of OD. They quickly learned that calling something "new OD" was unacceptable to those in the field since it implied other forms of OD were "old" and out of date. This forced them to sharpen their thinking and triggered a search for different terminology to describe what they were conceptualizing and culminated in their article "Revisioning Organization Development: Diagnostic and Dialogic Premises and Patterns of Practices" (Bushe and Marshak 2009) that won the Douglas McGregor Memorial Award for the best article in 2009 in *The Journal of Applied Behavioral Science*. Over the following years, these two change thinkers contributed a series of articles, book chapters, special issues of journals, and in 2015 an edited book elaborating the theory and practice of this new form of OD.

In their book Bushe and Marshak (2015c) introduce the concept of a "Dialogic OD Mindset" that they define as "the combination of theories, beliefs, assumptions, and values that shape how one sees and engages the world" (p. 11). They assert that how OD practitioners approach a specific situation is a product of these variables. They describe the Dialogic OD Mindset with a combination of eight key premises (see Table 5) and three underlying change processes.

These key premises represent assumptions about organizations and change. In addition, they include three core principles that Bushe refers to as the "secret sauce": emergence, narrative, and generativity (Bushe and Marshak 2015a). See Table 6 for a description of these core principles.

Table 5 Key Premises of the Dialogic OD Mindset

1. Reality and relationships are socially constructed
2. Organizations are meaning-making systems
3. Language, broadly defined, matters
4. Creating change requires changing conversations
5. Structure participative inquiry and engagement to increase differentiation before seeking coherence
6. Groups and organizations are continuously self-organizing
7. Transformational change is more emergent than planned
8. Consultants are a part of the process, not apart from the process

Bushe and Marshak (2015b, pp. 17–18)

Table 6 Three Core Processes of Organizational Change in Dialogic OD

Emergence is when a disruption in the ongoing social construction of reality is stimulated or engaged in a way that leads to a more complex reorganization
Narrative is when there is a change to the main story lines people use to explain and bring coherence to their organizational lives
Generative images are when words or symbols are introduced or emerge that allow people to see old things in new ways

Bushe and Marshak (2015a)

See www.dialogicod.net for a list of comments about their book and ideas. Later in this chapter the discussion returns to possible next steps in the development of theory and practice to flesh out the new Dialogic OD.

Contribution as a Leader, Educator, and Practitioner in the Field of OD

Marshak's thinking and writings have always been stimulated by something experienced as a practitioner, teacher, or contributor to the field of OD and its supporting organizations. He has made significant contributions to the field and institutions of OD by assuming numerous leadership roles: cochair of the 1984 OD Network Annual Conference; cofounder of the Chesapeake Bay OD Network in 1984; vice chair of the board of trustees, NTL Institute in 1990; founding faculty member for the AU/NTL MSOD program in 1979–1980; trustee of the OD Network Board of Directors (2003–2008); acting editor, *The Journal of Applied Behavioral Science* in 2004; and cofounder of the OD Educational Association (ODEA) in 2007.

Not to be overlooked is the personal impact he has had on thousands of students he taught through NTL workshops in the US and overseas and as adjunct faculty at several universities including American University, Georgetown University, University of Texas, and Johns Hopkins University. As a faculty member at American University's School of Public Affairs between 1977 and 2016, Marshak has served as both an adjunct professor and most recently as Distinguished Scholar in Residence, teaching both in the masters in public administration and in the AU Masters of Science in Organization Development Program, which was previously known as the AU/NTL program. As one of the founding faculty, Marshak has taught more than 70 cohorts since 1980 and well over 1500 students have experienced Marshak's engaging, yet challenging, teaching style. With an insistence on the importance of theory to the practice of OD, the ability to present complex information succinctly, and his experience as both a practitioner and thinker about OD, students continually give Marshak's class the highest ratings in the AU MSOD program.

Some insight into Marshak's unique approaches to learning in the classroom can be found in an early article he wrote explaining his approach in the classroom titled "Cognitive and Experiential Approaches to Conceptual Learning" (Marshak 1983), in which he argues that as cognitive creatures we employ a "conceptual system to understand phenomenon and guide behavior" (p. 72). He explains that our conceptual system consists of theories and concepts; these theories are of two types: personal and formal. Our personal theories develop from our childhood and life experiences and inform us as to how the world works; the downside is that our personal theories are usually unexamined and out of our conscious awareness. Not coincidentally this also forms a foundational idea that he revisited and expanded upon in his later work on covert processes more than a decade later. In the classroom one of Marshak's gifts to students is to make them aware of these personal, unconscious theories and to encourage them to question whether these unconscious theories are hurtful or helpful, all while teaching them formal theories of organizational behavior.

Marshak seeks to develop students to be strong, thoughtful practitioners. Today, alumni of AU's MSOD program are in positions of leadership and influence in all of the OD academic and professional associations as well as multiple sectors, including government, industry, and the nonprofit where they are observing and applying insights into organizations and organizational change that they learned from Marshak. One recent cohort of students in the AU MSOD program spoke about the "Pocket Marshak" (B. Hall, personal communication, May 1, 2016), which represented a desire to have in your pocket Marshak's ability to listen to the language being used; to observe the situation for clues of the underlying meaning; to form assumptions based on the language used, the observed behavior, augmented by relevant theories or models; and, within seconds, to ask riveting, insightful questions that shift the person or system to a new perspective.

Having reviewed Marshak's key contributions to the field of organizational change, what new insights have illuminated and shifted how academics and practitioners view the field of organizational change?

New Insights: Influencing Theory and Practice

This section reframes Marshak's key contributions and presents the derivative insights that have influenced the field for more than 30 years. The section begins with a narrative of how Marshak illuminated the author's view of organizational change.

Impact of Marshak's Thinking, Teaching, and Mentoring on This Author

Reflecting on Marshak's contribution to the field of organizational change, I begin with the impact his thinking, teaching, and mentoring has had on me as an OD practitioner and educator. In 1994 my mentor was Fred Nader, a former president of NTL Institute and an OD change practice leader whom I met when he was consulting to American Management Systems where I was an information technology (IT) professional. With Nader's encouragement and support, I applied to and enrolled in the AU/NTL master's degree program in OD with cohort 33 in 1996. As Nader taught in the AU/NTL program, I shared with him that I had some misgivings about our next professor, Dr. Marshak, who had a reputation as being exceedingly challenging and demanding; many of my classmates were quite anxious about taking Marshak's course in organization theory. Nader pointed out that I had a choice: I could let Marshak's reputation intimidate me and hinder my learning, or I could reframe it as an opportunity to spend two weekends with one of the cleverest minds in the field of OD. I chose the latter option and even 20 years later, Marshak's course was one of the most memorable and powerful learning experiences I have had. In class we explored the classical literature with Weber (1946), Burns and Stalker (1961), Katz and Kahn (1978), Lawrence and Lorsch (1969), and Thompson (1967), as well as more recent writings on metaphors (Morgan 1986). What surprised me was being challenged to be aware of my own perceptions of organizations and my personal assumptions and beliefs about the world. Marshak stimulated my curiosity about human systems.

With the encouragement of another professor in the program, Charlie Seashore, I subsequently chose to pursue a Ph.D. in human and organizational systems at Fielding Graduate University, where Seashore was the dean of faculty. When I approached the dissertation phase, I knew I wanted to focus on exploring how people in complex organizations made sense of planned organizational change. I needed an external reader for my dissertation and asked Marshak to be that reader because of his focus on change, language, and meaning making, his insights into large, bureaucratic organizations, and his academic and professional rigor. My research (Wagner 2006) was focused on how different stakeholder groups experienced and made sense of Secretary Donald Rumsfeld's intended transformation of the US Department of Defense (DOD) in the early 2000s as part of the second President Bush administration. Marshak's review and feedback on what I had hoped was my close to final draft was both devastating and insightful; he encouraged me to look deeper into the study. When he gave me positive feedback on my revisions, I was delighted and knew that I had a good product as later indicated by the fact that a summary of my dissertation received a Best Paper Award from the OD&C Division of the Academy of Management (Wagner 2006). After obtaining my PhD, I returned to the AU/NTL program with a friend and colleague, Dr. Kathleen Cavanaugh, where we offered to redesign the one course that had least prepared us for our doctoral work: Methods of Problem Solving (MOPS), which at the time focused on only quantitative, not qualitative, data collection and analysis. Marshak offered to mentor us through the design phase and to co-teach the first course with us; under his tutelage I learned much about designing experiential learning and structuring activities to reinforce the readings through activities in the classroom.

With Marshak's ongoing support, I have continued to teach in this program since 2006, became the Interim Director in 2014, and the next year the Director and an Executive in Residence in the School of Public Affairs. Marshak continues to challenge my thinking, heightening my awareness of language and metaphors, and encourage me to strive for excellence. I have felt blessed to have Marshak's continued support in my quest to grow and develop as an educator and administrator in higher education.

New Insights and Contributions to OD and Change Theory and Practice

Throughout his work Marshak has led us to view change in organizations in new and surprising ways. He has challenged the dominant OD model of change (1993a), shifted the focus on language from being how it reports reality to how it creates reality (1993b), provided a model for seeing the hidden or subconscious factors that can impede a change initiative (2006a), highlighted how we implicitly privilege action over talk (1998a) and stability over change (2002a), and conceptualized and introduced the Dialogic OD mindset (Bushe and Marshak 2009, 2014, 2015a, b, c). Each of these new insights and contributions are reviewed briefly below.

Expanded the Lewinian paradigm on organizational change from "the" paradigm to "a" paradigm. When Marshak's acclaimed article "Lewin Meets Confucius: A Review of the OD Model of Change" (1993a) was published almost a quarter of a century ago, it raised some important ideas and challenged the then dominant OD model of change (unfreeze, movement, refreeze (Lewin 1951)). He asserted that this foundational OD model was based in Western culture and argued that alternative conceptions of change existed in other cultures. He presented and described contrasting world views: the linear, start-stop nature of the Lewinian perspective on change with the continuous cycle of change in the Confucian and Taoist perspectives. Marshak's insight – change is both continuous and cyclical rather than just episodic and linear – enables us to step out of the prevailing paradigm in order to see our paradigm of change not as "the" paradigm but as "a" paradigm. The following year, Marshak adapted and expanded these insights for practitioners in "The Tao of Change" (Marshak 1994). See Table 2 for how a practitioner might understand the difference between the Lewinian and the Confucian views of change.

In the process of presenting these new insights at conferences and in both academic and practitioner journals, Marshak quickly learned that "the possibility that there might be something outside of, and different from, the dominant OD model of change seemed to be an unacceptable proposition" (Marshak 2009, p. 66). Years later, he would encounter similar pushback when he and Bushe proposed that there was an alternative to the foundational OD mindset and models of change.

Highlighted the importance of nonrational and hidden aspects of change in partnership with Judith Katz. Marshak and Judith Katz integrated a range of ideas in the social sciences into a single model of hidden dynamics, signaling the importance of paying attention to the nonrational and hidden dynamics of a change effort. As practicing scholar/practitioners, they developed their insights into how nonrational factors (e.g., politics, inspirations, emotions, ways of thinking, and psychodynamics) have important influences in change efforts. They began by presenting these insights at organization development network conferences (Marshak and Katz 1990, 1991) and in articles in the *OD Practitioner* (Marshak and Katz 1997, 2001). Marshak documented these insights in his book *Covert Processes at Work: Managing the Five Hidden Dimensions of Organizational Change* (Marshak 2006).

Katz observes that one of Marshak's strong skills is his brilliance at integrating different ideas and concepts, a recent example being detecting the shifts in OD, pulling them together, and drawing the distinction between the traditional OD, calling it "Diagnostic OD" and the new, emerging practices that he and Bushe labeled "Dialogic OD" (J. Katz, personal communication, April, 20, 2016). In discussing her experience working with Marshak, she reflected that he was not a "stop and start guy" meaning that once something caught his attention he would stay focused on it across the decades. His tenacity has brought the field an increased awareness of language, symbolism, and metaphors as discussed below.

Galvanized the importance of language, symbolism, and metaphors of change. Marshak provided the field with the insight that people hold different formal and informal conceptions of change and that these different conceptions directly influence how people see and respond to change. In so doing he encouraged practitioners and academics to reflect on their implicit assumptions and then try to experience the world through a different set of assumptions. This line of thinking and questions ran through much of his work and was a central theme in his classic article, "Managing the Metaphors of Change." Starting with his first practitioner publication about the difference between magicians and shamans of OD (Marshak 1982), a significant portion of his work was intended to raise awareness of the conceptual confines of the field as revealed by word images, prevailing narratives, embedded meanings, and other forms of symbolic expression and to then suggest things beyond existing confines. Some of his key insights for the field of organizational change related to language, symbolism, and metaphors include the following (R.J. Marshak, personal communication, May 5, 2016):

- Language socially constructs and both enables and limits how we think about and experience change.
- Metaphors, story lines, and other forms of symbolic expression reveal explicit and implicit ways of thinking.
- Intervening through language can reframe mindsets and lead to both new behaviors and actions.
- Talk is a form of action, and talk contains action.

Marshak's views from the edge have challenged our conceptions of consulting and change for almost 35 years and led him to his most recent set of insights and collaboration with Bushe on conceptualizing an emerging form of OD they call, Dialogic OD. As Marshak notes, when one perceives language as constructive and change as continuous it begins to lead one's thinking away from traditional OD assumptions to a different conceptualization of OD focused on continuous, emergent change, the role language and symbols play in change, and the unplanned spontaneity of systems that recreate themselves (R.J. Marshak, personal communication, May 5, 2016).

Identified and brought coherence to a new form of OD: Dialogic OD. In 2010 NTL sponsored a special conference titled "The New OD" where Marshak challenged the status quo in his keynote address in which he shared his observations about the emergence of a new form of OD and potential consequences for the field as a whole. In a subsequent article, "OD Morphogenesis: the Emerging Dialogic Platform of Premises" (Marshak 2010), he captured the central concern: "...how the underlying premises that historically formed the field of OD have been expanded to allow a broader range of new communities of OD practice to emerge" (2010, p. 5). In the title Marshak borrows the term "morphogenesis" from biology where it refers to a biological process that "deals with the form of living organisms" (Brown et al. 1993). In the article he applies the concept of morphogenesis to the field of OD and proposes a platform of premises upon which the original OD was built. He then contrasts that with a set of premises that he identifies as creating a platform for an emerging, new form of OD. The two platforms of premises are presented in Table 7.

In the article Marshak also builds on an earlier presentation of metaphors of change (see Table 3) and expands it to the influence on change theories (see Table 8).

Three important insights presented in the morphogenesis article are that the emergent "dialogic" form of OD "offer[s] different possibilities and practices than found in foundational OD," "both [forms] currently exist and that OD, as a field, would benefit from a clearer differentiation," and "that people are more and more drawing on and combining the newer premises such that some practices now include a combination of several or even all of them" (Marshak 2010, p. 8). As the story of Dialogic OD emerges, there is still much work remaining.

Table 7 Contrasting Premises in OD

Foundational Premises in OD	More recent premises in OD
1. Positivism and Univocality	1. Social Construction and Plurivocality
2. Social Psychology and the Primacy of Small Groups	2. Large Group/System Events
3. Open Systems Theory	3. Meaning-Making Systems
4. Humanistic Psychology	4. Participative Action Inquiry
5. Action Research and Process Consultation	5. Discursive Studies
6. Planned Change	6. Complexity, Self-Organizing, and Continuous Change
7. Humanistic and Democratic Values	7. Humanistic and Democratic Values

Marshak (2010, pp. 6–8)

Table 8 Influences on Change Theories

	Mechanical Sciences (1900 to Present)	Biological Sciences (1960s to Present)	Interpretive Sciences (1980s to Present)	Complexity Sciences (1990s to Present)
Organizations are:	Determinate, closed systems	Contingent, open systems	Generative, meaning-making systems	Complex adaptive systems
Focus on:	Efficiency, plans, structure, IT, productivity	Alignment, congruence, strategic plans	Discourse, meaning making, culture, consciousness	Chaos, self-organization, emergent design
Change by:	Fix and Re-engineer	Adapt and Re-position	Reframe and Rename	Flux and Emergence

Marshak (2010, p. 5)

Legacies and Unfinished Business: Advancing the Dialogic Mindset

In concluding this chapter, the reader is invited to reflect on what inspiration or insights he or she has derived from Marshak's body of work and how to apply these learnings in his or her practice as an OD scholar/practitioner or as an OD-enabled leader. In addition, readers are challenged to consider how they might build upon Marshak's contributions.

Legacies for Scholars and Practitioners

Marshak has collaborated with many scholar/practitioners throughout his career. Several who shared their stories of working with Marshak described him as a generous colleague; their comments helped identify the key contributions discussed earlier in this chapter. When asked about his legacies, the conversations focused on his heightened skills at observation, analysis, and synthesis; his gifts as a theorist, cognitive linguist, and writer; and his exceptional presence as a classroom teacher. First, so many commented that Marshak is one of the great intellects in our field; one reason is because he is brilliant at integrating disparate things and creatively pulling them together into a coherent whole (J. Katz, personal communication, April 20, 2016). Another said his brilliance played out in his strong contribution to theorizing in both organizational discourse studies and Dialogic OD (D. Grant, personal communication, June 7, 2016). Marshak's ability as a writer was a theme that came through; several mentioned his style of including vignettes in his writing; one colleague observed that the "vignettes give his writing so much energy. . .his language comes alive" (D. Grant, personal communication, June 7, 2016). Practitioners commented that when they read

Marshak's description of conversations with clients, they recognized similar conversations from their own practice and this helped reframe everyday conversations and provided new insights.

Many discussed Marshak's contributions to the field of OD. One colleague asserted that Marshak's work in organizational discourse studies and Dialogic OD has "reinvigorated the field of OD" and that Marshak was a "bridge" between the foundational forms of OD and the newer forms of OD (D. Grant, personal communication, June 7, 2016). Grant went on to say that without Marshak's bridging role the field might have lost some of its traditions and values of OD if Marshak had not reminded them of its origins. Others also described his commitment to the field of OD, but commented that he embraced it with a tough love and that he was not one to "drink the Kool-Aid," which enabled him to cast a critical eye on the field (M. Minahan, personal communication, April 2016). One colleague wrote "A sense of hopeful anticipation may not be unwarranted when we reflect on the possibility of receiving Bob's next effort, contribution or 'humble inquiry' into organizational dynamics, enterprise performance, and 'wise' actions for improved change leadership" (D. LaCour, personal communication, April 15, 2016).

In the classroom, the first Director of the AU/NTL program remembers Marshak as "a remarkable, extraordinary classroom instructor... the best" (D. Zauderer, personal communication, April 25, 2016). One colleague provided insight into Marshak's philosophy in the classroom, which is to teach the direct relationship between theory and practice; noting that he has a "high-bar" desire for students to deeply understand theory because that directly influences the effectiveness of their practice (J. Katz, personal communication, April 20, 2016).

Unfinished Business: Creating Theory and Practice for Dialogic OD

Bushe and Marshak's book (2015c) – *Dialogic Organization Development: The Theory and Practice of Transformational Change* – is viewed as a paradigm shift in the field of organizational change. The authors have hosted webinars, presented at conferences, held book signings at various universities, and sponsored the First Annual Dialogic International Conference held in Vancouver, BC, Canada in August 2015 as a prelude to the annual Academy of Management Conference. Other such events will likely follow. However, the work that they have started continues. In the conclusion of their book, they propose a series of questions that will need to be addressed:

- How do dialogic processes of transformation work in practice?
- When is a Dialogic OD approach called for?
- What are the key choice points Dialogic OD practitioners routinely face?
- What choices do they and organizational leaders make and why?
- What skills and knowledge are needed for successful Dialogic OD practice? (Bushe and Marshak 2015c, p. 402)

In closing, it seems appropriate to highlight Marshak's decades of bringing to the field his integration of ideas from different theories, practices, and traditions. Almost everything he has done has brought together ideas that might have been previously disjoint, such as magicians and shamans (Marshak 1982), Lewin and Confucius (Marshak 1993a), talk and action (Marshak 1998), overt and covert (Marshak 2006), and finally Diagnostic and Dialogic OD (Bushe and Marshak 2009).

References

Bartunek, J. M., & Woodman, R. W. (2015). Beyond Lewin: Toward a temporal approximation of organization development and change. *Annual Review of Organizational Psychology and Organizational Behavior, 2*, 157–182.

Berger, P. L., & Luckmann, T. (1966). *The social construction of reality: A treatise in the sociology of knowledge*. New York: Doubleday.

Brown, L., Hughes, A. M., Sykes, J., Trumble, W. R., Hole, G., Knowles, E. M., ... & Stevenson, A. (Eds.). (1993). *The new shorter Oxford English dictionary*. New York: Oxford University Press.

Bunker, B. B., & Alban, B. T. (1997). *Large group intervention: Engaging the whole system for rapid change*. San Francisco: Jossey-Bass.

Burns, T., & Stalker, G. M. (1961). Mechanistic and organic systems. In J. M. Shafritz & J. S. Ott (Eds.), *Classics of organization theory* (3rd ed., pp. 207–211). Belmont: Wadsworth Publishing.

Bushe, G. R., & Marshak, R. J. (2009). Revisioning organization development: Diagnostic and dialogic premises and patterns of practice. *Journal of Applied Behavioral Science, 45*(3), 348–368.

Bushe, G. R., & Marshak, R. J. (2014). The dialogic mindset in organization development. *Research in Organizational Change and Development, 22*, 55–97.

Bushe, G. R., & Marshak, R. J. (2015a). *Dialogic organization development: Recapturing the spirit of inquiry*. Paper presented at the First International Dialogic OD Conference, Vancouver.

Bushe, G. R., & Marshak, R. J. (2015b). Introduction to the dialogic organization development mindset. In G. R. Bushe & R. J. Marshak (Eds.), *Dialogic organization development: The theory and practice of transformational change* (pp. 11–32). Oakland: Berrett-Koehler.

Bushe, G. R., & Marshak, R. J. (Eds.). (2015c). *Dialogic organization development: The theory and practice of transformational change*. Oakland: Berrett-Koehler.

Goffman, E. (1961). *Asylums: Essays on the social situation of mental patients and other inmates*. Garden City: Anchor Books.

Grant, D., & Marshak, R. J. (2009). *A discourse-based theory of organizational change. Best Paper Award, Organization Development and Change Division*. Paper presented at the Academy of Management., Chicago.

Grant, D., & Marshak, R. J. (2011). Toward a discourse-centered understanding of organizational change. *Journal of Applied Behavioral Science, 47*(2), 204–235.

Grant, D., & Oswick, C. (Eds.). (1996). *Metaphor and organization*. London: Sage.

Heracleous, L., & Marshak, R. J. (2004a). Conceptualizing organizational discourse as situated symbolic action. *Human Relations, 57*(10), 1285–1312.

Heracleous, L., & Marshak, R. J. (2004b). *Organizational discourse as situated symbolic action: Application through an OD intervention. Best Action Research Paper Award, Organization Development and Change Division*. Paper presented at the Academy of Management, New Orleans.

Katz, D., & Kahn, R. (1978). *The social psychology of organizations* (2nd ed.). New York: Wiley.

Keenoy, T., Marshak, R. J., Oswick, C., & Grant, D. (2000). The discourses of organizing. *Journal of Applied Behavioral Science, 36*(2), 133–135.

Lamb, Y. S. (2008). Morley Segal, 74: Innovator in group dynamics at AU. *Washington Post*. Retrieved from http://www.washingtonpost.com/wp-dyn/content/article/2008/04/21/AR20080

Lawrence, P. R., & Lorsch, J. W. (1969). Organization-environment interface. In J. M. Shafritz & J. S. Ott (Eds.), *Classics of organization theory* (3rd ed., pp. 229 233). Belmont: Wadsworth Publishing.

Lewin, K. (1951). *Field theory in social science*. New York: Harper & Row.

Marshak, R. J. (1982). Magicians and shamans of OD. *OD Practitioner, 14*(3), 8–9.

Marshak, R. J. (1983). Cognitive and experiential approaches to conceptual learning. *Training and Development Journal, 37*(5), 72–79.

Marshak, R. J. (1993a). Lewin meets Confucius: A review of the OD model of change. *Journal of Applied Behavioral Science, 29*, 393–415.

Marshak, R. J. (1993b). Managing the metaphors of change. *Organizational Dynamics, 22*(1), 44–56.

Marshak, R. J. (1994). The Tao of change. *OD Practitioner, 26*(2), 18–26.

Marshak, R. J. (1996). Metaphors, metaphoric fields, and organizational change. In D. Grant & C. Oswick (Eds.), *Metaphor and organizations* (pp. 147–165). London: Sage.

Marshak, R. J. (1998). A discourse on discourse: Redeeming the meaning of talk. In D. Grant, T. Keenoy, & C. Oswick (Eds.), *Discourse and organization*. London: Sage.

Marshak, R. J. (2002). Changing the language of change: How new contexts and concepts are challenging the ways we think and talk about organizational change. *Strategic Change, 11*, 279–286.

Marshak, R. J. (2006). Emerging directions: Is there a new OD? In J. V. Gallos (Ed.), *Organization Development: A Jossey-Bass Reader*, pp. 833–841. San Francisco: Jossey-Bass Publishers.

Marshak, R. J. (2006). *Covert processes at work: Managing the five hidden dimensions of organizational change*. San Francisco: Berrett-Koehler.

Marshak, R. J. (2008). In memoriam: Morley Segal. *PS: Political Science and Politics, XLI*(3), 638–639.

Marshak, R. J. (2009). *Organizational change: Views from the edge*. Bethel Maine: The Lewin Center.

Marshak, R. J. (2010). OD morphogenesis: The emerging dialogic platform of premises. *Practicing Social Change, 2010*(2), 4–9.

Marshak, R. J. (2013a). Generative conversations: How to use deep listening and transforming talk in coaching and consulting. In J. Vogelsang, M. Townsend, M. Minahand, D. Jamieson, J. Vogel, A. Viets, C. Royal, & L. Valek (Eds.), *Handbook for strategic HR: Best practices in organization development from the OD network* (pp. 161–167). New York: AMACOM, a division of the American Management Association.

Marshak, R. J. (2013b). Leveraging language for change. *OD Practitioner, 45*(2), 49–55.

Marshak, R. J. (2015). My journey into dialogic organization development. *OD Practitioner, 47*(2), 47–52.

Marshak, R. J., & Heracleous, L. (2005). A discursive approach to organization development. *Action Research, 3*(1), 69–88.

Marshak, R. J., & Katz, J. H. (1990). *Covert processes and revolutionary change*. Paper presented at the Forging Revolutionary Partnerships: 1990 National OD Network Conference, Philadelphia.

Marshak, R. J., & Katz, J. H. (1991). *Keys to unlocking covert processes*. Paper presented at the Building Ourselves...Our Work... Our Organizations...Our World: Proceedings of the 1991 National OD Network Conference, Long Beach.

Marshak, R. J., & Katz, J. H. (1997). Diagnosing covert processes in groups and organizations. *OD Practitioner, 29*(1), 33–42.

Marshak, R. J., & Katz, J. H. (2001). Keys to unlocking covert processes: How to recognize and address the hidden dimensions of individuals, groups and organizations. *OD Practitioner, 33*(2), 3–10.

Marshak, R. J., Keenoy, T., Oswick, C., & Grant, D. (2000). From outer words to inner worlds. *Journal of Applied Behavioral Science, 36*(2), 245–258.

Morgan, G. (1986). *Images of organization*. Newbury Park: Sage.

Oswick, C., & Marshak, R. J. (2012). Images of organization development: The role of metaphor in processes of change. In D. Boje, B. Burnes, & J. Hassard (Eds.), *The Routledge companion to organizational change* (pp. 104–114). London: Routledge.

Oswick, C., Keenoy, T., Grant, D., & Marshak, R. J. (2000). Discourse, organization, and epistemology. *Organization, 7*(3), 511–512.
Oswick, C., Grant, D., Marshak, R. J., & Cox, J. W. (2010). Organizational discourse and change: Positions, perspectives, progress, and prospects. *Journal of Applied Behavioral Science, 46*(1), 8–15.
Thompson, J. D. (1967). *Organizations in action: Social science bases of administrative theory.* New York: McGraw-Hill.
Wagner, R. S. (2006). *The human element of organizational transformation: A phenomenographic study of how internal stakeholders in federal defense organizations experience and make sense of planned organizational change.* (PhD), Fielding Graduate University, Santa Barbara.
Watkins, J. M., Mohr, B. J., & Kelly, R. (2011). *Appreciative inquiry: Change at the speed of imagination* (2nd ed.). San Francisco: Pfeiffer & Co.
Weber, M. (1946). Bureaucracy. In J. M. Shafritz & J. S. Ott (Eds.), *Classics of organization theory* (3rd ed., pp. 81–86). Belmont: Wadsworth Publishing.
Weick, K. E., & Quinn, R. E. (1999). Organizational change and development. *Annual Review Psychology, 50*, 361–386.
Wheatley, M. J. (1992). *Leadership and the new science: Learning about organization from an orderly world.* San Francisco: Berrett-Koehler.

Further Reading

This final section includes a short list of books and journal articles that enable readers to take their interests further. The readings are organized by the identified themes in Marshak's work.

Classic Articles: Lewinian, Western with Confucian, Eastern Perspectives of Change

Marshak, R. J. (1993). Lewin meets Confucius: A re-view of the OD model of change. *The Journal of Applied Behavioral Science, 29*(4), 393–415.
Marshak, R. J. (1994). The Tao of change. *OD Practitioner, 26*(2), 18–26.

Presenting a Framework for Analyzing the Hidden Dimensions of Changes: The Covert Processes Model™

Marshak, R. J. (2006). *Covert processes at work: Managing the five hidden dimensions of organizational change.* San Francisco: Berrett-Koehler Publishers.

Focusing on Language, Symbolism, and Metaphors of Change

Marshak, R. J. (1993). Managing the metaphors of change. *Organizational Dynamics, 22*(1), 44–56.
Marshak, R. J. (1998). A discourse on discourse: Redeeming the meaning of talk. In D. Grant, T. Keenoy, & C. Oswick (Eds.), *Discourse and organization* (pp. 15–30). London: Sage.
Marshak, R. J. (2002). Changing the language of change: How new contexts and concepts are challenging the ways we think and talk about organizational change. *Strategic Change, 11*(5), 279–286.
Marshak, R. J. (2013). Leveraging language for change. *OD Practitioner, 45*(2), 49–55.

Marshak, R. J., & Grant, D. (2008). Organizational discourse and new organization development practices. *British Journal of Management, 19*, S7–S19.
Heracleous, L., & Marshak, R. J. (2004). Conceptualizing organizational discourse as situated symbolic action. *Human Relations, 57*(10), 1285–1312.

Conceptualizing and Describing a New Form of Organization Development: Dialogic OD

Bushe, G. R., & Marshak, R. J. (2009). Revisioning organization development: Diagnostic and dialogic premises and patterns of practice. *Journal of Applied Behavioral Science, 45*, 348–368.
Bushe, G. R., & Marshak, R. J. (Eds.) (2015). *Dialogic organization development: The theory and practice of transformational change*. Oakland: Berrett-Koehler Publishers.
Marshak, R. J. (2015). My journey into dialogic organization development. *OD Practitioner, 47*(2), 47–52.

Writings for Practitioners in the Field of OD

Many of Marshak's best works for practitioners are included in a section in *Views from the Edge* in "Part Four: Insights for Organization Development Practitioners."

Marshak, R. J. (2009) *Organizational change: Views from the edge*. Bethel: The Lewin Center.

A 30-Year Collaboration of Victoria Marsick and Karen Watkins: Learning in the Workplace

50

Michael Beyerlein, Khalil M. Dirani, and Lei Xie

Abstract

A field in the social and organizational science grows in richness of perspective, methods, and tools, the same way a field in the hard sciences does: new ideas emerge from the rich conversation of the members. Sometimes, a rich flow of ideas emerges from a special subgroup, such as collaborative partnerships. This chapter focuses on such a partnership: the 30-year collaboration of doctors Victoria Marsick and Karen Watkins. It is a story of discovering new ways to view learning in the workplace, but it did not start with that focus. The content of our chapter is based on interviews with Marsick and Watkins and with seven of their colleagues, who read much of their work and related material and interacted with them for several decades. Interviews included former students, colleagues, coauthors, and fellow board members for the Association for Talent Development (ATD, formerly ASTD) and the Center for Creative Leadership (CCL). Those individuals had known the two scholars 15–25 years.

Keywords

Collaboration • Informal and incidental learning • Learning organization • Human resource development • Performance Learning • Organization development • Problem-solving

M. Beyerlein (✉) • K.M. Dirani • L. Xie
Educational Administration and Human Resource Development Program, Texas A&M University, College Station, TX, USA
e-mail: beyerlein@tamu.edu; dirani@tamu.edu; xlaizhzh1@tamu.edu

D.B. Szabla et al. (eds.), *The Palgrave Handbook of Organizational Change Thinkers*,
DOI 10.1007/978-3-319-52878-6_98

Contents

Introduction

In 1985, one of those rare collaborations between scholars was born that influenced both research and practice in multiple disciplines around the world. Victoria Marsick and Karen Watkins began a 30-year partnership of thinking and writing that resulted in focusing the attention of scholars on workplace learning and provided them with frameworks and tools. This chapter traces the evolution of their collaboration and the impact of their work on organizational change, human resource development, and adult learning. Twenty-first century organizations depend on constant learning for generating constant adaptive change at a level unprecedented in prior centuries. Marsick and Watkins' work provides insight and guidelines for development of learning organizations.

Influences and Motivations: Marsick and Watson's Development as Scholars

Marsick is currently the professor of adult learning and leadership for the department of organization and leadership, and codirector of a research institute at Teachers College (TC), Columbia University, which studies learning in organizations. Marsick's scholarship includes work on informal learning, action learning, team learning, system learning culture, strategic organizational learning, and knowledge management.

Watkins is currently the professor and program coordinator in the Department of Lifelong Education, Administration and Policy (Learning, Leadership, and Organization) at the University of Georgia. Her scholarship focuses on learning organizations, action learning, action science, workplace learning, reflective learning, informal learning, incidental learning, human resource development, organizational change, and learning at the core.

During three decades of shared thinking and writing, doctors Marsick and Watkins have produced more than 50 joint publications, including five books and one significant measurement instrument (the Dimensions of the Learning Organization Questionnaire, *DLOQ*). Those publications have had a significant impact on both the research and practice of human learning at the individual, team, and organizational levels in all kinds of organizations. Our chapter will trace the development of those ideas, their impact and the legacy of this team of two exceptional individuals, and their notable collaboration.

Marsick and Watkins started their careers in different fields and different locations, although their commencement dates for BS, MS, and PhD show that they were on parallel schedules. Marsick grew up in Cleveland, Ohio, and noticed that its many ethnic neighborhoods each represented distinct cultures with "stick-to-your-own-kind" norms about boundary crossing. She became interested in socialization, particularly its influence on "unspoken, tacit assumptions about what is or is not possible in society (Marsick, personal communication, April 10, 2016)." This led to her interest in the works of Chris Argyris and Donald Schön (whom she discovered in graduate school) on single-loop and double-loop learning, tacit assumptions, and societal suppression. Her interest in cross-cultural dimensions of socialization originated when – as part of her master's degree in international public administration at Syracuse – she spent a little more than a year in India – an "eye opening" experience that enabled her to examine her own unspoken assumptions about society. A classroom assignment that grew out of this internship experience upon her return to Syracuse to complete her degree was used by a nonprofit organization, World Education, with which she subsequently worked, including 3 years as a field representative in Southeast Asia (and on whose advisory board she has served). Through that assignment, she met Jack Mezirow, Len Nadler, Bob Luke, and other adult educators who had interests in adult learning and change. Marsick learned about training and development by working with Nadler, among others, on training design and implementation, and through working with nonprofit organizations in Asia and Africa as a consultant.

Victoria Marsick's Career

Marsick's PhD studies in adult education were completed at Berkeley, under the mentorship of Jack London, who had an interest in equity and in international adult education. While at Berkeley, Marsick collaborated with Mezirow and others on a grounded theory study of higher education programs designed for women who returned to their studies after raising families or earning a living. This research led to Mezirow's (1978) seminal theorizing about how adults critically examine assumptions, leading to transformation of their views, perspectives, and actions. Marsick worked with Mezirow as a graduate student and then as a colleague through his retirement at Columbia in 1992. She described Mezirow as a major influence on her thought and work, particularly transformative learning (personal communication, April 10, 2016). Her understanding of society's role in shaping lives grew while working on her dissertation – a comparative analysis of experiential learning designs for training programs preparing field workers in health and family planning (Nepal, Taiwan, and the Philippines). Another key influence was the 5 years she spent in a staff development position at the United Nations Children's Emergency Fund (UNICEF) after earning her PhD, where she honed her training and development (T&D) design skills. She learned organization development (OD) skills from her supervisor, Eigil Morch, who utilized an OD framework in supporting organizational learning at UNICEF. Marsick's extensive international work provided her with the opportunity to refine a focus on experiential learning design to support individual and organizational development, and to gain an appreciation of the complexities of change in nested systems through the management of system dynamics. That rich experience was the prelude to meeting Watkins.

Karen Watkin's Career

Watkins began her academic career as a teacher of English at Miami-Dade Community College, where Carol Zion's mentorship involved her in faculty and organization development (Watkins, personal communication, April 10, 2016). Watkins became frustrated with how difficult it was to get faculty to change, so she began to develop an interest in learning and organizational change. Oscar Mink convinced her to complete her doctoral work at the University of Texas at Austin (UT Austin), and played a significant mentoring role for her in OD. She worked with Mink on OD in workshops, in developing a new Human Resource Development (HRD) program, on conference presentations, on book chapters, in consulting through the National Institute for Staff and Organizational Development, and in the cochairing of dissertations – frequently during the early 1980s, but continuing on into the 1990s. She joined the Human Resource OD Program at UT Austin to teach OD, and discovered the work of Argyris and Schön. Watkins read Schön's book *Beyond the Stable State* for her dissertation work. She invited Argyris and Schön to speak at UT, which led to a long-term relationship with Schön and his students, to develop curricula in action science. In 2001, she and Jackie Wilson coauthored a paper about Argyris for a book on influential twentieth century authors in adult and continuing education.

Launching a 30-Year Collaboration

In the 1980s – in the early days of HRD as a field – a debate to decide whether or not HRD was "adult education" because of its focus on behavioral change and skills training was arranged between Mezirow and Nadler at the Commission of Professors of Adult Education Conference. By contrast, the field of adult education – with its roots in community development – advocated for a view of social justice that did not include organizations that were considered anti-worker. Watkins facilitated a small group to discuss the debate remarks, and Marsick was in her group. She spoke to Marsick during the break, and the two women immediately discovered how parallel their histories and interests were. Marsick invited Watkins to coauthor a chapter on approaches to researching workplace learning in the book she was editing, *Learning in the Workplace* (1987). That led to their first coauthored book, *Informal and Incidental Learning in the Workplace* (1990), which focused on learning outside the classroom; that volume was reissued in 2015. The continued development of those ideas led to the realization that informal learning strategies were central to HRD and that they differed by level and by how individuals deal with the system dynamics of the organization.

Through the 1990s, Marsick and Watkins each published books with other coauthors, but their key contributions linked their scholarship on informal and incidental learning with organizational learning. Over time, they have updated their model of informal and incidental learning to recognize its interactive, social nature (Marsick and Watkins 1990). In 1993, they coauthored *Sculpting the Learning Organization*, followed in 1996 by an edited book that illustrated what learning organization looked like *(In action: Creating the Learning Organization*). In 1999, they published a follow-up to *Sculpting*, called *Facilitating the Learning Organization*, which was followed in 2003 by *Making Learning Count: Diagnosing the Learning Culture in Organizations* as an issue of *Advances in Developing Human Resources*. How did these ideas coevolve over time?

Their early conversations were about informal and incidental learning, based on common interests in action science (Argyris and Schön), learning (John Dewey and Mezirow), OD (Kurt Lewin), and action research. They realized later that they had both written dissertations on organizational change but had different foci and contexts. The subsequent intermingling of these ideas formed a part of their intellectual scaffolding. They conceptualized the outline for their first book on informal and incidental learning while traveling by train in England to participate in an international conference. They continued to develop their ideas in joint workshops and conference presentations as they worked on *Sculpting the Learning Organization*, drawing on research they were carrying out independently or with other coauthors, such as the studies of team learning that Marsick undertook with Kathleen Dechant and Elizabeth Kasl in the 1990s. Their work with other colleagues often enriched their work together. The writing process for *Sculpting* published in 1993 radically differed from the process for *Informal and Incidental Learning*. For the 1990 book, they each wrote chapters by themselves and shared the results for editing by email between Austin, Texas, and New York City. They did the same with chapters for *Sculpting*, although they had worked together on the arguments in the book and the outline for its chapters. When they received reviewer feedback about the manuscript for *Sculpting*, they realized that they needed to refocus and do a significant rewrite on several chapters. They found ways to work together in blocks of time, but this go-round, each of them rewrote the other's chapters after extended conversations about the necessary changes, leading to the publisher's observation that this book seemed to have a single voice.

Their primary areas of shared scholarship include the learning organization and informal and incidental learning. The impact of that scholarship has been global with their key measurement instrument, the *DLOQ*, and learning organization conceptual framework, translated into at least 15 languages and used in studies in a number of countries. Another major impact of their work was its key role in influencing research directions in the field of HRD. They are widely recognized for providing the field with a research-based set of theories, tools, and practices that have influenced how scholars and practitioners think about and study learning in organizations – a multilevel process that represents the cornerstone of sustainability in the turbulent times of the twenty-first century workplace. Their work together continues today. The next section provides an overview of the more critical ideas they have cocreated.

Key Contributions: Informal and Incidental Learning and the Learning Organization

In the following section, we will discuss two of Watkins and Marsick's main scholarly contributions, namely informal and incidental learning and the learning organization.

Informal and Incidental Learning

Informal and incidental learning gained researchers' interest during only the past 20 years; efforts started with defining and describing both types of learning. Marsick and Watkins pioneered this field by providing a model for informal and incidental learning and through the publication of their book, *Informal and Incidental Learning in the Workplace* (first published in 1990 and reprinted in 2015). Marsick and Watkins knew that traditional structured approaches to training were not effective when it came to learning in the workplace. They believed that informal and incidental learning were more effective approaches to helping people in the workplace, and they developed a theory that captured their concepts and provided strategies for understanding and capturing informal learning. At that time, they did not think that in 25 years, their work would become central for scholars, practitioners, and students of the field of HRD.

Marsick and Watkins (1990) said that they wrote their book for "those who are interested in informal and incidental learning in the workplace, which [they] contrast with more highly structured workshops, seminars and courses that are often referred to as training and development (1990, p. 3)."

Marsick and Watkins said that they believed that, unlike formal learning, informal and incidental learning were learner-driven and were intentional, self-directed, and not highly structured. They suggested that organizations can deliberately encourage such forms of learning and that individuals can learn informally or incidentally, irrespective of their organization's environment.

Informal and Incidental Learning Origins and Model

Informal learning can be traced back to the works of Lindeman (1926) and Dewey (1938), who emphasized the importance of learning from experience and the role of reflective thought in the learning process. Marsick and Watkins (2001) noted that their theory of informal and incidental learning was rooted in concepts such as formal and nonformal learning (Jarvis 1987), social modeling (Bandura 1986), experiential learning (Kolb 1984), self-directed learning (Knowles 1950), action and experiential learning (Revans 1982), action science (Argyris and Schön 1978), reflection in action (Schön 1983), critical reflection and transformative learning (Mezirow 1991), tacit knowing (Nonaka and Takeuchi 1995), situated cognition (Lave and Wenger 1991), and communities of practice (Wenger 1998).

Marsick and Watkins' (1990) model describing informal and incidental learning has been empirically tested in numerous studies that represent a variety of organizational contexts. Based on that model, researchers have (a) identified catalysts for informal learning (Ellinger et al. 2003); (b) examined learning strategies, techniques, and outcomes and consequences for organizations (Cseh et al. 1999); and (c) explored the importance of context on informal and incidental learning (Marsick and Watkins 2001).

Marsick and Watkins (1997) characterized their model as a problem-solving approach that commences with an event or situation as a trigger, stimulating the need to develop a solution to a problem and to find the meaning in a situation. Triggers often challenge an individual's presently held frame of reference and require a nonroutine response (Marsick and Watkins 1990). The informal learning process continues through phases that include the individual's interpreting the trigger, considering alternative solutions, identifying appropriate learning strategies, and implementing the chosen strategy – followed by an evaluation of anticipated and unanticipated consequences of the chosen solution (Cseh et al. 1999). The concluding phase of the informal and incidental learning model provides a foundation for further learning, and shapes expectations for future experiences. The entire process is embedded in "context," or the complex environment in which the informal learning occurs (Marsick and Watkins 1990).

Figure 1 depicts the Marsick and Watkins model of informal and incidental learning. The model shows a progression of meaning making – for each new insight individuals may have to go back and question earlier understandings. According to Marsick and Watkins (2001), the model is arranged in a circle, but the steps are neither linear nor necessarily sequential.

Figure 2 presents the reconceptualized model of informal learning. In this newest version of the Marsick and Watkins model, the doctors integrated the incidental learning process, since "it was clear to us that it is always occurring, with or without our conscious awareness (Marsick and Watkins 2001, p. 29)." Both models of informal and incidental learning show the genuine evolution of Marsick and Watkins as scholars and students of learning in the workplace through the integration of research and practice within HRD.

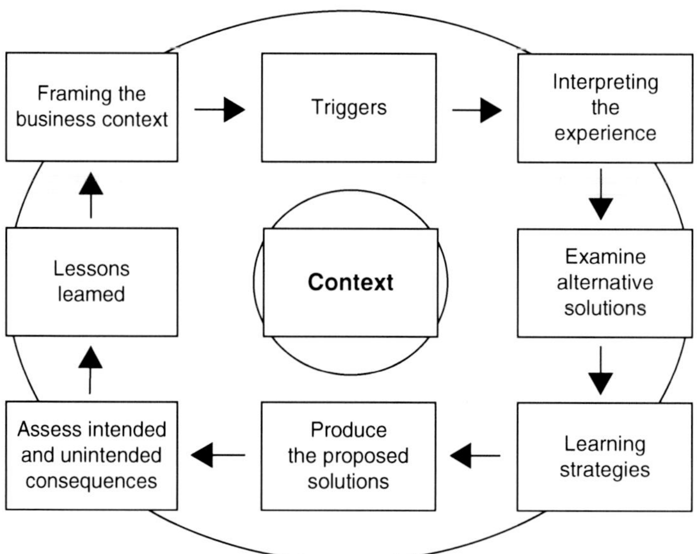

Fig. 1 Informal and incidental learning model (Reprinted from *Informal and Incidental Learning* (Marsick and Watkins 2001) and *New Directions for Adult and Continuing Education* (Marsick and Watkins 1989, p. 29). Copyright 2001 by Marsick and Watkins)

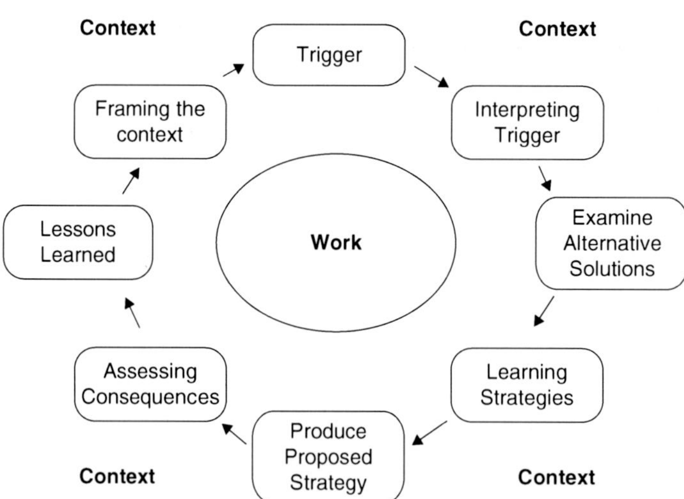

Fig. 2 Marsick and Watkins' reconceptualized model for enhancing informal and incidental learning (Adopted from Cseh et al. 1999. Reprinted with permission)

The Learning Organization

The early work of Watkins and Marsick on incidental and informal learning has generated a huge impact in the world of adult and continuing education. Interweaving that work with their study of organizational learning created a unique perspective impacting both scholarship and practice. Three books later, the ideas on "sculpting" and "facilitating" the learning organization continued to evolve. This is such an important piece of organizational change because of its influence on organizational readiness for change and continuous improvement. Dr. Marie Volpe, a former senior employee at Exxon and current adjunct assistant professor of adult learning and leadership at TC, Columbia University, contributed a comment for the book cover of Watkins and Marsick's (1993) book, *Sculpting the Learning Organization: Lessons in the Art and Science of Systemic Change:* "This is not a 'flavor of the month' management book; this is a blueprint for organizations in the 21st century."

In *Sculpting the Learning Organization*, Marsick and Watkins defined a learning organization as "one that learns continuously and transforms itself. Learning is a continuous, strategically used process – integrated with, and running parallel to, work (Watkins and Marsick 1993, p. 8)." With a profound understanding of informal and incidental learning and considerable professional experience in organizational change consulting, they offered "analysis of the characteristics, qualities, and efforts of emerging learning organizations that will help ... set a course and develop practices to create ... learning organization (Watkins and Marsick 1993, p. xv)." They captured the characteristics of a learning organization at four different interacting levels: individual, group, organization, and society.

The essence of the book stems from the question of how to improve organizational change effectiveness and increase continuous learning capacity. With the intention of helping organizations succeed, their conceptualization of learning organizations draws on relationships among learning culture, leadership, and strategy. As an important part of "sculpting" a learning organization, organizational learning culture becomes a cornerstone for organizational change readiness. Learning culture supports employees in planned and unplanned change via continuous learning opportunities, collaboration, and work toward a clear vision (Haque 2008). A learning organization also constantly creates learning opportunities for employees to hone their learning skills, which changes them to become more adaptive toward future organizational change (Argyris and Schön 1978). Learning occurs at multiple levels and is both cognitive and behavioral. Initially, Marsick and Watkins identified six action imperatives for the creation of a learning organization that occur at four levels (individual, team, organization, and society), as shown in Fig. 3. Based on those six action imperatives, recommendations are drawn to guide the creation of learning organizations. Unlike researchers focused primarily on theory-building, this model thus also supports implications for practice.

Although they are two independent "sculptors" for their first book, their long-term collaboration made one unified masterpiece with obvious value. The similarity

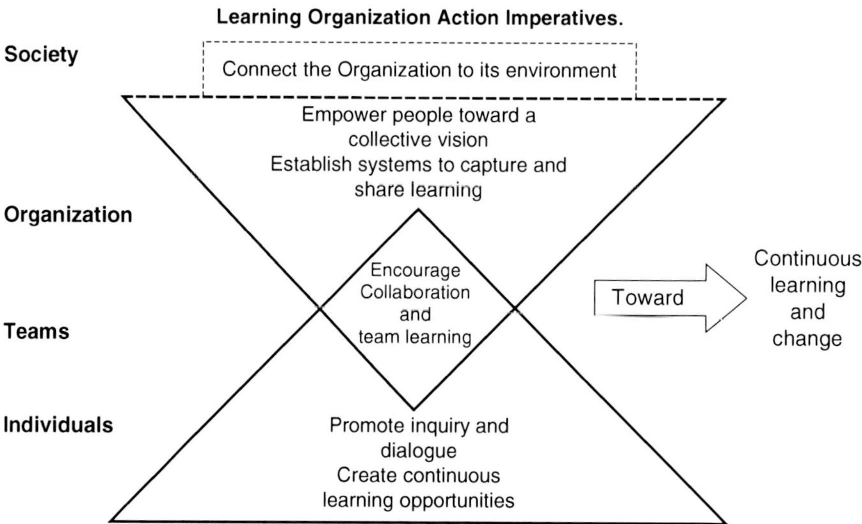

Fig. 3 Learning organization action imperatives (Adopted from Sculpting the Learning Organization: Lessons in the Art and Science of Systemic Change (p. 10) by K. E. Watkins and V. J. Marsick (1993), San Francisco, CA: Jossey-Bass, Copyright 1993 by Watkins, K. E., & Marsick, V. J. Reprinted with permission)

of their professional experiences enhanced their relationship for writing and combining thoughts. Both Marsick and Watkins have applied these ideas in their work with organizations, especially through action learning and action research, both in the United States and in other countries. In using the metaphor of sculpture, they acknowledge the differences between a work of art and the dynamic work of organizations that are dealing with ever-changing people and ever-evolving goals (Watkins and Marsick 1993). The core dimensions of learning organizations are thus expressed in many different ways. To illuminate what this looks like, in 1996, they published another book, *In Action: Creating the Learning Organization*, through the American Society for Training and Development (ASTD), which sent out more than 7,500 invitations to submit cases, from which Watkins and Marsick selected 22 examples of real-world organization learning applications. Each company employed unique means of managing change and promoting continuous learning, respectively. This book illustrated the action imperatives in Fig. 3. Watkins and Marsick showed that learning organizations are socially created: "the visionary leader serves a role not unlike that of the sculptor who releases the inner essence of the creation (Watkins and Marsick 1996, p. iii)." Intuitively, it is not hard to notice that building a learning organization is as much an art as it is a science (Watkins and Marsick 1993).

With heated competition from companies around the globe, organizations with learning cultures react faster than traditional organizations to business environment change, such as economic downturn or unplanned economic consequences. Therefore, the biggest change in the 1996 book from the doctors' previous publication was not only a greater focus on examples from case studies – instructing readers about how to facilitate building a learning organization – but also the learning level change from "society" to "global," due to increasing international influence. They wrote, "Learning at the global level is thinking globally; crossing boundaries of environmental or societal impacts, including those that affect the quality of life afforded organizational members by the organization (Watkins and Marsick 1996, p. 7)."

Watkins and Marsick (1996) said that the vision of key leaders is primary. Marsick and Watkins later developed their third book, *Facilitating Learning Organizations: Making Learning Count* (1999), adding one more imperative to the previous six: "provide strategic leadership for learning." This showed their evolving understanding of the role that leadership has been playing in organizational change (Fig. 4). Therefore, they adapted their original model by adding leadership as a seventh action imperative.

In most cases, as the first step, changing leaders' roles supports all of the organizational learning interventions that take place during organizational change (Marsick and Watkins 1999). Cases in the writers' second book have shown a close relationship between leadership and organizational learning, as Senge (1990) also emphasized. There is no doubt that leaders in the executive level are key in the early phases of organization change (Burke 2002). Many argue the important role that leaders play in organization change, even though there is little scientific support for that impact of leadership (Burke 2002).

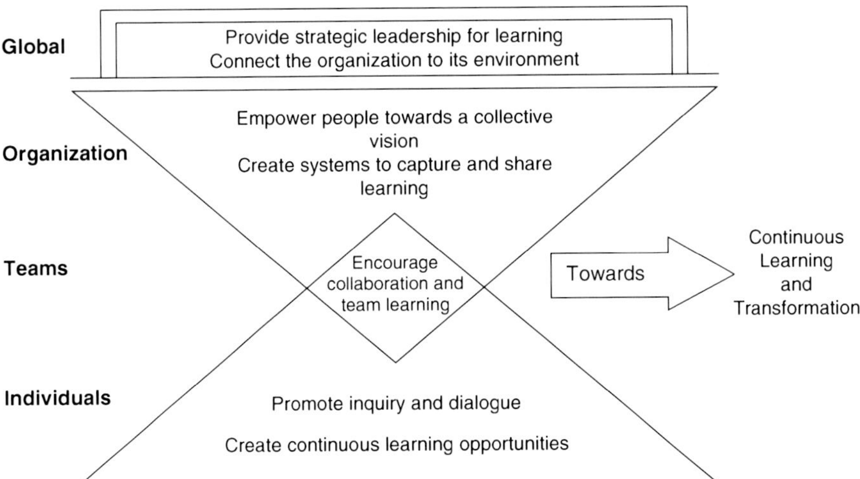

Fig. 4 Learning organization imperatives (Adopted from *Facilitating Learning Organizations: Making Learning Count* (p. 11), by V. J. Marsick and K. E. Watkins (1999), London: Gower Press, Copyright 1999 by Marsick, V. J., & Watkins, K. E. Reprinted with permission)

Bridging Theory and Practice

In their book *Facilitating Learning Organizations*, Marsick and Watkins (1999) proposed that leadership should be a mindset for *everyone* in the learning organization, not only those on the executive level. They wrote, "Leadership spurs learning individuals that spreads out in ever-widening waves through teams, larger groups within the organization, and in some cases, the entire organization (Marsick and Watkins 1999, p. 209)." The leadership resides in employees that empower them to actively bring in new ideas from the outside environment, and thus to absorb, digest, and spread what they have learned to the whole organization. Successful organizational learning interventions must grow within the organization to fit in the special context with right and timely guidance from the leadership level. To summarize, Marsick and Watkins wrote, "The learning organization is a living, breathing organism that creates the space that enables people and systems to learn, to grow and to endure (Marsick and Watkins 1999, p. 210)."

Along the learning organization research journey, Watkins and Marsick advocated that people and companies enact these ideas by working through action technologies such as action learning, action research, and action science. Action research brings action and theory together, enabling practitioners to produce effective actions that stem from theories. At the same time, researchers develop theory with real applications (Dickens and Watkins 1999). Brown and his colleagues (1988) said that action research is most effective when participants immerse themselves in objective problems, and critically reflect on those issues. Action technologies emphasize personal inquiry, self-reflection, and critical thinking. Its essence matches one of the seven imperatives for a learning organization: promoting inquiry and dialogue. The learning organization model provides a map for employees to change cognitively. Meanwhile, action technologies create an inquiry environment at the larger organizational level. Thus, action techniques "add a strong dose of behavioral practices and affective changes of heart and will (Marsick and Watkins 1999, p. 5)."

In their 1999 collaborative book *Facilitating Learning Organizations*, Marsick and Watkins built the connection between the leaders' role as facilitators and the learning organization by using recent, vivid, practical examples. An increasing number of managers – undergoing changes in leadership roles – play more of a facilitator role in order to foster organizational learning (Ellinger et al. 1999). Implications for facilitators are the keys to this book. Separating itself from many that focus primarily on theory, this book emphasizes translating theory into practice.

To summarize, the concept of the learning organization is an important area of interest for HRD scholars and is a valuable framework for managers of organization change. Marsick and Watkins' body of research about learning organization theory and practice during the past 25 years has had a major impact in the area of research and practice. Watkins and Marsick (1993, 2003) provided a framework of seven dimensions for the learning organization and constructed a 43-item questionnaire to measure these dimensions. Scholars have used different variations of the learning organization questionnaire – i.e., a 21-item *DLOQ* or a seven-item *DLOQ* – in many contexts. Today, scholars have validated and employed the *DLOQ* in various national and organizational contexts and produced more than 100 related studies around the world (Watkins and Dirani 2013). For example, based on the *DLOQ* framework, Dirani (2013) worked on validating the *DLOQ* and measured how a learning culture impacts theory and practice in the Lebanese culture. Based on Dirani's work, several researchers are already using the *DLOQ* in the other Arab countries such as Jordan, Saudi Arabia, the United Arab Emirates, and Egypt. The *DLOQ* has recently been added to the APA PsychTests database.

New Insights: Continuous Development of Conceptual Models

More than 150 studies using the informal and incidental learning model and more than 100 studies using the learning organization model have examined learners from varied organizational settings and professional contexts. Scholars have adopted, adapted, or utilized different versions of these models (such as 21-item DLOQ with Egan et al. (2004), or the informal and incidental learning model with Cseh et al. (2000)). Time and time again, Marsick and Watkins have indicated that these models need to be further examined within other professions and cultures, and have collaborated with other coauthors on such initiatives such as Marsick and Yates' (2012) work on communities of practice in various contexts; Marsick et al.'s (2013) work on schools; and Marsick et al.'s (2015) work in the public sector in Spain.

Holistic View on Divergence and Convergence of the Two Models

While most perspectives on informal and incidental learning models are focused on the individual level, Watkins and Marsick see interactions among the individual, group, and organizational learning levels. Scholars have attempted to provide a holistic view of learning and connect learning models at different levels (see for example, Yang 2003). The divergence of those learning models is that each makes a unique contribution to learning practice in HRD as well as organization development and change. The convergence between the models is striking. Both informal and incidental learning and the learning organization (a) emphasize dialogue, inquiry, and reflection, (b) are largely supported by constructivism or emphasis on how adults make meaning of new incidents and/or information by relating them to previous experiences, and (c) stress ownership of the learning process by learners. Both models have contributed to learning theory at the individual level (supported by Mezirow 1991) and fit with individual learner development goals. At the same time, both models are equally powerful in developing better institutions with the ultimate goal of systematically using learning activities to improve the institution sponsoring the learning activity.

How the Thinkers Impacted Our Work and Why We Want to Write a Chapter

Marsick and Watkins' impact on the three authors of this chapter has been substantial, as it has on the field. We represent three differing perspectives on their work: full professor from a different field, associate professor with a HRD focus (and 6-year colleague of Watkins'), and doctoral student in HRD. As a result, our combined perspectives represent the long-range influence of the two thinkers, covering more than 20 years and the current impact that continues to spread. The impact has been tangible and intangible, direct and indirect. For example, impacts include influences such as Beyerlein's move as a full professor from industrial/organizational (I/O) psychology and organizational leadership departments and foci into the field of HRD 3 years ago, Dirani's choice of major field as a doctoral student and assistant professor to focus much of his scholarly work on further development of the Watkins–Marsick framework and instrument and expand its use into Middle Eastern countries, and Xie's recognition as a doctoral student of the importance of the framework for explaining innovation in organizations and committing to the study of companies in central China that would benefit from it.

Legacies and Unfinished Business: Impact on Theory and Practice

During more than three decades of professional work, Marsick and Watkins have had a significant impact in a variety of ways, including (a) students they mentored; (b) research publications; (c) practice-oriented publication; (d) development and validation of the DLOQ and related instruments; (e) contributions as officers and board members in professional organizations such as Academy of HRD, Association for Talent Development, CCL, and World Education; (f) contributions to not-for-profit organizations such as UNICEF, the International Red Cross, and the Organization for Economic Cooperation and Development (OECD); (g) consulting with corporations; and (h) administrative roles on campus, including department chair and center director. The work in all of those forms of contributions typically focused on an increasing capacity for learning in organizations (O'Neil, personal communication, April 25, 2016), which aligned with their definition of HRD as "enhancing the learning capacity of both individuals and the organizations (Russ-Eft et al. 2014, p. 10)," a role they have contributed to for more than three decades, directly through consulting and indirectly through students, publications, and service.

For example, Walter McFarland (personal communication, April 28, 2016) included Marsick on his dissertation committee for a study of collective learning. Later, he started a division at the consulting firm Booz Allen focused on learning in organizations. It grew to 600 people building learning cultures that increase resilience over time. McFarland found the Marsick and Watkins approach to the learning organization more appropriate for his large projects than the Senge model was, saying that "they gave the concepts some rigor," "accelerated the evolution" and "elevated the discourse," as well as creating a measuring tool. He said that he sees a trend toward a greater valuing of learning as a central process in organizations and so, in his role as chairman of the board of ATD, recently launched a new journal for chief learning officers. Competitive advantage goes to the organization that "learns faster, better, cheaper."

Professor Andrea Ellinger completed her dissertation under Watkins, and coauthored publications with her and Marsick (personal communication, May 6, 2016). She agreed with McFarland that "through learning, you can get performance." She suggested that one of the values of the *DLOQ* was an "exponential impact" for use in practice and as a focus in research spread around the globe, partly because there is no fee for its use. She said that the *DLOQ* reflects both the informal and incidental learning and the learning organization streams of research. Watson and Marsick's influence on her and the way she works as an academic was substantial; "working with both of them is just fun," she said. "It energizes you."

As a member of the board of directors for the Center for Creative Leadership (CCL), Bill Pasmore (personal communication, April 28, 2016), said that he was "trying to shift focus from individual development to organizations and societies at CCL." Marsick served on the board with him, and so brought a perspective that emphasized a multilevel view of learning in organizations. Pasmore said, "Good strategy is a continuous process ... based on learning," and "the organization change people and strategy people are converging and learning is the bridge." However, he added that in spite of several decades of research and practice about the learning organization, many of today's firms continue to focus only the individual's learning. Watkins and Marsick's legacy "is still being built."

Lyle Yorks had worked as a consultant for Drake, Beam, and Morin when he entered the Adult Education Guided Intensive Study (AEGIS) doctoral program at TC, Columbia University that Marsick directed. As a faculty member at Eastern Connecticut State University, Yorks worked with Marsick and Judy O'Neil to research action learning programs. He later joined the TC faculty as a colleague, and now directs the AEGIS program. He said that he sees the shift toward a learning emphasis in major organizations, "companies increasingly relying more on informal and self-directed learning. Companies identify who they need to develop; they make the resources available ... but the emphasis is on employees ... to actually take the initiative. Companies ask, 'How do we track the incidental learning? How do we document that and provide for it?'" Therefore, there is a declining use of formal workshops (personal communication, April 28, 2016). Yorks and McFarland both spoke about the fact that new partnerships are emerging on campuses between colleges of education and business colleges to focus on the practical value of scholarly knowledge about learning processes. That bridging of disciplines is also reflected in York's course and text on strategy development as an organizational learning process.

The impact of that scholarship has been global with Watkins and Marsick's key measurement instrument, the *DLOQ*, and its conceptual framework, which has been translated into 15 languages and used in studies in many countries. Their work has been influential in building the young field of HRD and in examining the relationship between the fields of HRD and adult education that – over the years – have often experienced tension over boundaries. Since Marsick and Watkins worked across the boundaries and challenged them through writing, speaking, and example, they contributed to the emergence of a more collaborative spirit (O'Neil, personal communication, April 25, 2016). The timing of Marsick and Watkins' early work correlated with the evolution of organizational designs from the dominantly hierarchical – where decision-making was reserved for higher levels in the hierarchy – to flatter structures with increased empowerment because of the essential involvement of individual workers in processing information, sharing it effectively, collaborating on local decisions, and feeding critical insights upward.

The work that Marsick did with Watkins influenced Marsick's early work with ASTD Vice President of Research Martha Gephart, who had invited Watkins, Marsick, and others to a workshop to examine similarities and differences among models and instruments that assess and measure organizational learning. Gephart and Marsick eventually won a competitive grant to fund and codirect a research center at Columbia University in 1999, the J. M. Huber Institute for Learning in Organizations. Gephart's work with Marsick emphasized research into organizational system dynamics underlying learning and performance. Gephart and Marsick's book *Strategic Organizational Learning* (2016) features framework and assessment tools for diagnosis and assessment that, as Gephart summarized, "jointly optimize learning and performance (personal communication, April 29, 2016)" for adapting to the changing environment rapidly and for crafting a strategy that enables management of the environment.

Rob Poell in the Netherlands – with whom Marsick, York, and others at TC are collaborating to develop a new integrative framework for researching work-based learning – summarized their impact from his perspective as a student in the 1990s and a collaborator in later years (personal communication, April 26, 2016): "They have shown the world that there is an immense world of learning outside of formal training. They pre-empted 70:20:10 by about 25 years. They have drawn organizations to seeing the importance of a learning culture for performance. They have opened up so many avenues for new research in HRD, not to mention avenues for new researchers' careers in HRD."

Impact on Theory and Practice

The next stage for this remarkable collaborative team represents their recent shift toward the support of schools, human service, and not-for-profit organizations. This humanitarian focus is not new for either of them. They both completed work with such organizations in the 1980s and occasionally every decade, but now it seems to be a greater focus. For example, in a conversation with Marsick upon her return home from a trip, McFarland (personal communication, April 28, 2016) asked what she did there in Bermuda. Her answer was, "I worked with academic and Bermudian colleagues on a story-based conversational approach to improving education in Bermuda." Watkins, on the other hand, has been working with the Red Cross to use the *DLOQ* to improve its humanitarian initiatives, and with the Organization for Economic Cooperation and Development (*OECD*) to create an international measure of schools as learning organizations. These are a few examples of their service-oriented attitudes and concern about human and organization development on the global stage, as is their project work and visiting-professor assignments in nearly two dozen countries. There may be a shift in the focus of their energies, but there is no loss of momentum as they continue their impactful collaboration with book chapters and journal articles that are in progress or in press this year.

A snapshot of their impact is visible in the list of awards they have received, ranging from scholar of the year; induction into the International Adult and Continuing Education Hall of Fame and the Academy of Human Resource Development Scholar Hall of Fame the Robert L. Dilworth Award for Professional Achievement in Action Learning; a number of best paper awards at conferences; and, of course, teaching awards. The caliber of their work with graduate students can be inferred from the number of dissertation awards won by those students, and by the impact they have had as scholars and practitioners continuing to apply, refine, and expand the ideas they learned from their mentors, Watkins and Marsick.

Conclusion

The 30-year partnership of Marsick and Watkins has been profiled in this chapter to provide an example of long term collaboration's value and to summarize their joint work and its impact. They enriched the understanding of learning in the workplace by emphasizing the key roles of informal and incidental learning and its role in building learning organizations. They also provided the field of organization change with an assessment tool for implementing their ideas in the workplace that has been used around the world. The important ideas of their mentors found new expression and made impactful development through more than 50 joint publications. Their legacy of work together continues through the many successful students they mentored. Many organizational and societal challenges will be handled with more insight when their work forms a cornerstone for future research and application.

References

Argyris, C., & Schön, D. A. (1978). *Organizational learning: A theory of action perspective* (Vol. 173). Reading: Addison-Wesley.

Bandura, A. (1986). *Social foundations of thought and action: A social cognitive theory*. Englewood Cliffs: Prentice-Hall.

Brown, L., Henry, C., Henry, J., & McTaggart, R. (1988). Action research: Notes on the national seminar. In S. Kemmis & R. McTaggart (Eds.), *The action research reader*. Geelong: Deakin University Press.

Burke, W. W. (2002). *Organization change: Theory and practice* (1st ed.). Thousand Oaks: Sage.

Cseh, M., Watkins, K. E., & Marsick, V. J. (1999). Reconceptualizing Marsick and Watkins' model of informal and incidental learning in the workplace. In K. P. Kuchinke (Ed.), *Proceedings, academy of human resource development conference* (Vol. I, pp. 349–356). Baton Rouge: Academy of Human Resource Development.

Cseh, M., Watkins, K. E., & Marsick, V. J. (2000). Informal and incidental learning in the workplace. In G.A. Straka (Ed.), Conceptions of self-directed learning: Theoretical and conceptual considerations (pp. 59–74). New York, NY: Waxmann.

Dewey, J. (1938). *Experience and education*. New York: Collier Books.

Dickens, L., & Watkins, K. (1999). Action research: Rethinking Lewin. *Management Learning, 30* (2), 127–140. doi:10.1177/1350507699302002.

Dirani, K. M. (2013). Does theory travel? Dimensions of the learning organization culture relevant to the Lebanese culture. *Advances in Developing Human Resources, 15*(2), 177–192. doi:10.1177/1523422313475992.

Egan, T. M., Yang, B., & Bartlett, K. R. (2004). The effects of organizational learning culture and job satisfaction on motivation to transfer learning and turnover intention. *Human Resource Development Quarterly, 15*(3), 279–301. doi:10.1002/hrdq.1104.

Ellinger, A. D., Watkins, K. E., & Bostrom, R. P. (1999). Managers as facilitators of learning in learning organizations. *Human Resource Development Quarterly, 10*(2), 105–125. doi:10.1002/hrdq.3920100203.

Ellinger, A. D., Ellinger, A. E., & Keller, S. B. (2003). Supervisory coaching behavior, employee satisfaction, and warehouse employee performance: A dyadic perspective in the distribution industry. *Human Resource Development Quarterly, 14*(4), 435–458. doi:10.1002/hrdq.1078.

Gephart, M., & Marsick, V. J. (2016). *Strategic organizational learning*. Berlin: Springer.

Haque, M. M. (2008). *A study of the relationship between the learning organization and organizational readiness for change*. Doctoral dissertation. Retrieved from ProQuest Dissertations & Theses Global. (Order No. 3311367).

Jarvis, P. (1987). *Adult learning in the social context*. London: Croom-Helm.

Knowles, M. (1950). *Informal adult education*. New York: Association Press.

Kolb, D. A. (1984). *Experiential learning: Experience as the source of learning and development*. Englewood Cliffs: Prentice-Hall.

Lave, J., & Wenger, E. (1991). *Situated learning – Legitimate peripheral participation*. Cambridge: Cambridge University Press.

Lindeman, E. C. (1926). *The meaning of adult education*. New York: New Republic.

Marsick, V. J. (Ed.). (1987). *Learning in the workplace*. Beckenham, Kent: Croom-Helm.

Marsick, V. J., & Watkins, K. E. (1990). *Informal learning in learning organizations*. London: Routledge.

Marsick, V. J., & Watkins, K. E. (1997). Lessons from informal and incidental learning. In J. Burgoyne & M. Reynolds (Eds.), *Management learning: Integrating perspectives in theory and practice* (pp. 295–311). Thousand Oaks: Sage.

Marsick, V. J., & Watkins, K. E. (1999). *Facilitating learning organizations: Making learning count*. London: Gower Press.

Marsick, V. J., & Watkins, K. E. (2001). Informal and incidental learning. *New Directions for Adult and Continuing Education, 2001*(89), 25–34. doi:10.1002/ace.5.

Marsick, V. J., & Yates, J. L. (2012). Informal learning and complex problem solving of radiologic technologists transitioning to the workplace. In H.-T. Hou (Ed.), *New research on knowledge management models and methods* (pp. 171–194). Rijeka: InTech. doi:10.5772/1799.

Marsick, V. J., Watkins, K. E., & Boswell, S. A. (2013). Schools as learning communities. In R. Huang & J. M. Spector (Eds.), *Reshaping learning. New frontiers of educational research* (pp. 71–88). Berlin/Heidelberg: Springer.

Marsick, V. J., Fernández-de-Álava, M., & Watkins, K. E. (2015). Valuing and evaluating informal learning in workplace communities of practice. In O. Mejiuni, P. Cranton, & O. Táíwò (Eds.), *Measuring and analyzing informal learning in the digital age* (pp. 215–232). Hershey: IGI Global. doi:10.4018/978-1-4666-8265-8.ch015.

Mezirow, J. D. (1978). Perspective transformation. *Adult Education Quarterly, 28*(2), 100–110. doi:10.1177/074171367802800202.
Mezirow, J. D. (1991). *Transformative dimensions of adult learning*. San Francisco: Jossey-Bass.
Nonaka, I., & Takeuchi, H. (1995). *The knowledge creating company*. New York: Oxford University Press.
Revans, R. W. (1982). *The origins and growth of action learning*. Bromley: Chartwell-Bratt.
Russ-Eft, D., Watkins, K. E., Marsick, V. J., Jacobs, R. L., & McLean, G. N. (2014). What do the next 25 years hold for HRD research in areas of our interest? *Human Resource Development Quarterly, 25*(1), 5–27. doi:10.1002/hrdq.21180.
Schön, D. (1983). *The reflective practitioner*. New York: Basic Books.
Senge, P. M. (1990). *The fifth discipline: The art and practice of the learning organization*. New York: Doubleday.
Watkins, K. E., & Dirani, K. M. (2013). A meta-analysis of the dimensions of a learning organization questionnaire looking across cultures, ranks, and industries. *Advances in Developing Human Resources, 15*(2), 148–162. doi:10.1177/1523422313475991.
Watkins, K. E., & Marsick, V. J. (1993). *Sculpting the learning organization: Lessons in the art and science of systemic change*. San Francisco: Jossey-Bass.
Watkins, K. E., & Marsick, V. J. (Eds.). (1996). *In action: Creating the learning organization*. Alexandria: American Society for Training & Development.
Watkins, K. E. & Marsick, V. J. (Eds). (2003). Making learning count! Diagnosing the learning culture in organizations. Advances in developing human resources 5, 2. Newbury Park: Sage/ Academy of Human Resource Development.
Watkins, K., & Wilson, J. (2001). Chris Argyris: The reluctant adult educator. In P. Jarvis (Ed.), Twentieth century thinkers in adult and continuing education (pp. 139–205). Revised Edition. London: Routledge
Wenger, E. (1998). *Communities of practice*. Cambridge: Cambridge University Press.
Yang, B. (2003). Identifying valid and reliable measures for dimensions of a learning culture. *Advances in Developing Human Resources, 5*(2), 152–162. doi:10.1177/1523422303005002003.

Further Reading

Marsick, V., & Watkins, K. (1990). *Informal and incidental learning: International perspectives on adult and continuing education*. London: Routledge.
Marsick, V., & Watkins, K. (1994). The learning organization: An integrative vision for HRD. *Human Resource Development Quarterly, 5*(4), 353–360. doi:10.1002/hrdq.3920050406.
Marsick, V., & Watkins, K. (2001). Informal and incidental learning. In S. Merriam & R. Caffarella (Eds), *Update on adult learning: New directions in adult and continuing education* (pp. 25–34). San Francisco: Jossey-Bass.
Marsick, V., & Watkins, K. (2003). Demonstrating the value of an organization's learning culture: The dimensions of the learning organization questionnaire. *Advances in Developing Human Resources, 5*(2), 132–151. doi:10.1177/1523422303005002002.
Marsick, V., Volpe, M., & Watkins, K. (1999). Theory and practice of informal learning in the knowledge era. In V. Marsick & M. Volpe (Eds.), *Informal learning on the job: Advances in developing human resources* (pp. 80–95). San Francisco: Berrett-Koehler.
Watkins, K., & Marsick, V. (1992). Toward a theory of informal and incidental learning in organizations. *International Journal for Lifelong Learning, 7*(4), 287–300. doi:10.1080/0260137920110403.
Watkins, K., & Marsick, V. (1992). Building the learning organization: A new role for human resource developers. *Studies in Continuing Education, 14*(2), 115–129. doi:10.1080/0158037920140203.

Watkins, K., & Marsick, V. (1993). *Sculpting the learning organization.* San Francisco: Jossey-Bass. [Translated into Japanese, 1994; Chinese, 2001].

Watkins, K. E., & Marsick, V. J. (1997). *Dimensions of the learning organization questionnaire.* Warwick: Partners for the Learning Organization.

Yang, B., Watkins, K., & Marsick, V. (2004). The construct of the learning organization: Dimensions, measurement, and validation. *Human Resource Development Quarterly, 15*(1), 31–56. doi:10.1002/hrdq.1086.

The Human Side of Douglas McGregor

51

Peter F. Sorensen and Therese F. Yaeger

Abstract

This biography covers the life and contributions of one of the most significant contributors to management and organizational thinking. Douglas McGregor set the stage for a new wave of management with his Theory Y managerial assumptions. McGregor's work influenced a generation of scholars and practitioners who changed the practice of management and created the foundation for the twenty-first century of management thinking. This chapter presents and discusses the forces that influenced and motivated McGregor's thinking. It reviews McGregor's basic contributions particularly his best-known contribution of Theory X and Theory Y. In addition, it reviews McGregor's key insights and their impact on theory and practice that have led to organizational change being viewed in new and surprising ways. Finally, a discussion of McGregor's legacies, unfinished business, and further readings is provided.

Keywords

Theory X and Y • Human side of enterprise • Organization development • Douglas McGregor

Contents

P.F. Sorensen (✉) • T.F. Yaeger
Organization Development Department, Benedictine University, Lisle, IL, USA
e-mail: psorensen@ben.edu; tyaeger@ben.edu

D.B. Szabla et al. (eds.), *The Palgrave Handbook of Organizational Change Thinkers*,
DOI 10.1007/978-3-319-52878-6_18

Introduction

Theory X and Theory Y and the *Human Side of Enterprise* are classics, which shaped the thinking of both practitioners and scholars into the twenty-first century. The organizations that McGregor envisioned more than a half-century ago in his original work are now the norm.

The scholars who have shaped the field who worked with and were influenced by McGregor represent a "Who's Who" in the field of organization development. Through his writing, McGregor brought the field of management theory to the everyday manager. He had the ability to translate new and emergent concepts in management into a language that appealed to practitioners. It is no accident that the BNA film (a film series dedicated to highlighting the most influential behavioral science approaches to management) on McGregor's thinking was presented by an exceptional academic (Bennis), an exceptional OD scholar (Beckhard), and an exceptional practitioner (John Paul Jones).

Influences and Motivations: Culminating Life Experiences

There are several sources for understanding McGregor's history and background that discussed the influences and motivations of McGregor's work, in particular, two chapters on McGregor in Weisbord's *Productive Work Places Revisited: Dignity, Meaning and Community in the 21st Century* (2004) and the introductions to two of McGregor's early works: *Leadership and Motivation* (1966) and *Human Side of Enterprise* (1960). An additional source for understanding what influenced McGregor is the work of Heil, Bennis, and Stephens, *Douglas McGregor, Revisited* (2000). A number of direct quotes are included from his colleagues and students to better capture the influences and motivations underlying McGregor's work.

Douglas McGregor was born in 1906 and died suddenly in 1964 at the age of 58 from a heart attack. Weisbord (2004) describes McGregor as "being born into a strict Scotch Presbyterian family in Detroit, Michigan, on September 16, 1906." McGregor's early years were spent in the McGregor Institute, an organization dedicated as a shelter, a mission for homeless men founded by McGregor's grandfather, and later led by McGregor's father. McGregor, as an early student, spent time in the office there as well accompanying gospel songs on the piano.

As a student, McGregor spent time at Detroit City College and Oberlin, completed graduate work at Harvard, earned a doctorate in social psychology, and joined the faculty at Harvard. Several years later, he joined the faculty at MIT in the Industrial Relations program.

In 1948, McGregor became the president of Antioch College. While at Antioch, the college became one of the first to welcome students of color. At that time, McGregor also had to deal with pressures from the American Activities committee to expel student activists. After serving as president of Antioch College, he returned to MIT as faculty in the Sloan School of Management where he wrote *The Human*

Side of Enterprise (1960). In the preface to his book, *Human Side of Enterprise*, McGregor describes the initiating factor in his work. In 1954, he received, along with Alex Bavelas, a grant from the Alfred P. Sloan Foundation to explore the question of what makes a good manager. Studies from the Sloan Foundation grant led to the following comments:

> It seems to me that the making of managers, in so far as they are made, is only to a rather small degree the result of management's formal efforts in management development. It is a much greater degree the result of management's conception of the nature of the task and of all the policies and practices which are constructed to implement this conception. The way a business is managed determines to a very great extent what people are perceived to have 'potential' and how they are developed. (p. vi).

Weisbord (2004) describes McGregor's work as developing between 1937 and 1949, a time characterized by World War II. During this period, his work involved conflicts between management and labor. Weisbord cites a quote from one of McGregor's work from that time, a quote which in a way predicts what the field of OD was to become, "It is not the fact of change but the method of bringing it about which is important if we are going to achieve a greater degree of cooperation between management and labor" (2004, p. 123).

McGregor was certainly influenced not only by his early childhood experiences in a strict Scotch Presbyterian family who had a mission for homeless men but also by the characteristics of the behavioral sciences of that time. McGregor's thinking is described as maturing during a time of major new developments in the behavioral sciences (Weisbord 2004, p. 138). Kurt Lewin, Abraham Maslow, and Frederick Herzberg are described as being part of those new developments. McGregor is described as being deeply committed to the ideas of Maslow and Herzberg, in particular Maslow's hierarchy of needs and Herzberg's concept of job enrichment. He believed that the higher level needs that Maslow touted needed to be built into jobs through the redesign of work systems that promote dignity, meaning, and community into work (2004).

In relation to the field of Organization Development, Weisbord (2004) writes, "Organization Development professionals are indebted to him not only for his ideas and exemplary practices but for the people he encouraged and inspired. McGregor helped Kurt Lewin found the Research Center for Group Dynamics at MIT. He was one of the earliest appliers of Lewin's ideas in academia . . . McGregor recruited the extraordinary MIT organization group, Richard Beckhard, Warren Bennis, Mason Haire, Joseph Scanlon, Edgar Schein, all who played major roles in setting the boundaries, practices, and values behind systematic organizational change" (p. 118). In describing the friendship between Beckhard and McGregor, Weisbord (2004) attributes the origin of the term Organization Development to McGregor and Beckhard, while the two of them were working together consulting at General Mills.

McGregor's childhood influences and his later influences are related again by Weisbord (2004) in citing a 1981 interview with Jerry Harvey: "All the biggies like Argyris, Likert, and Blake suddenly disappeared. I peeked through the door to the next room and saw them huddled around the piano singing gospel songs, accompanied by Doug McGregor" (p. 116). This narrative demonstrates how McGregor's early childhood experiences later allowed him to create an unanticipated and shared experience among the top people in the field, all of whom shared a common motivation – the improvement of the human condition at work.

One way of identifying those who influenced Doulas McGregor, or who were influenced by McGregor, is to review persons identified in his last publication, *The Professional Manager* (1967). This book was in progress at the time of his death and completed by Warren Bennis. Included in the preface are Edgar Schein, Richard Beckhard, Mason Haire, Rensis Likert, Charles Myers, John Paul Jones, Eric Trist, Robert Blake, Edwin Boring, Gordon Allport, Irving Knickerbocker, Leland Bradford, and Jay Forester, while the contents of the book include references to such familiar names as Larry Greiner, Wendell French, Kenneth Benne, Robert Guest, Fredrick Herzberg, Katz and Kahn, Hal Leavitt, Ron Lippitt, J. Loft, Floyd Mann, Abraham Maslow, Jane Mouton, Donald Pelz, and Eric Trist, all familiar names in the field of Organization Development. A number of these names cited included the early MIT group, industry experts, and organizational scholars, who shared Theory Y beliefs with McGregor, helping to redefine the field of organizational change.

In summary, what were the dominant influences and motivations that created the foundation for McGregor's work? For an answer to that question, we defer to one of his closest friends, colleague, and student, Warren Bennis. Bennis writes in his introduction to McGregor's *Leadership and Motivation* with reference to McGregor's early family life:

> The kind of an 'upbringing' using that word in the old fashioned sense, puts into focus the dominant chords in Doug's intellectual origins: religion, the search for meaning, music and the firmly embedded idea that through productive work man will find his salvation. (1967, p. xi)

Again Bennis writes:

> It was no accident that Doug's central theoretical worry, the last few years, was the 'management of conflict'. There is no doubt in my mind that his intellectual contribution was based on his uncanny capacity to use himself so splendidly. The fallout from his management of (and learning from) his own conflicts have given us an enhanced and more realistic vision of man's potential. (1967, p. xii)

Key Contributions: Translating for the "Human Side"

McGregor's work had profound and multiple influences on the field of Organization Development and management in general. In the following section, we address two of his major contributions: (1) his contributions to theory and (2) his influence on a generation of OD scholars who were to become the OD giants. There is no way that we can do justice to the contributions of Douglas McGregor, but at least we can give a glimpse of what he accomplished. Again, we use quotes from McGregor himself and those who knew him in an effort to give "life" to our description of his work. In a way, McGregor's contributions need to be assessed as a "translator." In other words, it was his ability, his gift, to be able to communicate to a larger audience, the audience of managers, that which was taking place as the new discipline of the behavioral sciences was beginning to have a significant impact on the changing field of management and the emerging field of Organization Development. We begin with a quote from McGregor, followed by a brief description of his contribution to the field of OD, which leads us to transition to his influence on the next "first" generation of ODers. We complete this section with a review of his major conceptual contributions and illustrations of what we call his role as a "translator."

In the preface to the 25th Anniversary printing of *The Human Side of Enterprise*, Warren Bennis quotes McGregor in 1950, when McGregor wrote:

> Out of all this has come the first clear recognition of an inescapable fact: we cannot successfully force people to work for management objectives. The ancient conception that people do the work of the world only if they are forced to do so by threats or intimidation, or by the camouflaged authoritarian methods of paternalism, has been suffering from a lingering fatal illness for a quarter of a century. I venture the guess that it will be dead in another decade.

Contributions to Theory: X and Y. There is no question that McGregor is most closely associated with his Theory X and Theory Y, but he also had the ability to translate behavioral science practices that were having a profound impact on management and how organizations were structured. He had the ability to translate these activities into a form that was both attractive and understandable to managers. He used emerging applications to illustrate his Theory Y. We briefly present his Theory Y and Theory X, a related concept called the self-fulfilling prophecy, followed by a brief summary and discussion of four of the Theory Y practices identified by McGregor.

We would like to let McGregor speak for himself as he defines the concepts that were to make such a profound impact on management, and he ultimately defines his concept of Theory Y (McGregor 1957). He writes:

> The conventional conception of management's task in harnessing human energy to organizational requirements can be basically stated in three propositions. In order to avoid complications introduced by a label. I shall call this set of propositions 'Theory X'.
>
> 1. Management is responsible for organizing the elements of productive enterprise...
> 2. With respect to people, this is a process of directing, their efforts, motivating them, controlling their actions, modifying their behavior to fit the needs of the organization.
> 3. Without this active intervention by management, people would be passive – even resistant to organizational needs. They must therefore be persuaded, rewarded, punished, controlled...
>
> ...we require a different theory of the task of managing people based on more adequate assumptions about human nature and human motivation ... Call it 'Theory Y' if you will. (1957, p. 6)

McGregor presented Theory Y using another set of propositions:

- People are not by nature passive or resistant to organizational needs. They have become so as a result of experience in organizations.
- The motivation, the potential for development, the capacity for assuming responsibility, and the readiness to direct behavior toward organizational goals are all present in people. Management does not put them there. It is a responsibility of management to make it possible for people to recognize and develop these human characteristics for themselves.
- The essential task of management is to arrange organizational conditions and methods of operation so that people can achieve their own goals best by directing their own efforts toward organizational objectives (1960).

Although McGregor is best remembered for his Theory X and Theory Y, another one of his contributions directly related to Theory X and Theory Y is the concept of the self-fulfilling prophecy, the idea that a manager's assumptions determine and shape a manager's managerial style and that this style creates a set of reactive behaviors on the part of subordinates, reactive behaviors that reinforce the manager's original assumptions. In other words, Theory X assumptions create Theory X management behavior, which in turn creates Theory X behavior on the part of employees, and that Theory Y assumptions, in turn, create Y styles of management resulting in more positive and productive employee behavior, again, reinforcing the manager's original assumptions.

McGregor's contributions also rest on his work that relates Theory Y to certain management styles and organizational practices, which included management by integration and self-control, a critique of performance appraisal, administering salaries and promotions, the Scanlon Plan, participation, the managerial climate, staff-line relationships, and improving staff-line collaboration.

His original presentation of his thinking, "The Human Side of Enterprise," was first published in *Adventures in Thought and Action*, Proceedings of the Fifth Anniversary Convocation of the School of Industrial Management, Massachusetts Institute of Technology, Cambridge, April 9, 1957. In it, he presents Theory X and Y, refers to Maslow theory of motivation, and discusses four approaches to management that are consistent with Theory Y. They are performance appraisal, decentralization and delegation, job enlargement, and participation and consultative management.

McGregor was highly critical of the manner in which performance appraisals were conducted. He felt that they raised issues of integrity, placing managers in a position of judgment of others. McGregor's answer to traditional performance appraisal was a more collaborative system based on goal setting, which became known as Management by Objectives. Management by Objectives moved control of the job from the manager to the employee and created conditions under which employees had greater control over their own activities – a move from external control to employee control and intrinsic motivation.

Decentralization and delegation represented another example of Theory Y practices. For McGregor, decentralization and delegation were ways of freeing employees from external control and a way of increasing a sense of responsibility and satisfying higher level needs. He cited the work at Sears, Roebuck, and Company where delegation approaches were implemented to increase employee's sense of responsibility. He also thought of decentralization and delegation as being closely related to Management by Objectives, in that both were a means of enhancing employee responsibility and decreasing management control.

McGregor cited work at IBM and Detroit Edison as illustrations of job enlargement, work redesign that enhanced opportunities for satisfying higher level needs and acceptance of responsibility. Here McGregor was influenced by the work of Herzberg, another way for increasing employee responsibility and the satisfaction of Maslow's higher level needs.

Participation and consultative management, for McGregor, served as an additional approach consistent with Theory Y. This was another way of increasing employee responsibility and the fulfillment of higher level needs. However, McGregor noted that these Theory Y approaches to management experienced a number of failures. He attributed these failures to the fact that frequently management had "bought" the ideas but had implemented and applied them within a Theory X context.

The work of Woodman (1965) relating organization form to technology and the work of Burns and Stalker (1961) and Lawrence and Lorsch (1967) have helped us to understand the number of forces mandating new organizational forms. The rapidly changing field of technology and a rapidly changing environment were forces that required increased delegation and decentralization, which are forms of McGregor's Theory Y (Sorensen and Minahan 2011, p. 179). The further development of the field of Organization Development over the years has also served to strengthen and develop these McGregor "Theory Y" approaches. For example, the work of Hackman and Oldham and the Job Diagnostic Survey have significantly furthered and developed the concept of job enrichment and job redesign. Specifically, the work by Hackman and Oldham gave us a way of measuring changes in job redesign.

At the time of McGregor, many of McGregor's concepts were counterculture. But his ideas have continued to gain momentum and are reflected in, for example, the popularity of *In Search of Excellence* by Peters and Waterman (1982) and, more recently, for example, in *Built to Change: How to Achieve Sustained Organizational Effectiveness* by Lawler and Worley (2006). In addition, while at McKinsey, Tom Peters notes that Douglas McGregor's theory of motivation known as Theory X and Theory Y was directly influential on the direction of his projects.

Influence on the First Generation of OD Scholars

There is no question that McGregor's work had a significant influence on the field of management and Organization Development. He wrote at a time when the social sciences were providing data that supported McGregor's thinking, but McGregor had the ability and language to present a concept of management that was emerging in a way that was more attractive to managers and changed the way organizations were managed. In short, McGregor made the behavioral sciences relevant to the world of management.

Clearly, it is impossible to adequately assess McGregor's influence on a generation of ODers and managers, but here we provide illustrations of his influence on the "first generation," the creators and developers of the field. We provide illustrations from this first generation through Warren Bennis, Edgar Schein, Dick Beckhard, Marvin Weisbord, and Edith Seashore.

McGregor influenced Bennis, Schein, and Beckhard directly through their interaction at MIT. Marvin Weisbord was influenced indirectly through his application of Theory Y concepts as a manager. In a different way, Edith Seashore was influenced by McGregor as her mentor and at a more personal level, as she stated, "Doug was my mentor and very good friend, and Charles and I planned our wedding date around the availability of Doug" (Schein et al. 2007).

Warren Bennis became Distinguished Professor of Business Administration at the University of Southern California and was a major contributor to the literature and practice of Leadership and Organization Development. He published numerous books including *Douglas McGregor Revisited*, as well as several books with McGregor.

Edgar Schein became the Sloan Fellows Professor of Management in the Sloan School of Management and is one of the major figures in the field of Organization Development. Schein is also a Fellow of the American Psychological Association and the National Training Laboratories (NTL). He is author of numerous books in the field, from the classic *Process Consultation* (1987) to *Humble Consulting* (2016), and he is a major contributor to our understanding of organizational culture with *Organizational Culture and Leadership* (1985).

Dick Beckhard became an adjunct professor of management at the Sloan School of Management. He was author of several books and articles including the classic "The Confrontation Meeting," in the *Harvard Business Review*, March–April, 1967, and is coeditor with Warren Bennis and Edgar Schein of the Addison-Wesley Series in OD. Marvin Weisbord became a major contributor to the field and an internationally recognized consultant and writer in the field. Weisbord is probably best known for his contribution to large group methods for organizational change with his technique called Future Search.

Edith Seashore became a woman pioneer in the field at a time when a woman's role was perceived quite differently than it is today. She became president of the NTL Institute, received a Lifetime Achievement Award from the Organization Development Network (NTL), and was one of the cofounders of the American University/NTL Institute Master's Degree Program in Organization Development. One telling illustration of McGregor's influence is reflected in comments by Edith Seashore to Marvin Weisbord (2004, p. 119) in reference to McGregor's inaugural address as Antioch College President, "Two minutes before he started to speak I had no idea of what I wanted to do with my life. At the end of his talk, I knew."

It is no accident that one of the most influential book series in the field of Organization Development, the classic Addison-Wesley "six-pack," was edited by persons significantly influenced by McGregor, namely, Warren Bennis, Edgar

Schein, and Dick Beckhard. Each contributed a volume to the "six-pack." Other contributors included Blake and Mouton, creators of the Managerial Grid, and major influencers on the emerging field of Organization Development and the field of management.

In his discussion of the roots of Organization Development and the work of Douglas McGregor, Weisbord cites the meaning of McGregor's work for himself (Weisbord), a meaning which is also a fitting description, not only of McGregor's major conceptual contribution Theory Y but a description of the fundamental values of the field Organization Development which is "an expression of life's purposes – affirming dignity in every person, finding meaning in valued work, achieving community through mutual support and accomplishment" (Weisbord 2004, p. 122).

New Insights: Illustrating McGregor's Impact

Douglas McGregor has clearly had a profound effect on the field of management. His thinking became part of, and laid the foundation for, today's organizations – and many would argue for organizations and management of the future. In *Douglas McGregor Revisited* (2000), Heil, Bennis, and Stephens identify the trends that have determined the necessity for McGregor's concept of management. These trends include technology, environmental turbulence, need for innovation, and more powerful consumers, among other changes. To quote Heil, Bennis, and Stephens:

> One of McGregor's most important contributions to management today underlies all of these movements. He asked every manager to view management not merely as a toolbox of tasks but as an integrative function that asks them to examine their deepest held beliefs about people and the nature of work. (2000, p. 15)

McGregor's impact on management was not immediately realized. For us, two significant contributions are of particular importance. First, his tenure as president of Antioch College, where he created an environment of learning and experimentation, in what was to become the foundation of the emerging field of OD: participation, action research, and group dynamics. Second, McGregor was instrumental in bringing Kurt Lewin to MIT, the establishment of the Research Center for Group Dynamics, as well as the recruitment of Beckhard, Bennis, Haire, Scanlon, and Schein to MIT (Weisbord 2004, p. 118).

The influence of McGregor continues to be reflected in the work of a significant number of contributors to the field of management, most significantly the contributors that were cited earlier in our discussion on the influence of McGregor. They also include the work of Michael Beer in *High Commitment High Performance* (2009); Marvin Weisbord's, *Productive Workplaces Revisited* (2004); and Edgar Schein's, *Process Consultation* (1969) and *Humble Consulting* (2016) to name but a few.

Below, we share the role that McGregor's work has played in our personal development, both in our practitioner life (Therese was Director of Global for

Motorola and Peter began his OD career as Assistant Director of Organizational Analysis for CNA Financial) and our academic careers. We include illustrations of McGregor's influence on our academic work over the years (for Peter, articles and publications that began over 50 years ago) with selected references of our work at the end of this section.

SORENSEN: In 1959, I joined a newly formed corporate department called "Organizational Analysis" in a major insurance and financial organization. I was invited to join this group by my mentor Dr. Bernard Baum who had just completed his PhD at the University of Chicago. Much of the work dealt with defining the formal organization structure, but we were also free to collect data and publish studies related to the behavioral sciences and management. The department became a mecca for university studies, with researchers from the University of Chicago, MIT, Michigan, IIT, and a number of others. Much of the early work and publications had to do with the distribution of power and influence in organizations. In fact, the first publication was the reporting on the power and influence studies at an insurance conference (a little bit different from the usual presentations at an insurance conference). In a way, the department became one of the early internal Organization Development departments. My first paper at the Academy of Management in 1970 was on perceptions of influence by students in several universities, with colleagues from the University of Illinois who had joined the department. As part of our education in organizational analysis, we created an informal study group within the department. The first required reading on our list of readings was *The Human Side of Enterprise* by Douglas McGregor (1960) and, later, the work of Warren Bennis. There were several aspects of McGregor's work that were of particular interest, particularly Theory X and Y and how these concepts were reflected in such management practices as performance appraisal, Management By Objectives, and participatory management and delegation.

I cannot say that the company at that time was a model of Theory Y, but with degrees and education in sociology, these were concepts that clearly resonated with members of our department. This period was a time of turbulence, recognition of gender discrimination, discrimination involving people of color, the Weathermen (an American left wing extremist organization in the 1960s and 1970s), the SDS (Students for a Democratic Society), Kent State, sit-ins at major universities, chaos in Chicago's Grant Park as part of the presidential election activities, and Chicago's Mayor Daley at the Democratic Convention. Along with the turbulence, there was also an element of optimism. McGregor's writing was popular in management but frequently misinterpreted as being "soft management," while just the opposite was true. Somehow, out of all of this, things were moving in the direction of Theory Y.

After leaving corporate to complete my dissertation, my interests in McGregor's ideas continued as I joined the faculty at George Williams College, truly a Theory Y College. There, a newly formed department of administration staffed by faculty from NTL, highly familiar with the concepts of McGregor and Theory Y management was growing. At George Williams, studies and publications related to management power and participation continued, but this time on an international basis, more studies were done on Management by Objectives and the role of organizational culture in determining the extent to which MBO was truly Theory Y, and the seeds of Appreciative Inquiry were planted, as David Cooperrider, a student in the George Williams program, was introduced to McGregor's concepts and Organization Development. McGregor's influence was also part of the Contemporary Trends Lecture Series in Change Management, which included a number of scholars and practitioners influenced by, and who were also students of, McGregor including Edgar Schein, Marvin Weisbord, and Edith Seashore. The Lecture series continues today as does the influence of McGregor's work on me and on the PhD program in Organization Development, now at Benedictine University.

YAEGER: As a new graduate student in Management and Organization Behavior, I entered my MGMT530 Organizational Behavior course in the early 1990s at Illinois Benedictine College (now Benedictine University), having read the appropriate textbooks. I loved my OB reader – it had contributions from Blake and Mouton, Lawler, Likert, Lawrence, and Lorsch, just to name a few. But one particular reading was McGregor's article "The Human Side of Enterprise" first published in *Adventures in Thought and Action*, in the Proceedings of the Fifth Anniversary Convocation of the School of Industrial Management at MIT in 1957. The article was a short ten-page piece, describing how management thinking should merge more with the social sciences (more than just the physical sciences) to make human organizations effective. In the article, McGregor stated, "we are becoming quite certain that, under proper conditions, unimagined resources of creative human energy could become available within the organizational setting."

I realized that in 1957 when McGregor wrote this thought piece (which culminated into his 1960 book), there were no formal Organizational Behavior or Organization Development programs to share this thinking with. This thinking was shared among Industrial Management thinkers and managers, who probably thought that these Theory X and Y concepts were too soft. I wondered how this thinking was working today and how (or if) it was received in the management arena. In short, had Theory caught on as I think it should have?

I let go of the reading in class just long enough to watch a two-part BNA Video entitled "Theory X and Theory Y: The Work of Douglas McGregor" created with Saul Gellerman in 1969. The video provided a description of Theory X and Y in Part One, the assumptions that managers make about workers, and the self-fulfilling prophecy. Part Two was more application oriented with role playing in a factory setting and a response to the factory illustration by Dick Beckhard (of MIT) and John Paul Jones (then with Federated Department Stores). The film, which went from film reel in the 1970s, to VHS in the 1990s, to DVD after 2000, and finally to thumb drives today, is still shown in introductory OB courses today. For me, it evidences how groundbreaking McGregor's Theory X and Y were, yet it drives the discussion of "why aren't we more Theory Y yet."

I share this story because, after understanding Theory X and Y and the self-fulfilling prophecy, I was introduced to Cooperrider's work on Appreciative Inquiry. In Cooperrider's famous 1990 article, "Positive Image, Positive Action," he opens by paraphrasing McGregor stating, "Modern management thought was born proclaiming that organizations are the triumph of the human imagination. As made and imagined, organizations are products of human interaction and mind rather than some blind expression of an underlying natural order" (McGregor 1960). This reminded me of McGregor's statement about unimagined resources of creative human energy, which, in essence, is indication that McGregor's Theory Y is thriving via Appreciative Inquiry! Still today, both McGregor's Theory X and Y, along with Cooperrider's Appreciative Inquiry, have been two of the most resonant theories in my work and writing. My alignment with both of these scholars merely affirmed my passion to live in the Organizational Behavior and Organization Development disciplines.

Unfinished Business: McGregor's Legacy

In this article, we have discussed McGregor's major contributions and the later thinkers that McGregor influenced who have carried his concepts forward. Here again we reference works by those scholars that McGregor has influenced as they describe, in their own words, the major intellectual legacies of McGregor. We also present a discussion of how McGregor's legacy is still to be fully investigated, the extent to which McGregor's concepts are universal, and the extent to which the thinking of a person shaped by a Scotch Presbyterian background extends across international boundaries. This question, of course, has significant implications for the true legacy of McGregor's work.

The legacy of McGregor's work is reflected in Marvin Weisbord's classic work *Productive Workplaces Places* and *Productive Workplaces Revisited*, subtitled Dignity, Meaning, and Community in the twenty-first century, in which Weisbord devotes three chapters to McGregor, the first chapter of the book "A Personal Prologue: Discovering Theories X and Theories Y" and two later chapters, "McGregor and the Roots of Organization Development" and "The Human Side of Enterprise Revisited."

But for us, and specific to Weisbord, McGregor's legacy is captured in a single Weisbord quote: "Douglas McGregor, a gifted professor, wrote *The Human Side of Enterprise* (1960) and changed forever the way managers view their own assumptions and behavior" (Weisbord 2004).

One of the most comprehensive discussions is by Warren Bennis, in *Douglas McGregor Revisited*, in which the authors discuss the legacy and continued relevance of McGregor's work.

According to Bennis, Heil, and Stephens, McGregor matters, and they capture McGregor's legacy in a single quote:

> The world that Douglas McGregor spoke of is here. In today's inter-connected economy of bits and bytes, of wired companies and real-time business, the spread of technology has made the human side of enterprise more important than ever. (Heil et al. 2000)

Another comprehensive discussion of his legacy can be found in Sorensen and Minahan's article in the *Journal of Management History* with guest editor Therese Yaeger and later in the *Oxford Bibliography* by Yaeger and Sorensen. Sorensen and Minahan explain:

> Most recently, McGregor's concepts have been reflected in one of the most popular and influential new approaches to organizational performance – Appreciative Inquiry. Appreciative Inquiry is founded on the philosophy of social construction and incorporates one of McGregor's important concepts – the concept of the self-fulfilling prophecy. The tremendous influence and effectiveness (Yaeger et al. 2005) of Appreciative Inquiry stands as probably the strongest testimonial to the continued validity of McGregor's work. (Sorensen and Minahan 2011)

Without question, one of the most important questions in the field today, and clearly for the future, is the question of globalization and the role of national cultural values as they relate to and influence the field of Organization Development. Some of the most influential work in this area is the work of Geert Hofstede (1980, 1991). Hofstede discusses the limitations of management approaches developed in the USA (including the work of Douglas McGregor), in countries characterized by different national cultural values. Hofstede (1980) directly addresses a number of management approaches presented in McGregor's classic works, namely, motivation, leadership, decision-making, Management by Objectives, Management of Organization Development, and humanization of work. Hofstede's work is based primarily on four concepts representing issues that are characteristic of societies and different countries in general, power distance, uncertainty avoidance, individualism, and masculinity.

To quote Hofstede, in terms of the applicability of Organization Development across different cultures:

> American-style Organization Development meets, for example, with formidable obstacles in Latin European countries...Latin countries lack the equality ethos which is an important motor behind OD....OD processes creates insecurity which in a high uncertainty avoidance culture is often intolerable. OD represents a counterculture in a Latin environment. (1980, pp. 266–267)

On the other hand, more recently, there has been considerable discussion concerning the applicability of OD across national cultural boundaries. Golembiewski et al. (2005) present an array of extremely impressive data that OD works well across national boundaries in general.

In addition, one of the most successful and influential approaches to OD today is Appreciative Inquiry. Appreciative Inquiry is highly consistent with the principles of McGregor's Theory Y and the self-fulfilling prophecy. In a comprehensive review of the literature of AI (Yaeger et al. 2005), a review which included over 400 publications, the review reports a high degree of success across highly diverse national cultures including, for example, the USA, Brazil, Canada, Australia, Nepal, the UK, Africa, Mexico, and the Netherlands.

Conclusion

It is our impression that over the last half-century, the world in many respects has become more Theory Y. In fact, based on reviews of OD by Golembiewski, and reviews of AI by Yaeger, Sorensen, and Bengtsson, we repeat a sentiment expressed by Golembiewski that somehow, national cultural values serve as a veneer over basic, fundamentally shared universal values, values reflected in the work of Douglas McGregor and the field of Organization Development.

But we believe McGregor's Theory X and Theory Y are far reaching, even broader than OD, as McGregor's concepts remain an indelible part of contemporary management thinking. This is evidenced in one example, by management scholars Bedeian and Wren who published the "Most Influential Management Books of the 20th Century" in *Organizational Dynamics* (2001). In their review, they ranked McGregor's *The Human Side of Enterprise* as number four of the 25 most influential management books of the twentieth century. Clearly, this book popularized the idea that managerial assumptions about human nature and human behavior are all important in determining managers' styles of operating. We agree.

References

Golembiewski, R. T., et al. (2005). Informing an apparent irony in OD applications: Good fit of OD and Confucian work ethics. *Research in Organization Change and Development, 15*, 241–273.

Heil, G., Bennis, W., & Stephens, D. C. (2000). *Douglas McGregor revisited: Managing the human side of the enterprise*. New York: Wiley.

Hofstede, G. (1980). Motivation, leadership, and organization: Do American theories apply abroad? *Organizational Dynamics, 9*(1), 42–63.

McGregor, D. (1957). The human side of enterprise in adventures in thought and action. In Proceedings of the fifth anniversary convocation of the School of Industrial Management. Cambridge, MA: MIT.

McGregor, D. (1960). *The human side of enterprise*. New York: McGraw-Hill.

Schein, E. H. (1969). *Process consultation: Its role in organization development,* Addison Wesley OD series. Reading: Addison Wesley.

Schein, E. H. (2016). *Humble consulting. How to provide real help faster*. Oakland: Berrett-Koehler Publishers.

Schein, E., Seashore, E., Yaeger, T., Sorensen, P., Ovaice, G., Goodly, T. (2007). Doing well by doing good: The legacy of Douglas McGregor in today's corporate world. Joint Symposium, National Academy of Management, Philadelphia, Aug 2007.

Sorensen, P. F., & Minahan, M. (2011). McGregor's legacy: The evolution and current application of theory Y management. *Journal of Management History, 17*(2), 178–192.

Weisbord, M. R. (2004). *Productive workplaces revisited: Dignity, meaning, and community in the 21st century*. New York: Wiley.

Yaeger, T. F., Sorensen, P. F., & Bengtsson, U. (2005). Assessment of the state of appreciative inquiry: Past, present, and future. *Research in Organizational Change and Development, 15*, 297–319.

Further Reading

Babcock, R., & Sorensen, P. (1976). *Strategies and tactics in management by objectives*. Champaign: Stipes Publishing Company.

Bedeian, A. G., & Wren, D. A. (2002). Most influential management books of the 20th century. *Organizational Dynamics, 29*(3), 221–225.

Beer, M., Eisenstat, R. A., & Foote, N. (2009). *High commitment high performance: How to build a resilient organization for sustained advantage*. New York: NY John Wiley & Sons, Inc.

Bennis, W. G. (2011). Chairman Mac in perspective. *Journal of Management History, 17*(2), 148–155.

Cooperrider, D. L. (1990). Positive image, positive action: The affirmative basis of organizing. In S. Srivastva & D. L. Cooperider (Eds.), *Appreciative management and leadership* (pp. 91–125). San Francisco: Jossey-Bass.

Cummings, T., Buono, A., Sorensen, P., & Yaeger, T. (2014). Management consulting and organization development: Divergent origins and convergent lives/strange bedfellows, arranged marriage or mutual partners? Panel presented at the Organization Development International Conference of the Academy of Management, June 2014, Lyon.

Drucker, P. (2000). In G. Heil, W. Bennis, & D. C. Stephens (Eds.), *Douglas McGregor revisited: Managing the human side of the enterprise*. New York: Wiley.

Hofstede, G., Hofstede, G. J., & Minkov, M. (1991). *Cultures and organizations: Software of the mind* (Vol. 2). London: McGraw-Hill.

Sorensen, P., & Yaeger, T. (2015). *Theory X and theory Y.* Oxford, UK: Oxford Press, Bibliography. doi: 10.1093/obo/9780199846740-0078.

Sorensen, P., Yaeger, T., Bengtsson, U. (2006). *The current state of action research in the U.S.* In: European Group and Organizational Studies Conference (EGOS), Bergen, July 2006.

Yaeger, T. (2011). Honoring Douglas McGregor and the 50th anniversary of 'the human side of enterprise'. *Journal of Management History, 17*(2), 144–147.

Yaeger, T., & Sorensen, P. (2010). Advancing appreciative inquiry: AI Temadag, presented to OD Talks/Denmark Postal Conference, Sept 2010, Albertslund.

Yaeger, T. (Chair), Cummings, T., Fry, R., Lorsch, J., Schein, E., Sorensen, P., & Tjosvold, D. (2015). *Governing OD growth and history: Re-Visiting the Addison-Wesley 6-Volume Series with OD Scholars*. In: Showcase Symposium, National Academy of Management, Vancouver, Aug 2015.

Eric J. Miller: Practicing Scholar in Action 52

Jean E. Neumann and Antonio Sama

Abstract

This chapter traces Eric Miller's early career from social anthropologist in industry through four decades as a second-generation social scientist for the Tavistock Institute of Human Relations (TIHR). We assert that each decade can be understood as emphasizing one of Eric's contributions within four categories that sustain our field today. (1) *Systems of Organization* (Miller and Rice 1967) stands as a seminal contribution to *organizational theory and work organization design*. Not only does Eric's original research with Ken Rice in Indian weaving sheds embody the emerging principles of socio-technical systems, but their ideas about boundaries, levels of analysis, representational meetings, and differentiation between subsystems led to extending systems thinking into other sectors. (2) Eric's extensive *action research* shaped social policies in a range of "people processing institutions": for example, geriatric and psychiatric hospitals; the education, treatment, and support of people with disabilities; and role changes for nurses, occupational health specialists, and wives in diplomatic service. His "working notes" and "working hypotheses" technique helps outsiders and insiders to mutually negotiate action, bringing together organizational development with action research. (3) By his third decade at TIHR, Miller demonstrated explicit concern with *systems change and societal analysis*, applying social science for social problems (e.g., workers' strikes, relations between immigrant communities); he began using cross-boundary developments that required both systems design and psychodynamic interpretation (e.g., mergers and acquisitions, a Mexican water system). An outcome of this concern was an Organization for the Promotion of Understanding of

J.E. Neumann (✉)
The Tavistock Institute of Human Relations, London, UK
e-mail: j.neumann@tavinstitute.org.uk

A. Sama
Canterbury Christ Church University, Canterbury, UK
e-mail: antonio.sama@canterbury.ac.uk

D.B. Szabla et al. (eds.), *The Palgrave Handbook of Organizational Change Thinkers*,
DOI 10.1007/978-3-319-52878-6_19

Society (OPUS). (4) While Eric directed TIHR's *group relations and experiential learning* offerings from 1970, he emphasized that culturally appropriate dissemination needed to be led by people within their own countries. Thus, while avoiding hero worship, Miller encouraged the formation of two dozen institutions scattered around the world, each identifying somehow with Tavistock schools of thought.

Keywords
Action research • A. K. Rice • Anthropologist in industry • Cultural change • Group relations • Role analysis • Societal analysis • Socio-technical systems • Systems psychodynamics

Contents

Introducing Eric J. Miller

Eric John Miller (1924–2002) was most closely associated with The Tavistock Institute of Human Relations (TIHR), London, UK. In search of a career in applied social science, he joined the staff of this small yet globally influential R&D center in 1958, working steadily for over four decades until his death at 78. As a part of the second generation recruited by TIHR founders, Eric's substantive impact can be tracked over several categories of scholarship and practice that still underpin organizational change thinking today. The titles of those categories have varied over the years, depending on fads, funding, and geographical application. Here, we trace Eric Miller's publications and practice relevant to developments and dissemination of organization theory and work organization design, action research, systems change and societal analysis, and group relations and experiential learning.

Influences and Motivations: Anthropologist in Industry

Eric J. Miller was born in 1924 (between the two world wars) in the then small town of High Wycombe, located in the county of Buckinghamshire, which is northwest of London. Both of his parents encouraged his intellectual precociousness. His father was a schoolteacher and his mother had ambitions for her first-born son to become a classics scholar. At the age of 17, he won a scholarship in classics to Jesus College, Cambridge University. In 1941, with WWII heating up, Eric anticipated a year of university before joining the army. In his own words, "I did a minimum of study, rowed and worried about the future" (Miller 1993, p. ix).

Once he joined the army and completed basic training, Eric was sent in 1943 to participate in a War Office Selection Board – this was, unbeknownst to him, a social innovation in which founding members of the Tavistock Institute had been involved. Its purpose was to enable soldiers from a wide range of socioeconomic backgrounds to be assessed in groups on their potential to become military leaders. Eric was selected to be a junior officer in the Royal Artillery, serving initially in North Central India and then in Burma toward the end of the war. For the next 3 years, his military roles were immersed in "the cultural mélange" of troops who were Hindus, Muslims, Sikhs, and Gurkhas complicated by "surrendering cohorts of Japanese" (Miller 1993, p. x).

These wartime and cross-cultural experiences motivated Miller to switch from classics to anthropology once he returned to Cambridge University in 1946. He achieved a first class degree and funding for doctorate field research where he spent 2 years in a southwestern region of India studying "change in the traditional social system in Kerala, where substantial Muslim and Syrian Christian minorities lived alongside the highly stratified caste structure of the Hindu majority" (Miller 1993, p. x). Subsequent funding for 18 months of postgraduate research, based on a contrasting social system in northern Thailand, came from the Foreign Office.

Miller had been enacting "social anthropology" in the footsteps of leading early-twentieth-century anthropologists. His professor, Meyer Fortes, had studied under Bronislaw Malinowski at London School of Economics. This British anthropological approach blended structuralism and functionalism – a distinction defined in a history of anthropology text as follows: "social structure was the matrix, or enclosing form, of society, while social function was the role that individual parts of society played in maintaining the structural whole" (Erickson and Murphy 2013, p. 91). Malinowski, widely accepted creator of participant observation as ethnographic method, is associated with Emile Durkheim's notion that functionalism is rooted in biology (ibid: 94).

By 1952, Miller was in his late 20s and eager to find something other than field anthropology, yet he was reluctant to consider academic anthropology. Eric wanted to do something to address the social problems he had seen. He wrote to his professor asking for guidance; Fortes activated a British-American network on Eric's behalf. This search for a role included the Chief Executive of Glacier Metal Company, Lord Wilfred Brown, whose manufacturing firm was the subject of the Tavistock Institute's first major action research project. Also contacted was Peter Jones, Executive Vice-President of Ludlow – a family-owned jute (a fiber used in making burlap, hessian, etc.) company with several mills particularly in Eastern India. Jones was looking for an anthropologist to work internally on several outstanding issues of cultural change.

At this point, Wilfred Brown introduced Eric to the Tavistock Institute of Human Relations (TIHR), wherein he met four of the founding social scientists: Tommy Wilson, Eric Trist, Harold Bridger, and Ken Rice. Rice (who eventually became his mentor, colleague, and boss) had begun his well-known study at the cotton mills in Ahmedabad, Western India. Eric writes about his first direct contact with TIHR: "I met a strange set of people, who seemed to be mixed up with psychoanalysis as well as with 'proper' social science"; about Ken Rice (also a social anthropologist), he says, "This was the kind of applied social science that I was looking for, and I badly wanted to know more" (Miller 1993, p. xii).

Eric was hired at the progressive and innovative Ludlow Company. Initially, he spent a year at the USA headquarters in Massachusetts preparing for relocation to Eastern India, as well as learning about the industry in general and about jute processing in particular. With his anthropological field sensitivities, Miller absorbed much about Northeast USA culture of the early 1950s. Simultaneously he was reading publications from the Tavistock Institute, being introduced to the American "human relations school" (e.g., Roethlisberger and McGregor), having his first experience as a "management trainer" with groups in New York, and visiting other mills in Mississippi and Pennsylvania. He also shadowed Tom Harris (a consultant with both Ludlow and Polaroid) who used his own psychometric tests "to predict the cultural adaptability of expatriates to work in the Indian culture" (ibid.).

Thus began Eric's formative, 3-year stint as an internal consultant or change agent with an overall focus on cultural change. Early on, he assisted public health officers in culturally aware approaches for encouraging Indian workers to take anti-malaria medication. Once in India, he focused on what would later be understood "as a transition from Theory X to Theory Y" in a situation ambivalent at best toward "the proposition that workers who were treated as responsible would behave more responsibly" (Miller 1993, p. xiv). Eric made a point to visit Ken Rice in Western India to study the experiments in semiautonomous working groups in weaving. He found it possible to apply what Rice was learning to Eastern India by "designing the work organization for new, very broad looms for carpet-backing that Ludlow had just acquired" (ibid.).

Miller's additional challenge was to consider how to work with the cross-cultural tensions affecting relationships between expatriate US and UK managers and engineers and the more qualified Indians. While the corporation had a manifest policy to hire more Indians, there was an inconsistency between the status hierarchy and the managerial hierarchy. Eric helped to work through the various issues by consulting to the senior management group (ibid.).

Apparent in his formative period in applying social science to business challenges, Eric out of necessity and circumstance enacted the dual emphases that would characterize his career for decades to come: action research with work organizational design, and group consultation in situations wherein issues of difference blocked progress. In 1956, 2 years into these change processes, a shift in US corporate ownership meant the internal role was finished. Eric accepted another internal consultant role at the Ahmedabad Calico mills – this time as "a full-time counterpart to Rice's visiting consultancy from the Tavistock Institute" (ibid.). Two years later, now aged 34, Miller moved back to London to join the TIHR staff working in the small unit led by Ken Rice.

Key Contributions: Organization Theory and Systems Psychoanalysis

1958–1969: Organization Theory and Work Organization Design

Eric's publications during his first few years at the Tavistock Institute built on his practical experiments within the two Indian mills and tested related ideas within UK manufacturing settings along with other industrial sectors new to him. His transition into TIHR culminated with *Systems of Organization: The control of task and sentient boundaries* (Miller and Rice 1967), a book that established his credibility as an organizational theorist in the emerging discipline of systems approaches to complex organizations. Additionally, it exemplifies the close collaboration that he and Ken Rice transferred from Ahmedabad back to London and the intensity to which social scientists at TIHR were engaged in the early days of developing socio-technical systems (STS) theory and practice.

Initially, Miller – the social anthropologist with experience as an internal consultant for 5 years – crafted a detailed description and analysis of principles of ways in which work in an organization can be grouped. He asserted "three possible bases for clustering of role-relationships and thus for the internal differentiation of a production system" (Miller 1959, p. 249): technology, territory, and time are shown as essential "dimensions of difference in the context of transition from a primary or simple production system to a complex system" (Miller 1959, p. 245). Further, "differentiating a complex system into sub-units means breaking down the kind and quality of management required" (ibid: 257).

Around the same time, Ken Rice published a detailed case analysis about the Ahmedabad experiments focusing on productivity and social organization, as well as the process and implications for organizational change (Rice 1958). Subsequently, a second more theoretical book appeared introducing the concept of primary task to open systems theory (Rice 1963) and illustrating the undeniable relevance of the enterprise's environment as a force in organizational change.

Systems of Organization (Miller and Rice 1967) brought together into an overall framework central concepts and logically connected learning from both men. We think that the major contribution delivered by Miller and Rice was that this book summarized a pivotal point in the creation of a systems approach to organizations. Their scheme could be applied within, across, and between levels of analyses of social systems, including individuals, pairs, trios, small groups, intergroups, large groups, subunits, across units, departments, divisions, organizations, and their environments as enterprises. The open systems model echoed the idea of functionalism being rooted in biology and biological metaphor. Their overall conceptual framework introduced four broad angles: systems of activity and their boundaries; individuals, groups, and their boundaries; task priorities and constraints (including primary task); and organizational model building – "the patterning of activities through which the primary task of the enterprise is performed" (Miller and Rice 1967, p. 33).

Miller and Rice struggled over organizational boundaries such as theoretical and practical interfaces through case analyses of building a new steel works, open systems and boundary controls applied to a research institute, and a full-blown application of the systems approach to the flying and ground systems of an airline. They illustrated a fairly new concept of transactions within and across organizational boundaries by providing case material from selling and sales forces, as well as from a dry cleaner's shop with his backstage technical cleaning process. They also showed how task roles and functional boundaries within a family business had become tangled up with the psychodynamics of the family members holding most roles.

The final two parts of the book address how computer systems were beginning to eliminate organizational boundaries within enterprises, ending with a snapshot of learnings about task and sentient groups (think about those anthropological kinship networks at different levels of social analysis) and their boundary controls. In later years, Miller felt that an important contribution of *Systems of Organization* were the values that he and Rice had explored. He identified two issues that echo the human relations movement of the time, of which TIHR was a part: (1) what "led to effective forms of group working – semi-autonomous groups – which optimized the psycho-social needs of the workers and the demands of the technical system" (Miller 1993, p. 27); and (2) that the manager's job was "not to tell individual workers what to do, but to provide the boundary conditions which enabled the work groups . . . to get on with their task" (ibid.: 15). These values may seem a bit underwhelming now, but they were ground breaking in the 1960s through 1980s.

Indeed, Miller and Rice (1967) remained a classical text for three generations of academics of work organization, organizational consultants, and change agents (managerial and employee representative) who were involved in applying socio-technical systems (STS) to improve the quality of working life (QWL) and to design and implement improvements and innovations in the technical and technological aspects of all sorts of work. A list (much too long to mention of edited books and collections in organizational theory, in general, and the systems approach to organizations particularly) includes selections from *Systems of Organization* and related publications from others at TIHR. Eric himself put together just such a collection in a two-volume series entitled, *The Tavistock Institute Contribution to Job and Organizational Design* (1999).

By the new millennium, much of the core values and concepts became so widespread that newer generations did not consider the need to cite Miller and Rice. Their TIHR colleagues Trist and Emery – better disseminated to both US and Australian audiences – might still be mentioned today as representatives of the TIHR socio-technical systems approach. Even so, the impact of this school of thought persists to the extent that many of the tools, techniques, and design outcomes were taken up, often without the values of optimization of workers' needs and incorporated into such approaches as cellular working, lean management, interdisciplinary care teams, patient and student pathways, etc.

1970–1979: Action Research

At the age of 46, Eric's second decade at the Institute began with the sudden death of Ken Rice from a brain tumor. Shortly thereafter, Miller published twice in Rice's honor: an evaluation of the STS work at the weaving shed and a compilation of papers in the spirit of Rice's last 10 years (Miller 1976). He also accepted a role, previously held by Rice, as Director for the Tavistock Institute's Group Relations Programme. As far as publications go, the 1970s saw Eric using his action research and consulting more within the health, social care, and public service domains, and, with one notable exception, less directly with industry and commerce.

In the early 1970s, results became available from a major stream of action research concerning the application of the systems theory of organization to residential institutions for physically handicapped (Miller and Gwynne 1972). Along with TIHR social scientist, Geraldine Gwynne, the colleagues had worked within and across five such organizations in collaboration with residents, staff, and management. Their nomenclature contrasted a warehousing approach centered on dependency based on a purpose of prolonging physical life, with a horticultural approach emphasizing independence based on a purpose of developing and using remaining abilities. The project aimed to develop organizational models catering to these mixed needs, experimented with implications for staff's role definition and development, including exploring ambivalent attitudes all around. The question driving the action research was how to manage the work of both subsystems in a way that residents and staff could retain integrity in their own functioning egos.

This stream of projects – *A Life Together* (Miller and Gwynne 1972) and subsequently *A Life Apart* (Dartington et al. 1981) – helped shape social policy in the education, treatment, and support of people with disabilities. The researchers had to grapple with cultural issues underpinning the primary task of different models of care, as well as ways of thinking and communicating about the personality and behavior of staff and residents. Subsequent opportunities to use an open systems approach to organizational analysis in, what Eric called "people-processing institutions," arrived from a geriatric hospital, handicapped persons in the community, a psychiatric hospital, and a diocese of the Church of England.

Simultaneously, the topic of changing occupational roles, and the organizational changes necessary to address same, became an increasingly important arena for Eric's scientific research and consultancy practice. In the opening pages of the book edited in honor of Rice, Miller focused on role analysis and organizational behavior (1976, pp. 1–18). The interconnection of roles and structure was showing up in the social anthropology literature at the time. As his second decade at TIHR unfolded, Eric had completed two projects on role change for professional associations in occupational health and in nursing leading to an influential study concerning the role of wives in the diplomatic service.

Eric's work on diplomatic wives made waves (Miller 1993, pp. 132–145). There was a diversity of stances apparent between traditional roles for UK diplomats' wives around the word that was being questioned by some women who did not want to be required to take on embassy roles and by others who wanted to work elsewhere. These tensions seemed to coincide with age, phase of family development, and stage of husband's career. More consultancy than action research, the study's impact was substantial as change unfolded right into the early 1990s. The report itself constitutes, in our view, Miller at his most blended as anthropologist and systems thinker and most entertaining in observing and analyzing while standing a bit back so that the network of determined stakeholders could work things out on their own without his input.

1980–1989: Systems Change and Societal Analysis

During his very busy second decade at TIHR, Eric participated in three other substantial action research projects. While the actual client engagement took place in the 1970s, subsequent contributions only became apparent later. One involved a large manufacturer suffering with merger and acquisition problems, the notable exception to his extensive experimentation with nonindustrial sectors in the 1970s. The other two took place in Mexico and demonstrate Miller in social anthropologist mode applying open systems to the complexity of societal issues. Over several years, he consulted on (a) the conceptualization of a socioeconomic process of integrated rural development and (b) the macro-design of regional water authorities tied to hydrological systems.

After some thought, we have placed these three projects under systems change and societal analysis, a substantial area of interest in Eric's third decade at TIHR. A cluster of publications between 1977 and 1980 illustrate his preoccupation with making sense of how psychoanalysis and power could be brought into ways of thinking about the processes of development and change. Within the context of the UK at the time, there was a great deal of turmoil going on in the society (e.g., conflict in Northern Ireland, multiple trade union strikes affecting public services, a controversial female Prime Minister). It was also a period in which ideologies of employee involvement and participative management were being used within corporations, sometimes alongside STS-inspired semiautonomous working groups.

Keeping in mind that Eric had been functioning as Director of TIHR's Group Relations Programme, the incorporation of applied psychoanalysis in his publications increased gradually and always in relation to what could be labeled role analysis or cultural analysis. That is, Miller's observations of behavior were described and interpreted in a way that spelled out challenges being experienced by the people within the social system under study. Attempts were made to propose actions that allowed those implicated to work out the challenges themselves, in the light of an analysis.

Eric's writings about processes of change and development increased. Heavily drawing on group relations thinking as applied to consultancy practice, he argued in favor of seeing the relationship between the individual and enterprise as "a relationship between two systems" and of "the reciprocal dependence of the boundary role-holders on the role-holders inside [the boundary that] goes unrecognized; it gets forgotten that there can be no leaders without followers" (Miller 1977, pp. 38–39). Based on a merger-acquisition industrial case, he asserts that the use of group relations events as an intervention serves the dual purposes of organizational development and industrial democracy. "Authority, by becoming detached from rank and status, and attached instead to task and role, is available to each member of the organization" (ibid: 60). In related writing, Eric puzzled over why UK trade unions turned down the opportunity to join the rest of the European Union in mandated workers' councils (1985). He concluded that "British industry and society generally are moving out of that dependency culture, through a phase of failed dependency and toward 'post-dependency'... shifting into a more genuinely instrumental ... relatedness to the employing organization" (Miller 1993, p. 313).

Clearly, Miller was going through a period of thinking bigger systems change, like his extensive rural development project in Mexico. Combining open systems thinking with social anthropology, he proposed that even something large and complex (like integrated rural development aiming at reaching 20,000 rural communities) could be considered a system and, therefore, subject to processes of thoughtful development. "A change in the relatedness of a system to its environment requires internal changes within the system: it must shift to a new steady state if it is to survive" (Miller 1979, p. 218).

Eric's Mexican clients were inquiring about how to coordinate organizationally such an intervention that cuts across state and local levels, with many different federal ministries and agencies involved. For 3 years, he helped them "identify the kind of relationship, at the interface between the 'developers' and their 'client systems' that would enable" a self-sustaining process of rural development (ibid: 220). He used a four-model template to help the clients consider how their project might unfold: top-down, bottom-up, enlightened paternalism, and negotiated model. Action research cycles were undertaken to achieve the primary task of the negotiated model: "to provide resources to help each community to formulate, negotiate and implement its own community development programme" (ibid: 224).

Back in the UK, Eric assisted in the creation and development of a registered charity, the Organisation for the Promotion of Understanding of Society (OPUS). Together with its first executive director, Olya Khaleelee, they wrote an influential paper that brought together this emerging concern for what was happening in society and communities (Khaleelee and Miller 1985). The goal of the paper was implied in the title, *Beyond the small group: Society as an intelligible field of study* (ibid.; see also Miller 1993, pp. 243–272).

Apparently, Miller's central theme in his third decade at TIHR was integrating power, psychoanalysis, and systems approaches into community change and societal analysis. His work with an extensive community conflict and resolution project in Northeast London was characterized by the sort of multiracial, multi-immigrant, multi-socioeconomic population that echoed his earlier years in India and Burma. He subsequently consulted to two extensive action research projects on the effectiveness and complexity of a Self-Help Alliance in health and social care. Both projects brought him into relationship with voluntary organizations struggling with public sector agencies. And he felt drawn into writing explicitly about organization consultation and dynamics.

1990–2002: Group Relations and Experiential Learning

When Miller joined the Tavistock Institute in 1958, the group relations program had started and was gearing up. In parallel with furthering socio-technical systems, Ken Rice, who had participated in Wilfred Bion's small study groups, was active in the creation and development of these conferences. Indeed, he wrote the seminal text, *Learning for Leadership* (Rice 1965), and emerged as Director of TIHR's Group Relations Programme in these early days. Eric would have been subjected to TIHR's policy of scientific staff undergoing psychoanalysis; and, he was involved as participant and staff for these experiential learning conferences.

Despite taking over as Director of TIHR's Group Relations Programme in 1970, there are few publications from Miller that exclusively address the conference work itself. As a part of his preoccupation with integrating power with psychoanalysis and systems change, he spoke to a 1980 annual meeting of the US-based A.K. Rice Institute on the politics of involvement (Miller 1985) as well as the politics of identity "a subject which has long intrigued me" (Miller 1993, p. vii). Eric asserted three levels active in the micro-politics of any situation (macro, inter-institutional, and intra-institutional) indicating that "it is a subject that nestles on the boundaries of micro-sociology, social psychology, psychodynamic psychology and political science" (ibid.).

We consider this preoccupation to be one of Miller's contributions to group relations and experiential learning. Sama recalls Eric speaking with him about "how the here and now can be used, at times, to ignore the political nature of power" (personal communication, January 1996). Miller insisted that, within the conference design, the interpersonal level of study constituted work on the politics of identity – "the me, not me" (ibid.). He clearly had been motivated to take up this issue in the light of a debate going on within the US group relations community of practice at the time. He places himself firmly with one foot in the camp supporting the integrity of the conference model as a place for socio-psychological-political study of systems dynamics. On the other foot, he calls for an increase in the emotional and cognitive capability in studying politics within the conferences including those between staff and participants. "The political dimension of group relations conferences, at both micro and macro levels, has been relatively neglected, to the detriment of our understanding both of the processes that occur within the conferences themselves and also of the processes involved in the transition of members to their roles in external institutions" (Miller 1985, p. 387). He challenges consultants working in the group relations tradition to search for interpretations related to what systemic political function might be served by the behaviors they are observing and considering already in a socio-psychological light.

This was a strong statement, coming as it did during his tenth anniversary as Director of TIHR's Group Relations Programme, that harmonizes with the intensive action research and consulting he was doing with community systems change and societal analysis. Early in his fourth decade at TIHR, aged 66, Miller wrote two short papers (1990a, b) about experiential learning in groups, focused specifically on the Leicester model. Leicester is a city in the UK wherein the Tavistock Institute's intensive 2-week residential group relations conference takes place annually as it has done since 1957. The experiential study conference provides configurations at multiple levels of system: individual, small group, intergroup, large group, and institutional – interwoven with individual review and application to external roles and situations.

Miller's two papers on Leicester conferences (1990a, b) had been requested by Eric Trist and Hugh Murray. Trist and Murray were editing three volumes about the Tavistock Institute of Human Relations' contributions to the social engagement of social science (1990, 1993, 1997). The group relations innovations were essential to the first volume on socio-psychological theory and practice, wherein TIHR social scientists were experimenting with integration of the British psychanalytic tradition (e.g., Bion, Bowlby, and Klein), Kurt Lewin's principles of analysis, and a systems approach to organizational analysis. Two aspects of Miller's papers stand out.

Firstly, while containing a density of information, the writing invites the reader to engage simultaneously with the educational and historical value they represent. The initial paper introduces the group relations conference as a long-established, still vibrant approach. Eric offers historical origins and developments in design, explores the interplay between theory and method (including conceptual framework, the practice and role of staff, theory, and phenomenology), and ends with the role of participant and the nature of learning (Miller 1990a). The subsequent paper addresses dissemination and application of group relations conferences in the UK and across the world. Eric begins with institutional reproduction and adaptation, summarizes applications as interventions at the organizational and the societal level, and ends with reflections on – what was then – current experiences with the model (Miller 1990b).

The second aspect of these papers worth noting is that Eric writes as if he has been on the boundary of the group relations conferences. He takes no credit for the maintenance, enhancement, and adaptations of the TIHR Leicester conferences since 1970; nor does he insert himself into the narrative of institutional reproduction (a term he credits with Rice's 1965 *Learning for Leadership*) within the UK and around the world. Such a stance is consistent with both values and concepts underpinning the group relations model and the experiential learning of a community of practice. During a celebration of Eric's life after his death in 2002, his international colleagues (Gould et al. 2001, 2004) spoke eloquently of Eric as an institution-builder globally who was a master of leading from behind.

In addition to TIHR's own Group Relations Programme and the Advanced Organizational Consultation (AOC) program (Neumann 2007), Eric played roles in the formation and development of most of the national institutes of human relations dotted around the world. These included, but are not limited to, AKRI (USA), OFEK (Israel), OPUS (UK), MundO (Germany, Austria, and Switzerland). Remember back to his first TIHR publication wherein he proposed a notion that the job of a manager or a leader was not to tell individuals what to do, "but to provide the boundary conditions which enabled the work groups . . . to get on with their task" (Miller 1959, p. 15). Apparently, Miller's institutional building capacity enacted this idea at the level of community of practice and cross-institutional and cross-national boundaries!

New Insights: Both Macro- and Micro-collaboratively

In a posthumous publication, Eric states that by the mid-1960s, "a set of four frameworks – psychodynamic, psychosocial, socio-technical and systemic – was available and being used in the Institute's action research and consultancy with organizations" (Miller 2002, p. 193). We consider that Eric's career before and during his time at the Tavistock Institute of Human Relations (TIHR) embodies a steady taking on of each of these frameworks until a full set constituted his own scholarly practice.

Our understanding of his 1940s experience in the military and subsequent training at Cambridge in social anthropology suggests that the psychosocial already was intimately apparent during his fieldwork studies of social stratification in India and Thailand. Surely, his formation in the 1950s as an applied social scientist – from the role of internal consultant during work organizational redesign processes in manufacturing – can be understood predominately as immersion in the early evolution of socio-technical systems. By the late 1960s, Miller and Rice had created a significant book on systems of organization, from which clearly grew a workload manifested in Eric's 1970's extraordinary action research into nonindustrial sectors.

Miller convincingly asserts that "the psychodynamic is never irrelevant" (ibid.). Yet with few exceptions, he did not set the psychodynamic off on its own, away from the systemic, socio-technical, and psychosocial (see, e.g., Miller 1998). He clearly considered "that a psychodynamic perspective is a necessary but not sufficient condition for effective organizational consultancy" (ibid: 186).

In his 1993 collection of papers, Eric clusters his selection into five sections: toward a conceptual framework, three studies of "people-processing institutions," analysis and diagnosis, processes of development and change, and societal processes. We have used this book, which includes a bibliography of his publications, to map and then trace his evolution as an applied social scientist. In reviewing Miller's own chosen papers, we were struck by the sheer volume of action research projects and a pattern of gradually evolving toward a way of thinking that integrated those four frameworks.

As people closely associated with TIHR ourselves, it is worth mentioning that some of the frameworks were taken as separate specialties by different units within the Institute. To strive for (and achieve to some extent) a type of integration across the four frameworks was not necessarily a shared institutional task. In the 1970s, there seemed for a while to be a dissemination split by sectors: socio-technical systems disseminated through industrial and commercial organizations and group relations disseminated through health, social care, and public sector organizations. Even in the 1980s, it was possible to glimpse how these frameworks had been adopted by different academic disciplines and related occupations, for example, systems of organization and socio-technical being taken on by industrial sociologists, business strategists, and management schools and group relations, psychosocial, and psychodynamic being taken on by psychologists, micro-sociologists, psychiatrists, and not-for-profit scholarly practitioners.

In Fig. 1, we indicate something of the integration that we think emerges from Miller's action research publications. At the center of the figure, a diagram from

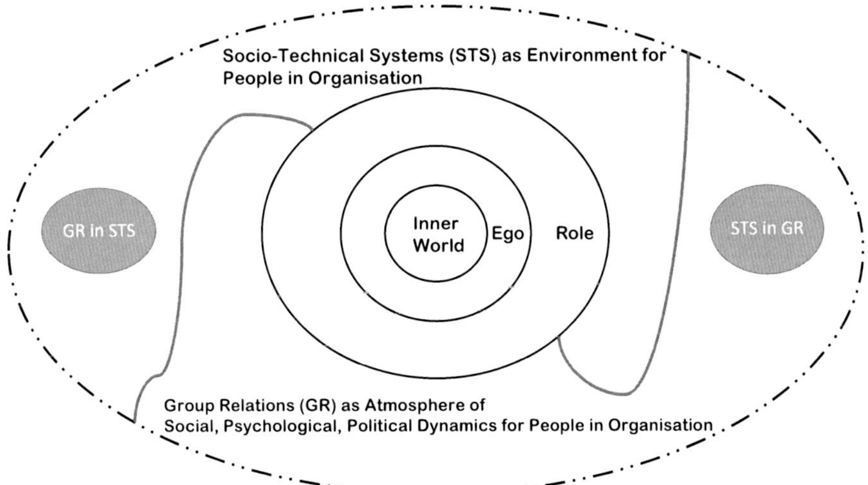

Fig. 1 Integrating socio-technical systems and psychodynamics

Systems of Organization (Miller and Rice 1967, p. 17) illustrates the authors' lowest level of analysis: "the individual … represented on the pattern of a system of activity" (ibid: 16). To this, we have added a third concentric circle entitled, "role," as an element of analysis that Eric increasingly used as necessary for understanding people-processing systems. We set this individual down into the middle of a context – a total situation to use Kurt Lewin's concept – depicted by a larger systemic circle (the social system relevant particularly to this person or people) with a dotted-line boundary, indicating an environment wider than and surrounding the visible relevant social system.

In that final concentric circle, we assert our experience of Eric Miller's contribution as a change thinker: that is, manifesting theoretically and practically both separate and simultaneous aspects of socio-technical systems and group relations. Elsewhere in this paper, we also have used different phrases: "organization theory" in recognition of the importance of the *Systems of Organization* book (Miller and Rice 1967) and "systems psychodynamics" in the light of Eric's social anthropological bias of attending simultaneously to both social structure and social function. Eric claimed a unique consolidation of these two frameworks, while explicitly respecting a genealogy that combined systems theory and psychoanalysis (Miller 1997, p. 188). He defined systems psychodynamics as meaning, "a model of open socio-technical systems informed by a psychoanalytic perspective" (ibid.: 187).

From 1993, Eric worked as part of a trio to create the Advanced Organizational Consultation (AOC) program with the explicit purpose of experimenting with an integration of organizational theory, systems psychodynamics, and consultancy competence. While it was possible to locate and work with original TIHR socio-technical and socio-ecological theory (e.g., Neumann et al. 1995; Trist and Murray 1993, 1997), it is fair to say that much had been taken into the established academic domains of organizational theory, business strategy, and operations management. AOC faculty found it necessary to draw on other contemporary literatures to illustrate and flesh-out aspects of TIHR organizational theory. Fortunately, it was possible to locate and work with original TIHR socio-psychological theory (e.g., Trist and Murray 1990).

An integrated lens of systems psychodynamics, however, required additional publications (Holti 2011; Miller 1993; Neumann 1999, 2010). It was readily possible to find scholarly practice and academic publications in this area (e.g., writers like Gould et al.). In terms of consultancy competence, methodologies, and practices related to action research, work organization design and group relations had much to offer (e.g., Armstrong et al.; Pasmore et al.). Miller usefully wrote up his "working note" methodology (Miller 1995), and much was accomplished through experiential learning (Neumann 2007). A focus on the consultant's role helped motivate participants to bring many angles on consultancy competence into their learning community, thereby introjecting Eric's strong stance of inviting collaboration while avoiding the creation of dependency.

Legacies and Unfinished Business: Accessible and Normal Integration

Integration of Applied Social Science

In the 2000s, there has been a rise of approaches that define themselves against systems of organization in favor of conversations, dialogue, strength-based approaches, etc. These politics of identity are very strong: systems is the "not me," and one of these "new paradigm" approaches is the "me." Apparently, that which was unique and exciting in 1960s, has become taken for granted within organizational theory and work organization design. This could have something to do with many examples of systems thinking being applied without the human optimization values! Some vocal and well-published academics among current generations of practitioners (including a few baby boomers) are holding the term, "systems," accountable for abuses in consultancy and change management practice. The essential critical theory aspects of the TIHR traditions seem less understood.

Perhaps this is a point where the historical split caused trouble. We refer to a split between the group relations tradition, in which talking and working through is a central methodology of a soft side, and the socio-technical tradition, in which the application of specialist knowledge to jobs, roles, technology, work flows, and industrial relations constitutes a hard side. Theoretically, there is still much to be done that addresses integration. Those working within a systems approach to organizations perhaps need more exposure to group relations thinking, which legitimizes thoughts and feelings and politics without looking for premature solutions. Many in the group relations community of practice may rely primarily on *Systems of Organization* for organizational theory and could benefit from understanding how improved structures can free up emotions including anxiety.

If we take Eric's action research as example, it could well be that we need another round of intensive study within nonlinear STS work, along the lines of the people-processing systems that Miller investigated. Combined with information technologies as the central form of coordination and management, impact on roles and the structure of work can be examined in the light of the social, psychological, and political issues. Certainly, current changes within the environment of enterprises must be taken into consideration. These studies may be there but seem difficult to find with explicit reference to these TIHR integrated theories of practice.

There are many reasons why elements of the "me" methods in the "new paradigm" could be used to encourage and reveal the range of system psychodynamics at play in today's settings. Further, both group relations and STS methods can be adjusted, even customized, for contemporary purposes of cross-boundary OD. For example, service departments contracted outside the boundaries of main organizations may not live up to their anticipated financial benefits (valued by the people in core decision-making departments) while redefining belonging and task concerns of people on the front line in the contracted suppliers. Enforced matrix and project management routines suffer from inadequate shared cultures across various boundaries (e.g., functional, occupational, geographic, etc.). That, which is considered sacrosanct from so-called rational viewpoints, may be addressed more effectively when influenced by so-called emotional viewpoints. Methodologies for emotional-rational collaboration might well heal unnecessary splits within economic-technological logics.

Writing and Publishing Action Research

We think Miller's use of action research to report specifics of systems issues integrated with psycho-social-political dynamics is still important. People respond to stories that show how environmental challenges put people in difficult positions and how finding ways to air the issues and work things through within the boundaries of their own groups can make a difference. Miller clearly had a professional knack for applying theory in practice and then summarizing it in a working note (e.g., Miller 1993, 1998) to enable basic dialogue with clients. Then, he could write it up again as a case scenario for scholarly practitioners and then incorporate more than one such case to illustrate more theoretical points for academe.

We puzzle over the degree to which this capability might be rooted in social anthropological ethnography. Such "narrative analysis" methodology – in the form of case studies and storytelling – powerfully evokes the qualitative richness of both particularities and totalities of client and scientific situations. However, current publication conventions can work against such methodology being published in organizational and managerial academic journals. Scholarly practitioners often find it difficult to impossible to move beyond the writing and submitting stages. A master of the form (like Eric Miller) does not necessarily make for a functioning role model. Differentiation within the action research publishing community further complicates that as an outlet. Similarly, clinical research of such a narrative form is not widely distributed outside – for example – psychotherapeutic communities of practice. This suggests it is no accident that books of papers have become a norm of dissemination in these arenas.

Differentiation and Integration of Consultancy Methodologies

While there has been a plethora of publications on systems-based psychoanalysis, there is a paucity of publications on action research and consultancy from that perspective. Of concern for us is the education and development of scholarly practitioners in this regard. In addition to the publication issue above, there is the need to differentiate from and integrate with both the expert-oriented management consulting role/methodology and the collaboratively oriented group relations consulting role/methodology. It seems that idiosyncratic solutions to polarities between these two roles can be observed in individuals but not so much in a way that the field of organizational change benefits.

Eric Miller is a good example: he was a management consultant when working with organizational clients (usually managers or leaders) and used the working note to input his ideas to those who had to live with the problem and implement solutions. In contrast, as a group relations consultant, Eric spoke very little and kept in mind a particular attitude toward the role that enacted his integrated notions of what he was doing (see Fig. 1). He was committed to studying factors that gave people substantial difficulty in thriving in modern organizations and society. Active as both an applied social science researcher and management consultant, Miller's brilliance was to point people toward emotional attitudes and ways of thinking that worked against their taking power through accessible systemic actions in their idiosyncratic situations.

Ideas within the systems psychodynamic communities of practice that are crying out for attention point to current "appropriate dependency" in relation to the 1980s values of "autonomy." This seems even more serious in the light of cutbacks in governmental programs, the "on your bike" and "go it on our own" societal dynamics, and projection of hatred toward those who are visibly different – all present as we write. The emotional downsides of "primary task" and "primary risk" and how it relates to cultural change could suggest applications of altered group relations methodologies. And, finally, the need for mechanisms for on-going learning in the applied social sciences – originally created as face-to-face and time-consuming – now seem too costly to operate with any certainty. What might contemporary practicing scholars in action do?

Conclusion

Eric John Miller (1924–2002) entered the fields that have evolved into what we now label, "organizational change," as a nascent social anthropologist in industry. Coming of age during WWII in India and Burma, Eric's scholarship capabilities emerged through his ability to study practical challenges being experienced at the boundaries of society, social systems, and organizations. He arrived at the influential Tavistock Institute of Human Relations (TIHR) in London, UK, under mentorship of A.K. Rice, already steeped in the innovations that became socio-technical systems and systems psychodynamics. As we have shown into this chapter, Eric's substantial impact from that base can be traced across the multiple, interconnected domains of organization theory and work organization design, action research, system change and society analysis, and group relations and experiential learning.

We assert that Eric Miller's publishing output over four decades at TIHR shows how his practical scholarship developed in relation to a massive volume of action research and consultancy projects. He considered that his learned aim combined "a model of socio-technical systems informed by a psychoanalytic perspective" (Miller 1997, p. 187). This blend can be seen repeatedly in his preoccupation with integration of micro- and macro-level of social analysis, with the integration of accessible models for action with deep theoretical frameworks, and with the integration of collaborative working with consultancy clients for change as well as offering publications and presentations that coach academics into the social engagement of social science.

References

Dartington, T., Miller, E. J., & Gwynne, G. V. (1981). *A life together: The distribution of attitudes around the disabled*. London: Tavistock Publications.

Erickson, P. A., & Murphy, L. A. (2013). *A history of anthropological theory* (4th ed.). Toronto: University of Toronto Press.

Gould, L. J., Stapley, L. F., & Stein, M. (Eds.). (2001). *The systems psychodynamics of organizations: Integrating the group relations approach, psychoanalytic, and open systems perspectives*. London: Karnac Books.

Gould, L. J., Stapley, L. F., & Stein, M. (Eds.). (2004). *Experiential learning in organizations: Applications of the group relations approach*. London: Karnac Books.

Holti, R. (2011). Understanding institutional change in project-based organizing. *The Journal of Applied Behavioral Science, 47*(3), 360–394.

Miller, E. J. (Ed.). (1976). *Task and organization*. Chichester: Wiley.

Miller, E. J. (1977). Organizational development and industrial democracy. In C. L. Cooper (Ed.), *Organizational development in the UK and USA: A joint evaluation* (pp. 31–63). New York: PBI Books.

Miller, E. J. (1979). Open systems revised: A proposition about development and change. In W. G. Lawrence (Ed.), *Exploring individual and organizational boundaries: A Tavistock open systems approach* (pp. 217–233). London: Karnac Books.

Miller, E. J. (1985). The politics of involvement. In A. D. Coleman & M. H. Geller (Eds.), *Group relations reader 2* (pp. 383–397). Washington, DC: A.K. Rice Institute.

Miller, E. J. (1990a). Experiential learning in groups I: The development of the Leicester model. In E. Trist & H. Murray (Eds.), *The social engagement of social science: The socio-psychological perspective* (Vol. I, pp. 165–185). London: Free Association Books.

Miller, E. J. (1990b). Experiential learning in groups II: Recent developments in dissemination and application. In E. Trist & H. Murray (Eds.), *The social engagement of social science: The socio-psychological perspective* (Vol. I, pp. 186–198). London: Free Association Books.

Miller, E. J. (1998). A note on the proto-mental system and 'groupishness': Bion's basic assumptions revisited. *Human Relations, 51*, 1495–1508.

Miller, E. J. (1999). *The Tavistock Institute's contribution to job and organizational design (two volumes)*. Aldershot: Aldgate.

Miller, E. J. (2002). The strengths and limitations of a psychodynamic perspective in organizational consultancy. In S. F. Nolan & P. Nolan (Eds.), *Object relations and integrative psychotherapy: Tradition and innovation in theory and practice* (pp. 186–198). London: Whurr Publishers.

Miller, E. J., & Gwynne, G. V. (1972). *A life apart: A pilot study of residential institutions for the physically handicapped and the young chronic sick*. London: Tavistock Publications.

Neumann, J. E. (1999). Systems psychodynamics in service of political organizational change. In R. French & R. Vince (Eds.), *Group relations, management and organization* (pp. 54–69). Oxford: Oxford University Press.

Neumann, J. E. (2007). Becoming better consultants through varieties of experiential learning. In M. Reynolds & R. Vince (Eds.), *The handbook of experiential learning and management education* (pp. 258–273). Oxford: Oxford University Press.

Neumann, J. E. (2010). How integrating organizational theory with systems psychodynamics can matter in practice: A commentary on critical challenges and dynamics in multiparty collaboration. *The Journal of Applied Behavioral Science, 46*(3), 313–321.

Neumann, J. E., Holti, R., & Standing, H. (1995). *Change everything at once: The Tavistock Institute's guide to developing teamwork in manufacturing* (p. 2000). Didcot: Management Books.

Rice, A. K. (1958). *Productivity and social organization: The Ahmedabad experiment*. London: Tavistock Publications.

Rice, A. K. (1963). *The enterprise and its environment*. London: Tavistock Publications.

Rice, A. K. (1965). *Learning for leadership*. London: Tavistock Publications.

Further Reading

Khaleelee, O., & Miller, E. J. (1985). Beyond the small group: Society as an intelligible field of study. In M. Pines (Ed.), *Bion and group psychotheraphy* (pp. 354–385). London: Routledge & Kegan Paul.

Miller, E. J. (1959). Technology, territory and time: The internal differentiation of complex production systems. *Human Relations, 12*, 243–272.

Miller, E. J. (1993). *From dependency to autonomy: Studies in organization and change*. London: Free Association Books.

Miller, E. J. (1995). Dialogue with the client system: Use of the 'working note' in organizational consultancy. *Journal of Management Psychology, 10*(6), 27–30.

Miller, E. J. (1997). Effecting organizational change in large systems: A collaborative consultancy approach. In J. E. Neumman, K. Kellner, & A. Dawson-Shepherd (Eds.), *Developing organizational consultancy* (pp. 187–212). London: Routledge.

Miller, E. J., & Rice, A. K. (1967). *Systems of organization: The control of task and sentient boundaries*. London: Tavistock Publications.

Trist, E., & Murray, H. (Eds.). (1990). *The social engagement of social science: The socio-ecological perspective* (Vol. I). London: Free Association Books.

Trist, E., & Murray, H. (Eds.). (1993). *The social engagement of social science: The socio-technical perspective* (Vol. II). Philadelphia: University of Pennsylvania Press.

Trist, E., Emery, F., & Murray, H. (Eds.). (1997). *The social engagement of social science: The socio-ecological perspective* (Vol. III). Philadelphia: University of Pennsylvania Press.

53 Frederick A. Miller: Leveraging Inclusion as a Breakthrough Organizational Development Strategy

Monica E. Biggs

Abstract

Frederick A. Miller has contributed to the theory and practice of organization change by challenging and reframing how organizations understand and leverage differences to create inclusive workplaces. With Judith H. Katz, he published the first comprehensive model and framework for implementing diversity and inclusion as a lever for strategic culture change, moving diversity from a compliance-driven set of programs to a breakthrough OD strategy linked to higher operational and bottom-line performance. Miller came of age during a period heavily influenced by the Civil Rights Movement in the United States, which significantly shaped his vision not only of what society could be but also of the role organizations needed to play in moving society toward a greater equality of opportunity and participation. His work reflects a lifelong commitment to pushing back on the status quo to help change organizations into places where human beings can be fully human and where each person can grow, do their best work, and have a meaningful experience. Many of Miller's insights come from observing and learning from his clients, engaging with peers on corporate and not-for-profit boards, and studying what is happening in the world. In collaboration with Katz and others in his firm, he has developed several simple models and practical tools and processes that make it easier for clients to move toward a workplace in which people can do their best work in service of the organizational mission, vision, and strategic objectives. Miller believes that, fundamentally, organizations are only as productive as the interactions between people. Significant organizational change for today's organizations requires an adjustment in the quality of interactions between people. Conscious Actions for Inclusion is a tool that provides a set of behaviors communicated in simple, common language that opens the door to greater clarity and enhanced ways of interacting.

M.E. Biggs (✉)
The Kaleel Jamison Consulting Group Inc., Troy, NY, USA
e-mail: monicabiggs1242@gmail.com; monicabiggs@kjcg.com

D.B. Szabla et al. (eds.), *The Palgrave Handbook of Organizational Change Thinkers*,
DOI 10.1007/978-3-319-52878-6_65

Keywords
Civil rights • Culture change • Diversity • High-performing organizations • Inclusion • National Training Laboratories • Organization development

Contents

Introduction

An organizational heretic is "someone who sees a truth that contradicts the conventional wisdom of the institution to which she or he belongs – and who remains loyal to both entities, to the institution and the new truth" (Kleiner 2008). Much of what Frederick A. Miller has done to advance the field of diversity, inclusion, and organizational transformation has been done as a heretic (Kleiner included Miller in *The Age of Heretics* (2008)). A black activist, he chose to be a change agent working *inside* major US corporations. In many of his early client engagements, he was the first African-American to interact in a consultant capacity with members of senior management.

Throughout almost 45 years of organization development (OD) practice, he has facilitated large-scale organizational change without undermining the cultural values that made the organization successful: acknowledging the contributions of the founding "white male" culture, while at the same time aggressively challenging the institutionalized "isms" that have kept other groups down. He rejected change efforts that sought to level, or even raise, the playing field for all groups to the current level of white men as *insufficient*, saying the treatment many white men receive is not good enough either. The real challenge was to raise the playing field *for all* by creating an inclusive culture in which everyone felt valued as an individual and where differences were leveraged in support of the enterprise's goals (Miller and Katz 2002).

To raise the playing field, organizations needed an "inclusion breakthrough," a level of culture change that involved the rethinking and redesigning of many aspects of organizational culture: policies, practices, and sometimes structure. With Judith H. Katz, he published the first comprehensive model and framework for implementing diversity and inclusion as a lever for strategic culture change, moving it from a compliance-driven set of programs to a breakthrough OD strategy linked to higher operational and bottom-line performance.

Influences and Motivations: The Civil Rights Movement and OD - Aligning Personal and Professional Values

Miller came of age during a period heavily influenced by the Civil Rights Movement in the United States, which significantly shaped his vision not only of what society could be but also of the role organizations needed to play in moving society toward a greater equality of opportunity and participation.

He was born in 1946, into a lower middle-class neighborhood in West Philadelphia, Pa., the only son and youngest child of four. With a 13-year gap in age between him and his next older sister, his experience growing up was more like that of an only child. He was also introverted by nature and liked spending time alone or with a close friend or two, playing make-believe battles with miniature plastic soldiers or competitive board games. He also learned to play chess, a pastime he still loves. Miller's extraordinary ability to strategize and position organizational change interventions, always thinking two or more steps ahead, was born out of these early play experiences.

His mother Clarice, whom he described as "the first activist I ever met," was resolute in overcoming any barrier her son faced as an African-American child in the 1940s and 1950s, as he made his way through school and life in the inner city. She was indomitable and would not let anyone, regardless of her or his title or level of authority, limit her son's potential. When the school counselor put Fred – along with most of the other African-American children in his class – on the vocational-technical track, Clarice demanded that he be moved into the college entrance courses. The counselor resisted, explaining the unlikeliness that Miller could manage the workload, as he was "not college material," to which Miller's mother retorted, "You are not going tell me what my son can't do. You do your job and get him into those classes, and I will make sure he does what he needs to get to college" (Miller, personal communication, May 12, 2016).

Even then, Miller knew that he was lucky; he did not feel he deserved more breaks than his friends, he knew he was not the smartest in the group, and he did not feel superior to his friends and others of his peers. What he did feel was a deep responsibility to pay back the support and love of his parents and the kindnesses shown by neighbors and peers, by doing something big that would make the world a better place. He dedicated *The Inclusion Breakthrough*, a book he wrote with Katz, to his parents, who gave him "the wings to fly out of the box that was supposed to be the destiny of an inner city child whose birth certificate indicated Negro" (Miller and Katz 2002, preface). In 1946, the word "negro" on a person's birth certificate was more than a description of his or her racial group. It defined – and limited – who a person was and what she or he could become.

His father, for whom he was named, died suddenly when Miller was a high school senior. It was an enormous blow in many ways. Miller had no way to pay for college until a local pastor, the Rev. Leon H. Sullivan, recommended him for a scholarship set aside for fatherless boys. He reflected on this turn of events as the last gift his father gave him. Sullivan, a clergyman and civil rights leader, would become famous in 1977 for drawing up the Sullivan Principles, guidelines for American businesses operating in South Africa under apartheid (Lewis 2001).

Learning from Great Black Thinkers and Activists

In 1968, Miller arrived at Connecticut General Insurance Corporation (now CIGNA) as a management trainee, with a degree from Lincoln University (Pennsylvania), the country's first degree-granting historically black university. Founded in 1854, the school provided a springboard for many notable African-Americans who became pioneers in their fields. These included US Supreme Court Justice Thurgood Marshall, Harlem Renaissance poet Langston Hughes, music legend Cab Calloway, Medal of Honor winner and editor Christian Fleetwood, Emmy Award-winning and Tony Award-nominated actor Roscoe Lee Browne, first President of Ghana Kwame Nkrumah, and first President of Nigeria Nnamdi Azikiwe. In the 1960s, Lincoln was a place that awakened and sharpened Miller's social justice and Black Power activism and expanded his worldview.

He recalled, "At Lincoln I was exposed to some of the great black thinkers and activists of the decade. Charles V. Hamilton was the dynamic chair of the political science department. He and civil rights activist Stokely Carmichael (later changing his name to Kwame Ture) were coauthoring their groundbreaking book *Black Power: The Politics of Liberation in America*, and they would come into class and 'rap' about their ideas" (Miller, personal communication, May 12, 2016).

Miller was also inspired by civil rights leader James L. Farmer Jr., who had joined the faculty in 1966 after becoming disenchanted with the growing militancy of the Congress of Racial Equality (CORE), which he had cofounded. He was known as one of the Big Four, along with Dr. Martin Luther King Jr. of the Southern Christian Leadership Conference, Whitney Young of the Urban League, and Roy Wilkins of the National Association for the Advancement of Colored People. Farmer was a pioneer in the development and use of nonviolent direct action as a tactic for fighting racial discrimination; he helped develop the concept of affirmative action and was one of the first blacks to serve in a high-ranking government position (Connell 1999).

Becoming an Organizational Change Agent

Unlike many of his college friends, who were eager to become community activists, Miller felt he could be most effective as a change agent inside organizations. When he joined Connecticut General in 1968, the insurance industry was still reeling from the riots of the early 1960s. The devastating riots that erupted in 125 cities nationwide after Martin Luther King, Jr.'s assassination on April 4, 1968 reinforced the need for change. When the 1968 riots were over, some 39 people were dead, more than 2,600 injured, and 21,000 arrested. The damages were estimated at $65 million, approximately $385 million today (Risen 2008). While King's death may have ignited the riots, black people's frustration with de facto segregation, workplace discrimination, police brutality, and urban poverty had been building for decades. Connecticut General, recognizing that things needed to change, both in society and inside the corporation, increased its commitment to affirmative action. Miller was recruited to join a pioneer cohort of African-American professionals in the company. He eventually became the first person of color in the company's 100-year-plus history to rise from management trainee to the rank of officer.

Miller said, "I was brought into a corporate setting eager to work hard and be successful. I soon learned that it was not a level playing field – that it was not fair for everyone in the organization, and especially not for our group of black professionals. For example, after a round of performance evaluations, I realized that every single one of us was rated lower than our white peers. The organization just had a culture that very much supported certain people and groups, and did not support others" (personal communication, May 12, 2016). His career was interrupted in October 1968 when he was drafted for military service. Miller served for 2 years in the US Army in Korea during the Vietnam War. He returned to his position at Connecticut General in 1972 with a greater awareness and appreciation for the value of all people and a determination to eliminate discrimination.

In spring 1972, Miller was introduced to what would become his life's work in OD when he attended a company diversity education session. OD was a natural career path for this black activist and change agent at heart because, for Miller, the underlying values of the Civil Rights Movement and OD were fully aligned:

> Civil Rights: To create both a society and organizations in which people are treated fairly and with respect.
> OD: to create workplaces in which people matter, are valued, and participate in and influence their work experience (Katz and Miller 2014).

Fortunately for the work that Miller was to do, Connecticut General was a progressive organization led by CEO Henry Roberts, who valued individual and system change. Miller transferred from the group pension department to work with his white colleague, Richard H. Kremer, in human resources. With Kremer, he facilitated, and then directed, the Intergroup Cooperation and Understanding (ICU) Program. The ICU Program, one of the first diversity initiatives in a major US corporation, was the management's response to black employees' increased pressure on Connecticut General to make good on its commitment to equal employment. Thousands of employees participated in 3-day residential and experiential workshops that taught them how to work across racial and gender differences. This training shook up the status quo. Black-white, and later, woman-man, workshops brought people together across hierarchical levels for honest and emotional discussions about race relations and gender stereotypes. The workshops impacted all three levels of the system: building personal awareness, interpersonal understanding and group collaboration, and mobilizing employee action groups to challenge organizational norms and practices that kept some people "down." It is important to note how revolutionary the concept of partnering across racial and gender differences was during this period. It would be another decade before works such as Thomas Kochman's *Black and White Styles in Conflict* (Kochman 1981) and Alice Sargent's *The Androgynous Manager* (Sargent 1981), among others, would describe new paradigms for workplace communication and partnership.

At the black-white workshops, Miller originated the practice of starting every session by having people say "hello" to each other. Greeting another person and shaking hands in a sincere manner are a very simple intervention, but one that Miller believed was fundamental to interacting across differences in an honest and authentic way. For some whites, this "hello" activity was the first time they had ever touched a black person's hand. Since that time, "hellos" have been a keystone in Miller's work; he continues to use the practice to help people connect across differences, whether in the workplace or community gatherings.

NTL, Kaleel Jamison, and Other OD Pioneers

Miller's facilitation style and methods were influenced by the National Training Laboratories' (NTL) T-group methodology in which the facilitator creates a safe "container" that encourages participants to share emotional reactions (as opposed to judgments or conclusions) that arise in response to their colleagues' actions and statements. The focus on suspending judgment, to deeply listen to others, foreshadowed Miller's and Katz's later work on the impact of shifting from a judging to a joining mind-set as the first step toward improving the quality of people's interactions (Katz and Miller 2013). As an NTL member facilitating public workshops, Miller would find great satisfaction facilitating more than 20 T-groups, deeply impressed with the power and the effectiveness of the T-group as a means of fostering positive change in individuals and teams and the potential impact on organizations.

Miller also participated in Will Schutz's Esalen encounter groups, which encouraged people to face their fears and express themselves honestly and directly. Later, with Kaleel Jamison, he taught and continued to develop her model of straight talk, which was one of the first to identify direct, honest, and clear communication as a precursor to real systems change (Jamison 1985). Straight talk was a radical proposition for the time by presuming that conflicting views, values, cultures, and styles were best addressed openly and that those differences – properly resolved – will enhance rather than detract from the organization and its success.

After meeting in 1973 at a Living School women-men working together lab, Miller hired Kaleel Jamison as a consultant to facilitate woman-man and transactional analysis workshops at Connecticut General. Kaleel's workshops encouraged vigorous disagreement so that people in these groups could be heard and self-empowered. She was also one of the first to talk about self-empowerment in organizations. In their book, *Be Big*, Miller and Katz expanded on Kaleel's idea of the "big circle" by offering ways for people to show up more fully as individuals and in their interactions with others and to find ways to be big together in organizations (Katz and Miller 2008). Miller left Connecticut General in 1979 to join Jamison's OD practice, to partner with, and continue to learn from her.

Miller's role at Connecticut General afforded him the opportunity to immerse himself in personal growth and OD workshops led by a variety of theorists and practitioners, including Jack Gibb, Robert Bales, Peter Block, John Weir, Sherman Kingsbury, Moshe Feldenkrais, Peter Vaill, Rose Miller, John Scherer, Jimmy Jones, Edith Seashore, and Marvin Weisbord. (Weisbord and Seashore both consulted to Miller as he formed his firm, The Kaleel Jamison Consulting Group Inc.; Seashore continued to provide coaching, support, and entry for Miller into the OD professional network, throughout her life.) What Miller took from these experiences significantly influenced his thinking about group process, OD, and his use of self as an instrument of change.

When Block came to Connecticut General to co-facilitate his consulting skills workshops with Miller, he was still formulating what would later become *Flawless Consulting: A Guide to Getting Your Expertise Used* (Block 1981). While Miller practiced Block's process for engaging clients in an empowered and direct way, Block observed. Miller also went to visit Herb Shepard at Fort Courage, his home in Connecticut, to "inhale his wisdom," and then asked Shepard to lead a life planning workshop. When a senior vice president heard that people were being encouraged to plan their lives beyond the company, he blew his top and demanded that Miller be fired. This was tantamount to organizational sabotage and not to be tolerated. Luckily for Miller, CEO Roberts intervened and Miller's job was saved. That would not be the last time Miller would be threatened with termination. He joked, "I used to keep a letter of resignation in my back pocket for the day when either the company or I would be ready to end it. (personal communication, May 18, 2016)."

Partnership with Judith H. Katz

Miller met Katz at a NTL board meeting when Miller was a board member and Katz – along with colleague Bailey Jackson – conducted a workshop on racism. Katz's seminal work, *White Awareness: Handbook for Anti-Racism Training*, is still used as a resource for consultants and educators (Katz 1978). They stayed connected through NTL. Immediately after Jamison's untimely death in 1985, Miller invited Katz to become his business and thinking partner as he formed The Kaleel Jamison Consulting Group (KJCG) to continue Kaleel's work and legacy.

Miller and Katz's shared set of values and their passion to make organizations places where all people can do their best work – places that leverage the differences, as well as similarities that all people carry – have sustained their creative partnership for more than 30 years. Both were influenced by NTL values and methodologies. Both instinctively seek out people in the organization who are on "the fringe" or are not given the opportunity to do their best work and therefore cannot add their value to the mission and vision of the organization. Their work creates environments that enable those voices to be heard. Both try to follow Lewin's counsel that there should be no research without action and no action without research. Their client interventions are followed by intense reflection and discussion, leading to the development of theoretical constructs, models, and practical tools that help their clients create more inclusive cultures.

Key Contributions: Inclusion as a Strategy to Achieve Higher Organizational Performance

Miller has made his major contributions to the theory and practice of organization change by challenging and reframing how organizations understand and leverage differences to create inclusive workplaces and how change agents facilitate strategic culture change using inclusion as a means to achieve higher organizational performance and accelerate bottom-line results.

A New Definition of Inclusion

In September 1991, NTL Institute asked Miller to bring together the voices of 40 leaders, researchers, and practitioners who were working to address issues of diversity in organizations. Little had been written to date to make this topic accessible for managers and the general public. The result was the landmark book *The Promise of Diversity* (Cross et al. 1994), coedited by Elsie Y. Cross, Katz, and Seashore. The book was a call to action for leaders and OD change agents to eliminate oppression which, despite the advances made in the 30 years since the Civil Rights Act, remained a daily struggle for many in organizations. It proposed that practitioners find ways to hear, understand, and appreciate both the individual difference perspective (which held that the fundamental issue of diversity was to create understanding between different individuals, to discover, and celebrate "common ground") and the social justice perspective (which called for addressing discrimination and oppression at the group and system levels).

In the chapter "Forks in the Road: Critical Issues on the Path to Diversity," Miller went a step further by calling for a radical rethinking, redefining, and restructuring of many aspects of institutions and people's lives. At a time in which diversity was presented in organizations as a human resource problem to be managed, overcome, neutralized, or minimized, he was one of the first to describe the organizational change driven by diversity as a *revolution*. Organizations could not realize the benefits of a diverse workforce without fundamental changes in how people led, communicated, planned, solved problems, and designed organizational structures, policies, and practices. Leaders also needed to surface and address conditions, some subtle and "invisible," that blocked and oppressed people due to their differences. Miller did not think that people understood the magnitude of the changes involved. "Inclusion," he wrote, "turns comfortable upside down and inside out" (Cross et al. 1994, p. 39).

Miller and Katz were among a few practitioners who pioneered the use of the term *inclusion* in 1990, in part because it more fully described the goal for strategic culture change and in part to differentiate between true culture change and mere change in head count. Proponents of the value-in-diversity perspective advocated a "business case for diversity," linking a more diverse workforce to improvements in customer service, product quality, and bottom-line profitability; however, few management practices, policies, and accountabilities changed to make diversity a core business success factor (Cox 1993). Miller recognized that diversity without inclusion did not work. A definition of inclusion was developed and popularized that linked directly to enhanced individual, team, and business performance, standing apart from other definitions in the literature which generally overlooked the system-level element of improving collective work.

> Inclusion is a sense of belonging: feeling respected, valued and seen for who we are as individuals. There is a level of supportive energy and commitment from leaders, colleagues and others so that we – individually and collectively – can do our best work. (Katz and Miller, 2010)

Historically, discussions of organizational development ignored diversity and inclusion as a means by which to position and drive strategic culture change (e.g., Tichy 1983; French et al. 1989; Sikes et al. 1989; Bolman and Deal 1984; Kezar 2001). In *Inclusion Breakthrough: Unleashing the Real Power of Diversity* (Miller and Katz 2002), Miller and Katz introduced a comprehensive model, the inclusion breakthrough cycle, and change implementation technology, the KJCG methodology for strategic culture change, that synthesized their insights, experiences, frameworks, and interventions from three decades of OD practice. Inclusion is framed as the *HOW* – the means for transforming people's connections and interactions as they do their work and achieve results.

The Inclusion Breakthrough Cycle and Methodology for Strategic Culture Change

The inclusion breakthrough cycle (see Fig. 1) focuses on five key elements for leveraging differences and creating a culture of inclusion: (1) new individual and

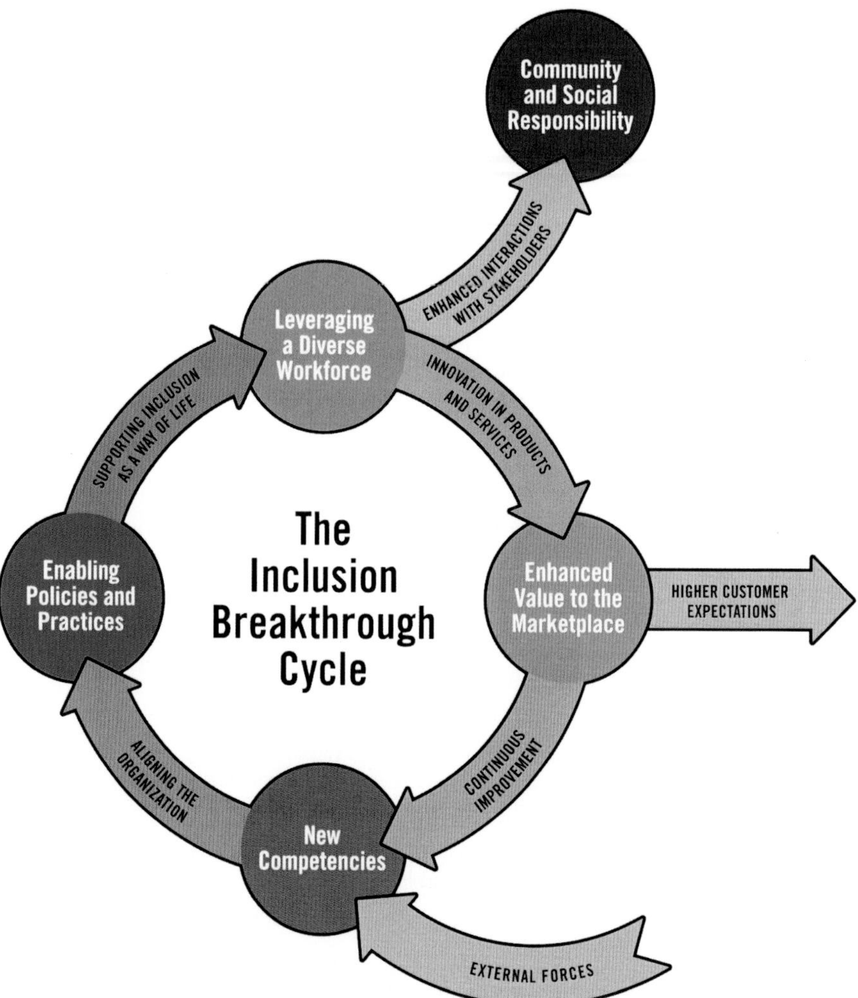

Fig. 1 The inclusion breakthrough cycle describes five key elements for leveraging differences and creating a culture of inclusion (Reprinted from Miller and Katz (2002). Copyright 2002 by The Kaleel Jamison Consulting Group, Inc. Reprinted with permission)

team competencies, (2) enabling policies and practices, (3) leveraging a diverse workforce, (4) community and social responsibility, and (5) enhanced value to a diverse marketplace.

- New competencies: Individual and team competencies for communicating across differences, addressing and working through conflict, and creating a safe and supportive environment for all. The competencies were further refined as 12 conscious actions for inclusion (Katz and Miller 2012b).

- Enabling policies and procedures: New baseline for how policies and practices support individuals and address all social identity groups.
- Leveraging a diverse workforce: Nine guidelines for becoming a worthy organization that retains key talent.
- Community and social responsibility: Ways to develop mutually beneficial partnerships with the people and organizations that furnish their workforce, customers, suppliers, and distributors and to support economically healthy and safe communities.
- Enhanced value to a diverse marketplace: Capitalizing on the full range of differences of people in the organization's home country before "going global."

Recognizing that the marketplace is becoming increasingly diverse, therefore, the ability to partner across differences needs to be core competency of the organization.

The KJCG methodology for an inclusion breakthrough has four phases:

- Phase I – Building a platform for change: Develop a bottom-line business case for change, position the effort, and conduct an organizational assessment.
- Phase II – Creating momentum: Develop a critical mass of people modeling the new culture.
- Phase III – Making diversity and inclusion a way of life: Link the inclusion breakthrough to operations and business process improvement initiatives; inclusion becomes how business is done and how people interact.
- Phase IV – Leveraging learning and challenging the new status quo: Measure progress and reassess.

Through the implementation of the KJCG methodology, many organizations have been able to connect the inclusion culture change effort to achieving their higher business objectives. The methodology also introduced several innovative change interventions developed, tested, and refined in large client systems (Dun & Bradstreet, Eastman Kodak, Ecolab, United Airlines, Mobil Oil Company, Allstate Insurance, Toyota Motor Co., Merck & Co. and Apple Inc., among others). Some examples include cocreation with senior leaders of the "from-to culture vision" (see Fig. 2) to provide a gap analysis and concrete vision of the desired future state, pockets of readiness strategy to engage business units or functions to be the first to model and act as "proof of concept" for the new culture, and group interventions such as learning partners and core inclusion and change partners designed to inform, enroll, and build a critical mass of people in the organization to reach the tipping point for change.

Pockets of Readiness Strategy

Miller developed the pockets of readiness strategy to increase buy-in from clients who were more willing to invest in a systemic culture change effort once they saw

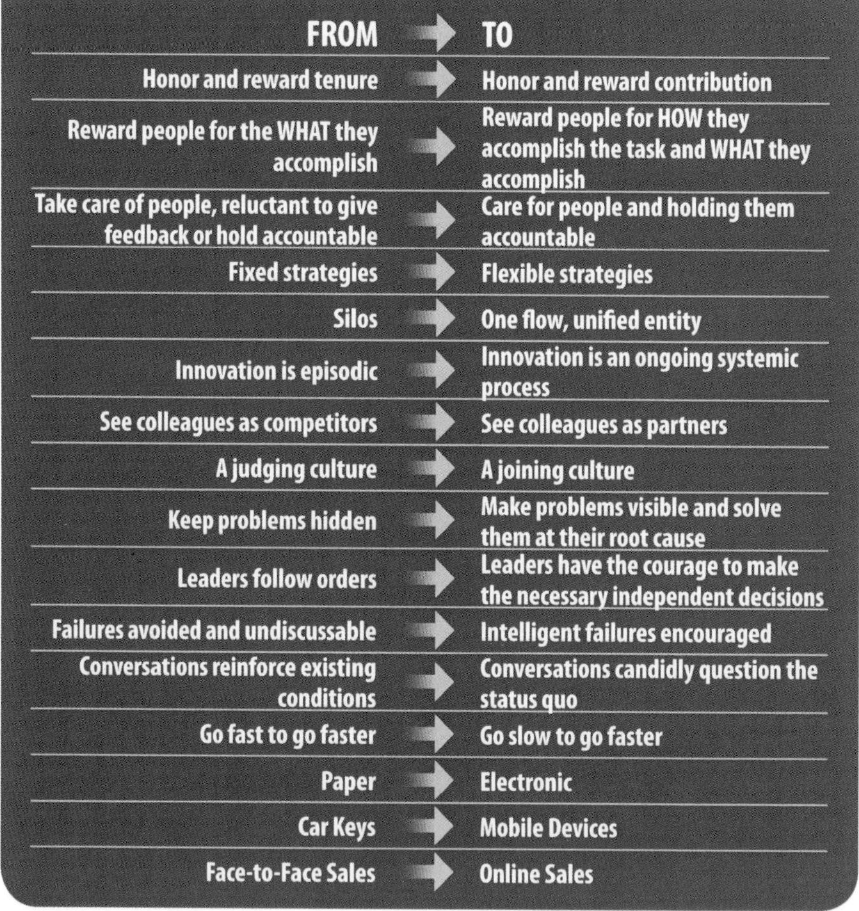

FROM → TO Challenges and Opportunities for Today's Organizations 2.1

FROM	TO
Honor and reward tenure	Honor and reward contribution
Reward people for the WHAT they accomplish	Reward people for HOW they accomplish the task and WHAT they accomplish
Take care of people, reluctant to give feedback or hold accountable	Care for people and holding them accountable
Fixed strategies	Flexible strategies
Silos	One flow, unified entity
Innovation is episodic	Innovation is an ongoing systemic process
See colleagues as competitors	See colleagues as partners
A judging culture	A joining culture
Keep problems hidden	Make problems visible and solve them at their root cause
Leaders follow orders	Leaders have the courage to make the necessary independent decisions
Failures avoided and undiscussable	Intelligent failures encouraged
Conversations reinforce existing conditions	Conversations candidly question the status quo
Go fast to go faster	Go slow to go faster
Paper	Electronic
Car Keys	Mobile Devices
Face-to-Face Sales	Online Sales

Fig. 2 Examples of a from-to culture vision that provides a gap analysis and concrete vision of the desired future state (Reprinted from F. A. Miller and J. H. Katz (2014). Copyright 2014 by The Kaleel Jamison Consulting Group, Inc. Reprinted with permission)

evidence of successful transformation in a business unit or function. Miller knew senior leaders needed a concrete picture of the "end state" – what a more inclusive organization that leverages differences will look and feel like, how people would interact differently, and, most importantly, how inclusion would impact the bottom line. From his experience, Miller also knew that there were parts of the organization that could move a lot faster toward the new culture. Why not leverage these pockets of readiness as "proof of concept?"

It is common for organizations to cascade or "roll out" change initiatives from the top down through the organization, a slow and unpredictable way of building critical mass for change. Some organizations invest in large group interventions (e.g., search conference, future search, and open space technology), engaging the "whole system" to describe current state and identify targets for change (Bunker and Alban 1997). These technologies give voice to all the organization's stakeholders and can create common ground to move the entire organization forward, but they can be time-consuming and the implementation of the change – new state – can be uneven.

In contrast, the pockets of readiness strategy has proven advantageous because it provides observable and measureable benefits of an inclusion breakthrough quicker in order to inspire and enlist the rest of the organization. Both approaches have their place, but the proof-of-concept model creates a "pull" in the organization as leaders see the success and bottom-line impact and say, "I want some of that."

Learning Partners

Miller believes that the most critical component of any culture change effort happens in Phase I: the positioning of the organization and its leaders to create and support a structured, systematic inclusion breakthrough. When an organization's senior leaders realize that a culture change effort will affect every dimension of the organization, big questions arise: "How can we make changes of this scope, intensity and depth?" "Where do we start?" "How can we ensure success (Miller and Katz 2002)?" They often need to develop a new perspective on the organization's current state and how it is suboptimizing many in the organization, not just those who are different from the founding group. To that end, Miller enhanced the impact of the organizational assessment process by developing learning partners, a diverse cross section of high-performing team members who interview their peers and share with senior leaders – in a direct and personal way – the different experiences people in the organization are having. Learning partner sessions provide powerful insight for leaders about why change is needed and prepare them to create a culture change strategy that everyone can understand. Learning partners continue to support the change effort, acting as credible witnesses to the leaders' learning process and commitment to action.

Peer-to-Peer Leadership

As important as positioning the change with senior leaders is for the success of any culture change effort, an exclusively top-down approach can lead to skepticism and resistance. Core inclusion and change partners is a peer-to-peer leadership model that involves selecting, educating, and supporting groups of internal change advocates focused on accelerating change through peer-to-peer education, interaction, and modeling. Momentum for change increases as each change advocate initiates and leads peer groups. People throughout the organization come to trust the change because they learned it from team members they trust. From a systemic standpoint, including more people in this way accelerates the creation of a tipping point for culture change (Katz and Miller 2012).

Four Corners Breakthrough Model

Miller developed the four corners breakthrough model (see Fig. 3) to help clients recognize that, to meet the challenges of an increasingly complex and changing environment, they need the wisdom of everyone, not just leaders, greater speed in knowledge transfer and knowledge application across the organization, and breakthroughs, not just incremental change. The model grew out of consulting work with Digital Equipment Corp. in the 1980s, when Japanese competition was threatening US market leadership. The four corners breakthrough suggested that the wider diversity of perspectives, thinking styles, and skills among US workers, if sought out and valued, would allow for a 360-degree vision of business problems and create conditions in

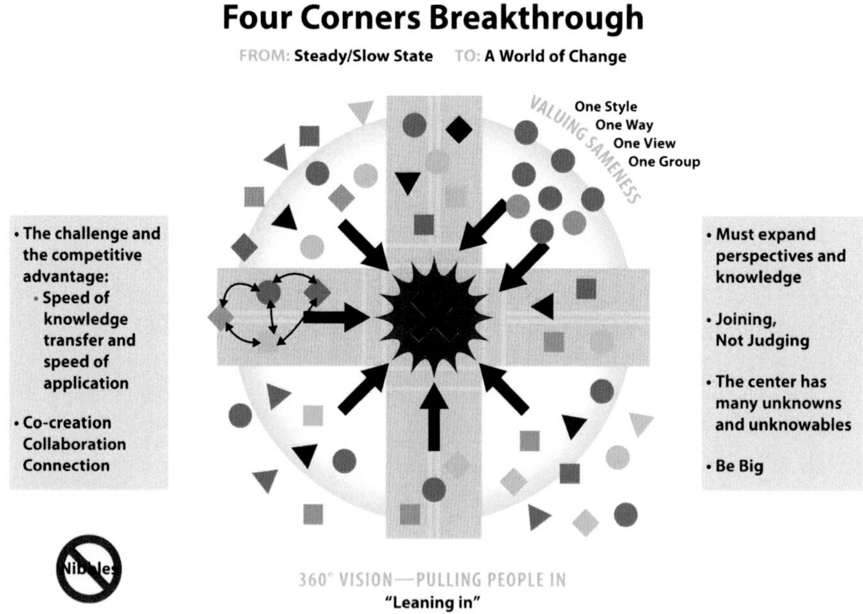

Fig. 3 Four corners breakthrough model describes the mind-set shifts necessary for organizations to thrive in a steady state of change (Reprinted from Miller and Katz (2010). Copyright 2010 by The Kaleel Jamison Consulting Group, Inc. Reprinted with permission)

which innovation could flourish, providing a strong competitive advantage over what Japanese companies could accomplish with their value on sameness.

Conscious Actions for Inclusion

Miller believes that, fundamentally, organizations are only as productive as the interactions between people. Significant organizational change requires an adjustment in the quality of interactions between people. With others in KJCG, he cocreated Conscious Actions for Inclusion (see Fig. 4), behaviors communicated in simple, common language that describe and open the door to greater clarity and enhanced ways of interacting.

One example of a Conscious Action for Inclusion is "state your intent and intensity: notions, stakes, boulders and tombstones," language that helps people both signal their intent to join with the other person and clarify intent at the onset. When people clearly state what they mean and how committed they are to an idea – ranging from a low level of commitment or "notion" to a level of the greatest investment or "tombstone" – others are better able to act quickly, decisively, and correctly. This simple model has been adopted as standard work by client organizations globally, to eliminate the guesswork that creates so much waste in effort, resources, and time in people's interactions. Its application has resulted in organization behavioral change at all three levels of system: individual, group, and system.

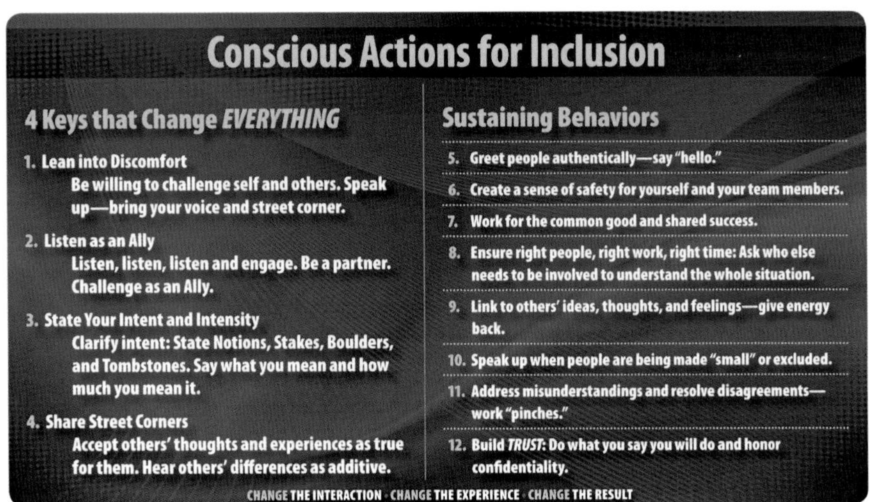

Fig. 4 Conscious actions for inclusion are 12 behaviors that describe and open the door to greater clarity and enhanced ways of interacting (Adapted from J. H. Katz and F.A. Miller (2012). Copyright 2012 by The Kaleel Jamison Consulting Group, Inc. Reprinted with permission)

New Insights: Client-Focused Models and Tools Grounded in Multiple Change Ideologies

Many of Miller's insights come from observing and learning from his clients, engaging with peers on corporate and not-for-profit boards, and studying what is happening in the world. Most often in collaboration with Katz, he derives actionable theories from these experiences and then develops simple models and practical tools and processes that make it easier for clients to move toward the desired "TO" state, a workplace in which people can do their best work in service of the organizational mission, vision, and strategic objectives.

As a practitioner, his approach is grounded primarily in OD, described most often as part of the teleological or planned change theoretical tradition, but the models and change technologies he cocreates reflect many different ideologies of change, each with its own assumptions about the nature of human beings and social systems. In addition to the theories of planned change, these include dialectical or political theories; social cognition; environmental theories such as contingency, open systems, and chaos theory; and cultural theories (Van de Ven and Poole 1995).

The Inclusion Breakthrough Cycle model and the KJCG methodology for strategic culture change added to the conceptual knowledge base on OD by providing the first comprehensive framework and set of interventions that leaders and change agents can utilize to position, implement, and sustain culture change related to leveraging differences and inclusion as the *HOW*. Both models reflect the application of teleological theories, specifically planned change, in that the organization is presented as purposeful and adaptive and relies on leaders and change agents to plan and implement change in a manner that is aligned with the organization's external environment, vision, mission, and goals and enables people to do their best work.

The methodology also draws from dialectical or political theories that include change processes such as persuasion, influence and power, and social movements. Embedded in the approach are many strategies for positioning the effort with senior leaders through consciousness-raising education; defining the business case for inclusion, which links the change to stakeholders' self-interest; developing a critical mass of agents of change; and creating networks to spread influence and support the change effort. The approach rejected "diversity for diversity's sake," making the case for the investment in culture change only if the new state supports and advances the mission, vision, and strategies of the organization.

New Language Supports New Mind-sets and Behaviors

In numerous client engagements, Miller and his colleagues in KJCG have demonstrated that significant culture change requires a change in the conversational dialectic. The rhetoric that emerged in the field of diversity in the 1990s replaced the term "diversity" with "inclusion." This created substantial confusion: in many organizations, "diversity" became synonymous with US affirmative action, which by definition excluded white men. In other cases, there was no material change in diversity management practices that continued to focus on how to assimilate the newcomers into the current culture. A new definition of inclusion was offered that differentiated it from diversity. The term "leveraging differences" was also introduced, allowing for a broader range of differences beyond race, color, age, and gender, such as thinking style, background, skills, and experiences.

Conscious Actions for Inclusion is a model of inclusive language and behaviors, introduced and refined over the course of many years. It provides people with an easy way to signal their intent to "be different." The model supports the emergence of new meaning and helps rechannel people's energy to create more inclusive partnerships on individual, group, and system levels. In this way, it represents a blend of the dialectical and cultural perspectives described by Shein (1985) and others.

Informed by Chaos Theory

Miller has adopted several concepts from open systems and chaos theory, i.e., organizations are systems operating in a constantly changing context and environment; therefore, they must find ways to stay open to information "from everywhere, from places and sources people never thought to look before" (Wheatley 2006, p. 83). Meg Wheatley's application of chaos theory to organizational change (Wheatley 2006) informs the four corners breakthrough model, which describes environmental complexity as "unknowns and unknowables" and offers simple language like "street corner" as a metaphor for different perspectives, world views, and experiences that can be brought to bear on the complex problems faced by organizations. The idea that all organizations are fractal in nature is applied in a new way in the pockets of readiness strategy, i.e., one business unit or function not only represents a microcosm of the culture but also can initiate a new and repeatable pattern of behaviors to help accelerate whole system change.

Presence Consulting

In chaos theory, "you can never tell where the system is headed until you've observed it over time" (Wheatley 2006, p. 132). This holds true within the newer dialogic OD practices, as well. As organizations become composed of more diverse people operating in a more dynamic environment, the assumption that there is some singular social reality "out there" to be diagnosed and changed becomes less useful for OD practitioners (Bushe 2010). Miller developed presence consulting, an intervention in which external change agents become fully integrated into the day-to-day work life of the people inside the organization, "being present" at meetings, on the shop floor, etc. to support them as they learn and experiment with new inclusive mind-sets and behaviors in their daily interactions (DaRos 2011). By being present in this way, consultants learn from the variety of realities that exist in the system and then intervene to help create the enabling conditions for successful interactions to take place.

As a point of illustration, several presence consultants were deployed during a 5-year cultural transformation of the manufacturing division of a global pharmaceutical company, under Miller's direction. It became evident that continuous quality improvement, safety, and reduction of waste were strongly held values in this organization's lean environment. One of the most impactful interventions was the introduction of inclusive mind-sets and behaviors that enhanced the quality of day-to-day interactions and reduced the waste typically generated by unresolved conflict, nonproductive meetings, and a pervasive fear of being blamed for errors.

As the new mind-sets and behaviors took hold, people gained the sense of emotional safety needed to speak up, make problems visible more quickly, and leverage different people's ideas to come up with innovative solutions. Leaders attributed the accomplishment of a major global corporate business objective, including reduced cost and improved efficiency, to the culture change effort. Inclusion linked to what mattered most in the organization: corporate values and goals of quality, safety, and reduction of waste, resulting in a positive impact to the bottom line for a key division and the overall corporation.

Legacies and Unfinished Business: Creating a New "We" in Society and Organizations

Miller has changed how leaders and OD practitioners conceptualize and implement diversity and inclusion as a strategic lever for large-scale organizational change. The KJCG framework and methodology, cocreated with Katz, provide clients with the means to identify cultural barriers to inclusion, establish the organizational imperative for change, build critical mass, and accelerate the adoption of new mind-sets and behaviors needed to sustain the new culture.

When asked about "unfinished business," Miller speaks first about the need for people to create a new *we* in society and in our organizations. History is rife with examples of how not to approach differences. All too often, we have identified with a narrow version of *we*: immediate family, village, clan, social identity group, and – in our organizations – department, function, level, and team. Differences continue to be met with mistrust, isolation, fear, and oppression. Miller challenges this mind-set and initiates social change as part of every role he holds: OD consultant, member of the boards of directors for numerous corporate and not-for-profit organizations (e.g., Ben & Jerry's, Day & Zimmermann, Sage Colleges and One World Everybody Eats), and as a business owner and citizen leader in community, church, and civic groups.

In 2017, The Sage Colleges awarded Miller an honorary doctorate of Humane Letters for his lifelong efforts to move society and organizations toward greater equality of opportunity and participation.

In 1990, he led one of the first major diversity efforts in a large US municipality, City of San Diego, CA, that focused on the inclusion of white women, people of color, and gay, lesbian, bisexual, and transgendered (GLBT) people in the police and fire departments. During his firm's consulting with Mobil in 1997, it became the largest company to implement domestic partner benefits, setting the precedent for many companies to follow. In ODN, Miller initiated the first people of color conference and gained board sponsorship for what is now the LGBTQ (lesbian, gay, bisexual, transgendered, queer) affinity group. As a board member of One World Everybody Eats Foundation, he contributes his thinking to the sharing economy through the "pay what you can café" model as a way to address hunger. And in Troy, NY, where his firm is located, he founded the Troy 100 Forum, which brings together leaders in different sectors of the community to share perspectives on topics of public concern to the city.

He raises the question of how OD practitioners can help organizations go beyond traditional social responsibility initiatives to create a new *we* that includes their local communities. Safer, more inclusive, and sustainable communities benefit organizations in many ways, including attracting and retaining the best talent, which will continue to be a competitive advantage for most organizations.

Artificial Intelligence

Looking into the future, Miller sees artificial intelligence (AI) and its impact on organizations and organizational change as the next frontier for the field, both in terms of theory development and practice. While AI applications are increasingly being integrated into the workplace, we know little about their impact on work processes, organization design, and culture. Compared to previous technology-driven social changes, AI is expected to transform how we work at a rate that is exponentially faster. AI will present significantly new challenges for OD theorists and practitioners who will need to mediate between humans and intelligent machines to create more inclusive workplaces where everyone (and everything) can contribute their best thinking.

A final thought about unfinished business is the need to develop more heretics. Miller said, "We just can't have enough of them, given the changes we need to make to move to a much better state for all humans."

Conclusion

Frederick A. Miller was one of the first to recognize that diversity efforts in organizations, without inclusion, did not work. With Judith H. Katz, he developed a new definition of inclusion and published the first comprehensive model and framework for implementing diversity and inclusion as a lever for strategic culture change, moving it from a compliance-driven set of programs to a breakthrough OD strategy linked to higher operational and bottom-line performance. His contributions to the field reflect a lifelong commitment to the underlying values of both the Civil Rights Movement and OD: to create both a society and workplaces in which people are treated fairly and respectfully, feel valued, and can participate in meaningful ways.

References

Block, P. (1981). *Flawless consulting: A guide to getting your expertise used*. San Francisco: Jossey-Bass/Pfeffer.

Bolman, L. G., & Deal, T. E. (1984). *Modern approaches to understanding and managing organizations*. San Francisco: Jossey-Bass.

Bunker, B. B., & Alban, B. T. (1997). *Large group interventions: Engaging the whole system for rapid change*. San Francisco: Jossey-Bass.

Bushe, G. R. (2010). Dialogic OD: Turning away from diagnosis. In W. J. Rothwell, J. M. Stavros, R. L. Sullivan, & A. Sullivan (Eds.), *Practicing organization development: A guide leading change* (3rd ed., pp. 617–623). San Francisco: Wiley.

Bushe, G. R., & Marshak, R. J. (Eds.). (2015). *Dialogic organization development: The theory and practice of transformational change*. Oakland: Berrett-Koehler.

Connell, R. (1999). James S. Farmer; Was top civil rights leader. *The Los Angeles Times*. Retrieved from http://www.articles.latimes.com

Cox, T. (1993). *Cultural diversity in organizations: Theory, research and practice*. San Francisco: Berrett-Koehler.

Cross, E. Y., Katz, J. H., Miller, F. A., & Seashore, E. W. (Eds.). (1994). *The promise of diversity: Over 40 voices discuss strategies for eliminating discrimination in organizations*. New York: Irwin.

DaRos, D. J. (2011). Presence consulting creates lasting change (online community post). Retrieved from https://www.td.org/Publications/Newsletters/Links/2011/06/Presence-Consulting-Creates-Lasting-Change.

French, W. L., Bell, C. H., & Zawacki, R. A. (Eds.). (1989). *Organization development: Theory, practice and research*. Homewood: Irwin.

Jamison, K. (1985). Straight talk: A norm-changing intervention. *Organization Development Practitioner, 17*(2), 1–8.

Katz, J. H. (1978). *White awareness: Handbook for anti-racism training*. Norman: University of Oklahoma Press.

Katz, J. H., & Miller, F. A. (2008). *Be BIG: Step up, step out, be bold*. San Francisco: Berrett-Koehler.

Katz, J. H., & Miller, F. A. (2010). Inclusion: The HOW for organizational breakthrough. In W. J. Rothwell, J. M. Stavros, R. L. Sullivan, & A. Sullivan (Eds.), *Practicing organization development: A guide for leading change* (3rd ed., pp. 436–445). San Francisco: Pfeiffer.

Katz, J. H., & Miller, F. A. (2012a). How human dynamics create winners and losers: Using inclusion as the HOW for successful mergers and acquisitions. *Organization Development Practitioner, 44*(3), 63–67.

Katz, J. H., & Miller, F. A. (2012b). Inclusion: The HOW for the next organizational breakthrough. *Practicing Social Change, 5*, 16–22.

Katz, J. H., & Miller, F. A. (2013). *Opening doors to teamwork and collaboration: 4 keys that change everything*. San Francisco: Berrett-Koehler.

Katz, J. H., & Miller, F. (2014). Learning from the journey: OD values. *Organization Development Practitioner, 46*(4), 39–43.

Kezar, A. (2001). Understanding and facilitating organizational change in the 21st century: Recent research and conceptualizations. In *Jossey-Bass higher and adult education series* (Vol. 28(4), pp. 25–56). San Francisco: Jossey-Bass.

Kleiner, A. (2008). *The age of heretics*. San Francisco: Jossey-Bass.

Kochman, T. (1981). *Black and white styles in conflict*. Chicago: The University of Chicago Press.

Lewis, P. (2001). Leon Sullivan, 78, dies; fought apartheid. *The New York Times*. Retrieved from http://www.nytimes.com

Marshak, R. J. (2006). *Covert processes at work: Managing the five hidden dimensions of organizational change*. San Francisco: Berrett-Kohler.

Miller, F. A., & Katz, J. H. (2002). *The inclusion breakthrough: Unleashing the real power of diversity*. San Francisco: Berrett-Koehler.

Miller, F. A., & Katz, J. H. (2010). *The four corners breakthrough: A key to the future*. Troy: The Kaleel Jamison Consulting Group, Inc. Unpublished.

Risen, C. (2008). The legacy of the 1968 riots. *The Guardian*. Retrieved from http://theguardian.com

Sargent, A. (1981). *The Androgynous manager*. New York: Amacom.

Shein, E. H. (1985). *Organizational culture and leadership*. San Francisco: Jossey-Bass.

Sikes, W., Drexler, A., & Gant, J. (1989). *The emerging practice of organization development*. Washington, DC: NTL.

Tichy, N. M. (1983). *Managing strategic change: Technical, political and cultural dynamics*. New York: Wiley.

Van de Ven, A. H., & Poole, M. S. (1995). Explaining development and change in organizations. *Academy of Management Review, 20*, 510–540.

Wheatley, M. J. (2006). *Leadership and the new science: Discovering order in a chaotic world*. San Francisco: Berrett-Koehler.

Further Reading

Cline, E. (2011). *Ready player one*. New York: Crown Publishers.

Coates, T. (2015). *Between the world and me*. (First edition.). New York: Spiegel & Grau.

Katz, J. H. and Miller, F. A. (Fall 2013). "Judging Others Has Not Worked...So Let's Join Them," *Leader to Leader. 70*, 51–57.

Katz, J. H. and Miller, F. A. (Winter 2014). "4 Keys To Accelerating Collaboration," OD Practitioner. 46(1), 6–11.

Webb, J. H. (1978). Fields of fire: a novel. New York: Bantam Books.

X, M. & Haley, A. (1965). The autobiography of Malcolm X. New York: Grove Press.

Philip Mirvis: Fusing Radical Humanism and Organizational Spirituality in a Boundaryless Career

54

Tojo Thatchenkery and Param Srikantia

Abstract
This chapter explores the distinctive contributions of Phil Mirvis, an organizational psychologist who has skillfully fused radical humanism and organizational spirituality in what can be best described as a boundaryless career. The boundaryless label captures the character of his contributions that defy categorization as they seamlessly weave together theoretical imagination, research-oriented creativity, and practical ingenuity while integrating multiple epistemologies and methods, including within his ambit individual, group, and societal levels of functioning, in addition to attending to both the tangible and intangible dimensions of organizational functioning. After reviewing some dominant influences and defining moments that shaped his career, the chapter explores Mirvis's contributions in five thematic dimensions of organizational life, namely (a) large-scale organizational change, (b) mergers and acquisitions, (c) the character of the workforce and workplace, (d) leadership development, and (e) the role of business in society. The chapter concludes with a discussion of Mirvis's key insights and legacies that include but are not limited to his work on failures in OD work as opportunities for new understandings, his elaboration of learning journeys as an instrument of promoting emotional and spiritual self-actualization in business contexts and his amplification of the compatibility of organizational cultures as a determinant of success in mergers and acquisitions.

T. Thatchenkery (✉)
George Mason University, Arlington, VA, USA
e-mail: thatchen@gmu.edu

P. Srikantia
School of Business, Baldwin Wallace University, Berea, OH, USA
e-mail: psrikant@bw.edu

D.B. Szabla et al. (eds.), *The Palgrave Handbook of Organizational Change Thinkers*,
DOI 10.1007/978-3-319-52878-6_48

Keywords
Organization development • Change management • Spirituality • Scholar-practitioner • Large systems transformation • Mergers & acquisitions • Workforce development • Business & society • Leadership development

Contents

Introduction

Philip H. Mirvis is an organizational psychologist who has built bridges between research, theory, and practice to make deep and enduring contributions in five thematic dimensions of organizational life: (a) large-scale organizational change, (b) mergers and acquisitions, (c) the character of the workforce and workplace, (d) leadership development, and (e) the role of business in society. In each of these domains he has introduced new concepts and frameworks while also inventing organizational interventions and dynamic action research practices. A self-described "jack of many trades," he has studied and helped to stimulate different kinds of organizational sense-making not dependent on any particular methodological device or epistemology. Much of his change scholarship is drawn from his consulting work and field research with large and innovative organizations around the world. He has operated in academic, business, consulting, and research roles, freely navigating the unique challenges of each of these domains with energy and insight (see his writings on issues in scholarship and practice). He situates himself today, first and foremost, as a reflective practitioner.

Mirvis has a B.A. from Yale University and a Ph.D. in Organizational Psychology from the University of Michigan. In early career, he was a professor in the School of Management at Boston University and held research posts at the Institute for Social Research at the University of Michigan, the Center for Applied Social Science at Boston University, and (part time a decade ago) at the Center for Corporate Citizenship at Boston College. He has been a visiting professor at Jiao Tong University in Shanghai, China, and the London Business School, and has contributed to executive education programs at universities and in businesses on six continents. For the past 25 years, Mirvis has operated as an "independent" consultant and researcher. He is relocating to Santa Fe, New Mexico, with his wife, Mary Jo Hatch, a renowned organizational theorist, prolific author of influential books, and recently retired professor from the McIntire School of Commerce at the University of Virginia.

Influences and Motivations Artful Creative Rebellion

As scholarship is to some extent autobiographical, the tenor of Mirvis's independent, nonconforming, and antiauthoritarian orientation was evident early in his life when, for example, he refused to document his long division calculations to his insistent fourth grade teacher in a Catholic grammar school and was later expelled for failing to comply with what appeared to him to be rigid and mindless rules. This orientation continued to grow during the 1960s when his public high school in Columbus, Ohio, was racially integrated, and Mirvis was suspended for running an "underground" student newspaper that challenged prevailing taboos on everything from interracial dating to wearing blue jeans to school. After he joined the undergraduate program at Yale, this "us-against-them" world view was expanded into activism by consciousness raising from faculty and students and participation in campus teach-ins and the "May Day" protests over the dubious murder trial of Bobby Seale of the Black Panthers in New Haven (where he also learned of the shootings of antiwar protestors at Kent State University). These experiences and the general climate of anti-establishment protest met by state repression appear to have ignited a strong desire in him to not only rail against but also to reform social and institutional realities.

Mirvis was first initiated into the field of organizational change during his undergraduate years as a psychology and administrative science major. He was introduced to more humanistic organizational psychology concepts through a directed reading course with Richard Hackman, participated in various T-group experiences, and was exposed to organization development (OD) and change practices by Yale faculty (including Chris Argyris and Clay Alderfer) and campus visitors such as Harvey Hornstein and Saul Alinsky. His "revolutionary" zeal (an attribute that would exercise a subterranean influence in his organizational change work later on) became focused through his coursework on "freeing" workers from the tyranny of oppressive managers and organizations. At the same time, he came to realize that OD was a "double-edged sword" that was capable of both energizing human emancipation and potentially pacifying working people, thus serving the interests of the so-called ruling elite.

Tough and troubling questions about supposedly "value-free" organizational concepts and the varied "uses" and "misuses" of OD interventions appear in Mirvis's writing about ethics in organizational research, values in change efforts, and consciousness raising in executive development (see *Company as Total Community*). His own personal dilemmas on these fronts (on teaching in a business school, advising senior managers, and consulting on large-scale mergers) are reported in his autobiographical writings (see *Midlife as a Consultant*) and more recently in a book on "intellectual shamans" by Sandra Waddock (2015).

Right after graduating from college, Mirvis sought to enact his "save the worker" aspirations by joining the US Department of Labor and participating in a study led by Neal Herrick to assess the economic costs of "bad" management in employee absences, grievances, and the like. Mirvis was joined in this investigation by colleague Barry Macy, a former Alcoa executive, and also met regularly Labor Department advisors Eric Trist, Warren Bennis, and Edward Lawler. Connecting with these luminaries, learning how they wrestled with questions of reform versus cooptation in their own work, and seeing them as role models led Mirvis toward an academic career path. Lawler encouraged him to apply to the Ph.D. program in the organizational psychology department at the University of Michigan and to join his Quality of Work Life (QWL) program based at the Institute for Social Research.

Mirvis was deeply influenced by Lawler's capacity to mix research and consulting fluently within the context of his academic career and also was his tenant (in Lawler's home) for several of his graduate study years. He benefitted immensely from the creative tension between schisms in the doctoral program at Michigan. One camp of students favored rigorous empirical research in established topic niches while another was more discovery-oriented, exploratory, and engaged in more qualitative studies that were higher on practical relevance. Lawler had blazed his trail betwixt these poles as an "action researcher" with his well-known studies of plant start-ups at TRW, Procter & Gamble, General Foods, and Honda and as a practical scholar in studying the impact of Quality of Work Life programs on working people and their organization.

A seminar at Michigan led by psychoanalyst Michael Maccoby became a pivotal point for Mirvis's self-definition. Maccoby argued passionately about how the "interior life" of managers shaped their actions and how context was crucial in understanding organizational dynamics. These ideas resonated and further reinforced Mirvis's appetite for activism and applied work that aimed at broad, meaningful change rather than addressing microscopic questions. Mirvis began to inhabit the role of a "reflective practitioner," exploring "artful" change methodologies and gaining insights into the interplay of one's own psyche and the role of social construction in how action research projects are selected, framed, executed, and interpreted.

After earning his Ph.D., Mirvis went to Boston University where he taught in the management school while simultaneously working at the Center for Applied Social Science with senior faculty Gerry Gordon, Mike Useem, and Robert Chin (who would be another mentor and guide him on his first overseas teaching and research in China). His research in these years examined multiple levers of organizational change including the impact of computer technology on office and factory workers, work-life balance initiatives, and his first studies of corporate mergers and acquisitions (M&A). He designed and executed several survey feedback and action research projects with Amy Sales and Edward Hackett.

It was perhaps a blessing in disguise that Mirvis was denied tenure at Boston University in what appears to have been a process influenced by political differences and tensions related to his activism against University President John Silber and his involvement in the faculty union as a steward for the School of Management (though Mirvis also notes that his antiauthoritarian streak led him challenge proposals by the School's associate dean and a department chair which would hamper the promotion prospects of any nontenured faculty member). The denial of tenure marked his full-blown entry into the world of what he would call "scholarly practice," initiating a string of consulting assignments in M&A, human capital development, and the social responsibilities of business.

His writing also reflected a different style relative to mainstream academic research literature in organizational behavior and change. The style was more spontaneous, organic, incorporating qualitative information and case study material and demonstrating a greater concern with questions of practical impact. Mirvis's scholarship demonstrates methodological eclecticism, featuring case studies, interviews, and shared reflections that take on a story telling quality, capturing significant lessons derived from organizational interventions. His research studies have involved an extensive array of collaborators from multiple continents drawn from universities, business, and consulting. The research is typically focused on investigating real world issues, talking with organizational participants, and constructing comprehensive learning histories that capture the social, emotional, and task-centered dimensions of change interventions undertaken in their companies.

Another event of great importance in Mirvis's life was a workshop that he attended led by Scott Peck, M.D., author of the best-selling book, *The Road Less Travelled: A New Psychology of Love, Traditional Values and Spiritual Growth.* Mirvis remembers this as a very important part of helping him to confront his knee-jerk antiauthority reactions and to "heal" from the denial of his tenure. Through his 10-year association with Peck and colleagues in the Foundation for Community Encouragement, Mirvis gained skills in dealing with powerful male authority figures and also introduced a spiritual dimension into his work. It expanded his epistemology and ontology, making him more open to varied forms of sense-making and stimulated his writing on *Soul Work* and *Community Building* in organizations.

Key Contributions: The Transformation of Consciousness in Large Systems

As noted in the introduction, Mirvis has integrated and made meaningful contributions to theory, research, and practice along five thematic dimensions of organizational life. In this section, the discussion of key contributions is organized according to these five thematic dimensions, namely: (a) large-scale organizational change, (b) mergers and acquisitions, (c) the character of the workforce and workplace, (d) leadership development and consciousness-raising, and (e) the role of business in society.

(a) **Large-scale organizational change:** Mirvis has been a prolific contributor to enriching our understanding of large-scale organizational change. He has approached this domain from multiple angles and through multiple lenses. One of his early provocative contributions to the OD and change discipline was the book he coedited with David Berg titled *Failures in Organizational Development and Change: Cases and Essays for Learning*. It pointed out very correctly that while OD scholars had written extensively on the failings of organizations, the field had not been very reflective on its own failures. The *Failures* book speaks to the minds and hearts of OD scholars and practitioners as it features first-person essays chronicling failures by leading figures in OD, identifies where they went wrong and why, and highlights specific lessons learned. The various chapters explore some of the most important sources of OD failure including the absence of shared understandings during entry, resistance to change embedded in cultural hostility, intergroup conflict, hidden authority relationships, and bureaucratization of change processes. The volume helped to promote critical self-examination and a learning-from-errors orientation to the field. By focusing on failings, it also sought to promote healthy skepticism and continuous improvement to the field of OD, the very qualities that OD strives to entrench in organizations.

Mirvis has also fashioned himself as an "amateur" historian and presented useful and insightful perspectives on the evolution of OD from the 1960s to 1980s. OD in the 1960s represented more of a human relations perspective and philosophy, a set of values celebrating human potential in organizations, consistent with Theory Y assumptions of McGregor and self- actualization insights drawn from Maslow. The OD consultant's focus in that era was on creating a deeper alignment between the individual needs and organizational needs. Mirvis traces how this emphasis shifted in the 1970s during the "technostructural" era in which the perceived looseness of the field was rejected in favor of more formalized organizational interventions that attempted to increase the synergy between technology, organizational structure, and the sociotechnical dimensions. This was also the period in which university departments for training OD professionals were established.

According to Mirvis, the evolution of OD continued with another swing of the historical pendulum, this time in favor of recognizing and according the environment a much bigger role in organizational effectiveness and resilience. Changes in technology, ownership, structure, and strategy demanded significant developments in environmental scanning, stakeholder analysis, and business planning. The firm level focus of OD had to be expanded to allow for a greater recognition of interorganizational networks involving mergers, acquisitions, and other cooperative arrangements. In projecting the future of OD through the 1990s, Mirvis was remarkably accurate in forecasting greater integration of seemingly contradictory perspectives that would strive to embody and transcend the apparent paradoxes in organizing such as the ones between internal and external aspects of the organization or control and flexibility as the basis of culture (Denison and Spreitzer 1991).

Mirvis also wrote two papers about "revolutionary" developments in the field celebrating, for example, the innovative contributions of Barry Oshry with his power labs, Bill Torbert's Theatre of Inquiry, and more recent contributions concerned with art-based and spiritual forms of intervention. Of particular interest is his distinction between evolutionary and revolutionary perspectives on the history of OD. Evolutionary perspectives and revolutionary perspectives can be contrasted according to four dimensions. For example, evolutionary perspectives have represented a *knowledge base* that is cumulative and universalistic, a *movement* that has been scientific and utilitarian, a *client base* that has been logical and pragmatic, and *OD practice and practitioners* that have been market-driven and professional. In sharp contradistinction to this is the depiction of a revolutionary perspective to OD in which the *knowledge base* is contextual and particularistic, a *movement* that is humanistic and value-based, a *client base* that is explorative and experimental, and *OD practice and practitioners* that are visionary and free-spirited. These four bipolar categories structure two sharply contrasting perspectives on the history of OD and reflect a deep understanding of the need for integrating and embracing seemingly contradictory orientations. A recent paper on 50 years of contributions to the *Journal of Applied Behavior Science* (*JABS at 50*) provides at more expansive summary of the academic side of the field.

(b) **Mergers and acquisitions:** Early on in his career when Mirvis was at Boston University, he and his colleague Mitchell Marks were invited by W. Michael Blumenthal, then CEO of Burroughs Corporation, to facilitate the human integration in what was the largest hostile takeover in US corporate history at that time. This engagement, involving the creation of Unisys, marked the beginning of what would become a storied career in M&A consulting. His scholarly work in this domain concerned the "merger syndrome" – a term coined to highlight a range of merger dynamics including: human resistance; explication of the integration of structures and processes involved in a merger; the much publicized concept of the clash of company cultures, and insight into the subsequent acculturation phase that mark several successful mergers. He has coauthored (with Marks) several books such as *Managing the Merger* and *Joining Forces: Making One Plus One Equal Three in Mergers, Acquisitions and Alliances*, and scholarly research articles capturing the lessons learned (outlined in the bibliography ending this chapter).

Marks and Mirvis (2001) analyzed their experience in over 70 mergers and acquisitions to discern characteristics that differentiate successful from unsuccessful combinations. While noting that three of four mergers fail in terms of their core financial and strategic objectives, the study pointed to importance of managing the strategic and psychological elements in the "precombination phase." In their words:

> The strategic challenges concern key analyses that clarify and bring into focus the sources of synergy in a combination. This involves reality testing of potential synergies in light of the two sides' structures and cultures and establishing the desired relationship between the two companies. And the psychological challenges cover actions required to understand the mindsets that people bring with them and develop over the course of a combination. This means raising people's awareness of and capacities to respond to the normal and to-be-expected stresses and strains of living through a combination. (p. 80)

To this point, most of the focus in M&A scholarship and practice concerned "post-merger" integration. This experience-based study also stimulated scholars and practitioners to give fuller attention to "premerger" issues (which, as the authors point out, is complicated because of legal requirements for secrecy and the inability to bring the two parties together). Mirvis writes about several premerger sessions with companies that helped them forestall culture clashes and, in a couple of cases, back out of the deal because of cultural misfits. All of this highlights the value of insights gained from "hands-on" engagement with practitioners.

(c) **The character of the workforce and workplace:** Mirvis also explored characteristics of the workforce and the workplace from his early days of working with Edward Lawler to more recent investigations of the "boundaryless" career with Douglas (Tim) Hall. Along the way he studied the financial impact of employee attitudes, the import of demographic changes on work attitudes, the rise of cynicism in the US workforce and society, and matters of work-life integration. Many of his writings provide useful pointers to practitioners on these strategic human resources management issues and themes.

One of Mirvis's enduring contributions was contributing to the Organizational Assessment Package (OAP) at Michigan and coediting a volume on methods and measurement tools for assessing organization change. His leadership in two national surveys of US employee attitudes and the Louis Harris and Associates' *Laborforce* 2000 survey also yielded data-based understandings of conditions in the workforce and workplace and documented the impact of progressive work designs, management practices, and employee engagement strategies.

While schooled in traditional research designs and survey methods, Mirvis came to question the merits of "scientific" research methods during his graduate study years. Guided first by Donald Michael, who wrote provocatively about the limits of technology assessments, Mirvis authored a series of papers reframing assessment as an art rather than as a science. In these, he goes about systematically taking apart the often unacknowledged fallacies and absurdities of the logical positivist assumptions that have bedeviled approaches to assessment. For example, in an early contribution titled "The Art of Assessing the Quality of Life as Work: A Personal Essay with Notes," Mirvis (1980) makes some conceptually elegant and intriguing arguments for embracing artistic imagination, empathy, and intuition as a necessary and legitimate component of a valid, reliable, and holistic evaluation.

The essay is a critique from a philosophy of science perspective on how the study of organizations, workers, and work itself has been distorted to fit into the Procrustean bed of the organization scientist's templates and rational mental models. A more ecologically grounded and holistically expansive perspective could emerge if only the researchers would allow the organic phenomenology of the worker, the nonrational and unconscious forces at work in organizations, and the recognition of workers and organizations as entities imbued with unique characteristics of their own. His recommendation that we unabashedly "rely on our intimate and personal knowledge of human behavior to derive models of work and working people" (p. 472) represented a bold departure from the canons of standard scientific research at that time while demonstrating how this expansion of our attitude would actually result in more valid and accurate depictions of organizational and worker realities.

In one of the most significant reinterpretations of a classic study, Mirvis revisits the results and analysis of the classic Hawthorne experiments and demonstrates how the researchers missed very important lessons from the bank wiring room experiments because of the narrowness engendered by their academic socialization. In Mirvis's (1980) words:

> Had they gone further...they would have conceived of the changes as an emergent work form and experienced the euphoria of the women as an indication of their quality of life at work...Moreover, if it is to be believed that the Hawthorne studies and the ensuing predictions that better "care" of workers would lead to human and economic improvements helped to stimulate the human relations movement in organizations, an alternative and more compelling interpretation of the findings might have changed the quality of work life itself in the subsequent four decades! (p. 483)

His vision of assessment as a subliminal integration of the artistic and scientific appreciation of work and his detailed elucidation of how to carry out such assessments is a powerful blueprint for a revolution in assessment studies that incorporates the imagination and lived experience of the workers themselves and is carried out by researchers who are real human beings, fully inhabiting their subjectivity, as opposed to dispassionate, passive observers of the objects of their studies.

(d) **Leadership Development and Consciousness Raising:** Informed by his exploration of the spiritual and aesthetic dimensions of organization life and practice, Mirvis began to incorporate these dimensions consciously into his intervention work in the late 1990s. *To the Desert and Back: The Story of One of the Most Dramatic Business Transformations on Record* describes his work with the British/Dutch consumer product conglomerate, Unilever. During his 1-year stint at the London Business School at the invitation of Sumantra Ghoshal, Mirvis was contacted by Louis "Tex" Gunning, who was running the Dutch side of Unilever foods, and invited to design and conduct community building retreats in the Ardennes, Scotland, and Middle East. Mirvis's experience at facilitating these "journeys" represents a radically innovative methodology, linking community building with deep "soul work" and consciousness raising in executives and in organizations. These journeys involve actual instances of travel of intact divisions or management teams to distant locations, sets of both planned and spontaneously occurring events and activities during the sojourn all of which would then become a springboard for new insights relevant to grasping underlying organizational dynamics.

Through a "behind the scenes" perspective, he was able to identify multiple ways in which performing arts can provide the impetus for large-scale organizational change. As one example, nearly 1600 of the Unilever employees were taken in buses, without prior indication of destination, to a factory setting in which they witnessed aisles and aisles of food that was wasted and spoiled. The team then disposed of the food through a burial ceremony. This incorporation of such scripted as well as spontaneous sequences and ceremony interspersed with collective sharing and sense-making processes breathed dynamism, emotion, and vitality into their workplace. Speaking of this interweaving of performance arts into management consulting, Mirvis et al. (2001) write:

> In the language of the arts and the emerging discipline of performance studies, the events described might be termed performances. In each instance, the actions of the leaders and staff are more or less scripted and unfold through scenes. The events themselves are staged, with scenery and actors in place, costumes and props ready, and the chairman cum director exerting a strong or light hand, depending on the performance. The parallels between process and performance are striking: the latter also involves an arrangement of activities across time and space, dramatization with a beginning and end, and activity, termed by scholars of the genre as performativity, that pulls it all together (Carlson 1996). This distinction may seem moot. In everyday language, people speak easily of the "art of leadership," read about management as a "performing art," and move toward craftsmanship in labor, harmony in teamwork, and "world-class performance. But to lift up and focus specifically on the performative aspects of leadership, we believe, offers a fresh, useful way to see, understand, and undertake organizational change. (p. 24)

His work is an invitation to organizational change practitioners to expand their creativity in leveraging dramaturgy and the performing arts more powerfully in their work even while seeking to unravel the mystery of organizational change through the metaphor of change as theater.

Mirvis also collaborated with Karen Ayas, from the Society for Organizational Learning, to work with Gunning in Unilever's operations in Asia, further developing what is a unique contribution to organizational studies, namely cutting edge experiential learning work in which participants live through shared organizational experiences, internalizing them and living them in the "here and now" followed by phases of storytelling about what is happening to them. In the words of Mirvis:

> One intervention of interest is a "learning journey" in which hundreds of leaders in a company travel together to inform their strategies and intentions. The journeys, lasting up to a week, are multilayered, multisensory experiences that engage the head, heart, body, and spirit. They are tribal gatherings in that we typically wake at dawn, dress in local garb, exercise or meditate together, hike from place to place, eat communally, swap stories by the campfire, and sleep alongside one another in tents. In our daily experiences, we might meet monks or a martial arts master, talk with local children or village elders, or simply revel in the sounds and sights of nature. We spend considerable time in personal and collective reflections about who we are as a community, what we are seeing, and what this means for our work together. Throughout a journey, a team of researchers prepares a "learning history" that documents key insights for continued reflection. (Mirvis 2006, pp. 81–82)

These methods have also been incorporated into the design of innovative leadership development programs. Mentored by Noel Tichy in the use of action learning in "project based" leadership development programs, Mirvis has championed the design and development of these programs in Intel, Ford Motor Co., Shell Oil, Novo Nordisk, Wipro (India), and CP (Thailand). His ability to inject theater and the performing arts into organizational interventions and to lead outdoor leadership experiences has led to a number of extremely creative consulting interventions in exotic locations spanning all the way from the Rockies, Pyrenees, Alps, and Himalayas. He has developed and orchestrated corporate learning and growth journeys coupled with community service projects in the "urban" USA, Paris, London, Sao Paulo, Tallinn, Estonia, rural India, China, Vietnam, in Greenland, and among aboriginal people in Borneo, Paraguay, and Australia.

In bringing "soul work" to corporations that are thought to be essentially devoid of soul and obsessed with the bottom line, Mirvis's contribution demonstrates the potential for community and spirituality at the workplace. It is a very promising indication that organizations and their leaders can be responsive to radically humanistic interventions.

(e) **Role of business in society:** Mirvis's scholarly and consulting career reflects an enduring interest in the role of business in society, beginning with his early, defining experiences with Ben and Jerry's, then with Royal Dutch Shell amidst the Brent Spar crisis, and finally with Unilever as it embarked on its sustainability journey. One of his "academic" stints was to join with Bradley Googins at the Center for Corporate Citizenship which afforded him a unique opportunity to study hundreds of companies in the development of their relationship to society. Mirvis has written extensively on the stages of development of corporate social responsibility (CSR), enhancing employee engagement through CSR and social innovations that simultaneously promote both societal and business objectives. He conducted the International Survey of Corporate Citizenship (2003–2009) and was the author of an annual ranking of the top corporate citizens in the world and in the USA in association with the Reputation Institute (2008–2010). His scholarly work has been paralleled by real world engagement at senior levels of corporate leadership working with Ben and Jerry's Ice Cream, Unilever, the SK Group (Korea), IBM, PepsiCo, and Mitsubishi (Japan) among others.

New Insights: Synergistic Integration of Divergent Modalities

In terms of Burrell and Morgan's (1979) *Sociological Paradigms of Organizational Analysis*, Mirvis's scholarship and practice can be situated in the Radical Humanist quadrant of organizational paradigms, espousing a conception of reality as socially constructed (not objectively constituted) and a commitment to exploring the potential for change in making organizations more responsive to human needs and aspirations (as opposed to continuity and maintenance of the existing order). For all of us whose scholarship and practices derives its inspiration from a Radical Humanist model of organizations, Mirvis's commitment to the potential for emancipatory scholarship has been a great source for inspiration. Given that the majority of scholars in the organizational studies field who undergo intellectual socialization in US business school espouse logical positivism, Mirvis's work blazes a trail from which all of us who are committed to an alternative framing of organizations can find intellectual and spiritual nourishment. He has by his prolific scholarship, imaginative theorizing, and creative consulting demonstrated the intellectual vitality, generativity and aliveness of a radically humanist view of organizations. His scholarship can be used as a model to help embryonic researchers in doctoral programs to see for themselves the unique insights that can emerge from qualitative research that embraces methodological pluralism and multiple epistemologies.

Mirvis's contribution lies at the intersection of at least five distinct well-defined literature streams within the discipline of organizational studies, and his work enriches each one of these tributaries of specialized scholarship in research, theory, and practice. First, there is the organization change and development (ODC) literature that focuses on the effective management of planned organizational changes designed to enhance the problem-solving capabilities of organizations. Mirvis's exploration of different organizational change interventions, his studies of failure in OD, and his research into large-scale organization change would align appropriately here. Second, there is the organizational behavior and organizational theory streams (OB and OT) that deal with the micro and macro aspects of organizational life with the intent of studying existing processes from a research and scholarly perspective. Mirvis's numerous studies on the character of the workforce and workplace summarized earlier exemplify and enrich these streams of scholarly literature in the organizational studies. Third, there is a growing movement exploring the spirituality dimensions of organizational life (MSR), and Mirvis's work on leadership and consciousness development reflects a profound appreciation of the spiritual dimension. His early work in this area is also tied to the recent emphasis on well-being in organizations (Davies 2016; Bishop 2016; Conyers and Wilson 2015; Bojanowska and Zalewska 2016). Fourth, his research connects with the strong literature arising from the recognition among scholars of the ways in which bureaucracies involve asymmetrical power relationships that privilege some constituencies and associated world views at the expense of some others. Mirvis's work, based on his early defining experiences, demonstrates a consistent commitment to creating egalitarian structures based on power equalization and this commitment is widely diffused throughout his research, scholarship, and practice. Finally, the proliferation of studies on corporate social responsibility (CSR) constitutes another clearly defined research stream that absorbs Mirvis's work on the role of business in society. CSR and the role of businesses in creating (or destroying) a sustainable environment and economy have become one of the most visible areas of research and action today (Moon 2015; Eichar 2015). Mirvis's work had a significant impact in stimulating interest in this topic when it was in its early stages.

Personal Reflections I (Thatchenkery) deeply resonated with Mirvis's work on several counts and I would like to highlight just a few of the broader similarities in orientation and conceptual spaces that Mirvis and I share at the level of core interests and commitments. Paralleling my interest in the social constructionist perspective on organizations, Mirvis is also comfortably aligned with a social constructionist perspective that examines organizations as sociocultural productions that arise from consensus and rooted in social processes and subjective meaning making processes. Reflecting my interest in Appreciative Inquiry and contributions in Appreciative Intelligence®, Mirvis is similarly committed to understanding what provides energy and vitality to organizational systems. I have also attempted to create synergy between action learning, sensitivity training, and experiential learning, a trinity that constitutes a very fertile area of creative experimentation for Mirvis in both theory and practice. Mirvis's foray into the social responsibilities of business is similarly echoed by my own intellectual excursion into the theme of positive design, sustainability, and sustainable value.

Equally important is another quality that Mirvis has modeled for all of us, namely professional courage. When faced with senior organizational leaders who may have a very narrow focus on bottom line profitability, Mirvis's work on learning journeys and performance art can help OD practitioners make a credible case for transcending the obsession with short-term or immediate measurable business outcomes and create a space for exploring alternative methods for reenergizing management teams. Similarly, Mirvis's work on failures in OD empowers us all to be more playful and adventurous in framing and designing interventions, and reminds us that without the permission to fail, no real creativity is possible. For all those of us who see ourselves as exponents of the Positive Organizational Scholarship tributary of organizational research, we can all build on the multiple ways in which Mirvis has dedicated his life to discovering the hidden life forces that give vitality and momentum to human organizing when the constraints of rationality, rigid bureaucracy, and mechanistic thinking are transcended.

On a more personal note, I (Tojo Thatchenkery) have known Phil since my doctoral studies at Case Western. My mentor Suresh Srivastva used to organize seminar series where leading thinkers in organization studies were invited to participate for a few days with doctoral students and invited scholars on the latest thinking in the field. All of us were assigned to "shadow" a scholar and I was lucky to be assigned to Phil. I still remember the excitement of meeting someone who spoke his mind and challenged everyone around him not to be afraid and to say what they were truly thinking. He taught me how to disagree with respect but not to give in. I observed that Phil had genuine credibility because he "walked the talk." He did not preach anything that he was not doing himself. While listening to my dissertation ideas which included appreciative inquiry, Phil encouraged me to listen with empathy and an open mind, and to be prepared for surprises.

Later on, as I moved to the Washington DC area to start my academic career at George Mason University, I was delighted to find that Phil lived in the area. Thus began our long-term friendship where I could meet him as frequently as I wanted (he was very generous with him time) and share what I was working on and receive insightful feedback. Phil believed in relationships rather than playing a formal role. He would invite me to watch the Washington Wizards game as his guest (he was an ardent fan of the team) and many of our productive dialogues happened during the dinner before or after the game. I felt Phil's presence most rewarding because he had a gift of offering feedback without judging. I was able to launch a few risky initiatives early in my academic career because Phil coached me in doing so. The courage I had gained since then stays with me today.

Personal Reflections As the coauthor, I (Param Srikantia) would like to register my deep gratitude to Mirvis for several facets of his work that have been a source of inspiration to me. I deliver a seminar titled *Beyond Emotional Intelligence: The Manager as an Enlightened Presence* which is based on the work of the legendary Indian mystic Osho, to managers of Fortune 500 companies in several cities through the international training organization, Institute of Management studies (IMS). The seminar, based on Eastern perspectives embodied in Osho's books and discourses, engages managers in inner work that crosses many of the same organizational and tacit boundaries that Mirvis describes in his experiments with the management teams of Unilever. Participants engage in deep emotional sharing, going beyond social masks and exploring how their managerial styles were shaped by the emotional challenges they encountered in their childhood.

Mirvis's work has given me enormous moral support, creative fuel, and professional courage in promoting this brand of inner self-exploration to managerial populations normally unaccustomed to such public displays of emotional authenticity. It has also given me a solid platform to stand on in speaking to business audiences, knowing that the modality of transforming managerial consciousness is one that has been successfully attempted in the history of OD.

Legacies and Unfinished Business: Transcending Polarities in a Boundaryless Career

Mirvis's distinctive accomplishment has been his ability to engage with the seemingly irreconcilable tensions between research and action and to craft a role as a scholarly practitioner. He has been able, by virtue of his own personal example, to demonstrate that it is possible for a scholarly practitioner to enjoy a level of recognized success within academia. He has been able to integrate the best of what the real world offers in terms of conceptually challenging consulting work with the theoretical heights that a scholar can scale by developing experientially grounded lessons derived from the field. Further, crafting novel and unusual interventions and learning events encourages OD professionals and change agents to think and act more creatively and provocatively. To sum his contributions:

- His book with Berg on Failures in OD moved the field away from the notion of failure as something to be feared to the idea that failure is something that can be celebrated for the useful insights that it may produce. Until the message that it is okay to fail was broadcast among OD practitioners, there was much less willingness in the field to engage in self-questioning and reflective practices that may call into question the consultant's mental models and intervention strategies. This book represents the potential for double loop learning that must be leveraged not just by the clients but also by the consultants themselves.
- Mirvis's work on M&A with Marks awakened organizations to the importance of compatibility (or lack thereof) between organizational cultures as a vitally significant determinant of success or failure in making deals. It is a perennial reminder

that due diligence is not merely a matter of business architectures and strategies but of attending to the underlying human variables that are much less tangible and much more complex.
- Mirvis's orchestration of learning journeys represents a creative response to the contemporary global epidemic of alienation in organizations. With the uncertainties of the global era and the competition, employees experience high levels of powerlessness, meaninglessness, cultural estrangement, social isolation, normlessness, and self-estrangement. Learning journeys are the perfect antidote to these states of alienated consciousness and represent a very lively intervention modality that embraces people in their wholeness and totality, allowing the entire system to be informed by the significance of the individual and for the individual to feel honored and affirmed in being contributed to by the whole system.

Notwithstanding these contributions, Mirvis agrees that his kind of work represents an anomaly to mainstream scholarship and practice and that there is plenty of "unfinished business" in the field of OD and change. For instance, the idea that assessment and change practices are both an art and a science is agreeable to many but the prevalence of pseudo-scientific assessment tools and standardized change management packages suggest that the field has yet to catch up to the level of organizational wisdom and scientific perspicacity represented by this integration of epistemologies. With a few notable exceptions, most graduate programs in organizational studies disproportionately inculcate the epistemology of a scientist among their students and do very little to help encourage the celebration of this work as both an art and a science.

While Mirvis's work carries with it a deep honoring of work/family integration and careers that represent a "path with a heart," a celebration of egalitarianism and power equalization within modern bureaucracies, and a radically humanistic vision of work, there are definite indications that the organizational zeitgeist may actually be evolving in precisely the opposite directions. Working people everywhere are treated as disposable assets and continuous job insecurity yields dependency, subservience, and serious work/family imbalance engendered by the fear of job loss.

In turn, Mirvis's work on CSR may be intellectually inspiring but evidence attests to strong corporate control of the world's food resources by a handful of conglomerates (including some that Mirvis has worked with and featured as icons of CSR), the displacement of indigenous people by corporations thirsting after natural resources on cooperatively owned land, and further threat of environmental degradation through fracking, global warming, and deforestation even as the global epidemic toward privatization of the commons leaves the average citizen ever more impoverished. And as Mirvis's writings on "best practices" in CSR stress laudatory conduct, such unflagging corporate optimism also carries with it the serious risk that CSR could be serving as the proverbial "opiate of the people" administered by people with high power in corporations to preserve and perpetuate the inequities of the status quo and the disenfranchisement of communities across the whole world.

Conclusion

There has been a longstanding tension in the organizational studies disciplines between the cynicism of critical theorists and the sometimes Pollyannaish perspectives of positive organization psychology (Davies 2016). The early Mirvis, through his revolutionary zeal, had been a trenchant champion of disaffection with the status-quo and much of his writing preserves a healthy level of skepticism including a deep awareness of the distortions caused by power structures. The positive psychology movement, on the other hand, seems to sweep power issues aside in calling for a focus primarily on the "good" side of the picture. Rather than seeing cynical realism and positive thinking as incompatible, the truly positive scholar will appreciate the idealism that fires the cynic and empathize with the sources of the cynic's wariness in the deep witnessing and understanding of how modern institutions frequently partake in and create impunity to extreme abuses of power. And perhaps the cynic as well might cast aside "miserablism" (especially prominent in business schools today, as the late Mirvis (2014) writes) in favor of exploration and experimentation aimed at uplifting the human condition. This level of transcendental integration of these seemingly divergent and antithetical stances is what will bring both tendencies into a condition of mutually beneficial dialogue and maybe even collaboration. And it would be perfectly in keeping with Mirvis's capacity to transcend polarities that has been one of the most distinguishing hallmarks of his boundaryless career.

References

Bishop, M. (2016). *The good life: Unifying the philosophy and psychology of well-being*. New York: Oxford University Press.

Bojanowska, A., & Zalewska, A. (2016). Lay understanding of happiness and the experience of well-being: Are some conceptions of happiness more beneficial than others? *Journal of Happiness Studies, 17*(2), 793–815.

Burrell, G., & Morgan, G. (1979). *Sociological paradigms and organisational analysis* (Vol. 248). London: Heinemann.

Carlson, M. (1996). *Performance*. London: Routeledge.

Conyers, M., & Wilson, D. (2015). *Positively smarter: Science and strategies for increasing happiness, achievement, and well-being*. New York: Wiley-Blackwell.

Davies, W. (2016). *The happiness industry: How the government and big business sold us well-being*. New York: Verso.

Denison, D., & Spreitzer, G. (1991). Organizational culture and organizational development: A competing values framework. In W. Pasmore & R. Woodman (Eds.), *Research in organizational change and development* (Vol. 5, pp. 1–21). Greenwich: JAI Press.

Eichar, D. (2015). *The rise and fall of corporate social responsibility*. New Brunswick: Transaction Publishers.

Mirvis, P. H., Ayas, K., & Roth, G. L. (2001). Learning in performance: How a Dutch company transformed itself. *Reflections, 2*(4), 21–38.

Moon, J. (2015). *Corporate social responsibility: A very short introduction*. New York: Oxford University Press.

Waddock, S. (2015). *Intellectual shamans*. Cambridge: Cambridge University Press.

Further Reading

Select Publications by Mirvis on...

a. Organization Change

Mirvis, P. H. (1988). Organization development: Part I – An evolutionary perspective. In R. W. Woodman & W. A. Pasmore (Eds.), *Research in organizational change and development* (Vol 2, pp. 1–58). Greenwich: JAI Press.
Mirvis, P. H. (2005). Large group interventions: Change as theater. *Journal of Applied Behavioral Science, 41*(1), 122–138.
Mirvis, P. H. (2006). Revolutions in OD: The new and new, new things. In J. Gallos (Ed.), *Organization development: A Jossey-Bass reader*. San Francisco: Jossey-Bass.
Mirvis, P. H. (2014). JABS at 50: Applied behavioral science and something more? *Journal of Applied Behavioral Science, 50*(4), 1–31.
Mirvis, P. H., & Berg, D. N. (Eds.). (1977). *Failures in organization development and change: Cases and essays for learning*. New York: Wiley Interscience.
Mirvis, P. H., Ayas, K., & Roth, G. (2003). *To the desert and back: The story of one of the most dramatic business transformations on record*. San Francisco: Jossey-Bass.

b. Mergers & Acquisitions

Marks, M. L., & Mirvis P. H. (1998). *Joining forces: Making one plus one equal three in mergers, acquisitions, and alliances*. San Francisco: Jossey-Bass. 2nd ed., 2010.
Marks, M. L., & Mirvis, P. H. (2001). Making mergers and acquisitions work: Strategic and psychological preparation. *Academy of Management Executive, 15*(2), 80–94.
Mirvis, P. H. (2008). Can you buy CSR? *California Management Review, 51*(1), 109–116.
Mirvis, P. H., & Marks, M. L. (1991). *Managing the merger*. Englewood Cliffs: Prentice-Hall. (Republished by Beard Books, Frederick, 2003).
Mirvis, P. H., & Sales, A. S. (1990). Feeling the elephant: Culture change following a corporate acquisition and buyback. In B. Schneider (Ed.), *Organizational climate and culture*. San Francisco: Jossey-Bass.

c. Workforce and Workplace

Kanter, D. L., & Mirvis, P. H. (1989). *The cynical Americans: Living and working in an age of discontent and disillusion*. San Francisco: Jossey-Bass.
Mirvis, P. H. (Ed.). (1993). *Building the competitive workforce: Investing in human capital for corporate success*. Wiley: New York.
Mirvis, P. H., & Hall, D. T. (1994). Psychological success and the boundaryless career. *Journal of Organizational Behavior, 15*, 365–380.
Mirvis, P. H., & Macy, B. A. (1976). Human resource accounting: A measurement perspective. *Academy of Management Review, 1*, 74–83.
Seashore, S. L., Lawler, E. E., Mirvis, P. H., & Cammann, C. (Eds.). (1983). *Assessing organizational change: A guide to methods, measures, and practices*. New York: Wiley.

d. Leadership Development & Consciousness Raising

Mirvis, P. H. (1997). 'Soul work' in organizations. *Organization Science, 8*(2), 193–206.

Mirvis, P. H. (2008). Executive development through consciousness raising experiences. *Academy of Management Learning & Education, 7*(2), 173–188.

Mirvis, P. H., & Ayas, K. (2008). Enhancing the psycho-spiritual development of leaders: Lessons from the leadership journeys in Asia. In J. Gallos (Ed.) *Business leadership: A Jossey-Bass reader*. San Francisco: Jossey-Bass.

Mirvis, P. H., & Gunning, W. L. (2006). Creating a community of leaders. *Organizational Dynamics, 35*(1), 69–82.

e. Role of Business in Society

Googins, B., Mirvis, P. H., & Rochlin, S. (2007). *Beyond 'good company': Next generation corporate citizenship*. New York: Palgrave.

Mirvis, P. H. (1994). Environmentalism in progressive businesses. *Journal of Organizational Change Management, 7*(4), 82–100.

Mirvis, P. H. (2000). Transformation at Shell: Commerce and citizenship. *Business and Society Review, 105*(1), 63–84.

Mirvis, P. H. (2012). Employee engagement and CSR: Transactional, relational, and developmental approaches. *California Management Review, 54*(4), 93–117.

Mirvis, P. H., & Googins, B. (2006). Stages of corporate citizenship: A developmental framework. *California Management Review, 48*(2), 104–126.

f. Issues in Scholarship and Practice

Mirvis, P. H. (1980). The art of assessing the quality of work life. In E. Lawler, D. Nadler, & C. Cammann (Eds.), *Organizational assessment* (pp. 471–489). New York: Wiley.

Mirvis, P. H. (1994). Human development or depersonalization? The company as total community. In F. Heuberger & L. Nash (Eds.), *A fatal embrace? Assessing holistic trends in human resources programs*. New Brunswick: Transaction.

Mirvis, P. H. (1996). Midlife as a consultant. In P. J. Frost & M. S. Taylor (Eds.), *Rhythms of academic life*. Beverly Hills: Sage.

Mirvis, P. H. (2014). Mimicry, miserablism, and management education. *Journal of Management Inquiry, 23*, 439–442.

Mirvis, P. H., & Lawler, E. E. (2011). Rigor and relevance in organizational research: Experiences, reflections, and a look ahead. In E. E. Lawler, S. Mohrman, et al. (Eds.), *Doing research that is useful for theory and practice – 25 years later*. San Francisco: Berrett-Koehler.

Mirvis, P. H., & Seashore, S. E. (1979). Being ethical in organizational research. *American Psychologist, 34*, 766–780.

Dr. Susan Albers Mohrman: Scholar and Agent of Effective and Meaningful Organizations

55

Ramkrishnan V. Tenkasi and George W. Hay

Abstract

Dr. Susan Albers Mohrman is a senior research scientist with the Center for Effective Organizations (CEO) at the University of Southern California Marshall School of Business. Many consider her to be a giant in the field of organization development and change (ODC) with her independent and joint contributions with other luminous colleagues from CEO such as Edward Lawler, Allan "Monty" Mohrman, Susan Cohen, and Christopher Worley. Mohrman has made several path-defining contributions during her illustrious and continuing 38-plus-year career at CEO. These contributions touch on multiple aspects of the field – teams, leadership, organizational design, organizational growth and development, rigorous research, theory development, useful research, and the cultivation of the future generation of scholar-practitioners.

Several core themes unite these diverse aspects. One integrative theme is her deep respect for and dedication to the constructive role that organizations can play in the lives of their members and the communities in which they are located. Another integrative theme is the need to build organizations that meet the multiple hurdles of effectiveness, efficiency, meaningfulness, and significance. A third is the multivocality of organizational expertise that rest in scholars, organizational leaders, employees, and other stakeholders. A fourth integrative theme is the persistent quest for models (and theories) of organizational functioning that better explain desired outcomes. As we reflect upon Dr. Mohrman's contributions, legacy, and unfinished business we are inspired to hold fast to the

R.V. Tenkasi (✉)
The Benedictine University, Chicago, IL, USA
e-mail: rtenkasi@ben.edu

G.W. Hay
Business Psychology Department, The Chicago School of Professional Psychology, Chicago, IL, USA
e-mail: GHay@thechicagoschool.edu

D.B. Szabla et al. (eds.), *The Palgrave Handbook of Organizational Change Thinkers*,
DOI 10.1007/978-3-319-52878-6_49

values of human dignity, meaningful work, sustainability, and scientific empiricism as we continue to cultivate powerful agents of change who fulfill the promise of the field of ODC.

Keywords
Teams • Leadership • Organizational design • Organizational growth and development • Rigorous research • Theory development • Cultivation of the future generation of scholar-practitioners

Contents

Introduction

Dr. Susan Albers Mohrman is one of the leading scholars, researchers and practitioners of Organization Development and Change (ODC) who has reached this point in her still active career after traveling a path filled with robust experiences in diverse organizations. Although there is much that differentiates these experiences from each other, there are also some patterns that repeat themselves and are therefore characteristically Dr. Susan A. Mohrman. Dr. Mohrman has always been engaged in serving society and helping to build better communities. She has also actively reflected upon her experiences and chosen to pursue the fulfillment of her vision for society by furthering her expertise as a change agent. She has shared what she has learned in books, articles, and workshops so that others might learn from her experiences. Last, and perhaps by far the most important, she works collaboratively with organizations, their leaders, and other scholars to apply this expertise and develop it further. These patterns are visible in the next sections that describe the influences, contributions, legacy and unfinished business that constitute her work.

Influences and Motivations: The Quest for Meaningful and Effective Organizations

Dr. Susan Albers Mohrman is a senior research scientist with the Center for Effective Organizations (CEO) at the University of South California, Marshall School of Business. Many consider her to be a giant in the field of organization development and change (ODC) with her independent and joint contributions with other luminous colleagues from CEO such as Edward Lawler, Allan "Monty" Mohrman, Susan Cohen and Christopher Worley. CEO is considered the first university-industry partnership of its kind in the United States, dedicated to carrying out collaborative social science research projects to generate useful knowledge.

Mohrman was born and raised in Lancaster, PA with a family focused on public service. Her father was a physician who provided support and care to the needy. Given a strong interest in societal good and the empowerment of human beings, Mohrman enrolled at Stanford University and completed her undergraduate degree in psychology. While at Stanford, she also met Monty Mohrman, her future husband, research colleague and life partner. The two eventually married in a dream wedding at the Stanford University Chapel. Given their penchant for public service and the progressive social change ethos of the 1960s, both decided to pursue a Master's degree in education at the University of Cincinnati as a way of giving back to society, particularly the public school system.

Sue Mohrman's first brush with ODC was in a course at the University of Cincinnati, where she was exposed to the avant-garde work of Bennis, Benne and Chin (1961) – in particular their ideas of democratic, planned change in the creation of meaningful work systems. These ideas seemed to hold the answers to some longstanding questions provoked by Mohrman's work experiences as a youth. She found organizations to be dehumanizing bastions of domination and control. Her quest henceforth was, "How can we make work and organizations more effective, satisfying, interesting, and meaningful?"

Mohrman's subsequent work as a secondary school teacher with the Cincinnati Public School System sparked her interest in furthering the development of social mission-driven organizations such as schools. She wanted to understand what drives individuals to join organizations like these that require its members to subjugate the pursuit of wealth, prominence, or fame, to the interests of the larger good. More importantly, she wondered how such organizations could become more effective by aligning and sustaining the interests of their members to promote their social mission in fulfilling and meaningful ways. Her experience was that many teachers join schools for altruistic reasons, but after a matter of time, their motivation to serve gets "beaten out of them" due to the constraining nature of hierarchical and segmented organizational structures that do not match the work that has to be carried out to educate and engage children (Mohrman and Wohlstetter 1994). In order to gain a deeper understanding of these early formative questions, Mohrman enrolled in the Ph.D. program in organization studies at Northwestern University in Chicago.

Her Ph.D. studies allowed her to further familiarize herself not only with the fields of Organization Behavior and Organization theory, but also with the field of Organization Development. This included further focus on Warren Bennis's work on values-based approaches to organizational change as well as the writings of other leading change scholars – like Ed Lawler and Chris Argyris – in making work more meaningful and interesting. Robert Duncan's mentorship at Northwestern helped complement micro-psychological approaches with macro-sociological organization theory understandings of organization design and change that were further influenced by Jay Galbraith's postulations on organization design. The Socio-

Technical Systems (STS) perspective that focused on the joint optimization of both human and technological systems were meso-level influences, since organization design approaches in that era entered ODC via STS. Her dissertation work focused on the impact of an intervention into the Waukegan School District, aimed at providing teachers with the opportunity to make changes in how the school district operated in order to improve the educational outcomes for students. Based on that work she developed the belief that school systems, like other organizations, could not be changed simply by motivating people to work harder and be told that they are empowered to make change. School districts had to be redesigned to fit with the requirements for educating "whole people". Her doctoral studies set the stage for Mohrman's lifelong work as a scholar-practitioner, focusing on how to participatively design and change organizational systems to accomplish human purpose.

Although Mohrman's intention post-Ph.D. was to return to work with public school systems as a change agent, she joined the business school at the University of Southern California (USC) as an assistant professor. Lawler arrived around the same time at USC with the vision of starting a research center that would redirect organizational research to actually influence practice, based on an understanding of the real issues organizations were facing. This was also a time when the discipline of organizational studies was devolving into a field of narrow perspectives and frameworks that lacked an appreciation for the systemic nature of organizations. Business schools were increasingly emphasizing a disciplinary-based approach toward research. It was in this context that Lawler and Monty Mohrman founded the CEO at USC with the explicit goal of doing rigorous theory-driven research in which practical usefulness was a major concern.

Sue Mohrman was inherently drawn toward the mission of CEO and transferred her services as assistant professor from the management and organization department to CEO as a research scientist, which, in her words, "shaped me as a scholar, researcher and change agent" (Mohrman, personal communication, May 2016). This was an opportunity for her to actively engage in field research doing experiments, case studies and evaluation studies to help organizations become more effective by combining rigor with relevance.

Dr. Mohrman's career also includes substantial service to professional associations such as the Academy of Management (AOM) where she was Chair of the ODC Division, and a member of the governing board. In these roles she championed the importance of bridging knowledge to action and research to practice.

Key Contributions: Building Meaningful and Effective Organizations Through Research, Theory Development, and Application

Dr. Mohrman has made several path-defining contributions during her illustrious and continuing 38-plus-year career at CEO. The following are examples of the key research studies, theoretical developments, and practical applications that characterize her work.

An early contribution in collaboration with Tom Cummings was reconfiguring the STS model to a self-design process model (Mohrman and Cummings 1989). Putting into play the STS model in multiple factories that were undergoing transitions led to the realization that any model or framework can only be an initial tool within the target organizational system. The members of that system must go through a learning process to apply the model in their local setting. They must learn about incorporating their values in the change process because the self-design model is driven by the "engineering" piece of STS as well as the "values" piece of it. It is a critical step in self-design to map out the values of the people in the organization, since those values must be embedded in the STS redesign that have implications for the design itself and its' implementation effectiveness.

The work of CEO in terms of bridging rigorous research with relevant practice was at odds with how academia in general and organizational studies in particular were evolving with a narrow focus on disciplinary based research (Mohrman 2001). Mohrman and her colleagues were instrumental in organizing two conferences at the Center to legitimize translational research. The first one on useful research (Lawler et al. 1985) brought together several mainstream scholars who had moved their personal interests to having an impact on organizations, and captured their insights on how best to achieve such an impact. The second conference on managing large-scale change (Mohrman et al. 1989) was a congress of rigorous researchers and practical interventionists to draw insights on how best to combine rigorous research with practical interventions to effectively change organizations. The integration of research with practice has been a continuing quest for Mohrman, who is now recognized as one of the foremost world scholars in this domain (Mohrman et al. 2001; Jarzabkowski et al. 2010; Mohrman and Lawler 2011).

Designing team-based organizations (Mohrman et al. 1995; Mohrman and Mohrman 1997) came out of STS foundations, and Mohrman's interest in understanding how to design for this new form of organizing, was spurred by her firm belief that team based designs offered an antidote to the "tyranny of bureaucracy" (Mohrman, personal communication, May 2016). There were challenges associated with how teams learn across the organization, work laterally, and retain their unique capabilities while working in collaborative settings. Added to these challenges is the superimposing cultural context of Western societies, where teamwork does not come naturally to people.

Organizational redesign is a critical capability for organizations to develop in order for a system to adapt to the dynamic and rapid changes in both the business and societal environments. One of Mohrman's key contributions in this regard concerns the potential ways through which the gap between the theoretical understandings of ODC and the actual practice of design in organizations can be bridged. ODC needs to become a discipline (Mohrman and Mohrman 1997; Mohrman 2007). Organizations need to build into their core functioning the capacity to continually adjust, adapt, and redesign the organization with the involvement of multiple stakeholders (Mohrman et al. 2007). It is more important than ever to juxtapose theories of ODC with the actual organizational design process to cultivate organizations that are good for their stakeholders and for society (Mohrman, personal communication, May 2016).

Building networks, particularly self-designing and self-organizing networks involving multiple stakeholders, also needs to be an integral part of design. Networks have the power to solve problems, foster innovation, and deliver more effective services than traditional hierarchical organization designs (Mohrman et al. 2003, 2007; Wagner and Mohrman 2009). Note that the networks envisioned by Mohrman exist within the organization itself but also extend across organizations (inter-organizationally) and ultimately throughout communities at large.

Mohrman's interest in sustainability came about as a response to the changing micro and macroeconomic realities, and to the very personal realization that her grandchildren would inherit a world with seemingly intractable problems. In her view, the Western world has created a very dark manifestation of humanity with its undeniable adverse impact on the natural environment and on issues of social justice. The unfolding of the global economy that has brought many out of poverty (and allowed a small element of the population to become extremely wealthy) has been accomplished with the costs of environmental degradation, climate change, and burgeoning inequality. The pursuit of wealth has become the key driver for individuals and organizations at the expense of the common good. This economic ethos has become the sine-qua-non of organizational being and has placed other values such as sustainability at the margins (Mohrman et al. 2015). Her current work builds on a larger recognition that ODC (and organization studies in general) should help redirect the global economy toward a more sustainable and equitable trajectory that incorporates social justice and human meaning (Mohrman and Worley 2010; Mohrman and Shani 2011, 2012, 2014).

New Insights: New Forms of Organizing and New Roles for Change Agents

The contributions that Mohrman has made to ODC described in the prior section also demonstrate the broad reach of her insights. This section will highlight a few dominant insights that merit continued consideration and reflection.

Bridging research with practice has gained momentum in recent years, including the fields of medicine and public health in the increasing prominence of "translational research." Dr. Mohrman believes that we have not yet unearthed its full potential. There is not much premium placed on the usefulness and impact of research in many academic settings, and the field of organizational studies almost exclusively continues to support disciplinary-based research. The external environment for corporations is changing so fast that they rely on a process of invention through trial and error to counter these forces, and do not have the patience to consider the vast research and theory knowledge base available on designing and changing organizations. This need for translational work suggests the first insight to be highlighted – organizations will not reach their full potential in terms of effectiveness, efficiency, meaningfulness and social value until they move beyond trial and error modes of organizational design and into the thoughtful application of extant research and theory.

Furthermore, the field does not have a population of change agents who are able to appreciate, value, or critically assess this extensive store of knowledge for practical use. The charge then for ODC scholars (and a professional passion for Mohrman) is to find ways for the accumulated knowledge to be packaged in a practical fashion without sacrificing rigor, and for multi-disciplinary teams to provide knowledge and support for organizations as they face the challenges in our fast-paced world. Scholars need to imagine and experiment with research that can have an impact, utilizing questions such as "How do you do it?" and "What are the elements that go beyond theoretical understanding of the distal focus on organizations?" How do scholars combine research knowledge with the ideas of organizational practitioners on how organizations design to accomplish human purpose? This realization leads to a second insight – that organizations cannot thoughtfully apply research and theory without employees and consultants trained in those skills. Translational work is inherently human and people driven.

Dr. Mohrman has some contrarian insights about the role of the leader as a change agent. Some of her early publications attest to her thoughts on this matter (Mohrman 1998). There is an overemphasis on the leader as the primary agent of change that ties in with the whole lore around the "romance of leadership" (Meindl and Ehrlich 1987). While the leader may provide a vision and a path or direction and communicate the values embedded in the required change, the legions of people lower down in the organization bring the vision into fruition. Organizations need employees to emerge as leaders to make the change work. It is not accurate to give all of the attention and credit, good or bad, to the leaders and executives who are a small percentage of organizational members. Understanding the self-regulatory characteristics of organizations and organizational systems, and the role of lower participants in the dynamics of fundamental change is an important area for future research. A third insight is that effective translational work involves a redesign of the structure and culture of the organization to include not just the specialized knowledge brokers but also the other members of the organization. Translational work shifts the roles of leaders and followers.

Dr. Mohrman's 38-plus years of experience studying organizational change as a theoretician, researcher and scholar-practitioner has led to the personal recognition that change cannot really be managed. Hence the fourth and final insight – all we can do as change agents is create organizational enablers for change to happen. This approach – called "Beyond Change Management" (Worley and Mohrman 2016) – in some ways harkens us back to Herbst's (1974) thoughts on designing with critical minimum specifications. In a paradoxical fashion, the outcomes of efficiency, effectiveness, meaningfulness and social value may come from doing less rather than more.

Legacy and Unfinished Business: Harnessing the Integration of Theory and Practice for Future Good

Dr. Mohrman's contributions and insights touch on multiple aspects of the field – teams, leadership, organizational design, organizational growth and development, rigorous research, theory development, and the cultivation of the future generation of scholar-practitioners. Several core themes run through these and serve as her legacy within the field of ODC. One core theme is her deep respect for and dedication to the constructive role that organizations can play in the lives of their members and the communities in which they are located. Another core theme is the need to build organizations that meet the multiple hurdles of effectiveness, efficiency, meaningfulness, and significance. A third is the multivocality of organizational expertise that rests in scholars, organizational leaders, employees, and other stakeholders. A fourth core theme is the persistent quest for models (and theories) of organizational functioning that better explain desired outcomes. The following areas of work in ODC form a short list of the unfinished business of her legacy.

Consider the role of technology in human work systems. A trend that started in the early 1990s and continues until today is the technological imperative that appears to guide organizations at the expense of human values. Technological capability – whether it is business process reengineering, enterprise-wide information systems, or powerful IT platforms and applications – have become the key underpinning of designing and redesigning modern organizations. It is only recently that we have been dealing with the values piece of this change, whether that requires being on call 24/7 due to instantaneous global communication or working from late at night until early morning to synchronize with virtual team partners across the globe. The direction humanity wants to go is not well understood, and many workers are going where technology takes them. A big challenge for ODC – and the first area of unfinished business – is to understand and grapple with the question of how organizations can allow their employees to reassert control over their lives, given the dominant technological imperative.

Likewise, there is a dominant technology focus with teaming. The way teaming was formerly understood has disappeared; the emphasis is now on newer forms of computer-supported collaborative work with "smart teams". "Smart teams" are temporary and often virtual, and with an increasingly transactional nature of employment. Investigating and understanding the development of collaborative systems in the context of technology-mediated communication versus intact teaming may better serve organizations, but only if their leaders develop a profound understanding of how to make this new form of work and employment address the needs of people. This introduces a challenge and a second area of unfinished business for ODC scholars as they search for ODC models that maximize the potential of collaborative systems.

Achieving global sustainability goals require collectives of people who can self-organize more effectively around desired human preferences. The chance of global sustainability happening organization by organization is more remote. Real development must move to the inter-organizational level – which is a third area of unfinished business. Dr. Mohrman's focus lately has been on how to design for such inter-organizational collaborations, building on her earlier work on trans-organizational development that began with Tom Cummings. ODC scholars have to create better understandings of how to build self-organizing networks around critical issues such as providing adequate global food supplies, mitigating the health inequities experienced by some populations, delivering wellness care that is tailored to the individual needs of specific patients, and addressing the human rights and social justice implications of how our global economy is unfolding. These challenges, in Mohrman's view, can only be addressed by many networks of stakeholders working together to focus on sustainable development while considering the various eco-systems that constitute our interconnected world.

Dr. Mohrman considers the most significant part of her legacy to rest with scholar-practitioners located in organizations, such as Stu Winby, formerly of Hewlett Packard. Stu Winby is now a scholar-practitioner working with many companies to merge the design of digital technology with the design of organizations. Mohrman is a founder and core faculty member in the CEO's Organizational Design Program, and has dedicated much of her time and energy to helping its participants learn how to lead their companies' complex redesigns aimed at developing the new capabilities required in the changing world. She feels that it is with this group that she is most directly able to bridge the gap between research and practice. This call to bridge the gap between research and practice is a fourth area of unfinished business.

In terms of impact on other scholars, Mohrman believes that her scholarship and mentorship has primarily influenced scholars who aspire to do useful research. These include several of her colleagues – past and present – at CEO, such as Susan Cohen, Cristina Gibson, David Finegold, Chris Worley, George Benson and an author of this chapter, Ram Tenkasi. From a broader angle, researchers working on teams and collaboration – such as Eduardo Salas – have found Mohrman's work useful. A significant contribution is getting academic researchers and scholar-practitioners in organizations to think about ways to bring in rigorous research and embed them in practical organizational projects. Toward this end, many of her publications and much of her contribution to the Academy of Management have focused on what it means to do useful research, and how to do it. This fifth area of unfinished business, clearly related to the fourth area of unfinished business, is the cultivation of scholar-practitioners within academia, for-profit, and not-for-profit organizations so that translational work can start, grow, and prosper.

As we reflect upon Dr. Mohrman's contributions, legacy, and unfinished business we are inspired to hold fast to the values of human dignity, meaningful work, sustainability, and scientific empiricism as we continue to cultivate powerful agents of change who can fulfill the promise of the field of ODC.

References

Bennis, W. G., Benne, K. D., & Chin, R. (Eds.). (1961). *The planning of change: Readings in the applied behavioral sciences*. Oxford: Holt, Rinehart & Winston.

Herbst, P. G. (1974). *Socio-technical design: Strategies in multidisciplinary research*. London: Tavistock Publications.

Jarzabkowski, P., Mohrman, S. A., & Scherer, A. G. (2010). Organization studies as applied science: The generation and use of academic knowledge about organizations [special issue]. *Organization Studies, 33*(9–10), 1189–1208.

Lawler, E., Mohrman, A., Mohrman, S., Cummings, T., & Ledford, G. (Eds.). (1985). *Doing research that is useful for theory and practice*. San Francisco: Jossey-Bass.
Meindl, J. R., & Ehrlich, S. B. (1987). The romance of leadership and the evaluation of organizational performance. *Academy of Management Journal, 30*(1), 91–109.
Mohrman, S. A. (1998). Top management viewed from below: A learning perspective on transformation. In J. A. Conger, G. M. Spreitzer, & E. E. Lawler (Eds.), *The leader's change handbook: An essential guide to setting direction and taking action* (pp. 271–300). San Francisco: Jossey-Bass.
Mohrman, S. A. (2001). Seize the day: Organizational studies can and should make a difference. *Human Relations, 54*(1), 57–65.
Mohrman, S. A. (2007). Having relevance and impact: The benefits of integrating the perspectives of design science and organizational development. *Journal of Applied Behavioral Science, 43*(1), 12–22.
Mohrman, S. A., & Cummings, T. G. (1989). *Self-designing organizations: Learning how to create high performance*. Reading: Addison-Wesley.
Mohrman, S. A., & Lawler III, E. E. (Eds.). (2011). *Useful research: Advancing theory and practice*. Berrett-Koehler: San Francisco.
Mohrman, S. A., & Mohrman, A. M. (1997). *Designing and leading team-based organizations: A workbook for organizational self-design*. San Francisco: Jossey-Bass.
Mohrman, S. A., & Shani, A. B. (Eds.). (2011). *Organizing for sustainability*. London: Emerald Press.
Mohrman, S. A., & Shani, A. B. (Eds.). (2012). *Organizing for sustainable healthcare*. London: Emerald Press.
Mohrman, S. A., & Shani, A. B. (Eds.). (2014). *Reconfiguring the eco-system for sustainable healthcare*. London: Emerald Press.
Mohrman, S. A., & Wohlstetter, P. (1994). *School-based management: Organizing for high performance*. San Francisco: Jossey-Bass.
Mohrman, S. A., & Worley, C. G. (2010). The organizational sustainability journey [special issue]. *Organization Dynamics, 39*(4).
Mohrman Jr., A. M., Mohrman, S. A., Ledford Jr., G. E., Cummings, T. G., Lawler III, E. E., et al. (1989). *Managing large scale organizational change*. San Francisco: Jossey-Bass.
Mohrman, S. A., Cohen, S. G., & Mohrman Jr., A. M. (1995). *Designing team based organizations*. San Francisco: Jossey-Bass.
Mohrman, S. A., Gibson, C. B., & Mohrman Jr., A. M. (2001). Doing research that is useful to practice. *Academy of Management Journal, 44*(2), 347–375.
Mohrman, S. A., Tenkasi, R. V., & Mohrman Jr., A. M. (2003). The role of networks in fundamental organizational change: A grounded analysis. *The Journal of Applied Behavioral Science, 39*(3), 301–323.
Mohrman, S., Mohrman Jr., A. M., Cohen, S., & Winby, S. (2007). The collaborative learning cycle: Advancing theory and building practical design frameworks through collaboration. In A. B. Shani, S. A. Mohrman, W. A. Pasmore, B. Stymne, & N. Adler (Eds.), *Handbook of collaborative management research* (pp. 509–530). Thousand Oaks: Sage Press.
Mohrman, S. A., O'Toole, J., & Lawler, E. E. (Eds.). (2015). *Corporate stewardship: Achieving sustainable effectiveness*. London: Greenleaf Press.
Wagner, C. S., & Mohrman, S. A. (2009). Science as a communications network: An illustration of nanoscale science research. In N. Vonartis & F. Malerba (Eds.), *Innovation networks in industries* (pp. 177–194). London: Edward Elgar Press.
Worley, C., & Mohrman, S. A. (2016). A new view of organization development and change competencies: The engage and learn model. In D. Jamieson, R. Burnette, & A. Buono (Eds.), *Consultation for organizational change, revisited* (pp. 29–48). Charlotte: Information Age Publishing.

Further Reading

Mohrman, S. A. (2001). Seize the day: Organizational studies can and should make a difference. *Human Relations, 54*(1), 57–65.

Mohrman, S. A., & Cummings, T. G. (1989). *Self-designing organizations: Learning how to create high performance*. Reading: Addison-Wesley.

Mohrman, S. A., & Lawler, E. E., III (Eds.). (2011). *Useful research: Advancing theory and practice*. San Francisco, Berrett-Koehler.

Mohrman, S. A, Gibson, C. B., & Mohrman, A. M., Jr. (2001). Doing research that is useful to practice. *Academy of Management Journal, 44*(2), 347–375.

Mohrman, S. A., Tenkasi, R. V., & Mohrman, A. M., Jr. (2003). The role of networks in fundamental organizational change: A grounded analysis. *The Journal of Applied Behavioral Science, 39*(3), 301–323.

Mohrman, S. A., Galbraith, J. R., & Monge, P. (2006). Network attributes impacting the generation and flow of knowledge within and from the basic science community. In J. Hage & M. Meeus (Eds.), *Innovation, science and industrial change: The handbook of research* (pp. 196–216). London: Oxford Press.

Mohrman, S. A., O'Toole, J., & Lawler, E. E. (Eds.). (2015). *Corporate stewardship: Achieving sustainable effectiveness*. London: Greenleaf Press.

Worley, C., & Mohrman, S. A. (2016). A new view of organization development and change competencies: The engage and learn model. In D. Jamieson, R. Burnette, & A. Buono (Eds.), *Consultation for organizational change, revisited* (pp. 29–48). Charlotte: Information Age Publishing.

David Nadler: A Life of Congruence

56

William Pasmore

Abstract
David Nadler was a scholar-turned-practitioner who left his mark on the field of organization development through his work with CEOs and his writing about organizational diagnosis, data feedback, organization design, transformation, and boards. The consulting firm he created, Delta Consulting, was the premier firm specializing in consulting to CEOs on matters related to their personal and organizational effectiveness. He is perhaps best remembered for creating, along with Michael Tushman, the congruence model, which serves as a guide for organizational diagnosis and design. However, his greatest impact was on those who knew him as clients, associates, and friends.

Keywords
Congruence model • Data feedback • Organizational architecture • Board effectiveness

Contents

W. Pasmore (✉)
Teachers College, Columbia University, New York, NY, USA
e-mail: pasmore@tc.columbia.edu

D.B. Szabla et al. (eds.), *The Palgrave Handbook of Organizational Change Thinkers*,
DOI 10.1007/978-3-319-52878-6_50

Introduction

It is my deep pleasure to reflect on the life of my friend, mentor, boss, and colleague David Nadler. He led an extraordinary life; one that sometimes seemed either blessed and cursed but was always remarkable. His impact on the field of organization development was huge, and yet the influence he had on his clients and contemporaries was greater still.

It would be hard to capture all that David thought and everything that David was in a series of volumes, let alone a short chapter. His mind was incredibly fertile, making a series of almost continuous groundbreaking contributions from the 1970s to the 2010s. As a consultant, he influenced others to change the course of their lives and their corporations. As a businessman, he became very wealthy and helped others to do the same. He had his quirks and hard sides; he was not a perfect human being. Yet, in retrospect, his quirks and hard sides made him who he was and were as important to his success as the generosity, brilliance, and fearless tenacity he displayed.

Influences and Motivations: Shaping Forces

I worked with David Nadler at Delta Consulting, the firm he founded, from 1997 to 2008. I knew him long before then, but only as a fellow academic attending Academy of Management conferences with some shared interests. David was teaching at Columbia in the late 1970s and had already established a reputation as one of the up and comers in our field.

David's transition into full-time consulting in the early 1980s probably came as a surprise to him, as did mine, although our paths there were different. David had been denied tenure at Columbia, not due to his lack of scholarly productivity but because he ran afoul of a senior member of the faculty who resented the fact that an assistant professor without tenure had created a consulting/research firm instead of focusing his full attention on teaching, scholarly publishing, and service to the school.

David modeled his firm largely after the Institute for Social Research at the University of Michigan, where David had done his doctoral work. It made perfect sense to him that he would use the firm to advance his research and to provide consulting to organizations based on that research, since he had seen the model work at Michigan. His senior colleagues at Columbia had different priorities in mind. They expected untenured faculty to focus their attention on research and publishing in scholarly journals, not on creating a "business." Noel Tichy, who hired David, was unable to stem the tide that turned against David in the tenure review process.

I, on the other hand, had been a tenured full professor at Case Western Reserve for 20 years before trying my hand at consulting full time, a move triggered by a desire to relocate to the Northeast. David welcomed me to Delta despite my being a passing acquaintance and remained a friend and mentor for the rest of his life. David died of cancer in 2015 at age 66, far too soon. By then, he had ascended to the position of Vice Chairman of Marsh McLennan, the huge corporation that purchased Delta

Consulting and also owned Mercer, Putnam Investments, Oliver Wyman, and many other subsidiary assets. As a result of the sale, David had become very wealthy, had homes in New York, Westport Connecticut, and Naples Florida and a sailboat named "Congruence" after the famous model that he developed with Michael Tushman. I have fond memories of sailing on that boat with David, which he captained as meticulously as he ran his affairs. "Perfect" was lowest the acceptable bar for David.

But let's go back to the beginning. David's father, Leonard Nadler, was an academic who taught at George Washington, with a focus in Human Resources Management. In fact, he is credited with coining the term, "Human Resource Development." He applied his scholarship in projects with the state department, and then in ASTD, setting an early example of the life of the scholar-practitioner for his eldest son. At first, David saw his career going in some other direction but when it came time to attend college, he chose his father's institution. Mark Nadler, his brother, recalls living with David as a freshman while David was a junior at George Washington. Mark said that during the Vietnam war years, David interned at IBM. The contrast between what seemed like a hopeless international quagmire and the relentless pace of action and excitement at IBM altered David's trajectory from a career in the Foreign Service to one related to business.

After George Washington, David enrolled in the MBA program at the Harvard Business School in order to familiarize himself with all aspects of business. The connections he made there and the emotional ties he felt to Harvard were among the strongest influences in his later career. For years, the consultants at Delta Consulting would hold regular all-hands meetings at the Harvard Club in New York, where David also met frequently with his colleagues, clients, and former classmates. In addition to the connections Harvard provided, his membership in the Harvard community provided David a patina of aristocracy, which he valued and used to maximum advantage.

David's time at Harvard convinced him that he was on the right path by focusing on both academics and business. Therefore, it was not as surprising as it may have seemed at the time that his next move would be to pursue his PhD at the University of Michigan.

Ed Lawler, who was David's chair, describes David as a terrific student, albeit business focused. David worked extensively with Ed on quality of worklife projects while at Michigan and became enamored with the Institute for Social Research (ISR) which had been founded by Rensis Likert and others and was being run by Bob Kahn, David Bowers, and Charlie Seashore during David's time as a graduate student. ISR served as the model for David's consulting firm, Organizational Research and Consultation (OR&C), which later became Delta Consulting.

Ed said that David was always happy to contribute to discussions in class but could become impatient or even rude at times if others were not prepared to do the same. David was on a mission to become a scholar-practitioner. He never imagined anything other than becoming a faculty member and turned down several opportunities with consulting firms that expressed interest in him. While Ed did not see the "pure researcher" in David that he saw in other students, he had no doubt about his motivation to succeed and become a part of the academic elite.

David had a natural ability to translate the complex work that others were doing on theory into practice. He was profoundly influenced by Katz and Kahn's book on the social psychology of organizations and systems theory in particular. It was clear to Dennis Perkins, a fellow doctoral student at Michigan and lifelong friend who also held a Harvard MBA, that the congruence model was based on the open systems thinking they had learned from Katz and Kahn. Michael Tushman, co-author of the congruence model, confirmed that David was the one who brought the open systems thinking to their work on the congruence model, without which the model would not have been nearly as powerful. David was also intrigued with Harold Levinson's work on organizational diagnosis and counted him among his key influences.

Perkins remembers David the doctoral student creating a reference location system out of computer punch cards and push rods that enabled him to find references about a specific topic by inserting the rods into the holes on the cards and using them to pull certain cards from the deck. He was far ahead of what Google Scholar would eventually allow the rest of us to do.

David was a person, according to Perkins, who had a knack for getting things done. He used checklists to track work details and kept his desk in immaculate order, while books and papers from his office-mate frequently overflowed into David's space, something David did not appreciate. David had an entrepreneurial orientation even then and took full advantage of the opportunities that Lawler, ISR, and its Survey Research Center (SRC) afforded. It was a fertile ground for what was to come.

Key Contributions: The Scholar-Practitioner in Action

Joining the faculty of the Columbia Business School upon earning his doctorate in 1976, David commenced what would be a productive, lifelong career in contributing to the literature in the field of organization development. Given that ISR and David Bowers in particular had pioneered the survey feedback method, it is understandable that one of David's earliest and best-known publications was a book in the Addison-Wesley series on organization development titled simply *Data Feedback*. It was a contribution that is as timely today as it was in its year of publication, 1977. I still use it in my consulting course; there simply is not a better resource on how to collect, prepare, and impart information of all kinds to clients. Later, David would use his expertise in data feedback to perfect methods for collecting and feeding back data to CEOs, a demanding audience who expected extremely high-quality analytics and value-added sensemaking.

It was at Columbia that David worked closely with Noel Tichy, Michael Tushman, and Warner Burke, the latter who was on the faculty of Teachers College. Tushman remembers that he and Nadler followed one another around for interviews at different institutions in the hiring process. Tushman was aware of Nadler, but the two did not really know each other until Tichy hired them both and brought them together for the first time in his home. The two hit it off immediately and began work on redesigning the core course on organizations which, according to Tushman, had

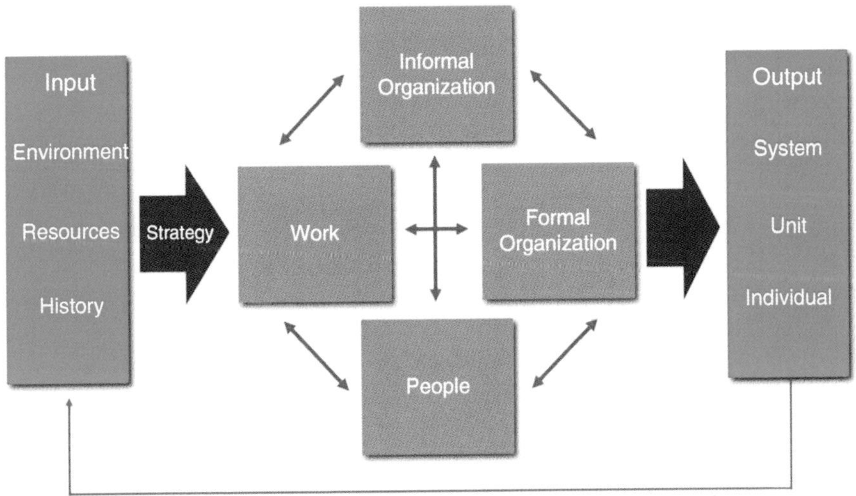

Fig. 1 The congruence model (From Nadler and Tushman 1980)

been a disaster. In the process of redesigning the course, David suggested that having a model around which to build the course would be a good idea. A few working lunches later, the now widely known congruence model was born (Nadler and Tushman 1977). Tushman's work had been on networks, social innovation, and culture. David brought Katz and Kahn's open systems thinking perspective (Katz and Kahn 1966), as well as Levinson's work on organizational diagnosis (Levinson et al. 1972) and Lawrence and Lorsch's work on organizations and the environment (Lawrence and Lorsch 1967). They combined these different scholarly traditions to create the congruence model, which has stood the test of time. Tushman says that the model was intended to help leaders solve problems they faced. It was more than an "academic theory" about how organizations worked. It was a tool that David and others would apply in organization development consultation from that point forward (Fig. 1).

Applying the congruence model started with examining the fit or "congruence" of an organization's environment and its strategy. A good strategy considered opportunities and threats, the resources at the organization's disposal, and its unique history, positioning, and capabilities. As we know, however, even good strategies do not always produce the results intended. When this happens, according to the congruence model, there can only be three explanations. First, the strategy can be at fault; what appeared to be sound strategic thinking needs to be reconsidered, either because the strategy was faulty or the environment changed substantially. If after review the strategy is deemed sound, there are two additional explanations for a lack of success. First, the formal organization design and processes used to perform the work may not be designed to execute the strategy. Second, the informal organization (culture) or people (talent) may not support success. It is the responsibility of leadership to determine what the cause of the problem is and to experiment with different solutions until the desired results are achieved at the overall system, business unit, and individual levels.

Some leaders believe that improving the culture or making strategic talent changes can overcome problems associated with poor organization design or work processes. The congruence model argues the opposite, based on the sociotechnical systems school. Poor work organization, structural barriers, and inappropriate use of power by virtue of position are more deterministic of outcomes than positive motivation or thwarted capabilities. The same point was recently made in a 2016 Harvard Business Review article by Lorsch and McTague.

If the work processes and formal organization are judged to be well aligned with a workable strategy but results are not forthcoming, only then should attention shift to the informal system (culture, teamwork) and people (talent, engagement, rewards). Once necessary improvements are made in all four elements of the organizational design (work, formal organization, informal organization, and people), the final step is to ensure that the four elements are designed to be mutually reinforcing. The arrows in the model represent the fit or "congruence" among the elements and are considered as important in their impact on outcomes as the individual elements. As Russell Ackoff explained so colorfully, identifying the best individual components of every automobile engine in existence would not permit one to build the world's best engine because the parts would not fit together. The implication is that rather than benchmarking each element of an organization against "best in class," it is better to assemble the elements in ways that fit well together and, by so doing, produce optimal overall results. In the sociotechnical systems school, which David studied, the process of improving the performance of a single element at the expense of the effectiveness of the overall system is known as "sub-optimization." David was against implementing changes in one part of an organization without considering their impact on the whole, especially if the changes were faddish or driven by the desire of a unit or individual to "one-up" others. If the HR department was about to roll out an employee engagement program, for example, David would ask why. It was not that he was against employee engagement, but he wanted leaders to understand how the entire system worked to produce results. If employees were more engaged, how would this contribute to the work being done better or the organization design more effectively supporting the strategy? It is safe to say that if the congruence model was understood and applied more often, leaders would save billions annually on implementing programs or changes that either have no impact or actually make matters worse.

Dennis Perkins, David's peer at Michigan and early colleague at Organizational Research and Consultation (which would later evolve into Delta Consulting), pointed out to David that "leadership" was missing as a separate variable in the congruence model. Perhaps because Nadler and Tushman were tasked with designing a course on organizations, they saw leadership as interspersed throughout the model rather than in a category of its own. Nevertheless, David conceded that adding leadership to the model might have been a good idea, had not OR&C just finished printing 4000 copies of the model for use with clients. Money was tight, and David could not bear to see the printed copies go to waste.

Michael and David worked together on developing cases for the course that featured managers dealing with issues of motivation, culture, and organization design. These topics later became the subjects of books or white papers produced by OR&C and then Delta Consulting. David felt that consulting included educating leaders on topics that every Columbia MBA would have learned in the course that he and Tushman taught. Nadler and Tushman continued to work together on a number of these publications, including *Strategic Organization Design* (1988), *Organizational Frame Bending* (1989), *Beyond the Charismatic Leader* (1990), *Competing by Design*, 1997, and, with Donald Hambrick, *Navigating Change* (1997).

In these works, Nadler and Tushman leveraged the congruence model to point toward ideas in the areas of organizational design and change that would consume David for the next decade. The idea of congruence, or alignment among the building blocks, was what produced excellence. The organization design process, as conceived by David, began with understanding which elements in the model needed to be better aligned with the strategy and with one another (using diagnostic methods modeled on Levinson's work). In strategic organizational design, the large pieces of the organization first needed to be grouped together according to function, product, geography, or processes, as dictated by strategic priorities. Then, these groups needed to be "linked" by mechanisms that would allow coordination across their boundaries, using both formal and informal mechanisms for sharing information and making decisions. Finally, after creating the strategic or high-level design of the enterprise, the work of operational, or within-unit design, would begin. Operational design includes the definition of work processes, roles, talent requirements, and other details that determine the efficiency and effectiveness of operations. Since organizational design is a process that involves change, Nadler and Tushman also addressed issues concerning power, anxiety, and control during the transition from one structure to another.

Tushman says that the scholar-practitioner model was clearly what guided David in his years at Columbia. David understood that publishing was an important part of the job but truly loved consulting and being an entrepreneur. He worked with Warner Burke to create a fabulous course on consulting to organizations which continues to be taught at Teachers College today. I have taught it and am amazed at both its complexity and design integrity. In addition, David collaborated with Tichy, Tushman, Jeff Pfeffer, and Charles O'Reilly on programs about change that are still being taught in executive education programs at Harvard and Columbia. David also guided the work of graduate students, including Deborah Ancona, who worked on research and consulting projects with David.

David valued research and recruited Tushman, who remained at Columbia, to be his part-timer at "research department" in the early years of OR&C and Delta Consulting. David also applied his own research skills to advance understanding and practice during his years at Delta. Tushman cites David's work on boards (2004, 2011) as being perhaps the most creative and groundbreaking of David's later career. This work helped CEOs and board members better understand the range of relationships that may exist between boards that are "passive" or inactive and boards that are overly involved, which he calls "operating boards." The ideal balance is one that David calls "engaged." The engaged board accepts its responsibility for overseeing the performance of the CEO and the success of the enterprise. To do this, they need relevant industry and financial expertise. Moreover, they must work hard at defining the way they will work with the CEO to ensure that the most important issues are addressed while the roles of the CEO and the Board are clear. The engaged state is difficult to maintain as issues arise, but it is helpful to remind both the CEO and the board that this ideal should be the goal, even if discursions from the ideal occur from time to time. In the book on *Building Better Boards* (Nadler et al. 2011), David and his colleagues leverage research that Delta conducted as part of a National Association of Corporate Directors (NACD) study to address issues such as the pros and cons of combining the CEO and chairman's role, succession planning, board composition, and board assessment.

David's other noteworthy contributions include books on *Organizational Architecture* with Marc Gerstein and Robert Shaw (1992), *Discontinuous Change* with Robert Shaw and Elise Walton (1994), *Champions of Change* (1997) and *Executive teams* with Janet Spencer (1998). *Organizational Architecture* (1992) included chapters by a number of Delta Consulting senior partners on the history of organizational architecture, managing acquisitions, building strategic partnerships and joint ventures, designing high-performance work systems, succession planning for the executive team, and collaborative strategic planning. A chapter by Robert Shaw on the capacity to act defined the steps that CEOs need to take to have the wherewithal to address problems and implement solutions, including such things as having a clear vision, prioritizing a vital few imperatives, assigning clear responsibility, and providing adequate resources. The concept of capacity to act was one that caught on with CEOs who often felt helpless in the face of what seemed to be overwhelming forces working against them. Likewise, the chapter by Shaw and Perkins outlined how CEOs can learn from "productive failures," a concept that we see embodied in design thinking today.

Discontinuous Change (1994) tackles the topic of organizational transformation, with particular attention to the leadership and cultural requirements to achieve success. Discontinuous change begins with a bold and courageous strategy that must be communicated so that the transformation can be carefully staged. Then, the executive leaders must engage in ways that impact the culture in the present and for the future. David writes about the need to go beyond the myth of the heroic leader, since the actions of the heroic leader only do so much and produce dependency which is not supportive of true engagement. While heroic leaders provide a vision, enable change to happen, and use charisma to create positive energy, leaders must work together to provide instrumental and institutionalized leadership. Instrumental leadership addresses how the new enterprise will be structured and measured, and people will be rewarded. Institutional leadership leverages the contributions of the members of the entire senior team and broadens the notion of leadership to extend beyond the senior team to include senior management.

Champions of Change (1997) delves into the role of the CEO in leading radical discontinuous change. Important actions include overcoming obstacles to change, developing a shared direction, building a new strategy, redesigning the organization, aligning strategy and culture, building a new senior team, and engaging senior leadership in sustaining the change. The book ends with important principles for CEOs leading discontinuous change, including ensuring appropriate involvement, exercising committed leadership, providing valid information, making informed choices, and constructing integrated change.

In *Executive Teams* (1998), David calls once again upon his colleagues to write about the unique nature of working at the top of complex enterprises, this time with a focus to how teams at the top differ. Since any executive team is a reflection of the CEO, the book begins with a look into the complexity of the role of the CEO and the many stakeholders and interests which the CEO, and by implication the senior team, must contend. In cases where a COO position exists, another article explores the different forms of relationships the COO holds to the CEO and to other members of the executive team. Following that, one of the most read pieces that David and his brother Mark ever wrote together is offered, entitled *Performance on the executive team: When to Pull the Trigger*. The subject is when to dismiss an underperforming member of the executive team. The criteria offered and advice on the process touches an area that has been an emotional sinkhole for many CEOs – making the call regarding a long-term team member and often personal friend who is no longer the right person for the job. Additional topics include trust and conflict among members of the team, providing feedback to the team on its performance, and the work of the executive team around strategy, culture, change and governance.

Several of David's later works were completed with his brother Mark, who joined Delta Consulting after a successful career in journalism. Mark remembers that David was always interested in making a reputation through his writing. While still an undergraduate student, David wrote a piece called the "New Orientation to Work" that was later published by ASTD in 1971. The premise was that baby boomers would be flooding the job market and that they would need to be managed differently than their predecessors, a conversation strikingly similar to that concerning millennials today. Mark said that there was never any doubt in David's mind that he would become an academic. David knew that before getting his MBA but felt that the MBA would better prepare him to work with executives and write about business. Mark speculates that had David been granted tenure at Columbia, the story of his career would have been different. His intention was to model his career after Lawler, Levinson, and others; he would have remained in academia rather than moving into consulting full time.

Mark said that David's writing was driven by a desire to translate practice into strategy. He was good at "connecting the dots." He would observe different clients as they struggled with similar issues and distill common themes and patterns. It was a gradual process of accumulating information and turning it into knowledge, not waking up in the middle of the night with a "flash of brilliance." As the pieces fell into place, the whole picture would gradually emerge. Mark helped David's thinking by pushing back on him, challenging him to think differently about the varied business issues his clients encountered. David had a tendency to "rediscover" the same idea several times, and Mark helped him to move past what he already knew to discover new insights. One example of this was the breakthrough that resulted in

David's *Harvard Business Review* article, "The CEO's Second Act" (2007), which was an entirely new perspective on what happens to CEOs who are hired to do one thing, accomplish that, and then are forced to do something they are not prepared to do.

The more they worked together, the more David took on the role of deciding the topic while Mark did a greater share of the writing. David found it increasingly difficult to find time to sit and write, with so much going on in the firm that demanded his personal attention. He told Mark that it was like his chair had springs; no sooner would he sit down than the chair would pop him back up. David did the consulting that provided the real-life examples that made the work come alive and invented the abstract concepts. Mark, using the talents he had honed in journalism, made the writing easily accessible to an executive audience.

David built a large research team at Delta Consulting and commissioned researchers to work with practicing consultants on projects that resulted in white papers on leading strategic combinations, CEO succession, and a variety of other topics. David maintained personal quality control on these publications, since each represented the Delta Consulting brand that David had worked so passionately to build and maintain. I can recall being assigned to a joint project with Mercer Management Consulting and Mercer HR on the topic of pre-merger assessment. After a year of collaboration, an article was published, but the assessment itself, which was the goal of the work, was scrapped because it did not meet David's standards. He knew what he wanted and was not afraid to say no to contributions that did not deliver to his specifications. It was an important lesson for me about not accepting the product of difficult collaboration with peers as the best that could be accomplished. David may have left academia, but he never lowered his standard for publishable work.

The research group, led by Carlos Rivero and later David Wagner and myself, produced tools and thought pieces that facilitated the work of the firm's consultants. These included a tool for assessing the effectiveness of executive teams (Executive Team Assessment Questionnaire), a tool for assessing lateral relationships (The Lateral Relationships Questionnaire), a tool for analyzing interview information (MIDAS), and material for the books and articles mentioned previously.

David's closest writing connections throughout his career were Michael Tushman and his brother Mark Nadler. Professionally, he teamed with Tushman, Noel Tichy, Don Hambrick, and Warner Burke while at Columbia and with Dennis Perkins, Carl Hill, Chuck Raben, David Bliss, Rick Ketterer, Elise Walton, Janet Spencer, Dan Plunkett, Rosalinde Torres, Terry Limpert, Peter Thies, Carlos Rivero, David Wagner, and others while at Delta Consulting.

As mentioned previously, David's thinking was most strongly influenced by Katz and Kahn (open systems), Harold Levinson (diagnosis), Ed Lawler (quality of worklife), Jay Galbraith (organization design), and Rensis Likert and David Bowers (survey feedback). David prided himself on translating behavioral science theories into understandable guidance to executives. In the process, he created the congruence model, a unique approach to organization design, novel thinking about boards, new approaches to succession planning and strategic planning, refined methods for approaching discontinuous change, tools for post-merger integration, ways to measure executive team effectiveness, and fresh perspectives about the CEO's role. While the congruence model and feedback remained at the core, David never stopped exploring frontiers and adding his own thinking to issues of interest to senior executives. The research team at Delta and his brother Mark did a lot of the heavy lifting as the years went by, but David always filled the role of chief scientist in addition to his other duties. He provided direction for the work, guided it along, and approved the final product. While many professors have the advantage of working with bright doctoral students, David had his own shop full of PhDs, and they were among the best and brightest. Many have since joined other consulting firms or started ventures of their own.

As Ed Lawler observed when reflecting on David as a graduate student, David was preoccupied with business and not as enamored with basic research. He did not build basic research into the agenda at Delta. Most of the thinking that he conceived was based on his own work in the field with executives and his personal creativity. While he was quite comfortable with advanced statistics, he recognized that executives would not understand them and therefore did not devote attention to publishing in rigorous academic journals. Practicality and impact outweighed empirical evidence in determining what was important to say. As a field, we continue to struggle with the relevance-rigor issue in much of what we publish. Are we writing for one another just to achieve tenure or academic credibility? David, after his time at Columbia, no longer struggled with the debate. For him, it was all about what would help executives achieve success.

Contributions to Practice

David initially wanted to create an ISR-like research consulting entity that he could run while maintaining a full-time faculty position at Columbia. Dennis Perkins remembers the initial organizing meeting for Organizational Research and Consultation (OR & C) held at the Delaware Water Gap hotel, where David outlined his vision for the firm. David recognized that his genius was in taking complex things and making them simple, which executives liked. He also felt that his own high need for control would resonate with executives. As an example, David often used the metaphor of a captain at the wheel of a sailing a ship that he was trying to steer through a storm, only to find that the wheel was not connected to the rudder. In this, he captured the deep fear that many executives have regarding their success being dependent upon others who are beyond their immediate control. David would then introduce the congruence model as a way to bring order to chaos.

In his consulting, David told executives that they were the architects of their organizations, from strategy to design, culture, talent, and work processes. He helped executives think about the changes they needed to make to align their organizations with their strategies and thereby achieve the critical outcomes by which their legacy would be measured. Over the years, David developed interview guides and surveys connected to the congruence model, making the connection between his research, change consultation, and organizational performance stronger and stronger. As he worked with the CEOs of notable companies, beginning with Xerox and continuing with many more over the next 30 years, his reputation and that of his firm grew.

David was one of the few founders of a successful consulting firm who recognized almost immediately that his own impatient, perfectionistic, low-tolerance-for-stupidity style would need to be buffered as he worked with clients who needed more coddling than David preferred to provide. He partnered with Carl Hill and later with David Bliss, who left Xerox to join David's consulting firm after having been David's client. Carl and David Bliss were like Tontos to the Lone Ranger, according to Perkins.

As is the case with many startups, the firm almost failed before it succeeded. During a meeting with a client, the firm's accountant burst in and announced that there was not enough money in the bank to meet payroll. Soon thereafter, Carl Hill surprised David by mortgaging his home to provide the working capital the firm needed to survive. A large contract with Xerox turned the tide and David never looked back.

At some point, David recognized that he was doing work with CEOs and that it would make sense to position the firm as one that was focused exclusively on CEOs as clients. This raised the visibility of the brand, attracting clients and top talent. It also allowed Delta Consulting (the "Delta" was the Greek symbol for change) to charge premium prices for its services. Unlike McKinsey and other competitors, Delta did not use a leveraged model in which senior partners sold the work and junior partners carried out the projects. Delta hired senior partners exclusively, and the partners themselves did the work. A few projects would require teams of senior people to work together but the norm was for the work to be carried out by one or two partners, working very closely with the CEO client and sometimes the head of HR.

By the time I joined the firm in 1997, David had most things down to a science. I, along with my eight new-hire classmates that year, spent a full 6 weeks in New York learning the "Delta Way" at the firm's expense. Senior consultants took responsibility for sharing their experience with us, following a curriculum designed by David that covered the firms intellectual property, approach to consulting, the world of the CEO, various tools, technology, and the right colors and fonts to use in creating documents. While no one "flunked out," it was clear that the expectations we were to meet were very high. In return, we became members of an elite community that enjoyed challenging work, excellent pay and benefits, and four offsite events a year at five-star resorts where we spent time learning from and teaching one another.

The work covered a variety of topics. Organization design was a staple, based upon the congruence model and a detailed methodology outlined in *Competing by Design* (Nadler 1997). Succession planning, board effectiveness, change leadership, change communications, executive team effectiveness, and post-merger integration were also frequent assignments. Later, Delta purchased CDR, a firm founded by Peter Cairo, David Dotlich, and Steven Rhinesmith to get into the leadership development business.

Most of the consulting work started with in-depth interviews of the executives involved, often based on questions that David had framed around the congruence model. These data were analyzed according to a rigorous process that was the secret to Delta consulting's success. Part of the "Delta Way" was learning how to analyze and then construct a detailed feedback report that pulled no punches when it came to telling executives exactly what work needed to be done.

When I think of David's contributions to practice, they consist of a combination of the business model that Delta was built to deliver, the intellectual property that positioned the brand on the forefront of practice, maintaining the highest standards of quality in serving clients, and employing methodologies that combined rigor with down-to-earth practicality. Yes, the topics of feedback, change, organization design, and boards are the ones for which David is known; as with his writing, it was his systems perspective that made him the great leader and practitioner he was. The pieces were important, but the way in which he combined them was the "secret sauce."

Executives appreciated the all-senior trusted advisor model and the seemingly 24/7 availability of their consultants who worked on a project-retainer model rather than daily or hourly rates. The logic was simple and appealing: the highest-level expertise at premium rates, delivered through a confidential trusted advisor or small team. In the time I was there, while the name of the firm was rarely mentioned, we saw plenty of the results of our work appear prominently in the Wall Street Journal. David was thrilled to see his picture included on the cover of Business Week among a short list of other consulting gurus. It was external validation of what we all knew to be true.

New Insights: Disruptive Change

As David's brother Mark noted, David had a knack for seeing what was important to executives and connecting the dots. He was constantly drawing upon his early thinking and later experience to offer new thoughts. He did not stand still but rather kept exploring new topics and challenges. Part of his personal brand was remaining in tune with business developments, always ready to offer a fresh perspective and provocative insights.

There are far too many things one could learn from working with David to record here. Some of these things are carved into my memory – the congruence model, strategic organizational design, and the CEO succession process – and others have simply become part of my scholar-practitioner DNA, no longer observations of David but part of who I am. For the moment, I will focus on his work on the topic of disruptive change.

Around 1997, David became concerned with helping leaders understand that not all changes were equal. Some changes were more far reaching and complex than others. Therefore, he argued, a different approach was needed for disruptive change as compared with more limited or straightforward change. This approach called for more direct sponsorship by the CEO, the creation of change structures to guide the transition and ultimately, fundamental changes to the organization's design. Little did David know in 1997 that disruptive change would move from the exception to the norm 20 years later. Yet even in 1999, he and Michael Tushman (Nadler and Tushman 1999) wrote about organizations of the future and the core competencies that would be needed for the twenty-first century. How on target were they with their projections?

Here are the major trends that they observed: (1) the effects of globalization, including increased competition and access to markets; (2) fully entering the information age; (3) the shift from manufacturing to knowledge work in the postindustrial economy; (4) continuous innovation and more rapid change; and (5) the fragmentation of consumer and business markets into specialized groups (mass customization). So far so good. Then, as a result of these trends, Nadler and Tushman called out six strategic imperatives:

1. Increasing strategic clock speed
2. Creating a business portfolio that contains varied business models
3. Abbreviated strategic life cycles
4. Go to market flexibility
5. Enhanced competitive innovation, including skills in innovating in strategy and organization design
6. Managing intra-enterprise cannibalism (replacing existing products with new ones)

These imperatives would require that organizations increase their strategic clock speed, adopt a variety of business designs simultaneously, focus on the right number of critical linkages to other organizations, accelerate the organizational design process, open up hybrid distribution channels, and construct conflict management processes. Although Nadler and Tushman could not fully appreciate the digital revolution that was yet to come, their precognition was not far off.

Today, the word "disruption" is included in almost every discussion of business trends or strategy. Clayton Christenson's work on *The Innovator's Dilemma* (1997) helped us understand that large, successful organizations are the least likely to disrupt their industry; rather, smaller, more nimble firms with little to lose are the ones that will push radically new products and solutions. Michael Tushman and Charles O'Reilly described the "ambidextrous" organization in their book, *Winning at Innovation* (2002), and more recently updated their thinking to address leading through disruption (O'Reilly and Tushman 2016). The number of books and articles on disruption is growing at an exponential pace. It is clear that disruption has caught our attention and will be with us as a topic of study and applied practice for some time to come.

Disruption is a topic that is keeping executives up at night and certainly would have been something that David would have addressed. In keeping with my learning from him that it makes more sense to study things that are important to leaders than ideas that are academically appealing but of little interest to CEOs, my own work on disruptive change has taken me on a learning journey. While I have always been a student of change, I think David was right about disruptive change being different. In my latest book, *Leading Continuous Change* (2015), I explore how models that have been helpful in leading single changes have broken down under the pressure of complex, continuous change. Currently, I am learning all I can about what is happening with disruptive change in Silicon Valley as well as its impact on organizations everywhere.

So far, I have come to understand that different kinds of disruption are taking place. Like David's thinking back in 1997 that all changes are not the same, I am seeing differences in the source of disruptions and in responses to them. Disruptions that are caused by technological innovation are different than disruptions caused by new business models, new organizational configurations, generational shifts, climate change, and global competition. These changes require different responses, although each type of change is still inherently disruptive, meaning that incremental adjustments will fall short of responding to the challenges or opportunities they present. Business model disruptions require shifting resources from previously successful but soon to be extinct products and services to something new and largely untested. Technical disruptions will demand new talent or new alliances to acquire expertise that can help frame technical opportunities. Organizational design disruption will force consideration of shifting leadership patterns, power distribution, and organizational culture. Since each of these disruptions involve radically different ways of working, all of the elements in the center portion of the congruence model will need to change and then realign with one another. This degree of change is rare and often unsuccessful as leaders find it difficult to throw out what is known in favor of what is unfamiliar. The fact that the people resisting the change may not be the right people to lead through the disruption is why the CEO's personal involvement is critical. Those with power will use it to hold for as long as they can if they feel threatened. CEOs need to understand this and make the tough calls regarding how to proceed in the face of this resistance. Responding to disruptive change is inherently risky. Disruptive change evokes extremely powerful politics and emotions, inside and outside the organization. Few CEOs and their senior teams are aware of what is truly required of them to lead through disruptive change.

When several disruptive forces converge and change becomes complex and continuous, extraordinary leadership is required to lead change of the magnitude that is required. The first thing that is needed is an openness to question the status quo. Options need to be explored and learning will be required. Design thinking and continuous rather than periodic strategy-making should be adopted in the face of uncertainty.

As new alliances and partnerships are formed, the importance of work outside the formal organization takes on increasing significance. To access expertise, a "staff on demand" model leveraging external talent may begin to replace the predominant full-time employment model. In this type of organization, leadership is very different; it has certainly less command and control and more influence by appeal to a common vision.

Thus, as we encounter disruptive change, we are exploring David's interests in leadership, change, and organization design. While the nature of the challenges have changed, the insights David offered continue to influence how we think and practice.

Legacies and Work Left Unfinished: Improving Boards

Near the end of his life, after retiring from his position at Marsh McLennan, David and his brother Mark created Nadler Advisory Services with a focus on CEOs and Boards. They were able to acquire the intellectual capital that had been created over the years at Delta Consulting from Marsh McLennan and continued to add to it. It was clear that David intended to stay on course for the remainder of his career. The wheel of the ship was firmly connected to the rudder.

Had David survived, the issues that we continue to see in the failures of boards to fulfill their oversight responsibilities would have attracted his attention. His interest in organizational design would have been peaked by the discussions that are occurring around organizations of the future, whether they be teal Laloux (2015) or holacracies (Robertson 2015), or something else. His love of technology would have drawn him into advising executives about our digital future and its implications for enterprise strategies, transformation, talent, and design. Wherever he went next, the congruence model and data feedback would have followed along. A stable core would provide the launching pad for continued exploration of the unknown.

References

Christensen, C. (1997). *The innovator's dilemma: When new technologies cause great firms to fail.* Boston: Harvard Business Review Press.

Laloux, F. (2015). *Reinventing organizations: A guide to creating organizations inspired by the next stage of human consciousness*. Brussels: Nelson Parker.

O'Reilly, C., & Tushman, M. (2016). *Lead and disrupt: How to solve the innovator's dilemma*. Stanford: Stanford University Press.

Pasmore, W. (2015). *Leading continuous change: Navigating churn in the real world.* Oakland: Berrett -Koehler.

Robertson, B. J. (2015). *Holacracy: The new management system for a rapidly changing world.* New York: Macmillan.

Tushman, M. L., & O'Reilly, C. A. (2002). *Winning through innovations*. Boston: Harvard Business School Publishing Corporation.

Further Reading

Conger, J. A., & Nadler, D. A. (2004). When CEOs step up to fail. *MIT Sloan Management Review, 45*(3), 50.

Hambrick, D. C., Nadler, D. A., & Tushman, M. L. (1997). *Navigating change: How CEOs, top teams and boards steer transformation*. Cambridge, MA: Harvard Business Press.

Katz, D., & Kahn, R. L. (1966). *The social psychology of organizations*. New York: Wiley.

Lawler, E. E., Nadler, D., & Cammann, C. (1980). *Organizational assessment: Perspectives on the measurement of organizational behavior and the quality of work life*. New York: Wiley.

Lawrence, P. R., & Lorsch, J. W. (1967). *Organization and environment: Managing differentiation and integration*. Cambridge, MA: Harvard University Press.

Levinson, H., Molinari, J., & Spohn, A. G. (1972). *Organizational diagnosis*. Cambridge, MA: Harvard University Press.

Lorsch, J., & McTague, E. (2016). Culture is not the culprit. *Harvard Business Review*, April, 2016.

Nadler, D. A. (1977). *Feedback and organization development: Using databased methods*. Boston: Addison-Wesley Longman.
Nadler, D. A. (1997). *Champions of change: How CEOs and their companies are mastering the skills of radical change*. San Francisco: Jossey-Bass.
Nadler, D. A. (2004a). Building better boards. *Harvard Business Review, 82*(5), 102–105.
Nadler, D. A. (2004b). What's the board's role in strategy development?: Engaging the board in corporate strategy. *Strategy & Leadership, 32*(5), 25–33.
Nadler, D. A. (2007). The CEO's second act. *Harvard Business Review, 85*(1), 66–72.
Nadler, D. A., & Lawler, E. E. (1983). Quality of work life: Perspectives and directions. *Organizational Dynamics, 11*(3), 20–30.
Nadler, D. A., & Spencer, J. (1998). *Leading executive teams*. San Francisco: Jossey-Bass.
Nadler, D. A., & Tushman, M. L. (1977). *A congruence model for diagnosing organizational behavior*. New York: Columbia University, Graduate School of Business.
Nadler, D. A., & Tushman, M. L. (1980). A model for diagnosing organizational behavior. *Organizational Dynamics, 9*(2), 35–51.
Nadler, D. A., & Tushman, M. L. (1988). *Strategic organization design: Concepts, tools & processes*. Glenview: Scott Foresman & Co..
Nadler, D. A., & Tushman, M. L. (1989). Organizational frame bending: Principles for managing reorientation. *The Academy of Management Executive, 3*(3), 194–204.
Nadler, D. A., & Tushman, M. L. (1990). Beyond the charismatic leader: Leadership and organizational change. *California Management Review, 32*(2), 77–97.
Nadler, D. A., & Tushman, M. L. (1997). *Competing by design: The power of organizational architecture*. Oxford: Oxford University Press.
Nadler, D. A., & Tushman, M. L. (1999). The organization of the future: Strategic imperatives and core competencies for the 21st century. *Organizational Dynamics, 28*(1), 45–60.
Nadler, D. A., Tushman, M. L., & Hatvany, N. G. (1982). *Managing organizations: Readings and cases*. Boston: Little, Brown and Company.
Nadler, D. A., Gerstein, M. S., & Shaw, R. B. (1992). *Organizational architecture: Designs for changing organizations*. San Francisco: Jossey-Bass.
Nadler, D. A., Shaw, R. B., & Walton, A. E. (1995). *Discontinuous change: Leading organizational transformation*. San Francisco: Jossey-Bass.
Nadler, D. A., Behan, B. A., & Nadler, M. B. (Eds.). (2011). *Building better boards: A blueprint for effective governance*. New York: Wiley.
Tushman, M. L., & Nadler, D. A. (1986). Organizing for innovation. *California Management Review, 28*(3), 74–92.

Jean E. Neumann: The Consultant's Consultant, Working Through Complexity in Organizational Development and Change

57

Francesca Falcone

Abstract

Jean Neumann is senior fellow in scholarly practice at The Tavistock Institute of Human Relations (TIHR), London. She works as both a practitioner and academic in the field of organizational change and development and provides professional advice and development to managers, leaders, consultants, and other organizational change practitioners. Her work is focused on integrating theory and practice to develop more realistic and sensible approaches to the organizational change. While the academy is still accustomed to split theory and practice, research, and action, Jean Neumann's contribution stresses the intimate and profound connection between them; as she demonstrates through her consultancy practice, it is not enough to try to explain things (as the traditional research methods do); the challenge is also to try to change them within a process of understanding and inquiry that involves all members of a given social system. In this sense, her (systemic) consultancy model for organizational change and development offers a learning architecture for a change process that challenges complex issues and supports participative solutions to entrenched problems enabling people to work with uncertainty.

Keywords

Action research • Organizational change and development • Consultancy relationship • Scholarly practice • Stakeholders involvement

F. Falcone (✉)
Department of Political and Social Sciences, University of Calabria, Arcavacata di Rende, Italy
e-mail: francesca.falcone@unical.it

D.B. Szabla et al. (eds.), *The Palgrave Handbook of Organizational Change Thinkers*,
DOI 10.1007/978-3-319-52878-6_51

Contents

Introduction

One of the most important changes in thinking organizational change in the last years has been the gradual acknowledgment of the importance of participative and bottom-up driven approaches with an emphasis on "processes."

The literature on organizational change is dominated by two conflicting approaches, the planned and emergent change approach (Burnes 1996). The planned change approach was initiated by Lewin who developed his general framework for understanding the process of organizational change at level of behavior change. Even though it was criticized, a significant number of scholars still continue to consider it a useful reference for promoting and supporting change; they tried to develop his work in an attempt to make it more practical specially looking at the role of change agent (Lippitt et al. 1958; Bullock and Batten 1985; Schein 1964, 1969).

Jean Neumann is one of those scholars and practitioners who was interested to Lewin's legacies, the cornerstone of the TIHR's tradition. She searched and wrote on the practical application of his principles for carrying out action research and, at the same time, for supporting scholarly practitioners and organizational consultants to expand the perspective from which they engage with their client system. These lewinian principles seem to echo with the emergent approach to organizational change – of which complexity theory is undoubtedly a conceptual evolution. This is the critical link which marks her approach. Jean's consultancy work interrelates the planned and emergent approaches, and doing so recomposes the debate showing how is possible to consult with such "dualities." She is aware that (a) change is a continuous and open-ended process of adaptation whose premise is the uncertainty and the complexity of the external and internal environment, (b) it is no more an hetero-directed but a self-directed process that emerges through the involvement and commitment of the various stakeholders, (c) and the consultant is an expert of the organizational processes and can help the client to develop diagnostic and intervention skills.

Her consultancy approach emphasizes participation, aims for organizational awareness and of the wider context, encourages empowerment process, and allows the experimentation of new intervention methodologies and organizational modalities. In other words, by supporting capacity building and providing "space" and "time" for reflection, Jean's approach is in its essence a learning process. Because the aim is to allow and make accessible "space for experimentation" through the involvement of all peripheries of the system (from "top-slice" to "whole system"), her "cycle of planned change" for organizational change and development can be understood as a support and "containment" process to enable the system the transition from the present to the future.

Much of Jean's seminal work is dedicated to integration: between theory and practice, organizational theory and psychodynamic, and organizational theory, system psychodynamics, and consultancy competences. A such integration echoes her specific intellectual and professional "tension" toward the development of the ability to work "across categories" that is the real challenge of the advanced organizational consultant.

This chapter will discuss her professional background looking at those influences and motivations that have shaped her theories, researchers, and practices in the field of organizational change and development, her specific contributions to the development of organizational change theory and practice, and her major intellectual legacy. One section, in particular, will be focused on the intellectual and inspirational impact of her work on the conceptualization of the organizational development and change approach, consultancy work, and organizational consultant's advanced competences.

Influences and Motivations. "How Can Human and Social System Change?" Professional Evolution Between Epistemic Issues and Consultancy Commitment

Jean Neumann works as an organizational development and change consultant, researcher, and educator. She entered the field of organizational development and change through the discipline of adult development and educational psychology in 1976. She graduated from the Union for Experimenting Colleges and Universities (a federal social experiment designed to encourage adult learners into postsecondary study, based in Ohio at the time) with a bachelor's degree in educational sociology and psychology. She later went on to achieve a master's degree in adult education, psychology, and learning theory from the University of Rhode Island in Kingston, Rhode Island. This first university experience played a profound role in Jean's vocational education. As an undergraduate student within the experimental "university without walls" program (a government program), she also worked as a registrar in the university management center where she became familiar with the sociopsychological challenges of flattened hierarchies and consensual decision-making. Positively influenced by that experience, she became inclined to learn more in order to develop herself professionally. For that purpose, she attended several residential workshops (associated with NTL Institute), the first of which was titled "Educational Design and Program Planning," which combined group processes and experiential learning. These experiences were so enlightening for her that she chose to write her undergraduate dissertation on "Facilitating self-direction in adult learners."

Thus Jean was also introduced to organizational development and change (OD&C) techniques. From her point of view, the educational design process, combined with other applied behavioral science, was a ground on which to build advanced competences in data feedback and planning, team building, problem-solving, and short-term OD&C interventions. The master's degree in adult development and education provided her a broader and deeper theoretical and practical base for OD&C. By extending and improving her knowledge and competences, Jean identified a connection between professional development and academic studies. After receiving her MA, she worked as part-time internal change agent for the Rhode Island Office of Higher Education, addressing issues of motivation and cooperation within community organizations, universities, and government agencies with the purpose of implementing social policy.

In 1982 Jean Neumann started a PhD program in Organizational Behavior at Case Western Reserve University in Ohio to improve her practice competence. After nearly 5 years of extensive and broad study, she emerged with an enhanced understanding of theories and methodologies underlying OD&C. During her doctoral studies, theories of open system and organizational design expanded her awareness of strategic change. Neumann was influenced greatly by three authors: Chin and Benne and their article on strategies for changing human systems, Kolb and Frohman and their contribution on the cycle of planned change, and Argyris and his three directions for professional diagnosis.

The central question at the core of her reflection on her consulting experience is "how can human and social system change?" She found that such systems can be understood and changed only through the participation and commitment of the people involved in the process of learning and change. From here, she was thrilled at the idea of change as a reeducative process (concept already present in Lewin's ideas, but rarely acknowledged) and her preference for action research as a strategy for changing.

Lewin saw a strong connection between action research and reeducation. He considered action, research, and training a triangle solidly unified and the participation as a way through which people can learn to plan and evaluate strategic action (Peters and Robinson 1984). Although Lewin has not explicitly talked about action research in terms of reeducation, in the essay "Forces behind food habits and methods of change" (1943), it is quite evident that his action research, whose goal was exploring and supporting ways through which people change their eating habits, has been a reeducation process itself: the result of this experiment led Lewin to state that people change when they develop a need for change (unfreezing), when they try to move toward the new values and behaviors (moving), and when they stabilize and solidify that new behaviors as the norm (refreezing). As Coghlan and Jacobs (2005) state, the Lewin's work on reeducation has received little attention even if "(...)

much of what he understood to be central to the complex process of reeducation is critical to the process of change and underlies the philosophical principles and practice of action research (p. 444)." Going back to this paper, they explore the ten general observations about the process of reeducation in order to demonstrate the profound transformational meaning of the action research process that Lewin had in mind.

In her approach to OC&D, Jean Neumann refers to Chin and Benne's chapter "General Strategies of Effecting Changes in Human Systems" (1969), in "The Planning of Change" (Bennis et al. 1985) which is for her one of the best contributions that helps organizational consultants conceptualize both the philosophical assumptions and the actual practices of the change process. Their work systematizes several approaches to organizational change into a theoretical and conceptual framework which helps to identify three main strategies for changing (Fig. 1).

While the empirical-rational strategy is prescriptive and focused on rational solutions to problems and the power-coercive strategy seeks to accumulate and maintain political and economic power behind the change objectives, the normative-reeducative strategy is diagnostic, so based on collaborative learning solutions that, in facilitating the process of change, result in (Chine and Benne 1969, p. 32):

- A dialogical relationship between client and consultant.
- The consultant's awareness that the client's problem cannot be defined a priori and unilaterally or solved through a technical intervention; it requires a psychosocial approach that facilitates cognitive and perceptive change.
- The necessary collaboration between client and consultant in defining and solving the client's problem as a basis for diagnosis and intervention.

The assertion of Chin and Benne that OD&C can be understood as a "normative-reeducative strategy" for changing human systems was for Jean meaningful for its

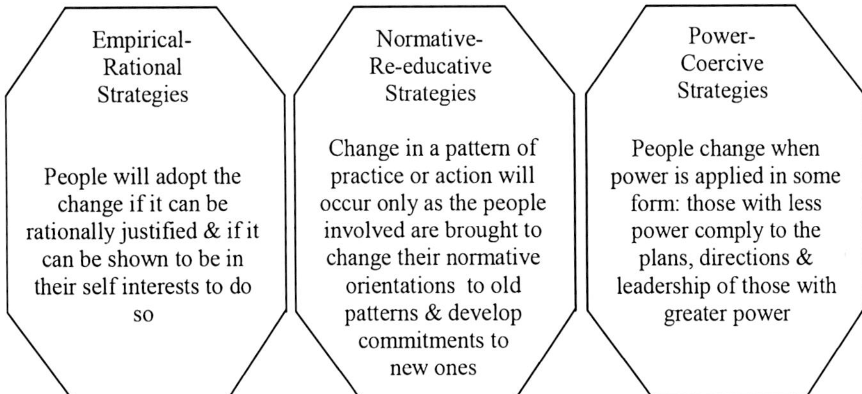

Fig. 1 Three strategies for change (Chin and Benne 1969, in Neumann 2013c)

emphasis on experience-based learning as an ingredient of enduring changes in human systems. Through this reading she felt that "learning for progress" (Neumann 2016) could be a methodology in OD&C practices. Some years later, her "Advanced Organizational Consultancy" program at the Tavistock Institute (which was a practice-based program) became the vehicle through which the principle "learning together for progress" (Ibid., p. 111) was enacted within practical scholarship for organizational consulting.

Jean Neumann's initial OD&C training was focused on the concepts of "contracting," "intervention," and "evaluation" as main phases of a "cycle of planned change" (the beginning, the middle, and the ending of the intervention) without any degree of awareness about other phases of the cycle as "scouting," "entry," and "mutual negotiation of intervention." In the same way, she did not ground her consultancy practice on a well-established diagnosis technique; the short duration of her initial consultancy work (one entire cycle of organizational development) required a small diagnosis aimed to a general understanding on how to proceed in the process of OD&C.

As the consultancy process became more complex with project work that required two or three rounds of the OD cycle, she felt that her OD&C techniques needed to be revisited and reinforced. She read a paper written by Kolb and Frohman on "An Organization Development Approach to Consulting" (1970) in the Sloan Management Review which still represents one the most accredited models in the field of organizational development.

Their model is focused on two important and interrelated issues: the relationship between client and consultant and the nature of the consultancy work through seven stages (scouting, entry, diagnosis, planning, action, evaluation, termination).

This OD&C approach and methodology was enlightening for Jean as it offered her a progressive approach to interacting with an organizational client and enabled a virtuous cycle where the professional application of theory was connected to practice. She found the "cycle of planned change" particularly useful in conceptualizing the first two stages (scouting and entry), and some aspects of the third (diagnosis), as constitutive of the early stages of crossing boundaries and building relationship with a client system (Neumann 1994). It must be said that for Kolb and Frohman in the phase "entry" "contracting" is implied. They maintain: "Once the entry point has been selected, the consultant and the client system, through the entry representative, begin to negotiate a contract. In its use here, the word "contract" implies more than a legal document agreed upon at the outset of the project" (1970, p. 55). In Neumann's terms, "crossing boundaries" means stepping across the geographical and social boundaries that constitute the organization and "building a working relationship" with the client that requires a negotiation about a formal agreement to work together and an informal one aimed to negotiate the role of both consultant and client to explore meanings and concepts that make sense of the situation (Neumann 1997). Having the entire cycle in mind, she learned to handle scouting, entry, and contracting in a way that diagnosis is the outcome, followed by a "mutual negotiation of intervention" which is an integral part of the intervention and as such needs to be faced at each round of OD&C (Neumann 2016).

Going back to the phase of diagnosis, during her OD&C training, Jean Neumann learned some techniques of data gathering drawing on the educational design process from both adult learning theory and practitioner books on data feedback and planning as alternative approaches for diagnosis. In this time span, she became more sensitive to the ethical dimension of data feedback and the reporting process. Reading Argyris on practical and ethical standards for applying theory was a further inspiration. She accepted Argyris' three conditions for professional diagnosis (1970) which form an integral part of any intervention activity. Making change in human system with integrity for Jean means (Argyris 1970, pp. 15–20; Neumann 2013c):

- *Generating valid and useful information*. Valid information describes factors and their interrelationship that create the problem for the client system. It is based on a diagnosis that represents the total client system and not the point of view of any subsystem and it includes variables that can be influenced by clients for effective change to follow.
- *Guaranteeing free and informed choice.* To have free choice, the client has to clarify a cognitive map of what he or she wishes to do. Free and informed choice implies voluntary and proactive decision-making by the client through a process of selection of alternative actions. In such a way, decision-making is placed in the client system which is responsible for any agreed upon choices of action.
- *Supporting internal commitment to the choice made.* The client's internal commitment to the choice and action (of change) has to be enduring and strong to be internalized by each member so that they feel the responsibility of the choice and its implications.

Two additional essential sources of knowledge and skills in Neumann's professional evolution were the Tavistock Group Relation Conference and the National Training Laboratory (NTL) program for OD&C specialists. Group Relation was a new and an unusual experience in which she felt to be in a "foreign land" (Neumann 2016, p. 117) where nothing seemed to be familiar and nothing made sense for her in the "here and now." What she experienced in the Group Relation event was how psychodynamics is applied to groups and organizations and concepts such as power, authority, leadership, boundaries, social differences, compliance, and resistances. Although at the beginning she was very confused about the methods used, she started to make sense of boundaries and authority relations and developed an intellectual and practical capability to use this approach, integrating it with socio-technical system theory in her consultancy work. In particular, she was able to identify the points where these two Tavistock Institute literature traditions can be used together in the wider OD&C process – the diagnosis, the design, and the delivery of cross-boundary interventions (Ibid., p. 118).

Focusing on power and influence during the change process and combining theoretical inputs with experiential learning, the NTL program was enlightening and reinforced Jean's notion of experiential learning. It gave her useful insights for the comprehension of the interconnections between different levels of analysis and for facing issues that may have an influence on the individual's capacity to participate effectively in the process of change (Ibid., p. 116). In London, Jean Neumann attended the Leicester Conference on authority relations and organizational behavior, where she expanded her awareness on the connection between psychological phenomena and political dynamics and sensed the power and influence of organizational culture during each stage of the change process (Ibid., p. 116).

As participant and staff member for the Group Relation Conference, she became even more aware of the literature and practices of applied psychodynamics. Jean began to work with categories and processes of system psychodynamics in her OD&C practice combining them with the socio-technical system theory. Thinking specifically at the issues characteristic of the initial stages of crossing organizational boundaries and building a working relationship, she states "there is no theory better than psychoanalysis applied to groups and organizations to help illuminate messy, stuck relationship. And, finally, organizational theory and sociology which explain resistance to organizational change strike me as a necessary piece to this puzzle" (Neumann 1994, p. 15). In her opinion, psychodynamic theory applied to social systems helps to understand "difficulties" and "confrontations" produced by unconscious reasons that explain messy dynamics between consultant and client (Ibid., p. 20).

The tension toward the integration between organizational theory and system psychodynamics even in practice pushed Jean Neumann to conceptualize a practical conceptual framework. With the "Advanced Organisational Consultation" (AOC) program within the Tavistock Institute, her challenge was to bring the Tavistock Institute of Human Relation School of thought together with the NTL Institute's practice theory and other contemporary organizational studies (Fig. 2).

The discussion of her background suggests how Jean professional development has been characterized by increasing degrees of theoretical and methodological complexity and highlights three ethical and professional "tensions" as invariable constants of her work: an authentic interest for integrating action research and human

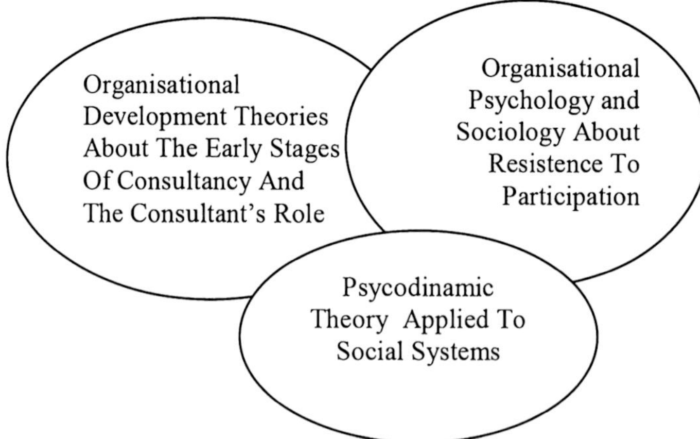

Fig. 2 Accumulated knowledge of logical relevance to difficult beginnings (Neumann 1994, p. 16)

system change, a preoccupation with the integration between theory and practice for more realistic and consistent approaches to organizational development and change, and a continuous commitment in a process of learning where challenging practice, reflecting and writing on the own professional experience, and going back and forth between theory and practice are an essential attitude to became an "advanced" consultant.

In the next session, Jean's key contributions will be presented and discussed in order to understand the essence of her work which consists in innovative and useful theoretical advancements in the field of organizational development and change and innovative and practical methodological approaches for the consultancy work.

Key Contributions. Integrating Conceptual and Practice Domain

Jean Neumann has made some very important practical and theoretical contributions to organizational change and development. Four interconnected aspects of her research and development can be specifically useful to organizational consultants and change managers:

1. Participation as a technique in order to reduce resistance to organizational change
2. The (reinterpreted) employment of the "Cycle for Planned Change" as a container to work with action research
3. The relevance of integrating psychodynamics and organizational theory in the early stages of the consultancy work
4. Education of the organizational consultant as a scholarly practitioner

Why People Do Not Participate in Organizational Change

Participation has always played an important role in Neumann's work, both as a subject of inquiry and a method of working. She defines participation as a "process-of-choice for overcoming resistance to change" and a "goal of the change effort in itself" (Neumann 1989, p. 182).

Although participation is considered essential for the development of human systems, and the willingness to participate is taken for granted, Jean notices that very often people chose not to participate in the processes of change. Her contribution is focused on nonparticipation, which has preeminently been explained in terms of personality study. Researches on organizational change and employee participation have assumed that the act of nonparticipation stems from some lack in the individual, denying the complexity of the participative behavior.

Influenced by Kurt Lewin's formula, which states that behavior is the result of the dynamic interaction between personality and environment, Jean challenges the historical emphasis on personality and shifts her focus to the working environment in order to understand why people choose not to participate in decision-making processes. She identifies three categories of explanations that are structural, relational, and social explanations. Structural explanations comprise organizational design, work design, and human resources management. These factors refer to "predetermined systems which shape human behavior by requiring specific socio-technical boundaries, flows of information, connections between subsystems, sanctions for activities, and strategies for motivation" (Neumann 1994, p. 24). From this point of view, Jean demonstrated that people do not participate in the process of change when (Neumann 1989, pp. 185–190):

- *Real decisions are made outside participative fora.* Most participative scheme runs parallel to the decision-making process of the organization. In these parallel processes, significant choices about strategy, organizing mode, and individuals are made. They represent the solution for managers or organizational leaders to deal with controversial issues via less formal political channels, bringing decisions to channels of formal participation simply for ratification (Ibid., p. 186).
- *The task does not require participation.* It can be said that when an invitation to participate appears to be legitimate or relevant for the nature of the individual's task, the individual perceives that participation as more effective. However, highly repetitive tasks tend to discourage people to be involved in decision-making process; they know that due to the nature of their task, their participation is not relevant. In case like this, an invitation to influence could meet disinterest (Ibid., p. 188).
- *Participation is not reinforced through mechanisms of human resources management conveying the fundamental norms of organization*, i.e., required behavior.

Relational explanations for nonparticipation include the management of participation, the dynamics of hierarchy, and the individual's stance toward organization. These factors refer to "relationship between individuals and groups which pose contradictions and dilemmas by introducing emotionally laden issues" (Neumann 1994, p. 24). From this point of view, people are less willing to participate when (Neumann 1989, pp. 191–196):

- *Participation is managed in a ways that discourage participative competences.* A participative scheme is defined by (a) properties (degree of formality, degree of directness, access to participation, content of decisions, and social range of participators), (b) organization's "participation potential" (values, assumptions, and goals of those who implement the participative scheme), and (c) dilemmas in managing participative scheme (dilemmas about beginning, procedures and rules, choice of issues, team work, connections between participative fora and the rest of organization). These factors shape the structure of the participative decision-making, and the ways through which that structure will be managed will encourage or discourage to participate (Ibid., pp. 191–192).
- *Rank and status are more important than competence at task and role.* Here the starting point is hierarchy as a dysfunctional approach to organizing authority and participative decision-making as a corrective to its (negative) dynamics – i.e., competition and conflict among organizational members. Successful

implementation of participative decision-making implies changes of hierarchy, but feelings and conflicts generated by hierarchy may block its successful implementation. Participation and hierarchy have to do with issues of authority in organization, but they differ in the way they conceive it; the former grounds the authority on competence, the latter defines authority as based on position and sees the competence as a threat for the organization. The hierarchical assumptions are so profoundly embedded in organizational life that any little progress toward participation provokes resistance. In a such situation where rank and status matter more than competences, it is more likely that individuals tend to disregard participation unless they are sure they can improve their rank and status through participation (Ibid., pp. 192–194).
- *Participation conflicts with nonwork role and need.*

Social explanations consist in primary and secondary socialization, ideology of work, and the social history of politics. These factors "exist prior to and outside the boundaries of a specific enterprise. They impact on organizational life through a steady, sometimes imperceptible influence on the individuals who make up the workforce. This cluster of explanation captures how individuals make sense of the structure and relationship in an organization" (Neumann 1994, p. 24). According to Jean, people might resist participation when (Neumann 1989, pp. 196–201):

- *They have been socialized successfully to avoid behavior which threaten hierarchical authority.* The secondary socialization to which young members are subjected tends to constrain the expression of those personal capacities that represent a threat to hierarchical authority. This means that such process makes them more passive and dependent, and in doing so, it negatively affects the willingness to participate unless the individual was socialized for a level of stratification which usually involves making decision. The larger the number of people who have learned to operate successfully as subordinate, the bigger the resocialization task required to convince them to participate (Ibid., p. 197–198).
- *Participation challenges values and beliefs.* Ideology of work is made of beliefs and assumptions about organizing work. Sometimes organizational members hold conscious attitude and beliefs about work: how work should be organized, how members should behave, or what kind of reward should be given for the good work. Generally speaking, some profound aspects of ideology are not always conscious and expressed. As an integral part of the own culture and the culture of reference group, they are a way of life and have to do with "what is real and what ought to be." In this sense, every choice an individual makes has to be congruent with his belief system. The ideology of work is not different. Members very often experience participative schemes as serving managerial ideology or as challenging their own ideology of work. By using a participative scheme, members might experience a mismatch with their socialized ideology, and instead of seeing it as something of positive for them, they could see it as a manifestation of a managerial ideology to which they have to adapt. Although participative decision-making requires individual autonomy, certain types of ideology (such

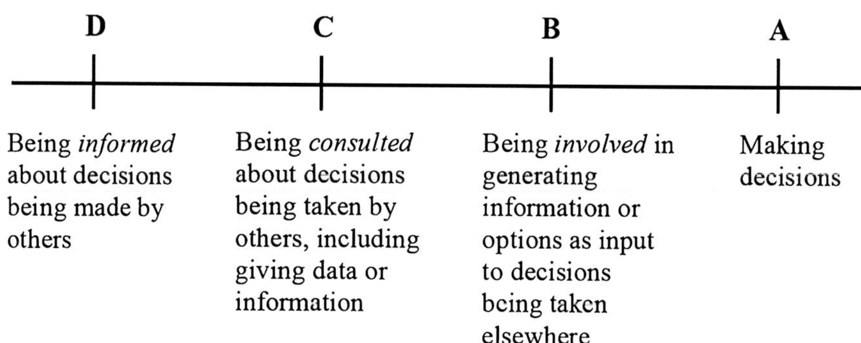

Fig. 3 A way to think about involvement and participation (Neumann 2000, p. 318)

as the dynamics of hierarchy) tend to support and reinforce not-autonomous stances. The decision to use participative scheme is usually made by top managers, so any kind of stance, not-autonomous or semiautonomous, is in its essence hierarchical. Hierarchy is a form of ideology and as such carries beliefs and assumptions perceived and experienced as natural, "the way things are." In this sense, ideology could increase or decrease willingness to participate (Ibid., p.198–199).

- *Adversarial politics, both in the past and present, have resulted in and continue to support protection of self and others.*

Later, Jean Neumann (2000) attributed two specific features to participation. Participation must be *genuine*: this means that managers, employees, or external stakeholders will be involved in the decision-making depending on the degree with which their participation will really produce changes (Ibid., p. 317).

The concept can be graphically summarized as follows (Fig. 3):

The range starts with a lower involvement (D), which is mere information about the decisions generally made by a person or a group at the higher level of the hierarchy. Slightly more managers and employees can be consulted about decisions taken by others (C) through the expression of some reactions to the proposal or mechanism for giving data or information. Active involvement (B) aims to generate information or make some proposals which will be used as input for the decision to be taken elsewhere. At the extreme of the continuum is the decision taken by people involved (A): their decision could be ratified at some other organizational level, but they have the power to decide.

According to Neumann, involvement is genuine if the level of participation of people corresponds to the real authority managers and staff have based on their hierarchical position. This is a critical point, since – as Neumann has demonstrated – one of the main reasons for which people do not participate in the process of change, despite having been given the possibility to, is that they perceive their participation will not be real and their opinion will not be taken into account.

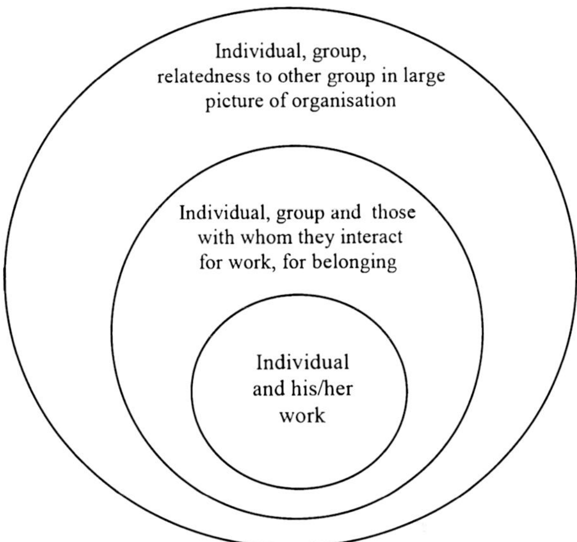

Fig. 4 Concentric circles of preferred involvement in contest issues (Neumann 2000, p. 319)

The second feature of participation is *appropriateness*. It refers to the degree of participation that makes sense according to the "content" of the decision and its effective pertinence for individuals and groups who are asked to participate (Ibid., p. 318). Jean Neumann considers that appropriateness develops on three levels, starting from individuals and their tasks up to the group and its issues (Fig. 4).

The definition of the issues and the identification of the potential solutions have an impact on individuals, and their tasks will probably be "areas" where individuals would like to have a say, so that such decisions are appropriate to specific areas of involvement. As a next step, working very close with other people, individuals develop a sense of concern for the group with which they work. Then, any change in the structure of the organization or in the models of interactions among individuals requires a significant degree of participation and involvement. As a final step, individuals desire appropriate participation when their position within the organization is affected by a specific decision. According to Jean, "position" does not just referred to occupational identities or status levels, but it can also include the "relatedness" (Miller 1990 – in Neumann 2000, p. 318) of groups to each other. In her opinion, some change decisions have an impact on relatedness, defined as "fantasies and projections that groups have about each other in a complex social system – those perceptions, feelings and opinions that are not necessarily based on face-to-face interaction but have to do with symbols and stories" (Ibid.). Because some issues connected to structural aspects of the organization can have implications for the relatedness affecting the individuals' morale, appropriate participation in a wider organizational perspective needs to be considered.

The Cycle of Planned Change in Organizational Development

Jean Neumann is one of the few authors who has expanded and deepened Kolb and Frohman's formulation (1970) of the seven basic stages of the "cycle of planned change." From her perspective "the cycle of planned change in organizational development" is the "container" where action research is implemented (Neumann 1997). Her model has a double goal, as Kurt Lewin stated: producing changes and developing knowledge within a reference context. In approaching action research, she has been influenced both by Lewin's assumptions, of which she evokes a reappraisal, and by the lessons of scholars and organizational consultants, such as Argyris, on the ethical-professional dimension and the operating modalities that facilitate and support changes in human systems.

As for the first point, Jean Neumann underlines that in the consulting practice, the principle-value of integrity drives the behavior of the consultant. In this case, integrity refers to professional reliability, fairness, and objectivity. All of these elements contribute to support the processes that the consultant should facilitate. In practical terms, she considers the three operational indications mentioned by Argyris – valid and useful information, free choice, and internal commitment – as indispensable tools for consultants aiming to give a professionally accurate diagnosis.

By making reference to Kolb and Frohman's model, Jean Neumann conceptualized a first model of planned change in organizational development (1997) made of six stages (scouting, entry and contracting, diagnosis, planning and negotiating interventions, taking action, evaluation), each of which has a set of activities that need to be undertaken by the client and consultant (Fig. 5).

The figure shows the cycle readapted from Kolb and Frohman's model adding two possible options: the termination of the consultancy relationship or the start of another iteration of the consultancy process as a result of the evaluation phase (Ibid., p. 10).

More recently, through a reflection on her consultancy experience, she has gone into detail of her model in order to emphasize the principle of (internal and external stakeholders) participation and involvement (Neumann 2013c). In this deepening and expanding, Jean brings both nonlinear STS and project-based working to bear on the OD&C cycle (Fig. 6).

This model outlines the interactive and dynamic stages through which both consultant and clients experience their shared research and action processes. Such a cycle is both a *process* and a *product* of learning for both of them. The learning process stemming from the model generates working hypotheses that are always temporary and negotiable. Jean believes that the problem-setting and the framing of the work hypotheses are generated and shared within some "points of mutual adjustment" (the stars depicted in the cycle). There are points where consultant and client come together to make sense of the difficulties and the organizational situation. They can be metaphorically understood as "time" and "space" of "meaningful conversations" (Neumann 2013c) that emerge as a result of a continuous and shared learning process.

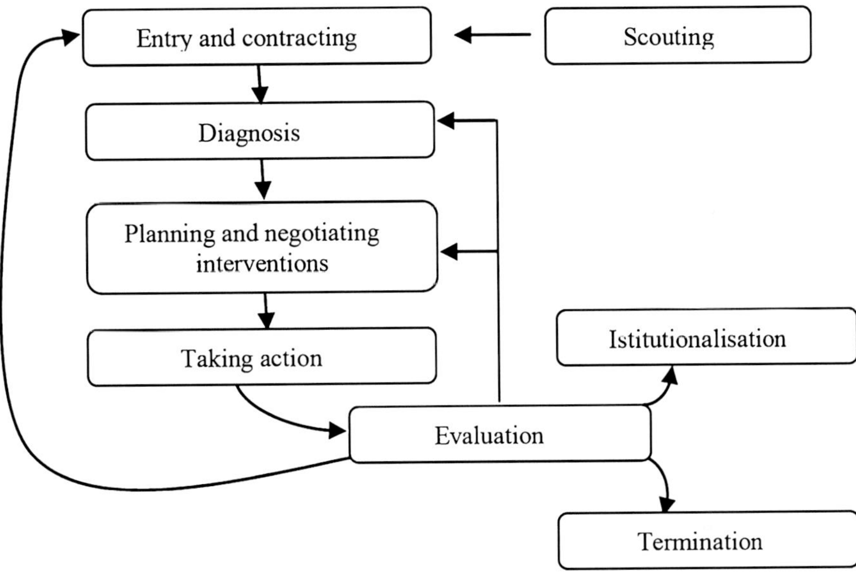

Fig. 5 The cycle of planned change in organizational development (Kolb and Frohman 1970) Adapted by Neumann 1997, p. 10

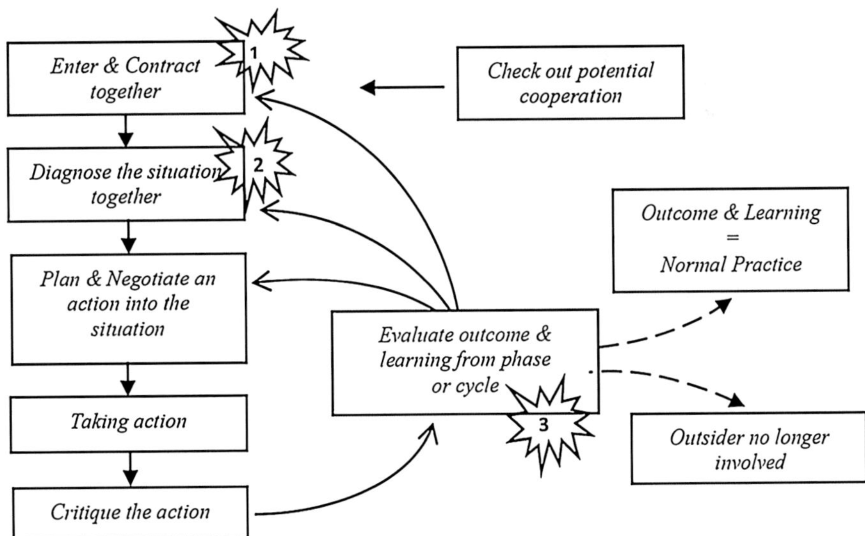

Fig. 6 A cycle of insiders and outsiders cooperating to plan and make changes with necessary points of mutual adjustment (Neumann 2013c)

In her approach, Jean bases the cycle of planned change on four of Kurt Lewin's principles/rules, which she has revised in order to make them practical and relevant for organizational consultants, who are facilitating and supporting the change processes (Neumann 2011a, b, 2012, 2013a).

The dynamic approach rule. Lewin's dynamic approach rule states that the "elements of any situation should be regarded as parts of a system" (Neumann 2011a). It implies a global approach and refers to the necessity of discovering multiple forces at work in each situation (Ibid.). According to Jean, when leading an organizational intervention, it is important to assume that all parts of the system as interrelated and forming a complex whole. For the organizational consultant, the challenge is understanding how these parts are connected with each other and how the nature of such interrelations affect the modalities through which a system reacts to changes.

The field theory rule. Lewin's field theory rule states that "analysis starts with the situation as a whole" (Neumann 2011b). It assumes that a person and his or her environment are closely related – "*one* constellation of interdependent factors" (Lewin 1946 – in Neumann 2011b). Drawing on Lewin, Jean Neumann clarifies that the concept of "field" includes all aspects of individuals in relationship with their surroundings and conditions that influence the behaviors and developments of concern at a particular time (Ibid.). In terms of an organizational intervention, Jean Neumann states that a representation of the field and of any forces at work in it is a worthy instrument of analysis for consultants, since such forces are able to facilitate or to slow down the process toward the goals of learning and changing.

The contemporaneity rule. Lewin asserted that "only conditions in the present can explain experience and behavior in the present" (Gold 1992 – in Neumann 2012). During an organizational change, this rule helps to understand the concrete elements within the time and field that may be influencing people in their environment (Ibid.) According to Neumann, the consultant should take into account the elements of the current situation (stay focused on the "here and now") that motivate people and their environment that make small steps of change possible.

The constructive method rule. According to this rule, the understanding of an organizational situation is possible by "making a proper translation from phenomena to concepts" through "the process of conceptualization" (Lewin 1997 – in Neumann 2013a). Jean asserts that the constructive method encourages the creation of the concepts necessary to explain a situation. The explanation and the conceptualization in itself provide a representation and a rich description of the total situation as it is experienced by the people involved (Ibid.). Conceptualization is the tool that allows consultants to formulate working hypotheses.

Jean Neumann has made a practical point and a diagnostic tip for each rule that can be useful for organizational consultants who are in the developmental steps of the change cycle (Neumann 2013b) (Table 1).

In particular, the first and the second rule, in conveying the concepts of "wholeness" and "interaction," introduce a precise working approach for the consultant, which Jean Neumann defines several times as "inclusive" (Neumann 2013b).

Table 1 Four principles for carrying out action research from Kurt Lewin (Neumann 2013b)

	Dynamic approach rule	Field theory rule	Contemporaneity rule	Constructive method rule
Lewin	*"All elements of any situation should be regarded as parts of the system"*	*"Analysis starts with the situation as a whole"*	*"Only conditions in the present can explain experience & behavior in the present"*	*"Create concepts however intangible, that seem necessary for explanation"*
Practice pointer	Describe the broad picture of group, inter-group, organizational and inter-organizational relationship that relate to issue under consideration	Keep in mind multiple causal conditions and interaction effects among causal elements	Identify what, within the present situation, contributes to behaviors and attitude held by clients; expressing empathy and understanding	Aim for useful conceptualization of the problem or challenge facing the client system
Diagnosis tip	Ask: *"What motivates this person or group to behave like this? From where is energy coming?"*	Ask: *"From whom or where does someone get a concern or help? Then what happens? To whom or where do they pass their work on next?"*	Ask:(in the face of historical stories) *"How does that show itself now and in what ways?"*	Ask: *"How are the environment and the people in this situation inseparably bound together?"*

For her, action research is a methodology that ultimately depends on individuals' participation and involvement. These elements underline the very democratic and empowering nature of this methodology, but also the specific feature of being able to better face the resistance to change that naturally emerges from the process.

Jean is the promoter of a systemic idea of change, where participation and involvement are considered as leading and unavoidable principles-values. The following is Jean's graphical representation of the process (Fig. 7):

The concentric circles indicate *who* should be involved in *which activities* in the starting, progression, and extension phases. The assumption is that the people involved in a specific circle should indicate, in turn, the people who should be gradually involved in a change. At any circle/level it is possible to proceed as follows:

- *Upward* (to a hierarchical and geographical level) and *outward* (horizontally toward departments or internal organizations or also toward powerful external stakeholders);

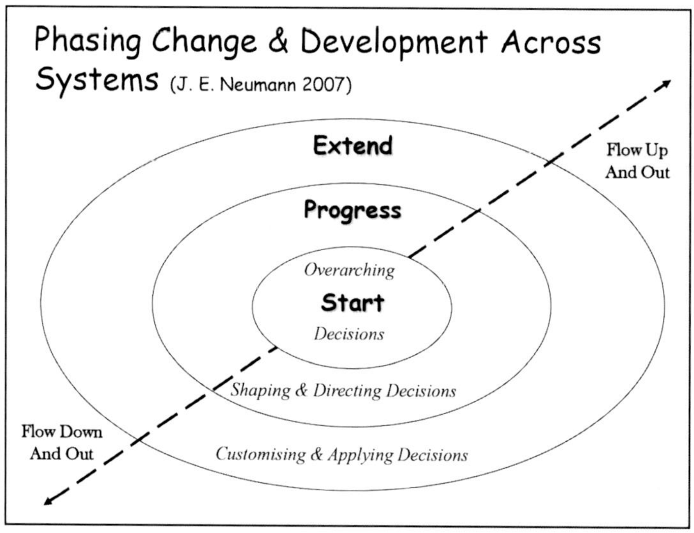

Fig. 7 The phasing model (Neumann and Sama 2009)

- *Downward* (toward usually excluded individuals) and *outward* (toward individuals whom the system refers to, such as clients, groups, and communities)

The practical implication of this "phasing model" is undoubted. It allows to "populate the space" (Neumann 2013c) identifying individual, groups, or organizations who ask to be heard and involved and that are usually excluded. The overall aim is to locate the stakeholders within each phase of the change process proceeding through multiple cycles where each interaction gets information from the previous one.

Conceptualizing Multiple Cycles

The cycle of planned change (in both versions – Figs. 4 and 5) describes an entire cycle of organizational development from the first contact with the client system to the end of the intervention. Jean asserts that, specially for short-term interventions, one single cycle is a rapid movement through the stages (Neumann 1997). She highlights a specific element in the cycle of change for organizational development – multiple and repeating cycles, one after the other, in a developmental and logical approach, where the end of each phase leads to knowledge and the new information instructs the next cycle. For this reason, consultants, besides supporting the relationships and decisions with the client at any phase of the process, must be able to conceptualize and develop multiple cycles through which change develops. Since the prerequisite is that the knowledge necessary to identify the problem and trigger changes is embedded in the organizational context and practice, conceptualizing, negotiating, and developing multiple cycles encourage "situated and outcropping" (Neumann 2013c) learning processes that support people in the discovery of original solutions to their organizational problem and foster the development of a "learning to learn" ability.

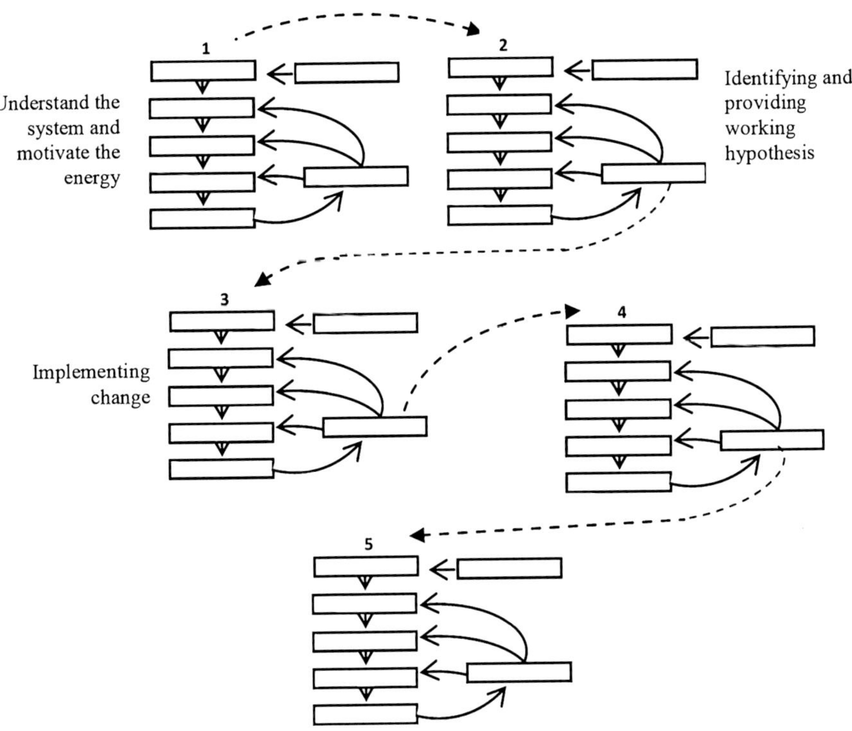

Fig. 8 Multiple iterations of action research (Neumann 2013c)

If the organizational change is seen within an incremental development perspective, few actions (of change) can be concluded within a single cycle. Jean Neumann asserts that it is necessary to conceptualize at least three cycles as part of the initial entry and contracting process (Ibid., p. 18). The first may generate significant learning for consultants since it allows them to understand how the system works (through what modalities and organizational processes) and to monitor the energy necessary to motivate people and the organization to change. The second may lead to the identification of some working hypotheses. Finally, the third cycle starts to implement (small) changes.

Therefore, after the first cycle, consultants should make sure that they have set the basis for the subsequent cycles of organizational development (Fig. 8).

The Relevance of Integrating Psychodynamics and Organizational Theory in the Early Stages of the Consultancy Work

Jean Neumann has paid much attention to the issue of integration between psychodynamics and organizational theory in relation to the "difficult beginnings" of a new consultancy relationship. Building a consultancy relationship requires a process of negotiation about the roles, phases, and activities of the change process. These negotiations, which can be a source of anxiety for both the consultant and client, certainly concern roles and responsibilities, but they also deal with crucial issues that have to do with the nature of authority and leadership in organizational change (Neumann 1994).

Scouting, entry, and contracting (with some elements of the diagnosis) constitute the initial stages of the consultancy process which often lead to difficulties and confrontations. Scouting is the phase in which the consultant decides whether to proceed with entry and contracting. To make this decision, the consultant needs to hear the presenting problem, identify the type of consultation requested, and assess the source of authorization of the client representative. If the decision is positive for both, an agreement needs to be reached in the next phase. The aim of entry and contracting is to negotiate a formal agreement to work together and an informal psychological contract of mutual needs and expectations (Neumann 1997).

As initial steps of crossing boundaries and building a working relationship, scouting, entry, and contracting are tricky phases in terms of expectations, roles, and responsibilities. Sometimes, despite formal and informal agreements that are reached, a renegotiation that takes the form of a confrontation may be necessary. Literature on organizational development consultancy addresses the client's expectation and identifies ways with which consultants and managers work together (Steele 1975; Block 1981 – in Neumann 1994). The attention and the amount of writing on such topics suggest that these early stages of the consultancy process provide the foundation on which these "difficult beginnings" may arise.

For Jean Neumann, the application of psychodynamic to the social system becomes the keystone to understand and identify the unconscious dynamics between consultant and client and try to work through them to advance the change. The concepts she finds relevant include task anxiety, individual and group defenses, transference, and countertransference (Neumann 1994).

One of the most important implications of the application of psychodynamic theory to the study of groups and organizations is the shift of attention from the individual to the group or organization as a whole. Lewin stated that the group to which the individual belongs is the ground on which his perceptions, ideas, and actions arise and develop. From such perspective, the individual acts not as an individual but as a member of the group. As Jean asserts, the group (and the group's behavior) has a pivotal role in shaping the individual's behavior because it is an important element in the working "life space" of the person (Ibid., p. 20). Since individuals search for a connection between their inner world and the organization to which they belong (Menzies Lyth 1989 – in Neumann 1994), Jean maintains that the result is an organization made of people with a strong tendency to join with others to create some socially structured defenses against shared feelings of threat (Ibid., p.20).

As Isabel Menzies Lyth demonstrated (1960; 1989), a group or an organization creates and enacts defense mechanisms when it is experiencing anxiety, fear, or uncertainty; they try to protect themselves by eliminating those situations, tasks, activities, and relationships that provoke, or evoke, anxiety. Following this seminal work, Neumann focuses her attention on the anxiety arising from the nature of the work. "Task anxiety can be understood as those policies, routines, structures and rituals which allow members to avoid fears, anxiety, doubt, guilt and uncertainty" (Neumann 1994, p. 21). It concerns the implementation of all those activities necessary for the primary task of the organization. If the group defends itself against this anxiety in a way that threatens its psychological survival, then its primary task is neglected.

Bion's definition of "basic assumption group" offers a useful interpretation to understand the socially created defenses between a group representing the client system and a consultant. The basic assumptions constitute "mental activities that have in common the attribute of powerful emotional drive" (Bion 1961 – in Neumann 1994, p. 21). Members of a group influenced by basic assumptions assume a common attitude toward the authority figure or consultant, "acting 'as if' such and such were the case" (Ibid., p. 22). The basic assumption group shares a joint fantasy of which the consultant needs to be aware.

An additional complex process at the beginning of the consultancy work is the interpersonal process of transference and countertransference that blocks and confuses the working relationship between client and consultant. As Jean points out, it is not unusual that the client, through a psychological unconscious process, transfers from the past to the present something of an unresolved experience (Ibid. p. 22). He or she can perceive and respond to the consultant "as if" the consultant were an important figure form the past – "an unconscious intrapsychic fantasy that distorts an individual's perceptions and interactions" (Kets de Vries and Miller 1984 – in Neumann 1994). The challenge for the consultant is not only to recognize this dynamic and the power of the transference but also to be aware of the countertransference, which is the same process from the consultant toward the client in reaction to the client projections (Ibid., p. 23).

Even individual defenses can come into play. According to Neumann, they are patterns of psychological behavior which are not necessarily caused, or evoked, by the presence of the consultant (Ibid., p. 23). Some of them, such as denial and reaction formation, are critical in the difficulties and confrontations of the early stages and appear in the members in relation to task anxiety.

If psychodynamic theory makes understandable what is happening "beneath the surface" of individuals, groups, and organizations, organizational theory addresses some issues that are significant for consultancy work. In order to understand confrontations and difficulties, Jean refers to some specific organizational variables on which she researched and wrote. She stated "My work focuses on those organizational changes which result in increased individual autonomy, greater group responsibility, and more effective system-wide influence" (Neumann 1994, p. 24); these three are areas of great interest in her research on (non)participation in organizational change, which identified three categories of explanations (structural, relational, and social – see above) for why people might resist participation in organizational change (Neumann 1989). It must be said that within the wider organizational theory, Jean's approach to consultancy competence is rooted in socio-technical system theory and socio-ecological perspectives of TIHR's tradition. For the purpose to understand potential conflicts and difficulties in the early stages of

Table 2 Grid for analysis of "difficult beginnings" (Neumann 1994, p. 26)

	Socio-psychological aspects of early stages			
Issues to be negotiated during the early stages which might be resolved		Mismatch between consultants' and clients' expectations of consulting relationship	Organizational issues relevant to consultancy brief	Psychodynamics
	Scouting Entry and contracting Initial phase of diagnosis and working with findings	Expert Pair of hands Collaboration Neutral observer Mutual engagement	Structure: Organizational design Work design Human resources management Relations: Management of participation Dynamics of hierarchy Culture: Primary and secondary socialization Ideology of work Social history of politics	Task anxiety Group defenses: basic assumption Transference and counter-transference Individual defenses

consultation process, she focuses on such explanations as significant data which challenge and make more complex the consultancy remit.

Neumann's contribution about the integration between psychodynamics and organizational theory in the initial stages of the consultancy relationship develops a practical framework for making sense of "what is going on" between client and consultant and for understanding "why" and "where" difficulties and confrontations arise. Combining them, she builds the following matrix as a "tool" for organizational consultant (Table 2).

The matrix summarizes, and makes visible, all those issues that need to be negotiated at the beginning of the consultancy: the client's expectations, the psychodynamics enacted in the interaction between client and consultant, and the organizational issues that are the "raw materials from which organizational change must be crafted" (Neumann 1994, p. 25).

Jean identifies three working hypothesis which are embedded in the matrix (Ibid., p. 26):

- Confrontation arises between client and consultant around overt and covert decisions in building the working relationship.
- The specific psychodynamics beneath difficult beginnings enact both client's expectations about the consultancy relationship and the organizational issues relevant to the consultancy process.
- From confrontations concerning diagnosis and roles, significant data emerge about the organizational issues which are relevant of the consultancy process.

- Successful working through difficult beginning requires the consultant to address every single aspect of such difficulties: the client's expectations of the consultant's role, the organizational issues, and the psychodynamics of the interactions.

The organizational Consultant as Scholarly Practitioner

Jean Neumann has been one of the first scholars to conceptualize the idea of the organizational consultant as a scholarly practitioner. In reflecting on the nature of the work of consultant, starting from her own professional experience, Jean considers the ability to learn from practice as crucial for the consultancy competence. Her starting point is that knowledge originates from (and is rooted in) experience and experience is built into knowledge within a cyclical relation of integration between theoretical and practical experience. So, in her professional evolution, she faced the practical necessity to commit herself in "self-directed learning" (Neumann 2007) to develop a high degree of consultancy competence. Considering the consultant as a "self-directed learner" means moving from consulting technique to scholarly practice (Neumann 2016). Jean acknowledges the importance of self-reflexivity as a crucial skill to support the process of professional growth. In her terms, self-reflexivity can be understood as having an ongoing conversation with oneself about what one is experiencing as one is experiencing it.

To be committed to a continuous learning process helps consultants to make sense of the situation in which they consult in relation to their working relationship and consultancy activities with clients. They fill the gap between what they are able to do or actually do and what they need to know or do. In this perspective, a consultant is a scholarly practitioner, an "advanced organizational consultant" (Neumann 2007; 2016) who is able to integrate theory and practice in his/her work to support both consultancy domain, which is the combination of organizational sectors, issues, and portfolio of approaches for which one offers one's services (Neumann et al. 1999, p. 220) and clients' requests.

In terms of professional development and organization-oriented consultancy, Neumann considers consultants' progress as an essential element – moving away from organizational consultancy as the sole application of known methods toward active self-study and development of new methods to address new organizational challenges (Miller 1993 – *cit.* in Neumann et al. 1999). This is the position of scholarly practice. Such transition is possible through a continuous and dynamic movement that combines theory and practice and that Jean Neumann graphically represents by means of an hourglass (Fig. 9):

Such a metaphor explains the process that generates learning (and changes) and makes the activity of consultant more mature. If theory allows the practitioner to learn methodologies, then practice becomes the "place" where (Neumann 2013c):

- "Good questions" are asked , i.e., those that allow to reflect on practice.
- Awareness is (re)generated.
- New abilities, linked to theory and practical experience, are developed.

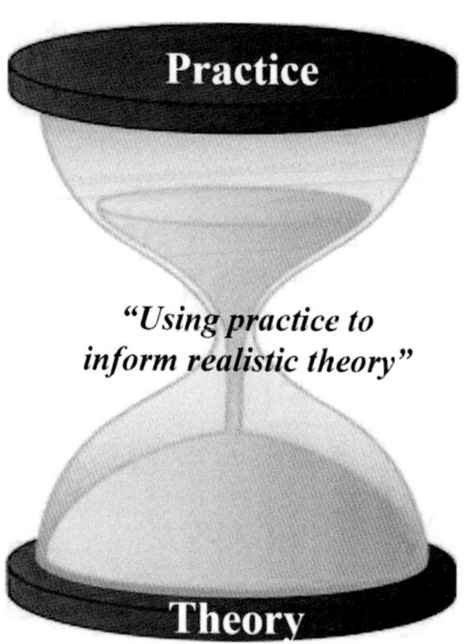

Fig. 9 Hourglass metaphor (Neumann 2013c)

However long-life learning, (self)reflection, and writing from experience as a sensemaking process – the use of "self" as a source of data – (Neumann 2017) are, according to Jean Neumann, equally significant components in the learning process for the development of the consultants' advanced professional skills. All these elements may help the organizational consultant to relearn "how" to do things – such as to describe and explain what happens in his/her role, how to analyze the professional experience from the point of view of several theories, and how to identify practical challenges not understood before.

New Insights. Consultancy as Scholarly Practice Through a Paradigmatic Shift

The reappraisal of Lewin's ideas by Jean Neumann and her explicit commitment to integrate the former with organizational and psychodynamic theories both pave the way to new approaches to organizational change and consultancy processes. In particular, the practical application of Lewin's principles provides consultants with tools of analysis that are useful to understand the system and its processes. It also highlights that through the consultancy process, rooted in action research principles (from diagnosis, through working hypotheses, to shared action planning), the clients' perspectives can be widened and their understandings increasingly enhanced. At the same time, clients can be more motivated toward change.

Jean Neumann's key insights about the consulting process can be described along three intertwined dimensions:

1. Moving from a top-slice to a whole system (consultant's approach)
2. Global configuration and interrelation among events (consultant's tool)
3. Space differentiation (consultant's skill)

The representation of the client system as a whole, the description of the factors and their interrelationship that create the problem for the client system, and the support of clients' reflection and growth through a sensemaking process of his organizational experience are three essential factors of the consultant's activity in all phases and iterations of the planned cycle of organizational change. Employing these factors is a challenge for consultants at an ontological, epistemological, and methodological level.

From a Top-Slice to a Whole System (Change) Approach

One of the major impacts Jean Neumann has had on the philosophies and practices of organizational change is the paradigmatic and methodological framework wherein she locates the process of consultancy: action research. In epistemological terms, action research introduces great changes in the way people "look at the world" and "are involved in researching". This goes beyond the positivist tradition by acknowledging the close link between theory and action and the natural and unavoidable interaction between the individual and the world – "the environment and the people involved are inseparably bound up together" (Lewin 1935 – in Neumann 2013a). In methodological terms, action research is a kind of social research that aims for changing the social system through the researcher/consultant acting on or in the social system and the participation and involvement of people in an immediate problematic situation (Neumann 2013c), a democratic and empowering action by definition.

The re-elaboration of Kurt Lewin's formula applied to action research that has been developed by Neumann in her models challenges the traditional approaches to organizational change and highlights how change should be (re)considered within a paradigmatic shift moving from a top-slice approach ("how to plan successful organizations?") to a whole system approach ("how to make sense of what we are experiencing?"). In the former, managers usually identify the necessary changes and plan them adopting incremental actions along with some defined and ad hoc control measure. In the latter, the leading principle for the consultant's action is "system thinking". Consultants must consider the whole system and the interdependence among each single component.

The rule of the dynamic approach by Lewin (i.e., to look at the elements of any situation as a part of the system) leads consultants to identify the complexity of the system and to consider the diversity of the "voices" populating it. A wider perspective is a critical diagnostic tool for the organizational consultant. It allows a better understanding of the (problematic) situation through the general description of the relationships and the identification of the practical points of inquiry that could be useful for the organizational intervention. The whole system approach, thus, positions consultants in a holistic perspective that is crucial, since complex issues cannot be fully understood if they are considered as detached from the wider system to which they belong. Whatever change occurs in a subsystem has an impact on other subsystems in the system and, in turn, is influenced by the changes occurring in other subsystems in ways that are not often initially easy to understand. The following is

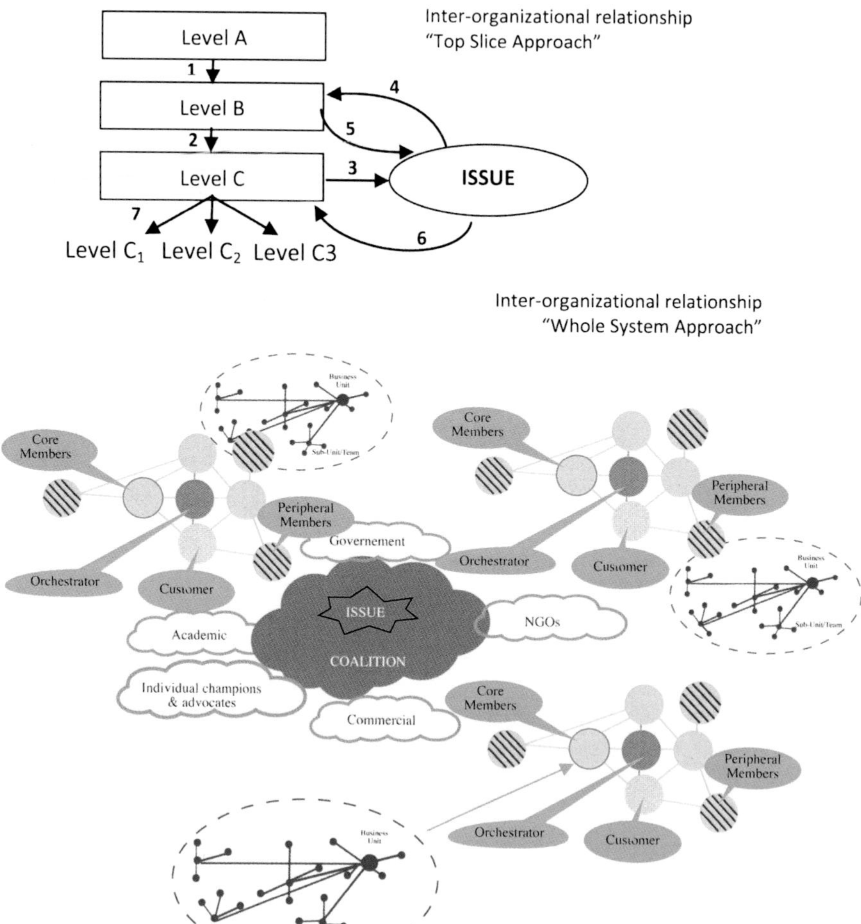

Fig. 10 Comparison between top-slice and whole system approaches

useful, graphical representation that simplifies the rules of the dynamic approach and makes the whole system approach immediately visible (Fig. 10).

Such a graphical representation is useful for consultants to approach the situation "as a whole" and seek meanings in the complex interrelational models among subsystems. The picture that shows the "whole system approach," which is named "issue-based ecosystem" (IBES), comes from the study of the STS Roundtable working group and was presented at the *STS Roundtable Annual Meeting*, in Canterbury (UK) on October 2012. What this comparison suggests is the challenge of "keeping in mind" the voices of the whole system that are part of the conversations and decisions of change.

In other words, the picture highlights dynamics that are not always visible if consultants focus on the analysis of interactions at an individual level. This is crucial for consultants since very often results (either positive or negative) are more linked to the interrelation among actions than to the effects of a single action.

Global Configuration and Interrelation Among "Facts" as a Tool for Consultants

Looking at the situation as a whole allows consultants to have a total representation of the field. Having a global configuration means being able to identify the forces at work that can support, hamper, or slow down the process of change.

In applying the rule of the field theory by Lewin, Jean Neumann introduces a new level of analysis for consultants: the close interdependence between the individual and the environment. If both are bound together, and they influence each other, then consultants need a clear representation of the field, i.e., they need to focus on the interaction between environmental and personal forces to understand why people, groups, or organizations behave in certain ways.

In the process of consultancy, force-field analysis can be conceived as an analytical tool employed by the organizational consultant within the problem-setting and problem-solving activities with the client. Force-field analysis can deepen a consultant's awareness of how tasks and relations are pivoted on a given problem or issue. From a graphical point of view, the following (synthetic and analytical) representations may help both consultants and clients to concretely describe several elements affecting a given situation, thus warning them that there is not a single cause to a certain event (Fig. 11).

Such a representation undoubtedly has practical value since it allows consultants to generate a comprehensive and exhaustive description of the whole situation and to see how single components are intertwined. In addition, it can be used to check the power of the forces at work and support clients in a process of "local sensemaking," which, in turn, helps them in the processes of decision-making, action planning, and implementation.

"Differentiation Space": A consultant's Ability

Once again, in considering Kurt Lewin's assumptions, Jean Neumann applies the topological concept of "life space" to organizational consulting. Drawing on Lewin's work, for which it was important to represent what is allowed in an individual's life space, Jean advances that "advanced" is that consultant who is aware of the degrees of free movement in a space populated by boundaries that could be trespassed.

Lewin proposed the formula B=f(P,E) – **B**ehavior is a **f**unction of the **p**erson and his environment (1936) – to indicate that a person's behavior can be understood and explained by considering person and environment inseparably bounded. In Lewin's

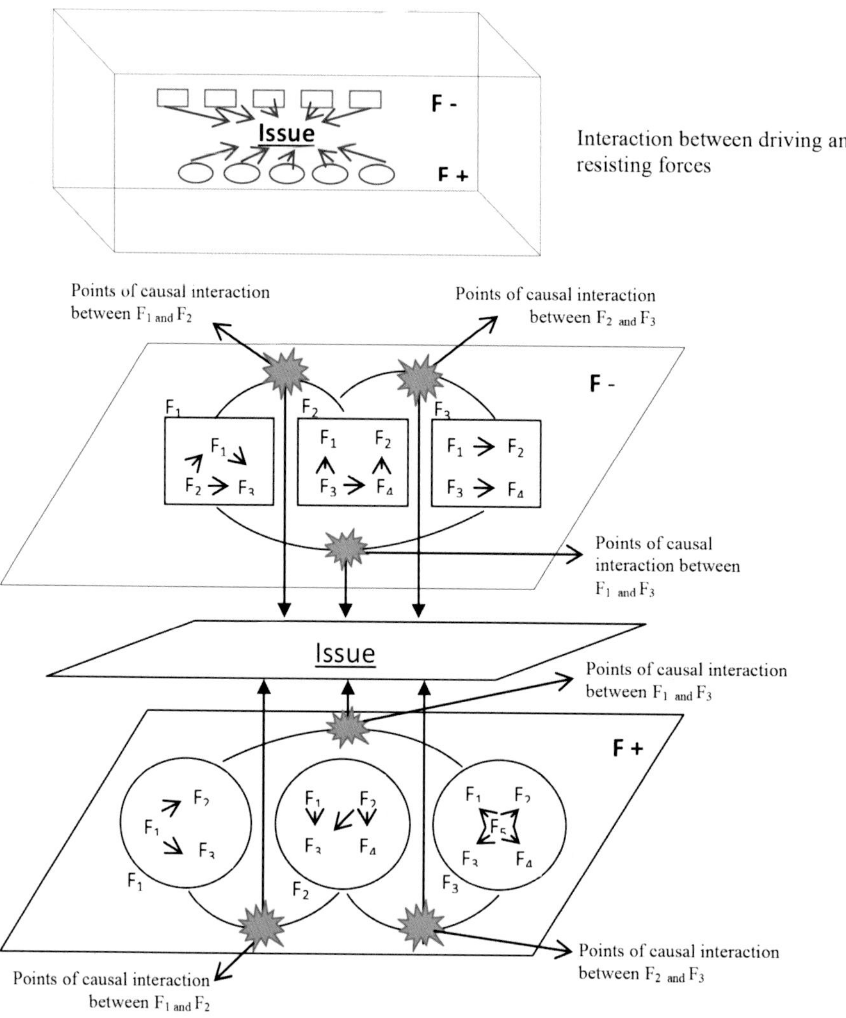

Fig. 11 Revisited force-field analysis model [author's own elaboration]

terms, they are interdependent and inseparable; in fact, he also created the eqs. E=f (P), according to which the environment is considered a function of the person, and P=f(E), which explains the person as a function of the environment. Such combination creates a complex and dynamic psychological field, defined as a totality of coexisting and mutually interdependent psychological facts. They are life space, environmental factors, and boundary zone. The life space is the person's subjective psychological representation of the environment; the environmental factors refer to what is objectively happening in that moment with no any influence in the person's life space; boundary zone is the point where life space and environment meet, and in this sense it is the boundary between objectivity and subjectivity. Lewin believed that objective facts are psychologically relevant as they have a subjective meaning. It is the person's subjective world and his personal perspective that shape the reality of psychological significance, and such reality includes the life space – that is, the totality of the elements that are personally significant in the external environment and in the person's internal world (Rummel 1975). The psychological field, or life space, has to be represented as it exists for a person, so including both physical settings and his needs, desires, and dreams. Needs, in particular, are crucial in Lewin's ideas as they organize the behavior and affect the space's cognitive structure (Ibid.). They are satisfied when the person achieves his goals. Goals are related to needs by a positive or negative valence (that is the degree of attraction or repulsion). According to Lewin, people tend to move psychologically toward goal in their life space that has a strong positive valence and away from it if a high negative valence is associated to it. "Locomotion" is the word used by Lewin to call these movements. It refers not just to a physical movement through the space but a movement through the psychological environment within the person's life space.

Because life space is divided into regions by boundaries, locomotion through the life space may be prevented by barriers. Barriers may be physical (i.e., a wall between oneself and the desired goal) or psychological (the goal or desired object is forbidden). To Lewin a barrier is anything that the person perceives as a block or resistance to locomotion toward goal. If barriers are impenetrable, the space of free movement can be limited; the more permeable a barrier is, the easier it is to perform locomotion through it. A change in a person's position is represented as a locomotion from one region to another.

In Neumann's perspective, freedom of movement is not only physical (i.e., moving around a concrete social space) but also psychological, i.e., reaching a goal, though the movement is not physical, it is a movement in space. The application of this concept to the role of the consultant not only expands the abilities of the organizational consultant but, more specifically, shows that growth consists in a progressive expansion of the life space in terms of possible movements toward boundaries to be crossed and barriers to be overcame.

In practical terms, the concept of life space poses a question: "what happens to consultants when, together with the client system, they try to reach a goal (of change)?" (Neumann 2013b). This is the crucial point: consultants find several different obstacles along the process. They are multifaceted and complex, and they can be perceived and experienced as positive and/or negative, according to the emotional condition that affects their capacity to see and choose one direction rather than another. According to Jean, the perception of an obstacle stimulates and enacts in the individual the sensory and perceptual skills, which produce insights, ideas, and plans aimed at overcoming it. Such capacity of overcoming or bypassing obstacles, i.e., choosing one direction instead of another, represents the consultants' ability to "differentiate space" (Ibid.). This ability allows to build new modalities of "being in" or "being related to" reality, and, thus, to reorganize and reconsider it, as well as to rebuild their own system of strategies and behavior (Fig. 12).

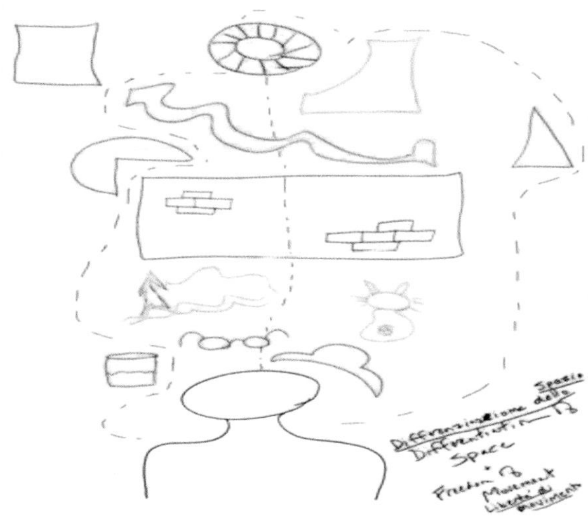

Fig. 12 Differentiation space and freedom movement (Neumann 2013c)

The graphical representation by Neumann simplifies the concept so well that it has become a heuristic tool through which consultants can imagine and represent their "space" and "movement": the *person* (i.e., the consultant) willing to overcome obstacles to reach the goal; the *hat*, as a metaphor of the role one has, or of the roles one has to face; the *drinking glass*, as a greater of lower ability to being propositional toward an intervention (the half full, half empty glass logics); the *spectacles* as a symbol of learning; and the *wall* as the greatest obstacle to be overcome. The other elements scattered in the diagram are obstacles that can be found along the path toward the goal. The practical aspect of such an approach lies in the ability to identify those void spaces among the elements in the space that are "spaces in motion" and allow consultants to make a choice or another, depending on the positive forces leading to action and/or negative forces inhibiting it. In these "spaces in motion" or of differentiation of space, there is the discovery of degrees of freedom of movement that allow consultants to slightly progress toward the change goal.

Legacies and Unfinished Business: Advanced Organizational Consultancy

The most important intellectual legacy by Jean Neumann is the concept of the "advanced organizational consultant" which aligns with the concept of the organizational consultant as a scholarly practitioner. She assumes that organizational consultants need to enhance and reinforce their own consultancy abilities and competences through professional training that relies on experiential learning methodologies. To address contemporary organizational challenges, consultants need to develop a wider theoretical and practical approach. This could originate both from the integration of the three specific pillars of applied social sciences (the organizational theory, the consultancy competence, and the system psychodynamics perspective) and from the consultants' domain.

As for the first point, by integrating the consultancy work in a wider theoretical perspective, organizational consultants avoid the risk of being hyper-specialized in a single field and of assuming their approach as the best in absolute terms. As for the second, increased knowledge about organizations, system psychodynamics, and the consultancy practice in organizational sectors and issues, as well as about the system of their own approaches, makes organizational consultants more responsive and innovative vis-à-vis the peculiar features of the client system. In other words, according to Jean Neumann, the width and depth of a consultant education determine his/her "professionalization," which is an increased ability to understand and work with those organizational complexities that represent challenges to be faced.

With the aim to guarantee a complex and holistic approach to the profession of the organizational consultant, Jean Neumann directed academic studies for the Advanced Organisational Consultation (AOC) program for the Tavistock Institute of Human Relations (Neumann 2007). For the AOC, this was a double challenge: educating consultants at a higher level and designing and providing a learning environment that encompassed approaches and methodologies from applied social sciences (Neumann 2017). Such a challenge has pragmatically solved the conceptual and professional issue that privileged the psychodynamic approach as a leading theory-methodology for some communities of practice. Merging organizational theory, psychodynamic approach, and consultancy competence (i.e., the TIHR schools of thought with NTL Institute's practice theory and contemporary organizational studies) was Neumann's practical solution to an unresolved issue. The term "advanced" represents for Jean Neumann the practical need to integrate theories and practices in a way that could be operationally useful for both consultants and clients. This need leads the consultant to engage in a continuous self-directed learning toward the development of a cognitive approach able to "bridge" disciplines and conceptual categories.

Offered by TIHR between 1993 and 2009, the AOC was organized into seven modules, each incorporating five modalities of experiential learning: curriculum and module design, experiential activities and reflection, consultancy experience and reflection, vicarious learning, and institutional reflexivity. For Jean Neumann, this practice-based program enacted the principle of "learning together for progress," but at the same time, it tested practice as a source of knowledge for organizational consultancy (Neumann 2017).

Conclusion

Jean Neumann is not just a "change thinker," but she is scholarly practitioner and consultant's consultant.

Her approach to the OD&C theory and practice and organizational consultancy can be defined as "dynamic," since it is rooted in a learning process aimed to identify and evaluate solutions to practical organizational problems, and "systemic" in consideration of the relevance of stakeholder participation and involvement in any stage of the change process. By integrating "learning for progress" with deep reflection, Jean's consultancy approach holds the promise of an embedded learning process that can simultaneously inform and create change.

Jean's seminal work connects complexity, organization, and change and offers a holistic approach to changing complex social and organizational systems showing how complex issues cannot be properly understood in isolation from the wider system of which they are a part. In terms of organizational change, the concept of "whole system" that emerges from her contribution suggests the idea that there are not actions (of change) that can be centrally planned and outcomes exactly predictable.

From a methodological point of view, Jean's theoretical and practical framework helps practitioners, action researchers, organizational consultants, managers, or change agents to reconceptualize the organizational change as a process of collaborative and in-depth inquiry where all stakeholders are involved and practical knowledge is produced for the express purpose of taking action to promote change; in this sense, her systemic consultancy approach increases the ability of the involved organizational members, or external stakeholders, to research, understand, and resolve problems of mutual interest, and it opens up the possibility for them to meaningfully engage with the complexities of the real-life organization. From a theoretical point of view, "complexity" becomes a new paradigm that poses new challenges and new working hypotheses for organizational consultant. Complexity theories provide a conceptual framework, a way of thinking and of seeing the organizations. Although Jean Neumann does not make any explicit reference to it, her work precisely gets the point: the organizational consultant needs to understand social and organizational systems in terms of heterogeneity of their structures, (inter) relationship, and properties that emerge from local interactions. Complexity, then, means "taking into account the whole" and seeks meanings in the complex pattern of interrelationship between people, groups, and organizations as they emerge. The organizational consultant has to be able to see "enough" and understand "enough" to make sense of the situation such that he can act meaningfully and purposefully within it.

Jean's extensive work also identifies an implicit connection between complexity and her consultancy process based on action research principles. It could be said that "complexity" provides a valuable theoretical support for action research, which, in turn, provides a valid methodological approach to the study of complexity. The capacity of action research to address complex issues or to manage complex situation is undoubted, as several definitions on action research literature asserted. The principles Jean speaks of, and the work she cites (Kurt Lewin's four practical principles as guideline in her "cycle of planned change in organizational development"), have relevant point of (inter)connection with some principles of complexity theories. A such connection poses new organizational challenge about how enhancing change in human systems and offers new paths for reflecting on the nature of organizational consultant's role.

The two concepts that make explicit such connection are global configuration and interrelation system. Lewin asserted that the study of social facts requires a dynamic and global perspective to analyze the situation at the level of the interdependence of the factors working in that situation; he strongly believed in an in-depth analysis of social phenomena and rejected the mechanical, positivistic ontological models, which assume linear causality between events and effect. Lewin formulated the "field theory" where the field is understood as both "whole dimension" – in which factors coexist in their interdependence (*global configuration*) – and "dynamic dimension," characterized by a circular causality produced by relationship among the factors present in the field (*interrelations system*). The field is not the container of bodies and forces but is defined by the people (bodies) and relationships (forces) that it contains; so, the field is a global, dynamic, and nonlinear system defined by the person, environment, and behavior, whose structure changes continuously according to the changes of the individuals and their relationships.

With reference to the consultant role, the challenge is evident: shifting in thinking about how change happens implies a reflection on new ways of working and engaging with organizations. It is within this context that Jean's consulting approach can be seen as the more appropriate methodological "landing place" that allows emerging processes through a local sensemaking process, the reformulation of mental schemes, and the ability to "contain" the contradictions and the ambivalences of complexity. Her key contributions and her professional commitment show how her approach to OD&C can be framed as an emancipatory endeavor, capable of supporting and achieving individual and social change in today's complex environment which is demanding a move toward paradigms that are able to hold holistic, dynamic, and systemic views.

References

Argyris, C. (1970). *Intervention theory and method: A behavioural science view.* Reading: Addison-Wesley Publishing Company.

Bennis, W. G., et al. (1985). *The planning of change* (4th ed.). New York: Holt, Rinehart and Winston.

Chin, R., & Benne, K. D. (1969). General strategies for effecting change in human systems. In W. G. Bennis, K. D. Benne, & R. Chin (Eds.), *The planning of change* (4th ed., pp. 22–45). New York: Holt, Rinehart and Winston.

Kolb, D. A., & Frohman, A. L. (1970). An organisation approach to consulting. *Sloan Management Review, 12*(1), 51–65.

Neumann, J. E. (1989). Why people don't participate in organisational change. In R. W. Woodman & W. A. Pasmore (Eds.), *Research in organisational change and development* (Vol. 3, pp. 181–212). Greenwich: JAI Press.

Neumann, J. E. (1994). Difficult beginnings: Confrontation between client and consultant. In G. D. Casemore, A. Eden, K. Kellner, J. McAuley, & S. Moss (Eds.), *What makes consultancy work – Understanding the dynamics* (pp. 3–47). London: South Bank University Press.

Neumann, J. E. (1997). Negotiating entry and contracting. In J. E. Neumann, K. Kellner, & A. Dawson-Shephers (Eds.), *Developing organisational consultancy* (pp. 7–31). London: Routledge.

Neumann, J. E. (2000). Managerial and employee involvement in design processes. In D. Clements-Croome (Ed.), *Creating the productive workplace* (pp. 310–322). London: Taylor & Francis.

Neumann, J. E. (2007). Becoming better consultants through varieties of experiential learning. In M. Reynolds & R. Vince (Eds.), *The handbook of experiential learning in management education* (pp. 258–273). Oxford: Oxford University Press.
Neumann, J. E. (2011a). Kurt Lewin – 'Dynamic approach rule'. Lectures & Presentations. http://www.tavinstitute.org/projects/kurt-lewin-dynamic-approach-rule-2/
Neumann, J. E. (2011b). Kurt Lewin – 'Field theory rule'. Lectures & Presentations. http://www.tavinstitute.org/projects/field-theory-rule/
Neumann, J. E. (2012). Kurt Lewin – 'Contemporaneity rule'. Lectures & Presentations. http://www.tavinstitute.org/projects/kurt-lewin-contemporaneity/
Neumann, J. E. (2013a). Kurt Lewin – 'Constructive method rule'. Lectures & Presentations. http://www.tavinstitute.org/projects/kurt-lewin-constructive-method-rule/
Neumann, J. E. (2013b). *Action research and four practical principles selected and interpreted from Kurt Lewin*. Paper presented at the "Learning to Change: Capacity Building for Action Research" workshop, held on 7–10 May 2013, Lamezia Terme.
Neumann, J. E. (2013c). *Action research and a cycle for planned change*. Paper presented at the "Learning to Change: Capacity Building for Action Research" workshop, held on 7–10 May 2013, Lamezia Terme.
Neumann, J. E. (2016). From consulting technique to methodology to scholarly practice. In B. Burnes & J. Randall (Eds.), *Perspective on change: What academics, consultants and managers really think about change* (pp. 109–127). London: Routledge. [Kindle version]. Retrieved from amazon.com
Neumann, J. E., Miller, E. J., & Holti, R. (1999). Three contemporary challenges for OD practitioners. *The Leadership & Organization Development Journal, 20*(4), 216–221. doi:10.1108/01437739910277028.

Further Reading

Bion, W. (1961). *Experiences in groups*. London: Tavistock Publications.
Block, P. (1981). *Flawless consulting: A guide to getting you expertise used*. Austin: Learning Concepts.
Bullock, R., & Batten, D. (1985). It's just a phase we're going through: A review and synthesis of OD phase analysis. *Group & Organization Management, 10*(4), 383–412. doi:10.1177/105960118501000403.
Burnes, B. (1996). *Managing change: A strategic approach to organisational dynamics* (2nd ed.). London: Pitman Publishing.
Burnes, B. (2004). Kurt lewin and the planned approach to change: A re-appraisal. *Journal of Management Studies, 41*(6), 977–1002. doi:10.1111/j.1467-6486.2004.00463.x.
Burnes, B. (2009). *Managing change: A strategic approach to organisational dynamics* (5th ed.). Harlow: Pearson Education Limited.
Coghlan, D., & Jacobs, C. (2005). Kurt Lewin on reeducation. Foundations for action research. *The Journal of Applied Behavioral Science, 41*(4), 444–457. doi:10.1177/0021886305277275.
Gold, M. (1992). Metatheory and field theory in social psychology: Relevance or elegance? *Journal of Social Issues, 1*(2), 67–78. doi:10.1111/j.1540-4560.1992.tb00884.x.
Kets de Vries, M. F. R., & Miller, D. (1984). *The neurotic organization*. San Francisco: Jossey-Bass Publisher.
Lewin, K. (1935). *A dynamic theory of personality – Selected papers*. New York: McGraw-Hill.
Lewin, K. (1936). *Principles of topological psychology*. New York: McGraw-Hill.
Lewin, K. (1943). Forces behind food habits and methods of change. In *The problem of changing food habits. Report of the committee on food habits* (pp. 35–65). Washington, DC: National Academy of Sciences. https://www.nap.edu/read/9566/chapter/8
Lewin, K. (1946). Action research and minority problems. *Journal of Social Issues, 2*, 34–46. doi:10.1111/j.1540-4560.1946.tb02295.x.

Lewin, K. (1997). Constructs in field theory. In D. Cartwright (Ed.), *Field theory in social science & selected theoretical papers* (pp. 191–199). Washington, DC: American Psychological Association. (Original work published 1944).

Lippitt, R., Watson, J., & Westley, B. (1958). *The dynamics of planned change*. New York: Harcourt, Brace & World.

Menzies Lyth, I. (1960). A case-study in the functioning of social systems as a defence against anxiety. A report on a study of the nursing service of a general hospital. *Human Relation, 13*(2), 95–121. doi:10.1177/001872676001300201.

Menzies Lyth, I. (1988). *Containing anxiety in institutions. Selected essays* (Vol. 1). London: Free Association Books.

Menzies Lyth, I. (1989). *The dynamics of the social. Selected essays* (Vol. 2). London: Free Association Books.

Neumann, J. E. (2005). Kurt lewin at the Tavistock institute. *Educational Action Research, 13*(1), 119–135. doi:10.1080/09650790500200271.

Neumann, J. E. (2010). How integrating organisational theory with system psychodynamics can matter in practice: A commentary on critical challenges and dynamics in multiparty collaboration. *The Journal of Applied Behavioral Science, 46*(3), 313–321. doi:10.1177/0021886310373464.

Neumann, J. E., & Hirschhorn, L. (1999). The challenge of integrating psychodynamic and organizational theory. *Human Relations, 52*(6), 683–695. doi:10.1177/001872679905200601.

Neumann, J. E., & Sama, A. (2009). *Beyond the top slice: discovering how to enable integrated health and social services through a network of providers, workforce, cares and people who use services*. Paper presented at the STS round-table annual meeting, Chicago.

Peters, E., & Robinson, V. (1984). Origin and status of action research. *The Journal of Applied Behavioral Science, 20*(2), 113–124. doi:10.1177/002188638402000203.

Rummel, R. J. (1975). Psychological field theories. In *Understanding conflict and war, volume 1, the dynamic psychological field*. Beverly Hills: Sage. https://www.hawaii.edu/powerkills/DPF.CHAP3.HTM#*

Schein, E. (1964). The mechanism of change. In B. Burke, D. Lake, & J. W. Paine (Eds.), *Organization change. A comprehensive reader* (pp. 78–88). San Francisco: Jossey-Bass. (2009).

Schein, E. (1969). *Process consultation: Its role in organization development* (Vol. 1). Reading: Addison-Wesley.

Steele, F. (1975). *Consulting for organizational change*. Amherst: University of Massachusetts Press.

Debra A. Noumair: Understanding Organizational Life Beneath the Surface

58

Frank D. Golom

Abstract
Debra A. Noumair is Associate Professor of Psychology and Education at Teachers College, Columbia University, and Founding Director of the college's Executive Masters Program in Change Leadership. A contemporary leading voice in organization change and development, Dr. Noumair's key intellectual contributions can be found in her work applying psychodynamic and systems theories to group and organizational behavior. This chapter reviews her intellectual contributions to change research, theory, and practice, including the application of group relations to organizational settings, the integration of group relations and organization development, the creation of a systems psychodynamic framework for organizational consultation, and the development of executive education in leading and managing change. The chapter also reviews the early influences and motivations that led to her career as an organizational psychologist, as well as the impact of her teaching, writing, and professional practice on thousands of students, clients, and colleagues over the last two decades. The earliest outlines of her intellectual legacy in the field are also considered.

Keywords
Group relations • Organization development • Systems psychodynamic consulting frameworks • Executive education • Leading change

F.D. Golom (✉)
Department of Psychology, Loyola University Maryland, Baltimore, MD, USA
e-mail: fgolom@loyola.edu

D.B. Szabla et al. (eds.), *The Palgrave Handbook of Organizational Change Thinkers*,
DOI 10.1007/978-3-319-52878-6_85

Contents

Introduction

Several years ago, administrators at Teachers College, Columbia University (TC), embarked on a new development campaign centered around tribute scholarships for the institution's greatest "teacher-scholars." The campaign allows alumni and other individuals to donate significant funds to create endowed scholarships in honor of the many great thinkers, teachers, and scholar-practitioners to walk the hallowed halls of Columbia University's graduate school of education, the first and largest graduate school of education in the United States. Given TC's rich 100-year history in education, psychology, and health, it is not surprising that such social science luminaries as Morton Deutsch, Jack Mezirow, Maxine Greene, and Donna Shalala all have scholarships in their honor. In fact, a quick perusal of the list of endowed scholarships reveals that many of those chosen to participate in the inaugural campaign are preeminent thinkers in their field, some of whom are at the twilight of their careers, while others, long since passed, continue to captivate all of us with their scholarly legacies.

Yet one of the names on the list of tribute scholarships is not like the others. At the top of the scholarship website sits an endowed scholarship fund in honor of Debra A. Noumair, Associate Professor of Psychology and Education at Teachers College, Columbia University, who is neither at the end of her career nor long passed her prime, but whose impact has certainly been substantive, steadfast, and profound. The founding director and creator of one of the premiere organization change and development training programs in the country and current coeditor of the annual volume *Research in Organizational Change and Development*, Debra Noumair has contributed such insight and thought leadership to the field of organization change and development through her teaching, mentoring, writing, and professional practice that alumni of the college took it upon themselves to create a tribute scholarship in her name and honor a legacy to the field that is very much still being written. As the introduction to her scholarship fund indicates, Debra Noumair is the guiding force behind the college's Executive Masters Program in Change Leadership, where she is known for flouting conventional, rational thinking about change and organizational life. What the introduction and her articles, chapters, and books do not tell you, however, is that Debra Noumair is also the guiding force behind decades of thinking, training, and organizational consulting from a systems psychodynamic perspective, the heart of where her scholarly and applied contributions reside. This is her story.

Influences and Motivations: Nontraditional Roots and Routes

Today, Debra A. Noumair is an accomplished teacher, scholar, consultant, and executive coach, having served on the faculty at Teachers College, Columbia University, since 1991. In addition to her work as founding director of the college's Executive Masters Program in Change Leadership, Debra is also on the faculty of the graduate programs in social-organizational psychology, where she was in charge of the practice component of masters and doctoral training from 1999 to 2011. Originally trained as a counseling psychologist, Debra's route to organizational psychology and change leadership has been equal parts preordained and circuitous. And, like any great thinker in any field, she is, through her uncanny abilities for reflection and self-insight, the sum total of the influences and experiences that have led her to this point.

Debra was born in New Jersey to a working-class family of mixed Italian and Lebanese backgrounds. Her father was not particularly keen on her going to college, instead wanting her to do something that could be perceived as more useful to the family restaurant business. The irony that she would, decades later, become an organizational psychologist is not lost on her, and it is fair to say that she came to be the organizational psychologist she is not because she learned about the field in some textbook or because her parents studied it in college, but because she saw firsthand, through her own formative experiences, the significant complexities and irrationalities of group and organizational life. She did for a time try to please her father directly, enrolling in a junior college and majoring in retail until her experiences in a group dynamics course and an internship working with the severely drug addicted in a community mental health clinic led her to attend Boston University (BU), where she would start down the path of becoming the psychologist and thinker many of us know her to be.

At BU, Debra would major in rehabilitation counseling and would find herself heavily immersed in clinical work despite lacking any advanced education in the fields of clinical and counseling psychology. As a result, she sought strong theoretical and conceptual graduate training, which led her to apply to the counseling psychology program at Teachers College, Columbia University, an institution known for its emphasis on the scholar-practitioner model and on promoting theoretically grounded and social justice-minded application, intervention, and practice in the real world. It was at Teachers College that Debra first became exposed to dueling theoretical frameworks for understanding group and organizational life, particularly the interpersonal approach advocated by the National Training Laboratories and a psychodynamic approach based on the work of Wilfred Bion and Melanie Klein and promoted by the Tavistock Institute in the United Kingdom. It is fair to say that the Tavistock approach to group dynamics better appealed to the human complexity and irrationality that Debra witnessed through her lived experience and her counseling psychology background, and she adopted this psychodynamic framework as her lens of choice for understanding group and organizational behavior.

Her accomplishments as a graduate student in the counseling psychology program at Teachers College earned her a spot on the tenure-track faculty shortly after completing her doctoral work. Not surprisingly, she began teaching courses in group dynamics, which she had developed into both a passion and an area of expertise since her time at the junior college. Debra credits her involvement with the A. K. Rice Institute for the Study of Social Systems with fine-tuning her psychodynamic understanding of groups and organizations and launching her as a national expert in the field of group relations. "The world made sense," Debra said of her experience with her first group relations conference, which is now a curricular staple and key differentiator of the organizational psychology training received by thousands of graduate students at Teachers College, Columbia University, over the years.

In the early 1990s, the various programs in psychology were housed in the same academic department at Teachers College, and Debra's work teaching group dynamics from a systems psychodynamic perspective caught the attention of W. Warner Burke, founder, creator, and long-serving director of the graduate programs in social-organizational psychology and, as this volume can attest, one of the preeminent leading voices in organization change and development. As the story goes, Warner asked to co-teach group dynamics with Debra to "see what she does," and together their partnership would launch a number of joint ventures that would become critical both to the training of organization development practitioners and psychologists and to the perspective each would take on organizational life in their scholarly and academic work. Warner, ever the quintessential social psychologist, would emphasize a linear, rational, and positivistic understanding of organizational dynamics that felt venerable, scholarly, and straightforward, but somehow incomplete. And Debra, with her strong counseling psychology training and her expertise in psychodynamic theory, would emphasize the chaotic, irrational, and socially constructed nature of group and organizational behavior that more reliably and validly resembled the modern workplace, but was much harder to navigate, both intellectually and in practice.

Debra, however, was up to the challenge, finding her time with the organizational psychology students to have more of a basis in actual work experience than the group therapy concerns of the counseling psychologists in training. As she put it, organizational life offered a live laboratory for the application of systems psychodynamic principles and an immediate flash point for intervention and reward that was harder to come by in a therapy context. Her belief in the immediate applicability of systems thinking to groups and organizations in the real world was further confirmed by several early experiences in executive education at the Columbia University Business School and by a burgeoning executive coaching practice. Intellectually, and personally, a career transition was complete. Debra would leave the counseling psychology program to join the social-organizational psychology faculty in the fall of 1999.

Originally, Debra joined the graduate programs in social-organizational psychology to start a practice-oriented Psy.D. program in organizational psychology. Yet rather than head a separate practice-oriented program, Debra instead supported the integration of science and practice within the masters and Ph.D. programs already in existence. She took over responsibilities for teaching the main practice courses in the organizational psychology curriculum – group dynamics and a practicum course in organizational consultation and change. She also set out to design and develop a set of new courses based on her training as a counseling psychologist, but with strong organizational applicability, including executive coaching. She became director of executive education programs in change and consultation in 2005 and, most notably, in 2011, launched an intensive, year-long masters program in change leadership that has garnered recognition as one of the leading training programs in organization change and which TC's provost has dubbed the most innovative program at the college. For nearly three decades, countless practitioners and organizational psychologists owe their training in systems psychodynamics to her intellectual vision born of an integrated understanding of the overt and covert aspects of group and organizational life. By facilitating a conceptual discussion between organizational psychology and counseling psychology in the service of deepening our understanding of leading change, Debra has trained an army of psychologists in a way that few can – hence the Debra A. Noumair Endowed Scholarship Fund.

Key Contributions: Dynamic, Systems Approaches to Organization Change and Development

Although Debra had a successful career as a counseling psychologist, both at Teachers College and within the American Psychological Association's counseling psychology division, her key contributions as an academic and as a practitioner can be found in her work applying psychodynamic and systems theories to group and organizational behavior, as well as the related training models that she has developed and put into practice over the last few decades. Taken together, her intellectual contributions can be found in four main areas: group relations theory, the integration of group relations and organization development, the creation of a systems psychodynamic framework for organizational consultation, and executive education in leading and managing change.

Group Relations Theory and Application

In many ways, group relations was and is Debra's first love. Originating in the United Kingdom at the Tavistock Institute and based on Wilfred Bion's (1961) work on the collective unconscious of groups, group relations theory attempts to explain the ways in which unconscious forces frequently interfere with rational group behavior and decision making (Stokes 1994; Noumair et al. 2010). According to Bion, who is also described in this volume, group behavior can be classified into overt, task-oriented activity, which he termed the work group, and covert, task-avoidant activity, which he termed the basic assumption group. Debra's earliest writings were concerned with this basic assumption activity, the underlying psychodynamic processes that fuel it, and the interplay of psychodynamic defense mechanisms and social identity variables, including race, gender, class, and sexual orientation. In fact, the organizational complexities, authority dynamics, irrationalities, and resistances surrounding issues of difference and diversity in groups and organizations are a main foci of a number of Debra's scholarly publications, many of which seem prescient given the national climate around issues of diversity and social justice that would emerge decades later in the United States under the Presidency of Barack Obama. In her article, *The Tiller of Authority in a Sea of Diversity*, she and a colleague write, "we can expect that authentic work on diversity and authority will be challenging, will take a long time, will be a process and is likely to involve change that will be experienced as catastrophic and will be strongly resisted" (Reed and Noumair 2000, p. 27). The projections and stereotypes received by certain groups within organizations (i.e., women, gay individuals, racial minorities), the implications of those projections for dysfunctional authority and leadership dynamics, and the group and organizational interventions necessary to correct such dysfunctions are some of the key contributions Debra has made to the study and understanding of group relations (Connolly and Noumair 1997; Noumair et al. 1992; Noumair 2004; Reed and Noumair 2000). In fact, her work in this area led to her coediting the third and latest installment of the A. K. Rice group relations reader series, *Group Dynamics, Organizational Irrationality, and Social Complexity* (Cytrynbaum and Noumair 2004).

The Integration of Group Relations and Organization Development

Given her firm theoretical foundation in group relations, it is not surprising that Debra's second contribution to the field of organization change and development is born from her expert knowledge of psychodynamic theory and principles and reflects her continued professional work to integrate group relations and organization development. As a teacher, mentor, and professional role model to decades of organizational psychologists, her many students and disciples are already practicing with the integrated approach that Debra and her colleagues continue to develop, test, and refine. Her intellectual contributions in this area began in the field when she started teaching the practicum in organizational consultation and change course at Teachers College, Columbia University, where she sought to integrate key concepts from group relations and organization development and help students use them to consult to various corporate and not-for-profit clients. Debra describes this integration in some detail in a 2013 article on organizational dynamics (Noumair 2013) as well as in her recounting of a challenging client engagement (Noumair et al. 2010) that highlighted the importance of infusing organization development with psychodynamic theory, a group-as-a-whole level of analysis (Wells 1995) and social-structural concepts from group relations (Noumair 2013). In both articles and in her work training students as change practitioners, Debra frequently notes that group relations is necessary but insufficient for diagnosing and intervening in complex organizational systems and for leading change. In fact, to work effectively as consultants, individuals need to integrate their understanding of group relations with models and frameworks from organization development for a fuller understanding of organizational life. This integration, which is evident in her recent writings, is perhaps the hallmark of her intellectual career thus far, representing a differentiating approach to the training adopted by the graduate programs in organizational psychology at Teachers College as well as a challenge to both group relations and OD practitioners to attend to the blind spots in their respective fields (Burke and Noumair 2015). Her 2010 article in the *Journal of Applied Behavioral Science* (*JABS*) lays out the competing foci of group relations and organization development well:

> An OD consultant true to Lewin would take behavior at face value and operate accordingly, whereas a group relations (GR) consultant would observe the same behavior and wonder what else a person was meaning but not saying... Understanding a given situation for the GR practitioner is a matter of observing behavior, then interpreting the words and actions (or silence and passivity) for deeper meaning. Understanding a given situation for the OD practitioner is a matter of asking selected questions, summarizing the responses to the questions, feeding the summary back to the client, and assuring that the client reowns the data. (Noumair et al. 2010, p. 493)

Not surprisingly, Debra's courses, executive education programming, and consulting engagements are infused with this artful blend of psychodynamic and organizational psychology principles, including training modules she developed to teach doctoral students to serve as process consultants in the tradition of Edgar Schein (1999) but with explicit, structured attention to social-structural concepts from the world of group relations, including group boundaries, authority relations, and role and task assignments (Green and Molenkamp 2005; Noumair 2013; Burke and Noumair 2015).

Systems Psychodynamic Frameworks for Organizational Consultation

A third and related contribution Debra Noumair has made to the field of organization change is the development of an explicit systems psychodynamic conceptual framework for consulting to and navigating unconscious dynamics in organizational systems. Dually influenced by the work of Robert Marshak (2006) on covert processes and Warner Burke on rational models of organizational performance and change (Burke and Litwin 1992), this framework provides practitioners with a specific tool that can be used to understand and diagnose behaviors and emotions that may operate out of the conscious awareness of organizational members. More specifically, the tool expands the well-regarded organization development model designed by Warner Burke and George Litwin (1992) by incorporating specific psychodynamic processes thought to influence each of the factors in the model and of which traditional organization development practitioners might be unaware. As Debra notes in the updated third edition of the classic *Organization Development: A Process of Learning and Changing*, "beneath the surface of the Burke-Litwin model lie what may be unconscious and irrational aspects of an organization. For example, an overt conflict between two individuals may appear rational on the surface but might also be evidence of competitive dynamics related to leadership succession; that is, power and authority issues and unspoken conflict beneath the surface" (Burke and Noumair 2015, p. 168). Until recently, no conceptual model in the US OD tradition has attempted to link actual overt organizational variables like leadership, management practices, and climate to specific psychodynamic and emotional processes, including splitting, scapegoating, task avoidance, and anxiety. Debra's emerging work in this area provides a level of specificity around covert process that should advance the field beyond its historical emphasis on distinctly rational and positivistic approaches, potentially bridging not only organization development and group relations but also more diagnostic vs. dialogic approaches to OD (Noumair et al. 2017).

Executive Education and Development

For all that Debra Noumair's scholarly work has been about the application of group relations theory and the integration of group relations and organization development, its true impact remains in the executive education programs she has designed, led, and facilitated over the last two decades. In fact, not only has executive education provided her with a living, breathing laboratory to build curriculum and design pedagogy around her intellectual perspective on change and her views of organizations; it has also allowed her to come full circle in her own life. As Debra will tell you, nothing she has done in her career up to this point has afforded her the opportunity to marry her early business experiences with her love of psychology more than her pioneering work in executive education and in the design of the Executive Masters Program in Change Leadership (XMA) at Teachers College, itself the culmination of decades of teaching, coaching, and mentoring business executives from various sectors. There is much to say that is unique about the beloved XMA program, but as contributions go, its impact on the field moving forward is likely threefold. First, the program itself was a massive organization change project, requiring data-based interventions around some of the overt aspects of organizational life and a careful attention to the politics, motives, mindsets, and psychodynamic forces that often derail a change effort. The very study of how the program came into existence is a model for program development in both higher education and the corporate world. Second, the program curriculum is designed around a set of specific professional competencies culled from all of the major professional associations in change, organization development, and group relations in the United States, thereby continuing to emphasize and integrate training in both the overt and covert aspects of organizational life in ways that few other industrial/organizational psychology or organization development graduate programs have been able to do (Golom and

Noumair 2014). Finally, the program uses the latest thinking on organization change to inform the ways change is taught, relying less on didactic lecture and more on innovative pedagogical techniques and delivery formats, including cohort-based, contextualized, experiential learning (Burke and Noumair 2009). As a result, the program is as transformative to its intended audience as it is advertised, a rare feat made possible both because of Debra's intellectual vision of an integrated curriculum and because of the incredible degree of integrity with which she approaches the task of teaching about change. To date, her biggest contribution to the field may be best summarized by the tagline of the XMA program, itself a simple way to summarize her thinking on organization change and her decades of writing, teaching, mentoring, and coaching thousands of future leaders and practitioners. Effective change is not simply about clearer and more robust strategic plans or new organizational structures. Effective change is also about the covert and subtle forces that impinge upon people, often without their knowledge, that they may be unable to see or escape from. Thus, as the tagline goes, how you see it will set you apart.

New Insights: Organizational Life Beneath the Surface

The new insights that have been generated by Debra's approach to organizational consultation and change are many and varied, but they reside most notably in the minds, hearts, and works of the many clients, colleagues, and students who have been fortunate enough to learn with and from her over the last few decades, many of whom also had the great fortune of studying traditional models of organization development and organizational psychology under her esteemed colleagues, Warner Burke and Bill Pasmore, both featured in this volume. What many of these individuals will tell you is that Debra's perspective on the power of covert processes and her ability to integrate objective, overt, and rational data with subjective, discursive, and often symbolic information related to unconscious dynamics is significantly responsible for the ways in which many of us now frame, understand, and navigate our own client systems. At the start of the chapter on covert processes in her recent organization development text, Debra writes: "OD models and frameworks alone are not always sufficient to surface underlying forces that influence the behavior of individuals, groups and entire systems" (Burke and Noumair 2015, p. 161). Although this perspective is not particularly surprising for anyone who has been exposed to her integrated training models or her ability to traverse and link the overt and covert aspects of organization life, the realization that traditional organization development may be insufficient continues to slowly dawn on organization change and development practitioners (Bushe and Marshak 2009), and there is a growing acknowledgment that supplemental frameworks may be necessary (Burke 2011). Perhaps this is why Warner Burke decided to coauthor the new addition of his esteemed organization development text with her, for as Debra says, behavior in organizations may not always make rational sense, but it will always make psychological sense (Burke and Noumair 2015). What she has illuminated for many of us is the idea that all organizational behavior is "rational" in some way, even when it is not.

Of course, Debra Noumair is not the first thinker, in this field or otherwise, to point out that many of our organizational behavior models are overly rationalized and linear, while the organizations of the real world remain anything but. For example, in 1987, Howard Schwartz wrote an essay on the meaning of teaching organizational behavior to his students. In the essay, he contrasted the clockwork model of organizations, which dominated his textbooks and his classrooms, with the snakepit model of organizations, which he believed was a much more accurate depiction of organizational life. Despite nearly all of his students saying that the snakepit was a more accurate metaphor for the organizations they knew personally, all of them reported wanting to learn the rational models and strategies for textbook clockwork organizations. As Schwartz noted:

> The snakepit that each of them knew was not an exception to the rule, it *was* the rule. We could forget about the clockwork picture presented by the texts – organizations aren't like that. So now we could turn to the study of the snakepit with a clear conscience. We were, after all, there to study organizational behavior... In this case, though, the feelings did not take long to come out. This demonstration, impressive enough to me, had no impact on the bulk of my students. Facts be damned. They wanted to know the techniques for managing clockworks. (Schwartz 1987, p. 20)

Although Schwartz' speculation as to the reasons for his students' wishes are entirely psychodynamic, one could make the argument that the students wanted to learn the techniques for managing the clockwork because no parallel frameworks existed for understanding the snakepit. The insights Debra Noumair has generated, in her writing, her practice, and her work with students and colleagues, rest almost exclusively on providing us with such frameworks.

Because not many individuals are as facile with the integration of psychodynamic theory and organization development as Debra, to truly see her insights in action is to read her case work where she describes what consulting from a systems psychodynamic framework looks like, feels like, and entails. Her work with the Luminary Institute (a pseudonym) described in Noumair (2013) and in Burke and Noumair (2015) is a case in point and would remind anyone who has ever had the pleasure of working with Debra about the many layers of data, hypotheses, and interventions, both overt and covert, that she is able to hold and synthesize in her mind at the same time. These sources are worth a perusal for anyone interested in experiencing the insightful and simultaneous application of the components of her systems psychodynamic framework, namely, psychodynamic theory (Gould et al. 2006), a group-as-a-whole lens (Wells 1995), and social-structural aspects of group life (Green and Molenkamp 2005). Yet the real lesson in the chapter can be found in Debra's postmortem after her case analysis. Ever the consummate educator and mentor, she ends the chapter with a call to personal change and growth for those who wish to use this systems psychodynamic framework and see organizational reality as she sees it:

> Consulting to an organization, using this framework, requires a core capacity to reflect on one's emotional experience, interrogate that experience, make meaning of it, inquire about

> the emotional experience of others, and trust that emotional experience constitutes valid data (Argyris 1965). The issues a consultant faces at the outset of a consultation may not make immediate rational sense. Once the consultant experiences the underlying reasons she was hired in the first place, her experience becomes perhaps the first useful data point in the discovery process. (Burke and Noumair 2015, p. 182)

Everything is data, I hear the former counseling psychologist in her say. And the field of organization change and development is better for it.

Legacies and Unfinished Business: Mapping the Unconscious Terrain

Writing about the legacy of someone very much midcareer is like judging a movie when you are only halfway through it. There is clarity around what you have already seen and, of that, what you have found novel, insightful, and worthy of continued discussion, but beyond that, you have no certain idea how it ends. Nevertheless, the work of Debra A. Noumair and her contributions to the field of organization change and development thus far have left an indelible enough impact on those of us who have worked with and been trained by her that the earliest outlines of her legacy are certain. Without question, the key contribution of her work in all its forms is the integration of group relations and organization development, which has resulted in countless organizations, practitioners, and fellow colleagues experiencing and witnessing organizational reality in profoundly unique and powerful ways. Her students are convinced that the group relations and practicum components of their training differentiate them from other consultants and practitioners, making them both better diagnosticians of and effective locksmiths for the intractable dynamics deeply embedded far under the surface of most organizations. And her clients, whether they be individual C-suite executives, corporate leadership development programs, or national nonprofits, have all benefited greatly from her ability to surface undiscussable and deeply psychological processes in the context of the strategic business frame that the rational side of organization development routinely provides.

While those who have worked with her continue to think, write, and teach about organizations steeped in her legacy, Debra continues to examine the unconscious processes underneath traditional organization change and development frameworks, exploring the issues of power, authority, and social identity that appeared in her earliest scholarship and seeking additional specificity and precision in linking the overt and covert aspects of organizational life. To that end, Debra recently coedited a special issue of the *Journal of Applied Behavioral Science* that attempts to frame diversity and inclusion from an organization change perspective, and she and her research team are planning a series of papers aimed at exploring and validating more thoroughly the covert organization development model she proposed in her recent article in *Research in Organizational Change and Development* (Noumair et al. 2017). As she seeks additional specificity and precision in linking overt and covert organizational factors and as she and her research team apply clinical and qualitative research methods (Schein 2015) to map the hidden psychodynamic terrain of organizations more completely, Debra's model will likely gain additional validity in scientific and practitioner circles, and her intellectual contributions to the field of organization change and development will only grow.

As she says in her most recent paper outlining the development of this model, "it is our stance that a thorough exploration of the covert dynamics at play in the past and present, when coupled with overt data, will yield a deeper understanding of the organization, as well as the potential future direction(s) it may take" (Noumair et al. 2017, p. 42). What Debra has not said, but we can, is that this is the view she has cultivated now for three decades, intellectually and in practice, from her father's restaurant to the hallowed halls of Teachers College and so many classrooms and executive training centers in between. How she sees change in organizations has certainly set her apart, and as she continues to share that view through her teaching, mentoring, writing, and professional practice, as she works to integrate the fantasy of organizational rationality with the reality of our diverse, chaotic, and irrational times, her wish is that this view sets all of us apart and makes us better thinkers and change leaders, now and into the foreseeable future. Were the story to conclude with that as her legacy, I believe it would be the only tribute that Debra A. Noumair would ever need.

References

Argyris, C. (1965). Explorations in interpersonal competence, II. *The Journal of Applied Behavioral Science, 1*, 255–269.

Bion, W. R. (1961). *Experiences in groups*. New York: Basic Books.

Burke, W. W. (2011). A perspective on the field of organization development and change: The Zeigarnik effect. *The Journal of Applied Behavioral Science, 47*, 143–167.

Burke, W. W., & Litwin, G. H. (1992). A casual model of organizational performance and change. *Journal of Management, 18*, 532–545.

Burke, W. W., & Noumair, D. A. (2009). Action learning and organization development. In R. L. Dilworth & Y. Boshyk (Eds.), *Action learning and its applications*. Basingstoke: Palgrave MacMillan.

Burke, W. W., & Noumair, D. A. (2015). *Organization development: A process of learning and changing* (3rd ed.). New York: Pearson.

Bushe, G. R., & Marshak, R. J. (2009). Revisioning organization development: Diagnostic and dialogic premises and patterns of practice. *The Journal of Applied Behavioral Science, 45*(3), 348–368.

Connolly, M., & Noumair, D. A. (1997). The white girl in me, the colored in you, and the lesbian in us: Crossing boundaries. In M. Fine, L. C. Powell, L. Weis, & M. Wong (Eds.), *Off-white: Essays on race, culture, & society* (pp. 322–332). New York: Routledge.

Cytrynbaum, S., & Noumair, D. A. (Eds.). (2004). *Group dynamics, organizational irrationality, and social complexity: Group relations reader 3*. Jupiter: A. K. Rice Institute for the Study of Social Systems.

Green, Z.G., & Molenkamp, R. (2005). *The BART system of group and organizational analysis: Boundaries, authority, role and task*. Unpublished manuscript.

Golom, F. D., & Noumair, D. A. (2014). No add-ons necessary: Cultural and pedagogical implications of a competency-based approach to training I/O psychologists. *Industrial and Organizational Psychology: Perspectives on Science and Practice, 7*(1), 18–21.

Gould, L. J., Stapley, L. F., & Stein, M. (2006). *The systems psychodynamics of organisations*. London: Karnac Books.
Marshak, R. (2006). *Covert processes at work: Managing the five hidden dimensions of organization change*. San Francisco: Berrett-Koehler.
Noumair, D. A., Fenichel, A., & Fleming, J. L. (1992). Clarence Thomas, Anita Hill and us: A group relations perspective. *The Journal of Applied Behavioral Science, 28*(3), 377–387.
Noumair, D. A. (2004). Diversity and authority conferences as a social defense. In L. J. Gould, L. Stapley, & M. Stein (Eds.), *Applied experiential learning: The group relations training approach* (pp. 63–84). Madison: Psychosocial Press.
Noumair, D. A., Winderman, B. B., & Burke, W. W. (2010). Transforming the A. K. Rice Institute: From club to organization. *The Journal of Applied Behavioral Science, 46*(4), 473–499.
Noumair, D. A. (2013). Cultural revelations: Shining a light on organizational dynamics. *International Journal of Group Psychotherapy, 63*(2), 153–176.
Noumair, D. A., Pfaff, D. L., St. John, C. M., Gipson, A. N., & Brazaitis, S. J. (2017). X-ray vision at work: Seeing inside organizational life. In A. B. Shani & D. A. Noumair (Eds.), *Research in organization change and development, volume 25*. UK: Emerald Group Publishing Limited.
Reed, G. M., & Noumair, D. A. (2000). The tiller of authority in a sea of diversity: Empowerment, disempowerment, and the politics of identity. In E. Klein, F. Gabelnick, & P. Herr (Eds.), *Dynamic consultation in a changing workplace* (pp. 51–79). Madison: Psychosocial Press.
Schein, E. H. (1999). *Process consultation revisited: Building the helping relationship*. Reading: Addison-Wesley.
Schein, E. H. (2015). Organizational psychology then and now: Some observations. *Annual Review of Organizational Psychology and Organizational Behavior, 2*, 1–19.
Schwartz, H. S. (1987). The clockwork or the snakepit: An essay on the meaning of teaching organizational behavior. *Journal of Management Education, 11*(2), 19–26.
Stokes, J. (1994). The unconscious at work in groups and teams: Contributions from the work of Wilfred Bion. In A. Obholzer & Z. G. Roberts (Eds.), *The unconscious at work: Individual and organizational stress in the human services* (pp. 19–27). New York: Routledge.
Wells, L. (1995). The group as a whole: A systemic socioanalytic perspective on interpersonal and intergroup relations. In J. Gillette & M. McCollom (Eds.), *Groups in context: A new perspective on group dynamics* (pp. 49–85). Lanham: University Press of America.

Further Reading

Burke, W. W., & Noumair, D. A. (2002). The role of personality assessment in organization development. In J. Waclawski & A. H. Church (Eds.), *Organization development: A data drive approach to organizational change* (pp. 55–73). San Francisco: Jossey-Bass.
Noumair, D.A. & Burke, W.W. (2002). The multiplicity of roles and demands for the leader as partner. In L. Segil, J. Belasco, & M. Goldsmith (Eds.), *Partnering: The new face of leadership*, New York: AMACOM.
Noumair, D. A., & Shani, A. B. (Eds.). (2016). *Research in organization change and development, volume 24*. UK: Emerald Group Publishing Limited.
Shani, A. B., & Noumair, D. A. (Eds.). (2017). *Research in organization change and development, volume 25*. UK: Emerald Group Publishing Limited.

Shaul Oreg: Disentangling the Complexity of Recipients' Responses to Change 59

Marlene Walk

Abstract

Shaul Oreg contributes to contemporary thinking in organizational change research in significant ways. In his early research, Shaul established the construct of dispositional resistance to change, which captures affective, cognitive, and behavioral aspects of individuals' personal orientation toward change. Building on this work, Shaul shows that dispositional resistance to change predicts reactions to specific change, which are subsequently related to individual- and work-related outcomes. Overall, his research provides an in-depth view of reactions to change and an integrative approach to understanding the antecedents and consequences of these reactions. Through the holistic approach that characterizes his research, Shaul is able to uncover nuances at play in the interactions between individual and contextual factors and, thus, contributes to a better understanding of the complexity involved in recipients' responses to change. This chapter describes Shaul's personal background and motivation for this line of research, discusses the key contributions of his research and how it impacted other scholars, and outlines his future research trajectory.

Keywords

Dispositional resistance to change • Reactions to change • Change recipients

M. Walk (✉)
School of Public and Environmental Affairs, Indiana University-Purdue University Indianapolis, Indianapolis, IN, USA
e-mail: mwalk@iupui.edu

D.B. Szabla et al. (eds.), *The Palgrave Handbook of Organizational Change Thinkers*,
DOI 10.1007/978-3-319-52878-6_86

Contents

Introduction

Shaul Oreg's research focuses on the interaction between personality characteristics and contextual factors, with a particular interest in the theme of organizational change. In his early research, Shaul contributed to contemporary organizational change theory by establishing the construct of dispositional resistance to change, capturing affective, cognitive, and behavioral aspects of individuals' personal orientation toward change. Building on this work, Shaul shows that dispositional resistance to change predicts reactions to specific change, which are subsequently related to individual- and work-related outcomes. More broadly, his research has helped uncover the complexity involved in recipients' responses to change. The holistic approach, which characterizes most of his work, combines individual and contextual factors and thus provides an integrative understanding of reactions to organizational change.

Influences and Motivations: Personal Background and Research Companions

Shaul holds a PhD in Organizational Behavior from the School of Industrial and Labor Relations (ILR) at Cornell University (2003), an MA in Clinical Psychology from Ben-Gurion University (1997), and a BA in Psychology and Computer Sciences from Tel-Aviv University (1994). After receiving his PhD in 2003, Shaul moved back to Israel and started his career as Lecturer in the Department of Sociology and Anthropology at the University of Haifa. He worked at the University of Haifa until 2011 (since 2008 as Senior Lecturer with tenure) before moving to The Hebrew University of Jerusalem, where he is now Associate Professor at the School of Business Administration. Between 2015 and 2017, Shaul has been on sabbatical as a Visiting Associate Professor back at Cornell University.

When asked how he became interested in change research, Shaul says "my interest in this field was entirely coincidental" and begins to tell the following story, with which he had opened his first job talks, back in 2002: Shortly after having moved to Ithaca, New York, from Be'er Sheva, Israel, in 1999, Shaul's parents back in Israel have begun to experience problems receiving emails. It soon became clear that the problem was related to their Internet service provider and so, Shaul urged his father to switch providers. His father, however, was very reluctant about switching providers; in fact, he adamantly resisted the idea, giving a series of excuses that seemed irrational to Shaul. As this was not the first time Shaul has come across these kinds of responses from his father, he became very curious about the reasons for his behavior. After realizing that "resistance to change" was an actual field of study, Shaul approached his PhD advisor, Professor Tove Hammer, about the possibility of taking on an independent study on this topic. During his research for the independent study, Shaul grew increasingly surprised that despite the fact that a lot had been written about the topic, a significant psychological explanation of resistance seemed to be missing. As is the case in some of his later work, Shaul often uses dispositional approaches to tackle research questions relying on his background in clinical psychology. Because only a few research studies came close, but not close enough, to how he conceptualized the notion of "resistance to change," Shaul, encouraged by Dr. Hammer, had not only found a topic for his dissertation but also an important construct – dispositional resistance to change – that helps researchers and practitioners to better understand the notion of resistance to change.

Shaul identifies a few key scholars that helped shape his research and thinking in various ways. Two of Shaul's early mentors while at ILR were Tove Hammer (from the department of Organizational Behavior) and Daryl Bem (from the Psychology department), who – besides many other things – taught him the craft of writing. Both of them, Shaul says, "were artists and had impressive writing skills . . . stressing the importance of simple writing." Further, when asked about who and what influenced his thinking, Shaul mentions being impressed by Tim Judge's (Ohio State University) work, especially with respect to the dispositional approach and its application to a large variety of phenomena. Upon starting to consider a broader approach to the study of reactions to change, Shaul was especially inspired by Jean Bartunek's (Boston College) emphasis on the change recipient's perspective. Even though he had always thought about change from the recipient's perspective, it was only through Jean's (and others who adopted a similar approach) work that this perspective became explicit. The inspiration Shaul drew from her work is mutual as Jean points out that she had "been impressed with his resistance to change scale . . . and his leadership about change" (Bartunek, personal communication).

After starting to collaborate with others, Shaul felt particularly inspired by two of his collaborators: Yair Berson (Bar-Ilan University) and Noga Sverdlik (Ben-Gurion University of the Negev). Yair describes their collaborative work as focusing "on interactions between personality and situations as well as work that highlighted the personality of the leader and its manifestations in organizational processes and outcomes" (Berson, personal communication). Both scholars describe a very strong mutual influence their collaboration and friendship has had on them over the past 10 years. Whereas Shaul "learned everything he knows about leadership and broader contextual approaches to explain behavior from Yair," Yair says "until I met Shaul, personality has been mostly a control variable in my research . . . however, Shaul's greatest impact on me has to do with how he approaches science. The strictly rational, methodical, and meticulous approach to research and writing makes him not only a great colleague but also a mentor. Planning, conducting, and, in particular, writing with him has always been a source of learning for me" (Berson, personal communication). The collaborative work with Noga Sverdlik has focused on the interaction between personal values and type of change. According to Shaul, Noga taught him to appreciate new complexities in phenomena, well beyond those he had considered. This sentiment is mutual as Noga describes: "Whenever we work together I learn from and with him something new about theory, methodology and writing. He is the perfect partner for development and exploration" (Sverdlik, personal communication).

It will become clear in later sections of this chapter how these influences and motivations impacted Shaul's research.

Key Contributions: Disentangling the Complexity of Recipients' Responses to Organizational Change

Shaul's work broadly falls into two clusters: "Reactions to Change in Organizations" and "Effects of Personality and Values on the Behavior of the Self and Others." Given that the main focus of this handbook is on organizational change, I will emphasize contributions within the first cluster. Specifically, I will be highlighting three contributions to the organizational change literature and some observations that are relevant across research clusters.

Holistic Perspective of Individuals and Their Environment

Throughout most of his research, Shaul applies a holistic focus while integrating individual characteristics alongside social and contextual factors, which provides rich insights into the particular area of study. For instance, Shaul considers the combined role of individuals' dispositional resistance to change and the organizational environment as factors that predict individuals' attitudes to change (Oreg 2006). Similarly, in research with Karen van Dam and Birgit Schyns, the authors establish that the characteristics of the daily work context (operationalized through leader–member exchange and perceived development climate) are related to change process characteristics (such as information, participation, and trust in management) and that these, in turn, significantly predict individuals' resistance to change, alongside the influence of individual characteristics on resistance to change (van Dam et al. 2008). Moreover, in a review of studies of change recipients' reactions to organizational change, Shaul, Maria Vakola, and Achilles Armenakis consider change recipients' characteristics, the organizational context as well as specific aspects of the organizational change, such as the change process, perceived benefit/harm, and the change content as predictors of reactions to change (Oreg et al. 2011). Similar trends can be found in work within Shaul's second cluster of research. For instance, in a study with Yair Berson and Tali Dvir, the researchers investigate organizational culture as a mechanism that mediates the effects of CEO dispositions on organizational outcomes (Berson et al. 2008). In other research with Oded Nov, Shaul explores both dispositional and conceptual antecedents of motivations to contribute to open source initiatives (Oreg and Nov 2008).

Dispositional Resistance to Change

A significant contribution to theory and research on organizational change is the notion of dispositional resistance to change due to the explicit focus on the role of personality in shaping responses to change. Whereas most of the earlier scholarship on resistance to change has focused on the organizational context, Shaul emphasizes the individual as source of resistance and conceptualizes the construct of resistance to change as a personality trait (rather than an attitude) consisting of multiple dimensions (affective, cognitive, behavioral) (Oreg 2003). This theorizing has been appraised as one of four influential theories since the earliest and most prominent work on the topic by Coch and French (1948) (Burnes 2015).

After reviewing the literature on sources of resistance that originate in an individual's personality, Shaul engaged in a thorough scale development process as a means of uncovering the nature of dispositional resistance to change. In seven studies, he developed and validated a scale that is "designed to tap an individual's tendency to resist or avoid making changes, to devalue change generally, and to find change aversive across diverse contexts and types of change" (Oreg 2003, p. 680). Dispositional resistance to change, and its corresponding RTC scale, consists of four factors: Routine-seeking (behavioral component) pertains to individual's inclination to adopt routines, emotional reaction (affective component) encompasses the degree to which individuals are uneasy and experience stress when faced with change, short-term focus (a second affective component) reflects the extent to which individuals focus on the short-term inconveniences rather than long-term outcomes of change, and cognitive rigidity (cognitive component) taps onto the frequency and ease with which individuals change their minds. The construct's content and structure has been validated across 17 countries in subsequent work (Oreg et al. 2008) and both the trait as a whole and its separate dimensions have been shown to predict change-related outcomes. The construct is particularly valuable in predicting individuals' reactions to specific organizational changes (Oreg 2006; Sverdlik and Oreg 2009). For example, dispositional resistance to change has been linked with affective and behavioral responses to an organizational restructuring (Oreg 2006). Moreover, leaders' dispositional resistance to change is associated with followers' intentions to resist change (Oreg and Berson 2011). Even outside the area of organizational change, dispositional resistance to change provides useful insights into occupational choices (Oreg et al. 2009) as well as the adaption of innovations (Oreg and Goldenberg 2015).

Conceptualizations of Reactions to Change

Another contribution of Shaul's research has been to the conceptualization of change recipients' reactions to change. Here, two distinct angles are especially noteworthy: (1) reactions to change as multidimensional attitudes and (2) inter-attitude conflicts and complex responses to change.

First, part of Shaul's earlier work addressed the conceptualization and measurement of reactions to organizational change as multidimensional attitudes. Shaul built on Piderit's (2000) three-dimensional conceptualization of these reactions to develop a measure of negative attitudes toward change, and empirically tested the antecedents and consequences of affective, cognitive, and behavioral reactions to change (Oreg 2006). The three-dimensional construct adds nuance to the understanding of individuals' reactions to organizational change. Especially notable is that the individual components are related to different change outcomes, highlighting the importance of a multidimensional view. Specifically, the affective component of attitudinal resistance to change relates to an affective outcome (job satisfaction), the behavioral component to change to a behavioral outcome (intentions to quit), and the cognitive component to a cognitive outcome (continuance commitment). This particular contribution has not only conceptual but also strong managerial implications as it provides managers with a better understanding of the relationship between employees' reactions to change and subsequent outcomes. As such, this perspective emphasizes the need for an in-depth approach to understanding and addressing organization members' responses to organizational change.

Second, in research with Noga Sverdlik, Shaul focuses on the interaction of the type of change (voluntary vs. imposed), change recipients' predispositions, and the orientation toward the change agent on individuals' responses to change (Oreg and Sverdlik 2011; Sverdlik and Oreg 2009, 2015). The underlying assumption is that voluntary changes provide individuals with opportunities for self-expression and autonomy, whereas imposed change inhibits these opportunities and, thus, restricts self-expression and autonomy. Imposed change therefore leads to value conflicts such that "individuals who emphasize openness to change are predisposed to support imposed change because it presents opportunities for renewal, but at the same time are predisposed to resist it because it threatens their sense of autonomy" (Sverdlik and Oreg 2009, p. 1441). As such, individuals tend to experience internal conflicts, as manifested in the experience of ambivalence, when change is imposed. Feelings of ambivalence are especially likely to occur in situations of conflict between the orientation toward change and the orientation toward the imposing change agent (Oreg and Sverdlik 2011). Specifically, the relationship between dispositional resistance to change and ambivalence is weaker among those who hold a negative orientation toward the imposing agent. Moreover, the nature of change influences the relationship between personal values and organizational identification, especially in cases where anxiety levels are high (Sverdlik and Oreg 2015). When change is imposed and when change recipients experience anxiety due to the change, individuals' conservation values are positively, and their openness values are negatively, related to their organizational identification following a change.

Building on this, Shaul and his colleagues (Oreg et al. 2016) have recently proposed a model in which they outline the main mechanisms through which individuals' responses to change emerge, with a particular focus on emotional episodes (that include appraisal, affect, and behavior). These emotional episodes map onto two dimensions of valence and activation that comprise four response types. This circumplex of recipients' affective and behavioral responses to change highlights the variety of potential responses to change, ranging from change resistance, through change disengagement and change acceptance, to change proactivity. Based on their initial theorizing, the authors discuss the mechanisms through which recipients form their responses to change. Here Shaul and colleagues draw on appraisal theory, describing how primary appraisals (evaluation of the relevance of the change to the self) and secondary appraisals (evaluation of the ability to cope with the change) predict the valence and activation of recipients' affective and behavioral responses. Specifically, they argue that goal congruence, a form of primary appraisal, influences the valence of recipients responses, and goal relevance, a second form of primary appraisal and coping potential, a form of secondary appraisal, influence the activation of recipients' responses. With this particular work, the authors (1) highlight the role of activation, in addition to the valence of recipients' responses (which dominated past research), (2) integrate the role of emotional episodes during change into a holistic view, incorporating affect, cognition, and behavior, and (3) critically evaluate the assumptions that change recipients are passive and that resistance to change is solely negative.

Overall, Shaul's research provides an in-depth view of reactions to change and an integrative approach to understanding the antecedents and consequences of these reactions. The cumulative effect of his work on change recipients provides a richer understanding of why and when individuals resist change. Whereas earlier views of reactions to change tended to be monolithic, Shaul's research helped to uncover the intricacies involved in recipients' responses to change and to demonstrate how personal and contextual factors interact in shaping these multidimensional responses.

New Insights: Inspiring Others

It is a challenging task to fully capture the impact that a scholar has on others. The approach I have chosen attempts to provide both a quantitative and qualitative indication of the new insights generated based on Shaul's research. For the quantitative evaluation, I considered articles that cited Shaul's works using his Google Scholar citation count (Google Scholar – Shaul Oreg 2016). Table 1 displays the citation counts of the five most cited articles in each of the two research clusters (see section "Key Contributions: Disentangling the Complexity of Recipients' Responses

Table 1 Top 5 citations per cluster

Cluster 1: Reactions to change in organizations			Cluster 2: Effects of personality and values on the behavior of the self and others	
Article	**Citation count**	**% of articles extracted**	**Article**	**Citation count**
(Oreg 2003)	736	13.59	(Oreg and Katz-Gerro 2006)	298
(Oreg 2006)	529	18.90	(Oreg and Nov 2008)	251
(Oreg et al. 2011)	234	32.86	(Berson et al. 2008)	246
(van Dam et al. 2008)	213	29.91	(Oreg and Berson 2011)	112
(Oreg et al. 2008)	90	44.44	(Herzog and Oreg 2008)	47

Source: Google Scholar – Shaul Oreg (2016)

to Organizational Change"). As indicated earlier, Shaul's work on dispositional resistance to change (Oreg 2003; Oreg et al. 2008) and the development and test of a model with antecedents and outcomes of multidimensional attitudes to change (Oreg 2006) have received the most attention.

Beyond the degree of impact, as is assessed by looking at number of citations, I also aimed to gain some insights into the content of the impact that Shaul's work has on others. I therefore reviewed those articles that are based most heavily on his work. To do this, I used Google Scholar's "cited by" function. Google Scholar's ranking algorithm sorts citations according to relevance, whereby articles with higher citation counts are listed in higher positions than those that have been cited less frequently (Beel and Gipp 2009). Moreover, according to their *About Us* page, Google Scholar "aims to rank documents the way researchers do, weighing the full text of each document, where it was published, who it was written by, as well as how often and how recently it has been cited in other scholarly literature" (Google Scholar 2016). Unfortunately, it is less clear how much weight Google Scholar puts on any of these individual criteria.

Given the focus of this handbook on organizational change, I limited my review to articles falling into cluster 1 "Reactions to Change in Organizations." For each of the articles I proceeded as follows: First, I sorted articles that cited Shaul's work according to relevance (rather than date). Second, to account for the time since publication, I weighted Shaul's more recent work more heavily. For research with a citation count of >500, I extracted the first 100 citing articles; for articles with a citation count of >200, I extracted the first 70 citing articles; for articles with a citation count of >100, I extracted the first 50 citing articles; for works with a citation count of >50 I extracted the first 40 citing articles; and for articles with fewer than 50 citations I extracted all citing articles (see Table 1). This resulted in a total of 242 articles that have cited Shaul's articles, which I then perused for their content (see below). It is important to note that I limited my search to academic

Table 2 Citation distribution within cluster

Citation count	Cluster 1 (n=242)	
	#	%
≥20	7	2.89
10–19	17	7.02
5–9	36	14.88
2–4	67	27.69
1	115	47.52

articles in English; as such, I did not consider books, book chapters, dissertations, conference papers/proceedings, or working papers. I also excluded self-citations.

As the extracted articles differed immensely in how often they cited Shaul's work (1 to 59), I focused on articles that build off Shaul's work in a substantive way. Specifically, these were articles in which Shaul's work has been referenced more than five times within the article (see Table 2).

After engaging in an inductive review of the extracted articles, the areas of impact largely mirror the identified main contributions: (1) dispositional resistance to change, (2) holistic approach of individuals and their environment, (3) conceptualizations and measurement of reactions to change.

Dispositional Resistance to Change

The diversity of applications of the dispositional resistance to change construct is notable. Besides being used in organizational change contexts (e.g., Michel et al. 2013; Turgut et al. 2016), dispositional resistance to change has also been incorporated in various other contexts such as technology acceptance (Laumer et al. 2016; Meier et al. 2013) and technology use (Mzoughi and M'Sallem 2013; Nov and Ye 2008, 2009), and innovation resistance (Heidenreich and Spieth 2013). It was also used among different sets of participants, including students (Michel et al. 2013; Nov and Ye 2008), public sector (Battistelli et al. 2013; Michel et al. 2013) and private sector employees (Mulki et al. 2012), as well as customers (Mzoughi and M'Sallem 2013). As part of these research efforts, the RTC scale has been used and further validated in other languages such as Russian (Stewart et al. 2009), Turkish (Saruhan 2013), Chinese (Hon et al. 2014), and German (Kunze et al. 2013).

In the various models proposed, dispositional resistance to change has been conceptualized as an independent, moderating, and mediating variable. Across studies, it has been identified as a reliable direct predictor of various reactions to change, such as emotional exhaustion in a longitudinal study (Turgut et al. 2016), affective commitment to change (Michel et al. 2013), felt stress (Mulki et al. 2012), perceived ease of use of digital libraries (Nov and Ye 2008) and mobile health services (Guo et al. 2013), and individual (Kunze et al. 2013) as well as creative performance (Hon et al. 2014).

In a few studies, dispositional resistance to change was used as a moderator. For instance, Michel et al. (2013) investigated the moderating role of dispositional resistance to change on the relationship between change characteristics (benefit and extent of change) and commitment to change among four samples drawn in the German context, but only found evidence for the trait's moderating effect in one sample. Similarly, Lamm and Gordon (2010) were unable to support the moderating role of dispositional resistance to change between psychological empowerment and behavioral support for organizational change among US MBA students.

Dispositional resistance to change was also conceptualized as a mediator in one study. In particular, Kunze et al. (2013) found that dispositional resistance to change mediated the relationship between age and individual performance. In addition, occupational status and tenure served as moderators for the age-dispositional resistance to change relationship.

All the cited papers in this subsection use the RTC scale in some form. Most often, scholars use RTC as a summated rating scale with all (e.g., Battistelli et al. 2013; Michel et al. 2013; Saksvik and Hetland 2009) or a selection (Guo et al. 2013; Mzoughi and M'Sallem 2013) of the initial 17 items. Researchers have also used RTC as second-order construct where the four dimensions load on a latent factor representing the overall RTC disposition as initially conceptualized (e.g., Mulki et al. 2012). Whereas most of those studies reported good fit using US American (Foster 2010) and Indian (Mulki et al. 2012) samples, some studies report lack of salience of the cognitive rigidity factor using samples from Germany (Michel et al. 2013) as well as Russia and the Ukraine (Stewart et al. 2009). Moreover, other scholars have incorporated individual dimensions of the RTC scale as variables into the models (Dyehouse et al. 2017). Finally, recent research in the domain of innovation adoption has suggested and empirically demonstrated that dispositional resistance to change can be part of a higher-order "passive innovation resistance" construct (Heidenreich and Handrich 2015; Heidenreich and Spieth 2013).

Besides its influence on theory in the area of organizational change (Burnes 2015) and empirical investigations of the construct as discussed above, dispositional resistance to change was frequently used to establish conceptual arguments in other management topics (e.g., Boohene and Williams 2012; Talke and Heidenreich 2014), as well as in political science (Owens and Wedeking 2012) research. For example, Owens and Wedeking (2012) draw on the notion of cognitive rigidity to argue that justices who show that cognitively rigid justices are less likely to suffer from ideology drift as compared with those who are more cognitively flexible.

Even though this analysis focused on academic articles, one paper – targeted to inform organizational change practice – referred to the value of dispositional resistance to change research for practitioners (Erwin and Garman 2010).

Overall, this brief discussion illustrates how the notion of dispositional resistance to change contributes to a better understanding of the complex nature of resistance to change.

Holistic Approach

Most of the articles I reviewed emphasize individuals as the main source of resistance rather than focusing on contextual factors (Burnes 2015; Michel et al. 2013).

However, organizational change and reactions to change have also been said to be context dependent (Burnes 2015), which has led Shaul and his colleagues to argue for the incorporation of both individual and contextual aspects for explaining responses to change (Oreg et al. 2011). This more holistic approach is not as prevalent among the papers I reviewed; there was only one study that considered both individual level as well as contextual factors when investigating dispositional resistance to change. In particular, Hon et al. (2014) in their study of working adults in Chinese companies show that dispositional resistance to change is negatively related to creative performance but that this relationship is moderated by organizational modernity, supportive coworkers as well as empowering leadership.

The holistic nature of the conceptual framework Shaul and his colleagues have offered (Oreg et al. 2011) has also sparked recent research independent of the interest in dispositional resistance to change. Specifically, van der Smissen et al. (2013) explored how organizational change and the attitudes toward change impacted psychological contract fulfillment, operationalizing four of the five proposed antecedent categories in (Oreg et al. 2011) model. Using a series of hierarchical regression models, the authors show that transformational changes are negatively related to affective attitudes toward change and, subsequently, affective attitudes toward change are positively associated with psychological contract fulfillment. The framework has also been used to generate new research in areas that have been understudied. Holten and Brenner (2015), for example, aim to better understand the intermediate phases of change (i.e., change antecedents and explicit reactions to change) by applying a change process perspective in their study of followers' attitudes and reactions to change. Finally, Ghitulescu (2013) draws on the Oreg et al. (2011) framework to investigate the impact of the work context on change-oriented behaviors such as adaptive and proactive behavior among special education teachers during organizational change.

My own work has also been influenced by Shaul's holistic approach to organizational change. My coauthor, Femida Handy (University of Pennsylvania), and I adopt the conceptual framework of change recipients' reactions to organizational change. Specifically, we conceptualize job crafting as reaction to change in a proactive and participative fashion and, by doing so, provide an alternative to most of the contemporary research that focuses on resistance to change. Building on (Oreg et al. 2011) theoretical framework, we investigate the relationships between the individual, interpersonal, occupational, and organizational antecedents of job crafting as well as subsequent work-related and individual outcomes during organizational change. We find support for our conceptual model using multilevel data from a recent radical change affecting the German education sector (Walk and Handy 2016).

Conceptualization of Reactions to Change

Besides Shaul's work on dispositional resistance to change, the notion of attitudinal resistance to change as discussed above also gained attention in the literature. For instance Georgalis et al. (2015) find that perceived justice (interpersonal, informational and procedural) can be conceptualized as a mediator between the organizational context in the form of LMX, information, and participation and attitudinal resistance to change. Similarly, in two papers, van den Heuvel and colleagues investigate psychological contract fulfillment and attitudinal resistance to change (van den Heuvel and Schalk 2009; van den Heuvel et al. 2015). Findings indicate that psychological contract fulfillment is related to affective resistance to change, but not to behavioral or cognitive resistance (van den Heuvel and Schalk 2009). Moreover, the authors confirmed the mediating effect of psychological contract fulfillment, trust, and perceived need for change between change information and the three dimensions of attitudinal resistance to change (van den Heuvel et al. 2015).

As indicated in this section, Shaul's scholarship has inspired researchers to venture into new areas of organizational change. However, the approach I have chosen has some distinct limitations. First, it establishes the academic impact of Shaul's work, but might not adequately reflect the impact that his work has had on practitioners. Second, even though this method accounts for some of the "time since publication"-bias, newer works, especially articles that were recently published (e.g., Oreg et al. 2016), are not reflected here.

Legacies and Unfinished Business: Future Steps and Research Trajectories

So far, I have addressed Shaul's inspirations and influences, summarized his key contributions, and assessed the impact of his work on others. This final section is dedicated to possible future trajectories for these lines of research.

Some of Shaul's ongoing work further builds on the notion of dispositional resistance to change. For instance, together with Noga Sverdlik, Shaul translates the individual-level resistance to change disposition to the cultural level, exploring the dimensionality of societies' orientation toward stability versus change. They use this societal concept to predict national indexes of economic, technological, and social change (Sverdlik, personal communication). In another, ongoing, project Shaul is focusing on the conceptualization of context and has adopted a lexical approach for identifying the fundamental dimensions of psychological situations. One particular direction this line of work could take would be to explore the core attributes of change situations (rather than of the responses to change). Moreover, as noted above, Shaul and colleagues (Oreg et al. 2016) developed a new conceptual framework in which they present a circumplex of responses to change. Moving forward, this conceptual model sets the course for several future avenues for exploration and testing.

This most recent work also exemplifies Shaul's development as a critical thinker. In his earlier work he has used the term "resistance to change" which corresponded with how the literature had discussed responses to change at that time. Over the years, however, inspired by other scholars (Bartunek et al. 2006; Dent and Goldberg

1999; Ford et al. 2008), Shaul adopted other terms such as "attitudes toward change," "reactions to change," "ambivalence toward change," and more recently, "responses to change," to account for the possibility change recipients are not simply passive "reactors."

A fascinating aspect of Shaul's research trajectory is the fact that his father's resistance to change Internet providers constituted the initial spark for his research career. And Shaul confirms, "Despite my belief in the role of personality, clearly so much of what happens to us is determined by luck and circumstances." When asked how his father scored on the resistance to change scale, Shaul responded: "He has not taken the RTC, but maybe he should."

Conclusion

This chapter outlined how Shaul Oreg's theorizing and research significantly contributes to contemporary thinking in organizational change research. Shaul is a promising emerging thinker and I am sure that his curiosity for understanding individual behavior during change processes will continue to drive him to explore organizational change research in creative and innovative ways.

References

Bartunek, J. M., Rousseau, D. M., Rudolph, J. W., & DePalma, J. A. (2006). On the receiving end: Sensemaking, emotion, and assessments of an organizational change initiated by others. *The Journal of Applied Behavioral Science, 42*(2), 182–206.

Battistelli, A., Montani, F., & Odoardi, C. (2013). The impact of feedback from job and task autonomy in the relationship between dispositional resistance to change and innovative work behaviour. *European Journal of Work and Organizational Psychology, 22*(1), 26–41.

Beel, J., & Gipp, B. (2009). *Google Scholar's ranking algorithm: The impact of citation counts (an empirical study).* Paper presented at the 2009 third international conference on research challenges in information science.

Berson, Y., Oreg, S., & Dvir, T. (2008). CEO values, organizational culture and firm outcomes. *Journal of Organizational Behavior, 29*(5), 615–633.

Boohene, R., & Williams, A. A. (2012). Resistance to organisational change: A case study of Oti Yeboah complex limited. *International Business and Management, 4*(1), 135–145.

Burnes, B. (2015). Understanding resistance to change–building on Coch and French. *Journal of Change Management, 15*(2), 92–116.

Coch, L., & French, J. R. P. J. (1948). Overcoming resistance to change. *Human Relations; Studies Towards the Integration of the Social Sciences, 1*, 512–532.

Dent, E. B., & Goldberg, S. G. (1999). Challenging "resistance to change". *The Journal of Applied Behavioral Science, 35*(1), 25–41.

Dyehouse, M., Weber, N., Fang, J., Harris, C., David, R., Hua, I., & Strobel, J. (2017). Examining the relationship between resistance to change and undergraduate engineering students' environmental knowledge and attitudes. *Studies in Higher Education, 42*(2), 390–409.

Erwin, D. G., & Garman, A. N. (2010). Resistance to organizational change: Linking research and practice. *Leadership and Organization Development Journal, 31*(1), 39–56.

Ford, J. D., Ford, L. W., & D'Amelio, A. (2008). Resistance to change: The rest of the story. *Academy of Management Review, 33*(2), 362–377.

Foster, R. D. (2010). Resistance, justice, and commitment to change. *Human Resource Development Quarterly, 21*(1), 3–39.

Georgalis, J., Samaratunge, R., Kimberley, N., & Lu, Y. (2015). Change process characteristics and resistance to organisational change: The role of employee perceptions of justice. *Australian Journal of Management, 40*(1), 89–113.

Ghitulescu, B. E. (2013). Making change happen the impact of work context on adaptive and proactive behaviors. *The Journal of Applied Behavioral Science, 49*(2), 206–245.

Google Scholar. (2016). About Retrieved from https://scholar.google.com/intl/en/scholar/about.html

Google Scholar – Shaul Oreg. (2016). Shaul Oreg – Google Scholar Profile. Retrieved from https://scholar.google.de/citations?user=-hah7M4AAAAJ&hl=en, 7 July 2016.

Guo, X., Sun, Y., Wang, N., Peng, Z., & Yan, Z. (2013). The dark side of elderly acceptance of preventive mobile health services in China. *Electronic Markets, 23*(1), 49–61.

Heidenreich, S., & Handrich, M. (2015). What about passive innovation resistance? Investigating adoption-related behavior from a resistance perspective. *Journal of Product Innovation Management, 32*(6), 878–903.

Heidenreich, S., & Spieth, P. (2013). Why innovations fail: The case of passive and active innovation resistance. *International Journal of Innovation Management, 17*(05), 1350021-1 – 1350021-42.

Herzog, S., & Oreg, S. (2008). Chivalry and the moderating effect of ambivalent sexism: Individual differences in crime seriousness judgments. *Law & Society Review, 42*(1), 45–74.

Holten, A.-L., & Brenner, S. O. (2015). Leadership style and the process of organizational change. *Leadership and Organization Development Journal, 36*(1), 2–16.

Hon, A. H., Bloom, M., & Crant, J. M. (2014). Overcoming resistance to change and enhancing creative performance. *Journal of Management, 40*(3), 919–941.

Kunze, F., Boehm, S., & Bruch, H. (2013). Age, resistance to change, and job performance. *Journal of Managerial Psychology, 28*(7/8), 741–760.

Lamm, E., & Gordon, J. R. (2010). Empowerment, predisposition to resist change, and support for organizational change. *Journal of Leadership and Organizational Studies, 17*(4), 426–437.

Laumer, S., Maier, C., Eckhardt, A., & Weitzel, T. (2016). User personality and resistance to mandatory information systems in organizations: A theoretical model and empirical test of dispositional resistance to change. *Journal of Information Technology, 31*(1), 67–82.

Meier, R., Ben, E. R., & Schuppan, T. (2013). ICT-enabled public sector organisational transformation: Factors constituting resistance to change. *Information Polity, 18*(4), 315–329.

Michel, A., Todnem By, R., & Burnes, B. (2013). The limitations of dispositional resistance in relation to organizational change. *Management Decision, 51*(4), 761–780.

Mulki, J. P., Jaramillo, F., Malhotra, S., & Locander, W. B. (2012). Reluctant employees and felt stress: The moderating impact of manager decisiveness. *Journal of Business Research, 65*(1), 77–83.

Mzoughi, N., & M'Sallem, W. (2013). Predictors of internet banking adoption: Profiling Tunisian postponers, opponents and rejectors. *The International Journal of Bank Marketing, 31*(5), 388–408.

Nov, O., & Ye, C. (2008). Users' personality and perceived ease of use of digital libraries: The case for resistance to change. *Journal of the American Society for Information Science and Technology, 59*(5), 845–851.

Nov, O., & Ye, C. (2009). Resistance to change and the adoption of digital libraries: An integrative model. *Journal of the American Society for Information Science and Technology, 60*(8), 1702–1708.

Oreg, S., & Goldenberg, J. (2015). *Resistance to innovation: Its sources and manifestations*. Chicago: University of Chicago Press.

Oreg, S., & Katz-Gerro, T. (2006). Predicting proenvironmental behavior cross-nationally values, the theory of planned behavior, and value-belief-norm theory. *Environment and Behavior, 38*(4), 462–483.
Oreg, S., & Nov, O. (2008). Exploring motivations for contributing to open source initiatives: The roles of contribution context and personal values. *Computers in Human Behavior, 24*(5), 2055–2073.
Oreg, S., Bayazit, M., Vakola, M., Arciniega, L., Armenakis, A., Barkauskiene, R., et al. (2008). Dispositional resistance to change: Measurement equivalence and the link to personal values across 17 nations. *Journal of Applied Psychology, 93*(4), 935.
Oreg, S., Nevo, O., Metzer, H., Leder, N., & Castro, D. (2009). Dispositional resistance to change and occupational interests and choices. *Journal of Career Assessment, 17*(3), 312–323.
Owens, R. J., & Wedeking, J. (2012). Predicting drift on politically insulated institutions: A study of ideological drift on the United States supreme court. *The Journal of Politics, 74*(02), 487–500.
Saksvik, I. B., & Hetland, H. (2009). Exploring dispositional resistance to change. *Journal of Leadership and Organizational Studies, 16*(2), 175–183.
Saruhan, N. (2013). Organizational change: The effects of trust in organization and psychological capital during change process. *Journal of Business Economics and Finance, 2*(3), 13–35.
Stewart, W. H., May, R. C., McCarthy, D. J., & Puffer, S. M. (2009). A test of the measurement validity of the resistance to change scale in Russia and Ukraine. *The Journal of Applied Behavioral Science, 45*(4), 468–489.
Talke, K., & Heidenreich, S. (2014). How to overcome pro-change bias: Incorporating passive and active innovation resistance in innovation decision models. *Journal of Product Innovation Management, 31*(5), 894–907.
Turgut, S., Michel, A., Rothenhöfer, L. M., & Sonntag, K. (2016). Dispositional resistance to change and emotional exhaustion: moderating effects at the work-unit level. *European Journal of Work and Organizational Psychology, 25*(5), 735–750.
van Dam, K., Oreg, S., & Schyns, B. (2008). Daily work contexts and resistance to organisational change: The role of leader–member exchange, development climate, and change process characteristics. *Applied Psychology, 57*(2), 313–334.
van den Heuvel, S., & Schalk, R. (2009). The relationship between fulfilment of the psychological contract and resistance to change during organizational transformations. *Social Science Information, 48*(2), 283–313.
van den Heuvel, S., Schalk, R., & van Assen, M. A. (2015). Does a well-informed employee have a more positive attitude toward change? The mediating role of psychological contract fulfillment, trust, and perceived need for change. *The Journal of Applied Behavioral Science, 51*(3), 401–422.
van der Smissen, S., Schalk, R., & Freese, C. (2013). Organizational change and the psychological contract: How change influences the perceived fulfillment of obligations. *Journal of Organizational Change Management, 26*(6), 1071–1090.
Walk, M., & Handy, F. (2016). *"Doing it my way" – Job crafting during organizational change.* Paper presented at the third Israel organizational behavior conference, Tel-Aviv.

Further Reading

Oreg, S. (2003). Resistance to change: Developing an individual differences measure. *Journal of Applied Psychology, 88*(4), 680.
Oreg, S. (2006). Personality, context, and resistance to organizational change. *European Journal of Work and Organizational Psychology, 15*(1), 73–101.
Oreg, S., & Berson, Y. (2011). Leadership and employees' reactions to change: The role of leaders' personal attributes and transformational leadership style. *Personnel Psychology, 64*(3), 627–659.

Oreg, S., & Sverdlik, N. (2011). Ambivalence toward imposed change: The conflict between dispositional resistance to change and the orientation toward the change agent. *Journal of Applied Psychology, 96*(2), 337–349.

Oreg, S., Vakola, M., & Armenakis, A. (2011). Change recipients' reactions to organizational change a 60-year review of quantitative studies. *The Journal of Applied Behavioral Science, 47*(4), 461–524.

Oreg, S., Bartunek, J., Lee, G., & Do, B. (2016). An affect-based model of recipients' responses to organizational change events. Academy of Management Review, amr. 2014.0335.

Sverdlik, N., & Oreg, S. (2009). Personal values and conflicting motivational forces in the context of imposed change. *Journal of Personality, 77*(5), 1437–1466.

Sverdlik, N., & Oreg, S. (2015). Identification during imposed change: The roles of personal values, type of change, and anxiety. *Journal of Personality, 83*(3), 307–319.

William A. Pasmore: Navigating Between Academy and Industry – Designing and Leading Change

60

Abraham B. (Rami) Shani

Abstract

William "Bill" A. Pasmore's journey to date is all about the joy of navigating between academy and industry. Since completing his B.S.I.M at Purdue University in 1973, he held positions and had appointments in both universities and firms. As this chapter is written, Bill holds a professor of practice, organization, and leadership appointment at Teachers College, Columbia University, and senior vice president and advisor to CEOs, boards, and executive team position at the Center for Creative Leadership. Bill is recognized by scholars and practitioners alike for his continuous contributions. His contributions during the past four decades to the field of organizational science, applied behavioral science, and managerial practice are both extensive and deep. The first book that he co-edited with Jack Sherwood *Sociotechnical Systems: A Sourcebook* (1978) was one of the first books to clearly define the field of sociotechnical systems. In 1988 and 1994 he further advanced his contribution to sociotechnical system theory and practice by completing two books titled *Designing Effective Organization: The Sociotechnical System Perspective* and *Creating Strategic Change: Designing the Flexible Hugh-Performing Organization.* The annual volumes Research in Organization Change and Research that were co-edited by Bill and Dick Woodman (the first volume was published in 1987) established a special platform for scholars, practitioners, and scholar-practitioners to share new thought-provoking research-based insights that continue today (with Volume 25 planned to be published in 2017). He continued his contribution by serving as the editor for the *Journal of Applied Behavioral Science* 2011–2016. Bill has devoted the last

A.B. R. Shani (✉)
Drop Faculty and Research, California Polytechnic State University, San Luis Obispo, CA, USA
e-mail: ashani@calpoly.edu

D.B. Szabla et al. (eds.), *The Palgrave Handbook of Organizational Change Thinkers*,
DOI 10.1007/978-3-319-52878-6_52

forty years to studying change, assisting with change, and leading change in organizations as a scholar-practitioner. This manuscript captures Bill's past and present trajectory with some promising future milestones as he continues to navigate in the borderland of academy and industry.

Keywords
Sociotechnical systems • Action research • Collaborative management research • Strategic change • Social innovation • Research in organizational change and development • Leadership development • Leading continuous change • The 4D continuous change model

Contents

Introduction

The contribution of William "Bill" A. Pasmore, a professor of practice, organization, and leadership at Teachers College, Columbia University, and senior vice president and advisor to CEOs, boards, and executive teams for the Center for Creative Leadership, is recognized by scholars and practitioners alike. The first two articles that he published in Decision Sciences on group decision making and the *Journal of Applied Behavioral Science* in 1976, a comparison of the effectiveness of different approaches to change, established the trajectory for Bill's contribution and impact that continues. The annual volumes Research in Organization Change and Research that were co-edited by Bill and Dick Woodman (the first volume was published in 1987) established a special platform for scholars, practitioners, and scholar-practitioners to share new thought-provoking research-based insights that continue today (with Volume 25 planned to be published in 2017). Bill continued his contribution by serving as the editor for the *Journal of Applied Behavioral Science* 2011–2016. Bill worked and collaborated with many colleagues and CEOs of global Fortune 1000 firms on a wide array of challenges such as change, leadership, senior team development, and organization design. Throughout his career he traveled and worked in the border between academy and industry and as such had an impact on both. His contribution to the field was recognized recently by the Academy of Management that institutionalized an Annual Pasmore-Woodman Award in honor of change scholars who have exhibited exceptional collaboration in their work together.

Influences and Motivations: Collaboration as the Source of Learning and Change

Great thinkers in the field of organization development and change have had diverse connections, experiences, and academic backgrounds that triggered and influenced their motivation. In Dr. William (Bill) A. Pasmore's case, the initial attraction was the desire to do something to address the quality of work life for people in manufacturing in the 1970s. In his first organizational behavior class, his professor and later mentor Don King taught a session that delved into life on the assembly line and pointed out that it did not have to be that way. Bill was moved by the issues and felt compelled to do something to help if he could. Eventually, it led to his study of sociotechnical systems and the groundbreaking work of Eric Trist and his colleagues in the UK who had explored alternatives to traditional work arrangements.

Bill has devoted the last forty years to studying change, assisting with change, and leading change in organizations as a scholar-practitioner. Following the completion of his Bachelor of Science in Aeronautical Engineering and Industrial Management at Purdue University, the invitation to join Purdue's doctoral program provided the early exposure to the field of organization development (OD) theory, practice, and consulting. Bill received his doctorate in administrative sciences from the Krannert Graduate School of Management at Purdue University in 1976. Early on, Don King, a professor at Purdue active in OD consulting, and Jack Sherwood became Bill's mentors, close colleagues, and collaborators. For the next 15 years, Jack and Bill published together, designed, and led sociotechnical systems (STS) workshops and worked on a variety of change efforts in organizations.

As part of his early exposure to the field of STS, Bill also made a number of trips to visit the Tavistock Institute in search of more information about the research that Eric and others had done. Eric, by then, had moved to the USA, where Bill met him in a project they were both involved in at General Foods. At the Tavistock, Hal Murray and others were helpful in explaining the dual focus of the Tavistock on groups and sociotechnical systems. By the time Eric departed, it seems the group side, initiated by Bion, had "won out," and there was little to be found in writing about the early research on work systems. Fortunately, Eric filled this gap by publishing two volumes on the work-related research of Tavistock which tell the story.

Eric Trist became an intellectual inspiration. In Bill's words, "Eric Trist was a mentor, although I didn't get to spend as much time with him as I would have liked." Learning with Eric Trist and Fred Emery about the history and ideas behind STS established the theoretical foundation for Bill's work over the next four decades.

Joining the faculty at the Department of Organizational Behavior, Weatherhead School of Management, Case Western Reserve University (CWRU), served as a key milestone. Professor Suresh Srivastva was an early influence on Bill's writing (his advice was quality, not quantity) and consulting. Suresh saw "the potential in me and supported me in his role as chairman." Other colleagues were also influential: especially Frank Friedlander from an OD perspective and Dave Brown from a global social change perspective. The collaboration with Frank resulted in a milestone study about an action research project at GE that was published in Administrative Science Quarterly (ASQ) (Pasmore and Friedlander 1982). Later, David Cooperrider and Bill began to work collaboratively on both appreciative inquiry and social innovation (see Cooperrider and Pasmore 1991a, b). Partnership with Paul Tolchinsky (a colleague from the Purdue days; see Pasmore and Tolchinsky 1989), Al Fitz, Gary Frank, Barry Morris, and Bob Rheem evolved in the formation of consulting firms that led to inventions of change and development interventions, such as the "Fast Cycle Full Participation Process," to transform workplaces. Two sabbatical periods at INSEAD, Fontainebleau France, and Stanford University provided additional insights about the role that OD can play in transforming the workplace. At INSEAD, Bill taught a course with forty students from twenty-five different countries but not a single American. At a time when everyone was writing about taking businesses global, it was clear that American MBA students were missing the opportunity to *be* global. Learning from people who lived a different cultural experience became a passion for Bill. At Stanford, Bill taught a T-group-based course in human relations with David Bradford, which was the most popular elective in the MBA program at the time. It was interesting to Bill that the extremely bright students at Stanford were interested in developing self-awareness, while his Midwestern students at Case tended to view self-reflection as torture. Bill realized that there are people in the world who are ready for change and there are those who are not. The same applies to leaders in industry, of course, and Bill sought to work with leaders who were change oriented versus change resistant whenever he could.

Following twenty years as an academic at CWRU, Bill embarked in 1997 on a transition from mostly academic-based to more consulting-based work (see, e.g., Carucci and Pasmore 2002a, b; Pasmore and Torres 2004, 2006a, b). Ten years with the Delta Consulting Group, where David Nadler became a friend and mentor to Bill, then led to taking on a new challenge in 2008 as senior vice president and global organizational practice leader for the Center for Creative Leadership (CCL). Former Admiral John Ryan, CCL's president, supported Bill's efforts to build the new practice there (see, e.g., Pasmore et al. 2010; Cross et al. 2013).

Later, ongoing conversations with Warner Burke, a friend and a mentor who was instrumental at several points in Bill's career, resulted in an invitation to return to academia. In 2010, after a brief negotiation with his boss at CCL that allowed him to keep his position there on a part-time basis, Bill joined the faculty at Teachers College at Columbia University as a professor of practice. Bill claims, "Now, I'm fortunate to have great colleagues like Debra Noumair and Warner Burke at Columbia, and Rami Shani at Cal Poly." Throughout the last four decades, Dick Woodman (another friend from Purdue) has remained Bill's closest writing/publishing colleagues.

Key Contributions: Sociotechnical Systems and Beyond

Bill started out in the area of sociotechnical systems design. "The sociotechnical system perspective considers every organization to be made up of people (the social system) using tools, techniques and knowledge (the technical system) to produce goods or services valued by customers (who are a part of the organization's external environment" (Pasmore 1988, p. 1). His concerns for quality of working life issues have drawn Bill to explore insights from the applied behavioral sciences (see, e.g., Pasmore 1976; Pasmore and King 1978; Pasmore and Nemiroff 1975; Ford et al. 1977; Pasmore et al. 1978). His vast contributions to the field can be clustered into six categories: his contribution to STS thinking and practice, the theory of action research, the theory of non-routine/knowledge work design, leadership strategy and leading complex organizations, training students in OD at different levels and in different institutions, and editorial work on the *Research in Organizational Change and Development* series (20 volumes, 1987–2012; see Pasmore and Woodman and Woodman and Pasmore 1987–2012) and the *Journal of Applied Behavioral Science* (2011–2016; see Pasmore 2011–2016).

The early work of Kurt Lewin regarding change and planned change, coupled with the work of Eric Trist, Fred Emery, and Lou Davis on sociotechnical systems, served as the foundation and point of departure for Bill's work. His contributions to STS theory and practice provided both empirical rigor and practical relevance. For example, the comprehensive comparative review of 132 STS experiments provided an empirical illustration of the impact of STS interventions (Pasmore et al. 1982); the compilation of STS manuscripts as a source book provided a conceptual map of the field. The source book was organized into six sections: organizations as socio-technical systems, working with the organization as open system, STS theory, STS diagnosis, STS change, and STS studies – what do we really know and perspectives on STSs (Pasmore and Sherwood 1978). Pasmore's book *Designing Effective Organizations: A The Sociotechnical Systems perspective* provided conceptual clarity of STS theory and practice and made the concepts accessible to a wider audience while summarizing the research evidence to demonstrate its effectiveness (Pasmore 1988).

The emerging challenges of knowledge work resulted in the need to develop a new theory of organization, management, design, and change. Building on the basic notion that social plus technical change is more powerful than social change alone provided a platform from which the design of non-routine/knowledge work can be explored. Dr. Pasmore illustrated in a set of studies that by applying STS thinking to the design and redesign of knowledge work enhanced collaboration and outcomes (see, e.g., Pasmore and Gurley 1991; Pasmore and Woodman 1997; Pasmore and Purser 1993; Purser and Pasmore 1992; Purser et al. 1992; Pasmore 1994a).

For Bill, the evolution of STS, action research (AR), and collaborative management research (CMR) theory and practice have a lot in common. The STS school was heavily influenced by Lewin's approach to action research, with Bion's theories about leaderless groups and Bertalanffy's work on system thinking. As such, Pasmore contributed to STS, AR, and CMR both theoretical and practical development by making the links and the interplay clearer (see, e.g., his article titled "AR in the workplace: The STS perspective," Pasmore 1982a, and other works (Pasmore 1982b, 1983, 1994a, 1998; Pasmore and Khalsa 1993; Pasmore 2001). The study that Pasmore and Friedlander conducted at GE also illustrated the fact that AR is a foundational pillar of an STS intervention (Pasmore and Friedlander 1982). In collaboration with Rami Shani, Pasmore also advanced a theory of the AR process

(Shani and Pasmore 1985). This collaboration served to trigger the quest to gain new insights about "collaboration" and "action" while conducting an engaged research process. In an STS change effort, a high level of engagement occurs between the scholar-practitioner and the system. Staying true to AR and collaborative management research (CMR), this collaboration means that researchers and practitioners co-design, co-implement, co-evaluate and engage in joint sensemaking, and co-generate knowledge (Coghlan 2011). Researchers and practitioners are both co-researchers and co-subjects, in that they research together as partners, and what they research is their collaborative endeavor. This orientation was further crystalized in the commentary that Dr. Pasmore wrote describing ten different change effort partnerships between industry-academia based on a variety of collaborative approaches reported in the *Collaborative Research in Organizations* book (Pasmore 2004) and the *Handbook of Collaborative Management Research* that he co-led and co-edited (see Pasmore et al. 2008; Shani et al. 2008).

Bill's continued fascination with change and leading change led to the development of major contributions with new perspectives about the development of organizational agility capability, leadership strategy, and most recently, leading complex, continuous change. His shift to the application of sociotechnical systems thinking to non-manufacturing settings, involving knowledge work and non-routine tasks like R&D, also led to a book on organizational agility called *Creating Strategic Change: Designing the flexible, high-performing organization*. This contribution was intended as a resource to guide thinking about evolving organizational forms. Pasmore claims that building the capability to create flexible, high-performance, learning organization is the secret to gaining competitive advantage in a world that will not stand still (see, e.g., Simendinger and Pasmore 1984, Pasmore 1986, 1994a, 2011; Rao and Pasmore 1989). After joining The Center for Creative Leadership, Pasmore authored a paper on leadership strategy that argued that leadership development efforts had to tie directly to an organization's future strategy. Today, this assertion has become widely accepted across the leadership development industry (Pasmore and Lafferty 2009; Horney et al. 2010).

More recently, Bill wrote a book on leading continuous change and how that requires different approaches than classic OD (Pasmore 2015). The book presents a "4D" framework (discovering, deciding, doing, and discerning) that can enable leaders and their organizations to deal with multiple changes simultaneously.

His most recent publication is a measure of change leadership behaviors that can be used to provide leaders with feedback and development (Stilwell et al. 2016). He is currently working on a book about how organizations can use technology to enable collaboration in the digital age, with two colleagues from the French consulting firm Theano, Michel Zarka, and Elena Kochanovskaya.

One of Professor Pasmore's major contributions to the field and a common thread of the past four decades is his high level of engagement in training, developing, and mentoring students in OD – both in university-based programs and executive education. For example, he was the director of the masters in OD program at CWRU and director of undergrad education in management for two years at CWRU. Pasmore also supervised over 25 doctoral theses and served on the committees of over

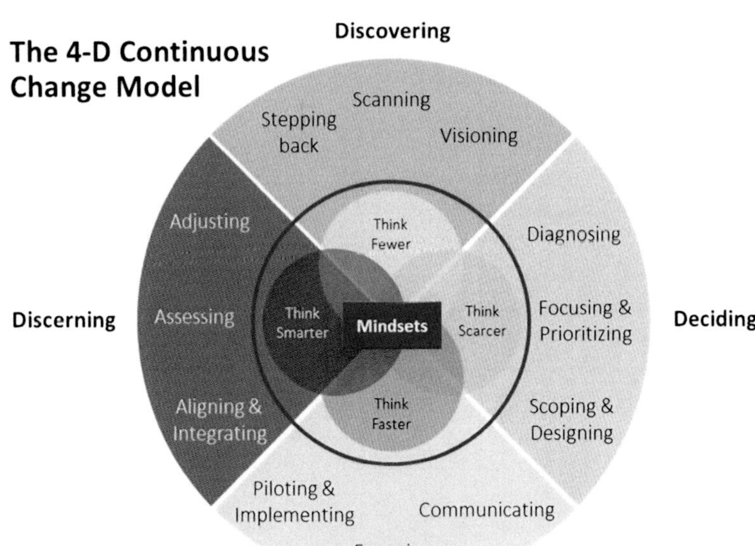

Fig.1 The 4D change model (From Pasmore 2015)

50 doctoral theses. He taught in the MBA and executive program in organizational change at Stanford and the MBA program at INSEAD. Bill organized and led many seminars and workshops, for example, the NTL Senior Managers' Conference with his colleague John Carter for four years (1987–1992), the Sociotechnical System Design for Total Quality workshop that was offered over 50 times (1979–1994), and the Fast Cycle Full Participation STS Design workshop (1993–1996). Pasmore also co-led seminars on collaborative research methodologies at the Stockholm School of Economics, Stockholm, Sweden, and the Politecnico di Milano, Milan, Italy (Fig. 1).

Many of his doctoral students and colleagues have extended Dr. Pasmore's work. For example, Ram Tenkasi, today a full professor, is producing work around knowledge work; Professor Ron Purser conducted research and produced a book on search conferences with Merrilyn Emery; Jean Neumann has continued to publish on work and organization design and enhancing meaningful participation in change; and Rami Shani, a full professor, continues to push the boundaries in STS, AR, and CMR while working in the USA and the global arena. Many of Professor Pasmore's master's students and a few doctoral students are working in organizations as OD change agents. Recent students Alan Friedman (master's student) and Kate Roloff (doctoral student) are studying the traits that make physician leaders effective, and Rebecca Stilwell and DaHee Shon (doctoral students) have written about assessing change leader behaviors.

Perhaps Professor Pasmore's most influential contribution to the field is the editorial and developmental role that he has played in the creation and diffusion of knowledge. Out of many, two major contributions stand out: co-editor of *Research in Organizational Change and Development* and serving as the editor of the *Journal of Applied Behavioral Science*. Together, he and Dick Woodman were the founding editors of the series *Research in Organizational Change and Development* and co-edited 20 volumes over 25 years (1987–2012). The first annual research volume in *Organization Change and Development* was published by JAI Press in 1987. Since then, *ROCD* has provided a special platform for scholars and practitioners to share new research-based insights. In conjunction with the new volume every year, Pasmore and Woodman also led a symposium at the Academy of Management annual conference that has become an integral part of the ODC division program in which division members have the opportunity to meet with authors of the upcoming volume. The symposium participants ranged from 75 to 150 division members, and the sessions created lively engagement and dialogue with the authors in small groups. The "give and take" at these symposia sessions over the years has advanced our collective understanding of current issues facing the field and triggered ongoing conversations throughout the meeting. Due to Pasmore and Woodman's tireless effort, *Research in Organization Change and Development* developed a tradition of providing insightful, thought-provoking, and cutting-edge chapters. The chapters in each volume represent a commitment to maintaining the high quality of work that members of the OD&C community have come to expect from this publication.

Pasmore also served as the editor of the *Journal of Applied Behavioral Science*. He took on the role of *JABS* editor in 2010 and served in this position between 2010 and 2016. Under Pasmore's leadership, *JABS* continued to develop, enhanced its quality and distribution, and increased its place in the journal ratings. *JABS* continues to serve as one of the leading journals in the field of organization development and change today. Being engaged as a developmental coach and mentor work while editing a journal is a complex and challenging task. Beyond the added value to the field's knowledge, according to some, Professor Pasmore has set the bar at a higher level and created a new standard.

Emerging New Insights: The Impact of Collaboration

As a scholar-practitioner, Dr. Pasmore led a wide variety of collaborative projects. Some of the projects that shaped his ideas, theories, and future paths include a project with the Army Research Institute; the R&D Forum that included a number of companies including P&G, where a long-term study was undertaken; the USAID-sponsored Social Innovations in Global Management project with David Cooperrider; a five-year consulting project with Unilever; various CEO succession and board projects; a leadership strategy development project with Kao brands; the GE project with Frank Friedlander; and work redesign efforts at Polaroid, General Foods, and Levi Strauss.

The work with GE to understand and prevent injuries was instrumental in gaining some new insights about integrating STS thinking with AR practice (see Pasmore and Friedlander 1982). The project funded by the Army Research carried out a study about the utilization of STS thinking in the design and redesign of military units. The Institute funded the project with the U.S. Army to experiment with STS design in an IT unit in Germany for three years. This collaborative effort also resulted in new theoretical insights on using STS in knowledge work environments (see, e.g., Pasmore et al. 1983; Pasmore 1982a, b, 1984). Some of the collaborators on the academic side included Marty Kaplan, Barry Morris, Rami Shani, and David Cooperrider (see, e.g., Pasmore et al. 1982; Pasmore 1983; Pasmore et al. 1983). The new insights about STS design for non-routine work led in part to the creation of the R&D Forum, which was established to bring together R&D firms interested in improving knowledge work. P&G was a member, and the work with them spanned 10 years and produced a couple of dissertations. Ron Purser, Ram Tenkasi, Kathy Gurley, and Bruce Hanson were engaged at various times (see, e.g., Pasmore and Fagans 1992, 1994; Pasmore and Purser 1993; Purser and Pasmore 1992; Purser et al. 1992).

The social innovation project co-led with David Cooperrider and funded by USAID took the research team to India and Africa on numerous occasions to understand how to apply a combination of appreciative inquiry and future search methods in order to strengthen NGO (non-governmental organizations) leadership (see Cooperrider and Pasmore 1991a). Using appreciative inquiry, leaders of NGOs were brought together to learn how to strengthen the aspects of their organizations that gave them life and purpose. Bill also used search conference methodologies to help NGOs in India, Africa, and Sri Lanka collaborate more effectively with government and industry partners.

The work that Bill carried out while at Delta Consulting with Unilever on organization redesign and post-merger integration evolved into a 5-year project that involved facilitating change at every level. The CEO (Charles Strauss) and head of HR (Nigel Hurst) were tremendous client partners (see, e.g., Carucci and Pasmore 2002a, b). The project involve the post-merger integration of three companies into one, which involved organizational redesign at the strategic and operational level, resulting in significant improvements in processes, product innovation, consumer insights, and profitability.

Bill also worked on various CEO succession and board projects while with Delta. This work brought Bill into the world of the executive and more strategic change. David Nadler, Rick Ketterer, Roselinde Torres, Rick Hardin, and others were guides and collaborators during these engagements. Bill helped clients understand that succession and board decisions of various kinds involved both rational and emotional elements and that to ignore either was a mistake. Today, we would use the language of covert processes to describe the emotional component of these important group processes.

Finally, while at CCL, the work with Kao Brands demonstrated the power of creating a leadership strategy that went beyond leadership development as a series of programs, but instead looked at leadership in a holistic way, and integrated work on the organization's culture and talent to adapt to evolving business strategies. A former client from Unilever (Jim Conti) moved to Kao and became Bill's client, along with one of the CCL sales people who went to Kao to take an internal HR position (Martin McCarthy). This work allowed Kao to expand its operations globally without losing a sense of what made its leadership culture unique. In addition, the focus placed on leadership development had the added benefit of greatly increasing the retention rate of individuals hired into new leadership positions.

The common denominator across all the key projects and the diverse and numerous corporations was the commitment to gain new insights about current challenges in the workplace. Some examples of these include STS/work design projects with Levi Strauss, Polaroid, General Foods, Nabisco, and Amoco Pipeline that impacted both practice and theory development; action research with GE; knowledge work/ R&D with P&G, BMS, Goodyear, Monsanto, and Corning; organization redesign with Unilever, US Navy, United Airlines, GE, and Storage Tek; CEO succession/ board effectiveness with Massachusetts Mutual, Compuware, PepsiCo, Thrivent Financial, and Walmart; and leadership strategy with Kao, Nova Chemicals, Kauffman Foundation. Another common denominator across the projects is that they all explored alternative solutions, carried out work relevant to practice, were reflective in nature, and met scientific rigor. Bill's collaborative inquiry style, the humble inquiry orientation (see Schein 2013), and the establishment of collaborative learning communities led to projects that had major impact both on knowledge creation and practice.

Bill's practice is true to his view and definition of collaborative management research, namely, "Collaborative management research is an effort by two or more parties, at least one of whom is a member of an organization or system under study and at least one of whom is an external researcher, to work together in learning about how the behavior of managers, management methods, or organizational arrangements affect outcomes in the system or systems under study, using methods that are scientifically based and intended to reduce the likelihood of drawing false conclusions from the data collected, with the intent of both proving performance of the system and adding to the broader body of knowledge in the field of management" (Pasmore et al. 2008, p. 20).

The CMR approach refers to a stream within the action research family that has been identified as a potent method for advancing scientific knowledge and bringing about change in organizations. At the most basic level, CMR orientation claims that by bringing management and researchers closer together, the rate of progress in understanding and addressing issues such as creativity, innovation, growth, change, organizational effectiveness, economic development, and sustainable development will be faster than if either managers or researchers approached these topics separately.

Legacies and Unfinished Business: The Joy of Continuous Impact of Meaning Creation

As noted previously, Bill's unfinished work is focused on the future. Some of the issues facing many organizations today include digital disruption, a change in working arrangements to "contributors" versus employees, faster and more significant technological advances, global competition, and the real threat of climate change. To face these challenges will require completely new thinking about organization design, which in turn will make new demands on leaders that will change the ways in which they think and behave. Working with the innovation team at CCL, colleagues in the French consulting firm Theano, and his students at Columbia, Bill is undertaking an ambitious effort to build centers for the future in both healthcare and industry. The purpose of the centers will be to promote collaborative research and practice in creating future ways of working. The centers, which operate virtually now, would become physical locations where people could gather to learn and share insights from practice if Bill has his way. Of course, he recognizes that life does not go on forever and that there is "So much to do with so little time." Bill doesn't anticipate retiring any time soon and has books, consulting projects, and research underway. He enjoys his multiple affiliations and values his colleagues above everything else with regard to his professional life. "As long as I can work on interesting projects with great people, I'm happy," he says.

Proudest Moments as a Scholar-Practitioner

Bill identified key moments in which he was proud as a scholar-practitioner. One such moment was when an assembly line worker came to him at a conference and thanked him personally for changing his life, because of what he had written and how his company had used it to make his work more meaningful. Another was when one of his students wrote to tell him about the success they were having in their career. Yet another was when a CEO client told him that she so looked forward to their time together.

One of the standout moments was being honored by his colleagues at the Academy of Management with the creation of an annual award to be given in Dick Woodman's and his name, to researchers who do outstanding, long-lasting collaborative work together. In his words, "It's really something when your colleagues notice the effort you have put in. For me, it was like the Academy Awards, only they named the Oscar after us."

One thing that Bill hopes people would remember about his contribution to OD is that he never stopped learning, exploring what is new, and trying to add more to the field. He did not get stuck in a single paradigm or methodology. In his own words, "I think I have always been a teacher and a learner and tried not to let my success go to my head. There's so much more we need to know. Of course, I'm not finished – I'm as excited now about what I'm working on as anything in my career."

Bill believes that the challenges the field faced at the beginning are still out there. "It's hard for us to be critical about what needs improvement in organizations and the world and not have that make people in positions of authority a little nervous." He argues that people in the field can and should appreciate what's good and empathize with leaders but still have to make it better; and that's not always easy. He wishes the next generation greater resourcefulness, greater wisdom, and the continued courage to avoid taking the easy way out. The world is full of significant challenges to tackle, from global warming to peace, poverty, and hunger. "Maybe the next generation, with its attitude that anything is possible and with the help of technology, can do what we've as yet been unable to do." Bill is working with his long-time colleague Dick Woodman on a chapter for Research in Organization Development and Change that will spell out issues the field needs to address. "Too much of what we are researching and writing about in our journals is based on questions that were asked in the 1960s. It's time we advanced our thinking to make the issues critical to the future, not the past," he says.

Of course, he is also an editor, along with David Szabla and Mary Barnes, of this volume on Great Thinkers in the field. Despite Bill's critique of the current state of the field, he believes the field has a proud history and that new students should know more about the people and ideas behind it.

References

Carucci, R., & Pasmore, W. (2002a). Driving change through advocacy. *Mercer Management Journal, 14*.

Carucci, R., & Pasmore, W. (2002b). *Relationships that enable enterprise change*. San Francisco: Jossey-Bass/Pfeiffer.

Coghlan, D. (2011). Action research: Exploring perspectives on a philosophy of practical knowing. *The Academy of Management Annals, 5*(1), 53–87.

Cooperrider, D., & Pasmore, W. (1991a). The organization dimension of global change. *Human Relations, 8*, 763–787.

Cooperrider, D., & Pasmore, W. (1991b). Global social change: A new agenda for social science? *Human Relations, 10*, 1037–1055.

Cross, R., Ernst, C., & Pasmore, W. (2013). A bridge too far? How boundary spanning networks drive organizational change and effectiveness. *Organizational Dynamics, 42*, 81–91.

Horney, N., Pasmore, W., & O'Shea, T. (2010). Leadership agility: A business imperative for a VUCA world. *People and Strategy, 33*(4), 32–38.

Pasmore, W., & Tolchinsky, P. (1989). Doing it right from the start: Merging total quality and sociotechnical systems design. *Journal for Quality and Participation, 12*, 56–59.

Pasmore, W., & Torres, R. (2004). Choosing the next best CEO. *Mercer Management Journal, 16*, 67–75.

Pasmore, W. (1976). The Michigan ICL study revisited: An alternative explanation of the results. *Journal of Applied Behavioral Science, 2*, 245–251.

Pasmore, W. (1982a). Sociotechnical systems interventions. In E. Pavlock (Ed.), *Organization development: Managing transitions*. ASTD: Washington, DC.

Pasmore, W. (1982b). Overcoming the roadblocks in work restructuring. *Organizational Dynamics, Spring*, 54–67.

Pasmore, W. (1983). Turning people on to work. In D. Kolb, I. Rubin, & J. McIntyre (Eds.), *Organizational psychology*. Englewood Cliffs: Prentice Hall.

Pasmore, W. (1984). A comprehensive approach to planning an OD/QWL strategy. In D. Warrick (Ed.), *Contemporary organization development: Current thinking and applications* (pp. 204–217). Glenview: Scott, Foresman.

Pasmore, W. (1986). Power and participation: The coming shakeup in organizational power structures. In S. Srivastva et al. (Eds.), *Executive power* (pp. 239–256). San Francisco: Jossey-Bass.

Pasmore, W. (1988). *Designing effective organizations: The sociotechnical systems perspective*. New York: Wiley.

Pasmore, W. (1994). *Creating strategic change*. New York: Wiley.

Pasmore, W. (2001). Action research in the workplace: The socio-technical perspective. In P. Reason & H. Bradbury (Eds.), *The handbook of action research* (pp. 38–47). New York: Wiley & Sons.

Pasmore, W. (2004). Collaborative research mechanisms: Some lenses and mechanisms, a commentary. In A. Adler, A. B. (Rami) Shani, & A. Styhre (Eds.), *Collaborative research in organizations: Foundations for learning, change, and theoretical development* (pp. 167–172). Thousand Oaks: Sage Publications.

Pasmore, W. (2011). Tipping the balance: Overcoming persistent problems in change. In A. Shani, R. Woodman, & W. Pasmore (Eds.), *Research in organizational change and development* (Vol. 19, pp. 259–292). Bingley: Emerald Publishing.

Pasmore, W. (2015). *Leading continuous change: Navigating churn in the real world.* Oakland: Berrett-Koehler.

Pasmore, W., & Fagans, M. (1992). Participation, individual development, and organizational change: A review and synthesis. *Journal of Management, 18*(2), 375–397.

Pasmore, W., & Friedlander, F. (1982). An action research program for increasing employee involvement in problem solving. *Administrative Science Quarterly, 2*(7), 343–362.

Pasmore, W., & Gurley, K. (1991). Enhancing R&D across functional areas. In R. Kilmann & L. Kilmann (Eds.), *Making organizations more competitive* (pp. 368–396). San Francisco: Jossey-Bass.

Pasmore, W., & Khalsa, G. (1993). The contributions of Eric Trist to the social sciences. *Academy of Management Review, 18*(3), 546–569.

Pasmore, W., & King, D. (1978). Understanding organizational behavior through change: A comparative study of multifaceted interventions. *Journal of Applied Behavioral Science, 4*, 455–468 . Reprinted in D. Katz & R. Kahn (Eds.). (1980). *The study of organizations*. San Francisco: Jossey-Bass.

Pasmore, W., & Lafferty, K. (2009). *Developing a leadership strategy.* Greensboro: Center for Creative Leadership Publication.

Pasmore, W., & Nemiroff, P. (1975). Lost at sea: A consensus seeking task. In J. W. Pfeiffer & J. E. Jones (Eds.), *The 1975 handbook for group facilitators*. La Jolla: University Associates.

Pasmore, W., & Purser, R. (1993). Designing work systems for knowledge workers. *Journal for Quality and Participation, July/August,* 78–84.

Pasmore, W., & Sherwood, J. (Eds.). (1978). *Sociotechnical systems: A sourcebook*. San Diego: University Associates.

Pasmore, W., & Torres, R. (2006a). The board's new roles in CEO succession. In D. Nadler, B. Behan, & M. Nadler (Eds.), *Building better boards* (pp. 172–191). San Francisco: Jossey-Bass.

Pasmore, W., & Torres, W. (2006b). How to make sure your next CEO is a winner. *Corporate Board Journal, March-April.*

Pasmore, W., & Woodman, R. (Eds.). (1997). *Research in organizational change and development* (Vol. 10). Greenwich: JAI Publishing.

Pasmore, W., Srivastva, S., & Sherwood, J. (1978). Social relationships and organizational performance: A sociotask approach. In W. Pasmore & J. Sherwood (Eds.), *Sociotechnical systems: A sourcebook*. San Diego: University Associates.

Pasmore, W., Francis, C., Haldeman, J., & Shani, A. B. (Rami). (1982). Sociotechnical systems: A North American reflection on empirical studies of the seventies. *Human Relations, 12*, 1179–1204.

Pasmore, W., Stymne, B., Shani, A. B. (Rami)., Mohrman, S., & Adler, N. (2008). The promise of collaborative management research. In A. B. (Rami) Shani, S. Mohrman, W. Pasmore, B. Stymne, & N. Adler (Eds.), *Handbook of collaborative management research* (pp. 7–32). Thousand Oaks: Sage Publishing.

Pasmore, W., Shani, A. B. (Rami)., & Woodman, R. (Eds.). (2010). *Research in organizational change and development* (Vol. 18). Bingley, UK: Emerald Publishing.

Pasmore, W., Shani, A. B. (Rami)., & Mietus, J. (1983). Technological change and work organization in the US Army: A field experiment. In G. Mensch & R. Niehaus (Eds.), *Technology and work organization* (pp. 153–166). Plenum: New York.

Purser, R., & Pasmore, W. (1992). Organizing for learning. In W. Pasmore & R. Woodman (Eds.), *Research in organizational change and development* (Vol. 6, pp. 37–114). Greenwich: JAI Press.

Purser, R., Pasmore, W., & Tenkasi, R. (1992). The influence of deliberations on learning in new product development teams. *Journal of Engineering and Technology Management, 9*, 1–28.

Rao, H., & Pasmore, W. (1989). Knowledge and interests in organizational studies: A conflict of interpretations. *Organizational Studies, 2*, 225–240.

Schein, E. (2013). *Humble inquiry*. San Francisco: Berrett-Koehler Publishers.

Simendinger, E., & Pasmore, W. (1984). The development and destruction of cooperation in physician-management teams. *Journal of Hospital Administration, 6*, 21–35.

Stilwell, R., Pasmore, W., & Shon, D. (2016, Forthcoming). Change leader behavior inventory: Development and validation of an assessment instrument. *Journal of Applied Behavioral Science*. doi: 10.7916/D8SJ1KNM.

Shani, A. B. (Rami)., & Pasmore, W. A. (1985). Organization inquiry: Towards a new model of the action research process. In D. D. Warrick (Ed.), *Contemporary organization development: Current thinking and applications*. Glenview: Scott, Foresman . [Reproduced in Coghlan, D., & Shani, A. B. (Rami) (Eds.). (2010). *Fundamentals of organization development* (Vol. 1) (pp. 249–260). London: Sage].

Woodman, R., & Pasmore, W. (Eds.). (1987). *Research in organizational change and development* (Vol. 1). Greenwich: JAI Publishing.

Further Reading

Nemiroff, P., Pasmore, W., & Ford, D. (1976). The effects of two normative structural interventions on established and ad-hoc decision-making groups: Implications for the improvement of decision-making effectiveness. *Decision Sciences, 7*(4), 841–855.

Pasmore, W. (1998). Organizing for jazz. *Organizational Science, 9*(5), 562–568.

Pasmore, W., & Fagans, M. (1994). Old science, new values? *Vision Action, 12*(4).

Pasmore, W. (1995). Social science transformed: The socio-technical perspective. *Human Relations, 48*(1), 1–21.

Pasmore, W., & Woodman, R. (Eds.). (1988). *Research in organizational change and development* (Vol. 2). Greenwich: JAI Publishing.

Pasmore, W., & Woodman, R. (Eds.). (1995). *Research in organizational change and development* (Vol. 8). Greenwich: JAI Publishing.

Pasmore, W., & Woodman, R. (Eds.). (2003). *Research in organizational change and development* (Vol. 14). Greenwich: Elsevier.

Pasmore, W., & Woodman, R. (2007). *Research in organizational change and development* (Vol. 16). Oxford, UK: Elsevier.

Pasmore, W., & Woodman, R. (Eds.) (n.d.). Greenwich: JA1 Publishing.

Pasmore, W., Petee, J., & Bastian, R. (1987). Sociotechnical systems in health care: A field experiment. *Journal of Applied Behavioral Science, 3*, 329–340.

Pasmore, W., & Woodman, R. (Eds.). (1992). *Research in organizational change and development* (Vol. 6). Greenwich: JAI Publishing.

Pasmore, W., & Woodman, R. (Eds.). (1999). *Research in organizational change and development* (Vol. 12). Greenwich: JAI Publishing.

Shani, A. B. (Rami)., Woodman, R., & Pasmore, W. (Eds.). (2011). *Research in organizational change and development* (Vol. 19). Bingley, UK: Emerald Publishing.

Shani, A. B. (Rami)., W., & Woodman, R. (Eds.). (2012). *Research in organizational change and development* (Vol. 20). Bingley, UK: Emerald Publishing.

Shani, A. B. (Rami)., Morhman, S., Pasmore, W., Stymne, B., & Adler, N. (Eds.). (2008). *Handbook of collaborative management research*. Thousand Oaks: Sage Publishing.

Srikantia, P., & Pasmore, W. (1996). Conviction and doubt in organizational learning. *Journal of Organizational Change Management, 9*(1), 42–53.

Woodman, R., & Pasmore, W. (Eds.). (1989). *Research in organizational change and development* (Vol. 3). Greenwich: JAI Publishing.

Woodman, R., & Pasmore, W. (Eds.). (1991). *Research in organizational change and development* (Vol. 5). Greenwich: JAI Publishing.

Woodman, R., & Pasmore, W. (Eds.). (1993). *Research in organizational change and development* (Vol. 7). Greenwich: JAI Publishing.

Woodman, R., & Pasmore, W. (Eds.). (1996). *Research in organizational change and development* (Vol. 9). Greenwich: JAI Publishing.

Woodman, R., & Pasmore, W. (Eds.). (1998). *Research in organizational change and development* (Vol. 11). Greenwich: JAI Publishing.

Woodman, R., & Pasmore, W. (Eds.). (2001). *Research in organizational change and development* (Vol. 13). Oxford, UK: Elsevier.

Woodman, R., & Pasmore, W. (2002). The heart of it all: Group and team-based interventions in organization development. In J. Waclawski & A. Church (Eds.), *Organization development: A data-driven approach*. San Francisco: Jossey-Bass.

Woodman, R., & Pasmore, W. (Eds.). (2005). *Research in organizational change and development* (Vol. 15). Oxford, UK: Elsevier.

Woodman, R., Pasmore, W., & Shani, A. B. (Rami)., (Eds.). (2009). *Research in organizational change and development* (Vol. 17). Bingley, UK: Emerald Publishing.

Andrew M. Pettigrew: A Groundbreaking Process Scholar

61

Harry Sminia

Abstract

This chapter positions Andrew Pettigrew as a process scholar. It describes his work of catching "reality in flight" as he investigated the continuity and change, which is involved in subject areas like the politics of organizational decision-making, organizational culture, fundamental strategic change, human resource management, competitiveness, the workings of boards of directors, and new organizational forms. The chapter also describes the research methodology of contextualism that Andrew Pettigrew developed to capture "reality in flight." It discusses the extent to which Andrew Pettigrew succeeded and how his research program could be developed further.

Keywords

Process • Contextualism • Strategic change • Politics • Impact

Contents

Is Andrew Pettigrew a "change thinker"? Asking this question is not meant to start an argument whether he should be included in this book or not. It actually serves the purpose of pinpointing why he should be included. Pettigrew is not a "change thinker" in that he aimed to understand the phenomenon of "change" in its own right.

H. Sminia (✉)
Department of Strategy and Organization, University of Strathclyde Business School, Glasgow, Scotland, UK
e-mail: harry.sminia@strath.ac.uk

D.B. Szabla et al. (eds.), *The Palgrave Handbook of Organizational Change Thinkers*,
DOI 10.1007/978-3-319-52878-6_53

His prime motivation was to understand "process" as it happens. His research questions are not about how or why change happens or what change is in a general sense. They are about why particular change did happen while other change did not. In doing so, he conducted research on decision-making, organizational culture, organization development, strategy formation, human resource management, competitiveness, health services, public management, corporate governance, and new organizational forms. He is interested in the larger process of continuity and change, as the subtitle of Pettigrew's landmark book, *The Awakening Giant: Continuity and Change in ICI*, aptly indicates (Pettigrew 1985a). In doing so, he generated a number of insights that are relevant for understanding change and change management. And he developed the research methodology of contextualism as a way to investigate change.

Influences and Motivations: Close Scrutiny of Real Problems

Andrew Pettigrew's research career started properly in 1966. In the UK, business schools were in the process of being established. He had graduated with a sociology degree and a postgraduate diploma in industrial administration from the University of Liverpool. His first academic job was as research fellow on a project instigated by Enid Mumford, who had just moved from Liverpool to the newly established Manchester Business School (MBS). She also acted as his dissertation supervisor with Andrew earning his PhD in 1970. In this project, he uncovered the political nature of organizational decision-making (Pettigrew 1970, 1973).

In those early years, there were various influences that affected Pettigrew's research orientation. In fact, his first experience as a researcher was on an anthropological expedition to Uganda when the young Andrew was still at school. He helped charting cultural change among the Musopisiek people of the Sebei. It was this experience that taught him the importance of getting close to the action to understand what is going on, but also about the contextual nature of social phenomena. This was perpetuated at Liverpool, where the sociology that was being established there was theoretically informed but problem-orientated empiricism but also assumed the presence of conflict and change. It continued at MBS with Enid Mumford doing her research in coal mines and the port of Liverpool in this tradition. Pettigrew's study of managers while they were making their decisions was conducted in a similar manner. He went in and observed managers and their decision-making activity while it was going on, as Enid Mumford had done with the coal miners and with the Liverpool dockers. What he observed was far removed from the rationalistic ideal that was being propagated. He came out with a clear understanding of the inherently politicized nature of management.

Another profound influence was his time spent at Yale from 1969 to 1971, at the invitation of Chris Argyris. This he considers to be the most significant period of his career and indeed life (Pettigrew 1998). It strengthened Andrew Pettigrew's conviction that true understanding comes from being close to the phenomenon under study, as Chris Argyris always insisted that any new theoretical and therefore abstract idea has to be explainable through concrete examples. Yale also exposed Andrew Pettigrew to a completely different research culture that was simultaneously collegial and competitive, and where status and success for an academic were indicated through a stream of journal publications.

If his PhD research taught Andrew Pettigrew about the politicized nature of management, his next project revealed the influence and importance of culture. It was set up as a study of change. It concerned the Gordonstoun School in Scotland, which changed from single sex to coeducation in 1972. He conducted a multi-method study, doing interviews with key people – including members of the Royal Family, conducting a survey among students and staff, analyzing documents, and investigating the history of the school, all to get close to the action and to find out how and why things were going on as they did. The findings pointed at the interactions between entrepreneurship/leadership and organization culture (Pettigrew 1979). Andrew Pettigrew again was ahead of the curve here, being one of the first to introduce the notion of organization culture, indicating that if we talk about organizational change, we can conceptualize it as cultural change.

One of the things that Andrew Pettigrew has urged people to do is to not only conduct research for its own sake but to also engage with and propagate the findings among management practitioners. One way of doing this is to publish articles in practitioner journals. In fact, it was a publication in a practitioner journal on the basis of his PhD thesis, which had attracted the attention of an OD consultant who was working in ICI. ICI at the time was the largest manufacturing firm in the UK, working mainly in the chemical industry. The process that Andrew Pettigrew had investigated for his PhD project concerned a succession of decisions about investing in and replacing computer systems. As part of this, he focused on the role of computer experts in the firm and their interactions with the managers who were making the decisions. One of the findings pointed at the phenomenon of the "experts" gaining influence and legitimacy on the basis of their involvement in the decisions and their effect on the outcome. The OD consultant reckoned a similar process was going on with the OD specialists and their effectiveness in ICI. OD was introduced to ICI in an attempt to make its management more effective, but the extent to which OD was taken up varied across the various ICI divisions. He asked Andrew Pettigrew whether he was interested to investigate.

The ICI project originally was about this question of how OD's influence and effectiveness varied across the various parts of ICI. It quickly grew into the larger question of how strategic change is realized. This project was eventually published in book form (Pettigrew 1985a) but with various other publications written on the back of it (e.g., Pettigrew 1987a, d, 1990). If anything, the ICI study put Andrew Pettigrew on the map. It also linked him with the strategic management field, contributing to making strategy process and strategic change research objects in their own right. Furthermore, it solidified his methodological approach of contextualism as a way to investigate change.

The "fame" and recognition that came with the ICI study allowed Andrew Pettigrew to establish a research center. After he came back from the USA in

1971, he became a lecturer at London Business School. In 1976, he took up a professorship in organizational behavior at the University of Warwick. This is where he established the Centre for Corporate Strategy and Change (CCSC) in 1985.

The center embarked upon a range of research projects, all utilizing his contextualist methodology. These projects were conducted by research teams, with many of its members going on to become well-recognized management scholars in their own right. These projects took on big questions like the usefulness and development of strategic human resource management (Pettigrew et al. 1990), competitiveness and strategic change (Pettigrew and Whipp 1991), continuity and change in the British National Health Service (NHS) (Pettigrew et al. 1992), new public management (Ferlie et al. 1996), the functioning and effectiveness of boards of directors (McNulty and Pettigrew 1999; Pettigrew and McNulty 1998), and new and innovative forms of organizing (Pettigrew and Fenton 2000; Pettigrew et al. 2003). All these projects were very timely, in effect investigating phenomena in the making but also right at the heart of what were then contemporary issues in management scholarship and in (British) society. Apart from conducting relevant research, in this way Andrew Pettigrew was also able to generate interest and secure funding.

Andrew Pettigrew expressed his eagerness of getting close to understanding what is going on as wanting to "catch reality in flight" (Pettigrew 1998). It is about getting to grips with the process by which things emerge. This implies change but also continuity. The way to do this, he reckons, is to engage with these phenomena in the making (i.e., Schwarz and Stensaker 2014). Management scholarship should not be this detached activity that just aims to explain. It should be about cocreation and engagement, about solving problems and generating insight that is relevant (Pettigrew 1997a, 2001a, 2005). This is reflected in his choice of research topics. He asks big questions. Only explicitly explained as such with the research project on innovative forms of organization (Pettigrew 2003), all of these topics were scrutinized for their progress (is the phenomenon spreading and what shape does it take?), process (how is the phenomenon coming into being?), and performance (what are its effects?). Ideally, it is about "big themes" investigated by "big teams." It is about how particular changes are brought about, instead of how change in a general sense can be achieved.

Andrew Pettigrew left Warwick in 2003, taking up the position of Dean of the University of Bath School of Management. CCSC had been dissolved in 2001. He moved to the University of Oxford Saïd Business School in 2008, becoming a Professor of strategy and organization, from which he retired in January 2016. At Bath, he would say, he had to practice what he preached. He saw his tenure there as having to reinvigorate what was essentially a good school into a world-class business school. He also became a bit more reflective, involving himself with an EFMD initiative on the future development of business schools (Pettigrew et al. 2014), as well as publishing on the relevance of management scholarship (Pettigrew 2001a, 2011b).

Key Contributions: Contextuality in Process Courses and Outcomes

It is not easy to pick Andrew Pettigrew's main contributions, as there are so many. Yet all his works center on two interrelated themes. One is theoretical in wanting to understand the course and outcome of processes of continuity and change. The other one is methodological in developing contextualism as a research methodology to generate this understanding.

Starting with his dissertation (Pettigrew 1970, 1973), he found the process of continuity and change to be very much of a political-cultural nature. What he observed was that decision-making is an essentially social and political process. It features complexity, uncertainty, and diverging interest and demands. This he captured later with the expression "*politics as the management of meaning*" (Pettigrew 1985a, p. 44). He recognizes that people basically act to further a cause they have an interest in, but do so within the confines of an existing social structure or context. However, this context does not just act to channel people's activities. It is actively drawn upon to legitimize claims and interests, and in doing so becomes a target and subject for change as well.

Management activity is therefore stratified in that it aims to achieve certain ends – the surface layer – and in doing so confirms or changes the social structure or context, the deeper layer, within which this takes place (cf. Sminia and de Rond 2012). People who want to be effective as a change agent have to be proficient in playing this politics of meaning game. It also turns management and the ongoing process of continuity and change into a continuous contest between people who are content with how things are going on and people who favor a different way of how things could and should be going on. Recognizing that we are dealing with a struggle here, the way in which this is allowed to play out affects the outcome. For instance, a firm's competitiveness was found to depend on how it deals with this contest between change and continuity (Pettigrew and Whipp 1991). Likewise, the effectiveness of boards of directors depends on how the board process is allowed to play out, with boards that feature debate about the future direction of the firm getting better results than boards that just rubber-stamp decisions made by the executive team (McNulty and Pettigrew 1999; Pettigrew and McNulty 1998).

Andrew Pettigrew was arguing against the many management scholars who expected managers to be rational decision-makers and who saw organizational change as designing and implementing new organizational structures. The dominant understanding of how decision-making is and should be done was one of information processing and choice. He was also arguing against the behavioral approach (Cyert and March 1963; March and Simon 1958). To him, the behavioral approach put too much emphasis on the individual manager and on cognitive limitations. He observed decision-making as a social-cultural-political process, involving an organization's social structure as much as the interests and cognitive abilities of the participants.

This basic finding of continuity and change playing out within a context but also shaping the context resonates with other observations that distinguish between incremental and more fundamental and radical strategic change (e.g., Anderson and Tushman 1990; Argyris and Schön 1978; Burgelman 1983; Greenwood and Hinings 1988; Johnson 1988). Incremental change takes place within the confines of the social structure. "Real" strategic change involves alterations to the social structure. It reflects a dialectic (Van de Ven and Poole 1995) and structuration-like theory of process. It is remarkable that Andrew Pettigrew sketched out the contours of a structuration-like theory of management in his 1970 dissertation (Pettigrew 1970, 1973), well before Giddens (1976) was published. Andrew Pettigrew (1985a) later associated his stance with structuration sociologists like Giddens (1979), Sewell (1992), and Sztompka (1991).

Structuration refers to an approach in sociology that tries to marry the what appear to be contradictory explanations of social order as being a consequence of either individual initiative (agency) or collective interests and norms and values (social structure). Giddens (1976, 1979, 1984) developed the notion of "duality of structure," proposing that social structure constrains but also enables agency while simultaneously social structure only persists if the actions it specifies continue to be enacted. From a structuration point of view, agency and social structure therefore are seen as mutually constitutive.

It is therefore not surprising that Andrew Pettigrew is critical of much change research that he considers as being "ahistorical, acontextual, and aprocessual." He is wary of change methods and methodologies that claim to be universally applicable, as management in general, and therefore change management in particular, is very context sensitive and plays out as a unique concurrence of events. This is particularly apparent in his conclusions about the spread and use of OD in ICI (Pettigrew 1985a). He points at a paradox first put forward by Warmington et al. (1977) that to design an effective change program, one has to understand an organization's culture and power configuration, which one can only learn about in the course of embarking upon a change program. This is also apparent in his research into change in the British National Health Service (Pettigrew et al. 1992), where he develops the concept of a receptive context to change. In a similar vein, he contextualizes competitiveness within the way in which a firm deals with change over time (Pettigrew and Whipp 1991). The more sensitive the management of change is to the specific circumstances in which the change is playing out, the more effective the process will be.

In the course of doing his research into continuity and change – attempting to catch reality in flight – Andrew Pettigrew developed a research methodology that he labeled as contextualism (Pettigrew 1985a, b, 1987c, 1990, 1992, 1997b), a term derived from Pepper (1942). It is most succinctly described by way of the "Pettigrew triangle" (see Fig. 1). It requires the researcher to investigate the process of change over time while relating it to the context in which it plays out as well as the content of what is being changed, treating all three angles of the triangle as mutual constitutive. The methodology is longitudinal in nature, utilizing multiple methods to gather data while the process takes place, supplemented with historical data to understand where the process under observation is coming from. There is a direct link between

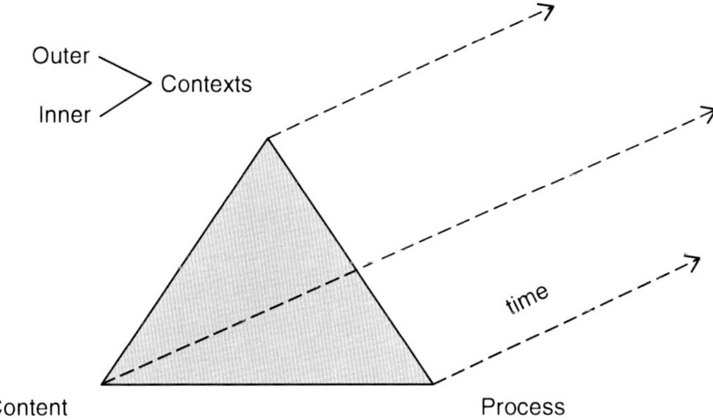

Fig. 1 Framework for analyzing change (Source: Pettigrew lecture slides (April 2009))

contextualism as a methodology and the structuration-like process theory that Andrew Pettigrew employs.

The requirements of multisource, multi-data, and also multi-researcher teams, as the size and the scope of a project tend to exceed the capacities of a single investigator, however, are not a license to simply collect everything that comes into sight. This, as Andrew Pettigrew puts it, will only lead to data asphyxiation (Pettigrew 1990). To prevent this, firstly, data collection has to focus on the context and how it impinges on but is also affected by the course of events, on the process and how the course of events takes shape over time, and the content of what exactly is changing and what remains constant (Pettigrew 1985a, c).

Secondly, any data gathering exercise needs to be accompanied by a careful consultation of the existing literature, drawing on various different approaches to provide a first conceptual sketch about how the phenomena under study is currently understood. As was said earlier, Andrew Pettigrew prefers big questions about issues and problems that in effect refer to phenomena in the making like, for instance, strategic human resource management, new public management, or innovative organizational forms. Similarly, he is interested in how things like managerial decision-making, OD, strategic change, competitiveness, or board process actually play out while being enacted. The consultation of the literature generates a first understanding with regard to the phenomenon under study as well as expectations about its effects. It will also generate more specific questions, as it is not uncommon that the literature holds conflicting accounts, often features widely exaggerated claims about the effects, and very likely is ahistorical, acontextual, and aprocessual. These more specific questions then inform as well as limit the data collection efforts. Andrew Pettigrew favors a comparative case study design where similar processes of continuity and change but with different outcomes are scrutinized for differences in the course of the process.

A contextualist analysis consists of six activities (Pettigrew 1985a, c). To start, you are required to draft a detailed chronological description of the process under study. Once that is done, you expose the continuity and change as it occurs in the course of the process. This then allows you to compare existing theoretical insights with the course of events to identify where current theory falls short. In the course of this, you have to distinguish between the various contextual levels at which the process plays out. As this is done, the initial chronology is redrafted to separate out what is occurring at each contextual level for the period under investigation. Finally, the outcome of the process has to be evaluated on the basis of how the course of the process has taken shape as interplay between these various contextual levels. Such an analysis is not a mechanical exercise of processing data to arrive at a conclusion. It requires judgment and skill. The criteria by which a contextualist analysis is judged center on the balance between description and analysis, whether there is new theoretical understanding, whether this new understanding is based on how the course of the process has taken shape, and how well the abstracted theoretical process account connects with the process data (Pettigrew 1985c).

These six activities then allow you to report on the findings in the way that Andrew Pettigrew normally does (Sminia 2016). For instance, in Pettigrew and Whipp (1991), the literature review in effect is a consultation of various strands of literature about competitiveness, with its limitations explained in a way that anticipates the findings of the research project. These findings and explanations in turn take shape in the form of providing short answers and long answers. The long answer here contains in-depth and mostly chronological accounts of the five cases that were investigated for the competitiveness project. This long answer illustrates, demonstrates, and justifies the short answer.

The short answer of how firm competitiveness relates to strategic change ability then introduces the new theoretical understanding that has come out. In this project, this is explained by way of a mechanism consisting of five interrelated factors (see Fig. 2; Pettigrew and Whipp 1991, 1993; Whipp and Pettigrew 1992; Whipp et al. 1989a, b). The five factors are "environmental assessment," "leading change," "linking strategic and operational change," "human resources as assets and liabilities," and "coherence." It refers to a process pattern that is shared among higher-performing firms. With regard to environmental assessment, organizations should be "open learning systems" that reinterpret the circumstances in which they operate. It should not be regarded as a technical exercise of information processing and dissemination. Leading change is about both providing small, incremental directions and generating legitimacy for change. Linking strategic and operational change is about emergent activity being embraced but linked with evolving intentions. A firm's human resource management should not treat people as liabilities but as assets. Finally coherence is about consonance, advantage, and feasibility and about safeguarding the integrity of the organization while it changes.

Another example presents a novel theoretical understanding about innovative forms of organizing (a verb) by way of a short answer in the form of a set of nine complementary activities (see Fig. 3; Pettigrew and Fenton 2000; Pettigrew et al. 2003; Whittington et al. 1999). Andrew Pettigrew found that these nine activities tend to have a mutually reinforcing effect and that the benefits of such an innovative organizational form will only be present when a firm goes for it wholeheartedly. This

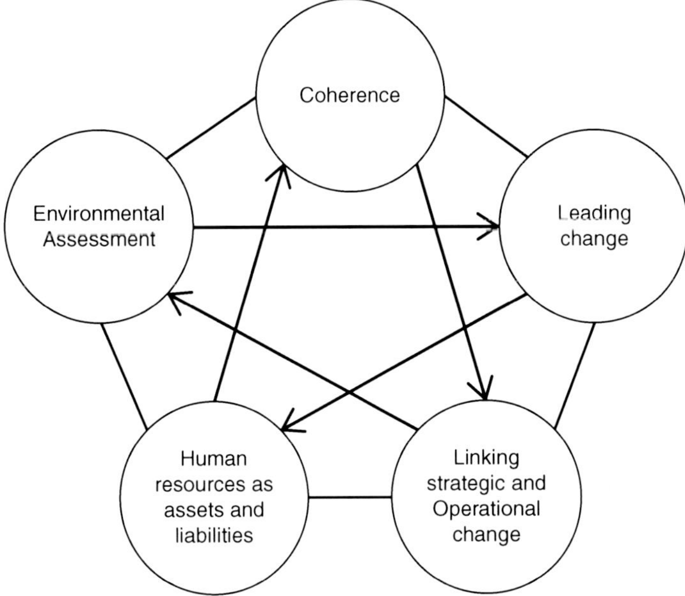

Fig. 2 Managing change for competitive success: the five central factors (Source: Pettigrew and Whipp (1991, p. 104))

is because there is a positive complementarity, involving all of the elements of the new organizational form. There is a negative complementarity when firms limit themselves to only one or a few aspects, with the benefits failing to materialize and things even becoming worse. Again, there are also extensive long answers that provide the details of the various case studies, as well as theory reviews that consult and interrogate different strands of literature, expose their weaknesses, and to which the findings are compared.

New Insights: Generality in the Specifics

Elaborating continuity and change in a structuration-like manner, putting (change) management forward as a process of politics of meaning, and developing a contextualist methodology that reflects the highly specific nature of each change process yield a number of new insights that on occasion contradict the prevailing orthodoxy.

The emphasis on context and the uniqueness of each process course plays down the importance of generalizability of research outcomes. There is a questioning of the presumption that management knowledge eventually will take on the form of generalizable theory and universally applicable change tools and methods. Very early on he argues against the variance approach and the expectation that "proper" research has to be about developing constructs, variables, and indicators, which have to be tested for

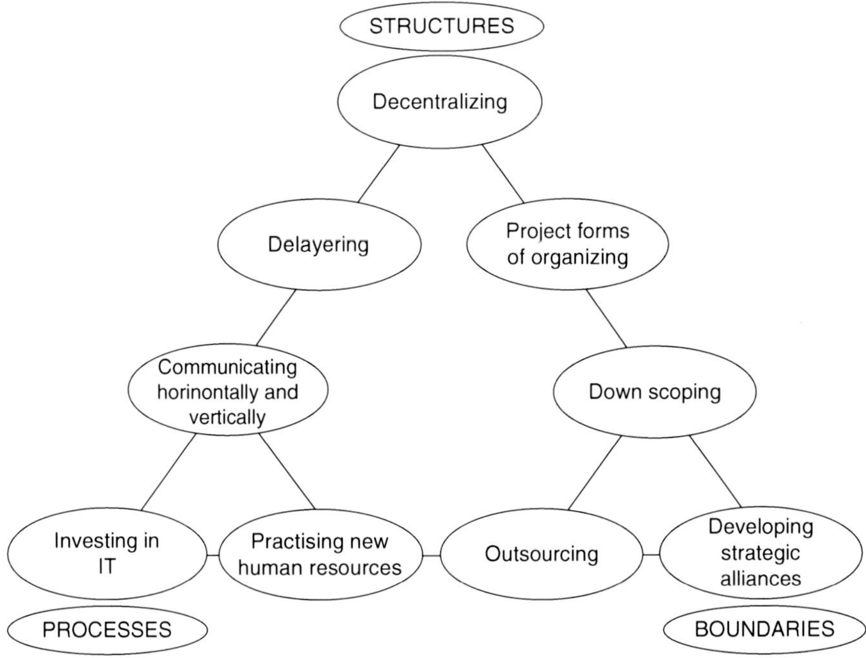

Fig. 3 New forms of organizing: the multiple indicators (Source: Pettigrew and Massini (2003, p. 12))

their hypothesized relationships (Pettigrew 1973). Later in his career, he comments on the irony of this kind of research, not arriving at any definitive conclusions but instead prompting further research on more specific and fine-grained questions and boundary conditions, in effect validating his contextualist perspective (Pettigrew et al. 2002). It makes you wonder why generalizability is considered to be such a key indicator of research quality. Contextuality does not mean that management research is incapable of generating insights that are of relevance beyond the cases under investigation. It should be more about transferability and versatility than generalizability (Van de Ven 2007), about looking for the general in the specific than the generalizability of the specific. Some of Andrew Pettigrew's close collaborators in a number of his research projects have argued for external validity in terms of relevance for the people for whom the research is conducted (Ferlie and McNulty 1997).

It also puts the utilization of change management tools and techniques in perspective. The specific and contextual nature of (change) management means that any claim about an inherent and universal effect of a specific tool or technique has to be questioned. If there is an effect, it is a consequence of the interaction between the tool or technique, the way in which it was deployed, and the circumstances in which it was used. For instance, we found the utilization of large-scale intervention (LSI) – a bottom-up approach of realizing change throughout an organization as a whole (Bunker and Alban 1992) – in effect perpetuated the top-down culture that existed in the organization in which it was applied (Sminia and van Nistelrooij 2006). The supposed effects inherent in LSI of generating change through dialogue were counteracted by contextual and emergent factors that shaped the course of the process. In another instance, despite carefully formulating a strategic plan as well as setting out and embarking upon the various steps by which it should be implemented, I observed that some skillful politics of meaning meant that the whole thing was abandoned within a year (Sminia 2005).

Cases like this can be easily dismissed as instances of bad management. Yet on reflection, they reveal the possibility of highly skillful change management practices by which a specific tool or technique is utilized in a context-sensitive manner (van Nistelrooij and Sminia 2010). For instance, dialogue can improve mutual understanding in an organization that is entrenched in various noncommunicating factions. The same exercise can also infuse an organization with a bit more variety and spice things up, when it is suffering from groupthink. In different contexts, with the change management tool keyed in differently, the process will generate different, albeit possibly favorable outcomes for each specific situation.

Contextuality not only refers to place but also to time. And as "times change," the problems and situations that managers have to deal with change as well. To Andrew Pettigrew, management scholarship therefore is not about uncovering universal truths. It is about engaging with the realities that managers have to deal with. He propagates engaged scholarship (Van de Ven 2007) that queries phenomena as they occur and emerge (Schwarz and Stensaker 2014) instead of filling gaps in existing theory. Scholarship therefore comes with the double requirement of rigor and relevance (Pettigrew 1997a, 2005). This he expresses by way of the five I's of Impact by offering "how to" knowledge, of Innovation in theory and method, of Interdisciplinary openness, of Internationalism through investigation and collaboration, and of Involvement with but independence from fellow researchers and users. Impact is an increasing concern in the UK because of its rising prominence among the criteria according to which university research is assessed. He claims that contextualist methodology is ideally suited to deliver (Pettigrew 2011b).

Legacies and Unfinished Business: Change Beyond the Confines of the Organization

The "Pettigrew triangle" has informed many research projects, either just as a means to clarify the object of enquiry has a process, context, and content aspect or by embracing the full contextualist research methodology. Moreover, Andrew Pettigrew's research has helped to introduce and further legitimize qualitative research, especially in the realm of strategic management. It has also helped to effectively falsify the effectiveness of too linear and objectivist approaches to management.

Yet Andrew Pettigrew is not without his critics. For instance, Cray et al. (1991) and Rajagopalan and Spreitzer (1997) criticized Pettigrew's work for its lack of generalizability, but this is beside the point for a contextualist. More essentially, he has been criticized for not being contextual enough. Andrew Pettigrew (1985a, pp. 36–37) urges us to elaborate context as more than "*just a descriptive background, or an eclectic list of antecedents*." Caldwell (2005) argues that this is exactly what Andrew Pettigrew has been doing. In fact, Caldwell points at a more fundamental problem that is present in all research that adopts structuration-like theory. This is the problem that it is empirically very difficult to distinguish whether specific events in the course of a process are primarily due to management agency or to the surrounding context or social structure. Moreover, by arguing, as Andrew Pettigrew has done, that change processes are to a large extent indeterministic, Caldwell reckons that a contextualist approach has become irrelevant to practicing managers. As there apparently is so much impinging on a situation, what difference can a manager make? Such impracticality is also brought forward by Buchanan and Boddy (1992) and Dawson (1994). Ironically, others have criticized Andrew Pettigrew's uncritical stance toward (top) management and the implicit assumption that they are ultimately in charge (Morgan and Sturdy 2000; Willmott 1997).

Andrew Pettigrew has also been criticized for not being sufficiently processual (Chia and MacKay 2007; Hernes 2014; Tsoukas and Chia 2002). This also relates to his structuration-like conceptualization of the change process in that these authors decline the mutual constitutive nature of agency and structure, and therefore the distinction between change and continuity. To them process is always a matter of emergence and change, with agency and structure both arising out of the inherent dispositions and logics of practice (Schatzki 2001). It is fair to say that, despite being critical of Andrew Pettigrew's elaboration of process and change, his work did pave the way for the introduction of the "practice turn" in management and organizational scholarship, specifically with regard to the strategy-as-practice movement (Jarzabkowski and Spee 2009; Whittington 1996, 2006).

Andrew Pettigrew's contextualist methodology is also in need of further elaboration in terms of contextualist methods (Sminia 2016). He provided extensive guidance in how to design and conduct a contextualist research project (Pettigrew 1985b, c, 1987b, 1989, 1990, 1995, 1997b, 2011b, 2013). Nevertheless, replicating his approach is not without difficulty because of a lack of more detailed descriptions how all that data that comes with a contextualist research project has been gathered and especially analyzed. He only indicates that this requires skill, judgment, and lots of discussion among research team members.

Andrew Pettigrew retired from Saïd Business School, University of Oxford, in January 2016. The Pettigrew project is far from finished and still worth pursuing, despite the criticism. One avenue would be to extend research in change as well as the reach of the management of change well beyond an organization's boundaries. There are at least two reasons for doing this. Firstly, as is already implied in his elaboration of context as social structure, whether its constraining and enabling effect is due to something inside or outside the organization is not a necessarily important aspect for understanding what is going on. What is important, though, is that the contextuality of the change process is taken into account.

Secondly, there is a need to be more ambitious with change management and change research in that its reach should extend beyond the organization's boundaries. There is a somewhat implicit understanding that organizational change is about adapting an organization to changing (external) circumstances. This is notwithstanding that many change initiatives, although originating within an organization, generate effects well beyond it. This is especially apparent in studies into institutional change and institutional entrepreneurship (e.g., Gawer and Phillips 2013; Greenwood and Suddaby 2006; Johnson et al. 2000; Leblebici et al. 1991; Lounsbury and Crumley 2007). Conceptually, many of these studies share Andrew Pettigrew's structuration-like approach to process (e.g., Barley and Tolbert 1997; DiMaggio and Powell 1983; Hirsch and Lounsbury 1997; Lawrence et al. 2009). Furthermore, the accounts and explanations of institutional change and institutional entrepreneurship resemble Andrew Pettigrew's "politics as the management of meaning" in that they combine politics and power with culture. It stands to reason to integrate research in organizational change and institutional entrepreneurship by treating it as one and the same process. In doing so, it would be possible, for instance, to open up strategy content research by adding considerations about how a firm can be competitive in specific circumstances with considerations about how a firm can generate and change the circumstances that are responsible for its competitiveness.

One of my current research projects takes up this challenge of investigating continuity and change well beyond the confines of a single organization. It looks at the emergence of High Value Manufacturing. Apart from being a phenomenon in the making as managers and policy makers look for a solution for manufacturing firms to find a viable way of operating in a world where competition appears to be mostly focused on price, manufacturing appears to become more and more a matter of simultaneous cooperation and competition, with continuity and change taking shape concurrently in both the intraorganizational and the interorganizational realms.

References

Anderson, P., & Tushman, M. L. (1990). Technological discontinuities and dominant designs: A cyclical model of technological change. *Administrative Science Quarterly, 35*, 604–633.

Argyris, C., & Schön, D. A. (1978). *Organizational learning: A theory of action perspective*. Reading: Addison-Wesley.

Barley, S. R., & Tolbert, P. S. (1997). Institutionalization and structuration: Studying the links between action and institution. *Organization Studies, 18*(1), 93–117.

Buchanan, D. A., & Boddy, D. (1992). *The expertise of the change agent: Public performance and backstage activity*. London: Prentice-Hall.

Bunker, B. B., & Alban, B. T. (1992). Editors' introduction: The large group intervention – a new social innovation? *Journal of Applied Behavioral Science, 28*(4), 473–479.

Burgelman, R. A. (1983). A process model on internal corporate venturing in the diversified major firm. *Administrative Science Quarterly, 28*, 223–244.

Caldwell, R. (2005). Things fall apart? Discourses on agency and change in organizations. *Human Relations, 58*(1), 83–114.

Chia, R., & MacKay, R. B. (2007). Post-processual challenges for the emerging strategy-as-practice perspective: Discovering strategy in the logic of practice. *Human Relations, 60*(1), 217–242.

Cray, D., Mallory, G. R., Butler, J. E., Hickson, D. J., & Wilson, D. C. (1991). Explaining decision processes. *Journal of Management Studies, 28*(3), 227–251.

Cyert, R. L., & March, J. G. (1963). *A behavioral theory of the firm*. Englewood Cliffs: Prentice Hall.
Dawson, P. (1994). *Organizational change: A processual approach*. London: Paul Chapman.
DiMaggio, P. J., & Powell, W. W. (1983). The iron cage revisited: Institutional isomorphism and collective rationality in organizational fields. *American Sociological Review, 48*(2), 147–160.
Ferlie, E., & McNulty, T. (1997). "Going to market": Changing patterns in the organization and character of process research. *Scandinavian Journal of Management, 13*(4), 367–387.
Ferlie, E., Ashburner, L., Fitzgerald, L., & Pettigrew, A. M. (1996). *The new public management in action*. Oxford: Oxford University Press.
Gawer, A., & Phillips, N. (2013). Institutional work as logics shift: The case of Intel's transformation to platform leader. *Organization Studies, 34*(8), 1035–1071.
Giddens, A. (1976). *New rules of sociological method: A positive critique of interpretative sociologies*. London: Hutchinson.
Giddens, A. (1979). *Central problems in social theory: Action, structure and contradiction in social analysis*. Basingstoke: Macmillan.
Giddens, A. (1984). *The constitution of society: Outline of a theory of structuration*. Cambridge: Polity Press.
Greenwood, R., & Hinings, C. R. (1988). Organizational design types, tracks and the dynamics of strategic change. *Organization Studies, 9*(3), 293–316.
Greenwood, R., & Suddaby, R. (2006). Institutional entrepreneurship in mature fields: The big five accounting firms. *Academy of Management Journal, 49*(1), 27–48.
Hernes, T. (2014). *A process theory of organization*. Oxford: Oxford University Press.
Hirsch, P. M., & Lounsbury, M. (1997). Ending the family quarrel: Towards a reconciliation of "old" and "new" institutionalisms. *American Behavoral Scientist, 40*(4), 406–418.
Jarzabkowski, P. A., & Spee, P. (2009). Strategy-as-practice: A review and future directions for the field. *International Journal of Management Reviews, 11*(1), 69–95.
Johnson, G. (1988). Rethinking incrementalism. *Strategic Management Journal, 9*, 75–91.
Johnson, G., Smith, S., & Codling, B. (2000). Microprocesses of institutional change in the context of privatization. *Academy of Management Journal, 25*(3), 572–580.
Lawrence, T. B., Suddaby, R., & Leca, B. (2009). Introduction: Theorizing and studying institutional work. In T. Lawrence, R. Suddaby, & B. Leca (Eds.), *Institutional work: Actors and agency in institutional studies of organization* (pp. 1–28). Cambridge: Cambridge University Press.
Leblebici, H., Salancik, G. R., Copay, A., & King, T. (1991). Institutional change and the transformation of interorganizational fields: An organizational history of the US radio broadcasting industry. *Administrative Science Quarterly, 36*, 333–363.
Lounsbury, M., & Crumley, E. T. (2007). New practice creation: An institutional perspective on innovation. *Organization Studies, 28*(7), 993–1012.
March, J. G., & Simon, H. A. (1958). *Organizations*. New York: Wiley.
McNulty, T., & Pettigrew, A. M. (1999). Strategists on the board. *Organization Studies, 20*(1), 47–74.
Morgan, G., & Sturdy, A. (2000). *Beyond organizational change*. London: Macmillan.
Pepper, S. C. (1942). *World hypothesis: A study in evidence*. Berkeley: University of California Press.
Pettigrew, A. M. (1970). *A behavioural analysis of an innovative decision* (Doctoral Dissertation, University of Manchester).
Pettigrew, A. M. (1973). *The politics of organizational decision making*. London: Tavistock/Van Gorcum.
Pettigrew, A. M. (1979). On studying organizational cultures. *Administrative Science Quarterly, 24*, 570–581.
Pettigrew, A. M. (1985a). *The awakening giant: Continuity and change in ICI*. Oxford: Basil Blackwell.

Pettigrew, A. M. (1985b). Contextualist research and the study of organizational change processes. In E. Mumford (Ed.), *Research methods in information systems* (pp. 53–75). Amsterdam: Elsevier.

Pettigrew, A. M. (1985c). Contextualist research: A natural way to link theory and practice. In E. Lawler III, A. M. Mohrman Jr., S. A. Mohrman, G. E. Ledford Jr., T. G. Cummings, et al. (Eds.), *Doing research that is useful in theory and practice* (pp. 222–274). San Francisco: Jossey-Bass.

Pettigrew, A. M. (1987a). Context and action in the transformation of the firm. *Journal of Management Studies, 24*(6), 649–670.

Pettigrew, A. M. (1987b). Researching strategic change. In A. M. Pettigrew (Ed.), *The management of strategic change* (pp. 1–13). Oxford: Basil Blackwell.

Pettigrew, A. M. (1987c). Theoretical, methodological and empirical issues in studying change. *Journal of Management Studies, 24*(4), 420–426.

Pettigrew, A. M. (Ed.). (1987d). *The management of strategic change*. Oxford: Basil Blackwell.

Pettigrew, A. M. (1989). Longitudinal methods to study change: Theory and practice. In R. M. Mansfield (Ed.), *New frontiers of management* (pp. 21–49). London: Routledge.

Pettigrew, A. M. (1990). Longitudinal field research on change: Theory and practice. *Organization Science, 1*(3), 267–292.

Pettigrew, A. M. (1992). The character and significance of strategy process research. *Strategic Management Journal, 13*, 5–16.

Pettigrew, A. M. (1995). Longitudinal field research on change. In G. P. Huber & A. H. Van de Ven (Eds.), *Longitudinal field research methods* (pp. 91–125). San Francisco: Sage.

Pettigrew, A. M. (1997a). The double hurdles for management research. In T. Clark (Ed.), *Advancement in organizational behaviour: Essays in hounour of Derek S Pugh* (pp. 277–296). London: Dartmouth Press.

Pettigrew, A. M. (1997b). What is processual analysis? *Scandinavian Journal of Management, 13* (4), 337–348.

Pettigrew, A. M. (1998). Catching reality in flight. In A. Bedeian (Ed.), *Management laureates* (pp. 171–206). Greenwich: JAI Press.

Pettigrew, A. M. (2001). Management research after modernism. *British Journal of Management, 12*, S61–S70.

Pettigrew, A. M. (2003). Innovative forms of organizing: Progress, performance and process. In A. M. Pettigrew, R. Whittington, L. Melin, C. J. Sánchez-Runde, F. A. J. van den Bosch, W. Ruigrok, & T. Numagami (Eds.), *Innovative forms of organizing* (pp. 331–351). London: Sage.

Pettigrew, A. M. (2005). The character and significance of management research on the public services. *Academy of Management Journal, 48*(6), 973–977.

Pettigrew, A. M. (2011). Scholarship with impact. *British Journal of Management, 22*, 347–354.

Pettigrew, A. M. (2013). The conduct of qualitative research in organizational settings. *Corporate Governance, 21*(2), 123–126.

Pettigrew, A. M., & Fenton, E. (Eds.). (2000). *The innovating organization*. London: Sage.

Pettigrew, A. M., & Massini, S. (2003). Innovative forms of organizing: Trends in Europe, Japan and the USA in the 1990s. In A. M. Pettigrew, R. Whittington, L. Melin, C. J. Sánchez-Runde, F. A. J. van den Bosch, W. Ruigrok, & T. Numagami (Eds.), *Innovative forms of organizing* (pp. 1–32). London: Sage.

Pettigrew, A. M., & McNulty, T. (1998). Sources and uses of power in the boardroom. *European Journal of Work and Organizational Psychology, 7*(2), 197–214.

Pettigrew, A. M., & Whipp, R. (1991). *Managing change for competitive success*. Oxford: Basil Blackwell.

Pettigrew, A. M., & Whipp, R. (1993). Managing the twin process of competition and change: The role of intangible assets. In P. Lorange, B. Chakravarthy, J. Roos, & A. H. Van de Ven (Eds.), *Implementing strategic change processes* (pp. 3–42). Oxford: Basil Blackwell.

Pettigrew, A. M., Hendry, C., & Sparrow, P. R. (1990). *Corporate strategy change and human resource management*. Sheffield: The Department of Employment, Training Agency.
Pettigrew, A. M., Ferlie, E., & McKee, L. (1992). *Shaping strategic change: Making change in large organizations, the case of the NHS*. London: Sage.
Pettigrew, A. M., Thomas, H., & Whittington, R. (2002). Strategic management: The strengths and limitations of a field. In A. M. Pettigrew, H. Thomas, & R. Whittington (Eds.), *Handbook of strategic management* (pp. 3–29). London: Sage.
Pettigrew, A. M., Whittington, R., Melin, L., Sànchez-Runde, C. J., van den Bosch, F. A. J., Ruigrok, W., & Numagami, T. (Eds.). (2003). *Innovative forms of organizing*. London: Sage.
Pettigrew, A. M., Cornuel, E., & Hommel, U. (Eds.). (2014). *The institutional development of business schools*. Oxford: Oxford University Press.
Rajagopalan, N., & Spreitzer, G. M. (1997). Toward a theory of strategic change: A multi-lens perspective and integrative framework. *Academy of Management Review, 22*(1), 46–79.
Schatzki, T. R. (2001). Introduction. In T. R. Schatzki, K. Knorr-Cetina, & E. von Savigny (Eds.), *The practice turn in contemporary theory* (pp. 1–14). London: Routledge.
Schwarz, G. M., & Stensaker, I. G. (2014). Time to take of the theoretical straightjacket and (re-) introduce phenomenon-driven research. *Journal of Applied Behavioral Science, 50*(4), 478–501.
Sewell, W. H. (1992). A theory of structure: Duality, agency, and transformation. *American Journal of Sociology, 98*(1), 1–29.
Sminia, H. (2005). Strategy formation as layered discussion. *Scandinavian Journal of Management, 21*, 267–291.
Sminia, H. (2016). Pioneering process research: Andrew Pettigrew's contribution to management scholarship, 1962–2014. *International Journal of Management Reviews, 18*(2), 111–132.
Sminia, H., & de Rond, M. (2012). Context and action in the transformation of strategy scholarship. *Journal of Management Studies, 49*(7), 1329–1349.
Sminia, H., & van Nistelrooij, A. (2006). Strategic management and organization development: Planned change in a public sector organization. *Journal of Change Management, 6*(1), 99–113.
Sztompka, P. (1991). *Society in action: The theory of social becoming*. Cambridge: Polity Press.
Tsoukas, H., & Chia, R. (2002). On organizational becoming: Rethinking organizational change. *Organization Science, 13*(5), 567–582.
Van de Ven, A. H. (2007). *Engaged scholarship: A guide for organizational and social research*. Oxford: Oxford University Press.
Van de Ven, A. H., & Poole, M. S. (1995). Explaining development and change in organizations. *Academy of Management Review, 20*(3), 510–540.
van Nistelrooij, A., & Sminia, H. (2010). Organization development: What's actually happening? *Journal of Change Management, 10*(4), 407–420.
Warmington, A., Lupton, T., & Gribbin, C. (1977). *Organizational behaviour and performance: An open systems approach to change*. London: Macmillan.
Whipp, R., & Pettigrew, A. M. (1992). Managing change for competitive success: Bridging the strategic and the operational. *Industrial and Corporate Change, 1*(1), 205–233.
Whipp, R., Rosenfeld, R., & Pettigrew, A. M. (1989a). Culture and competitiveness: Evidence from two mature UK industries. *Journal of Management Studies, 26*(6), 561–585.
Whipp, R., Rosenfeld, R., & Pettigrew, A. M. (1989b). Managing strategic change in a mature business. *Long Range Planning, 22*(6), 92–99.
Whittington, R. (1996). Strategy as practice. *Long Range Planning, 29*(5), 731–735.
Whittington, R. (2006). Completing the practice turn in strategy research. *Organization Studies, 27* (5), 613–634.
Whittington, R., Pettigrew, A. M., Peck, S., Fenton, E., & Conyon, M. (1999). Change and complementarities in the new competitive landscape: A European panel study, 1992–1996. *Organization Science, 10*(5), 583–600.
Willmott, R. (1997). Structure, culture and agency: Rejecting the current othodoxy of organization theory. *Journal for the Theory of Social Behaviour, 27*(1), 93–123.

Further Reading

The best way to get to know Andrew Pettigrew's work is to read it, with the list of references below providing the information when and where his books and articles have been published. To get 'inside the man', there are a few occasions where he reflected on his own work (Mintzberg, Waters, Pettigrew, & Butler, 1990; Pettigrew, 1998, 2001a, 2011b, 2012). Apart from that, concise introductions to his body of work can be found in Sminia (2009, 2016; Sminia & de Rond, 2012). Finally, two of his major publications, his dissertation project (Pettigrew, 1973b) and the ICI study (Pettigrew, 1985d) have been re printed recently as Pettigrew (2001b) and (Pettigrew, 2011a) respectively.

Mintzberg, H., Waters, J. A., Pettigrew, A. M., & Butler, R. J. (1990). Studying deciding: An exchange of views between Mintzberg and Waters, Pettigrew, and Butler. *Organization Studies, 11*(1), 1–16.

Pettigrew, A. M. (2001). *The politics of organizational decision-making* (reprint ed.). London: Routledge.

Pettigrew, A. M. (2011). *The awakening giant: Continuity and change in imperial chemical industries* (reprint ed.). Abingdon: Routlegde.

Pettigrew, A. M. (2012). Context and action in the transformation of the firm: A reprise. *Journal of Management Studies, 49*(7), 1304–1328.

Sminia, H. (2009). Process research in strategy formation: Theory, methodology and relevance. *International Journal of Management Reviews, 11*(1), 97–125.

Out of the Poole and into the Ocean: Understanding Processes of Organizational Change Through the Work of Marshall Scott Poole

62

Paul M. Leonardi

Abstract
Marshall Scott Poole's research on processes of organizational change has been influential across multiple fields. Few scholars have drawn inspiration from such interdisciplinary sources and had such impact across various disciplines. For four decades, he has developed metatheoretical approaches, specific theories, and novel over a career of nearly methodologies for studying the process of organizational change. His work on group decision development, technology use, and virtual organizing has opened up new lines of inquiry for organizational researchers. In his current work, Poole continues to demonstrate that change is not something that happens to organizations, but rather that by their very nature organizations are continuously changing.

Keywords
Process theory • Technology • Organizational change • Decision making

Contents

P.M. Leonardi (✉)
Technology Management Program, University of California, Santa Barbara, CA, USA
e-mail: Leonardi@ucsb.edu

D.B. Szabla et al. (eds.), *The Palgrave Handbook of Organizational Change Thinkers*,
DOI 10.1007/978-3-319-52878-6_88

Introduction

I have a friend who is a competitive open-water swimmer. He prefers to race in the ocean because he says the swift currents provide great physical and mental challenges. Although he lives just a few blocks from the beach on a fairly warm part of the coast, he does the bulk of his training in a local swimming pool. I found it curious that he did not train in the ocean given that he lives so close to it and that it is the site of his favorite competitions. So 1 day I asked him about his choice. He replied:

> When you train in the ocean there's too many things to worry about. It's too cold. The current is pushing you this way and that. And, you're always wondering about your distance and speed. I can focus in the pool. I work on my strokes and my breathing and my timing. When I train in the pool it makes be a better competitor in the ocean because it really allows me to focus on the process of how I can change my approach to get better.

Just like the ocean, organizations are always moving and changing. It is hard to understand their dynamics while we are working in them. In much the same way that it makes sense for an open-water swimmer to train in the pool to prepare for competition in the ocean, to understand the dynamics of organizational change requires a removal from them that provides the perspective to understand the processes by which those change occur. Once we understand the processes of organizational change, we can then go into organizations while their swift currents are pulsating and make them better.

To understand and prepare for the process of organizational change, organizational theorists have been very lucky to have a pool of their own: Marshall Scott Poole. Since the late 1970s, Poole's interdisciplinary work on organizational change has helped scholars across a number of fields to conceptualize, measure, and theorize about change as a communication process. Poole's main theoretical contribution to the field has been to build an approach to organizational change that casts change not as an event or an outcome but a process. Poole's processed-based thinking about change emerged at the time when organizational theorists were developing fixed sequence models of change that treated organizational changes as if they proceeded in a lock-step fashion in predetermined directions. Poole's legacy has been to demonstrate that change processes can occur in multiple sequences, that they are often recursive, and that they typically produce as many unintended outcomes as they do intended outcomes. Beyond this important contribution, Poole has developed specific theoretical frameworks for building process-based models of organizational change and various methodological techniques for capturing and assessing it, and he has done so in a variety of empirical contexts whose study has sparked the entire new areas of research.

To develop such thinking, Poole has drawn on ideas and concepts from across disciplines. Not surprisingly his work not only evinces and enviable interdisciplinary character, but it is also used widely across disciplines including management, organization studies, communication studies, information systems, and network science, just to name a few. His research exemplifies some of the best theoretical and methodological work across these various disciplines. To understand how his contributions emerged and what we can learn from them for the study of organizational change as a process, let's dive into Poole.

Influences and Motivations

Early Years

Marshall Scott Poole (known by his friends and colleagues as Scott) grew up in Amarillo, Texas. In the eighth grade, Poole became interested in a career in science after becoming inspired by his biology teacher. Always ambitious, a young Scott Poole decided that he wanted to become a biochemist. To learn more about biology, he began to compete in science fairs, and as a high school student, he competed in an international science fair with a project that involved synthesizing peptides. The project caught the attention of the US Department of Agriculture who offered him a prestigious internship that allowed him to work on an odiferous project: analyzing manure samples.

Poole enrolled in Michigan State University to study chemistry. This was the era of massive student revolt, and outside of the classroom, Poole became involved in protests of US intervention in Vietnam and the Michigan State debate team. His friends and mentors on the debate team encouraged him to take classes in the Department of Communication, which was, at the time, arguably the top Communication department in the country. Sitting in his communication classes, Poole began to realize that solving problems involving people was much more difficult than solving the hardest problems that he experienced in his biochemistry classes. Donald Cushman was a professor of Communication and Poole's debate coach. On long drives to and from tournaments, he would talk with Poole and the other debaters about philosophy, science, ethics, rhetoric, and its place in public affairs. These conversations led Poole to become so intrigued by the challenge of predicting human behavior and furthered his desire to make the world a better place in a time of global turmoil. Cushman told Poole that if he wanted to become a strong social scientists, he needed to first study rhetoric. But Michigan State's Communication department had purged all their rhetoricians. Cushman advised Poole to transfer to the University of Wisconsin and complete a Communication degree there so he could gain a solid foundation in rhetoric. Poole decided to follow Cushman's advice and he moved to Wisconsin.

After completing his Communication degree at Wisconsin, Poole moved back to Michigan State to study with Cushman for a master's degree, then we went back to Wisconsin to complete his Ph.D. in Communication with an all-star committee of Joseph Cappella, Dean Hewes, and George Huber. He also took classes with Andre Delbecq in Wisconsin's business school. During his time at Wisconsin, Poole read French structuralists like Levi-Strauss (1976) and Barthes (1975) who wrote about deep structure. He also read rhetoricians who treated argumentation as an inventional system (Thompson 1972). These influences led Poole to conceive of structures as phenomena that were at the surface level, maintained through communication, but that also existed at a deeper cultural level that had long-lasting impacts on the way groups and organizations operated.

Multiple Sequence Models of Group Decision-Making

Upon moving to his first faculty position in the Department of Speech Communication (now the Department of Communication) at the University of Illinois at Urbana Champaign, Poole began to publish a series of papers (1981, 1983a, b) that were among his first attempts at creating a process-based theory of change. These papers focused on the phenomenon of group decision-making. In them, Poole explicitly compared existing unitary and multiple sequence models of group decision-making through an analysis of decision development in student and physician groups. The first paper in this series (Poole 1981) found that different groups followed different phases of development. Even though most groups did share ideas and clarify information, invite others to participate, attempt to reduce tension, muddled around in uncertainty and ambiguity, antagonized each other, developed and critique ideas, and finally reinforced each other and integrated ideas, they did so at different moments in their history and also took varying amounts of time to do so. The second paper in the series (Poole 1983a) attempted to show why different phases in the development emerged by identifying breakpoints that pushed one phase into the next. This study also showed that groups often repeat phases rather than progress through them linearly as most unitary sequence models suggest. The third paper (Poole 1983b) set forth a series of propositions that pointed to a contingency theory of multiple sequences. This paper argued that a variety of environmental factors affect each group differently, thus causing certain breakpoints, which lead to the progression toward a new phase or the repetition of a previous phase. Taking these three studies together, Poole (1983b: 340) suggested that there are "two sets of explanatory factors representing fundamental parameters of group activity: the group's task and its historical context."

This set of studies laid the early groundwork for the foundation Poole would later build around process-based change. Poole demonstrates that this phenomenon of group decision-making is fundamentally communicative. In other words, decision-making begins and ends with communication among individuals. Poole also explains what communication does – it structures sequences of decisions – and how it does so, through the cumulative structuring of tasks and the accretion of prior communication activity into implicit and explicit rules that guide future communication. In developing his theory of decision development, Poole did not attempt to hive off communication as one part of decision-making. Rather in making clear the importance for scholars to study decision-making and how decisions develop in groups and organizations, Poole's theory of decision development has had a major impact. It has set the foundation for many other studies, not just in the field of Communication but in other disciplines as well (e.g., Gersick 1988). At this same time, Poole worked with David Seibold and Robert McPhee to explore the dialectical processes of deep structure and surface structure in changes in group decision-making over time. Drawing on Giddens' (1979, 1984) work on structuration theory, Poole et al. (1985) argued that change took place as the agency of actors, and the structure of the group decision environment implicated one another in a dialectical process, over time. Their structurational theory of group decision-making offered an alternative to accounts of structure in the social sciences as fixed. Engaging with Giddens' work allowed the authors to demonstrate that structure was produced in action – through communication – and that change was, therefore, a natural property of the organizing process.

In 1985, Poole left the University of Illinois to join the faculty of the Department of Speech Communication at the University of Minnesota. In addition to continuing to refine his studies of group decision development (Poole and Roth 1989a, b), Poole began two new collaborations.

Adaptive Structuration Theory

The first collaboration was with Gerardine DeSanctis in the Management Sciences department. Poole and DeSanctis began to work together to develop a group decision support system (GDSS) technology that would aid groups in the decision-making process. What is most notable about this collaboration was its attempt to bring a design science orientation to theories of change. Poole had been working on his theories of decision development in groups and had amassed a weight of evidence suggesting how groups might make better decisions. The GDSS was built following these theories and evidence. In more contemporary theoretical parlance, one might argue that rules for good decision-making were inscribed (Holmström and Robey 2005) into the technology. In this project, theory informed technology design.

But, things did not go quite as planned. In early work, Pool and DeSanctis and their students studied undergraduate students using the Software Aided Meeting Management (SAMM) system, the non-chauffeured (there was no moderator) GDSS system they developed (Watson et al. 1988). The authors found that the use of the system led to several intended outcomes for which the system was implemented including enhancing post-meeting consensus as compared with groups that did not use the technology, but also to some unintended outcomes including the fact that compared to the control group, users of the system did not experience more equal influence from across the group in terms of the final solution.

The results of these studies, coupled with similar results generated by other researchers studying GDSS systems (e.g., Dennis et al. 1988), led Poole and DeSanctis to the conclusion that the presence of intended and unintended effects of the use of the technology were "attributable to the fact that various groups use the GDSSs differently" (1990: 176). This observation served as the basis for their formulation of adaptive structuration theory (AST), a variant of Giddens'(1984) structuration theory that took seriously the interactions between the deep structures that constitute technological artifacts, organizations, and work groups. The main insight of this theory was that "advanced technologies bring social structures which enable and constrain interaction to the workplace" (DeSanctis and Poole 1994: 125). As the authors argued, a new technology can be described in terms of its structural features and the general spirit of the feature set. Structural features are the specific types of rules and resources or capabilities offered by the system. The spirit is "the 'official line' which the technology presents to people regarding how to act when using it, how to interpret its features, and how to fill in gaps in procedure which are not explicitly specified" (DeSanctis and Poole 1994: 126). To sum succinctly, the authors argued that individuals who use a technology directly experience its "spirit." They appropriate the features of a technology in ways either that are consistent with the spirit in which it was designed and implemented (a faithful appropriation) or that are inconsistent with this spirit (an ironic appropriation).

To provide empirical support for their propositions, Poole and DeSanctis (1992) embarked on a slightly modified program of study. Rather than looking simply for effective use, they began to explore the process by which the appropriation of group structures led to changes in how the technology was used and how appropriations of the technology's features led to changes in group structure. Using micro-coding techniques, they found support for nine types of appropriations of the features of the technology: direct appropriation, substitution, combination, enlargement, constraint, contrast, affirmation, negation, and ambiguity. The findings indicated that 11 of the 18 groups were faithful appropriators of the technology. The groups that appropriated the features faithfully – in-line with the spirit with which the technology was designed and implemented – had a higher consensus in group decisions than those that did not. Further analysis by the authors (DeSanctis and Poole 1994; Sambamurthy and Poole 1992) confirmed that simply using the technology did not guarantee improvements in decision-making within a group, but that improvements were directly tied to *how* the groups appropriated the technology into their ongoing stream of interaction. More specifically, DeSanctis and Poole (1994) found that although the same technology was used by different groups, its effects were not consistent due to differences in each group's appropriation moves.

Metatheoretical Accounts of the Processes of Innovation and Change

The second collaboration was with Andrew Van de Ven in the Carlson School of Management at the University of Minnesota. Poole was introduced to Van de Ven by

Andre Delbecq who was Van den Ven's dissertation adviser. Poole showed his methods on process research that he had been developing in his studies of group decision-making, and also in the early stages of GDSS use to Van de Ven, Van de Ven observed that they could be quite useful for analyzing case studies of innovation.

Whereas Poole's studies of change so far had focused on specific empirical contexts, his work with Van de Ven attempted to build metatheoretical insights about studying the process of change within groups and organizations. Drawing on Poole's training in inventional systems and topoi from rhetoric, he and Van den Ven began to conceive of various theoretical toolkits for the study of innovation and change. Paradox emerged as an early way to begin this metatheoretical conversation. Drawing from work on tensions and paradoxes from rhetorical studies, Poole and Van den Ven (1989) outlined a set of theory-building strategies that would help researchers take advantage of, rather than fall victim to, theoretical tensions. Their work proposed four modes of working with paradoxes: (1) accept the paradox and use it constructively; (2) clarify levels of analysis; (3) temporally separate the two levels; and (4) introduce new terms to resolve the paradox. Not surprisingly, given Poole's prior work, he and Van de Ven illustrated these approaches by interrogating a theme core to Poole's previous process studies of change: the action structure paradox – the relationship between communication structures and deep structure in organizing.

As he and Van de Ven continued to collaborate in building theory about the process of organizational change and innovation, they also began to develop new methodological techniques to study change processes within organizations (Van de Ven and Poole 1990). The continued interplay between metatheoretical stances on processes of innovation and change, the development of methodological toolkits with which to study process, and Poole and Ven de Ven's own empirical work brought them to a view that organizational change and development had to be explained by multiple theoretical perspectives in order to capture the multiple motors that powered change at multiple levels of analysis. Much like he had done when advocating for a move from unitary to multiple sequence models of group decision-making, Poole, now together with Van de Ven, argued that the search for a unitary theory of organizational change was a fool's gambit; instead, the most trenchant insights about organizational change would arise from a multiplicity of theoretical perspectives because change itself was a multifaceted process. Together, Poole and Van de Ven argued that change could occur in different units – such that change could include multiple entities of a single entity of change and that change also could occur across different modes – change could either be prescribed in advance or could be constructed out of the ongoing interaction between various events and processes. The now famous two by two that resulted from these contrasting dimensions evinced four types of theories that exemplified change as a process: (1) evolutionary theories that modeled change as a process of variation, selection, and tension; (2) dialectic theories which held that change was the results of the synthesis of conflict produced by theses and antitheses; (3) life-cycle theories that depicted change as a cyclical process of birth, growth, harvesting, and termination; and (4) teleological theories that charted a recursive course from search for alternatives, to the creation and implementation of goals, to dissatisfaction with certain processes, which resulted in new opportunities for search (Van de Ven and Poole 1995).

It is clear that Poole's influences stretched back to his early days at the bench in his biochemistry classrooms. The hard sciences taught him that the world is not at rest but always moving and changing and that to understand and describe that change, the investigator had to work constantly to develop new methods. His study of communication and rhetoric taught him the value of exploring a phenomenon from multiple view points and through multiple theoretical lenses and that the outcome of this epistemological flexibility was a realization that important phenomena in the world happened at unique levels of analyses and in distinct temporal orders. As Poole learned early in his education and throughout the formative years of his career as a professor, an embrace of paradox and of interdisciplinarity can go a long way to building insights about change that have lasting impact.

Key Contributions

At the time that Poole began publishing his most influential papers on adaptive structuration theory and on the processes of innovation and change, he moved to Texas A&M University where he held appointments in the Department of Communication and the Department of Information and Operations Management in the Business School. Poole began applying the theoretical lenses he had developed in his prior work to understand the change process in a variety of areas, including brainstorming (Jackson and Poole 2003), virtual collaboration (Brown et al. 2004), and telemedicine (Deng et al. 2005). In 2006 he moved back to the Department of Communication at the University of Illinois at Urbana Champaign, where he also became the director of the Center for Computing in the Humanities, Arts, and Social Science (I-CHASS). As director of I-CHASS, Poole began to collect and analyze a number of extremely large data sets of virtual organizations. With several colleagues, he created the Virtual Worlds Exploratorium – a collection of large data sets of virtual gaming communities that would allow him to chart the process of change in groups and organizations as it occurred in the moment-by-moment interactions that were captured on the digital gaming platforms (Williams et al. 2011). With such data in hand, Poole and his colleagues had to create and refine new methods, such as relational event modeling (Pilny et al. 2016) to make sense of the processes of change occurring in them. Poole remains at the University of Illinois to this day.

Throughout his distinguished career of groundbreaking empirical research and theoretical advance, Poole has made many contributions to the theory and methods associated with studying the process of organizational change. From among the many, I highlight four key contributions here.

Conceptualizing Organizing as a Process of Continuous Change

Perhaps his greatest contribution is that Poole has altered the field's understanding of organizational change through his work showing that change is not an event that happens in organizations, but that organizing is itself a process of change. Although today with perspectives like structuration theory and practice theory so widely diffused, the idea that organizing is a process that is continually in flux may not seem new, this was not always the case. Poole's work has been among the most influential in making the case that organizing is a process. In Poole's view that process is driven by communication. Individuals, groups, and collectives communicate in particular ways and that not only respond to but also produce the demands of their communication environments. As communication patterns shift, so to do the surface and deep structures that underlie them.

When organizations are seen as always in the making, change becomes a matter of course. For this reason, Poole has argued that a process-based approach to the study of organizational change provides a strong ontology for understanding organizing. Of course, as Van de Ven and Poole (2005) have argued, change processes take on different forms and different temporal trajectories and are of different magnitudes at different levels of analysis and as different elements become involved. But, these differences notwithstanding the process of organizational change never stop so long as organizations continue in their existence.

Processes Are Driven by Generative Mechanisms

Poole has always been a strong advocate for using multiple theoretical lenses for understanding the change process. His reason for this stance is simple. When a researcher studies processes of change, they collect a prodigious amount of data over time. Those data are dense and complex. A traditional solution to the problem of process complexity was for researchers to focus on one part of the process in their analysis, or one specific time frame (Monge and Poole 2008). But by reducing the focus in this way, researchers run the risk of missing the multiple forces that push organizing in one direction rather than another. As Poole has argued, processes are driven by various generative mechanisms, or what he and Van de Ven have called "motors" (Van de Ven and Poole 1995). To understand how these motors operate requires a broad rather than a narrow focus. Poole's strong belief is that when studying a complex messy process like change, a research cannot let theory dictate what data are collected or analyzed or else the researcher may find him or herself producing a self-fulfilling prophecy. Instead, Poole argues that researchers must collect and test their data with multiple theoretical schemas to see which are generative.

Although this approach may sound common when dealing with data collected inductively, it is a radical departure for data analyzed from a deductive vantage point – as most of Poole's work has done. Poole's early influences in rhetoric taught him that although theory should drive the analysis of data, there is no guarantee that any one theory is correct. Thus, one of Poole's major contributions to the study of process has been to model an ability to explore multiple generative mechanisms simultaneously by interrogating the data with multiple theories. As Poole and his colleagues have recounted (Poole et al. 2000), this catholic approach to theoretical analysis is one of the reasons that the Minnesota Innovation Research Program was so successful.

Methods for Studying Organizational Change Processes

In studying organizational change processes, Poole and his colleagues have developed a variety of methods for capturing change in action and charting it as it occurs. At the broadest level, Van de Ven and Poole (2000: 31) have described four requirements for process analyses of longitudinal event data:

1. A clear set of concepts for selecting and describing the objects to be studied
2. Systematic methods for observing change in the objects over time
3. Methods for representing raw data to identify process patterns
4. A motor or theory to make sense of the process patter and a means of determining whether the theory fits the observed patterns

What is novel about this set of four steps is the constant interplay between theory and method. As Poole's work has shown over the years, the development of theory and methodology go hand in hand. Without theories to inform methodological choices, researchers who study the process of change would be grasping in the dark. But without the appropriate data analyzed into consistent temporal patterns, researchers would be unable to test theories and identify their generative potential for explaining processes in the data.

At a more granular level, Poole's work on sequences in group decision development and on GDSS use has led to more fine-grained methodological innovations for studying the process of organizational change. These include but are not limited to (Van de Ven and Poole 2000: 38–48):

1. Producing a chronological listing of qualitative events
2. Coding chronological events into conceptual tracks
3. Analyzing process patterns or cycles in activity tracks
4. Developing a vocabulary of describing processual progressions, which includes types of relations between developmental events, and an understanding of whether the progression was simple or unitary, cumulative, or conjunctive
5. Identifying causal relationships among event tracks
6. Making an assessment of tracking methodology

Together, these broad and granular recommendations drawn from nearly three decades of work on processes of organizational change have provided researchers with a sophisticated set of tools with which to examine and explain their phenomena of interest.

The Role of Technology in the Process of Change

Another key contribution of Poole's work has been to show how new technologies contribute to the processes of change that occur in organizations. Poole's research has shown that certain structures for use are built into a technology and that when individuals encounter those structures, they appropriate them in ways that are consistent with existing organizational and group requirements. According to Poole and DeSanctis (1990: 184), the concept of "appropriation" may be defined as "the mode or fashion in which a group uses, adopts, and reproduces a structure." In this stream, a technology is socially constructed as organizational members appropriate its features to support or change group and organizational dynamics. His work developing adaptive structuration has shown that technologies play a key role in the change process because they provide capabilities to organizational actors as their features are appropriated in the context of use. Most current studies of technology use in organizations build on these foundational insights (for review see Leonardi and Barley 2010; Rice and Leonardi 2013).

It is hard to overestimate the influence of this line of research. Scholars who study organizational change have long considered new technologies to be ancillary to the change process (for more information see Jackson et al. 2002). But in showing how new technologies provide motors for change, his work has helped to legitimize and catalyze research and theory about technology's role in the change process. As new technologies continue to infiltrate organizations at an increasing pace, Poole's contributions in this area become more salient.

New Insights

Poole's contribution to scholarship has taken many forms. From his important contingency models of decision-making to theories of adaptive structuration, to developing frameworks and methods for the study of change processes, and to his current work on networks and evolutionary theories of change, Poole's work continues to inspire scholars across multiple disciplinary domains. In the field management, his work on change processes continues to influence the way that scholars conceptualize, measure, and theorize organizational dynamics, especially as they approach them longitudinally. In the field of information systems, Poole's work on adaptive structuration and its attendant concepts of appropriation and spirit are continually discussed, tested, and revised as scholars attempt to grapple with understanding the role that technologies play in the organizing process. And, in the field of communication, Poole's work on decision-making and group dynamics is inspiring fresh thinking about how teams form, operate, and dissolve in various contexts, including virtual organizations.

Poole's work has been extremely influential in my own development as a scholar. Since I was a graduate student, Poole's work has served as a source of ideas that have led me to ask important questions and to which I have reacted. I first got to know Poole's work on adaptive structuration theory because I was trying to understand how designers and managers influenced the way that workers interpreted new technologies and used their features to change the way they worked. One of my first published papers (Leonardi 2007) drew on Poole and DeSanctis' notion of appropriation to argue that as individuals make different kinds of appropriations of a new technology's features, they activate information available in the technology in different ways. As new information become available, workers then shift their patterns of interaction in ways that create changes that lead to new appropriations – and the cycle continues. These same insights led me to consider that the features of technologies themselves mattered a great deal for the interpretations people made about a technology's functionality (Leonardi 2009b) and to develop theory that the development and use of a new technology were not two separate periods in the life cycle of technological and organizational change; rather, that new technologies and organizations co-evolved through a series of activities that rendered them mutually constitutive (Leonardi 2009a).

Paying so attention to Poole's work on adaptive structuration, I began to notice important differences in the way that Poole articulated technology's role in the organizing process from other scholars. Steve Barley and I (Leonardi and Barley 2010) showed that Poole's work on adaptive structuration theory respected the materiality of technology to a greater degree than most other theories and that it was likely to lead to better predictions about the affects technology would have on organizational changes than other theoretical perspectives. Building on these insights, I developed a theory of imbrication, which suggested that the human agency of actors and the material agency of technologies became interlocked (or imbricated) in sequences of changes in routines and artifacts that define the organization process (Leonardi 2011a, b, 2012). Based on this work, I have attempted to show how theorizing the affordances of new technologies can help organizational scholars to take seriously the role of technology and material agency in the unfolding of organizations without falling victim to the tendency to resort to inadequate deterministic or constructivist stances on technologically induced organizational change (Leonardi 2013b, c; Leonardi et al. 2013; Leonardi and Vaast 2017).

Reflecting on Poole's program of research on group decision development has also allowed me to articulate a number of guidelines for how scholars who study organizational communication might develop deeper, better theory about the role of communication in the organizing process (Leonardi 2017a). As I examined the way that Poole constructed his program of research and developed theory about group decision development, I began to realize that this set of studies clearly follows a strategy of discovery. Poole demonstrates that this phenomenon of group decision-making is fundamentally communicative. In other words, decision-making begins and ends with communication among individuals. Poole also explains what communication does – it structures sequences of decisions – and how it does so (through the cumulative structuring of tasks and the accretion of prior communication activity into implicit and explicit rules that guide future communication). In developing his theory of decision development, Poole did not attempt to hive off communication as one part of decision-making. Rather in making the importance for scholars to study decision-making and how decisions develop in groups and organizations, Poole showed that decision-making is a phenomenon that is nothing more than sequences of communication. Poole's theory of decision development has had a major impact. It has set the foundation for many other studies of group decision-making both within and out of the discipline. And outside of the discipline, especially, it has lead scholars to understand that decision-making is communication, plain, and simple.

A final idea with which I have been working over the past several years has arisen by combining Poole's work on technology use in organizations with his meta-theoretical writings on process. One way to think about the role of materiality in organizational life is to suggest that materiality is itself a process (Contractor et al. 2011). This idea may seem strange because we (myself included) tend to think that materiality is something that exists as a substance – even in those instances where it is digital (Leonardi 2010; Leonardi and Rodriguez-Lluesma 2012). Poole's work suggests that from a radical process perspective, one might even think of materiality as a process. He recommended to me that I read the work of the process philosopher Nicholas Rescher to consider how one might theorize materiality as a process. Blending Poole's work with Rescher's has led me to begin theorizing how materiality is itself an organizing process (Leonardi 2013a, b) that organizational scholars should take seriously in their accounts of organizational change. I view this radical shift to a process-centered view of materiality as an exciting new area for theory building that is inspired by the combination of several areas of Poole's incredible body of work.

Legacies and Unfinished Business

Scott Poole has spent his career developing metatheoretical frameworks, specific theories, and methodological tools for studying organizing as a process of change. The tremendous number of citations to his articles, the awards he has one for his work, and the ways that his theories and methods have diffused across multiple disciplines provide evidence of a strong legacy in studies of organizational change. But just like the phenomenon he studies, Poole is ever in motion. In conversation with me, Poole outlined three areas of unfinished business that continue to draw his effort and that he hopes will capture the interest of other change researchers.

Identifying Basic Structural Forms

Poole claims that most of the work on the process of change over the last 30 years has been devoted to discovery – attempting to uncover and describe how and why organizations change as they do. Yet there is little formalization of knowledge into basic structural forms. Poole would like to see change researchers develop an algebra that formalizes and expresses change processes in a way such that they can be easily compared, contrasted, and expanded.

Create More Opportunities for Action

To develop metatheoretical perspectives on organizational change, Poole acknowledges that his work and the work of others has had to move to high levels of abstraction. The downside of such abstraction is that much of what we know about processes of change is not actionable. Vocabularies for describing change do not often help managers and leaders of organizations to directly change or deal with it effectively. Throughout his research into processes of change and the forces that drive them, Poole has become aware of how relatively powerless managers actually are. They often try to create methods or techniques that counteract natural processes of organizing. Helping to unveil these processes and their motors might help managers and leaders to ride the wave of changes much better than they can attempt to alter its course.

Articulate Multiple Possibilities

Poole's career has played out against a strong belief that scholars need to adopt multiple perspective to understand phenomena as complex as the change process. If one believes that there is no single truth out there to be discovered, then the smartest move is to articulate multiple possibilities about how process unfolds and compares and contrasts them. Approaches like structuration theory are attractive precisely because they allow ways to integrate various perspectives simultaneously. One goal for future work is to create and identify other approaches that will allow researchers to articulate multiple possibilities for how change unfolds and to test those possibilities through processes of comparison and abstraction.

Conclusion

Marshall Scott Poole has developed an inspiring program of research on the process of organizational change. Organizations are difficult to study because they are always in motion. But it is their very motion – the continuous process of change – that makes them exciting and dynamic and makes researchers want to dive in. But before we dive in, we might take a tip from my friend the open-water swimmer: To most effectively navigate the waves in the ocean, we'd better spend some time at the Poole.

References

Barthes, R. (1975). *The pleasure of the text*. New York: Macmillan.

Brown, H. B., Poole, M. S., & Rogers, T. (2004). Interpersonal traits, complementarity, and trust in virtual collaboration. *Journal of Management Information Systems, 20*, 115–138.

Contractor, N. S., Monge, P. R., & Leonardi, P. M. (2011). Multidimensional networks and the dynamics of sociomateriality: Bringing technology inside the network. *International Journal of Communication, 5*, 682–720.

Deng, J., Poole, M. S., Miller-Scheideman, C., & Brown, H. B. (2005). Learning through telemedicine: Case study of a wound care network. *International Journal of Healthcare Technology and Management, 6*, 368–380.

Dennis, A. R., George, J. F., Jessup, L. M., Nunamaker, J. F., & Vogel, D. R. (1988). Information technology to support electronic meetings. *MIS Quarterly, 12*(4), 581–624.

DeSanctis, G., & Poole, M. S. (1994). Capturing the complexity in advanced technology use: Adaptive structuration theory. *Organization Science, 5*(2), 121–147.

Gersick, C. J. (1988). Time and transition in work teams: Toward a new model of group development. *Academy of Management Journal, 31*(1), 9–41.

Giddens, A. (1979). *Central problems in social theory*. Berkeley: University of California Press.

Giddens, A. (1984). *The constitution of society*. Berkeley: University of California Press.

Holmström, J., & Robey, D. (2005). Inscribing organizational change with information technology. In B. Czarniawka & T. Hernes (Eds.), *Actor-network theory and organizing* (pp. 165–187). Malmo: Liber.

Jackson, M. H., & Poole, M. S. (2003). Idea-generation in naturally occurring contexts. *Human Communication Research, 29*(4), 560–591.

Jackson, M. H., Poole, M. S., & Kuhn, T. (2002). The social construction of technology in studies of the workplace. In L. A. Lievrouw & S. Livingstone (Eds.), *Handbook of new media: Social shaping and consequences of icts* (pp. 236–253). London: Sage.

Leonardi, P. M. (2007). Activating the informational capabilities of information technology for organizational change. *Organization Science, 18*(5), 813–831.

Leonardi, P. M. (2009a). Crossing the implementation line: The mutual constitution of technology and organizing across development and use activities. *Communication Theory, 19*, 278–310.

Leonardi, P. M. (2009b). Why do people reject new technologies and stymie organizational changes of which they are in favor? Exploring misalignments between social interactions and materiality. *Human Communication Research, 35*(3), 407–441.

Leonardi, P. M. (2010). Digital materiality? How artifacts without matter, matter. *First Monday, 15*(6), Available from: http://www.uic.edu/htbin/cgiwrap/bin/ojs/index.php/fm/article/viewArticle/3036/2567

Leonardi, P. M. (2011a). Innovation blindness: Culture, frames, and cross-boundary problem construction in the development of new technology concepts. *Organization Science, 22*(2), 347–369.

Leonardi, P. M. (2011b). When flexible routines meet flexible technologies: Affordance, constraint, and the imbrication of human and material agencies. *MIS Quarterly, 35*(1), 147–167.

Leonardi, P. M. (2012). *Car crashes without cars: Lessons about simulation technology and organizational change from automotive design*. Cambridge, MA: MIT Press.

Leonardi, P. M. (2013a). The emergence of materiality within formal organizations. In P. R. Carlile, D. Nicolini, A. Langley, & H. Tsoukas (Eds.), *How matter matters: Objects, artifacts, and materiality in organization studies* (pp. 142–170). Oxford: Oxford University Press.

Leonardi, P. M. (2013b). Theoretical foundations for the study of sociomateriality. *Information and Organization, 23*(2), 59–76.

Leonardi, P. M. (2013c). When does technology use enable network change in organizations? A comparative study of feature use and shared affordances. *MIS Quarterly, 37*(3), 749–775.

Leonardi, P. M. (2017a). How to build high impact theories of organizational communication: Strategies of discovery and reconceptualization. *Management Communication Quarterly, 31*(1), 123–129.
Leonardi, P. M. (2017b). Materiality as an organizing process: Toward a process metaphysics for material artifacts. In A. L. H. Tsoukas (Ed.), *Sage handbook of process organization studies*. Thousand Oaks: Sage.
Leonardi, P. M., & Barley, S. R. (2010). What's under construction here: Social action, materiality, and power in constructivist studies of technology and organizing. *Academy of Management Annals, 4*, 1–51.
Leonardi, P. M., & Rodriguez-Llucsma, C. (2012). Sociomateriality as a lens for design: Imbrication and the constitution of technology and organization. *Scandinavian Journal of Information Systems, 24*(2), 79–88.
Leonardi, P. M., & Vaast, E. (2017). Social media and their affordances for organizing: A review and agenda for research. *Academy of Management Annals, 11*(1), 150–188.
Leonardi, P. M., Huysman, M., & Steinfield, C. (2013). Enterprise social media: Definition, history, and prospects for the study of social technologies in organizations. *Journal of Computer-Mediated Communication, 19*(1), 1–19.
Levi-Strauss, C. (1976). *Structural anthropology* (Vol. 2). New York: Basic Books.
Monge, P., & Poole, M. S. (2008). The evolution of organizational communication. *Journal of Communication, 58*, 679–692.
Pilny, A., Schecter, A., Poole, M. S., & Contractor, N. (2016). An illustration of the relational event model to analyze group interaction processes. *Group Dynamics: Theory, Research, and Practice, 20*(3), 181–195.
Poole, M. S. (1981). Decision development in small groups i: A comparison of two models. *Communication Monographs, 48*, 1–24.
Poole, M. S. (1983a). Decision development in small groups ii: A study of multiple sequences in decision making. *Communication Monographs, 50*, 206–231.
Poole, M. S. (1983b). Decision development in small groups iii: A multiple sequence model of group decision development. *Communication Monographs, 50*, 321–341.
Poole, M. S., & DeSanctis, G. (1990). Understanding the use of group decision support systems: The theory of adaptive structuration. In J. Fulk & C. Steinfield (Eds.), *Organizations and communication technology* (pp. 173–193). Newbury Park: Sage.
Poole, M. S., & DeSanctis, G. (1992). Microlevel structuration in computer-supported group decision making. *Human Communication Research, 19*(1), 5–49.
Poole, M. S., & Roth, J. (1989a). Decision development in small groups iv a typology of group decision paths. *Human Communication Research, 15*(3), 323–356.
Poole, M. S., & Roth, J. (1989b). Decision development in small groups v: Test of a contingency model. *Human Communication Research, 15*(4), 549–589.
Poole, M. S., & Van de Ven, A. H. (1989). Using paradox to build management and organization theories. *Academy of Management Review, 14*(4), 562–578.
Poole, M. S., Seibold, D. R., & McPhee, R. D. (1985). Group decision-making as a structurational process. *The Quarterly Journal of Speech, 71*, 74–102.
Poole, M. S., Van de Ven, A. H., Dooley, K., & Holmes, M. E. (2000). *Organizational change and innovation processes: Theory and methods for research*. Oxford: Oxford University Press.
Rice, R. E., & Leonardi, P. M. (2013). Information and communication technologies in organizations. In L. L. Putnam & D. K. Mumby (Eds.), *The sage handbook of organizational communication: Advances in theory, research, and methods* (pp. 425–448). Thousand Oaks: Sage.
Sambamurthy, V., & Poole, M. S. (1992). The effects of variations in capabilities of gdss designs on management of cognitive conflict in groups. *Information Systems Research, 3*(3), 224–251.
Thompson, W. N. (1972). Stasis in Aristotle's rhetoric. *The Quarterly Journal of Speech, 58*(2), 134–141.

Van de Ven, A. H., & Poole, M. S. (1990). Methods for studying innovation development in the Minnesota innovation research program. *Organization Science, 1*(3), 313–335.

Van de Ven, A. H., & Poole, M. S. (1995). Explaining development and change in organizations. *Academy of Management Review, 20*(3), 510–540.

Van de Ven, A. H., & Poole, M. S. (2000). Methods for studying innovation processes. In A. H. Van de Ven, H. Angle, & M. S. Poole (Eds.), *Research on the management of innovation: The Minnesota studies* (pp. 31–54). Oxford: Oxford University Press.

Van de Ven, A. H., & Poole, M. S. (2005). Alternative approaches for studying organizational change. *Organization Studies, 26*(9), 1377–1404.

Watson, R. T., DeSanctis, G., & Poole, M. S. (1988). Using a gdss to facilitate group consensus: Some intended and unintended consequences. *MIS Quarterly, 12*, 463–468.

Williams, D., Contractor, N., Poole, M. S., Srivastava, J., & Cai, D. (2011). The virtual worlds exploratorium: Using large-scale data and computational techniques for communication research. *Communication Methods and Measures, 5*, 163–180.

Joanne C. Preston: Integrating Disciplines, Expanding Paradigms

63

Jeanne D. Maes and Kenneth L. Wall

Abstract

Motivated by her father at an early age to be her best, Joanne C. Preston has emerged on the forefront as a scholar-practitioner in her quest to "make the workplace healthier." Building on her Russian, French, and German language skills and her solid foundation in developmental psychology, she has pushed the boundaries of traditional organization development and change (ODC). Preston has taken the best of family therapy practice and applied its interventions to small business and workplace problems, producing results sufficiently substantial to catch the attention of international business owners. Her interventions in large systems change and her astute ability to create superordinate goals were instrumental in South Africa's transformation from apartheid and in Poland's change from communism to a free market society. Her work with governmental leaders has improved Kenya's educational system. On the home front, Preston has introduced an international dimension to ODC education. She has cut across the typical discipline boundaries of psychology, business, and education and, by using technology, she has created new models of education for graduate students, linking global teams in workplace settings. Similarly, she has been influential in the creation of new types of business and professional network organizations. Preston has the rare gift of blending theory into practice on six continents, affecting academic audiences, businesses, nonprofit organizations, and governments.

J.D. Maes (✉)
Mitchell College of Business, University of South Alabama, Mobile, AL, USA
e-mail: jmaes@southalabama.edu

K.L. Wall
Epic Investments, Inc., Colorado Springs, CO, USA
e-mail: kwwall@yahoo.com

D.B. Szabla et al. (eds.), *The Palgrave Handbook of Organizational Change Thinkers*,
DOI 10.1007/978-3-319-52878-6_89

Keywords
Cultural change • Democracy • Network organizations • New models of education • Organization Change Alliance • Potential model of transformational change • Power and politics • Sustainable organizational structures • Superordinate goals

Contents

Introduction

Great thought leaders share several common traits. They are approachable, transparent, and collaborative – and they make things happen (Brosseau 2016). This description epitomizes Joanne C. Preston, who has taken the theories of several disciplines and integrated them to "reach beyond the traditional scopes of influence to guide the growth of organizations (Boyer 1990; Ghani 2006, p. 246; Gordon 2007)" in multicultural settings. She has also advanced the whole-person paradigm (Covey 2006) in her research and consulting for more than four decades. Building on her language skills and her solid foundation in developmental psychology, she has pushed the boundaries of traditional organization development and change. Preston has the rare gift of blending theory into practice on six continents, affecting academic audiences, businesses, nonprofit organizations, and governments.

Influences and Motivations: Early Challenge to Excellence

Strongly influenced by her family and her father's encouragement, "Be the best that you can be, whatever that is," Preston sets out as an undergraduate to major in foreign languages but quickly fell in love with psychology. She graduated from

Louisiana State University with one of the first doctorates in the discipline of developmental psychology ever earned in the United States and one of the first women accepted in the program. In 1973, she and her husband, David, arrived in Richmond, Va., where Preston became affiliated with the University of Richmond, her new home from 1973–1991. It was during this time that she evolved from the psychologist frame of mind into a fully engaged management and organization development (OD) specialist. Her training in psychology provided a solid foundation in individual and group work, experiential design and analysis, and developmental approach to healthy adults, and the clinical studies enabled a better understanding of conflict management and complex problem solving (Watson 1968).

Her desire to make the workplace healthier for everyone became insatiable, and she poured herself into learning everything she could about organization development and change. She soon realized that she needed to gain experience as an ODC practitioner, and she began attending the annual information exchanges of the Organization Development Institute (ODI) in Williams Bay, Wis., where she met many of the friends who would influence her life's course. One of these, Don Cole, O.D. Institute president, candidly spoke about his experiences applying ODC to social change and motivated Preston to participate in interventions to create nonviolent social change in communist Poland, Russia, and eventually South Africa.

During this time, Preston's husband decided to change his career focus and return to school. Preston took a sabbatical to join him and received a visiting professorship at Pennsylvania State University. There, she spent the entire year handling family therapy groups, little realizing that this experience would commence her practice of organization development and change. To illustrate, in one of her family therapy groups, Preston worked with the owner of a medium-size business. When this man saw improvements in the way his family functioned, he decided to hire Preston to help make improvements in his business.

Upon returning to Richmond, she acquired a large multinational corporation client with an assembly line problem. The lines were extremely aggressive toward each other to the point of one team's sabotaging another that was doing well. After careful listening, Preston suspected that competition was rewarded instead of cooperation. She suggested two interventions: (1) a one-day team-building session for all three lines simultaneously and (2) changing the reward system so that half of Group A was paired with half of Group B; the other half of Group B was paired with half of Group C and half of Group C was paired with half of Group A. In this way, all lines and shifts were paired, and cooperation was the only route to rewards.

The client was so pleased with Preston's work that he sent her to a supply factory in communist Russia, one that also had an assembly line problem. Preston spoke to the factory director, explaining her need to be able to interview the line bosses alone, in order to receive better information. The director would not allow it; he wanted to hear what his employees were saying, and Preston interviewed the line bosses with the director present. This experience was a turning point for Preston. Rather than viewing the director's behavior as a client problem, she discovered her own cultural blinders as a consultant regarding democracy and confidentiality.

With the Russian factory experience fresh in her mind, Preston developed a presentation (later an article) for the International O.D. Institute Conference in Zeist, the Netherlands (Preston 1987). She shared the stage with Ed Schein and assumed that everyone would leave after his presentation concluded. Instead, the audience gave Preston a standing ovation for her disclosure of learning of her own consulting blinders, evidently a rare thing for an American to admit. At the Zeist conference, she met two other consultants, Ian Barber from Spain introduced her to Louw DuToit from South Africa. These relationships turned into long-standing friendships and led to much of Preston's international work. She was impressed by DuToit's genuine belief in ODC values and ethics, coupled with his love for his country, and especially his willingness to personally fund ODC interventions.

DuToit invited Preston and a colleague, Terry Armstrong, to participate in an intervention in South Africa. Recognizing this as an opportunity of a lifetime, Preston requested backing from the president of the University of Richmond. He fully supported this and many other trips during her tenure there. Interestingly, meanwhile a dean told Preston that she would have to stop her work in South Africa for two reasons – first, it was not hard science, and second, it would ruin her reputation as a psychologist "working in such a horrible place that condoned apartheid."

With her practice of OD underway, Preston decided to transfer from psychology to business management. In 1991, she became chair of management and entrepreneurship at Kennesaw State University. There, she polished her leadership skills and basked in the stimulating intellect and mentoring of her friend, Bob Golembiewski, an OD practitioner and researcher, at the University of Georgia.

Kennesaw opened a new area of involvement for Preston – the Family Enterprise Center – and she began applying ODC skills to business and family dynamics (Preston 1993a). While there, she helped found the Organization Change Alliance (OCA) along with Golembiewski, Don Carter, Joel Finlay, and Tom Myers. This group accomplished much for ODC. It became a well-known forum in the greater Atlanta area for ODC professionals, regularly bringing in recognized ODC academics and practitioners to speak. It also provided opportunities for its members to give back to the community as well as hone their skill sets in workplace settings.

In 1994, three occurrences influenced Preston's career. First, she met Dean Bob Canady of the Pepperdine School of Business, who recruited her to become director of the MSOD program and to develop a doctorate in OD; second, Nelson Mandela became president of South Africa; and third, she received the prestigious O.D. Consultant of the Year Award from the Organization Development Institute for her work in international social development. This award was doubly special, as her husband David lived long enough to know about it before he lost his battle with brain cancer.

In 1994, Pepperdine was a Mecca of ODC and offered a unique opportunity for Preston to lead this group into the future – redesigning the MSOD program to include engaging master's degree students in international ODC work in France, Mexico, and China. Development was challenging, as many of the business faculty did not want a PhD program; additionally, there were difficulties with accreditation.

Only a limited number of the faculty was publishing, and the ODC program turned into an EDDOC because the Graduate School of Education and Psychology already had doctorates. There were many conflicts causing hard feelings all around, and those years at Pepperdine were a mixture of opportunity and political battles. Despite the challenges, the EDDOC doctoral program had its first cohort in 1995.

Preston's days at Pepperdine ended in 2000, and in early 2001, she went to the University of Monterrey in Monterrey, Mexico, to work with Daphne DePorres and Nancy Westrup, two graduates of the Pepperdine EDDOC program. At Monterrey, she taught, encouraged the faculty to write, and supported the extended Pepperdine doctoral program begun at the University of Monterrey.

From Monterrey, Preston briefly returned to California before moving to New Orleans to open a bed and breakfast, Chateau du Louisiane, and continue her international consulting. With her late husband's family there, Preston viewed New Orleans as the closest culture to Europe. She provided some consulting work for the City of New Orleans and Mayor Ray Nagin. In one planning meeting, the mayor asked if there was anything that could be done with the gangs, drug dealers, and prostitutes near the French Quarter. Preston remarked that something needed to come along and implode the entire system. That implosion came 2 weeks later, with Hurricane Katrina (J. Preston, personal communication, October 29, 2016).

Forced to evacuate, Preston left New Orleans for a few months. Upon her return, she became involved in the hurricane recovery efforts with Carolyn Lukensmeyer and the United New Orleans Plan. Several citywide town hall meetings were televised to cities all over the United States and Alaska, where New Orleans residents had been evacuated. This was an exciting project and many of the evacuees did return. However, for Preston, it was bittersweet, as her bed and breakfast was the only house destroyed in the Garden District, and she knew that she needed to look for new opportunities. Meanwhile, she taught in several university master's degree and doctorate programs.

That opportunity came when she received an email from Colorado Technical University (CTU) in Colorado Springs, Colorado. Though Preston had had no previous contact with CTU, the person running the program requested that she teach a hybrid class and serve as keynote speaker for one of its residencies. She enjoyed the experience so much that she accepted the fulltime position as Dean of the Doctorate of Management Program in 2007 and moved to Colorado Springs. This was a new start.

Key Contributions: International Change, Organizational Innovation, ODC Education, and Academic Journal Editor

Four areas in which Preston has made significant contributions to the field of ODC stand out. These include applying ODC to large-scale country change, improving ODC education, founding new types of organizations, and serving as editor of the *Organization Development Journal*.

Brought New Sensitivity to International ODC

Although she participated in many other international and domestic interventions, Preston's greatest contributions were in South Africa, Poland, and Kenya. The interventions in South Africa were of major bottom-up nature, while those in Poland and Kenya were top-down.

South Africa Louw DuToit created a bottom-up intervention that helped move South Africa out of apartheid, and his message made South Africa an obsession for Preston. To be successful, this intervention had to address the following issues: (1) There would never be a top-down intervention because leadership did not want it; (2) Government could not control the power; (3) Government was resistant to change; (4) Blacks were not involved; (5) Communication was both ineffective and lacked credibility; (6) Foreign pressure made the existing government more reactive; (7) There was a lack of understanding about democracy; and (8) There were too few behavioral scientists to help bring about the needed change (Preston 1996).

Taking the initiative for change upon himself, DuToit established a group, the Leadership for the Future, to train leaders about democracy and its benefits for South Africa. Additionally, he conducted workshops focusing on peaceful change, and established a group of community, educational, and government leaders called the Community and Development Association of Africa (CDMAA), targeting the white, black, and colored (race designation then), a group needed to build a superordinate goal of multi-nationality. DuToit knew that it would take a strategic meeting of this group to build momentum.

In 1986, DuToit invited Preston and Armstrong to a meeting, but did not reveal the nature of the meeting (Preston 1996). When they got off the plane, DuToit asked them to speak to a small group of people about cultural synergy (Preston and Armstrong 1987). They did not know that they were going to be the keynote speakers for the CDMAA meeting until they arrived at Johannesburg on the Sunday evening of the event. Upon their arrival, DuToit announced that Armstrong and Preston were in charge of a 300-person meeting. Not only were attendees strangers to each other, but also because of their tribal backgrounds, they hated each other (Preston and Armstrong 1991). This was a complicated situation. Because the government defined the participants as "multiracial," it was actually against the law for such a group to assemble. More importantly, these attendees were going to plan strategies for eliminating apartheid nonviolently.

Even though this was a time before large group interventions were used in ODC, Armstrong and Preston decided to use basic OD rather than lecture about cultural synergy. They needed to find a positive superordinate goal immediately and framed it as "creating a safe South Africa for our children." The atmosphere became electrified with enthusiasm and strangers became friends through this discussion. Later, Preston reflected that had they used something like "do this for the love of your country" nothing would have worked (J. Preston, personal communication, October 29, 2016).

The Johannesburg meeting was both serious and volatile as were many others that involved, DuToit, Barber, Armstrong, and Preston. Conflict could arise from anywhere, and during this time, some were hurt and others killed. DuToit's home was burned down and Tammy Saloma, a leader of the CDMAA, was stabbed 30 times by a rival tribe for his involvement in nonviolent ODC work. Every intervention meant walking the line between violence and nonviolence, and the remaining ODC practitioners had to use power and politics carefully (Preston 1988; Preston and DuToit 1991). Although using power and politics was habitually avoided in ODC work or had negative implications in those days, the situation in South Africa made its use imperative since the culture was authoritarian, and aggressive behavior was endemic (Preston and DuToit 1993). There was a very clear hierarchy in the tribal culture that dictated what its members should do. It did not afford tribal members the opportunity to learn or develop and practice problem-solving skills under parental guidance; instead rigid, inflexible behaviors developed as members reached adulthood. Therefore, many of the planned interventions were entwined around workshops that helped participants develop sorely needed problem-solving skills, conflict resolution skills, flexibility, and an understanding of democracy (Preston and DuToit 1991; Preston, DuToit, Van Zyl and Holscher 1993; Preston et al. 1996; Preston 1993b).

DuToit and associates even taught conflict resolution skills to high-ranking tribal leaders to minimize aggressive behaviors. One such incident was at a school in Pietermaritzburg in the heart of Zululand. When colleagues arrived to conduct the workshop at the hotel, they saw a note that a school was under attack. Without delay, they went to the school and saw the school director trying to protect the building, the fathers and sons Toi-toing (performing a tribal threat dance), and the police surrounding the group, guns drawn and ready for action. The tribal leaders had a megaphone and were trying to control the crowd. Immediately, the consultants split their efforts between the school leaders, the police, and the crowd.

One example of using power and politics in this event stood out in Preston's memory. While the threat of violence was at its peak, Van Zyl was told to go into the school building rather than try to reason with the fathers and sons – who likely would have harmed or killed him. Zulu tribal leaders and the Zulus respected their regular consultants, and consequently it was better that a non-Afrikaner go with the outside group. This action worked (J. Preston, personal communication, October 29, 2016).

During the summer of Mandela's inauguration (1994) as the new head of South Africa's government, Preston was invited to return to work with DuToit and Barber on projects involving the government, major organizations about to become independent from the government, and nonprofits evolving to help assist the new government. Many interventions and meetings took place with the eventual outcome of a South African democracy.

Poland Preston's experiences in Poland stemmed primarily from team interventions led by Don Cole. Cole had at least two general interventions and Preston was invited to participate on several others. The first of these was a trip to communist Russia to determine if social scientists from the USSR and other countries could work together. The session was held on a boat and the scientists enjoyed a cruise on the Volga River. The participants met in the morning, and though Preston never saw the Russians meet, she suspected they somehow managed to do so as they spoke with one voice. After a few days, she spoke to the steward in his own Russian language and inquired how the Russian scientists got organized. He told her that they met in the bar "with the good vodka" after the bar closed. That evening, Preston stayed after closing and spoke Russian the entire evening. In the morning, she had breakfast with the rest of the participants and shared her information. Her ability to fit in culturally gave her consulting a tremendous advantage (J. Preston, person communication, October 29, 2016).

This advantage was demonstrated in another dramatic example of the importance of cultural acceptance. Preston and Cole were invited by the National Academy of Sciences to help resolve a conflict between Russian communists, Polish communists, and Solidarity scientists. Cole, the more experienced consultant, was on stage with the president of the National Academy of Science, and Preston was relegated to the back of the audience. Each division chair felt it imperative to tell the entire history of his respective division, beginning in 900 A.D. From 8 a.m. until approximately 11 a.m., the stories droned on until Cole became impatient. Wanting to start an intervention and have the participants discuss how they could cooperate, he stood up and announced, "Enough wasting time. I want you to get into groups and talk about how to cooperate with each other." Immediately, the scientists walked out. The president approached Preston, saying, "You are on." "Can you convince them to return?" she asked. "Only if I order them," he said, and did just that. Once the scientists returned, Preston continued the stories until lunch break at 1 p.m. By working through the existing authoritarian culture structure rather than using the more informal approach of open participant discussion commonly associated with ODC interventions in the United States, Preston was able to have the president ask the group to work on the issues, which they did (J. Preston, personal communication, October 29, 2016).

After the Academy of Sciences meeting with Cole, Preston was invited to facilitate a meeting between Russian communist leaders, Polish communist leaders, Solidarity leaders, Lech Walesa, and Walesa's interpreter (Preston 1989b). The meeting's purpose was to identify how these groups could cooperate effectively, if there was a change in the government from Russian domination to a Polish government. For years, each of these groups had considered the others' nuisances, especially Solidarity. In this typical ODC intervention, that of – discussing goals and visions for the future and strategizing how the groups could work together – Preston sensed the existence of an "elephant" in the room, some issue that was impeding communication and which everyone recognized but no one would directly address. She asked the group to air the issue, but no one would say anything. Finally, through the translator, Walesa told Preston to keep going because she was doing fine. Preston realized that she was going to anger Walesa and the others if she pressed the issue any further and continued the facilitation. However, she left the meeting feeling like the overall intervention was a failure because although some communication had occurred along with a few possible strategies for working together, the groups never surfaced the mysterious underlying issue. It was not until she left Poland and reached her next destination that she realized what had transpired during the intervention when she read in the newspaper that Solidarity had taken over the government and Walesa was leading Poland (J. Preston, personal communication, October 29, 2016).

Afterward, Preston returned to Poland several times, conducting workshops for small business owners and influential community members on changing to a free market economy and developing transformational leaders using ODC training. On one trip to Warsaw, she worked with a small hotel owner to develop more effective business strategies; she taught others how to set up small business. On another trip to Warsaw, she worked with teachers and other influence leaders to identify skill sets and specific action items to help their communities (J. Preston, personal communication, October 29, 2016).

Kenya On several occasions, Preston worked with governmental leaders on strategies to improve the Kenyan educational system. On her first trip to Kenya, she provided strategy training for business and nonprofit owners in Nairobi. During the training for the nonprofit group, a woman arrived very late and Preston spent some personal time updating the woman. On the second day of training, the woman mentioned that Preston knew her husband who wanted to meet with Preston after the session. The woman's husband was Dr. Taatia arap Toweet, past Prime Minister of Education for Kenya and a participant in the meetings to make Kenya independent from England.

Another significant meeting for her was a meeting with President Mwai Kibaki. Preston asked him to outline his vision for Kenya. When his response was a non-corrupt government, Preston explained that a non-corrupt government was not a vision. She noted that since Kenya had one of the highest education levels for an African country, it could become the think tank of Africa. The president liked the idea and engaged her in helping to create more strategies for education (J. Preston, personal communication, October 29, 2016).

Arap Toweet also introduced Preston to Daniel arap Moi, his friend and co-tribal leader. Although arap Moi had a negative reputation during his presidency, he desired to leave a positive legacy through education and wanted to build his university into one of the best in his country. Preston discussed ways he could achieve his goals. Today, Moi University is one of the best in Kenya.

Since arap Toweet's death, Preston has returned to Kenya a few times working with arap Toweet's son and encouraging women to stay in school. She also dealt with community issues, tribal conflict, and educational issues.

Designed New Models of ODC Education

Preston has left a distinct footprint on the very nature of ODC education, both in the United States and internationally. For many years, the literature regarding the effectiveness of formal ODC education programs, along with training new ODC practitioners, has been controversial. An early study by Head et al. (1996) showed that graduate education is a major component for the development of ODC skills, but it ranked second to personal growth evolving from professional workshops, mentoring, and team consulting. These authors believed that universities needed to design programs that included courses teaching ODC skills, providing opportunities to participate in ODC research, offering opportunities to test character and promote personal growth, making available team consulting and mentorships, and requiring students to attend ODC conferences.

Adding Global Focus: Expanding the Pepperdine MSOD; Constructing the EDDOC In 1994, Pepperdine University's MSOD was one of the few university programs with a focus on personal growth. As Preston launched a redesign, she made sure to retain the program's best parts: personal growth, sensitivity groups, teamwork, a thesis, and mentoring. Since the program offered little to no international experience, three trips were added to help students develop a global perspective. These included working with organizational clients and faculty members in France, Mexico, and China.

In Monterrey, Mexico, MSOD students worked with a glass company client, an experience providing special language challenges for the primarily English-speaking students. During the week, the students observed the production line, interviewed designated employees, analyzed the data, and presented their findings to the senior management team with recommendations for the future. This was a significant step forward in ODC education because the redesigned program included international consulting experience with seasoned faculty.

With the MSOD program a success, Preston, with the help of Kurt Motamedi and Chris Worley, developed an OD doctorate program featuring an international aspect. The program designers knew that many students would come from the MSOD and further build on their existing skills. Therefore, they inserted a required team-building experience for all doctoral students prior to starting classes and that included a high ropes course, a sensitivity group, and a team-choosing exercise.

The Pepperdine doctorate program was designed for working adults rather than typical traditional OD programs existing in 1995. Throughout the calendar year, students worked individually or by the Internet with their team; additionally, they had a seven-day meeting once a semester. This design was an extension of the already classic MSOD experience and included international activities to provide these advanced students with the same global skills in their consulting experience.

Monty Miller, a member of the first Pepperdine Cohort in EdD Organizational Change, observed of Preston, "She inspired, motivated and set the bar, all in a matter of minutes. It started with her deeply inspiring story of conducting a teambuilding-program with the group from the National Academy of Sciences." He continued, "We were motivated to excel. The more we invested into the program, the more exponential multipliers we would receive out of the program; that was true. And her final words were, 'You are not done till you have published'" (M. Miller, personal communication, April 4, 2016). The program was so successful that Peter Sorensen invited Preston to consult with him when he was designing his PhD program for Benedictine University. She also taught in the program for him several times.

Designing a New ODC Model for Working Adults: Colorado Technical University (CTU) As a major contribution to its ODC education process, Preston became Colorado Technical University's Dean of the Doctorate of Management. This program was totally designed for working adults as a hybrid program (Preston 2014). For a time, it was a diamond in the crown of ODC education. While primarily online, this hybrid program had a required residency – the powerful heart of the program (Preston 2014).

The purpose of the first residency was socialization into the program. Students met as a group to get to know each other and their first faculty member. From the second residency onward, half the cohorts attended at any one time. Students were required to attend three residencies a year, but many came to all four because of their desire to learn. At the program's peak, there were 240 new students every year – 30 to 60 students every quarter – and the residencies were filled with class time, famous keynote speakers, workshops, and a large town meeting to discuss issues. Online education has had a very poor reputation, especially at the doctorate level, but during its glory days, this program was far superior to any doctoral online program or even full residence program available.

The program degree was business management and incorporated 12 classes. It also consisted of a solid ODC background as a base for all students (Preston 2014). Additionally, there were specializations (composed of four classes) in such areas as ODC, Global Leadership, Environmental and Social Sustainability, Homeland Security and Emerging Media. Mike McCoy and Preston interviewed major constituencies for these specialties and designed them based on constituency needs and requirements. According to Preston et al. (2012), Homeland Security is one such example.

The most popular specialty was ODC, followed by Global Leadership and then Environmental and Social Sustainability. The Global Leadership specialty was the first doctoral program in this area. It was a combination of ODC skills, social media, culture, international/global business, and environmental and social sustainability (Preston 2014). For the ODC, Global Leadership, and Environmental and Social Sustainability specialties, an advanced research class taken outside the United Stated was required and included a major team project within the host country.

To illustrate, Kenneth Wall and Preston took a large group to a location near Beijing, China, and worked with the human resource department in a major sporting goods corporation. In order to be ready for their action research project, the students refreshed their knowledge of action research and learned about Chinese culture and the specific business organization's culture prior to their departure to China. During their brief stay, they were officially introduced to the culture, gathered one cycle of data, analyzed it, and prepared a report for the HR senior staff.

The CTU online hybrid program is the only one that ever attempted such an extensive project. Other students conducted interventions in several countries, including South Africa and India. The faculty ultimately made this program special (Preston 2014). Each faculty member was a star in ODC in his or her own right, and they came to this program because it was like a mini-academy of management meeting. They were stimulated, not only by the teaching but also by each other outside the classroom. While these well-known faculties came worldwide to CTU residency, the program's powerful component was that they themselves designed and taught the online classes. Moreover, they came because they truly enjoyed seeing each other four times a year and felt stimulated with the new ideas from the information meetings with their professional colleagues. The same faculty were mentors of the dissertation committees. (To be a mentor, a faculty member had to have at least 20 peer-reviewed publications, although many far exceeded the requirement.)

One of Preston's former students, Tonya Henderson, said, "Dr. Preston made sure her students learned several different methods. Not only did she fill our consulting toolboxes, but she shared her network in a way that gave us direct access to some of the great thinkers in our field. You simply can't put a price on that kind of learning, or the confidence that comes with it" (T. Henderson, personal communication, April 5, 2016).

Thus, the program design, the residency, and the faculty were the factors moving ODC education forward in a major way for several very meaningful years. Unfortunately, CTU was a for-profit university, and its corporate leadership made the decision to standardize classes and eliminate the faculty-designed ones, shorten residency, reduce the number of residencies, and vary the faculty brought for residency. The program exists today, but it is not the same.

Founding Sustainable Organizations on ODC

Three new types of organizations exist today partly because of Preston's influence. These include the Organization Change Alliance (OCA) in Atlanta, bed and breakfasts of New Orleans, Louisiana (BBNOLA), and the International Society for Organization Development and Change (ISODC).

The Organization Change Alliance (OCA) The OCA came into existence when Preston moved to Atlanta. It was formed officially on January 11, 1993 (Preston 1993b), and grew out of several concurrent forces. First, there was a lament by Golembiewski (1993) that the national training labs no longer had the influence needed to help train new professionals in the field and that there was no platform or good way to transfer basic ODC values to newcomers. Additionally, not many university programs were available in which to train ODC professionals, – especially in the South.

At that time, there was a cadre of OD academics and practitioners in the Atlanta area who wanted to do something about this inability to socialize new people to the profession. Finlay, Carter, Golembiewski, and Preston became a steering committee for a new OD professional organization and were supported by initial members like Myers.

The visioning process developed the basis for this new organization and included mentoring, affiliations, service, improving professional skills, certification, OD research, OD marketing, and "what is in it for me" (Preston 1993b, p. 80). Its foundation was learning and service, something that made this organization unique. The members all participated in community projects and assigned designated mentors for new people in the field. Workshops were conducted at regular meetings to reinforce or learn new skills, theory, and/or practice. This organization continues today.

Bed and Breakfasts of New Orleans, Louisiana (BBNOLA) When Preston arrived in New Orleans in 2002, many bed and breakfasts and small family restaurants existed in the French Quarter, Garden District, and surrounding tourist areas (Preston 2012a, b). These groups were not organized nor were they motivated to join forces.

Preston bought a bed and breakfast (B&B) and quickly saw a need for working together. Most of the B&Bs could manage quite well during the high season, as could the family restaurants. During the hot, sticky summers, the larger corporate hotels and corporate restaurants had all the customers. By joining forces, there was an opportunity to get some of the business for the smaller hotels, B&Bs, and family restaurants through joint marketing, coordinating meals with stays, and discounts on tourist attractions. The problem was that these owners were fiercely independent entrepreneurs who thought first about competition, rather than working together.

Preston decided to develop a network organization to combat the problem (Chisholm 1998). By using a network, owners of these organizations could remain independent and yet work together for their mutual interests. Thus, in 2002, after much negotiation and compromise, the BBNOLA was born (Preston 2012a).

In 2005, Hurricane Katrina devastated the city of New Orleans. With the subsequent failure of their businesses, many of the BBNOLA group members left. Preston was among them. Upon her return, playing the consultant facilitator once again, she convinced BBNOLA members to persist and try new techniques to attract tourists and save their businesses (Preston 2012b). The group developed a website that showcased the B&Bs, small hotels, and restaurant locations. Tourists could view pictures of the location, prices, and rooms and even register online. This positive energy was generated from establishing a network organization that still exists today (Preston 2012b).

International Society for Organization Development and Change (ISODC) This professional organization was founded by Terry Armstrong, Jeanne Maes, Lena Neal, Peter Sorensen, and Preston. Prior to its formation, numerous discussions occurred about the future of the *Organization Development Journal*, founded by Joseph Cangemi in fall 1983 and owned by the Organization Development Institute (ODI). Cole was quite ill by now and it seemed clear that if the ODI dissolved, something needed to be done to save the journal or let it go.

Thus, the International Society for Organization Development came into being in January 2011. Two years later, the word "change" was added to its name.

While the ISODC emerged from the ODI, it was an entirely new entity. Its founders realized that to serve a truly global constituency, it had to become a network organization (Chisholm 1998). These founders wanted to develop an organization that would not have chapters, but rather be a joining force for the many splintered groups in the field. They wanted people from disciplines beyond ODC and the social sciences to join and help the field grow and change.

Editor of the *Organization Development Journal* Cole's encouragement to write for the *Organization Development Journal* attracted Preston to follow the track to eventually becoming its editor. From 1988 to 1990, she served as its peer review editor under then-editor Armstrong's tutelage. During this brief apprenticeship, Preston developed the peer review system for manuscript review – something that was previously missing.

In 1991, Preston assumed the editorship for the first time. As of this writing, she has served as editor three times. Under her editorship during the years, she has tried to keep the journal balanced between theory, practitioner, case study, experimental research, action research, and how-to articles. Her goal has been twofold: (1) provide the field with solid theory and research and (2) feed the practitioner with new ways to increase practice effectiveness.

In its life cycle, the *Organization Development Journal* is currently in the early maturity stage, and it now is one of the best international journals in ODC. It is Preston's goal to maintain that position while she remains editor. In finding writers, selecting appropriate articles for issues, encouraging guest editors for special issues, and maintaining a top-flight editorial staff, she realizes that she has had an impact on the ODC field and its thinking.

New Insights

As a scholar-practitioner, Preston's focus has been consistent in applying ODC theory to the field, integrating and expanding it through her practice and writing. Her keen ability to penetrate situations has resulted in greater understanding using superordinate goals, creating cultural change democracy, designing sustainable organizational structures, and applying new models to ODC education.

Superordinate Goals: Alleviating Hostile Situation in Large South African Groups

In her work in South Africa, Preston was able to draw from her experiences in her family therapy groups and later, entrepreneurial family business consulting to address often hostile situations and work with large disparate groups. In one visit to South Africa, Preston and Armstrong were surprised to learn that they were responsible for bringing together a 300-person meeting, and lecture was out of the question. They somehow had to use the group to create the needed cultural synergy to move forward. On the spot, Preston and Armstrong crafted a superordinate goal to unite the groups, "creating a safe South Africa for our children." It worked and

Armstrong and Preston received a standing ovation and were invited to facilitate the remaining few days in the same manner.

These two pioneers used OD in large groups before it became conventional. They also created positive superordinate goals to unite groups before there was Appreciative Inquiry (Cummings and Worley 2015).

Cultural Change Democracy: Visioning Possibilities in South Africa

Analyzing the impacts of culture and the potential of conflict as a catalyst for change, Preston has focused on helping leaders understand the dynamics of their situations and what is possible.

For example, South Africa's culture was quite rigid with no opportunity to learn, make mistakes, or develop problem-solving skills (Preston, DuToit, Van Zyl and Holscher 1993). Children were raised with strict obedience to their parents and authority figures, and tribal culture consisted of a distinct hierarchy producing rigid, inflexible behaviors. To address these cultural challenges, Preston and Armstrong conducted workshop interventions helping participants develop an array of needed skills: problem solving, conflict resolution, flexibility, and an understanding of the use of cultural change democracy, a foreign concept at the time (Preston, DuToit, Van Zyl and Holscher 1993; Preston et al. 1996; Preston 1993b; Preston and DuToit 1991).

Creating Sustainable Organizational Structures

Preston has educated and helped others to navigate changing organizational structures and natural disasters and changing economic conditions (Pierce 2006). One striking example mentioned above was the network organization, BBNOLA. Building on a superordinate goal, that of attracting more business for everyone, Preston persuaded the small business owners that working together was truly beneficial. She used the concept of trans-organizational change, due to the owners' alliance as under-organized systems (Brown 1980). She knew that they would go through the process of identification, convention, organization, and evaluation (Brown 1980). Then, she established a design team to create the structure of BBNOLA. Using the work of Rupert Chisholm in some of his community work in Pittsburgh as a model, Preston encouraged the group to explore the environment, identify the current community structure, vision a desirable future, plan broad action steps, and follow through with additional work (Chisholm 1998).

Daphne DePorres and Steve Fazio both recounted her amazing ability to "get to the heart of a matter" and create spaces in which forward movement can occur (DePorres, personal communication, April 6, 2016; S. Fazio, personal communication, April 8, 2016). BBNOLA illustrates one of these instances.

New Models and Applications for ODC Education: Preston's Mark on Theory and Practice

Preston's forward thinking in requiring international experiences of ODC students ensured that global thinking will be solidified in the literature. Her many articles regarding the importance of self-knowledge and culture have provided the basis on which others have continued to build.

She realized the importance of integrating conflict resolution skills into her practice very early on. Her reports of this use in South Africa have been foundational in applying conflict-handling skills to create change in other areas.

Legacies and Unfinished Business

Legacies: Potential Model for Transformational Change – South Africa

During Preston's career, she has demonstrated the use of self-as-instrument, far ahead of its popularity in the literature (Cheung-Judge 2012). Additionally, she has labeled her ability to observe herself, an organizational (or situational) culture, its leaders, its people, and any interventions simultaneously as "synergistic action research" (Preston 1989b).

Her ability to engage in synergistic action research is exemplified by her work in South Africa, using Dick Beckhard and Harris's organizational transition model (Beckhard and Harris 1987) and realizing the need to modify it. The model focused on five specific areas in the change process: (1) evaluating the need for change, (2) defining the desired future state, (3) describing the present state, (4) moving from the present to the future, and (5) managing the transition.

For example, while working in South Africa, Preston's team became aware that the Beckhard and Harris model did not explain everything that was going on in the situation. They observed that the "organization" did not make this transition by its own efforts, but that the people had a great deal to do with it (Preston et al. 1996). The team observed the "present state," and within that present state, the people had an old reality that contained the thoughts, beliefs, feelings, and behaviors necessary to be successful *in the present state* of the organization. As the leaders developed a new organizational vision and desired future state, in order to be successful, the people would have to change their reality to fit the future. Thus, they would go through a transition, while the people – the real catalysts for helping the organization reach the future state – would go through a transformation stage.

Preston had the opportunity to meet Beckhard at an academy of management meeting and discuss the article about the South Africa situation. Beckhard appreciated the new thinking and recognized the need to modify the model.

In the potential model of transformational change applied to South Africa, the people and the organization go through eight corresponding substages of change, to move from the present state with its old reality to the future state and its new reality

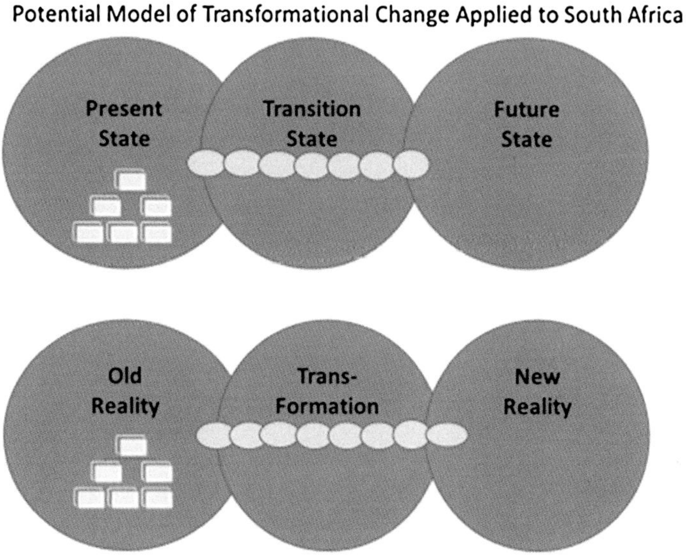

Potential Model of Transformational Change Applied to South Africa

Fig. 1 Transition and transformation: A vital interdependency (Preston et al. 1996) (Reproduced with permission)

(Preston 1996). The leaders envision a desired new future and begin the transition (see Fig. 1 below).

The leadership needs to plan interventions in stage 1 of transition to help develop the people in the first stage of transformation. Next, the organization moves to the second state of transition and the leaders plan interventions to bring the people along to that new level of reality. This process continues with each step in the transition in which the people must be brought along. If this process is consistently followed, the people in the organization would have the thoughts, beliefs, feelings, and behavior appropriate for the new organization's success when the future state is obtained.

In South Africa, the organization made the transition successfully to the *new* South Africa, but the people were left behind. While Mandela realized what was happening, he felt that it was necessary to change the country. This decision may have been appropriate at the time, but in retrospect, the cultural training in problem solving and conflict resolution should have reached all segments of society instead of the leaders only.

Unfinished Business: Using Social Media in Traditional OD Practice and Education

Preston's intellectual curiosity continues to seek new applications to the field of ODC. She is currently interested in social media and its untapped potential in three areas: (1) exploring more about using social media in traditional ODC practice, (2) how it might be applied in social change situations, and (3) how can it enhance

ODC education. For example, social media could be used to build global Internet teams and could also make interesting interventions and enhance mentoring new people in the field.

In recent years, Preston has harnessed the power of webinars in traditional ODC practice and research. Between 2013 and 2015, she produced popular webinars for the Academy of Management Consulting and organization development divisions on the topic of preparing manuscripts for submission to the academy. She has also used webinars to address such topics as consulting skills (with Armstrong and David Jamieson), and how to break into global consulting, using stories and audience questions to make skills more transferable. She is exploring their use in small groups to promote personal growth.

She has postulated about the power of using social media as an intervention to promote social change. Her interest was piqued when she attended an ISODC conference in Amsterdam, the Netherlands, in 2014. There, she made a presentation on the history of OD as applied to social change and lamented that there is not much of this being done today, even though there are opportunities. A young couple that had just returned from Ukraine was in the audience. Instead of delivering their planned presentation, they shared what they did in Ukraine to promote peace, revealing how they used social media to design the intervention, to train facilitators, and to attract people in Ukraine to participate in the intervention (later written as an article in the *Organization Development Journal* (Fursman and Fursman 2014).

Preston immediately saw the possibilities and wondered what else could be done in other situations. As she continues to explore this area, she will encourage others to become involved.

Finally, there is a use for social media in formally educating and training future leaders. At present, there are master's programs in this specialty area, but no full PhD programs. As an example, the Global Leadership specialty area created at CTU is filled with use for social media as a combination of organization development and change, cultural awareness, environmental and social sustainability, and global business. This program can prepare leaders for business, international corporations, government, nonprofit, nongovernmental, and Internet organizations. Students gain much experience by interacting with thought leaders across the world. It is Preston's dream to further such a program; it only needs a university home that realizes the need for global leaders, coupled with an appreciation for social media as a tool for education.

Conclusion

Ultimately, great thought leaders make things happen through their approachability, transparency, and collaborative style. This description characterizes Joanne C. Preston who, over the course of her career, has integrated the theories of several disciplines into practice. With a foundation in developmental psychology, she set forth to make the workplace healthier. To date, she has influenced the growth of organizations and left her imprint on academia, nonprofits, businesses, and governments on six continents.

Echoing her father's encouragement to "be the best that you can be, whatever that is," Preston felt the exhilaration of exploring and experimenting. This has become her mantra to her students and clients as she moves ahead to greater contributions. Certainly, as the world becomes a smaller place through globalization, it will take great thought leaders like Preston to persevere integrating and applying interdisciplinary theories to new horizons of practice with the goal of making the workplace healthier.

References

Beckhard, R., & Harris, R. T. (1987). *Organization transitions: Managing complex change* (2nd ed.). Reading: Addison Wesley.

Boyer, E. L. (1990). *Scholarship reconsidered: Priorities of the professoriate*. Princeton: Carnegie Foundation for the Advancement of Teaching.

Brosseau, D. (2016). 6 characteristics great thought leaders share. *Entrepreneur*. Retrieved from http://www.entrepreneur.com/article/230696

Brown, L. D. (1980). Planned change in underorganized systems. In T. Cummings (Ed.), *Systems theory in organization development* (pp. 181–201). Chichester: Wiley.

Cheung-Judge, M. Y. (2012). The self as instrument: AA cornerstone for the future of OD. *O.D Practitioner, 44*(2), 42–48.

Chisholm, R. (1998). *Developing network organizations: Learning from practice and theory*. Reading: Addison-Wesley.

Covey, S. R. (2006). Leading in the knowledge worker age. In F. Hesselbein & M. Goldsmith's (Eds.), *The leader of the future 2: Visions, strategies, and practices for the new era* (pp. 215–246). San Francisco: Jossey-Bass.

Cummings, T. G., & Worley, C. G. (2015). *Organization development and change*. Mason: Thomson Southwestern.

Fursman, R., & Fursman, I. (2014). Winning the peace in Ukraine by combining OD practices with technology. *Organization Development Journal, 32*(4), 53–62.

Ghani, U. A. (2006). The leader integrator: An emerging role. In F. Hesselbein & M. Goldsmith's (Eds.), *The leader of the future 2: Visions, strategies, and practices for the new era* (pp. 241–254). San Francisco: Jossey-Bass.

Golembiewski, R. T. (1993). What's ahead for OD and ODI? Some informal guessing that rests on caring as well as analysis. *Organization Development Journal, 11*(2), 15–22.

Gordon, M. (2007, May). What makes interdisciplinary research original? Integrative scholarship reconsidered. *Oxford Review of Education, 33*(2), 195–209.

Head, T. C., Armstrong, T., & Preston, J. C. (1996). The role of graduate education in becoming a competent organization development professional. *OD Practitioner, 28*(1), 52–60.

Pierce, P. (2006). Leading in a constantly changing world. In F. Hesselbein & M. Goldsmith's (Eds.), *The leader of the future 2: Visions, strategies, and practices for the new era* (pp. 113–120). San Francisco: Jossey-Bass.

Preston, J. C. (1987). Cultural blinders: Take them off before attempting international O.D. *Organization Development Journal, 5*(l), 50–58.

Preston, J. C. (1988). Power and politics: A necessity in large systems change. *Organization Development Journal, 6*(4), 46–52.

Preston, J. C. (1993a, February). Clarify family values first. *Nation's Business, 54*, 46–52.

Preston, J. C. (1993b). A new model for local OD professional groups. *Organization Development Journal, 11*(2), 75–84.

Preston, J. C. (1996, Winter). South Africa: My journey on the river of transformation. *Academy of Management ODC Newsletter, 11*, 6–8.
Preston, J. C. (2012a, December). The evolution of a tourism network in the tourist industry. In G. D. Sardana & T. Thatchenkery's (Eds.), *Positive initiatives for organizational change and transformation* (pp. 120–138). New Delhi: MacMillan Publishers.
Preston, J. C. (2012b). Increasing local tourism through network organizations. *Global Management Journal, 4*(1), 37–42.
Preston, J. C. (2014). Online doctoral programs: Can they produce the business scientists and leaders needed for the 21st century? *International Journal of Learning and Change, 2*(1), 39–47.
Preston, J. C., & Armstrong, T. R. (1987). Cultural synergy: A dynamic opportunity for nonviolent problem-solving in South Africa. *The Organization Development Practitioner, 19*(4), 12–16.
Preston, J. C., & Armstrong, T. R. (1991). Team-building in South Africa: Cross cultural synergy in action. *Public Administration Quarterly, 15*(l), 65–82.
Preston, J. C., & DuToit, L. J. (1991). Violence in South Africa: A possible endemic problem that has a feasible solution. *Proceedings of the 21st. Annual OD Information Exchange*, Williams Bay, pp. 83–86.
Preston, J. C., DuToit, L., Van Zyl, D., & Holscher, F. (1993). Endemic violence in South Africa: An OD solution applied to two educational settings. *International Journal of Public Administration, 16*(11), 1767–1792.
Preston, J. C., DuToit, L., & Barber, I. (1996). A potential model of transformational change applied to South Africa. In R. W. Woodman & W. A. Pasmore (Eds.), *Research in organizational change and development* (pp. 175–200). Greenwich: JAI Press.
Preston, J. C., Armstrong, T. R., & McCoy, J. M. (2012). Developing a doctoral program in the emerging field of home land security: An OD approach to curriculum development. In R. R. Sims (Ed.), *Change (transformation) in government organizations* (pp. 191–208). Charlotte: Information Age Publishing.
Watson, R. I. (1968). *The great psychologist: From Aristotle to Freud.* New York: J. B. Lippincott and Company.

Further Reading

Preston, J. C. (1988). Power and politics: A necessity in large systems change. *Organization Development Journal, 6*(4), 46–52.
Preston, J. C. (1989a). Synergistic action research in large systems change: The ideal, the plan, and the reality. *Organization Development Journal, 7*(3), 61–68.
Preston, J. C. (1989b). Perestroika in Eastern Europe as a challenge to O.D. paradigms: One person's view of the team visit to Poland. *Research/Study Team Newsletter on Nonviolent Large System Change, 4*(l), 17–18.
Preston, J. C. (1993a, February). Clarify family values first. *Nation's Business,* p. 54.
Preston, J. C. (1993b). A new model for local OD professional groups. *Organization Development Journal, 11*(2), 75–84.
Preston, J. C. (1996, Winter). South Africa: My journey on the river of transformation. *Academy of Management ODC Newsletter*, 6–8.
Preston, J. C. (2010). Developing a doctoral program in the emerging field of Homeland Security: an OD approach to curriculum development. In R. R. Sims (Ed.), *Change (transformation) in government systems*. Charlotte: Information Age Publishing.
Preston, J. C. (2011). The evolution of a tourism network in the tourist industry. In G. D. Sardana & T. Thatchenkery's (Eds.), *Positive initiatives for organizational change and transformation* (pp. 120–138). New Delhi: MacMillan.
Preston, J. C. (2012). Increasing local tourism through network organizations. *Global Management Journal, 4*(1/2), 39–43.

Preston, J. C. (2014). Online doctoral programs: Can they produce the business scientists and leaders needed for the 21st century? *International Journal of Learning and Change, 2*(1), 3947.

Preston, J. C., & Armstrong, T. R. (1987). Cultural synergy: A dynamic opportunity for nonviolent problem-solving in South Africa. *The Organization Development Practitioner, 19*(4), 12–16.

Preston, J. C., & Chappell, K. E. (1990). Teaching managers leadership. *Leadership & Organization Development Journal, 11*(5), 11–16.

Preston, J. C., & Armstrong, T. R. (1991). Team-building in South Africa: Cross cultural synergy in action. *Public Administration Quarterly, 15*(l), 65–82.

Preston, J. C., & DuToit, L. J. (1991). Violence in South Africa: A possible endemic problem that has a feasible solution. In *Proceedings of the 21st annual OD information exchange*, Williams Bay, pp. 83–86.

Preston, J. C., & DuToit, L. (1992). Large systems change: issues related to the strategy. *Journal of Organizational Change Management, 5*(3), 7–17.

Preston, J. C., DuToit, L., Van Zyl, D., & Holscher, F. (1993). Endemic violence in South Africa: An OD solution applied to two educational settings. *International Journal of Public Administration, 16*(11), 1767–1792.

Preston, J. C., DuToit, L., & Barber, I. (1996). A potential model of transformational change applied to South Africa. In R. W. Woodman & W. A. Pasmore (Eds.), *Research in organizational change and development* (pp. 175–200). Greenwich: JAI Press.

Inspiring Positive Change: The Paradoxical Mind of Robert E. Quinn

64

Gretchen M. Spreitzer

Abstract

This chapter focuses on the work of Robert E. Quinn. He has devoted his professional and personal life to developing himself and others into understanding what it means to be an inspiring change agent. From his life lessons as a child to his unconventional insights as a college student to his work in church life, and especially in his scholarship, Quinn has used key life experiences to learn and grow. Every step of the way, he has sought to understand, document, and ignite transformational experiences. In this way, he is an exemplary applied behavioral scientist, continually integrating scholarship and practice. Quinn's major contributions include (1) the development of the competing values model which embraces the role of tension and paradox to understand organizational life, (2) articulating the essential role of self-empowerment in inspiring positive change, and (3) challenging the assumption that leadership is less about having a position of authority and more about having a mind-set (the fundamental state of leadership). In the last decade, Quinn has brought these different contributions together as a cofounder of a new field of organizational studies, named positive organizational scholarship, which focuses on the science for bringing out the very best in organizations, teams, and individuals. Quinn's contributions extend beyond these content areas as he is also a masterful teacher and mentor who helps others envision their full potential. For all of these reasons, Quinn's personal vision to inspire positive change has been fulfilled on many dimensions.

Keywords

Transformational leadership • Positive leadership • Moral power

G.M. Spreitzer (✉)
Ross School of Business, Center for Positive Organizations, University of Michigan, Ann Arbor, MI, USA
e-mail: spreitze@umich.edu

D.B. Szabla et al. (eds.), *The Palgrave Handbook of Organizational Change Thinkers*,
DOI 10.1007/978-3-319-52878-6_54

Contents

Introduction

In this chapter, I consider the work of an empowered and empowering man Robert E. Quinn. To transform an individual is to bring about a deep change in meaning, awareness, and capacity. Transformed individuals take on a new identity. They become more empowered and empowering. Something similar is true at the collective level. To transform a group or organization is to bring about a deep change in the culture. In this case numerous people become empowered and empowering. Exercising transformational influence also results in another kind of change. The change agent, who inspires and facilitates the transformational process, also engages in deep learning and becomes more empowered and empowering.

Quinn has dedicated five decades of his life to understanding, documenting, and igniting the process of transformation. As an applied behavioral scientist, Quinn has an unusual ability to integrate scholarship and practice and to inspire positive change in students, executives, and organizations. This distinctive capability has been the foundation for Quinn's major academic contributions, which I preview below:

- He has introduced and developed the Competing Values Framework and the paradoxical approach to understanding and pursuing excellence in social systems.
- He has articulated the deep change or slow death dilemma in human systems and the essential role of self-empowerment and moral power in inspiring positive change.
- He has challenged the assumption that leadership is about position, knowledge, or skills and has introduced the notion that leadership is a fundamental state of being that each of us can learn to enter.
- He is one of the cofounders of the new and growing field called positive organizational scholarship which researches what brings out the very best in organizations, teams, and individuals.

In this chapter, I share some crucial developmental experiences that have shaped Quinn: I outline his core contributions, capture key elements of his legacy as a change thought leader (as seen through the eyes of prominent change scholars), and share the direction of where Quinn's work is going next.

Influences and Motivations

I interviewed Quinn to learn more about his early life experiences, and how they shaped him and his orientation to change. Quinn's early experiences profoundly shaped his eventual choice of study. His father died shortly after he was born, and he was raised in a blue-collar neighborhood in Newport, Rhode Island. His mother remarried, and his relationship with his stepfather was often trying. Throughout his childhood, he felt like he was on the outside of every group, trying to get in, whether in the family, classroom, or on the sports field. Like many people operating on the edge, he became an informal student of social dynamics.

When he was in eighth grade, his parents and sister joined the Mormon Church. He considered this decision appalling but gradually came to value the Mormon lifestyle as he began to see how it enriched lives. As a freshman in college at Brigham Young University (BYU), he made the decision to join the church. Nine months later he began serving a 2-year mission in Hawaii, which had a profound influence on his ability to understand himself and others.

The task of finding and converting people seemed impossibly difficult. Despite intense effort, he initially had little success. After a year of struggle, he received help from a young man named Stephen R. Covey who would later become known for his book, *The Seven Habits of Highly Successful People*. Quinn was touched by a speech Covey gave, and Covey later coached him in a long, disciplined process of spiritual self-surrender and personal purification.

The result was a transformation in which Quinn describes being filled with the "pure love of Jesus Christ." Centering himself in a higher power, he began to operate at a level of influence he could not have previously imagined. As he transcended his own ego, and became more virtuous, he discovered moral power, or choosing to empower oneself to do the right thing, regardless of external forces. As he taught with love, he began to operate with vision, individual consideration, and constant challenge. He was then able to engage and facilitate the conversion of other people.

At 20 years old, Quinn had experienced deep change and discovered an important key to transformational influence; knowledge and skill were necessary but insufficient. He learned that to change to others, one must also undergo deep self-change. Transformational change agents must transcend the ego and the transactional assumptions that structure conventional thinking and normal social life. Transformational change leaders must continually enlarge their own moral power and live from it. This discovery would have lasting impact.

After the change, Quinn was less driven by the assumptions of survival he learned as a child in a tough neighborhood. He learned that while survival is necessary to life, the purpose of his life is to grow and progress and help others do the same. Given this orientation, he made the important discovery that he wanted to dedicate his professional and personal life to inspiring positive change.

After his mission, Quinn returned to BYU and found the usual choice of majors to be limiting and uninspiring. So, he created his own major in "change." He improvised a major by seeking out professors and topics related to change, no matter what department they happened to be in. He formally graduated with a degree in sociology, but, in fact, he was "a change major." He continued his education with a master's degree in Organization Development at BYU. He then went on to complete a Ph.D. in Organizational Behavior and Applied Behavioral Science at the University of Cincinnati.

In reflecting on his education, Quinn told me, "I studied change constantly. If I took a course on X, I would turn it into a course on X and change. I read about change, I practiced change, I did research on change, I wrote about change and I taught about change. That one word integrated everything in my life. It created enormous synergies."

When I asked him about specific individuals who shaped him along the way, he mentioned his mission president and two faculty members at BYU. Orin R. Woodbury, his mission president, was a potent role model who Quinn sought to emulate. At BYU, Reed Bradford was a teacher of the purpose-driven life. Keith Warner introduced him to literature on organizational effectiveness. While these men were most influential, Quinn told me that the biggest influence on his intellectual development came from two of his peers – Kim Cameron and David Whetten. "We supported and cared for each other, professionally and personally. We made sacrifices for each other." All three eventually became fellows of the Academy of Management and today remain very close friends.

In 1975, Quinn finished his Ph.D. and took his first academic job in the Department of Public Administration at the State University of New York in Albany. After receiving tenure, he took on a leadership role as the Executive Director of the Institute for Government and Policy Studies. Kim Cameron invited him to spend 2 years as a visiting professor at the University of Michigan, School of Business in 1988. It was such a good fit that Quinn joined the Michigan faculty. He became a gifted teacher of executive education, and his research program thrived.

These life experiences powerfully shaped the change scholar Quinn has become over his 40-year career. In the next section of the chapter, I outline the key contributions of his work related to change.

Key Contributions

Some scholars have made their contributions in one or two related areas of inquiry. Quinn is unique. He has made contributions in a number of different areas of inquiry, yet, all of his work ties back to the question of how to inspire positive change. In this section, I fast forward to examine key contributions that have emerged from the pursuit of his life purpose, inspiring positive change.

Contribution 1: The Competing Values Framework (CVF) and the Paradoxical Perspective

Quinn became interested in organizational effectiveness while pursuing his master's at BYU. In the early 1980s, organizational effectiveness was a hot topic. Working with John Rohrbaugh, the two decided to shift the focus of study from the analysis of how people in organizations observed effectiveness to the study of how academic experts thought about effectiveness (Quinn and Rohrbaugh 1983). After the two gathered data, Rohrbaugh did a multidimensional analysis which produced a spatial map of the criteria of organizational effectiveness. He dropped it on Quinn's desk and asked, "Does this make any sense to you?"

Quinn recounts "I couldn't take my eyes off the printout. I headed off to vacation that afternoon, and I couldn't stop thinking about it. I was consumed by it. I was deeply joyful, because I knew we're onto something profoundly important."

The spatial map, which became known as the Competing Values Framework, juxtaposes two dimensions (internal/external and stability/change) to create four quadrants that reflect the key set of values that are often assumed to compete with each other in organizational life (see Fig. 1). The human relations (or collaborate) quadrant with its values of community, teamwork, and trust is often viewed as conflicting with the rational goal (or compete) quadrant, with its values of performance, speed, and competition. A second tension is reflected in the other two dimensions. Here the adhocracy (or create) quadrant, with its values of innovation, transformation, and change, is often viewed as contrasting with the hierarchy (or control) quadrant, with its values of efficiency, process, and systems.

All four quadrants contribute in important ways to organizational effectiveness, yet each is in tension with the others, especially the quadrant diagonal to it. A highly effective leader or culture transcends or even embraces those tensions. An ineffective leader or culture overemphasizes one or two of the quadrants and gives short shrift to the others. It is the interplay between the competing values across the quadrants that unleashes the potential of a system or a leader.

The four-quadrant framework has been applied by Quinn and colleagues to understand and improve organizational culture (Quinn and McGrath 1985; Cameron and Quinn 1999), organizational effectiveness (Quinn and Cameron 1983), communication styles (Quinn et al. 1991a), management information systems (Quinn and Cooper 1993), and teaching effectiveness (Quinn et al. 2015).

In each of the above areas the framework is an attractive tool because it allows people to easily and efficiently differentiate. To say, for example, "This organization is high on the values of the compete quadrant and low on the values of the collaborate quadrant," is to communicate a very complex observation in a very few words. When the culture framework, for example, is introduced to a team of executives, and they profile their organization, they immediately gain new insights. The clear categories make it easier to talk about where the organization is and how they might move in new directions.

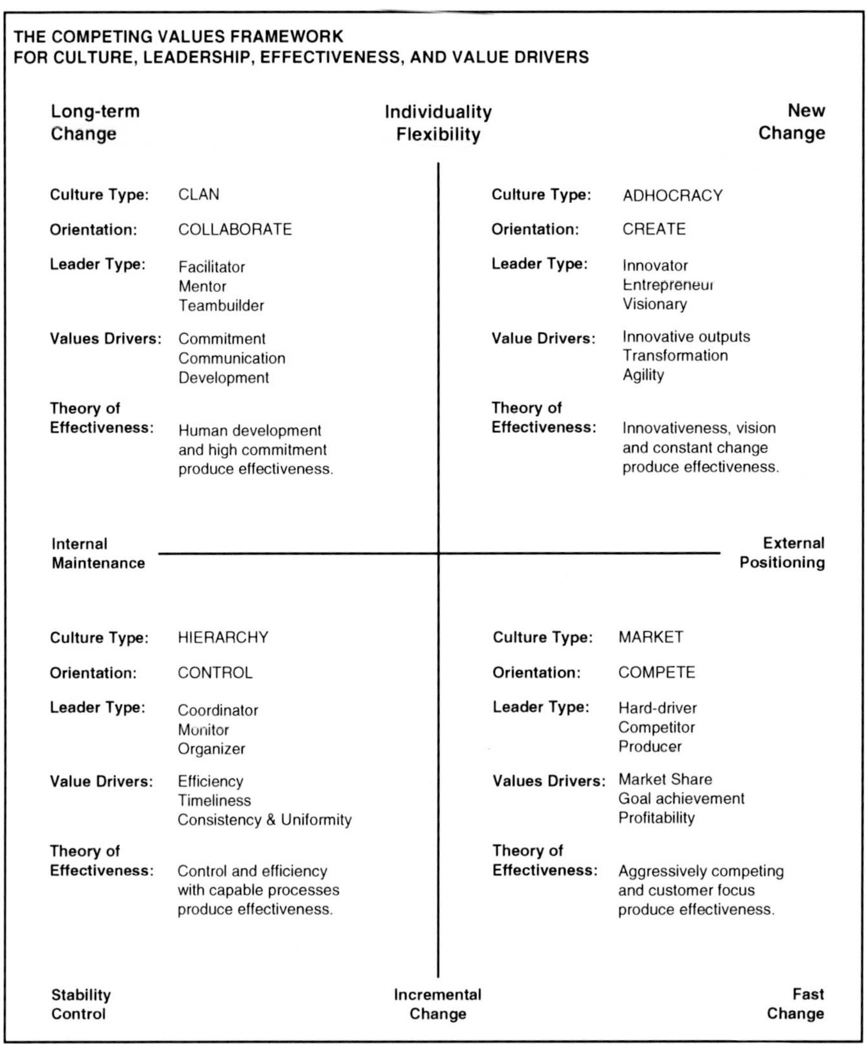

Fig. 1 Competing Values Framework (Reprinted with permission of the publisher. From Diagnosing and Changing Organizational Culture: Based on the Competing Values Framework, copyright© (2011) by D. B. Szabla, W. Pasmore, M. Barnes, Berrett-Koehler Publishers, Inc., San Francisco, CA. All rights reserved. "http://www.bkconnection.com")

So the model helps people clarify their intentions and clarify how to pursue them. This means the Competing Values Framework is similar to many other tools that can assist with analysis and decision-making. Yet the Competing Values Framework has two characteristics that make it different from other frameworks and can greatly elevate conventional thinking.

First it helps users understand and avoid the major vulnerability of conventional thinking, which Gregory Bateson (2002) referred to as schismogenesis which means

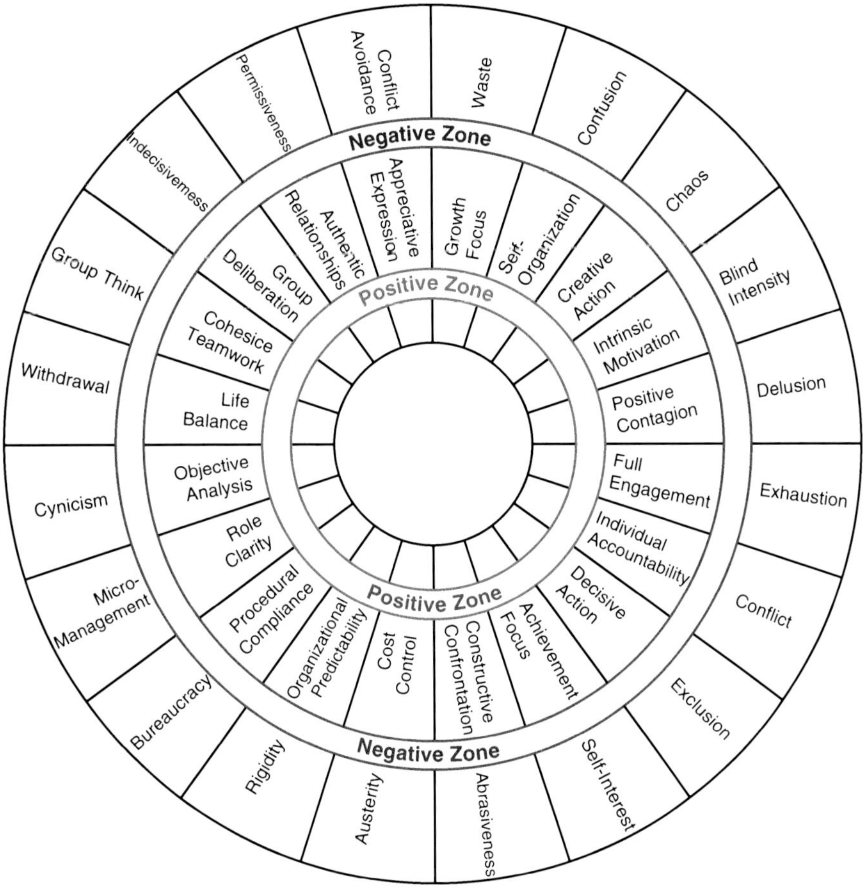

Fig. 2 A framework of organizational tensions (Borrowed from Quinn (2015))

split at birth (See Cameron et al. 2014, pp. 60–61). When people develop an intention of any kind, such as the pursuit of achievement, they often do so at the cost of some positive, opposite value, something that is completely ignored like the maintenance of authentic relationships. At the genesis of the intention, achievement and authentic relationships can become mutually exclusive. One is pursued, while the other is ignored or even denigrated. The actor cannot see that the opposing, positive values can operate together.

As a given value is pursued, it often leads to initial positive outcomes, but then, paradoxically the effort become dysfunctional. The pursuit of achievement, for example, results in a culture of self-interest, and trust and collaboration both collapse so that the pursuit of individual achievement also collapses. The point is that all positive values, pursued in a monistic fashion, turn negative. Figure 2 illustrates some positive values and the negative values that may arise when one positive value is pursued in isolation.

The second characteristic of the framework is that it makes the complex ecology of positive and negative values explicit and invites the actor to do something that is unconventional, that is, to think in both/and terms and pursue the integration of differentiation. In nature interpenetration of differentiated systems, like an acorn and the soil, or a sperm and an egg, can give rise to the emergence of a new and more complex system. Likewise in social action, major breakthroughs emerge from insights that integrate unlike categories (See Cameron et al. 2014, pp. 52–53).

People who master the Competing Values Framework begin to see organizations and other systems, not as nouns but as verbs; they see others, not as nouns but as verbs; they see themselves, not as nouns but as verbs. In other words, they begin to see the dynamic complex whole. When they do, they also recognize the paradoxical nature of excellence in the social world and the importance of integrating differentiation (Quinn et al. 1995a). When asked about how this actually works in organizations, Quinn provided this example:

> Organizations and people become excellent when they operate across the categories in the model. Great leaders, for example, are high on task and high on people, they maintain stability while leading change. They integrate differentiated categories. While conventional thinkers are trapped into the use of mutually exclusive categories, generative leaders are bringing about the integration of differentiated categories. Generative people accept and use the conventional perspective. Yet, they also embrace the more complex and dynamic integrative perspective. They become bilingual. They become able to see and integrate paradoxical tensions.

Such notions come into play in research on the development of leaders. While there was an existing stream of work on cognitive complexity in the literature, Quinn and his colleagues developed the notion of behavioral complexity (Quinn 1984; Quinn et al. 1991b, 1995b; Quinn and Hooijberg 1993; Quinn and Hart 1993; Lawrence et al. 2009). Behavioral complexity is the ability to exhibit contrary, opposing, or competing behaviors and roles as managers and leaders while still having coherence and integrity.

A person with high behavioral complexity is able to engage in a wider and more complex array of behaviors than a person with low behavioral complexity. A behaviorally complex leader both maintains continuity and leads change (one dimension of the CVF). A behaviorally complex leader also is able to look bidirectionally to embrace internal and external demands (a second dimension of the CVF). As leaders display complex behaviors from across the quadrants of the framework, their effectiveness goes up.

The framework has not only had an impact on scholarship but also on the world of practice. The competing values assessment of culture, first created by Kim Cameron and further developed together with Quinn, has been used in interventions for organizational culture change by hundreds of consultants and change agents (Cameron et al. 2014). The book (Cameron and Quinn 1999) that published the assessment is now in its third edition (2011). Quinn (along with Michael McGrath, Michael Thompson, Sue Faerman, Lynda St. Clair, and David Bright, 2015) also produced a textbook, now in its sixth edition, using the Competing Values

Framework to help students develop competencies associated with each dimension, in order to become more effective leaders.

Quinn's paradoxical insights led to a number of new efforts on paradox. In 1988, he published the book, *Beyond Rational Management: Mastering the Paradoxes and Competing Demands of High Performance.* In it, he began to articulate the link between the Competing Values Framework and excellence. That same year, he and Kim Cameron published a book called *Paradox and Transformation: Towards a Theory of Change in Organization and Management.* In it, they brought together leading organizational theorists and began to articulate the role of the paradoxical perspective in organizational theory. Today, organizational theorists show much interest in the paradoxical perspective, and much of the work ties back to these early efforts.

Contribution 2: Deep Change, Self-Empowerment, and Moral Power

Many of Quinn's research and writing efforts take root in his efforts to bring change in individuals and organizations. In the late 1980s he began to believe that both individuals and organizations are constantly confronted by something he called the "deep change or slow death dilemma." People and organizations are constantly required to change in various ways. Some of the pressures are ignored or denied. The unwillingness to face reality leads to increasing dysfunctional behavior patterns. Energy is lost, and the process of slow psychological death sets in. Psychological death is more than emotional exhaustion or burnout; instead, it involves being worn-down and disillusioned to the point of making a conscious choice to let an unaddressed organizational problem fester. His book, *Deep Change* (1996), articulated the difficulty and how to deal with it. The volume has been a long-term best seller for Jossey-Bass publishers.

After the publication of *Deep Change*, hundreds of people sent Quinn accounts of how they used the book to make deep change in their lives or in their organizations. These accounts ranged from people indicating how they used the book to reframe how they were managing a painful divorce to how they were using the book to alter how they were leading the transformation of the Army.

The authors of these accounts particularly described how the book inspired them to act courageously. The reader's stories of moral power became the foundation to three other books: *Change the World: How Ordinary People Can Accomplish Extraordinary Results* (Quinn 2000); *A Company of Leaders: Five Disciplines for Unleashing the Power in Your Workforce* (Spreitzer and Quinn 2001); and *Building the Bridge as You Walk On It: A Guide for Leading Change* (Quinn 2004). In the first, Quinn examined the lives of Jesus, Gandhi, and Martin Luther King Jr. and shows how self-examination and personal change give rise to moral power and social change. In the second, he and Spreitzer reviewed the empirical work on empowerment and show that self-examination and personal change lead to empowerment and impact. Empowerment begins with the self and involves a clear sense of meaning or purpose about one's work. In the third volume, Quinn used numerous cases to show how deep change leads to increased behavioral complexity, and he provides a language of paradox for helping observers to see and describe that complexity.

The common theme in the three books is that as people learn to fulfill and transcend the need for independence, and become effectively interdependent, they begin to see relationships more deeply and the sense of accountability changes. For example, when an authority figure encounters a resistant employee, the conventional assumption is that the employee is a problem to be fixed. A key insight from these books is that instead, if an employee is resistant, the problem is not in the employee but in the authority figure. He or she is not providing a vision inspiring enough to attract the employee into the process of commitment, learning, and change. To do so the authority figure must go through an episode of learning and change in order to understand that people are not merely objects. They have agency. Empowered leaders are empowering to others because they have learned to empower themselves and create effective interdependence.

Contribution 3: The Fundamental State of Leadership

The literature on leadership is extensive, and most of it focuses on the need for knowledge and skills. In the conventional view of leadership, a leader tends to be a person in a position at the top of some hierarchy. Effectiveness is a function of expertise and the ability to act competently. In the book, *Building the Bridge as You Walk On It: A Guide for Leading Change* (2004), Quinn began to argue that leadership is influence and that everyone has the capacity to act as a leader. The key is to move oneself into an elevated state of influence called the fundamental state of leadership.

A paper on the fundamental state of leadership was published in the *Harvard Business Review* (Quinn 2005). It quickly became a classic and was included in the *HBR's Ten Must Reads in Managing Yourself in 2011.* With his son Ryan, also an organizational behavior/change scholar, Quinn published a book called *Lift: Becoming a Positive Force in Any Situation* (Quinn and Quinn 2009). It provided an extensive discussion of the concept and the scientific foundations.

The essential argument is that it is natural for all of us to be comfort centered, externally directed, self-focused, and internally closed. In each case we can learn to move ourselves to a more positive orientation. When we clarify the result we want to create, we move from being comfort centered to being purpose centered. As we take ourselves into a self-determined and challenging intent, we more fully focus our attention and we increase our own energy; this also signals the importance of the purpose to others (See Quinn and Quinn 2015, Chap. 4).

When we move from being externally directed to being internally directed, we clarify our values and find the courage to live our values. We experience increased dignity, strength, and capacity to act for ourselves, and we operate from increased moral power (See Quinn and Quinn 2015, Chap. 6).

When we move from being self-focused to being other focused, we transcend the transactional assumptions of social life, and we orient to people and relationships with empathy. Genuine consideration builds trust and helps others to overcome self-justifications, increase their energy, and feel secure enough to explore, learn, and innovate (See Quinn and Quinn 2015, Chap. 8).

When we move from being internally closed to being externally open, we embrace a growth mind-set. We are willing to hear from, learn from, and cocreate with others. Externally open people invest more effort, persist longer, look for and use feedback, believe in themselves, and have higher aspirations (See Quinn and Quinn 2015, Chap. 10).

The personal change process is executed as people learn to ask four questions:

- What result do I want to create?
- Am I internally directed?
- Am I other focused?
- Am I externally open?

By focusing on some ordinary future event, and asking these questions, a person can become more purposive, more authentic, more empathetic, and more humble. In the process, the mind opens to new strategic alternatives. By proactively selecting and implementing a given new alternative, the leader creates a positive variation of the old self. By engaging in new experiences, the leader also accelerates personal learning and growth. Learning the concept can be enhanced by a number of individual and collective processes and tools (the tools can be found in Quinn and Quinn 2015, Chaps. 11–13).

New Insights: Positive Organizational Scholarship

In 2001, Quinn collaborated with his colleagues to address an important gap in the field of organizational studies. His frequent collaborator and friend, Kim Cameron, had returned to the University of Michigan after several years away as the Dean at Case Western Reserve University and was starting a research program on organizational forgiveness. Another Michigan colleague, Jane Dutton, was beginning a new research stream on compassion organizing. She and colleagues define compassion organizing as a "collective response to a particular incident of human suffering that entails the coordination of individual compassion in a particular organizational context" (Dutton et al. 2006, p. 61).

The three began to have conversations about the limitations of conventional organizational research. They began to argue that the bias in social science is toward the examination of normal patterns. People are normally found to be self-interested, reactive, and alienated. Organizations are naturally filled with conflict and distrust. The gloomy messages of social science turn into a self-fulfilling prophecy. The findings become implicit justification to pursue results while treating people poorly.

The natural outcome is that the other people act in self-interested, reactive, and alienated ways, creating organizations of conflict and distrust. The three began to argue that there is value in examining individuals, relationships, groups, and organizations at their very best. Findings from such studies would raise alternative views of how to lead.

In December of 2001, the three organized a research conference of like-minded academics at Michigan and beyond. Their edited book, *Positive Organizational Scholarship: The Foundations of a New Discipline* (Cameron et al. 2003), put a stake in the ground. Many researchers began to adopt the "positive lens." Thus was born a new discipline within organizational studies. Soon after, the three founded the Center for Positive Organizations at the Ross School of Business, and momentum grew. Today, the Center has eight fully engaged senior faculty members. There are more than 25 faculty at Ross associated with the Center and over 300 individuals listed in the Center's Community of Scholars.

In 2006, Quinn left the Center for 3 years to serve as a mission president in Australia. There, he applied the principles of positive organizational scholarship to the administration and leadership of the mission. He put great emphasis on the notion of engaging and changing others by first changing self. Young missionaries proved quite capable of understanding and internalizing the message. He says that the transformation of the mission became "one of the highlights of my life."

He returned to Ross in 2009, and published *Lift: Becoming a Positive Force in Any Situation* (Quinn and Quinn 2009) with his son Ryan. In 2014, he and his colleagues published a book about excellent public school teachers, *The Best Teacher in You: How to Accelerate Learning and Change Lives* (Quinn et al. 2014). It turns out that the best teachers are people who internalize the basic principles of transformational influence. Their classrooms become positive organizations, where students can flourish and exceed expectations. The book received the Ben Franklin Award, naming it the best book in education for 2015.

In 2015, Quinn published *The Positive Organization: Breaking Free from Conventional Cultures*. It documents how some executives evolve from operating within the conventional mind-set to operating within the positive mind-set. In doing so, they gain the capacity to create a sense of purpose, nurture authentic conversations, see possibility, embrace the common good, and trust the emergent process. These capacities seep into others, and they give rise to positive organizations. His research in positive organizational scholarship has been one of the most fulfilling and impactful parts of his more than 40-year career as a change agent and researcher.

Quinn's Legacy as a Thought Leader on Inspiring Positive Change

I invited several scholars, including some being profiled in this volume, to share their thoughts on Quinn's legacy as a change scholar: Jean Bartunek, Phil Mirvis, and Dick Woodman. I also drew input from two more junior scholars who have been mentored by Bob: Ryan Quinn (University of Louisville) and Ned Wellman

(Arizona State University). The responses corroborate the contributions noted above but articulate some additional insights on the legacy Quinn has created.

1. *Competing Values Framework*: "This work is groundbreaking, in that it provided a complex and dynamic foundation for examining and transforming organizations." The original 1983 article has been cited almost 3,000 times, and the related book with Kim Cameron is now in its sixth edition and has been cited almost 4,000 times. Scholars and consultants around the world use the Competing Values Framework to study and transform organizations to become their best.
2. *Paradox*: "Quinn can be viewed as a forefather of the role of paradox in organizational studies, particularly building on Gestalt psychology and Janusian thinking." Today, we see notions of paradox embedded in many scholarly theories, such as ambivalence, ambidexterity, and exploration/exploitation. Rather than seeing paradox as something negative that requires immediate resolution, paradox is a tension that can be harnessed for more creative, innovative, and transformative solutions.
3. *Deep Change*: "The thinking in *Deep Change* not only led to many individual and organizational transformations, it also became one of the taproots for the emergence of positive organizational scholarship and the fundamental state of leadership concept." The *Deep Change* book made it clear that nature pulls human systems toward decay. We can expect it; unless work is done to the contrary, people and organizations break down. The work to the contrary is called leadership. Leadership of self and of organizations surfaces conflict and transforms it. Effective leaders unify and energize. They bring life to others and to the organization.
4. *Positive Organizational Scholarship*: "Positive Organizational Scholarship is a movement that has successfully shone light on areas of organizational inquiry that have been ignored or given short shrift." In just over 10 years, positive organizational scholarship has moved from a fringe perspective to a key stream of research in organization studies. There have been special issues of prominent journals, like the *Academy of Management Review*, dedicated to positive organization scholarship and related themes. The *Handbook of Positive Organizational Scholarship* (Cameron and Spreitzer 2012) was published by Oxford University Press. At the Academy of Management, every year, more than 150 interested scholars come together to share insights, and at least two themes of the annual meeting have been on topics related to positive organizational scholarship: compassion and meaning. The Academy of Management has even bestowed its award for Most Impactful Research Center on the Center for Positive Organizations, and the faculty were awarded the "Joanne Martin Trailblazer" recognition, by the Organization and Management Theory (OMT) Division of the Academy in 2010. Moreover, many classes in the Ross School of Business curriculum, and around the globe, are grounded in positive organizational scholarship.
5. *Cultural Transformations*: "Quinn has an uncanny ability to integrate scholarship and practice." His personal mission of "inspiring positive change" brought transformation to numerous corporations, universities, and governmental

agencies. Over the years, he was a major force in extended cultural transformation efforts at places like Ford Motor Company, Prudential, Reuters, Whirlpool, and the US Government. In addition, he has played a lead role in shorter change efforts at hundreds of companies and agencies through Ross Executive Education and in his own consulting engagements.

6. *Student Transformations*: "Quinn is not only high in demand by executive audiences but also by degree students." He has taught a very popular course entitled *Becoming a Transformational Leader*. It attracts students from around the campus and has a perpetual waiting list. Many describe the course as life changing. In executive education, he has worked with thousands of professionals, and many of them claim similar impacts. He is also a highly sought-after guest speaker in classrooms around the university and the world. Students often come back to share their gratitude for how Quinn's teaching has transformed them in important ways.

A former doctoral student offered the following about how Quinn had impacted him: "I enjoyed working with Bob for two reasons. First, he is very thorough and thoughtful. When he addresses a question he looks at all possible angles of the question and is open to revising his thinking over time as he gets more information. The second thing is that I always got the sense that our relationship was personal – that he really cared about me as an individual and what I thought. For that reason, I always felt like I could trust his advice and that I could open up to him about things that I found confusing or frustrating. I always left our meetings feeling better about being a doctoral student then I did before."

7. *Developer of Teaching Tools*: "Quinn has a knack for innovative pedagogies for transformation that engage people in deep ways, very quickly." In his educator role, he has developed many teaching tools; some have turned into widely used products.

Reflected Best Self Feedback: With Jane Dutton, Laura Morgan Roberts, and Gretchen Spreitzer, he developed a transformational tool called the Reflected Best Self Exercise (HBR paper) that helps people see glimpses of their own greatness: (http://positiveorgs.bus.umich.edu/cpo-tools/reflected-best-self-exercise-2nd-edition/). The exercise has individuals solicit stories of when they have added value or made a positive difference, from 10 to 20 individuals, who know them well from different aspects of their lives (work, family, friends, etc.). Students then go through a process to weave themes drawn from their stories into the best self-portrait that coalesces their unique strengths, talents, and passions (Roberts et al. 2005b). The tool is now used widely around the globe for leader development in courses and corporations, to help individuals see pathways for becoming extraordinary (Roberts et al. 2005a).

Positive Leadership Game: Quinn also created a tool called *The Positive Leadership Game* with Gretchen Spreitzer (for more information on the game and where to purchase it, see this site: http://positiveorgs.bus.umich.edu/cpo-tools/positive-leadership-the-game/). The game engages small groups in a collective helping exercise, to release new ideas inspired by principles of positive organizational scholarship. The card game has more than 80 idea cards, each drawing from research-based findings. Players each make a request on something they would like help with, and then the players use the cards to generate new ideas relevant to the issue. Once they experience it, executives, in particular, show enthusiasm for the game and tend to suggest other ways the cards could be used.

Positive Organization Generator: In executive education classes, Quinn began to observe that participants would deeply resonate with the concepts from positive organizational scholarship. Yet on the last day, Quinn would ask what they were going to do at home and do differently, and the majority would look mystified. As he began to investigate the consistent pattern, Quinn concluded that the mature executives were like fearful high school students. In high school, the prime objective is to never be seen as uncool. The executives were fearful of embarrassment. They knew that taking new positive practices back to a conventional culture was dangerous. Quinn concluded that the problem did not belong to the participants as students but to him as a teacher. So he invented the positive organization generator (Quinn 2015).

The positive organizational generator provides 100 positive practices from real organizations. Participants have to review the hundred select the few that are most interesting and then "reinvent" them to their own context. In the process of reinvention, the executives come to "own" their ideas. They walk away with a small list of practices in which they are fully invested. They are willing to go home to implement, fail, learn, revise, and implement again.

Unfinished Business

Most recently, Quinn has been focusing on the role of purpose in the transformation of people and organizations. He and Anjan Thakor, an economist at Washington University in St. Louis, have worked on an issue that is central to the process of creating a positive organization. Economists assume that a narrow focus on value creation produces wealth. An emphasis on relationships and culture is a distraction that reduces the creation of wealth.

At the heart of microeconomics is the principal-agent problem in which a principal, or employer, contracts with an agent or employee. The amount of pay and the amount of effort are specified. If the principal is present to observe and control, then the effort is rendered. If the principle is not observing, the agent underperforms the transactional contract.

The two authors created a mathematical model of an organization based on conventional, transactional assumptions. They then introduced a higher purpose into the model. The organization was transformed. As the agent embraced higher purpose, they became principles or owners, and the organization produced more wealth. The paper provides an economic argument for the role of higher purpose in wealth creation.

Writing this paper led the two authors to question how CEOs think about purpose and wealth creation. This led to interviews of CEOs who head purpose-driven organizations. One of the surprising outcomes was the discovery that a sizable subset of the CEOs, when they entered the role, did not believe in purpose, people, or culture. As result of some crisis or life trauma, they discovered the power of purpose while serving as a CEO.

Quinn and Thakor are currently working on a book based on the analysis and on the interviews. The book is being written to assist the reader in bringing higher purpose to their life, their leadership, and their organization.

Given the many things Quinn has done, there are numerous areas where researchers can extend his work. When I asked Quinn what he would most like to see done, he replied as follows:

> My major concern is with the creation of a theory of positive organizing. I would like to see researchers extend the competing values model and empirically create an atlas of values. This would particularly include negative values. Without including the negative we cannot have a theory of positive organizing. All possible positive and negative values would be included in the analysis. The final result would be a comprehensive model that greatly expands the theoretical Fig. 2 that is shown in this chapter. With such a product, we could more clearly see how too much emphasis on any given positive value is likely to turn the organization in a negative direction and we could see what positive oppositions we need to simultaneously embrace. This would produce a framework that could guide much research and a framework that would guide more thoughtful practice.

Conclusion

I was honored to be invited to write this chapter for a person who has been my mentor for almost 30 years. I have benefited in so many ways by Quinn's paradoxical mind. When I first met him, his warmth and humanity shone through in all of our interactions. He is the kind of person that makes time to really listen to understand a person's perspective and mind-set. He wants to know you as a human being not just as a professional colleague. These behaviors epitomize the collaborate quadrant of the CVF. But here is where the paradox comes in. Quinn isn't just warm; he also sets very high expectations and seeks to help develop people into their best selves. When I asked him to chair my dissertation committee, he was constantly pushing me out of my comfort zone. Sometimes I wanted to take an efficient route or would sell myself short in terms of what I might be able to accomplish, but he would have nothing of it – he nudge me to keep aspiring for more and making a bigger contribution. This is the essence of the compete quadrant of the CVF, the polar opposite of the collaborate quadrant qualities and behaviors. Quinn is a master at transcending these opposites in his own behavior and interactions.

And it's not that he treats me specially, this is how he operates with all of his students (even executive education participants) or colleagues. We are better people for having Quinn in our lives, empowering us to be our best selves. And rather than keeping the secret to this ability to operate in paradoxical ways, he has conducted the research and developed the teaching pedagogies to help others learn how to become more paradoxical themselves, transcending and integrating the competing tensions in their own lives. If you are not already familiar with Quinn's work, I encourage you to start with one or two of the readings highlighted below. But beware, you will likely become a different, better person for having been exposed to his ideas.

References

Bateson, G. (2002). *Mind and nature: A necessary unity*. New York: Hampton Press.

Cameron, K., & Quinn, R. (1999). *Diagnosing and changing organizational culture*. Reading: Addison-Wesley Longman.

Cameron, K., & Quinn, R. (2011). *Diagnosing and changing organizational culture: Based on the competing values framework* (3rd ed.). San Francisco: Jossey-Bass.

Cameron, K., & Spreitzer, G. (2012). *Oxford handbook of positive organizational scholarship*. New York: Oxford University Press.

Cameron, K. S., Dutton, J. E., & Quinn, R. E. (Eds.). (2003). *Positive organizational scholarship: Foundations of a new discipline*. San Francisco: Berrett-Koehler.

Cameron, K., Quinn, R., DeGraff, J., & Thakor, A. (2014). *Competing values leadership* (2nd ed.). New York: Edgar Elger.

Dutton, J., Worline, M., Frost, P., & Maitlis, S. (2006). Explaining compassion organizing. *Administrative Science Quarterly, 51*, 59–96.

Lawrence, K., Quinn, R., & Lenk, P. (2009). Behavioral complexity in leadership: The psychometric properties of a new instrument. *The Leadership Quarterly, 50*(2), 189–205.

Quinn, R. (1984). Applying the competing values approach to leadership. In J. Hunt, D. Hosking, C. Schriesheim, & R. Steward (Eds.), *Leaders and managers: International perspectives on managerial behavior and leadership*. New York: Pergamon.

Quinn, R. (1996). *Deep change*. San Francisco: Jossey-Bass.

Quinn, R. (2000). *Change the world: How ordinary people can accomplish extraordinary results*. San Francisco: Jossey-Bass.

Quinn, R. (2004). *Building the bridge as you walk on it: A guide for leading change*. San Francisco: Jossey-Bass.

Quinn, R. (2005). Moments of greatness: Entering the fundamental state of leadership. *Harvard Business Review, 83*(7), 75–83.

Quinn, R. (2015). *The positive organization: Breaking free from conventional cultures, constraints and beliefs*. San Francisco: Berrett Koehler.

Quinn, R., & Cameron, K. (1983). Organizational life cycles and shifting criteria of effectiveness: Some preliminary evidence. *Management Science, 29*(1), 33–51.

Quinn, R., & Cooper, R. (1993). Implications of the competing values model for management information systems. *Journal of Human Resource Management, 32*(1), 175–201.

Quinn, R., & Hart, S. (1993). Roles executives play: CEO's, behavioral complexity, and firm performance. *Human Relations, 46*, 543–557.

Quinn, R., & Hooijberg, R. (1993). Behavioral complexity and the development of effective managers. In R. Phillips & J. Hunt (Eds.), *Strategic leadership: A multi-organizational – level perspective* (pp. 161–176). Westport: Quorum Books.

Quinn, R., & McGrath, M. (1985). The transformation of organizational culture: A competing values perspective. In P. Frost, L. Moore, M. Louis, C. Lundberg, & J. Martin (Eds.), *Organizational culture and the meaning of life in the workplace*. Beverly Hills: Sage.

Quinn, R., & Quinn, R. (2009). *Lift: Becoming a positive force in any situation*. San Francisco: Berrett-Kohler.

Quinn, R. W., & Quinn, R. E. (2015). *Lift: The fundamental state of leadership* (2nd ed.). San Francisco: Berrett-Koehler.

Quinn, R., & Rohrbaugh, J. (1983). A spatial model of effectiveness criteria: Towards a competing values approach to organizational analysis. *Management Science, 29*(3), 363–377.
Quinn, R., Hildebrandt, H., & Rogers, P. (1991a). A competing values framework for analyzing presentational communication in management contexts. *Journal of Business Communication, 28*(3), 213–232. Summer.
Quinn, R., Spreitzer, G., & Hart, S. (1991b). Challenging the assumptions of bipolarity: Interpenetration and managerial effectiveness. In S. Srivatva (Ed.), *Executive and organizational continuity*. San Francisco: Jossey-Bass.
Quinn, R., Kahn, J., & Mandl, M. (1995a). Perspectives on organization change: Exploring movement at the interface. In J. Greenberg's (Ed.), *Organizational behavior: The state of the science* (pp. 109–134). Hoboken: Lawrence Erlbaum Associates.
Quinn, R., Denison, D., & Hooijberg, R. (1995b). Paradox and performance: Toward a theory of behavioral complexity in managerial leadership. *Organization Science, 6*(5), 524–540.
Quinn, R. E., Heynoski, K., Thomas, M., & Spreitzer, G. (2014). *The best teacher in you: Accelerating learning and changing lives*. San Francisco: Jossey-Bass.
Roberts, L. M., Dutton, J., Spreitzer, G., Heaphy, E., & Quinn, R. (2005a). Composing the reflected best self-portrait: Building pathways for becoming extraordinary in work organizations. *Academy of Management Review, 30*(4), 712–736. Fall 2005.
Roberts, L. M., Spreitzer, G., Dutton, J., Heaphy, E., & Barker, B. (2005b). How to play to your strengths. *Harvard Business Review, 83*(1), 75–80.
Spreitzer, G., & Quinn, R. (2001). *A company of leaders: Five disciplines for unleashing the power in your workforce*. San Francisco: Jossey-Bass.

Further Reading

Cameron, K. (1988). *Paradox and transformation: Towards a theory of change in organization and management*. Cambridge: Ballinger.
Quinn, R. (1988). *Beyond rational management: Mastering the paradoxes and competing demands of high performance*. San Francisco: Jossey-Bass.
Quinn, R. (2012). *The deep change field guide: A personal course to discovering the leader within*. San Francisco: Jossey-Bass.
Quinn, R. (2015). https://thepositiveorganization.wordpress.com/2015/10/26/a-golden-opportunity/
Quinn, R., & Cameron, K. (1988). *Paradox and transformation: Towards a theory of change in organization and management*. Cambridge: Ballinger.
Quinn, R., & Thakor, A. (2014). Imbue the organization with a higher purpose. In J. Dutton & G. Spreitzer (Eds.), *How to be a positive leader*. San Francisco: Berrett-Koehler.
Quinn, R., Spreitzer, G., & Fletcher, J. (1995). Excavating the paths of meaning, renewal and empowerment: A typology of managerial high performance myths. *Journal of Management Inquiry, 4*(1), 16–39.
Quinn, R., Spreitzer, G., & Brown, M. (2000). Changing others through changing ourselves: The transformation of human systems. *Journal of Management Inquiry, 9*(2), 147–164.
Quinn, R., Faerman, S., Thompson, M., McGrath, M., & Bright, D. (2015). *Becoming a master manager: A competency framework* (6th ed.). New York: Wiley.
Weick, K., & Quinn, R. (1999). Organizational change and development. *Annual Review of Psychology, 50*, 361–386.

Reginald Revans: The Pioneer of Action Learning

65

Mike Pedler

Abstract

This chapter describes the philosophy and approach of Reginald Revans (1907–2003), a UK scientist and educational innovator. It traces the influences on his thinking, from his early imbibing of Christian and Quaker traditions to the later impact of world philosophies especially including Buddhism. His contribution to our understanding of change management processes gives a central place to learning, both personal and institutional. Revans' approach emphasizes the practical and moral significance of personal involvement in action and learning, as a means of resolving the intractable social and organizational problems that we find around us. Over a long life, Revans was ceaselessly active in testing his ideas which were always in a state of emergence. He leaves a rich heritage of proposals and possibilities for present practitioners. Five of the legacies of his work are discussed in this paper: Virtual Action Learning, Critical Action Learning, The Wicked Problems of Leadership, Unlearning, and the Paradox of Innovation.

Keywords

Action learning • Leadership • Wicked problems • Innovation • Unlearning

With many thanks to my colleagues who commented and contributed to this paper – Yury Boshyk, Tom Bourner, John Burgoyne, Ghislaine Caulat; David Coghlan, John Edmonstone, Jeff Gold, Bernhard Hauser; Jim Stewart & Russ Vince.

M. Pedler (✉)
Henley Business School, University of Reading and Centre for Action Learning Facilitation (CALF), Reading, UK
e-mail: mikepedler@hotmail.co.uk

D.B. Szabla et al. (eds.), *The Palgrave Handbook of Organizational Change Thinkers*,
DOI 10.1007/978-3-319-52878-6_20

Contents

Introduction

Reginald Revans (1907–2003) was successively an Olympic athlete, a nuclear physicist, an educational administrator, and one of the UK's first professors of management. He is best known as the pioneer of action learning (Revans 1982, 2011), an approach to social and organizational development through engaging people in learning from their attempts to change things. Drawing on ancient sources of wisdom and more recent forbears such as Dewey and Lewin, action learning is aimed at the improvement of human systems for the benefit of those who depend on them (1982, pp. 280–286). It is a pragmatic but moral philosophy with a strongly humanistic view of human potential that commits us, via experiential learning, to addressing the intractable problems of organizations and societies.

This chapter traces Revans' early influences and the sources of his personal and professional motivation, before summarizing his contributions to our understanding of change management and learning. After a description of his ideas and insights, the legacies of his work are discussed along with recent developments in practice.

Influences and Motivations: Understanding the Difference Between Cleverness and Wisdom

Revans was born into Edwardian England, a short age basking in post-Victorian achievement and surety but darkened by a growing anticipation of turmoil and change. If there were war clouds over Europe, then there was also political change afoot at home with the rise of working class awareness and the Labor movement. His early memories included meeting a delegation of seamen with his father as part of the inquiry into the sinking of the Titanic. It particularly impressed him that some of the seamen had bare feet. When he later asked his father what had been the most important lesson learned from this disaster, the reply was "What I learned from the Titanic inquiry was to discriminate between cleverness and wisdom" (Boshyk and Dilworth 2010, p. 50). Revans held this as one of the most important incidents in his life, and his father's insight became a touchstone of action learning. (NB Detailed descriptions of Revans' early life and influences and also of the historical development of action learning can be found in Boshyk and Dilworth 2010, especially Chaps. 2, 3, 4, and 6, which include contributions from some of his family and friends. Chapter 3: "Reg Revans: Sources of Inspiration, Practice and Theory" is especially useful.)

He was driven by strong values which included Christian and Quaker influences. In old age, he could still recite long passages from the Bible, read to him as a child by his mother. He attended Society of Friends meetings during his years at Cambridge University (1928–1935), and the Quaker influence was important in terms of his beliefs and practices. As a researcher in nuclear physics in the Cavendish Laboratory, but also a pacifist connected to the Campaign for Nuclear Disarmament, Revans was troubled by the military implications of the work at the Cavendish and eventually gave it up. Quaker practices can also be seen as influencing his ideas about action learning as it emerged over the next 30 or 40 years. The emphases on the fundamental equality of people, the importance of private indwelling or reflection, the centrality of inquiry, and the tradition of the "clearness committee" to help members with difficult problems and dilemmas are all visible in most current action learning practice (Dilworth and Boshyk 2010, pp. 54–59).

Yet Revans' moral and ethical influences are not limited to Christianity and Quakerism. In making it clear that he did not see himself as the inventor of action learning, which he regarded as ancient wisdom, he drew widely from many world philosophies: from Aristotle and Sophocles to the Enlightenment philosophers and Marx and in the teachings of Confucius and the Buddha. The mature Revans was "struck by the astonishing similarity between Buddhism and action learning" (1982, p. 529) and thereafter quotes the Buddha on the causes of suffering and how they can be eased. Revans wanted to heal the split between thinking and doing that he identified as toxic in the social structures of businesses, hospitals, and universities. In presenting action and learning as enjoined with each other, he proposes both a therapeutic process to encourage people to overcome the problems that immobilize them and as a means of invigoration and renewal through grasping the opportunities and challenges of social and organizational change.

Revans carried many of these beliefs and practices into his own life. He was uninterested in money and famously willing to go anywhere to talk to anyone "for the price of the bus fare." He lived simply and ate sparingly and did not own a car and preferred to walk, including on journeys between Manchester Airport and his Altrincham home, carrying his small suitcase. A man of great humility, always willing to listen and to learn, he was also iconoclastic, impatient, and critical of those he saw as exploiting rather than helping their fellow humans. This put him often outside establishment institutions, sometimes made him enemies, and perhaps contributed to a lack of the wider recognition of his work.

Key Contributions: Putting Learning at the Heart of Managing Change

Revans' contribution to managing change through action and learning is deceptively simple and not easily encapsulated. There is no single theory, no "hierarchy" or "universal model" to convey his message. Action learning is not presented as an organizational change model but as a practice for bringing about desired changes including in oneself. What he taught is that change and learning have to be practiced and cannot be learned secondhand. In placing learning at the heart of his ideas, Revans questions the predictability and linearity of change models that follow Lewin's unfreezing – moving – refreezing perspective. He rejects as illusory the many models and recipes which propose that change can be managed successfully this way or that, whatever the context. Change is an inevitable and natural condition of human organization; the question is: will we be overwhelmed by it or can we learn our way through so as to improve things?

Revans is a radical and his writings are based upon a moral philosophy, involving:

- *Honesty about self*
- *Starting from ignorance* – from not knowing in order to find fresh questions
- *Action as imperative for learning* – not just thought
- *In a spirit of friendship*
- *For the purpose of doing good in the world*

The essential preconditions for learning are honesty with self and the admission of ignorance. Action learning is not for the resolution of *puzzles* "or difficulties from which escapes are thought to be known" but for *problems* and *opportunities* "about which no single course of action is to be justified" (Revans 2011, p. 4). If we know how to proceed, then we just follow the recipe and little new learning takes place. Action learning on the other hand does not offer recipes, but starts from the acknowledgment of being lost or stuck, and from not knowing what to do next. For the big challenges in work and life, learning starts in first being able to admit to ignorance and loss of direction.

Revans' key contributions to learning theory consist of a network of elements which are bound up with each other. As action learners start with questions based on not knowing what best to do next, I started this chapter by asking some of my practitioner and academic colleagues for their views and with their help produced the following principal elements of his theory. These are, as discussed below, as follows: Action, Learning, The Principle of the Insufficient Mandate, Problems Not Puzzles, The Risk Imperative, Questioning, Sets, and The Ambiguity of Facilitation.

Action

> There can be no learning without action, and no (sober and deliberate) action without learning

Revans used this epithet, perhaps, as a conscious alternative to Lewin's dictum "No action without research; no research without action," to emphasize the interdependence of action and learning. Learning comes about through doing and "is cradled in the task" (2011, p. 3), but equally all learning is for the sake of action. The power of action learning stems from its philosophy of action and emphasis on the practice of change; no one can say they have learned anything until they have tried to change or improve something.

Learning

Revans used an equation to show that learning was the key to managing change:

$$L \geq C$$

holds that, in any organism, including individuals and organizations, the rate of learning has to be equal to, or greater than, the rate of change. Unless we adapt through learning, we become extinct. A colleague remembers hearing this "ecological equation" for the first time: "*It was simplicity itself – even obvious in retrospect – but it certainly made a major impact on me at the time (1970s)*" (Personal communication). Revans' second learning equation:

$$L = P + Q$$

holds that learning (L) is a combination of P, *programmed knowledge* or traditional instruction, and Q, *questioning insight*, the insight that comes from fresh questions and critical reflection. The Q factor is of particular importance because action learning is intended for work on difficult problems without known solutions.

The Principle of Insufficient Mandate

> Those unable to change themselves cannot change what goes on around them.
> (Revans 2011, p. 76)

Revans insisted that learning was always a voluntary activity. Managers and other people change their observable behavior only when they wish to; they may be "cognitively aware of the need to behave differently and yet remain determined not to do so in practice" (2011, p. 5). The *Principle of Insufficient Mandate* is another simple proposition with profound implications because it means that the starting point for any change management is with each individual. Everyone, regardless of rank or experience, becomes responsible for their own self-development in this process. It also means that there is a direct connection between the development of people and the development of organizations and that the former is a necessary condition of the latter. Linked to this insight is another: that a person's past experience, however wide, is of limited relevance in periods of rapid change. More than this, the "idolisation of past experience" (Revans 2011, p. 42) is a potent block to new learning.

Problems Not Puzzles

Action learning is not intended for puzzles – "difficulties from which escapes are thought to be known" – but for addressing problems or opportunities, "about which no single course of action is to be justified by any code of programmed knowledge, so that different managers, all reasonable, experienced and sober, might set out by treating them in markedly different ways" (2011, p. 4). Action learning is for intractable or novel situation where there is no single right answer. The biggest danger in such situations is to act on the basis of thinking we know what to do or to act on the advice of those who think they know, instead of starting from a process of inquiry. Revans reserved much of his scorn for experts (as distinct from expertise) who treat problems as if they were puzzles and for prescribing formulae in situations where learning is the first essential (Revans 2011, p. 8).

The Risk Imperative

Action learning is to "attack real problems . . .. or fertile opportunities" which "carry significant risk of penalty for failure" (Revans 2011, p. 6). Without this element of risk, no significant learning is likely to happen. In contrast to the emphasis on cognition in many learning theories, heart is as vital as head in Revans' thinking. His *Risk Imperative* is a recognition that people who tackle situations with no known solutions must essentially risk failure. To take risks in order to learn demands personal courage and is helped greatly by the encouragement of others, especially of fellow set members (see below).

Questioning

> The idea of setting questioning insight alongside programmed knowledge seems so obvious now, but it remains such a powerful perception about learning with peers. (Colleague – personal communication)

The importance of Q, or *questioning insight*, links to the distinction between puzzles and problems. While puzzles have "best" solutions and can be resolved by applying P with the help of experts, problems lack known answers and are best approached through the search for fresh questions. For any person, stuck with a difficulty or dilemma, or confronted by an opportunity they cannot grasp, the questions to open up new possibilities can be, once again, surprisingly simple: "What are you trying to do? What is stopping you? What can you do about this?"; and especially in relation to organizational problems: "Who knows. . .. Who cares . . .. and Who can . . ." (Revans 1982, p. 715). To provoke such questioning, and to help with new lines of thinking, action learning invokes the power of the small groups of peers or Set (see below). Questioning or the Q factor also informs Revans' broader thinking about organizational learning, which he sees as depending upon "the upward communication of doubt" (1982, pp. 280–286). In his discussions with managers, he would often restate this principle as: *"doubt ascending speeds wisdom from above"* – an aphorism that undermines the hierarchical assumptions that underpin so many change models.

Sets

As a small group of colleagues meeting regularly over time to help each other act and learn, the set is "the cutting edge of every action learning programme" (Revans 2011, p. 7). Sets are made up of volunteers who help each other to address difficult tasks, by listening, questioning, both supporting and challenging, exploring alternatives for action, and reflecting together on the learning from these actions. The peer group of the set is a deliberate strategy to encourage us to trust our own judgments and resist putting our fates in the hands of others (including facilitators see below). As an autonomous unit, the set can also be seen in the broader context of organizational change management: it "*provides the core process. . . where change is understood in pluralistic terms rather than as the will of one or a few people; in this way action learning can ensure the consideration of many voices and a dynamic for alignment*" (Colleague – personal communication).

The Ambiguity of Facilitation

Because action learning is about self-development (as part of social development), and because its aim is to encourage people to act on their own challenges, it is vital to avoid dependency on any external authority or expert. Facilitators can be classed as experts in this context, as unlike the set members, they do not put themselves at risk by carrying "personal responsibility for real life problems." Revans does allow that some "supernumerary" may be needed to get action learning programs started, but he is always very wary of what he refers to as "ambiguous facilitators" (2011, p. 9).

New Insights: Against Facilitation for Autonomous Learning

In the professional world of management and organizational development, nothing has caused more resistance to Revans' ideas than these strictures on facilitation. It is one of his most contentious claims and the one most often ignored in practice. Most action learning programs have facilitators, operating with varying degrees of expert power and control. Those who find themselves in this role and who wish to follow Revans' teaching should remember his injunction that it is the action learner who is important: the facilitator is dispensable.

As a developmental innovation, action learning emerges in the late 1960s, especially through initiatives undertaken in a consortium of London hospitals (Clark 1972; Wieland and Leigh 1971; Wieland 1981) and in the UK engineering conglomerate General Electric Corporation (GEC) (Casey and Pearce 1977). Though not limited to either organization development or management education, action learning gained prominence through its opposition to expert consultancy and traditional business school practice. In 1965, Revans resigned his chair at Manchester having lost his battle to make action learning the modus operandi of the new Manchester Business School (MBS). The installation of the MBA as the flagship program represented a victory for the "book" culture of the traditional university over the "tool" culture of the new College of Technology, which he saw as being more appropriate for the needs of managers (1980, p. 197).

I first heard him in the 1970s when he came to address a large group of management teachers in a newly formed Polytechnic Management Centre. Revans announced that management development was a moral practice and that we teachers were responsible for developing people and seeking to influence their conduct, their direction, and their actions. Most of those present found hard to engage with this. At that time, we were busily preoccupied with teaching marketing, operations management, and strategy and finance on business management programs, yet Revans argued that, to resolve our own problems and moral dilemmas, we should consider such questions as "What is an honest man (sic)?" and "How do I become one?" (Revans 1971, p. 69). Unsurprisingly this uncompromising prophet did not take everyone with him on that day – or indeed in the 40 years since. Still today many management teachers focus their energies instead on P, "the stuff of traditional instruction" (Revans 2011, p. 3).

Revans' practice can be traced back to the 1950s when he was Director of Education for the newly established UK National Coal Board. Eschewing the standard staff management programs with their learning from experts and lecturers, he encouraged the colliery managers to research their own problems as encountered in their pits and brought them together periodically to learn with and from each other. The term action learning did not appear in his writings until 1972 when he presented it as bringing together a number of key principles. Beyond this he resisted definition, liking instead to say what action learning is ***not***: "*job rotation.... project work.... case studies, business games and other simulations.... group dynamics and other task-free exercises....business consultancy and other expert missions.... operational research, industrial engineering, work study and related subjects . . .(or). . .. simple common-sense*" (Revans 2011, pp. 77–93).

Action learning is part of a wider growth of interest in action approaches or modalities in management and organizational research which contrast with more positivist approaches. It can thus be seen as part of a wider family of action-based approaches to research and learning, including action research and action science, which focus on "knowledge (as) produced in service of, and in the midst of, action" (Raelin 1999, p. 117). It has been described as an unusual "nondirective" form of action research (Clark 1972, p. 119) and is distinguished by the sovereignty it gives to the problem holders and its skepticism on the views and advice of experts of all kinds, including facilitators, academics, and professional researchers. This non-directiveness reflects Revans' belief in self-help, and skepticism regarding experts of all kinds includes academics and other external advisers.

At the same time, it is a family of approaches in itself. Revans was a good listener and always wanted to hear what people had to say. He was impatient for change and social progress and wanted to see action following the words. His response to the stories of those he met would usually include the question: ". . .. and what are you going to do about it?"

Action learning is perhaps best understood as an *ethos* rather than a single method and, while there is broad agreement on the main features of the idea, there are wide variations in its practice (Pedler et al. 2005, pp. 64–65). Partly because he resisted any single definition of action learning, including how it could be practiced, Revans' seminal ideas have stimulated a variety of methods and approaches, some of which are discussed below in section "Legacies and Unfinished Business: A Rich Heritage of Ideas and Provocations".

Revans welcomed these different interpretations as long as they observed his basic principles and supported the purposes of alleviating problems and improving lives. However, some practice developments in action learning since Revans are controversial in terms of his basic principles. Different practice communities have developed their own versions of action learning which can either be construed as departures from, or as developments of, "Revans Classical Principles" or the "Action Learning Gold Standard" (Willis 2004). The most obvious example is the widespread use of facilitators and even – in their strong form – action learning "coaches" (Marquardt 2004; Leonard and Marquardt 2010). Many current action learning practices regard facilitation as routine and ignore the power and sovereignty issues inherent in this stance. Some programs, such as those modeled on GE's Workout in the USA (Dotlich and Noel 1998), have been critiqued for departing from Revans' principles. Dixon (1997) has suggested that such designs lack key aspects of the action learning idea such as personal responsibility for action and space for reflection and are more appropriately seen as task forces or action projects. Some practitioners have argued that facilitation is necessary or appropriate to particular cultures or in working with particular forms of action learning, such as virtual action learning (VAL) and critical action learning (CAL) – discussed in section "Legacies and Unfinished Business: A Rich Heritage of Ideas and Provocations."

Revans' writing displays a morally charged and sometimes Biblical flavor that reveals his early influences. He can be both discursive and declamatory and also dismissive. A Welsh colleague of mine, whose family background had made him a connoisseur of nonconformist thinking and preaching, used to say that Revans reminded him of William Hazlitt, possessing the same love of words and of language filled with passion and power. This is not to everyone's taste and does not always make for accessible reading. Revans' books in fact did not sell well and are now with one exception out of print. His ideas however have spread widely through the efforts of his followers and borrowers. The ideas of action learning have had a significant effect on the practices of management, leadership, and organizational development in many different settings around the world, and Revans' words continue to offer stimulation, encouragement, and inspiration to practitioners and scholars grappling with the intractable problems of human development.

Legacies and Unfinished Business: A Rich Heritage of Ideas and Provocations

Revans left a rich heritage of ideas, provocations, and invocations. His writings and those of his successors continue to stir invention and experiment. Five of the legacies of his work are discussed below:

- Virtual Action Learning [VAL]
- Critical Action Learning (CAL)
- The Wicked Problems of Leadership
- Unlearning
- The Innovation Paradox

Virtual Action Learning [VAL]

VAL or Virtual Action Learning (Dickenson et al. 2010; Caulat 2012a, b) is "action learning which takes place in a virtual environment... via a range of enabling, interactive and collaborative communication technologies" (Dickenson et al. 2010, p. 59). As a development of Revans' approach which he could not have anticipated, VAL is a recent response to the realities and requirements of dispersed organizations. It can be glimpsed here in an audio form courtesy of a colleague's recent experience:

> I have been working with a German bank which acquired several other smaller banks in 2012. The Bank wants the managers to reflect on their leadership practice and to identify how they can lead remotely without having to travel every week to see their employees. First I ran a Virtual Leadership training for them, specifically tailored to their needs. Then we engaged in groups of 5 to 6 participants into Audio Action Learning sessions (3 sessions of 3 hours each). During the sessions participants share the plans that they made at the end of the training (what they wanted to do differently, what they wanted to start doing and what they wanted to stop doing) and how they are progressing on their plans as well as what they learn about themselves as "remote" leaders. We are working with 50 managers in an intensive way and with a further 100 further in a lighter way, and the changes are starting to make a difference. The Bank will make a qualitative assessment of the changes resulting from the initiative In September. The audio action learning is working well because the managers realized that the Bank is serious about the

changes – the initiative was also kicked-off with an article from the Board explaining that it was about achieving concrete results – and also because it helps them to persist in their plans and to deepen their learning as small groups.

Critical Action Learning (CAL)

As in the VAL example above, the protean nature of action learning makes it easily adaptable to local agendas, and the downside of this is that it can be employed by those in power to preserve existing conditions rather than to change them. Critical theorists such as McLaughlin and Thorpe (1993) and Wilmott (1994, 1997) have posed this challenge to action learning; given its versatility, how can action learning avoid the trap of being "selectively adopted to maintain the status quo?" (Wilmott 1994, p. 127). CAL aims to critique social and organizational conditions and in particular to question how power is distributed and used and how this influences events. An example of the CAL approach is offered by Reynolds and Vince: "Do ideas brought into action-based discussions help to question existing practices, structures and associated power relations within the organisation?" (2004, p. 453).

CAL is perhaps the most important development in post-Revans action learning. While consistent with his view that attempts to manage organization change are always political, and that any change attempt involves uncertainty and risk, a "critical turn" focuses less on individual motivations and actions toward more relational and contextual views of power. The pervasive presence of power relations applies even to action learning sets themselves; Vince (2001, 2004, 2008) shows how political and emotional dynamics can impact on sets and produce, not the desired learning in action but instead a stultifying "learning inaction."

In practicing CAL, a question arises: How can set members acquire the ideas that enable them to critique existing practices, structures, and associated power relations? Those seeking to practice CAL often find themselves providing inputs in one way or another so that set members can "get" the idea in order to use it; as a colleague puts it: in "*including critical reflection in our facilitation we probably do more than Revans might have suggested us to do, (but) it still is a central advice for me to leave the responsibility for solving problems in the set.*"

CAL also marks a shift in the epistemological basis of action learning. Pedler et al. (2005) use Lyotard's "triangle" (Burgoyne 1994) to speculate on the shifts in how action learning has been interpreted (Fig. 1). In response to the question What is knowledge for?, Lyotard has proposed three types of knowledge – speculative (S), performative (P), and emancipatory (E):

Mapped against these three types of knowledge, Revans' early work in schools, mines, factories, and hospitals was focused on resolving practical problems through scientific logic. In the 1950s and 1960s, Revans had not yet fully realized hi idea of action learning, and he was in what can be called "operational research" mode seeking rational solutions to organizational problems. By the 1970s, individual learning and personal development have become central to what is now called action

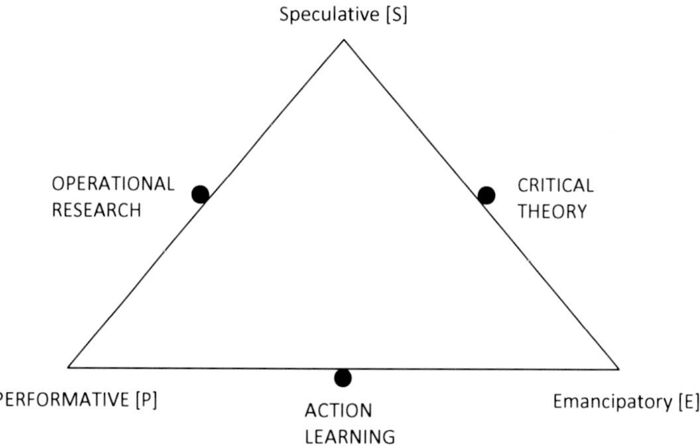

Fig. 1 Lyotard's triangle

learning, and his personal journey can thus be pictured as starting as a physicist from the top of the triangle (S), then moving to a point between P & S as he becomes concerned with practical problems, and then moving again to a point between P & E as he becomes convinced of the influence of human action and learning in the improvement of organizations and systems.

A shift to CAL requires a move toward critical and emancipatory theory, indicated by a point between S and E. The danger here is of gaining analytical power at the expense of a focus on action and reality testing; the continuing challenge for a CAL is to be critical while also being constructive. This is not easy, because CAL is achieved not just with the aid of critical theory but in drawing on the emotional power of the experience of being dominated, oppressed, or otherwise affected by power relationships. As Russ Vince comments (personal communication) "*To put this simply, I think that it is advisable in practice to balance power relations surfaced through critical reflection with acknowledgement of the emotional experience of learning together in the face of opportunities to both make and resist change. Therefore, in addition to the questions that are evoked when listening to others, I find that it is useful to connect with the emotions that are evoked in me as I listen. My assumption is that these are not usually my emotions... but are rather feelings being communicated by the action learning set member that he or she is barely aware of and finds difficult to own. Such feelings always have a profound effect on learning-in-action/learning inaction. Helping set members to trust that the feelings that are evoked in them as they listen to others is as important (to me) as helping them to learn how to formulate and intervene with questions.*"

This gets close to the essence of the action learning experience and illuminates the truth that while this may be a simple idea, it is a different matter to enact it. In an echo of the injunction I heard from Revans in the 1970s, Reynolds puts it thus (2011,

p. 12) "… . *.these complications of a critically reflective practice should not prevent action learning professionals applying it to their work. The impact which managers and professionals have on the workplace, working relationships and the social and physical environment demand it.*"

The Wicked Problems of Leadership

CAL may be especially relevant to the wicked problems of leadership (Brook et al. 2016). First proposed by Rittel and Webber (1973) in the context of urban planning, problems of drug abuse, homelessness, or crime in a neighborhood are termed wicked because they are hard to fully describe, because actions often provoke unintended consequences due to complex interdependencies, and because they usually require complex multiagency collaborations to address them. The idea has recently been applied to leadership concerning issues such as managing change or developing innovation. Grint (2005, 2008) proposes a leadership model (Fig. 2) in which the progression from "critical" to "tame" to "wicked" problems is marked by an increase both in uncertainty about solutions and the need for collaboration:

While "critical" (used specifically by Grint as denoting a crisis) problems are the domain of *command* and "tame" problems, which can be very complex, as in timetabling a school or building a new hospital, are the natural domain of *management*, "wicked" problems defy rational analysis and are the domain of *leadership* (Grint 2008, pp. 11–18). Revans' word "intractable," used to describe the problems best addressed via action learning, conveys a similar meaning. For Revans such problems require leadership: while puzzles may yield to expertise, the task of leadership concerns the "unanswerable questions as well as the unformulated ones" (Revans 1982, p. 712).

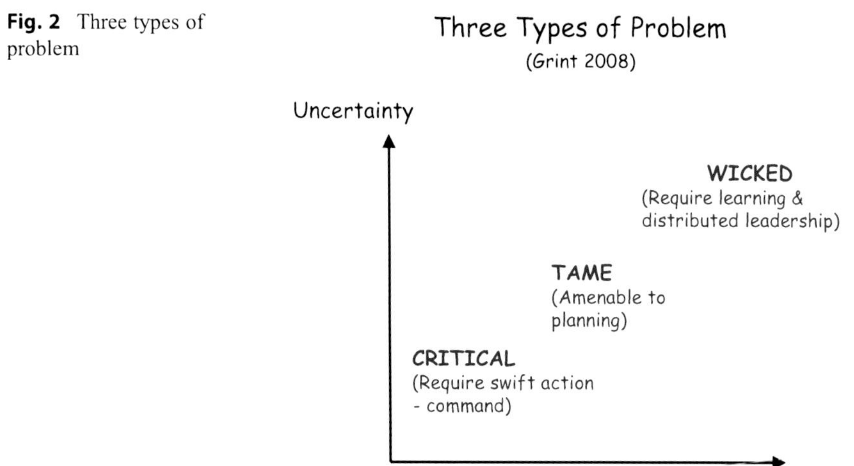

Fig. 2 Three types of problem

Much if not most action learning practice today takes place as part of leadership development programs (Conger and Toegel 2002, p. 332). The now widespread recognition of the uncertainty and risk of leadership decisions makes this highly appropriate. However, many leadership development programs remain largely taught, and where action learning is "tacked on" to such persuasive efforts, the warnings of the critical theorists are relevant. In such circumstances, action learning may be shaped to contribute to acculturation or "cultural doping" (Raelin 2008). In such circumstances, CAL might be of special value in managing change, although this might also be where it is least likely to be applied.

Unlearning

Several colleagues nominated this as a key aspect of Revans' thinking. Unlearning is implicit in Revans' ideas about learning, and this is of particular interest in the context of the wicked problems of leadership. A colleague said he had learned especially "*the limited relevance of past experience as a guide to action in a period of change (especially accelerating change*" whilst another reflected on how important it was for undergraduates to unlearn what they had been taught: "*I am stunned in every semester how surprising this is for many students, who so far successfully have passed their school and Bachelor classes thinking the learning process means to be able to reproduce theories from their textbooks*."

Revans' emphasis on learning as a voluntary activity implies the possibilities for not learning. This can be because learning is painfully elusive, and also where it is doggedly resisted: "there are also those who *soberly and deliberately refuse to learn*" (2011, p. 60 original italics). Learning in adults is "more likely to follow on the re-interpretation of past experiences than the acquisition of fresh knowledge" (2011, p. 6), but the "idolisation of past experience" (2011, p. 42) can hinder this reconfiguration, resulting in stuckness, avoidance, and "learning inaction" (Vince 2008). Revans stresses the need to start from ignorance and not knowing; the position from which questions may be asked. It also explains why he is so critical of misplaced expertise and the dangers of expert approaches whereby intractable problems are turned into puzzles with solutions.

Managing change and innovation depend upon escapes from old mindsets, and action learning, and CAL in particular, can provide helpful contexts for unlearning. Awareness of not knowing also opens up possibilities of nonaction – of attending, noticing, and being present without the compulsion to act. Wicked problems may often include elements of self-causation (Brook et al. 2016), and in these situations where knowledge is insecure and the consequences of actions unpredictable, the decision not to act, especially in previous and predictable ways, might be a good idea. It is not possible to know in advance what new possibilities might attend the refraining from habitual actions. By asking different questions so as to inquire into the unknown, deciding not to act maintains an openness to the emergence of possibilities not yet apparent (Hsu 2013; Antonacopolou 2009).

The Innovation Paradox

Unlearning thus has a pivotal role in creating opportunities for new thinking. Innovation is at the heart of Revans' thinking, manifest in his proposal of the need for "fresh questions" to match or surpass the pace of environmental change. The pursuit of innovation in mature economies is a current example of a widespread and wicked problem. The UK, for example, has a long-standing problem of low productivity, and while innovation accounts for up to 70% of economic growth, only a "relatively small proportion of firms (are) engaged in innovative activity" (BIS 2014, p. 3). The traditional way to resolve this problem is "creative destruction," the process described by Schumpeter in 1942 whereby new firms with new methods, markets, and ways of doing things drive out and destroy the old. But this is very destructive, not only of inefficient firms but of lives, communities, and economies. Moreover, the pattern of innovation in mature economies in recent years has led to lower levels of wages, either due to market forces or as a "result of employers deliberately shaping the innovative process in ways which enhance their wellbeing at the expense of workers" (Stiglitz and Greenwald 2014, p. 164). "Creative destruction" also neglects the role of government policy and the place of learning, which have a key role in increasing productivity in modern knowledge-based economies: "creating a learning society should be one of the major objectives of economic policy" (Stiglitz and Greenwald 2014, p. 6).

Revans' thinking could prove helpful to those seeking to resolve the problem of innovation through policy and learning rather than through destruction and coercion, His "Innovation Paradox" (1971, p. 75) recognizes the difficulties of overcoming inertia and resistance, especially from top managements (2011, pp. 63–62): "any new or specialist solution ... has to be integrated back into the total system of the enterprise" (1971, p. 90). This points to the gap between invention and implementation, which is not a puzzle to be addressed through "best practice" initiatives, because "Every effort to resolve this innovation paradox must be almost entirely situational" (1971, p. 90). Knowledge can be shared and technical advances replicated, but changes in practices and ways of working have to be uniquely realized in situ. In the context of managerial and organizational routines, this views Innovation as a practice not as an event. As Bourner puts it, the question is not whether an innovation works, but, in practice, "who can work it?" (2011, p. 122).

To address the Innovation Paradox, Revans proposes a "praxaeology" or general theory of human action with three overlapping systems of organizational decision, project cycles, and individual learning (1971, pp. 33–67). Success in integrating individual with organizational learning depends greatly on the quality of management and leadership practices, including good communication, and top management support (1971, p. 176). More recent writers using Revans' ideas to address the innovation problem include Kuhn and Marsick (2005), Wyton and Payne (2014), and Olssen et al. (2010), who argue that action learning can increase "innovation capability" in an organization.

However, the problem remains intractable. Recent reliance on organizational learning and knowledge creation to fuel innovation ignores the "institutional inhibitors," because it involves risk it is often a low priority for both line and senior managements (Kalling 2007). Another recent case bears this out; Dovey and Rembach (2015) detail the resistances experienced to an action learning initiative in an Australian university, noting that "innovation is a notoriously difficult strategy to execute. Given its intention to transform the status quo, it is not surprising that in most organizations the rhetoric of innovation substitutes for its practice" (2015, p. 280). This is a very common representation of the innovation paradox: people encouraged to come up with new ideas but also warned not to rock the boat. The notion of the "tempered radical" (Meyerson 2003) suggests that commitment to the organization can be combined with being determined to change it, a concept that Attwood (2007) sees as very appropriate to action learning. Less encouraging is Vince et al.'s (2016, p. 8) manager who says of his company: "*Everyone wants to be a little bit more innovative, but not very much*."

In the context of organizations established as stable entities, the idea of innovation is perhaps inherently paradoxical. Andriopoulos and Lewis (2010) see innovation as a process embedded, even mired, in paradoxes. Achieving it means simultaneously managing conflicting processes such as the pursuing of short-term survival and long-term sustainability. This in turn requires paradoxical approaches to managing and a certain "ambidexterity" (Andriopoulos and Lewis 2010, p. 104). Whether the innovation paradox is ever "resolved" is open to dispute. Paradox theory suggests that the contradictory elements that make up the paradox are not resolvable but persist and are enacted and re-enacted over time, as in Vince's (2008) "learning in action" and "learning inaction" which are dynamic and opposed tendencies always present as two sides of the same coin. Action learning however is both an optimistic and a pragmatic creed, and Vince et al. (2016) consider how CAL might help here, noting that the contradictory dynamics created when action learners collide with the innovation paradox provide opportunities for critical reflection. This can bring about a recognition of "the inseparability of both the transformational potential of action learning and the political purposes it serves as a process for reasserting compliance to a set of established norms" (2016, p. 12).

In response to the question: "Who can make this innovation work?", Bourner argues that "those who wish to share an innovation need to be explicit about the beliefs and values that underpin it, since only those who share those beliefs and values are likely to be able to make the new practice work well" (2011, p. 122). Innovation is – like learning – a voluntary activity, one that cannot be imposed or made mandatory. CAL is one means for addressing the innovation paradox head-on, through confronting the inherent tensions via critical reflection and allowing for some larger questions to be put. A voluntary practice of innovation means addressing those mundane but usually unasked questions at the forefront of the minds of all those contemplating any change; "Who benefits from this change? . . .and who loses? What will the new practices look like? . . . and what will be their impacts on jobs, privacy, autonomy? What is the function of the present discourses of innovation? … and whose interests are being served?" Those who can make innovations work, or unwork, will make their decisions based on their estimates of the answers.

References

Andriopoulos, C., & Lewis, M. W. (2010). Managing innovation paradoxes: Ambidexterity lessons from leading product design companies. *Long Range Planning, 43*(1), 104–122.

Antonacopolou, E. P. (2009). Impact and scholarship: Unlearning and practising to co-create actionable knowledge. *Management Learning, 40*(4), 421–430.

Attwood, M. (2007). Challenging from the margins into the mainstream: Improving renal services in a collaborative and entrepreneurial spirit. *Action Learning: Research and Practice, 4*(2), 191–198.

BIS Annual Report on Innovation. (2014). UK Department of Business. *Innovation & Skills, London, 2014*, 3.

Boshyk, Y., & Dilworth, L. (2010). *Action learning: History and evolution*. Basingstoke: Palgrave MacMillan.

Bourner, T. (2011). Self-managed action learning. In M. Pedler (Ed.), *Action learning in practice* (4th ed., pp. 113–123). Farnham: Gower.

Brook, C., Pedler, M., Abbott, C., & Burgoyne, J. (2016). On stopping doing those things that are not getting us to where we want to be: Unlearning, wicked problems and critical action learning. *Human Relations*, *69*(2), 369–389.

Burgoyne, J. (1994). Managing by learning. *Management Learning, 25*(1), 35–55.

Casey, D., & Pearce, D. (Eds.). (1977). *More than management development: Action learning at GEC*. Aldershot: Gower Press.

Caulat, G. (2012a). *Virtual leadership: Learning to lead differently*. Faringdon: Libri.

Caulat, G. (2012b). Virtual action learning: A new genre for powerful learning. In S. Voller, E. Blass, & V. Culpin (Eds.), *The future of learning: Insights and innovations from executive development* (pp. 72–87). Basingstoke: Palgrave.

Clark, P. A. (1972). *Action research & organisational change*. London: Harper & Row.

Conger, J., & Toegel, G. (2002). Action learning and multi-rater feedback as leadership development interventions: Popular but poorly deployed. *Journal of Change Management, 3*(4), 332–348.

Dickenson, M., Burgoyne, J., & Pedler, M. (2010). Virtual action learning: Practices and challenges. *Action Learning: Research and Practice*, *7*(1), 59–72.

Dixon, N. (1997). More then just a task force. In M. Pedler (Ed.), *Action learning in practice* (3rd ed., pp. 329–338). Aldershot: Gower Press.

Dotlich, D., & Noel, J. (1998). *Action learning: How the world's top companies are re-creating their leaders and themselves*. San Francisco: Jossey-Bass.

Dovey, K., & Rembach, M. (2015). Invisible practices, innovative outcomes: Intrapreneurship within the academy. *Action Learning: Research & Practice, 12*(3), 276–292.

Grint, K. (2005). Problems, problems, problems: The social construction of 'leadership'. *Human Relations, 58*(11), 1467–1494.

Grint, K. (2008). *Leadership, management and command – rethinking D-day*. Basingstoke: Palgrave.

Hsu, S.-w. (2013). Alternative learning organization. In A. Örtenblad (Ed.), *Hand-book of research on the learning organization: Adaptation and context*. Cheltenham/Northampton: Edward Elgar Publishing.

Kalling, T. (2007). The lure of simplicity: Learning perspectives on innovation. *European Journal of Innovation Management, 10*(1), 65–89.

Kuhn, J., & Marsick, V. (2005). Action learning for strategic innovation in mature organizations: Key cognitive, design and contextual considerations. *Action Learning: Research and Practice, 2*(1), 27–48.

Leonard, S., & Marquardt, M. (2010). The evidence for the effectiveness of action learning. *Action Learning: Research and Practice, 7*(2), 121–126.

Marquardt, M. (2004). *Optimizing the power of action learning*. Palo Alto: Davies-Black.

Mclaughlin, H., & Thorpe, R. (1993). Action learning – A paradigm in emergence: The problems facing a challenge in traditional management education and development. *British Journal of Management, 4*(1), 19–27.

Meyerson, D. (2003). *Tempered radicals: How everyday leaders inspire change at work*. Boston: Harvard Business School Press.

Olssen, A., Wadell, C., Odenrick, P., & Norell Bergendahl, M. (2010). The action learning method for increasing innovation capability in organisations. *Action Learning: Research & Practice, 7*(2), 167–179.

Pedler, M., Burgoyne, J. G., & Brook, C. (2005). What has action learning learned to become? *Action Learning: Research & Practice, 2*(1), 49–68.

Raelin, J. (1999). Preface to a special issue "The Action Dimension in Management": Diverse approaches to research, teaching and development. *Management Learning, 30*(2), 115–125.

Raelin, J. (2008). Emancipatory discourse and liberation. *Management Learning, 39*(5), 519–540.

Revans, R. W. (1971). *Developing effective managers*. New York: Praeger.

Revans, R. W. (1980). *Action learning: New techniques for managers*. London: Blond & Briggs.

Revans, R. W. (1982). *The origins & growth of action learning*. Bromley: Charwell Bratt.

Revans, R. (2011). *ABC of action learning*. Farnham: Gower.

Reynolds, M. (2011). Reflective practice: Origins and interpretations. *Action Learning: Research & Practice, 8*(1), 5–13.

Reynolds, M., & Vince, R. (Eds.). (2004). *Organizing reflection*. Aldershot: Ashgate/Gower.

Rittel, H., & Webber, M. (1973). Dilemmas in a general theory of planning. *Policy Sciences, 4*, 155–169.

Stiglitz, J., & Greenwald, B. (2014). *Creating a learning society: A new approach to growth, development, and social progress*. New York: Columbia University.

Vince, R. (2001). Power and emotions in organizational learning. *Human Relations, 54*(10), 1325–1351.

Vince, R. (2004). Action learning and organisational learning: Power, politics, and emotion in organizations. *Action Learning: Research and Practice, 1*(1), 63–78.

Vince, R. (2008). 'Learning-in-action' and 'learning inaction': Advancing the theory and practice of critical action learning. *Action Learning: Research and Practice*, 5(2), 93–104.

Vince, R., Abbey, G. Bell, D., & Langenhan, M. (2016) *Finding critical action learning through paradox: The role of action learning in the suppression and stimulation of critical reflection*. Working Paper, University of Bath.

Wieland, G. F., & Leigh, H. (Eds.). (1971). *Changing hospitals: A report on the hospital internal communications project*. London: Tavistock.

Wieland, G. F. (1981). *Improving health care management*. Ann Arbor: Health Administration Press.

Willis, V. (2004). Inspecting cases: Prevailing degrees of action learning using Revans' theory and rules of engagement as standard. *Action Learning: Research & Practice, 1*(1), 11–27.

Wilmott, H. (1994). Management education: Provocations to a debate. *Management Learning, 25*(1), 105–136.

Wilmott, H. (1997). Critical management learning. In J. Burgoyne & M. Reynolds (Eds.), *Management learning: Integrating perspectives in theory & practice* (pp. 161–176). London: Sage.

Wyton & Payne. (2014). Exploring the development of competence in Lean management through action learning groups: A study of the introduction of Lean to a facilities management function. *Action Learning: Research & Practice, 11*(1), 42–61.

Further Reading

Heifetz, R. (1994). *Leadership without easy answers*. Cambridge: Harvard University Press.

For More on Revans and the Development of His Ideas

Boshyk, Y., & Dilworth, L. (2010). *Action learning: History and evolution*. Basingstoke: Palgrave MacMillan.

Pedler, M. (Ed.). (2011). *Action learning in practice* (4th ed.). Farnham: Gower.

Raelin, J. (2009). On seeking conceptual clarity in the action modalities. *Action Learning: Research and Practice, 6*(1), 17–24.

Revans, R. (2011). *ABC of action learning*. Farnham: Gower. (This is the only text by Revans which is in print and easily available).

The journal *Action Learning: Research & Practice* from Routledge, Taylor & Francis. www.tandtonline.com/actionlearning

Yorks, L., O'Neil, J., & Marsick, V. (Eds.). (1999). *Action learning: Successful strategies for individual, team & organizational development*. San Francisco: Berrett-Koehler.

For More on Revans' Legacies

Brook, C., Pedler, M., Abbott, C., & Burgoyne, J. (2016). On stopping doing those things that are not getting us to where we want to be: Unlearning, wicked problems and critical action learning. *Human Relations, 69*(2), 369–389.

Caulat, G. (2012). Virtual action learning: A new genre for powerful learning. In S. Voller, E. Blass, & V. Culpin (Eds.), *The future of learning: Insights and innovations from executive development*. Basingstoke: Palgrave.

Dickenson, M., Burgoyne, J., & Pedler, M. (2010). Virtual action learning: Practices and challenges. *Action Learning: Research and Practice, 7*(1), 59–72.

Vince, R. (2008). 'Learning-in-action' and 'learning inaction': Advancing the theory and practice of critical action learning. *Action Learning: Research and Practice, 5*(2), 93–104.

66 Otto Scharmer and the Field of the Future: Integrating Science, Spirituality, and Profound Social Change

Patricia A. Wilson

Abstract
Claus Otto Scharmer has dedicated his life work to helping individuals and institutions collaboratively shape the emerging future for the healing of the whole – a process that unfolds through collective inquiry, holistic knowing, and co-creativity. Beginning with the question "why do our systems produce results that no one is happy with?," Scharmer has integrated systems thinking, action research, phenomenology, and inner awareness into a multidimensional matrix of processes and practices called Theory U. As a social technology, Theory U facilitates a shift in individual and collective awareness of the systems and social fields in which we are embedded. The resulting collective shift in awareness fosters collaborative action for systems change motivated by a shared sense of higher purpose.

Otto Scharmer has applied Theory U not only to systems change in teams, organizations, and institutions but also to addressing the major economic, ecological, and cultural schisms threatening the future of our planet today. Scharmer's work will likely be remembered for its guidance in the transition to a new epoch of spiritual openness, organizational fluidity, and social transformation. Theory U is more than an intervention tool – it is a way of being and doing in organizational life. Today this way of being and doing is an imperative, not only to address intensifying fundamentalism but to build the foundation of the next epoch that is already emerging.

Dr. Scharmer is a Senior Lecturer at MIT, a Thousand Talents Program Professor at Tsinghua University, Beijing, and a cofounder of the Presencing Institute.

P.A. Wilson (✉)
Graduate Program in Community and Regional Planning, University of Texas, Austin, TX, USA
e-mail: patriciawilson@utexas.edu

D.B. Szabla et al. (eds.), *The Palgrave Handbook of Organizational Change Thinkers*,
DOI 10.1007/978-3-319-52878-6_90

Keywords
Otto Scharmer • Theory U • Presencing • Systems change • Co-sensing • Action research • Phenomenology • Spiritual development • Inner awareness • Leadership • Organizational change • Social transformation • Consciousness

Contents

Introduction

Otto Scharmer introduced Theory U in 2004 in a coauthored volume with Peter Senge, Joseph Jaworski, and Betty Sue Flowers entitled *Presence: Human Purpose and the Field of the Future*, published by the Society for Organizational Learning. The following excerpt from a review of *Presence* that I wrote in 2005 captures the essence of Theory U:

> Have you experienced that special moment in a group when the bickering and dissension stop and the impasse is broken? Suddenly there is a felt shift in the room, a new shared understanding of what needs to happen; someone articulates the sense of the whole, and everyone is on board. *Presence* aims to find an intentional and sustainable path to those moments.
>
> Beneath the conversational text lies a logical structure of a model of collective knowing, called the U model. Prying open the black box of participation, the U model addresses how wisdom emerges in a group and how a group can discern, learn, and create the emerging future together. The model is informed by extensive interviews with selected scientists, business leaders, and spiritual masters about how they create and invent, and how they discern their sense of larger purpose. The common denominator is a shift in the sense of self, from the isolated individual struggling to accomplish, to that of a lightning rod for grounding the energy and wisdom of a larger whole.

Theory U provides guideposts to link the intimately personal and experiential to large scale, even global, systems change. The key is "presencing": individually and collectively accessing the source of knowing that arises from awareness of a larger whole. See Fig. 1.

Otto Scharmer has spent the last 25 years developing, testing, prototyping, and cultivating Theory U as a means to transform leadership and inquiry in organizations around the world. His 1990 diploma thesis on *Aesthetics and Strategic Leadership* and his 1994 doctoral dissertation on *Reflexive Modernization of Capitalism as Revolution from Within* at Witten/Herdecke University in Germany sowed the seeds for the conceptual basis and structure of Theory U.

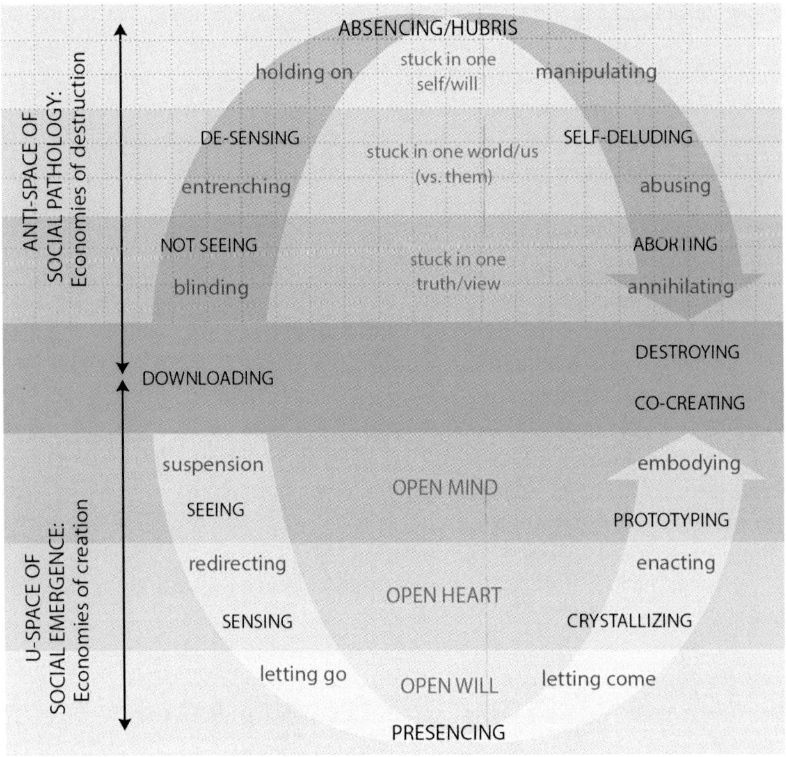

Fig. 1 Theory U: The U curve and its shadow (Source: Scharmer 2007, Fig. 17.3, p. 282)

Over the next decade, based at the MIT Sloan School of Management, Otto observed and participated in multiple organizational change processes, developed practical tools and methods, and wrote his signature book *Theory U: Leading from the Future as It Emerges*, first published in 2007. Over the following decade Otto put Theory U to work prototyping action projects with global corporations, governmental agencies, international development organizations, and local nonprofits. He and his wife, Dr. Katrin Kaufer, harvested the lessons from these action projects in their coauthored book on institutional systems change at the societal level, *Leading from the Emerging Future: From Ego-System to Eco-System Economies* (2013).

Looking ahead, Otto aims to create a platform for activating large scale cross-sector change in institutional leadership. In 2015 he and his colleagues at MIT and the Presencing Institute launched this new phase with a massive open online course (MOOC) called u.lab. In its first year u.lab reached 75,000 registered users from 185 countries and spawned at least 600 face-to-face hubs. Yet this is just the beginning, Otto asserts, of a "multi-local, global eco-system of societal renewal that operates from an awareness of the whole."

Otto Scharmer and Katrin Kaufer live near Cambridge, Massachusetts, with their teenaged daughter and son. Otto gives classes in the fall, including his global

MOOCs, and chairs the MIT IDEAS program, a 9-month action learning lab with change-makers in Indonesia and China. He also engages with other action learning projects in Asia, Europe, Brazil, and the USA. Katrin is a Senior Research Fellow at MIT's Community Innovators Lab (CoLab) and executive director of the Presencing Institute, which she and Otto cofounded with other action research colleagues. Both received their doctorates in management from Witten/Herdecke University near Dortmund, Germany.

In this chapter I take you through the high points of Otto's learning journey – the pivotal moments of discovery and the formative influences. These intellectual, spiritual, and social encounters shaped not only Theory U but Otto's sense of self and purpose. I describe the five key contributions he has made to the field of organizational development and beyond. I offer a personal account of how insights from his work have influenced my own awareness as an action researcher in the civic arena. Finally, I describe the next phase of Otto's trajectory going forward and conclude with a high level appreciation of how his work fits into the historic imperative for institutional transformation that we face today.

For this chapter, Otto and I conducted four recorded conversations of one- to two-hours each from October to December of 2016. I have put verbatim quotes from these conversations in italics or quotation marks. Otto reviewed the manuscript for accuracy.

Influences and Motivations: Otto's Learning Journey

Spirit and purpose Born in 1961 near Hamburg, Germany, Otto grew up in a family guided by a clear sense of purpose with values that honored the interconnectedness and mystery of life. His parents were pioneers in biodynamic farming, an approach to organic agriculture developed by Rudolf Steiner, the founder of the anthroposophical movement for social and spiritual renewal. Otto would transfer his father's love of cultivating the field to the social and organizational terrain, along with the same sensitivity and commitment:

> *I grew up in a context where a spiritual mindset was something very normal – basically a certain wonderment and appreciation that nature is not just a dead body of material waiting to be used, but has its own being and sacredness. . . . I was blessed that my parents sent me to a Waldorf school. While Waldorf School is really not about spiritual education, it is a holistic education – a holistic orientation in terms of head, heart, and hand. (It) means you know how creative processes work. You know that when you run into roadblocks. . ., then the real process is starting, not ending. It gives you more confidence . . . to stay with it.*

Sensing the field Otto's first conscious experience of a social field came in the late 1970s at age 16 as a participant in the massive antinuclear student movement. More than 100,000 protestors had gathered to fight the construction of a nuclear power plant at a site not far from the family farm. When the police blocked them a violent confrontation ensued. The protesters ultimately retreated as one body in stunned silence, Otto recounts. As shadows lengthened, the officers attacked once again "cutting through our collective body like a knife through butter." The protestors, in unspoken agreement, offered no violent resistance to the aggressors. While Otto was not hurt physically himself, he felt the pain of the onslaught as intimately real, as his own pain, because in that moment he was *one* with the *collective body* that was being violated.

Otto came away from that experience a different person. A new sense of purpose had awakened. He had felt part of a larger whole, in this case a global generational movement inspired by a shared sense of future possibility. Moreover, he had seen "the enemy" – the old system of exclusion that needed to transform. Otto came away from that day with a deepened sense of purpose and self. He had felt the power of connection to the collective field and through that doorway had found what was his to do for the rest of his life.

Letting go Later that same year (1977) came another turning point, the day he arrived home from school and witnessed the walls of his life-long home going up in flame. As three generations of his family watched their home burn down, the collective field of grief, loss, and mourning was palpable. But Otto felt something different: "an enormous inner void as though your whole self is gone except for one tiny little aspect, the self who is taking all of this in, not turning away from it, but being present and open to its unfolding."

The moment he came to that place of profound presence, he knew that life is not something to cling to and that identity (self) is not bound up in the experiences of the past nor the material context of the present. He realized that life is something far greater, that the universe is benign and will carry us, despite unimaginable apparent loss, if we simply step across the threshold to future possibility. The future was calling Otto. He let go of the attachments to his past and present identities to pass through the eye of the needle. Buoyed by that realization, while feeling almost ashamed that he was not fully sharing the field of grief, he looked forward – not back.

The power of intention Otto moved to Berlin in the early 1980s to join the Green Party and the East-West peace movement. He attended the Free University in West Berlin, a mecca for student activists. By 1984, Otto was convinced that the levers to systems change in our age lay in the economy. Otto felt a strong calling to join a new experimental university near Dortmund, called Witten-Herdecke, where he majored in economics and management, and, after organizing a year-long global Peace University, returned for doctoral studies in the same field. The first privately funded university in Germany, it emphasized student-initiated learning, action research, social responsibility, and cross-disciplinary studies.

Otto invited Norwegian peace researcher Johan Galtung, whom he had met in Berlin, to a student-organized conference at Witten-Herdecke. The students were galvanized by Galtung's vision for his next step: to create a mobile peace university for students to witness first-hand the global system as a living whole and from multiple cultural and systems perspectives. Otto and four peers set their intention to create such a global learning journey. "I knew this was what I was meant to do."

(Scharmer 2016, p. 194). With the go-ahead from the dean, the five students pulled it all together in a few months: a consortium of twelve universities, 290 lecturers, thirty-five students from ten countries, and a half-million dollars in private sponsorships (pp. 194–195). The creative power of intention manifested in the synchronicity and flow the student team experienced in organizing the journey:

> Our joint commitment to this project empowered us in a way that none of us had ever experienced before. We felt part of a larger field, a formative field of intentional creation. When we were operating in that field, we knew that nothing would prevent us from succeeding. ... Each time we encountered a setback, we knew... some kind of door would open up or helping hand would show up and lead us onward." (ibid, p. 195)

The subsequent global study trip, led by Galtung in 1989–1990, introduced Otto to Gandhian nonviolent conflict transformation, Buddhist practices for inner peace, and Daoist and Confucian philosophies on being and change. The resulting integration of Western analysis and Eastern holism would influence his Theory U.

European intellectual roots of Theory U Otto has always been an avid reader of philosophy, from classical to modern. He and his young peers formed study circles to read and discuss original texts, from pre-Socratic, Plato, and Aristotle to Nietzsche and the German phenomenologists, which included those in the tradition of Johann Wolfgang von Goethe and Rudolf Steiner. Otto cites Goethe and Steiner as the taproots of Theory U:

> Among the philosophical sources, perhaps most influential was the work of the educator and social innovator Rudolf Steiner, whose synthesis of science, consciousness, and social innovation continues to inspire my work and whose methodological grounding in Goethe's phenomenological view of science has left the most significant imprint on Theory U. The simplest way of locating Theory U in the landscape of intellectual traditions is to identify it as applied phenomenology – a mindful phenomenological practice for investigating the social field. ...To paraphrase Steiner, we have to investigate ...our own *thought process* – but then *follow that train* of observation all the way back to its source, exactly as Husserl and Varela advocated in their work on the phenomenological method. (Scharmer 2016, pp. 30–31)

In *Philosophy of Freedom*, Steiner had focused his phenomenology on individual knowing. Otto applied it to both individual and collective patterns of knowing and change, in teams, organizations, and society. Through Husserl (drawing on Goethe's holistic conception of seeing), Heidegger, Hösle, and Habermas, Otto explored the terrain of intra- and intersubjective experience. He traced the influence of awareness on perception, specifically how the structures of individual and collective attention (i.e., the source from which we operate) influence our ways of knowing and interacting.

Otto drew on Heidegger's concept of technology as applied art and *aletheia* as the opening to presence, Buber's work on dialogue (*I-Thou*), Bortoft's conception of presencing the whole, Joseph Beuys's concept of social sculpture, Nietzsche's work on aesthetics (viewing science through the lens of the artist and art through the lens of life), and Kitaro Nishida's formulation of place as presence. These influential writers helped Otto articulate the letting go and letting come at the deepest moment in the U curve – that pivotal moment when a group lets go of limiting beliefs and opens to the call of a higher emergent possibility.

The ground-breaking work of twentieth century German-born social psychologist Kurt Lewin linking Gestalt theory, practice, and change to social fields had a major influence on Otto. At MIT in the 1940s Lewin developed the study of group dynamics and the practice of action research as a participatory approach to change management. Otto was particularly captivated by Lewin's conceptualization of field theory, which posited the existence of a social field that was created by, but different from, the individuals in it, and at the same time exerted its own influence on the members.

The work of Bernard Lievegoed, Friedrich Glasl, and others at the Dutch NPI Institute for Organizational Development during the 1960s and 1970s served as another source of inspiration for Otto, as they were among the first to apply the evolutionary thinking and processes of Goethe and Rudolf Steiner to organizational development (Lievegoed 1973, 1996; Glasl and de la Houssaye 1975; Glasl 1997).

Otto received his diploma in management (with distinction) from Witte/Herdecke in 1990 and his Ph.D. (*summa cum laude*) in 1994. His undergraduate thesis and doctoral dissertation were both published in Germany as books in 1991 and 1996. Together they carried the seeds of the future Theory U. By the time Otto left Germany for MIT in 1994, he referred to himself as an action researcher.

Intellectual influences in the USA Upon completing his doctorate in management, Otto sought a way to ground his thinking in action – how could his ideas actually add value to real change makers in the world of business? He was attracted by the joint work of action researchers at the MIT Center for Organizational Learning, including Peter Senge, the founding director, Ed Schein, Chris Argyris, and William Isaacs at the Sloan School and Donald Schön in Urban Studies. So one day in 1994 he showed up to apply for a postdoc position. They invited him to come as a visiting researcher *if* he could bring his own research funding.

What seemed like a problem turned out to be an opportunity. Otto received a grant from the research arm of McKinsey, Europe, to interview 30 global business leaders and create a website making the results available to all. Those interviews were the chance to observe whether the moments of the U curve could be seen in action. His new colleagues at the MIT Sloan School of Management opened multiple doors to corporations where he could observe and participate in concrete change efforts. The McKinsey grant led to another three rounds of funded change-maker interviews, one of which was sponsored by Joseph Jaworski's Generon International, a business consulting group, to interview 150 corporate leaders and hold a thought leaders salon. Otto was now a senior lecturer and cofounder of the Presencing Institute at MIT.

Social psychologist Ed Schein was pivotal for Otto in learning how to add value to a business. First he reframed the question: how can you create a helping *relationship* with the leaders of a company? Schein helped Otto become an empathetic and other-directed practitioner. "I have never met anyone who lives his own principles to the degree that Ed Schein does," Otto said. "He talks about building helping relationships and that's what he is doing." Otto considers Ed Schein's approach to process consultation as "the mother of Theory U." Schein offered Otto a way of transforming his intellectual learning into a helping relationship with individuals, companies, and organizations through process consultation aimed at making better decisions and learning from action.

Peter Senge, Otto's other mentor at MIT, opened the doors to systems thinking and personal mastery. Drawing on the reflective practices of Argyris and Schön, Senge also addressed the link between leadership, collective inquiry, and the co-creative process, a central theme in Otto's work.

William Isaacs, Otto's colleague at the MIT Learning Center in the late 1990s, was applying Bohmian dialogue and field theory to the creative cycle through practices of deep listening, empathic connection, and collective inquiry. Isaacs's work informed Otto's use of generative dialogue in the U curve and vice versa: Otto's four quadrant model of dialogue, from polite conversation and downloading to reflective and generative dialogue, directly informed Isaac's 1999 book on dialogue.

Through his interview projects at MIT, Otto encountered other influential thinkers. When I asked him which he considered the most impactful, he began with cognitive scientist Francisco Varela and cognitive psychologist Eleanor Rosch. With their colleague, Humberto Maturana, Varela and Rosch developed the neurophenomenology of individual consciousness on a subjective, experiential, embodied level. Varela spoke to Otto of the blind spot of cognition – the inability to become aware of our awareness. Varela then described a process of introspection and contemplative practices that could illuminate the blind spot. He described the experience as one of increasing depth and interiority, a slowing down of time toward stillness, moving from head to heart to emptiness. So there it was – a neuroscientific explanation for presencing, the same phenomenon that Otto had identified from his philosophical inquiry and practical change experiences. Rosch added an even more subtle distinction: From that place (of presencing), she said, you are not looking out at the interconnected whole around you. You are seeing it from the inside as you experience it. In other words, you **become** the social field. That is the place of real knowing, the heart of the heart, the source of wisdom.

Ikujiro Nonaka, the Japanese organizational theorist, introduced Otto to his blend of Eastern (tacit) and Western (explicit) approaches to knowledge creation. From working with Nonaka and integrating Donald Schön's concept of reflection-in-action, Otto published his 2001 article on self-transcending knowledge that distinguished two types of tacit knowing: embodied and not-yet-embodied (i.e., aesthetic).

Otto cites Brian Arthur of the Santa Fe Institute for articulating a dynamic process of discovery in three stages: "observe, observe, observe," "allow inner knowing to emerge," and "act in an instant." Otto would reframe them into the three movements of the U curve: co-sensing, presencing, and co-creating.

Starting in the late 1990s, Otto and Katrin co-hosted for several years a circle called *S3 group* that focused on reinventing the twenty-first century university by integrating science, spirituality, and social change. The small informal group included Peter Senge, Arthur Zajonc, physicist at Amherst College, Diana Chapman Walsh, then President of Wellesley College, and Dayna Cunningham, director of the MIT CoLab, and occasionally Jon Kabat-Zinn, among others. The group met alternating between Walsh's home in Wellesley and Katrin and Otto's in Cambridge. Many ideas discussed in this group became foundational for Theory U's deeper intention of bending the beam of scientific observation back onto the observing self – both individually and collectively.

Key Contributions: Theory and Practice

Otto has noted that various experienced practitioners responded to his workshops on Theory U saying that they were deeply moved yet the content was not entirely new to them: "I just didn't know that I know." Otto takes this as the highest compliment for an action researcher, when accomplished practitioners can see themselves and their own best experiences in the mirror of the Theory U framework:

> *I'm actually just giving some lenses that allow people to make sense of something that they already have within them and among them – the living experience of some of the most significant moments of their lives, as a community, as an individual, or as a team.. What I really try to do is illuminate something that's already there – already embodied in our own best practice, where we step into some higher possibilities and begin to actualize what wasn't accessible and now it is.*

Belying Otto's modesty are five powerful contributions that Theory U makes to the field of organizational change, leadership, and action research:

The paradigm-changer Theory U is a consciousness-based framework for systems change. It brings together inquiry, spiritual development, and systems change. It views systems thinking, leadership, and change from the perspective of an evolving human awareness. By bringing these domains together Theory U offers a path-breaking insight: the pivotal importance of field awareness, i.e., a social field knowing itself. This knowing does not result from simply "getting the whole system in the room." It results from deepening the interior place from which the members (or stakeholders) in a system perceive each other and the whole. The resulting collective shift in awareness is the fertile ground that enables systems change to emerge. Theory U distills these insights into a social technology reflected in Otto's trademark U curve (see Fig. 1).

A new mode of cognition and learning The widely used Kolb reflective learning cycle is based on learning from the past – applying patterns from the past to future action choices. Theory U offers an emergent learning cycle, involving accurate observation, empathic connection with the field, stillness, emptying, and allowing inner knowing to emerge, then ideating and acting immediately on that inner knowing, learning while doing. This mode of knowing integrates spiritual development – i.e., deepening the inner place from which we attend – with observation, action, and reflection.

Integration of European phenomenology Theory U integrates the analytical rigor and deep insights of the twentieth century European philosophical discourse and phenomenological practice to illuminate the process of knowledge creation as it relates to shifts in spiritual awareness, linking deeper levels of consciousness to greater holistic perception. Specifically, Theory U contributes a vertical spectrum for understanding consciousness characterized by four different levels, or evolutionary states, of spiritual awareness that Otto has identified: (1) I-in-me, (2) I-in-it, (3) I-in-you, and (4) I-in-we/I-in-now. For me, reading *Theory U* with soft eyes and open mind is a spiritual journey of self-discovery guided by the insights of these philosophers.

Integration across systems Theory U extends the phenomenological focus on individual consciousness to groups, organizations, and larger living systems. Theory U was the first to link the micro, meso, macro, and mundo (i.e., global) scales, as he calls them. In their 2013 book, Otto and Katrin extend the analysis to the current ecological, social, and spiritual-cultural systems we have created and identify the levels of awareness that perpetuate the disconnects in each. The Matrix of Social Evolution they provide may prove to be a watershed contribution, as it allows the reader to grasp the whole system we are enacting at once (See Fig. 2.).

Tools and practices for transformation Theory U provides a unique practical social technology with a well-organized toolbox of experiential and reflective practices. The methods correspond to each of the moments on the U curve and include both group practices for creating a generative field and individual practices for spiritual deepening. Various of the tools are inspired by Goethean-based practices used in anthroposophy and Waldorf education. Some are familiar to group process facilitators; others are familiar to spiritual practitioners. They are methods to deepen individual and group consciousness, open the mind and heart, connect with one's larger purpose and sense of Self, and build an empathic field capable of transforming itself.

An example that Otto highlights is Social Presencing Theater, created by Otto and his colleague Arawana Hayashi at the Presencing Institute. This practice blends mindfulness, movement, and participatory social science theater in a way that surfaces the invisible dynamics of a social field, revealing both its current state and emerging future possibilities. As I have witnessed it, a group roleplays the stakeholders in their system and, after a silent freeze frame, reenacts the system to collectively build the desired future they have presenced.

Sectors of the Current Institutional Transformation

Stage	Government	Health	Schools	Companies	NGOs	Banks
1.0 Traditional Awareness: *Hierarchy*	Dominating state	Authority and input-centered: *institution-driven*	Authority and input-centered: *teacher-driven*	Centralized: hierarchy: *owner-driven*	Program-focused: *reactive-driven*	Traditional banking: *owner-driven*
2.0 Ego-System Awareness: *Markets and Competition*	Dormant state	Outcome-centered: *managed care–driven*	Outcome-centered: *testing-driven*	Decentralized: divisions: *shareholder- and target-driven*	Policy-focused: *advocacy- and campaign-driven*	Casino banking: *speculation-driven*
3.0 Stakeholder Awareness: *Networks and Negotiation*	Welfare state	Patient-centered: *need-driven pathogenesis*	Student-centered: *learning-driven*	Matrix or network: *stakeholder-driven*	Strategic initiative–focused: *stakeholder-driven*	Socially responsible banking: *stakeholder-driven*
4.0 Eco-System Awareness: *Awareness-Based Collective Action (ABC)*	D-4: direct, distributed, democratic, dialogic	Citizen-centered: *well-being-driven salutogenesis*	Entrepreneurial-centered: *co-sensing- and co-creating-driven*	Co-creative eco-system: *intention-driven*	Eco-system-focused: *intention-driven*	Transformative eco-system banking: *intention-driven*

Fig. 2 Ego- to eco-system awareness: *The matrix of social transformation* (Source: Scharmer and Kaufer 2013, Table 9, p. 196)

As Otto says about the practical application of Theory U tools and methods such as Social Presencing Theater:

> *They help change-makers take larger systems on a journey of making the system sense and see itself and thereby shift the state of consciousness. The focus is on ... looking at a situation through the eyes of another person or stakeholder in the system, something that turns your heart into an organ of perception that allows you to move outside of your own bubble.*

New Insights from Theory U: From Presencing to Absencing

Two major insights about consciousness define Theory U: presencing and absencing. Presencing refers to letting go at the deepest moment of the U curve (see Fig. 1), i.e., releasing the ego structures that block the possibilities for creativity, flow, wholeness, and love. The cycle of presencing entails deepening the place from which we listen to others, engage in dialogue, appreciate and know the larger living social field, recognize the whole in each part, and connect with our greater purpose. Presencing itself is the state of emptiness, openness, stillness, and connection to Source and Purpose, in which we can sense the highest future that is wanting to emerge through us. Presencing requires an open mind, an open heart, and the will to disregard our inner voices of judgment, cynicism, and fear, so that we can let go and let come. Presencing is not only an individual journey but a collective one of deepening connections to each other and the larger systems in which we are embedded.

Absencing (see Fig. 1) is the cycle of fundamentalism: entrenchment around one truth, denying or demonizing other, and closing the mind and heart. Social reality at the level of families, communities, organizations, institutions, and society emerges from the interplay of the two different social fields of absencing and presencing. Otto and Katrin (2013) apply these concepts to map how our economic and societal institutions could evolve toward presencing in order to address the economic, social, spiritual, and ecological disconnects facing the planet (see Fig. 2).

I first learned of Otto's work in 2003 when my colleague at UT, Betty Sue Flowers, handed me the prepublication proofs for the *Presence* book. Theory U seemed to integrate everything I was passionate about: dialogue, group process, field awareness, social change, and spiritual development. I attended Otto's 5-day workshop at the Shambhala Institute of Authentic Leadership that summer and was able to take in deeply for the first time the profound distinction between observing a system from without and sensing it from within.

It was that experience of holistic knowing and heart-connection that Otto led us toward, beyond mechanistic cause and effect to the deeper integrative mind that saw interconnected wholes, and beyond that to a felt sense of being that whole, experiencing oneness as a coparticipant in a vital living field. Emergence became not just a concept but an experience, as we witnessed it first in ourselves, in our own lives and trajectories, then in pairs, and finally in the whole group. I saw the power of conscious connection to Purpose, the energy of a charged and aligned social field, and the collective wisdom that was possible. I saw how a group with an open mind and heart and a sense of safety and trust could generate such a field.

Perhaps the most significant insight from Theory U is the idea of "playing the macro violin" (Scharmer 2016, p. 216). A famous violinist, given his first chance to play at the Chartres Cathedral, focused on playing his violin well. His performance flopped. He learned that the secret is not to play the violin but to play the surrounding whole – in this case, the cathedral. He called it "playing the macro violin" – moving your listening and performing to beyond yourself. That is what I see Otto Scharmer doing. When I do that myself I feel a shift in my attention, an alignment with purpose, and an opening of my heart.

Legacies and Unfinished Business: Activating a Global Platform for Healing the Whole

When Otto speaks of his objectives going forward, I feel the power of his alignment with higher purpose. Otto is committed to using Theory U as a catalyst for the institutional transformation he sees as necessary to heal the ecological, social, and spiritual-cultural divides threatening the planet. Since the publication of the first edition of *Theory U* in 2007 to the publication of the updated edition in 2016, Otto focused on taking the theory to practice. Through the Presencing Institute, he, Katrin, and their core group of collaborators organized workshops and learning journeys with government, industry, and civil society leaders, as well as young change makers. These efforts, such as the Global Wellbeing Lab and the MIT IDEAS program, spawned multiple pilot projects around the world: e.g., a four year project on institutional innovation with Namibian government leaders, an ongoing project on economic democracy in the Bronx, a program to regenerate local food production in Sao Paulo, a sustainable seafood industry initiative in Indonesia, and a collaboration with government and civil society leaders in China.

Otto could see that Theory U was having a practical impact in the world and developing a cadre of leaders imbued with the message and methods of Theory U. But for Otto that was not enough.

The question now, Otto said, is this:

> *Can you create something that is actually a healing force for the whole? The world is full of prototypes, but more often than not they are incapable of transforming the larger systems. What is it we can do that would allow these prototypes to transform the whole? That's the question of scale and sustainability for the transformation of a larger system: a world-wide ecosystem of innovation where all the pieces, even though they are autonomous in their own element, begin to work together in a global context based on a shared intention. A shared global ecosystem where everyone, all the elements, are supporting each other. Making what we have been learning and developing relevant to our current moment of disruption*

globally, a moment where the forces of absencing and presencing are stronger than ever before – that's what this next phase is about.

It is *our* generational imperative, he says, to be that healing force for the whole, to bring about the necessary transformational change. Toward that end Otto, Katrin, and their colleagues at the Presencing Institute launched a global enabling platform in 2015: the u.lab MOOC, a massive online course through MITx and edX.org. About 25,000 people participated in the first u.lab in early 2015 and another 50,000 newcomers in the second u.lab that fall. At least 600 local face-to-face hubs were created. Impact Hubs, a global network of hubs for social entrepreneurs, sponsored dozens of local u.labs. A few major hubs are now in the process of consolidation in Brazil, Scotland, Indonesia, and China.

In the following exchange we witness Otto's thinking in the moment about the emergent future:

O.S. *What's emerging from this* [2 year initial effort] *is an enabling platform and a global community. Now we are consolidating the learning from last year and this year and creating the foundation for the next evolutionary jump.*

P.W. What does that next level look like? How would the cooperation among these different self-organizing nodes or hubs show up in the world? What's the connectivity there that multiplies the leverage to a mundo level?

O.S. *That's exactly what we need to find out! I think we have in u.lab something that works for individuals – grassroots change-makers and social entrepreneurs – and it's wonderful. But I'm not sure that we really have found the right way of bringing in the big institutions. . . . What's missing in the social change world is a platform that links social entrepreneurs outside of the large institutions with the change-makers inside the large institutions. They need each other in order to change how the larger system operates.*

When you go into large boring institutions and work with the younger leaders there, what do you find? It's the same type of people [as the grassroots change-makers and social entrepreneurs who have a sense of purpose and want to make a difference]. *It's just that they made slightly different choices and ended up inside a boring institution. But in their soul, when you listen, they have the same deeper aspirations.*

So we must create those connections, but then also provide the learning journeys, the environments, the methods and tools that allow people to move from ego- to eco-awareness, from a siloed to a more holistic view of the system. We really need new infrastructure for that. We have done it occasionally, but we don't have an enabling infrastructure that could take that to scale. But in principle we have the elements, the components. We just haven't put them together. That's what makes me confident that we could, moving into this third stage now, actually make quite significant progress there.

In my view the forces of presencing are at least as strong and present in the current moment as are the forces of absencing. [We just don't see them.] *The public conversation in mass media and social media is all about absencing. We do not see the other side at all. That's where our role is because we need a new bottom-up platform, with* [local] *community and* [a global] *ecosystem that allows this other awareness to have a genuine holding space. In a word, what's the thing that's missing in the third stage? It's a holding space for this deeper awareness-based systems change.*

P.W. The fact you are already connecting change-makers electronically around the globe is a step in that direction, allowing people to step out of isolation and connect with others. That is big right there. Is it not helping to create that holding space?

O.S. *Frankly, what we have had in the MIT MOOC is not even that first step. It's just a tenth of that first step. That's why we are currently working on creating something that hopefully is much better and will be launched in April 2017 to create a more adequate and appropriate online holding space that allows this kind of collective awareness to land and manifest in the way it wants. The potential is there, but we have not had the right landing spots as yet. . . . Also the electronic connection is not sufficient because we need the offline elements* [local face-to-face communities] *as much as we need the online elements. Real place-based, in-person community experiences are the real holding space and landing strips for this kind of movement.* [We will want to] *leave a lot of initiative and autonomy on a local level, yet connect people to something much larger than themselves.*

P.W. Tell me more about the nature of the holding spaces that are so key to transformation.

O.S. *The larger holding space from which collective knowing and collective innovation can take place is the container for co-sensing across boundaries. Most institutional change processes fail because they miss that starting point: co-sensing across boundaries. Because they don't, organized interest groups go out and maximize their special interests against the whole, instead of engaging the whole system in co-sensing together. Most people, when they take learning journeys and benchmarking tours, just keep projecting their own views. Or we do sense-making in our own siloes. We don't have the co-sensing mechanisms where we as a distributed community in a city or in a larger system, begin to see reality together and then unearth the deeper mechanisms generating that reality.*

P.W. What do we need to activate the holding spaces?

O.S. *You need data to use as a mirror by which a system can see itself; you need dialogue; and you need heart intelligence. . . . Dialogue really is the capacity of a system to see itself. But it's not just seeing, it's also sensing – the feeling aspect* [the deep dive into the phenomenon, seeing from within it]. *And then the collective reflection and so on. Not easy to do, because you need experiential foundations, data foundations, a process, and the right kind of people. That's often where the quality is missing. With new technologies and with the new public challenges that we face in many communities, I think we have a wonderful opportunity to really create innovations there.*

In sum, Otto is focused on the long game, powered by connection to a higher purpose: large scale systems change for healing the whole, starting with the individual and collective capacity to perceive, know, and care about the dynamic, evolving whole of which we are a part. To that end, he is developing and testing platforms to create the necessary social infrastructure using the Theory U framework and technology of awareness-based action research on a global scale (Scharmer and Kaufer 2015).

He and his team at the Presencing Institute are themselves following the creative cycle of Theory U: building the feedback loops to see and sense the results of their rapid innovations. Thus, we can expect to see more attention to rigorously documenting the outcomes and impacts of the social technology of presencing, both individual and institutional, under different conditions, by sociodemographics, and longitudinally. We may also see more of the feminine qualities of soulfulness, playfulness, love, and nurturing brought forth in Theory U. And we may begin to see how to address the conundrum between connection to Purpose and work/life balance – i.e., how to practice what we want to create.

Conclusion: Fulfilling Our Generational and Spiritual Imperatives

To conclude I wish to put Otto Scharmer's work in the large sweep of history, looking back at its roots and looking forward to discern its potential role in history, and then bring the pendulum to rest in the present moment:

"Form follows consciousness." "As within so without." These two insightful propositions undergirding Theory U, often repeated in Otto's workshops and writing, echo the Hermetic teachings of the ancient wisdom traditions, passed down through the ages to the modern mystery schools that informed Goethe and Steiner and inspired phenomenological philosophy. Valuing spiritual knowing (*gnosis*), the phenomenological philosophers applied these insights to different domains of science and society, providing a humanizing and contemplative counterweight to the predominant Newtonian world view.

In the twentieth century, existential phenomenology gave rise to Gestalt psychology, from which arose Kurt Lewin's articulation in the 1940s of group dynamics, field theory, and action research – the foundations of organizational development. A spiritual dimension of OD with phenomenological roots started to appear in the 1950s with Lievegoed, followed by Glasl in the 1960s, Torbert in the 1970s, Cooperrider in the 1980s, and Peter Senge and Allan Kaplan in the 1990s. The introduction of complexity science and emergence, along with escalating interest in Eastern spiritual traditions, ushered in further development of spirituality and organizational development in the 1990s (e.g., Capra, Wheatley). The spiritual thread intensified in the first decade of the twenty-first century with Positive Organizational Scholarship and a panoply of popular books on holistic thinking, consciousness, chaos, and collaboration in the workplace along with practices for quieting the mind and fostering group resonance. Into this milieu came Otto Scharmer's *Theory U* in 2007, grafting OD back onto its strong ontological and epistemological roots in early phenomenology.

Looking back a century from now, people may see the first half of the 2000s as the birth canal of a new era of spiritual openness and organizational fluidity and feel grateful that our generation fulfilled its purpose to realize the future that was wanting to emerge through us, as Otto would say. Our mission was twofold: spiritual and generational. First, we had to deepen our own inner capacity to let go of our sense of a separate self and recognize our indivisible interconnectedness. This was our spiritual imperative. Only then could we learn to "co-sense" – i.e., together the needs of the whole and our future wholeness that was calling. Those needs were the three deep divides of today that threaten our future: the concentration of wealth, the ecological survival of the most vulnerable parts of the planet, and the cultural/ political schisms that divide us. Addressing those needs could not be postponed. This was our generational imperative: to activate the collective field to address the deep divides.

The field is fertile for Theory U and other approaches that recognize our spiritual and generational imperatives to take root. With unwavering intention, Otto Scharmer has provided theoretical precision, practical rigor, and a nuanced language for spiritual and organizational transformation that, while complex, is entering the global discourse of transformation through a platform for electronic and face-to-face hubs across multiple systems and cultures.

Otto Scharmer's Theory U, like Cooperrider's Appreciative Inquiry, is more than an intervention tool – it is a way of being and doing in organizational life. Today this way is an imperative, not only to address the absencing and fundamentalism intensifying today but to build the foundation of the next epoch that is already emergent.

Otto Scharmer reminds us that the real change starts with paying attention to our attention: "Experience is not what happens to us but what we do with what happens to us." This doing can be performed from a mind and heart that is closing (absencing) or from a mind and heart that is opening (presencing). The call of our time is about waking up to this source level of choice and agency that every human being is engaged in – moment to moment. Theory U is a mirror that facilitates that awakening both individually and across systems.

References

Glasl, F. (1997). *The enterprise of the future: Moral intuition in leadership and the organization's development*. Stroud: Hawthorn Press.

Glasl, F., & de la Houssaye, H. (1975). *Organisatie-ontwikkeling in de pracktijk*. Brussels/ Amersterdam: Elsevier. Also published in same year in German as *Organisationsentwicklung*. Bern/Stuttgart: Haupt Verlag.

Lievegoed, B. (1973). *The developing organization*. London: Tavistock.

Lievegoed, B. (1996). *Man on the threshold: The challenge of inner development*. Stroud: Hawthorn Press, Social Ecology Series.

Scharmer, C. O. (2007). *Theory U: Leading from the future as it emerges*. Cambridge: Society for Organizational Learning.

Scharmer, C. O. (2016). *Theory U: Leading from the future as it emerges* (2nd ed.). San Francisco: Berrett-Koehler.

Scharmer, O., & Kaufer, K. (2013). *Leading from the emerging future: From ego-system to eco-system economies*. San Francisco: Berrett-Koehler.

Scharmer, O., & Kaufer, K. (2015). Awareness-based action research: Catching social reality creation in flight. In H. Bradbury (Ed.), *The Sage handbook of action research*. Thousand Oaks: Sage.

Further Reading

Isaacs, W. (1999). *Dialogue and the art of thinking together*. New York: Currency Doubleday.

Jaworski, J., & Scharmer, C. O. (2000). "Leadership in the new economy: Sensing and actualizing emerging futures" (The Red Book). Generon International and Society for Organizational Learning, pdf, 53 pp. www.generoninternational.com/download/red-book-2/?wpdmdl=1834

Kaplan, A. (1996). *The development practitioners' handbook*. London: Pluto.

Scharmer, C. O. (2000). *Presencing: Learning from the future as it emerges. On the tacit dimension of leading revolutionary change*. Paper presented at the conference on knowledge and innovation, 25–26 May 2000, Helsinki School of Economics, Finland. http://www.welchco.com/02/14/01/60/00/05/2501.HTM

Scharmer, C. O. (2001). Self-transcending knowledge: Sensing and organizing around emerging opportunities. *Journal of Knowledge Management, 5*(2), 137–151.

Senge, P., & Scharmer, C. O. (2001). Community action research. In P. Reason & H. Bradbury (Eds.), *Handbook of action research*. Thousand Oaks: Sage.

Senge, P., Scharmer, C. O., Jaworski, J., & Flowers, B. S. (2004). *Presence: Human purpose and the field of the future*. Cambridge: Society for Organizational Learning.

Edgar H. Schein: The Scholar-Practitioner as Clinical Researcher 67

David Coghlan

Abstract

Edgar H. Schein's contributions to the field of organizational studies are far reaching. He was one of the first to formulate the field of organizational psychology in 1965, and he led the development of the field of organization development (OD) through his editorship of the pioneering Addison-Wesley OD series in 1969. He framed a philosophy of being helpful through process consultation and humble inquiry, articulated the experience of the organizational career, and framed a model of organizational culture and how it operates in complex systems.

Keywords

Edgar H. Schein • Organization development • Clinical research • Scholar-practitioner

Contents

D. Coghlan (✉)
Trinity Business School, Trinity College Dublin, Dublin, Ireland
e-mail: dcoghlan@tcd.ie; david.coghlan@tcd.ie

D.B. Szabla et al. (eds.), *The Palgrave Handbook of Organizational Change Thinkers*,
DOI 10.1007/978-3-319-52878-6_56

Introduction

The contribution of Edgar H. Schein, Society of Sloan Fellows Professor of Management Emeritus and Professor Emeritus at the Massachusetts Institute of Technology's (MIT) Sloan School of Management to the field of applied behavioral science is both extensive and deep. The first edition of his *Organizational Psychology* (1965) was one of the first books to define the field. In 1969, along with Warren Bennis and Richard Beckhard, Schein cofounded and edited the seminal Addison-Wesley series on the then emerging field of organization development. Between 1969 and 2000, over 30 books were published in that series by many of the leading figures in the field. His *Process Consultation* books (1969, 1987a, 1988, 1999) and their successors, *Helping* (2009a), *Humble Inquiry* (2013a), and *Humble Consulting* (2016a) are best sellers and widely used and cited. He is the founding editor of *Reflections*, the journal of the Society for Organizational Learning. Schein is a Fellow of the Academy of Management and of the American Psychological Association and has received many awards, including the Lifetime Achievement Award for Workplace Learning and Performance from the American Society of Training Directors; the Marion Gislason Award for Leadership in Executive Development, Boston University; the Everett Cherrington Hughes Award for Career Scholarship, Careers Division of the Academy of Management; the Academy of Management Scholar-Practitioner Award and the Lifetime Achievement Award from the International Leadership Association. He has an honorary doctorate from the IEDC Bled School of Management in Slovenia.

A notable feature of Edgar Schein's life is that he has penned several autobiographical reflections (1993, 2006, 2016b) and has been generous in giving interviews about his life and work (Sashkin 1979; Luthans 1989; Quick and Gavin 2000; Lambrechts et al. 2011; Mike 2014). What he has said about himself and how he understands his personal and professional development are readily available.

Schein was born in Zurich, Switzerland in 1928. His father was a physicist. The family moved to Odessa for 3 years, and then to Prague and in 1938 to Chicago where his father obtained a faculty position at the University of Chicago. As an undergraduate in the University of Chicago, he heard about Carl Rogers which sparked an interest in psychology. He attended Stanford where he wrote a master's dissertation on social influence. He did his Ph.D. in social psychology at the Department of Social Relations at Harvard. At the same time, as part of his 5-year military service, he entered the clinical psychology program of the US Army, which required him to complete a 1-year internship at the Walter Reed hospital as a clinical psychologist.

When he had completed his doctorate and military service Schein joined the MIT School of Industrial Management in 1956. Schein remained at MIT until his retirement in 2008. Between 1968 and 1971, he was the undergraduate planning professor for MIT, and in 1972 he became the chairman of the Organization Studies Group of the MIT Sloan School, a position he held until 1982.

Influences and Motivations: Institutions and Mentors

Schein joined the Department of Social Relations in Harvard for his doctoral studies. This was a powerful interdisciplinary program where he was exposed to Gordon Allport, Richard Solomon, Freed Bales, George Homans, Jerome Bruner, David McClelland and Talcott Parsons, among others. Each of these was engaging in pioneering social psychology research. At a daily sandwich lunch Schein (2016b, p. 81) reported that he was "thrilled to eavesdrop as different faculty members from different departments engaged in lively discussion and debates during these lunches." Through the interdisciplinarity of the group, he developed an eclectic view of social psychology. Allport was his first important mentor who taught him to locate issues in their historical context and who emphasized the adage that if you can't write about something, then you don't know it. Solomon taught him about good experimentation and the value of following interesting problems that affect theory and practice. Bruner's research on the effect of social class on perception taught him how the perceptual system is an active process of seeking out and attending to things that concern us. During his doctoral studies, Schein took a course in group dynamics at MIT that was delivered by Alex Bavelas. Bavelas's ability "to stimulate excitement and his creativity in the design of experiments were unbelievable" (Schein 2016b, p. 95). Schein was exposed to the famous Bavelas and Leavitt communication experiments that mapped the effects of different communication patterns on task performance. Schein (2016b, pp. 97–98) reflected "I became aware that the field of group dynamics was flourishing and that much of the work of people like Festinger, Schachter, Thibaut, Back, and Deutsch were actually conducted in and around MIT. This was experimental psychology at its best. Alex Bavelas became then and has remained one of my all-time heroes in the field. But alas I was in the army and committed to at least 3 years of service as an army psychologist. Kurt Lewin and his theories stayed very much on my mind even though I had never met him. I would continue as an experimental group dynamics researcher and I resolved to pursuit the Bavelas or Leavitt types of experiments in the future." In 1952, Schein completed his Ph.D. in social psychology under the direction of Allport and Solomon. His interest in social influence had led him to conduct an experimental study of imitation, on the question that if people learned to imitate someone performing one task, would they to continue to imitate that person on other tasks. His results demonstrated clearly that that people would learn to imitate someone who was shown to be correct on many trials of an ambiguous task and would continue to imitate that person on a similar other task, but not on a different one. He had access to army inductees in the Walter Reed Army Institute of Research and was able to conduct his experiments and his analysis readily.

From 1952 to 1956, Schein spent four postdoctoral years at Walter Reed where he joined an interdisciplinary team led by the psychiatrist, David Rioch. Rioch who was his second most important mentor and the one who taught him that if he wanted to find out something not to ask directly about it but to invite a story that would reveal what he wanted to know. This maxim became a central approach in process consultation and humble inquiry. Schein reflects that Rioch believed in stimulating his staff with other points of view, and he regularly invited Leon Festinger, Fred Fiedler, and Erving Goffman to consult with them on their projects. These were pioneering researchers in the field of social psychology. Festinger was developing his dissonance theory. Fiedler was engaging in leadership studies and Goffman was studying socialization. Schein notes that Goffman's "influence was deep and lasting" (2006, p. 291).

In 1953, during his tenure in the military psychology service, he was assigned to a project that evaluated and treated military personnel who had been captured by the North Koreans. These personnel were considered to have been indoctrinated and had allegedly collaborated with the enemy. Repatriates were returned to the USA from Korea by ship, and on the voyage, they were assessed psychologically and given therapy by psychiatric teams. Schein's ship was delayed for 3 weeks, and during that time, he set up a booth and interviewed repatriates about their experiences in the prison camps. Here he followed Rioch's maxim and essentially asked the soldiers to tell the stories of their imprisonment. They described very sophisticated techniques for manipulating the prisoners, controlling information, and using cellmates, who unbeknownst had already confessed, as apparent friendly persuaders. From these interviews and subsequent research, he framed his sociopsychological model of coercive persuasion that described the methods in terms of Lewin's model of change and influence (Schein et al. 1961). Schein described coercive persuasion as a process of physical and psychological unfreezing and how the unfreezing forces changed some of prisoners' beliefs and attitudes toward themselves and the Communists and make a sincere confession in the manner desired of them by the Communists.

Schein's decision to join the MIT School of Industrial Management (later the MIT Sloan School of Management) in 1956 came from an invitation from Douglas McGregor and through meeting and being impressed by Alex Bavelas. McGregor had built up psychology at MIT and been instrumental in bringing Lewin to MIT in 1945. Through his choice to join a professional school rather than a traditional psychology department, Schein was opting for a focus on applied research rather than one of experimentation, the then favored research model in social psychology.

As a young academic starting out at MIT, Schein's mentor was Douglas McGregor who encouraged him to bring his social psychology to the field of management. As Schein wrote up the work he had done with the prisoners of war, he reflected how these coercive persuasion methods were similar to those used in religious training and organizational socialization. He published his reflections in a provocative article titled, "management development as a process of influence" (Schein 1961). McGregor was what Schein later came to understand as a "clinical researcher." He was a careful observer of the situations in which he found himself and drew out ideas that he tested in the field, rather than by survey or by experimentation. McGregor also pushed him to be a teacher of executives.

In Schein's first year at MIT, McGregor suggested that he attend a T group at the National Training Laboratories (NTL). There and subsequently, as he became a staff member at NTL, Schein was exposed to a new approach to learning by being in an unstructured group that studied its own process. He reports on several insights from these experiences. One insight was the notion of experiential learning and its emphasis on the here-and-now and direct interpersonal feedback, which was so different from his academic training and teaching background in social psychology. Another insight came from his experience as a T group trainer whose role was not to offer expert advice but to facilitate participants' own understanding of themselves and what was going on in the group. This insight led to the articulation of process consultation, an approach to consulting that aimed to help client help themselves. A third insight was the use of the "lecturette," a short input that laid out some key process issues that participants could relate to their experience. His 1965 book with Warren Bennis on learning in groups became one of the classics on the subject of laboratory learning (Schein and Bennis 1965).

From his base in MIT and his experiences in NTL and encouraged by McGregor, Schein learned to consult with organizations and to focus on process as a way of trying to be helpful. From a caustic remark made by an academic colleague to the effect of asking him when he was going to do real research instead of teaching pop psychology to managers, he wrote *Process Consultation* (1969) to articulate the underlying philosophy of his work. Schein defines process consultation as the creation of a relationship with a client that permits the client to perceive, understand, and act on process events that occur in the client's internal and external environment in order to improve the situation as defined by the client. Over the following 60 years, Schein engaged in organizational consulting around the world and reflected on his experience and on the articulated learning of his clients.

As Schein engaged with two particular companies, Digital Equipment Corporation (DEC) (2003) and Ciba-Geigy, he received insights into the structure and role of culture in organizations. His framework of artifacts, espoused values, and tacit basic assumptions developed from his clinical observation of these firms and what emerged as he was trying to be helpful to them. He later consolidated these insights in other settings.

At NTL and then at MIT, Schein became acquainted with Dick Beckhard, with whom he developed a close relationship. Beckhard taught him that being a consultant, a teacher, and a researcher was about intervening to improve and to enable change. From Beckhard, he learned the practice of an "educational intervention," a dialogue with managers in an organization that would stimulate managers' thinking and possibly lead to a consulting relationship.

Schein engaged in a study of how organizations socialize their employees and began an analysis of the careers of MIT master's graduates. Out of this study came the construct of the career anchor, which captures what might be termed the "inner career," a set of self-identified competences, motivations, and values that guide occupational and role choices. He designed a method of self-assessment and interviews to identify an individual's career anchor. Interestingly, Schein identified his own career anchor as autonomy.

To try to summarize what Schein says shaped his academic life and to map those influences, his early life and the influences of Allport, Rioch, McGregor, and Beckhard are significant. About his early life, he (2006, p. 288) notes that "by the age of ten I had learned Russian, Czech, and then English and had made four cultural transitions. I also learned how to adapt quickly to new situations, a skill which I now realize was essential to doing effective consulting with organizations. This adaptive capacity shaped my career in many ways." During his doctoral studies, he learned from Allport to understand the history of his own field and to engage in good writing. Rioch taught him to inquire through story. McGregor brought him to MIT and changed the direction of his life from becoming an experimental social psychologist to becoming an applied organizational psychologist. McGregor also mirrored a method of working that was grounded in observation and engagement with the world of management practice. Finally, Beckhard taught him to be a consultant, and his many clients, especially in DEC and Ciba-Geigy, taught him the complex dynamics of organizational culture.

Key Contributions: Organizational Culture, Helping, Clinical Inquiry/Research, Career Dynamics, Organizational Change, Scholar-Practitioner

Schein's contributions to the field of organizational studies are far reaching. His formulation of the field of organizational psychology in 1965 and his lead in developing the field of organization development (OD) through his editorship of the pioneering Addison-Wesley OD series in 1969 opened up new fields of study. He framed a philosophy of being helpful through process consultation and humble inquiry that has become mainstream in both the academic and practitioner literatures. Schein articulated the experience of organizational careers and articulated a model of organizational culture and how it operates in complex systems. Each of these contributions is treated in his books. Other contributions that are found in articles, book chapters, and interviews are his notions of organizational therapy, organizational socialization, dialogue, and the role of anxiety in organizational change.

Many of his concepts are seminal in several fields.

- Organizational culture: Schein's *Organizational Culture and Leadership* (five editions), the two editions (with a further one in progress) of *The Corporate Culture Survival Guide*, and numerous articles and book chapters have shaped much of the understanding of this notion. In these writings, he challenges simplistic notions of culture that are portrayed in the popular literature. His insight is that culture shapes organizations much like personality does the individual and that therefore it needs to be taken seriously as it shapes how an organization survives and thrives. He provides a method for researchers to decipher an organization's culture, a method that takes explicit account of the different schools of research from which researchers operate (Schein 2017). Schein's study (1996) of the Singapore Economic Development Board demonstrates an account of a detailed inquiry into how that board that transformed Singapore into a world economic power.

- Helping: Schein's work on the process of helping, whether in the normal process of everyday living or in a role as a manager or consultant, has been formulated across seven books – the four *Process Consultation* books, *Helping, Humble Inquiry*, and the recent *Humble Consulting*. These books are best sellers and are widely cited. Through the notion of process consultation and humble consulting, he challenges and offers an alternative to the dominant prescriptive helping mode (which he calls the doctor-patient model) used by consulting companies. In theoretical terms, the notion of process consultation is a standard inclusion in books on organization development and change and is part of the construct of organization development. In the world of practice, process consultation is widely practiced in the field of consulting. He developed the notion of process consultation as clinical inquiry/research that has been influential in the field of action research (Schein 1987b). Here, he locates the process of trying to be helpful as the heart of organizational research.
- OD as clinical inquiry/research: In the third edition of *Organizational Psychology* (1980), Schein discussed action research within the context of OD as being grounded in Lewin's two dictums – there is nothing so practical as a good theory, and if you want to study an organization, try to change it. He also emphasized that "before a researcher can justify any particular research intervention in an organization that researcher should be able to justify that particular intervention from a consultant or therapist perspective" (1980, p. 242). In a substantive paper (2008), he located clinical inquiry/research in relation to other research approaches in terms of levels of researcher and system initiation of and involvement in the research, and he elaborated the clinical perspective of the researcher as focused on helping the system. Schein (1989/2010) explored the question of whether OD is a science, a technology, or a philosophy. Here, he put Lewin's work in the perspective of being rooted in the practical social science that Lewin practiced. Schein explores how action research is one of the distinctive features of OD and one of its core origins. Action research was based on two assumptions which are the cornerstones of OD. One is that involving the clients or learners in their own learning not only produces better learning but more valid data about how the system really works. The other is that one can only understand a system when one tries to change it, as changing human systems often involves variables which cannot be controlled by traditional research methods. Accordingly, as Schein argues, a central element of the OD approach is a reflexive approach which goes with the story as it evolves, rather than imposing predefined programs. Schein concluded that OD is a philosophy, and he points to his own articulation of process consultation/clinical inquiry as a philosophy of helping and later refers to it as organizational therapy (Schein et al. 2010; Schein 2013b).
- Career dynamics: Schein has written extensively on the dynamics of careers and job planning (1978, 1987c, 1995). His 1971 article in the *Journal of Applied Behavioral Science* was one of the first to define the field (Schein 1971). As described above, he analyzed the careers of MIT master's graduates from which he developed the construct of the career anchor. His workbook on career anchors is in its fourth edition (Schein and Van Maanen 2013).

- Organizational change: After his coercive persuasion research with the prisoners of war and his work on organizational socialization, Schein extended Lewin's social change and learning model to the field of organizational change. He found that change begins with some sort of disconfirmation, a disconfirmation that has to be accompanied by a concern, such as anxiety or guilt and that a sense of psychological safety needs to be created. The process of changing can work by scanning multiple sources of information or through a relationship with a single source, such as a tutor, therapist, or a consultant who acts as a facilitator of learning and change. Change then needs to be consolidated into the personality and into significant relationships. Lewin's three-step model of change is often criticized as being an oversimplification and irrelevant in the contemporary age of constant, discontinuous complex change. On the other hand, Cummings et al. (2015) argue that how the change management literature has adopted Lewin's stages, including Schein's, is not what Lewin himself developed and that the adoption, rather than what Lewin himself wrote, is the point of the contemporary criticism. Nevertheless, Schein's presentation (1979) of his model of learning and change enabled through interpersonal relationships, as derived from Lewin, holds a consistency with organization development, process consultation, and humble inquiry as a philosophy and as an intervention practice.
- Scholar-practitioner: For a special issue of the *Journal of Applied Behavioral Science* in 2009 to commemorate Schein's 80th birthday, Rami Shani and I, as the special issue coeditors, wrote to him to draw him into the process. We asked him if he preferred any of the areas of his contributions to be the theme of the special issue. Schein replied that his preference was the scholar-practitioner. He noted (2009b) that scholar-practitioners represent two subcultures, straddling what is science and what is practice. Enabling dialogue between the two worlds to cocreate knowledge that is useful for practice and robust for scholars is the challenge for the scholar-practitioner.

New Insights: Humble Inquiry

If I were ever asked to contribute to a series on books that changed people's lives, I would have little hesitation in selecting *Process Consultation* (1969) as one that changed mine. That little book opened up a perspective of working with people on task-focused issues in a manner that allowed them to understand what was going on and develop their own actions to deal with them. It provided insights that led me into OD and action research. After over 60 years of emphasizing process, Schein has moved to emphasizing the disposition of being "humble," which he defines as "the fine art of drawing someone out, of asking questions to which you do not already know the answer, of building a relationship based on curiosity and interest in the other person" (2013a, p. 2). His focus on humble inquiry brings together the threads of his previous work in being helpful and in building collaborative relationships.

At the same time, as focusing on building a helping relationship with a client, Schein also focuses on the need for self-reflexivity by the consultant/inquirer. He provides practical tips for the helper to enable self-awareness to unlearn old habits to develop the skills of "humble inquiry" (2009a, 2013a).

Process consultation/humble inquiry/humble consulting and its expression as clinical inquiry shapes my work as an OD/action research scholar-practitioner. Clinical inquiry is an orientation to research that views the researcher as one who helps clients understand their organizational challenges and works with them to help address those challenges. In doing so the clinical researcher is helped by the clients to generate the relevant data and build relevant theory that is useful to both practice and scholarship. Clinical inquiry provides a theoretical and practical philosophy for those who engage in OD through action research and collaborative management research (Coghlan 2009).

Legacy and Unfinished Business: Clinical Inquiry/Research

In 2011, Schein was asked what he considered to be his most important contribution (Lambrechts et al. 2011). He replied that, while he didn't think that he had a single thing that he considered to be the most important, "I've always been obsessed with the relationship between the individual and the system, the individual, and the organization. You can say that the career anchors idea is all about the individual, culture is really about the organization, and process consultation and helping are about the relationship. So the contribution is the total package rather than one element of it" (p. 141).

From my perspective, the unfinished business is clinical inquiry/research. Through being in a helping role, clinical inquiry/researchers bring a research attitude to the process as they collaborate with practitioners in sharing projects and fostering mutual inquiry that aims to cocreate knowledge that benefits both the scholar and practitioner. It characterizes doing research *with* people rather than doing research *on* or *for* them. This approach generates practical knowledge, a form of knowledge that has been largely excluded from the academy (Toulmin 1990; Coghlan 2016). While the links are not generally made explicitly, clinical inquiry/research provides a solid philosophical grounding for action research (Coghlan 2009, 2011) and collaborative management research (Werr and Greiner 2008). It frames a notion of authentic organization development as a philosophy as it engages with both elements of the dual identity of OD as a professional field of social action and an area of scientific inquiry.

Understanding the researcher as an engaged helper is a radical alternative to the research philosophies that dominate management and organizational research. Schein has been stridently critical of the research paradigm that dominates business schools and how that paradigm is increasingly irrelevant to the world of practice in its focus on predetermined questions and emphasis on quantitative rigor. In his view, he accords with the many critiques of how research is viewed and enacted in the field of management and organizational studics. He suggests that "inquiry" be a preferred term rather than "research," as research in OD undermines the powerful, basic assumptions about what science is – assumptions that dominate business schools' research and so enable the emphasis to shift to being helpful. In that vein, Schein suggests that, as part of their research training, organizational researchers do internships in organizations where their task is to be helpful and that they learn observational and interviewing skills, rather than focusing on learning to analyze surveys.

On this subject, Schein is not listened to and his voice is not heard. He made following astute observation: "We are still uncertain whether we should (1) be scientific and rigorous, allying ourselves with our academic colleagues who are concerned with knowledge production or (2) be helpful, allying ourselves with our clients and with other practitioners for whom data production is secondary to learning and change" (2008, p. 421). This observation continues to hold, and there is little evidence to suggest that those who lead doctoral research programs in business schools are addressing or even posing this question.

Conclusions

As this chapter has explored, Edgar H. Schein's contribution to the field of applied behavioral science is both extensive and deep. For over 60 years, he has creatively and systematically shaped theory and practice in areas such as organization development, career dynamics, the cultural dynamics of complex systems, leadership, process consultation, and clinical research. Now in his 88th year, he continues to be creative and reflective. A recent book, *Humble Consulting* (2016a), provides not only a rich reflection on the consulting process out of his extensive experience but is also creative in providing a new framework for developing theory and practice. In that book, he promises that there are other books to come.

I conclude with Schein's own words that capture his stance as a scholar-practitioner and which provoke our field to continue to reflect to on itself.

> After 60 years in this arena, I am convinced that we are still at a Darwinian stage of searching for constructs and variables worth studying and are still waiting for some Mendelian genius to organize the field for us. In other words, I still think that good observation, phenomenology, fieldwork, ethnography, and careful case analyses are more important than quantitative statistical hypothesis testing. Clinical analyses of cases come naturally from our work as consultants and interveners, which led me to propose clinical research as an important method in our field. I believe that good theory is still to be discovered by careful observation and analysis. (2015, p. 3)

References

Coghlan, D. (2009). Toward a philosophy of clinical inquiry/research. *The Journal of Applied Behavioral Science, 45*(1), 106–121.

Coghlan, D. (2011). Action research: Exploring perspective on a philosophy of practical knowing. *Academy of Management Annals, 5*, 53–87.

Coghlan, D. (2016). Retrieving a philosophy of practical knowing for action research. *International Journal of Action Research, 12*(1), 84–107.

Cummings, S., Bridgman, T., & Brown, K. G. (2015). Unfreezing change as three steps: Rethinking Kurt Lewin's legacy for change management. *Human Relations, 69*(1), 33–60.

Lambrechts, F. J., Bouwen, R., Grieten, S., Huybrechts, J. P., & Schein, E. H. (2011). Learning to help through humble inquiry and implications for management research, practice and education: An interview with Edgar H. Schein. *The Academy of Management Learning and Education, 10* (1), 131–147.

Luthans, F. (1989). Conversation with Edgar H. Schein. *Organizational Dynamics, 17*(4), 60–76.

Mike, B. (2014). Footprints in the sand: Edgar Schein. *Organizational Dynamics, 43*, 321–328.

Quick, J. C., & Gavin, J. H. (2000). The next frontier: Edgar Schein on organizational therapy. *Academy of Management Review, 14*(1), 31–48.

Sashkin, M. (1979). Interview. *Group & Organization Studies, 4*(4), 400–417.

Schein, E. H. (1961). Management development as a process of influence. *Industrial Management Review, 2*, 55–77.

Schein, E. H. (1965). *Organizational psychology* (1st ed.). Englewood Cliffs: Prentice-Hall.

Schein, E. H. (1969). *Process consultation: Its role in organization development*. Reading: Addison-Wesley.

Schein, E. H. (1971). The individual, the organization and the career: A conceptual scheme. *The Journal of Applied Behavioral Science, 7*(4), 401–426.

Schein, E. H. (1978). *Career dynamics: Matching individual and organizational needs*. Reading: Addison-Wesley.

Schein, E. H. (1979). Personal change through interpersonal relationships. In W. Bennis, J. Van Maanen, E. H. Schein, & F. I. Steele (Eds.), *Essays in interpersonal dynamics* (pp. 129–162). Homewood: Dorsey Press.

Schein, E. H. (1980). *Organizational psychology* (3rd ed.). Englewood Cliffs: Prentice-Hall.

Schein, E. H. (1987a). *Process consultation vol 1: Its role in organization development*. Reading: Addison-Wesley.

Schein, E. H. (1987b). *The clinical perspective in field work*. Newbury Park: Sage.

Schein, E. H. (Ed.). (1987c). *The art of managing human resources*. New York: Oxford University Press.

Schein, E. H. (1988). *Process consultation vol 2: Lessons for managers and consultants*. Reading: Addison-Wesley.

Schein, E. H. (1989/2010). Organization development: Science, technology or philosophy? MIT *Sloan School of Management working paper*, # 3065-89-BPS. [Reproduced In: D. Coghlan & A. B. (Rami) Shani (2010). *Fundamentals of organization development,* (Vol. 1, pp. 91–100). London: Sage].

Schein, E. H. (1993). The academic as artist: Personal and professional roots. In A. Bedeian (Ed.), *Management laureates: A collection of autobiographical essays* (Vol. 3, pp. 31–62). Greenwich: JAI Press.

Schein, E. H. (1995). *Career survival: Strategic job and role planning*. San Diego: Pfeiffer.

Schein, E. H. (1996). *Strategic pragmatism: The culture of Singapore's economic development board*. Cambridge, MA: MIT Press.

Schein, E. H. (1999). *Process consultation revisited: Building the helping relationship*. Reading: Addison-Wesley.

Schein, E. H. (2003). *DEC is dead. Long live DEC*. San Francisco: Berrett-Kohler.

Schein, E. H. (2006). From brainwashing to organizational therapy: A conceptual and empirical journey in search of 'systemic' health and a general model of change dynamics. A drama in five acts. *Organization Studies, 27*(2), 287–301.

Schein, E. H. (2008). Clinical inquiry/research. In P. Reason & H. Bradbury (Eds.), *The Sage handbook of action research* (2nd ed., pp. 266–279). London: Sage.

Schein, E. H. (2009a). *Helping*. San Francisco: Berrett-Koehler.

Schein, E. H. (2009b). Reactions, reflections, rejoinders and a challenge. *The Journal of Applied Behavioral Science, 45*(1), 141–158.

Schein, E. H., & Van Maanen, J. (2013). *Career anchors: The changing nature of careers* (4th ed.). New York: Wiley.

Schein, E. H. (2013a). *Humble inquiry: The gentle art of asking instead of telling*. San Francisco: Berrett-Koehler.

Schein, E. H. (2013b). Notes toward a model of organizational therapy. In L. Vansina (Ed.), *Humanness in organizations* (pp. 91–100). London: Karnac.

Schein, E. H. (2015). Organizational psychology then and now: Some observations. *Annual Review of Organizational Psychology and Organizational Behavior, 2*, 1–19.
Schein, E. H. (2016a). *Humble consulting: How to provide real help faster*. San Francisco: Berrett-Koehler.
Schein, E. H. (2016b). *Becoming American*. Bloomington: iUniverse.
Schein, E. H. (2017). *Organizational culture and leadership* (5th ed.). San Francisco: Jossey-Bass.
Schein, E. H., & Bennis, W. (1965). *Personal and organizational change through group methods*. New York: Wiley.
Schein, E. H., Schneier, I., & Barker, C. (1961). *Coercive persuasion*. New York: Norton.
Schein, E. H., Ogawa, J., & Bond, J. S. (2010). *Organizational therapy: Multiple perspectives*. Andover: Alternative Views Publishing.
Toulmin, S. (1990). *Cosmopolis: The hidden agenda of modernity*. Chicago: University of Chicago Press.
Werr, A., & Greiner, L. (2008). Collaboration and the production of management knowledge in research, consulting and management practice. In A. B. Shani, S. A. Mohrman, W. A. Pasmore, B. Stymne, & N. Adler (Eds.), *Handbook of collaborative management research* (pp. 93–117). Thousand Oaks: Sage.

Further Reading

Schein, E. H. (2006). From brainwashing to organizational therapy: A conceptual and empirical journey in search of 'systemic' health and a general model of change dynamics. A drama in five acts. *Organization Studies, 27*(2), 287–301.
Schein, E. H. (2008). Clinical inquiry/research. In P. Reason & H. Bradbury (Eds.), *The Sage handbook of action research* (2nd ed., pp. 266–279). London: Sage.
Schein, E. H. (2013). *Humble inquiry: The gentle art of asking instead of telling*. San Francisco: Berrett-Koehler.
Schein, E. H. (2016). *Humble consulting: How to provide real help faster*. San Francisco: Berrett-Koehler.
Schein, E. H. (2017). *Organizational culture and leadership* (5th ed.). San Francisco: Jossey-Bass.

Learning and Change in the Work of Donald Schön: Reflection on Theory and Theory on Reflection

68

Magnus Ramage

Abstract

Donald Schön was a deeply original thinker working on change, education, design, and learning. He is perhaps best known for his work on the reflective practitioner, in which he formulated a new epistemology of practice founded on knowing-in-action and reflection-in-action, a theory which has had considerable impact. He also made huge contributions to the field of organizational learning, working with Chris Argyris on theories in action and on single/double loop learning. Underlying all these contributions was a theory of change grounded in Dewey's theory of inquiry and deeply concerned with how institutions and professionals deal with a world beyond the stable state. An educator as well as a theorist and practitioner, Schön was highly interested in how professionals can be taught in ways that reflect the reality in which they work rather than the traditional forms of technical rationality. This chapter examines Schön's key contributions, the influence of philosophy and music upon his work, and the many ways his work has been used.

Keywords

Professionalism • Epistemology • Reflective practice • Stable state • Change • Organizational learning

Contents

M. Ramage (✉)
School of Computing and Communications, The Open University, Milton Keynes, UK
e-mail: magnus.ramage@open.ac.uk

D.B. Szabla et al. (eds.), *The Palgrave Handbook of Organizational Change Thinkers*,
DOI 10.1007/978-3-319-52878-6_57

Introduction

Donald Alan Schön (1930–1997) was an extraordinarily original thinker, working at the boundary between the theory and practice of change, design, and education, and constantly pushing those boundaries. He is perhaps now most widely read as the originator of the concept of the "reflective practitioner," a concept that he originated in urban planning and design but has been extremely influential in education, management, social work, law, and many other fields. Indeed, the concept of reflective practice is now so well known that it risks eclipsing Schön's other conclusions; yet it sits within a set of other ideas that are just as important and influential.

Just a few of those other contributions included: his work on change and the idea of the stable state; the concept of learning systems; his development with Chris Argyris of the concepts of organizational learning, and of Model I and Model II change; his work on generative metaphor; and his work with Martin Rein on frame reflection.

Underlying all this work was a fascination with the epistemology of practice: of how professionals learn and make sense of the world, and how they might do it better. One of Schön's long-time collaborators, scholar of music and education Jeanne Bamberger, wrote in a reflective piece after his death of the notes she had made over 23 years of conversations with him:

> And running through all of these was a continuing search which I can now see as one way of grappling with that "persistent image". If one must give up, go beyond the stable state, one must also ask: How do we learn anything really new? How do we come to see in a new way? (Bamberger 2000, p. 10)

If those sound like theoretical concerns, for Schön they were deeply practical, and it was his life's work to show their practicality to others. In the process he shaped more than one field of practice as well as theory in very profound ways.

Influences and Motivations: Philosophy, Practice, and Music

Given his influence on concepts of practice, it is appropriate that Donald Schön blended both theory and practice throughout his working life, combining academic rigor and practical grounding. He began his academic life with a strong philosophical training, studying that field at Yale, the Sorbonne, and Harvard. Indeed Waks (2001, p. 37) refers to him as a "displaced philosopher" and observes that "philosophy was his first professional tongue."

A major philosophical influence upon all his later work was the theory of inquiry of John Dewey, the American pragmatist theorist of education. In a late paper, Schön heralded Dewey's theory of inquiry as a revolt against "dualisms of thought and action, research and practice, science and common the academy and everyday life" (Schön 1992, p. 121). This focus on an epistemology which breaks through dichotomies between theory and practice was crucial to everything he would later do.

Dewey's writings are quoted throughout Schön's work, and he stated quite explicitly that he wrote his doctoral thesis in 1955 based on Dewey (1938), and 30 years later reworked its ideas "now on the basis of empirical studies professional practice that would have been out of order in the Harvard philosophy department of the mid-1950s ... [to] make my own version of Dewey's theory of inquiry, taking 'reflective practice' as my version of Dewey's 'reflective thought'" (Schön 1992, p. 123). Those reworked ideas formed the basis for *The Reflective Practitioner* (Schön 1983).

Although Dewey was important throughout Schön's life, other philosophers also had a considerable influence on his thinking. He wrote himself (Schön 1992) that his early training was in logical empiricism (the Anglo-American analytic tradition, also known as logical positivism), but he largely moved beyond this approach in most of his work, and took on ideas from broader philosophical schools. In particular he was later influenced by the theory of tacit knowledge of Michael Polanyi, and as we shall later see by the ancient Greek philosopher of change Heraclitus – his second book (Schön 1967) was subtitled *The New Heraclitus*, and it could be considered a good description of Schön himself.

The combination of research and practice served Schön well throughout his life. Following his PhD (and a short time in the army), he spent 15 years in professional practice: first as a product design consultant at Arthur D. Little, then working in government for the National Bureau of Standards, and finally as the director of the Organization for Social & Technical Innovation (OSTI). Three of his major books were written while working in practice. Indeed, while working at OSTI he was invited to be the youngest person ever to give the British Broadcasting Corporation's prestigious annual lecture series, the Reith Lectures for 1970, subsequently published as his book *Beyond the Stable State* (Schön 1971).

When he returned to academia in 1972, as a professor of Urban Studies and Education at the Massachusetts Institute of Technology (MIT), he nonetheless retained close links with practice, and his later books are founded on a conversation between ideas and practice. He continued to be based at MIT for the rest of his life. It was while working at MIT that he developed some of the collaborations briefly mentioned above – with Jeanne Bamberger and Martin Rein, but most especially with Chris Argyris (based at nearby Harvard), with whom he developed so many important ideas.

Argyris brought a number of influences of his own that would prove to be important to their collaboration, notably his strong allegiance to the work of Kurt Lewin, the founder of the field of organizational development. Through his work with Argyris, Schön would also become influenced by some of the lessons of cybernetics, notably the work of Ross Ashby and Gregory Bateson, two profoundly original thinkers on learning whose work fed directly into the theory of organizational learning.

A further profound influence on his work came through his love of music. Schön was deeply musical, as a player of the clarinet and piano, and as a composer. While studying philosophy at the Sorbonne, he was equally engaged in studying the clarinet at the Conservatoire de Paris, and he practiced and played the clarinet on an almost daily basis for the rest of his life. Music for Schön was more than a hobby – it had a deep influence upon the way he thought and wrote, as Richmond argued: "it was perhaps the structure of musical composition that inspired the profound harmony of his written output . . . the unifying theme of all his oeuvres was a finale that left those he had so powerfully engaged refreshed and with hope for the future" (Richmond et al. 1998, p. 3).

Indeed, Schön's musical experience formed the basis for one of his most vivid description for perhaps his most celebrated concept, that of "reflection-in-action":

> When good jazz musicians improvise together, they similarly display reflection-in-action smoothly integrated into ongoing performance. Listening to one another, listening to themselves, they "feel" where the music is going and adjust their playing accordingly. A figure announced by one performer will be taken up by another, elaborated, turned into a new melody. Each player makes on-line inventions and responds to surprises triggered by the inventions of the other players. But the collective process of musical invention is organized around an underlying structure. There is a common schema of meter, melody, and harmonic development that gives the piece a predictable order. In addition, each player has at the ready a repertoire of musical figures around which he can weave variations as the opportunity arises. Improvisation consists in varying, combining, and recombining a set of figures within a schema that gives coherence to the whole piece. As the musicians feel the directions in which the music is developing, they make new sense of it. They reflect-in-action on the music they are collectively making – though not, of course, in the medium of words. (Schön 1987, p. 30)

Schön often compared himself to a giraffe – an obituary called him "long-necked, graceful, curious, aloof" (Warsh 1997) – but from his height he was able to look over a wide range of different areas of life. The same obituarist described him as "interested in anything and everything: the design of a washing machine agitator; the pension system in Germany; the computer wiring-up of MIT; a program for homelessness in Massachusetts; the process by which corporations present themselves through the use of space" (Warsh 1997). That image of a giraffe was taken up by his wife, the celebrated sculptor Nancy Schön, as a posthumous tribute: she has made several sculptures under the name of "the reflective giraffe."

Although seen as somewhat aloof in professional life, he was a mentor to a large number of students as well as practitioners: one former student described him as "tough but flexible, blunt yet understanding, he challenged us to do our best work" (Fischler, in Richmond et al. 1998, p. 8).

In his personal life he was anything but aloof. He was deeply devoted to his family – with his wife Nancy he had four children and several grandchildren. At the time of his death, he was preparing one of his grandsons for his bar mitzvah ceremony (Schön was Jewish), and building a puppet theatre for his grandchildren, "who he taught the essence of reflection by having them critically conceive a theory of how a puppet theatre ought to work" (Richmond et al. 1998, p. 3).

Music and family came together at the end of his life. Sanyal (in Richmond et al. 1998, p. 7), drawing on accounts by Don's son Andrew, writes that

> it was a fitting farewell for his family to stand surrounding his bed holding hands and singing rounds of songs . . . as Don's eyes closed for the last time, the family members lowered their

voices in sorrow only to be urged by Don who raised his right palm to request them to continue singing so he could listen to his favourite Brahms as he gently embraced death.

It was this combination of influences and motivations – of Deweyan philosophy, professional practice, deep curiosity, music, and concern for the world – which led Donald Schön towards the profound contributions that he made in such a variety of different fields.

Key Contributions: Change, Learning, and Reflection in Individuals and Organizations

Schön's first lasting contribution (or perhaps we might better say, set of contributions) centered around models of change in organizations, society, and technology. He published this work in two books, *Technology and Change: The New Heraclitus* (Schön 1967) and *Beyond the Stable State* (Schön 1971). Although the first of these was published 50 years ago, it remains very fresh and relevant to today's concerns. Schön contrasts the approach to two understandings of reality from two classical philosophers, Parmenides and Heraclitus – the first grounded in the permanence of stability, the second in the permanence of change.

In the view of Parmenides, as Schön (1967, p. xi) puts it, "stability was the only reality; being was continuous, changeless, one; change, in the form of creation or passing away, was inherently contradictory and therefore illusory." Organizations and society behave, argued Schön, as if Parmenides was correct: "we conceive of our institutions – nations, religions, business organizations – as enduring" (ibid., p. xii).

This conception of stability is summarized in Schön's concept of the **stable state** – the idea that our lives, our institutions, and our societies have fundamentally unchanging elements, values, and theories (an idea first introduced in Schön 1967, but developed at greater length in Schön 1971). As Schön wrote, "belief in the stable state is belief in the unchangeability, the constancy of certain central aspects of our lives, or belief that we can obtain such a constancy" (1971, p. 9). This kind of belief is attractive to many people and it is a guard against many forms of uncertainty. The stable state behaves homeostatically, as Schön identified – it self-regulates to preserve its form.

In particular, organizations are frequently dependent on the concept of the stable state. They tend to act as if they will continue to exist in their current form, with their current ownership and management, indefinitely. This is clearly false – to take just one counter-example, if we consider the Fortune 500 companies from 1970 and look at their status in 1983, one third had been merged or taken over with other companies, or split in some form (De Geus 1997, p. 51).

Moreover, organizations act according to Schön's principle of dynamic conservatism, an active and elastic approach to remain in the same form, which Schön (1971) described as "a tendency to fight to remain the same" (p. 32). Dynamic conservatism is not wholly negative – it is the process "through which social systems keep from flying apart at the seams ... our systems need to maintain their identity, and their ability to support the self-identity of those who belong to them, but they must at the same time be capable of transforming themselves" (Schön 1971, p. 60).

Notwithstanding the widespread nature of this belief in, and deliberate action to reinforce, the stable state, Schön regarded it as an insufficient description of the nature of organizations and society. Rather than siding with Parmenides in his view of change, he supported the view of Heraclitus, the Greek philosopher of constant change who famously argued that "one can never step in the same river twice" (strictly speaking, a later paraphrase of his words). In Heraclitus' view, stability is only achieved in the river through the rapidity of change in the flowing of the water.

In a similar way, Schön (1971) argued that "throughout our society we are experiencing the actual or threatened dissolution of stable organizations and institutions, anchors for personal identity and systems of values . . . the stable state itself is becoming less real" (p. 15). It affects a wide variety of institutions – he mentioned governments, labor movements, churches, and universities as four types of institutions which are radically affected by a loss of stability. This loss of the stable state, Schön argued, came partly from technological change and partly from social factors – exponential growth in technology had reached the point where it had become pervasive in all parts of the world, and changing at a speed that made it hard to ignore. (As a side note: in today's society we equate "technology" and "technological change" with computers and communications; Schön was talking about a wide range of technologies, and the widespread importance of the digital computer was only beginning in 1967.)

Schön identified three typical "anti-responses" to the loss of the stable state, each in turn essential attempts to refuse to recognize it: an attempt to *return* to the previous stable state, as best as possible; a *revolt* which is apparently against the past state, but in such a way that the past is enabled surreptitiously to return; and a state of *mindlessness*, which seeks to escape from the reality of change through drugs, violence, or other techniques. He saw each of these as unconstructive, as failures "to confront what might be like to live without the stable state" (Schön 1971, p. 29).

Instead, he argued that:

> The loss of the stable state means that our society and all of its institutions are in continuing processes of transformation. We cannot expect new stable states that will endure even for our own lifetimes.
>
> We must learn to understand, guide, influence, and manage these transformations. We must make the capacity for undertaking them integral to ourselves and to our institutions.
>
> We must, in other words, become adept at learning. We must become able not only to transform our institutions, in response to change situations and requirements; we must invent and develop institutions which are "learning systems", that is to say, systems capable of bringing about their own continuing transformation. (Schön 1971, p. 30)

This concept of a **learning system**, then, was Schön's key response to the loss of the stable state, to widespread change. A learning system needed to be heavily decentralized both in terms of geography (enabled by new communications) and in terms of decision-making (so that its leadership would be ad hoc and fluid rather than fixed and hierarchical). He argued that both businesses and governments had the potential to be take on the character of learning systems, but that he most clearly saw them occurring in nascent form through two very different institutions – the newly prominent business consultancy firms, and the youth movement that occurred in the United States during the late 1960s. Both forms of institutions had proved themselves to be decentralized, with shifting leadership, and both to be effective at learning and adaption.

Schön discusses the behavior of a learning system that is working well, in his concept of governments as learning systems, although the lessons apply just as well to other forms of organization: "The opportunity for learning is primarily in discovered systems at the periphery, not in the nexus of official policies at the centre. ... central [government] comes to function as facilitator of society's learning, rather than as society's trainer" (Schön 1971, p. 177). This concept would directly feed into his later work on organizational learning, but in itself can already be seen as the template for the decentralized governance that is so frequently seen as important in contemporary organizations.

In Schön's next key work (working with Chris Argyris), he developed the concept of **theories of action**, which they outlined in their first joint book (Argyris and Schön 1974), where they observe that "theories constructed to explain, predict, or control human behaviour are in many ways like other kinds of theories. But insofar as they are about human action – that is, about human behaviour that is correctable and subject to deliberation – they have special features" (p. 5). The concept of theories of action appears to build upon Schön's earlier work on metaphors and Dewey's theory of inquiry, although neither is directly cited in the book.

They make a crucial distinction between espoused theory, "the theory of action to which [someone] gives allegiance, and which, on request, he communicates to others" (p. 7) and theory-in-use, "the theory that actually governs his actions ... which may or may not be compatible with his espoused theory." This distinction between espoused theory and theory-in-use is crucial in their joint work – much of Argyris and Schön (1974) is concerned with analyzing the nature of theories-in-use, which they note are highly difficult to express in explicit models or concrete statements.

They observe that in practice, two basic forms of theories-in-use are found, which they term Model I and Model II. The first of these, Model I, is based on the following assumptions: "a win/lose world, other people behave according to the assumptions of Model I, rational behaviour is most effective, public testing of assumptions is intolerably risky" (Argyris and Schön 1974, pp. 79–80); they contend that this is the commonest model in practice, despite being significantly dysfunctional. The second form, Model II, is based on the goals of: "maximize valid information; maximize free and informed choice; maximize internal commitment to decisions made" (ibid., pp. 87–89). They also discuss ways of enabling individuals to transition from Model I to Model II, and the implications of this theory for professional education.

Building on the idea of theories of action, which has a largely individual focus, Argyris and Schön moved on to look at the concept of **organizational learning**. Their books on this subject (Argyris and Schön 1978, 1996) were among the first to consider the topic, which has later become extremely important. Their starting point is to ask what it means for an organization to learn: "it is clear that organizational learning is not the same as individual learning, even when the individuals who learn are members of the organization" (Argyris and Schön 1978, p. 9). Their answer drew heavily on the earlier idea of theory-in-use. They argue that "organizational learning occurs when individuals, acting from their images and maps, detect a match or mismatch of outcome to expectation which confirms or disconfirms organizational theory-in-use" (ibid., p. 19).

There is a strongly cybernetic flavor to this approach – it is deeply founded on feedback loops, the central concept both of cybernetics (Wiener 1948) and of the related field of system dynamics (Forrester 1961), much of this work having been carried out at MIT where Schön was based. Argyris and Schön drew even more explicitly on cybernetics in their use of the concept of single-loop and double-loop learning, which is often taken to be original to Argyris and Schön but which they attribute to the early cybernetician Ross Ashby (1960).

They define single-loop learning as occurring when "members of the organization respond to changes in the internal and external environments of the organization by detecting errors which they then correct so as to maintain the central features of organizational theory-in-use" (Argyris and Schön 1978, p. 18). This kind of learning is sufficient if the parameters for judging which errors to detect and correct are clear and constant. Circumstances may arise when those parameters are seen to be insufficient, and in that case double-loop learning is occurring: "a double feedback loop [which] connects the detection of error not only to strategies and assumptions for effective performance but to the very norms which define effective performance" (ibid., p. 22). The distinction between this single-loop and double-loop learning, and Gregory Bateson's theory of proto-learning and deutero-learning (which he originated in 1942 – see Bateson 1972), is quite a fine one, but Argyris and Schön place double-loop learning somewhere between proto- and deutero-learning.

Argyris and Schön are modest in the level of their contribution to this work. They do not claim to have originated the concept of organizational learning, and their 1978 book contains an appendix entitled "A Review of the Literature of Organizational Learning," based on six theories of organizational learning (organization as group, agent, structure, system, culture, and politics). This modesty notwithstanding, their joint work on organizational learning hugely advanced the field, putting it on a much sounder intellectual basis, and it is to Argyris and Schön (1978) that the huge majority of organizational learning researchers look as the basis for their work. In particular, Senge's (1990) concept of a learning organization rests heavily on Argyris and Schön's ideas.

Last (in terms of the time it was produced) we come to the contribution for which Schön may be best remembered: the concept of the **reflective practitioner**. In this work (Schön 1983, 1987) he drew together many of his earlier concerns, taking them forward in a new direction. His starting point is a "crisis of confidence in professional knowledge" (Schön 1983, p. 3), arising from a mismatch between the needs of professionals and the skills gained through traditional education processes. These traditional forms of professional education are dominated by a teaching model that Schön terms "technical rationality," which stresses "instrumental problem solving made rigorous by the application of scientific theory and technique" (Schön 1983, p. 21).

This starting point resembles some of the critique of society's response to change he presented in *Beyond the Stable State*. In a vivid passage, he writes of the disparity between the requirements of practice and the approaches that are possible under technical rationality:

> In the varied topography of professional practice, there is a high, hard ground where practitioners can make effective use of research-based theory and technique, and there is a swampy lowland where situations are confusing "messes" incapable of technical solution. The difficulty is that the problems of the high ground, however great their technical interest, are often relatively unimportant to clients or to the larger society, while in the swamp are the problems of greatest human concern. (Schön 1983, p. 42)

The reason for this disparity in professional education, which makes it unsuitable for work within this swamp, arises from insecurity. In the establishment of a series of applied professional schools, such as social work, education, architecture, and urban planning, there was a widespread sense that these essentially applied fields needed to become "proper" academic disciplines with grounding to resemble established professions such as medicine and law. The result, Schön argued, was a form of teaching which stressed rigor and scientific foundations, rather than the direct needs of professional practice – making them well-grounded academically but poorly grounded in practice.

Schön worked to build "an inquiry into the epistemology of practice ... based on a close examination of what some practitioners – architects, psychotherapists, engineers, planners, and managers – actually do" (Schön 1983, p. viii). Working with similar techniques to his earlier examination of metaphors in use (Schön 1963) and on the nature of theories in action (Argyris and Schön 1974), and again drawing on Dewey's work, he studied in depth the behavior of professionals as they operate.

The two key ideas in this epistemology of practice as Schön presents it are knowing-in-action and reflection-in-action. The first is a way of understanding how we actually embody and work with knowledge: "when we go about the spontaneous, intuitive performance of the actions of everyday life, we show ourselves to be knowledgeable in a special way ... our knowing is ordinarily tacit, implicit in our patterns of action and in our feel for the stuff with which we are dealing. It seems right to say that our knowing is *in* our action" (Schön 1983, p. 49).

Schön moves on to consider the ways that we can both "think about doing [and] that we can thinking about doing something while doing it" (ibid., p. 54). It is this process, where professionals improvise in the moment based on their past experience, that he terms reflection-in-action. One who reflects-in-action "is not dependent on the categories of established theory and technique, but constructs a new theory of the unique case" (ibid., p. 68).

Schön frequently used jazz musicians (given his own musical interests) as an example of reflection-in-action, and I have earlier quoted him at some length writing on this form of reflection. This way of changing practice based on based experience is crucial to his epistemology. As he wrote: "when a practitioner makes sense of a situation he perceives to be unique, he sees it as something already present in his repertoire. . . . The familiar situation functions as a precedent, or a metaphor, or. . . an exemplar for the unfamiliar one" (Schön 1983, p. 138).

Examples such as the jazz musicians serve as a useful corrective to a misunderstanding that has arisen around Schön's work: that he is encouraging a different sort of reflection, the quiet kind that might occur at the end of the day through a journal or in conversation with a mentor or close friend. This too is an important part of reflective practice – Schön refers to it as reflection-*on*-action – but it is less critical to his vision of the epistemology of practice.

The concept of reflection-in-action was thus critical to Schön's alternative model of professional education: it needed to be one that drew upon the real nature of professional knowledge, action, and reflection. In a striking observation, Schön argued that a focus on reflective practice could lead to a "demystification of professional expertise . . . to recognize that the scope of technical expertise is limited by situations of uncertainty, instability, uniqueness and conflict . . . when research-based theories and techniques are inapplicable, the professional cannot legitimately claim to be expert, but only to be especially well prepared to reflect-in-action" (Schön 1983, p. 345).

Ultimately, Schön's vision of the reflective practitioner, as an expert in practice as much as in theory, drew upon all of his earlier insights in philosophy, change, and learning, and presented a radical alternative view to that of the dispassionate expert. It is a vision that remains radical and important today.

New Insights: One Person, Many Influences

Without a doubt, Schön's influence upon academic and professional practice has been huge. However, it is striking that there seem to be several Donald Schöns who have influenced different communities. There is Schön the change theorist, with his potent understanding of the stable state and what lies beyond it. There is Schön the organizational theorist (here always cited as the second part of a pair with Argyris), founder of organizational learning and concepts of single-loop and double-loop learning. There is Schön the theorist of professional practice, with his concept of knowing-in-action, and the related (but not identical) Schön the theorist of education, champion of reflection-in-action. Lastly there is Schön the design theorist, influential originally within planning but increasingly taken up into the growing importance of design thinking.

All of these Schöns are overlapping of course – how could they not be when they were a single person? The many authors who cite and draw upon his work will often focus on one part but acknowledge the rest. But there is a sense, in authors drawing on his work, that they most clearly care about one of these Schöns. This is surprising in the sense that he himself saw his work as coherent, with a strong narrative thread running through it; although he wrote a lot, and contributed a large number of new ideas, he did so carefully and clearly. This is in contrast to an author such as the anthropologist and cybernetician Gregory Bateson (1972), who has also had an influence upon many disciplines – but in his case that was partly because he operated in several different disciplinary spaces during his lifetime, and only in later life came to see his work as a unified whole.

In my own experience, I encountered two Schöns first, then a third, and lately have become captivated by a fourth. While working on my doctorate in the evaluation of information systems (Ramage 1999), I read widely and worked with practitioners of organizational learning, as I took a view of evaluation as a learning process. It was clear in this reading that Argyris and Schön had a special place in the formation of organizational learning as a concept, and I found their work useful as a starting point. Running alongside this approach, I had further encounters with Schön as he was gradually taken up in the area of human-computer interaction (an important aspect of information systems), as a theorist of design – he was interviewed in late life for a book on the importance of design in the software process, at a time when design was just beginning to be a key concept in a range of fields (Schön and Bennett 1996).

When I moved from research to teaching, taking up a post at The Open University (the UK's largest university and a pioneer in distance learning) I came to know a third Schön: the reflective educator. Colleagues across the university, especially in professional areas, drew heavily on Schön's concepts of reflection. His ideas were taught in many fields, and the idea of reflection-in-action was central to the pedagogic model of many different areas. At one time at the Open University (OU), it was hard to find a teaching program that did not have some reference to Schön's work, frequently coupled to the learning cycle of David Kolb (1984). This was true in vocational fields where Schön has been taken up elsewhere, such as social work, nursing, teacher education, and management (all important areas for the OU). But it was also very much the case in the Faculty of Technology which for 35 years developed sociotechnical and reflective courses on highly technical subjects (until two successive internal mergers weakened that culture). Some of the this was a probably a misuse of Schön's ideas – on occasions reflection was presented as an after-thought within assessment activities, referred to scathingly by students as "the R word" – but much of it gave a richness to distance education of professionals that can sometimes be lacking.

In my own work I encountered a fourth Schön more recently: the Schön of *Beyond the Stable State*. I spent several years writing an overview of the life and work of 30 key systems thinkers (Ramage and Shipp 2009), including Donald Schön, and it was the Schön who wrote about widespread systemic change that struck me very much in producing that work. Re-reading Schön's many works in preparing this chapter, it is that Schön that still strikes me today. A statement such as the one quoted above that "the loss of the stable state means that our society and all of its institutions are in continuing processes of transformation" (Schön 1971, p. 30) was highly innovative in 1970 when he first gave his Reith Lectures. Today, in a period of huge political, economic, and social turmoil, it remains just as relevant. I think it is this Schön that could perhaps better be rediscovered than any of the other Schöns.

Two remaining images from Schön's writing have been important to me as an educator and scholar, and to my colleagues in the Systems group at the Open

University. Both have appeared above in this chapter. This first is the image of reflection-in-action as jazz: anyone who has sat in a jazz concert and seen the shift from one instrument to another, the spontaneity of solo works, will find this familiar. The second is the idea of the swamp: the messy real world of practice, into which theorists need to tread with care; this is an image which has inspired a number of systems colleagues (e.g., Ison 2010) and which continues to challenge us today.

Legacies and Unfinished Business: Power and Public Policy

Schön's legacy has been huge, as I have already explored: in particular in professional education of all kinds (through the reflective practitioner), in design, and in organizational learning. So many authors have drawn upon his work, and he is extremely widely cited.

He is not without critique. A curious phenomenon is that which Fischler (2012, p. 322) describes as "the widespread diffusion but limited impact of Schön's ideas." Fischler is especially talking about Schön's impact within planning theory, where he had his academic home for 25 years, and where he is more respected than used. Nonetheless, the same could be said for a number of other fields where Schön's name, and the concept of the reflective practitioner, is widely cited but at quite a superficial level, where "very few represent an attempt to apply Schön's theory in novel ways, to test his propositions as hypotheses, to expand on his ideas, or otherwise to engage his work in a direct manner" (ibid.). There is a sense in reading some of those citing Schön that it is done because everybody cites Schön, but that the main concerns in the work are elsewhere.

One of the concerns that Fischler raises is that Schön's work takes (or is read as taking) a largely individual approach. The theories-in-action he presents are largely those of individuals; the reflective practitioners are individuals. Of course, he also has a theory of organizational learning, but this too does not have a high degree of engagement with power. There is a sense in some of Schön's work of a lack of context. Newman, for example, contrasts reflection-in-action with the critical educational work of Paolo Freire, arguing that: "Freire envisages praxis as a process with the potential of bringing about social, even revolutionary, change. Schön's reflection-in-action is also seen as capable of bringing about change in both the practitioner and the organisation, but it is not presented as a process that might challenge the society of which the practitioner and the organisation are parts" (Newman 1994, p. 90).

Schwartz (1987), in a book review of *The Reflective Practitioner* which also drew on earlier criticisms he had made of *Theory in Practice*, took a slightly different angle, arguing that: "on the whole it seems to me to offer a view of man and of human institutions that is naively optimistic in that it assumes that impediments to reflectivity are simply the result of bad habits and are easily corrected through a change in behaviour" (p. 616).

These issues of a lack of concern for power and social change in Schön's work are well described, although they can be defended in other ways. It is clear from writings such as *Beyond the Stable State* that he had a great concern for policy issues, and he returned to this quite explicitly in one of his last books, on the idea of institutional frames. He and Martin Rein, his coauthor and another long-time collaborator, argued there that: "policies are sometimes reframed in action, and their reframing sometimes results from the actors' reflection on frame conflicts that arise in the evolving, politically coloured process of policy design" (Schön and Rein 1994, p. viii). Moreover, his colleague Niraj Verma defended him from the charge of a lack of appreciation for power dynamics, arguing that "Don was deeply interested in issues of power – not the power of holding a gun over someone, but a subtle form of intellectual power that grips us and forces us to act in particular ways ... in its consequences it is as dangerous as more conventional forms of power" (Richmond et al. 1998, p. 9).

Perhaps the final statement to be made about Schön's legacy is that it is still a slightly unfinished one in terms of its effects. The ideas of reflection-in-action, of moving beyond the stable state, and his conceptions of design, in particular, are rich ones which need to be read and applied more carefully than hitherto; and with a particular eye to the issues of individualism, context, and power.

Donald Schön led a deep and reflective life, and taught us much about change, learning, and practice; there are many things we can still learn from his work today.

References

Argyris, C., & Schön, D. A. (1974). *Theory in practice: Increasing professional effectiveness*. San Francisco: Jossey-Bass.

Argyris, C., & Schön, D. A. (1978). *Organizational learning: A theory of action perspective*. Reading: Addison-Wesley.

Argyris, C., & Schön, D. A. (1996). *Organizational learning II: Theory, method, and practice*. Reading: Addison-Wesley.

Ashby, W. R. (1960). *Design for a brain: The origin of adaptive behaviour* (2nd ed.). London: Chapman & Hall.

Bamberger, J. (2000). Unanswered questions. *Cybernetics & Human Knowing, 7*, 9–16.

Bateson, G. (1972). *Steps to an ecology of mind*. Toronto: Chandler.

De Geus, A. (1997). The living company. *Harvard Business Review, 75*, 51–59.

Dewey, J. (1938). *Logic: The theory of inquiry*. New York: Henry Holt and Company.

Fischler, R. (2012). Reflective practice. In B. Sanyal, L. J. Vale, & C. D. Rosan (Eds.), *Planning ideas that matter: Livability, territoriality, governance, and reflective practice* (pp. 313–332). Cambridge, MA: MIT Press.

Forrester, J. W. (1961). *Industrial dynamics*. Cambridge, MA: MIT Press.

Ison, R. (2010). *Systems practice: How to act in a climate change world*. London: Springer.

Kolb, D. (1984). *Experiential learning: Experience as the source of learning and development*. Englewood Cliffs: Prentice-Hall.

Newman, D. (1994). *Defining the enemy: Adult education in social action*. Sydney: Stewart Victor Publishing. Retrieved from http://www.michaelnewman.biz/pdf/defining_the_enemy-COMP.pdf

Newman, S., & van der Waarde, K. (2015). Donald A. Schön: Bibliography. Retrieved from http://www.graphicdesign-research.com/Schon/bibliography.html

Ramage, M. (1999). *The learning way: Evaluating co-operative systems*. Unpublished Ph.D. thesis, Lancaster University.

Ramage, M., & Shipp, K. (2009). *Systems thinkers*. London: Springer.

Richmond, J., Sanyal, B., Rodwin, L., Fischler, R., & Verma, N. (1998). Donald Schön – A life of reflection. *Journal of Planning Literature, 13*, 3–10.
Schön, D. (1963). Displacements of Concepts. London: Tavistock Publications.
Schön, D. (1967). *Technology and change: The new Heraclitus*. Oxford: Pergamon.
Schön, D. (1971). *Beyond the stable state: Public and private learning in a changing society*. London: Temple Smith.
Schön, D. (1983). *The reflective practitioner: How professionals think in action*. New York: Basic Books.
Schön, D. (1987). *Educating the reflective practitioner: Toward a new design for teaching and learning in the professions*. San Francisco: Jossey-Bass.
Schön, D. A. (1992). The theory of inquiry: Dewey's legacy to education. *Curriculum Inquiry, 22*, 119–139.
Schön, D., & Bennett, J. (1996). Reflective conversation with materials: An interview with Donald Schön by John Bennett. In T. Winograd (Ed.), *Bringing design to software* (pp. 171–184). Reading: Addison-Wesley.
Schön, D., & Rein, M. (1994). *Frame reflection*. New York: Basic Books.
Schwartz, H. S. (1987). The reflective practitioner: How professionals think in action (book review). *Administrative Science Quarterly, 32*, 614–617.
Senge, P. M. (1990). *The fifth discipline: The art and practice of the learning organization*. New York: Doubleday.
Smith, M. K. (2001, 2011). Donald Schön: Learning, reflection and change. In *The encyclopedia of informal education*. Retrieved from www.infed.org/thinkers/et-schon.htm
Waks, L. J. (2001). Donald Schön's philosophy of design and design education. *International Journal of Technology and Design Education, 11*, 37–51.
Warsh, D. (1997, December 28). The giraffe. *The Boston Globe*, p. F1.
Wiener, N. (1948). *Cybernetics: Or control and communication in the animal and the machine*. Cambridge, MA: MIT Press.

Further Reading

Argyris, C., & Schön, D. A. (1996). *Organizational learning II: Theory, method, and practice*. Reading: Addison-Wesley.

Schön's writing was extremely clear and worth reading in its own right. Much of his key work was contained in books rather than articles, and is of a nature that the whole book needs to be read to gain full comprehension. The following works are of particular significance:

Schön, D. (1970). Change and industrial society. British Broadcasting Corporation Reith Lectures. Retrieved from http://www.bbc.co.uk/radio4/features/the-reith-lectures/transcripts/1970/
Schön, D. (1971). *Beyond the stable state: Public and private learning in a changing society*. London: Temple Smith.
Schön, D. (1983). *The reflective practitioner: How professionals think in action*. New York: Basic Books.

Works about Schön by others:

Bamberger, J. (2000). Unanswered questions. *Cybernetics & Human Knowing, 7*, 9–16.
Newman, S., & van der Waarde, K. (2015). Donald A. Schön: Bibliography. Retrieved from http://www.graphicdesign-research.com/Schon/bibliography.html
Smith, M. K. (2001/2011). Donald Schön: Learning, reflection and change. In *The encyclopedia of informal education*. Retrieved from www.infed.org/thinkers/et-schon.htm

Note that Schön's name is sometimes written as 'Schon' in library catalogues and bibliographies, which is incorrect but an easy mistake to make. It is sufficiently common that when searching for him online, it is best to look for both 'Schön' and 'Schon'.

69 Edith Whitfield Seashore's Contribution to the Field of Organization Development: Theory in Action

Barbara Benedict Bunker

Abstract
Edie Seashore was a protégé of Douglas McGregor and a pioneer in the small group dynamics training movement that emerged from the work of Kurt Lewin (founder of the field of social psychology) and developed by the National Training Institute (NTL) at its summer campus at Bethel, Maine. She led the movement that integrated NTL and became its first woman president. NTL also created the first OD training program for consultants. During her more than 60 years as an independent consultant, she founded the American University master's degree program in OD (with Morley Segal) and taught in many of the other OD graduate degree programs in the United States. She had a profound influence on the hundreds of OD consultants that she taught and trained. She believed that diversity and inclusion were central values in OD practice. She embodied this value in her work and life. Seashore wrote one of the earliest articles on gender in the workplace. As a gifted practitioner, she believed that taking action produced data that led to effective interventions. She emphasized the use of self as critical to effective practice. Her choice awareness matrix helped practitioners interact with clients effectively, learn from the situation, and take next steps. Her wonderful sense of humor and deep practitioner insight helped many OD consultants over many years.

Keywords
Action theory • Feedback • Reframing • Gender • Choice awareness matrix • Support systems • Diversity

---

B.B. Bunker (✉)
Department of Psychology, The University at Buffalo, Buffalo, NY, USA
e-mail: bbunker@buffalo.edu

D.B. Szabla et al. (eds.), *The Palgrave Handbook of Organizational Change Thinkers*,
DOI 10.1007/978-3-319-52878-6_23

Contents

Influences and Motivations: Carving Out Space for Women and Diversity in OD

Edith Whitfield Seashore graduated from Antioch College in 1950 with a Bachelor of Arts Degree in Sociology. Antioch was a "nontraditional" college with a work study program and deep commitments to participation in a democratic society. Both of Seashore's parents were lawyers, although her mother never practiced. Before she went to college, Seashore attended a progressive (Dewey) school, but was aware of her minority status as a Jew when she was ignored socially on some occasions. The Antioch students were active in college governance. During her junior year, she was part of the search committee for a new president. Douglas McGregor was selected. During her senior year, she was elected "community manager" (i.e., president of the student body), which meant that she spent most of her year running and influencing college affairs (she often remarked with a wide smile that her challenger for this office was Warren Bennis – and she won!). McGregor became Seashore's mentor. He took her to her first T-group experience in the college lab at Bethel, Maine, the summer home of the National Training Laboratory for Applied Behavioral Science (NTL). Seashore's college experiences and McGregor's ideas in particular (theory X and theory Y) had a profound influence on her values and worldview. She left college deeply committed to making a difference in this world.

During the 1950s, as research on small group processes blossomed, Seashore returned to Bethel every summer to co-train T-groups. At the same time, she lived and worked in New York City and earned a master's degree in social psychology at Columbia University. After Seashore co-trained at Bethel for 10 years, Jack Glidewell took her aside in 1960 and told her that she was just as good – or better than – the men who were NTL trainers and that she should not return to Bethel unless she was recognized as a full trainer. She took his advice, and by the next summer, she was thereafter recognized as an equal and increasingly as one of the most competent trainers. But sexism was everywhere in the 1960s. There were very few women on university faculties, and NTL was essentially a white male club of social science professors. Seashore became an important presence on the Bethel summer NTL campus. She worked with and absorbed the ideas and theories of virtually all of the early OD thinkers who were part of the Bethel summer community, including Ed Schein, Chris Argyris, Bob Tannenbaum, Lee Bradford, Ron Lippitt, Herb Shepard, Ken Benne, Dick Beckhard, Shel Davis, and John and Joyce Weir. Seashore and her husband Charlie spent their summers in Bethel during the 1960s, as Charlie was working for NTL. Seashore was a role model and a beacon of hope for other aspiring women in mostly male professions.

The 1960s brought sit-ins and protests about racial discrimination, the women's movement, and the Vietnam War. In group dynamics, the emphasis shifted from group process to encounter groups focusing on interpersonal feedback and individual development. The Organization Development Network began in an informal meeting in 1965 of industrial trainers in California. After a stint at the Ford Foundation, Seashore worked for Richard Beckhard Associates for several years, developing skills and experience dealing with business organizations and consulting to systems.

The 1960s was a time of upheaval and change, during which women took on challenges to change the culture of work. For example, NTL ran a "Presidents Labs" that was open only to chief executives. The men who came often brought their wives, so NTL offered a "wives group" experience for them. Initially, Seashore was allowed to train only the wives group, although she was then one of the most experienced and accomplished trainers at NTL. Finally, she broke through the barrier. Once she successfully trained a presidents group, the norms changed.

This was a period of time in which the few women working at Bethel met informally out of earshot to compare notes, support each other, and invent strategies to challenge the sexism that surrounded them. For example, Seashore, Billie Alban, and Barbara Bunker were the three women that NTL was willing to hire as competent trainers for T-group labs. In our informal conversations in the early 1970s, we three were able to make a list of approximately 20 women who – by NTL standards – were competent to lead T-groups. When the NTL staff would complain that there were not any competent women for them to hire, we presented our list, but nothing happened. We asked, "Why aren't there more women on staffs?" "We don't know any," they replied. "What about the list we gave you?" we asked. "What list?" they said. They lost at least three lists before the hiring practices actually changed to include more women.

Consciousness Raising and Empowering Women to Act

I got to know Seashore at Bethel in the late 1960s. We spoke about the women's movement, which was just taking off when we worked as part of several lab staffs. During this time, women often caucused in private to reflect on their experiences with male colleagues and figure out how to act to shift situations in which they were not listened to and were treated disrespectfully or unfairly. Even the Bethel culture was white male dominated and not particularly interested in changing. Seashore's propensity to work with situations through action is captured in this experience:

We were part of an eight-person lab staff meeting to plan our work the day before the participants arrived. We were brainstorming about where in the schedule to put a theory session, and a man proposed that we hold the session right after lunch. I commented that people generally have low energy after a meal and that maybe it would be a good idea to have an experiential activity then. No one responded, and the group continued to talk about ideas for the theory session. Then, about 10 min later, a guy named Bill said, "People are generally low energy after a meal and maybe it would be a good idea to have an experiential activity then." There was an immediate positive response from another man, and the whole group began to actively discuss which activity to use. I was stunned and shocked. When we took a break, I pulled Seashore aside and asked her if my suggestion was unclear, or what she saw happen. She said, "Barbara, they don't expect women to have good ideas, so they didn't hear what you said, but you were perfectly clear!" We then cooked up a plan to change the situation. We agreed that when either of us proposed something, if there was no group response, the other would say "That's a really interesting idea. Let's talk about it!" We didn't have to agree with the idea itself. We just needed to get it onto the floor for discussion. We discovered that this worked like a charm in many situations, without distracting or accusing the group and stopping the work process.

Over time, Seashore and I had this kind of conversation about many of the key issues that created problems for women entering the field of OD. We talked about our ideas at national OD meetings and finally wrote them up in an article that named the major issues: "Power, Collusion, Intimacy-Sexuality, Support: Breaking the Sex Role Stereotypes in Social and Organizational Settings (Bunker and Seashore 1976)." In this article, we described the behaviors that were part of the old world of sexism and the process we used to increase our own awareness. Our old responses were making it easy for sexism to continue! Then we described our process for becoming more aware and changing our behavior in situations where we experienced sexism. This piece circulated informally through many organizations in mimeographed and ditto format long before it was officially published. Women used it to reflect on and chart their own journey and as the basis for discussions with colleagues and clients, both male and female.

Seashore was a big presence in the field of group training and OD from the very beginning of her career in the 1950s. She was articulate about her views, but had great humor and warmth. She was always in action about the issues that stemmed from deeply held values. If a direct approach did not work, she figured out how to get what she wanted done in another way. She trained and influenced hundreds of people who entered the field of OD. In the 1970s, she was the consultant who worked on integrating several of the military academies that began accepting women. Her stories about her interventions there are the stuff of legends. Here is a brief version of the well-known story about her first meeting with the captain in charge of the integration of women into the United States Naval Academy. The captain (also known informally as "Boomer" to his men because of his loud voice) decided to interview Seashore after they found several other male consultants to be wrong for the task. Upon her arrival, Seashore was told that there would be very little time for the interview. She remembered McGregor's story about how consultants need to have one good idea to be successful with their clients. After the preliminaries, the captain described the situation. Women would arrive that summer for training and be part of the academy, which was then all male. "What should I do?" he asked. "You should have some women on the summer orientation staff," she shot back. He turned to his staff and said, "Get some women on our summer staff." "Yes, sir!" they said. Seashore was hired and worked for 8 years on many issues involving the real integration of women into the academy (Seashore 2006).

In the process of writing this article, I talked with many of Seashore's OD colleagues. These conversations have added to my thinking and to the information in this article. I am grateful for the help from Michael Broom, Katherine Farquhar, Darya Funches, Harvey Hornstein, Brenda Jones, Lennox Joseph, Judith Katz, Robert Marshak, Fred Miller, Beverly Patwell and Ruth Wagner. Becky May Seashore and Kimberly Seashore, Edie's daughters, read early drafts of this manuscript and generously shared memories and materials from their family history.

Key Contributions: Diversity, Inclusion, the Use of Self, and the Choice Awareness Matrix

Diversity and Inclusion Are an Essential Part of Organization Change and Development

The ferment about gender and race affected organizations in the 1970s. In response to what was happening, some organizations instituted training programs like assertiveness training for women and diversity training for Caucasians. Seashore saw these issues as fundamental to organization change, not as separate training programs. She had a core belief that only when all voices were heard and responded to could an organization really fulfill its potential. Her personal world had always included people of color and other minorities, and she believed that this was both right and valuable. These were deeply held values that she consistently enacted as an important part of her life. They can be seen in how she chose to use her time, the diversity of the people she worked with, and those whom she mentored.

This contribution to the field became very visible in 1975, when she and three other NTL members (Hal Kellner, Peter Vail, and Barbara Bunker) convinced the NTL board members to resign rather than declare bankruptcy and close. Those individuals were replaced with a new board that was half women, half men, half people of color, and half white. Seashore became the new president of NTL, and Elsie Cross, a woman of color, became the first chair of the new board. The "four horsepersons," as they were often called, did this by convincing 75 very competent trainers to donate 2 weeks of their time doing NTL labs so the organization could pay off its debts and transform itself in a new beginning. This included changing the old membership criteria to become much more inclusive. The invited new members became the core of the new organization, while others had to apply for membership. Membership intake was controlled by categories so that people were admitted in groups of four – one from each category. The $250,000 debt was paid off in 2 years. For people in the newly developing field of OD consulting, the fallout from these events was positive for some and very upsetting for others. But the message was very clear: diversity is an important part of our work in organization development and change.

The Civil Rights Act of 1964 caused organizations like AT&T to realize that they needed to address issues of diversity in their own organizations. Seashore, Cross, Kellner, and others worked within the organization to create awareness and change. One such change project was allowing women to "climb the poles." These had been "men-only" positions, but the female employees at AT&T wanted access to these jobs. The consultants worked with the whole system during this transition. Their early efforts became a model for working within the whole organization rather than just sending people off for diversity training.

Use of Self and the Choice Matrix

The expression "use of self" developed and was prominent in the training of T-group trainers in the 1950s and 1960s. It called for trainers to be aware of their own motivations and the impact of their behavior on others. This was a period in which psychoanalysis and psychotherapy were popular as part of professional training. For the participants, an important part of the T-group experience was becoming more aware of the impact of their own behavior on others. The group became a vehicle for collecting data about that impact, via a carefully defined process known as "feedback," a practical translation of the social psychological understanding of perception and action taking (Seashore et al. 1991). As the feedback process became popular and the word entered the general vocabulary, the basic steps and process often became distorted, as in "Let me give you a little feedback" – meaning "Let me tell you what I don't like about you!" This popular distortion of a carefully calibrated psychology-based process occurs too frequently. As a needed corrective, the Seashores' thinking refocused on what wanting to give someone *feedback* said about the giver's own internal state and perception. The impulse to give feedback provides data about what is going on inside. It needs to be attended to particularly by people in the helping professions.

Seashore's choice matrix (Patwell and Seashore 2006) is a 2-×-2 matrix that expands the 1960s' use of self-concept by focusing on a person's state of awareness as he or she takes action (Fig. 1). For a number of years, Seashore developed these ideas about the "conscious use of self" in her work with Michael Broom and their Triple Impact Consulting program. She expanded it to include the coaching relationship in her work with Beverley Patwell and their Canadian clients. The matrix contrasts automatic socially determined behavior with what today might be called "mindfulness," i.e., awareness of our thoughts, feelings, and motivations, as we prepare to act. This process can lead to personal growth and increased competence as a practitioner. It is also a formidable defense against the well-known tendency (especially in western countries) to blame the situation or anything but ourselves for the outcomes of our behavior.

Seashore's natural penchant toward action as a way to clarify and change situations led her to think about how to help developing OD practitioners not get

Choice Awareness Matrix

©Edie Seashore

AWARENESS	CHOICE ATTRIBUTED TO SELF	CHOICE ATTRIBUTED TO OTHERS
AWARE	ACCOUNTABLE Deliberate Intentional	BLAME
UNAWARE	AUTOMATIC Robotic Habitual	SOCIETAL INHERITANCE Adapt Assimilate

Fig. 1 Choice matrix

paralyzed in situations of ambiguity. As she mentored developing practitioners, she saw them getting stuck trying to translate theory into useful action. The choice matrix was an important conceptual first step in expanding the range of choices for action when a person could not see possibilities for action. Her own consulting style was based on action research theory. She understood that when you take action, a reaction provides information that can be the basis for your next action. Seashore engaged situations of uncertainty or ambiguity in this manner; she treated the reactions as data that informed her next move. You could say that she was the embodiment of action research. Her behavior was often intuitive and experimental. She believed that if you want to understand what is going on, you need to act and pay close attention to the reactions. For her, the key issue was not "the right intervention," but allowing the situation to speak so that she could learn from it and respond.

Briefly review her insights and how they affected both you and others – see sample chapters to learn how authors are developing this section.

New Insights: Theory in Action

Seashore's contribution was to help OD practitioners move past their sense of "stuckness," i.e., not being able to envision alternatives or invent new ideas or behaviors to change the current situation. She conceptualized this skill in her choice awareness matrix. She embodied this skill throughout her life in groups and with her clients. Her wonderfully funny stories about consulting and her life were another way that she made theory come to life for others.

Edie Seashore was a consummate practitioner in the tradition that Donald Schon describes in *The Reflective Practitioner* (1983). Schon talks about "practitioner knowledge" as intuitive and based in experience. It is the ability to be effective in action in particular situations. OD practitioners continually find themselves in complex situations with clients and groups where they need to act and the options are not always immediately apparent. Creating new options by taking action is critical to unfreezing the situation and promoting change. Seashore was a genius at this type of intervention. Her "rule of thumb" was to keep moving, to take some action, and to never get frozen in place. When you were able to do that, new options almost always appeared. The one thing she believed you should not do was to do nothing. For example, if a group participant got very angry and attacked her, as the leader she needed to engage that person, acknowledge and work with the anger, and see what happened next. The one thing that would create real trouble was to ignore that feeling or respond to it with anger.

Her "rule of thumb" was to keep moving, to take action in the face of any situation that is problematic or frustrating when it is not clear what to do. My personal example is our time in airports together at a time when we were both traveling frequently. She had an action strategy for dealing with delays or cancellations. The minute they were announced, she got on her phone making tentative alternative arrangements while most others grumbled and waited passively to see what would happen next. She did not assume that things would work out or that the airline would take care of her. She took action to assure that she had other options. I have used her strategy for years with great results.

Some of her contributions to the field of OD are in the many practitioners she trained in master's degree programs or in the Triple Impact Consulting program for experienced practitioners which she created with Michael Broom. In each of these programs, people practiced dealing with complex organizational situations and honed their intervention skills. "Don't just stand there, do something!" is an essential skill for an OD practitioner in interpersonal, group, and organizational settings, but not one that can be learned from reading. Her hundreds of students and colleagues saw her taking effective action in all kinds of difficult situations and carry that rule of thumb with them in their own practice.

Seashore's Legacy: Influencing the Training of OD Practitioners

We generally think about important ideas in currency as the product of the well-published academics and practitioners in the field of OD. Seashore had a huge impact on how practitioners think and do their work by a different route. In the late 1970s, when she was president of the NTL Institute, she began to plan for a master's degree program in OD that would have NTL partnering with a major university. Morley Segal was teaching at American University in Washington, DC, and was an NTL member. Seashore and Segal developed the Master of Science in Organizational Development (MSOD) at American University as a joint program between the university and NTL. The program – which began in 1980 and is now training its 71st cohort – included NTL lab experiences and courses at the university. It has graduated at least 1,700 students with master's degrees in OD. The *use of self* concept is deeply embedded in the program and distinguishes it from other MSOD programs. Seashore taught in the program for 30 years. She also brought her ideas to many other master's and doctoral level programs by teaching in programs at Johns Hopkins University, Concordia University, Fielding Graduate University,

Georgetown University, the University of Massachusetts, McGill University, Sonoma State University, Benedictine College, and Pepperdine University.

As a result of her interactions with students in all of these programs, she was a hub in a large network of OD consultants who considered her their mentor and would turn to her for advice about client situations. These were talented people who had their degrees, knew the theories, and were working on their distinctive contribution as practitioners. There are always situations in practice when it helps to have consultation from peers. Seashore saw that need and with Broom – established the Triple Impact Program for people in practice. It would meet for a day once a month in major cities on both coasts and deal with the consulting issues that individuals in the group were experiencing. Seashore used her choice matrix to help people move from being stuck or seeing no possibilities to clarifying what they could do in the situation. The dynamics of the process are close to what is described as "reframing" (Bolman and Deal 2013; Brummans et al. 2008). In fact, Seashore also used the language of reframing to help people develop a new set of possibilities. She became known for suggesting to people describing a current dilemma that they begin their description of their situation with the words "*Until now...*" This "reframing" shifts the perspective from current stuckness to the possibilities of what could happen next and invites new possibilities for action. Seashore's "until now" intervention is a good example of how she understood theory, but translated it in her consultation into useful interventions on behalf of her clients.

A Model for Navigating a Career and a Family

When Seashore entered the OD field as an independent consultant in the 1960s, she was a pioneer in an emerging profession comprised of men. The model of women staying home to raise children and maintain the family was still in place. Most married women did not work, and if they did work, they certainly did not travel for work. Seashore did both with two young children at home. Her male clients were unaware of her family dynamic for the most part, since the 1960s was a time in which work and personal life were kept separate. If they did happen to find out, their reactions were usually negative.

Other professional women, however, were intrigued to understand how Seashore was able to value, enjoy, and manage her roles as wife, mother, home manager, and professional OD consultant. She became a role model for new possibilities in their lives, and so they studied what she was doing.

With the strong support of her husband, Seashore created an extensive support system that allowed her to both work away from home and be very present in it. In those days, preschools, public childcare, au pairs, video home monitors, and delivery services were mostly nonexistent, except for the very wealthy. Seashore hired a woman who was working for friends and brought her into her home to be her ears, eyes, and extra pair of hands. Her main responsibility was the children, but she coordinated other functions as well, including the business phone calls that were essential to their consulting practices. When she was away, Seashore talked with her children as they got up, after school, and before they went to bed. She was deeply and directly involved in their everyday lives and at the same time in touch with the now highly valued and respected woman who was her helper at home and who gradually became a special and cherished part of the family. As the children grew older and needed transportation, Seashore taught the woman to drive and bought her a car. The Seashores created a retirement plan for her and supported her buying her own home.

The Seashores had other warm relationships with people who provided support services for their intense lifestyle. They always had a cab driver who was part of their system and who could be counted on to appear and take them to the airport. The cleaners and the grocers would go out of their way for the Seashores because of the relationships they created. We now call this a support system or a support network. Charles Seashore developed this support matrix idea into a conceptual diagnostic map (Seashore 1982) that is used by many OD consultants. Although he got it into conceptual shape, many of the ideas came from his life with Edie Seashore and their joint journey to create a family that would allow them both to work and travel and still be strongly and securely connected to life at home.

I decided to volunteer to write about Seashore's contribution because I believe she was much more influential in the field of OD than her publication list suggests. Over the years, she was a regularly featured speaker and presenter at professional meetings. Her sessions at these meetings attracted large and appreciative audiences. Her work was deeply influenced by her values and ideas that she converted into actions. She had a wealth of tacit knowledge characteristic of the consummate practitioner (Schon 1983). Her ideas have deeply influenced many whom she mentored, taught, or were part of her network of friends and colleagues. Seashore was an active independent consultant and teacher well into her 80s. I can remember people asking her, years ago, "When are you going to retire, Edie?" She replied, "I am retired! This is it!" She was again a pioneer as she grew older. Her death in 2013 was a profound shock to the OD community, which responded with large memorial gatherings on both coasts.

In Summary: The Essential Edie Seashore

Edie Seashore was an OD pioneer and a force to be reckoned with in the lives of those she taught, befriended, and loved. Her core belief in social justice was fundamental to who she was. She engaged the world with a clear purpose, a willingness to take action, and a wonderful sense of humor that included herself. She valued diversity as a core part of OD. It can be said of her that her "theory in use" matched her "espoused theory," most of the time. She used storytelling as an intervention before books were written about it. She was the hub of an extensive network before networking became an intervention. She valued what women could bring to the workplace before gender became a research topic. She was ahead of her time and absolutely in your corner!

References

Bolman, L. G., & Deal, T. E. (2013). *Reframing organizations: Artistry, choice, and leadership* (5th ed.). San Francisco: Jossey Bass/Wiley.

Bunker, B. B., & Seashore, E. W. (1976). Power, collusion, intimacy-sexuality, support: Breaking the sex role stereotypes in social and organizational settings. In A. G. Sargent (Ed.), *Beyond sex roles* (pp. 356–370). St. Paul: West.

Brummans, B. H. J. M., Putnam, L. L., Gray, B., Hanke, R., Lewicki, R. J., & Wiethoff, C. (2008). Making sense of intractable multiparty conflict: A study of framing in four environmental disputes. *Communication Monographs, 75*(1), 25–51.

Patwell, B., & Seashore, E. W. (2006). *Triple impact coaching: Use-of-self in the coaching process*. Columbia: Bingham House Books.

Schon, D. (1983). *The reflective practitioner: How professionals think in action*. New York: Basic books.

Seashore, C. N. (1982). *Developing and using a personal support system: NTL reading book for human relations training*. Arlington: NTL Institute.

Seashore, E. W. (2006, winter). One good idea. *OD Seasonings, 2*(1). Retrieved from http://c.ymcdn.com/sites/www.odnetwork.org/resource/resmgr/Updated_SeasoningsPDFs/Seashore,_Seasonings,_Just_O.pdf

Seashore, C. N., Seashore, E. W., & Weinberg, G. W. (1991). *What did you say?: The art of giving and receiving feedback*. North Attleborough: Douglas Charles Press.

Further Reading

Bunker, B. B., & Seashore, E. W. (1976). Power, collusion, intimacy-sexuality, support: Breaking the sex role stereotypes in social and organizational settings. In A. G. Sargent (Ed.), *Beyond sex roles* (pp. 356–370). St. Paul: West.

Cross, E. Y., Katz, J. H., Miller, F. A., & Seashore, E. W. (1994). *The promise of diversity: Over 40 voices discuss strategies for eliminating discrimination in organizations*. Arlington: NTL Institute.

Jones, B. B., & Brazzel, M. (2014). *The NTL handbook of organization development and change: Principles, practices, and perspectives*. New York: Wiley.

Patwell, B., & Seashore, E. W. (2006). *Triple impact coaching: Use-of-self in the coaching process*. Columbia: Bingham House Books.

Seashore, C. N., Seashore, E. W., Weinberg, G. W. (1991). What did you say?: The art of giving and receiving feedback. North Attleborough: Douglas Charles Press.

Peter Senge: "Everything That We Do Is About Shifting the Capability for Collective Action. . ."

70

Kathryn Goldman Schuyler

Abstract

Peter M. Senge is an author, organizational consultant, and systems thinker whose writings and workshops have influenced scholars and managers around the world. From his base at MIT in what was originally the Organizational Learning Center, which became the Society for Organizational Learning (SoL), Senge has contributed to a fundamental shift in the way that many look at the nature and scale of change. His initial book, *The Fifth Discipline,* brought together practices for generating the inner shift in awareness that he originally termed *metanoia,* from the ancient Christian term for movement of mind or awakening, supporting people in developing practical, interlinked capacities to reflect, learn together, and think systemically about how to have sustainable organizations in a sustainable world. His writings and collaborative work with leaders in schools, not-for-profit organizations, and corporations continue to contribute to organizational and societal evolution.

Keywords

The Fifth Discipline • Systems thinking • *Metanoia* • Sustainability • Awareness-based system change • Consciousness • Cultivation • System sensing

Contents

K. Goldman Schuyler (✉)
California School of Professional Psychology, Alliant International University and Coherent Change, San Francisco, CA, USA
e-mail: kathryn@coherentchange.com

D.B. Szabla et al. (eds.), *The Palgrave Handbook of Organizational Change Thinkers*,
DOI 10.1007/978-3-319-52878-6_100

> *I am part of a larger reality, and if I am unaware of it, I will take actions that might make a lot of sense to me at the individual level or even my tribe or local group, but they'll be counterproductive in the larger world in which we're operating.*
>
> *(Peter Senge, in conversation with Otto Scharmer, U-Lab* 2015*)*

Peter Senge's work, from the initial publication of his best-selling book *The Fifth Discipline* (1990/2006) to the present time, has aimed to address what he first sensed as a teenager: that our society was "destroying the conditions for our own wellbeing, and we're all doing it..." (Peter Senge, in conversation with Otto Scharmer, ULab, 2015). He has provided systems perspectives, tools, and learning environments that have made it possible for people in business, education, government, and other communities of practice to think about the whole systems in which their work is embedded, so as to generate change that addresses underlying trends, rather than simply fixing current issues. His books, articles, and the organizations he has inspired or cofounded have already led to significant change in how people think about change, how organizations perceive their strategic direction, and how many business leaders understand the importance of shifting the impact of their business on the planet toward creating a more sustainable world.

At the heart of this is his recognition of the importance of self-development or "cultivation" for leaders, so that they never think that they have "the answer" but instead continually seek to listen to excluded voices in their worlds and develop sufficient personal mastery so that they can sustain both listening and deep commitment to what they value over long periods of time. In this chapter, I describe what inspires Peter in his work as a change leader and writer, highlight the most influential aspects of his work, indicate how this has been important to my own development as a scholar-practitioner, and finally, having spoken with him and several people who have been influenced by him in different ways, suggest what his lasting uniqueness may be – as I feel he is quite distinct among social and behavioral scientists.

Influences and Motivations: History, Engineering, and Consciousness

Describing the personal journey that led him to his work, Peter spoke of his teen perceptions.

> I remember conversations with my mother. I was probably 13, 14, 15 years old. I grew up in Los Angeles, and I watched Los Angeles go from paradise to really not such a nice place . . .,

> and so, I was very acutely aware of the adverse effects that are occurring when people take their individual actions with little awareness of the larger system.
>
> At some level we create all these problems. It's not bad luck. It's not random. Somehow, our handprint is on every one of these problems. But of course, for most of us, most of the time it's somebody else's handprint, right? It's not . . . my handprint. I'm not destroying species; somebody else must be destroying species, but then if you look where is this somebody else, you will not find them, because that somebody else is the plural us. (Peter Senge, in conversation with Otto Scharmer, ULab, 2015)

Although he believes that this blindness to our part in the collective has been true throughout history, he sees our current moment as a critical one because the scale at which humans impact the planet has shifted from local to global.

Unlike most social scientists and change practitioners, Peter was trained as an engineer. He chose to attend MIT as a graduate student to build on his undergraduate education in understanding systems. Intrigued by the systems view, he wondered how to apply it to social systems and to "how we understand human connectedness" (Peter Senge, in conversation with Otto Scharmer, ULab, 2015). During his first semester as a student in 1970, he met his mentor Jay Forrester. Forrester had impressive credentials as an engineer. In the 1940s and 1950s, he had invented core memory – a key technical breakthrough that enabled digital computation. Reflecting back, Peter pointed out to me that Forrester and his team supervised the construction of the first 28 general purpose digital computers that were installed around North America in the early 1950s to coordinate the first coordinated defense system for North America – and that many of these continued to work into the 1980s, 30 years later.

What impressed him in Forrester's work shows the nature of his focus throughout his career. As Peter described the importance of this project, "*Doing the whole of it* was meaningful to me. They do breakthrough, kind of prototyping stuff. But they don't just do that. They supervise the construction – the full production, manifestation, and implementation of the computers by IBM (which is how IBM got into the computer industry)" (Peter Senge, in conversation with Otto Scharmer, ULab, 2015). In other words, even before he published his first books or founded the organizations that have influenced scholar-practitioners and managers around the world, Peter looked at societal systems change in the context of historical perspectives. He was intrigued by questions of how to design practical systems that work beyond typically expected lifetimes of usage and fascinated by the unseen interconnectedness of our human actions.

Describing himself, as far back as he can recall, he wondered how we as humans might shift the thousands-of-years-old pattern of societies coming into existence, growing, and either depleting their resources or being unable to settle their conflicts and then disappearing. He saw this as recurring throughout human history, but with larger implications in the present period, since humans can now destroy not just their local environment but the conditions for life of the whole species. The way he has brought together historical perspectives, an engineering can-do mindset, and an awareness that the roots of genuine transformational change lie in deep processes of mastering consciousness is core to Peter's uniqueness as a scholar-practitioner of organizational change. Over the decades of his professional life, he has meditated regularly, regarding this as fundamental for his capacity to listen, which he sees as an essential capacity for any leader (Senge 2012). He perceives all problems as rooted in the way we as human beings use our consciousness, which shapes how we act.

> . . .the human being exists with one foot in the infinite and one foot in the manifest or the phenomenological. . . .all of this [systemic global problems] starts in some sense as mental distress or confusion, then it manifests in ways of acting that produce huge problems in the world. . . .You've got to deal with the lack of understanding and the lack of cultivation that all of us have in this world that shapes how and what we perceive. . . .Everything that we do is about shifting the capability for collective action, which starts with a different quality of conversation, a different collective awareness. (Senge 2012, pp. 316–317)

He is convinced that unless we cultivate our awareness through a practice of contemplation such as meditation, we project our own fears on the world:

> It's really that commitment to cultivate yourself, your ability to be quiet, your ability to be present, your ability to control your ego and your fear and self-centeredness, your ability to listen, your ability to suspend your own thoughts, to distinguish what's happening from what you're projecting – all of that is foundational for being an effective leader who can actually do some good. (Senge 2012, p. 327)

The extent to which his work is grounded in the importance of what he initially called *personal mastery* (*The Fifth Discipline*, 1990/2006) and more recently has referred to simply as *cultivation* is affirmed by various key collaborators of his, notably Roger Saillant (see *The Fifth Discipline*, p. 266) and Otto Scharmer (see comments, which appear later in this chapter).

From the start of his professional life, Peter combined practical application projects with theory development, writing for the general public, and teaching. He grounded this work in collaborations with different people at different times, always working with others. Initially, he developed workshops entitled *Leadership and Mastery* with Bob Fritz and Charles Kiefer of Innovation Associates. Coleading 40–50 of these 3-day workshops over 10 years was a practice field for developing and refining ideas and tools, which he then honed in writing *The Fifth Discipline* (1990/2006). As he describes himself, when he wrote this book that launched his global level of influence, he was not a theorist, but a practitioner writing from experience.

> Most people write books about their ideas. Sometimes, people write books based on their experience, and this was very much the latter. We were confident, because we'd seen so many examples of dramatic improvement in results and deep learning and growth by people, teams, and individuals. There wasn't any question of whether or not this would be useful: if it could be done well, it would be useful. (Interview for this chapter, May 30, 2016)

He repeatedly emphasizes both the collaborative nature of his own thinking and the way that the success of his books is embedded in communities of practice where people from business, education, government all work to use the ideas (Senge et al.

2015b). In fact, he wrote *The Fifth Discipline* (1990/2006) in order to launch the Organizational Learning Center at MIT (Senge et al. 2015b).

He has been influenced by colleagues from varied disciplines. For example, he built on Chris Argyris' ideas about Model I and Model II change as well as his use of the ladder of inference and was influenced by Chilean biologist Humberto Maturana's work about cognition and autopoiesis in change processes. He considers his understanding that there is no "reality" separate from the observer to have been influenced by Maturana, who as Peter said was "a very rigorous biologist who became famous for his work as an experimental biologist, trying to understand how a frog sees a fly" – which eventually became Nobel Prize winning research (Interview for this chapter, May 30, 2016) . It was out of this grounding in the "hard sciences" that Peter developed his perspectives on consciousness and the social creation of "reality" – not out of philosophy, although his thinking has also been influenced by his decades of Buddhist practice. As he commented, "everything that exists in the physical world exists in a web of interconnectedness, and it's always continually in flux," but somehow humans tend not to perceive this, since "most of us perceive things, and we perceive things as being more less fixed" (Interview for this chapter, May 30, 2016). This tendency to perceive fixity strongly influences how people work to "drive" change and is probably fundamental to why so many change programs are ineffective.

Peter's work can be distinguished from that of many influential social scientists, not only by its interdisciplinary nature but also by his unique combination of engineering, societal focus, and grounding in awareness or consciousness. All of his writing has been for the public, rather than being published initially in scholarly journals, making for a different type of career than many. Based at MIT, one of the US's foremost scholarly institutions, he crafted a path that let him remain in the academy without playing by its normal rules – something that is hard to do in any field.

Key Contributions: Bringing Awareness-Based Systems Change into the World of Business

Peter Senge's main contributions to transformational change can be viewed from various perspectives: conceptual, practical, and role modeling.

Conceptual

Often referred to as one of the top 25 business books of the twentieth century, *The Fifth Discipline: The Art and Practice of the Learning Organization* (1990/2006) brought together the simultaneous and interactive importance of five fundamental disciplines that had not previously been seen as a consolidated group of success skills for organizations or businesses. He called them *disciplines* meaning "a body of theory and technique that must be studied and mastered to be put into practice... (from the Latin *disciplina*, to learn)" (Senge 1990/2006, p. 10).

These are

- *Personal mastery* – "the discipline of continually clarifying and deepening our personal vision, of focusing our energies, of developing patience, and of seeing reality more objectively";
- *Mental models* – "deeply ingrained assumptions, generalizations, or even pictures or images that influence how we understand the world and how we take action";
- *Team learning* – teams where "the intelligence of the team exceeds the intelligence of the individuals in the team, and where teams develop extraordinary capacities for coordinated action";
- *Systems thinking* – situations where the component parts are so interdependent that events "distant in time and space" have hidden influences on one another so that one can only understand what is happening by contemplating it as a whole;
- *Shared vision* – "the capacity to hold a shared picture of the future we seek to create" (Senge 1990/2006, pp. 7–9).

While none of these disciplines were new, in this book Peter presented them in their interdependence with one another in a way that made them practical and usable for managers and organizational consultants, opening a deeper space for executives and scholars to think together about change, grounded in personal practices of meditation and awareness. Concepts and practices that had existed but had been rarely used in the business world became popular: they are increasingly discussed in boardrooms around the world and used by both external and internal organization consultants.

Peter's unique contribution is in the way he discussed these tools, showing their practicality and urgency for the world of leaders. Even now, decades later, although both scholars and practitioners more often address the value of contemplation for leaders, it is still rare to bring together ancient practices of mind training with collaborative systems thinking focused on global change as well as organizational performance. Where much management thinking has led people to emulate others' leadership or the way other organizations have done things (e.g., benchmarking), Peter has always emphasized how people need to master their own minds, perceptions, and ways of interacting in order to generate creative actions.

The kind of change he sought and continues to seek involves *metanoia*: a deep inner shift in awareness about the systemic way things unfold in life and how that is influenced by how we think about and see life (see Senge 1990/2006, p. 13). In his second edition of this major work, he described how the disciplines work together: "The five disciplines represent approaches (theories and methods) for developing three core learning capabilities: fostering aspiration, developing reflective conversation, and understanding complexity" (Senge 1990/2006, p. 2). These capabilities work together to enable the kind of creative, generative leadership that is needed in all organizations.

Revised in 2006, with considerable material added to illustrate the impact of the ideas in the book, *The Fifth Discipline* (1990/2006) is one of the best-selling leadership books ever published and has been for a long time. For example, when it was re-translated and re-published in China in 2012, 15 years after its first translation, "it was the best-selling business book in the country," and in 2013 "it was the number two" (Senge et al. 2015b, p. 2). Peter has published several other highly influential books, all of which were written collaboratively, showing his strong orientation toward interaction. *Presence: Human Purpose and the Field of the Future* (Senge et al. 2004) introduced the notion of *presencing*, which is understanding oneself not only as an individual but as part of a larger social field, an idea elaborated further by Otto Scharmer (2009) in *Theory U*. Building on notions introduced earlier as personal mastery, *Presence* was revolutionary for many managers and organization consultants in looking at how consciousness could be foundational for dramatic societal change. In *The Necessary Revolution: How Individuals and Organizations are Working Together to Create a Sustainable World* (Senge et al. 2007), Senge and his colleagues focused on how companies around the world were developing products and processes that would allow the planet and human society to flourish. He returned to another area he perceives as foundational for lasting change – education – in coauthoring *The Triple Focus: A New Approach to Education* with Daniel Goleman in 2014, which was written to support schools in developing programs that simultaneously develop skills of understanding self, relating to others, and thinking systemically in students of all ages, from kindergarten to high school. In other words, to appreciate Peter Senge's contributions about transformational change, one needs to seek not particular concepts, but the way his publications show what he finds important, and to appreciate his combined emphasis on personal reflection, engaging in systemic thinking, and concretely putting ideas into practice.

Practical

Among organizational consultants, Peter has made two sets of choices that are uncommon. He increasingly chose clients driven by his insights about what needs to change globally: his initial focus on business transitioned over time to a focus on generating sustainable food chains, healthy water, and the development of community-based schools that use his five disciplines to create classrooms that are learning organizations. In addition, rather than establishing a boutique consulting firm, as so many have, he created a series of network-based organizations in which knowledge is shared and people are encouraged to work collaboratively. Initially, his organizational change center was based within MIT, but it transitioned, becoming the independent Society for Organizational Learning (*SoL*) in 1997, with structural changes developed by a design team led by visionary thinker and executive Dee Hock. As Senge described the reason for transitioning out of the university, at the core was the way that universities fragment the development and application of knowledge (Senge and Kim 1997, reprinted 2013). As Senge and Kim, a cofounder of the MIT center, had explained in 1997, "Because research, practice, and capacity-building each operate within the walls of separate institutions, the people within these institutions feel cut off from each other, leading to suspicion, stereotyping, and an 'us' versus 'them' mindset" (p. 6). Instead, as a global membership organization, SoL was intended to foster cross-institutional collaboration through its journal, workshops, and community gatherings.

Rather than focusing mainly on research or theory development, as many change theorists have done, Peter has focused on presenting concepts so they will be used in impactful ways. *The Fifth Discipline Fieldbook* (Senge et al. 1994) was the first of several books modeled on the *Whole Earth Catalogue* (Brand 1971, 1980), a hugely popular book that offered tools for change on a global level. Patterning his books on these books and working with Art Kleiner, one of the original editors of the *Whole Earth Catalogue*, Peter and his collaborators gathered tools and thinking that helped corporate managers, school administrators, and teachers put the core concepts of the five disciplines into practice in their organizations. This orientation toward publishing action-oriented, story-based, coauthored books continued with *The Dance of Change: The Challenges to Sustaining Momentum in a Learning Organization* (Senge et al. 1999), *Schools that Learn: A Fifth Discipline Fieldbook for Educators, Parents, and Everyone Who Cares About Education* (Senge et al. 2000), and *The Necessary Revolution: How Individuals and Organizations are Working Together to Create a Sustainable World* (Senge et al. 2007).

Peter has been catalytic in the formation of a number of organizations based on the principles he explicated and in addition has been dedicated to long-term efforts developed collaboratively by people from different parts of the world working in business, academia, and government. He supported the founding of the Sustainable Food Lab by Oxfam and Unilever in 2003, bringing together many of the world's largest food companies and key NGOs to develop outcome-oriented collaboration (Senge et al. 2015b). The Food Lab takes leaders from these very different worlds on learning journeys where they experience firsthand what farmers face in various parts of the world, where the existing food production process is fueling the cycle of poverty. People who would not have been willing to sit down at the same table to negotiate find themselves learning together, and as one Target executive said, "...every single assumption I came here with has been turned upside down" (Hamilton 2015, NP). The Academy for Systemic Change focuses on developing next-generation leaders who are already accomplished in awareness-based systemic change and can work together to advance this emerging field of know-how (see http://www.academyforchange.org/). They have created a virtual systems design center that connects, leverages, and enables the transfer of know-how. "We are a global community of individuals, organizations, and networks who are deeply involved in developing living examples that show what is possible in creating social systems that foster biological, social, and economic well being" (http://www.academyforchange.org/no page). The Academy has become a major focus of Peter's energy, as he sees it as a foundational place for developing and extending the lineage of what he has come to call "awareness-based systems change" – which is also being developed and promoted through Otto Scharmer's Presencing Institute, in which Peter is a key collaborator. Among its activities, the Academy for Systemic Change sponsors use of the five disciplines in schools and school systems through a project named Camp Snowball, which brings together educators and students for a week each summer, to showcase and share examples of effective uses of each of the tools and to build community among them (see http://www.campsnowball.org/).

Role Modeling

Peter is seen by many as a role model for a new way of being a change agent rooted in scholarship and knowledge. He has worked side by side with people from many fields – working actively with corporate, NGO, and community leaders, as well as with people from the academic world. When he arrives to participate in any group, he tends not to speak, but to listen, often preferring to be the last to speak when he is on a panel at a conference. His collaborative way of developing practice-oriented books and methods has supported others in taking action while he works alongside them. By quietly making time in his own life for decades to meditate regularly and only occasionally discussing this in public, he has helped people in the social sciences to appreciate the connection of individual reflection and systems change. He presented this initially in *The Fifth Discipline* as personal mastery, which he now sees as "standing between the worlds of phenomena and consciousness in service of living one's life as an ongoing process of creating (bringing into reality) what matters most to you" (Personal communication, July 13, 2016). By his actions, he has made space for others to think, lead, and consult from a place of deeper awareness of principles like interdependence and impermanence.

In addition, his actions have modeled how consultants can choose to focus on the issues that they believe are most important, rather than those that pay the most, as many consultants do. Peter chose sustainability (including food systems and water), education, and developing the next generation of leaders. By making such choices and acting on them, his actions speak to many across the worlds of organization change.

New Insights: Change and Learning Are Inseparable

Taking a 500-foot up "helicopter" view of organizational change literature, Peter Senge can be seen to have nourished a unique body of work that lives at the intersection of theory and practice. Bringing together the five disciplines of change in the context of learning as active shaping and doing, rather than as just taking in new information, is fundamental to his worldview. In the second decade of the twenty-first century, many speak and write about consciousness and the value of mindfulness for leaders, whether or not they understand it from decades of meditation practice, as Peter does, but few thought about this in the 1980s and 1990s. Fewer still make it practical and accessible to corporate executives.

I was an organization development consultant when I first read *The Fifth Discipline*. I had been personally involved with what he now calls awareness-based change since the 1980s, but it was not easy to bridge the world of "personal growth" (as we called it then) and the nature and structure of organizations. As far back as the late 1970s, I noticed that the societal change processes of the 1960s and 1970s seemed to have generated two forces moving in opposite directions within American culture: large numbers of people "dropping out" to create lives based on alternative values, while "the actual power residing in the largest, most complex, least-regulated organizations – the multinational organizations – increased" (Goldman 1979, p. 24).

To explore bridging this gap, my doctoral research assessed how studying in more open institutions (meaning those with clear purpose, considerable inclusion of all voices in decision-making, and openness to the surrounding community) was connected with fostering a sense of autonomy among students (Goldman 1979). Like Peter has done over the years, I focused on education because I suspected that students who experienced an open, person-centered college environment could reasonably expect other social organizations to function similarly. "This underlines the potentially catalytic impact of open organizations within community colleges" (p. 12, emphasis added here). As I wrote in the dissertation, I was seeking organizational change foundations for the possibility of encouraging "societal renewal, expanded consciousness, and increased use of latent human potential" (Goldman 1979, p. 14).

Since Peter had not yet written about personal mastery, it was not easy to speak about how organizations contributed to or inhibited the development of human consciousness. I struggled to find conceptual foundations for the type of change I wished to help happen in the world. When I read *The Fifth Discipline,* I felt that here, finally, was a mainstream path for action in this area, something that had been so lacking. I have used many aspects of the book in consulting with corporate management teams, specifically referring clients to the way Peter described alignment and its value and also to his description about when to shift from decision-making to dialogue.

For me, as I sense is true for many others, *The Fifth Discipline* legitimized talking about dialogue and the importance of practices of personal mastery in the corporate setting – something that had previously been difficult, if not impossible. During the late 1980s and early 1990s, it was highly controversial to offer workshops within corporations on skills related to reflection and meditation. Articles in *Fortune* and major newspapers like the *NY Times* presented accusations from people within such corporations, alleging that training in meditation was "brainwashing" them (see for example, Ciulla 2004, pp. 69–70; Main and Riley 1987; Sink 2007). To have a positive and respected source discussing personal mastery as a core discipline for managers was a first step in legitimizing what has now become widely accepted.

His work made space for me and for many organizational consultants to support managers in developing personal reflection processes and made them comfortable in doing such personal development work. Several years ago, I interviewed Peter about his meditation practice, strongly influenced by the Buddhist-Taoist-Confucian synthesis of Chinese teacher, Nan Haui-Chin, and the implications of having such a practice for organizational and social change (Senge 2012). There are few other places where he has shared his personal experience and perspectives on spiritual practice. A later discussion with him encouraged me to develop *Creative Social Change: Leadership for a Healthy World* (Goldman Schuyler et al. 2016). His comments about how he prioritized "catalyzing and influencing collective action in reshaping systems" and "deeper exploration of systemic change" (Personal communication, March 7, 2014) shifted my focus from writing about individual practices back to my earlier emphasis on collective change toward a healthy society. He and his writings have helped me to hold lightly to two themes, neither of which has been dominant in organization change and development: deep, disciplined personal awareness practice and the potential for systemic change. As chair of the Practice Theme Committee of the Academy of Management, I led the committee in giving Peter its prestigious Lifetime Career Award in 2012 for all the reasons described above.

Legacies and Unfinished Business: Awareness-Based Change Toward a Sustainable World

I see Peter Senge as a leader in creating a new role for people focused on societal change. He personally bridges the gaps between engineering, management, organizational behavior, systems change, and Eastern wisdom traditions and practices, as he can write and speak from personal experience in all of these areas. His unassuming style and self-confidence allowed him to nourish collaborative networks of practice and collaborative books, all focused on practitioners wishing to make change in key arenas of society: sustainable food and water, as well as education and the development of businesses to serve such purposes. His recent focus has been the creation of the Next Generation Leaders program in the Academy of Systemic Change, which brings together people in their late twenties and thirties who are already doing good work related to change to help them go further and support them in taking on broader leadership in such systemic change.

Perspectives on Peter Senge's Legacy

Because Peter speaks so much about the importance of collaboration, I sought out the views of several people with whom he has worked recently, so as to bring other voices into this chapter and to add their perspectives on Peter's influence on them and the field. I spoke with Otto Scharmer, coauthor of *Presence: Human Purpose and the Field of the Future* (Senge et al. 2004); Daniel Goleman, coauthor of *The Triple Focus: A New Approach to Education* (Senge and Goleman 2014); and Stacey Tank, VP of Corporate Communications and External Affairs, The Home Depot, who is a participant in the Next Generation Leaders program. I sought to glean how their work with Peter has influenced them as people, authors, and leaders and also how they perceive his legacy.

Daniel Goleman has focused on leadership and the importance of social and emotional learning (SEL) for decades (e.g., see *Primal Leadership: Realizing the Power of Emotional Intelligence*, 2002; *Healing Emotions: Conversations with the Dalai Lama on Mindfulness, Emotions, and Health,* 2013; *The Emotionally*

Intelligent Workplace, 2001). Ever since writing *Emotional Intelligence* (1995), he has emphasized how much children need such development, which he believes is ignored by standard curricula. To encourage such learning, he founded the Collaborative for Academic, Social, and Emotional Learning (CASEL) at Yale University (now at the University of Illinois in Chicago) to get such programs into schools. Since he and Peter have known one another for years and were each inspiring attempts to influence the schools, they decided to join forces by writing a book together, with Senge focused on the need for systems thinking and Goleman focused on social-emotional learning. It seemed clear that "this would be a very complete education and would beautifully complement the standard curriculum" (Personal communication, July 28, 2016). *The Triple Focus* (2014) describes the three skill sets that they see as essential: developing self, tuning in to other people, and understanding the larger world and how systems interact. They saw value in bringing together their lines of work so as to maximize the influence on school systems, as both agreed that:

> the factory model we have inherited through the Industrial Age School was never about tapping and cultivating this innate potential. It was never about growing human beings – it was designed to train factory workers en masse. Though almost everything has changed in the reality for our students since this model was implemented almost 200 years ago, the basic design of school has only been adjusted incrementally, not fundamentally. [An] important synergy between SEL and systems thinking has to do with transforming pedagogy and the culture of school. For example, a key to making such a spiral view of cognitive-emotional development practical in real educational settings is profound respect [for the learner]. (Senge and Goleman 2014, pp. 31–32)

Together, they focused on the *how* (the approach to pedagogy) as much as the *what* (SEL and systems learning), knowing that how anything is taught completely colors what is learned. In closing, Goleman commented to me "I find Peter a superb collaborator – it is his specialty. He listens, he's thoughtful, he adds insight. His thinking has long been a part of my way of looking at things, and his interest in education is really from the heart" (Personal communication – Interview for this chapter, July 28, 2016).

When I asked him to reflect on Peter's legacy and influence upon his own work, Otto Scharmer emphasized how Peter has created a very unique blend of theory and practice that was transformational for him with regard to how he has approached learning and change. Otto described how Peter:

> with his own presence, uses himself as a gateway for accessing a deeper level of knowing and creating a different atmosphere in the room that allows people to experience and sense themselves in a different way. It's a very visceral impression. …it was as if somebody opened a new set of eyes for me about what you can do. Even today, most learning environments are just talking heads, whereas what I saw him doing was entirely different. And it had a major influence on me: the whole thing of creating a more generative learning environment and an atmosphere that allows you to access a different level of your own awareness. (Personal communication – Interview for this chapter, September 2, 2016. All the following quotes are from this interview).

By shifting the structure from a university-based learning center to a global community – when Senge formed SoL – he helped those around the world begin to self-organize. This inspired Otto's sense of what could be possible globally, so his collaboration with Peter helped him to birth *Theory U*, both on a conceptual level and on what he considers to be a "systems sensing level." "In Peter's journey, you can see how gifts of the mind are more and more connected with the heart and finally with the hands."

What underlies everything, in Otto's experience of him, is that:

> Peter is a practitioner who with the greatest sincerity cultivates his inner self as a vehicle to be more effective in serving the whole. You can see and sense this. It shines through in how he interacts with everyone. And this has had a real impact on my life.

Finally, he has been pioneering a new type of academic career "that redefines the relationship between theory and practice" for coming generations. For most academics, practice is something one looks at from outside, but:

> as an action researcher, you're involved with your whole being in actual transformation and practice. Practice plays a primary role and is much more intertwined with theory. . . .we are interested in knowledge that is helpful to the evolution of society. We are interested in healing, in catalyzing developmental potential – and that's our core essence, that's our DNA.
>
> Peter shows that when you have the courage to stand outside the well-worn path, you can actually create your own path that is much more interesting and relevant. From our very first conversations, I sensed how deeply connected he was with his own inspiration and intention in life. Meeting him and sensing this gave me permission to establish this connection within myself. So he created a role model for a different kind of teaching and learning, where you create an environment that allows people to connect more deeply with their own purpose in life. Peter has done this for many, many people.

Finally, looking at Peter's influence from the perspective of a young executive who has been participating in the current Next Generation Leaders program, his sense of history and value for reflection are evident. According to Stacey Tank:

> Growing up in business and in a US context, I was taught to jump immediately to action. Get it done. Quickly! Playing with pacing is one of my personal learning edges. Peter, on the other hand, has an innate ability to look across time. Across generations. To hold the creative tension. To find the deeper meaning and solution. I can think of many circumstances in which the world would have benefited from a longer-term view. It may be the most absent capability in the world today – and a lot is at stake because of it.
>
> Peter shared the attached quote with me a few years ago, from the Iroquois Confederacy Peacemaker (comparable to the US Declaration of Independence) first written about 1000 A.D. It reads, "Think not forever of ourselves, nor of our own generation. Think of continuing generations of our families. Think of our grandchildren. And of those yet unborn whose faces are coming from beneath the ground." This has stayed with me along with the question of how we can encourage more people to think and act this way. (This and the following comments are from a personal communication, September 13, 2016)

Tank, too, commented about how she listens and works with people. She emphasized the importance of systems thinking tools in business today, given the complexity and level of challenge in all companies, and sees these spreading. Finally, she too noted the way his being makes a difference that can be felt:

> Peter has a calm, thoughtful energy that immediately makes you feel at peacc. In my first conversations with him, I was struck by how he approaches every single person as an equal. Every question and idea matters. Every person is valued and safe.

Unfinished Business: Embedding Mindful Practices in Institutions

From my conversations with Peter, I know he would laugh at the thought of there *not* being unfinished business, given the nature of change that he has focused on throughout his life. I see two areas to reflect on.

Why Has There Not Been More Change?

Having seen and felt the enormous impact of Peter's work and his books over the last 25 years, I found myself wondering why there has not been more change and why things seem worse in many ways in organizational life, despite all the skillful efforts of so many people around the world. In the 1990s, there was huge excitement about this work, and many serious managers and consultants devoted considerable thought and time to it. While there have been many successful projects in some companies and parts of the world, in some ways it seems as though life has become more complex, and leaders still regard such approaches as existing on the fringes of business and social science. The need for cross-sector collaboration, which was suspected but not developed in the early years, is not yet widely recognized. I have no easy answer to this question, but it is an important one for those dedicating themselves to facilitating societal transformation.

One answer can be found in a comment Peter made in a recent article, reflecting on a trend he has observed over the years:

> Someone who just picked up the tools of *The Fifth Discipline* and said, "Hey, we can make more money if we use these tools" generally accomplished very little. But someone who had a deep intent to transform the prevailing organizational culture or the nature of work itself or people's relationship to their work could have amazing results. So, where the practitioner is coming from in terms of intent, spirit, and openness is important. (Senge et al. 2015b, p. 4)

As systems science shows, change takes time and includes delays, so cross-institution, cross-sector, and planetary change will take decades and perhaps centuries. In addition, deep change unfolds in ways very different from a linear progression. As Peter sees it:

> We live in a time of profound cross-currents: things are getting much worse *and* embodiments of a different future now being born can be seen all around us. If you think about this just a little, you realize it could not really be different. This same "dance of change" characterizes deep change in the natural world as well – the new emerges in the midst of the systems that have prevailed for a long time, and how the two interact shapes the change process.

As Maturana says, "All change occurs while it is being inhibited." It is naïve to think that one day everyone wakes up and says, "We have been doing it all wrong," and then sets out to change en masse. So, it should not surprise any of us that as the inner contradictions and destructive side effects of our traditional industrial–age ways of thinking and operating become more evident, people and institutions fight harder to preserve them. We all have a core choice – we can either put our attention on the battle with the status quo or on shepherding the new being born. (Personal communication, December 12, 2016.) For more discussion of these perspectives, see Scharmer et al. (2014) and Senge et al. (2015a, Winter).

Awareness-Based Systems Change Takes Time

Most of what Peter Senge has helped to catalyze is still being developed. As he and his coauthors described the current state of "system leaders," people who foster collaboration for crossing thresholds none previously believed could be crossed, such leaders are needed but rare (Senge et al. 2015a). What they have in common, whatever their style or cultural basis, is that "their profound commitment to the health of the whole radiates to nurture similar commitment in others" (p. 28). This requires the kind of personal cultivation that Peter speaks and writes about and which has always been at the core of his work.

From Peter's own perspective, what remains to be developed for awareness-based change to spread and take root globally can be called "the interpenetration of collective reflection and action" – having reflection shift from primarily an individual event to one that focuses on the social field. When the world has leaders who are able to lead from a space of self-cultivation, nourished by deep, ongoing reflection, or meditation practices and who excel at nurturing networks of collaboration and larger generative fields, it will gradually become more possible for "the whole to become aware of itself as a whole." In a recent conversation, Peter commented that:

How to really embed mindful practices in institutions is a work of many, many decades and even generations. Really, we are just at the beginning. If you put it in a perspective of cultural change, when did human culture start to drift so far away from a generative connection with nature? Over the last several thousands of years! So, that's not going to be reversed overnight. I like the term *system sensing*: it orients us toward the capacity that we have to become present in the moment and really sense into the group and larger systems as a whole.

[To do this] I think collectively practicing silence is important.... Bringing together people who are very active in diverse change leadership networks into a culture of silence can help to cultivate and maintain an awareness of the whole. Silence as collective practice is a lost art in modern society, but it's an ancient idea that opens lots of important doors. It brings us in touch with subtle energies and how they manifest in the physical environment. There are groups who work this way, but few. We haven't talked much about this, because it has been premature. ...we have to learn how to move back and forth between silence and words, reflection and action, in ways that conserve mutual awareness of both. For the modern mind, silence is the absence of noise. But for cultivation traditions, silence is the presence of something – it's not about absence, it's about presence. Once people experience this, they tend to fall in love with it: they become more and more able to allow awareness to rest in itself. (Personal communication, July 13, 2016)

Twenty-five years after the publication of *The Fifth Discipline*, Peter Senge's influence has been felt on the issues he most values: sustainability, food and water, and education. It is acknowledged in many countries, including China, where he now spends considerable time each year. He and Otto Scharmer are part of China's "Thousands Talents" program, aimed to prioritize critical new capabilities for the country and its possible role in the world. Since his influence comes from his writing, his collaborative projects, and his own self-cultivation, I feel that the most powerful impacts will live and grow, as those influenced by him continue to live and lead in ways colored by deep value for awareness-based systemic change, serving the needs of generations not yet imagined.

References

Brand, S. (1971). *The last whole earth catalogue*. New York: Random House.

Brand, S. (1980). *The next whole earth catalogue*. New York: Point.

Ciulla, J. (2004). *Ethics, the heart of leadership*. Westport: Praeger.

Goldman, K. L. (1979). Organizations and autonomy: An exploration of the relationship between organizational openness and personal autonomy in American community colleges (Unpublished doctoral dissertation). Columbia University, New York.

Goldman Schuyler, K., Baugher, J. E., & Jironet, K. (Eds.). (2016). *Leadership for a healthy world: Creative social change*. Bingley: Emerald Group Publishing.

Goleman, D. (1995/2006). *Emotional intelligence*. New York: Random House.

Goleman, D. (2001). *The emotionally intelligent workplace*. San Francisco: Jossey-Bass.

Goleman, D. (2013). *Healing emotions: Conversations with the Dalai Lama on mindfulness, emotions, and health*. Boston: Shambhala.

Goleman, D., Boyatzis, R., & McKee, A. (2002). *Primal leadership: Realizing the power of emotional intelligence*. Cambridge: Harvard Business Press.

Hamilton, H. (2015, Winter). System leaders for sustainable food. *Stanford Social Innovation Review*. NP.

Main, J. & Riley, C. A. (1987, November 23). Trying to bend managers' minds. Fortune, http://archive.fortune.com/magazines/fortune/fortune_archive/1987/11/23/69878/index.htm

Scharmer, C. O. (2009). *Theory U: Leading from the future as it emerges*. San Francisco: Berrett-Koehler.

Scharmer, O., Saxena, S., & Goldman Schuyler, K. (2014). Connecting inner transformation as a leader to corporate and societal change. In K. Goldman Schuyler, J. E. Baugher, K. Jironet, & L. Lid-Falkman (Eds.), *Leading with spirit, presence, and authenticity* (pp. 13–38). San Francisco: Jossey-Bass/Wiley.

Senge, P. (1990/2006). *The fifth discipline: The art and practice of the learning organization*. New York: Doubleday.

Senge, P. (2012). "Leaders should be people who are deeply involved in their own realization of being a human being" – An interview with Peter Senge. In K. Goldman Schuyler (Ed.), *Inner peace – Global impact: Tibetan Buddhism, leadership, and work* (pp. 317–327). Charlotte: Information Age Publishing.

Senge, P., & Goleman, D. (2014). *The triple focus: A new approach to education*. Florence: More Than Sound.

Senge, P. & Scharmer, O. (2015). Conversation on U-Lab. https://courses.edx.org/courses/course-v1:MITx+15.671x+3T2015/courseware/ca9d93b968ee4a1cb07fa46b703a93834c3b5740632c4b60998158b75db30006/

Senge, P., Kleiner, A., Roberts, C., Ross, R. B., & Smith, B. J. (1994). *The fifth discipline fieldbook*. New York: Crown Business.

Senge, P., Kleiner, A., Roberts, C., Ross, R. B., Roth, G., & Smith, B. J. (1999). *The dance of change: The challenges of sustaining momentum in learning organizations*. New York: Crown Business.

Senge, P., Cambron-McCabe, N., Lucas, T., Smith, B., Dutton, J., & Kleiner, A. (2000). *Schools that learn: A fifth discipline fieldbook for educators, parents, and everyone who cares about education*. New York: Doubleday Currency.

Senge, P., Scharmer, O., Jaworski, J., & Flowers, B. S. (2004). *Presence: Human purpose and the field of the future*. New York: Crown Business.

Senge, P., Smith, B., Kruschwitz, N., Laur, J., & Schley, S. (2007). *The necessary revolution*. New York: Doubleday.

Senge, P., & Kim, D. H. (2013). From fragmentation to integration: Building learning communities. *Reflections, 13*(4), 3–11.

Senge, P., Hamilton, H., & Kania, J. (2015a, Winter). The dawn of system leadership. *Stanford Social Innovation Review, 13*(1), 26–33.

Senge, P., Schneider, F., & Wallace, D. (2015b). Peter Senge on the 25th anniversary of *The Fifth Discipline*. *Reflections, 14*(3), 1–12.

Sink, R. (2007, Autumn). My unfashionable legacy. *Strategy + Business*. Downloaded September 11, 2016 from http://www.strategy-business.com/article/07302?pg=0

Further Reading

For those new to Peter Senge's writings, as a starting place I would recommend looking at both his early book *The Fifth Discipline* (1990/2006) and his recent co-authored article "The Dawn of System Leadership" (2015). In The *Fifth Discipline*, be sure to read the recent edition and focus on Peter's new introduction (pp. ix–xvi), the overall description of the five disciplines (Part III, pp. 128–252), and the newly-added chapter based on interviews with people who have used this approach over the years (pp. 255–282). You may also find it helpful to see his recent thinking about creating a healthy world, as juxtaposed with the views of Margaret Wheatley, Otto Scharmer, Ed Schein, and Robert Quinn in *Creative Social Change: Leadership for a Healthy World* (Goldman Schuyler et al. 2016, Chap. 1, and esp. pp. 65–88).

All of his writing, as listed in the references, will interest those who wish to go deeply into this area. Those reading more selectively may particularly enjoy the following:

Goldman Schuyler, K. with Wheatley, M., Scharmer, O., Schein, E., Quinn, R., & Senge, P. (2016). Visions of a healthy world: Views from thought leaders. In K. Goldman Schuyler, J. E. Baugher, & K. Jironet (Eds.), *Creative social change: Leadership for a healthy world* (pp. 23–90). Bingley: Emerald Group Publishing.

Senge, P. (1990/2006). *The fifth discipline: The art and practice of the learning organization*. New York: Doubleday.

Senge, P. (2012). "Leaders should be people who are deeply involved in their own realization of being a human being" – An interview with Peter Senge. In K. Goldman Schuyler (Ed.), *Inner peace – Global impact: Tibetan Buddhism, leadership, and work* (pp. 317–327). Charlotte: Information Age Publishing.

Senge, P., Hamilton, H., & Kania, J. (2015, Winter). The dawn of system leadership. *Stanford Social Innovation Review, 13*(1), 26–33.

Senge, P., Scharmer, O., Jaworski J., & Flowers, B. S. (2004). *Presence: Human purpose and the field of the future*. New York: Crown Business.

71 Abraham B. (Rami) Shani: A Journey from Action Research and Sociotechnical Systems to Collaborative Management Research and Sustainable Work Systems

Michael W. Stebbins

Abstract

Abraham B. (Rami) Shani, a professor of management and organization behavior at the Orfalea College of Business, California Polytechnic State University, San Luis Obispo, is a recognized scholar in the organization development and change field. The first book that he coauthored with Gervase Bushe, a pioneering articulation of parallel learning structure theory in the Addison-Wesley Organization Development Series, was written at a time when the rapidly growing field was not well understood or well-defined. The book, *Parallel Learning Structures: Increasing Innovation in Bureaucracies*, was hailed by Richard Beckhard and Edgar Schein as "a seminal theory of large-scale organization change based on the institution of parallel systems as change agents." The book has been widely quoted in contemporary times in line with new attention to diverse learning mechanisms within the field of organization design. As of this writing, Rami continues to publish and serve as an editor of journal articles, books, and book chapters at a record pace. In 2008, he joined Richard Woodman and William Pasmore in editing the annual volumes of *Research in Organizational Change and Development*, which establishes a special opportunity for academics and practitioners to share research findings and emerging trends in OD. Over the years, Rami has worked with consultants, scholars, clients, and leaders within the organization development academic community to found the subfield of collaborative management research and to document the evolution of sociotechnical systems theory toward sustainable work systems thinking and the development of new organizational capabilities. The chapter sections below will explore these collaborations and contributions. After a brief look at influences and motivations, the chapter will expand on three contribution categories along with ties to the relevant scholarly literature. It will be noted that beyond a phenomenal

M.W. Stebbins (✉)
Orfalea College of Business, California Polytechnic State University, San Luis Obispo, CA, USA
e-mail: mstebbin@calpoly.edu

D.B. Szabla et al. (eds.), *The Palgrave Handbook of Organizational Change Thinkers*,
DOI 10.1007/978-3-319-52878-6_91

publication record and active involvement in organization development research societies and consortiums, Dr. Shani plays a key role in shaping the academic research agenda in action research, collaborative management research, and organization design.

Keywords
Action research • Sociotechnical systems • Collaborative management research • Parallel learning structure theory • Learning mechanisms • Academic/industry partnerships • Organization design • Sustainable work systems

Contents

Influences and Motivations: From Experimental Design to Lewinian Action Research

The issue of influences that motivate interest in the field of organization development and change is fascinating, given that great thinkers often have very different backgrounds, training, and connections to the field. In Dr. A. B. Shani's case, the attraction is rooted in his early experiences as an undergraduate student, early mentorship by experimental design (Mode 1) researchers (Gibbons et al. 1994), his experiences as an officer in the Israeli military, and master's and first-year doctoral experiences. Mode 1 and Mode 2 research will be briefly defined in the "Advancements in Action Research Theory and Practice Through Establishment of the New Field of Collaborative Management Research" section under "Key Contributions: Collaborative Management Research and Beyond." The examples provided below demonstrate his early focus on involving research participants in real-world problem-solving, along with his initial thinking about action research processes.

As an undergraduate student at Tel Aviv University during the early 1970s, Rami was trained by psychologists in rigorous experimental research. Emphasis was on adoption of appropriate field research methods and coursework on statistics and data analysis. During his senior year, he worked at an absorption center within a private high school. The center focused on integrating students coming to Israel from different parts of the world. Over 200 incoming students at the high school relied on the center around the clock, as they lived in campus dorms. Rami saw an opportunity to conduct a mini-thesis on cultural influences and personal space. That is, Rami wanted to know how Russian, Argentinian, Israeli, and other people at the school felt about proper buffer zones and how they positioned themselves in social situations. The study would also track sex, family size, and other influences related to notions of personal space. The main focus of data collection was on "meet in the street" encounters and accurate measurements of distances between participants. Findings from this first study were eventually published in the *Journal of Cross-Cultural Psychology* (Ziv et al. 1975). His early experiences with Mode 1 research both in college and later in the military produced interesting findings and publications, but especially with the military studies, he was troubled that the work did not produce many practical changes.

Dr. Shani's formal education was interwoven with military service. As he advanced to officer status, Rami observed that the army gathered an enormous amount of data from cadets and soldiers using survey research methods. He observed that the data was shared at the command level but rarely trickled down to lower levels or served any real use in personal development of officers. As a part of his master thesis, Rami initiated his second research study. This study was patterned after the pioneering Rosenthal and Jacobson Pygmalion study on the importance of teacher expectations. The Pygmalion effect associated with the Rosenthal and Jacobson study is the phenomenon whereby higher expectations lead to an increase in performance. This time, the study involved adults rather than children, with more safeguards regarding ethics (human subjects). Dr. Shani identified an opportunity to conduct similar research with soldiers, but this time, manipulating military trainer expectations during 3-month and 6-month leadership training courses. As with his first study, the research involved rigorous experimental design, including attention to human subjects. Experimental and control groups imitated the design used in the Rosenthal Pygmalion study. During the experiment, Dr. Shani participated as an observer, with an announced role as developer of future training programs. Professor Dov Eden, his academic mentor and advisor, emphasized from the start that data collected during the project should be used in feedback/discussion sessions with the sponsors. The study showed that high expectations led to lower attrition rates and improved performance. Presentations were made at the Base level and at Headquarters offices responsible for leadership development. In short, despite clear results and implications for changing hundreds of courses, the military had little interest in replicating the studies or following up with course changes. In stark contrast, the researchers were excited about the studies, identifying three "A" publication possibilities. Dr. Shani wondered, "What's wrong with this picture?" The hands-on field research experience, as well as frustrations over such limited use of the findings, led Rami to reconsider the ways that sponsors and participants were engaged in research programs. There had to be better ways to collaborate with clients and include them in research programs (Eden and Shani 1982).

During the first year of the Ph.D. program in Organizational Behavior (OB) at the Weatherhead School of Management, Case Western Reserve University, some of

Dr. Shani's work was published, and he continued to build his research knowledge and skills. As a junior member of the doctoral program and at the same time adjusting to a new country, he was also wrestling with doubts about traditional experimental research (Mode 1), the mix of courses he was taking, and whether to continue with the OB doctoral program. Following a break after the first year, Rami began to work with professors experimenting with Mode 2 qualitative research amid growing interest in action research programs at the Weatherhead School. In major studies conducted by Case professors at the Cleveland Clinic, there was more emphasis on engaging participants at all stages of the research program cycle. The research did not start with traditional hypotheses but instead focused on significant problems facing leaders at the medical centers. Also, the new work featured lively conversations with medical providers and direct attention to patient care issues. In the Clinic and other studies, Don Wolfe, Suresh Srivastva, and Bill Pasmore placed research in the context of the Lewinian action research tradition. About that time, Rami was also taking an organization theory class from David Brown and was frustrated with studying a wide range of macro models that seemed distant from practical application to real-world problems. David Brown, seeing Rami's frustration with course content, led him to explore sociotechnical systems (STS) theory. The macro theory, combined with field applications, seemed suited to Rami's preoccupation with relevance and action. These new associations and research projects essentially put Rami on a new path that led to his dissertation focus.

Bill Pasmore was determined to keep Dr. Shani at Case Western. He included Rami in a pending proposal to the Pentagon around support for the implementation of a sophisticated computer system designed to assess NATO combat readiness. Honeywell Corporation had developed the system in question but encountered serious problems in getting it to work properly. There was an urgent need to identify the problems and integrate technical and human systems in order to make progress. Pasmore and his team responded to the Pentagon RFP with a proposal to research the topic while utilizing a sociotechnical system (STS) framework and action research (AR) orientation. Rami joined the project and participated in a massive literature search focused on AR and STS while preparing the research design phase of the study (see for example, Pasmore et al. 1982). Some of the leading STS people in the country were asked to join an advisory board for the combat readiness project. In meetings and informal sessions, Rami gained exposure to Jack Sherwood, Dave Hanna, Jim Taylor, David Feldman, Harvey Kolodny, and other leading scholar practitioners. Several other STS projects were underway at the time within Proctor and Gamble, the World Bank, and Bailey Controls, creating a stimulating climate at Case that emphasized solid relationships and deeper level of engagement with partners, including clients (Pasmore and Friedlander 1982).

In part based on the literature search for the Pentagon, Rami vowed to take a holistic look at action research studies completed through 1981. This became the focus of his doctoral dissertation and paved the way for early theory building on parallel groups, parallel learning structures, and parallel learning systems. Initial collaboration with Gervase Bushe on parallel learning structures proved promising. The work evolved over the years to produce strong contributions in organization development and change theory related to a wide variety of learning mechanisms. This is one of the three advancements reported in section two of this chapter.

After he completed the doctoral program in 1981, Dr. Shani moved to North Dakota University as a tenure track faculty member in organization behavior. In contrast to the larger projects at Case, Rami was able to partner with other social scientists at North Dakota to start his own action research projects. This provided Rami the opportunity to establish different relationships with clients at all phases of action research (see for example, Eberhardt and Shani 1985; Shani and Eberhardt 1987).

Key Contributions: Collaborative Management Research and Beyond

Conversations with Dr. Shani and examination of his published works uncovered three clear themes that provide a framework for this section of the chapter. First, Professor Shani has contributed to literature concerning alternative modes of knowledge creation. The main contributions are advancements in action research theory and practice through establishment of the new field of collaborative management research. Emphasis has been on creation of collaborative, engaged forums within collaborative management research programs. Second, Dr. Shani has participated in the evolution of sociotechnical systems theory (STS) within international research consortiums. The shift has been toward sustainable work systems (SWS) design and the attention to creating new organizational capabilities. This evolution has spanned two decades and survives in multiple forms, including work with colleagues at the USC Center for Effective Organizations, the FENIX Executive Ph.D. program at the Stockholm School of Economics, Chalmers University of Technology's Institute for Management of Innovation and Technology in Sweden, and graduate programs at Politecnico di Milano in Italy. Finally, along with Gervase Bushe and Peter Docherty, Dr. Shani has clear contributions to the OD&C literature in articulation of parallel learning structure theory and the expansion to consideration of diverse learning mechanisms within the field of organization design.

While the above list contains main contribution categories, it must also be said that Rami's CV reveals a fourth theme that his research partners can readily identify. This theme is that Dr. Shani is the coeditor (since 2008) of the annual research series *Research in Organizational Change and Development*, the co-series editor of *Organizing for Sustainable Effectiveness*, and has coauthored diverse book chapters, articles, and presentations both within the organization development and change field and outside this field. Multidisciplinary collaboration on change research topics, as well as similar collaboration on marketing, information systems, production, healthcare, human resource management, innovation, product development, sustainability, and other change-related topics, has been part of his research agenda for the past four decades. Rami maintains a wide array of memberships in long-standing research centers, as well as associations with multiple university programs and transitory research groups. While this might fit within the first category listed above, it is nonetheless important that Dr. Shani has been a force for professional development in his partnering and encouragement of diverse scholarly contributions to the OD&C literature.

Advancements in Action Research Theory and Practice Through Establishment of the New Field of Collaborative Management Research

Gibbons et al. (1994) notes that new research practices are being introduced and the mode of knowledge creation is being changed in significant ways. Two modes of knowledge creation, mode 1 and mode 2, are each connected with distinctive sets of research practices. Mode 1 knowledge production – a complex of ideas, methods, values, and norms – has evolved to control the diffusion of the Newtonian model. Researchers who follow the rules are by definition professional practice, "scientific." Mode 1 problems are set and solved in a context governed by the academic interests of specific disciplines and communities. In contrast, Mode 2 knowledge is worked out in a context of application and is often interdisciplinary. Typically, Mode 2 includes a wider set of researchers, practitioners, and clients working together on a problem defined in a specific, local context. Various aspects of the Mode 1/Mode 2 distinction will be revisited throughout this chapter.

The point that Rami appreciates both Mode 1 and Mode 2 research orientations has been mentioned above, but more will be said about his support for Mode 2 knowledge creation. As coeditor of the first volume entitled *Collaborative Research in Organizations: Foundations for Learning, Change, and Theoretical Development* (Adler et al. 2004), Rami brought together diverse European and North American scholar practitioners. The intent was to provide alternative lenses and mechanisms to support academic-industry partnerships in conducting action research. Partnering and collaboration between people in university/institute settings and those in other organizational settings is increasingly part of knowledge production in management-related fields. While there is a belief that this partnering can add tangible value if carried out with attention to scholarly quality, there is still much to be learned about the emergence of Mode 2 (Gibbons et al. 1994) research. Mode 2 research often features involvement of a greater range of participants in the knowledge development process, along with greater variance in research processes and practices. Bonds are formed between academic researchers and organizational representatives that result in adoption of unique methodologies that are thought to be appropriate for the specific setting and presenting problems.

More complexity through involvement of different stakeholders and consideration of alternative research orientations can lead to disagreements about research processes and outcomes. On a higher level, collaborative management research (CMR) can be critiqued based on four different clusters of questions or perspectives. Rami and his coauthors point out epistemological, political, ethical, and efficiency bases for initiating a dialogue about the contributions of CMR. Also, in his seminal first volume on collaborative research (Adler et al. 2004), Rami and his coauthors identified five different facets of collaborative research: different schools of thought or orientations used during collaborative management research, different types of academic organizations that facilitate partnerships and collaborative research, the emerging role of insider researchers, the associated learning mechanisms, and documentation of scientific and actionable knowledge. The key contribution was to map the subfield of CMR within action research as a body of knowledge and to generate discussion about the merits of CMR frameworks in terms of scholarly quality and practical relevance. As will be further documented below, much of Rami's work has involved meta-analysis of trends in OD&C theory and practice.

In a second handbook, Dr. Shani and his colleagues provide a more in-depth look at the promise of collaborative management research. The second handbook includes additional scholar/practitioner, management consulting, and client perspectives concerning CMR (Shani et al. 2008). It also includes case examination of research centers specifically designed to conduct collaborative management research and more in-depth treatment of CMR mechanisms and processes used in more complex and diverse organizational settings during change programs. Dr. Shani's specific contributions to AR and CMR theory are partly summarized in his contribution to the handbook (Coghlan and Shani 2008). Teaming with David Coghlan, Dr. Shani discusses the issues that managers and researchers must address to create a healthy community of inquiry that is appropriate for the particular task situation, research process, and culture (both academic and organizational). Both research task and relational issues, such as quality of participation and engagement in cycles of action and reflection, must be addressed. The authors further articulate the knowledge and skills required to create a community of inquiry and build it as the community evolves (see for example, Schein 2013) to produce tangible project outcomes and desired academic outcomes. Quality in CMR communities of inquiry seems to depend upon the nature of the real-life issue studied, the quality of collaboration, the quality of the reflective process, and whether the results are significant and the knowledge actionable.

Rami has regularly contributed to action research, OD&C, and collaborative management research handbooks, and journal articles on the promise of CMR. Together with David Coghlan, he coedited two four-volume series: *Fundamentals of Organization Development* (Coghlan and Shani 2010) and *Action Research in Business and Management* (2016). Some specific contributions can be found in the coauthored Chapter 45 of the *Sage Handbook of Action Research* (2008), second edition, and chapter four of the *Sage Handbook of Action Research*, third edition (2015). The authors address issues in developing new capabilities when programs are mainly driven and carried out by insider action researchers. Building on prior research on how organizations develop capabilities via CMR, insider action research initiatives, and learning mechanisms, Rami engaged doctoral students in research projects that further explore the meaning and practice of the Mode 2 research orientations in diverse organizational settings (see for example, Roth et al. 2007; Mitki et al. 2008; Fredberg et al. 2011; Shani et al. 2012; Cirella et al. 2012; Radaelli et al. 2014; Coghlan et al. 2016; Canterino et al. 2016).

Parallel Learning Structure Theory and Expansion to Consideration of Diverse Learning Mechanisms Within the Field of Organization Design

In the 1980s, Rami worked with Gervase Bushe to publish *Parallel Learning Structures* (PLMs) in the Addison Wesley OD Series. In the preface, the authors describe a PLM as "a technostructural intervention that promotes system-wide change in bureaucracies, while maintaining the advantages of bureaucratic design." Technostructural intervention refers to a change in the technology and/or structure of an organization with the purpose of improving or stabilizing the entire sociotechnical system in the organization (Bushe and Shani 1991). The book as a whole was a refreshing shift in OD away from the usual preoccupation with an organization's social system to include attention to technical system factors (technology, structures, rules, and regulations) and organization design approaches such as STS. At the time of publication, *Parallel Learning Structures* was only one of a few books in the OD series that focused on the growing field of organization design within OD&C. Others included the book by Blake et al. (1989), *Change by Design*; Mohrman and Cummings (1989), *Self-Designing Organizations*; David Hanna's (1988) *Designing Organizations for High Performance*; Galbraith's (1973) *Designing Complex Organizations*; the Davis and Lawrence (1977) book, *Matrix*; and the Hackman and Oldham (1980) book, *Work Redesign*.

Bushe and Shani did not invent the notion of parallel learning structures, as they existed in different forms in a host of OD cases and other publications. But they did coin the term as a generic label for interventions where a structure is created, the structure operates parallel with the formal hierarchy and formal structure, and has the purpose of increasing an organization's learning (new thoughts and behaviors by employees). The PLS would vary with the type of OD intervention, but the "generic" intervention process would include purpose and scope of the project, formation of a steering group, communicating the steering group's vision and expectations to members of the organization, formation of study or other working groups, conducting the inquiry process and identifying options, experimental implementation, system-wide diffusion, and evaluation. The book paved the way for close examination of organizational learning and blocks to learning what change agents must deal with during an OD intervention.

Dr. Shani's work in the late 1980s began to shift more centrally to organization design. He teamed with Michael Stebbins to write a series of articles comparing different academic-based design approaches that manifest significant differences from design approaches used by leading management consulting firms in industry. The academic approaches all included a guiding conceptual model for change, design principles, a clear redesign process, and empirical records of applications in different settings (see for example, Stebbins and Shani 1989). For the next two decades, Dr. Shani's publications began to emphasize two trajectories: a broad examination of learning mechanisms beyond PLS, and evolution of a STS-based theory of organization design toward the sustainable work systems view of organization design. The SWS branch will be covered in the section below.

Based on a sabbatical at the Stockholm School of Economics in 1991–1992, Rami began to link with European research centers devoted to quality of working life and work design. Along with Peter Docherty, he began to examine the diverse ways that people in organizations seize upon ways to learn. In his foreword to the Shani and Docherty book, *Learning by Design*, Bill Pasmore (Shani and Docherty 2003) notes that the authors provide a window through which the reader can catch a glimpse of organizations in the act of learning, in the process of improving. Moreover, he notes that through cases offered by Docherty and Shani, we learn that learning is not unidimensional, replicable, or even translatable from one organization or one country to the next. Learning processes and learning structures seem to coevolve in organizations.

In completing *Learning by Design*, the authors relied on colleagues at their prior institutions. For Rami, this included Frank Friedlander, Bill Pasmore, David Kolb, and Gervase Bushe at Case Western. Additional support included first exposure to Torbjorn Stjernberg, Docherty, Bengt Stymne, and Jan Lowstedt at the Stockholm School of Economics. Many others, including Mariano Corso at Politecnico de Milano, Armand Hatchel at Ecole de Mines in Paris, Paul Lillrank, and Harvey Kolodny, contributed to discussions about action research and learning by design. Peter Docherty's perspective on *Learning by Design* stemmed originally from the Swedish Work Environment Fund's program on "New Technology, Work Organization, and Management," which occurred between 1982 and 1987. This work involved over 50 projects and with opportunities for interaction with a large number of his Scandinavian colleagues. This was followed by a program for Learning Organizations, 1990–1996, and eventually the SALTSA Work Organization program project on sustainable work systems, which established a strong network with colleagues in over 10 countries. Members of the SALTSA network met face to face during 1999–2004, producing a variety of books, research proposals to the EU, journal articles, and conference papers. Peter Docherty established the SALTSA network from his bases at the National Institute for Working Life and the Royal Institute of Technology in Stockholm.

The critical contribution of *Learning by Design* was to track organizational learning to prior theories and definitions, to pose a conceptual model that links learning mechanisms to strategy and design, resources and capabilities, the context, and sustainability. The vital link is said to be learning mechanisms. To a great extent, learning mechanisms determine change program success. Learning mechanisms, at and across different levels of the organization, are the internal ways of organizing, acting on, and developing the firm's differentiated capabilities. While individual, team, and organizational learning mechanisms are examined, perhaps the strongest contribution was to identify and analyze *organizational* learning mechanisms (Lipshitz et al. 1996), as well as linkages among the context, learning requirements, and choices among learning mechanisms. In later publications, cognitive, structural, and procedural categories of learning mechanisms are articulated in much greater depth (see for example, the rather comprehensive listing of the categories in terms of types and examples in Docherty and Shani (2008), and discussion found in Shani and Docherty (2008)). Cultural or cognitive mechanisms are the bearers of language, concepts, symbols, theories, frameworks, and values for establishing thinking, reasoning, and understanding consistent with the organization's strategy. Cognitive learning mechanisms are management's main means for creating an understanding among employees on the character, need, and priority of the strategy and the learning and changes required to realize it. Structural learning mechanisms are organizational, physical, technical, and work-system infrastructures that facilitate research and practice-based learning. Examples include communication channels, the establishment of lateral structures, formal and informal forums, and learning-specific structures such as parallel learning structures and process improvement teams. Procedural learning mechanisms concern the rules, routines, methods, and tools that can be institutionalized to promote learning. They include processes and methods for collective learning, such as action learning or debriefing routines. Docherty and Shani have also made contributions in the way of advice for those who are to design learning mechanisms or make choices among existing learning mechanisms during change programs. For more on first-person voice/practice skills, second-person voice/practice communities of inquiry, and third-person learnings about how to learn to manage change while being in the middle of it, see Docherty and Shani (2008) and Shani and Docherty (2008). More recent publications provide additional development, illustrations, and empirical testing of learning mechanisms (see for example, Fredberg et al. 2011; Cirella et al. 2012).

The Evolution of Sociotechnical Systems (STS) Theory Toward Sustainable Work Systems and the Creation of New Organizational Capabilities

Early efforts to advance theory and practice on organizational learning and learning mechanisms moved in tandem with sociotechnical systems advancements in the 1990s and beyond. The byline for the book *Learning by Design* is "Building Sustainable Organizations." At Case and through continuing collaboration with Bill Pasmore and other STS experts, Rami was schooled in STS theory and applied projects to build more effective organizations. During the Swedish-led SALTSA programs of 1998–2000, a diverse mix of scholars met at least twice a year to focus on design of work systems that could achieve a balance between employee involvement and engagement on the one hand and work-life balance on the other. In other words, how might organization and work be designed to ensure both high performance and employee development and quality of life? The project was called "From Intensive to Sustainable Work Systems," and most European and American members of the network contributed to the network's book, *Creating Sustainable Work Systems: Emerging Perspectives and Practice* (Docherty et al. 2002). Many of the contributors had backgrounds in organization development and change, organization and work design, and in particular, STS design. The STS designers included Frans M. van Eijnatten at Eindhoven University of Technology, Jan Forslin at the Royal Institute of Technology, Stockholm, and Rami Shani from California Polytechnic State University, San Luis Obispo. Many of the other 16 contributors had extensive experience guiding organization and work design projects based upon alternative action research-based design theories.

Rami's contribution to the first SALTSA-based book, beyond being a coeditor, was to set the context for the book and the vision for SWS design, including a clear focus on regeneration and development of human resources and the dual emphasis on promotion of quality of working life and competitive performance. He teamed with Michael Stebbins to write "Eclectic Design for Change," the first attempt to articulate the network's version of reflective design. Borrowing from Mackenzie (1986), SWS design is thought to be a blend of theory (organization science), knowledge embedding in the particular industry/sector and work situation, and the contributions of those who participate in the design or redesign process. Given the trend to inclusion of more stakeholders in design projects, SWS design recognizes that there is potentially a wide separation from a science-based solution that a manager might hope to use and one that will meet the needs of different constituents and work well in practice (Stebbins and Shani 2002). In this first effort at theory-building, the authors felt that as with STS and other design approaches, design processes would emerge separately by country contexts and the nature of the industry and firm.

The authors believe that while design processes will differ, it is possible to articulate requirements for the design process. Requirements refer to the pressures that stem from external and internal business conditions – the things that require change (Lillrank et al. 1998). Requirements are not the same as design criteria, but they eventually lead to development of criteria that will guide different change programs. Key requirements for the design process include exploring alternative design approaches at the outset; self-application of theory, methods, and practices; encouraging participants to take ownership of the change process through high involvement at all stages; exploring dilemmas identified during design work; recognizing the iterative nature of design work, continuous modification of designs during projects, including transitions and implementation; and exploration of intended and unintended consequences of design work. As with other leading design approaches, SWS design would have a guiding macro model, design principles, design requirements, and design criteria. Design criteria are statements that describe, in ideal terms, those functions that the new design should perform. Design criteria usually have action verbs; they state that the design should facilitate, promote, encourage, provide for, or motivate (Nadler and Tushman 1988). Design criteria reflect the values of the different stakeholders and are written in response to competitive conditions, the tasks to be executed, the collective sense of current problems, the perceived cause of problems, and other constraints.

The authors have recognized action research, STS, and self-design contributions to SWS theory. For example, while STS was originally developed to work in production settings, it has been significantly modified to work in services (Adler and Docherty 1998) and nonroutine situations (Pava 1983; Pasmore 1988; Mohrman and Cummings 1989). Self-design is also an outgrowth of STS theory and practice. The initial self-design work by Karl Weick (1977) has been captured and enhanced by Mohrman and Cummings (1989). The ideas of design as an ongoing process and design as a recipe are part of both self-design and SWS design. The recipe idea does not mean a blueprint, but rather, recipes that require varying amounts of improvisation. Through action learning, the organization is prepared for continuous adjustment and redesign. SWS theory incorporates much of self-design thinking and also extends it through collaborative involvement of stakeholders in establishment of design requirements, design criteria, and homegrown creation of diagnostic tools used during the redesign process.

A second SWS design book, *Creating Sustainable Work Systems: Developing Social Sustainability* (2009), edited by Peter Docherty, Mari Kira, and Rami Shani, moved design thinking further by providing definition of what is meant by human and social sustainability in work organization. The second book also reveals more about the connections between business design and organizational design in the context of the environment and ongoing change management efforts. Stebbins and Shani (2009) propose Concurrent design as a way to integrate *business design* choices (selection of customers, creation of value for customers, assuring profit, and deciding which activities to perform in the value chain) with *organization design* choices (see for example, Slywotzky and Nadler 2005). Concurrent design featuring strong dialogue among those managing the business design, the organization design, and change management processes that guide both efforts. There are some strong connections here to modern architectural design (Weick 2004; Gehry 2004). In each case, a skeletal framework is created early with the idea that users can gradually complete the design work. Designers should underspecify structures and processes in the early going. Instead, self-organizing activities will flesh out the skeleton. This type of thinking is opposite to many past approaches to strategic organization design and in fact, more closely follows innovation that occurs in new product development. In brief, Concurrent design infuses a capability to self-organize around changing business design and organization design decisions. For more on this thinking, see Kelley and Littman (2005).

In Concurrent design projects, diverse stakeholders participate in deliberations about the vision and design criteria. The work is done by self-design groups, and the learnings from self-design experiments are discussed in light of perceived outcomes. Discussions with stakeholders are based on design principles underlying SWS change programs and of course, design criteria established by those involved in the project at hand. Beyond this basic model, not much is specified on Concurrent design process. For more on the topic of eclectic SWS design processes, see Stebbins and Shani (1995, 2009). For more on SWS design cases and the learning mechanisms that build employee skills in self-design, see Docherty et al. (2009). For more on a systematic view of outcomes and conducting impact analyses during design, see Nadler and Tushman (1997). For a discussion on the promise of creating collaborative organizations with a greater level of power equalization based on dialogue and collective learning, see Docherty et al. (2009, chapter 17).

During the past 10 years, Dr. Shani has been one of the leaders (with Peter Docherty, Sue Mohrman, and Chris Worley) of a growing network concerned with the design of sustainable organizations, which evolved to be "organizing for sustainable effectiveness." The inaugural meeting took place in October 2008, followed by five workshops held around the globe. The first volume stemming from the meetings summarizes the extensive literature on sustainability. Members of the network draw on pioneers in the field to examine how the topic of sustainable effectiveness has been approached and what has been learned (Mohrman and Shani 2011). Particular focus is on purpose and capabilities development, which leads to the notion that organization design and learning processes are critical to building a sustainable world. It involves simultaneous focus on economic, social, and ecological outcomes.

Subsequent workshops focused on organizing for sustainable healthcare (Mohrman and Shani 2012), building networks for sustainable effectiveness (Mirvis and Worley 2013), reconfiguring the ecosystem for sustainable healthcare (Mohrman and Shani 2014), and organizing supply chain processes for sustainable innovation in the agriculture and food industry (Cagliano et al. 2016). In the volumes on healthcare, the authors examine healthcare systems that are building the foundations for sustainable, high-quality healthcare. Case-based analyses cover organization design changes that take advantage of new knowledge and medical advances needed to generate positive impacts on the health of individuals and societies. The chapters also explore the change capabilities and learning mechanisms that healthcare systems can adopt to focus on implementation and continuous improvement. The focus on design of sustainable organizations in healthcare will continue to occupy Rami's time, given the importance of the topic. All nations are grappling with problems of rising consumer demands for high quality care, in the face of limited resources and competing claims on government sources of income.

New Insights: Knowledge and Skills Needed to Conduct Collaborative Management Research Programs

Dr. Shani's unique experiences with Ph.D. programs in Sweden and Italy have provided special insights about academic/industry partnership issues, along with the knowledge and skills needed to carry out collaborative management research programs. His participation on the faculty at FENIX required intense involvement with doctoral students as they conceived and carried out projects within sponsor companies (see for example, Coghlan and Shani 2015). As early as 2002, Rami introduced David Coghlan from Trinity to lead the FENIX seminar on insider action research. Students needed special knowledge and skills concerning the unique roles that action-researchers play and how to conduct themselves during projects. At FENIX, the foundations for training in CMR and Mode 2 research were diverse. They included action research theory and practice, use of specific methodologies within action research, and understanding of various models of organization design. For example, doctoral students explored Schein's Clinical Inquiry approach and cases and Hatchuel's theories on work intensity and work design. Rami contributed action research and CMR seminars at FENIX.

While the FENIX Executive Ph.D. program no longer exists per se, faculty at both Chalmers and the Stockholm School of Economics continue to advise single doctoral students in the FENIX tradition and in Mode 2 methods. At Politecnico di Milano, Rami continues to teach the Ph.D. course on CMR theory and practice. Also, through projects with industry partners and doctoral students, Rami continues the dual focus on OD practice and scientific inquiry. This follows the Lewinian heritage of action and collaboration, scholarship and practice, as being core values of OD.

The FENIX executive Ph.D. model featured unusual cooperation between researchers and managers and high commitment of resources from both sides. Executives at the four partner companies nominated Ph.D. candidates, paid for their attendance at courses and seminars in the Ph.D. program, and paved the way for original research within the companies. Essentially, students/managers were paid full time by their respective companies while they worked half time on their normal company endeavors. The FENIX faculty carried high student project loads and had to be available to meet with senior management partners, as well as the research teams. In navigating the issues involving sponsors, FENIX instructors had to show how projects would be science-based and benefit both OD&C and the companies. Knowledge and skills about handling insider/outsider issues gained during the FENIX and Milan projects have been shared in numerous scholarly works (see for example, Shani et al. 2012; Coghlan et al. 2016; Canterino et al. 2016; Cirella et al. 2012). In these and other publications, Coghlan and Shani and their students explore unique issues with CMR as a modality of action research in diverse settings.

As Coghlan and Shani (2017, in press) point out, Mode 2 knowledge production characteristics provide attention to both OD practice and scientific inquiry. The instructors as outside action researchers team with the students and inside teams to address specific organizational challenges. The researchers are to generate knowledge within a particular organizational context. Shani and Coghlan extended this profile to consider four other characteristics of Mode 2 research. For example, in the FENIX practice and other similar arrangements, the insider and outside researchers are accountable to management. There must be assurance that learning mechanisms will be created to sustain change. But at the same time, for the science of OD and CMR, the researchers are accountable to the academic community. For example, the faculty must certify the research and analysis methods used during projects and must be comfortable with both Mode 1 and Mode 2 research. The research team must learn to demonstrate how the work is rigorous, reflexive, and relevant (Coghlan and Shani 2014). We are beginning to understand that CMR can be judged by its own criteria and standards, which are different from traditional research standards (Canterino et al. 2016, in press). Moreover, in some instances, action research and CMR initiatives can be institutionalized through careful selection of learning mechanisms (Coghlan and Shani 2015). It is highly likely that Dr. Shani will continue to advance the three main themes of knowledge creation through CMR, the OD&C theory's new emphasis on learning mechanisms, and enhancement of sociotechnical systems theory to include the emerging literature on organizing for sustainable effectiveness.

Legacies and Unfinished Business: Three Interrelated Areas of Organization Development Research

As observed in the chapter sections above, Rami has been a leader in advancing theory in three interrelated areas of organization development research. Manuscripts currently in the works highlight innovation in Mode 2 research processes and practices as well as bonds formed between academic researchers and managers. Through two major handbooks, Dr. Shani provides an in-depth look at the promise of collaborative management research and the challenges faced in creating healthy communities of inquiry in particular task situations. Future publications will continue to explore the unique methodologies created by researchers and managers that are appropriate in specific organizational settings. Together with David Coghlan, Rami will build on prior work on building new capabilities via CMR when the change programs are mainly driven and carried out by insider action researchers. As shown in the first section of this chapter (see section "Advancements in Action Research Theory and Practice Through Establishment of the New Field of Collaborative Management Research"), contributions in this area are already diverse and full of insights on unique methodologies.

For mainstream OD practitioners, Dr. Shani's legacy is tied to his initial postdoctoral research on parallel learning structure theory and the expansion to consideration of diverse learning mechanisms within the OD subfield of organization design. The book *Parallel Learning Mechanisms* remains a classic in exploring PLMs as technostructural interventions that promote system-wide change. The book also supports a shift within the OD field to consider technical system factors and comprehensive organization design approaches such as the most recent literature on sustainable work systems design. Rami has had a strong role, along with Peter Docherty in shaping the research agenda on action research and learning by design. His most recent contributions take the form of theory building, illustrations, and empirical testing of learning mechanisms.

Dr. Shani has also been a leader in building the body of literature on sustainable work systems, recognizing action research, sociotechnical systems, and self-design contributions to SWS theory. Two SWS books explore human and social sustainability in work organization, highlighting connections between business design and organizational design in the context of ongoing change management efforts. Dr. Shani will continue to be involved in the evolution of concurrent design thinking and projects focused on developing capabilities to self-organize in the face of changing business design and organization design decisions. His efforts to publish literature on the topic of organizing for sustainable healthcare and reconfiguring the ecosystem for sustainable healthcare are just beginning but show great promise for solving problems complex healthcare settings.

In summary, Dr. Shani will continue to be a highly visible contributor on scholarly books and journal articles related to issues in collaborative management research, action research, and innovation in the field of organization design. Through his efforts as a reviewer and editor of books and journals Rami will have a vital role in building the worldwide organization development research agenda.

It has been my treat in retirement to meet monthly with Rami and our friend Jim Sena in beautiful Morro Bay, California, to catch up on family, college, and community news. Our extended lunch conversations have continued for over 10 years, and it paves the way for collaborations on diverse research, writing, and editorial projects. Rami has this unique friendship and collaborative relationship with many others. He is most animated when recognizing the ideas and accomplishments of diverse faculty within the Orfalea College of Business as well as when he shares information related to new and old associations with scholars and students in Europe. Much of the conversation relates to collaboration with colleagues in Italy, Sweden, Canada, Ireland, and Israel, but his personal network in his adopted USA is also vast. People who know Rami well recognize his limitless energy and affection for players in the field of organization development and change. It is clear that Rami will continue to be an excellent colleague at the Orfalea College of Business and a vibrant force in the worldwide organization development community.

References

Adler, N., & Docherty, P. (1998). Bringing business into sociotechnical systems theory and practice. *Human Relations, 51*(3), 319–345.

Adler, N., Shani, A. B., & Styhre, A. (Eds.). (2004). *Collaborative research in organizations: Foundations for learning, change, and theoretical development*. Thousand Oaks: Sage.

Blake, R., Mouton, J.S., & McCanse, A. A. (1989). *Change by design*. Reading: Addison-Wesley.

Bushe, G. R., & Shani, A. B. (1991). *Parallel learning structures: Creating innovation in bureaucracies*. Reading: Addison-Wesley.

Cagliano, R., Caniato, F., & Worley, C. G. (2016). *Organizing supply chain processes for sustainable innovation in the agri-food industry*. UK: Emerald.

Canterino, F., Shani, A. B., Coghlan, D., & Brunelli, M. S. (2016). Collaborative management research as modality of action research: Learning from a merger-based study. *Journal of Applied Behavioral Science, 52*(2), 157–186.

Cirella, S., Guerci, M., & Shani, A. B. (2012). A process model of collaborative management research: The study of collective creativity in the luxury industry. *Systematic Practice and Action Research, 25*(1), 281–300.

Coghlan, D., & Shani, A. B. (2008). Insider action research: The dynamics of developing new capabilities. In P. Reason & H. Bradbury (Eds.), *The Sage handbook of action research: Participatory inquiry and practice* (pp. 643–655). Thousand Oaks: Sage.

Coghlan, D., & Shani, A. B. (Eds.). (2010). *Fundamentals of organization development: Emerging issues and challenges* (4 Vols.). Los Angeles: Sage.

Coghlan, D., & Shani, A. B. (2014). Creating action research quality in organization development: Rigorous, reflective, and relevant. *Systemic Practice and Action Research, 25*, 523–536.

Coghlan, D., & Shani, A. B. (2015). Developing the practice of leading change through insider action research in: A dynamic capability perspective. In H. Bradbury (Ed.), *Handbook of action research* (pp. 47–55). Thousand Oaks: Sage.

Coghlan, D., & Shani, A. B. (Eds.). (2016). *Action research in business and management* (4 Vols.). Los Angeles: Sage.

Coghlan, D., Shani, A. B., & Roth, J. (2016). Institutionalizing insider action research initiatives in organizations: The role of learning mechanisms. *Systemic Practice and Action Research, 29*, 83–995.

Coghlan, D. & Shani, A. B. (2017 in press). Inquiring in the present tense: The dynamic mechanisms of action research. *Journal of Change Management*.

Davis, S. M., & Lawrence, P. (1977). *Matrix*. Reading: Addision-Wesley.

Docherty, P., & Shani, A. B. (2008). Learning mechanisms as means and ends in collaborative management research. In A. B. Shani, S. A. Mohrman, W. A. Pasmore, B. A. Stymne, & N. Adler (Eds.), *Handbook of collaborative management research* (pp. 163–182). Thousand Oaks: Sage.

Docherty, P., Forslin, J., & Shani, A. B. (Eds.). (2002). *Creating sustainable work systems: Emerging perspectives and practices*. London: Routledge.

Docherty, P., Kira, M., & Shani, A. B. (Eds.). (2009). *Creating sustainable work systems: Developing social sustainability*. London: Routledge.

Eberhardt, B., & Shani, A. B. (1985). The effects of full-time vs. part-time employment status on attitudes toward specific organizational characteristics and overall job satisfaction. *Academy of Management Journal, 27*(4), 893–900.

Eden, D., & Shani, A. B. (1982). Pygmalion goes to boot camp: Expectancy, leadership, and trainee performance. *Journal of Applied Psychology, 67*(2), 1179–1204.

Fredberg, T., Norrgren, F., & Shani, A. B. (2011). Developing and sustaining change capability via leaning mechanisms: A longitudinal perspective on transformation. In A. B. Shani, R. W. Woodman, & W. Pasmore (Eds.), *Research in organizational change and development* (Vol. 19, pp. 117–161). Bingley: Emerald.

Galbraith, J. (1973). *Designing complex organizations*. Reading: Addison-Wesley.

Gehry, F. O. (2004). Reflections on designing and architectural practice. In R. Boland Jr. & F. Collopy (Eds.), *Managing as designing* (pp. 19–35). Stanford: Stanford University Press.

Gibbons, M., Limoges, C., Nowotny, H., Schwarzman, S., Scott, P., & Trow, M. (1994). *The new production of knowledge*. London: Sage.

Hackman, J., & Oldham, G. (1980). *Work redesign*. Reading: Addison-Wesley.

Hanna, D.P. (1988). *Designing organizations for high performance*. Reading: Addison-Wesley.

Kelley, T., & Littman, J. (2005). *The ten faces of innovation*. New York: Doubleday.

Lipshitz, R., Popper, M., & Oz, S. (1996). Building learning organization. *Journal of Applied Behavioral Science, 32*:292-305.

Lillrank, P., Shani, A. B., Kolodny, H., Stymne, B., Figuera, J. R., & Liu, M. (1998). Learning from the success of continuous improvement change programs. An international comparative study. In R. Woodman & W. Pasmore (Eds.), *Research in organization change and development* (Vol. 13, pp. 47–72). Greenwich: J&I Publications.

Mackenzie, K. (1986). *Organization design: The organizational audit and analysis technology*. New York: Ablex.

Mitki, Y., Shani, A. B., & Stjernberg, T. (2008). Leadership, development and learning mechanisms: Systems transformation as balancing act. *Journal of Organizational Change Management. 29*(1), 68–84.

Mirvis, P. H., & Worley, C. G. (2013). Building networks for sustainable effectiveness. In A. B. Shani, S. A. Mohrman, & C. G. Worley (Eds.), *Organizing for sustainable effectiveness* (Vol. 3). London: Emerald.

Mohrman, S., & Cummings, T. (1989). *Self-designing organizations: Learning how to create high performance*. Reading: Addison-Wesley.

Mohrman, S., & Shani, A. B. (2012). Organizing for sustainable healthcare. In A. B. Shani, S. A. Mohrman, & C. G. Worley (Eds.), *Organizing for sustainable effectiveness* (Vol. 2, pp. 113–146). Bingley: Emerald.

Mohrman, S. A., & Shani, A. B. (2014). Reconfiguring the eco-system for sustainable healthcare. In A. B. Shani, S. A. Mohrman, & C. G. Worley (Eds.), *Organizing for sustainable effectiveness* (Vol. 4). Bingley: Emerald.

Nadler, D., & Tushman, M. (1988). *Strategic organization design: Concepts, tools, and processes*. Glenview: Scott Foresman.

Nadler, D. A., & Tushman, M. L. (1997). *Competing by design: The power of organizational architecture*. New York: Oxford University Press.

Pasmore, W. A., & Friedlander, F. (1982). An action research program for increasing employee involvement in problem solving. *Administrative Science Quarterly, 27*, 343–362.

Pasmore, W. A. (1988). *Designing effective organizations: The sociotechnical systems perspective*. New York: Wiley.

Pasmore, W. A., Francis, C., & Shani, A. B. (1982). Sociotechnical systems: A North American reflection on empirical studies of the seventies. *Human Relations, 35*(12), 1179–1204.
Pava, C. H. (1983). *Managing office technology: An organizational strategy*. New York: Free Press.
Radaelli, G., Guerci, M., Cirella, S., & Shani, A. B. (2014). Intervention research as management research in practice: Learning from a case in the fashion design industry. *British Journal of Management, 25*(1), 335–351.
Roth, J., Shani, A. B., & Leary, M. (2007). Insider action research: Facing challenges of new capability development within a biopharma company. *Action Research, 5*(1), 41–61.
Schein, E. H. (2013). *Humble inquiry: The gentle art of asking instead of telling*. San Francisco: Berett-Koehler.
Shani, A. B. & Eberhardt, B. (1987). Parallel organization in health care institution. *Group and Organization Studies, 12*:147–173.
Shani, A. B., & Docherty, P. (2003). *Learning by design*. Oxford: Blackwell.
Shani, A. B., & Docherty, P. (2008). Learning by design: A fundamental foundation for organization development change programs. In T. Cummings (Ed.), *Handbook of organization development and change* (pp. 163–181). Thousand Oaks: Sage.
Shani, A. B., Mohrman, S., Pasmore, W. A., Stymne, B., & Adler, N. (Eds.). (2008). *Handbook of collaborative management research*. Thousand Oaks: Sage.
Shani, A. B., Coghlan, D., & Cirella, S. (2012). Action research and collaborative management research: More than meets the eye? *International Journal of Action Research, 8*(1), 45–67.
Slywotzky, A. J. & Nadler, D. (2005). Strategy and organization consulting. In L. Greiner & Poulfelt (Eds.), *Management consulting today and tomorrow*. New York: Routledge.
Stebbins, M. W., & Shani, A. B. (1989). Moving away from the 'mafia' model of organization design. *Organizational Dynamics, 17*(3), 18–30.
Stebbins, M. W., & Shani, A. B. (1995). Organization design and the knowledge worker. *Leadership and Organization Development Journal, 16*(1), 23–30.
Stebbins, M. W., & Shani, A. B. (2002). Eclectic design for change. In P. Docherty, J. Forslin, & A. B. Shani (Eds.), *Creating sustainable work systems: Emerging perspectives and practice* (pp. 201–212). London: Routledge.
Stebbins, M. W., & Shani, A. B. (2009). Toward a sustainable work systems design and change methodology. In P. Docherty, M. Kira, & A. B. Shani (Eds.), *Creating sustainable work systems* (pp. 247–267). New York: Routledge.
Weick, K. (1977). Organization design: Organizations as self-designing systems. *Organizational Dynamics, 6*, 30–46.
Weick, K. (2004). Rethinking organizational design. In R. Boland Jr. & F. Collopy (Eds.), *Managing as designing* (pp. 36–53). Stanford: Stanford University Press.
Ziv, A., Shani, A. B., & Nebenhaus, S. (1975). Adolescents educated in Israel and in the Soviet Union: Differences in moral judgment. *Journal of Cross-Cultural Psychology, 6*(1), 108–121.

Further Reading

Coghlan, D., & Shani, A. B. (2005). Roles, politics, and ethics in action research design. *Systemic Practice and Action Research, 18*, 533–546.
Popper, M., & Lipshitz, R. (1998). Organizational learning mechanisms: A structural and cultural approach to organizational learning. *Journal of Applied Behavioral Science, 34*(2), 161–179.
Zand, D. (1974). Collateral organization: A new change strategy. *Journal of Applied Behavioral Science, 10*(1), 63–89.

Peter F. Sorensen: Influences, Influencer, and Still Influencing 72

Therese F. Yaeger

Abstract

Peter F. Sorensen, PhD, is professor and program chair of the Organization Development and Organizational Behavior Programs at Benedictine University just outside Chicago in Lisle, Ill. This profile contains information that emerged through numerous interviews and document searches. It confirms that Sorensen is still an emerging thinker in the field of organizational change, with his contributions spanning more than 50 years. Sorensen's background, contributions, and insights are explored, with the intent of aligning his work and background with that of Dr. Kurt Lewin, the father of social psychology. From these sharings, it may be concluded that Sorensen follows a Lewinian approach to life – providing insights to colleagues, removing obstacles in change, exploring the global populations, teaching concepts in social psychology, and influencing students (Lewin, Field theory in social science. New York, Harper & Row, 1952; Marrow, The practical theorist: The life and work of Kurt Lewin. New York, Teachers College Press, 1977). One such student of Sorensen's is Dr. David Cooperrider, creator of Appreciative Inquiry (AI) who wrote to Sorensen, "The Benedictine OD program you created and have built is so solid and so key to our entire field. You inspired my passion for a field that is becoming increasingly relevant and critical to human being's lives everywhere."

Keywords

Influence • Power • Benedictine University • Global OD • Appreciative inquiry

---

T.F. Yaeger (✉)
Organization Development Department, Benedictine University, Lisle, IL, USA
e-mail: tyaeger@ben.edu

D.B. Szabla et al. (eds.), *The Palgrave Handbook of Organizational Change Thinkers*,
DOI 10.1007/978-3-319-52878-6_92

Contents

Influences: Education and Environment

In some ways, Sorensen's influences and motivations parallel those that influenced the field of Organization Development with the work of Lewin during World War II and the Nazi occupation of Europe. Sorensen grew up in a family dedicated to working with the youth of the West Side of Chicago, what was referred to as the "inner city." His father was an executive of the YMCA and director of a YMCA camp. His summers at camp were a shared experience for his entire family.

Sorensen's father and grandfather emigrated from Denmark in the late 1920s and early 1930s, prior to the Nazi invasion of Denmark. In fact, Sorensen's early childhood was characterized by conversations concerning the welfare of relatives in Denmark, stories of the Nazi decree that all Jews were to wear the Star of David, and how the Danish King appeared the next morning for his horseback ride wearing the Star of David. Sorensen remembers stories of how the Nazis attempted to destroy the Danish pride and the destruction of the beautiful Tivoli Gardens that was done in retribution for sabotage by the Danish underground. After WWII, Sorensen was told about how one of his relatives died in a Nazi concentration camp because he was a Danish policeman who worked to help the Danish Jews escape to Sweden. Other relatives provided a "safe house" for members of the Danish underground and those who escaped Nazi-occupied Denmark. From then on, people all over the world who had escaped Nazism with the help of the Sorensen family contacted his relatives every 4th of July.

After graduating from high school, amidst his extreme introversion, Sorensen entered Chicago's City College on the south side of Chicago but was drafted into the Army in 1955 before he completed his degree. Sorensen's limited college experience served him well in the military; because of his education, he was made a clerk-typist and was sent to Germany as part of the 11th Airborne Division (even though he absolutely refused to jump out of planes). Thanks to the educational services of the Army, he was able to complete 2 years of college while in the service.

Sorensen claims that there were two developments in his early career that influenced his OD work: his education and his experiences at CNA. After leaving the service in 1957, he returned to college under the GI Bill. While taking a class in social psychology, he first watched the film by Lewin, Lippitt, and White regarding an experiment with the Boy's Club. He still remembers how he sat in the dark after the film ended, waiting for the lights to come back on, thinking, "My god, this is not just a study of young boys. This is a study which encompasses all of the stories that I heard as a young boy about WWII and Nazism." Also at college, he met his mentor, Dr. Bernie Baum, an adjunct professor who had just completed his PhD at the University of Chicago with his dissertation on the decentralization of authority in a bureaucracy. Dr. Baum recognized Sorensen's shyness but also appreciated his military experience and maturity.

While still a student, Baum asked Sorensen if he would join him as he was starting a department at CNA Financial centered on organizational analysis (in a way, one of the early internal OD departments). Even here, the impact of World War II continued to play an important role in Sorensen's career, as Baum's family – like Lewin's – had seen the "handwriting on the wall" and escaped Nazi Germany with his family in the 1930s.

At CNA, Sorensen experienced firsthand the potential of good organizational change and analysis efforts. The department of organizational analysis became a "mecca" for organizational studies with researchers from MIT, Northwestern, Michigan, and the University of Chicago, to name a few. As early as 1965, Sorensen and his CNA colleagues studied the works of Douglas McGregor, Warren Bennis, Kurt Lewin, and others in the emerging field of OD. According to Sorensen, he was able to "work with the best in the field," presenting papers at regional management and sociological meetings, attending executive meetings of the Academy of Management. Both Whisler and Burack influenced Sorensen's thinking in terms of computer technology and its impact on the influence and control in organizations, and Sorensen had the opportunity to coauthor with both scholars on the topics of managerial training and organizational control (see Whisler et al. 1967; and Baum and Sorensen 1970).

There, he was also introduced to and worked with Douglas McGregor's Theory X and Theory Y concepts; the work from the University of Michigan group with Dr. Rensis Likert and his four systems of management; Arnold Tannenbaum's work on the measurement of power and influence in organizations; and Floyd Mann, Donald Pelz, and the rest of the great University of Michigan research team. These organizational researchers shaped Sorensen's thinking by modeling how good measurement and research can be translated to the corporate audiences while still making contribution to management research, and they provided models of organization research that served as a standard through Sorensen's career.

Beyond his work, at the societal level, it was a time of turbulence: of recognition of discrimination involving gender and people of color, the Weathermen (an underground American organization that carried out jailbreaks and riots), the Students for a Democratic Society (SDS), the 1970 Kent State shootings and sit-ins at major universities, and Chicago's Mayor Daley at the 1968 Democratic Convention. This turbulent period reinforced Sorensen's interest in power and influence in organizations and organizational change. The 1960s and 1970s for Sorensen became a time of great realization – he saw the link between employees in organizations, and people broadly, stating, "We all want to be involved, with goals and development for our own future."

Along with the turbulence, there was also an element of optimism. Sorensen does not claim that CNA at that time was a model of Theory Y, but with his colleagues' education and degrees in sociology, the OD concepts clearly resonated with members of the organization analysis department. Although McGregor's writings were popular in management, they were frequently misinterpreted as being "soft management," when just the opposite was true. Sorensen believes that somehow, out of all of this, things were moving in the direction of Theory Y, as both management and employees were embracing the concept of increased employee involvement and commitment.

Baum later left CNA for a faculty position to establish a PhD program in public health at the University of Illinois, and Sorensen again returned to school, completing his PhD with the help of his wife Nancy Evans (whom he had met while working at CNA) and Dr. Elmer Burack, whom he had met as part of a research project at CNA and who was starting a PhD program at Illinois Institute of Technology. Sorensen's 1971 dissertation entitled "Management development under conditions of change," pertained to the role of computer technology and the redistribution of power and influence in organizations, which is a topic still of interest to Sorensen today. His doctoral research continued with a 1976 *Academy of Management Journal* publication with Burack entitled "Management preparation for computer automation: emergent patterns and problems," where he claimed that "management's computer preparation often seriously lags installation, is narrowly conceived, is incomplete or may never even take place" (p. 318).

According to Lewin, the father of OD, "Every psychological event depends upon the state of the person and at the same time on the environment, although their relative importance is different in different cases." (1936). Consistent with Lewin's quote above, Sorensen believes that his state and the state of his environment at the time contributed to his future in work, OD, and education. Clearly, the increasingly turbulent environment and the rapidly increasing technology were shaping the future for Sorensen and the field of OD.

Opportunity knocked before Sorensen even finished his PhD. While still a student, he received a phone call from the dean of George Williams College in Illinois, asking if he would be interested in joining the faculty (which he did), as part of a new graduate program with a college and faculty that later formed the Mecca for sensitivity training in the Midwest. He joined with two faculty members (Bennett and Perlmutter) who were major influencers in National Training Laboratories (NTL). Sorensen was greatly influenced by these two faculty who were instrumental in creating this Mecca for sensitivity training – Bennett and Perlmutter provided expert knowledge on sensitivity training, and "introverted" Sorensen balanced the OD curriculum with concepts on measurement, power, and organizational theories. This exposure to new change concepts further provided the basis for his interest in the field of Organization Development. Later, the George Williams OD program was cited in an early group book as one of the first programs to offer coursework in group work, sensitivity training, and other concepts that later served as a foundation for OD. In 1986, Sorensen and the OD master's program at George Williams moved to Benedictine University, where the Masters of Science in Management and Organizational Behavior Program served as a foundation for one of the first PhDs in Organization Development.

Sorensen as Influencer Through Programs and Publications

Sorensen's upbringing, education, and exposure to corporate OD work in his 20s allowed opportunities for contributions in later years. Equipped with good values (work and family) and the ability to publish provided fodder for major contributions in organization development and change research. Two of Sorensen's key contributions include his influence with students as part of the creation of the PhD program at Benedictine University and his research interests as reflected in five decades of publications.

PhD Program at Benedictine University

Sorensen is reminded of the challenges and changes necessary when starting a new doctoral program at a traditionally undergraduate private college – in short, truly understanding the system where change is introduced. This undertaking was monumental in that the development and startup of the PhD program in OD was the first of its kind in the OD field and the first doctoral program at any Benedictine college or university. The change was successful in that it remains a critical turning point for Benedictine University; in the more than 20 years of the program's existence, it maintains a successful PhD completion rate, and two doctoral programs have since started at Benedictine University. Designed as a scholar-practitioner program to provide a bridge between the academic scholar and corporate practitioners, it has created a large number of alumni who stay in the corporate/practitioner world, as well as many who transitioned into academic careers, at schools such as Northwestern University and Purdue University. Today, alumni of Benedictine University and the former George Williams College programs reach into the 10,000 range.

The PhD program at Benedictine University has served as a model for two additional doctoral programs at Benedictine, and alumni of the program are now faculty in and chairs of a number of doctoral programs in the United States and internationally. The initial faculty were two graduates of the Case Western Reserve University program – Dr. Ram Tenkasi and Dr. Jim Ludema, and later Therese Yaeger, director of global OD for Motorola. Ludema went on to establish a PhD program at Benedictine in values-driven leadership, Tenkasi continues with the program as a major contributor and as a Fulbright senior research scholar, and Yaeger continued with the program with major contributions to international OD. Every member of the OD PhD program served as chair of a major Academy of Management division, and Yaeger served both as the chair of the consulting division and as president of the Midwest Academy of Management.

Reflecting on the impact of his contributions at Benedictine University, Sorensen can be assured of his success, as he has been honored by Benedictine University with the highest faculty award (The Whinfrey Award) and the naming of the OD lecture hall as the Sorensen Hall of Leaders.

Publications: Power, Structure, and Technology

Sorensen's contribution to OD research encompasses more than five decades of publications. His earliest publications in the 1960s involved the concepts of power and influence; a second research focus involved international and global OD; and a third focus involved appreciative inquiry and positive cultures.

Much of Sorensen's work on power and influence was dedicated to the concept of the total amount of influence in an organization – that the total amount of influence could be increased or decreased dependent upon the management system. He continuously studied, researched, and reported on the positive relationship between the total amount of influence in a system (indicated by the level of collaboration and shared influence) and organizational effectiveness. Amidst his introversion, Sorensen was encouraged by Baum to copresent their CNA research at the 1965 Annual Meeting of the American Risk and Insurance Association (ARIA). Their paper entitled "Influence Relationships as Administrative Organizational Data" was presented by the timid Sorensen, but he got quickly hooked on presenting strong research in an effort to identify next research topics.

While still in the corporate world, he continued to publish and present on his concept of influence and attitudes (Baum and Sorensen 1970). Also in 1970, he presented at the Illinois Sociological Association and the Midwest Academy of Management conferences, and he was invited to the Academy of Management. While there, he had the opportunity to sit in on an Academy of Management Planning Committee session, and the following year, at the National Academy of Management, he presented his first award-winning paper with Baum on the topic of student power and influence in universities. Sorensen's publications on influence and control included "The effect of managerial training on organizational control: An experimental study," in *Organizational Behavior and Human Performance* with Baum et al. (1970), and "The measurement of intraorganizational power: The application of the control graph to organization development," in *Group & Organization Studies* in 1977 with Baum. When he assessed managerial training and its effect on distribution of influence, his findings were consistent with the early work of Arnold Tannenbaum (1962) as his results indicated an increase in total amount of influence which indicated greater shared influence as a result of training efforts.

This work was followed by a period of studies on Management by Objectives (MBO), based on the concepts of McGregor's Theory Y and the implications of MBO for enhancing the total amount of influence in an organization – a concept introduced earlier by Tannenbaum. Peter always felt that Management By

Objectives (MBO) was one of the most important applied concepts consistent with McGregor's Theory Y. His research over time indicated that organization culture was an important intervening variable and that organizations which were essentially Theory X (hard management) in orientation simply used MBO as another technique for exercising control and centralized decision-making. Conversely, Theory Y organizations used MBO as a meaningful and effective way of enhancing collaboration and focusing on enhanced organizational performance. Working with his colleague Richard Babcock, they published "Organizational Variables and the Success of MBO: A Research Note," in the *Journal of Management Studies* with Straub in 1976; and "Some difficulties in longitudinal assessment of need satisfaction related to management by objectives," in *Psychological Reports* (Sorensen Babcock and Hasher 1977). These studies reaffirmed the notion that continued organizational support over time for MBO programs was necessary for ongoing sustainability of the programs.

Research in technology in the 1960s and 1970s was unfolding and Sorensen captured this opportunity. Peter's early work on technology began at CNA with a collaborative research effort involving Tom Whisler from the University of Chicago, as Whisler and Leavitt in a 1958 *Harvard Business Review* article predicted that computer technology would lead to increased centralization of decision-making. This work included an article by Whisler, Meyer, Baum, and Sorensen "Centralization of organizational control: An empirical study of its meaning and measurement" in *Journal of Business* (1967). Afterwards, as part of his PhD dissertation, Sorensen was involved in a research project at the Illinois Institute of Technology exploring the relationship between technology and organization structure and design. This project allowed him to experience different organizations and their respective technological structures. Peter's later work on the topic of influence demonstrated that Theory X cultures used technology to centralize decision-making and that Theory Y cultures used information technology to strengthen decentralization. Sorensen's work on computers and technology appeared with his dissertation chair Elmer Burack in the *Academy of Management Journal* (1976) and *Organization Design* (1977).

Influencing and Integrating Global Perspectives

Peter's continued research in power and control in organizations took an interesting twist as he explored the relationship between national cultural values and the use of power embedded in those cultural values. This data also resulted in some of the first international survey data reporting on national differences in the distribution of power and influence in organizations. Sorensen's findings actually preceded and closely paralleled the 1980 culture work of Geert Hofstede. Sorensen's findings, consistent with Hofstede research, indicated that the Scandinavian countries were the most egalitarian of cultures. Later, Alfred Jaeger furthered Hofstede's dimensions (power distance, uncertainty avoidance, individual vs. collectivism, and masculinity vs. femininity) and indicated that the Scandinavian cultural values were closest to the values of OD. In short, Jaeger's findings confirmed that Sorensen's Danish heritage made him a perfect fit for the world of OD!

Through the 1980s and 1990s, Sorensen expanded his work on international and global OD. In 1991, he coedited one of the first books on Global OD entitled *International Organization Development* with Thomas Head, Nick Mathys, and Keith Johnson (he later published *Global Organization Development*, coauthored with Head and Yaeger et al. 2006).

For this book, Sorensen's early research and publications involving a seven-country case study (Head and Sorensen 1993) provided exposure and expertise on global change issues, so that when he decided to create the first OD book on global challenges, colleagues were willing to share their cases for Sorensen's book, based on their OD and global experiences. This resulted in more than a dozen chapters for their first book, with cases involving countries that were not compatible to OD values to chapters on the most compatible countries, such as Denmark, Norway, and Sweden.

Peter's doctoral students have continued to expand the topic of global OD with dissertations and publications on OD studies from Africa, Latin and South America, Europe, Scandinavia, and the Far East. Publications also included early OD work in China (i.e., "Chinese executives' assessment of organization development interventions" in the *Organization Development Journal*, 2006).

Beyond publications, Sorensen was involved in expanding global OD knowledge. After serving as the chair of the ODC Division of the Academy of Management, in 2002 Sorensen proposed an international conference sponsored by the division. The proposal was initiated and cosponsored (with the management consulting division) at the biennial international conference at the University of Lyon 3 in France. This conference was attended by students and faculty members from more than 20 countries. At the early 2001 conference with the management consulting division, Sorensen presented a paper involving an international study on the concept of bridging from corporate strategy to implementation of strategy across the globe. This conference still continues today, in collaboration with the ISEOR Research Center (University of Jean Moulin). Beyond France, Sorensen has also presented papers at conferences in Denmark, Norway, France, the Netherlands, Switzerland, Austria, Mexico, and China, and his work has been published in French, Spanish, and Mandarin.

Applying Appreciative Inquiry to Practice

A third focus of Sorensen's research emerged in the 1990s – concept of Appreciative Inquiry. This interest was stimulated by the fact that Appreciative Inquiry (AI) was a concept initiated by his former George Williams master's student, David Cooperrider.

To further Cooperrider's AI concept, Sorensen attempted to share AI to the practitioner community. As a result, in 1996 Sorensen was the guest editor of a special 1996 double issue of the *OD Practitioner*, presenting the topic Appreciative

Inquiry for the first time to the OD Network. A quick 3 years later, with Cooperrider, Sorensen with Therese Yaeger and Diana Whitney, created an AI reader entitled *Appreciative Inquiry: Rethinking Human Organization Toward a Positive Theory of Change* (Champaign: Stipes Publishing). Again in 2001, the team of Cooperrider, Sorensen, Yaeger, and Whitney created a second reader entitled *Appreciative Inquiry: An Emerging Direction for Organization Development*; finally a third reader by the four authors was entitled *Appreciative Inquiry: Foundations in Positive Organization Development* in 2005.

Much of Sorensen work on Appreciative Inquiry was devoted to creating and presenting empirical studies of the implementation of AI. His commitment to the assessment of the effectiveness of AI is captured in an article published in Woodman and Pasmore's *Research in Organization Change and Development* Annual entitled "Assessment of the State of Appreciative Inquiry: Past, Present, and Future," with Yaeger et al. (2005). Here, the most important finding was that the more rigorous the study's design, the more favorable the outcome was. In essence, where there may be an aversion to do quantitative AI research, the data indicated that the more rigorous the AI design, the stronger the positive outcomes.

However, Sorensen's own research studies with Appreciative Inquiry combined AI with the assessment of organization change using a measure of organization culture, the Organization Culture Inventory (OCI), and the use of survey feedback. One particular area of interest was initiated by a reviewer of the 2005 *ROCD* article who suggested the concept of latent positive change (LPC), a finding that organizations with which Sorensen studied were characterized by a period of strong positive cultures. The concept of latent positive culture is reported in several articles, including "Appreciative Inquiry Meets the Logical Positivist" (Sorensen et al. 2005) and "Appreciative Inquiry in Bureaucratic Settings" (Stroyberg et al. 2005).

Additionally, in 2005 Sorensen envisioned a book series where the Addison Wesley 1970 series ended. The field of OD had expanded tremendously, and Sorensen with Yaeger identified more than a dozen topics worthy of publication. To that end, the Contemporary Trends in Organization Development book series was created and ten books already exist in the series, with topics such as large scale change, OD in health care, global organization development, optimizing talent, and the education of the scholar practitioner.

Still today, Peter continues to publish and present on global OD and appreciative inquiry. But Sorensen remains proud that almost all of this work has been in collaboration with his mentors (Baum and Burack), his colleagues (Head, Yaeger, and Richard Babcock), or his countless students.

Sorensen has been a member of a number of academic and professional organizations, including the National Academy of Management, the Midwest and Southwest Regional Academy of Management, and Chair of the OD division of the academy, and two alumni of the Benedictine PhD program have served as presidents of the Midwest Academy. He is a member of the OD Network and the International Society for Organization Development. The OD Network honored Sorensen for his contribution to OD education (titled the Kathy Dannemiller Sharing the Wealth Award), and the International Society for Organization Development (formerly

O.D. Institute) presented him with the Consultant of the Year Award. He is currently an international director of the International Society for Organization Development. He was the keynote speaker at the first OD conference in China, and one of the graduates of his PhD program was instrumental in the development and implementation of the first PhD program in organization development in Asia.

New Insights: Involved Influencer

Upon reflection, Sorensen realizes now how his contributions to OD education (although common practice today) were formerly "novel" for typical, more traditional classroom practice in the 1960s, 1970s, and later. As a former student, coauthor, and current collaborator with Sorensen, I have witnessed his teaching approach to be in alignment with Lewin's approach to learning and collaborating among students. He is reminded of two novel educational concepts that were cutting-edge in the 1970s, namely, the application of experiential adult learning and the creation of doctoral OD education.

Experiential Learning

Sorensen, like Lewin, believes that learning is more effective when it is an active rather than a passive process (Marrow 1977). Similarly, whereas Lewin (Weisbord 2012) pointed out that all problems have social consequences that include people's feeling, perceptions of reality, self-worth, motivation, and commitment, Sorensen believes that the awareness of both of these Lewinian concepts – active learning and understanding the social consequence – not only support OD philosophy but enhance the teaching and better prepares adults for real world work involving teamwork and collaboration.

A former masters-level student of Sorensen claimed that it was Sorensen's approachable style that made him a better student, claiming, "Sorensen's demeanor is one of humility, never drawing a focus on him but on others. He brings this unassuming characteristic and humor to informal conversations and to formal meetings, lectures, and discussions. Although never posing as an authoritative figure, the impact of his work is widely acknowledged, experienced, and appreciated by those who have studied and collaborated with him or read the body of his publications. His remarkable contributions deserve the recognition he has long deflected to doctoral students and colleagues." Other students disagree, insisting that Sorensen's approach to learning, while experiential, is one of academic excellence, claiming that Sorensen would never settle for second-rate graduate work.

Another indication of Sorensen's experiential learning style is the Contemporary Trends in Change Management Lecture Series. In 1977, with a seminar style approach to experiential learning, the first Lecture Series was presented at George

Williams and with Drs. Robert Blake and Dr. Jane Mouton of the Managerial Grid, and Dr. Edgar Schein as first year speakers. This semi-annual event led by Sorensen and his colleague Dr. Judi Strauss became the intellectual conduit for OD, as the lecture series and soon became a mecca for the Chicago OD community. The lecture series continues today in its 40th year, featuring major figures in the field such as Michael Beer, Susan Mohrman, W. Warner Burke, and David Cooperrider, among others. It is interesting that Sorensen today realizes he has had the opportunity to work with approximately 50% of the named thinkers in this book and as many as 75% of contemporary thinkers.

Doctoral Education for OD

Sorensen, like Lewin, recognizes the meaningfulness of applied research and practical theory. While Lewin argued that applied research could be conducted with rigor and that one could test theoretical propositions in applied research (Rogers 1994), similarly Sorensen credits this research/theory concept to the scholar/practitioner design of the Benedictine University Doctoral Program. The scholar-practitioner design is what attracts the eager OD practitioner. One such practitioner is corporate executive and PhD alumni Dr. Mary Lou Kotecki who reminds us of Sorensen's passion to create the finest scholar-practitioner program, stating:

> Through Sorensen's program students are inspired and challenged by national and international thought leaders. Distinguished Visiting Scholars have included five Academy of Management Presidents (Bartunek, Cummings, Van deVen, Rousseau, and Huff); and other visiting scholars included Worley, Cappelli, Boje, Weisbord, Torbert, Beer, Burke, Argyris, Coghlan, Stacey, Gergen, and Cooperrider among many others. Additionally, he brought in more historical practitioners such as Blake and Mouton, Schein, and Dannemiller.
>
> As professor and director of this Ph.D. program Dr. Sorensen also serves as its linchpin. Sorensen lectures and serves as a student advisor, advocate, and motivator thus galvanizing student learning, participation, and performance. And, most remarkably, Peter consistently recognizes student contributions to the field and to their organizations.
>
> Through the years, Peter's Benedictine University students have come from very large corporations and institutions, through small for-profit and non-profit organizations, NGOs, consulting groups, energy and retail companies, and medical, educational, federal, financial, and religious institutions. Their positions ranged from CEOs, corporate officers, and executives to medical professionals and human resource directors. Three of his students served as officers within Academy of Management divisions; others serve on journal review boards or as journal editors.

Although she is an early graduate of the PhD Program in Organization Development at Benedictine University, Kotecki reminds Peter that he has now graduated more than 200 doctoral students in 20 years (but Sorensen is too humble to mention this!)

Sorensen parallels Lewin's willing collaboration with colleagues and students and sees this as a contribution to future OD scholars. Clearly, Sorensen's 50 years of OD work has spurred not only a passion for OD student learning but the power of the novel student learning through the lecture series and how the scholar-practitioner doctoral program illuminates the innovative approaches to OD for future scholars.

Unfinished Business: Still Influencing and Unfinished

Sorensen realizes now that he was destined for a career in OD based on his early exposure to humanistic values in his Danish family. Values around power in organizations such as autonomy, participation, and shared leadership – which are at the core of OD – were part of the family values with which he grew up. His exposure to disruptive societal changes of the 1960s aligned with what Lewin observed in Germany during his formative years. For Sorensen, the fundamental values of OD and the egalitarian values of the Scandinavian countries continue to influence him today more than ever.

Sorensen does not ponder about his legacy, stating "that's too far away to think about." In short, his thinking around unfinished business is still evolving. But three primary topics of unfinished business keep Sorensen busy – global OD, positive change, and education of the scholar-practitioner.

Global OD

Sorensen emphasizes that we have yet to begin to understand the true significance of OD and change work in a global setting. He and the late Thomas Head shared that each international OD case as a grain of sand, but the beach has yet to be created to see a more holistic picture. He has reiterated to students that OD and change efforts can be very different in different cultures, and yet OD consultants may be too focused on their intervention to realize this important factor.

Sorensen is proud that his first book on global OD actually reported on unsuccessful change efforts in different countries – he would like to see more learning and reporting of lessons learned for failed change efforts in other countries.

Positive Change

In 1996, when Sorensen was the guest editor of a double issue of the *OD Practitioner* on the topic of Appreciative Inquiry to the OD Network, he thought Appreciative Inquiry would be a powerful concept to share Cooperrider's work with OD practitioners. Having been a masters-level student of his, Sorensen was now familiar with Cooperrider's work at Case Western Reserve University and saw this issue as an opportunity to share new concept with the world of practitioners. Cooperrider willingly agreed to contribute to this undertaking. To date, this one 1996 issue is the most reprinted volume of the *OD Practitioner*, Sorensen insists. "What David Cooperrider has started (ignited, Sorensen says is more appropriate) is simply the beginning of our knowledge of positive science in organizations," Peter contends.

Tangentially, Peter continues to look for the connection between AI and positive organizational concepts and is currently exploring the potential relationship between positive change and the increasingly popular notion of thriving and agile and how these concepts are changing the former concepts of influence and control in organizations.

Scholar Practitioner Programs

One of the challenges of the future will be to optimize the opportunities and challenges presented by the increasing number of scholar-practitioner doctoral programs. Optimizing these opportunities can be realized by finding ways of sharing and collaborating on building the knowledge of the field sometimes by collaborating with other doctoral programs!

With the concept of the scholar-practitioner is the need of role models to aspiring OD consultants. Here, Sorensen believes there can be better role modeling in publishing, in practice, and in consulting. For example, Sorensen's role modeling to students is evidenced by his insistence that the Benedictine OD doctoral students' participate and present at the local and national Academy of Management meetings. As his mentor Baum stressed to him, Sorensen believes that the sharing and dissemination of one's research is necessary and often provides a promising future. According to Dr. Kathy Schroeder, a corporate OD executive and alumna of the Benedictine University PhD Program, "My research and publications are evidence of Peter's influence on my OD work. My published works on OD research and knowledge have strengthened my capabilities exponentially."

Sorensen realizes from his students that awards not only make a difference for the future of a new doctor's vitae but that they also make a difference in measuring success of the doctoral programs they attended.

So while Sorensen claims that he has unfinished business, many of his students and colleagues agree that he continues to influence OD research and countless students. As a former student of Peter myself, we all welcome his future contributions.

Further Readings

Baum, B., & Sorensen, P. (1965). *Influence relationships as administrative organizational data.* Paper presented at the 1965 Annual Meeting of The American Risk and Insurance Association (ARIA).

Baum, B., & Sorensen, P., (1970). *Contemporary student attitudes and the future of management.* Paper presented at the Annual National Meeting of the Academy of Management.

Baum, B. H., Sorensen, P. F., & Place, W. S. (1970). The effect of managerial training on organizational control: An experimental study. *Organizational Behavior and Human Performance, 5*(2), 170–182.

Burack, E., & Sorensen, P. F. (1976). Management preparation for computer automation: Emergent patterns and problems. *Academy of Management Journal, 19*(2), 318–323.

Burack, E. H., & Sorensen Jr., P. F. (1977). Computer technology and organizational design. *Organizational Design, 8*, 223–235.

Cooperrider, D., Sorensen, P., Whitney, D., & Yaeger, T. (1999). *Appreciative inquiry: Rethinking human organization toward a positive theory of change*. Champaign: Stipes Publishing.

Cooperrider, D., Sorensen, P., Yaeger, T., & Whitney, D. (2001). *Appreciative inquiry: An emerging direction for organization development*. Champaign: Stipes Publishing.

Cooperrider, D., Sorensen, P., Yaeger, T., & Whitney, D. (2005). *Appreciative inquiry: Foundations in positive organization development*. Champaign: Stipes Publishing.

Head, T. C., & Sorensen, P. F. (1993). Cultural values and organizational development: A seven-country study. *Leadership & Organization Development Journal, 14*(2), 3–7.

Head, T. C., et al. (2006). Chinese executives' assessment of organization development interventions. *Organization Development Journal, 24*(1), 28.

Hofstede, G. (1980). Culture and organizations. *International Studies of Management & Organization, 10*(4), 15–41.

Jaeger, A. M. (1986). Organization development and national culture: Where's the fit? *Academy of Management Review, 11*(1), 178–190.

Johnson, H., Sorensen, P., & Yaeger, T. (2013). *Critical issues in organization development: Case studies for analysis and discussion*. Charlotte: Information Age Publishing. ISBN-13: 978-1623963255.

Lewin, K. (1936). *A dynamic theory of personality*. New York: McGraw-Hill.

Lewin, K. (1945). The research center for group dynamics at Massachusetts Institute of Technology. *Sociometry, 8*(2), 126–136.

Lewin, K. (1952). *Field theory in social science*. New York: Harper & Row.

Likert, R. (1961). *New patterns in management*. New York: McGraw-Hill.

Marrow, A. J. (1977). *The practical theorist: The life and work of Kurt Lewin*. New York: Teachers College Press.

Rogers, E. (1994). *A history of communication study: A biological approach*. New York: The Free Press.

Sorensen, P. F. (1971). Management development under conditions of change. Unpublished PhD dissertation, Illinois Institute of Technology, Chicago.

Sorensen Jr., P. F. (1976). Control and effectiveness in twenty-seven Scandinavian voluntary organizations. *Journal of Management Studies, 13*, 183–190.

Sorensen, P. F., Babcock, R., & Hasher, B. (1977). Some difficulties in longitudinal assessment of need satisfaction related to management by objectives. *Psychological Reports, 41*, 646.

Sorensen Jr., P. F., & Baum, B. H. (1977). The measure of intra-organizational power: The application of the control graph of organization development. *Group and Organization Studies, 2*(1), 61–74.

Sorensen, P., & Yaeger, T. (2004). Appreciative inquiry as a large group intervention: An innovation in organizational consulting. In A. Buono's (Ed.), *Creative consulting: Innovative perspectives on management consulting* (pp. 229–242). Greenwich: Information Age Publishing.

Sorensen, P., & Yaeger, T. (2015). Theory X and theory Y. *Oxford Press Bibliography*. doi:10.1093/obo/9780199846740-0078.

Sorensen, P., Head, T., Mathys, N., & Johnson, K. (1991). *International organization development*. Champaign: Stipes.

Sorensen, P., Head, T., Sharkey, L., & Spartz, D. (2005). Appreciative inquiry meets the logical positivist. In D. Cooperrider, P. Sorensen, T. Yaeger, & D. Whitney (Eds.), *Appreciative inquiry: Foundations in positive organization development*. Champaign: Stipes Publishing.

Sorensen, P., Head, T., Yaeger, T., & Cooperrider, D. (2011). *Global and international organization development* (5th ed.). Champaign: Stipes Publishing. ISBN1-58874-398-5.

Straub, A., Sorensen, P. F., & Babcock, R. (1976). Organizational variables and the success of MBO: A research note. *Journal of Management Studies, 13*(1), 84–86.

Stroyberg, L., Yei, T., Akinyele, A., Sorensen, P., & Yaeger, T. (2005). Appreciative inquiry in bureaucratic settings. In D. Cooperrider, P. Sorensen, T. Yaeger, & D. Whitney (Eds.), *Appreciative inquiry: Foundations in positive organization development*. Champaign: Stipes Publishing.

Tannenbaum, A. S. (1962). Control in organizations: Individual adjustment and organizational performance. *Administrative Science Quarterly, 7*(2), 236–257.

Weisbord, M. R. (2012). Productive workplaces, dignity, meaning and community in the 21st Century. 25th anniversary. *Jossey-Bass, San Francisco (CA)*, 506.

Whisler, T., Meyer, H., Baum, B., & Sorensen, P. (1967). Centralization of organizational control: An empirical study of its meaning and measurement. *Journal of Business, 40*(1967), 10–26.

Yaeger, T., Sorensen, P., & Bengtsson, U. (2005). Assessment of the state of appreciative inquiry: Past, present and future. In R. Woodman & W. Pasmore (Eds.), *Research in organizational change and development* (Vol. 15, pp. 297–319). London: Elsevier Ltd.

Yaeger, T., Head, T., & Sorensen, P. (2006). *Global organization development: Managing unprecedented change*. Charlotte, NC: IAP – Information Age Publishing Inc. ISBN1: 978-1-59311-559-3.

Ralph Stacey: Taking Experience Seriously 73

Chris Mowles

Abstract

Ralph Stacey is one of the pioneers in taking up insights from the complexity sciences in organizational theory. Trained in South Africa and the London School of Economics as a macroeconomist, and latterly as a group therapist, Stacey has combined abstract analytical thinking with an interest in experience, the emotions, a sense of self, and belonging, which make us human. From his interdisciplinary education and experience in industry he has developed a perspective on organizations which combines insights from both the natural and social sciences. This has led to a substantial body of publications with international renown. From the sciences of complexity he argues by analogy that organizations are iterating patterns of human interaction, never in equilibrium, which cannot be controlled by any individual or group. From the social sciences he focuses on the importance of our interdependence, expressed through power relations, and daily conversational activity. Sixteen years ago, and with two close colleagues, he founded a group-based professional doctorate, which runs psychodynamically. The program encourages practicing managers and leaders to focus on their daily experience of managing in uncertainty. In starting this program, he has recreated the best traditions of the Academy dating back to the ancient Greeks, where students and staff engage together in reflective conversation about the things which matter to them, provoking each other to think. Though he is well past retirement age Ralph is still a faculty member, raconteur, and conversationalist, participating in ways which make us all, faculty and students alike, more fully ourselves.

C. Mowles (✉)
Hertfordshire Business School, Hatfield, UK
e-mail: c.mowles@herts.ac.uk

D.B. Szabla et al. (eds.), *The Palgrave Handbook of Organizational Change Thinkers*,
DOI 10.1007/978-3-319-52878-6_93

Keywords
Complexity sciences • Complex responsive processes of relating • Experience • Ralph Stacey • Doctor of Management • Process sociology • Pragmatic philosophy

Contents

> We must not begin by talking of pure ideas – vagabond thoughts that tramp the public roads without any human habitation – but must begin with men and their conversation
> (Peirce 1958, Vol. 8, p. 112).

Introduction

Ralph Stacey was one of the first organizational scholars to appreciate the revolutionary potential of insights from the complexity sciences for theories of organizing. Highly trained in mathematics and statistics as a macroeconomist, the original appeal of the sciences of complexity for him were mathematical models demonstrating stable instability, or regular irregularity, a state known as "on the edge of chaos." This seemed to him to parallel his own experience in industry that managers are often in control and not in control both at the same time. His working experience had taught him that politics and power also figure prominently in how managers come to make decisions, particularly in conditions of uncertainty. Over time, and coterminous with his development as an academic and group therapist, he moved further and further away from the idea that organizations are complex systems to argue instead by analogy drawing on pragmatic philosophy and process sociology. Pragmatic philosophy is a broad discipline but is preoccupied with experience and action as the opening quotation shows. Process sociology is concerned with the flux and change of human interaction and how society arises from figurations of power and interdependence. This led him to develop the perspective known as "complex responsive processes of relating," a body of theories which combines insights from both the natural and social sciences. It is an account of how the complex phenomenon we refer to as "organization" arises from everyday conversational activity of human bodies responding to each other, engaged in the game of organizational life, cooperating and competing to get things done. So human beings are involved in complex activity and are responding to each other in continuous processes of interaction: hence the name of the perspective, complex responsive processes of relating. Key to understanding the perspective is a highly social view of mind, self and society, a complex understanding of time, a pragmatic understanding of experience and values, an appreciation of paradox, and a figurational view of human relating based on power. His legacy rests not just in the complex body of theory, which he has developed, but also in his recreation in the Academy and beyond of a different, and ancient, tradition of deliberating together about what it means to be human.

Influences and Motivations: Thinking About the Game of Organizational Life

Ralph Stacey tells the story that when he was chief strategist for a stockbroker and fund manager in the City of London, his job was to brief all the traders at the start of the day about significant financial trends in the markets so that they had a better idea about how they might trade. Quite soon into the job, he realized that he had no idea which trends were significant and which were not and so had very little insight about how best to advise them about what to do. He approached each new day with increasing dread, traveling from his home to the office and reading the *Financial Times* on the underground for clues about what he might say when he got there. Standing up in front of the traders, his managers, and the whole staff team, he found himself stuttering and stumbling over what he told them. His mouth was dry, his confidence at rock bottom: all he was doing was regurgitating what anyone else could have said if they had read the same newspapers, simply refracted through his own training as an economist. He had a deep experience of impostor syndrome.

It was a big crack in the confidence of someone who had always excelled as scholar, who had won prizes at the University of Witwatersrand in Johannesburg for his work on economic modeling, and who had gone on to take both his Masters and PhD at the London School of Economics in London in economic model-building and forecasting using sophisticated statistical models. Stacey was someone who had always succeeded and held important jobs in the planning departments of British Steel and the construction company John Laing. It was a great relief to him when he was made redundant from the financial company after about a year, and this event probably was a big impetus in his scholarly journey to work out why social life is unpredictable and impervious to many of the theories that he had learnt as a macroeconomist.

However, one quarter from which he found some support while still in the firm was from listening to a senior, older trader who took little interest in macroeconomic trends but treated the whole performance of trading as a game to be studied. Instead of just relying on financial reports and stock prices, the trader paid as much attention to his colleagues and the waves of enthusiasm or desperation that swept through them. One of the most important clues for discerning what might play out on the trading floor, as far as he was concerned, was how the traders responded to each other, amplifying some trends and damping down on others, how stock prices affected traders, and thus how traders affected stock prices. The market was being created and recreated on a minute-by-minute basis through trades and responses to trades, so that it was difficult to identify the beginning and the end, the cause and the effect.

Joining the Academy

The idea of ensemble human performance as game, the amplifying and dampening effects of patterns of human behavior, and the interweaving of intentions are themes that Stacey returned to repeatedly during his thirty-year career as an academic. This he resumed when he left the private sector to join Hatfield Polytechnic, latterly and henceforward the University of Hertfordshire (UH), in 1985 and in his early 40s to run the MBA program there. He directed the MBA with other colleagues in a highly participative way, teaching theory to the students who were practicing managers, but also encouraging them to describe and make sense of their daily experience of managing in organizations. He was also exposed at the time to the thinking of the Tavistock Institute in London, which was involved in the development of the MBA program and which had a long tradition of thinking about organizational life from a psychoanalytic perspective. So his intellectual preoccupations continued to be congruent with Peirce's injunction in the opening quotation that in order to make progress together we should pay attention to people and their conversation: what they do, what they say about what they do, and how they come to say it. His ideas developed into a body of thought he and colleagues have termed "complex responsive processes of relating," which draws parallels between the predictable unpredictability of social life and the stable instability of complexity models which first fascinated him when he began to write books in the early 1990s.

Complex Responsive Processes: The Movement of Thought

It would be easy to categorize Stacey's oeuvre as having a clear epistemological break between the scholarship he produced in the 1990s and his output post-2000. From the millennium onwards, after joining together with Doug Griffin (2001) and Patricia Shaw (2002), he took a radical social turn toward the pragmatism of G. H. Mead (1934, 1938) and the process sociology of Norbert Elias (2000, 2001). (The developing friendship resulted in their starting a professional doctorate together, named the Doctor of Management (DMan), which still runs to this day). That is to say, having mined the complexity sciences as a source domain for thinking about complex social processes in organizations from a realist perspective, sometimes claiming that organizations were complex adaptive systems, latterly his work took a turn to the social sciences, arguing the link with the complexity sciences by analogy and taking the step that social complexity needs to be understood with the help of sociology, philosophy, and psychoanalytic theory. However, quite a number of themes and interests permeate both early and later periods, so it may prove an instructive exercise to explore what has changed and what has stayed the same in his intellectual development. (It is interesting to note that when other scholars reference Stacey's work, it is often the first, more realist period to which they predominantly refer).

In three books written over a period of nearly 16 years, Stacey set out to understand learning processes in organizations and the genesis of knowledge and creativity. *Complexity and Creativity* (1996) was Stacey's fourth book, having already established himself as a pioneer in the complexity sciences, particularly with his second book *The Chaos Frontier* (1991). His next book attempting to describe learning and knowledge creation, *Complex Responsive Processes in Organizations: Learning and Knowledge Creation*, was published in 2001 as one of a series of books published by Routledge from colleagues at UH establishing the turn to social science in working with complexity ideas, as outlined above. And the third book tackling learning and knowledge, *Complexity and Organizational Reality* (2010), was ostensibly the second edition of *Learning and Knowledge Creation* but was so extensively rewritten that it took on a life of its own. I take each of these books sequentially to explore how each is located in Stacey's thinking and how they link together in the development of the body of the thought which takes the experiential component of the process of organizing, bound by power relations, values, and ethics, as its focus of study. As I outlined earlier, this focus on responsive experience, brought together in a perspective entitled complex responsive processes, links together insights from the complexity sciences, hence complex, with pragmatic theories of experience and communication, and the process sociology of Norbert Elias focusing on power and interdependence.

Ideas Which Contributed to the Publication of Complexity and Creativity

The Chaos Frontier, Stacey's second book, explores in detail a variety of manifestations of the complexity sciences, in particular mathematical chaos. In mathematics "chaos" describes a particular state of behavior of models based on nonlinear equations. Nonlinear models can demonstrate perfectly stable and symmetric patterns with certain parameter values and completely random patterns at others. But there is also a state in between, where the parameter values are such that they produce graphed patterns of regular irregularity: at "the edge of chaos," the concept informing the title of the book. They are neither perfectly stable nor random, but both stable and unstable at the same time. They are fractal in nature, symmetrically unsymmetrical, and Stacey goes on to indicate how these fractal patterns turn up everywhere in nature in the shape of coastlines, firs, and snowflakes. Stacey makes the case that the increasing instability of the business environment means that managers need to look for alternative models for developing their companies over the longer term rather than relying on equilibrium models. While over the short-term, conventional control mechanisms work, more appropriate models are required, mirroring the environment they find themselves in, because organizations are subject to nonlinear feedback mechanisms. Stacey makes the link here between the linear or nonlinear models that scientists use to model reality and the mental models that managers use to understand the world. He implies that a change in the former brings about a change in the latter and enables a greater ability to make sense of the turbulence managers need to navigate in conditions of open-ended change. In stable conditions, more orthodox management methods pertain.

Stacey sets out a rather binary argument to make the case for a strategic management approach based on the mathematical chaos. On the one hand, he says, conventional strategic management paradigms emphasize alignment, control, stability, and predictability. It is a paradigm that privileges top-down control often based on charismatic leadership, rationality, value-agreement, and sequential planning; however, for Stacey these are precisely the approaches that will disable managers when they face conditions of uncertainty because they prevent organizations from adapting to fast-changing circumstances and an evolving future. He stresses that he is not suggesting that managers should give up on control mechanisms, nor should they simply react to what arises. Rather, he states that learning processes in conditions of uncertainty are essentially political and depend upon a degree of conflict and an exploration of difference among colleagues. Strategy evolves from groups of managers continuously exploring what is new and different about the current situation working with analogous reasoning, a pattern of reasoning which mirrors the fractal patterns to be found in nature, to feel their way forward comparing the difficulties "in here" with the environment "out there." In other words, and harking back to his experience of the trading floor and his work with managers on the MBA at Hertfordshire Business School, it is important to pay attention to what managers find themselves doing every day at work as they compete and cooperate with their colleagues to get things done, and to find out what is similar and different about the circumstances they now face.

The publication of the *Chaos Frontier* led to Stacey being invited to join a cadre of scholars similarly interested in the complexity sciences. He attended a restricted membership complexity symposium in Canada where he met and conversed with Meg Wheatley (1992) and Jeff Goldstein (1989), among others, and went on to join something called the "Chaos Network," which held annual conferences. At one of these conferences, Stacey came across the work of the Santa Fe Institute and, in particular, Waldrop's book *Complexity: the Emerging Science at the Edge of Order and Chaos* (1992), which set out the history and development of the complexity sciences.

So by the time he came to write *Complexity and Creativity in Organizations*, the book on learning and knowledge under discussion, he had established himself as a scholar in a group at the forefront of what was perceived to be a new discipline in organizational studies. He had mounted a critique of what he termed the conventional orthodox strategic management discipline and had begun to investigate the social, psychological, and political dimensions of organizing in conditions of uncertainty, which he set alongside a more formal, systemic, and realist understanding of organizational structures and control in conditions of stability. Stacey grafted together the conventional and the unconventional, the traditional and the new.

Complexity and Creativity: Principal Arguments

One of the first shifts in the book from the previous work is to identify one of the manifestations of the complexity sciences, complex adaptive systems theory (CAS), as being the richest example for thinking about social and organizational life. Rather than the edge of chaos example dominant in the *Chaos Frontier*, Stacey turns instead to CAS and claims that organizations are complex adaptive systems. A CAS is a computer-based model populated by agents, which interact according to rules designed by a computer programmer. Over time, the agents begin to develop patterns of interaction which are not reducible to or predictable from the rules given at the outset. The agents and their interactions evolve in surprising ways.

Stacey's first claim in the book, then, is that human brains are complex adaptive systems where neurons are the agents manipulating symbols and images. Together with other human beings, they in turn are complex adaptive systems to form organizations and institutions, which in turn are complex adaptive systems forming the wider society. These nested CAS have an inherent order, which is simply waiting to be unfolded through the experience of the system, but no one can know what that order will be until it unfolds in real time. In previous work, Stacey had already produced a dualism that one form of management is required in conditions of certainty and another in conditions of open-ended change. In this book he creates another, that of the formal and informal, the legitimate and the shadow organization. It is in the shadow system where people engage in necessary politics and use their intuition and practical judgment. And it is a self-organizing, bottom-up process, which interacts with the formal, procedural top-down legitimate system to create organizational stable instability. The quality of the crash between the legitimate and shadow systems in organizations creates the space for creativity and novelty to emerge; he describes this as being the space at the edge of system disintegration. The injunction for managers, drawing on Stacey's increasing exposure to psychoanalytic literature and experience, is to develop the capacity to hold onto enough of the anxiety generated by the ambiguity of uncertain situations to enable them to play and be creative. This play is both self-organizing and emergent.

Stacey's perspective on learning and creativity arises directly from CAS, which are manifestations of the complexity sciences that demonstrate self-organizing and emergent behavior. In organizational terms, this leads him to take an interest in organizational politics, anxiety and unstructured conversational exploration of possibilities in conditions of uncertainty, which he understands as analogous to CAS. Arguing against what he takes to be the dominant paradigm in organizational scholarship (the idea that we depend upon charismatic leaders to set organizational direction), he argues that we need not fear these "unstructured" processes. They will not lead to anarchy because they are constrained by our need for each other, the requirements of the task, and our common humanity. Stacey still presents his theory of learning and creativity as contingent, that is to say applicable in some circumstances and not in others. It rests on a series of dualisms: formal and informal organizations, top-down and bottom-up processes, legitimate and shadow systems, and ordinary and extraordinary management. It still also depends upon a systemic understanding of organizations. Leaders and managers practice what he terms "extraordinary management" when they take up a position on the boundary of stability and chaos, contain the anxiety of their peers and better articulate potentially creative thought, discoveries, and behaviors, although there are no guarantees that this will be effective. He stresses the importance of what he describes as self-reflection, a lack of complacency and the need to keep things "on the boil," but still insists that managers as capable of "installing appropriate psychological and emotional conditions to encourage spontaneous self-organization that might produce creative outcomes" (Stacey 1996, p. 279). He argues that this is not the same as giving prescriptions for what works.

Key Contributions: The Radical Challenge to Systemic and Contingency Theories of Organization

In the mid-1990s, Stacey had persuaded the university authorities, against some opposition, to start a PhD group at UH rather than supervising students individually. This was directly related to his training as a group analyst at the Institute of Group Analysis (IGA), fascinated as he had been by his exposure to the experience of working with the Tavistock Institute and having attended a number of Leicester conferences. (Leicester Conferences have been run by the Tavistock since 1957 and are large group events, lasting for 2 weeks, which attempt to study human interaction in real time. The role of the consultant in the Tavistock tradition and the role of the group conductor in group analysis are very different). There is not space here to describe the differences between Tavistock and IGA traditions except to say that the IGA has a much more social therapeutic tradition. The IGA was founded by S. H. Foulkes (1964), who was both a psychiatrist and a psychoanalyst but who reinterpreted Freud to understand human interaction in highly social terms, after Hegel. Influenced by his friend and colleague Norbert Elias (2000), Foulkes developed a body of theory and working methods, which placed the group at the heart of therapeutic intervention. It challenged the assumption that there are individuals at one ontological "level" and society at another, and it privileged neither one nor the other. For Foulkes, the whole of society could be represented in a group of 8–10 people and that is where its therapeutic potential for individuals lies. There are no individuals without society and no society without individuals in Elias' terms (2001); they are two sides of the same coin.

As I mentioned previously, two students who were attracted to UH because of Stacey's publications on complexity and organizations were Doug Griffin (2001) and Patricia Shaw (2002), and Stacey became their supervisor. Both Griffin and Shaw had a great deal of experience in organizational consulting and had worked together, and Griffin had a long history of philosophical inquiry, having moved to Germany from the USA to pursue his doctorate on the phenomenology of Husserl while working under Gadamer (1960). All three became friends and spent long hours together working out the weaknesses and lacunae of taking up theories from the complexity sciences and applying them directly to social life, talking of organizations as though they were CAS. Stacey had already come across the ideas of Norbert Elias from his training at the IGA, and Griffin introduced the thinking of the pragmatists, in particular the communicative theories of G. H. Mead (1934). Together they wrote *Complexity and Management: Fad or Radical Challenge to Systems Thinking?* (Stacey et al. 2000), which became something of a manifesto for a new perspective they termed "complex responsive processes of relating." (They coined the term complex responsive processes to signal that it was derived from CAS, but that they were not taking a systemic view, and that human beings were responsive and not just adaptive). It also coincided with the founding of the professional doctorate, the DMan, at UH, which has continued for the last 16 years and has produced more than 50 doctorates. The program draws on the expanding body of theories originating in the combination of complexity and social science insights and is based on the working methods of the IGA. It is a research community which socializes the learning process in small and large groups, and where students iterate, then reiterate, their theses as a series of projects in response to comments and reactions from their peers and their supervisors. At bottom it tries to do justice to the idea of emergent learning, overcoming the dualisms of theory and practice, subjective and objective, and individual and social.

New Insights: No Inside, No Outside, and the Paradox of Forming and Being Formed

I explore the ideas in the developing perspective more thoroughly below in the next step of the discussion of Stacey's theories of learning and knowledge creation, but for now it is sufficient to say that the *Fad* book marks a radical shift in thinking from the earlier work. Firstly, it abandons a systemic view of organizations altogether, arguing after Elias that to think of organizations as parts and wholes with boundaries is simply to use a mystery to solve a mystery. Stacey et al.'s (2000) argument is that thinking systemically about organizations assumes that the researcher is somehow outside the organization understood as whole, while at the same time it covers over human interaction with abstractions. Instead, Stacey et al. place social interaction at the heart of organizational research, the gesture and response of feeling human bodies, which create patterns of relating and then more patterns. These patterns emerge according to themes organizing the experience of being together. There are no systems, no wholes, no boundaries, no inside and no outside, no formal or informal systems, or no top-down or bottom-up: just patterning and then further patterning of experience. The second major shift is to abandon the direct link between CAS, selected as the most helpful manifestation of the complexity sciences, and organizations but to argue by analogy drawing principally on the arguments of Hegel, Mead, and Elias that we are intersubjectively formed. Stacey et al. (2000) abandon dualisms and argue paradoxically instead that individuals are formed by social life; at the same time they form social life. Neither the individual nor the social are prior but arise both at the same time in a paradoxical movement of dialectic.

The *Fad* book sets out a theory of what it calls "transformative causality" to explain social evolution in distinction to the rationalist if-then causality of Newton, the formative causality of systems theory (unfolding what is already there) or the adaptionist causality of neo-Darwinism (change occurs because of chance mutation and survival of the fittest). The term "transformative causality" is an attempt to explain evolution endogenously, arguing that it occurs without external cause but simply and only because of its own activity.

Learning and Knowledge Creation: A Complex Responsive Processes Perspective

The publication of the *Fad* book and the founding of the DMan led to a productive 8 years of publications in the Complexity and Emergence series by Stacey, Griffin, and Shaw, and the graduates of the DMan program, either as monographs (Fonseca 2001; Streatfield 2001) or as edited volumes investigating concepts of emergence (Stacey 2005), research (Stacey and Griffin 2005a), public sector organizations (Stacey and Griffin 2005b), improvisation (Shaw and Stacey 2006), and values (Stacey and Griffin 2008). Alongside these, Stacey completed the fifth edition of his textbook (now published as *Strategic Management and Organizational Dynamics: The Challenge of Complexity*, Stacey and Mowles 2016), the first edition of which he wrote in 1992 and produced an edited collection of complexity readings upon which he comments with Griffin, MacIntosh et al. (2006). Additionally, having qualified as a group analyst, Stacey wrote an extended critique of psychoanalytic theory in his book *Complexity and Group Processes: A Radically Social Understanding of Individuals* (2003).

The second book on learning and knowledge explores some of the complex responsive ideas in more depth. In doing so, it deepens Stacey's critique of cognitivist theories of mind and knowing, systems thinking, and sender/receiver models of communicative exchange. For example, he critiques the idea that new knowledge is created in organizations by making the tacit explicit, an idea originated by Polanyi (1960) and then further developed by Nonaka and Tekeuchi (1995). To argue in this way assumes a cognitivist position that knowledge is somehow stored in individuals' heads, Stacey argues. As an alternative, he posits that tacit and explicit knowledge can never be separated. And by drawing on Mead's (1934) ideas that the evolution of mind is a social process and that neither mind nor knowledge is stored in an individual brain in any straightforward sense, he argues instead that knowledge is replicated and potentially transformed in communicative interaction between people. This is a process which cannot be captured, stored, or owned by anyone, thus making the idea of "leveraging knowledge assets" highly problematic, although this is not to say that knowledge cannot be stored in organizations in abstract form. This leads Stacey to recommend attaching much greater importance to every day conversations in organizational life, since it is in these exchanges that potentially valuable knowledge is created and recreated.

From this argument, he critiques what he deems to be a contemporary ideology of recruiting an exceptional professional elite to enhance knowledge creation. For Stacey, focusing on the quality of relating is as important as the attributes of the particular individuals engaged by organizations. He thinks that simply emphasizing the role of an elite cadre is likely to set up harmful insider/outsider dynamics, which are likely to cause stress and resentment. In terms of educating the workforce, Stacey argues that the contemporary emphasis on curriculum design and quality assurance replicates the dominant assumption that thought precedes action and that learning proceeds in linear fashion. As an alternative, he argues that learning in organizations, or in universities, arises from the potential transformation of identity of both individuals and the group and cannot be predicted in advance. It arises from communicative processes of meaning making arising in figurations of interdependent people – changes in meaning also reflect changes in power relations and the ability of people to break out of stuck patterns of communication and live with their anxiety.

Stacey's understanding reflects a different understanding of ethics. He argues:

> From this perspective, accountability and responsibility do not mean achieving targeted consequences, they mean the ethical, moral requirement to take responsibility for one's actions and account to one's fellows for what one is doing . . . Quality actions are actions that both those carrying them out and those affected by them can accept as ethical and moral in themselves, and acceptance implies a process of negotiation. The social is co-operative and competitive interaction as moral order. (2001, p. 230)

Uncertainty requires a pragmatic response to thinking about ethics since we cannot know the outcome of our actions, no matter how well motivated we are. Nonetheless, we are still responsible for what happens following our actions and need to proceed by keeping ends and means in view and negotiate what our actions mean to us.

Here are some similarities in thinking between Stacey's reflections on knowledge and learning in 1996 and those from 2001. In both books, Stacey draws on the complexity sciences, to argue for the importance of nonlinear dynamics in organizations coping in situations of uncertainty. But before 2000, he argues that organizations are complex systems, and after he argues by analogy. His favored manifestation of the complexity sciences in both cases is CAS. In both, he is concerned with microinteractions, which are shaped by power and politics and the psychosocial effects of anxiety and stuck patterns of behavior. But by 2001, he has turned to the social sciences in the form of philosophy and sociology to interpret key insights. This means taking up the radically social philosophy of G. H. Mead and the process sociology of Norbert Elias in particular. From Mead he takes the central insight that we are social through and through. Mind is the activity of an individual able to take herself as an object to herself, while communication is a series of gestures and responses between the self and others, where meaning emerges in the flow of the conversation of gestures. Meaning, then, is not a packet of data unproblematically communicated from one to another, nor is it determined by one party alone. From Elias he adopts the idea that society arises as the patterning of activity of highly interdependent social beings, a pattern which is controlled by no one and by no powerful group. Order arises from the interweaving of intentions. In taking a perspective informed by these ideas, he has challenged a number of assumptions about social life. The first is that any one person or group of people can ever be in control of ongoing interaction. This may influence it strongly, but they cannot control it. Then he drops cognitivist assumptions that mind is contained in an individual and that, from there, it is possible to assume an objective position "outside" an organization looking "in." This does away with the need for mental models. He has also dropped the dualisms of inside/outside, formal/informal, ordinary/extraordinary management in favor of paradox; as humans we are formed by social processes and form them both at the same time and these result in dynamics of inclusion and exclusion. He adopts a pragmatic theory of action and ethics, which takes uncertainty seriously, arguing that ethical behavior is to be found in negotiation of how a group understands the particular application of general principles. And he adopts Mead's (1938) complex understanding of time, which held that we anticipate the future by drawing on the past in the living present. He has developed this position by elaborating a critique of systems thinking derived from Kant, and which he argues covers over human interactions with abstractions. Rather, Stacey argues that social patterns of stable/instability arise in the interweaving of intentions of responsive human bodies. The patterning of interaction, which we call "experience," creates nothing outside itself but further patterning, which is what he terms "transformative causality."

The Later Period: Deepening the Perspective of Complex Responsive Processes

The period (2008 to the current day) saw a number of changes to the DMan, where students are now working actively with narrative research methods, pragmatic philosophy, and process sociology. They write narratives about what is happening to them at work, drawing on pragmatic theories of experience, communication and action, and social theories, which take an interest in power, culture, and identity. One of the cofounders of the DMan program, Patricia Shaw, left faculty in 2009 to pursue other projects. Ralph Stacey himself stepped down as director of the program in 2011 and was replaced by Chris Mowles, although he has continued as a member of faculty. Meanwhile, the other original founder of the DMan, Doug Griffin, died after a short illness in December 2015 and is missed by the wider research community. During this period, Stacey wrote two further books, the one under discussion here (2010) *Complexity and Organizational Reality: Uncertainty and the Need to Rethink Management after the Collapse of Investment Capitalism* and *The Tools and Techniques of Leadership and Management: Meeting the Challenge of Complexity* (2012) and two further editions of his textbook, the last of which was updated and revised with Chris Mowles (Stacey and Mowles 2016). Taking these three volumes together gives the most comprehensive statement of Stacey's thinking, but consistent with the enquiry into learning and knowledge creation, this chapter deals with the first volume.

Complexity and Organizational Reality

The first thing to note is that Stacey does not stick simply to revising and updating the 2001 volume but paints a much wider canvas to understand the financial crisis from a complex responsive processes perspective. He links the crisis to the dominant and impoverished understanding of what leaders and managers do in organizations from the perspective of what gets taught in many business schools. It is still the case, he argues, that we have an expectation that leaders and managers can control the futures of their organizations and choose their "direction." Even a cursory consideration of what happened during the financial crises would lead all but the most committed of managerialists to assume the opposite, that leaders might be in charge, but they are certainly not in control. The book makes an extensive argument critiquing the notion that there could ever be an evidence-base for management, based on the sciences of certainty. This is because these depend upon generalized propositions, which apply irrespective of context. Rather, he restates why the complexity sciences, what one might term the "sciences of uncertainty," are a better source domain for thinking about stability and change, and how global patterns of human activity arise simply and only because of what everyone is doing together in their local interactions. They also account for the contextual nature of organizational knowledge, which is not universally applicable. No doubt influenced by process sociologist Elias, Stacey traces the historical development of leadership and management, the historical development of a sense of self (Taylor 1992), the development of the state and abstract ways of thinking (Scott 1998), and the evolution of concepts derived from the complexity sciences and how they have been taken up by organizational scholars.

In the last of these, he notices how a majority of complexity scholars still operate from within a paradigm of control, assuming that complex processes can be harnessed by leaders and managers for the good of the firm. He sides with Zhu (2007), who argues that many scholars drawing on the complexity sciences offer very little difference from the paradigms they claim to be replacing, because they are still stuck within a paradigm of control. Anything radical or different has a tendency to be absorbed into existing patterns of thinking and has to show that it aspires to scientific abstract mathematical modeling (McKelvey 2003), a helpful discipline, but not one which can say much about what human beings get up to on a daily basis in organizations. Focusing on what people are doing equates to taking an interest in processes of communicative interaction, the dynamics of inclusion and exclusion as this plays into the repetition or potential transformation of our identities, and the flux and change of power figurations sustained and potentially transformed through norms, values, and ideology.

Stacey offers no prescriptions for how to get ourselves out of the muddle that we find ourselves in implementing vast schemes of improvement in the UK for education and health, for example. These have yet to demonstrate their effectiveness, yet we continue to insist that visionary leaders and managers can lead us to utopia. Instead, he offers more humble insights. Firstly, and whatever we mean by leadership, it manifests itself as the ability to endure the anxiety of uncertainty longer than others. It also involves an enhanced capacity to notice one's own habitual patterns, and the habitual reactions of the group, to complex and demanding situations, and perhaps to draw these to people's attention. The reasons for doing so are that the general complexity of the environment is also present in the local day-to-day interactions taking place in every day organizational life. This observation points to the importance of cultivating reflexivity in leaders and managers, so that they become more detached about their involvement in the game of organizational life. He also draws attention to the importance of depathologising conflict, which arises inevitably in a situation calling out different goods. For Stacey, a leader is someone who is able to bring a group of people into a different relationship with themselves and thus with the leader; they are able better to recognize themselves and their situation, and understand themselves anew. Leaders are better able to articulate emerging patterns, or experiential themes, which are evolving in the experience of being together. Finally, change arises in everyday conversational activity and the capacity to notice, engage with, and make this more nuanced, enhancing our understanding of who we are and what we are doing together, offers greater hope for enduring uncertain and complex situations. Leadership is a highly social activity practiced in groups, and improving our ability to pay greater attention to this practice, finding more subtle ways to describe how it is playing out and how we might participate in it, may offer more opportunities for creating the futures we desire.

Legacies and Unfinished Business: Focusing on Experience

Ralph Stacey was part of a small cohort of scholars in the early 1990s who were the first to identify the potential of the complexity sciences for informing a different approach to understanding processes of stability and change in organizations. Gradually, and over time, scholars drawing on the complexity sciences have proliferated, and it has almost become taken for granted that leaders and managers have to take complexity seriously if they are to do their jobs well. To a degree, this is often synonymous with a modernist narrative that increasing globalization and advances in information technology have meant that old paradigms of management no longer pertain. The taking up of insights from the complexity sciences are then seen as a contingent response to the emergence of new environments and pressures and enable leaders and managers to continue to exercise control in conditions of uncertainty. Complexity is a new tool in the managerial armory. These are precisely the assumptions that Stacey had abandoned by the end of the 1990s.

To illustrate the difference between Stacey's perspective and those of his contemporaries, let me draw on a paper from 2007 by Mary Uhl-Bien, Russ Marion, and Bill McKelvey, three eminent scholars who bring in the complexity sciences extensively in their work. The paper argues that top-down bureaucratic forms of management were effective for the industrial age, but a new form of leadership is needed for the knowledge age. This requires the development of a new framework for leadership, which the authors term complexity leadership theory (CLT). They then draw on

CAS to argue that organizations are complex adaptive systems, which have a unique and socially constructed "persona." What is needed is a theory of leadership, rather than merely focusing on leaders, which encourages adaptive and emergent outcomes. The required leadership framework needs to distinguish between administrative leadership that serves to coordinate organizational activity and adaptive leadership to refer to the leadership that occurs in emergent, informal adaptive dynamics throughout the organization. Finally, the authors claim that the framework needs to address adaptive challenges rather than technical problems, since the former and not amenable to authoritative fiat and involve managers trying to find their way out of problems they may not have encountered before. They adapt Ashby's (1960) law of requisite variety to argue for a law of requisite complexity, i.e., that the degree of complexity inside an organization needs to match the degree of complexity outside the organization. So complex problems demand complex responses, and it is the role of the leadership framework to:

> [seek] to foster CAS dynamics while at the same time enabling control structures appropriate for coordinating formal organizations and producing outcomes appropriate to the vision and mission of the system. It seeks to integrate complexity dynamics and bureaucracy, enabling and coordinating, exploration and exploitation, CAS and hierarchy, and informal emergence and top-down control. (2007, p. 304)

The point of bringing in this example is not so much to critique it but to demonstrate the difference Stacey brings as he joins together both the natural sciences of complexity and social sciences into a radically social view of organizations. Stacey no longer claims that organizations are CAS, as do Uhl-Bien, Marion, and McKelvey (2007) – in fact he argues that they are not systems at all. Moreover, he has dropped many of the dualisms prevalent in Uhl-Bien et al.'s (2007) article. Stacey challenges the idea that there is a clear distinction between leadership and management, that there would be no difference between administrative and adaptive leadership for contingent conditions, and that there are bureaucratic structures and emergent processes (which he originally formulated as the legitimate and shadow organization until he changed his mind). Nor does he consider emergence to be a special category of human activity, which is the opposite of something planned or structured. Whatever emerges emerges because of the activity of feeling human bodies acting locally, whether they are planning or undertaking some other kind of activity. Human beings are constantly responding and adapting to each other all the time, in Stacey's view. In his books of 2010 and 2012, particularly alluding to the financial crisis, he has challenged the assumption that emergent processes are inevitably creative and innovative; for Stacey, they may also be destructive and regressive. Only time will tell, and the judgment depends on who is judging.

In sum, Stacey's work has moved to a position that calls into question the paradigm of managerial control and assumes that complexity helps us understand all human relating and always has. It may be that we are currently bombarded by rapid and complex change for a variety of reasons, but people in all ages have complained about the increased tempo of change afflicting their particular era and have bemoaned the threats to identity and existing ways of doing things which result. It would be safe to say that Stacey's oeuvre has little in common with many of his contemporaries who still draw on the complexity sciences to produce new managerial frameworks to intervene instrumentally in organizations understood as systems. Instead, it probably has more family resemblances with process theories of organizational becoming (Tsoukas and Chia 2002; Langley and Tsoukas 2012; Langley et al. 2013; Hernes 2014), or critical management studies (CMS), although there are also clear differences with both traditions of thought. What the perspective of complex responsive processes shares with process theories of organization is a preoccupation with organizational becoming, with intersubjectivity and with complex theories of time. What it shares with CMS is interest in power, politics, and the creation and recreation of identity, what one might understand as a theory of culture or *habitus*. The perspective is critical, rather than realist, pragmatic rather than instrumental and above all values reflexivity and the dialectical exploration of difference. Although it encourages a focus on microinteractions to understand how global patterns are being functionalized, it is a perspective which claims to account for micro and macrosocial phenomena understood paradoxically. It does not require, as some critics have argued, a macrosocial theory at another level of observation: this is to completely misunderstand one of Stacey's central insights, following Elias (2000), that local and global arise simultaneously, forming and being formed.

Ralph Stacey was a successful working economist and has latterly achieved international eminence in organizational scholarship and in the domain of group therapy. But it would also be true to say that he has done so by highly unorthodox means according to the current standards of the academy, and particularly in the domain of organization studies. He has not been an assiduous publisher of journal articles, he has not been active on the conference circuit, he has not founded a research center in order to host waves of visitors and delegations, nor has he developed franchisable tools, frameworks, and techniques from which to make money. There is no copyrighted Stacey method – he did once design a two-by-two matrix, with one axis charting high agreement to low agreement and the other mapping close to certainty or far from certainty to map the conditions in which extraordinary management is required. Stacey had dropped this contingency theory of management by the millennium, although the diagram persists with a life of its own. The first two factors leave him open to the accusation that he has not sufficiently tested his ideas in peer review.

Instead he founded the modest DMan program of around 16 students at any one time, which still attracts participants from all over the world, and he has taken delight in working with consultants, managers, and leaders from all sorts of organizations to help them toward their doctorates. He also started the annual complexity and management conference, which is unlike most academic conferences; it is not structured around the presentation of academic papers but creates maximum opportunity for delegates to talk to each other about things which matter to them. As mentioned previously, the DMan is a professional doctorate, which aims to make a contribution to practice as much as theory, and students produce theses which are highly engaging, complex, practical, and reflexive, but ultimately hard to derive articles from to publish in journals. Nonetheless, Stacey states that the thing which gives him most professional pleasure is to see ordinary managers, some of whom are less formally educated than many doctoral students, walking onto stage to collect their doctorates from the university's Vice Chancellor after a number of years of intellectual struggle in the research community. What is more, because the DMan is run as a group, faculty and students develop a degree of engagement with each other, which is highly unusual in an academic setting. In follow-up surveys, the 60 or so graduates of the program have described their experience as profound and transformational, and this is also true of the broader community of consultants, academics, and managers who have attended the annual conference over the years. One way of understanding Stacey's legacy, then, is not just to restrict it to an explanation of a complex body of ideas, which have proved very influential, but to note how he has consistently created space and time, on the DMan, at the conference and in the many public talks he is invited to give and for the contemplation of and engagement with what it means to be human and live a good life. In this sense, Stacey is part of a much more ancient tradition dating back to the Greeks and beyond of bringing people face to face to take their experience seriously, to question each other, to deliberate, and to demonstrate through that activity what we mean to each other.

References

Ashby, W. R. (1960). *Design for a brain* (2nd ed.). New York: Wiley.

Elias, N. (2000). *The civilizing process: Sociogenetic and psychogenetic investigations*. Cambridge, MA: Blackwell.

Elias, N. (2001). *The society of individuals* (trans: Jephcott, E. & Ed. Schröter, M.). New York: Continuum International Publishing Group.

Fonseca, J. (2001). *Complexity and innovation in organizations*. London: Routledge.

Foulkes, S. H. (1964). *Therapeutic group analysis*. London: George Allen and Unwin.

Gadamer, H. G. (1960). *Truth and method*. New York: Continuum Books.

Goldstein, J. (1989). A far from equilibrium systems approach to resistance to change. *Organizational Dynamics, 17*(2), 16–26.

Griffin, D. (2001). *The emergence of leadership: Linking self-organization and ethics*. New York: Taylor & Francis.

Hernes, T. (2014). *A process theory of organization*. Oxford: Oxford University Press.

Langley, A., & Tsoukas, H. (2012). Introducing "perspectives on process organization studies". In T. Hernes & S. Maitlis (Eds.), *Process, sensemaking, & organizing* (pp. 1–26). Oxford: Oxford University Press.

Langley, A., Smallman, C., Tsoukas, H., & Van de Ven, A. (2013). Process studies of change in organization and management: Unveiling temporality, activity, and flow. *Academy of Management Journal, 56*(1), 1–13.

MacIntosh, R., MacLean, D., Stacey, R., & Griffin, D. (2006). *Complexity and organization: Readings and conversations*. London: Routledge.

McKelvey, B. (2003). From fields to science: Can organization studies make the transition? In R. Westwood & S. Clegg (Eds.), *Point/counterpoint: Central debates in organizational theory*. Oxford: Blackwell.

Mead, G. H. (1934). *Mind, self, & society: From the standpoint of a social behaviorist*. Chicago: University of Chicago Press.
Mead, G. H. (1938). *The philosophy of the present*. Chicago: Chicago University Press.
Nonaka, I., & Tekeuchi, H. (1995). *The knowledge-creating company: How Japanese companies create the dynamics of innovation*. New York: Oxford University Press.
Peirce, C. S. (1958). In A. Burks (Ed.), *Collected papers of Charles Sanders Peirce* (Vols. VII–VIII). Cambridge, MA: Belknap Press.
Polanyi, M. (1960). *The tacit dimension*. London: Routledge, Kegan and Paul.
Scott, J. C. (1998). *Seeing like a state: How certain schemes to improve the human condition have failed*. New Haven: Yale University Press.
Shaw, P. (2002). *Changing conversations in organizations: A complexity approach to change (complexity and emergence in organizations)*. London: Routledge.
Shaw, P., & Stacey, R. (2006). *Experiencing spontaneity, risk & improvisation in organizational change: Working live*. London: Routledge.
Stacey, R. D. (1991). *The chaos frontier: creative strategic control for business*. London: Butterworth-Heinemann.
Stacey, R. D. (1996). *Complexity and creativity in organizations*. San Francisco: Berrett-Koehler Publishers.
Stacey, R. D. (2001). *Complex responsive processes in organizations: Learning and knowledge creation*. Abingdon: Routledge.
Stacey, R. D. (2003). *Complexity and group processes: A radically social understanding of individuals*. London: Routledge.
Stacey, D. (Ed.). (2005) *Experiencing emergence in organizations: local interaction and the emergence of the global pattern*. London: Routledge.
Stacey, R. D. (2010). *Complexity and organizational reality: Uncertainty and the need to rethink management after the collapse of investment capitalism*. Abingdon: Routledge.
Stacey, R. D. (2012). *Tools and techniques of leadership and management: The challenge of complexity*. Abingdon: Routledge.
Stacey, R., Griffin, D., & Shaw, P. (2000). *Complexity and management: Fad or radical challenge to systems thinking?* London: Routledge.
Stacey, R., & Griffin, D. (Eds.). (2005a). *A complexity perspective on researching organizations: Taking experience seriously*. London: Routledge.
Stacey, R., & Griffin, D. (Eds.). (2005b). *Complexity and the experience of managing in the public sector*. London: Routledge.
Stacey, R., & Griffin, D. (2008). *Complexity and the experience of values, conflict and compromise in organizations*. London: Routledge.
Stacey, R. D., & Mowles, C. (2016). *Strategic management and organizational dynamics: Strategic management and organizational dynamics*. London: Pearson Education.
Streatfield, P. (2001). *The paradox of control in organizations*. London: Routledge.
Taylor, C. (1992). *Sources of the self*. Cambridge, MA: Harvard University Press.
Tsoukas, H., & Chia, R. (2002). On organizational becoming: Rethinking organizational change. *Organization Science, 13*(5), 567–582.
Uhl-Bien, M., Marion, R., & McKelvey, B. (2007). Complexity leadership theory: Shifting leadership from the industrial age to the knowledge era. *The Leadership Quarterly, 18*(4), 298–318.
Waldrop, M. (1992). *Complexity: The emerging science at the edge of order and chaos*. London: Viking.
Wheatley, M. (1992). Leadership and the new science (Rev. ed.). San Francisco: Berrett-Koehler.
Zhu, Z. (2007). Complexity science, systems thinking and pragmatic sensibility. *Systems Research and Behavioral Science, 24*(4), 445–464.

Further Reading

The most recent and comprehensive statement of Stacey's work is to be found in the 7th edition of the textbook published in 2016 (Stacey and Mowles 2016). Meanwhile for a lighter and briefer overview of some of the key ideas, readers may be interested in: Mowles, C. (2011) *Rethinking Management: radical insights from the complexity sciences*, London: Gower. For an exploration of one of the key concepts of complex responsive processes, paradox, then Mowles' next book (2015) *Managing in Uncertainty: Complexity and the Paradoxes of Everyday Organisational Life,* London: Routledge, might be helpful, as might a chapter he wrote on one of the key contributors to the theory of complex responsive processes, Norbert Elias: Mowles, C. (2015) The Paradox of Stability and Change: Elias' Processual Sociology, in Garud, R., Simpson, B., Langley, A., and Tsoukas, H. (Eds) *The Emergence of Novelty in Organizations*, Oxford Oxford University Press :pp.245–271. For an insight into how the DMan program is run as a research community drawing on the ideas of the pragmatists and methods from group analytic practice then there are two articles in press. These explore the potential contribution of group analytic thinking to critical management education based on 16 years' experience running the DMan, and, inversely, explain critical management thinking and practice to group analysts: Mowles, C. (in press 2017) Experiencing uncertainty – on the potential of groups and a group analytic approach for making management education more critical, *Management Learning,* and **Mowles, C. (in press 2017) Group analytic methods beyond the clinical setting – working with researcher-managers, *Group Analysis*.**

Robert Tannenbaum: An Examined Life

74

Christopher G. Worley, Anthony Petrella, and Linda Thorne

Abstract
This chapter chronicles Robert Tannenbaum's life and contributions to organization development and change. Considered one of the founding fathers of OD, Tannenbaum's shift from accounting to industrial relations marked an increasing emphasis and passion for humanistic psychology. He was a champion for personal growth within a systems perspective, always recognizing the specific situation within which people were embedded. Although his publications on leadership, decision-making, and change were considerable and influential, it was his affirming impact in person – with each individual and audience he met – that defines his legacy in organizational change.

Keywords
Organization development • Humanistic psychology • Personal growth

Contents

C.G. Worley (✉)
Strategy and Entrepreneurship, NEOMA Business School, Reims, France
e-mail: Christopher.worley@neoma-bs.fr

A. Petrella • L. Thorne
Arnold, MD, USA
e-mail: tony.petrella@verizon.net; lindathorne@verizon.net

D.B. Szabla et al. (eds.), *The Palgrave Handbook of Organizational Change Thinkers*,
DOI 10.1007/978-3-319-52878-6_25

> Many organizations today, particularly those at the leading edge of technology, are faced with ferment and flux. In increasing instances, the bureaucratic model – with its emphasis on relatively rigid structure, well-defined functional specialization, direction and control exercised through a formal hierarchy of authority ... and relative impersonality of human relationships – is responding inadequately to the demands placed upon it from the outside and from within the organization. There is increasing need for experimentation, for learning from experience, for flexibility and adaptability, and for growth. (Tannenbaum and Davis 1969, p. 67)

Introduction

Anyone could be forgiven for attributing the opening quote to some modern-day management guru. It was, in fact, written in 1969 by the subject of this chapter, Robert "Bob" Tannenbaum, and his client at TRW Space Systems, Sheldon Davis. The paragraph appears in the introduction to an article that proposed and defended a set of fundamental values that differentiated the growing social movement known as human relations and the practice of organizational development (OD). It was a watershed moment in the field provided by one of its leaders. For many, the article captured a zeitgeist; for others, it still does.

The purpose of this chapter is to reflect on Tannenbaum's life and contributions. He was highly regarded within the field of OD, the specialized niche of organization change that relies on the application of behavioral science to improve organization effectiveness (Cummings and Worley 2015). Tannenbaum is considered a founding father of OD and, in particular, a champion for personal growth and self-awareness. For Bob, separating personal growth from organizational change was like separating yin from yang.

In as much as this volume is oriented toward scholars and scholar-practitioners who made important contributions to change theory, the role of the scholar-practitioner – the one who not only develops but applies concepts and theories in practice – should be recognized and given special consideration. It is, in many ways, a more difficult task. Helping managers solve organizational problems and develop solutions in ways that transfer knowledge, build capacity and capability, improve performance, and contribute to an individual's growth and learning is inordinately and profoundly complex. Rigorous practitioners have contributed much to our understanding of the organization change phenomenon (Beckhard and Harris 1977; Kleiner 1996).

As authors and chroniclers of Tannenbaum's history and contribution – and knowing him the way we did – we also see the purpose of this chapter as including a strong practitioner orientation in addition to Bob's academic achievements. For all of Tannenbaum's conceptual developments and publications on the role of managers, managerial decision-making, leadership, and group dynamics, he was always connected to practice. Relevance and effectiveness were important watchwords. In addition to our descriptions of Tannenbaum's contributions to change thinking, we also will be focused on his contributions to change practice.

The chapter proceeds as follows. We first provide a chronology of Tannenbaum's early life, upbringing, education, and professional accomplishments. We then discuss three "arcs" in his academic and practitioner career, including his views of humanism, his views regarding the role of individuals in the course of organization change, and his application of systems theory. We conclude with observations about his insights and impacts on the field and our sense of how Tannenbaum would view the world today.

Influences and Motivations

Bob Tannenbaum was born to Henry and Nettie Tannenbaum in Cripple Creek, Colorado, in 1915. He remembered his early years as "a very happy period of my life" (Tannenbaum 1995, p. 36). He reflected that many of his psychological strengths "may have been built in that early period" (Tannenbaum 1995, p. 36).

In 1923, his family moved to Santa Ana, Calif. Southern California was to be an important context in his life and the setting of important experiences. For example, shortly after the move, he was confronted while walking home from school and called a "Jew" and "Christ killer." He described that event "as deeply central to the later years. It was a terrible rejection for me" (Tannenbaum 1995, pp. 39–40). Two years later, Bob had climbed a tree in front of his house, and as school let out, a boy saw him in the tree and yelled out to others, "Hey, do you want to see a Jew?" Several kids gathered around the tree, staring and taunting him. Tannenbaum stayed in the tree. Instead of coming down to fight, he "cowered in the tree and *took* it" (Tannenbaum 1995, p. 41). The tree experience became an important story for him; it was a central theme in his 1977 OD Network Conference speech. One outcome from these two experiences was Tannenbaum's identification with and empathy toward minorities or "anything that sets a person off as separate from the others" (Tannenbaum 1995, p. 41).

In 1932, Tannenbaum entered Santa Ana Junior College, taking leadership roles as president of his freshman class and of the student body. He entered the University of Chicago as a junior in 1935 and graduated with his Bachelor of Arts degree in 1937. Tannenbaum placed second out of 103 at the end of his senior year and was invited to join the Phi Beta Kappa Society. He believed that Chicago's comprehensive testing process worked well for him. "With my kind of systems sense, if I saw a problem or a case in a question, that characteristic of mine helped me to pick out very quickly the material from many different places that would be relevant" (Tannenbaum 1995, p. 60). Tannenbaum believed that had the exams been more traditional, requiring memorization of facts and details, he would not have done as well.

In that same year, he began teaching accounting at Oklahoma A&M College, postponing work on his master's degree, also in accounting, to replace a professor on leave. However, in January, Tannenbaum's father became ill. Although Tannenbaum continued his teaching and received updates, by the time he was able to get to Santa Ana, his father had died, and he was only able to attend the funeral.

Tannenbaum returned to the University of Chicago in 1938 to begin his master's degree in accounting and soon began having anxiety attacks. They would usually occur when he was alone in the evening. Despite receiving support from a cousin and a very good friend, he decided to seek more help from the student health services office. Their counseling approach was based on a behavioral science theory, which Tannenbaum stopped finding helpful after just a few weeks. As his first attempt at "seriously trying to cope with my feelings," he considered it "a major life experience . . . and its impact has carried forward dramatically in both my personal life and my professional life" (Tannenbaum 1995, p. 71).

He began his doctoral studies in Chicago in the fall of 1939. His declared major was personnel management and industrial relations. While at Oklahoma A&M College, he decided to change his major from accounting and described this as "my first move toward people" (Tannenbaum 1995, p. 75). There was no epiphany, just a gradual change in focus. But World War II put that work on hold.

Tannenbaum joined the US Navy in 1942 and was accepted into its V-12 program, which quickly trained officers. He was assigned to the Combat Information Center (CIC) and to Destroyer Squadron 22. Tannenbaum's job was "going from ship to ship and training and helping in developing effective CIC operations." Because he went to different ships, he "had a chance to observe nine commanding officers and their leadership styles, [which] were markedly different, ranging from very democratic to . . . very authoritarian and non-consultative" (Tannenbaum 1995, pp. 88–89). Tannenbaum saw this experience as a significant influence in the creation of his views on leadership.

During this time (1945), he met and married Edith (nee Lazaroff) Tannenbaum. The courtship lasted all of 28 hours. "Her centeredness and emotional maturity, given the kind of conflicted inner psyche that I have – with my drive for achieving, for accomplishing – has just been terribly important to me, because she's been there as a rock, giving me a sense of peace, perspective, and balance" (Tannenbaum 1995, p. 102).

Bob Tannenbaum received his doctorate in 1949 with a dissertation titled "A Rational Synthesis of the Manager Concept with Application to the Managerial Decision-Making Process."

In the fall of 1948, Tannenbaum joined the University of California, Los Angeles, with a joint appointment to the College of Business Administration and the Institute of Industrial Relations. He started as acting assistant professor as he was finishing his Ph.D. and became an assistant professor after the Ph.D. was awarded. The school's dean, Neil Jacoby, knew Tannenbaum from the University of Chicago and held the goal to "build a modern personnel management/industrial relations area" (Tannenbaum 1995, p. 162). Bob eagerly began that process by changing the curriculum and hiring faculty. By 1950, he had become the personnel management/industrial relations area chair at the school and continued in that position until 1963.

Under his guidance and leadership, UCLA's business school – now the Anderson School – became a leading center of research and practice in organizational development and leadership.

Tannenbaum took an early retirement from UCLA in 1977 for health reasons and moved to Carmel, California. During his career, he was awarded an honorary doctorate from the Saybrook Institute, elected as a fellow of the NTL Institute, admitted as a diplomate from the American Board of Professional Psychology, and recognized as a distinguished member of the OD Network. He also received the first ASTD's Lifetime Achievement Award and was regarded as a leading figure in the field of humanistic psychology, where his oral history and papers are archived at University of California, Santa Barbara, along with those of Rollo May, Carl Rogers, James Bugental, and Virginia Satir.

Key Contributions to the Field of Organizational Change

Tannenbaum's contributions to organizational change include strong views about the importance of humanistic values, the related belief that individuals are the source of ideas, energy and change in organizations, and early advocacy of systems thinking. His publications, teaching, speeches, and practice provide important grounding to these contributions.

Humanistic Values

Bob's early writing, based mostly on his doctoral dissertation, explored the definitions and functions of management and the processes of decision-making. These articles were written in a positivist, rationalist, and scientific style at a seminal time in the evolution of organization theory. They reflected important contributions to what would become known as the human relations movement (Scott 1981; Perrow 1979). Over time, however, his orientation changed dramatically to psychological, humanistic, and behavioral.

Tannenbaum's initial descriptions of management and formal organization were clearly influenced by the researchers of the time. His first two articles – "The Manager Concept: A Rational Synthesis" (Tannenbaum 1949) and "Managerial Decision-Making" (Tannenbaum 1950) – were heavily influenced by Chester Barnard's (1938) *The Functions of the Executive*, as well as Herbert Simon's (1947) views of administrative behavior. In "The Manager Concept," Tannenbaum aimed to understand the functions of management. In addition to Barnard and Simon, he reviewed, among others, the writings of Stene (1940), Mooney and Reiley (1939), and Mary Parker Follett (1940) to determine the most parsimonious set of management functions. He concluded that "managers are those who use formal authority to organize, direct or control responsible subordinates . . . in order that all service contributions be coordinated in the attainment of an enterprise purpose"

(Tannenbaum 1949, p. 240). His definition appears a full five years before the widely accepted definition by Koontz and O'Donnell (1955).

"Managerial Decision-Making" is a tutorial on the types and processes of rational decision-making in organizations. After classifying and describing his terms, Tannenbaum turned to an analysis of authority as a central part of his definition of management. "The real source of the authority possessed by an individual lies in the acceptance of its exercise by those who are subject to it" (Tannenbaum 1950, p. 26). This perspective on power and authority was enormously popular among the human relations crowd but would be challenged by Emerson (1962), who argued power was a function of dependency.

While his first two articles were decidedly rational extensions of existing theory, the two follow-on articles, "Participation by Subordinates in the Managerial Decision-Making Process" (Tannenbaum and Massarik 1950) and "Job Satisfaction, Productivity and Morale" (Tannenbaum et al. 1961) began to explore the implications of these views on practical matters. In the participation article, Tannenbaum described the opportunity and logic for participation. He did not see participation as a "normatively" good thing. Participation was a "contingency" that needed to be understood. Adding additional knowledge, experience, and perspective directly addressed a weak assumption in the rational decision-making model regarding the manager's knowledge of alternatives. Participation was thus an interesting possibility in terms of contributing to better decision quality and execution. In the job satisfaction article, Tannenbaum attempted to connect and integrate these concepts in terms of organizational effectiveness.

With the publication of "Some Current Issues in Human Relations" (Tannenbaum 1959), however, he left the rationalist view behind and fully embraced a humanistic one. In the article, Bob responded to especially caustic criticisms of the human relations movement (Schoen 1957; McNair 1957, 1958). He suggested that in an area exploding as quickly as human relations, the broad range of opinions, perspectives, arguments, and controversies should be unsurprising. Training group (T-group) and sensitivity training programs had caught fire and liberated (brainwashed, according to the detractors) executives, social workers, engineers, mothers, and steel workers. Many of those were becoming apostles and advocates. It radically increased the number and diversity of voices from a variety of backgrounds, perspectives, experiences, education, and motivations.

Looking across this tangle of claims and techniques, Bob argued that human relations was a set of skills, competencies, knowledge (developed through research), tools, and processes for understanding how people get along with each other. Like any set of skills, knowledge and understandings, it could be used for good or ill, and he agreed that some people had used these tools badly, while others had inappropriate objectives or motivations. However he also clearly stated that it was important to keep focused on the right issues. That a few people were misusing the tools should not distract managers and researchers from the potential for human achievement. Both the seller and the buyer in a transaction have responsibilities to ensure a product's productive use. Tannenbaum demonstrated a nuanced understanding of the social movement of which he was a part. He was aware of how powerful these tools, methods, and knowledge were, and he tried to diffuse irrational fears with rational arguments.

By the mid-1960s, human relations, humanistic psychology, T-groups, and sensitivity training were in full bloom. Organizational development had emerged as an important and applied manifestation of these perspectives, theories, and techniques and McGregor's *The Human Side of Enterprise* (McGregor 1960) had catalyzed much of its promise. But riding on the coattails of human relations, the field of OD was more a movement than a disciplined professional activity. Tannenbaum believed that the field needed to be more explicit about its foundations. "Very often in our field, when people are talking about change, they don't deal explicitly in terms of, 'Toward what?' Wouldn't you say that Hitler brought about organizational transformation in Germany? It's not enough to talk about change or transformation, but . . . to say, 'For what?' Or, 'In what direction?' 'Why?' And what are the values involved?" (Tannenbaum 1995, pp. 4–5).

After working for more than four years with Sheldon Davis, a senior personnel manager, at TRW Space Systems, Tannenbaum and Davis presented a paper at the MIT/Sloan School's McGregor Conference that would become "Values, Man and Organizations" (Tannenbaum and Davis 1969). The 13 values clarified and differentiated how a humanistic view of people in organizations could be applied. We chose seven as illustrative:

- Away from utilizing an individual primarily with reference to his job description toward viewing him as a whole person
- Away from walling off the expression of feelings toward making possible both appropriate expression and effective use
- Away from maskmanship and game playing toward authentic behavior
- Away from distrusting people toward trusting them
- Away from avoiding facing others with relevant data toward making appropriate confrontation
- Away from avoidance of risk-taking toward willingness to risk
- Away from a primary emphasis on competition toward a much greater emphasis on collaboration

More than any other statement of its time, the article became an important touchstone for the field. "In our view, McGregor was overly cautious and tentative in calling the Theory Y tenets 'assumptions' and in limiting them to being his 'interpretations'" (p. 68). Tannenbaum and Davis declared this as the way to unleash the untapped potential of both individuals and organizations.

Tannenbaum was a vocal proponent of the humanistic values he believed appropriate for the OD profession, and he continued to refine them. By the 1983 ODN Conference, he was challenging the field with additional values, including recognition and acceptance of differences, awareness of and concern for our social and ecological environments, the pursuit of peace, holding a sense of the sacred, and loving unconditionally beginning with one's self.

Tannenbaum's critics believed that his position – and perhaps more importantly his advocacy of the values – was overly directive. This is an enduring issue, as the field of OD remains mired in debates about its "values" and how they should be expressed and used (Church and Jamieson 2014; Worley 2014). In particular, interventionists are often reluctant to share their beliefs, knowing that it is crucial for people to discover and articulate their own value systems. This belief springs from experience and asserts that it is especially important for leaders with formal authority to understand and acknowledge their own values and mission.

Individuals as the Source of Ideas, Energy, and Change

Why or when Tannenbaum developed the view that everyone was a unique individual and that this mattered greatly to organization change is unknowable. But he would certainly have agreed with the quote from Walt Kelly's famous Pogo comic strip, "we have met the enemy and he is us!" (http://www.thisdayinquotes.com/2011/04/we-have-met-enemy-and-he-is-us.html). It is also a safe bet that this perspective was connected to his experiences in and commitments to sensitivity training.

The first National Training Laboratory (NTL) in Group Development was held in Bethel, Maine, in the summer of 1947. NTL had been established to study the T-group as an alternative to traditional forms of learning and education. Paul Sheets, the head of UCLA's Extension Services, was involved with this early training and wanted to start a similar program in the West. In 1951, Sheets invited Tannenbaum to be part of a planning committee that would eventually launch the Western Training Laboratories. "For me, these [planning sessions] were very exciting. I was with people who were very behavioral science-oriented and all humanistically oriented. I was in the process of making a transition myself, from personnel management and industrial relations into the behavioral sciences. I was in a learning mode" (Tannenbaum 1995, pp. 196–197). The first Western Training Laboratories program was held in 1952. In 1958, the Western Training Laboratories moved to the UCLA conference center near Lake Arrowhead, California.

Tannenbaum served as the dean of faculty, and during his involvement with T-groups, he continually experimented with different models. He was always focused on personal learning. Reflecting Bob's emerging views on the individual's role in change, the Western Training Laboratories focused on the person – on the self – rather than interpersonal relationships. Without polarizing the differences, the NTL laboratories focused on group dynamics. Staff exchanges between the two groups began in the early 1960s and afforded important cross-pollination opportunities. Tannenbaum's first trip to NTL's Bethel was in 1963. As the dean of an advanced lab, he invited Will Schutz, Herb Shepard, and Charlie Seashore to be on his staff. Tannenbaum also worked with Abraham Maslow at a Western lab.

But Bob's interests in this subject extended beyond Western Training Laboratories and NTL. In 1953, with the help of Irving Weschler and Fred Massarik, Tannenbaum started "Leadership Principles and Practices," an undergraduate course in sensitivity training. It was probably the first sensitivity course offered in any management school. The title was deliberate. Tannenbaum was aware that most academic courses focused on the intellect and any course that dealt with the emotional and intuitive would be looked upon with suspicion (Tannenbaum 1995, p. 219). In 1966–1967, Tannenbaum – along with Art Shedlin – also developed the first university-based OD training program, a ten-week residential "Learning Community in Organization Development" course for OD practitioners. It was sponsored by UCLA's Graduate School of Management and its university extension. It lasted for two years in that form and then was shortened to a six-week, full-time program that continued until Tannenbaum's heart attack in 1971 (Tannenbaum 1995, pp. 298–299). Tannenbaum also contributed to the Master of Science in Organization Development (MSOD) program at Pepperdine University, which was created by one of his students, Pat Williams, in 1975. Tannenbaum was a central figure in that program, advising faculty on curriculum design and teaching in every cohort until the year before he died. In addition, Tannenbaum partnered with Williams in Mexico, where he helped to build the University of Monterrey's OD program and the Mexican Association of Professionals in OD.

The culmination of Tannenbaum's interest in individual change as key to organizational change came in his collaboration with Bob Hannah, a former student, with whom he developed the "Holding On and Letting Go" program at NTL. It was first held in 1976, and Tannenbaum stayed with it until 1985. The lab was entirely focused on intrapersonal matters, matters of deep, emotional, and generally unconscious blockages. The basic premise underlying the workshop was that individuals in the context of social organizations become increasingly unwilling to change when the change gets closer to their core identity. In referencing this work, Tannenbaum quoted Ernest Schachtel, a psychoanalyst:

> The anxiety of the encounter with the unknown springs ... from the person's fear of letting go of the attitudes to which he clings for safety, of the perspectives which these attitudes give him on the world, and of the familiar labels for what he sees in the world. So man is afraid that without the support of his accustomed attitudes, perspectives, and labels he will fall into an abyss or flounder in the pathless. Letting go of every kind of clinging opens the fullest view. But it is this very letting go which often arouses the greatest amount of anxiety". (Tannenbaum 1976, p. 4)

It's no wonder we are inclined to hold on to the "safety" of our old and familiar ways of being. Emotions and their source are neither easy to acknowledge nor deal with. In this lab, people encountered confusion, shock, fear, helplessness, depression, and loss of meaning. Understanding this process was an important step in discovering one's "inner voice" and of the connection between the self and change.

The insights gained through these personal development and educational experiences helped Tannenbaum develop a better understanding of how difficult it is for a person to change. He admonished overly enthusiastic "change agents" to be more aware and respectful of the difficulties people have with change. The need for safety, stability, and continuity were – and are – a powerful force for "holding on," and powerful feelings need to be explored and "let go" if leaders expect deep change in their organizations.

Tannenbaum thus developed the belief that self-knowledge and self-awareness could liberate and mature a person and that, in the end, this path allowed the individual to make appropriate choices regarding his or her identity rather than be chained to past experience. Tannenbaum believed that for an individual to break the bonds of the past and confront the responsibility of free choice, the greatest strength that person could have was faith in his or her real self and that the self was an inner being of feelings and emotions that could be understood only through work. It was a journey that took time, required a growing maturity, and was unique to every individual.

In his search for ways to raise a person's consciousness, Bob learned that feelings were most often the doorway to personal discovery, insight, and change. He said, "I frequently used this phrase: "in personal learning, feelings are our best friends" (Tannenbaum 1995, p. 140). Feelings needed to be acknowledged, examined, learned from, and appropriately expressed. He was convinced that thinking is always accompanied by a parallel stream of emotion that there is an indivisible connection between thoughts and feelings. A friend recognized this capacity in Bob:

> "I see how beautifully you combine thought and feeling.
> Thought without feeling sits like a stone on the brain,
> on the page, or on the tongue.
> But with warmth and compassion it takes wing and flies
> straight to the heart."
>
> A gift from Liz Bugental, wife of James Bugental, on the occasion of Tannenbaum's 80th birthday

When a person consciously embraces this awareness, he or she is much more likely to take the right action. Carl Rogers supported such a view. He wrote that a person emerging from therapy "increasingly discovers that his own organism is trustworthy; that it is a suitable instrument for discovering the most satisfying behavior in each immediate situation" (Moustakas 1956, p. 206).

This was one of Tannenbaum's biggest contributions to the field of organization change: the understanding and realization of the complex role emotions make to effectiveness, which is the output of a system composed of a situation and some people (Tannenbaum and Massarik 1957). Tannenbaum focused his considerable intellect on the people part of that equation and how the complexities of life contributed to dysfunctional behaviors. While never denying the contribution of the situation (see below), it was Tannenbaum's belief that with effort, individuals could understand themselves well enough to make increasingly conscious and responsible choices to engage in new behaviors, move in new directions, and provide the impetus to make organization changes.

In his work with T-groups, with intact teams, teaching and speaking, and in his consulting/coaching, Bob worked to bring people's limiting scripts into consciousness, thereby freeing them to make more enlightened and appropriate choices in their lives. He believed that clients must ultimately find the courage to freely face existential questions and act in accordance with their inner compass. He encouraged and equipped people to take responsibility for their future.

Tannenbaum's beliefs always guided his counseling conversations with clients and mentees. He was both patient and optimistic that, given the right environment, it was within the power of most people to reach their full potential. Tannenbaum accepted this belief as an article of faith. He worked hard to help his clients and students develop a level of confidence in their inner voices that allowed them to come out from behind the masks they wore. Working toward this courageous faith and freedom of choice in people, in their being and becoming, was the foundation of his work.

Tannenbaum was, in many ways, swimming upstream against a society and culture that actively discouraged the expression of feelings, especially negative feelings, and his psychodynamic perspective was not a widely shared view in the world of organization development. Very few, if any, people in the field of OD approached the depth of self-exploration that Bob proposed. In this regard, he was a pioneer.

He followed this path in his own life; it was a signature of his work in the field of organizational change. He deeply believed that the individual was *the* major source of ideas, energy and change. He believed that the pursuit of self-knowledge and free choice were important values. They were also a doorway to greater effectiveness in the individual's life: with family, organization, and beyond.

Systems Thinking

In a 1982 interview with Dave Jamieson for the *Training and Development Journal*, Tannenbaum was asked what concept or framework could move the practice of organizational development forward. He responded, "To me, the most powerful framework available is systems theory, which is also a way of thinking about the world. I think this view is particularly appropriate for practitioners. An organization's relationships with its environment ... is becoming more important as determinants of what happens inside the [organization]. We will need to devote more attention to problems which exist at this boundary" (Jamieson and Tannenbaum 1982).

As much as he believed in the single individual as the source for change, Tannenbaum also believed that significant change at any social system level, from interpersonal, to group, to organization and beyond, was likely to trigger insecurity and stress. Managers and OD practitioners must be prepared to respect, live, and work with this reality. Thus, Tannenbaum's focus on self-development was complemented by an interest in the practical application of systems thinking.

In particular, there was an emerging understanding that the T-group/sensitivity training experience, while powerful, was limited in its transferability. Maintaining the new behaviors developed in a T-group environment was impossible in the context of the organizational environment where structures, systems, processes, power, and culture were at play. In the late 1960s, for example, Tannenbaum supported Lou Davis – whose focus was job design – in bringing Eric Trist to UCLA. Tannenbaum knew and respected Trist from their experiences at Bethel and

NTL. Because of Trist's pioneering work in sociotech work, "we became much more aware of the importance of technology in the unfolding of organization work and, in other important ways, had our horizons widened" (Tannenbaum 1995, p. 188).

One of the first interventions using systems awareness occurred in 1952–1953 at the US Naval Ordnance Test Station in China Lake, California. Extending the ideas learned in sensitivity training about the role of the individual in change and group dynamics, Tannenbaum and his colleagues facilitated "vertically structured" groups, a manager and his/her direct reports, to explore group dynamics, interpersonal communication, and task issues. These sessions are generally regarded as the first examples of what would become team building (French and Bell 1993, pp. 26–28; Tannenbaum 1995, pp. 281–282) and were chronicled in two publications (Tannenbaum et al. 1954; Kallejian et al. 1955). It was the first demonstration of group dynamic's pragmatic utility in the business world. Team building and team development would eventually become a broadly accepted organization practice (Dyer 1977).

For organization development, this was the "thin edge of the wedge." It opened up the view that the system, and not just the individuals in it, needed to change. Eventually, a small number of OD practitioners would take on an entire organization as the client. The consultant and client, often the CEO, would start with a complete examination of the organization's environment before addressing the internal dynamics of the organization. This was a radical departure from the "human relations" approach used to bring about organizational change by a focus on the personal and interpersonal organizational dynamics. It was a marriage of the practice of business consulting and organization development and a logical extension of systems thinking.

It also led Tannenbaum to extend his original thinking about leadership. In "Leadership: A Frame of Reference," Tannenbaum and Fred Massarik (1957) defined the term as "interpersonal influence, exercised in situation and directed, through the communication process, toward the attainment of a specified goal or goals" (p. 3). In other words, leadership was a process that involved an influencer (a leader), someone being influenced (a follower), and a situation. Although this article was not widely read, Tannenbaum believed that the ideas in the article formed many of the beliefs that were reflected in his later work (Tannenbaum 1995, p. 164).

His second leadership publication was based on a talk to California state administrators. Warren Schmidt encouraged him to write it up, and together they produced the HBR Classic "How to Choose a Leadership Pattern" (1958). It remains one of the most copied and downloaded articles of all time. While standard leadership training at that time was focused on a right way and a wrong way to be a leader, Tannenbaum's view was different. "We weren't the first to begin talking about leader, follower, and the situation, but we gave heavy emphasis to this. And as many of these things work out, the time [was] right for something" (Tannenbaum 1995, p. 166). In the article, Tannenbaum and Schmidt suggested that leadership was not some monolithic set of competencies to be pursued and followed mechanistically. Instead, leaders may choose between extremes of top-down pronouncements and participation or involvement from subordinates. They labeled this as boss-centered versus subordinate-centered leadership. "It was one of the first statements in the management literature of what 10–15 years later came to be known in the management theory area as contingency theory" (Tannenbaum 1995, p. 167).

Later in Tannenbaum's career, his counseling work with CEOs was done with a systems framework. CEOs, usually with their spouse, would visit him at his home in Carmel. They would spend a couple of days talking about the problematic issues facing the client. To prepare himself for these conversations, with the permission of his clients, Tannenbaum would contact their colleagues, subordinates, and adult family members. In these conversations, he inquired about their relationship with the client as well as how the client behaved in various situations. Tannenbaum showed a keen awareness of the importance of the practical and psychological environment of the client and how that environment impacted his or her behavior.

Insights for the Field

Tannenbaum's influence on us as individuals, practitioners, and researchers and his influence on the field can be seen in the way much consulting work gets done. Although Tannenbaum was a productive writer/researcher early in his career, his legacy to organizational change is unlikely to be tightly connected to his writing. In that sense, one might say that he left a light footprint. Instead, his influence on change will be personal – and rightly so. His footprint resides in the people who learned from and experienced him when he was still alive. These people were deeply affected, and they carry this energy forward in the world today.

For us as individuals and practitioners, Tannenbaum was instrumental in launching or encouraging us to have committed lives of personal growth in service of being effective consultants and members of society. He was convinced that an OD practitioner would be a better organizational consultant if the practitioner was clear about, understood, and was able to know when a client said or did something that stirred an emotion, defensive routine, or other reaction. Importantly, however, Tannenbaum was clear about the boundaries of this work for practitioners and clients.

For practitioners, personal growth work was important to improve the consulting process; it was never about training practitioners to be therapists. In fact, Tannenbaum was quick to admonish practitioners, smitten by the personal growth bug after attending a T-group or other personal growth experience, who wanted to practice such tactics on clients. Personal growth was first about sharpening the consultant as an instrument of change, a process that each of us takes personally and seriously. Similarly, and in keeping with his views of systems theory as a central part of OD, coaching clients through difficult emotional experiences was always contextual. Finding the appropriate and relevant expression of feelings, emotions, thoughts, and ideas was always a part of organizational change, not some separate activity. Thus, while he advocated for personal growth in general, he was clear that OD was an organization process of which becoming more emotionally mature and integrated was only a part. This integrated perspective of the change and consulting process is core to how we operate as practitioners and action researchers.

In thinking about how Bob influenced our own practice, our thoughts also center on the importance, power, and limits of affirmation. Bob's presence and expression was almost always affirming. He had a calm and considerate manner; we, and in fact almost anyone he interacted with, invariably felt that Bob was interested in their experience in the moment. When he spoke, he usually presented his thoughts and feelings in an open-ended way and sought a response from those listening. He was patient and could attentively listen to another person for a long time. It is no wonder that so many OD practitioners, including us, considered Bob a mentor and looked forward to the opportunities to be with him.

But affirming a person's worth or ability to change is not the same thing as encouraging someone to change. Bob's work on holding on and letting go raised an essential truth about change that transcends systems levels. The closer a system – individual or organizational – gets to issues of core identity, the more frightening change becomes. We fear that too many people in our field too easily and indiscriminately go for the "transformation" button without regard for the nature of the change. When change involves core identity, and it is incumbent on the OD practitioner to know when that is, the need for continuity must be appreciated. In our own personal growth work, each of us recognized a critic. That part of us which was eager to find different ways of being confrontational and all-too-willing to raise difficult issues with authority figures. But understanding the reality of core identity allowed us to become more patient, more accepting, more tolerant, and more caring. It allowed us to see reality and legitimate paths to wholeness in new ways.

Thus, much of Tannenbaum's impact came through an educational process and often through the many seminal speeches he gave to the US and Canadian OD networks. He used these opportunities to share his current thinking and raise issues that he saw in the profession, and they were always thought provoking. One of the themes he returned to numerous times was the abuse of "techniques, methodology, and procedures as being almost the be-all and end-all of OD work" (Tannenbaum 1968, p. 1). It was not techniques themselves that bothered him. It was people's dependency on their use and eventually to their overuse. Tannenbaum's plea was to develop and use one's self in consulting. He emphasized the need for behavioral flexibility and social sensitivity, for understanding the other, and for ways of being achieved only through self-understanding.

For example, Tannenbaum gave a keynote speech to the OD Network Conference in Pasadena, California, in 1983. After a statement of his credentials and accomplishments, the convener introduced him this way: "Bob's relationship to this network and to those whose lives he has touched is far deeper and richer than mere professional credentials. To walk and talk with Bob is to get more in touch with the spirit and the values of our profession. When you meet and share with Bob, you are more aware than ever that OD is not a set of techniques or workshop designs, nor is it a group of behavioral theories, not even a set of principles. OD, when you meet Bob, you learn [is] a matter of personal orientation, a matter of heart, a matter of toughness, a matter of modesty, a matter of grace, a matter of the power and the pain of love." His insights, questions, and comments were challenging, wise, and helpful. People who were fortunate enough to have spent time with him benefited in their practice and their lives. One man working with one person inevitably produced change.

Anyone who was at the OD Network Conference in April, 1973 remembers – and many of those who were not there have either heard about, read about, or know about – the presentation that Tannenbaum gave, entitled "Does this Path have a Heart?" During the speech, he quoted Carlos Castaneda's "The Teachings of Don Juan: A Yaqui Way of Knowledge" to express his belief in the importance of individual choice:

> I warn you look at every path closely and deliberately. Try it as many times as you think necessary. Then ask yourself, and yourself alone, one question: Does this path have a heart? If it does, the path is good; if it doesn't, it is no good. One path makes you strong. The other one weakens you.

Although Bob was obviously talking about the practice of organization development, he was also asking this question in the most personal way. He confronted individual OD practitioners with the practical, moral, and spiritual question of how they wished to conduct their life as a way to give themselves and their work meaning. Tannenbaum was telling us that we all have this question to answer. Each of us and *each of us alone* must make the existential choice in everything that we do.

Every individual in every generation has to address this question. It is an unending odyssey, and it will never be done once and for all. Isaiah Berlin wrote, "values – ethical, political, aesthetic – are not objectively given, not fixed stars in some Platonic firmament, eternal, immutable, which men can discover only by employing the proper method – metaphysical insight, scientific investigation, philosophical argument, or divine revelation. Values are generated by the creative human self. Man is, above all, a creature endowed not only with reason but with will" (Berlin 2013, p. 43). Bob urged people to take the path of deep vocation, not simply a means of livelihood. This depth of caring was his signature message and perhaps his greatest legacy.

Legacies and Unfinished Business

We believe that Tannenbaum would be an outspoken critic of today's approaches to leadership development and personal growth. We feel confident that he would have liked Jeff Pfeffer's 2015 book "Leadership BS." He would agree that too much leadership development is naïve regarding power and unconnected to results. With regard to personal growth, we think he would say that popular methods are too technique driven, too shallow, and too fickle with respect to fads. Knowing your Myers-Briggs Type Indicator (MBTI) score is not personal growth. For Tannenbaum, and on this point the authors completely support his view, personal growth was (and is) deep work, hard work, often painful work, and perhaps most importantly, not an end in itself, but a powerful means to more effective lives both in an out of the office.

Tannenbaum was an optimistic humanist. He deeply cared for people, and individual development was a major focal point of his long career. He believed that all social system change was mediated through individuals. He encouraged leaders and organizational development professionals to make a commitment to becoming "more whole, more complete, more mature human beings who are in touch with themselves and their environment" (Tannenbaum 1980). Bob embodied this quest for deep self-awareness and maturity. This was his North Star, his meta-goal, and he pursued it in many settings and in many roles.

Tannenbaum died in his sleep of congestive heart failure on March 15, 2003. In his obituary, Sam Culbert, a former student and longtime colleague at UCLA, wrote, "but you don't have to believe that [he is dead] if you don't want to. If you choose not to, you'll have plenty of company. Why erase from your mind the presence of a man who constantly affirms you!"

References

Barnard, C. (1938). *Functions of the executive*. Cambridge: Harvard University Press.

Beckhard, R., & Harris, R. (1977). *Organization transitions: Managing complex change*. Reading: Addison-Wesley.

Berlin, I. (2013). *The crooked timber of humanity: Chapters in the history of ideas*. Princeton: Princeton University Press.

Cummings, T., & Worley, C. (2015). *Organization development and change* (10th ed.). Mason: Cengage Publishing.

Church, A., & Jamieson, D. (2014). Current and future state of OD values. *OD Practitioner, 2*(46), 2.

Dyer, W. (1977). *Team building: Issues and alternatives*. Reading: Addison-Wesley.

Emerson, R. (1962). Power-dependence relations. *American Sociological Review, 27*(1), 31–41.

French, W., & Bell, C. (1993). *Organization development: Behavioral science interventions for organization improvement* (4th ed.). Englewood Cliffs: Prentice-Hall.

Jamieson, D., & Tannenbaum, R. (1982). Development in an era of paradigm shifts, changing boundaries, and personal challenge. *Training and Development Journal, 36*(4), 32–42.

Kallejian, V. J., Weschler, I. R., & Tannenbaum, R. (1955). Managers in transition. *Harvard Business Review, 33*(4), 55–64.

Kleiner, A. (1996). *The age of heretics: Heroes, outlaws and the forerunners of corporate change*. New York: Currency Doubleday.

Koontz, H., & O'Donnell, C. (1955). *Principles of management: An analysis of managerial functions*. New York: McGraw-Hill.

McGregor, D. (1960). *The human side of enterprise*. New York: McGraw-Hill.

McNair, M. P. (1957). Thinking ahead: What price human relations? *Harvard Business Review, 35* (2), 15–39.

McNair, M. P. (1958). Too much human relations? *Look, 22*(28), 48.

Metcalf, H., & Urwick, L. (Eds.). (1940). *Dynamic administration: The collected papers of Mary Parker Follett*. New York: Harper and Brothers.

Mooney, J., & Reiley, A. (1939). *The principles of organization*. New York: Harper and Brothers.

Moustakas, C. (Ed.). (1956). *The self: Explorations in personal growth*. New York: Harper & Row Publishers.

Perrow, C. (1979). *Complex organizations: A critical essay* (2nd ed.). New York: Random House.

Pfeffer, J. (2015). *Leadership BS*. New York: Harper Business.

Schoen, D. R. (1957). Human relations: Boon or bogle. *Harvard Business Review, 35*(6), 41–47.
Scott, W. R. (1981). *Organizations: Rational, natural and open systems*. Englewood Cliffs: Prentice-Hall.
Simon, H. (1947). *Administrative behavior.* New York: Macmillan.
Stene, E. (1940). An approach to a science of administration. *American Political Science Review, 34* (6), 1124–1137.
Tannenbaum, R. (1949). The manager concept: A rational synthesis. *Journal of Business, 22*(4), 225–241.
Tannenbaum, R. (1950). Managerial decision-making. *Journal of Business, 23*(1), 22–39.
Tannenbaum, R. (1959). Some current issues in human relations. *California Management Review, 2* (1), 49–58.
Tannenbaum, R. (1968). Using self in the consulting process. Excerpts from a presentation given by Robert Tannenbaum on July 24, 1968 to the Program for Specialists in Organization Development (PSOD), National Training Laboratories, Bethel.
Tannenbaum, R. (1976). Some matters of life and death. *OD Practitioner, 8*(1), 1–7.
Tannenbaum, R. (1980). This I believe. *Liaison: The Journal for the Association of Canadian OD, 4* (Special Edition), 1–26.
Tannenbaum, R. (1995). Bob Tannenbaum: An unfolding life integrating the personal and professional. An oral history produced by UC Santa Barbara's Oral History Program for the Humanistic Psychology Archive, Santa Barbara.
Tannenbaum, R., & Davis, S. A. (1969). Values, man and organizations. *Industrial Management Review, 10*(2), 67–86.
Tannenbaum, R., & Massarik, F. (1950). Participation by subordinates in the managerial decision-making process. *The Canadian Journal of Economics and Political Science, 16*(3), 408–418.
Tannenbaum, R., & Massarik, F. (1957). Leadership: A frame of reference. *Management Science, 4*(1), 1–19.
Tannenbaum, R., & Schmidt, W. H. (1958). How to choose a leadership pattern. *Harvard Business Review,* (March-April), 3–12.
Tannenbaum, R., Kallejian, V., & Weschler, I. R. (1954). *Training managers for leadership*. Los Angeles: University of California Press.
Tannenbaum, R., Weschler, I., & Massarik, F. (1961). *Leadership and organization*. Milton Park: Routledge.
Worley, C. G. (2014). OD values and pitches in the dirt. *OD Practitioner, 46*(4), 68–71.

Further Reading

DeCarvalho, R. (1991). *The founders of humanistic psychology*. New York: Praeger.
Freedman, A. (1999). The history of organization development and the NTL institute. *The Psychologist-Manager Journal, 3*(2), 125–141.
Hirsch, J. I. (1987). *The history of the National Training Laboratories 1947–1986, American University Studies Series VIII, Psychology*. New York: Peter Lang Publishing.
Miller, J. G. (1978). *Living systems*. New York: McGraw-Hill.
Schmidt, W., & Tannenbaum, R. (1960). Management of differences. *Harvard Business Review, 38* (6), 107–115.
Tannenbaum, R., Weschler, I. R., & Massarik, F. (1961). Assessing organizational effectiveness: Job satisfaction, productivity, and morale. In R. Tannenbaum, I. Weschler, & F. Massarik (Eds.), *Leadership and organization: A behavioral science approach* (pp. 333–345). New York: McGraw-Hill.
Weschler, I. R., Massarik, F., & Tannenbaum, R. (1962). The self in process: A sensitivity training emphasis. *Issues in Human Relations Training, 5*, 33–46.

75 Frederick Winslow Taylor: The First Change Agent, From Rule of Thump to Scientific Management

Søren Henning Jensen

Abstract

This chapter describes Taylor from a perspective that appears to have been much neglected – his role as a change agent. Throughout his life and career as a manager and management consultant, Taylor worked with organizations to make positive changes, making them better, more efficient, and less reliant on rules of thumb. He changed the notion of the modern organization to one driven and managed by scientific principles. This chapter interprets his work through this lens. It is not intended as a celebration or critique, but rather as an alternative perspective – one that offers or inspires new insights and views on change and on Taylor and his work. The chapter sets out a general introduction before going on to discuss Taylor's main influences and sources of motivation – what was fueling his thinking and driving his actions? From there, we consider Taylor's key contributions, or more precisely his key contributions in his role as a very early proponent of change. This leads us on to a new view of Taylor, from which we ask what can be learned from him today; what new insights, if any, does he bring to perspectives on organizational change? In this context, we review examples of his influence in areas that may be surprising to readers. The chapter ends with a discussion of some unresolved issues – unfinished business and harder-to-transfer ideas that must be addressed if we are to truly harness the potential of Taylor's work and deliberations. The chapter ends with a short list of suggested further reading.

Keywords

Taylorism • Change • Organizing • Scientific management • Workflow • Knowledge

S. Henning Jensen (✉)
Department of Management, Politics and Philosophy, Copenhagen Business School, Copenhagen, Denmark
e-mail: shj.mpp@cbs.dk

D.B. Szabla et al. (eds.), *The Palgrave Handbook of Organizational Change Thinkers*,
DOI 10.1007/978-3-319-52878-6_24

Contents

Introduction

This chapter considers Frederic Winslow Taylor from a perspective that has not been well studied: his role as a change agent. Most people would not think of Taylor as a change scholar. He is best known for having given birth to scientific management, which has historically been seen as an objectivist and functional approach to improvement, an old and *static* approach to doing things better – whereas *change* is seen as dynamic and modern. Yet, in this chapter I assert that Taylor was the first modern change scholar and indeed one of the greatest. Much of his thinking was by no means modern. To a large extent, his ideas and beliefs were rooted in his time. His view of workers was very far from modern-day human resource management (HRM) practices, and many aspects of his approach and the ontological assumptions of his methods are outdated and appear naive at best. His theories have also been misused, misunderstood, and taken out of context. But he was among the first to realize that change, and management, in general, should be carried out with a view of the context of the whole organization. His approach included all levels of the organization and had a strong focus on personnel. He understood that implementation and follow-up were key elements in any change process and that these do not happen of their own accord.

Frederick Winslow Taylor was in many ways an enigma, even in his own time. In quite a few areas, he was very much a product and steward of his time. He was also a man of progress and in several ways considerably ahead of his time. Around the turn of the twentieth century, he was concerned about nature going to waste or disappearing altogether. It seemed to him that the vast majority of people were focused on producing goods and services at unprecedented speed and in unprecedented numbers with little or no concern for the impact on the environment. Resources, both natural and human, were plentiful so there was no concern for conservation. But Taylor had a strong drive. He was concerned about waste in general and the waste of human effort in particular. This feels to be at the very heart of his motivation. Taylor was keen to ensure that work was carried out with little or no waste, that functional labor was not carried out in a haphazard manner, that no slack or "soldiering" was allowed, and that work was well structured and monitored. Only in this way would wealth and welfare be secured. "Soldiering" was a term Taylor used often. It is a military term, referring to the time soldiers spent doing nothing between their chores; to Taylor it epitomized the waste of resources –

inefficiency: "Underworking, that is, deliberately working slowly so as to avoid doing a full day's work, 'soldiering' as it is called in this country" (Taylor 1919, p. 13). (It should be noted that while Taylor first published his book in 1911, the references made in this chapter are from the 1919 version from Harper & Brothers.)

Taylor was convinced that the organized company, and indeed society, would not come about unless overseen by solid middle managers like him, as the vital link connecting upper management with manual laborers. This was a new way of thinking and behaving, which promised to ensure that efforts and resources were not wasted. But the approach to planning, organizing, and managing organizations had to be *changed*. In this respect, scientific management clearly deals with the management of change, and it is in this light that we will consider Taylor and his work as a change scholar and practitioner. Be warned, the literary trick of repetition I employ is no accident: it is intended to drive home central points and highlight change elements for which Taylor was a strong advocate. It also reinforces how the same simple elements and ideas expressed with Taylor's clarity, to a large extent contributed to the immense impact of his ideas, which still endure today.

I am neither a proponent for scientific management and Taylor in general nor an opponent. But I am curious about the person, practitioner, and scholar that Taylor was, and I am captivated by the complexity, range, clarity, and impact of his thinking and his work. I am convinced, too, that seeing him as a change scholar adds much-needed depth to our understanding of him.

Influences and Sources of Motivation: What Drove Taylor's Thinking?

With a background as a machinist and engineer, at a time when the role and impact of technology was on the rise and engineers were seen as a new class helping society to secure growth and prosperity, Taylor set out to lead change at the very beginning of this new era. Engineers were meant to drive change. But few, if any, brought about change as Taylor did.

When we are writing about historical persons, parts of the description will inevitably be based on guesswork. Even if there is meticulous documentation or access to letters and diaries, these only give us a part of the whole picture. We're also bound to interpret these clues in the context of current standards, having not experienced the environment as it was. This means that we will never fully understand Taylor and the motives behind his work. It is important to acknowledge this before I go on to discuss how I perceive Taylor as a change management scholar. We cannot conclude categorically that this is who or how he actually was; we can only surmise this, drawing on his life experiences and his impact in the organizations he worked for.

It is always difficult to say what exactly shapes people. Looking at Taylor's early years, the shift in plan from studying to become a lawyer at Harvard (one of the most prestigious universities in America) to working as an apprentice patternmaker and machinist at the Enterprise Hydraulic Works in Philadelphia must have had a significant impact on his life. Missing out on a place at one of the very best universities and a promise of a prominent career may have been what attuned him to the notion of lost opportunities and wasted resources.

Perhaps it was his nature and background, which differed considerably from those he worked with even from the start, that enabled Taylor to observe work on the shop floor with analytical clarity and some detachment, in turn spurring his interest in efficiency and waste reduction. The groundwork he did in studying how organizations worked, and how they should work, led to his role as one of the first management consultants, continuously striving to identify what could and should be changed, improved, and made more efficient. It is evident that right from the start of his career that Taylor wanted to improve efficiency. Not just in the narrow scope dictated by the firm he was working in, but in a wider and more general context. He used the term "nationwide efficiency," noting that inefficiency was not a local but a general problem. "This paper has been written: First. To point out through a series of simple illustrations, the great loss which the whole country is suffering through inefficiency in almost all of our daily acts" (Taylor 1919, p. 15).

During his early years, Taylor witnessed inefficiency at both an individual employee level and at a managerial level. He was much more focused on the former than the latter, which had more to do with the design of the work. This required that workers and management were aligned for the system to work. In practice it usually meant that workers should do as explained to them by their superiors. But, it also required that management worked and planned efficiently, so that workers had efficient routines to follow. In this regard, professionalism was an implicit requirement of management. This was also evident from the incentive structure, where rates favored high-quality products: the result of carefully planned work procedures and work processes broken down into smaller parts which could be better observed, measured, and optimized.

Whatever the reason, Taylor had both an eye and a talent for improving efficiency in organizations. He was leading change efforts in the organizations he worked for, and the changes caught on and inspired others to follow his example. Eventually his methods went country-wide, even before he wrote his famous book on scientific management and gained international recognition in the early twentieth century (Guillen 1997). It seems that what really caught on was the promise at the core of his work: that we can do better, waste fewer resources, and get more out of the resources we already possess; that we can and we must change! Though this exact formulation does not appear in *The Principles of Scientific Management*, it is one of the key messages in the introduction to the book and a strong theme that runs through the work. In the introduction, Taylor asserts "the search for better, for more competent men from the presidents of our great companies to our household servants was never more vigorous than now" (Taylor 1919, p. 6). This feels like an early reference to the need to create a sense of urgency, something Kotter (1996) highlights in his approach to change. Later in the introduction, Taylor cites scientific management as the tool that "can bring together and reconcile the interests of employers and employees" (Taylor 1919, p. 10).

Key Contributions: Taylor's Impact on Change in Theory and Practice Through a Hands-On Approach

Although this chapter is not dedicated to the technicalities of scientific management, it makes sense to offer a brief overview of the method of change Taylor used and for which he became famous. Even for readers who are familiar with his work, this is an important backdrop for understanding him as a change agent.

Taylor's approach to change encompassed the whole organization. The process involved several steps; the image most associated with Taylorism (or scientific management), time studies of individual workmen using a stopwatch, came relatively late in the process. First, he made revisions and adjustments to the management group, designed to coordinate and systematize the manufacturing process. He made sure management had well thought-out plans for manufacturing in all its stages and related activities. This was the starting point: without this, the subsequent steps would have little impact. The next step was to ensure that the machinery was operating properly. This was accomplished by making necessary adjustments to enhance machine performance. In this step of the process, it was important that the adjustment of the tools and machines was in alignment with the production plans laid out by the management. Finally, when the production company was functioning at a high level of efficiency, Taylor introduced changes to the way labor was carried out, to increase the output of the workers. Adjustments to the way the work was carried out were put in motion to secure a smooth process without any bottlenecks. The adjustments and recommendations were directed both at workers directly involved with production and those handling the constituent materials and finished goods. In particular Taylor emphasized two groups of employees in his change process: those in charge of operating the machinery, being at the very core of productivity, and those who organized and managed the work on the shop floor. The people on the shop floor were in charge of the layout of the plant and ensured that the orders coming from the planners at the management level were carried out. This, according to Taylor, was one of the cornerstones of his work. He makes clear that, "to work according to scientific laws, the management must take over and perform much of the work which is now left to the men; almost every act of the workmen should be preceded by one or more preparatory acts of the management which enable him to to do his work better and quicker than otherwise" (Taylor 1919, p. 26).

This was how real change was implemented. It was crucial to engage both parties in the change efforts. It was also important to change and develop the surrounding organization to ensure that the impact carried over would not be compromised by suboptimal practice or the creation bottlenecks when products moved out of the process. In other words, Taylor's approach was all-encompassing. To add value, the process of eliminating waste from all parts and functions of the organization was essential. While focus was on the shop floor – where the production was carried out and where the new efficient methods would be visible and tangible – the process started at the top of the organization, concerning the overall layout and management systems. This is described in some detail by Taylor: "Perhaps the most prominent single element in modern scientific management is the task idea. The work of every workman is fully planned out by the management at least one day in advance and each man receives in most cases complete written instructions, describing in detail the task which he is to accomplish as well as the means to be used in doing the work" (Taylor 1919, p. 39).

Taylor's approach was to methodically divide and break down the process into smaller parts with the goal of increasing efficiency and reducing waste. Planning, strategy, and design were all seen as managerial tasks, while the workers carried out the work exactly as dictated by management.

Taylor's theories and applications helped change many aspects of how work takes place in modern factories. He changed the way production of goods and services is executed and the way we approach the design of work. This includes, but is not limited to time studies, work planning, incentive schemes, and the role of the middle manager. Scientific management is now an active part of how work is conceived, planned, managed, and executed. This is possibly best expressed in the quote: "In the past man has been first; in the future the system must be first" (Taylor 1919, p. 7). In other words, the management system is more important than the needs and ideas of any individual.

I believe that a significant contribution of Taylor's legacy, both good and bad, is rooted in the clarity of his approach. He reduced complexity by applying a stringent, linear approach to how organizations should work. His methods break down entire work processes, including management functions. Processes are observed, measured, and modified to achieve high-performance modes in all functions. Processes are changed until perfection is achieved. Although Taylor's methods were initially developed and implemented in production companies, his approach was quickly accepted to be so simple and universal that it was applied to all types of companies. It was not so much *context* specific as *mindset* specific. All industries involving some kind of production could use the approach in some way. It had scalability and embodied the philosophy that "This company can do better/be more productive/optimize its use of resources." It held the promise that the optimal organization could be created: nothing would have to be left to guesswork; there would be no more rule of thumb. In this way Taylor's approach served as the mechanism by which firms could transition from guesswork or unreliable contribution to science-driven rules.

Taylor objectified production processes. He relied heavily on data, observations, measurements, and careful planning and goal alignment. In time, his methods even spread to the service industries and from the private to the public sector. As we will see below, his influence even reached architecture and the aesthetic, *avant-garde* movement. In this sense, the change he brought about was on a much grander scale than that of most other scientists and practitioners. Taylor's biggest contribution of all, perhaps then, is the simple fact that his theories could be applied system-wide.

Wren (2011, p. 12) notes that Taylor's conclusions have not survived unchanged. I am not sure how far I agree with this. It is true that the application and understanding of how to work with the principles of scientific management have changed over time and have adapted to a modern way of understanding workers. Still it should also be noted that much of the later controversy of scientific management does not come from the source, from Taylor, but rather from later and often rather loose interpretations of his methods. So the by the book interpretation of his thought have clearly not survived unchanged. But the very core of the thoughts brought forward still remains intact to this day.

The enduring elements of scientific management from Taylor's ideas were largely driven by a keen interest in eliminating waste and focusing all labor on achieving optimal production. Progress and change should be driven by data, analysis, and a clear and consistent methodology, not the rule of thumb. (The term "rule of thumb," in use since the seventeenth century, refers to rules and measurements based on guesswork and rough practice, rather than exact and scientific measurements.) This need is more pronounced today than when first evidenced by Taylor. Its importance to change is reflected clearly in change management disciplines and tools, such as Lean Six Sigma and Business Process Re-engineering. The idea that everything that *can* be measured in relation to work processes *should* be measured can be traced back to Taylor. While "data-driven management" may be a more recent association, work tasks – no matter how mundane – were to be carefully scrutinized and designed to optimize utility. In other words, effort should never be wasted. This principle of Taylor's theory has survived unchanged. The concept of methodical, empirically driven improvements of work processes is here to stay, and all methods and management tools that are built on this principle owe this to Taylor. His introduction of science – of correct measurements, of a carefully planned stepwise approach – to change, taking into consideration the whole organization from top management to the shop floor, can thus be seen as Taylor's most important contribution to his field.

Taylor's approach to change extended above and beyond looking at the manual labor aspect and how this was carried out. It was a new way of thinking, planning, and executing work – from its organizing to its execution and gradual improvement. There should be no more guesswork or rule of thumb, but objective measurements and observations of work, always striving to decrease waste and increase output. Taylor's approach resulted in optimization of the work process by breaking this down into manageable parts. In many ways, what would have been seen as the "new rules," based on the principles of scientific management, appear to have been in direct opposition to apprenticeships. Taylor wanted work and management to be objective and impersonal and for knowledge to be shared where it was needed. Apprenticeship, on the other hand, emphasized passing on craft skills, with a focus on personal knowledge and judgment. This tended to promote knowledge hoarding and *individual* rather than collective processes, which in turn meant less reliable approaches to work across an organization. Taylor saw the value of knowledge as being at an organizational level, rather than an individual level. He valued the knowledge that existed on the shop floor as much as the knowledge residing with top management. But he also valued the new knowledge generated by carefully measuring and subsequently changing work processes. To Taylor, this vastly outweighed the knowledge embedded in rules of thumb, which assumes by and large that the same routines will be followed, without any real insight into how well they work or what could and should be improved. Taylor describes this under "The Finest Type of Ordinary Management" (Taylor 1919, pp. 30–34). In the greater scheme of things, he maintains that only knowledge that has been carefully collected through scientific measurements and methods provides real value to companies and in turn to society as a whole. Taylor set out to show "the enormous gains which would result from the substitution by our workmen of scientific for rule of thumb methods" (Taylor 1919, p.16). The downside is that knowledge is rarely neutral: it usually reflects a particular perspective, most often the perspective of the management (Nonaka 1994). Knowledge can used to wield power over workers, ultimately creating inequality in the workplace. Much of the criticism leveled at Taylor is directed precisely at these power dynamics of his model, and yet he seemed oblivious to them. Still, Taylor was among the first to demonstrate and document the effect of using knowledge systematically in the management process. Although it is light-years away from knowledge management as we know it today, his influence in this area is still one of his major achievements.

New Insights: What Can We Learn from Taylor Today?

Change is an inherent part of the life of an organization, which is why it is so important to understand and try to manage it and why the tools and managerial approaches we create must be able to cope with the changes firms encounter. Some approaches will change, some will perish, and others will persist over time. So to what extent have the contributions of Taylor – a change scholar who practiced over 100 years – stood the test of time?

Clearly the time in which Taylor lived and worked had a bearing on his standpoint. His work contains scant mention of the empowerment or involvement of workers, with much greater emphasis on maintaining class and power structure. He refers to the vast majority of knowledge in a company being on the shop floor, rather than in the boardroom: "Now in the best of ordinary types of management, the managers recognize frankly the fact that the 500 or 1000 workmen included in the twenty or thirty trades, who are under them, possess this mass of traditional knowledge, a large part of which is not in the possession of the management" (Taylor 1919, p. 26). But he is clearly referring to workers' aggregate knowledge, his point being that this knowledge must be gathered by the middle management and sent up the hierarchy for analysis with the purpose of productivity improvement. Workers needed to be obedient and pliable; otherwise, they were of no use. Orders were to be followed, not questioned: the labor force could easily be replaced. Taylor's was a world divided by class, and in that world, those with a proper education and position possessed more personal knowledge than the individual worker. This argument goes right back to our earlier observations, that the change Taylor and his fellow engineers were supposed to bring about was one that kept the class divisions intact yet ensured that resources were utilized optimally and that there would be no "soldiering." This era-specific emphasis has a bearing on the applicability of Taylor's approach in the modern world where the role and impact of class and class consciousness differ significantly in the workplace. Technologies aimed at keeping the working class efficient but docile are frowned upon now, for good reason. Yet Taylor also advocated that when a worker could not do as instructed, he or she should be replaced, because such a person would not feel at home as they would never realize his or her potential as they might do other places. There is no dismissing of individuals who fall short of the requirements imposed by Taylor's regime. They are not seen as "bad," but simply as not being right for that particular job. This is a perspective that has retained its currency – recognition of the need to match personal skills and qualities with the job in hand. In this sense Taylor was an early proponent of job specialization based on skills and requirements to increase efficiency and reduce waste. Once he implemented changes in an organization, even menial tasks were changed to fit the overall plan and layout. The primary skill was the ability or willingness to learn new ways of doing things and to accept the new ways of organizing and carrying out the work.

Critics are quick to accuse Taylor of dehumanizing the work process: they accuse him of everything from ineptitude to being a charlatan, the devil incarnate, responsible for the exploitation of workers through demeaning work practices. (See, e.g., Wrege and Perroni 1974, whose article focuses on the famous "pig iron" case – which we will examine more closely later in the chapter.) Several of his detractors suggested that Taylor had fabricated or sugarcoated (e.g., Wrege and Perroni 1974) the results that had made him and his method famous; others (e.g., Govekar and Govekar 2012) argue that Taylor was simply employing a parable to bring his teachings to life. In reexamining the legacy of Taylor's work, Wrenn (2011) asserts that too much attention has been paid to finding flaws in his arguments and to demonizing Taylor and not enough placed on his contributions of how work processes are designed, organized, performed, and improved. Others consider the wider-reaching influence Taylor has had – in the case of Guillen (1997) – on modern architecture.

Taylor's theories may have seemed extreme, with their focus on weeding out all of the slack from an organization. However, taken as an approach, philosophy, or set of guidelines, it would be left up to the management to reflect on their application and choose where to set the limit. We can opt to focus on the rigidity of Taylor's ideas, his insistence on one best way to do pretty much anything, or we can also choose to see his theories as an open offer to management to decide how tightly organized they want their company to be. In an open, competitive economy, this could also become a parameter when attracting investors, resources, and talent. I believe that this is a new insight that has been lost in the "either/or" debate of Taylor's theories.

If we adopt Taylor's approach to eliminating waste as the driver for change, we must also apply this to the waste of human efforts. Taylor would argue that it is a waste of resources if the wrong person is assigned to a specific task. He advocated that attention be given to matching the individual worker to the task at hand, both with the aim of increasing efficiency and of ensuring that the skills of the individual worker were not wasted (i.e., by being put into a context where their skills could not be sufficiently utilized). To my mind, this aspect of Taylor's approach to change has been overlooked: matching "skills required" with "skills possessed." If we look at how companies today ask employees and managers to apply for their own jobs as a part of a major change process, we can see that this vital element of change management is alive, well, and being increasingly widely adopted. Its application today may be miles away from Taylor's original application to coal shoveling and pig iron carrying, but the mechanism and the underlying assumption are much the same. If a worker's skills do not meet the organization's needs, neither party will be satisfied in the long run, and skills and human efforts will be wasted.

We should remember, however, that the attention to personnel handling came late in the change process, after machine calibration and the overhaul of managerial processes including work planning, This seems to be in line with the statement that with scientific management, the system came first. We are not given much insight into this part of the process, and it is doubtful that the same candor was displayed in terms of staffing at a managerial level in Taylor's day as it is today. However, Taylor's change process did take into account the idea that tasks and skills needed to be matched, and that change was not isolated to the shop floor – an insight that is too often overlooked in Taylor's work, perhaps because of his overall emphasis.

It is evident how Taylor's thinking has brought about change in classical production including heavy industry, the railways, and – in due course – services. All of this is well-known and documented. However, to properly show how far Taylor's thinking reached and affected the actions of others, and how far his approach to change reached, we will go on to explore its application and impact in the field of modernist architecture in the early part of the twentieth century, with reference to Guillen (1997). While this may not be the most known or scrutinized area of Taylor's influence, it highlights the breadth of impact his thinking on change had for society as a whole. Therefore it is seen a fitting to include here rather than focusing on his influence in organizations, which is rather well-known.

A quite surprising area of influence Taylor was the impact he had on European modernistic *avant-garde* architecture. This began soon after *The Principles of Scientific Management* was published and endured until the 1930s. Nothing could be further apart than the rigid principles of scientific management and the experimental and vibrant ideas and principles of *avant-garde* modernism. It was the purity of Taylor's ideas that caught on and felt very close to some of the basic principles of *avant-garde* architecture. The new idea was that the only proper approach to progress was to abandon guesswork and embrace measurements and science. Science (psychology, engineering, physiology) should dictate how to plan and execute work as a way out of the old orthodoxy when planning and developing society overall and its buildings. There was focus on hierarchy or hierarchies as a means to an end when it came to establishing the control of work (Guillen 1997). Ideas including those suggesting that conflicts could be avoided or reduced through planning and controlling and that knowledge should be collected, analyzed, and used for the good of all, rather than be hoarded by individuals or even worse overlooked, underused, and neglected, also came from Taylor's work and found their way into the new *avant-garde* modernism. The idea that progress came from planning and executing in iterations, and that technology should be embraced and actively used, was another area where modernism and Taylor's theories intersected. Scientific management is often seen as uniformity, which is not entirely correct given Taylor's emphasis on the need to carefully match workers with the right task and then carefully monitor and instruct that person to help improve his or her skills. This fitted well with the concept of talent and talent development in modern architecture at that time. As noted by Guillen (1997, p. 689), the list of similarities and inspiration between the two goes even further. After initially seeing Taylorism as "an inevitable and horrible path towards the future" (Guillen 1997, p. 689), Le Corbusier soon after embraced the concept wholeheartedly. Even to the degree where he encouraged Taylorization and standardization to his fellow architects (Guillen 1997, p. 696). Possibly Le Corbusier and the other modern architects of the era saw the clean, methodical, and rational approach as something they could use to create their visions. The new architecture was all about clean lines, space optimization, and minimalism with no waste: through Taylor they saw a way to accomplish their ideals and achieve the desired aesthetics. The compatibility of Taylor's ideals and those of this artistic profession were surprisingly strong.

This example illustrates how the influence of Taylor with his clean scientific approach to change, and focus on strict planning and resource efficiency, can be traced across the modern economy and society – perhaps to a greater degree than many have realized. It also highlights the importance of perspective. It is easy to see Taylor's scientific management as nothing but a nitty-gritty approach to organizing work processes. Whether or not you agree with his theories and approach to change, it is important to acknowledge that he was, to no small degree, responsible for a scientific approach to the study and improvement of organizations more generally – inspiring research, practice, and new ideas with wide-ranging impact. (Next time you admire early twentieth-century modernistic architecture, or Le Corbusier's designs, remember that they have been inspired by Taylor!)

Looking more closely at Taylor's work, we soon see that there is more than meets the eye. He was an inspiration for change in many areas, and his theories still provide valuable insights, as long as we see *The Principles of Scientific Management* as a source of inspiration – of new thinking about rationalization – and not just as stale and dusty manual.

Yet Taylor's theories also leave some unfinished business: issues that he did not address and aspects of thinking about the organization of work that do not carry over so easily into current practice.

Legacies and Unfinished Business: Landmarks and Room for Improvement

Thanks, in part, to Taylorism, society has benefited from fine-tuned production of goods and services which in turn paved the way for increased wealth and reduced prices. This has not been without cost to individuals however, and even now – more than 100 years after Taylor's work was published – there are still significant outstanding issues in the pursuit of optimal change management. It is important not to overestimate Taylor's influence, and it would be wrong to state that all modern attempts and approaches to modify and improve the workplace in a systematic way are somehow borne out of or rooted in Taylorism. It would also be misleading to attribute all positive and negative elements that have grown out of increased work specialization, and efficiency gains and division of labor, to Taylor's work and thinking. So let us focus the remaining discussion on some of the remaining issues that are most significant, both in terms of legacies and unfinished business from a change perspective.

As mentioned earlier in this chapter, Taylor cites the now-famous case of "the pig iron" in his book *The Principles of Scientific Management* (Taylor 1919, pp. 42–47). In this example, a laborer named Schmidt was used to demonstrate how to instruct workers to follow the precise instructions of their supervisors to significantly increase productivity. The story illustrates several points Taylor was not exactly known for, most notably his people skills, particularly when dealing with ordinary workers. In this case, Schmidt the pig iron carrier is given rather direct and somewhat harsh orders by Taylor, which Taylor justifies as being "appropriate and not unkind" for a man of Schmidt's "mentally sluggish type" (Taylor 1919, p. 46). Taylor's description of what ensues is rather less generous:

> The pig iron handler stoops down, picks up a pig weighing about 92 pounds, walks for a few feet or yard and then drops it on the ground or upon a pile. This work is so crude and elementary that in its nature the writer firmly believes that it would be possible to train an intelligent gorilla so as to become a more efficient pig iron handler than any man can be. (Taylor 1919, p. 40)

Imagine a modern manager uttering something even remotely similar today – and during a change process! Taylor was very much a man of his time – characterized by strict class divisions and class consciousness. Those who performed menial labor were expected to follow orders and to do so blindly. In the early 1900s, it was assumed that those with no formal education or position in society were simple and lacked the personal motivation and wit to direct themselves. Consequently to the elite, both the old and the new class of engineers, where Taylor belonged perfectly, were perfectly natural to talk to, think about, and treat manual workers in a manner that would be frowned upon today. So comparing manual laborers to Gorillas would be considered reasonable. When Taylor (1919) notes that there is more knowledge on the shop floor than at the managerial level, he is referring merely to information that middle managers could collect, analyze, and act upon. There is no thought given to empowerment of those shop floor workers, as would be the case in today's change management movements. Whatever potential laborers might hold, this would have been deemed latent until made manifest by managers and consultants. *This* was what needed to happen to effect change and reduce waste. This is one of the most important areas of unfinished business in Taylor's theories. For his ideas here to have relevance and value in today's knowledge economy, they must be applied to all groups of employees. The idea that shouting orders or treating people like they are mindless drones is long gone in most societies – we simply know better now. Taylor did not. But had he still been around today, that thought process would undoubtedly have developed – in this sense the lack of focus on the individual is merely unfinished business. If brought up to date, I would assert that Taylor's work and method would fit well with the contemporary view on human resource management, and management in general – and could be tested as such.

Closely related to this issue is the relative lack of consideration to work breaks in Taylor's proposed method. In his book he tells a story about women visually inspecting ball bearings at the Simonds Roller Bearing Company. This was done using old rule-of-thumb management. Then a Mr. Sanford E. Thompson took over the management of this work and applied scientific management to the process. Interestingly, one of the main components was to reduce the number of work hours and introduce mandatory breaks. It was noted that, contrary to what might be expected, "with each shortening of the working day the output increased instead of diminishing" (Taylor 1919, p. 88). This was done to reduce stress and ensure that the women could work with a high predictable level of quality over time (Taylor, p. 92). Breaks were to be organized and carefully managed to avoid the current situation where, despite the long hours, "the girls spent a considerable part of their time either in partial idleness, talking and halfworking, or in actually doing nothing" (Taylor 1919, p. 92).

Taylor notes in detail how the women's work is carefully monitored to determine how to organize the work: "guarding against giving her a task so severe that there was danger from over fatigue or exhaustion" (Taylor 1919, p. 92.)

The story and its implications are interesting because it shows that Taylor did factor in issues such as job boredom and the cognitive aspect of work in addition to the physical and physiological aspects. It also illustrates that Taylor looked for optimal work designs for all the involved elements. Numbers were to be respected as absolute, whether units per time, steps walked or in this case the length of the breaks. Today, the idea that it should be possible to achieve this level of scientific accuracy for all types of manual work seems implausible in the modern world and, to my knowledge, has not been tried and tested in a proper workplace setting.

However, this is not the unfinished business we are focusing on here. Rather I wish to address the insufficient attention paid to workers' breaks in Taylor's methods. Yes, he does write that optimal conditions need to be set otherwise productivity will decrease and workers be worn prematurely down. However, there is little elaboration of this and even less consideration of the likelihood of his rules being kept to as rigidly as he prescribes once he has changed an organization. As the companies Taylor changed were all driven by profit, surely there would always be the temptation to crank up the pace just a "little" more. And yet it seems that Taylor did not anticipate that his method carried inherent scope for exploitation. Possibly he had a strong belief in his own authority and was confident that his words would weigh heavier than the drive to increase profits or even that the logic was self-evident and needed no further elaboration. Another explanation could be that he lacked the human insight to anticipate the risk of potential exploitation. Whatever the reason, Taylor's approach to change and the principals of scientific management need an efficient management tool to protect workers from exploitation. Simply stating that breaks are important without properly embedding this in this change approach as he did with the observation and planning is not sufficient. This lack of sufficient attention to a point that has since been a central point of criticism for those who see scientific management as inhumane makes for another piece of unfinished business in Taylor's work.

The famous (or infamous) "pig iron" case described above effectively illustrates the very core of his work. As it turned out, there never was a worker named Schmidt employed at the factory: it is not a "true" story (Wrege and Perroni 1974; Wrege and Hodgetts 2000). Some critics argue that this demonstrates that Taylor was not honest or that the whole thing was a sham (Wrege and Perroni 1974). Yet, as suggested above and has been referenced by Govekar and Govekar (2012), the most likely explanation is that Taylor intended the use of the story to function as a parable; indeed, he used it as an example both in his book and in his speeches. In Govekar and Govekar (2012), the authors go on to show the parable as a literary concept and analyze the story according to these terms. I agree wholeheartedly with the underlying analysis they present – and that the parable is intended to show both the reason for implementing scientific management and its impact, by way of example, even if this is made up. I would argue further that the parable does not simply illustrate how scientific management works; it also clearly demonstrates how Taylor worked with change. In this sense, the "pig iron" case is a very powerful parable, which boils down his approach to changing organizations and making workers more efficient, by using a methodical approach. Parables are simple stories; therein lies their impact. The pig iron story as a parable underscores Taylor's impact, which lies in the simplicity of his message. Organizations can be changed to function more effectively, to be optimal, to eliminate waste of all kinds – just follow his prescription for scientific management and the results will follow. This, as I see it, is Taylor's legacy.

Conclusion

In this chapter we have journeyed through Taylor's life and works from his early years and influences, which ultimately led to a lifelong study and pursuit of change and improvements, including his legacy and the unfinished business he left behind.

The picture I wanted to show was one of Taylor as a change scholar rather than merely a rationalist. It is true that he is credited with inventing and promoting the method used to rationalize work, making it manageable in order to improve and optimize it. However, if we look at this in a broader context, all the steps in Taylor's approach to achieving efficiency are elements in a change process. It is the change that creates the efficiency. Further, I believe that without the greater message concerning the need for organizations to change in a systematic and manageable manner, the tools would have been long forgotten. Today we do not use the actual methodology Taylor proposed, and we certainly don't use the approach to managing or "coaching" employees as he did. Taylor saw this need to improve efficiency early on in his career and he pursued it relentlessly. To him, change was about reducing and eliminating waste, and Taylor detested waste in any shape or form. He argued that change and efficiency improvements were a means to an end for eliminating waste.

As I see it, the impact of Taylor's work came from the simplicity and clarity of his message. All organizations can be improved, can reduce resource waste, and can change – as long as they approach the problem scientifically. They need to reduce complexity by breaking down assignments into smaller parts, by acknowledging that the parts of the organization need to be aligned, and by accepting the limitations of imperfect knowledge. Through Taylor's theories, the change process becomes simple and manageable without sacrificing the big picture. He promises that the potential of change and improvement embedded in all organizations can be realized through what is essentially change management. Below I will try to illustrate the complexity of his work and the influence it has had.

When we look at the range of his contribution, it is obvious that Taylor inspired change in more ways than most probably realize. I have put together some of the most prominent insights and shortcomings in the works of Taylor to illustrate my point that in order to truly understand Taylor's work and its impact, we need to see the full picture.

Taylor indirectly criticized contemporary organizations and their management for not paying attention to the total flow of the work process and partly for not creating alignment throughout the organization's activities. He was also critical of their inability to recognize the value of the collective knowledge of workers and the role of the middle manager. He recognized that knowledge about organizations came from the shop floor more than from the management floor and that planning and execution were intertwined. He identified the middle manager as a key player in successful change initiatives – in fact Taylor practically invented the modern version of the middle manager function as imperative to the process of improving organizations. "This close, intimate, personal cooperation between the management and the men is of the essence of modern scientific or task management" (Taylor 1919, p. 26).

However, he forgot to formally build a break into his change process, other than a friendly reminder of not overdoing it.

Taylor was also naive in his trust in management to create optimal production rather than cannibalize resources. He created incentive schemes that strongly favored the owners and managers over the workers. He was overbearing and condescending in his reference and approach to the workers. He was an elitist and a rationalist, forgetting or overlooking any personal motivation beyond money. Yet Taylor's work has been read as having been deeply influenced by Christian thinking. Indeed his rather short book, written in a straightforward language, has inspired several interpretations of possible subtexts and metaphors. Even if few people have actually read *The Principles of Scientific Management*, every business school student and most managers know about Taylorism. This is a clear indication of its importance.

His method influenced production and service, both public and private, and it carried over into a context not foreseen by Taylor or any of his contemporaries. Despite being seen as the epitome of uniformity, Taylor's work inspired *avant-garde* architecture to the extent that Le Corbusier strongly encouraged young architects to read Taylor's work. While the approach Taylor proposed is seen as obsolete by today's standards, the underlying methods and logic are very much present in most modern efficiency tools. In short, even if Taylor's methods and approach to scientific management are simple, his theories are not. There is so much more than meets the eye once we abandon what we think we know about him and look deeper. It is

Taylor's ability to explore the complexity of change which I believe allowed him to express the clarity of how to manage change effectively.

References

Govekar, P. L., & Govekar, M. A. (2012). The parable of the pig iron: Using Taylor's story to teach the principles of scientific management. *Journal of Higher Education Theory and Practice, 12* (2), 73–83.

Guillen, M. F. (1997). Scientific management's lost aesthetic: Architecture, organization, and the Taylorized beauty of the mechanical. *Administrative Science Quarterly, 683*, 682–715.

Kotter, J. P. (1996). *Leading Change*. Boston: Harvard Business School Press.

Nonaka, I. (1994). A dynamic theory of organizational knowledge creation. *Organization Science, 5*(1), 14–37.

Taylor, F. W. (1919). *The principles of scientific management*. New York: Harper & Brothers.

Wren, A. D. (2011). The centennial of Frederick W. Taylor's the principles of scientific management: A retrospective commentary. *Journal of Business and Management, 17*(1), 11–22.

Wrege, C.D., & Perroni, A.G. (1974). Taylor's Pig-tale: A Historical Analysis of Frederick W. Taylor's Pig-Iron Experiments. *Academy of Management Journal, 17*, 6–27.

Wrege, C.D., & Hodgetts, R.M. (2000). Frederick W. Taylor's 1899 Pig Iron Observations: Examining Fact, Fiction, and Lessons for the New Millennium. *Academy of Management Journal, 43*, 1283–1291.

Further Reading

For those who find they would like to know more about Taylor, I have provided a list of proposed additional reading. It is not an exhaustive or authoritative list. The volume of literature on Taylor and his works is extensive. Rather, it is a list that I have compiled based on my own research into his life and work. It shows the breadth of his influence which extends in many directions. His influence begins with his own work, *The Principles of Scientific Management*, which stands out as the one book that those of us who have worked with him use to underscore the impact of his thinking and conclusions. Next, there is a list of articles, many of which were written in relation to the centennial for the publication of Taylor's book in 1911. They are chosen because I feel that they all deal with the author and his work in a manner displaying curiosity, academic rigor, and a genuine interest in seeing more than just the obvious. The articles look at Taylor with a view to understanding his thinking and his actions, to identify underlying patterns in his writing.

Blake, A. M., & Moseley, J. L. (2010). One hundred years after *The Principles of Scientific Management*: Frederick Taylor's life and impact on the field of human performance technology. *Performance Improvement, 49*(4), 27–34.

Boddewyn, J. (1961). Frederick Winslow Taylor revisited. *Journal of Administrative Management, 2*, 100–107.

Kuleza, M. G., Weaver, P., & Freidman, S. (2011). Frederick W. Taylor's presence in 21st century management accounting systems and work process theories. *Journal of Business and Management, 17*(1), 105–121.

Monin, N., Barry, D., & John, M. D. (2003). Toggling with Taylor: A different approach to reading a management text. *Journal of Management Studies, 40*(2), 377–401.

Ramkrishnan (Ram) V. Tenkasi: Expanding and Bridging the Boundaries of Theory, Practice, and Method

76

Eric J. Sanders, George W. Hay, Bart Brock, and Elise Barho

Abstract
In the field of organization development and change, Dr. Ramkrishnan (Ram) V. Tenkasi is an emergent thinker with contributions to scholarship and practice. Woven throughout the career of this academic and Fulbright senior research scholar is a recurrent theme of dialectical synthesis and boundary expansion along with frequent collaboration across a spectrum of advisors, peers, and doctoral students. Tenkasi's scholarship has influenced the field with contributions to its understanding of organizational knowledge and communication, scholar-practitioners and the linkage of thought and action, and models of organization development – particularly large-scale change. He continues to expand his own learning and boundaries through immersion in cross-disciplinary methodologies while expanding both the rigor and relevance of our field.

Keywords
Scholar-practitioner • Cognition • Communication • Social networks • Large-scale change • Longitudinal • Socio-technical systems • Learning • Research

E.J. Sanders (✉)
College of Business and Management, Cardinal Stritch University, Milwaukee, WI, USA
e-mail: ejsanders@stritch.edu; eric.sanders@ODeconomist.com

G.W. Hay
Business Psychology Department, The Chicago School of Professional Psychology, Chicago, IL, USA
e-mail: ghay@thechicagoschool.edu

B. Brock
Concordia University, Mequon, WI, USA
e-mail: Bart.Brock@cuw.edu; brockwb@hotmail.com

E. Barho
Huron Consulting, Chicago, IL, USA
e-mail: ebarho@huronconsultinggroup.com; ebarho@gmail.com

D.B. Szabla et al. (eds.), *The Palgrave Handbook of Organizational Change Thinkers*,
DOI 10.1007/978-3-319-52878-6_94

Contents

Introduction

Ramkrishnan (Ram) V. Tenkasi's contributions and insights as an emergent thinker within the field of organization development and change are broadly recognized and encompassing. His success in reaching across philosophical and disciplinary boundaries is characterized by a dialectical synthesis of theoretical paradigms and the integration of managerial action into those paradigms. His recognition as an emergent thinker is evidenced by the broad range of scholarship conducted by others citing his research. This Fulbright senior research scholar and professor of organization development at Benedictine University strengthens the field of organization development and change with rigorous research, with the transformation of that rigor into relevance as actionable knowledge for management practitioners and with the development of the next generation of management scholar-practitioners.

Influences and Motivations: Eastern, Western, and Dialectical Synthesis

Born in India, the third son of a successful, well-educated couple, Ramkrishnan (Ram) V. Tenkasi's early years occurred within the philosophical paradigms of a pluralistic society, perhaps the foundational elements for a propensity of dialectical synthesis evident throughout his career. Early education included readings in classical Indian scripture, such as the Bhagavad Gita, still found on his office bookshelf, and contemporary Eastern philosophies including the writings of Tarthang Tulku, a Tibetan Buddhist author and teacher. Formative grounding in the broader, subjectivist philosophies of the East are clearly balancing influences to his later studies of objectivist philosophy prominent in Western social sciences.

Doctoral Education. Tenkasi conducted his doctoral studies at Case Western Reserve University (R. Tenkasi, personal communication, February 7, 2015). Some of his most influential advisors were those serving as his dissertation committee: William Pasmore (chair), Richard Boland, Suresh Srivastava, and David Cooperrider. Influential traces of each are found throughout his later work.

Pasmore provided mentoring in large organizational consulting and its requisite understanding of systems theory. Jointly, Tenkasi and Pasmore obtained a grant for socio-technical research of knowledge work at Procter & Gamble, concluding with new theory development about how teams are hampered in generating knowledge due to cognitive over-simplification processes. This journey into grounded theory, mixed methods, and scholar-practitioner work initiated Tenkasi's path toward being a scholar-practitioner – living in the worlds of both academia and practice (Tenkasi and Hay 2008). Cooperrider and Srivastava also served as early influencers. As Tenkasi studied and conducted fieldwork with them at the Cleveland Clinic, development occurred for the theory and methodology of appreciative inquiry (AI). Here Tenkasi learned to apply abstract theory to practice, taking the concepts of appreciative, positive psychology that Cooperrider and Srivastava developed to support AI, and applying them to organizational change including large-group interventions comprised of many stakeholders. Interestingly, Cooperrider conducted his master's-level studies at George Williams College with Peter Sorensen who Tenkasi later joined in developing the Benedictine University Ph.D. program in organization development.

Boland was Tenkasi's strongest influencer in terms of organizational theory and is a frequent coauthor in the intervening postdoctoral years. Boland brought exposure to the original articles of theory builders not only in organization theory but also in various social sciences and the philosophy of science in particular. Tenkasi learned philosophy of science through studying Socrates, Aristotle, and Plato; Wittgenstein, Kuhn, Popper, and Latour, organization theory from the writings of Mooney and Reiley and Richard Scott; management theory based on the arguments of Frederick Taylor, Chester Barnard, Max Weber, and Henri Fayol, and change theory from Lewin (1947); economics from the writings of Adam Smith; systems theory from the writings of von Bertalanffy, and its application in open systems from the work of Henderson, Parsons, and Taylor. He studied evolution from the work of Darwin and its derivative, population ecology a deterministic theory while also absorbing more agential organizational approaches such as decision theory, resource dependence, and contingency theory as noted by Hall (1987). He also studied the systems-resource model (Yuchtman and Seashore 1967) and participant-satisfaction models (Cummings et al. 1977), followed by more theory, including learning and social theory from Giddens (1979), Archer (1995), and Bhaskar (1998). This framing provided a strong foundation for Tenkasi's own theory building and the framework he has used to teach organization theory and philosophy of science to hundreds of doctoral students over the past 20 years. This theory building and framework rests on essentially three points made in one of his early chapters, "Knowing and Organizational Being" (Tenkasi 1993):

- theoreticians can no longer claim an exclusive right to knowledge ... exploration of the 'consciousness' of an organization – and the capacity to imagine alternatives – should be open to the contributions of each and every organizational participant;
- ...within such a pluralistic, 'active' structure of knowing, successive depths of questions make themselves available to be examined;

- active inquiry and imagination may be able to break the knowledge barrier and support new ways to address key issues such as peace, prosperity, and social justice.

(Tenkasi 1993, pp. 172–175)

These three points appear as themes throughout this chapter.

Early Scholar-Practitioner Focus. Upon completing his doctorate, Tenkasi became an assistant professor in the Center for Effective Organizations (CEO) at the Marshall School of Business in the University of Southern California (USC). He worked for 6 years at CEO in what Jay Galbraith described as a halfway house for scholar-practitioners who are working both in academia and industry (R. Tenkasi, personal communication, February 7, 2015). Tenkasi taught and conducted a number or research projects, most often working with Sue Mohrman, and they ultimately developed a theory of change as a learning process, noting that change comes from new cognition inducing new behaviors that also enable structural coordination mechanisms (Tenkasi and Mohrman 1999; Tenkasi et al. 1998).

Perhaps most important in his years at USC, Tenkasi became a true scholar-practitioner, developing his already strong research skills through both longitudinal and cross-sectional studies with clients including AlliedSignal, Hewlett-Packard, Kaiser Permanente, Motorola, Shell Oil, and Texas Instruments. This high-level work and exposure allowed him to build both skill and credibility as a researcher and consultant. It also taught him to work quickly and effectively to generate results that were useful to both the client and the knowledge community at large.

Leadership in Academia. Tenkasi advanced as an active researcher with grants from the National Science Foundation (NSF), the Fulbright foundation (where he was named a senior research scholar for a longitudinal study encompassing 40 years of the Indian software industry analyzing the determinant factors for its unprecedented growth), and many other government and nongovernmental sources. Meanwhile, he developed as a leader in academia. He served as an officer of the Organization Development and Change Division of the Academy of Management starting in 2002 and culminated as its chair in 2007. He has also served on Funding Panels for the National Science Foundation regularly since 1998, Netherlands Foundation of Scientific Research Institutes (NWO, the equivalent of NSF for the Netherlands), the Department of Defense, American Association for the Advancement of Science (AAAS), Fulbright awards, as well as the National Institutes of Health. Since 1998, Tenkasi has helped build Benedictine University's doctoral program in organization development. Working closely with Peter Sorensen and Jim Ludema initially, and later with Therese Yaeger, he codeveloped the curriculum and process used in this executive doctoral program focused on creating scholar-practitioners. Pushing and pulling working professionals through a doctoral program in just 3 years is a formidable challenge to which Tenkasi rose easily. Leveraging his strong research background, Tenkasi took the lead in teaching philosophy of science, organization theory, qualitative methods, quantitative methods, the scholar-practitioner journey, and mixed research methods.

Tenkasi serves on the editorial boards of many journals, including the *Journal of Applied Behavioral Science* (associate editor), the *Journal of Organizational Change Management*, the *Open Business Journal Bentham Science Series*, the *International Biopharmaceutical Association*, and the *International Journal of Management Practice*. He has led in terms of both his own research development and his service to the academic community.

Development of New Scholars. Tenkasi is actively engaged in teaching students in a variety of doctoral programs, primarily at Benedictine University. The graduate students he has taught carry with them his imprint in terms of conducting rigorous research. The dissertations he has chaired have added to the field and their authors continue to do so – witness the dissertations he has chaired that are cited and referenced in this chapter. The four authors of this chapter have benefited from having Tenkasi as their chair; most of their subsequent publications convey actionable knowledge for use by scholar-practitioners. Furthermore, three of the chapter authors have moved from being full-time practitioners to being academic scholar-practitioners with undergraduate, masters, and doctoral students of their own.

Although the development of new scholars is part of Tenkasi's legacy, it also brings into sharp focus the nature of scholar-practitioners. The challenge of transforming business managers and organizational leaders into scholar-practitioners requires a different andragogy from those within traditional research-focused doctoral programs. The "outside-in" approaches of didactic instruction where knowledge is poured into students are eschewed in favor of "inside-out" approaches of constructivist learning where knowledge is grasped as it is produced. Comprehension occurs as students give voice to their emerging understanding of theory; expertise emerges as students enact their research. Tenkasi's classes are a learning laboratory for the development of a deeper understanding of the fundamental nature of scholar-practitioners and of the processes used to gain and produce actionable scientific knowledge. As beneficial as this is for the doctoral students, this also continually deepens Tenkasi's appreciation and insight into organizational knowledge and action.

Key Contributions: Perspective Making and Perspective Taking, Process Models of Theory-Practice Linkage, Scholar-Practitioner Development, Validating Models of Large-Scale Change, and Expanding Longitudinal Methods

Not unexpectedly for an emergent thinker on organizational change, Tenkasi's growing work has yielded diverse, multiple, and substantial contributions to the field of organization development and change. Five broad contributions are highlighted in this section: perspective making and perspective taking, process models of theory-practice linkages, scholar-practitioner development, validating models of large-scale change, and expanding longitudinal methods. The influences and motivations discussed in the preceding section are visible in these five contributions.

Perspective Making and Perspective Taking. Tenkasi approaches organizational knowledge with the concepts of perspective making and perspective taking. Along with coauthor Dick Boland, he advances the critical role that perspective making and perspective taking serve as "...the basis for transformation within and between communities of knowing..." (Boland and Tenkasi 1995, p. 352). (Note: this article is one of Tenkasi's leading publications with 517 Web of Science citations to date and a broad scope of referencing conferences and articles.)

Perspective making and perspective taking offered a different view on knowledge work (e.g., innovation and new product development) from the dominant paradigm at that time, the conduit paradigm. The conduit paradigm held that innovation could be accomplished with the linear sharing of organizational knowledge and is evidenced by the deployment of knowledge warehouses to store the intellectual capital of an organization. Under the conduit model, knowledge warehouse users merely access the stored knowledge to be on the way to successful innovation. The problem with the conduit model, as Tenkasi and Boland point out, is that is ignores the symbolic and interpretative dimensions of any knowledge element.

Perspective making and perspective taking are based on Wittgenstein's model of language games (1953), a model that allows knowledge to be studied in terms of its symbolic and interpretative dimensions. Knowledge does not exist only at an abstract level but is situated at a concrete level within the activities and conversations of the knowers. Perspective making is the ability of knowledge workers to make explicit their concrete level knowledge on some aspect of their work. Since perspective making is only the externalization of knowledge, perspective taking is needed to complete the knowledge work within an organization. Perspective taking is the ability of the knowledge worker to internalize the knowledge held by others – to play in the language game as if a member of that knowledge community. Successful innovation and new product development require the synergistic use of perspective making and perspective taking to leverage and extend the knowledge that is being developed within the organization. Boland and Tenkasi (1995) end with an emphasis on narrative as the means to further perspective making and perspective taking as it is experientially grounded, enriched with language and action. Perhaps innovation could be furthered with more emphasis on the essentially human capacities for storytelling and less emphasis on the rather sterile knowledge warehouses.

Process Models of Theory-Practice Linkage. Around the turn of the current millennium, there was a renewed call within the management literature for academics and practitioners to bridge knowledge and action. Stemming from continued observations of a "great divide between theory and practice" (Astley and Zammuto 1992; Lawler et al. 1996; Rynes et al. 2001), many professionals were questioning their discipline and its future. As Austin and Bartunek (2003) pointed out, what is the lasting value of management scholarship if it does not translate into management practice that makes a difference – management knowledge and practice are inextricably linked. Huff and Huff (2001) proposed the creation of "boundary spanners" who would "potentially close the relevance gap from both ends" of science and business (p. 50). Boundary spanners are tasked with the securement of actionable scientific knowledge – the knowledge that meets the criteria of the scientific community and the business needs of the organization (Adler et al. 2004, p. 84).

Tenkasi and Hay (2004) completed one of the first studies documenting how boundary spanners bridged knowledge and action. Based on the work of Mohr (1982) that differentiated between process and variance approaches to empiricism (Van de Ven and Poole 2005), the study adopted a process lens, while most extant research depended on variance approaches to examine this divide. The main result of this inductive study of scholars, practitioners, and scholar-practitioners was a process mode of theory-practice linkages.

The process model shows us that theory-practice linkages occur within all phases of organizational work. Linkage across knowledge and action happens in the beginning (project definition), the middle (project execution), and the end of scholar-practitioner work (project realization). Furthermore, there appears to be a causal order to these phases. Actionable scientific knowledge does not occur without linkages being present in the earlier phases. Theory-practice linkages in project definition and in project execution precede boundary spanning in project realization.

Theoretical contributions from this study provide us with understanding of the nature of *bridging processes* across knowledge and action as scholar-practitioners move from theory to practice and from practice to theory in separate phases across time. They may begin with the use of a *theory* to frame upcoming actions that need to be taken later, or they might *collect data on the results of an intervention (practice)* to inform a subsequent theoretical discussion. Scholar-practitioners also use *coordinative* linkages involving the presence of both theory and practice at the same time. For example, scholar-practitioners are adept at achieving actionable scientific knowledge through one form of practice, action research, allowing the simultaneous movement of organizations forward via action while generating greater depths of understanding, be it practical or scholarly.

Scholar-Practitioner Development. Tenkasi's synthesis of thought-action provided insight for Hay in the development of a scholar-practitioner process model and later Sanders in its extension into a functional model of scholar-practitioner work. Under Tenkasi's guidance, Sanders (2015) compares the work of highly experienced scholar-practitioners in organization development (including Edgar Schein, Warner Burke, Thomas Cummings, and Michael Beer – all profiled in this volume) and in medical translational research to reveal that scholar-practitioners in the two fields are far more similar than different in thought-action application. It verifies the roles of scholar, practitioner, and scholar-practitioner over time (Tenkasi and Hay 2004; Wasserman and Kram 2009) and adds the important role of teacher. It further shows that both groups not only move between segmented roles of scholar, practitioner, and teacher but also integrate roles, blending two or even all three of those roles together. The study also confirms and expands on the strategies and tactics used to connect theory and practice introduced by Tenkasi and Hay (2004) and develops the personal characteristics these boundary spanners share. Combined, this thought-action insight better describes the work of scholar-practitioners in both fields than traditional theory of a linear model of academic development: basic science to hypothesis generation, then limited trial testing, and finally larger population application with limited feedback from the field to the academy.

Validating Models of Large-Scale Change. Social networks are the stuff of both popular acclaim and derision, but Tenkasi went deeper to examine their efficacy as tools in implementing large-scale organizational change. Tenkasi and Chesmore (2003) chose to examine the validity of *strong ties* through a social network lens of intraorganizational units when studying 40 units of a large, multinational corporation implementing large-scale organizational change. Quantitatively confirmed hypotheses show that strong ties between the change initiator and the change recipient supported more successful change efforts than those with weaker ties. Further contribution highlights the importance of strong ties at not just the group (or unit) level but also the individual level in large-scale change.

Tenkasi with his frequent coauthors, Sue and Alan Mohrman, further illustrates the power of informal social network configurations to better facilitate deep, fundamental organizational change as compared to change efforts dependent on hierarchical, formal implementation networks. Mohrman et al. (2003) is a widely cited article that provided a key contribution to our understanding of large-scale change by further revealing that informal networks of relationships among *individuals* are the conduits through which organizational information and resources are exchanged, work is accomplished, and decisions are made. And these informal networks are critical for conveying a message of change, as well as enacting it throughout an organization.

Throughout the first decade of the twenty-first century, Tenkasi continued his research on large-scale change as a Fulbright senior research scholar studying the computer software industry in India from its founding in 1966 to 2003. His quantitative application of negative binomial regression to data from over 1,000 of the software firms provides clear significance for growth factors which are broadly categorized as institutional or entrepreneurial. Institutional factors incorporate governmental policy liberalization, technical institution infrastructure, ecological effects, software technology parks, and venture capital effects – the latter two having a negative effect, perhaps due to competitive density. Entrepreneurial factors include caste/community, business house, premier institutions, replication, and nonresident Indian effects.

The growth of the software industry within India cannot be modeled without the inclusion of the Indian caste system and its impacts regarding an entrepreneurial effect. The traditional Indian business community includes the Vaishyas, Syrian Christians and Sindhis' and Parsees' groups while excluding Brahmins, Kshatriyas, other Hindus, other Christians, and Muslims. Traditionally, firms were also most likely to be founded by people from business houses (families or organizations) such as the Tatas, Birlas, TVS, and government organizations. Tenkasi found that a key entrepreneurial determinant of software industry success was the large-scale entry of nontraditional business communities that included artisans who were lower in terms of significance in the traditional Indian caste system. This industry matched their values and interests while others did not, and while established industries had imperfect market conditions with structural advantages that favored stronger business houses and the traditional business-oriented castes such as the Vaishya's, the nascent software industry eliminated those advantages and enabled nontraditional business communities to thrive along with those founded by the traditional business houses and castes.

In addition to documenting the historical growth of the software industry in India, there are two key contributions of this research to organizational theory. At an institutional policy level, Tenkasi showed that government should facilitate evaluation and investment in areas where both human and physical capital are available and maintain that investment over time. Additionally, bureaucratic barriers should be minimized, practices to involve the masses over favoring elitism should be applied, and policymakers should assess, learn, and revise these policies over time. On an entrepreneurial level, he showed that policymakers should encourage people to challenge societal norms to promote the entrepreneurial spirit. This involves ensuring that people obtain the necessary skills and education, encouraging role models for people to follow (especially successful Indian entrepreneurs in the USA who returned to India), and enlisting the assistance of external community and ethnic resources to be key sources of knowledge spillover and entrepreneurial stimulation.

Expanding Longitudinal Methods. Tenkasi continually seeks to build new insights within the field, particularly through strengthening the rigor and richness of our evaluations of organizational change efforts. His efforts in this area led to new insights for Brock as the rigor in longitudinal studies was challenged by accessing methods of a field most familiar with longitudinal work – epidemiology (Brock and Tenkasi 2014). While some of his work has been theoretical in nature, Tenkasi confronted the applied complexities of generalized estimating equations (GEE) often used in epidemiological studies in response to troubling characteristics that plague much of longitudinal data, namely, non-Gaussian and noncontinuous data, repeated measurements issues, and within-variable autocorrelation (Ballinger 2004; Hardin and Hilbe 2003; Liang and Zeger 1986; Zeger and Liang 1986).

His further insights into the need for ensuring rigor when evaluating field work in organizational change led us to an additional cross-disciplinary methodology designed for confirmation of variable manipulation in medically based observational studies – propensity scoring. This methodology enables field researchers to *in effect* retrospectively achieve the impact of experimental randomization through examining the conditional probability that a subject *would have received* a particular treatment based on a vector of observed covariates (Rosenbaum and Rubin 1983). Propensity scoring extends the rigor of observational field studies by allowing rigorous confirmation of treatment effect, which is otherwise elusive yet quite necessary in longitudinal work.

As Tenkasi and Brock utilized these cross-disciplinary methodologies to rigorously evaluate fieldwork over a 3-year, longitudinal period, they discovered strong evidence that a synthesis of diagnostic and dialogic organizational change paradigms was not only possible but also likely more fruitful than either change paradigm acting independently (Brock and Tenkasi 2015). These findings are yielding new insights about the conduct of observational and longitudinal studies, yet even this finding on the efficacy of synthesizing diametric paradigms may be linked to his earlier theoretical contribution in combining paradigmatic and narrative cognition (Boland and Tenkasi 1995).

New Insights: Ontology, Epistemology, and Praxis of Organization Development and Change

The diverse, substantial, and multiple contributions of Tenkasi to organization development and change contain several overarching insights relevant to the discipline. These insights deepen our understanding of the discipline beyond the surface level content of the contributions to generate new possibilities for the discipline. The understandings and new possibilities stem from consideration of the ontology, epistemology, and praxis of organization development and change.

Ontological Insights. Complementing Tenkasi's scholarship are two insights into the nature of organizational reality. These are classified as ontological insights due to how they reframe foundational assumptions on organizational reality. The first insight concerns organizational knowledge and the fundamental assumptions about its nature. The second insight focuses on scholar-practitioners and the fundamental assumptions regarding the relationship between their thoughts and actions.

The work by Tenkasi on organizational knowledge is based on a rejection of the assumption that such knowledge exists independent of the knowers who created it. Rather than viewing knowledge workers as craftspeople who assemble new ideas based on the objective qualities of prior knowledge, they view knowledge work as innately subjective and filled with interpretation. The strong form of the insight into the ontology of knowledge is that knowledge does not exist outside of the knowers but rather rests within the processes of knowing that characterize human beings. It is more accurate, from this ontological perspective, to discuss organizational knowing rather than organizational knowledge. Organizational knowing puts the necessary people and meaning making back into the picture.

The work by Tenkasi on scholar-practitioners is based on a rejection of the Cartesian separation of thought and action that forms an untested assumption behind most of the research on scholars and leaders. He advances a premise that thought and action co-occur and that to deny their coexistence is to minimize the critical role that each plays together in successful scholarship and practice. Tenkasi brought the work of the Russian cognitive psychologist, Lev Vygotsky (1962), into the conversation to effectively frame how thought can mediate action. And in doing this, he provides historical context to the call to bridge knowledge and action by linking the early 1900s to the early 2000s. This lasting interest in scholar-practitioners is not just about actionable scientific knowledge; it searches for deeper understanding of how we as human beings can leverage our powers of cognition and agency to make a difference with our professions and lives. This insight is one of the contributions that has distinguished Tenkasi as a great thinker on Organization Change and Development.

Epistemic Insight. Clearly integrated into the work of Tenkasi are the insights that there are multiple forms of knowing and that expertise is not the sole domain of scholars or presidents and CEOs of organizations. There is an Aristotelian philosophy of knowledge that underpins Tenkasi's model of the scholar-practitioner as an epistemic technician (Tenkasi and Hay 2008). Scholar-practitioners have experiential knowledge, technical know-how, theoretical understanding, and wisdom to solve dilemmas. The significance of the epistemic insight is that it democratizes the formal and informal inquiries into organization development and change – the perspectives of all employees, stakeholders, clients and customers, and interested parties have value. This democratic assumption to knowing mitigates the damage that can result from privileged truth imposed on an organization by vested interests and the powerful. It is this epistemological insight that furthers the ability of an organization to be an agent of community wellness and social change.

Praxis Insight. The process model of theory-practice linkages highlights the high level of skill required of successful scholar-practitioners. Scholar-practitioners who generate actionable scientific knowledge use theory-practice linkages as organizational tools across a broad range of their capacities. Master scholar-practitioners are active agents in the linkage process – they construct the conditions and the forms of the theory-practice linkages. The master scholar-practitioner uses theory-practice linkages as framing devices to give direction to a broadly expressed change mandate from top leadership, as influencing and legitimizing devices to argue for a course of action, as sensemaking devices to bring into focus the ambiguity and confusion of organizational life, and as demonstrative devices to indicate the practical and theoretical value of the results. Most significantly, scholar-practitioners use these tools within academia as well as organizations. They are adept at moving strategically between these two worlds.

The significance of this insight for praxis rests in its implications for change agents. Change agents are not confined to operate just within the current tasks and conditions of the organization nor are they solely responsible for generating development out of nothing on their own. Rather the change agent is a skilled craftsman who constructs the conditions and forms of development out of the material within the organization. The change agent cultivates and nurtures the growth of the organization, not as a bystander but as an active catalyst for emergence.

Legacies and Unfinished Business: Advancing the Ontology, Epistemology, and Praxis of Scholar-Practitioners of Organizational Change

As an emerging thinker of organizational change, Tenkasi's legacy is growing and there is much unfinished business. Many of those profiled in this volume are still actively contributing to the knowledge community well into their eighties. Assuming Tenkasi will have similar longevity, there are 30 years of contributions yet to come. Consider this a mid-career review of his growing body of work.

The Legacy of Tenkasi's Scholarship. We identify four ways in which Tenkasi's scholarly agenda has created a legacy for other scholar-practitioners to follow. First is his legacy of theoretical contributions as noted in the previous sections. His doctoral dissertation on cognition and how it impacts team development and research and development grew into the work on organizational knowing and how organizational learning impacts organizational change (e.g., Tenkasi et al. 1998; Tenkasi and Mohrman, 1999). Second, his work on large-scale change, especially the research on the determinant factors of the growth of the Indian software industry, has been presented globally and has impacted policy and development of the software industry in other countries (e.g., India, China, Australia). A third legacy is Tenkasi's methodological ambidexterity and reflexivity. His work demonstrates how innovative research paradigms (e.g., process and epidemiological models of analysis) can be brought to bear on the field to tease out new insights.

Fourth, and finally, his work on and with scholar-practitioners may be his greatest legacy. His research over the years has brought us models of how scholar-practitioners create useful knowledge (Tenkasi 2011; Tenkasi and Hay 2004, 2008) and the strategies and tactics that they use to translate theory to practice (Tenkasi and Hay 2004; Sanders 2015). This work continues to evolve and will engender further scholarship on how boundary spanners work between knowledge communities as the worldwide economy grows increasingly based on organizational learning and knowing.

The Unfinished Business of Tenkasi's Scholarship. Two areas within Tenkasi's scholarly agenda rise to significance as generative of major research initiatives and define his unfinished business to date. First, and in addition to being his greatest legacy, scholar-practitioners form a primary area for further study. This ongoing research centers on the challenges of being boundary spanners, as the worlds of scholarship and practice are hard to bridge. As difficult as it is to succeed in one of them, it is even more difficult to succeed in both. The production of actionable scientific knowledge is a rare outcome; more executive doctorates of OD wind up contributing to practice or scholarship but not both. This finding merits continued investigation to identify the originating conditions and operating mechanisms for actionable scientific knowledge. Additionally, more research is needed to extend the existing research to other communities of practice. Who are the boundary spanners of these disciplines and how do they bridge knowledge and action?

The second avenue of unfinished business concerns the investigation of the ontology of organizations. This avenue of research seeks to challenge the taken-for-granted assumptions on the nature of organizations and their functioning. Tenkasi and Boland questioned the status quo on knowledge management with the use of Wittgenstein and Giddens to reframe the nature of organizational knowing. Critical realism (Bhaskar 1998) and morphogenetic theory (Archer 1995) played a key role in the development of the process model of theory-practice linkages because of their openness to the dialectical synthesis of thought and action that makes scholar-practitioners possible.

More of this ontological work needs to be done to further our understandings of organization development and change by testing our assumptions on the mechanisms and agents of such change. And there are a host of topics to investigate: the role of dialogue versus shared action in organizational change, how an individual change agent mobilizes a system toward change, the interleaving of replication and emergence as change unfolds, and, lastly, what is the nature of change that is permanent.

It is to these ontological, epistemic, and praxis challenges that we look to continue the legacy of Ramkrishnan (Ram) V. Tenkasi.

References

Adler, N., Shani, A. B., & Styhre, A. (2004). *Collaborative research in organizations: Foundations for learning, change, and theoretical development*. Thousand Oaks: Sage Publications.

Archer, M. (1995). *Realist social theory: The morphogenetic approach*. New York: Cambridge University Press.

Astley, W. G., & Zammuto, R. F. (1992). Organization science, managers, and language games. *Organization Science, 3*(4), 443–460. doi:10.1287/orsc.3.4.443.

Austin, J. R., & Bartunek, J. M.. (2003). Theories and practices of organizational development. *Handbook of psychology*.

Ballinger, G. A. (2004). Using generalized estimating equations for longitudinal data analysis. *Organizational Research Methods, 7*(2), 127–150. doi:10.1177/1094428104263672.

Bhaskar, R. (1998). Philosophy and scientific realism. In M. Archer, R. Bhaskar, A. Collier, T. Lawson, & A. Norrie (Eds.), *Critical realism: Essential readings* (pp. 16–48). New York: Routledge.

Boland Jr., R. J., & Tenkasi, R. V. (1995). Perspective making and perspective taking in communities of knowing. *Organization Science, 6*(4), 350–372.

Brock, B., & Tenkasi, R. V. (2014, August). *Unlocking the temporal power of words: GEE in qualitative-quantitative, longitudinal change research*. Professional Development Workshop presented at the Academy of Management Annual Meeting, Philadelphia.

Brock, B., & Tenkasi, R. V. (2015, August). *A comparative study of organizational change: Dialogical, diagnostic, and diagnostic-dialogical*. Paper presented at the Academy of Management Annual Meeting, Vancouver, British Columbia, Canada.

Cummings, T. G., Molloy, E. S., & Glen, R. (1977). A methodological critique of fifty-eight selected work experiments. *Human Relations, 30*(8), 675–708.

Giddens, A. (1979). *Central problems in social theory: Action, structure, and contradiction in social analysis* (Vol. 241). Berkeley: University of California Press.

Hall, R. H. (1987). *Organizations: Structures, processes and outcomes*. Englewood Cliffs: Prentice-Hall.

Hardin, J. W., & Hilbe, J. M. (2003). *Generalized estimating equations*. Boca Raton: Chapman & Hall/CRC.

Huff, A., & Huff, J. (2001). Refocusing the business school agenda. *British Journal of Management, 12*, S49–S54.

Lawler, E. E., Mohrman, S. A., Ledford, G. E., & Lake, D. G. (1996). Creating high performance organizations. *Human Resource Management-New York, 35*(2), 251–254.

Lewin, K. (1947). Frontiers in group dynamics concept, method and reality in social science: Equilibria and social change. *Human Relations, 1*, 3–41.

Liang, K.-Y., & Zeger, S. L. (1986). Longitudinal data analysis using generalized linear models. *Biometrika, 73*(1), 13–22.

Mohr, L. B. (1982). *Explaining organizational behavior* (Vol. 1). San Francisco: Jossey-Bass.

Mohrman, S. A., Tenkasi, R. V., Mohrman, J., & Allan, M. (2003). The role of networks in fundamental organizational change: A grounded analysis. *The Journal of Applied Behavioral Science, 39*(3), 301.

Rosenbaum, P. R., & Rubin, D. B. (1983). The central role of the propensity score in observational studies for causal effects. *Biometrika, 70*(1), 41–55.

Rynes, S. L., Bartunek, J. M., & Daft, R. L. (2001). Across the great divide: Knowledge creation and transfer between practitioners and academics. *Academy of Management Journal, 44*(2), 340–355.

Sanders, E. J. (2015). *A comparative analysis of the roles, strategies and tactics used by scholar-practitioners in organization development and medical translational research to simultaneously create research knowledge and help clients achieve results*. Dissertation. Lisle: Benedictine University.

Tenkasi, R. V. (1993). Knowing and organizational being. *Mastery of mind: Perspective on time, space and knowledge, 111*, 180.

Tenkasi, R. V. (2000). The dynamics of cognitive oversimplification processes in R&D environments: An empirical assessment of some consequences. *International Journal of Technology Management, 20*(5–8), 782–798.

Tenkasi, R. V. (2011). Integrating theory to inform practice: Insights from the practitioner-scholar. In S. A. Mohrman, E. E. Lawler III, & a. Associates (Eds.), *Useful research: Advancing theory and practice* (p. 456). San Francisco: Berrett-Koehler.

Tenkasi, R. V., & Chesmore, M. C. (2003). Social networks and planned organizational change: The impact of strong network ties on effective change implementation and use. *The Journal of Applied Behavioral Science, 39*(3), 281.

Tenkasi, R. V., & Hay, G. W. (2004). Actionable knowledge and scholar-practitioners: A process model of theory-practice linkages. *Systemic Practice and Action Research, 17*(3), 177–206.

Tenkasi, R. V., & Hay, G. W. (2008). Following the second legacy of Aristotle: The scholar-practitioner as an epistemic technician. In A. B. Shani, S. A. Mohrman, W. A. Pasmore, B. Stymne, & N. Adler (Eds.), *Handbook of collaborative management research* (pp. 49–72). Los Angeles: SAGE.

Tenkasi, R. V., & Hay, G. W. (2013). Understanding the essential principles for integrating theory and research knowledge to the realm of practice: Lessons from the scholar practitioner. In G. D. Sardana & T. Thatchenkery (Eds.), *Reframing human capital for organizational excellence* (pp. 224–241). New York: Bloomsbury Publishing.

Tenkasi, R. V., & Mohrman, S. A. (1999). Global change as contextual collaborative knowledge creation. *Organizational dimensions of global change: No limits to cooperation, 114*, 138.

Tenkasi, R. V., Mohrman, S. A., & Mohrman Jr, A. M. (1998). Accelerated learning during organizational transition. *Tomorrow's organization: Crafting winning capabilities in a dynamic world*, 330–361.

Van de Ven, A. H., & Poole, M. S. (2005). Alternative approaches for studying organizational change. *Organization Studies, 26*(9), 1377–1404.

Vygotsky, L. S. (1962). *Thought and language*. Cambridge, MA: MIT Press.

Wasserman, I. C., & Kram, K. E. (2009). Enacting the scholar practitioner: An exploration of narratives. *The Journal of Applied Behavioral Science, 45*(5), 12–38.

Wittgenstein, L. (1953). *Philosophical investigations*. New York: MacMillan.

Yuchtman, E., & Seashore, S. E. (1967). A system resource approach to organizational effectiveness. *American Sociological Review*, 891–903.

Zeger, S. L., & Liang, K.-Y. (1986). Longitudinal data analysis for discrete and continuous outcomes. *Biometrics, 42*(12), 121–130.

Further Reading

The following publications will help the reader to explore in more depth the overarching themes from Tenkasi's work.

Understanding the essential principles for integrating theory and research knowledge to the realm of practice: lessons from the scholar practitioner (Tenkasi & Hay 2013).

Integrating theory to inform practice: Insights from the practitioner-scholar (Tenkasi 2011).

Following the second legacy of Aristotle: The scholar-practitioner as an epistemic technician. (Tenkasi & Hay 2008).

Actionable knowledge and scholar-practitioners: A process model of theory-practice linkages. (Tenkasi & Hay 2004).

Social networks and planned organizational change: The impact of strong network ties on effective change implementation and use (Tenkasi & Chesmore 2003).

The role of networks in fundamental organizational change: A grounded analysis (Mohrman et al. 2003).

The dynamics of cognitive oversimplification processes in R&D environments: An empirical assessment of some consequences (Tenkasi 2000).

Perspective making and perspective taking in communities of knowing (Boland Jr & Tenkasi 1995).

Knowing and organizational being. (Tenkasi 1993).

Tojo Thatchenkery: Concept Champion, Engaged Educator, and Passionate Practitioner 77

Param Srikantia

Abstract

The chapter reviews the scholarly and practical contributions of Tojo Thatchenkery as a concept champion, engaged educator, and passionate practitioner to the discipline of organizational change management. After briefly reviewing some of the dominant influences that have shaped Thatchenkery's work, the chapter focuses on his contribution (a) as a scholar-practitioner elucidating the construct of Appreciative Intelligence®, (b) as a thought leader and a champion of the social constructionist and hermeneutic perspective on organizations, (c) as a scholar-practitioner generating original, bold, and creative extensions of the appreciative inquiry approach to knowledge management, sustainable value, and economic development, (d) as a champion of multiculturalism and diversity, (e) as an exceptionally creative pedagogic innovator who has fused action learning, sensitivity training, and experiential learning into a graduate program that equips a new generation of organizational development professionals, and finally (f) as an effective and creative consultant with an extensive array of high-powered clients who have benefitted from innovative organizational interventions interweaving elements such as Appreciative Intelligence®, social constructionism, sustainable value, and invisible leadership. The chapter concludes with an exploration of Thatchenkery's key insights and legacy to the field of organizational change.

Keywords

Organizational development • Change management • Appreciative inquiry • Appreciative intelligence • Social constructionism • Learning organizations • Invisible leadership • Hermeneutics • Management consulting • Entrepreneurship • Sustainable value • Knowledge management • Multiculturalism and diversity

P. Srikantia (✉)
School of Business, Baldwin Wallace University, Berea, OH, USA
e-mail: psrikant@bw.edu

D.B. Szabla et al. (eds.), *The Palgrave Handbook of Organizational Change Thinkers*,
DOI 10.1007/978-3-319-52878-6_95

Contents

Introduction

Dr. Tojo Thatchenkery is a transnational scholar and practitioner and a prolific contributor to multiple domains of organizational development and change theory, research, and practice. He is best known for elucidating the construct of Appreciative Intelligence® and is widely recognized as a thought leader and a champion of the social constructionist perspective on organizations. He is particularly celebrated for his conceptual development of a hermeneutic approach to organizations and for undertaking original, bold, and creative extensions of the appreciative inquiry approach to multiple frontiers such as knowledge management, sustainable value, and economic development. Drawing upon his transnational experiences, he has also been a champion for recognizing and valuing diversity, reminding organizational decision makers to be sensitively attuned to the unique leadership patterns of a range of cultural groups through his work on invisible leadership of Asian Americans. He has demonstrated exceptional ingenuity in organizational consulting, with an extensive array of high-powered clients who have benefitted from innovative organizational interventions interweaving elements such as Appreciative Intelligence®, social constructionism, sustainable value, and invisible leadership.

Influences and Motivations: Local Pathways to a Global World

Tojo Thatchenkery's organizational worldview was decisively shaped by at least three distinct forces: His upbringing in India which connected him to an ocean of wisdom free of Western overreliance on technical analytical rationality; the intellectual climate in the doctoral program in Organizational Behavior at Case Western Reserve University; and a handful of mentors from across the world.

Thatchenkery's upbringing in India has been a significant force in his scholarship, teaching, and consulting, in both explicit and implicit ways. Tojo was born in Kerala,

India, in 1959 to a family strongly rooted in the values of education. His mother, a longtime high school teacher and later the head of various educational institutions in Kerala instilled the values of liberal education for her five children. The state of Kerala has the distinction of having elected the first communist government anywhere in the world (instead of by revolution). Kerala stands out as one of the best examples of social engineering for creating income equality among people and this focus on social justice influenced Tojo for rest of his life.

Thatchenkery's work on Asian immigrants and their enacted styles of invisible leadership and his formulation of the notion of Hindu social capital are direct expressions of the cross-cultural influence on his scholarly output. Furthermore, since the entire notion of bureaucracy is a colonial import to the Indian context under British rule, Thatchenkery also benefited from a healthy skepticism towards the dominant Western organizational model, namely, ubiquitous yet stultifying bureaucratic structures and culture. This skepticism supported his creative exploration of alternatives to dominant organizational theories, models and practices.

From Kerala, Tojo decided to move to the capital city of New Delhi for his undergraduate and Master's studies in Psychology. While being a student at the University of Delhi, he was active as a member of the academic council of the University, representing the whole student body. He was instrumental in fighting for and creating several student-centered initiatives at the conservative University of Delhi. He earned his BA in Psychology in 1980 and MA in the same subject in 1982. Soon after that, he was appointed as a research associate at the University of Delhi Business School and during this time he became active at the Indian Society for Applied Behavioral Sciences, an organization devoted to fostering social justice in India through education and training.

Thatchenkery's talent for research began emerging even as an undergraduate student studying psychology in India. Responding to the clash of epistemologies that was such a hallmark of postcolonial Indian society, as a young teenager Thatchenkery conducted a carefully designed study to explore the scientific validity of astrological predictions. By the time he was a graduate student, he had published research papers in India in the applied behavioral sciences and had already begun a successful career at New Delhi University in the social sciences. The organizational studies community in the United States was very fortunate to be able to import a young scholar who had shown so much early promise in India and who already had the breadth of perspective and experience to conduct meaningful scholarship and practice, formulate bold questions, explore courageous approaches, and bring an original and creative mind, without succumbing to the limiting forces of the dominant logical positivist zeitgeist prevailing in the US context.

Thatchenkery was subsequently also influenced by the Case Western Reserve University's Organizational Behavior department, which was the first ever in the world to award a Ph.D. in Organizational Behavior and has been known for its commitment to methodological pluralism and for encouraging nonpositivistic research in the discipline. Historically, it is equally well known for its commitment to developing scholarly practitioners and practical scholars who explore the interplay among theory, research, and practice, in contrast to many other doctoral programs in the discipline that tend to intellectualize organization behavior while devaluing attention to practical, everyday conundrums of organizational life.

In his scholarship, teaching, professional services, and consulting, Tojo Thatchenkery embodies and extends the highest aspirations for scholarship and practical effectiveness that inspired the founding members of the Case Western Reserve University's Organizational Behavior department. Whereas most organizational behavioral departments in the United States are restrictively positivistic in their orientation, encouraging incremental and largely verification-oriented research, the Case Western Reserve University's Organizational Behavior program actively challenged doctoral students to pursue bold, discovery-oriented research and to experiment with a broad range of paradigms and qualitative research techniques. Based on Gibson Burrell and Gareth Morgan's *Sociological Paradigm's of Organizational Analysis*, one can clearly discern Thatchenkery's commitment to the paradigmatic quadrant of radical humanism, embodied in two distinct streams of scholarship. First, Thatchenkery has made important scholarly contributions to social constructionism, a paradigm of research and thought that has been significantly underrepresented in business schools, despite its centrality in many social science and humanities disciplines. Like other social constructionists, Thatchenkery posits that organizations cannot be understood merely as objective entities discoverable by a positivistic science, but irreducibly as socially constructed entities whose meaning and dynamics are generated through social processes involving individual and group mental models, practices, values, norms, enactments, and relationships. This ontological frame invites a range of approaches to understanding and intervening in organizations, including attending to the phenomenology of organizational members.

Secondly, Thatchenkery is implicitly aligned with another tenet of radical humanism in rejecting the current status quo and zeitgeist of the organizational world. He embraces not maintenance of existing organizational forms but a deep commitment to exploring organizational systems and processes that are significantly more responsive to human aspirations and that are better suited to unleashing the full potential of human beings. Thatchenkery's scholarship combines the optimism of social constructionist perspectives in viewing organizations not as rigid entities resembling machines but as cooperatively constructed realities amenable to continuous reinterpretation and transformation with the reformist zeal captured in a commitment to change and novelty rather than to continuity and maintenance. Radical humanist perspectives are conspicuously absent in most business school education perhaps because of the conservative nature of corporations and the vested interests that silently shape mainstream business discourse. It is against this intellectual context of a profound scarcity of creative theorizing in the radical humanist tradition that Thatchenkery's significant contribution to organizational studies can be better understood and appreciated.

Thatchenkery was also influenced by a constellation of mentors consisting of creative organizational behavior thinkers who, in combination with his substantial native talents and intellect, helped to springboard his conceptual imagination. Abab Ahmad, an eminent management scholar at the Faculty of Management Studies, University of Delhi, was a seminal influence on Thatchenkery and mentored him during Thatchenkery's time as a research associate and later as lecturer. Deepankar Roy, a prominent organization development consultant, introduced Thatchenkery to T-groups and facilitation techniques, an initiation that has been a vital part of Thatchenkery's creative learning, practice, teaching, and scholarship ever since.

Chief among Thatchenkery's mentors at the Case Western Reserve University was Dr. Suresh Srivastva, who encouraged his students to be fiercely and unapologetically original and courageous in their formulation of research questions, the selection of research methodology and in transcending disciplinary boundaries, nudging them to read classical philosophers, world literature and multiple social sciences so as not to be limited by the intellectual horizons of business theorizing. Together, Dr. Suresh Srivastva and Dr. David Cooperrider developed what became known as appreciative inquiry, and Dr. Cooperrider's consistent focus on positive organizational imagery was another source of influence. Dr. William Pasmore, through his contributions both to knowledge work and to a sociotechnical perspective on organizational change, helped to inspire Thatchenkery to explore the continuous potential for organizational learning and the reiterative realignment of technology and social processes especially in the context of knowledge management. Dr. David Kolb, an eminent theorist and researcher on adult learning, exposed Thatchenkery to a very broad range of readings and intellectual orientations that expanded his culturally ingrained potential for non-linear learning. Dr. Richard Boyatzis was Thatchenkery's first year advisor and helped reinforce Thatchenkery's focus on applied scholarship. Kenneth Gergen, the doyen of social constructionist perspectives on organizations, was Thatchenkery's intellectual collaborator who provided encouragement to build conceptual bridges between social constructionism, hermeneutics, and appreciative inquiry.

Key Contributions: Appreciative Intelligence and Dynamic Workplaces

Thatchenkery has been a prolific contributor to multiple domains of theory, research, and practice. This section summarizes his key contributions in the following areas: (a) as a scholar-practitioner elucidating the construct of Appreciative Intelligence®, (b) as a thought leader and a champion of the social constructionist perspective on organizations, most particularly with the conceptual development of a hermeneutic approach to organizations, (c) as a scholar-practitioner generating original, bold, and creative extensions of the appreciative inquiry approach to multiple frontiers such as knowledge management, sustainable value, and economic development, (d) as a champion for recognizing and valuing diversity, reminding organizational decision makers to be sensitively attuned to the unique leadership patterns of a range of cultural groups through his work on invisible leadership of Asian Americans, (e) as an exceptionally creative pedagogic innovator who has fused action learning, sensitivity training, and experiential learning into a graduate program that equips a new generation of organizational development professionals to take on the organizational challenges posed by increasingly complex, unstable, conflicted, and chaotic environments, (f) as an effective and creative consultant with an extensive array of high-powered clients who have benefitted from innovative organizational interventions interweaving elements such as Appreciative Intelligence®, social constructionism, sustainable value, and invisible leadership.

Elucidation of the Construct of Appreciative Intelligence®

Thatchenkery's development of the construct of Appreciative Intelligence® (Thatchenkery and Metzker 2006) bears eloquent testimony to his own Appreciative Intelligence® and his capacity for creative conceptual innovation by sensing an intellectual opportunity, extrapolating themes from one intellectual domain to another and developing ideas that embody his deep commitment to making a practical and positive difference in the mindset of contemporary managers and the surrounding organizational milieu. Thatchenkery invokes a powerful and naturalistically grounded metaphor of "seeing the mighty oak in the acorn" to describe this form of intelligence that enables some people "to perceive the positive potential in a given situation and to act purposively to transform the potential to outcomes" (Thatchenkery and Metzker 2006).

Appreciative Intelligence is defined by Thatchenkery as "The ability to reframe a given situation to recognize the positive possibilities embedded in it that were not initially apparent. . .to perceive the positive potential in a given situation and to act purposively to transform the potential to outcomes." Thatchenkery's conceptualization involves three components, namely reframing, appreciating the positive, and seeing how the future unfolds from the present. Thatchenkery's work provides numerous examples of Appreciative Intelligence, some even involving reframing a situation for a new possibility even in the face of extreme deprivation. For example, Muhammad Yunus, distinguished economist and founder of the Grameen Bank who was awarded the Nobel Peace Prize saw entrepreneurial creativity and spark even among homeless, disenfranchised people too poor to own the shirt on their back. They would not have the financial capacity to qualify for traditional bank loans. But rather than seeing them through the denigrating lens that the middle class and the elite see them, he decided to boldly advance them sums of money to establish entrepreneurial projects and to pay back the loans. While customary belief would lead us to expect that such loans not backed by collateral would not be returned, Yunus stumbled upon the surprising discovery that the abysmally poor, when advanced small sums of money, actually paid back their loan obligations at a more impressive rate than their middle class and upper class counterparts. This revolutionary finding enabled him to establish the Grameen Bank and through its success, the global microcredit movement which has proved to be a popular, though now controversial tool in the armamentarium of poverty alleviation measures.

Conceptualized in this manner, Appreciative Intelligence® can be understood as a very important new form of intelligence to be added to the range of intelligences identified by Gardner (1983) as part of his theory of multiple intelligences. At the same time, Appreciative Intelligence® goes beyond Gardner's formulations because

Gardner's eight types of intelligence (namely: linguistic, bodily-kinesthetic, spatial, musical, logical-mathematical, intrapersonal, interpersonal, and naturalist) still appear as static, discrete, trait like dimensions that operate independently of each other. Thatchenkery's construct of Appreciative Intelligence® is more a dynamic way of being than a static trait and one that is not confined to a particular dimensions but cuts across categories and domains of existence to enable the individual to powerfully inhabit a certain ontological space (Thatchenkery 2015).

In theorizing this special ontological space, Thatchenkery drew on his cultural upbringing and early socialization in India, which helped him to distinguish and resonate with a particular constellation of possibilities. Thatchenkery believes that, growing up in the extremely resilient culture of India, one continually experiences the dynamic vitality of the human spirit that never seems to be depleted in its celebration of life even in the face of the greatest hardships of everyday living. Recognition of these possibilities and realities of "being" fostered an intellectual consciousness in Thatchenkery that enabled him to exercise the very faculty that the construct of Appreciative Intelligence® illuminates. In addition, the theory behind Appreciative Intelligence® also draws on social constructionist philosophy highlighting the role of language and mental models in shaping one's perceptions of reality.

The exploration of Appreciative Intelligence® in the context of entrepreneurship, innovation, social capital, knowledge management, economic development, and leadership has been a recurring theme in Thatchenkery's work beginning with Thatchenkery and Metzker (2006) and continuing through countless research papers and books (listed in the bibliography that follows this chapter). The construct has attracted the attention of practicing managers at the highest levels of strategy formulation, and Thatchenkery has unveiled this concept in multiday seminars conducted in all the major cities of the United States, Europe, Asia, and South America. Thatchenkery's work has impacted tens of thousands of people at all levels of organizations. His ability to translate the theory and practice of Appreciative Intelligence® and to present it in an engaging manner that inspires practicing managers to apply it readily in their organizational contexts makes him a scholarly entertainer of world class repute and explains the overwhelming contagion of enthusiasm for his seminars and texts. His book *Appreciative Intelligence®: Seeing the Mighty Oak in the Acorn* enjoys the distinction of endorsement by the Harvard Business Review that placed the book on their recommended reading list in 2006. It is an important contribution to the sets of approaches committed to supporting the unfolding of human potential in its multiform manifestations because it joins a chorus of voices that are helping to retire the anachronistic conceptions of intelligence as a unitary phenomenon. Taken to its logical conclusion, it has the power to help create a world in which every child can come to be appreciated for their uniqueness and special talents in a noncompetitive celebration of multiple capabilities that nature has generously sprinkled and distributed.

Given the impact of the book and the construct of Appreciative Intelligence®, it would be appropriate to indicate a little about its history and the influences that inspired Thatchenkery to develop it fully. It was through his inductive research into the phenomenal success of entrepreneurs in the Silicon Valley region and the transformation of that region into a powerhouse of entrepreneurial innovation that he began to discern a pattern that led to his adumbration of the concept of Appreciative Intelligence®. He was fascinated by the manner in which venture capitalists, immigrant entrepreneurs, and educated professionals gathered in this region, making possible a magnitude of innovation that amounted to nothing short of "history making," culminating in such wonders of the entrepreneurial world as the Internet, social media, and the marvel of a networked world. Thatchenkery coined the term "Appreciative Intelligence®" to account for this explosion of entrepreneurial innovation, demonstrating the centrality of this schema of apperception and its embodiment as an identifiable form of intelligence among these outstanding entrepreneurs that made the degree of innovation, risk taking, and creativity possible (Thatchenkery and Metzker 2006). He was building on his 1990s research on the dynamism of Indian entrepreneurs in that region to suggest that multiple ethnic groups felt supported in the Silicon valley community that successfully led to opportunity recognition, persistence, resilience, and anticipation of positive outcomes, the essential ingredients of Appreciative Intelligence®. The development of Appreciative Intelligence® reflects Thatchenkery's creative capacity to synthesize and transform diverse streams of thought and experience into a powerful new theory and practice, as he brings together research into entrepreneurial successes of the Silicon Valley subculture, appreciative inquiry, social constructionism, and the theory of multiple intelligences to create both a construct and an accompanying set of organizational interventions to help unleash and transform organizations and individuals into generative entities capable of achieving dramatic breakthroughs in innovation and entrepreneurial resilience.

Thatchenkery's book on Appreciative Intelligence® has been exceptionally well received and translated into five languages. In addition to it being selected by *Harvard Business Review* for inclusion in their 2006 recommended book list, a number of other reputed, cutting-edge practitioner outlets have featured a discussion of the book, including Canada's *Globe and Mail*, the ASTD publication *Training + Development*, and other management magazines such as *Ode* (Europe and United States), *Management Next* (India), *Organisations and People* (United Kingdom), and *Transformation* (a publication of the World Business Academy).

Thatchenkery makes it abundantly clear that even though the construct of Appreciative Intelligence® may appear like an individual competency, it has a profound impact on groups, organizations and at the broader societal level, and he explores how it can be applied in all of these contexts. For corporations, its application can result in enhanced performance through new products, improved work arrangements, and an explosion of creativity and innovation. For the governmental organizations, Appreciative Intelligence® would pave the way for new forms of governance, perhaps less based on power-over and more based on power-with and a celebration of the positive potential of recognizing that we are all deeply interconnected, leading to a more enlightened way of being in relationship with each other.

Thought Leadership of the Social Constructionist Perspective on Organizations

True recognition of the significance of Thatchenkery's contributions requires an understanding of the intellectual context of the discipline at the time Thatchenkery aligned himself with the social constructionist viewpoint and challenged the ascendency of logical positivist approaches to organizational behavior (Gergen and Thatchenkery 2014). The most eloquent testimony to the powerful impact and enduring relevance of his contribution is evident from the impact made by three of his seminal pieces that converge to form a very solid body of conceptual work on the social constructionist viewpoint on organizations (Thatchenkery 1992; Gephart et al. 1996; Gergen and Thatchenkery 2004). We will now explore the essential features of this aforementioned trinity. Thatchenkery's *Organizations as texts: Hermeneutics as a model for understanding organizational change* has come to be cited more than 400 times in various publications that explore the role of language in organizational studies including an intellectual endorsement of its centrality by *The Annual Review of Psychology* (1999) which indicated the significance of his work for the field of organization change and development. In *That's Moving: Theories that Matter*, Karl Weick (1999), past editor of the *Administrative Sciences Quarterly* states, "Thatchenkery's use of hermeneutics to understand what happens when people fold appreciative inquiry into their ready-to-hand action" exemplified precisely the kind of scholarship that represent theories that truly matter.

Another element that made up this intellectual trinity of powerful papers that shaped and supported the social constructionist perspectives in organizational theory is a paper titled *Organization Science as Social Construction* that Thatchenkery coauthored with Kenneth Gergen, one of the leading exponents of social constructionism (Gergen and Thatchenkery 2004). This paper was truly foundational and built conceptual linkages between hermeneutics and social constructionist philosophy within the realm of organizational studies. Ever since its appearance, Thatchenkery's *Organization Science as Social Construction* has been consistently ranked among the most frequently cited papers especially by scholars who are dedicated to exploring the role of language, assumptions, and self-referentiality in organizations. It also enjoyed the distinctive honor of winning the prestigious *McGregor Award*, awarded jointly by the *Journal of Applied Behavioral Science* and Sage Publications for the best articles published in *JABS* from 1990–1999. Regarding the third element of the trinity, it was in 1996 that Thatchenkery coedited with David Boje and Robert Gephart another definitive work, also widely cited, *Postmodern Management and Organization Theory*, which helped inject a broad variety of postmodern perspectives into organization theory (Gephart et al. 1996).

Collectively speaking, this trinity described above gave a tremendous scholarly impetus to the proliferation of social constructionism in research in organizational studies and management. Although postmodernism had begun to percolate into the social sciences as early as the 1980s, its dynamic application within the field of organizational studies and management theorizing and research is clearly one of

Thatchenkery's flagship scholarly accomplishments. This has helped unleash an intellectual revolution in the world of organizational theorizing, helping to humanize both the organizations themselves and the intellectual reservoir from which they draw their inspiration for change and transformation. The introduction of postmodern perspectives into the Academy of Management (AOM), the very bastion of highly valued scholarly research on management, was also accomplished at the initiative of Thatchenkery. A showcased paper symposium that Thatchenkery arranged in 1992 entitled *Postmodernist readings of managerial abilities, learning organizations and information systems* became the very first time that a symposium championing the postmodern perspective was featured on the AOM program.

Extensions of Appreciative Inquiry to Knowledge Management, Sustainable Value, and Economic Development

Thatchenkery has been extensively involved with the refinements and subsequent developments in the appreciative inquiry approach in terms of theory, research, and practice (Thatchenkery et al. 2010; Thatchenkery and Chowdhry 2007; Thatchenkery and Stough 2005; Thatchenkery 2005). His numerous books, some authored and others edited by him, have significantly expanded the frontiers of appreciative inquiry and applied the method to new settings and contexts, significantly enriching the understanding of the potential appreciative inquiry brought to varied areas of business, nonprofit, and research environments.

Consistent with his interest in enhancing the creativity of knowledge work environments, Thatchenkery adapted the general principles of appreciative inquiry to knowledge work environments, resulting in the articulation of an approach he pioneered called the Appreciative Sharing of Knowledge (ASK) (Thatchenkery 2005). Equally significant and to be discussed more extensively later in this chapter is the creative use that Thatchenkery has made of appreciative inquiry and sensitivity training in educating students in the art and science of designing knowledge work environments of great intellectual vitality. In combining these approaches, Thatchenkery gives concrete expression to the fact that the cognitive effectiveness and conceptual vitality of groups is powerfully shaped by the emotional and social architecture underlying their functioning.

Another noteworthy extension of appreciative inquiry created by Thatchenkery is in the area of sustainable value. A landmark contribution in this domain has been his coedited book *Positive Design and Appreciative Construction: From Sustainable Development to Sustainable Value*, bringing together contributions from various scholars and practitioners of appreciative inquiry in developing a new design-based approach to creating sustainable value, replacing the older notions of sustainable development (Thatchenkery et al. 2010).

Thatchenkery has been the very epitome of scholarly productivity in the prolific manner in which he has gone about the business of building bridges between the concepts of Appreciative Intelligence® and appreciative inquiry on the one hand and the vast array of domains to which he has applied the appreciative processes.

Bridging together appreciative inquiry, knowledge management, sustainable development, social capital, organizational development, postmodernism, and information technology and economic development, he has been able to create a collage of new possibilities hitherto unexplored in organization studies. Not only has he independently authored and coauthored myriad books, but also, through books edited by him, he has also created spaces to which he has attracted scholars and practitioners engaged in these frontiers of research to pool together their insights and key learning and advance entire fields of application. A list of these scholarly books will give the reader a glimpse into the variety and vastness of his conceptual endeavors: They include *Managing Complex Organizational Change* (2016), *Optimizing Business Growth: Strategies for Scaling Up* (2016), *Leveraging Human Factors for Strategic Change: An Organizational Culture Perspective* (2015), *Understanding Work Experiences from Multiple Perspectives* (2015), *Organizational Transformation: Change Management Perspectives* (2014), *Strategic Initiatives for Competitive Advantage in the Knowledge Society* (2014), *Reframing Human Capital for Organizational Excellence* (2013), *Positive Initiatives for Organizational Change* (2012), *Positive Design and Appreciative Construction: From Sustainable Development to Sustainable Value. Leveraging Global Competiveness for Organizational Excellence* (2010), *Enhancing Organizational Performance Through Strategic Initiatives* (2009), *Handbook on Management Cases* (2008), *Appreciative Inquiry and Knowledge Management* (2007), *Information Communication Technology and Economic Development: Learning from the Indian Experience* (2006), and *Appreciative Sharing of Knowledge: Leveraging Knowledge Management for Strategic Change* (2005).

Multiculturalism and Invisible Leadership

Thatchenkery's contributions as a transnational scholar who is in a vantage position to address issues related to cultural diversity and to educate scholars and practitioners globally about the possibilities and challenges associated with international diversity in a global world found further expression in his book (coauthored with Keimei Sugiyama) *Making the Invisible Visible: Understanding the Leadership Contributions of Asian Minorities in the Workplace* (2011). The book examines the significant impact made by Asian minorities in the United States and elsewhere but in doing so elucidates a construct of "quiet leadership," referred to also as "invisible leadership," a self-effacing style of leading people unobtrusively, often from behind the scenes, that may pass unnoticed in organizational cultures more attuned to detecting and recognizing self-promotional styles of leadership widely practiced by white males and embedded as the dominant zeitgeist of Western or Western-styled organizations.

While Western notions of leadership imply a high degree of visibility, personal charisma, and the creative use of power, one of the distinctive hallmarks of the Eastern traditions is a conception of leadership as entailing ego-transcendence. In the Eastern traditions, a leader is someone who makes a contribution to the well-being of the collective but does so in a very self-effacing manner because he or she has transcended their ego and is able to subordinate their quest for visibility to the collective needs of the group they belong to. The prolific Indian mystic, Osho, whose discourses have been captured in several thousand books covering all the wisdom traditions of the world, explains that in the West, the leader is trying to be the metaphorical wave while in the East, the leader is one who has come to understand the ephemeral nature of the wave and therefore disappears as the wave only to be resurrected as the ocean itself, embodying its immense power and vastness. Thatchenkery's work on invisible leadership explores the leadership style of many Asian Americans whose values and outlook are rooted in collectivism rather than in individualism and who prefer to lead quietly and unobtrusively. It is the style of leadership captured by Nelson Mandela in his autobiography, *Long Walk to Freedom* when he states: "A leader is like a shepherd. He stays behind the flock, letting the most nimble go out ahead, whereupon, the others follow, not realizing that all along they are being directed from behind." Similar sentiments are echoed in the Taoistic tradition by its founder Lao Tzu who says of the best leaders, that when their work is done, the people say "we did it ourselves."

It is appropriate to indicate that Thatchenkery's interest in the notion of invisible leadership appears to have its roots in his own cultural experiences. He recalls vividly a speech delivered by a former President of India, Abdul Kalam. In this famous speech, Kalam recounted a time when he was the mission director of India's first satellite launch that unfortunately failed. Kalam described how the Chairman of the Indian Space Research Organization at that time, Mr. Satish Dhawan took full responsibility publicly for the failure. A few years later when the launch was completed successfully, Dhawan stepped out of the way and attributed the credit for the success of the launch to Kalam who directed the mission and had Kalam announce the success to the media. Thatchenkery was very moved by this example and quotes the words of Kalam who characterizes the ideal leader as one who "takes the full brunt of failure, but shies away from the sunshine of success, handing over the glory to teammates and believing that success belongs to the whole and not to one individual, therefore, the whole should benefit and the success is mutually owned." It is hardly surprising that Thatchenkery became intrigued by the styles of leadership among the Asian minority in the United States who import similar ideals of making quiet contribution, choosing to stay behind the scenes and be somewhat anonymous they have imbibed from the collectivism of their culture of origin.

In this book (Thatchenkery and Sugiyama 2011), Thatchenkery brings together research, theory, and anecdotal data that highlights one of the major challenges of managing organizations in which many subcultures with their own distinctive personal, managerial, and leadership styles coexist. His book is a wake-up call for all those managers and leaders who are genuinely concerned about tapping into the creative talent, particular capabilities and authentic styles of minorities and the multiple ways in which their contributions may come to be eclipsed by a more dominant, vocal majority more at ease with more visible and strident ways of declaring their contribution. Thatchenkery's work is a powerful response with significant insight into the marginalization that many Asian managers and professionals experience in their organizations (Thatchenkery and Sugiyama 2011). Much organizational change theory has often implicitly assumed a homogenous cultural context and his work is an important rejoinder helpful in reversing this blindness to diversity that has unwittingly crept into the field. In so many ways, Thatchenkery's groundbreaking work serves as a useful reminder to organizational decision makers, power centers, and architects of organizational change to be sensitively attuned to the idiosyncratic, self-effacing, quiet, and invisible leadership patterns of minority groups like the Asian Americans (Cheng and Thatchenkery 1997). He is recognized as one of the very first researchers to shed the analytic spotlight on the human and social capital dynamics and patterns unique to Asian Americans in federal agencies and in US corporations, and his reputation has led him to the US Congress to testify for the *White House Initiative on Asian Americans*.

Thatchenkery's contribution to multicultural understanding and insight is predicated, among other things, on his notion of a communal or social rationality in sharp contradistinction to the conception of human beings as self-contained, rational individuals. In the context of corporate globalization, this viewpoint offers a very important alternative to the culturally disembedded notion of a society formed of self-interested individuals that is wreaking havoc on the cultural integrity of societies globally. Thatchenkery replaces this with a recognition of communal reality that shows a genuine appreciation for persons and communities as conditioned by and organically rooted in historical and social contexts. His research on information communication technology (ICT) and economic development of India (Thatchenkery and Stough 2005) is a powerful example of the significance of communal rationality.

Prior to Thatchenkery's research, no one had predicted that India would emerge as a major center of excellence in terms of information technology because most models based on technical rationality highlighted the lack of a sound infrastructure, excessive governmental regulation, and an unresponsive investment climate (Thatchenkery and Stough 2005). As Thatchenkery's analysis pointed out, most of these accounts failed to acknowledge the significance of communal rationality that was firmly rooted in a collectivist culture that was resilient enough to transcend problems and embrace creative solutions through a cooperative consciousness. Unconstrained by self-interested individualism and its liabilities, the culture promoted active knowledge sharing because ideas were not seen as privately owned but communally shared and exchanged. Thatchenkery coined the term *Hindu Social Capital*, which "signifies the positive characteristics and competencies attributed to the Indian professionals (in software, banking, engineering, etc.) in India and overseas based on the common perception of Indians as good with abstractions (The term *Hindu* is used, for want of a better one, to explicate the Indian mind-set and is not meant to be a religious attribute)."

Pedagogic Innovation in the Institutionalized Fusion of Action Learning, Sensitivity Training, and Experiential Learning

After earning his Ph.D. in Organizational Behavior from the Weatherhead School of Management at Case Western Reserve University, Thatchenkery joined the brand new department of Social and Organizational Learning (PSOL) at George Mason University, a department that was established with the goal of promoting interdisciplinary work involving faculty from diverse academic backgrounds including economics, anthropology, sociology, computer science, management, and cultural studies. Thatchenkery excelled at institution building and early in his career at George Mason, he collaborated with faculty across schools and created the Master of New Professional Studies program which became a prolific incubator for about half a dozen masters programs that were developed out of this initiative.

One of Thatchenkery's sterling accomplishments is that in 1996 he became the founder of a professional Master's degree program with a focus on organizational learning and knowledge management (ODKM) at George Mason University, the first of its kind anywhere. The program was renamed M.S. in Organization Development & Knowledge Management in 2008 and celebrated its 20th year of growth this year. He is currently the program director of this Master of Science in Organization Development and Knowledge Management at the Schar School of Policy & Government at George Mason University, Arlington, Virginia. This professional degree that Thatchenkery founded has produced a very impressive cadre of practitioners, consultants, entrepreneurs, and scholars who are leaders in education, public service, change management, and organizational transformation in business, government, global and US-based NGOs, and international financial institutions.

It would be instructive to explore the unique, "blue ocean" features of the program that Thatchenkery founded because significant dimensions of his approach to organizational change have been woven into the design of the program and integrated in a most spectacularly innovative manner. The three required core courses he teaches for the ODKM program are Group Dynamics and Team Learning, Organizational Learning Laboratory, and Learning Community. All three of these courses have significant experiential grounding and are designed to foster pragmatic, intellectual, social, emotional, and spiritual competencies in both the experienced and embryonic organizational development professionals who participate as students. Thatchenkery believes that many different kinds of knowledge are integrated in communities and institutions and that every community develops over time a set of shared *practices*, resulting in a community of practice.

Each of the three courses is distinctive. In the Group Dynamics and Team Learning course, students go through an intense T-group type experience that is ingeniously cross-fertilized with methods and perspectives drawn from adult and experiential learning theories, organizational learning methodologies, and encounter groups. In the Learning Community course, Thatchenkery focuses on communities of practice, helping students identify, surface, and play with both tacit and explicit group practices and norms, while also generating new ones, through an innovative course design in which small groups of students design and deliver professional-quality, full-day learning experiences for the benefit of their colleagues, the professors, alumni, and guests, and then reflect on the experience (both of codesigner and participant) through a structured process. In the Organizational Learning Laboratory, students acquire mastery of organizational learning interventions and conduct real-world consulting projects designed to promote breakthroughs in organizational effectiveness, learning, and renewal.

A core hallmark of Thatchenkery's approach is the personal reflection application essay (PRAE), "where students describe their experiences from intense group interactions, simulations, exercises, case studies, or role play, reflect on them, conceptualize/theorize them using readings, and propose concrete new behaviors they would engage in based on the new learning." Although many students find this level of integration of experience, observation, conceptualization, and experimentation initially challenging, they readily see the value of the exercise because of its direct relationship to the competencies of being an organizational change agent. Another novel dimension of the program is that students are often invited back to facilitate small group laboratory learning within the program.

In addition to his role designing programs, curricula, and courses, Thatchenkery has been a committed and supportive mentor to his students. He has advised and chaired many Ph.D. dissertations and master's students both at GMU and at other institutions. Thatchenkery goes well above and beyond to help his students in the directions they most seek to develop. For students with a practitioner focus, he analyzes what the student needs and helps the student develop the knowledge, skills, competencies, experience, networks, and qualities of being necessary to be effective and successful in organization development and change (or wherever their careers take them). For students with a scholarly focus, he helps the students develop the conceptual and analytical rigor, knowledge, skills, and experience necessary to excel. For students with a combined focus, he provides both types of guidance. In all cases, Thatchenkery goes far above and beyond for his students, both while they are students and also whenever needed afterwards as alumni. For example, as part of giving students experience and opportunity, three of his books were coauthored with his students: Carol Metzker for *Appreciative Intelligence*®, Keimei Sugiyama for *Making the Invisible Visible*, and Dilpreet Chowdhry for *Appreciative Inquiry and Knowledge Management*. Students routinely seek out Thatchenkery for guidance, and alumni routinely stay in touch with him for decades on end.

In addition to his role at George Mason University, he is also a doctoral faculty at Fielding Graduate University, Santa Barbara, California, and a member of the NTL Institute of Applied Behavioral Science and the Taos Institute. The NTL institute is the pioneering organization for applying insights from the behavioral sciences to awaken people to possibilities for creating egalitarian and more socially just workplaces that embrace power equalization and celebrate and promote diversity. The Taos Institute focuses on bringing the benefits of a social constructivist paradigm and insights to organizational and other human contexts. In all of these pedagogic roles, Thatchenkery's core philosophy of teaching and the accompanying set of practices outlined above permeate his pedagogy, student interaction and mentoring, and design of programs, curricula, and courses.

Impactful Consulting Integrating Multiple Methods and Perspectives

Thatchenkery's impact in the field of organizational development and change reaches an acme in his consulting work. His consulting has had a salubrious influence on tens of thousands of managers globally. Thatchenkery's consulting draws on Appreciative Intelligence®, social constructionism, knowledge management, sustainable value, invisible or quiet leadership, organizational learning, group dynamics, and mindfulness. In these presentations and interventions, he shows an extraordinary conceptual and training agility in applying his vast reservoir of insights in each of the aforementioned thematic areas to the design and delivery of high impact programs and workshops. Through the Institute of Management Studies (IMS), a membership organization of Fortune 500 companies providing training and management development seminars for corporations in nearly 30 cities around the world, Thatchenkery has reached hundreds of global managers at all levels of management offering a uniquely integrated blend of expertise in Appreciative Intelligence®, knowledge management, mindfulness, and organizational learning. Additionally, Thatchenkery has an extremely impressive array of clients globally who invite him to offer his expertise in enhancing the effectiveness of their organizations. His seminars and interventions lie within the domains of change management, leadership development, organization design and strategy, and knowledge management. Past and current clients include Food and Agriculture Organization (FAO) of the United Nations, IBM, Fannie Mae, Booz Allen, PNC Bank, Lucent Technologies, General Mills, 3 M, British Petroleum, the International Monetary Fund, the World Bank, United States Department of Agriculture, United States Environmental Protection Agency, Pension Benefit Guarantee Corporation, US Department of Treasury, USPS OIG, US Department of Housing and Urban Development, Akbank (Turkey), and the Tata Consulting Services (India).

New Insights: Unleashing Human Potential Through Appreciative Intelligence

Thatchenkery's contribution to the scholarly and practical dimensions of organizational development has been extremely catalytic in unleashing creative currents that have helped thaw the somewhat rigid edifice of logical positivism in the disciplines of public policy, knowledge management, and organizational learning and development. His elaboration of social constructionist and hermeneutic approaches to organizational theory have added to our appreciation of the fluidity of organizations and their capacity for dynamic vitality, interplay, and continuous rejuvenation that occur between and among organizations, actors, observers, and environments (Gergen and Thatchenkery 2014). He has helped remind us constantly of the creative power of human subjectivity in the design of organizations through the iterative mechanisms of interpretation, sensing, and meaning making (Thatchenkery 1992).

It is impossible to overestimate the extent to which the epistemological stance he has inhabited across multiple thematic areas of scholarship has fueled viable alternatives to mainstream approaches in how organizational processes are understood conceptually and managed through creative interventions predicated upon social constructionist appreciative sense-making.

Just as one illustration of the very profound real-world impact of Thatchenkery's work, the articulation of the construct of Appreciative Intelligence (Thatchenkery 2015) represents both, a significant conceptual refinement and extension of appreciative inquiry and an applied lever of transformation that is highly generalizable to a plethora of real world problems. It has had very significant consequences reaching the shores of countless organizations globally. Through the seminars of the Institute of Management Studies (IMS) mentioned earlier, Thatchenkery has reached literally thousands of participants who have rated his impact extremely highly and have noted the carryover effects of his teaching into everyday practices in their own organizational context in diverse, geographically dispersed global organizations. From a more personal standpoint, I can provide one direct example among hundreds of organizational change efforts inspired by Thatchenkery's work every year. It was not uncommon at this international financial institution that I consulted with to arrange for the "training" of leaders of so-called Third-World countries by inviting economists from leading American universities to impart the training. The reality was that much of this training delivered by academic experts was far removed from the realities of the leaders of the various countries. Several economists from the so-called First World were perceived as largely disconnected from the ground-level realities of the various countries. Thatchenkery and Appreciative Intelligence® inspired the author to reframe the challenge away from providing expert opinion of eminent economists and toward unleashing the appreciative intelligence of the participants themselves by designing spaces for the profound insights, experiences, talents, and capacities of the diverse participants to be freely shared. Participants were invited to bring glowing examples of economic rejuvenation from their local contexts and to serve as faculty, inspiring each other through powerful sharing with the other participants from different regions of the world. This promoted transfer of learning and insights across the world based on an appreciative valuing of what appeared to be working best in the ground level realities as opposed to abstract theories taught by the so-called First world experts. The concept of "Appreciative Intelligence®" thus enabled the conscious pursuit and focus on positive examples from different regions of the world and the replacement of the expert paradigm with a celebration of the local knowledge available. The concept of Appreciative Intelligence® and the powerful implications of organizational realities as socially constructed have influenced and shaped theory, research and practice tremendously (Thatchenkery and Metzker 2006). In business schools and in schools of public policy it has introduced to the teaching of organizational change an extremely tangible set of methods and techniques to help overcome the logical positivist conception of organizations as rigid entities not very amenable to change and transformation.

Legacies and Unfinished Business: Multiple Tributaries, Unknown Destiny

While many organizational and management specialists have taken the level of the firm as the fundamental unit of analysis and have consequently attempted to develop concepts and interventions that optimize organizational outcomes within a firm level competitive advantage mindset, Thatchenkery enjoys a somewhat different but impressive reputation in the general field of management and in the specialty of Organization Development (OD). He is often recognized as a consummate scholar and practitioner who has transcended the narrowness of the firm level focus of organizational development and instead taken the focus of his efforts to be the creative unleashing of human potential within larger social collectivities. His contributions on appreciative intelligence, social constructionism and hermeneutics, sustainable value, appreciative sharing of knowledge (ASK), and invisible leadership go beyond firm level competitive dynamics and seek to unleash the creative splendor inherent in human nature in the service of human flourishing, enhancing the synergistic potential among human beings, and maximize cooperative consciousness and entrepreneurial creativity. Within OD, he is especially recognized in the area referred to as Positive Organizational Behavior, which examines the multiple ways in which language, particularly positive language, generates organizational realities. His paper, "Organizational Sciences as social construction," coauthored with Kenneth Gergen, has now come to be recognized as a classic and has been cited more than 400 times and has been reprinted half a dozen times in different scholarly journal outlets. Similarly, his book *Appreciative Intelligence®* is a Harvard Business Review recommended reading. In the area of knowledge management, which is centrally important in today's information society, Thatchenkery has developed Appreciative Sharing of Knowledge (ASK). When it comes to questions of planetary well-being and responsible stewardship of the planet's resources, Thatchenkery has contributed through his book *Positive Design and Appreciative Construction: From Sustainable Development to Sustainable Value.*

Thatchenkery intends to spend the next few years studying the relationship between entrepreneurial cognition, opportunity recognition, and Appreciative Intelligence®. While most research on entrepreneurship focuses on the macro level using knowledge spillover theory and regional advantage strategy frameworks, Thatchenkery's contributions explore entrepreneurship at the micro, individual level, studying the interrelationships between entrepreneurial cognition, opportunity recognition, and Appreciative Intelligence®. He is articulating a comprehensive, multilevel research agenda examining entrepreneurship in a holistic manner. Similarly, Thatchenkery's work on quiet and invisible leadership among Asian Americans is blazing a new trail as the first major piece of research to identify and document leadership styles that may be unique and idiosyncratic to specific ethnic minorities. In a global, multicultural world, the study is an extremely valuable reminder of the importance of not merely giving lip service to diversity but to understanding the unique leadership patterns, styles of engagement, and forms of contribution that may be relatively distinct to and prevalent among people who share a collective identity.

Conclusion

Thatchenkery's scholarly and professional contributions to the organizational development field demonstrate the potential for synergy between scholarship and practice and the interplay between the three identities that he has been able to inhabit in a fluidly integrative manner, namely that of concept champion, an engaged educator and a passionate practitioner. As a concept champion, he has demonstrated relentless commitment to upholding the intellectual significance of Appreciative Intelligence, social constructionism, and invisible leadership. As an engaged educator, Thatchenkery has been able to create and sustain a dynamic institutional architecture for one of the world's leading graduate programs in organizational development and knowledge management at George Mason University, a program that has already produced twenty cohorts of practitioners who are in so many ways shaping the field of organizational development and its emerging contours in the Washington D.C. metropolitan areas and elsewhere, globally. As a passionate practitioner, he has crafted a variety of creative interventions involving Appreciative Intelligence, he has extended appreciative inquiry to challenges of knowledge management and sustainable development and he has shaped the organizational cultures of countless organizations through his seminars that have had an extraordinary impact.

Imparting extraordinary vitality to Thatchenkery's scholarly and practitioner work is a tremendous gift for weaving together seemingly disparate elements into coherently integrated wholes and leveraging the concomitant synergies in knowledge work. In his world, appreciative intelligence, social constructionism and hermeneutics, knowledge management, entrepreneurial creativity, invisible leadership, action learning, sustainable value, and cross-cultural identity formation in fostering leadership excellence don't exist in splendid isolation but freely flow into each other like multiple tributaries coming together, mixing, colliding, dissolving, and disappearing as individual thematic entities only to be reconstituted in a oceanic space of transformative energy capable of enhancing the resilience of individuals, organizations, and societies for planetary well-being. They come together as seamlessly and with the same degree of integrative synergy as the three facets of Thatchenkery himself- a concept champion, an engaged educator and a passionate practitioner, each one fortifying the other, adding layers of multidimensional richness to his presence as an organizational development practitioner who is leaving an indelible imprint on the profession.

References

Cheng, C., & Thatchenkery, T. (1997). Why is there a lack of workplace diversity research on Asian Americans? *The Journal of Applied Behavioral Science, 33*(3), 270–276.

Gephart Jr., R., Boje, D., & Thatchenkery, T. (1996). Postmodern management and the coming crises of organizational analysis. In D. Boje, R. Gephart, & T. Thatchenkery (Eds.), *Postmodern management and organization theory*. Newbury Park: Sage.

Gergen, K., & Thatchenkery, T. (2004). Organization science as social construction: Postmodern potentials. *The Journal of Applied Behavioral Science, 40*(2), 228–249.

Gergen, K., & Thatchenkery, T. (2014). Organization science as social construction: Postmodern potentials. In E. Bell & H. Willmott (Eds.), *Qualitative research in business and management: Challenges and prospects* (Vol. 4). London: Sage.
Thatchenkery, T. (1992). Organizations as "texts": Hermeneutics as a model for understanding organizational change. *Research in Organization Development and Change, 6*, 197–233.
Thatchenkery, T. (2005). *Appreciative sharing of knowledge: Leveraging knowledge management for strategic change.* Chagrin Falls: Taos Institute Publishing.
Thatchenkery, T. (2015). Appreciative intelligence®. In D. Coghlan & M. Brydon-Miller (Eds.), *Encyclopedia of action research.* Thousand Oaks: Sage.
Thatchenkery, T., & Chowdhry, D. (2007). *Appreciative inquiry and knowledge management: A social constructionist perspective.* Cheltenham: Edward Elgar.
Thatchenkery, T., & Metzker, C. (2006). *Appreciative intelligence®: Seeing the mighty oak in the acorn.* San Francisco: Berrett-Koehler.
Thatchenkery, T., & Stough, R. (2005). *Information communication technology and economic development: Learning from the Indian experience.* Cheltenham: Edward Elgar.
Thatchenkery, T., & Sugiyama, K. (2011). *Making the invisible visible: Understanding leadership contributions of Asian minorities in the workplace.* New York: Palgrave MacMillan.
Thatchenkery, T., Cooperrider, D., & Avital, M. (Eds.). (2010). *Positive design and appreciative construction: From sustainable development to sustainable value.* Bingley: Emerald.

Further Reading

Thatchenkery, T. (2007). Postmodernity. In S. Clegg & J. Bailey (Eds.), *International encyclopedia of organizational studies* (pp. 1283–1285). Thousand Oaks: Sage.

78 William Rockwell Torbert: Walk the Talk

Steven S. Taylor

Abstract
Bill Torbert's career has combined being a leader, teaching leadership, consulting to leaders, and researching leadership. Above all else he has been intent on embodying and explicating what he came to call his "collaborative developmental action inquiry" (CDAI) approach to life, social science, and leadership. CDAI sees every action as an inquiry and every inquiry as an action. That is to say, we are constantly inquiring into the social world and also acting to change that social world. Torbert's response to this is to suggest a social science that is based in multiplicity. Rather than a single set of practices, he suggests that social science research can have a first-, second-, or third-person research voice; have first-, second-, or third-person practice as its subject; and be about the past, present, or future; with single-, double-, or triple-loop feedback. CDAI represents a different paradigm that holds that the primary aim of social science research is to generate moments of deep inquiry amidst action and create capacity for and practice of mutual exercises of power, leading to patterns of timely action. In order to "do" CDAI, Torbert has created various ideas and tools for practice. For first- and second-person practice of CDAI, Torbert has developed two powerful tools, the four territories of experience and the four types of speech. In third-person research, he led the use of adult developmental theory in organization change and extended the theory to create stage models of organizational development and of social scientific development.

Keywords
Action inquiry • Developmental theory • First-person research • Second-person research • Third-person research • Action research

S.S. Taylor (✉)
Foisie School of Business, Worcester Polytechnic Institute, Worcester, MA, USA
e-mail: sst@wpi.edu

D.B. Szabla et al. (eds.), *The Palgrave Handbook of Organizational Change Thinkers*,
DOI 10.1007/978-3-319-52878-6_59

Contents

Bill Torbert's career has combined being a leader, teaching leadership, consulting to leaders, and researching leadership. Above all else he has been intent on embodying and explicating what he eventually came to call his "collaborative developmental action inquiry" (CDAI) approach to life, social science, and leadership (moving from the general case to the specific). I say embody and explicate because Bill has always tried to walk his talk. His published works are efforts to talk his walk and to explain in text what Bill was trying to live, often drawing upon his own adventures (and misadventures) as illustrations of his ideas. And, unlike many action researchers, Bill has not rebelled against quantitative research. In fact, he is the first to have introduced the notion of integrating "first-, second-, and third-person" research (Torbert 1997, 2013) on the past, present, and future (Chandler and Torbert 2003), interweaving quantitative measures, qualitative data, and action interventions (Torbert 2000b, 2013).

Bill was one of my professors when I did my Ph.D. at Boston College. I was never his research assistant, nor was he my advisor (although he was on my Ph.D. committee). After I finished my Ph.D. and left Boston College, he and I were part of a small group that met regularly to inquire into our own practice for over a decade. Bill and I eventually wrote one chapter together (Torbert and Taylor 2008), and even though I have read most (but certainly not all) of his work, I primarily know Bill and his work from our efforts to walk our talk together, which in some ways continues to this day. The lessons I learned about living, social science, and leadership were profound, and in this chapter I hope to offer some small sense of that.

Influences and Motivations: Peace, Yale, and Action Research

Bill went to Yale as an undergraduate in the early 1960s and as a graduate student in the late 1960s. With the civil rights movement domestically and the Vietnam War abroad, it was a time of unrest when it seemed possible to question everything, and Bill was well situated to do so. His father worked for the State Department, and Bill spent time in several countries growing up, which may be where he first learned that there are many different ways of being and that our deepest cultural assumptions and rules about how to be in the world are not simply taken-for-granted facts of nature, but rather social constructions of a particular human culture.

His first great influence at Yale was the pastor and civil rights and peace activist William Sloane Coffin (cf. Coffin 2004). Through Coffin's influence, Bill played a leadership role, first in Yale in Mississippi, which led to the 1964 and 1965 civil rights acts, and then as director of Yale Upward Bound, an innovative war on poverty high school program, which cut New Haven's drop-out rate in half through the practice of "collaborative inquiry." Bill's second great influence at Yalewas Chris Argyris, whom Bill first met and studied with as an undergraduate and who chaired Bill's dissertation committee in graduate school. Like Coffin, Argyris' influence was not only intellectual but also behavioral and emotional. Argyris raised questions about whether one's actions were in fact consistent with one's values and introduced Bill to experiential learning in groups (Bethel T-groups, Tavistock group relations, Esalen encounter groups). The third great influence Bill encountered while he was at Yale was the Gurdjieff work (cf. Ouspensky 1949), based in New York and Paris, which Bill attended for 25 years. The central inquiry of this spiritual work is how one can develop an impartial, post-cognitive consciousness amidst the stresses of everyday action. In addition, while at Yale, Bill met, read the work of, and was significantly influenced by political theorists Hannah Arendt, Paul D'Entreves, Karl Deutsch, and Herbert Marcuse, psychologists Erik Erikson and Abraham Maslow, political economist Charles Lindblom, philosopher Donald Schön, and theologian Paul Tillich.

After Yale, Torbert taught at Southern Methodist University (SMU) in Dallas for 2 years and at the Harvard Graduate School of Education for 4 years. He chose to go to Harvard in part to learn more about developmental theory from Lawrence Kohlberg and Bill Perry and in the end learned even more from Carol Gilligan and Bob Kegan (who was then a grad student), as well as from the writings of John Rawls and Amartya Sen. After his time at Harvard, he was influenced primarily by several of his peers in our field – Ian Mitroff, Lou Pondy, Bob Quinn, Peter Senge, and Karl Weick – but most of all from his British action research colleague and coauthor Peter Reason.

After he resigned from Harvard, Torbert directed The Theatre of Inquiry for 2 years and then joined the faculty at Boston College, initially as Graduate Dean of the Management School. There he remained for 30 years until his retirement in 2008. At The Theatre of Inquiry, Bill led weekly hour and a half "Action Workshops," a 13-week "business/school" whose members first created a business together, and then went on to start their own businesses, and a monthly public performance which began as a theatrical play for an audience and gradually invited the audience into a profound action inquiry by the end of the evening. All of these exercises became fodder for the action-effectiveness MBA program that he later cocreated with faculty at Boston College. This unique approach transformed the BC MBA program from a rank below the top 100 to #25 nationally.

Later, in the late 1980s and until his retirement in 2008, Bill served as director of BC's Ph.D. program in organizational transformation, consulted to more than two-dozen organizations, served on the board of directors of unusual companies (e.g., Trillium Asset Management, the original socially responsible investing company, and Harvard Pilgrim Health Care, which became #1 HMO nationally at that time), and won local and national teaching prizes, as well as national research awards. His most well-known books during this period were *Managing the Corporate Dream*, *The Power of Balance: Transforming Self, Society and Scientific Inquiry*, and *Action Inquiry: The Secret of Timely and Transforming Leadership.*

Since 2008, he has functioned as principal of Action Inquiry Associates, continuing to sponsor and do research on the Global Leadership Profile, the psychometric measure that, since 1980, has served as the quantitative anchor for his and a number of his colleagues and students' third-person action research. He has also changed his focus from organizations to friendships; has cocreated the Action Inquiry Fellowship, wherein three-dozen highly diverse international scholar/practitioners sharpen their first- and second-person action inquiry capacity with one another; and, in 2015, coauthored with Hilary Bradbury, *Eros/Power: Love in the Spirit of Inquiry.*

Key Contributions: Collaborative Developmental Action Inquiry

Returning to the beginning of his career, Bill's senior undergraduate thesis "Being for the Most Part Puppets: Interactions Among Men's Labor, Leisure, and Politics" (Torbert and Rogers 1972), written in collaboration with his classmate Malcolm Rogers, became his first published book. This sociological field survey of 209 blue-collar workers in three industries showed that the relative amount of discretion a man had in his job directly predicted the degree of his creative leisure engagement and political action. These findings, along with Bill's direct experience of the poverty and mechanicity of assembly-line workers' jobs, motivated him to try to learn how organizations could be reorganized to encourage creativity and responsibility at all levels and how he himself could play a leadership role in such processes.

Argyris had agreed that Bill could do an action research dissertation on (a) his founding and leadership of Yale Upward Bound and (b) the school's evolution toward becoming a truly collaborative venture between faculty and students (as documented primarily by innumerable tape recordings of meetings and interviews of all participants). This eventually led to the explication of an eight-stage theory of organizational development at the end of Bill's third book, *Creating a Community of Inquiry: Conflict, Collaboration, Transformation* (1976), written largely in the first person. This book documented both how the author himself learned and changed as a collaborative leader and how each of six different sub-cycles of the program followed the same developmental sequence (the two spring staff selection and curriculum planning periods, the two distinct 7-week residential summer programs, the five-person core staff, and the overall 2-year endeavor). This theory of eight organizational development stages has proven to be the most differentiated in the field of organizational development. By showing what stage of development an organization was currently at, the theory also became key to Torbert's later, quantitatively verified successes (Torbert 2013) in generating organizational transformations in his action research/consulting interventions. One reason for this is that the theory shows how organizations alternate between more centralizing stages and more decentralizing stages suggesting radically different interventions at alternating stage transitions, whereas most OD consulting theory and practice focus on helping organizations decentralize.

But, why, you may be asking, was this Bill's third book (1976) and not his second? Because, after he had completed his 2-year study of Upward Bound during graduate school, just as he was about to write it up, the department's faculty concluded that it could not possibly be objective and scientific if the researcher was also an actor in the field experiment. Unfortunately for Bill, he had not yet generated the concept of how first-, second-, and third-person research can complement and strengthen one another. Faced with a choice between discontinuing the doctoral program and designing and executing a completely different study in 9 months, Bill chose the latter, doing a laboratory experiment on learning from experience, asking why it is so difficult to learn from experience in a way that transforms one's initial assumptions. Thus, this dissertation, *Learning from Experience: Toward Consciousness* (Torbert 1973), became Bill's second book.

Learning from Experience first introduces the notion that, contrary to the general modern view that the outside world is the "territory" that we attempt to "map" via social science, there are actually four distinct "territories of experience" – the outside world, our inner sense of our own embodiment and action, our thinking and feeling, and a post-cognitive attention that any of us can cultivate, but few do.

This laboratory study produced a reliable verbal behavior scoring system that was shown to be able to distinguish which of two educational processes generated the most moments in action when participants were conscious of all four territories at once. This quality of first-person awareness-in-action was shown to be necessary, in turn, for a person to learn whether his or her assumptions at the outset of an "action inquiry" process deserved to be transformed. In his later work, to which we now turn, Bill showed how second-person conversations, third-person organizations, and social science itself can gradually cultivate a conversational and organizational awareness-in-action that spans all four territories of experience, by evolving through analogous personal, organizational, and paradigmatic developmental trajectories.

We can date the second half of Torbert's career from his acceptance of the position of Graduate Dean at the Boston College School of Management in 1978 to his retirement from Boston College in 2008. His scholarly work has been the development of "collaborative developmental action inquiry" (CDAI), which although not often recognized as such is a fundamentally new and different paradigm for social science research. That is to say, Bill takes seriously the idea that we are co-constructing our social world as we act and interact. Bill's first articulation of this approach was to suggest that we need an "action science" (Torbert 1976 pp. 167–177). The term *action science* was picked up by Chris Argyris and eventually became the title of the book (Argyris et al. 1985) that lays out the philosophic and academic foundations for Argyris' approach. Meanwhile, Bill came to the conclusion that "science" was too cognitive a word and instead adopted the term "action inquiry" (Torbert and Associates 2004) to better convey the more holistic and embodied work he was trying to describe.

Argyris conceived of action science as a way of extending the naturalistic science tradition. Torbert conceived of action inquiry as a new paradigm that includes third-person, generalizable theory, data, and quantitative testing of hypotheses; but that also breaks away from many of the assumptions and methods that constitute empirically positivist scientific inquiry, in order to include first- and second-person inquiry into the very action settings in which we researchers are ourselves also participants. One of the most important ideas in Argyris' Action Science is the Popperian notion of disconfirmability – action science argues strongly for treating all of our mental models (Senge 1990) about the world as hypotheses that we should actively be trying to disconfirm, especially when those mental models lead us to act in ways that prove to be problematic in some way. This is the essence of Argyris and Schön (1974) Model II double-loop feedback as I understand it. Torbert is all for holding our mental models loosely and inquiring into them, but action inquiry does not rest on the same belief that that we can apply the processes of naturalistic scientific inquiry to our actions in the social world (indeed, action inquiry comes closer to a quantum understanding of physical science, and Torbert believes CDAI represents a paradigm change relevant to both the social and natural sciences).

The Popperian idea of disconfirmability implies both a certain stability and a certain distance. That is, you need a phenomena that is stable enough to be testing the same phenomena that you formulated the hypothesis about. And you need to be able to observe the phenomena from enough of a distance that you can see what it is. Often neither of these conditions are met in the case of social action (cf. Lehrer 2010). Instead, action inquiry sees every action as an inquiry and every inquiry as an action. That is to say, we are constantly inquiring into the social world and also acting to change (or not) that social world. When I see my colleague first thing in the morning and ask her or him how they are doing, it is an inquiry, a probe into the system (even when I intend it as a simple social ritual that doesn't require an answer). When my colleague responds with "same old, same old," I learn that the social world is much as it usually is. But when my colleague responds "my dog died last night," I have learned something else and our relationship has changed in some – perhaps small – way. Action inquiry is based on this understanding of the social world as something that is constantly shifting in which we are embedded, unable to assume either stability or distance.

Torbert's response to this is to suggest a social science that is based on multiplicity. Rather than a single set of practices, he suggests that social science research can have a first-, second-, or third-person research voice; have first-, second-, or third-person practice as its subject; and be about the past, present, or future; with single-, double-, or triple-loop feedback (Chandler and Torbert 2003). This results in 81 different research types – Torbert's argument is that modern social science includes a woefully small subset of these research types and that the more types that are included, the more powerful the research will be. I say powerful, because another way in which action inquiry represents a new and different paradigm is that Torbert holds that the primary aim of social science research is to generate more and more instances and patterns of timely action – not only to gain greater and greater certainty about a conceptual map of the world, supported by various sets of empirical facts, as is the aim of most modern social science.

In order to "do" action inquiry, Torbert has created various ideas and tools for practice. The idea of first-, second-, and third-person research/practice (Torbert 1997)

Table 1 Four territories of experience of an individual person (From Torbert and Taylor 2008)

The outside world	Objectified, discrete, interval units, of which "I" am actively aware when "I" notice the color and manyness of what "I" see or the support the outside world is giving me through the soles of my feet (focused attention)
One's own sensed behavior and feeling	Processual, ordinal rhythms in passing time, of which "I" am actively aware when I feel what I am touching from the inside or when I listen to the in and out of my breathing or the rhythms and tones of my own speaking (subsidiary, sensual awareness)
The realm of thought	Eternal nominal distinctions and interrelations, of which I can be actively aware if my attention "follows" my thought, if I am not just thinking, but "mindful" that I am thinking (witnessing awareness)
Vision/attention/intention	The kind of noumenal vision/attention/intention that can simultaneously interpenetrate the other three territories and experience incongruities or harmonies among them

has been perhaps the most popular, at least in terms of being adopted by the academic community (e.g., Reason and Bradbury 2001; Shear and Varela 1999; Velmans 2009). For first- and second-person practice of action inquiry, Torbert has developed two powerful tools, the four territories of experience, shown in Table 1 (Torbert 1972), and the four types of speech, shown in Table 2 (Fisher and Torbert 1995). The four territories of experience are (1) *the outside world*, (2) *one's own sensed behavior and feeling*, (3) *the realm of thought*, and (4) *the realm of vision/attention/intention,* and one of the practices of action inquiry is to pay attention and recognize feelings of fit and/or incongruity across the four territories. Is a given outcome congruent or incongruent with an organizations' vision?

It is probably not possible to always be paying attention to all four territories of experience at the same time – I know I have trouble being aware of more than one at a time, and in most of my life, I'm not consciously aware of any of them. However, the feelings in each of these territories are useful data that can help guide action. Here we can plainly see a difference between paying attention to a feeling of incongruity and seeking disconfirming data – a strict action *science* can't accept feelings of incongruity as legitimate data to disconfirm a mental model. Action *inquiry* requires paying attention to those feelings and inquiring further, that is, acting to further explore those feelings. Eugene Gendlin's *Focusing* (1982) and his subsequent work on exploring "felt sense" is another body of first-person research in the same spirit.

Torbert's four types of speech take the idea that speech is action (Austin 1962), or rather conversational interaction across the four territories of experience, which at its best includes (1) *framing* a joint intent, (2) *advocating* one or more strategies, (3) *illustrating* how specific behavioral tactics and contextual conditions favor a strategy, and (4) *inquiring* how one's conversational partners respond. Here the contention is that a balance of the four types of speech will be more effective in generating timely action and receptivity to feedback on the part of all participants

Table 2 Four parts of speech (From Torbert and Taylor 2008)

Framing refers to explicitly stating what the purpose is for the present occasion, what the dilemma is that you are trying to resolve, and what assumptions you think are shared or not shared (but need to be tested out loud to be sure). This is the element of speaking most often missing from conversations and meetings. The leader or initiator assumes the others know and share the overall objective. Explicit framing (or reframing, if the conversation appears offtrack) is useful precisely because the assumption of a shared frame is frequently untrue. When people have to guess at the frame, they frequently guess wrong and they often impute negative, manipulative motives ("What's he getting at?"). For example, instead of starting out right away with the first item of the meeting, the leader can provide and test an explicit frame: "We're about halfway through to our final deadline and we've gathered a lot of information and shared different approaches, but we haven't yet made a single decision. To me, the most important thing we can do today is agree on something. . . make at least one decision we can feel good about. I think XYZ is our best chance, so I want to start with that. Do you all agree with this assessment, or do you have other candidates for what it's most important to do today?"
Advocating refers to explicitly asserting an option, perception, feeling, or strategy for action in relatively abstract terms (e.g., "We've got to get shipments out faster"). Some people speak almost entirely in terms of advocacy; others rarely advocate at all. Either extreme – only advocating or never advocating – is likely to be relatively ineffective. For example, "Do you have an extra pen?" is not an explicit advocacy, but an inquiry. The person you are asking may truthfully say "No" and turn away. On the other hand, if you say "I need a pen (advocacy). Do you have an extra one (inquiry)?" the other is more likely to say something like, "No, but there's a whole box in the secretary's office." The most difficult type of advocacy for most people to make effectively is an advocacy about how we feel – especially how we feel about what is occurring right now. This is difficult partly because we ourselves are often only partially aware of how we feel; also, we are reluctant to become vulnerable; furthermore, social norms against generating potential embarrassment can make current feelings seem undiscussable. For all these reasons, feelings usually enter conversations only if the relationship is close and risk is low, in which case there is little likelihood of receiving corrective feedback. The other time when feelings enter conversations is when they have become so strong that they burst in, and then they are likely to be offered in a way that harshly evaluates others ("Damn it, will you loudmouths shut up!"). This way of advocating feelings is usually very ineffective, however, because it invites defensiveness. By contrast, a vulnerable description is more likely to invite honest sharing by others ("I'm feeling frustrated and shut out by the machine-gun pace of this conversation and I don't see it getting us to agreement. Does anyone else feel this way?")
Illustrating involves telling a bit of a concrete story that puts meat on the bones of the advocacy and thereby orients and motivates others more clearly. Example: "We've got to get shipments out faster [advocacy]. Jake Tarn, our biggest client, has got a rush order of his own, and he needs our parts before the end of the week [illustration]." The illustration suggests an entirely different mission and strategy than might have been inferred from the advocacy alone. You may be convinced that your advocacy contains one and only one implication for action and that your subordinate or peer is at fault for misunderstanding. But in this case, it is your conviction that is a colossal metaphysical mistake. Implications are by their very nature inexhaustible. There is never one and only one implication or interpretation of an action. That is why it is so important to be explicit about each of the four parts of speech and to interweave them sequentially, if we wish to increase our reliability in achieving shared purposes
Inquiring obviously involves questioning others, in order to learn something from them. In principle, the simplest thing in the world; in practice, one of the most difficult things in the world to do effectively. Why? One reason is that we often inquire rhetorically, as we just did. We don't give the other the opportunity to respond, or we suggest by our tone that we don't really want a TRUE answer. "How are you?" we say dozens of times each day, not really wanting to know.

(*continued*)

Table 2 (continued)

"You agree, don't you?" we say, making it clear what answer we want. A second reason why it is difficult to inquire effectively is that an inquiry is much less likely to be effective if it is not preceded by framing, advocacy, and illustration. Naked inquiry often causes the other to wonder what frame, advocacy, and illustration are implied and to respond carefully and defensively. If we are inquiring about an advocacy we are making, the trick is to encourage the other to disconfirm our assumptions if that is how he or she truly feels. In this way, if the other confirms us, we can be confident the confirmation means something, and if not, then we see that the task ahead is to reach an agreement

(Steckler and Torbert 2010; Torbert 2000a). Of course, in day-to-day life, it is not always easy to distinguish advocacy from framing, and it is not unusual for people to mask an advocacy as an inquiry (e.g., "why are you being such a jerk?" is usually really advocating that the other is being a jerk rather than being an honest inquiry). The more authentic the inquiry, the more likely it is to yield a valid response. The point is not to provide a precise analytic tool with which to map out interactions, but rather to provide a guide for the messy practice of interacting with other human beings in real time.

Torbert is best known (cf. McCauley et al. 2006) in academia for his use of the third-person idea of developmental theory (cf. Loevinger 1998). The theory suggests (and is supported by a great deal of empirical evidence (Torbert 1994, 2013) that as adults, we develop through various stages that are defined by having different governing action logics and that gradually lead toward a greater and greater capacity for continual four-territory awareness, for timely action, for receptivity to pertinent feedback, and for the development of organizations that support such personal development. Each action logic determines how we make sense of and act in the world. The stages are described in Table 3. Torbert adopted and adapted Loevinger's sentence completion test instrument for determining developmental level for business use (now referred to as the *Global Leadership Development Profile*). He is not the only scholar to use developmental theory (e.g., Kegan 1994; Kegan and Lahey 2009); however, he led the use of developmental theory in organization change and extended the theory to create stage models of organizational development (Fisher and Torbert 1995;Torbert 1976, 1987) and of social scientific development (Torbert 2000b, 2013).

Torbert's empirical work linking leadership development to organizational transformation includes one of the most stunning findings in the literature. Change leaders at the Transforming and Alchemical action logics predicted 58% of the variance of the success in organizational change (Torbert 2013). In modern social science where seemingly no variable ever explains more than a few percent of the variance, this is a truly incredible result. Couple it with Torbert's other empirical work which finds that only about 5% of managers in organizations are at the Transforming or Alchemical action logics (Fisher and Torbert 1995), and his work offers both a compelling explanation for the relative lack of success of organizational change efforts and a clear prescription for how organizations can more successfully manage change.

Table 3 Action logics (Adopted from the Action Inquiry Associates *Global Leadership Development Profile Report* created by Bill Torbert and Elaine Herdman-Barker in 2012)

Opportunistic	Short-time horizon, flouts power and sexuality, rejects feedback, hostile humor, deceptive, manipulative, externalizes blame, punishes, views luck as central, punishment rules, views rules as loss of freedom, *eye-for-an eye* ethic
Diplomatic	Observes rules, avoids inner and outer conflicts, conforms, suppresses own desires, loyalty to group, seeks membership, right versus wrong attitude, appearance and status conscious, tends toward clichés, works to group standard
Expert	Interested in problem solving via data, critical of others and self, chooses efficiency over effectiveness, perfectionist, values decisions based on merit, wants own performance to stand out, aware of alternative constructions in problem resolution but can be dogmatic, accepts feedback only from *objective* craftmasters
Achiever	Results and effectiveness oriented, long-term goals, concerned with issues of ethics and justice, deliberately prioritizes work tasks, future inspires, drawn to learning, seeks mutuality in relations, aware of personal patterns of behavior, feels guilty if does not meet own standards, blind to own shadow, chases time
Redefining	Collaborative, tolerant of individual difference, aware of context and contingency, may challenge group norms, aware of owning a perspective, inquiring and open to feedback, seeks independent, creative work, attracted by difference and change, may become something of a maverick, focuses on present and historical context
Transforming	Process and goal oriented, strategic time horizons, system conscious, enjoys a variety of roles, recognizes importance of principle and judgment, engaged in complex interweave of relationships, aware of own personal traits and shadow, high value on individuality, growth, self-fulfillment, unique market niches, particular historical moments
Alchemical	Alert to the theater of action, embraces common humanity, disturbs paradigms of thought and action, dispels notions of heroic action, deeply internalized sense of self-knowledge held with empty mind, sees light and dark, order and mess, treats time and events as symbolic, analogical, metaphorical (not merely linear, digital, literal)

New Insights: What I've Learned from Bill

The first thing I was told to read in my doctoral program was Gergen's (1991) *The Saturated Self*. It shook my taken-for-granted ontology of the social world to its core and led me to question the idea that the naturalist scientific tradition could ever "work" in the social world. Decades of reading management research have made it clearer to me that the naturalist scientific tradition is not enormously helpful, especially if Bill is right, and the aim of social science research is to generate deeper inquiry and more and more patterns of timely action.

I have tried to take seriously Bill's ontological idea that every action is an inquiry and every inquiry an action. The idea of speech as action comes easily to me because it was also part of my theater training (Stanislavski 1936a, b, 1961), and I have brought that into my own academic work (e.g., Taylor and Carboni 2008). Perhaps because of my theater training, I have been much more attracted to the first- and second-person practice of action inquiry and the tools, such as the four types of speech. I have worked on articulating how to teach action inquiry approaches (Taylor et al. 2008), and my latest book (Taylor 2015) is a how-to guide that brings together Bill's approach with other tools within the reflective practice tradition for leader development.

It has felt like a natural fit to take Bill's work and mix it with artistic methods. This is in part because there is a history of action research methods that use artistic forms and in part because of the way Bill has always welcomed art into his own practice (e.g., The Theatre of Inquiry) and in part because Bill's action inquiry paradigm for social science might more appropriately be called a paradigm for social art. One of the great lessons for me is that action inquiry is a craft for living – with the hope that if you master the craft, you might live artfully. Charlie "Bird" Parker said, "You've got to learn your instrument. Then you practice, practice, practice. And then when you finally get up there on the bandstand, forget all that and just wail" (quoted in Pugatch 2006, p. 73). Action inquiry provides tools and methods for practicing how we interact with each other. It offers developmental theory as an overarching pathway. But it is really about getting up there and just wailing in a way that produces more and more patterns of timely action in the service of social justice and human flourishing.

What does it look like to just wail when we interact with others? Isn't that what we do most of the time and often with disastrous results? The wailing that Bird speaks of isn't just doing whatever pops into your head and body. It is acting from a deeply embodied skill set and awareness of the context and situation. Below is a small example from a group of academics that had been meeting regularly for years to work on their action inquiry skills.

> On this cold November day, the members of the group had arrived and were exchanging greetings and catching up with each other. Faustina entered the kitchen where Paula was standing.
>
> "How are you doing, the super commuter?" said Paula.
>
> "I'm cranky," responded Faustina.
>
> "Oh what else is new, you are always cranky when you come to these meetings," answered Paula. And like after most "little things", they didn't engage with it further. However, a few minutes later when the group started to discuss their agenda for the meeting, Faustina suggested that they explore the interaction she had with Paula rather than working on the case that had previously been planned. Paula advocated that the group work on the originally planned case.
>
> "Why do you want to do it?" asks Faustina.
>
> "Because we said we were going to do it," replied Paula.
>
> "So what?" responded Faustina.
>
> Those two simple words, which we can imagine being said a hundred different ways, jolted the room. Robert had been feeling tired and frustrated with the way the group was being so nice to each other and not deciding which case to analyze and Faustina's "so what" brought him back to earth, back to feeling grounded. Robert thought, "ah, this is real and suddenly we're back to what matters." It was like a splash of cold water on his face.
>
> Meanwhile, Robin was excited by Faustina's "so what." She believed that Faustina had the self awareness and skill to say something very diplomatic and analytical, but had chosen to bluntly, emotionally, and somewhat confrontationally express what is going on for her

> with her "so what." Robin found her choice to be provocative, exciting and beautiful. It was not provocative enough to make Robin afraid – Faustina knew the group and had a sense of how much the group could take.
>
> It was also an effective action as it moved the group out of their wandering discussion of what they should do in their meeting to focusing on the sort of work that they all have previously agreed that they should be doing. (Taylor 2013 p 75–76)

This interaction is not earth shaking and it might not even be noteworthy for most people. But for this group, it was an example of mastery of the craft skill of interacting with others, an example of action inquiry performed at a high level – a purposive and strategically distinctive exemplar of double-loop feedback to both Paula and the group as a whole that changed the group's planned activity for the session. My great takeaway from working with Torbert's ideas and practices is that leadership is largely about the day-to-day interactions, these small moments and the immense craft skill that can be needed to navigate them well. And it is more than leadership; it is indeed an art of life. I tried to describe my understanding of my own creative process, and Bill commented to me that it was one of the best examples of action inquiry he had seen.

> I will describe my own process of creating an edge for a flower bed in my yard. The flower bed is between the front of my house and the lawn. When we bought the house there was no sharp edge to the bed, it just sort of ended and the grass began in what was more or less a straight line. My wife, Rosemary and I agreed that we wanted a more defined edge and that the edge should follow a more organic curve. Just reaching that sort of agreement was a complicated and creative process (that was spread out over a couple of years) of its own, but I'll start from having decided that much.
>
> With that in mind, we made a visit to our local stone yard and looked at what sort of materials they had that might make nice edging material. We walked around the yard, paying attention to our senses, what various materials looked like, what they felt like, and how they were being used in various displays. At this point what data I selected was based on the sensemaking I already had about the desired edge. I don't recall what the weather was like, or what either of us were wearing, but I do recall looking at various types of brick, rough-tumbled cobble stones in various sizes, and some manufactured paver products that were being used as edging in some sample patios. I looked at the colors, the weights, the sizes, the texture of the surface, the regularity or lack thereof, and how they fit together. In short I paid attention to what was important based on my thinking about the edging and I didn't pay attention to countless other things that were happening in the world around me.
>
> And as we looked at the materials, we talked about them. That is to say, I took action and commented upon what I was seeing and how I made sense of it. I said things like, "oh, this color is very nice" and "these granite chunks have a nice smooth edge." Rosemary also made comments like, "these would go well with the edging in the back yard" and "I'm a little creeped out by having someone's name on the edging." (The smooth granite pieces were from headstones that had broken during the engraving process and many of them did include parts of names of the dead on them.) This is the collaborative aspect of the creative process and my comments were actions that Rosemary attended to and her comments were actions that become sensory data I then selected and made sense of. As we talked, it became clear that brick was not appealing to either of us, so based on that sensemaking I stopped looking at different types of brick, I stopped selecting data about brick from the world I was in. As we talked I paid attention to the granite stones and how big they were, how they would fit in with existing edging, how regular they were and how they might fit together. Eventually we made a decision and bought a truckload of edging stone.

> We took the stone home and the next day laid out some rough curves of where the edge of the bed should be. This was a process of setting the stones out in a curved line and then looking at the edge and talking about it, "maybe out a little more here", "I think it's too straight there" and so on. Then making adjustments, moving the stones around, talking some more, making more adjustments until we were happy with the edge. During this process, we were selecting data about how the curve looked in relation to the house, the yard, and the existing plants in the bed and making sense of the whole of it in an intuitive and felt way. We would act by talking and adjusting and then consciously making sense of it again and based on that sensemaking (it's too straight here) make further adjustments. After several iterations of the process we were ready to move on to the next step, setting the stones into the dirt.
>
> The process of setting the stones in to the dirt is very much the same as the previous activities of selecting the stone and determining where the edge should be in terms of selecting data, making sense of it, acting and attending to particular data based on that sensemaking. However the craft skills involved and what data I attend to is different. What was fundamentally a problem in two dimensions has become a problem in three dimensions as I now have to work with the many ways in which my yard is not level. Where before I was looking at the big picture of the curving edge, I am now more focused on how each stone fits with the one before it, how deep the hole needs to be, and making sure the stone rests securely in the hole without wobbling. Every few stones I step back and look at the curves of the edge I am making and sometimes I pull a stone out and reset it in a slightly different position. I also think about pragmatic issues such as how high the edge should be and how that will affect drainage in a rain storm. There are also periodic conversations with Rosemary as we step back and talk about how the edge is going. The final edge is similar to the one we laid out in the previous stage, but it doesn't follow the same path exactly. (Taylor 2012, pp. 8–11)

Again, the interaction is hardly earth shaking, but that is part of the point. For me, the small, day-to-day process of acting, being open to what results from that action, then continuing to act while drawing upon highly developed craft skills, is the heart of action inquiry. Or at least the heart of the first- and second-person practices.

Legacies and Unfinished Business: Continuing Bill's Work

It is perhaps not surprising that, other than doctoral students writing their dissertations based on CDAI theory and the GLP instrument, the academic community as a whole has not (yet?) embraced Torbert's new paradigm for social science research – no existing paradigm ever yields easily (Kuhn 1962). However there are areas where his work is influential, notably in nontraditional educational programs that emphasize practice such as the Center for Creative Leadership, Fielding Graduate University, the California Institute of Integral Studies, the Integral Institute, or in the UK the Ashridge Business School, and in Canada the Shambhala Institute's Authentic Leadership in Action program.

It is also not surprising that the business world has not wholeheartedly embraced his work. Beyond the underlying aims of promoting social justice and human flourishing (both of which much of the business world has trouble serving), Torbert's approach is hard. It is not a quick fix, it cannot be applied en masse, and he asks people and organizations to walk the talk. It takes years to develop your own craft and practice of action inquiry.

The empirical findings from Torbert's developmental theory work also suggest that the challenge for businesses is large and cannot be easily addressed. Consistently successful change leadership requires post-conventional development. A small percentage of managers have reached this level of development. Generally it takes from 5 to 10 years to fully transition from one stage to the next. This implies that businesses need to spend decades to develop managers who will be able to consistently lead significant change efforts. Very few organizations work with those sorts of time frames.

Torbert calls for development into the post-conventional stages, the move from mystery/mastery to collaborative inquiry. It is very much the same movement as Argyris and Schön's (1974) move from Model I to Model II governing values. The *Difficult Conversations* (Stone et al. 2000) move from "A Battle of Messages" to "A Learning Conversation" is also essentially the same. In all cases the movement involves becoming curious about how you and the other are understanding the situation, why that is different, and how that leads you to act differently and in ways that are problematic for each other. In short, it requires what I call openness and deep curiosity toward ourselves and leaders.

The great remaining question is how do we develop leaders who have this openness and curiosity in a more timely way? How do we take timely action to develop people and organizations more capable of taking timely action? There is certainly a chicken-and-egg issue here or perhaps even something of a Catch-22, but it is the very real issue that Torbert's work has raised and not provided an answer for.

Maybe there isn't an answer; maybe there is only a dedication to practice over many years. Certainly the much ballyhooed 10,000-hours rule (Gladwell 2008) that tells us 10,000 hours of practice (dedicated practice of your practice really) is needed to develop expertise suggests that there are no shortcuts. The long history of master (or in some cases a coach) apprentice relationships in almost all embodied practices – from the arts to sports to spiritual practices – also suggests that as humans, this is how we develop. Perhaps the question then is why don't we pursue the craft of interacting with each other in a more disciplined and intentional way? Why aren't organizational leaders like master artists who constantly refine and develop their craft? Why aren't young managers like apprentices developing their craft under the direction of master leaders?

References

Argyris, C., & Schön, D. (1974). *Theory in practice – Increasing professional effectiveness* (1st ed.). San Francisco: Jossey-Bass Publishers.

Argyris, C., Putnam, R., & Smith, D. (1985). *Action science: Concepts, methods, and skills for research and intervention*. San Francisco: Jossey-Bass.

Austin, J. L. (1962). *How to do things with words*. Oxford: Clarendon Press.

Bradbury, H., & Torbert, W. (2015). *Eros/power: Love in the spirit of inquiry*. Tucson: Integral Publishers.

Chandler, D., & Torbert, W. R. (2003). Transforming inquiry and action. *Action Research, 1*(2), 133–152.

Coffin, W. S. (2004). *Credo*. Louisville: Westminster John Knox Press.

Fisher, D., & Torbert, W. R. (1995). *Personal and organizational transformations: The true challenge of continual quality improvement*. New York: McGraw-Hill.
Gendlin, E. T. (1982). *Focusing*. New York: Bantam.
Gergen, K. J. (1991). *The saturated self – Dilemmas of identity in contemporary life*. Philadelphia: Basic Books.
Gladwell, M. (2008). *Outliers: The story of success*. New York: Little, Brown and Company.
Kegan, R. (1994). *In over our heads: The mental demands of modern life*. Cambridge, MA: Harvard University Press.
Kegan, R., & Lahey, L. (2009). *Immunity to change: How to overcome it and unlock the potential in yourself and your organization*. Boston: Harvard Business Press.
Kuhn, T. (1962). *The structure of scientific revolutions*. Chicago: The University of Chicago Press.
Lehrer, J. (2010). The truth wears off: Is there something wrong with the scientific method. *The New Yorker*, 52–57.
Loevinger, J. (1998). *Technical foundations for measuring ego development: The Washington University sentence completion test*. Mahwah: Psychology Press.
McCauley, C. D., Drath, W. H., Palus, C. J., O'Connor, P. M., & Baker, B. A. (2006). The use of constructive-developmental theory to advance the understanding of leadership. *The Leadership Quarterly, 17*(6), 634–653.
Ouspensky, P. D. (1949). *In search of the miraculous: Fragments of an unknown teaching*. New York: Harcourt and Brace.
Pugatch, J. (2006). *Acting is a job: Real-life lessons about the acting business*. New York: Allworth Press.
Reason, P., & Bradbury, H. (2001). *Handbook of action research – Participative, inquiry & practice*. London: SAGE.
Senge, P. M. (1990). *The fifth discipline: The art and practice of the learning organization*. New York: Currency Doubleday.
Shear, J., & Varela, F. J. (1999). *The view from within: First-person approaches to the study of consciousness*. Thorverton: Imprint Academic.
Stanislavski, C. (1936a). *An actor prepares* (E. R. Hapgood, Trans.). New York: Routledge.
Stanislavski, C. (1936b). *Building a character* (E. R. Hapgood, Trans.). New York: Routledge.
Stanislavski, C. (1961). *Creating a role* (E. R. Hapgood, Trans.). New York: Routledge.
Steckler, E., & Torbert, W. R. (2010). Developing the 'Developmental Action Inquiry' approach to teaching and action researching: Through integral first-, second-, and third-person methods in education. In S. Esbjorn-Hargens, J. Reams, & O. Gunnlaugson (Eds.), *Integral education: New directions in higher education*. Albany: SUNY Press.
Stone, D., Patton, B., & Heen, S. (2000). *Difficult conversations: How to discuss what matters most*. New York: Penguin Books.
Taylor, S. S. (2012). *Leadership craft, leadership art*. New York: Palgrave MacMillan.
Taylor, S. S. (2013). Little beauties: Aesthetics, craft skill, and the expereince of beautiful action. *Journal of Management Inquiry, 22*(1), 69–81.
Taylor, S. S. (2015). *You're a genius: Using reflective practice to master the craft of leadership*. New York: Business Expert Press.
Taylor, S. S., & Carboni, I. (2008). Technique & practices from the arts: Expressive verbs, feelings, and action. In D. Barry & H. Hansen (Eds.), *The SAGE handbook of new approaches in management and organization* (pp. 220–228). London: Sage.
Taylor, S. S., Rudolph, J. W., & Foldy, E. G. (2008). Teaching reflective practice: Key stages, concepts and practices. In P. Reason & H. Bradbury (Eds.), *Handbook of action research* (2nd ed., pp. 656–668). London: Sage.
Torbert, W. R. (1972). *Experimental learning compared to previous learning theories Learning from experience – Towards consciousness*. New York: Columbia University Press.
Torbert, W. R. (1973). *Learning from experience: Toward consciousness*. New York: Columbia University Press.
Torbert, W. R. (1976). *Creating a community of inquiry: Conflict, collaboration, transformation*. London: Wiley.
Torbert, W. R. (1987). *Managing the corporate dream: Restructuring for long-term success*. Homewood: Dow Jones-Irwin.

Torbert, W. R. (1991). *The power of balance: Transforming self, society, and scientific inquiry.* Newbury Park: Sage.
Torbert, W. R. (1994). Cultivating postformal adult development: Higher stages and contrasting interventions. In M. E. Miller & S. R. Cook-Greuter (Eds.), *Transcendence and Mature Thought in Adulthood: The Further Reaches of Adult Development* (pp. 181–203). Lanham: Rowman & Littlefield.
Torbert, W. (1997). Developing courage and wisdom in organizing and in sciencing. In S. Shrivastva (Ed.), *Organizational Wisdom and Executive Courage* (pp. 222–253). San Francisco: The New Lexington Book Press.
Torbert, W. R. (2000a). The challenge of creating a community of inquiry. In *Transforming social inquiry, transforming social action* (pp. 161–188). New York: Springer.
Torbert, W. R. (2000b). Transforming social science: Integrating quantitative, qualitative, and action research. In F. Sherman & W. Torbert (Eds.), *Transforming social inquiry, transforming social action: New paradigms for crossing the theory/practice divide* (pp. 67–91). Norwell: Kluwer Academic Publishers.
Torbert, W. R. (2013). Listening into the dark: An essay testing the validity and efficacy of collaborative developmental action inquiry for describing and encouraging transformations of self, society, and scientific inquiry. *Integral Review: A Transdisciplinary & Transcultural Journal for New Thought, Research, & Praxis, 9*(2), 264–299.
Torbert, W. R., & Rogers, M. P. (1972). *Being for the most part puppets: Interactions among men's labor, leisure, and politics.* Cambridge, MA: Schenkman Publishing Company.
Torbert, W. R., & Taylor, S. S. (2008). Action inquiry: Interweaving multiple qualities of attention for timely action. In P. Reason & H. Bradbury (Eds.), *Handbook of action research* (2nd ed., pp. 239–251). London: Sage.
Torbert, W. R., et al. (2004). *Action inquiry: The secret of timely and transforming leadership.* San Francisco: Berrett-Koehler.
Velmans, M. (2009). *Understanding consciousness.* London: Routledge.

Further Reading

The Power of Balance. (William R. Torbert, 1991) – Torbert's mid-career masterwork that is the first full articulation of action inquiry, including a robust theory of power, as well as telling the story of his efforts (with successes and failures) to use Action Inquiryas a leader earlier in his career.

Action Inquiry. (William R. Torbert & Associates, 2004) – The final, mature articulation of Action Inquiry including tools, techniques and many different examples.

Eros/Power. (Bradbury & Torbert, 2015)–A jointly told Action Inquiryinto the nature of love, friendship, gender, and power over the course of the two authors' lives.

79 Eric Trist: An American/North American View (The Second Coming)

Paul D. Tolchinsky, Bert Painter, and Stu Winby

Abstract

Eric Lansdown Trist was born in 1909 and died in June 1993 in Carmel, California. Eric lived in a golden age of organization thinking and experimentation. While small in physical stature, Eric was a giant in his thinking and influenced many of the most prominent practitioners and theoreticians in his generation and the next in organization theory and organization design. The list of his protégé's reads a little like the subjects of this book. Those who knew him and learned from him were forever changed by his presence and thinking. This chapter reflects on Eric's second trip to the USA and North America, from the middle 1960s until his death. After experiencing America during the Great Depression, Eric returned to the UK, to carve out his career and explore the world of work and the social psychology of people at work. He loved America and often found himself defending her to his colleagues. When the opportunity came in the mid-1960s, invited by Lou Davis at UCLA, Eric returned and left an indelible imprint on his generation and the one to follow. Those of us who view organization design as our calling owe it mostly to Eric and his inspiration.

With special thank you to William Pasmore and Susan Wright

P.D. Tolchinsky (✉)
Performance Development Associates, Scottsdale, AZ, USA
e-mail: paultolchinsky@gmail.com

B. Painter
Consulting Social Scientist and Filmmaker, Bowen Island, BC, Canada
e-mail: bertpainter@gmail.com

S. Winby
SPRING Network LLC, Palo Alto, CA, USA
e-mail: paultolchinsky@gmail.com

D.B. Szabla et al. (eds.), *The Palgrave Handbook of Organizational Change Thinkers*,
DOI 10.1007/978-3-319-52878-6_27

Terms like "industrial democracy," "open systems," and most importantly "sociotechnical systems" became mainstream notions because of Eric. He pioneered the notion of organization ecosystems and predicted the turbulence of the last half of the twentieth century, with his colleague Fred Emery. Eric lived and breathed "action research" and "action learning. He fervently believed that the wisdom in the organization could solve most anything (a theme you might hear in other chapters, as well). Each person had a voice, and each voice had to be heard.

Keywords
Action learning • Action research • Sociotechnical systems • Open systems thinking • Industrial democracy • Jamestown • Rushton coal mine • Labour Canada • Quality of worklife • Turbulent environment • Self-managing work systems • Principle of redundancy • Adaptive work systems • Adaptive ecologies • Time to market • Ecosystems • Organization environments

Contents

Introduction

Eric Trist described his life as having roughly five phases, the first four in Britain and the last being in North America. *"The first phase was becoming a social psychologist with the study of the social and psychological factors in long-term unemployment in Dundee; the second was really in group dynamics, which I learned during the war and afterwards in a psychoanalytic context; third came the sociotechnical system ideas from the coal project; and the fourth, development of the idea of socio-organizational ecology which dates from a joint paper with Fred Emery on 'The Causal Texture of the Organizational Environment'"* (Emery and Trist 1967).

The fifth phase extended from 1966, Eric's appointment at UCLA, until his death in 1993. It was, in the view of these authors, his most productive years. During this span of approximately 30 years, Eric managed to write or inspire three books, several treatises on the Quality of Worklife and Socio-technical Systems, and numerous articles on the topic of organization design and organization ecology. He spawned an entire movement in the area of Quality of Worklife [or the Ecology of Worklife as it came to be known in the USA]; inspired labor organizations to participate in the co-creation of the workplace, in partnership with management; gave birth to a profession of "theory bound" practitioners in the field of organization design and organization change; and managed to write about the future we have today, in 2016!

Since Eric passed away in 1993, there have been numerous articles, chapters, video tributes, DVD's and even one book written about Eric (Trahair 2015; Kleiner 1996; Weisbord 2012 3rd Edition; Painter 1994). Given the wealth of reading material, both by Eric and others, it is difficult to find more to say about a man who influenced so many of us. We want to begin this article on the late 1960s and 1970s, picking up where Trahair (2015) leaves off in the story of Eric and his contributions to organization behavior, theory, and practice, the "second coming," if you will. Eric visited the USA in the 1930s, touring the USA and spending significant time in New England and the west coast. He returned to UCLA, at the invitation of Lou Davis in the mid-1960s, then moved to the University of Pennsylvania at the invitation of Russell Ackoff, lived for a short time in Minneapolis then moved to York University in Toronto at the invitation of Harvey Kolodny, and retired to Gainesville Florida and finally to Carmel, California, where he passed away.

Paul first met Eric at General Foods, in 1975, as a young, brash, internal consultant to the new product line start-ups. Eric had been hired to coach the leaders and guide the introduction of this more democratic, socially and technically integrated workplace. Eric impressed Paul as an unassuming Brit, almost frail, with a shy smile and enormous gift of inquiry. He was the first academic, research, practitioner Paul had ever met! He talked like a British laborer and connected with working class outrage, irony, empathy and unique humor, and profanity. At times, Eric could be in deep thought that he would run late to everything. He walked everywhere, often getting lost, and distracted by his own thought processes.

Influences and Motivations: Making the World a Better Place

Eric was a product of two world wars, although he was quite young during the first war. He lived through the Great Recession, and a period of great social upheaval and unrest. Eric was trained in group dynamics, psychoanalysis, and social psychology. As a group therapist, he could feel the energy within a group and could easily reflect what was from the heart and what was not.

In his first trip in the USA, Eric was struck by the socialist and communist movements. He empathized with the plight of workers. Eric saw the consequences of dysfunctional systems.

As a trained social psychologist, Eric engaged in appreciative inquiry, long before the term was invented by Cooperrider and others (1987). He was fully invested in the moment, always making you feel as though you were the only person in his universe. He was the consummate social psychologist, enamored with the workplace and making it better. He was not, nor did I ever hear him espouse to be, a business man or an engineer… although he was comfortable around both.

Eric was a tremendous listener, with the capacity to "hear" at multiple levels. In meeting, after meeting I attended with him, he could listen, cut through the words, and reflect immediately what was really important to individuals. As such, he had a deep empathy for people (much as others of his generation, i.e., Kathie Dannemiller).

In the mid-1940s, Eric saw a better way of managing the workplace (nearly stumbled on it, as some would say). A democratic approach that could lead to unparalleled performance. He spent his life testing and preaching this vision, building a worldwide network of devoted associates (including Kurt Lewin, Douglas McGregor, Eliot Jacques, William McWhinney, Bob Tannenbaum, and Fred Emery to name just a few), and mentoring disciples (such as Cal Pava, William Pasmore, Stu Winby, Bert Painter, Susan Wright, and multitudes more). This group, led by Eric, laid the groundwork for management innovations in the 1980s (many of which still exist in 2016 as elements of "holocracy" and "teal" organizations).

One of the most profound lessons to influence Eric's thinking and that of those he touched came from the now famous studies of the coal mines in the 1950s. The lessons Eric learned he applied over and over again. Two things stand out. First, the catalyst for the change was technology. This is still true today, possibly even more so. In 1949, a new technology to allow continuous longwall mining (vs. traditional hand-got methods) had been introduced. This technology was introduced differently in some locations than others. In mines that had problems installing the technology, engineers simply told miners how they should organize themselves and what to do. In mines where the technology was more productive, leaders enabled miners to decide for themselves how to organize the work. The more participative approach enabled a form of teamwork and self-control that had been lost in the "engineered" mines. Second, the teams literally designed themselves, what Trist and Ken Bamforth (his research colleague at the time) called "responsible autonomy" (Trist and Bamforth 1951). The results of the research were clear and significant, yet they were ignored by the British Coal Board, which refused to support self-organized approaches to mining. This resistance to new and more productive work arrangements that feature a shift of power from management to workers continues very much today and is something that drove Eric to fight for the rights of workers his entire life.

Eric had a tremendous affection for coal miners. He often related the story of the Rushton coal mine project outside of Philadelphia, PA. From Eric's perspective Rushton and his work with both Warren Spinks (owner/operator) and the United Mine Workers (Arnold Miller, President of the United Mine Workers of American) was a very meaningful experience for at least two reasons. First, of course, it brought back memories of his Durham days. And secondly, although the initial stages of the project were actually quite successful for both the workforce and the owner, it did break down over time. Union members were divided in whether or not to extend the autonomy to the rest of the mine. A myriad of issues arose, from perceived inequities to exclusion from some of the higher-paying jobs and experienced miners benefiting more than less senior coworkers. In the end, even the research team practices were called into question, 12 years later. Eventually the mine closed and the debate about what might have been continued (Goodman 1979).

Twenty-five years after the work in British mining, we witnessed the impact this had on Eric, many times within different client systems, as we worked with Eric in facilitating the design of several different production sites. Both his ability to connect with and relate to workers and his cautious way with leaders, who could undermine this shift in power, enabled Eric to inspire and motivate these around him.

Key Contributions: An Amazing Legacy

Eric (and his closest colleague, Fred Emery, who is also profiled in this collection of essays) gave the field terms and concepts that were both new and energizing. Terms like "industrial democracy," "open systems," and most importantly "sociotechnical systems" became mainstream notions because of them. Eric and Fred believed that organizations were living systems, and that as such, coped with turbulence by "generating their own order" from the bottom up. Eric treated every organization as an ecosystem that lived in relationship to the world around and the world within. In the coal mines, it was physical and visceral – the roof would collapse if workers did not have the skills and authority to do something about it, even if it was not part of their job description. In these organizations, Eric sought to build in the capacity of the people themselves to learn and change the system when it needed to change versus waiting to be told.

Let us explore several of Eric's contributions.

Each Person Has a Voice and the Ability to Influence

The notion of self-organizing: given the data, people will coalesce around solutions that will amaze you. Eric believed fervently that the wisdom in the organization could solve most anything. Each person had a voice, and each voice had to be heard. Combining these multiple realities into one cohesive solution was the most powerful way forward. This was true whether the workers were experienced in operating the technology or newly hired. "Greenfield" sites, started from scratch with new, self-organizing workforces, were among the most productive of all of the organizations that followed the sociotechnical system paradigm.

Open Systems and Systemic Thinking

In their seminal piece, "The Causal Texture of Organizational Environments" (see volume III: Trist/Tavistock Anthology 1997), Emery and Trist established that "the functioning of an organization can only be understood in its transactional relations with its environment." Further, the "environmental contexts in which organizations exist are themselves changing, at an increasing rate and towards complexity. As a result, one can only view, design, and adapt organizations with from a systemic perspective. Not seeing the whole enables what you do not see to undermine and potentially negate the rest (a sociotechnical point of view). It was important, in Eric and Fred's view, that organizations be designed with the capacity to adapt to whatever changes threatened their existence. This thinking was influenced by Ashby's law of requisite variety, which held that no biological system could survive a change in its environment without the ability to adapt to that change (Ashby 1957).

Sociotechnical Systems

Eric's greatest contribution to the field of organization behavior and design is in the understanding of the relationship between social systems and technology. Eric's insights into the interdependencies between these two concepts continue to influence and guide organization designs. Today many of those designers are software developers and knowledge workers who intuitively understand the dynamic relationship between the human system needs and requirements, the requisite technology, and the processes created to turn inputs into outputs.

The second principle of sociotechnical systems (shared first by Fred and expounded on by Eric) is the principle of redundancy of functions. *Any component system has a repertoire that can be put to many uses, so that increased adaptive flexibility is acquired. While redundancy of functions* (the essence of agility and adaptive systems) *holds at the biological level, as for example in the human body, it becomes far more critical at the organizational level where the components – individual humans and groups of humans – are themselves purposeful systems. Humans have the capacity for self-regulation so that control may become internal rather than external. Only organizations based on the redundancy of functions have the flexibility and innovative potential to give the possibility of adaptation to a rapid change rate, increasing complexity and environmental* uncertainty (International Conference on QWL and the 1980s, Toronto 1981). In practical terms, this often meant that workers should be multiskilled and broadly knowledgeable rather than able to perform only a single task or function.

Action Research or Action Inquiry

Three of the many definitions for action research are a "systemic inquiry that is collective, collaborative, self-reflective, critical and undertaken by participants in the inquiry" (McCutcheon and Jung 1990, p. 148); "a form of collective self-reflective inquiry undertaken by participants in social situations in order to improve the rationality and justice of their own social or educational practices, as well as their understanding of these practices and the situations in which these practices are carried out" (Kemmis and McTaggert 1990, p. 5); and "action research aims to contribute both to the practical concerns of people in an immediate problematic situation and to the goals of social science by joint collaboration within a mutually acceptable ethical framework" (Rapoport 1970, p. 499 as cited in McKernan 1991, p. 4).

Within all these definitions, there are four basic themes: empowerment of participants, collaboration between researchers and those in the system, acquisition of knowledge, and social change. The process that the researcher goes through to achieve these themes is a spiral of action research cycles consisting of four major phrases: planning, acting, observing, and reflecting (Zuber-Skerrit 1991, p. 2).

Put simply, action research is "learning by doing" – a group of people identify a problem, do something to resolve it, see how successful their efforts were, and, if not satisfied, try again. While this is the essence of the approach, there are other key attributes of action research that differentiates it from common problem-solving activities that we all engage in every day. A more succinct definition is,

> "Action research...aims to contribute both to the practical concerns of people in an immediate situation and to further the goals of social science, simultaneously. There is a dual commitment in action research to study a system and concurrently to collaborate with the members of the system in changing it into what is regarded as a desirable direction. Accomplishing these twin goals requires the active collaboration of researcher and client, and thus it stresses the importance of co-learning as a primary aspect of the research process" (Susman and Trist, SESS, 417–450). Eric rarely had a "plan" other than to engage with the client in an action research process, to discover what was next and how to proceed.

Eric believed, in his heart, that people should create their own futures and that people inherently knew the best answers and approaches; the notion is that no one knows better than those doing the work.

Academic/Researcher/Practitioner

Eric taught many of us coming out of the university in the late 1960s and 1970s the importance of teaching and continuous learning. He was a unique combination of the two. Always questioning and documenting, the researcher and writer part came easy. Applying the theory and testing it in reality were something else. Eric believed, as his mentor Kurt Lewin did, that "nothing is as practical as a good theory."

Eric's thinking and work first took hold in Procter and Gamble in the 1960s. Introduced to his concepts by McGregor, Procter embraced the notion of "open systems" and built their first sociotechnically designed factory in Augusta Georgia in 1963 (Kleiner 1996, p. 67). Augusta was so successful that by 1967, Procter had mandated that all new factories be designed this way.

In 1973, Eric began, what would be a 5-year effort, with the Jamestown Area Labor-Management Committee. Over this time frame, Eric and his doctoral students visited Jamestown regularly, helping to implement Joint Labor-Management Committees in the local factories in addition to a regional Area Labor-Management Committee to provide oversight and encouragement to local businesses and labor leaders. Eric found that having the commitment of this overall body had a stabilizing effect. Local small projects would go up and down, but they would hold because of the committee.

Jamestown was the first small town where innovative industrial cooperation took place. Over time, Jamestown became synonymous Labor-Management Innovation and cooperation. This effort was initiated by the then mayor, Stan Lundine. While he was Mayor, Jamestown received national attention for the labor-management strategy that Lundine implemented. Jamestown, which had long been a center of labor strife, became a national model for labor/management cooperation. Later as a Congressman, Lundine brought his labor/management ideas to Washington and was instrumental in developing legislation that created labor/management councils and employee stock ownership plans.

While Jamestown heralded a new way of collaboration and the Quality of Worklife movement, it also highlighted one of Eric's greatest frustrations: traditional resistance to these principles was always evident in these relationships. Acceptance to these principles was too tentative to alter the conventional management practices or encourage trade unions to divert their attention from traditional collective bargaining issues such as security and job seniority.

This led Eric to what he called "the function of a continuant." Introduced publicly in Oslo in 1987, the term came from a book on logic by W. E. P. Johnson, the Cambridge philosopher, written in 1924. Eric had a new use for it, namely, the need for a point of stability in a change-making organization. Today we call these joint groups "steering committees" or as John Kotter refers to them, "guiding coalitions."

Labour Canada: Quality of Worklife Takes Hold

Beginning in the early 1960s, Eric made frequent visits to Canada, for work and for pleasure – he said he had a "love affair" with Canada. After Eric moved to the University of Pennsylvania, his visits to Canada became more numerous, particularly for extensive work with Alcan at its smelter in Arvida, Quebec. During the 1970s, Eric consulted also with various federal government departments, including the federal Treasury Board, an interdepartmental system that aimed to promote public service-wide quality of worklife (QWL) practices. Eventually, in February 1977, Eric began his work as an advisor to a small QWL unit with the Canadian federal Department of Labour, promoting QWL ideas across Canada.

For the next 10 years, across Canada, Eric applied his master "network builder" skills in conferences, workshops, speeches, and films, encouraging grassroot innovation in quality of working life in individual workplaces, and, increasingly, in community-based developments. In Trist's words, the "new field of inquiry" was the extension of action research methods beyond the primary work system in individual organizations to the broader scale of "whole organizational systems" and "macro-social" contexts.

The application of this ecological framework depended upon center-periphery partnerships, where many of the "new directions of hope" to respond to the pressures of turbulent environments were to be found in the hinterlands of society. Thus, in Canada, Eric built on his experience from Jamestown, New York, and Craigmillar, Scotland, to help foster future-oriented development projects with employers, local and provincial governments, trade unions, educators, and individual citizens involved in joint efforts to revive their own communities in outlying regions of Canada such as Sudbury in Northern Ontario and in Cape Breton, Nova Scotia, on the Maritime coast.

Indeed, it was no accident that during the extended period of his engagement with Labour Canada, Eric "retired" from the University of Pennsylvania in 1978 and became Professor of Organizational Behavior and Social Ecology in the Faculty of Environmental Studies at York University, Toronto. Within this combination of academic and practitioner roles, Eric applied and developed new concepts of "management in turbulent environments," extended "search conference" methodologies throughout Canada, and in his last full-time teaching years at York was introducing an entirely new program on the study of the future.

At the peak of his involvement in Canada, Eric gave the closing address at the second International Conference on the Quality of Working Life in Toronto in 1981. Eric's theme was the re-thinking of QWL to take into account growing unemployment in developed economies, the emergence of knowledge work, and the impact of the microprocessor revolution. This was Eric Trist as a quiet but insightful "revolutionary...able to break out of old thought-systems and usher in a new paradigm" (Bennis 1978, p. 60). It was also the conviction of a person of intense passion with a nonjudgmental affection and devotion to the dignity of "the working man" (Painter 2016; Toronto 1981).

New Insights: Foreseeing the Future

If Eric were here today, he would likely be amazed at how right he and Fred got it, back then! Eric and Fred foresaw the turbulence of the 1970s and beyond as early as 1967 in their article... they began to write about "the salience of a turbulent environment." They predicted that the levels of interdependence, complexity, and uncertainty were rising so fast that traditional institutional forms would not be able to adapt or keep up. The notions of agility and adaptation, were first outlined in The Causal Texture of Organizational Environments, Human Relations, 20 (1967), pp. 199–237.

Eric held the view that "the more complex, fast-changing, interdependent but uncertain world growing up in the wake of the second industrial revolution is rapidly rendering obsolete and maladaptive many of the values, organizational structures and work practices brought about by the first. In fact, something like their opposite seems to be required. This is nowhere more apparent than in the efforts of some of the most sophisticated firms in the advanced science-based industries to decentralize their operations, to debureaucratize their organizational form and to secure the involvement and commitment of their personnel at all levels by developing forms of participatory democracy (Edinburgh 1971).

In the late 1980s, Eric again was early in identifying the value chain as a broader unit of analysis of the technical system, before the craze of reengineering. He defined the need for cross-functional, self-managing structures to align with parts of the value chain, like order fulfillment or product generation. Eric saw the necessity of STS to move upstream to product development and played a role in improving time to market performance by organizing complex human relations issues through new collaborative work designs. He understood the issues of task interdependence between functions and how empowered integrated teams could help manage coordination issues.

Eric continually sought the answer to the question, "how can we create adaptive ecologies in the workplace?" Twenty years later, in Silicon Valley, we can see that the new emerging work innovation is a self-managing work system that is comprised of members of the ecosystem who work together to improve the customer experience by linking wearable devices and big data technology from the customer to the multifunctional ecosystem work system. In the Valley the ecosystem is the new organizing unit. This essentially is a sociotechnical system.

Another innovation pervasive in the Silicon Valley and spreading worldwide is adaptive production systems which again have roots in Eric's work. Increasing turbulent environments requires increasingly more adaptive work organizations. Adaptive systems have highly attuned sensing and sense-making processes and the ability to rapidly prototype new solutions. These adaptive systems learn to fail fast, fix things quickly, and continuously interact with their ecosystems.

Eric was able to foresee the issues that would face society and organizations into the twenty-first century. Time to market, getting to market quickly, and really understanding what enables and gets in the way of moving faster were among these. He saw the world "speeding up" as far back as the mid-1970s. Further, as chaos occurs and situations become less predictable and faster, He saw the need for systems that can move as fast, become reconfigurable, and adaptive to the new situations.

Today, in 2017, in the world of digital the unit of analysis is the ecosystem. When you map a process (as Eric and Fred envisioned it), the touchpoints are other companies and function within them. The system contains multiple companies and multiple players, an ecosystem, or a constellation, much bigger than conceived by others during their time.

He foresaw the impact of the commuter age and the Internet.

He recognized that organizations were a part of an ecosystem. Today the boundaries between organizations have become blurred. Customers are competitors, and suppliers not exclusive and the product development, ideation to implementation cycles, are highly integrated across organizational boundaries. Design has become as much about the ecosystem of the organization, as it is about the roles, boundaries, interfaces, and interdependencies within the organization.

Unfinished Business: A Legacy of Things to Think About

To those who knew him, Eric was prone to depression and self-recriminations. People would describe him as humble to a fault. Often Eric felt that he had not had much of an impact and that his work made little difference. As he reflected on the world, it seemed to him that society had made little progress, even when the solutions were very obvious. Perhaps he never recovered fully from the rejection of his ideas by the British Coal Board in the 1960s.

Sometimes too trusting, often overlooked, he was Periodically not credited for his contributions to their thinking by colleagues like Elliott Jacques and Lou Davis (Pasmore 2016; Winby 2016). Academics viewed him as a competitor, while Eric always saw the opportunity for collaboration. Even trade unions did not always trust Eric's intentions and would renege on promises or fall back to traditional thinking. Eric, on the other hand, rarely criticized the ideas of others, instead finding the nugget or gem within that he could take and build on in an appreciative, helpful way.

One of Eric's greatest frustrations was the lack of sustainability of the changes he had helped introduce, even when these changes were demonstrably better than the old ways. Eric was at his best and most dynamic self when he was on the shop floor or in meetings with those doing the work. He was not a salesman nor particularly dynamic in a meeting with senior managers. As a result he worked a lot at the periphery of organizations, where he could affect the most change. The higher he tried to take his ideas, the more resistance he experienced. In the end, Eric could not explain how to make change happen (at the highest levels in a system) or how to embed it into the fiber of the organization.

Eric felt, toward the end of his life, that we had lost the thread that he had started with and that was the human condition. As the sociotechnical approach become more popular, it also become more codified and routinized. The core for Eric was unleashing the human spirit and human potential. Eric was reflecting on the "dark side," the "destructive" side of the human species. This darker perspective reflects perhaps Eric's own sense of not having accomplished as much as he would have liked, as well as his acknowledgement of what he saw as the challenges ahead (Wright 2016).

Full of self-doubt, Eric never got the academic recognition he deserved, even while publishing over 250 articles (either as sole author or in collaboration), numerous books, and working papers plus hundreds of speeches and guest lectures.

Conclusion

An important relationship in Eric's life was with his "best student" as Eric would fondly refer to Cal Pava. Cal met and studied under Eric at Wharton, and then later when Cal taught at Harvard, both he and Eric had ongoing collaborations and meetings. Cal extended social technical system theory and practice into the area of nonlinear work design and office work. He evolved social technical systems thinking by introducing such concepts as "deliberations" as a new unit of analysis for nonlinear work. In this respect, Cal was doing what Eric wanted, which was to evolve social technical system theory and practice beyond the manufacturing focus it had had over the last several decades. In the twilight of Eric's last years, unfortunately, Cal became gravely ill with an incurable brain tumor. Eric went to Stanford hospital in December of 1992 and spent an afternoon with Cal which became a seminal moment for Eric.

During the last few years of Eric's life, he was concerned that STS would fade away and never achieve the promise he felt it deserved. But during the last year of his life, he realized that his work was assimilated into the modern organization, that much of what he predicted were the issues of the day in management and organization science (Winby 2016). Cal Pava's work (1983) which was being integrated into Silicon Valley companies like Apple and Hewlett Packard, along with extensive use of STS concepts and practices in manufacturing and product development areas. The same holds for today, where STS has evolved into new models of work organization integrated with digital strategy.

In 1987, Eric went into semiretirement in Gainesville, Florida, with his wife Beulah, best friend, companion, secretary, and assistant on many projects (Weisbord 2012). In the last years of his life, he dedicated himself to his final and perhaps most lasting gift to us *The Social Engagement of Social Sciences: The Tavistock Anthology*, Volumes I and II with H. Murray (1990, 1993). The University of Pennsylvania would not publish Volume III. It was finished by Fred Emery (1997) and foretells of more than we are even aware of today.... Fred originally wanted no part in the SESS... seeing it as a look backward, and not about the future. When he finally read the first two volumes, he commented they were "even more amazing than I ever believed."

He died on June 4, 1993, in Carmel, California, at the age of 83. His close colleague Fred Emery died 4 years later, in Canberra, Australia, on April 10, 1997.

Many have described the importance of the relationship Eric and Fred Emery had. "Polar opposites" is the phrase Marv Weisbord (Productive Workplaces) used as an apt description. Eric would rarely take a compliment or credit, without acknowledging his kinship with Fred. Eric was fond of saying, Fred "was the smartest person I ever met!" Without Fred, much of the codification of Eric's thinking would be lost.

Finally, we would leave you with Eric's closing comments in his International Conference on QWL in the 1980s speech in Toronto, Canada, in 1981:

> *We must continue to create jobs of high quality and bring into being organizations and communities through new paradigms that provide the enabling conditions for such jobs to*

come into existence in both the market and social economies. Otherwise we are not likely to fare too well in countervailing the turbulent environment that increasingly surrounds us! How prescient. His challenge and legacy remain.

References

Ackoff, R., & Emery, F. E. (1972). *On purposeful systems: An interdisciplinary analysis of individual and social behavior as a system of purposeful events*. Chicago: Aldine-Atherton.

Ashby, W. R. (1957). *An introduction to cybernetics*. New York: Wiley.

Brown, S., & Eisenhardt, K. M. (1999). *Completing on the edge: Strategy as structured chaos*. Boston: HBR Press.

Cooperrider, D., & Srivastva, S. (1987). Appreciative inquiry in organizational life. *Research in Organizational Change and Development, 1*, 129–169.

Emery, F. E. (1972). Characteristics of socio-technical systems. In L. E. Davis & J. C. Taylor (Eds.), *Design of jobs* (pp. 157–186). Penguin Books.

Emery, F. E., & Trist, E. I. (1967). The causal texture of organizational environments. *Human Relations, 20*, 199–237.

Emery, F. E., & Trist, E. I. (1975). *Toward a social ecology: Contextual appreciations of the future in the present*. New York: Plenum Publishing.

Goodman, P. S. (1979). *Assessing organizational change: The Rushton quality of work experiment*. New York: Wiley.

Kemmis, & McTaggert. (1990). *The action research reader* (3rd ed.p. 1). Geelong: Deakin University Press.

Kleiner, A. (1996). *The age of heretics: Heroes, outlaws, and the forerunners of corporate change*. New York: Doubleday Publishing.

McCutcheon, G., & Jung, B. (1990). Alternative perspectives on action research. *Theory into Practice, 29*, 144–151. Merriam, S. B. (1988).

McKernan J. (1991). *Curriculum action research. A hand book of methods & resources for the reflective practitioner*. London, Kogan Page.

Painter, B. (2016). Personal conversations and interviews.

Painter, B. (1994). "Engineering for Commitment", 48-minute historical documentary on the Socio-Technical Design of Work. http://www.moderntimesworkplace.com/ for this and other articles and case studies from Eric Trist.

Pasmore, W. (2016). Personal conversations and interviews.

Pava, C. H. P. (1983). *Managing new office technology – An organizational strategy*. London: Free Press.

Rapoport, R. N. (1970). Three dilemmas in action research. *Human Relations, 23*(6), 499–513.

Susman, G., & Trist, E. I. (1993). Action research in an American underground coal mine. In *The social engagement of social science: A tavistock anthology. Volume II, the social technical perspective* (pp. 417–450). Philadelphia: University of Pennsylvania Press.

Trahair, R. (2015). *Behavior, technology, and organization development: Eric Trist and the Tavistock Institute*. New Brunswick: Transaction Publishers.

Trist, E. I. (1971). *A socio-technical critique of scientific management*. A paper contributed to the Edinburgh Conference on the Impact of Science and Technology.

Trist, E. I. (1979a). New directions of hope: Recent innovations interconnecting organizational, industrial, community and person development. *Regional Studies, 13*, 439–451.

Trist, E. I. (1979b). *Referent organizations and the development of inter-organizational domains* (pp. 23–24). 39th Annual Convention of the Academy of Management (Atlanta, 9/8).

Trist, E. I. (1981). *The evolution of socio-technical systems: A conceptual framework and an action research program*. Occasional paper no. 2, Ontario Quality of Working Life Centre.

Trist, E. I., & Bamforth, K. W. (1951). Some social psychological consequences of the longwall method of coal-getting. *Human Relations, IV*(1), 3–38.

Trist, E. I., & Murray, H. (1990). *The social engagement of the social sciences: A tavistock anthology. Vol. I: The social-psychological perspective*. Philadelphia: The University of Pennsylvania Press.

Trist, E. I., & Murray, H. (1993). *The social engagement of the social sciences: A tavistock anthology. Vol. II: The social-technical perspective*. Philadelphia: The University of Pennsylvania Press.

Trist, E. I., Emery, F., & Murray, H. (1997). *The social engagement of the social sciences: A tavistock anthology. Vol. III: The social-ecological perspective*. Philadelphia: The University of Pennsylvania Press.

Weisbord, M. R. (2012). *Productive workplaces: Dignity, meaning and community in the 21st century, 25th anniversary, Emery and Trist refine the workplace* (3rd ed.pp. 167–202). San Francisco: Jossey-Bass.

Winby, S. (2016). Personal conversations and email exchanges. Palo Alto.

Wright, S. (2016). Personal conversations and correspondence.

Wright, S., & Morley, D. (Eds.). (1989). *Learning works: Searching for organizational futures, a tribute to Eric Trist*. Toronto: The ABL Group, York University.

Zuber-Skerritt, O. (ED.) (1991). Action research for change and development. *Journal of International Development*, Wiley + Sons, V3.

Further Reading

International conference on QWL and the '80s. (1981). Toronto.

Lawrence, P., & Lorsch, J. (1969). *Developing organizations: Diagnosis and action*. Reading: Addison-Wesley Publishing.

Pasmore, W., Francis, C., Haldeman, J., & Shani, A. (1982). Sociotechnical systems: A North American reflection on empirical studies of the seventies. In *Human relations*.

Rothwell, W. J., Stavros, J. M., Sullivan. R. L., & Sullivan, A. (Eds.). (2009). *Practicing organization development* (3rd ed.).

Steele, F. (1975). *Consulting for organizational change*. Amherst: University of Massachusetts Press.

Tichy, N. M. (1974). Agents of planned social change. Congruence of values, cognitions and actions. *Administrative Science Quarterly, 19*(2), 164–182.

Tichy, N. M. (1975). How different types of change agents diagnose organizations.*Human Relations, 23*(5), 771–779.

Tichy, N. M., & Nisberg, J. N. (1974). Change agent bias. What they view determines what they do. *Group and Organization Studies, 1*(3), 286–301.

Trist, E. (1978). On sociotechnical systems. In W. Pasmore & J. Sherwood (Eds.), *Sociotechnical systems: A sourcebook*. San Diego: University Associates.

Haridimos Tsoukas: Understanding Organizational Change via Philosophy and Complexity

80

Demetris Hadjimichael

Abstract

Haridimos ("Hari") Tsoukas is a Greek organizational theorist whose work has been influential in introducing and popularizing a holistic, process-based conception of organizational change. Traditional accounts of change assume that entities (including organizations) are by nature static and only undergo change after external force is applied. In contrast, Tsoukas maintains that change is ever-present in the social world and that change itself is the intrinsic basis for organizing. As such for Tsoukas, organizations are not static entities but ongoing processes of organizing, embedded within social nexuses of practices and discourses, which are constantly mutating. He identifies two main sources of organizational change: (i) the world being an open-system and (ii) the reflexive agent. The assumptions and conclusions underlying his work have been strongly influenced by interpretative, phenomenological, and process philosophy, as well as complexity theory. To acquaint the reader with his ideas and work, the chapter is structured as follows: first it will describe Tsoukas' background, secondly it will summarize his key contributions to understanding organizational change, and thirdly it will discuss new insights from his work and it will conclude with his work's legacies and unfinished business.

Keywords

Organizational change • Process philosophy • Phenomenology • Interpretivism • Routines • Discourse • Reflexivity

D. Hadjimichael (✉)
Warwick Business School, University of Warwick, Coventry, UK
e-mail: phd15dh@mail.wbs.ac.uk

D.B. Szabla et al. (eds.), *The Palgrave Handbook of Organizational Change Thinkers*,
DOI 10.1007/978-3-319-52878-6_96

Contents

Introduction

Heraclitus famously remarked that "everything changes and nothing abides." This dictum may be argued to hold for both the physical and social strata of our world (see Prigogine 1992). On a physical level, change is evident, for instance, in the different geological layers of our planet. Each layer took millennia to form and signifies vastly different environmental circumstances overtime. On a social level, constant change is even more rapid. This is testified by both the constant mutation of different social institutions over the course of human history (e.g., tribalism, democracy, feudalism, communism, and capitalism) and by the endogenously created instability of each social institution (e.g., ever-changing financial and political circumstances in twentieth-century Capitalism) (e.g., see Cunha and Tsoukas 2015). On a micro-social level, that of the individual, change is apparent in the life history of each person which essentially is influenced by the evolving circumstances that exist during one's time. Ongoing change is something that Professor Haridimos Tsoukas came to recognize through his research and the trajectory of his own life. This may be illustrated by how his interest in exploring, thinking, and writing about organizational change had emerged through his life experiences.

Influences and Motivations: The Process of Becoming

Haridimos Tsoukas was born in 1961 in the small mountainous town of Karpenisi, in central Greece. He is often simply referred to as Hari, which is the Greek short form of the name Haridimos. He was the eldest child among three kids. His father worked as a shop keeper and his mother as a dressmaker. He grew up in a loving family, whose motto was "education, education, education." Family narratives of poverty, the Nazi occupation of Greece, the Greek civil war (1945–1949), and the persecution of left-leaning citizens after the end of the civil war (and the victory of the Right) shaped his upbringing. When the military dictatorship in Greece collapsed and democracy returned in 1974, Hari was in his early adolescence (13 years old).

He spent his late adolescent and early student years in an intensely politicized atmosphere, and as he admits, it has been impossible for him to shake off his long-held interest in politics and current affairs. As a student, he was involved in the left only to realize soon that his love of independent, open-ended thinking could not find a hospitable habitat in closed ideologies and intellectually unsophisticated political parties of the left. In the course of time, he came to describe himself as a progressive or communitarian liberal in the manner of Philip Selznick (2002). Civic engagement has always been important to him. As an intellectual, he always thought it important to contribute to public dialogue through his writing of opinion articles in Greek newspapers, a practice he begun even from his early student days through publishing a local newspaper in his home town.

Hari was originally educated as an electrical and industrial engineer. During the early-to-mid-1980s, he studied engineering on both an undergraduate (Ptychion) and postgraduate level (M.Sc.), at the Aristotle University of Thessaloniki (Greece) and the Cranfield University (United Kingdom), respectively. As he admits he was an "unhappy engineer by discipline" during the period of his undergraduate studies, and between 1985 and 1990, he grasped the opportunity to defect to the social sciences by undertaking a Ph.D. in organizational sociology at the Manchester Business School. While there, he received the Tom Lupton Doctoral Research Scholarship. During this time, he was supervised by the late Professor Tom Lupton, who subsequently retired, and his supervision was undertaken by Dr. Alan Thomas. His doctoral thesis was a piece of organizational sociology – "Explaining work organization: A realist approach (Tsoukas 1989a)" – involving the study of two plants, a chemical plant in northern Greece and another in northern England. Since his undergraduate days, he was strongly interested in the theory of knowledge, which later intensified during his doctoral research. The course on epistemology, on the first year of the Ph.D. program at the Manchester Business School run by Professor Richard Whitley, influenced him deeply. His concern with philosophy of science was manifested in the subtitled of his doctoral thesis ("A realist approach") – his research was explicitly based on a realist epistemology (Bhaskar, Harre), through which he attempted to explain the differences in the work organization of the two plants.

Another important influence during his doctoral years was the late Professor Stafford Beer – one of the leading post-World War II cyberneticians (Beer 1981). As he himself acknowledges, Hari took from Professor Beer a keen interest in systems, complexity, and cybernetics, which he has retained to the present day. Other intellectual influences were anthropologist Gregory Bateson (1979) and the philosopher Cornelius Castoriadis (2005). As Hari notes, from Bateson he learned to appreciate communication, metaphor, and connectedness, while he owes to Castoriadis his appreciation of indeterminacy and creative praxis. Looking back at his own intellectual development, he sees a decisive shift from rationalistic modes of thinking toward a greater appreciation of language, interpretation, and process. His encounter with the work of the late Professor John Shotter made him discover the eye-opening philosophies of Wittgenstein and Bakhtin while developing later an acute interest in phenomenology, existentialism, and Aristotelian philosophy. His strong interest in philosophy is evident throughout his work. Perhaps the best description of his own intellectual making is provided by him as follows (slightly paraphrased, see http://www.htsoukas.com): "I am not a philosopher but can't help but see everything from a philosophical point of view. I am not a complexity scientist but can't help but approach everything in terms of Gregory Bateson's memorable phrase "the pattern that connects." And I am not a politician but, as an engaged citizen, can't help but be passionate about the affairs of the 'polis'."

Between 1988 and 1990, he became an associate fellow of management studies at the University of Manchester. From 1990 until 1995, he was appointed as a lecturer in organizational behavior at the University of Warwick. Following 1995, he became an associate professor of organization and management at the University of Cyprus (1995–1998) and at the ALBA Graduate School (1999–2000). He was offered his first professorship at the University of Essex (1998–2000), which was followed by professorships at ALBA (2001–2003) and the University of Strathclyde (2000–2003). Since the early 2000s, thanks to his growing reputation and dedication to his profession, he was appointed as a scientific advisor to the Association of Chief Executive Officers in Greece and as a book series editor for the series "Management" by Kastaniotis Publishers in Greece (since 2003) and as series coeditor for "Perspectives on Process Organization Studies" by Oxford University Press (since 2010). Between the years 2003 and 2008, Hari became the editor in chief of the highly regarded journal *Organization Studies*. In conjunction with the above, Hari was promoted to George D. Mavros Research Professor of Organization and Management at ALBA (2003–2009). Throughout his career, Hari remained a strong believer in being an active citizen. As such, he regularly comments on Greek and Cypriot politics in major national media (i.e., currently "To Vima"; previously "Kathimerini," "EconomikosTachidromos") and his personal blog Articulate Howl (www.htsoukas.blogspot.co.uk – where he writes in Greek) (see Tsoukas 2015b). In 2015, to stay faithful to his beliefs on being an active citizen, he unsuccessfully ran for the Greek Parliament with a newly created social-democratic party.

As can be seen from the above, Hari has grown into becoming a highly esteemed member of the field of organizational and management studies. In 2009, his fascination with the notion of constant change led him to co-found (with Ann Langley) the annual International Process Symposium to which he has been a co-convener ever since. Currently he holds the positions of the Columbia Ship Management Professor of Strategic Management at the University of Cyprus (since 2010) and the Distinguished Research Environment Professor of Organizational Studies at the University of Warwick (since 2003). While holding these positions, apart from serving as the Dean of the Faculty of Economics and Management of the University of Cyprus (2012–2016), he received numerous awards for his teaching and research. Specifically, for the last 11 years Hari, has consistently received the Best MBA Teacher Award from Warwick Business School. Additionally, in 2014, he was awarded a higher doctorate (D.Sc.) from the University of Warwick in recognition of his lifetime contribution to his field of scholarship. Two years later, he was made the 18th EGOS Honorary Member and awarded the Joanne Martin Trailblazer

Award from the Academy of Management to recognize his work's contribution to organization and management theory, especially process thinking. During the same year, he was awarded the Cypriot Research Award from the Cypriot Research Promotion Foundation, in acknowledgment of conducting high-quality research in the Republic of Cyprus.

Key Contributions: Weaving Together Philosophy and Management

The aim of this section is twofold: firstly, I attempt to unpack the concepts that Hari uses to account for organizational change by referring to his research and influences; and secondly I seek to exemplify how his theoretical work enables a holistic understanding of organizational change. Indeed, the assumption that change is both perpetual and inherent in the social stratum is one of the most central aspects of Hari's research on organizational change. This is because this notion seems to underlie all the four pillars he relies on to account for change in organizations, which he and Robert Chia have termed as "organizational becoming" (Tsoukas and Chia 2002). The four pillars Hari builds on are (i) process, (ii) discourse, (iii) performativity, and (iv) the socially embedded self-reflexive individual. Despite referring to these concepts separately, it should be kept in mind that Hari's key contributions to understanding organizational change lay in their creative synthesis, which I seek to demonstrate below.

Process

Tsoukas (2012, p. 70) takes the ontological position that social phenomena (e.g., organizations) are not predetermined entities that await discovery via the utilization of quasi-Newtonian reasoning (see also Weick 1979). On the contrary, social phenomena are assumed to be the emerging interweavement of actions of sentient agents that have both intended and unintended consequences (Cunha and Tsoukas 2015, p. 229; Tsoukas and Chia 2011). He argues that to understand social phenomena in-depth (including organizational change), one must conduct detailed studies of the flow of activities in situated and temporal contexts (Langley et al. 2013; Tsoukas 1989b, 2009b, 2012, 2016b). Of course, the lack of determinacy in social interaction does not imply that the latter occurs randomly (i.e., without order/logic) (Tsoukas 2005b, p. 73). This is due to the fact that any interaction is inherently a part of both a broader social context as well as a local situation (Tsoukas 1998a, b). What this suggests is that although agents do not automatically execute a set of deterministic rules imposed on them by a social structure (Garud et al. 2015), these interactions are nevertheless regulated by tacitly attending from shared social expectations and understandings to the exigencies of each situation at hand (Dionysiou and Tsoukas

2013; Tsoukas 1996, 1998a, 2011). This understanding leaves open the possibility that new interactions may give rise to creative adaptation of what is socially expected, and this in turn may create new possibilities for future action which prior to an occurrence was unthinkable (Tsoukas and Chia 2002).

Hence, before Hari considers organizations, he sees that human action is essentially an ever-mutating flux of interaction (Tsoukas 1998b). Based on this, it is evident that he does not prioritize stability, to be able to conceptualize change (Tsoukas and Dooley 2011). In other words, he does not see change as a "fait accompli," but as a phenomenon that is always present. As such, he sees organizations as "secondary accomplishments" (Tsoukas and Chia 2002, p. 570). In Tsoukas and Chia (2002, p. 570) words: "Change must not be thought of as a property of organization. Rather, organization must be understood as an emergent property of change. Change is ontologically prior to organization." Put simply, change is the very condition for the existence of organizations – organization at large stabilizes human interaction. Nevertheless, despite their differences in ontological order, change and organizations are both conceived to share a similar nature: they are unfolding *processes* in which mutation over time is a given (Tsoukas 1998b).

Discourse

In their present form, organizations exist to impose order and hence direct the incessant flux of human interaction toward certain ends. They do so by imposing socially instituted rules and meanings on their members (Castoriadis 2005; Tsoukas 1998b; Tsoukas and Hatch 2001). By drawing on Weick (1979), it is asserted that organizations offer their members "a set of [generic] cognitive categories," which are meant to orient them in unfolding situations (Tsoukas and Chia 2002, p. 571). For example, the category "patient" is used in medical practices to signify that a person under this generalization requires treatment (Tsoukas 2016b, p. 149). Sharing categories is achieved by exposing organizational members to a specific way of talking about things – a discourse (Rorty 1989, p. 6; Taylor 1985b, p. 23; Tsoukas and Hatch 2001, p. 239). Discourse is given to members in narrative form (organized in stories) (see Bruner 1991). Thanks to this form, they are enabled to perceive what is salient in situations (Tsoukas 1998a). Each discourse highlights a specific aspect of the world that is tied to what is of importance to the community that uses it and, as such, signifies specific states of affairs and appropriate activity (Tsoukas 1998c, 2005a). This is because each discourse is centered around an imagery (see Shotter and Tsoukas 2011). For example, the development of chaos theory signifies that the until now dominant Newtonian imagery which had assumed that the cosmos is ordered and stable is simply one way of examining and thinking about it (see Tsoukas 1998b). The legitimation of the chaotic discourse essentially allows scientists to seek to understand the cosmos in ways unthinkable in the Newtonian conception. The reason is that the underlying imagery of the cosmos in chaos theory is one of unstable, dynamic, nonlinear behavior which is radically different from the Newtonian.

Performativity

Over time, agents take the organizational discourse and the way it presents the world (imagery), for granted, and engage in a patterned (i.e., organized) typology of actions. The performances that fall under a pattern of action for the sake of accomplishing an organizational goal are more commonly referred to as routines (Dionysiou and Tsoukas 2013; Weick 1979). But routines, like discourse, are seen at best only as "emergent accomplishments" (Feldman 2000). This is because they both have an element of stability and change. Both are open to modification, adaption, or even erosion (Tsoukas 2005a, p. 101). It should be noted, however, that language (which includes cognitive categories) and performance (i.e., practice/activity) are mutually constituted – if one changes so does the other (Tsoukas 2005a, p. 99).

The change of cognitive categories and routines can be explained by their contact with the world (Tsoukas and Chia 2002). In the world (which includes the organization) it is impossible to have definitional closure, because it is an open system (Prigogine 1992; Tsoukas 2016a). The world is an open system because events (especially in the social stratum) do not always follow a predetermined pattern – they are subject to unpredictable variation (Tsoukas 1989b, 1998b, 2013). In Tsoukas' (2016b, p. 145) words: "first-time events are not exception but the rule in human life." New events present members with new sets of circumstances. The uniqueness of the circumstances always has an element which has neither been articulated nor dealt with before (see Shotter 2011; Shotter and Tsoukas 2011). Hence, to express and deal with the new features of situations, organizational members must create new distinctions (Tsoukas 2009a, p. 942). To do so, they draw and apply existing cognitive categories and routines in new ways (Tsoukas and Chia 2002). If the new ways of expression and behaving are taken up by a number of people in the organization – this leads to new knowledge and organizational change (Tsoukas 2005a, p. 99, 2009a). Therefore, the constant performance of improvisation is required for the function and maintenance of the organization. This renders the organization as a process that is perpetually becoming something that it previously was not (Tsoukas and Chia 2011, p. 9; Weick 1993).

To illustrate the above, consider the ever-changing moving-in routine of the housing department of a U.S. university studied by Feldman (2000) and later discussed by Tsoukas and Chia (2002). Initially, the department specified that students could move into the university's halls of residence during three specific days at the beginning of the academic year. This routine resulted in angering the students and their parents, because it caused long queues and traffic jams. Their complaints triggered the department to change its routine in the following semesters. Specifically, an administrator was appointed to liaise with the local police department to manage traffic during those days. In parallel to this measure, new rules were instituted for the moving-in days. Cars stopping to unload in front of the halls were restricted to do so for just half an hour, and other specific parking spaces were allotted for the moving-in days. Change did not stop there. During a later year, the university's team was scheduled to play during the first move-in day. Because this caused serious complications to the housing department's process, further refinements were made to the department's routines. They decided to also liaise with the sports department prior to those moving-in days to ensure that they do not have a similar clash in the future.

Reflexive Agent

Of course, improvisation and thus change, cannot happen automatically. Sentient, knowledgeable individuals are required for organizations to perform effectively and achieve change in the light of the uncertainty and singularity of new circumstances (Sandberg and Tsoukas 2011, p. 342; Shotter and Tsoukas 2014b; Tsoukas 1996). According to Yanow and Tsoukas (2009), by relying on social/organizational significations, people are habituated to behave in certain ways (see also Tsoukas 2015a, p. 63). The habituation implies that when dealing with routine situations, people do so nonreflexively (Sandberg and Tsoukas 2011). Despite their nonreflexivity, their behavior always draws on collectively established significations of their social context (Shotter and Tsoukas 2014b, pp. 383–385; Tsoukas 1996). For example, when helping a customer with a common phone issue, an experienced employee is solicited by the situation to respond in a polite and helpful manner (as befits speaking to a customer) without having to think about it (Tsoukas and Vladimirou 2001). But, in unexpected situations, performances which under normal instances are fluid – break down.

Performance breaks down because the employee is likely to be "reflecting on" how to best deal with the unfamiliarity of the situation (Sandberg and Tsoukas 2011, pp. 344–346). But even in non-typical situations where the person is called upon to improvise, like in routine behavior, she/he necessarily draws on socially "established distinctions and standards of excellence" (Tsoukas 2015a; Yanow and Tsoukas 2009, p. 1345). The magnitude of a breakdown is related to how severe the unexpected situation is, and this in turn relates to the modification of the routines/categories required (Tsoukas 2016b; Tsoukas and Chia 2002). If the situation is only minimally different to a typical situation, then the employee is likely to only momentarily "reflect in action" and marginally adapt the normal procedure to deal with it. However, when the breakdown is a major deviation from typical situations, the employee is likely to have to "reflect on action" so as to find a new and appropriate ways to deal with the situation (Yanow and Tsoukas 2009). Consequently, one may see instituting a combination of a certain discourse, and a set of appropriate behaviors is not entirely pointless due to the open-endedness of the world (see Tsoukas and Dooley 2011). They both serve as the basis for their "imaginative extension" in ways that serve the organizational cause (Tsoukas and Chia 2002).

However, it should be noted that change is not only the result of organizational members encountering non-typical and unexpected situations (Tsoukas and Dooley 2011). People are inherently generators of organizational change (Tsoukas and Chia 2002). This is because agents are not simply puppets for the organization to achieve its goals. As explicated above, they are reflexive and, in addition, are emotional beings that have corporeality (Tsoukas 2005b, p. 380). Reflexivity is tied to narrative thinking, and this implies that all narratives have a narrator (Tsoukas 1998a; Tsoukas and Hatch 2001, p. 248). Due to their social nature, humans are reflexive narrators. Consequently, they can replicate what they do as agents in the form of stories. But far from being slaves to their perceptions and existing narratives, they can narratively reorganize what they perceive in ways that new possibilities for action are illuminated (MacIntyre 2007; Tsoukas and Hatch 2001). Therefore, due to having their own interests and views about the workplace, they themselves may use new narrative forms which in turn may serve as catalysts for change. In other words, they can exercise their ability to self-reflect (Yanow and Tsoukas 2009), so as to adapt their behavior by revising previously held beliefs in the light of new experiences (Tsoukas and Chia 2002).

An excellent example of the role of sentient individuals as a source of organizational change is the case of Rebecca Olson analyzed by Shotter and Tsoukas (2014a). Olson was appointed as the new CEO at a hospital in the United States. Shortly after her appointment, she realizes that along with the hospital's financial problems, she had to deal with a case of sexual harassment that had been ignored by her predecessor. The reason the case was ignored, despite the existence of an official process for dealing with such complaints was that the harasser was a member of a powerful family which could potentially cause problems to any CEO in the specific hospital. On top of that, it was not only one person that complained about the harasser but several over a sequence of years. Notice that like her predecessor, she could have opted to ignore the case and just focus on the financial aspect so as not to jeopardize her job. However, one of the victims, like Rebecca, had a physical disability. This spontaneously made her feel empathy for the victim. The "blend [of] judgment [disapproval] and feelings [disgust]" about the situation moved Rebecca to act against the harasser (Shotter and Tsoukas 2014a, p. 233). Unlike other similar cases she had dealt with in her previous work experience, the uniqueness of the circumstances predisposed her to approach this situation cautiously. For instance, she did not fire the person on the spot or take him to a tribunal. Due to the harasser's influence, she spent months deliberating and talking with people across the hospital. With this, over time she managed to acquire enough leverage to force the harasser to resign.

One can see that the actions of two single individuals and the inaction of several others effected change on the specific organization. In the case of the harasser, his influence and the inaction of other members allowed him to enact sexual harassment – undisturbed – in the organization for several years. This of course, changed the hospital's (not to mention his victims') morale and what behaviors were perceived as tolerable. However, with the intervention of the new CEO, she manages to change the status quo of the organization and reiterate that such behavior is unacceptable. Notice that to impose this change, she was not guided by the indifferent "processing" of hospital regulations (Taylor 1993). The process involved the unfolding of embodied emotions, reflection, and judgement. Her actions were the result of attending from what she considered to be socially accepted to how that type of behavior made her feel and think and consequently weave her narrative (Shotter and Tsoukas 2014a, p. 228).

In summary, by applying Hari's conceptual framework, it is noticeable that organizational change is not related to a particular aspect of an organization – but to the organization as a whole. The social realm is seen as an ever-evolving flux of human interaction that mutates on the basis of the nonlinear evolution of its institutions. Organizations are created to order the flux toward achieving a certain goal. Although, organizations are created to impose order, they are not stable entities. On the contrary, they are bundles of processes of organizing that are gradually differentiating their language (e.g., customer satisfaction, sales figures) and routines (e.g., safety, disciplinary procedures). Two reasons are identified as the main drivers of change. The first is the open-endedness of the world, which gives rise to unpredictable variation. Due to this, organizations are constantly called upon to deal with aspects of situations they have not dealt with before. As such, to deal with the uniqueness of each situation, they must "generate singularities" – tweak their practices and create new terminology to categorize arising peculiarities (Tsoukas 2016b, p. 246). The second is related to the organization's members. Specifically, as self-reflexive beings that experience the world emotionally via their bodies, they are seen to have their own perspective on how the organization "ought" to be. Therefore, by experiencing new situations, these may cause them to reflect on their beliefs. By doing so they may find that they would like the organization to be otherwise narratively rearrange events and thus take action that aims to change the organization (e.g., creation of new routines, organization of strikes, leadership initiatives). However, for any of the two discussed reasons to effect change, potential variations in routines or discourse must be taken up by a significant number of members of an organization.

New Insights: Beyond Determinacy and Rationalism

The new insights that can be derived from Hari's work on organizational change stem from the fact that it affords us to see this phenomenon in a completely new light. His work introduces a postmodern conception of the world (see Toulmin 1992, 2001), which emphasizes that "change is a fundamental ontological category of lived experience and that organization is an attempt to order and stabilize the intrinsic flux of human action" (Tsoukas 2005a, p. 101). Although, this view may be more accepted in the present, it was not common in the management literature when Hari started working with it in the 1990s. The vast majority of the management literature approached social phenomena (including organizational change) from the Cartesian-cum-Newtonian ontological perspective of static entities causally impacting each other (Shotter and Tsoukas 2011, p. 334). This perspective has been dominant for a very long time – its lineage can be traced as far back as Plato and Aristotle (see Tsoukas 1998b). In addition to the aforementioned perspective's assumption of "stasis" (being static), the literature on organizational change and strategy approached both from a rationalist perspective where they were portrayed as the result of premeditated planning (see Tsoukas and Chia 2011, pp. 8–9). The two most popular approaches that have relied heavily on rationalism and the ontology of determinacy to conceptualize organizational change are the behaviorist and cognitivist (Shotter and Tsoukas 2011, p. 334; Tsoukas 2005a). To understand how Hari's work spurred new developments in theory and research on organizational change, this section is structured as follows: I shall first briefly summarize how organizational change had been researched by the behaviorist and cognitive approaches prior to the popularization of Hari's work, and then I will aim to show how later research has incorporated Hari's insights.

One of the earliest and most prominent advocates of the behaviorist approach of organizational change is Kurt Lewin. This approach's underlying assumptions suggest that change is "episodic" and "other-directional" and that what is changed are objects with specific structures which can be calculatingly altered (Tsoukas 2005a, pp. 96–97). In particular, change is suggested to be essentially a sequence of movement between distinct states, e.g., moving from A to B and then to C (Tsoukas and Chia 2002, 2011, p. 9). Entities, such as organizations, are portrayed to be static by nature. Therefore, in this approach what is examined are the states but not the change that occurs between them (Tsoukas and Chia 2002). To effect change, a change agent (usually the management) must force a change on the organization by altering its members' behavior. The change agent can do so by issuing edicts that highlight a desired end which can be attained by the members behaving in a certain manner. To enforce edicts, change agents must rely on their hierarchical authority to reward or punish members. With the above rationale, it is obvious that the agents of change are seen as external forces that force organizations to change after considerable calculation on how to do so (Tsoukas 2005a).

Similarly, the cognitivist approach holds approximately the same assumptions about change as the behaviorist approach. However, the key difference between the two approaches lies with the fact that cognitivists focus on *why* people behave in certain ways (Tsoukas 2005a, p. 97). Behavior for them is a secondary phenomenon that depends on the meaning people have about something (see Healey et al. 2015). Meaning is equated with information processing. The latter is portrayed to mediate what a person perceives and how she/he responds to situations (for an extensive review, see Hodgkinson and Healey 2008). Information processing is seen to depend on a person's schemata of the external world (also referred to as representations). The latter are argued to be a form of stored knowledge which structures a person's perception of the world and the meaning it has for them. So, to enact organizational change, one must change the driver of behavior – the schemata. Merely applying a "stimulus-response" technique via the reinforcement or discouragement of behavior by rewarding or punishing people is highlighted to be inadequate (see Eden 1992, p. 261). Per the cognitivists, one must first understand individuals' schemata and then attempt to change them to successfully implement organizational change. Schemata are seen as measurable by using a technique referred to as cognitive mapping (see Pyrko et al. 2016). By doing so one can see the staff's beliefs and goals. Consequently, organizational change is again seen only as a matter of planning, applied in a series of steps by an external change agent (Eden and Ackermann 1998). Firstly measure the staff's schemata, secondly facilitate them to reflect and agree on "an aggregated map, and thirdly agree on a course of action for intervention" (Tsoukas 2005a, p. 97).

It is now easy to see the contrast of assumptions employed by the determinist-cum-rationalist perspective and Hari's as they are diametrically opposite. Whereas the first perspective holds that change is effected episodically on objects with determined structures (e.g., staff, behavior) by meticulous planning from external agents, the latter maintains that change is continuous and occurs intentionally and non-intentionally from within ever-mutating processes of organizing which rely on discursive distinctions that legitimize certain practices (Tsoukas and Chia 2002). These assumptions and the use of a process-cum-phenomenological language have opened up new avenues of researching organizational change by legitimizing the study of organizational discourses and practices as catalysts of change. For example, the *Journal of Organizational Change* had a special issue on how discourse is related to change in organizations, where Hari was called to write the afterword on how language matters in organizational change (Tsoukas 2005a). In this special issue, studies showed how discourse relates to organizational change and how a change of organizational routines relates to changes in discourse (e.g., see Anderson 2005; Tietze 2005). Similarly a further series of studies focusing on organizational change have further highlighted the role of marginal unplanned mutations in discourse, resources, and practices having cited Hari's work, ideas, and terminology (e.g., see Chiles et al. 2004; Feldman 2004; Reay et al. 2006; Weick et al. 2005).

Legacies and Unfinished Business: Different Language, Different World

Wittgenstein aptly remarked that "a picture held us captive. And we could not get outside it, for it lay in our language and language seemed to repeat it to us inexorably" (Wittgenstein 1986, para. 115). In the case of organizational change and organization studies, the picture of determinate entities with static natures has long held us captive (Tsoukas 2005a; Tsoukas and Chia 2002). This worldview paints a world of static objects and subjects that are locked together in quasi-causal relationships (Shotter and Tsoukas 2011). By uncritically adopting it, this perspective masks that the world is constantly subject to change and the process cannot be reduced to points on spatiotemporal lines. It masks what happens between the points and that change is not only effected from external forces (Tsoukas and Chia 2002, 2011). It masks that meaning is conceivable only from attending from the background of the vast nexuses of social meaning (Tsoukas 2005b, Chap. 16). It masks that change occurs from within the organization and that even Machiavellian change agents themselves are subject to change (Tsoukas 2005a).

The above is easily grasped if one realizes that no one, not even scheming change agents, possess what Thomas Nagel (1986) refers to as "the view from nowhere" – an objective, a-contextual, and a-temporal vantage point from which to peruse organizations and the world (Tsoukas 1997). Change agents and organizations themselves are immersed in social practices and imageries that orient them toward pursuing certain goals (Castoriadis 2005; Tsoukas 1998b). This is easily demonstrated by asking ourselves the question: toward what end is change consciously sought after by management of organizations that partake in modern capitalism? The answer is simple. It seeks to make the organization more efficient for it to attain the goal of infinite growth by infinitely reducing costs via the application of certain technological means (not necessarily material). If one accepts that societies institute certain goals which they take for granted and uncritically paint in positive colors (e.g., infinite growth and efficiency in modernity, God in the middle ages), then the notion of impartiality of change agents and organizations is a modern myth (Castoriadis 2005; Tsoukas 1997). A myth that was conceptualized in the Renaissance with Nicolai Copernicus's discoveries, the inception of Newtonian physics, and then popularized in the humanities by Descartes, Spinoza, and co; a myth which the Western world has enthusiastically strived to fulfil ever since. This myth's sphere of influence reached its climax in the first half of the twentieth century (e.g., the Vienna Circle, behaviorism, cognitivism) (MacIntyre 2007; Taylor 1985a; Toulmin 1992, 2001; Tsoukas 2011). But especially in the second half of that century, this view's accepted legitimacy had started to wane with the popularization of quantum physics, chaos theory, phenomenology, and re-engaging with pre-Socratic philosophers (Toulmin 2001; Tsoukas 1998b).

Following the above, the legacy of Haridimos Tsoukas lies with the fact that he has assisted in the making of a new worldview from which to examine organizational change. He has done so by helping scholars researching organizational change (and organization studies in general) to become familiarized with a new language early as the end of the 1980s (e.g., see Chiles et al. 2004; Feldman 2004; Garud et al. 2015; Reay et al. 2006; Weick et al. 2005). The language of complexity, phenomenology, and process philosophy are evident throughout most of his work (Tsoukas 1998b, 2016a; Tsoukas and Dooley 2011). In a recent keynote speech, he identified and urged researchers to import more vocabulary from the aforementioned fields in order to further investigate organizational change (Tsoukas 2015c). Specifically, these fields utilize an alternative language to describe emerging change, but process philosophy, in particular, has a unique way of signifying how temporality is linked to change (Garud et al. 2015, pp. 8–10). In his keynote address, Hari argued that especially the work of Herni Bergson can help us comprehend organizational change differently. As he noted:

> ...for Bergson and his interpreters...in the interest of action, attention is necessarily focused on the present, thus reducing the intensity of the whole past to a spatialized (extensive)

> conception of time. Insofar as we are typically interested in what we can do in the present, we assume that such a reduction is lasting, forgetting that the solidity of the actual is only apparent. However, the whole past does not go away. On the contrary, it may be selectively evoked in reconstructing present identity.

How does this help us better understand organizational change? As argued by Hari, it allows us to identify that organizational change is not only the result of deliberate managerial initiatives but also of a reality that is "continuous, indivisible, and qualitatively diverse," which unintentionally forges and reforges personal and organizational identities.

Hari identifies two promising avenues for future research on organizational change: firstly, he argues that we need to know more about how the past (societal, organizational, personal) influences how change is brought about by predisposing change agents and organizations to seek the attainment of certain goals. Secondly, and more importantly for Hari, new research should seek to adopt a language such as that used by Henri Bergson, William James, and Alfred North Whitehead (Tsoukas 2015c). This is because he argues that doing so would allow us to look beyond the ontology of static objects as implied in the language used to develop the until recently dominant stage-based models used that seek to account for organizational change. He is especially insistent on using a different vocabulary to think about phenomena because he takes seriously what Wittgenstein said over half a century ago: "the limits of my language mean the limits of my world" (Wittgenstein 2010, p. 74). Following numerous conversations with him, it is obvious to me that he is a fervent believer in the notion that the role of researchers in the social sciences is to push the boundaries of language to draw new distinctions that will allow us to perceive further nuances in our world or even to transform our view.

Conclusion

In conclusion, Hari has issued a call to arms – he is calling us to examine change and organizing from an entirely different perspective. By following the footsteps of his beloved philosophers – Cornelius Castoriadis, Charles Taylor, Alasdair MacIntyre, Richard Rorty, and Stephen Toulmin to name just a few – he has left us with a choice: we can follow suit and strive to cast off the shackles of the myths of modernity and take aim at creating new ways of perceiving the world (Tsoukas 1997, 1998b). Alternatively, we can continue to uncritically accept the mythology already in place in fear of anything different. Indeed, the new, the different – like the old can also prove to be a tyranny. Therefore, it should be stressed that Hari does not advocate blindly embracing different perspectives for the sake of them being different or new. Based on his political articles published in Greek media, he is acutely aware that dogmatism can only lead to sustaining old or creating new tyrannies of myths (see Tsoukas 2015b). By being lucky enough to have been Hari's student, I am certain that if he had to leave you with some remarks on how to further research organizational change or any other phenomenon, it would be to stay curious, be open-minded, and never stop being (self) critical.

References

Anderson, D. L. (2005). "What you'll say is...": Represented voice in organizational change discourse. *Journal of Organizational Change Management, 18*(1), 63–77.

Bateson, G. (1979). *Mind and nature: A necessary unity*. New York: E. P. Dutoon.

Beer, S. (1981). *Brain of the firm: The managerial cybernetics of organization*. Chichester: Wiley.

Bruner, J. (1991). The narrative construction of reality. *Critical Inquiry, 18*(1), 1–21.

Castoriadis, C. (2005). In K. Blamey (Ed.), *The imaginary institution of society*. Cambridge, UK/Malden: Polity Press.

Chiles, T. H., Meyer, A. D., & Hench, T. J. (2004). Organizational emergence: The origin and transformation of Branson, Missouri's musical theaters. *Organization Science, 15*(5), 499–519.

e Cunha, M. P., & Tsoukas, H. (2015). Reforming the state: Understanding the vicious circles of reform. *European Management Journal, 33*(4), 1–5.

Dionysiou, D. D., & Tsoukas, H. (2013). Understanding the (re)creation of routines from within: A symbolic interactionist perspective. *Academy of Management Review, 38*(2), 181–205.

Eden, C. (1992). On the nature of cognitive maps. *Journal of Management Studies, 29*(3), 261–265.

Eden, C., & Ackermann, F. (1998). *Making strategy*. Lodnon: Sage.

Feldman, M. S. (2000). Organizational routines as a source of continuous change. *Organization Science, 11*(6), 611–629.

Feldman, M. S. (2004). Resources in emerging structures and processes of change. *Organization Science, 15*(3), 295–309.

Garud, R., Simpson, B., Langley, A., & Tsoukas, H. (2015). Introduction: How does novelty emerge? In R. Garud, B. Simpson, A. Langley, & H. Tsoukas (Eds.), *The emergence of novelty in organizations* (pp. 1–24). Oxford: Oxford University Press.

Healey, M. P., Vuori, T., & Hodgkinson, G. P. (2015). When teams agree while disagreeing: Reflexion and reflection in shared cognition. *Academy of Management Review, 40*(3), 399–422.

Hodgkinson, G. P., & Healey, M. P. (2008). Cognition in organizations. *Annual Review of Psychology, 59*(1), 387–417.

Langley, A., Smallman, C., Tsoukas, H., & van de Ven, A. H. (2013). Process studies of change in organization and management: Unveiling temporality, activity, and flow. *Academy of Management Journal, 56*(1), 1–13.

MacIntyre, A. (2007). *After virtue: A study in moral theory* (3rd ed.). Notre Dame: University of Notre Dame Press.

Nagel, T. (1986). *The view from nowhere*. New York/Oxford: Oxford University Press.

Prigogine, I. (1992). Beyond being and becoming. *New Perspectives Quarterly, 9*, 4–11.

Pyrko, I., Dörfler, V., & Eden, C. (2016). Thinking together: What makes communities of practice work? *Human Relations*. http://journals.sagepub.com/doi/abs/10.1177/0018726716661040.

Reay, T., Golden-Biddle, K., & Germann, K. (2006). Legitimizing a new role: Small wins and microprocesses of change. *Academy of Management Journal, 49*(5), 977–998.

Rorty, R. (1989). *Contingency, irony, and solidarity*. Cambridge: Cambridge University Press.

Sandberg, J., & Tsoukas, H. (2011). Grasping the logic of practice: Theorizing through practical rationality. *Academy of Management Review, 36*(2), 338–360.

Selznick, P. (2002). *The communitarian persuasion*. Washington, DC: Woodrow Wilson Center Press.

Shotter, J. (2011). *Getting it: Withness-thinking and the dialogical...in practice*. New York: Hampton Press.

Shotter, J., & Tsoukas, H. (2011). Complex thought, simple talk: An ecological approach to language based change in organizations. In B. McKelvey, P. Allen, & S. Maguire (Eds.), *The Sage handbook of complexity and management* (pp. 333–348). Lodnon: Sage.

Shotter, J., & Tsoukas, H. (2014a). In search of Phronesis: Leadership and the art of judgment. *Academy of Management Learning and Education, 13*(2), 224–243.
Shotter, J., & Tsoukas, H. (2014b). Performing Phronesis: On the way to engaged judgment. *Management Learning, 45*(4), 377–396.
Taylor, C. (1985a). *Human agency and language philosophical papers* (Vol. I). Cambridge/London/New York/New Rochelle/Melbourne/Sydney: Cambridge University Press.
Taylor, C. (1985b). *Philosophy and the human sciences: Philosophical papers* (Vol. II). Cambridge/New York/Port Chester/Melbourne/Sydney: Cambridge University Press.
Taylor, C. (1993). To follow a rule . . .. In C. Calhoun, E. LiPuma, & M. Postone (Eds.), *Bourdieu: Critical perspectives* (pp. 45–59). Cambridge: Polity Press.
Tietze, S. (2005). Discourse as strategic coping resource: Managing the interface between "home" and "work". *Journal of Organizational Change Management, 18*(1), 48–62.
Toulmin, S. (1992). *Cosmopolis: The hidden agenda of modernity.* University of Chicago Press: Chicago.
Toulmin, S. (2001). *Return to reason.* Cambridge/Oxford, UK: Harvard University Press.
Tsoukas, H. (1989a). *Explaining work organisation: A realist approach.* University of Manchester: Manchester.
Tsoukas, H. (1989b). The validity idiographic explanations. *Academy of Management Review, 14*(4), 551–561.
Tsoukas, H. (1996). The firm as a distributed knowledge sytem: A constructionist approach. *Strategic Management Journal, 17*, 11–25.
Tsoukas, H. (1997). The tyranny of light: The temptations and the paradoxes of the information society. *Futures, 29*(9), 827–843.
Tsoukas, H. (1998a). Forms of knowledge and forms of life in organized contexts. In R. Chia (Ed.), *In the realm of organization: Essays for Robert Cooper.* London: Routledge.
Tsoukas, H. (1998b). Introduction: Chaos, complexity and organisation theory. *Organization, 5*(3), 291–313.
Tsoukas, H. (1998c). The word and the world: A critique of representationalism in management research. *International Journal of Public Administration, 21*(5), 781–817.
Tsoukas, H. (2005a). Afterword: Why language matters in the analysis of organizational change. *Journal of Organizational Change Management, 18*(1), 96–104.
Tsoukas, H. (2005b). *Complex knowledge: Studies in organizational epistemology.* Oxford/New York: Oxford University Press.
Tsoukas, H. (2009a). A dialogical approach to the creation of new knowledge in organizations. *Organization Science, 20*(6), 941–957.
Tsoukas, H. (2009b). Craving for generality and small-N studies: A Wittgensteinian approach towards the epistemology of the particular in organization and management studies. In D. Buchanan & A. Bryman (Eds.), *The Sage handbook of organizational research methods* (pp. 285–301). Los Angeles/London/New Delhi/Singapore/Washington, DC: Sage.
Tsoukas, H. (2011). How should we understand tacit knowledge? A phenomenological view. In M. Easterby-Smith & M. Lyles (Eds.), *Handbook of organizational learning and knowledge management* (2nd ed., pp. 453–476). Chichester: Wiley.
Tsoukas, H. (2012). Enacting reforms: Towards an enactive theory. In S. Kalyvas, G. Pagoulatos, & H. Tsoukas (Eds.), *From stagnation to forced adjustment: Reforms in Greece, 1974–2010* (pp. 67–89). New York: Columbia University Press.
Tsoukas, H. (2013). Organization as chaosmos. In D. Robichaud & F. Cooren (Eds.), *Organization and organizing: Materiality, agency and discourse* (pp. 52–65). New York/London: Routledge.
Tsoukas, H. (2015a). Making strategy: Meta-theoretical insights from Heideggerian phenomenology. In D. Golsorkhi, L. Rouleau, D. Seidl, & E. Vaara (Eds.), *Cambridge handbook of strategy as practice* (pp. 58–77). Cambridge: Cambridge University Press.
Tsoukas, H. (2015b). *The tragedy of the commons: Political wickedness, degradation of institutions, and bankruptcy.* Athens: Ikaros Books.

Tsoukas, H. (2015c). Thinking about organizational change as if change mattered: Insights from Bergson's process philosophy, ODC Division 2013 distinguished speaker. *Academy of Management ODC Newsletter*, (Winter), 10–15.
Tsoukas, H. (2016a). Don't simplify, complexify: From disjunctive to conjuctive theorizing in organization and management studies. *Journal of Management Studies, 54*(2) 132–153.
Tsoukas, H. (2016b). The power of the particular: Notes for an organisation science of singularities. In T. Corcoran & J. Cromby (Eds.), *Joint action: Essays in honour of John Shotter* (pp. 144–164). London/New York: Routledge.
Tsoukas, H., & Chia, R. (2002). On organizational becoming: Rethinking organizational change. *Organization Science, 13*(5), 567–582.
Tsoukas, H., & Chia, R. (Eds.). (2011). *Philosophy and organizational theory* (Research in organizational sociology, Vol. 32). Bingley: Emerald.
Tsoukas, H., & Dooley, K. J. (2011). Introduction to the special issue: Towards the ecological style: Embracing complexity in organizational research. *Organization Studies, 32*(6), 729–735.
Tsoukas, H., & Hatch, M. J. (2001). Complex thinking, complex practice: The case for a narrative approach to organizational complexity. *Human Relations, 54*(8), 979–1013.
Tsoukas, H., & Vladimirou, E. (2001). What is organizational knowledge? *Journal of Management Studies, 38*(7), 973–993.
Weick, K. E. (1979). *The social psychology of organizing* (2nd ed.). Reading: Addison-Wesley.
Weick, K. E. (1993). Organizational redesign as improvisation. In G. P. Huber & W. H. Glick (Eds.), *Organizational change and redesign* (pp. 346–379). New York: Oxford University Press.
Weick, K. E., Sutcliffe, K. M., & Obstfeld, D. (2005). Organizing and the process of sensemaking. *Organization Science, 16*(4), 409–421.
Wittgenstein, L. (1986). In G. E. M. Anscombe (Ed.), *Philosophical investigations.* (3rd ed.). Basil Blackwell: Oxford.
Wittgenstein, L. (2010). In C. K. Ogden (Ed.), *Tractatus logico-philosophicus*. Project Guttenberg: Urbana, Illinois. Retrieved from: https://www.gutenberg.org/files/5740/5740-pdf.pdf.
Yanow, D., & Tsoukas, H. (2009). What is reflection in action? A phenomenological account. *Journal of Management Studies, 46*(8), 1339–1364.

Further Reading

Tsoukas, H. (2005a). Afterword: Why language matters in the analysis of organizational change. *Journal of Organizational Change Management, 18*(1), 96–104.
Tsoukas, H. (2005b). *Complex knowledge: Studies in organizational epistemology.*Oxford/New York: Oxford University Press.
Tsoukas, H. (2015c). Thinking about organizational change as if change mattered: Insights from Bergson's process philosophy, ODC Division 2013 distinguished speaker. *Academy of Management ODC Newsletter,*(Winter), 10–15.
Tsoukas, H., & Chia, R. (2002). On organizational becoming: Rethinking organizational change. *Organization Science, 13*(5), 567–582.

Michael L. Tushman: A Practice-Informed Explorer and Organizational Scholar with a Focus on Viable Organizations

81

Sonja Sackmann

Abstract

This paper explores the contributions of organization theorist Michael L. Tushman to the field of organization change and development. The first section gives an overview of his early professional development and important professional stages followed by his key contributions to the field. These include his early focus on innovation and boundary spanning roles in innovation systems as well as an information processing approach for understanding and designing organizations also using network analysis. His quest for phenomena-driven and practically relevant work with a focus on the entire system and processes leads to the development of the congruence model – a general model to research, understand, assess, and further develop organizations. His work with doctoral students resulted in the punctuated equilibrium model that he applied to both organizations and technological changes as external forces of change. Another important contribution is his effort in solving Abernathy's productivity dilemma by developing the concept of ambidextrous organizations. These can deal with the apparent paradox of simultaneous exploitation and exploration. Ambidextrous organizations require, however, ambidextrous leadership – a concept that he explored in detail with his long-term colleague and friend Charles O'Reilley. The final section gives an overview of the many awards that he received up to this point as well as the way in which he worked. Most of his theories and frameworks were codeveloped with colleagues and doctoral students in a dialogical fashion. The paper closes with Michael Tushman's future concerns whether the developed theories, models, and recommendations regarding innovation will still hold in an increasingly web-based society.

S. Sackmann (✉)
Department of Economics, Management and Organization Sciences, EZO Institute for Developing Viable Organizations, University Bundeswehr Munich, Neubiberg, Germany
e-mail: sonja.sackmann@unibw.de

D.B. Szabla et al. (eds.), *The Palgrave Handbook of Organizational Change Thinkers*,
DOI 10.1007/978-3-319-52878-6_97

Keywords
Ambidexterity, ambidextrous organization, ambidextrous leader • Congruence model • Contradictions and paradoxes at the organizational level • Executive succession • Exploration, exploitation • Open system • Organizational evolution • Organizational innovation • Organizational transformation as punctuated change • Productivity dilemma • Punctuated equilibrium in technological change • Technological change, technological discontinuities

Contents

Introduction

Michael L. Tushman is an organization theorist who contributed and is still contributing to the theories of technological innovation and change as well as the design, management, and leadership of ambidextrous organizations. His most well-known and most influential work comprises the theory of punctuated change in technological innovation, leading change, organizational renewal, as well as the ambidextrous organization and the ambidextrous leader. His early work experience at General Radio and his work as a doctoral student with MIT Professor, Tom Allen, influenced him in that he wanted to have an impact as a research scholar and teacher in the real world. In all his endeavors, he was and still is motivated to solve Abernathy's (1978) "productivity dilemma (and associated paradoxical strategic challenges), innovation streams, ambidexterity, and senior teams" (Benner and Tushman 2015, pp. 497).

Rather than taking a functional approach, Michael Tushman always took an issue or problem focus in trying to develop theories that inform practice, teach those theories to students and executives, and learn from them to further enhance the development of viable theories, or discover in his observations of organizational issues, patterns that generate ideas for new theories. (Seong et al. 2015). Furthermore, most of his work was and still is collaborative work. As such, he was stimulated in his work by colleagues and especially doctoral students whom he inspired and most of whom became well-known scholars in their own right. Hence, Michael Tushman can also be considered a role model regarding the way in which he collaboratively generated and further developed his ideas, theories, and practice, in and for organizations who have to operate and survive in a complex world full of contradictions and paradoxes.

During his still very active professional lifetime, Michael Tushman received several awards and was recognized as an outstanding scholar (see last section). The following sections cover his influences and motivation for his work; his key contributions, especially regarding organizational change; new insights; his legacy; and the current focus in his research and executive teaching.

Early Influences and Motivations: A Quest for Relevant Work

Michael Tushman was born in 1947 in Worcester, Massachusetts, as the eldest of three children. His parents valued education but did not push him into any particular career. Even though his father was an engineer, his uncle who was a famous professor of materials sciences at MIT had a much bigger influence on Michael Tuchman's choices regarding his academic career.

At age 18, Michael Tushman started his studies in electrical engineering at Northeastern University in Boston. Being a co-op university at the time, he was able to earn money to pay for his education as well as get hands-on experience in this major field of study. His work experience at General Radio led directly to his interest in innovation and organizations. After receiving his BS in 1970 from Northeastern University, Michael Tushman decided to continue his graduate work in organizational behavior (OB) at Cornell University, which had a fine OB group and gave him a scholarship. Given his interest in organizations and innovation, he decided to pursue a PhD at the MIT Sloan School of Business in Organization Studies after having finished his MS in 1992 at Cornell. The Sloan School of Business had a great group of scholars in his area of interest at the time.

During his doctoral studies at MIT, Tom Allen and his work on social networks, organizations, and innovation had a great influence on Michael Tushman's early research direction and research, teaching, and practice as well as his values throughout his career. While Tom Allen was his chair, additional influences came from the members of his thesis committee Ralph Katz who worked on social systems, Paul Lawrence's and Edgar Schein's work in the area of organizational behavior, as well as Kurt Lewin's spirit and practical problem focus. Michael Tushman's thesis was entitled "Communications in Research and Development Organizations: An Information Processing Perspective."

His co-op work experience at General Radio (later renamed into GenRad), a broadline manufacturer of electronic test equipment, had lasting influences on him also during his doctoral work. In the early 1990s, the company experienced a financial crisis due to problems that had started with their entering the chip side of the testing market in the 1970s, due to a lack of focus on the mainstay board-testing business (www.fundinguniverse.com/companies-history/genrad-inc-history/) as well as increasing competition. These developments posed for Michael Tushman the puzzling questions *why* such a firm that employed many intelligent and excellent engineers could run into such financial problems that forced them to lay off a number of people.

During a job interview at Berkley University, Michael Tushman met Charles O'Reilly, who shared with him an interest in innovation and organizations, as well as an interest in connecting research to practice. This first meeting was the beginning of a still continuing friendship and very productive work relationship in the areas of research and executive education that lasts until today.

In 1976, Michael Tushman started his academic career as Assistant Professor of Business at the Columbia Business School in New York City. He became Associate Professor and Professor of Management in 1983. In 1982–1983, he went back to the MIT Sloan School of Management as Visiting Professor during his sabbatical. In 1989, he became the Phillip Hettleman Professor of Management. During this time, he developed productive work relationships with both colleagues and a number of doctoral students. Together with his colleague David Nadler, who became an assistant professor at Columbia Business School at the same time, Michael Tushman further explored the concepts of information processing (Tushman and Nadler 1978), organizational design and organizational architecture (Nadler and Tushman 1980), as well as frame bending (Nadler and Tushman 1989). Due to the interests of his doctoral students, Philip Anderson and Elaine Romanelli, he explored the topics of technological discontinuities (Tushman and Anderson 1986), organizational transformation as punctuated change (Romanelli and Tushman 1994), as well as the role of executive succession in turbulent times (Tushman et al. 1992).

In 1995–1998, Michael Tushman spent time as Visiting Professor at INSEAD, France. In 1998, he moved to Harvard Business School and in 1999 was appointed the Paul R. Lawrence MBA Class of 1942 Professor of Business Administration. He spent additional sabbaticals as Visiting Professor at MIT in 1996 and at Bocconi University, Milan/Italy, during 2010–2011. According to him, these sabbaticals deeply enriched his work and life as he mentioned in a personal conversation.

The collaboration with his colleagues David Nadler (Nadler and Tushman 1999) and especially with Charles O'Reilly and his doctoral students continued at Harvard. His work with his doctoral student, Mary Benner (Benner and Tushman 2003), continued to address and solve Abernathy's productivity dilemma (Abernathy 1978) by combining James March's concepts of exploration and exploitation (March 1991). This stream of research, in combination with the work at IBM during 2000 and 2008, inspired his work with James O'Reilley on tackling issues of organizational complexity by developing the concept and theory of ambidexterity (O'Reilly and Tushman 2004, 2008, 2016).

Michael Tushman's interest in teaching and working with many executives led to a number of teaching cases. These include Agrochemicals at Ciba-Geigy AG, the Swiss Watch industry, Greeley Hard Copy, SMA: Micro-Electronic Products Division, Corning Glass, Bedrock Productions, IBM, Compagnie Lyonnais, Artic Timber AB, BT Pl., Zurich Airport, Hema Hattangady and Conzerv, GE Money Bank, Lululemon, Zensar, HTC, as well as NASA.

Key Contributions: Taking a System's and Co-creation Approach to Developing Organization Theories, Models, and Frameworks

Michael Tushman contributed to the field of organization theory and change in his roles as practice-informed researcher and as teacher/educator/coach. The concepts and theories that he contributed to the field of organization theory and change are manifold. They include the importance of boundary spanning roles in organizations, the congruence model as a way of understanding and diagnosing organizations, the punctuated equilibrium model, technological innovation and change and the role executives play in change, as well as the concept of ambidextrous organizations that can deal with the contradictions inherent when combining exploration and exploitation in organizational designs. In addition, he promoted a phenomena-driven and process-oriented approach to the study and conceptualization of organizations.

In his role as teacher and educator, Michael Tushman developed and coached a number of doctoral students who became fine scholars in their own right such as Philip Anderson, Mary Benner, Adam Kleinbaum, Elaine Romanelli, Lori Rosenkopf, or Wendy Smith. He helped executives further improve their practice, and he codeveloped a large number of teaching cases some of which were mentioned above. In addition, the way in which he conducted his research and co-created organizational frameworks and models in a dialogical fashion can be considered a role model for developing the field of organization theory and change further (see the last section).

The following sections discuss these major contributions in more detail by taking a historical/biographical approach in their sequence as compared to starting with the one that received most citations.

Innovation and Boundary Spanning Roles in Innovation Systems

The topic of innovation as a means for organizational renewal and viability is a theme that runs through much of Michael Tushman's work. With his background in engineering, his early work as a researcher focused on the exploration of communication processes in research and development organizations with a focus on the innovation processes (Tushman 1977). This stream of research was based on the notion of organizations as open systems that need to be in exchange with their relevant environment and the critical issue of managing their boundaries. His research on innovation systems elucidated the importance of gathering and transmitting information to several external areas by special boundary roles that are contingent on the nature of the organization's work. His research results suggested a curvilinear relationship between the number of boundary spanning roles and project performance, in that too many boundary spanning roles may be redundant and actually impede coordination and control. Altogether, this stream of work supported the importance of taking a process-oriented perspective and creating linking pins across organizational boundaries both between the organization and its relevant environment as well as within organizations across functions and hierarchies.

Michael Tushman further specified the characteristics of boundary spanning individuals (Tushman and Scanlan 1981) as well as gatekeepers (Tushman and Katz 1980) and gatekeeping (Tushman and Katz 1982). He explored longitudinal effects of boundary spanning supervision on turnover and promotion in R&D (Tushman and Katz 1983) and contributed to the knowledge about communication networks in R&D (Tushman 1979). He also suggested ways to organize for innovation (Tushman and Nadler 1986) and manage strategic innovation and change (Tushman 2004).

Taking a (Information) Process Approach for Understanding and Designing Organizations

Designing organizations for long-term survival is a central problem in organizational change. At the time, most models of organizations and their research were static. In Michael Tushman's early work together with David Nadler, they suggested that organizations can be viewed as contingent information processing entities within the framework of open system theory. In their effort of dealing with work-related uncertainty, they considered critical tasks of organizations collecting, gathering, and processing information of all kinds on issues such as the functioning of different components, output quality, external technology, and market domains (Tushman and Nadler 1978). They proposed a contingency or fit model between information processing requirements facing an organization and its structural capacity in processing information, based on different kinds of coordination and control mechanisms as well as organic or mechanistic subunit designs. This work can be considered a pre-stage toward developing their congruence model of organizations.

A methodological contribution at that time was the use of social network analysis for the investigation of organizational issues (Tichy et al. 1979). The authors considered this method capable of capturing both prescribed and emerging processes as well as being a theoretical framework that both guide data collection and data analysis. Since then, network analysis has received wide attention in organizational analysis, especially with the growing importance of information (compared to material) flows, organizationaln processes and social networks.

Congruence Model

A central issue in organizational change is organizational analysis – the process of gaining an understanding of an organization's current mode of operation and its related problems, as a basis for deciding what kind of change is needed and most likely to be effective. In collaboration with David Nadler, Michael Tushman developed the congruence model as a general, dynamic model of organizations as shown in Fig. 1.

Their goal in developing this model was to reduce information complexity for managers. They wanted to help managers, "despite the mind boggling complexity

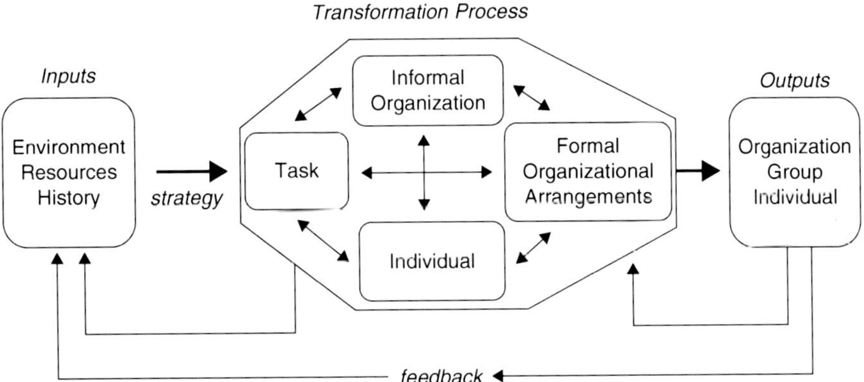

Fig. 1 Key components of the congruence model contingency model (Nadler and Tushman 1980, p. 47)

of organizations" (Nadler and Tushman 1980, p. 35) to "understand the behavior patterns of individuals, groups and organizations, to predict what kind of behavioral response will be elicited by various managerial actions, and finally, to use this understanding and these predictions to achieve control" (Nadler and Tushman 1980, p. 35). The congruence model indicates which kind of components is most important in unraveling "the mysteries, paradoxes and apparent contradictions that present themselves in the everyday life of organizations" (p. 36) and thus is a tool that guides managers and their own process in organizational problem analysis.

As mentioned above, this congruence model can be seen as an extension of their prior work on organizations as information processing systems. It is also based on the notion of organizations as open systems characterized with inputs that are transformed into outputs, including respective feedback loops. In addition to the key organizational input factors, Nadler and Tushman suggest critical features for the analysis of each key factor, such as what kind of demands does the environment make on the organization and on organizational action. In this model, they conceptualize strategy as "the stream of decisions about how organizational resources will be configured to meet the demands, constrains, and opportunities within the context of the organization's history" (p. 40).

Nadler and Tushman (1980) also define the four key organizational components with critical features for analysis. They conceptualized the informal organization as emerging arrangements with the following critical features: leader behavior, intra- and intergroup relations, information work arrangements, as well as communication and influence patterns. Regarding outputs, they differentiated the three levels of individual, group, and organization that contribute in combination to organizational performance. At the organizational level, they considered goal attainment, resource utilization, and adaptability the most critical.

As mentioned by Michael Tushman himself, he has been and still is using this model as a road map in his approach to organizations and in his work with executives in addressing their problems. The model is widely known as a useful framework in and for organizational diagnosis.

Organizational Evolution: The Punctuated Equilibrium Model

The work with his doctoral student, Elaine Romanelli, addressed the question of organizational evolution. With their general model of punctuated equilibrium at the organizational level, the researchers tried to integrate three existing frameworks of organizational evolution (population ecology, incremental, and transformational change) including predictive and nondeterministic models. Their model of punctuated equilibrium posits that organizations evolve through relatively long periods of rather stable, evolutionary phases called the equilibrium period. These are punctuated by short bursts of fundamental, discontinuous change characteristic for revolutionary periods. Revolutionary periods disrupt established activity patterns and create the basis for new equilibrium periods (Tushman and Romanelli 1985).

In testing the model, their research results refuted the idea that small organizational change could accumulate to produce nonrevolutionary transformations. Their data also revealed the mediating role of leaders, and especially executives, between these contrasting forces of change. More specifically, they found that major changes in the environment, as well as the succession of a CEO, significantly and positively influenced revolutionary transformations across three industries (Romanelli and Tushman 1994). Nevertheless, they considered these revolutionary transformations dangerous since they increase the risk for short-term failure.

Technological Change

Michael Tushman's work with his doctoral student, Philip Anderson, addressed the issue of environmental change building on the punctuated equilibrium model. More specifically, they investigated patterns of technological change as a major environmental force and their impact on environmental conditions that have an implication for organizations and their survival. They argued that technological progress is characterized by evolutionary, incremental changes punctuated by discontinuous, disruptive, radical change. These can be competence enhancing or competence destroying. The latter ones are associated with major changes in the distribution of power and control – both within firms and industries (Tushman and Anderson 1986). Their research revealed that the locus of technological innovations for competence-enhancing breakthroughs significantly differed from that of competence-destroying discontinuities.

Across three industries, Philip Anderson's data showed that competence-enhancing breakthroughs were significantly more likely to be initiated by existing firms, while new firms significantly more likely initiated competence-destroying breakthroughs. They also found that early adopters of technological breakthroughs grew more rapidly than the other firms and that successive competence-enhancing advances resulted in increased product-class maturity. Based on their findings, they suggested that technological discontinuities, regardless of being competence enhancing or competence destroying, may offer rare opportunities for competitive advantage for those firms that are willing to risk early adoption and hence are willing to take the risk of change under highly uncertain conditions. This stream of research led to recommendations for managing through cycles of technological changes (Anderson and Tushman 1991) and recommendations for organizational designs that influence technological process (McGrath et al. 1992).

Ambidextrous Organizations

In this stream of work, Michael Tushman addressed what Abernathy (1978) called the productivity dilemma. Based on his research and observations in the automobile industry, Abernathy (1978) suggested that the very focus on productivity gains by increasing efficiency caused its decline since this short-term focus inhibits flexibility and the ability needed for long-term survival. In addition, Abernathy considered both activities incompatible and questioned that they could be performed both simultaneously by an organization given their mutually exclusiveness. In his work with Mary Benner, Michael Tushman questioned the widely used process management focus of the 1990s for purposes of innovation. They expanded this focus and its related literature by arguing that organizations need both activities for their survival and that both can be performed simultaneously despite their contradictory nature. The organizational design answer was ambidexterity defined as the ability to sustain both efficiency and exploitation with exploration and especially technological innovation. Benner and Tushman (2003) explored how both technological and organizational contexts moderate the relations between process-focused activities and organizational adaptation. They argued that an ambidextrous organizational form or dual organizations having tight coupling with subunits and loose coupling across subunits could solve Abernathy's productivity dilemma.

Achieving such an ambidextrous organization requires, however, ambidextrous leaders (O'Reilly and Tushman 2011; Tushman 2014; Tushman et al. 2011) and ambidextrous leadership (Probst et al. 2011), an idea that grew during Michael Tushman's work with Charles O'Reilley at IBM. They argue that ambidextrous leaders cannot only deal with the contradictions and paradoxes inherent in organizational designs. Ambidextrous leaders can also recognize the importance of explicitly designing organizations that exploit and explore simultaneously. Hence, ambidextrous leadership is a framework in which all leaders across organizational levels can deal with the tensions and paradoxes associated with different kinds of strategies and innovation activities.

This stream of work had tremendous impact on research in strategy, organization theory, designing, and hence changing organizations as well as leadership development and recommendations for leaders and their decision-making.

New Insights: Gained and Further Developed in Dialogues with Colleagues, Doctoral Students and Executives

Michael Tushman has always focused on crucial issues or problems and raised fundamental questions to address in his research, rather than acting as a scholar trained in one field of expertise. His quest for relevance (Tushman and O'Reilly 2007) is probably one of the reasons why his work is so widely cited. His ideas start(ed) from careful observations of real-world phenomena, as was the case when he worked with General Radio. The question why a company with so many intelligent engineers was failing and had to lay off people was a real concern and puzzling question to him. Having been influenced by open systems theory and the relevance of organizational environments, their different degrees of turbulence and the critical issue of boundaries, including the impact on people by his mentors Ralph Katz, Paul Lawrence, and Edgar Schein, Michael Tushman developed a holistic approach to the study of organizations and their environment including organizational members. His need for a larger picture surfaced in the congruence model for organizational analysis. It contains all those components that he addressed in his later research – be it the environment and its technological change, innovation processes, evolution and the changing nature of organizations, the design and change of organizations facilitating positive performance, as well as the role of leaders in such a change process.

The exchange of ideas with colleagues and doctoral students was critical for Michael Tushman in developing these ideas further. In this process, he was always a curious explorer and reflective discussant, as reported by one of his doctoral students. Since he recommends working with smart doctoral students to colleagues for advancing organizational science (Seong 2014), I would like to cite a longer statement from Philip Anderson, one of his early doctoral students, about his mentor, teacher, and coach Michael Tushman. At the time, during his doctoral studies, Philip tried to make sense of what was driving cyclical patterns of destruction, followed by dominant designs.

> Mike and I had a series of discussions about this. One day in his office, I told him that having thought hard about the problem, it seemed to me that creative-destruction theories were mixing apples and bananas because two different types of technological change could kick off such waves. Some built on what the companies already knew how to do and amplified their strengths, even if they had to walk away from some sunk costs. Others fundamentally undermined what they knew how to do. This was why sometimes creative destruction destroyed incumbents but other times it did not. Mike immediately realized the importance of this idea—it was an *organizational* explanation for creative destruction [as compared to Schumpeter's economic one]. It transcended the "organizations are always inertial" mood of the times and linked punctuated-equilibrium approaches to technological and organizational change.
>
> I was a second-year doctoral student at the time; I was capable of coming up with an intriguing idea, but not developing it into a landmark paper. Mike took the lead in developing the concept into a theory, which became the basis for my doctoral thesis. He suggested we think of two papers on this subject, one that he would take the lead on and first-author, while I would take the lead on the other and first-author it. My real apprenticeship in learning how to write influential papers came from working with Mike over and over to refine what

became our most-cited paper, published in Administrative Science Quarterly in 1986, with the second paper appearing four years later.

This was the characteristic way in which Mike worked with doctoral students. Once they had spent some time becoming steeped in organization theory, he shared with them the many things he found interesting and discussed where he thought the field would go. Each doctoral student took up the torch in the area that he or she found most interesting. I am not an engineer, and I knew very little about technology before I went to Columbia, but the link between technological and organizational change is what interested me the most, so that's what I studied. The late and greatly missed, Beverly Virany, shared Mike's interest in executive teams. Lori Rosenkopf, a "real engineer" who knew much more about technology than I did, was interested in how communities shaped technological standards, so Mike expanded into that area with her. Mary Benner became interested in why an emphasis on process excellence (at that time, ISO 9000 qualification and the Baldrige Award for quality were all the rage) paradoxically constrains innovation. Wendy Smith became interested in how executives manage paradoxes. Adam Kleinbaum shared interests in organization design, combining that with insights into social networks. This is not an exhaustive list of his students, just illustrative.

This long quote is taken from an e-mail sent by Philip Anderson, in response to my question of how he experienced his work as a doctoral student with Michael Tushman. Not having worked with Michael Tushman myself, I could not do a better job in characterizing his way of developing new ideas and insights taking the field further in a process of co-creation with his doctoral students.

Legacies and Unfinished Business: Continuing the Path of Co-exploration, Exploitation, and Impact

Michael Tushman's legacy is well illustrated and documented in the list of many honors and awards that he received:

1996	He was elected Fellow of the Academy of Management
2005	He was named Lecturer of the Year at CHAMPS, Chalmers University of Technology
2008	He received an honorary doctorate from the University of Geneva explicitly for his work on the relationships between technological change and organizational evolution
2011	He received the Sumantra Ghoshal Award for Rigour and Relevance in the Study of Management from London Business School
2013	He received the Academy of Management Career Achievement Award for Distinguished Scholarly Contributions to Management
	He received the Academy of Management Review Decade Award for his paper with Mary J. Benner, "Exploitation, Exploration and Process Management: The Productivity Dilemma Revisited" (Academy of Management Review, 2003)
	The 2013 Apgar Award for Innovation in Teaching
2014	He received the Lifetime Achievement Award from the American Society for Training and Development (ASTD)
	He was recognized as Foundational Scholar in the Knowledge and Innovation Group of the Strategic Management Society
2016	He received the Distinguished Scholar Award from the Academy of Management's Organization Development and Change Division

Each one of the contributions discussed in the prior section was an innovation to the field of organization theory and change and set new standards. The work on information processes pointed out the importance of taking a process perspective for studying and conceptualizing organizations. The work on boundary spanners and gatekeepers illuminated the importance of managing organizational boundaries and connecting organizational subunits for innovation and effective performance. His curvilinear findings on the amount of information useful for performance were supported decades later in neurologically informed studies on information processing and decision-making at the individual level. The congruence model expanded open systems theory and combined it with contingency theory into a framework guiding managers and change practitioners in their effort to understand an organization's mode of functioning as a basis for the choice of most effective interventions.

His work on organizational evolution and the punctuated equilibrium model both expanded and specified existing phase models of planned organizational change (e.g., Lewin 1947; Lippitt et al. 1958) at the organizational level combining evolutionary and revolutionary phases of change (e.g., Greiner 1972) but refuting the idea that small changes could accumulate to transformational change. The research on technological innovation expanded his work to include environmental change and specified conditions under which organizations could actually use these rare conditions for competitive advantage.

The conceptualization of ambidextrous organizations solved Abernathy's productivity dilemma, by combining exploration with exploitation within the boundaries of an organization and thus reconciling apparent paradoxes and contradictions. This stream of research had implications not only for organizational design and change but also for strategy and management education, since ambidextrous organizations require ambidextrous leaders and ambidextrous leadership. It has stimulated work elaborating the concept, documenting its effects on organizational outcomes, and identified antecedents and boundary conditions (O'Reilley and Tushman 2013, 2016).

In addition to the broad range of contributions regarding research topics, the span of Michael Tushman's work and his diligence in approaching an interesting question is also remarkable. His research tended to start from an initial observation, discussing it with a close colleague or doctoral students to developing a model, testing it, expanding it to other areas, developing recommendations for managers, and teaching it to executives and future managers. Given this systematic approach and rigor, his work inspired many scholars to pick up questions he posed for further research, thus building on, elaborating, and differentiating his work. The following quote by Philip Anderson illustrates this process:

> ... I want to give you some insight into the way Mike works. He starts off orienting people toward interesting puzzles in organization theory. Unlike many people who

> specialized only in organization design or innovation or organizational change or executive team dynamics, his work has spanned the range of these things, and his broad interests inform one another, even though the people he works with (e.g. me) never are as broad as he is. Mike is an original thinker whose generosity of spirit allows him to bring out the best in other thinkers. He is remarkable in his ability both to create and co-create; when you work with him, he doesn't need to be pre-eminent yet he is much more than a catalyst, he is a master at recombining your ideas and his into something truly novel and significant.

Since Michael Tushman is still active, the question remains about unfinished or rather still to do business. Still being interested in the process of innovation, he has turned his interest toward the process of open innovation and its impact on organizational capabilities, its design, and leadership. The developments in the area of information technology have questioned organizational boundaries regarding the innovation process. This requires expanding the unit of analysis to the wider ecosystem. With communication costs decreasing, O'Reilley and Tushman (2013) posit that the locus of innovation will increasingly shift to the community. Hence, the larger community will become more relevant in the process of exploration and distributed innovation. What kind of leadership capabilities will be needed to lead across boundaries for long-term survival? What kind of implication will this shift have for an organization's culture and its identity?

In his recent reflection with Mary Benner on their Academy of Management Review Decade Award winning paper "Exploitation, Exploration and Process Management: The Productivity Dilemma Revisited" (Benner and Tushman 2015) and in his Distinguished Speaker address at the Academy of Management in 2016, he questions whether the developed models, theories, and recommendations still hold today and in the future. The radical environmental shifts and the new environmental conditions including our web-based societies will confront organizations with many more paradoxical pressures and dilemmas than just the productivity dilemma. With the community as becoming increasingly the focal unit for open innovation, "... our theories of innovation, organizational design, leadership, and organizational change must capture the tensions between these contrasting innovation modes" (Benner and Tushman 2015, pp. 508–509). In doing so, they suggest to move back from mature theory and research and "go back to basics – to go back to deeply study and carefully describing the phenomena of organizations and innovation. ... Such a phenomena-driven, problem-oriented research may be required again to help the field generate new constructs, mechanisms, and patterns associated with exploration and exploitation" (Benner and Tushman 2015). Such a phenomena-driven, problem-oriented approach to research can be considered one of the trademarks of Michael Tushman's work. About unfinished business, I want to conclude with his words: "While progress has been made, there remains much to do" (O'Reilley and Tushman 2013, p. 333). Being full of energy, my hunch is that Michael Tushman has still a lot to offer to the field of organization theory and change in the years to come.

References

Abernathy, W. J. (1978). *The productivity dilemma: Roadblock to innovation in the automobile industry*. Baltimore: Johns Hopkins University Press.

Anderson, P., & Tushman, M. L. (1991). Managing through cycles of technological change. *Research Technology Management, 34*(3), 26–31.

Benner, M. J., & Tushman, M. L. (2003). Exploitation, exploration and process management: The productivity dilemma revisited. *Academy of Management Review, 28*(2), 238–256.

Benner, M. J., & Tushman, M. L. (2015). Reflections on the 2013 Decade Award – "Exploitation, exploration, and process management: The productivity dilemma revisited" ten years later. *Academy of Management Review, 40*(4), 497–514.

Greiner, L. (1972). Evolution and revolution as organizations grow. *Harvard Business Review, 50*, 37–46.

Lewin, K. (1947). Group decisions and social change. In T. M. Newcomb & E. L. Hartley (Eds.), *Readings in social psychology*. New York: Henry Holt.

Lippitt, R., Watson, J., & Westley, B. (1958). *The dynamics of planned change*. New York: Harcourt, Brace and World.

March, J. G. (1991). Exploration and exploitation in organizational learning. *Organizational Learning, 2*(1), 71–87.

McGrath, R., MacMillan, I., & Tushman, M. L. (1992). The role of executive team actions in shaping dominant designs: Towards shaping technological progress. *Strategic Management Journal, 13*(1), 137–161.

Nadler, D. A., & Tushman, M. L. (1980). A model for diagnosing organizational behavior. *Organizational Dynamics, 9*(2), 35–51.

Nadler, D. A., & Tushman, M. L. (1989). Organizational frame-bending: Principles for managing reorientation. *Academy of Management Executive, 3*(3), 194–204.

Nadler, D. A., & Tushman, M. L. (1980). Beyond the charismatic leader: Leadership and organizational change. In *The training and development sourcebook, California Management Review, 32*(2), 77–97. DOI: 10.2307/41166606.

Nadler, D. A., & Tushman, M. L. (1999). The organizations of the future: Strategic imperatives and core competences for the 21st century. *Organizational Dynamics, 28*(1), 45–60.

O'Reilly III, C. A., & Tushman, M. L. (2004). The ambidextrous organization. *Harvard Business Review, 82*(4), 74–81.

O'Reilly III, C. A., & Tushman, M. L. (2008). Ambidexterity as a dynamic capability: Resolving the innovator's dilemma. *Research in Organizational Behavior, 28*(1), 185–206.

O'Reilly III, C. A., & Tushman, M. L. (2011). Organizational ambidexterity in action: How managers explore and exploit. *California Management Review, 53*(4), 5–21.

O'Reilley III, C. A., & Tushman, M. L. (2013). Organizational ambidexterity: Past, present, and future. *Academy of Management Perspectives, 27*(4), 324–338.

O'Reilley III, C. A., & Tushman, M. L. (2016). *Lead and disrupt how to solve the innovator's dilemma*. Stanford University Books. Standford: Stanford University press

Probst, G., Raisch, S., & Tushman, M. L. (2011). Ambidextrous leadership: Emerging challenges for business and HR leaders. *Organizational Dynamics, 40*(4), 326–334.

Romanelli, E., & Tushman, M. L. (1994). Organizational transformation as punctuated equilibrium: An empirical test. *Academy of Management Journal, 37*(5), 1141–1166.

Tichy, N., Tushman, M. L., & Fombrum, C. (1979). Social network analysis for organizations. *Academy of Management Review, 4*(4), 507–520.

Tushman, M. L. (1977). Special boundary roles in the innovation process. *Administrative Science Quarterly, 22*(4), 587–605.

Tushman, M. L. (1979). Managing communication networks in research and development laboratories. *MIT Sloan School Management Review, 20*(2), 37–49.

Tushman, M. L. (2004). *Managing strategic innovation and change: A collection of readings*. Oxford: Oxford University Press.

Tushman, M. L. (2014). The ambidextrous leader: Leadership tips for today to stay in the game tomorrow. *IESE Insights, 3*(4), 31–38.
Tushman, M. L., & Anderson, P. (1986). Technological discontinuities and organizational environments. *Administrative Science Quarterly, 31*(3), 439–465.
Tushman, M. L., & Katz, R. (1980). External communication and project performance: An investigation into the role of gatekeepers. *Management Science, 26*, 1071–1085.
Tushman, M. L., & Katz, R. (1982). Does gatekeeping make a difference? *ChemTech, 12*, 151–161.
Tushman, M. L., & Katz, R. (1983). A longitudinal study of the effects of boundary spanning supervision on turnover and promotion in research and development. *Academy of Management Journal, 26*(3), 437–459.
Tushman, M. L., & Nadler, D. A. (1978). Information processing as an integrated concept in organizational design. *Academy of Management Review, 3*(3), 613–624.
Tushman, M. L., & Nadler, D. (1986). Organizing for innovation. *California Management Review, 28*(3), 74–92.
Tushman, M. L., & O'Reilley III, C. A. (2007). Research and relevance: Implications of Pasteur's quadrant for doctoral programs and faculty development. *Academy of Management Journal, 50* (4), 769–774.
Tushman, M. L., & Romanelli, E. (1985). Organizational evolution: A metamorphosis model of convergence and reorientation. *Research in Organizational Behavior, 7*, 171.
Tushman, M. L., & Scanlan, T. (1981). Boundary spanning individuals. Their role in information transfer and their antecedents. *Academy of Management Journal, 24*(2), 289–305.
Tushman, M. L., Virany, B., & Romanelli, E. (1992). Executive succession, strategic reorientation and organization evolution. *Technology in Society, 42*(7), 297–314.
Tushman, M. L., Smith, W. K., & Binns, A. (2011). The ambidextrous CEO. *Harvard Business Review, 89*(6), 74–80.
Seong, S. (2014). A conversation with Michael Tushman on leadership, innovation, and strategic change. www.youtube.com/watch?v=QnwGw8OV_7M
Seong, S., Kim, Y., & Szulanski, G. (2015). Leadership, innovation and strategic change: A conversation with Michael Tushman. *Journal of Management Inquiry, 24*(4), 370–381.

Further Reading

Adler, P. S., Benner, M., Brunner, D. J., MacDuffie, J. P.; Osono, E., Staats, B. R., Takeuchi, H., Tushman, M. L., & Winter, S. G. (2009). Perspectives on the productivity dilemma. *Journal of Operations Management, 27*(2), 99–113.
Anderson, P., & Tushman, M. L. (1990). Technological discontinuities and dominant design: A cyclical model of technological change. *Administrative Science Quarterly, 35*(1), 604–633.
Binns, A., Harreld, B. J., O'Reilly III, C. A., & Tushman, M. L. (2014). The art of strategic renewal. *MIT Sloan Management Review, 55*(2), 21–23.
Hambrick, D., Nadler, D., & Tushman, M. L.(1998). *Navigating change: How CEO's, top teams and boards steer transformation*. Boston: Harvard Business School Press.
Henderson, R., Gulati, R., & Tushman, M. L. (Eds.). (2015). *Leading sustainable change: An organizational perspective*. Oxford: Oxford University Press.
Kleinbaum, A. M., Stuart, T. E., & Tushman, M. L. (2013). Discretion within constraint: Homophily and structure in a formal organization. *Organization Science, 24*(5), 1316–1336.
Nadler, D., & Tushman, M. L. (1988). *Strategic organization design*. Glenview: Scott, Foresman and Company.
Nadler, D., & Tushman, M. L. (1998). *Competing by design: The power of organizational architectures*. New York: Oxford University Press.
O'Reilly, III, C. A., Harreld, J. B., & Tushman, M. L. (2009).Organizational ambidexterity: IBM and emerging business opportunities. *California Management Review, 51*(4), 75–99.

Polzer, J., Gulati, R. Khurana, R., & Tushman, M. L. (2009). Crossing boundaries to increase relevance in organizational research. *Journal of Management Inquiry, 18*(4), 280–286.

Raisch, S., Birkinshaw, J. Probst, J., & Tushman, M. L. (2009). Organizational ambidexterity: Balancing exploitation and exploration for sustained performance. *Organization Science, 20*(4), 685–695.

Rosenkopf, L., & Tushman, M. L. (1992). On the organizational determinants of technological change: Towards a sociology of technological evolution. *Research in Organizational Behavior, 14*.

Smith, W. K., Binns, A., & Tushman, M. L. (2010). Complex business models: Managing strategic paradoxes simultaneously. Special Issue on Business Models. *Long Range Planning, 43*(2), 448–461.

Tushman, M. L. (1974). *Organizational change: An exploratory study and case history.* Ithaca: New York State School of Industrial and Labor Relations.

Tushman, M. L. (2007). On the co-evolution of knowing and doing: A personal perspective on the synergies between research and practice. *Journal of Management Inquiry, 16*(2), 132–138.

Tushman, M. L. (2014). The ambidextrous leader: Leadership tips for today to stay in the game tomorrow. *IESE Insight, 23*, 31–38.

Tushman, M. L., & Allen, T. J. (1979). Modes of technology transfer as a function of position in the research-development-technical service spectrum. *Academy of Management Journal, 22*(4), 694–708.

Tushman, M. L., & O'Reilly III, C. A. (2002). *Winning through innovation: A practical guide to leading organizational change and renewal.* Boston: Harvard Business School Press.

Tushman, M. L., O'Reilly III, C. A., & Nadler, D. (Eds.). (1989). *The management of organizations.* New York: Ballinger Publishing.

Tushman, M. L., Fenollosa, A., McGrath, D., O'Reilly III, C. A., & Kleinbaum, A. M. (2007). Relevance and rigor: Executive education as a lever in shaping practice and research. *Academy of Management Learning & Education, 6*(3), 345–365.

Tushman, M. L., Smith, W. K., & Binns, A. (2011). The ambidextrous CEO. *Harvard Business Review, 89*(6), 74–80.

Tushman, M. L., Lakhani, K., & Lifshitz-Assaf, H. (2012). Open innovation and organization design. Special Issue on the Future of Organization Design. *Journal of Organization Design, 1* (1), 24–27.

Peter B. Vaill: A Life in the Art of Managing and Leading Change

82

David W. Jamieson and Jackie M. Milbrandt

Abstract

Peter B. Vaill is both pioneer and thought leader in the fields of organizational behavior (OB) and organization development (OD). Over the past 60 years, Peter's ideas have influenced and informed numerous strands of thinking in the fields of management, leadership, and change. The common thread among these streams of thought: the relationship between organizational practice, theory, and learning. This chapter offers readers a glimpse into the career and work of Peter Vaill. Through several interviews with Peter, others who worked with him, and close readings of his writing, in this chapter we explore the themes and thinking that shaped Vaill's contributions to the field of change.

Keywords

Organization development • Organizational behavior • Permanent white water • High-performing systems • Theory and practice • Organizational learning • Scholar-practitioner • Management education

Contents

D.W. Jamieson (✉) • J.M. Milbrandt
Organization Development and Change, University of St Thomas, Minneapolis, MN, USA
e-mail: jami1396@stthomas.edu; jackiemilbrandt@stthomas.edu

D.B. Szabla et al. (eds.), *The Palgrave Handbook of Organizational Change Thinkers*,
DOI 10.1007/978-3-319-52878-6_60

Beyond all of the other new skills and attitudes that permanent white water requires, people have to be (or become) extremely effective learners. Peter B. Vaill-Learning as a Way of Being.

Introduction

Peter B. Vaill is described by colleagues and friends as an "innovator," "creative thinker," and "brilliant" human being. It's no wonder that he has been hailed the "poet laureate of management" (Kramer 2016). A pioneer in the fields of organization behavior (OB) and organization development (OD), Peter's ideas have influenced and informed numerous strands of thinking in the fields of management, leadership, and change. The common thread among these streams of thought: the relationship between organizational practice, theory, and learning.

Perhaps Vaill is best described as an original scholar-practitioner. His commitment, to what we later describe as "the field of practice," is reflected across his lifetime (over 60 years) writing, teaching, consulting, and thinking about human systems behavior and change. Leading various streams of thinking on organizational change and development (Vaill 1971) and executive and managerial learning (Vaill 1979) high-performing systems (Vaill 1982), process wisdom (Vaill 1984, 2008), and meaning and spirituality in organizations (Vaill 1998a) earned Peter notoriety and respect among scholars and practitioners alike. Throughout his career, three essential questions have become hallmarks of his work:

- How do organizations work?
- How do leaders, managers, and employees get things done?
- How can we (management educators) help them (managers, leaders, organizations, etc.) do what they are trying to do better?

In the following sections, we offer a narrative of Peter's life and career exploring these questions. We weave recent interviews (with Peter and others reflecting on his life and work) amidst Peter's essays and books, in an effort to create a semblance of a whole. And while these offerings are far from comprehensive, they offer the reader a glimpse into the depth of Vaill's experiences (events, relationships, ideas) and thinking (essays, books, and speeches) on his life in the landscape of management, leadership, and change.

Influences and Motivations: A Portrait of the Artist as a Young Man

In Peter Vaill's apartment in South Minneapolis nearby to where he attended high school pictures fill the wall. Photograph's of family; A photograph of Vaill, in younger years, arms raised above his head crossing a finish line; A painting of a young boy with a toy ship at the edge of a lake. Just below the painting, a piano-keyboard filled with pages of gospel music. Flanking a corner in the room, a writing desk with two bookshelves. One filled with a collection of his work (including his dissertation) the other filled with books that have been and remain influential to his thinking. A window next to his writing desk trimmed with a banner from months gone by, a reminder of the past moments of celebration reads "Happy Birthday!"

A Portrait of the Artist as a Young Man

Peter B. Vaill was born in St. Cloud Minnesota, on November 5, 1936, to Stanley and Elizabeth (Brown) Vaill. When Peter's father (who worked for the phone company) was transferred from St. Cloud to Duluth for 9 years, then later to Minneapolis. Peter went on to attend and graduate from high school in Minneapolis, and then went to the University of Minnesota, earning an undergraduate degree in psychology. At age 23, (1958) Peter left for Boston and admitted as a student in the Harvard MBA program.

In early and later essays on the field of OB (Vaill 1979, 2007), Peter reflected on his early days as a student at Harvard. It was at Harvard that he would first experience the field of organizational behavior (OB), where he would develop his early training and "case method" perspective and where he would meet with the people and ideas that would shape the trajectory of his career in the fields of management and change.

There may be dozens of experiences that informed Peter Vaill's thinking while at Harvard, but two events stuck out in his recent reflections (Jamieson and Milbrandt, May 2016a, June 2016b). The first was a class that he took during his MBA studies at Harvard, 1958–1959. The class was called "Human Relations" taught by a contemporary and close colleague of Fritz Roethlisberger – George Lombard. (George Lombard was described by Roethlisberger as one of his closest friends and later became editor of Roethlisberger's autobiography, "The Elusive Phenomena" (1977).) According to Vaill, Lombard's class was heavily influenced by the works of Roethlisberger and Dickson (1939) and Carl Rogers (1961) and built around practical application. It taught skills on listening and interpersonal relationships. As Peter described,

> . . .it [the course] was heavily oriented towards listening with acceptance, and empathy–Carl Rogers' hallmark. It was framed in a way to teach how to listen to the people around you, especially those who are reporting to you. . . . how to understand what their needs are. . . . how to understand what they are saying, what their feelings are. . . (Jamieson and Milbrandt, May 2016a)

The second major event was Vaill's decision to enter Harvard's newly named organizational behavior doctoral program. It was during Vaill's doctoral days that he became intimate with the perspectives of Roethlisberger and the case method.

In the 1960s Fritz Roethlisberger was the chair at Harvard and busy forming an exceptional OB department, attracting many of the future thinkers in the field. Roethlisberger had operated in the same era as Kurt Lewin, and both were researching various aspects of *human behavior in field settings* and exploring questions involving what we think of today as *engagement, motivation, turnover, productivity, and managing change.* Roethlisberger with mentor Elton Mayo was part of the classic Western Electric Company (Hawthorne Plant) studies in the 1920s–1930s where the field grew in its understanding about climate, motivations, and the *social systems of the workplace.*

Although Vaill was at Harvard for only 6 years, 1958–1964, his time there would prove formative. During his first year as a doctoral student (1960–1961), Vaill was introduced to a model of the field of OB conceived of by Fritz Roethlisberger. The model attempted to "map" the emerging field of organizational behavior. It was composed of six boxes that Vaill commented would likely be too simplistic for contemporary scholars, but at the time Roethlisberger presented it to the faculty and doctorate students at Harvard, it made a lasting impression. Nearly 45 years later, Vaill would write:

> In retrospect, this memo is perhaps of even more significance to a doctoral student and a relatively young working scholar than to a seasoned professional, for it urges us to think about how we are framing the field to ourselves, our students, our colleagues, and our professional reference groups. As we shall see, Roethlisberger wants to keep the practitioner in the picture. But the import of his memo is how keeping the practitioner in the picture then affects the theory and research that we do, and vice versa. (Vaill 2007, p. 323) (Fig. 1)

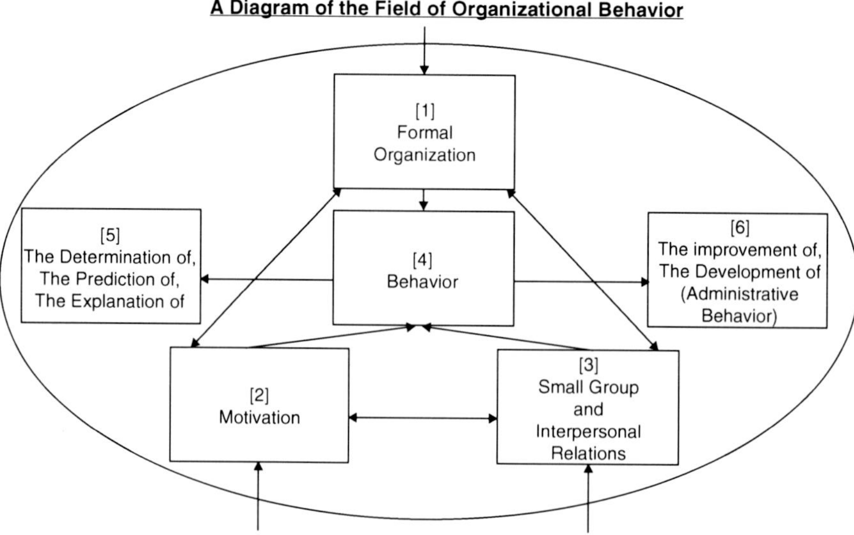

Fig. 1 A diagram of the field of organizational behavior

To enumerate on this "import" of the diagram and "keeping the practitioner in the picture," Peter concluded:

> As Roethlisberger well knew, the relations of theory and practice are themselves matters of a great deal of theorizing. The problem abides, partly because every new theory of theory and practice creates its own new problems of practice: How is this theory to be used in understanding it and working with it (i.e., practicing) to influence the world.... How does any new theory, any new idea about the relations of theory and practice, help? How does practice then influence the evolution of this new theory? .... As I noted, Roethlisberger himself could spin much more complex models of the field than this simple diagram. Yet he does offer it as a "diagram of the field" as a basis for asking what he considered questions of the most profound importance. (Vaill 2007, p. 323)

Vaill's reflection on his mentor, and early impressions of the field, allows us to see and understand the development of his unique "framework" of the managerial leader. It also informs how we may begin to differentiate the ideas which he would spend a lifetime exploring – which he would later describe as "Managing as a Performing Art," and the "Practice, with a capital P."

Impressions of the Organization and How It Functions

Vaill's early impressions of the field were situated in a time when "you could do no wrong" in the organization. The 1950s and 1960s were a golden era in which leaders and managers had the luxury of "good profit margins and stability." As a result, there were new innovations, ideas, and experimentation emerging under the banners of organizational behavior (OB) and organization development (OD): Peter was at the epicenter of both. He learned from the original thinkers, participated in early research and practice that led to many further developments in the fields, and began teaching the next generations of managers and other practitioners.

Paul Lawrence was Vaill's dissertation chair. Lawrence's early work was captured in *administering change* (Ronken and Lawrence 1952) and later he contributed to the quality of work life (QWL) movement. The major headline from *administering change* that stuck with Vaill was the idea that change goes better when people have a shared understanding. Peter later commented:

> He [Lawrence] had five propositions about the forces that facilitated change and inhibited it.... but the shorthand was that when people were all on the same page, change went more smoothly. When people were not, things were rocky and communication either didn't occur or it mis-occurred (sic)...but the most interesting thing was how the jobs they were doing influenced their perspectives on what the "page" even was. Compatible perspectives produced good communication, conflicting perspectives produced less effective communication. Understanding this "pin-pointed the "change problem." (Jamieson and Milbrandt, May 2016a)

These early learnings about the need for people to "get on the same page" (for change to work) were confounded by individual perspectives. The realization that your perspective of what the "page" was changed depending on your job would inform Peter fundamentally throughout his career. The early influences of Roethlisberger and others (Argyris, Likert, Lewin, Maslow, Rogers, and Lawrence) are traceably woven into Vaill's thinking and subsequent writing.

As Vaill worked toward his dissertation, he continued to refine his perspective. Ultimately, Vaill would reject the "scientific" ideals dominating the field of management – the notion of an absolute truth (based on what can be objectively measured). Instead he would embrace the idea that there are multiple truths (based on subjective experience and meaning). From then on Vaill's guiding question would be, "From whose point of view is this true?"

As Vaill pursued his dissertation work, thoughts around the dilemma of "multiple points of view" and the experience in organizations became more concrete. Namely, he was perplexed by the idea presented by Argyris (1957) that the needs of the healthy individual and the needs of the bureaucratic organization were incompatible. To Vaill these ideas revealed a need and passion to better understand (1) how "the hierarchies" within the organization worked and (2) how managers made meaning from their experiences and this meaning influenced their thinking and action (practice). It would be a mixture of good fortune and serendipity that he would be encouraged to work on a large-scale research project that provided him the opportunity to better understand the nature of these competing needs.

Paul Lawrence, who was teaching at Harvard was involved in a big research project at the time collecting data in 11 large organizations. What Vaill did was go into the companies, first with Lawrence and later on his own, to survey the different jobs and departments, using a questionnaire that had been developed to score different dimensions of the jobs, such as creativity, the amount of interaction they had with others, etc. As Vaill described it:

> Paul (Lawrence) was doing a large scale study on the relationship between the structure of industrial jobs, blue collar jobs, and the feelings and behaviors that people had in those jobs.... there was a lot of talk at the time on quality of work life and job design and that sort of thing. (Jamieson and Milbrandt, May 2016a)

As Vaill researched the various companies, he was looking at not only the organization and how it was structured but also observing how the people functioned in their environment and with each other. He commented on the process stating:

> We went around to several companies Paul had access to [a paper mill, a chemical plant, an IBM plant].... and we would go in and talk to the personnel people and they would take us down to the factory floor and we would walk around and look at different jobs and departments until we finally isolated a collection of jobs – a set we thought could be studied. (Jamieson and Milbrandt, May 2016a)

Peter wrote short cases on each of the organizations and for his dissertation wrote an in-depth analysis of one of the companies (the Fuller Brush Company and Brown Paper Company). These cases were never published; instead, they ended up being absorbed into the "Harvard system" and used for classroom teaching. Through his experience, researching in ways that combined theory with practice, Peter developed a point of view that would become instrumental to his life and work – that of a scholar-practitioner.

The Makings of a Scholar-Practitioner

A year after completing his dissertation, Peter was hired by Robert (Bob) Tannenbaum to teach at UCLA and who, according to Peter, thought he was getting a "systems and technology" expert. Vaill reflected:

> To an extent he (Bob Tannenbaum) did get that, because I was interested in the systems and technology, and I also had the desire and readiness to understand OD, and all that was being talked about it.... The Harvard point of view, the Case Method point of view, gives you a strong feeling of wanting to immerse yourself in some particular situation and that's what the OD consultant had to do is immerse in particular situations. (Jamieson and Milbrandt, June 2016b)

Working closely with Tannenbaum was a wonderfully rich experience and an opportunity to go deeper on the humans-in-organizations side of his interests. Bob was a proponent of "use of self" and the deep personal work needed to be healthy and capable of being your best. Without the humanistic values of *authenticity* and *intentionality*, organizations were designed to operate in ways that caused people to play games and behave in very unhealthy and inauthentic ways (Massarik et al. 1985).

Vaill's first year, 1964, as a professor at UCLA, under the leadership of Tannenbaum, placed him squarely in the mix of a very large-scale OD project at TRW Systems:

> Bob got me involved right away. Shel Davis, who was the main OD guy, had recruited a line-up of experts that included, (Richard) Dick Beckhard, Herb Shepard, Bob Tannenbaum, and there were a couple of other big names. Anyway it was a tremendous line-up.... and the consultant and department manager together were co-training. And after training all of the department managers in T-group facilitation, the OD consultant and the department manager would run T-groups for everybody.... and the whole idea was to get the people talking to each other... (Jamieson and Milbrandt, May 2016a)

As it would turn out, the experience of applying, innovating, and creating ways to help the leadership at TRW Systems develop their organization would prove to be another stroke of good fortune and serendipity for Vaill. According to Vaill, Sheldon Davis was a "scholar-practitioner." He was a leader who was ready to try new things and could integrate them. Davis had tremendous energy for this, and when asked how he kept it up quipped "Love the people, hate the system!" (Milbrandt 2017). In retrospect, this rare combination of qualities Davis embodied would be something Vaill would reflect on throughout his career. In these interactions at TRW with the externals (including Beckhard and others in the lineup) and the internals (Shel Davis and other managers) that Peter would see the "crystallization" of major innovations and concepts in the field of OD come into use.

Another notable influence during Vaill's time at UCLA was his interactions with Eric Trist. Trist had been instrumental in publishing a body of work in England involving the creation of the socio-technical systems theories and practices for improving workplaces and their effectiveness (Emery and Trist 1965). Trist's perspective on socio-technical theory – which involved the simultaneous optimizing of the technical and social aspects of organizations – had a huge impact on the emerging fields. Bringing to attention a need for research on outcomes of work and quality of work life, the socio-technical theories would later influence streams of thought on organizational engagement and satisfaction. While Vaill was at UCLA, Trist was a visiting professor in the Socio-Tech and Work Design Center led by Lou Davis. According to Vaill, he and Trist would become close colleagues. These interactions, no doubt, added greater depth to Peter's thinking on the systems view of organizations.

Throughout these experiences, informed by pioneers in the fields of organization behavior (Roethlisberger, Lombard, Lawrence, respectively) and organization development (Beckhard, Shepard, Tannenbaum, Trist), Vaill crystalized a line of thinking that would be unwavering – Peter would begin and end his career with an eye toward understanding leaders and the organizations from a perspective of experience, meaning, and practice.

On the Frontiers: Early Years in the Fields of Management and Change

It was 1966, Peter, in his later years at UCLA, found himself at an "Industrial Network" meeting at a Holiday Inn, in Montreal (Vaill 2005). Tannenbaum, who couldn't attend, asked Peter to go in place of him and represent the university. As Peter recounts it, there were two important things that took place at that meeting: (1) The network changed its name from the "Industrial Network" to the "Organization Development Network" (ODN) and (2) the leadership transferred from Jerry Harvey to Warner Burke. (The late Jerry Harvey, also a professor of management and later at George Washington with Peter, would become a lifelong friend and colleague.) Peter would go on to attend nearly every ODN meeting from the 1970s through the 1990s. Peter was also present when the leadership changed again from Warner Burke to Tony Petrella in the early 1970s. Peter recalled how during the Burke and Petrella years the organization grew from its founding, with about ten organizations represented in the Industrial Network, to more than 3000 members in the ODN when Petrella took over.

Peter also had many opportunities to work with NTL. Founded in the late 1940s by Kurt Lewin, with the help of Ron Lippitt, Leland (Lee) Bradford, and Ken Benne, NTL was a diverse mix of academics and practitioners from various backgrounds ranging from disciplines in the social sciences (psychology, social work, organizational behavior, sociology, political theory) to education (adult and organizational development). In its zenith, NTL was the place where scholars and practitioners who were interested in understanding "group dynamics" and social systems came to learn

(Kleiner 2008). It was in this context that the innovation of the "training group" otherwise known as the T-group flourished. Throughout the 1950s and 1960s, the T-group experience would be the dominate method used in Bethel labs. In many ways, these labs and the T-group infused the field of OD with its original energy (Bradford et al. 1964).

According to Vaill, his introduction to NTL was in the early 1970s. Peter was invited to study a subject that had received very little attention: "The world of the OD practitioner." The research involved several weeks at NTL's 1970 summer head quarters in Bethel, Maine, conducting in-depth interviews with consultants going through NTL's "Program for Organizational Training and Development." That summer, Beckhard was head of the program Peter was investigating.

A year later, Vaill completed his first on the topic of OD publication entitled, "Practice Theories in Organization Development" (Vaill 1971). According to Vaill, this study brought some attention to the field of OD and attempted to begin to define it from the bottom up. In understanding how OD professionals and managers made sense of their practice, Peter felt he was bringing some focus and clarity to defining OD. Themes found in Vaill's later writings are echoed in his conceptualization of "practice theory." Vaill writes:

> In the development to date of the OD field, two other subjects have received a great deal more attention then has the OD practitioner's own frame of reference. The first area is the study of organizations, and particularly what is wrong with them.... The second major area is how the OD practitioner, the agent of change SHOULD act if he wants to influence the system – an evolving body of prescriptions for effectively influencing organization events.... The basic thesis of this paper, however is that these two areas of OD should not continue to develop without being tempered and tested against the practical realities of the OD practitioners situation, that is against how the organization seemed to be TO HIM.... .practice theory is, literally, a personal theory guiding practice, bearing some relation to public, objective theories, about organizational situations, but in no sense identical with them. (Vaill 1971, p. 162)

Another key event during this period was that Vaill, shortly after receiving tenure at UCLA, and despite his deep admiration and love for Bob Tannenbaum, accepted a position at the University of Connecticut. This would prove to be a pit stop – as only a few years later, in 1973, an invitation would come from Gordon Lippitt (who Vaill had met at NTL) to interview for the deanship at George Washington University (GW) School of Government and Business Administration. At GW, Vaill would find a cohort of kindred spirts who would come to support him as a leader, colleague, and changemaker. Peter's entry into GW put him on the fast track to becoming a spokesperson for OB, OD, and management education.

In the Trenches: Middle Years Managing the Art of Change

Accepting a dean's position, in the School of Business and Public Administration, at George Washington (GW) moved Peter into a new phase of his career: administration. Although Peter only spent 5 years as dean, he spent another 20 years as a professor and director of what was initially called the "experimental doctoral program." According to his close colleague Erik Winslow, who was part of the team that received him at GW, Peter was part of a dream team that Gordon Lippitt had assembled which held enormous influence over the school at the time Vaill was there. The "team" was comprised of Peter Vaill, who studied with Roethlisberger and Tannenbaum, Erik Winslow who studied with Fredrick Herzberg (1976), and Jerry Harvey (1988) who studied with Robert Blake (Blake and Mouton 1964). It was a confluence of those influences (Tannenbaum, Herzberg, and Blake) along with Maslow (1943) and McGregor (1960) that really created the powerful team that shaped GW business school – which was one of the largest in the country (Dent 2002).

When Vaill accepted the deanship, he was only 37 years old.

In his first year as Dean, 1974, Peter delivered a commencement speech to the graduating class – entitled "Management as a Performing Art." Nearly 15 years later, Peter would publish his first book, with a similar title. Winslow reflected on the early development of Vaill's thinking:

> The three of us were talking- Jerry Harvey, myself and Peter once about managing and the roles managers have to play and he laughed and said, "Well, that's because managing is a performing art." And he wrote a speech about that. And Jerry Harvey kidded him and said, "How are you going to make a speech about managing as a performing art if you aren't going to do a performance?" And I couldn't believe it- Peter took a recorder- he took it with him to where he was giving the speech and before he started his speech he played a song on the recorder! And then he said, "That's to introduce my topic, "Management as a Performing Art." And I thought that was so creative. And quite frankly such a risk-taking behavior.... but was brilliant, just like Peter. (Milbrandt September 2016a)

Embedded in this early speech were the seeds for Vaill's central argument, then and now – business schools and business educators needed to change the way they were preparing the leaders of the future to lead future organizations. Vaill began to communicate, with urgency, this perspective pointing out quite early that the golden era in which the field of management was born would not return. Therefore, the concepts, theories, innovations, and checklists for how to manage it were ineffective. These models did not address the realities that managers were experiencing in "the trenches." These theories did not help leaders in their practice of leading organizations. Peter's advice to the teachers of management and change: *turn to practice to reinvigorate scholarship.*

Through Peter's various professional organizations (NTL, ODN, OBTS, ASTD), he would exercise and demonstrate his commitment to this end. Peter worked tirelessly to challenge and expand the boundaries of his own and others understanding of their practice. Longtime friend and colleague, Marvin Weisbord, recalled his work with Peter at NTL, first in workshops and later in sessions with the PSOD program. As Weisbord reflected, Vaill is, and was, an astounding designer of process, insightful on the social aspects of learning, and a creative idea stimulator. Having worked with Peter across decades, Weisbord offered key illustrations of Vaill in these areas. In describing a learning process Vaill designed (called ESAC –

an acronym for Educational System for Accelerated Comprehension), Weisbord laughed with joy:

> Oh, I haven't thought about this in years. Here is how it works: You are trying to teach something to a group. And you give them a presentation and instead of lecturing them for an hour or half an hour, you give them some of the basic concepts and a little task. Then you put them in small groups and you say, "What's your understanding of this and how to apply it?". (Jamieson and Milbrandt, June 2016c)

Later, Weisbord commented on the instrumental role that Peter played in leading and transforming the NTL, as an organization. He reflected:

> Peter was part of what we called the gang of four who re-organized NTL in 1975-which at that time was coming apart.... The social model- the whole idea that there was this elite group- called the fellows of NTL the 40 or 50 mostly academic members and then there were the grunts, like me, who were practitioners, and there were other issues around race and gender and other stuff – and so it really was a cultural re-organization.... and Peter was one of the four members who were asked to figure out how to organize NTL – it was Barbara Bunker, and Edie Seashore and Hal Kellner, and in 1975 they held a forum – So they got 60 of us together, and I don't know how they picked us, but we went to Washington and we spent two or three days thinking and re-organizing the future of NTL. Peter was really instrumental in the process. (Jamieson and Milbrandt, June, 2016c)

According to Weisbord, Vaill's's ability to stimulate ideas and new insights was an experience he had of Vaill time and time again. Vaill's creativity, his drive to experiment with design, was instrumental in Weisbord's development of his own process, *Future Search*.

As Weisbord explained it, the 1986 lab would be the last he and Peter ran together at Bethel. It was a 2-week lab designed for experts in the field of change. Weisbord commented he was anxious to experiment with the Future Search process, which was part of the design. The first week, they (Vaill and Weisbord) ran the lab according to the original plan, and it was the "worst lab ever." The second week (after making some adjustments) was the "best ever." As Weisbord described it, Vaill's ability to *experiment with experience in ways that he and others could use what they were learning* was a hallmark of working with him. Weisbord later reflected:

> In fact, Peter is the one who added "helpful mechanisms" to the six-box model (as found in "Productive Workplaces," 1986) as a catch-all to the things that I found didn't fit in the other boxes. He and I were talking one day, and I couldn't figure out what to do with these things that didn't fit. And I said, These things are helpful mechanisms... and he said "Then why don't you call it that?" And later he liked to say "that (helpful mechanisms) is the most useful box of all." That captures him in a nutshell...In the end it's what you do to help integrate.... (Jamieson and Milbrandt, June 2016c)

Weisbord concluded, Vaill's focus on what was useful stuck with him as he later helped developed his ideas on "acts of leadership" (being a good innovator, helping people collaborate across boundaries, etc.). Vaill's creativity with and concern for how things "worked" was one of his greatest gifts.

Key Contributions: A Life of Leading and Learning

Peter B. Vaill's life has been filled with writing and thinking but also leading in learning. As an educator for nearly 45 years, Vaill's interactions with others ranged from teaching in formal academic settings to presenting among peers. It is difficult to ascertain the impact of these interactions to those whose life Vaill touched. In speaking with a former student, Eric Dent, who is now an Endowed Chair in Ethics at Florida Gulf Coast University, we found a story that echoed Peter's own experiences as student at Harvard:

> I started an MBA program at George Washington University in 1984. I was planning to major in finance. So as you know every MBA student has to take the core courses and so I was taking a required organizational behavior class and he (Vaill) was my professor.... And while I was taking that class there were some things that were happening at work (related to what I was learning in the class) and that changed my interest from computer science and the physical sciences to human behavior. After that class the trajectory of my life changed from a career field in one area to a life-long interest in human behavior. (Milbrandt, July 2016b)

And later when describing Vaill's approach in the classroom, Dent reflected:

> You are going to get a pretty one sided story from me, I am a huge Peter Vaill fan. I think he is one of the wisest people I have ever met. I was always very impressed that he didn't teach from notes, which was different from the other faculty I had met at that time. He just seemed to know the material inside and out. He was able to place things in historical contexts and come up with incredible examples that seemed to illustrate in real ways the concepts that he was teaching. (Milbrandt, July 2016b)

In a different interview with William (Bill) Monson, who worked with Vaill in the executive MBA program at the University of St. Thomas (UST), Monson commented:

> I met Peter through a paper he wrote, the paper was titled "Notes on Running an Organization" and I made an immediate connection with him having never met him because he had such clarity on the topic. (Jamieson and Milbrandt, June 2016b)

Further reflecting on Peter's approach with students, Bill added:

> .... he was always careful not to privilege the art of management, or the science of management, but let's talk about the practice of management. What its really like for the person in the position called manager. And one of his core contributions, was his way is to go about this which was a reflexive process. (Jamieson and Milbrandt, June 2016b)

In Peter Vaill's own writing, he would eventually address the topic of teaching, identifying this role as both primary and important to his identity. In a reflective essay on his teaching, Vaill (1997) wrote:

> ....I have functioned as a teacher/speaker/presenter/workshop facilitator on the average of at least 2 or 3 times a month for my entire career....to capture the diversity of my experience in this chapter, I do not use the words teacher and student and classroom to talk about my work. I refer to myself as a presenter, to those I am presenting to as participants and to the setting in

> which I am doing it as sessions. These words for me do better justice to the range of my experience and to the fact that so many important learnings have occurred outside my role as a teacher of students in a classroom. (pp. 261–262)

In scope of Vaill's career, whether as the presenter or participant, this much seems true: Vaill's sense that good leading is learning and good learning is being aware of the opportunities and conditions needed to maximize learning for yourself and others.

Efficacy at the Point of Action

Perhaps it is in Vaill's earliest work and writings that we can see the greatest fire between his words, and we can see the solidification of his argument that leaders and organizations need to pay more attention to the experience, to the act of managing, to developing a consciousness and awareness which informs *how* things *happen* or *don't*.

In an article Vaill published on the field of OB, entitled "Cookbooks, Auctions, and Claptrap Cocoons" (short title, 1979), Vaill writes:

> I simply cannot imagine an academic field which lacks any of the components of OB: Its interest in action and its connection to the work of affairs; its eclectic intellect and relative freedom from preoccupation with the fine difference between psychology, sociology, philosophy, history, political science and economics... If we were more interested in action we would attach more importance to the experience.... We would be awed and humbled by the obvious fact that most of the time, most people make plans and are actually able to carry them out. We would ask, "How is that?" "How is that?" (Vaill 1979, p. 3)

This question and the preceding statements imply a train of thinking which would lay the foundation of Vaill's later work. The observation that leaders will need to let go of the formulas, the cooked up theories, and the "generalized" checklist of "what to do" in order to answer the better question, "how to do it?" To illustrate his concern for the "checklist trends" and often "impracticality" of theories that were constructed apart from practice, he offered the analogy:

> We've all heard managers and students ask for a cookbook (and among ourselves we speak condescendingly and even disdainfully of such needs). But what would the cookbook look like as written by a contemporary, OB professor? Well, it would probably take a systems view and discuss at great length the interactions of the cook, ingredients, utensils, sink, stove and diner. Reading it, one would not be able to tell if it was addressed to the spoon, the salt shaker, the cook or the dough.... As the field of cookbook theory matured, sub-specialists would emerge. We would produce a doctoral field in salt-shakers. Two-factor theories of the cook's motivation would be offered....ultimately the heavy-hitters in cookbook theory would be sitting in endowed chairs, satraps in a game which, long since, had relegated the cooks to the sidelines. (Vaill 1979, p. 4)

Vaill's laser-like focus on practice and study of how managers and organizations "got things done" would be consummate throughout his career and eventually prompt Peter to look at the role of leading and learning, in increasingly complex environments: in other words, twenty-first century organizations.

Midway into his career, Vaill set into motion his thoughts on this in what he described as "high-performing systems" (Vaill 1982). As Vaill conceived it, "high-performing systems" were ones in which the leaders "share three commitments – time, feeling, and focus – that enable them to project and maintain a clear and effective sense of purpose among all system members."

- *Time* refers to the observable and consistent long hours leaders devote – Vaill clarified in his later reflections on this that these leaders are not necessarily "workaholics" but typically stay longer hours than their counterparts who are not members of a high-performing system.
- *Feeling* refers to the clarity, respect, and devotion for which they express to the system and the people that work in it.
- *Focus* refers to an uncanny thoroughness of understanding of the work. Knowing what two or three things that need to get done and moving into action on them.

In these early comments, Vaill's sense of urgency and call for change is both unwavering and unapologetic: "Managing as a Performing Art" (1989) was a concept whose time had come.

Shifting the Paradigm

By the mid-1980s, Peter Vaill's sense that the management theory being taught in schools was outdated and the literature being used to teach MBAs was ineffective in preparing them for the "real world" was growing. It was at this time that he and a colleague were facilitating a session at the ODN conference called "My Practice." The session was meant to explore the current experiences of managers, leaders, facilitators, and other participants who attended.

As Peter reflected on this session and his growing observations of the increasing levels of change, uncertainty, and turbulence that management and leaders were facing, he offered that "leaders and managers are in a position of stepping into the dark with most of the initiatives they propose. They don't know what's going to happen next." In response to this suggestion, a participant who remains unknown offered his experience stating:

> Most managers are taught to think of themselves as paddling their canoes on calm, still lakes. . .they're led to believe that they should pretty much be able to go where they want, when they want, using means that are under their control. Sure there will be temporary disruptions during changes of various sorts – periods when you will have to shoot the rapids. . . .but the disruptions will be temporary, and when things settle down you will be back on calm lake mode. But it has been my experience, he concluded, that you never get out of the rapids. (Vaill 1989, p.)

Of course, hindsight is the best foresight. If today's readers pick up *Managing as a Performing Art* (1989), they may find themselves sucking air through their teeth as they shake their head in awe at the relevance "permanent white water" holds today.

Vaill's insights in Managing as a Performing Art are unchanged by time, and are as relevant now as when written. The metaphor and its meaning to organizations illustrate the feeling today's managers often talk of as "putting out fires," "going backward," and the feeling of being incapacitated in their ability to "get a handle on it." In permanent white water, leaders are sailing at breakneck speed into the unknown, propelled forward by forces they have no control over: the continuous, roaring white water beneath them. Peter's essential point is that it is incumbent upon leaders to stop putting their attention on how things got done on placid waters and turn their attention to how things are getting done in "white water."

In another well-known essay that followed, *Notes on Running an Organization* (Vaill 1992), Peter expanded upon his thinking on the need to learn from and observe the experience of practice commenting:

> Theory and practice do not "integrate"; they dance with each other, sometimes lustily, but just as often ploddingly or with one lording over the other or warily and with stony indifference. But it also must be said that in a school of administration, management, leadership, or practice, if theory and practice do not dance with each other somehow, the learner will graduate not knowing much about practice nor having gained any increment in concrete skill nor remembering any of the theories that were intended to be relevant in the future. (Vaill 1992)

Ultimately, in his writings, Vaill planted the seeds for a new paradigm: *Learning as a way of Being*. As Vaill points out, the model of the organization in which leaders can assume to know what to expect is becoming obsolete, that the emphasis on technical and rational solutions, or "off-the-shelf" remedies were no longer useful – if they ever were! Replaced with an increasing need to manage unknown thinking and action, organizations and the people in them need to learn how to manage the challenges of permanent white water, where the reality is chaos and uncertainty.

Vaill grounded this new paradigm in the following key assumptions:

- Reality is socially constructed.
- That the nature of "being" is subjective (there are many truths, perspectives, and meanings).
- The most effective leaders (in "permanent white water") will seek to understand and learn from their experiences and from the perspectives of those who report to them.

These key assumptions offer a compelling new vison of organization in the "new age" in his hallmark thinking on the art of managing permanent white water that came to maturity in his second book, *Learning as a Way of Being* (1996).

Toward a Human Image of the Organization

The value of *Learning as a Way of Being* (1996) lies not so much in the ready-made skills or steps offered to the reader but rather a perception of consciousness and the processes needed to develop it in future organizations. Vaill challenges his readers to consider these frames (old and new) of the needs of the individual and the organization stating:

> The permanent white water in today's systems is creating a situation in which institutional learning patterns are simply inadequate to the challenge. Subject matter is changing too fast. Learners are interweaving their learning with work responsibilities and expecting their learning to be directly relevant to these responsibilities. . .The problem is to envision what learning can be and how it can go on giving. . . while the traditional paradigm for conduction is not designed for the task and is in many ways inadequate under the current conditions. (Vaill 1996, p. 41)

Vaill goes on to define an approach and development of whole-person learning – or learning "that goes on all the time and extends to all aspects of a person's life. . . . " (Vaill 1996, p. 43) in seven types:

1. Self-directed learning
2. Creative learning
3. Expressive learning
4. Feeling learning
5. Online learning
6. Continual learning
7. Reflexive learning

In Vaill's typology, learning becomes the antidote to "white water." And Vaill is quick to point out that learning in organizations is necessary at all levels. To do this, Vaill suggests we must (collectively) shift our attention from understanding what has been (past performance metrics, ROI, profits, and loss) to what is becoming (new insights, synergies, invention) from the static (the tried and true, past successes, old pathways) to the dynamic (interactions, experiences, collaborations, innovation) from what is fixed (what we do) to what flows (how we are doing it). In this new frame of the organization, we can do better than surviving permanent white water – we can master the experience of it.

After writing *Learning as a Way of Being: Strategies for Survival in a World of Permanent White Water* (1996), Peter left GW for an appointment as an endowed chair in the newly forming Opus College of Business, at the University of St. Thomas (1997–2003), and helped develop a cutting-edge executive MBA program. Within that period at St. Thomas, Vaill would publish his third book, *Spirited Leading and Learning: Process Wisdom for a New Age* (1998), and various other commentaries on the field of OB and OD.

Process Wisdom: The Heart of Organizations

Vaill's early and later work on *process wisdom* is spread throughout his writings and teachings. He was regularly commenting on what managers did well (process), what didn't work well (process), and the need for new ways of acting (process) in the growing landscape of permanent white water. In one of Vaill's more recent chapters on "Process Wisdom" in Thomas Cumming's, *Handbook of Organization Development* (2008), he pulls together his earlier and current thinking on the role of process in social systems and organizations. In this chapter, Vaill emphasizes how process affects learning and subsequently all we do – and poses the question, if content is constantly changing, in what ways might our processes need to change too?

Vaill highlights eight virtues *process wisdom* brings to an organization in change. He Vaill argues that process wisdom:

1. Surfaces the *what* and the *how* in the organization, what the organization is trying to do, and the goal development and formal goal-directedness
2. Calls out the social (relationship) changes needed or implied by any change
3. Identifies the unintended consequences of leadership initiatives
4. Anticipates events that will need to happen as part of understanding how people may be affected by the changes
5. Helps to see beyond the immediate context of an action, into the larger system
6. Anticipates downstream disruptions to social process
7. Teaches others how to see and use process wisdom and provides a common language to more deeply explain what people are experiencing
8. Understands the element of the "unknown" when facing a "process frontier" and creates ways to authentically help people maintain experimentation and learning

In Vaill's *Spirited Leading and Learning* (1998), he continued to expand the challenge of the managerial leader being twofold – to recognize the importance of purpose and meaning in what people are doing (as they see it) and how to help one's self and others to determine what's missing and what needs to be worked on.

Themes in *Learning as a Way of Being* (1996) and *Spirited Leading and Learning* (1998), as well as in later essays (Vaill 2005, 2007, 2008), build to this general and final conclusion: Organizational life demands learning that is more personal, person-centered, and relevant to the needs of the individual, in order to serve the human system which Vaill contends is "the only side of the organization!" In this spirit Vaill rejects the dominant image of the organization, what he refers to as the "material-instrumental" perspective, offering an alternate vision of organizations, with a five-way bottom line (Vaill 1989). Vaill writes:

> I have concluded that it is possible, to talk about five ongoing and intertwined streams of valuing – a "five-way bottom line"... My alternative to the M-I model is a view of the organization, as an intertwined stream of energy that keeps it going from the individual and joint actions of people as they work out their sense of what is important, of what they need to do in their own present reality to fulfill and continue to pursue their sense of who they are. The five categories are simple and easily recognizable. I call them the economic, the technical, the communal, the adaptive, and the transcendent. (Vaill 2009 Conference Paper)

This highly "conscious" awareness on development was integral to Vaill's concepts of "Spirited Leading and Learning" (1998). As Vaill surmised, a leader's ability to understand meaning and purpose in their own life is the measure of their ability to develop such consciousness in others. And without this understanding of self – this whole-person consciousness – Vaill contends organizations cannot and will not survive the "rapids" of permanent white water. Ultimately, Peter invites us to become explorers, to abandon the idea of being learned to become *learning beings*, and to abandon the image and meaning of the organization as an economic engine and replace it with a construct that is more resilient, robust, whole, and humane. Peter points to key elements of this transformation:

- The practice of becoming *learners* versus *learned.*
- The practice of balancing what is technical (techniques, skills, competencies) with what is social (the social nature of human beings, our values, our assumptions, our desires and needs).
- The practice of valuing the process as much as the product. While work life has a utility, product, or service, leaders must attend to the process (purpose, meaning, and ways of working that honor the people who are and make up the organization).
- The practice of framing organizational scholarship and (i.e., management, OB, OD, ODC, HR, and all its various factions) management education in the landscape of application.

The culmination of the past 60 years of Peter's thinking on the topic of the person and the organization offers managers, educators, change agents, and change thinkers a compelling alternative: a new image of the person and the organization. In this new image, the needs of the organization are *not* conflicted with the needs of the individual but rather contingent on them. Vaill's thinking comes full circle in his final published thoughts in *Spirited Leading and Learning* and his chapter on *Process Wisdom* (2008).

Through his own self-study and observations of the field of management and change, Peter has offered a compelling bridge – to help the current and next generation of change thinkers begin to develop a body of consciousness around "practice wisdom."

New Insights: A Leader's Impact

In addition to the wide influence that Peter B. Vaill has had in scholarship (nearly 3000 citations from various articles are cited through "Google Scholar"), Vaill has also had impact in the field of practice and our own (the authors) work. Dave Jamieson reflected on Vaill's early influence, which for him began as early as 1970. Jamieson writes:

> As a young, new doctoral student at UCLA, we all had a desk in "student cubicles." On one vacant desk there were copies of many articles, working papers of faculty and previous students (most mimeographed!). Many of Peter's early essays were there, for students to read. The earliest concepts that I read about that stuck with me were "practice theory", the "*art* of managing" and "high performing systems" papers. (Some of which were recently

found in my personal archives, that have moved multiple times!) From my doctoral studies to today I had a strong orientation to practice and to develop the capability to lead change. And Vaill's earliest work resonated with me immediately. By graduation, I was already beginning a consulting career and working as a professional association leader.

Almost from the start, the image of the organization as a system was central in my thinking and speaking; additionally high performing teams became a mainstay in my work, as was my continual pursuit of my own "practice theory" which has never abated. In the beginning I chose to pursue a scholar-practitioner life and was passionate about exploring how theory could inform practice and vice-versa. As my experience accumulated, teaching provided the platform to clarify my own thinking on practice. Soon, I began to develop models and frameworks derived from my developing practice to help explain what I was observing. All of my work was informed and supported by others' theories and research, but was always slightly different based on the practice sources. This scholar-practitioner focus enabled me to successfully teach managers and later change agents, as they could relate to the 'practice theories' more easily and found great usefulness in the courses.

Although Peter and I did not meet one another at UCLA (we met much later) Peter's indirect influence on me can be in evidenced by the early writings on the topics mentioned above. Much of my own writing, alone and with others, is heavily influenced by practice or has been written to impact practice. Some of my current presentations express this: "How We Change Needs to Change," "Changing How We Change", "Why Organization Change is so Difficult and What We Can Do about It", "Learning Masterful Practice", "Mastering Consultation" and, "Suppose We Took OD Seriously" explore these current questions. Similar themes are evident in my other writing:

From books such as:

- *The Facilitators Fieldbook (1999, 2006, 2012)*
- *Consultation for Organization Change (2010)*
- *Consultation for Organization Change, Revisited (2016)*

To chapters and articles such as:

- *The Critical Role of Use of Self in Organization Development Consulting (2016)*
- *"Exploring the Relationship between HR and OD" (2015)*
- *"Exploring the Relationship between Change Management and OD" (2015)*
- *"The Practice of OD" (2008)*
- *"Values, Ethics and OD Practice" (2006, 2014)*
- *"Front-End Work: Effectively Engaging with the Client System" (2009)*
- *"Aligning the Organization for a Team-Based Strategy"(1996)*
- *"Design as the Bridge between Intention and Impact" (2015)*
- *"The Heart and Mind of the Practitioner: Remembering Bob Tannenbaum"(2003)*

- *"You are the Instrument"(1991)*
- *"What it Means to be a Change Agent"(1990)*

Finally, Peter and I were both embraced and inspired by Bob Tannenbaum and his central thinking about "use of self." And later, at the University of St. Thomas, although at different times and in different roles, I have continued to both concentrate on leadership, organization development and adult learning and, in the last 10 years, digging deeper into the "use of self" concepts – developing, writing, researching and teaching about it, especially as it relates to helping professionals of all types; and leaders and change agents, in particular. (Jamieson et al. 2013; McKnight and Jamieson 2016) As Peter wrote in his last book:

> ...all true leadership is indeed spiritual leadership, even if you hardly ever hear it put that flatly. The reason is that beyond everything else that can be said about it, leadership is concerned with bringing out the best in people. As such, one's best is tied intimately to one's deepest sense of oneself, to one's spirit. My leadership efforts must touch that in myself and in others." (Vaill 1998a)

For Jackie Milbrandt, who is currently a doctoral student in the field of organization development and change, Vaill's "permanent white water" and "learning as a way of being" have taken a prominent role in her early impressions in the overall field of study. Milbrandt writes:

> As a newcomer to the study of the field of OD and Change, I first learned of Vaill's work during my involvement with a project involving the *Journal of Management Inquiry's* "Six Degrees" podcast series (JMI Six Degrees 2016). The project involved a team of about a half-dozen interviewers and a list of 50 or more of the great thinkers in OD. The goal of the project was to capture various perspectives on the early and current thinking in the field of OD. Looking through the list, Peter Vaill's name jumped out at me. At the time, I had only really heard of his work through references to him – but that quickly changed. The more Peter and I talked, the more I became immersed in his writing and thinking about the nature of organizations and change. Of his many ideas, two have captivated my imagination and interest. Namely, the connectivity between personal experience and learning, and the perspective that change is not only continuous but accelerating.
>
> My current understanding of "permanent white water" and "learning as a way of being" have shaped my development and how I perceive the challenges of the time. In a world which I experience growing more diverse, complex, and turbulent – it is of critical importance to me to embrace the enormous challenge of learning and sharing what I learn in ways that help people collaborate across different perspectives, time zones, and cultures. This has presented a need for new models and ways of thinking about organizations and change. For myself and others in the field of OD and Change I find an urgent need to learn how to do this in order to function in today's volatile, unpredictable, complex, and ambiguous (VUCA) context (see Bennett and Lemoine 2014; Pasmore and O'Shea 2010). And, I have found myself reflecting on the broader questions – What are the intersections between learning and change? And how can I find ways to support both in organizations?
>
> In a recent presentation (co-facilitated with David Jamieson and Ken Nishikawa at the ODN 2015 titled "Connecting the Dots: Global Communities of Practice in the Field of OD") issues of globalization, the need to balance social and technical systems, and rapid change were at the forefront of the discussion. Reoccurring concerns over how to "develop conditions for psychological safety," "mechanisms to transfer and develop new knowledge" and how to

create spaces for "innovative" and novel approaches were discussed. The depth and attention to which Peter Vaill spent (a life-time) observing, thinking, and writing on these topics – and the insights he offers – in my view make his work relevant and valuable to my own understanding as a current scholar-practitioner and to generations in the foreseeable future.

Legacies and Unfinished Business: Reframing the Human-side of Enterprise

During and after Vaill's time at GW, he made key contributions to various networks and associations he was connected to as a consultant, scholar, and educator. People who worked closely with him over the years expressed their love and respect for him, and his incredible insights, generosity, and creativity he offered to them personally, and the organizations to which Vaill belonged.

As an active member, Vaill held various roles at the Center for Creative Leadership and continued to work with NTL. As a long-standing, active member at the OB Teaching Society (OBTS) and attendee of their annual conference (OBTC) and lifelong member of the OD Network (ODN), he received various honors and awards. In 2002, the OBTS awarded Peter with the "David L. Bradford Outstanding Educator Award." The same year, Peter received the ODN's "Lifetime Achievement Award." A few years later in 2007, he was awarded OBTS's "Peter Frost Mentoring Award." The people who knew him well commented on his ability to make the complex clearer, create spaces for personal reflection, show his own vulnerability, and approach all his work with humility. He was a critically thinking, reflective scholar-practitioner!

And like most good scholar-practitioners, he was integrative, bridging across disciplines, weaving perspectives and concepts together, and producing new understanding.

In a final interview with Peter, he presciently reflected on his current and developing thinking and observations – in three areas:

1. On transforming the image of people-in-the organization to people-as-the organization." Vaill offered:

> For almost 60 years we've been living with a massive misconstruction of the nature of organizations. Since Douglas McGregor published his famous book in 1960, the "Human Side of Enterprise," for the whole of the succeeding 56 years, we've accepted that construction – that there is a human side of enterprise.... and then there is all the business stuff; that's a misconstruction. The more correct construction is as follows: There is only one side to organizations and that's the human side. (Milbrandt, July 2016b)

2. On resurrecting the ideas of *spirit* and *purpose* into organizational thinking. On this, Vaill reflected:

> Since World War II almost no one, among the big names so to speak, in behavioral science has attached anything to the human being you might call a spiritual nature. That the feeling of being-that there is a higher meaning and higher purpose; the feeling of having a higher-

self that is up above all this craziness that is in the world. For some people it is the feeling of being blessed, processing or seeking God's grace – for others it is things to do with spirituality. (Milbrandt, July 2016b)

3. On defining leadership as a landscape of practice, Vaill concluded:

And finally, this whole field of practice – we just don't have a good understanding of what practice is – We have theory and then we have the trenches – that is not a deep understanding of practice – so I am working on a whole approach to practice that tries to transform that. (Milbrandt, July 2016b)

Conclusion

While so many in the field were building islands, Peter B. Vaill was building an arc made up of new ways of thinking, practicing, and approaching change through helping the "people who are the organization" renew hope, purpose and spirit in the work. We have some work ahead of us. But where do we begin?

As Vaill so often pointed out, we (as a field at large) have been asking the wrong questions. The vast majority have been looking at the outcomes in organizations "what happened" – instead we might be looking at the processes "what is happening?" We (as a field at large) have been trying to frame practice inside theory – instead we might try to frame theory in practice. As it would seem, in general, we have been barking up the proverbial wrong tree.

In essence, after nearly 60 years in the field of scholarship and practice, Vaill concludes that we have more questions than meaningful answers. He leaves us with some hints to what these may be:

- What do we really know about practice, if we do not question what *it* is?
- How can we support organizational learning and development if we do not more fully understand how *we* are learning and developing?
- How can we expect to understand the whole, if we do not understand ourselves?

As Vaill suggests, it is incumbent upon the next generation not only ask these questions (which are both timeless and timely) but to reflect on them and our experiences to inform our learning and leading change in the twenty-first century. For more than 60 years, Peter B. Vaill has dedicated his life to these questions and more. He has devoted a career to shaping the perspective of the fields of management, leadership, and change by creating "learning" and "learning spaces." Retired now, and no longer teaching formally, Vaill's essays and articles serve as a placeholder for others to explore. The questions posed and the insights shared, through numerous books, articles, and essays, gently beckon to us – inviting, challenging, and coaxing us to embark on a journey into the *art of learning, managing* and *leading change.*

References

Argyris, C. (1957). *Personality and organization: The conflict between the system and the individual.* New York: Harper and Row.

Bennett, N., & Lemoine, G. J. (2014). What a difference a word makes: Understanding threats to performance in a VUCA world. *Business Horizons, 57*(3), 311–317.

Blake, R., & Mouton, J. (1964). *The managerial grid: The key to leadership excellence.* Houston: Gulf Publishing.

Bradford, L. P., Gibb, J., & Benne, K. D. (1964). *T-group theory & laboratory method: Innovations in re-education.* New York: Wiley.

Dent, E. B. (2002). The messy history of OB&D: How three strands came to be one. *Management Decision, 40*(3), 266–280.

Emery, F., & Trist, E. (1965). The causal texture of organizational environments. *Human Relations, 18*, 21–32.

Harvey, J. B. (1988). *The Abilene paradox and other meditations on management.* San Francisco: Jossey-Bass.

Herzberg, F. (1976). *The managerial choice: To be efficient and to be human.* Homewood: Dow Jones-Irwin.

Jamieson, D., & Milbrandt, J. M. (2016a, May). Personal interview with Peter Vaill.

Jamieson, D., & Milbrandt, J. M. (2016b, June). Personal interview with Peter Vaill.

Jamieson, D., & Milbrandt, J. M. (2016c, June). Phone interview with Marvin Weisbord.

Jamieson, D., Auron, M., & Shechtman, D. (2013). Managing use of self for masterful professional practice. In J.V. Vogelsang, M. Townsend, M. Minahan, D. Jamieson, J. Vogel, A Viets, C. Royal, and L. Valek (Eds.), *Handbook for strategic HR: Best practices in organization development from the OD Network* (pp.127–136). NY:AMACOM.

Journal of Management Inquiry (Producer). (2016). Six Degrees: Jackie Milbrandt interviews Peter Vaill about his life and career [Audio podcast]. Retrieved from http://itunes.apple.com

Kleiner, A. (2008). *The age of heretics.* San Francisco: Jossey-Bass.

Kramer, R. (2016). Dialogic organization development: The theory and practice of transformational change. *Academy of Management Learning and Education, 15*(3), 639–643.

Maslow, A. H. (1943). A theory of human motivation. *Psychological Review, 50*(4), 370.

Massarik, F., Margulies, N., & Tannenbaum, R. (1985). The development of human systems: Basic themes. In R. Tannenbaum, N. Margulies, & F. Massarik (Eds.), *Human systems development: New perspectives on people and organizations.* San Francisco: Jossey-Bass.

McGregor, D. (1960). The human side of enterprise. New York: McGraw-Hill.

McKnight, L., & Jamieson, D. (2016). The critical role of use of self in organization development consulting. In D. Jamieson, R. Barnett, & A. Buono (Eds.), *Consultation for organization change, revisited.* Charlotte: Information Age Publishing.

Milbrandt, J. M. (2016a, September). Phone interview with Erik Winslow.

Milbrandt, J. M (2016b, July). Personal interview with Peter Vaill.

Milbrandt, J. M. (2017, February). Personal interview with Peter Vaill.

Pasmore, B., & O'Shea, T. (2010). Leadership agility: A business imperative for a VUCA world. *People and Strategy, 33*(4), 32.

Roethlisberger, F. J. (1977). In G. Lombard (Ed.), *The elusive phenomena: An autobiographical account of my work in the field of organizational behavior at the Harvard Business School.* Cambridge, MA: Harvard University Press.

Roethlisberger, F. J., & Dickson, W. J. (1939). *Management and the worker.* Cambridge, MA: Harvard University Press.

Rogers, C. R. (1961). *On becoming a person.* Boston: Houghton Mifflin.

Ronken, H., & Lawrence, P. (1952). *Administering changes: A case study of human relations in a factory.* Cambridge, MA: Harvard University Press.

Vaill, P. B. (1971). Practice Theories in Organization Development. In *Academy of management proceedings*, 161–170.

Vaill, P. B. (1979). Cookbooks auctions, and claptrap cocoons. *Organizational Behavior Teaching Review, 4*(1), 3–6.

Vaill, P. B. (1982). The purposing of high- performance systems. *Organizational Dynamics, 11*(2), 23–39.

Vaill, P. B. (1989). *Managing as a performing art: New ideas for a world of chaotic change*. San Francisco: Jossey-Bass.

Vaill, P. B. (1992). Notes on "running an organization". *Journal of Management Inquiry, 1*(2), 130–138.

Vaill, P. B. (1996). *Learning as a way of being: Strategies for survival in a world of permanent white water*. San Francisco: Jossey-Bass.

Vaill, P. B. (1998a). *Spirited leading and learning: Process wisdom for the new age*. San Francisco: Jossey-Bass.

Vaill, P. B. (2007). F. J. Roethlisberger and the elusive phenomena of organizational behavior. *Journal of Management Education, 31*(3), 321–338.

Vaill, P. B. (2008). Process wisdom – The heart of organization development. In T. Cummings (Ed.), *Handbook of organization development*. Thousand Oaks: Sage.

Vaill, P. B. (2009). The Second Great Commandment and the Leaders Golden Rule. Working conference paper form the seeing things whole and John A. Ryan Institute for Catholic Social thought partnership at Augsburg College.

Further Reading

Buono, A., & Jamieson, D. (2010). *Consultation for organization change. Research in Management Consulting & Research in organization development and change series*. Charlotte: Information Age Publishing.

Creasey, T., Jamieson, D., Rothwell, W., & Severini, G. (2015). Exploring the relationship between change management and OD. In W. Rothwell, R. Sullivan, J. Stavros, & A. Sullivan (Eds.), *Practicing organization development and change* (4th ed.). San Francisco: Pfieffer Publishing.

Jamieson, D. (1990). What it means to be a change agent. *OD Practitioner, 22*(1), back cover.

Jamieson, D. (1991). You are the instrument. *OD Practitioner, 23*(1), p. 20.

Jamieson, D. (1996). Aligning the organization for a team-based strategy. In G. Parker (Ed.), *The handbook of best practices for teams* (Vol. 1) (pp. 299–312). Amherst: HRD Press.

Jamieson, D. (2003). The heart and mind of the practitioner: Remembering Bob Tannenbaum. *OD Practitioner, 35*(4), 3–8.

Jamieson, D. (2009). Front-end work: Effectively engaging with the client system. In W. Rothwell, R. Sullivan, J. Stavros, & A. Sullivan (Eds.), *Practicing organization development and change* (3rd ed.). San Francisco: Pfieffer Publishing.

Jamieson, D., & Gellermann, W. (2014). Values, ethics and OD practice. In B. Jones & M. Brazzel (Eds.), *The NTL handbook of organization development and change* (2nd ed.). San Francisco: NTL/Jossey-Bass.

Jamieson, D., & Rothwell, W. (2015). Exploring the relationship between HR and OD. In W. Rothwell, R. Sullivan, J. Stavros, & A. Sullivan (Eds.), *Practicing organization development and change* (4th ed.). San Francisco: Pfieffer Publishing.

Jamieson, D., & Worley, C. (2008). The practice of OD. In T. Cummings (Ed.), *The handbook of organization development*. Thousand Oaks: Sage Publications.

Jamieson, D., Adelson, C., & Dye, L. (2015). Design as the bridge between intention and impact. *Organization Development Practitioner, 47*(2), 7–14.

Jamieson, D., Barnett, R., & Buono, A. (2016). Consultation for organization change, revisited. *Research in management consulting and research in organization development and change series*. Charlotte: Information Age Publishing.

Justice, T. & Jamieson, D. (1999, 2006, 2012). The Facilitators Fieldbook, 1st, 2nd & 3rd Ed. New York: AMACOM.
Milbrandt, J. M. (2016, August). Phone interview with Eric Dent.
Vaill, P. B. (1967). Industrial engineering and socio-technical systems. *Journal of Industrial Engineering, 18*(9), 530.
Vaill, P. B. (1971). Practice theories in organization development. In *Academy of management proceedings*, 161–170.
Vaill, P. B. (1976). The expository model of science in organization design. *The Management of Organization Design, 1*, 73–88.
Vaill, P. B. (1979). Cookbooks auctions, and claptrap cocoons. *Organizational Behavior Teaching Review, 4*(1), 3–6.
Vaill, P. B. (1981a). Exploration and discovery or how can you tell whether you're getting anywhere when you don't know where you're going? *Exchange: The Organizational Behavior Teaching Journal, 6*(2), 15–19.
Vaill, P. B. (1981b). Thoughts on using poetry in the teaching of OB. *Exchange: The Organizational Behavior Teaching Journal, 6*(3), 50–51.
Vaill, P. B. (1982). The purposing of high-performance systems. *Organizational Dynamics, 11*(2), 23–39.
Vaill, P. B. (1983). The theory of managing in the managerial competency movement. *Exchange: The Organizational Behavior Teaching Journal, 8*(2), 50–54.
Vaill, P. B. (1984a). Process wisdom for a new age. In J. Adams (Ed.), *Transforming work*. Alexandria: Miles River Press.
Vaill, P. B. (1984b). Management as a marital art. *Organizational Behavior Teaching Review, 9*(3), 96–97.
Vaill, P. B. (1985a). Integrating the diverse directions of the behavioral sciences. In R. Tannenbaum, N. Margulies, F. Massarik, et al. (Eds.), *Human systems development* (pp. 547–577). San Francisio: Jossey-Bass.
Vaill, P. B. (1985b). A personal statement. *OD Practitioner, 17*(1), 15.
Vaill, P. B. (1985c). OD as a scientific revolution. *Contemporary Organization Development*, 28–41.
Vaill, P. B. (1988). A note on the idea of courage. *Organizational Behavior Teaching Review, 12*(3), 9–11.
Vaill, P. B. (1989). *Managing as a performing art: New ideas for a world of chaotic change*. San Francisco: Jossey-Bass.
Vaill, P. B. (1989). *Seven process frontiers for organization development. The emerging practice of organization development*. La Jolla: NTL Institute.
Vaill, P. B. (1989). Lou Pondy and the organizational funny bone. *Journal of Organizational Change Management, 2*(2), 22–25.
Vaill, P. B. (1991). The inherent spirituality of organizations. In *Academy of management proceedings*, Miami Beach, 3–7 August 1991.
Vaill, P. B. (1992). Notes on running an organization. *Journal of Management Inquiry, 1*(2), 130–138.
Vaill, P. B. (1993). Visionary leadership. The Portable MBA in management, pp. 12–37.
Vaill, P. B. (1995). Best practices and organizational learning. *Organization Development Journal, 13*, 33–39.
Vaill, P. B. (1996). *Learning as a way of being: Strategies for survival in a world of permanent white water*. San Francisco: Jossey-Bass.
Vaill, P. B. (1997). Meditations on a poet's overall's. In R. Andre & P. J. Frost (Eds.), *Researchers hooked on teaching: Noted scholars discus the synergies of teaching and research*. Thousand Oaks: Sage.
Vaill, P. B. (1998a). *Spirited leading and learning: Process wisdom for the new age*. San Francisco: Jossey-Bass.
Vaill, P. B. (1998b). The unspeakable texture of process wisdom. In S. Srivastva & D. L. Cooperrider (Eds.), *Organizational wisdom and executive courage* (pp. 25–39). San Francisco: Jossey-Bass.

Vaill, P. B. (1998c). Executive development as spiritual development. In S. Srivastva & D. L. Cooperrider (Eds.), *Appreciative Management and Leadership: The Power of Positive Thought and Action in Organizations* (pp. 323–352). San Francisco: Jossey-Bass.
Vaill, P. B. (2000). Introduction to spirituality for business leadership. *Journal of Management Inquiry, 9*(2), 115.
Vaill, P. B. (2005). A Paradigm for Professional Vitality. In D. Bradford & W. Burke (Eds.), *Reinventing organization development: New approaches to change in organizations*. San Farncisco: Pfeiffer.
Vaill, P. B. (2007). F. J. Roethlisberger and the elusive phenomena of organizational behavior. *Journal of Management Education, 31*(3), 321–338.
Vaill, P. B. (2007). Organizational epistemology – Interpersonal relations in organization and the emergence of wisdom. In E.H. Kessler & J.R. Bailey (Eds.), *Handbook of organizational and managerial wisdom*. (pp. 327–356). Thousands Oaks, CA: Sage Publications
Vaill, P. B. (2008). Process wisdom – The heart of the organization development. In T. Cummings (Ed.), *Handbook of organization development* (pp. 219–236). Thousand Oaks, CA: Sage Publications.
Vaill, P. B. (2013). Towards a behavioral description of high-performing systems. In J.V. Vogelsang, M. Townsend, M. Minahan, D. Jamieson, J. Vogel, A Viets, C. Royal, and L. Valek (Eds.), *Handbook for strategic HR: Best practices in organization development from the OD Network* (pp. 234–240). NY: AMACOM.
Weisbord, M. (1987). *Productive workplaces*. San Francisco: Jossey-Bass.

Karl E. Weick: Departing from Traditional Rational Models of Organizational Change

83

Dave Schwandt

Abstract

Karl E. Weick is one of management's and organizational science's most influential social psychologists. He, more than most theorists, is responsible for pointing to the prevailing theories of management and organizational change and asking very pragmatic questions such as: "Is this plausible? What are we missing? What if we say this?" This chapter focuses on only four concepts within his large body of work: (1) organizing as a human process; (2) collective interpretation and loose coupling; (3) sensemaking; and (4) surprise and managing the unexpected. These concepts represent major departures from traditional rational models of organizational change. They are not necessarily labeled organizational change phenomena per se; however, each of them has been and remains critical to understanding human actions in the continuous flow of social change.

Keywords

Enactment • Human interaction • Loose coupling • Managing the unexpected • Sensemaking • Surprise

Contents

D. Schwandt (✉)
George Washington University, Washington, DC, USA
e-mail: schwandt@gwu.edu

D.B. Szabla et al. (eds.), *The Palgrave Handbook of Organizational Change Thinkers*,
DOI 10.1007/978-3-319-52878-6_62

Introduction

> Every experience enacted and undergone modifies the one who acts and undergoes, while this modification affects, whether we wish it or not, the quality of subsequent experience. (Dewey 1938, p. 35)

When Karl Weick reflects on his early days growing up in the Midwest, he usually recounts his adventures with locomotives and train yards. If he does not choose trains, he tells of his early love for music, and specifically jazz. His selection of these two remembrances as being significant was not based just on the excitement of travel or the beauty of jazz, but rather the processes that individuals were employing that made them important to him: "From the beginning I was hooked on the problem of coordination and collective improvisation" (Weick 1996b, p. 288).

For Weick, the "problems of coordination and collective improvisation" have provided a logical thread of conceptual continuity for his contributions to organizational change and management theory. His early perceptions have now become concepts such as organizing, enactment, sensemaking, interruptions, and mindful management of the unexpected. Although he has added differing venues for his perceptions, he remains concerned with the human condition and how we coordinate with each other and survive in unexpected situations in which surprise is always a possibility.

Surprise may occur differently for locomotive engineers than it does for jazz musicians; however, the combination of their cognitive processes with their contexts produces similar complex questions concerning the formation of human meaning. The complexity of the questions that interested him would require knowledge of both the individual and the collective level of analysis. He recognized early that knowledge of just psychology, or just sociology, would not be enough to understand human interactions and cognition.

Influences and Motivations: From Laboratory Psychology to the Management Sciences

After finishing his undergraduate degree in psychology at Wittenberg College, Weick attended Ohio State University (OSU) for his graduate studies (M.A. and Ph.D.). While at OSU, his curriculum spanned a broad spectrum of expertise including counseling and clinical psychology and organizational behavior. Weick's graduate work culminated in his dissertation research in human cognition and behavior.

Reflecting back on his early research (after 30 years), Weick noted its significance as a precursor to his later research concerning enactment and dealing with the unexpected:

> What continues to interest me about that study is that not only does it capture the effect of cognition on action. It also captures the effect of action on cognition. It does the latter more by accident than design. Even though I designed the study to create the cognitive dissonance, I also accidently created the conditions later found to induce strong behavioral commitment. (Weick 1993b, p. 6)

With Weick's initial interest in what people actually do and think, it is not surprising to find that he aligns with classical thinkers such as William James (1950) and John Dewey (1950). They offered him more than a worldview; in their writings they were using society to pose similar questions that Weick had concerning human behavior and cognition in organizations. Their commitment to the importance of the ongoing and recurring nature of human interactions, both at the individual and collective level, elevated the importance of human nature and conduct. Their pragmatic, and at times constructionist, philosophical or metaphysical ideas remain a part of Weick's ontology and epistemology today. He cites their work often in arguing for a need to understand not only why people act as they do in organizations but how they cognitively and emotionally cope with the puzzles of their environments.

After graduating with a Ph.D. in "organizational psychology" (the title of the degree is said to have been created at OSU for him and one other's plan of study because they were beyond the "standard curriculum"), Weick took academic positions at Purdue University and the University of Minnesota and was a visiting professor at the State University of Utrecht, the Netherlands. At Minnesota he was professor of psychology and also the director of the Laboratory for Social Relations. Much of his work during this period related to dissonance, perceived equity in pay, use of the laboratory as microcultures, and human productivity. It is also during this time period that he published the first edition of *The Social Psychology of Organizing* (1969).

In 1972, Weick accepted an appointment as professor of psychology and organizational behavior at Cornell University (receiving the Nicholas H. Noyes Endowed Chair in 1977). While there he became the editor of the well-known journal, *Administrative Science Quarterly*, and remained the editor from 1977 to 1985. After leaving Cornell and spending 4 years at the University of Texas as the Harkins and Company Centennial Chair in Business Administration, in 1988, he accepted the position of Rensis Likert Collegiate Professor of Organizational Behavior and Psychology in the Stephen M. Ross School of Business, University of Michigan, where he now serves as distinguished university professor, emeritus.

Each of Weick's career choices has moved him closer to the management sciences as opposed to the laboratory psychology that characterized his early career and education. His research and writing agenda have also increasingly reflected his early questioning of coordination and collective improvisation. The path that Weick selected for both his early preparation and his subsequent theorizing and research has allowed him to "change the conversations" in not only organizational sciences and social psychology but in how we see social change and human nature (Gioia 2006).

Through these various career moves, and many accolades such as Best Dissertation, Best Journal Article, Best Book, and Scholar of the Year, Weick has become one of the management and organizational science's most influential social psychologists. He, more than most theorists, is responsible for pointing to the prevailing theories of management and organizational change and asking, "Is this plausible? What are we missing? What if we say this?" He does this while motivating new discussions, elevating our concern for the human condition, and managing not to alienate other thinkers. It is important for him that humans are not portrayed as just environmental reactors or cultural dupes, but that they have choices that can, through their actions, enact their environments, thus creating different situations and new variations.

Key Contributions: Organizing as Respectful Interaction and Sensemaking

In this section, I discuss four advancements that stem from the work of Karl E. Weick. Each has had a direct impact on our understanding of organizational change (or, as Weick would say, "organizing"). The discussion that follows is couched in the theme of this volume, organizational change, and does not come close to representing the complete scope of Weick's long career achievements. There are risks involved in attempting to single out only four contributions from a career that spans five decades and has produced more than 200 journal articles, books, book chapters, and uncountable presentations. The same risk was mentioned by Weick in a review of Gerald Salancik's legacy (Weick 1996a), in which he provided the following caveat:

> What I underline, quote, and cite in Salancik's work may well be the very ideas that bored him and misrepresents what he felt were his best insights. I'm sorry if that is blatantly true. If it is, it probably means at a minimum, that I don't 'know' myself, nor did he. That notwithstanding, misrepresentation is an inherent risk in an understanding such as this and comprises its normal, natural trouble. (p. 565)

I invoke this same caveat for what follows.

Before we begin, it is important to note that Weick sees organizational change as a process that is continuous rather than episodic, nonlinear rather than linear, emergent as opposed to planned, and incremental rather than punctuated by the radical occurrence of a change action (Weick and Quinn 1999). In this context, he sees the role of change agents as facilitators that:

- Recognize, make salient, and reframe current patterns
- Shows how intentional change can be made at the margins

- Alters meaning by new language, enriched dialogue, and new identity
- Unblocks improvisation, translation, and learning (p. 366)

He believes that "what matters is the extent to which the program [of change] triggers sustained animation, direction, attention/updating, and respectful interaction" (Weick 2000, p. 233).

The four concepts that I have drawn from Weick's large body of work are (1) organizing as a human process, (2) collective interpretation and loose coupling, (3) sensemaking, and (4) surprise and managing the unexpected. These concepts represent major departures from traditional rational models of organizational change. They are not necessarily labeled organizational change phenomena per se; however, each of them has been and remains critical to understanding human actions in the continuous flow of change.

What follows is a description of these four concepts and their implications for our understanding of organizational change. It is my aim to (1) describe Weick's gentle but radical departure from prevailing thinking; (2) show that there is a consistency to his quest to understand how people coordinate and improvise – both at the individual and collective levels; and (3) demonstrate the resilience of these four concepts over the past 50 years of theorizing (Weick 2014). I allow the chronology of Weick's work to guide the sequencing of the four concepts to emphasize their interrelatedness over time.

Organizing as a Human Process

Weick's seminal work, *The Social Psychology of Organizing*, published in 1969 and significantly modified in 1979 (Weick 2015a), not only introduced a new way of using language but also turned the idea that "humans think then act" on its head. For Weick, it is "humans act then make sense of what they have experienced." He intentionally used the progressive tense (past, present, and future) of the verb form "organizing" in the place of the traditional noun form of "organization" to demonstrate the ever-changing and never-ending nature of the processes that humans employ to organize their actions and thinking. (As discussed later in this section, this use of language has in fact become one of Weick's signifiers.)

In the late 1960s, organizational development, strategy, systems planning, and human resource management promoted rational models to understand change in a rational world. Following appropriate steps of the models would lead to organizational effectiveness. (Of significance was the publication of Daniel Katz's and Robert Kahn's (1966) book titled *The Social Psychology of Organizations* that is a more rational, cause-effect, and research-based explanation of social behavior in organizations.) Weick's definition of organizing – "a consensually validated grammar for reducing equ – vocality by means of sensible interlocked behaviors" (Weick 1979, p. 3) – requires discussions of human interpretation, enactive processes, and humans' inability to predict outcomes as linear extensions of past behaviors. His process of organizing moved us away from the traditional objective, rational, and linear models of the 1960s and 1970s to one that requires interactive processes that are interpretive, subjective, and nonlinear in nature. Many have rightfully identified this book not only as seminal but as a game changer in thinking about organizations and their development (Czarniawska 2005).

Weick developed four subprocesses of "organizing," incorporating and extending the social psychological concepts of Don Campbell's (1965) evolutionary epistemology. These mutually interdependent sequential subprocesses are *ecological (environmental) change*, *human enactment* (Weick replaced Campbell's "variation" with "enactment" and added feedback loops among the subprocesses), *selection*, and *retention*. Weick's book devoted a full chapter to each process; however, here we focus on only one of the processes of organizing – the concept of *human enactment*.

Weick's inclusion of the concept of human enactment as part of the evolutionary process of organizing was game changing because it insisted that we understand ourselves as part of our environment and that we understand the environment as part of ourselves. The prevailing rational models focused on scanning the environment to identify threats to the organization's well-being and then reacting to the threat. Enactment, however, emphasized the mutually reciprocating relationships between human actions and the characteristics of our perceived environments. "People, often alone, actively put things out there that they then perceive and negotiate about perceiving" (Weick 1979, p. 165). This concept of enacting has been captured in one of Weick's better-known phrases, "How can I/we know what I/we think until I/we see what I/we say?" (p. 134).

Many of these ideas of organizing flew in direct opposition to those advocating rational decision-making models and planning, in which managers and employees would follow prescribed routines or recipes for a successful organizational change. In reality, many of those prescribed, planned changes failed (upward of 75%) (Burke 2011) because the focus was on the "plan," not on human processes:

> It is our contention that most "objects" in organizations consist of communications, meaning, images, myth, and interpretation, all of which offer considerable latitude for definition and self-validation. (Weick 1979, p. 157)

Before we leave Weick's concept of organizing, it is worth noting other concepts and language that were, at the time, "jolting" for the field of organizational change. Here is a sample of these jolting themes, with their page reference from *The Social Psychology of Organizing* (1979):

- People do not have to agree on "goals" to act collectively; **they first agree on means** (p. 91).
- **Ambivalence** is the optimal compromise. All actions embody "ambivalence" to deal with incompatible demands of flexibility and stability (p. 229).
- **Ecological change** provides the enacting environment the raw materials for **sensemaking** (p. 130).
- **Enactment** is to organizing as variation is to natural selection (p. 130).

- When things are clear, **doubt**; when there is doubt, treat things as if they are clear (p. 221).
- To doubt is to discredit **unequivocal information;** to act decisively is to discredit **equivocal information** (p. 221).
- Chaotic action is preferable to orderly inaction (p. 243).
- Enactment is the only aspect of the organizing process where the organism directly engages an external "environment" (p. 130).
- **Ignorance is functional** (p. 120).
- Everything flows, **adaptation can preclude adaptability**, and things keep falling apart (p. 120).
- **Loose coupling** promotes adaptation (p. 120).

The concepts listed in bold appeared time and again in Weick's later theorizing. As he moved closer to the management sciences, it became apparent that understanding these concepts required more understanding of the organization's environment, structure, and information. His later work not only focused on the level of human actions and cognition but also allowed him to integrate his consideration of collective cognition and structuring as part of organizing.

Collective Interpretation and Loose Coupling

To better understand organizing dynamics and change, one must understand the relationships between internal interactions, perceptions, beliefs, and the nature of the external environment. Weick's commitment to human enactment is found not only at the individual level of analysis but also at the collective level of the organization. Both levels are critical to the evolutionary process of making meaning of information and learning. This commitment was furthered in a paper he coauthored with Richard Daft (1984) in which they proposed organizations as "interpretive systems."

The authors defined interpretation as the organizational process by which information from the environment is given meaning based on managerial actions with the environment. The organization's ability to interpret its environment can be analyzed using a two-dimensional matrix. The first dimension of analysis is management's beliefs about the analyzability of the external environment (dichotomized into analyzable or unanalyzable), and the second dimension is the extent to which the organization intrudes to understand its environment (dichotomized into passive or active). With these two dimensions, the authors constructed a schema that delineates four modes of organizational (collective) interpretation (and samples of managers' scanning, decision-making, and interpreting behaviors): *conditioned viewing* (passive and analyzable, e.g., routine detection, formal data), *undirected viewing* (passive and unanalyzable, e.g., nonroutine detection, informal data, hunch, reactor), *discovering* (active and analyzable, e.g., formal search, surveys, active detection), and *enacting* (active and unanalyzable, e.g., experiments, inventing the environment, testing, learning by doing). This suggested framework allows managers to evaluate their actions in relation to their beliefs and an ever-changing environmental ecology. It characterizes interpretation as a distributed practice that must include the larger and more complex relationships of organizing and structuring.

Earlier, Weick (1976) turned to a more direct analysis of the impact of human actions on organizational structuring by expanding the concept of "loose coupling" (Glassman 1973). Using public educational organizations as his venue, he analyzed the concept by pointing out potential functions and dysfunctions of this mode of social coupling. He drew an image of loose coupling entities (events) that "are responsive, but that each event also preserves it own identity and some evidence of its physical or logical separateness" (Weick 1976, p. 3). This characterization of interacting systems allows for potential organizational change to occur through interactions, while also allowing for the preservation of entity identity. The loosely coupled system's coordination and interactions are dependent on "soft" structural mechanisms such as value congruency, flow of information, and modes of communications. He went on to explain that "these 'soft' structures appear to develop, persist, and impose crude orderliness among their elements" (p. 2) and that "loose coupling also carries connotations of impermanence, dissolvability, and tacitness, all of which are . . . potentially crucial properties of the 'glue' that holds organizations together" (p. 3).

Weick delineated seven assumptions about the configurations of loose coupling. Each assumption has both a function and a potential dysfunction, with the dysfunction shown in parentheses:

- Lowers the probability that the organization will have to – or be able to – respond to each little change in the environment (possibly not responsive)
- May provide a sensitive mechanism (possibly oversensitive)
- May be a good system for localized adaptation (may resist standardization)
- May be able to retain a greater number of mutations and novel solutions, in terms of the identity, uniqueness, and separateness of elements, than would a tightly coupled system (or may prevent diffusion of information)
- Allows any breakdowns in one portion of a loosely coupled system to be sealed off and not affect other portions of the organization (or possibly leads to isolation)
- Allows more room for self-determination by the actors (or actors may resist)
- Should be relatively inexpensive to run because it takes time and money to coordinate people (nonrational system of fund allocation) (Weick 1976, pp. 6–9)

The functions/characteristics of loose coupling were revisited in a review of the literature by Orton and Weick (1990), in which they developed a typology of loose coupling that incorporated causes of, types of, direct effects of, and compensation for loose coupling. In addition, the model addressed organizational outcomes such as persistence, buffering adaptability, and effectiveness. Their discussions refined the idea of loose coupling by considering both tight coupling and loose-tight coupling alternatives in their typology. However, they left us with one piece of advice, "To state that an organization is a loosely coupled system is the beginning of a discussion, not the end" (p. 219). Over the last four decades, the fields of management and organizational development have focused on these organizing dynamics by leaning toward organizations as ever-changing loosely coupled systems with less emphasis on managing loose-tight structuring (Burke 2014).

Weick's view of collective interpreting and structuring (coupling) as part of organizing has implications for what information is considered, how organizing impacts the meaning of that information, and how the cognitive process enacts, in a reciprocating manner, the ecology of the environment. It is in this context of meaning making that we see the importance of how managers (and others) communicate and make sense of their worlds.

Sensemaking

In the 1990s, Weick moved his organizing ontology into a more specific epistemology and comprehensive analysis of how people make sense of what is going on around them. Weick's sensemaking contribution emanates from his analysis of human venues that are characterized by the existence of multiple meanings, ambiguity, complexity, disintegrating structures, and, in many cases, unexpected interruptions to routine organizational life. In "The Collapse of Sensemaking in Organizations: The Mann Gulch Disaster" (Weick 1993a), he analyzed the tragic failure and death of 13 forest firefighters in 1949 (MacLean 1992).

Weick described sensemaking as a process of assigning meaning to what we observe. It "is about contextual rationality – it is built out of vague questions, muddy answers, and negotiated agreements that attempt to reduce confusion" (Weick 1993a, p. 636). In the collapse of sensemaking, Weick used contextual concepts such as interlocking routines, habituated action patterns, improvisation, respectful interaction, deviation amplification, and bricolage to convince us that the ideas of sensemaking are applicable to most organizations – independent of the severity of their missions.

Two years later, Weick expanded his sensemaking analysis into a book, *Sensemaking in Organizations* (Weick 1995a), where he made the concept available to a broader audience of managers and change agents. In his unobtrusive manner, he saw the book as "a developing set of ideas with explanatory possibilities, rather than as a body of knowledge" (p. xi). The book opens with a discussion of physicians making sense of, and discerning meaning from, the examination of injured children in emergency rooms and failing to consider the possibility of injuries due to parental child abuse. The use of this example, as opposed to firefighting, portrays the collapse of sensemaking as an outcome that all of us could suffer. His characterization of sensemaking reveals his past convictions concerning organizing and interpretation: "To talk about sensemaking is to talk about reality as an ongoing accomplishment that takes form when people make retrospective sense of the situation in which they find themselves and their creations" (p. 15).

He clarified the characteristics of sensemaking by delineating seven of its properties: (1) grounded in identity construction (through human interaction), (2) retrospective (thinking after we act), (3) enactive of a sensible environment (with the sensemakers part of their environments), (4) social (with people's actions shaping each other's meanings and sensemaking processes), (5) ongoing (with flows as the constants of sensemaking), (6) focused on and by extracted cues (which are simple, familiar structures that are seeds from which people develop a larger sense of what may be occurring), and (7) driven by plausibility rather than accuracy (with a focus on plausibility, pragmatics, coherence, reasonableness, invention, and instrumentality) (Weick 1995a, pp. 17–62).

For Weick, "sensemaking is grounded in both individual and social activity and whether the two are even separable will be a recurrent issue . . . , because it has been a durable tension in the human condition" (p. 5). For example, the sensemaking characteristic of *social* stems from his perceptions that "social order is created continuously as people make commitments and develop valid socially acceptable justifications for their commitments. Phrased in this way, individual sensemaking has the potential to be transformed into social structure and maintain those structures" (Weick 1993b, p. 26). This interaction between sensemaking and the collective structure (Weick and Roberts 1993) develops a language of organizational mind from the actions of heedful interrelations. "The concepts of heed, intelligent action, comprehension, recapitulation, and resocialization come together in the concept of collective mind as heedful interrelating" (p. 368).

It is important that we understand that Weick's sensemaking contribution redirects the focus from the traditional system's control over the individual to a situation that places more responsibility on the actions and thinking of the organization's members. It draws attention to the impact of our actions on others' meaning, the awareness of organizing cues, and the realization that plausibility is more the measure of our actions than accuracy. Incorporated into these characteristics is individual and collective interdependence. Weick's work in sensemaking highlights a lesson that organizational change professionals have learned: that is, both the individual and the collective levels of sensemaking are necessary for the development and maintenance of the capacity of an organization to adapt. If we want to prepare organizational members for a future that we cannot specifically predict, then we have to focus on their capacity to make sense of the unexpected.

Surprise and Managing the Unexpected

The development of the sensemaking concept from the analysis of disasters pointed to a failure of sensemaking by the individuals involved. In many respects, the failure was seen as not being able to, as a group or organization, understand the "unexpected" quickly enough – whether it was a change in the direction of a wildfire (Weick 1993a), a misunderstanding in the speech-exchange system (Weick 1990), or making sense of blurred images of a damaged space shuttle (Weick 2005). These cases contributed to Weick's interest in organizations that are confronted with complex situations and yet are successful in spite of the "unexpected" nature of their environments.

He turned his attention to types of organizations that have been labeled high-reliability organizations (HROs) to better understand the dynamics of sensemaking in environments of continuous change and potential surprise. It appears that what was missing in the case of the disasters was mindful organizing (Weick and Roberts 1993). This lack of mindful organizing was linked to the inability to detect error (Weick et al. 1999):

> While there has been some recognition that cognitive processes are important in high reliability functioning, what has been missing from these accounts is a clear specification of ways in which these diverse processes interrelate to produce effective error detection. (Weick et al. 1999, p. 36)

Weick and Sutcliffe again broadened the audience with the publication of *Managing the Unexpected: Sustained Performance in a Complex World* (3rd ed., 2015). In this work and prior editions of the book (Weick and Sutcliffe 2001, 2007), the authors stayed true to Weick's theoretical threads in earlier works (such as the concepts of sensemaking, heedfulness, enacting, and organizing) as they developed in more detail five principles of mindful organizing and management of the unexpected. They made it clear that these principles, although derived from HRO theory, are applicable to a wide range of cases and demonstrate the collective commitment and competence required for mindful organizing. Each principle is characterized by the cognitive actions of individuals and the collective and the increased importance of sensemaking:

- A preoccupation with failure, characterized by doubt as a mind-set and institutionalized wariness (p. 45)
- A reluctance to simplify, characterized by thinking and questioning out loud and reviewing assessments as evidence grows (p. 62)
- A sensitivity to operations, characterized by heedful interacting and integrated/shared mental maps (p. 77)
- A commitment to resilience, characterized by accelerated feedback, treatment of past experiences with ambivalence, and a mind-set of cure rather than prevention (p. 94)
- A deference to expertise, characterized by listening with humility, being wary of centralization and hierarchy, and creating flexible decision structures (p. 112)

In all organizational changes, we encounter interruptions as we manage the emergent, and many times unexpected, consequences of change. By evoking these principles, the authors challenge those theorists that profess a focus only on success, simplifying, standardizing, managing critical paths, planning, and centralizing control when confronted with the unexpected. If we are concerned with organizing and sensemaking and the human condition is always in flux, then one can argue that in all types of organizations, we have to learn to manage the unexpected. It is obvious that the five principles derived from HROs apply to most organizations. Weick and Sutcliffe (2015) provide us with insight as to "how" we might manage the unexpected aspect of human nature:

> Ask yourself, can I alter our ways of working so that it is easier for people to puzzle over small disruptions, question familiar labels, understand what they are currently doing, enhance their options, and identify the expertise that is needed? (p. 159)

New Insights: The Pragmatics of Theorizing

Weick's contributions, as briefly outlined above, have had a large impact on how we envision organizations, not as "things," but as people organizing, enacting, interpreting, loosely/tightly coupling, sensemaking, and managing the unexpected. However, I believe that one of Weick's most significant contributions to the field of organizational change and management has been the demystifying of the actions and thinking associated with theory building. I have come to value his epistemological contributions that "What Theory Is Not, Theorizing Is" (Weick 1995b, p. 385). That is, "theorizing" is a process rather than an end.

I came to academia in 1990 after 10 years of practice as the director of organizational development at a federal government agency. My experience in this role left me with observations and questions concerning the efficacy of our ability to change organizations: Why could not we reach a stable organizational state? Why had our "models" of change not achieved their stated goals? What happened to the "laws" governing social interaction? And, why did managers so vehemently discount the idea that managerial theory is useful?

It was my intent to explore these questions and to hopefully develop a network of scholar practitioners that would promote organizational change, not only from a "data"-driven perspective but also from a theory-practice foundation. Of particular concern was how I would be able to convince my students (managers and executives with 10–20 years of experience) that theory was not a bad word and that good theory could be useful, that social theory could provide an explanation for what we experience. I believed Kurt Lewin when he said that there was nothing so practical as good theory.

Of course, as new academics do, I turned to the literature. This is where I discovered a recent paper written by Weick entitled "Theory Construction as Disciplined Imagination" (1989). This paper (winner of the Best Paper of the Year Award from the *Academy of Management Review)* opened up new avenues to the world of building useful theory in the social sciences. Weick, again in opposition to traditional models (e.g., theory building as a logical problem-solving approach), introduced theory building in the social sciences not only as a "process" of *theorizing* but one in which imagination was seen as a positive, as opposed to a negative that required controls:

> Theorizing is viewed as disciplined imagination, where the 'discipline' in theorizing comes from consistent application of selection to trial-and-error thinking and the 'imagination' in theorizing comes from deliberate diversity introduced into the problem statements, thought trials, and selection criteria that comprise that thinking. (p. 516)

Weick equated theorizing to sensemaking (p. 519), with variation and conjectures being useful where " a greater number of diverse conjectures produces better theory than a process characterized by smaller numbers of homogeneous conjectures" (p. 522). Again disrupting prevailing thinking, Weick stated that plausibility is a substitute for validity, with plausibility being assessed by a variety of selection criteria such as what is "interesting, obvious, connected, believable, beautiful and/or real" (Weick 1989, pp. 523–527). With this new perspective, one must always be vigilant since the line between "that is interesting" and "that is in my best interest" can become very blurred in the world of organizing (p. 528).

The "theorizer" must keep in mind that "theories in organizational studies are approximations" (Weick 1995b, p. 386) and thus are always open to change. It means we have to be ready to "drop our tools" (Weick 1996b, 2007) and consider alternative explanations. This means that theorizing can be trying and hard work. Weick viewed the theorizing process as "cogitating and racking one's brain" – with brain racking taken from Talcott Parsons' idea of theory building (Isaac 2010). He felt that "racking is an appropriate description because it preserves the effortful struggles in theorizing between such dualities as variation and retention, living forward while understanding backward, perception and conception, and concreteness and abstraction" (Weick 2014, p. 178).

Returning to my entry into academia and my students, portraying social theory building as a process of theorizing or sensemaking changed the rules of engagement for scholar practitioners. Instead of a set of "laws" (nouns) that should explain behaviors in organizations, my students now could picture theory as an ongoing effort to understand relationships of action and cognition in complex environments. It provided a different perspective on the word "theory"; theory was now seen as theorizing (the action verb). This conceptualization became invaluable as my students were becoming scholar practitioners. Theory was no longer a dirty word. They saw what Weick meant in this statement:

> A disconfirmed assumption is an opportunity for a theorist to learn something new, to discover something unexpected, to generate renewed interest in an old question, to mystify something that had previously seemed settled, to heighten intellectual stimulation, to get recognition, and to alleviate boredom. (Weick 1989, p. 525)

It opened a window for them, not only into research and theory building (and their dissertations) but also into how they saw their practice as managers. This meant that they were capable of theorizing from their experiences as conjectures to be developed through diverse thinking, action, and imagination.

Legacy and Unfinished Business: Continue on the Journey of Understanding

Karl Weick's legacy continues to grow. He is actively pursuing a better understanding of people's thinking and actions in environments that are complex and self-organizing. For example, in a recent paper in which he explored the role of ambiguity, he opened his argument with the premise, "To increase ambiguity is to grasp more of the situation" (Weick 2015b, p. 1). Once again we see that he is challenging the traditional idea that simplifying ambiguity makes it more manageable. And once again, after five decades, he is still asking us to complicate ourselves, believe there is no one "best way," and appreciate the journey of understanding rather than seeing it only as a destination of our thinking.

Part of Weick's legacy is quite apparent in the contributions outlined above. In addition, his legacy includes those that have incorporated and built on his understandings. They include Sutcliffe on managing the unexpected in high-reliability organizations (Weick and Sutcliffe 2015), Barbara Czarniawska on organizational theorizing (Czarniawska-Joerges 1992), Dennis Gioia on sensegiving (Gioia and Chittipeddi 1991), Rob Stones on strong structuration (Stones 2005), and Taylor and Van Every on communication and emergence (Taylor and Van Every 2000).

What is not apparent from these discussions is that he has approached his quest for understanding people as they coordinate and collectively improvise with vigor, enthusiasm, and faithfulness to the concepts he professes. Let me share a brief example. We were very lucky that Karl agreed to visit and teach our scholar practitioners at George Washington University over the last 27 years. When he visited, he would start off by talking about his topic (sometimes organizing, sometimes sensemaking) and then he would grab a chair and sit down in front of the class and say, "I really would like to hear what you have to say about this topic." Of course, that started a conversation between the students and Karl that went on for hours. Sometimes he would even pull out his news reporter notebook from his coat pocket (he always has it with him) and would take notes on "interesting points that came up." Of course, the students would say, "Did you see that? Karl Weick took notes on what I had to say. Wow!"

Conclusion

Karl Weick has always been open to questioning his own work, listening to the world around him, and changing his perceptions and conceptions if he senses a different route. He is truly intrigued by potential variations in his own and others' conceptualization of organizing. The perceptions and concepts that he has pursued over the last five decades still urge him onto addressing his first interests in coordination and collective improvisation.

References

Burke, W. (2011). A perspective on the field of organization development and change: The Zeigarnik effect. *The Journal of Applied Behavioral Science, 47*(2), 143–167. doi:10.1177/0021886310388161.

Burke, W. W. (2014). Changing loosely coupled systems. *The Journal of Applied Behavioral Science, 50*(4), 423–444. doi:10.1177/0021886314549923.

Campbell, D. T. (1965). Variation and selective retention in social-cultural evolution. In H. R. Barringer, G. I. Blanksten, & R. Mack (Eds.), *Social change in developing areas* (pp. 328–348). Cambridge, MA: Schenkman.

Czarniawska, B. (2005). Karl Weick: Concepts, style, and reflection. *The Sociological Review, 53*, 267–278. doi:10.1111/j.1467-954X.2005.00554.x.

Czarniawska-Joerges, B. (1992). *Exploring complex organizations: A cultural perspective*. Newbury Park: SAGE.

Daft, R. L., & Weick, K. E. (1984). Toward a model of organizations as interpretation systems. *Academy of Management Review, 9*(2), 284–295.

Dewey, J. (1938). *Experience and education*. New York: Touchstone.

Dewey, J. (1950). *Human nature and conduct: An introduction to social psychology*. New York: Modern Library.

Gioia, D. A. (2006). On Weick: An appreciation. *Organization Studies, 27*(11), 1709–1721. doi:10.1177/0170840606068349.

Gioia, D. A., & Chittipeddi, K. (1991). Sensemaking and sensegiving in strategic change initiation. *Strategic Management Journal, 12*(6), 433–448. doi:10.1002/smj.4250120604.

Glassman, R. B. (1973). Persistence and loose coupling in living systems. *Behavioral Science, 18*(2), 83–98. doi:10.1002/bs.3830180202.

Isaac, J. (2010). Theorist at work: Talcott Parsons and the Carnegie project on theory (1949–1951). *Journal of the History of Ideas, 71*(2), 287–311. doi:10.1353/jhi.0.0079.

James, W. (1950). *The principles of psychology* (Vol. 1 and 2). New York: Dover.

Katz, D., & Kahn, R. (1966). *The social psychology of organizations*. New York: Wiley.

MacLean, N. (1992). *Young men and fire*. Chicago: University of Chicago Press. doi:10.7208/chicago/9780226501031.001.0001.

Orton, J. D., & Weick, K. E. (1990). Loosely coupled systems: A reconceptualization. *Academy of Management Review, 15*(2), 203–223.

Stones, R. (2005). *Structuration theory*. New York: Palgrave MacMillan.

Taylor, J. R., & Van Every, E. J. (2000). *The emergent organization: Communication as its site and surface*. Mahwah: Lawrence Erlbaum Associates.

Weick, K. E. (1969). *The social psychology of organizing*. Reading: Addison-Wesley.

Weick, K. E. (1976). Educational organizations as loosely coupled systems. *Administrative Science Quarterly, 21*(1), 1–19. doi:10.2307/2391875.

Weick, K. E. (1979). *The social psychology of organizing* (2nd ed.). New York: McGraw-Hill.

Weick, K. E. (1989). Theory construction as disciplined imagination. *Academy of Management Review, 14*(4), 516–531.

Weick, K. E. (1990). The vulnerable system: An analysis of the Tenerife air disaster. *Journal of Management, 16*(3), 571–593. doi:10.1177/014920639001600304.

Weick, K. E. (1993a). The collapse of sensemaking in organizations: The Mann Gulch disaster. *Administrative Science Quarterly, 38*(4), 628–652.

Weick, K. E. (1993b). Sensemaking in organizations: Small structures with large consequences. In J. K. Murnighan (Ed.), *Social psychology in organizations: Advances in theory and research* (pp. 10–37). Englewood Cliffs: Prentice Hall.
Weick, K. E. (1995a). *Sensemaking in organizations*. Thousand Oaks: SAGE.
Weick, K. E. (1995b). What theory is not, theorizing is. *Administrative Science Quarterly, 40*(3), 385–390. doi:10.2307/2393789.
Weick, K. E. (1996a). An appreciation of social context: One legacy of Gerald Salancik. *Administrative Science Quarterly, 41*(4), 563–573. doi:10.2307/2393867.
Weick, K. E. (1996b). Turning context into text: An academic life as data. In A. C. Bedeian (Ed.), *Management laureates: A collection of autobiographical essays* (Vol. 4, pp. 282–324). Greenwich: JAI Press.
Weick, K. E. (2000). Emergent change as a universal in organizations. In M. Beer & N. Nohria (Eds.), *Breaking the code of change* (pp. 223–241). Boston: Harvard Business School Press.
Weick, K. E. (2005). Making sense of blurred images: Mindful organizing in mission STS-107. In W. H. Starbuck & M. Farjoun (Eds.), *Organization at the limit: Lessons from the Columbia disaster* (pp. 159–177). Malden: Blackwell.
Weick, K. E. (2007). Drop your tools: On reconfiguring management education. *Journal of Management Education, 31*(1), 5–16.
Weick, K. E. (2014). The work of theorizing. In R. Swedberg (Ed.), *Theorizing in social science* (pp. 177–194). Stanford: Stanford University Press.
Weick, K. E. (2015a). Unplugged – my own book review. *Management, 18*(2), 189–193.
Weick, K. E. (2015b). Ambiguity as grasp: The reworking of sense. *Journal of Contingencies & Crisis Management, 23*(2), 117–123. doi:10.1111/1468-5973.12080.
Weick, K. E., & Quinn, R. E. (1999). Organizational change and development. *Annual Review of Psychology, 50*(1), 361–386. doi:10.1146/annurev.psych.50.1.361.
Weick, K. E., & Roberts, K. H. (1993). Collective mind in organizations: Heedful interrelating on flight decks. *Administrative Science Quarterly, 38*, 357–381.
Weick, K. E., & Sutcliffe, K. M. (2001). *Managing the unexpected: Assuring high performance in an age of complexity*. San Francisco: Jossey-Bass.
Weick, K. E., & Sutcliffe, K. M. (2007). *Managing the unexpected: Resilient performance in an age of uncertainty* (2nd ed.). San Francisco: Wiley.
Weick, K. E., & Sutcliffe, K. M. (2015). *Managing the unexpected: Sustained performance in a complex world* (3rd ed.). Hoboken: Wiley.
Weick, K. E., Sutcliffe, K. M., & Obstfeld, D. (1999). Organizing for high reliability: Process of collective mindfulness. In R. I. Sutton (Ed.), *Research in organizational behavior* (Vol. 21, pp. 81–123). Greenwich: JAI Press.

Further Reading

As Further Reading, I Would Suggest the Following Books that Provide a Scholarly/Research Perspective to Weick's Work (with Complete Citations Provided in the Reference Section):

The Social Psychology of Organizing (2nd ed., Weick 1979)
Making Sense of the Organization (Vol. 1, Weick 2001, and Vol. 2, Weick 2009)

The Following Books Provide a Broader Scope for the Scholar Practitioner:

Sensemaking in Organizations, 1995
Managing the Unexpected: Sustained Performance in a Complex World (3rd ed., 2015, with K. M. Sutcliffe)

The Following Papers Provide Insights for Change Agents:

"Fatigue of the spirit in organizational theory and organization development: Reconnaissance man as remedy" (1990)
"Collective mind in organizations: Heedful interrelating on flight decks" (1993, with K. H. Roberts)
"Drop your tools: An allegory for organizational studies" (1996)
"Drop your tools: On reconfiguring management education" (2007)

Weick, K. E. (1990). Fatigue of the spirit in organizational theory and organization development: Reconnaissance man as remedy. *The Journal of Applied Behavioral Science, 26*(3), 313–327.
Weick, K. E. (1996). Drop your tools: An allegory for organizational studies. *Administrative Science Quarterly, 41*, 301–313.
Weick, K. E. (2001). *Making sense of the organization* (Vol. 1). Oxford: Blackwell.
Weick, K. E. (2009). *Making sense of the organization* (Vol. 2). Malden: Blackwell.

Marvin Weisbord: A Life of Action Research 84

Martin D. Goldberg

Abstract

Marvin Weisbord's work – as professional author, business executive, organizational consultant, researcher, Future Search method founder, and cofounder of its global network – spanned 50 years. He was a partner in the esteemed consultancy, Block Petrella Weisbord Inc., and he was a prolific writer and thinker, as well as practical craftsman, in the field. He is widely known for his multi-edition, *Productive Workplaces: Dignity, Meaning and Community in the 21st Century* (2012), chronicling the history of organizational improvement, the rise of its seminal concepts, and how he absorbed them in his own personal and professional development and in case studies. He worked and learned from many of the greatest names in organization development (OD) and was influenced intellectually most profoundly by Kurt Lewin. He saw in Lewin's "action research" less of a technical change methodology than a way of thinking about and addressing organizational life and its dilemmas, using one's own and others' experience as the major source of change. This chapter describes the arc of his professional, conceptual, and practice development as an embodiment of action research. It also covers six enduring contributions of his – value-based perspectives, principles, and practices – and explores limitations and renewed possibilities of Weisbord's legacy to the future of the field.

Keywords

Action research • Business as a human enterprise • Facilitation principles and practices • Future search • Large-group conference methods • Organization productivity and performance • Sociotechnical approaches • Systems thinking • Values • Whole systems change • Work redesign

M.D. Goldberg (✉)
Distant Drummer LLC, Easton, MD, USA

Pepperdine University, Malibu, CA, USA
e-mail: mdg@distantdrummer.us.com

D.B. Szabla et al. (eds.), *The Palgrave Handbook of Organizational Change Thinkers*,
DOI 10.1007/978-3-319-52878-6_63

Contents

Introduction

I finally met Marvin Weisbord in November 2014 through a video interview I conducted with him as part of Pepperdine University's Master of Science in Organization Development (MSOD) Founders Video Series (Law et al. 2015). As a nonacademic organization development (OD) practitioner interested in theory, I had incorporated his ideas into my work for many years. We immediately connected, a tribute to his warmth, presence, and enthusiasm, qualities that have always shined through his books and articles. I set out to capture the evolution of his experience-based change learnings – the "whole elephant in the room," as he would say. This was no small task, given the scope of his 50-plus-year career as writer, business executive, researcher, and organizational consultant, as well as Future Search founder and codirector of its global, nonprofit network. Through all, he interwove eclectic threads of OD thinking in an emerging synthesis of concept and craft.

During his entire career, Weisbord sought to hear and bring together others' voices as part of a bigger picture "to help improve the conditions of things," both human and situational. He was keen on understanding how diverse schools of organizational thought informed his firsthand experiences. He avidly absorbed lessons from the sages of participative management, intrapersonal and group dynamics, sociotechnical redesign, systems theory, and large-scale change, but he never lost sight of basic common sense. He was equal parts practitioner, observer, sense-maker, and thinker, influenced by so many, as he lovingly credited in his professional odyssey, *Productive Workplaces: Dignity, Meaning and Community in the 21st Century* (2012), an unconventional work that evolved in successive editions over decades, much like Whitman's *Leaves of Grass*. It is a rich chronicle of Weisbord's experience, a history of the field, and a critique of his own work, in which he revisited cases and revised his thinking to follow-up on organizations' years after he had worked with them.

This chapter begins with a synopsis of Weisbord's career. Through a few "marker" stories, I want to convey a sense of his *personal* future search: the experiences, influences, and questions that impelled him from one career phase to another and from which his practical wisdom emerged. Moreover, I want to highlight his dedication to *action research* – even before he knew the term – immersing himself in experience, then letting his mind roam free on the implications for theory and practice. It is no wonder he found a special kinship with Kurt Lewin, "the practical theorist" (Marrow 1969). Looking back over the course of his professional life, Weisbord saw Lewin's action research less as a technical method than as a way of thinking about organizational dilemmas. In this sense, action research became the red thread running through his work. He also came to see it as a missing "ribbon" around much of how the field is practiced today, affecting its vitality and renewed future possibilities. But I anticipate the end of our story here. Let's begin at the beginning.

The Arc of Weisbord's Journey: Influences and Motivations

Weisbord did not set out to do the kind of work for which he eventually became widely known. His intent, from his early days growing up in Pennsylvania, was to be a professional writer. In the 1950s, he wrote and sold general interest magazine articles during college and graduate school at the University of Illinois and the University of Iowa, having studied journalism and social science; he also served as a US Navy journalist and taught journalism at Pennsylvania State University. Additionally, he took post-master's courses in American Civilization at the University of Pennsylvania. Having married and started a family, Weisbord supplemented his writing income by joining his father's family firm during the 1960s. But he continued to publish articles and wrote two books, *Campaigning for President* (1966) and *Some Form of Peace: True Stories of the American Friends Service Committee at Home and Abroad* (1968). These books sought to understand individual stories and how together they formed larger social patterns, reflecting his abiding interests in experience-based social inquiry and his ambitions as a professional writer.

Meanwhile, his experience as a business executive in his father's direct mail, business forms manufacturing firm led him to practical dilemmas in work organization and participative management. For example, he wrestled with how to incent shop floor workers to maximize productivity, how the effects of absenteeism on work output could be reduced, and how infighting between work groups could be alleviated. Weisbord experimented with self-managing work teams in the mid-1960s, on the counsel of a friend and compensation specialist, Don Kirchhoffer and his RCA training colleague Bob Maddocks. Weisbord witnessed firsthand how informal social factors and work design affected performance on the shop floor and how changes in wage-incentive schemes, his first hunch, were not enough. Kirchhoffer gave him a copy of Douglas McGregor's *The Human Side of Enterprise* (1960), which Weisbord said "blew his mind." Maddocks introduced him to systems thinking, a fundamental shift from his previous piecemeal way of addressing work problems. Moving the business from supervisory-led functional departments to self-managing teams – in which workers could directly coordinate and control their own work – Weisbord was struck by how a team of new, young workers learned, taught each other their jobs, and outperformed their peers, while some former supervisors complained about a loss of power and status, despite assurances of employment and no downgrade in pay.

There were pluses and minuses with the changes he introduced. Some of the reluctant supervisors eventually left, and some of the hourly workers who stayed did not take hold of the participative path. But some results proved remarkable. In order processing, throughput increased 40% and absenteeism and turnover went to nearly zero. Workers' self-esteem shot up when – after finishing their work early – they sought out and found other productive business contributions to make.

During this time with the family firm, Weisbord proceeded with trial and error, trying to make sense of what he saw. Deeply impressed with McGregor's *Human Side*, he also wanted "something more specific." He found it in McGregor's posthumous book, *The Professional Manager* (1967). A chapter on the redesign of a circuit board manufacturing plant, part of Non-Linear Systems Inc., informed Weisbord's practical efforts at establishing the self-led teams, and his trying out a pay-for-knowledge scheme to support multi-skill learning. This was his first acquaintance with sociotechnical approaches, which he would later delve into fully. He also read Rensis Likert's *New Patterns of Management* (1961), where he was attracted by how Likert quantified and systematically operationalized the management orientations of McGregor's Theories X and Y. Likert's work underscored what became Weisbord's central takeaway from McGregor: Business is a *human* enterprise and requires placing the existential human factor at the center of productive work. McGregor was also an eye-opener, because Weisbord saw how, without ever intending to, he had been caught up in bureaucratic, control-oriented Theory X assumptions in his management of the business. This recognition helped free him to experiment as he did with the self-managing teams. This first foray into sociotech also provided a root experience in which he began to see that, at bottom, the business and human dimensions of organizations are not antithetical, as they often become in practice and ideology. They are inextricable. Important technical tasks and business outcomes could not be obtained without real attention to the *inner quality* of the human experience, not just human behavior. By the same token, business, economic, market, and technological factors, along with flexible work design structures, were essential to address. After all, they were the *practical, dynamic context* in which purposeful work – and human growth in organizational settings – happened.

Weisbord left the family business in 1968 with the aim of dedicating himself to magazine and book writing. Despite his rich learning and accomplishments, he considered his years as a manager "wasted" for not doing what he really wanted. Later, he came to realize that his business experience laid the groundwork for a career in consulting, OD, and a new focus in his writing. This awareness began when his friend Bernard Asbell, a professional writer, asked Weisbord to join him in a consulting project with the Ford Foundation's Division of Education and Research. "Why me?" Weisbord asked. "I don't know anything about consulting." Asbell replied, "All we do is interview people and write a report – what you do all the time – and we can figure out the rest. Besides, they pay $100 day a day – each." Weisbord, having a family to support, thought, "Why not?" The two began the project, and one evening over dinner, Weisbord talked with Asbell about a new book idea he had been mulling over: the effects on a community when it is bypassed by the building of a superhighway. "Why would you write about that?" asked Asbell. "All you do is talk about those work teams in your business. That's what you should be writing about." Asbell was prescient, and there was Weisbord's future unfolding right in front of him.

He decided to explore the topic with a set of articles, the first of which was a 1969 assignment from *The New York Times Magazine* to write about NTL T-Groups, unstructured, experiential learning labs in human relations, radical in concept. He called NTL cofounder Bradford, who invited him to lunch along with then-NTL staffer Charlie Seashore. They agreed that Weisbord could participate in and write about a group, even though he imagined they thought him a bit naive. They introduced him to Bill Dyer, a then-top T-Group "trainer." With the participants' consent, Weisbord sat in the group as an observer, taking copious notes. He was captivated by what he saw and felt during the weeklong event. He identified with the mid-managers in attendance, as well as Dyer in his special facilitative role, attuned to what was happening moment-to-moment. As it turned out, the article was never published. But Dyer read the manuscript and wrote that he considered it the best ever written about T-Groups, aligned with what he was trying to accomplish descriptively and conceptually. The piece was not published until it was included in the third edition of *Productive Workplaces* (2012).

Weisbord began reading more deeply in the thinking and history of the emerging OD field that was burgeoning with new publications. In 1969 and 1970, he read the entire new Addison Wesley OD series, including books by Richard Beckhard, Ed Schein, Warren Bennis, and Paul Lawrence, all of whom he would subsequently meet and learn from. He read Chris Argyris' *Intervention Theory and Method: A Behavioral Science View* (1970) and Likert's *The Human Organization: Its Management and Value* (1967). He began writing articles on management topics for IBM's provocative *Think* magazine, the editor of which he knew from his graduate school days in Iowa. The Ford Foundation project led to consulting assignments, and he dove into Alfred Marrow's biography of Lewin, *The Practical Theorist* (1969). When he encountered Lewin, Weisbord was hooked. "This is where I knew I belong," he said.

Lewin's writings, from their first in the 1920s through the 1940s, were a huge influence on Weisbord. He saw the principles and practices of action research as not just a method but as a way of engaging with people and ideas. "Lewin's organizational change theories enormously attracted me after my experiences as a manager," Weisbord wrote. "And 'action research' soon formed the core of my consulting practice."

> Lewin conceived a novel form of problem solving that might be called "doing by learning." Lewin wed scientific management to democratic values and gave birth to participative management. And he did much more. He taught that to understand a system, you must seek to change it. This led to one of the key managerial insights of the last century: Diagnosis does not mean just finding the problem, but doing it in such a way as to build commitment for action. His was an unprecedented idea. While solving a problem, you could study your own process and thereby refine the theory and practice of change. He also pointed the way

> toward collaborative consultation. Lewin showed that even technical and economic problems have social consequences that include people's feelings, perceptions of reality, sense of self-worth, motivation and commitment. It is not given to consultants to sow the seeds for change (a screwy notion that spells trouble), but *to discover what seeds are present and whether they can be grown* [emphasis added]. We owe that precious insight to Lewin. (Weisbord 2012, pp. 80–81)

Weisbord saw Lewin's pioneering discoveries as profound: in interpersonal, group, organizational, and social dynamics; in fundamentally humanizing Frederick Taylor's insights (e.g., "scientific management") while still seeking precision; and in articulating a way to think, learn about, and encourage interdependent change *to the extent that conditions for change – themselves subject to discovery – were present.* Weisbord's appreciation of Lewin only deepened over time. He came to see Lewin's advances as permeating the entirety of OD.

Professionally, he came a member of NTL Institute and his consulting practice began to blossom. Weisbord partnered with many consultants, continuing to learn, co-learn, and try out many emerging techniques. At NTL, Warner Burke supported him in training workshops and facilitating labs. He also worked with Gail Silverman, Peter Vail, Allan Drexler, Ronald Lippitt, and Tony Petrella. During the 1970s, in consulting, he spent several years working with Paul Lawrence in nine academic medical centers. Their project evolved from Weisbord's first major change effort with Women's Medical College of Pennsylvania in its metamorphosis to a coeducational institution. Drawing upon Likert's ideas, he helped create a participative structure using "linking pin" planning councils, to rethink the mission, organizational structure, and budget process.

His lessons learned included appreciating the difference between relatively easy-to-grasp organizational change concepts and procedures and actualizing meaningful movement in the face of turbulent social conditions and real-world stakeholder constraints. Whether or not the change efforts produced the structural outcomes or "deliverables" as intended, the mutual support of the planning councils proved fertile for the medical school's future. This work resulted in several research studies that Weisbord copublished under the auspices of NIH and the Association of American Medical Colleges (1978). It also led to his provocative essay, "Why Organization Development Hasn't Worked (So Far) in Medical Centers (1976)." Of the latter, years after revisiting some of the key players of the case, Weisbord said that he had "learned the wrong lesson from experience" because there had been enduring value in the collaboration and connective tissue created by the intervention itself, notwithstanding the lack of immediate structural effects. In a similar vein, drawing upon the work of Likert and his colleague Floyd Mann from the University of Michigan's Institute for Social Research, Weisbord focused on other consulting projects that used survey research. He was struck by Mann's emphasis on the importance of feedback and dialogue in addition to the use of survey instruments, even though Weisbord was instinctively drawn to the measurement of "soft" factors like decision-making. At the end of the day, survey "findings" came alive only through their relevance to people's actual experiences. This thinking was also consistent with how Weisbord came away from his NTL training work. He found the human relations lab moments – critical as they were – to be meaningful only insofar as he was able to connect them back to his real-world experience of improving organizational life.

He first heard the cobbled expression "realife" (as in, "Yes, that's fine for a workshop but what happens when you try it back in *realife*?") from Peter Block. Weisbord had met Block and Petrella at an OD Network conference in 1970, and by 1974, he joined their partnership after working on projects with each of them and with Petrella at NTL team building labs. Block Petrella Weisbord Inc. became one of the most renowned OD and learning firms in the world, from the mid-1970s through the mid-1990s.

Despite differences in their areas of focus, the partners shared similar orientations as non-PhD practitioners strongly interested in ideas. As Weisbord put it, they were hard-nosed businessmen committed to improving work systems *and* their human dimensions. By nature, they were each imaginative innovators and design-thinkers. They found natural synergies to build on and learn from: Block the philosopher-advocate and teacher-trainer par excellence; Petrella the gifted practitioner, team builder, and large system change interventionist; and Weisbord ever the journalist-observer in the way he worked, bringing people together to coevolve a bigger future.

One of Weisbord's deep learnings came from seeing Petrella's innovations in team building technique, both of them having been influenced by the human dynamics of Mike Blansfield's "Team Effectiveness Theory (Weisbord 1985b)." The classical form of team building was that of interviewing each of the team members and summarizing the findings into themes that were then fed back to the team for consideration, deliberation, and action planning. This method in essence followed Lewin's course of providing feedback to "unfreeze" the system.

Petrella was struck by the oddity of the interventionist's being the one who summarized the findings and provided the feedback, since the team members were the ones with the perceptions in the first place. All the more, given that the aim of team building was for the members to get closer. He hit upon the idea of interviewing each member in front of the others, based on what he or she was willing to share. This way, the members owned responsibility for sharing their perspectives and engaging with each other directly, creating fuller unfreezing of the status quo, an immediate picture of the whole, and greater possibilities for the future. Each had to decide on the extent of his or her self-disclosure and willingness to trust others from the get-go. This illuminated the observations Weisbord had made while working with Asbell, when he wondered aloud, "Why are we as the consultants writing the reports when the participants are the ones who know what's happening?" With Petrella's innovation, the team building task could now be seen practically, as a matter of *structuring the context* in which the members could share their own thinking and put the bigger picture together for themselves. This influenced Weisbord to take another look at his more general consulting approach. Prior to his years with Block Petrella Weisbord, he had formulated his well-known "Six Box Model" published in *Organizational Diagnosis: A Workbook of Theory and Practice* (1978). The six-box model had roots in Weisbord's prior experience with the family firm and Maddocks' systems thinking influence. When Weisbord conceived it, the six-box model – purposes, structure, relationships, rewards, helpful mechanisms, and leadership – aimed to provide a practical assessment tool: where to look for issues and where to offer help. But as he continued his own development, he became uncomfortable with the idea of "diagnosis" as a more discreet phase of work that an OD "expert" performed. He found the concept of diagnosis to be too far removed from the necessary work that organizational members must do themselves to *own* the assessment, and he found the idea of diagnosis too fixed to deal with the increasing speed and dynamism of organizational change. Weisbord began to reframe Lewin's "unfreezing, moving, and refreezing" as part of a nonstop change process. He came to think of the six-box model as a set of snapshots depicting where a system is at any point in time. The model was most useful when clients collected their own data, developing commitment to act.

His understanding of systems thinking deepened as he met and worked with Eric Trist as part of his continuing work with Block Petrella Weisbord. Trist had studied Lewin's work and was a colleague of the pioneering social psychiatrist Wilfred Bion at London's Tavistock Institute of Human Relations. Weisbord grew close to Trist until the latter's death in 1993. Trist also introduced his collaborator Fred Emery and wife Merrelyn to Weisbord. Beginning in the late 1970s, Weisbord had many conversations with the Emerys about their and his work. He became immersed in sociotechnical and open-systems theory and practice, appreciating these approaches' revolutionary implications for the workplace. Among the many lessons he learned, Weisbord became more explicit in his grasp of work design as the central *task* focus of systemic change efforts (a key learning from the fiery, no-nonsense Fred Emery), as well as his understanding of human dynamics – some of which were unconscious – as the central *process* focus needed (a learning from the more empathic Trist). Trist and Emery's own collaboration provided Weisbord with a wide-angle lens for comprehending his experiences as a whole, helping him crystallize his lessons from business, consulting, and NTL around large-scale change.

Two more points about Emery and Trist are noteworthy to mention before turning to the final chapter of Weisbord's professional life, his work developing Future Search and the Future Search Network. His takeaway from Emery on the need for participants to transform objective work processes in no way diminished Weisbord's attention to the human dynamics always present as people worked the redesign tasks – for example, ways they would engage or disengage, project, and counterproject with each other and the change facilitator. He considered this subjective dimension the heart of transformation efforts. Emery thought this soft, but Weisbord persisted: Unless *inner* emotional experience was touched – not merely shifts made in work process and behavior – then the fuller productivity, meaningfulness, and motivating power of the change would be in question. "This was something the Emerys never quite got, despite their big contributions," Weisbord recounted (Law et al. 2015). Trist encouraged Weisbord toward "a conceptual emboldening" for *Productive Workplaces*, resulting in Weisbord's "learning curve" formulation (described more fully in the next section of this chapter). This was a conceptualization that not only framed the book but the entire evolution of the field. Even more was the personal effect of the relationship on Weisbord and the role model that Trist provided. Weisbord fondly remembered:

> Eric was my friend, colleague, mentor, gentlest collaborator and toughest critic. For 15 years I had enjoyed his calm presence, dry wit, boundless compassion and intellectual rigor. Eric had a quality shared with his mentor Kurt Lewin. That was the ability to find a kernel of truth in every statement, a seed of constructive possibility in every experiment, no matter how outlandish. I had seen Eric many times take a novel idea, turn it this way and that, and hand it back to its originator richer, fuller, and more insightful. (Weisbord 2012, p. 198)

Weisbord's interest in large-scale conference formats represented a culmination of his preceding work, as he brought people together to work on whole systems improvement themselves. He had already known Merrelyn Emery and her work with her husband and Trist in the search conference format. He got to know Lewin's student Lippitt, who had pioneered large-group, future-oriented community meetings with Eva Schindler-Rainman. Weisbord was especially struck by the opportunity to apply the conference approach to organizations and, before long, also applied it to wider social communities too. He came to realize that too much emphasis was placed on the "change agent" to sew an organization together through cascading interventions, teaching people, and the like. Rather, he saw that the issues needing tackling were imminent and from the start required a practical, holistic perspective that no one stakeholder group possessed. It was the dilemma of seeing the "whole elephant" in a way that connected to the real-world experience of everyone involved, up, down, and across organizations, and often those outside it. Later, he came to characterize this as "making systems thinking *experiential.*"

Moreover, he had found in his earlier consulting work that customary OD approaches seemed to take too long before people inevitably "hit a wall," where constructive movement at the enterprise level got stuck. This, too, reflected the truth of Lewin's maxim: "The way to understand a system is to try and change it." Only in action would the limits of what the system is really capable of be discoverable. Reciprocally, if the "field of action" was orchestrated in such a way that new kinds of interactions were possible (e.g., getting everyone in the room to address whole systems concerns), then the hold of some of the past limits could be let go of. From Lippitt, Weisbord learned that all parties with a stake in future success needed a way to get real with each other quickly, to let go of what was holding them back, and to focus on common ground. He connected with others concurrently working with large-group meetings, including Billie Alban and Kathleen Dannemiller. He also studied the Tavistock conference method from England that had especially influenced Trist. The Tavistock Institute of Human Relations was established in England at just the time NTL was being launched in the USA, influenced heavily by psychodynamic traditions employed in the social sphere, i.e., sociodynamics. Its experiential conference on group relations offers a somewhat more structured approach than T-groups to get at deep issues of power, authority, and human effectiveness in organizational life. Weisbord noted that Fred Emery, unlike his collaborator Trist, was "never a fan of the Tavi conference – it was too personal!" (Personal communication, 2016).

The distinctive Future Search approach is discussed in the next section. But it originally appeared in the first edition of *Productive Workplaces* in 1987. That year,

Weisbord took a leave of absence from Block Petrella Weisbord to be a senior research scientist at the Norwegian Institute of Technology in Trondheim, where he studied pioneering approaches to work design and large-group dialogue. He came to see the conference approach as different from OD – e.g., getting "everyone" in the room to improve whole systems themselves, integrating head and heart, body and soul in a larger environment than a single organization. Continuing his own development, he became involved with the body/mind integration work of John and Joyce Weir (1975) and their understanding of "self-differentiation," which would inform his stance as a facilitator in large-group conferences. In 1987, he met Sandra Janoff, a teacher in an experimental school where city and suburban children formed a self-managed learning community. Janoff's experience mirrored his own work with businesses, and together they began to refine Future Search principles and practices. By 1993, they had cofounded the Future Search Network. For the next 20 years, they conducted scores of conferences for businesses and communities around the world and trained more than 4,000 people in applying their principles for large-group success.

True to his original intentions, Weisbord continued writing throughout the consulting and Future Search phases of his long career. He captured his learnings in dozens of OD articles, many coauthored, and served as an associate editor of NTL's *Journal of Applied Behavioral Science* from 1972 to 1978. In 1974, with Howard Lamb and Drexler, he wrote *Improving Police Department Management Through Problem-Solving Task Forces*, based on their work with an urban police force, and he refined the six-box model in a textbook, *Organizational Diagnosis,* which was published in 1978. His magnum opus, *Productive Workplaces*, first appeared in 1987; his "revisited" version of it was released in 2004 (and voted by the OD Network as one of the most influential OD books written during the last 40 years); and the 25th anniversary edition was published in 2012. In 1992, he solicited work from 35 international authors and published *Discovering Common Ground.* He and Janoff jointly authored *Don't Just Do Something, Stand There! Ten Principles for Leading Meetings That Matter* (2007); *Future Search: Getting the Whole System in the Room for Vision, Commitment and Action* (2010); and *Lead More, Control Less: Eight Advanced Leadership Skills That Overturn Convention* (2015). Finally of note, continuing to innovate and reflect his enduring journalist sensibilities capturing life in action, he cofounded Blue Sky Productions with Allan Kobernick and Janoff in 1987, recording more than 30 videos on workplace improvement and case studies. Weisbord was indeed a prolific author and more. We now turn to a view of his most enduring and fundamental contributions.

A Distillation of Weisbord's Wisdom: Key Contributions

There is no question that Weisbord's contributions and influence on others in the field have been vast. But, for me, some contributions from his life's work stand out more than others, rising to a "first principle" order. For example, his six-box model was an innovative (and still widely studied) way to think about organizational diagnosis. However, I believe that the summit of Weisbord's journey yields a more fundamental set of six learnings – conceptual and practice methodology reflections that can be distilled from his lifetime of action research. Each of these contributions has a distinctive Weisbord "ring" to it, despite his comprehensive collaboration with others and his drive to learn from (and with) so many. They are:

1. "Everybody" Improves Whole Systems
2. Human Systems Facilitation: Don't Just Do Something, Stand There
3. Putting the Socio Back into Sociotech, the O back into OD
4. Techniques that Match Our Values
5. The Future Never Comes, It's Already Here
6. The Learning Curve: Organizational Improvement Past, Present, Future

"Everybody" Improves Whole Systems

This is the core principle behind the Future Search method. Weisbord's conception of the evolution of the field is treated in the final, sixth principle of this section. But suffice it here to say, Weisbord understood that if indeed we are confronted by what are inherently whole systems matters, then addressing them must be an all-hands effort *as a matter of principle.* Given the complexity and speed of organizational and other social system change, no one leader, person, stakeholder group, or constituency can grasp the whole of the systemic situation. All are needed to help one another see the situation, envision future possibilities, mobilize for action, and enact the future. The spirit of this, and a detailed approach, is captured in Weisbord and Janoff's *Future Search: Getting the Whole System in the Room for Vision, Commitment and Action* (2010), a work itself that evolved over three editions and 15 years of practice and learning. Regardless of the technical approach to large-group conference methods – Future Search, Open-Space Technology, Real-Time Strategic Change, or others – Weisbord came to see this principle as basic for meaningful, systemic change, one that did justice to both task achievement and human fulfillment.

In practice, getting everybody in the room for a Future Search conference means at least a "3-by-3" representation of those affected by a particular strategic concern – three functions wide and three functions deep, or more, where 60–100 people (with authority information, resources, expertise and need) are convened in a 3-day working session on the critical issue or opportunity at hand. People are invited to "come as you are," bringing their experience and thinking to bear. No prior effort to change them or train them in behaviors, skills, or systems models is needed, nor is the goal to "manage resistance" or advocate change on the part of the facilitators or meeting sponsors. Instead, it is to have the right people show up at an appropriately structured meeting in which they feel safe to share their experiences and speak heartfelt thoughts about the topic. This applies equally to executive leaders. In this, the preconference design task, done jointly with selected client partners, is to fashion a safe space for the collaborative work of the conference. This follows the general insight of Petrella's team building innovation discussed earlier, applied to the whole systems realm. The idea of getting "everybody" in the room as a large-scale meeting concept was derived from Lippitt and Schindler-Rainman. Related core ideas for Future Search that Weisbord and Janoff (2007) identified are:

- *Explore the global, "whole elephant" context for local action and before trying to fix any part.* Again, this is a task for participants in the conference, not the work of an "expert" diagnostician, allowing all parties to "talk about the same world" and codiscover that they all share the same basic dilemmas (derived from Emery and Trist and reflecting Weisbord's transcendence of his own Six Box Model).
- *Focus on common ground and future action, not problems and conflicts.* This energizes people for concerted action and limits taking participants back down the demoralizing path of irreconcilable differences (derived again from Lippitt and Schindler-Rainman, while also anticipating the later work of Appreciative Inquiry).
- *Have people self-manage their own groups and be responsible for action.* This means that people in relevant small groups within the large meeting format directly address their own piece of the puzzle once the bigger picture and common future priorities are identified. They then report out to the plenary for feedback, dialogue, and next steps (drawing on Weisbord's early experience with self-managing teams and influenced by Emery and Trist).

These core ideas directly inform the basic Future Search agenda: Day 1 addresses "where we've been" (past); Day 2 addresses "where we are" (present) and "what we want" (future); and Day 3 includes "how we get there" (common ground and action). Traditional and innovative conference techniques are used in the Future Search approach, including storyboarding individual, group, and the organization's (or community's) historical development; focusing on people's *experience* as the biggest source of useful information; and creatively imagining and dramatizing preferred futures for all to consider.

One notable feature of Future Search is that the time devoted to "action planning" gets considerably compressed compared to many other methods because of the immersive sharing of past and current experience and future thinking. Commitments for salient action are more immediately mobilized and zeroed in on by the process itself. Participants are "living into" the desired collaborative future by virtue of the conference design, which gives them room to experience it right in the room in the rapid, 3-day setting. The sought-after future is crystallized in the "here and now," with less gap between past and future to be analytically debated and bridged. Follow-on actions and reconvening to discuss and extend progress on priorities become natural outgrowths, assuming the right conditions and people's readiness to attend to them hold.

Because of their design, Future Search conferences have been successfully held in a wide variety of countries and cultures around the world and across sectors: arts and culture, business, communities, congregations, education, environmental, government, healthcare, social services, technology, and youth. Weisbord and Janoff (2007) described multiple examples with outcomes of Future Search conferences, including community building in a Northern Ireland city, reducing sectarian conflicts through alliances for economic renewal, work with UNICEF to demobilize child soldiers in Southern Sudan, global work connecting IKEA with NGOs to redesign its supply chain aligned with environmental sustainability, and dozens more, both commercial and social in impact. The Future Search Network site at http://www.futuresearch.net/network/videos/index.cfm also has several videos that show conferences in action and interviews with participants from across the globe. Reflections on some limitations and future possibilities of Future Search concepts can be found in the last section of this chapter, "Legacies and Unfinished Business: A Renaissance of Action Research?"

Human Systems Facilitation: Don't Just Do Something, Stand There

Throughout his career, Weisbord understood that those seeking to engage others in bettering organizational and social conditions are best served by a stance of genuine curiosity. His instinct was always to hear the myriad voices at play and follow where the emerging story led, as a whole and in its rich detail. This perspective completely informed his work in business, OD, and Future Search. As he gave up his Theory X assumptions as an executive, assumptions that never naturally suited him, he saw the results of his experiments with self-led teams and let them shape the next steps he took.

In his OD work at NTL and with Block Petrella Weisbord, he followed the course of people's experiences – including his own – as he carefully listened and intervened. So by the time he arrived at Future Search principles and practices, he had come to a different concept of the facilitator's role: The facilitator was not only *not* there to diagnose and "lead" change but he or she was to simply stand alongside those in the system who were seeking to improve their worlds and were ready enough to get in the room together and try. The facilitator's contribution was thus to help set the stage for people to do the work themselves – which also included a major contribution, as a consultant with expertise, in structuring and qualifying the context to promote collaborative dialogue. But Weisbord's stance as facilitator in the sessions, once begun, was reflected in the title of his 2007 book on facilitation principles and practices (written again with Janoff), *Don't Just Do Something, Stand There*. Weisbord and Janoff described it as "no ordinary meeting book."

> We aim to help you free yourself from the burden of having all the answers to the mysteries of human interaction. We will introduce you to a philosophy, a theory and a practice that is at once radical and simple. To apply our ideas, you will not need to worry about anybody's behavior but your own. (Weisbord and Janoff 2007, p. ix)

Ten principles for facilitating "meetings that matter" are covered in this pithy volume, starting with those for leading meetings and including those that will be familiar from Weisbord's Future Search concepts: Get the Whole System in the Room; Control What You Can, Let Go What You Can't; Explore the "Whole Elephant;" Let People Be Responsible; Find Common Ground; and more. But two of the principles in the book's second section, "Managing Yourself," deserve special attention because they capture deep aspects of "self as instrument," an uncommon bridge from the intra- and interpersonal to the practice of large-scale change: Make Friends with Anxiety and Get Used to Projections.

Understanding anxiety in oneself – and how it links to the anxiety those in the client system experience – is fundamental for Weisbord, especially given the complexity and uncertainty of large-scale change. Expecting anxiety (not trying to quell it for predetermined "success") is key. So is getting comfortable with the inherent projections and countertransferences that abound with all of the voices in the room. Both habits are essential to remain *present and helpful* – that is, to not simply do something out of anxiety and projection but to just stand there, really experience what is happening in the moment, and be of help. These are deep legacies from Weisbord's active years at NTL. While he and Janoff offered a range of practical suggestions to cultivate these practices, it is clear they are seen as self-mastered, emotional competencies.

For Weisbord, change readiness of system members and facilitators depends on recognition and acceptance of the inherent anxiety that change provokes. He cited Claes Janssen's concept (2011a, b) that people cycle through "four rooms of change": contentment, denial, confusion, and renewal (then back to contentment). Weisbord contended that it is only in confusion – the room of uncertainty, high anxiety, but also possibility – that people are most receptive to working together for change. Rushing people off of anxiety in order to have things tidy does not make for real interpersonal contact or headway on substance. Nor does pushing them when they are in the room of denial.

In a related way, those facilitating change are well served by staying aware of their own hot buttons to clearly recognize projections that others put on them, as well as their own tendencies to project. And they best allow the group to handle its own issues. This is one reason Weisbord came to see that the facilitator's role should be made smaller and smaller, not larger. This is a tough discipline, as all of us at times may be tempted to *talk* models and *make* things happen, which is the opposite of action research. One practice that Weisbord and Janoff found helpful was applying John and Joyce Weir's invention of "percept" language (1975), a technical way of thinking about what is being said in the room when one's own hot buttons – conscious or unconscious – are pushed, to get a clearer picture about what is "out there" versus inside our own heads.

But whatever the technique used, Weisbord saw the value in continuing to learn about oneself, coming to terms with uncomfortable, denied, "shadow" parts of the self. This allows facilitators to invite others to really share their views and not get triggered in overreacting to what is happening in the room, either through distorted perceptions or unhelpful actions. He wrote:

> There is a lifetime of personal work for each of us in contacting the shadow side of our natures, integrating the voices that tug us away from creative and humane impulses. We're never finished, and the right time to do it is every day. (Weisbord 2012, pp. 477–478)

In my interview with Weisbord, he shared a thought from his learning with John Weir: "If all human beings come from common ancestors – call it Adam and Eve or our species' evolution – we each have all the genes of everyone who has ever lived. So the more parts of ourselves we discover and truly integrate, that extends the range of humanity with which we can productively work (Law et al. 2015)." This reflected another Weisbord hallmark: the convergence of the deeply intrapersonal and being in the widest world outside of us.

Putting the Socio back into Sociotech, the O back into OD

Along with his business partners Block and Petrella, Weisbord shared the view that the human and actual work dimensions of an organizational system cannot really be pulled apart. They are not, as referenced earlier, antitheses, but twin aspects of a common, human systems root that must be dealt with to more surely move forward. In practice, many consultants and academicians specialize in one side or the other, with the human side frequently treated as behavioral, cognitive, or other "soft" matters and the work side seen as other "hard" factors – strategy, structure, technology, rewards, work design, and the like. Still many others will seek to combine them into a complex model (cognitive again). Regardless, for Weisbord, something is still missing: the *felt,* human side of enterprise – the world of what people actually experience and what they actually do. In fact, Weisbord said that the notion of an "organization" is a kind of reification; it is only people who make things happen, or, as the case may be, not. The "organization" acting is as much of a fiction as a desk jumping up to do the work. But that doesn't mean the *organizational context* is not in play, particularly "the real work" that goes on and how people perform it.

Some practitioners refashioned sociotechnical approaches – the robust theory for having people redesign their own work, which Weisbord learned from Emery and Trist – into a highly technical work variation analysis. The human behavior component became de-emphasized and lacked the vitality it had at the origins of the approach, going back to early Tavistock projects, grounded in Bion's sensibilities. Weisbord wrote, "Just as Taylor's sophisticated integration got reduced to time and motion study, so did sociotechnical systems become for many people a package to be installed like new software (Weisbord 2005, p. 6)." I found this in my own training in sociotech in the mid-1980s. It felt very mechanistic to me, with "human factors" tacked on for good measure. Weisbord recoiled at this trend, although he identified certainly with the way the actual work of an organization was performed. After all, it was his learning with Emery and Trist that gave him clearer insight into what he had done with the family firm work teams years earlier. But he continued to see and write about the human experience at the center of the equation. In this, we might say that Weisbord helped "put the socio back into sociotech." His lifelong practice of experiencing what is happening first and theorizing later also attests to this. So does his interest in the inner world of the facilitator, in the way he or she engages with a large work system or social community.

Conversely, Weisbord with his partners Block and Petrella held to the view that behavioral or personal growth activities, stripped of their "realife" organizational context, were unproductive for large-scale impact. "Alas, people improved themselves more than their organizations," he said.

> To remedy this, OD consultants invented team building to enable transfer of [T-Group] training (in the 1970s, I was a builder of some of the best losing teams in American industry). The strategic flaw of team building is exposed by systems theory. You can change a system only in relationship to the larger system of which it is a part – other functions, customers, suppliers, regulators and community. Don't misinterpret me. Team building and training are existentially valuable activities. In both settings, people can learn to be open, confront conflict, collaborate, appreciate differences, diagnose problems and set goals – all worthy activities. What people cannot get this way is influence, let alone power, over policy, procedure, system and structure. (Weisbord 2005, p. 5)

Human lab learnings, when not connected back to real work situations – and when the stakes of interaction are at their highest – may run counter to actual movement. As a field, OD could as quickly drift into fuzziness, "where the rubber meets the air," as some sociotech consultants characterized OD at the time. It was the polar opposite of sociotech's mechanistic drift. Weisbord articulated that it was important to "put the O back into OD (2012)." Real performance, task accomplishment, and organizational and market context mattered, as had been his instinct from the start. Moreover, as he became more learned about OD, he recognized that when the "human side" is isolated from practical consequence, the promise of the field is missed: *humanness is embedded in practice*, not cold theory, another trace from Lewin.

Techniques That Match Our Values

Seeing the tendency for sociotechnical approaches to become reduced to mechanistic models, Weisbord drew another important implication:

> Around [1990], I was invited to a manufacturing meeting in a famous paper company that is no more. The plant managers talked nonstop about the "multiskilled work team model" that a consulting group had put in – and how much resistance it stirred up. The company had *sacrificed participative values on an altar of canned techniques. We are always at risk to leave our values in the attic when we fall in love with great looking new techniques* [emphasis added]. (Weisbord 2005, pp. 6–7)

His understanding of the limitations of techniques, models, and the "science of organizational improvement" again owes a debt to Lewin. Weisbord came to see "social science" as an oxymoron, as elegant and precise a thinker that Lewin was, himself. Efforts to change large-scale human systems cannot proceed on classical scientific grounds, because their conditions are unique, dynamic, and non-replicable. As change facilitators, we are left with showing up as we *are*, with our presence, learning, and whole being. This requires us to keep our own baggage – attitudinal or intellectual – out of the way. Only in this way can we really meet clients where they are, a truism in OD (Shepard 1975).

But just here, a paradox arises. What we *are* includes our values. If our values truly are values – woven in the fabric of our being and not objects we can trade like so many interchangeable "parts" – then they remain with us when we are present to help organizations. This does not mean that all things that strike us as a "value" of ours may quite be core. They may stem from unrecognized shadow parts of the self, covering deeper issues, thus serving as a kind of pseudo value. This is why self-work for Weisbord, and so many other masters of the craft, is an enduring faith and act. So the trick for Weisbord is not simply casting aside techniques or models but understanding ourselves deeply in our core, so we make best use of "techniques that *match* our values." He put it this way:

> No matter what strategies we choose, if we organization designers want job satisfaction, *we still are stuck with finding techniques equal to our values*. Techniques cascade down the generations like Niagara Falls. Values move like glaciers. Techniques fill whole bookshelves. Values take up hardly room at all. I can still say mine in eight words: *Productive workplaces that foster dignity, meaning and community*. (Weisbord 2005, pp. 7–8)

These may not be values shared with all those in the field, but they are Weisbord's. And they doubtlessly resonate with many. Weisbord himself saw Future Search and other large conference methods as simply one type of strategy to meet these values, one that he expected would be eclipsed over time. The burden thus remains on today's and new generations of practitioners to innovate approaches that take us ever more to our largest aims.

The Future Never Comes, It's Already Here

Perhaps the grandest practical wisdom coming from Weisbord is his understanding that "the future never comes, it's already here." In a stunning passage in the last chapter of the same name in *Productive Workplaces* (2012), the innovator of Future Search wrote:

> Let me tell you about the future as I have experienced it for the last 50 years. The future never comes. Today is the future you imagined yesterday. It's slipping into the past by the second. When Frederick Taylor was born in 1857, every story in this book lay in the future. Now all are past. You cannot guarantee that what you wish for will happen. Improving companies, NGOs and communities can be existentially satisfying work if you avoid the megalomania of believing you build for the ages. There are no "secrets," whether from Attila the Hun, Socrates, Joan of Arc, Machiavelli, Freud, Mother Teresa or Vince Lombardi, that you do not already know. Leave tomorrow to the cosmos. Today's work requires every ounce of energy you have. (p. 472)

So if the future is now, how do better futures come into being? Weisbord's basic answer is that the future is *enacted* one step at a time in light of a bigger vision, dream, or goal we hold out there. Thus, better collective futures are based on what people practically do together today, then the next day, then the next day after that – all in light of a shared image of the future. Importantly, and contrary to what many consultants urge, that future image does not need to be worked out in great detail or lead to a blueprint. It should serve only as a reasonable facsimile of what a future *could be*, a *perceived* north star, as it were, to help inspire those on the journey to take steps each day, learning from them in real time as they move toward it. The journey can bring the destination more sharply into focus, uncover unexpected features, shaping and even shifting it. After all, we see the star only from the telescopes of today. In this way, better organizational and community futures *unfold* from the present, influenced by what happens today. They are coenacted by their players, not engineered – not simply cranked out from a plan. They happen, as Weisbord likes to say, "one meeting at a time." For this reason, he is skeptical of the language of "transformation" and "culture change," finding it grandiose. Similarly, his experience in complex change showed him that preplanned deliverables, detailed roadmaps, and project plans have little value. "We cannot go 20 moves down the chessboard," Weisbord declared (Law et al. 2015).

Practically speaking, then, for Weisbord, big change really amounts to a process of "getting to the next meeting." For example, when one productive conference is completed, leaders are wise to schedule, then convene, the next meeting, realizing that many smaller conversations, one on one or group, planned, and unplanned, would happen in between. Scheduling the next meeting itself shows commitment to the future, and a series of them provides a kind of glide path to the future as it is "lived into," real time.

Consultants can add the most value here through their support in orchestrating conditions for this, and for helping to design the meetings so that dialogue on matters that mean most to people can happen. One such effect in the large conference format is that people start to experience new possibilities, relationships, and shared commitments *right in the room*. The change is happening before their eyes, and they are in the thick of it! These same principles can apply to small group meetings as well, although their impact will be limited to the extent that the right people for systemic reach attend. Finally, one can see that the trajectory of this fits for individuals in their own development. I have tried to show how this can be seen in Weisbord's own career. Whether for an individual, group, or enterprise, this process represents another important facet of action research.

The Learning Curve: Organizational Improvement Past, Present, Future

When Trist reviewed a draft of *Productive Workplaces* in 1985 and suggested that Weisbord add a "conceptual emboldening" to the work, Weisbord was startled. He had not heard that phrase before and wondered if it was possible. He soon understood that Trist was asking him what overall conclusions could be drawn from his case experiences and his work with many of the field's pioneers.

> On a piece of scratch paper, I sketched what I had lived through in my work during the previous quarter century. Such was the origin of "The Learning Curve" that ties together the chapters of this book. (Weisbord 2012, p. xxvii)

Indeed, the learning curve does more than that: It provides a conceptual frame to understand the evolution of the field, past, present, and future. This is inclusive of OD, but broader still. Strictly speaking, OD – however one may define it – is part of a larger field of organizational improvement.

Overall, the concept depicts movement in four historical phases that build on each other. It represents basic ways that key organizational issues have been addressed, including the primary focus of improvement and who primarily attends to the issues. Weisbord termed the concept "a "learning curve," because he saw it reflecting the ever-widening insights of organizational stakeholders and improvement specialists. But, as discussed below, it will be apparent these are not strictly phases. Rather, they are ways of thinking about and acting on organizational improvement (Fig. 1).

Not everyone moves through these in the same manner or even at all. And each of these ways remains dominant for some, as well as situationally appropriate, to this

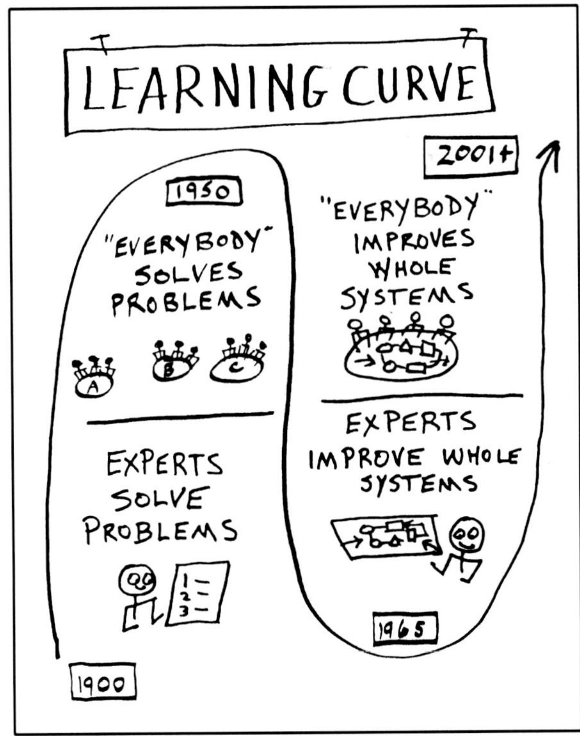

Fig. 1 Organization improvement learning curve (Weisbord 2012)

day. Still, the concept reflects a broad sweep of development over more than a century of efforts of organizational improvement.

The first phase, beginning at the turn of the last century, shows Taylor's influence on the application of "scientific" principles and practices to organizational improvement. Weisbord credited Taylor with an ethos to create a more democratic world that could lift the lot of all workers, based on the intervention of experts. In Taylor's day, these were industrial engineers, but they soon became experts of all kinds, doing interviews, conducting assessments, and performing analyses, then formulating solutions to problems of efficiency, work flow, technology, and the like. Many "expert" consulting firms of all sizes still operate with this approach.

Beginning in the 1950s, "human relations" insights began to take hold in practice, with employees' more broadly attending to solutions. This shift reflected earlier findings such as the Hawthorne studies, Lewin and Lippitt's discovery of "group dynamics," and the experiential learnings at NTL and Tavistock. The rise of team building, employee opinion surveys, behavioral and attitudinal training, interpersonal mediation, participative performance reviews, process consultation, and other similar activity came to the fore. Consultants with this orientation now served in more facilitative roles and helped participants address and tackle the issues themselves ("everybody solves problems"). The problem focus areas were, by and large, treated as discreet.

In the mid-1960s, as reflected in Weisbord's own journey, systems thinking started to break through in organizational improvement practice. Earlier work, such as Ludwig von Bertalanffy's general systems theory (1952), began to have an impact. Presenting problems in one area were increasingly seen as challenges of a "whole, open system," where economics, technology, strategy, structure, and other factors were now essential to consider. Weisbord succinctly summed up the definition of systems thinking: "Everything is hooked up to everything else!" (Weisbord 2005, p. 2). With employees and other stakeholders still involved, consultants tended to serve as experts to drive the work of change – given the complexity of the models – with increasingly sophisticated assessments and comprehensive solutions recommended to clients. This modality, where "experts improve whole systems," was dominant in organizational improvement strategies for the remainder of the century. It still characterizes many, if not most, of the large, worldwide consulting firms today. The economics and business models of these big consulting firms largely require this "expert" approach, as many of my colleagues and I found in years as partners with them.

The breakthrough of large-group process in which "everybody improves whole systems" began with the early conference methods in the 1970s; Weisbord worked more and more with that in the mid-1980s and beyond. As a more widely adopted way of addressing systems change, he dated the onset of this phase in the early 2000s, after groups such as the Future Search Network and other consultants concentrating on large-group methods made significant headway in achievements and use of the approach across the globe. The deep human dimension of the human relations movement returned, but now it was contextualized in what people did to work on large-scale strategies and actions that they drove. And instead of systemic information that consultants mined and complex models they introduced, the approach was now basically rooted in the experience of those in attendance and their sharing and making sense of that experience together for the future. The consultant's role was now to assist the client in preconference planning to structure the process and then stand back and let things happen. The aim was to enable all to fully own the change to the extent of their readiness – and then some, given the dynamics of the mobilized, forward looking community.

Weisbord saw the milestone where "everybody improves whole systems" as the frontier of thinking about organizational improvement. But he remained too much of a historian to think that anything lasts forever, so he believed the future of that improvement would doubtlessly lead elsewhere. Speaking at a forum on organization design, he said that large-group interventions are not "the end of history."

> Every method has its limits, as we all are destined to learn. Our ancestors have given us priceless gifts, but none has prepared us for a world of cellphones, email, virtual teams, the kind of BlackBerries that nobody but a dog would chew on and, more to the point, a global economy that is consuming resources at a rate far beyond our ability to replace them. Indeed, sustainable organizations may have no future in an unsustainable world. The future of organization design does not rest on any particular methods. It lies with the values of the people in this room. The pioneers whose work I have mentioned – Bion, Emery, Lewin, Likert, Lippitt, Maslow, McGregor, Taylor and Trist – all belong to the ages. They have no more to tell us. Look around you, friends and colleagues. *We* are the ones who are now up to bat. (Weisbord 2005, p. 8)

New Insights (Maybe Only Old Ones, Rediscovered)

Weisbord has influenced my own practice in OD in many ways. I first read his work after I began internal organizational consulting in the mid-1980s. His initial design efforts with work teams and pay for knowledge influenced an earlier project I had started: an employee-led effort to restructure a note center for mid-market Imperial Bank in California, where teams of specialists could process and document commercial loans with greater flexibility, speed, cooperation, and efficiency than if they had remained isolated specialists working through the conflicts of branch and headquarters offices. I had been impressed with both the task outcomes and human bonding that occurred in the effort. Weisbord's work added a conceptual understanding to what I was doing. The first article I read of Weisbord's was "Participative Work Design: A Personal Odyssey," *Organizational Dynamics* (1985a). This was an early piece that would become part of the first edition of *Productive Workplaces* (1987).

Not unlike Weisbord, I had first begun doing work at my company in task- and human-oriented change without formal training in the field, although I had studied theory in social science years earlier as a UCLA graduate history student. Weisbord's *Productive Workplaces* (1987) was first published as I attended Pepperdine's MSOD program after switching to business as a profession in the late 1970s. At Pepperdine, I was also introduced to large-scale methods by Dannemiller. I later applied large-group conference approaches in my work at the bank and in launching large client-consulting project teams when I joined KPMG Consulting in the mid-1990s.

As I worked over the years and began my own OD firm, I continued to experiment with large-group methods. I believe that two specific learnings are worth sharing, not because they are especially original but because they represent a kind of independent rediscovery through my own experience of conclusions at which Weisbord had arrived, thus validating his teachings for me.

The first of these has to do with a learning that *the promotion of confidentiality in team building and large-group intervention, far from fostering trust and group effectiveness, actually erodes trust and reinforces power distance between group members*. This occurred to me as I was doing interviews of a 30-member organizational unit for World Bank in preparation for a 2-day retreat of the entire team to consider its way of operating, given the constraints it faced in the institutional, operating environment. I had begun by interviewing unit members, assuring them confidentiality of what they were sharing with me and that I'd only report aggregate themes. But as I interviewed those from the top, middle, and bottom of the hierarchy, it dawned on me that the things they talked with me about were the very items they should be sharing directly with each other. After all, lack of trust and connecting with each other about what was happening in each of their worlds – and in a way they could do something constructively about – was the central issue that presented. Midway through the scheduled interviews, I began talking about the prospect of having each of the team layers – starting with the two co-leads – simply talk with each other, fishbowl style, about what their current worlds were like, with all others of the unit seated in a circle around them. Team members, including the co-leads, responded positively to that suggestion. I would sit to the side of the group in the middle, listening in, T-Group style. The only prompts were the few words hung around the room on flip chart paper – "Experience in your roles to date? Dilemmas? Frustrations? What you want from others in or outside the room?" – to guide their self-led discussions. After they concluded, those on the outside were invited to ask any questions for clarification and to say what they'd heard that they appreciated. No solutions or recommendation was invited. Those were reserved for day 2 of the retreat in structured rounds, where each of the natural work groups, in light of day one, would propose different operating models for the unit, drawing, describing, or dramatizing them in any way they'd like for wider discussion and next steps. For day one, as each of the hierarchical layers took their turns in the fishbowl, nothing about process was charted on the walls. But the entire unit left that first day – a day devoted to understanding, no action – with a rich picture of the status quo, dynamics, and all. There was no consulting interpretation. It was theirs. In day 2, they self-managed a discussion on the implications of day 1 thoughts, then crafted future operating model options and next steps. Notable in day 2 was how the co-leads stepped up to facilitate the whole unit in a way that shifted the perception of their power, their sincerity to share it, and the empowerment in the room. I didn't need to do a thing. I could just stand there. It was startling to behold!

Key takeaways from this case are twofold, each reinforcing Weisbord teachings. The first were the palpable shifts observable in the room, positively affecting the sensitivity of content shared, trust, leader-employee relationships, and the emergence of a shared systems perspective which drew from each of the participant's experiences. My role as consultant was significant in helping stage the basis for the conversations ahead of time and in between the days, but it was very understated in what was done during the retreat. The other takeaway, as noted above, was with understanding that confidentiality is not something to be reinforced in the consultant's method, but a phenomenon to be unpacked. This lays more solid ground for joint, owned action to happen.

The second key learning is how I have repurposed the use of an S-Curve framework when I work with large groups. I use it as a way to conceptually depict a systemic state of confusion during a period of watershed change – the gap period between the old maturing first curve and the yet-to-emerge second curve. I have found that this can help people recognize that current conflicts ascribed to others, rife in these situations, are indeed part of a systemic condition. This affects the way current dynamics are played out in efforts to reenvision and resist potential futures. Once seen, I have found this can be liberating for players in the room to move beyond symptomatic blame. And it provides a way to systemically portray Weisbord's understanding of confusion, as the "one room in change" where anxiety and possibility dwell and where actual movement, enacted together a step at a time, is possible.

Legacies and Unfinished Business: A Renaissance of Action Research?

Weisbord's legacy looms large. I have sought here to illustrate the ways his thinking unfolded and identify key contributions to the field, which, beyond being technically influential, have enduring importance to the *spirit* of our work. I want to focus now on two last things. First, his legacy of dialogue in organizations, including some reflections on ways it has been seen as limiting. Lastly, I want to take a moment and ponder Weisbord's legacy as a whole – how he embodied and breathed fresh life into Lewin's seminal idea of action research – and what it hopefully signifies for the future of the field.

Weisbord's Future Search encapsulated most of his prior learnings and was part of a line of work of others in large-scale organizational and community interventions. All relied on experience-based dialogue as primary fuel for change. Weisbord and Janoff's *Future Search* (2010) briefly compared and contrasted the method with others in the field, and a more comprehensive side-by-side comparison of approaches can be found in Barbara Benedict Bunker and Alban's *The Handbook of Large Group Methods: Creating Systemic Change in Organizations and Communities* (2006). Moreover, the language of "conversations" and "dialogue" in organizations today is widespread. One scholarly piece of work in this vein, Patricia Shaw's *Changing Conversations in Organizations: A Complexity Approach to Change* (2002), is especially noteworthy, given the nature of its radical critique.

Essentially, Shaw's approach to large-scale change is to think of it as a "temporal" process. She described Future Search, Open Space, and other methods of large-group dialogue as more "spatially" oriented; hence, their focus is on convening all the parties in a room, bounded by specific, often transformational intent. In contrast, she described an approach in which the consultant is invited into the world of work as it flows in time, without convening special meetings, to help people as they naturally meet to understand their work dilemmas in fuller ways. The consultant inquires into the stories people tell themselves about their organizational lives – e.g., What is happening? Why is it happening? For what importance? – so their narratives may be deconstructed or more fully threaded together across the organization. In effect, the consultant joins the team – not as an expert, nor as a neutral facilitator, but as a participant-observer, including sharing his or her own views and questions as may be deemed relevant. There are no "outside" systemic goals of sponsors, intents or tasks "superimposed" upon the groups. The process simply follows where the dialectic of the conversation leads. Shaw thus saw "conversing as a way of organizing" and as transformational activity in itself. She wrote:

> I am describing a mode of working that does not proffer a blueprint for practice; that does not define roles or select working models. Rather, I am describing how we may join ongoing conversations as participant sense-makers, helping to develop the opportunities inherent in such conversations. I am suggesting that this involves moving into the constraints, restrictions and premature closures as they materialize in communicative action so as to sustain exploratory meaning making. I am drawing attention to vital, informal, shadow processes that more dominant systematic perspectives render rationally invisible. These are the ordinary, everyday processes of organizational life that offer endless opportunity as we move from conversation to conversation. (Shaw 2002, p. 70)

And while Shaw maintained at least an implicit criticism of Future Search as being too structured and controlled – a critique that goes farther than Weisbord's own intentions to "let go," since Future Search amounted to an expert design to promote substantial dialogue in the first place – she ended with this note:

> Future Search events regularly [produce] the enthusiasm, collective focus and new action plans that its advocates suggest. The experience often generates optimism and goodwill. My question is not, "Is this worth doing?" Much may come of such events. Much *will* come of them and this will bear a complex relation to the hopes, fears and aspirations of the participants. My question is how to work with the ongoing conversational life of organizations in which such events may occasionally arise. (p. 151)

Shaw raises important questions for the sustainability of the conversation and action once it is evoked in a conference method. It is easier said than done to get commitments even to the next meetings, action teams, and the like. So Future Search, as Weisbord recognized, was no panacea. But his attraction to this approach in the latter part of his career was that he "never had to go to meetings again, where the right people, up and down and across, weren't in the room where meaningful work could occur" (Law et al. 2015). He had attended so many meetings that were dead ended or dead on arrival and that Future Search represented a step forward and hopeful alternative.

Regardless, Shaw provided for an interesting critique. On the one hand, she accepted, if even in subtle terms by virtue of her anthropological approach, Weisbord's principle of "everybody improves whole systems." But she then essentially rejected the strategy of getting the whole system in the room in specially structured ways as a means to that end. "I am not trying to gather in one place a 'microcosm of the whole' . . . but rather working as part of loose webs of relationship both legitimate and spun through a multitude of other kinds of relating" (p. 145).

It may be that Shaw's critique veered off too one dimensionally into dialogue, with the risk of no overarching work task driving the focus of conversations. It may be that such an approach to dialogue may be too loose and *not timely enough* for broad change, when needed under "realife" conditions – responding to the demands of markets, missions, and milestones and as felt by a mass of organizational or community members themselves. I have seen these flaws in large-scale dialogue efforts where there was either a failure to sufficiently stitch together heterodox dialogue for explicitly desired enterprise effect or where the dialogue itself broke down into programmatic vaporware. And it may be that this conversational flow does not create enough leverage for strategic or structural impact that can improve people's lives and collective outcomes. If so, the need for more concentrated interventions, Future Search and others, will persist. Indeed, perhaps Future Search, as a structured event, may in the end be but one in a battery of enterprise interventions – including coaching, counsel, strategy, team building, other pieces of work redesign, teaching, and he like, *conceived in terms of their systemic effects* – needing to be synchronized to help organizations move through large-scale change. I have often worked this way myself, and Weisbord's partner, Tony Petrella, was explicit in this in the course of his whole system consulting work. My own experience and graduate studies led me to see that the consultant, if he or she is to remain engaged, needs to follow the path of resistance as it presents, working backward until the core of the systemic difficulties, often denied, surface and can be more fully handled (Goldberg 1993).

Perhaps Shaw's understanding veers in the direction that Weisbord himself anticipated in his understanding that large-scale conferences are *not* the end of history. This may prove especially so in their ability to cope with the speed of change ushered in by ever-increasing technology innovations and the diversification of organizations into ever flatter, more dispersed, and complex network forms. And if Shaw can demonstrate that her approach helps people gain control over changes in work processes, policies, systems, structures, and technologies that benefit people widely, hers may be one of the voices at the new frontier.

One of Shaw's similarities to Weisbord is that her thinking arose from her queries to herself, working as a practitioner. Theory came after practice, including wrestling with the ideas of those who preceded her in light of her experience. So, in a way, we come full circle to Lewin, the practical theorist. This would have a certain joy for Weisbord, who embodied the very life of action research.

When I asked Weisbord what he saw as the future of OD, he gave me his frequent answer: that OD can be anything that anyone calls OD and that helps people in organization or community progress. "Who really knows what OD is?" he asked. "OD has had an 'identify crisis' as far as I can remember (Personal communication 2016)."

But Weisbord also has what might be called "a hope within a hope:" that OD, at its best, has something more to it than that. He told me that he thought OD, for all of its heterogeneity, lacked "a kind of ribbon around it" to give it shape and greater value. Amidst the scads of techniques and models, he thought that the missing ribbon was "action research," a way of approaching life with an open heart and mind, curiosity, and reflection on inner and outer things – helping people find greater meaning in their lives and work. That ribbon served him well throughout his own journey. With a little luck – and grace, perhaps – a kind of rediscovery of action research might be possible. Might today's very moment of massive economic, technological, and institutional change point to a renaissance of action research?

> Helping people study and improve their own situations seems to me worthy work, if someone will pay for it. We used to call that "action research," the part of Lewin's great legacy that remains for me fresh, flexible and adaptable. You can do action research on any aspect of organizational life. You just need people who want to do it. If the next generation learns how to adapt action research, that would be a great blessing.
>
> Making the world better one person, one meeting, one organization at a time could keep you psyched for a lifetime. I believe that all work that fulfills you and helps others is existentially valuable. (Personnel communication 2016)

References

Argyris, C. (1970). *Intervention theory and method: A behavioral science view*. Reading: Addison-Wesley.

Bunker, B. B., & Alban, B. T. (2006). *The handbook of large group methods: Creating systemic change in organizations and communities*. San Francisco: Jossey Bass.

Goldberg, M. D. (1993). Characteranalytic organization consultation. *Journal of Orgonomy, 27*(2), 218–231.

Janssen, C. (2011a). *The four rooms of change, part I: A practical everyday psychology*. Stockholm: Ander & Lindstrom.

Janssen, C. (2011b). *The four rooms of change, part II: Fifteen years of more experience*. Stockholm: Ander & Lindstrom.

Law, C. (Producer), Goldberg, M. D. (Writer/Interviewer), & Pile, S. (Videographer/Editor). (2015). Pepperdine university MSOD founders video series: Marvin Weisbord (Electronic video). Available from Pepperdine MSOD Alumni Council, c/o 4520 E. Rocky Slope, Phoenix, AZ 85044.

Likert, R. (1961). *New patterns of management*. New York: McGraw-Hill.

Likert, R. (1967). *The human organization: Its management and value*. New York: McGraw-Hill.

Marrow, A. F. (1969). *The practical theorist: The life and work of Kurt Lewin*. New York: Basic Books.

McGregor, D. (1960). *The human side of enterprise*. New York: McGraw-Hill.

McGregor, D. (1967). The organization of work at the worker level. In W. G. Bennis & C. McGregor (Eds.), *The professional manager* (pp. 83–96). New York: McGraw-Hill.

Shaw, P. (2002). *Changing conversations in organizations: A complexity approach to change*. New York: Routledge.

Shepard, H. A. (1975). Rules of thumb for change agents. *Organization Development Practitioner, 7*(3), 1–5.

von Bertalanffy, L. (1952). An outline of general systems theory. *British Journal for the Philosophy of Science, 1*, 114–129.

Weir, J. (1975). The human growth laboratory. In K. Benne, L. P. Bradford, J. R. Gibb, & R. D. Lippitt (Eds.), *The laboratory method of changing and learning: Theory and application*. Palo Alto: Science and Behavior Books.
Weisbord, M. R. (1966). *Campaigning for president: A new look at the road to the White House*. New York: Washington Square Press.
Weisbord, M. R. (1968). *Some form of peace: True stories of the American friends service committee at home and abroad*. New York: Viking.
Weisbord, M. R. (1976). Why organization development hasn't worked (so far) in medical centers. *Health Care Management Review, 1*(2), 17–28.
Weisbord, M. R. (1978). *Organizational diagnosis: A workbook of theory and practice*. Reading: Addison-Wesley.
Weisbord, M. R. (1985a). Participative work design: A personal odyssey. *Organizational Dynamics, D13*(4), 17–28.
Weisbord, M. R. (1985b). Team effectiveness theory. *Training and Development Journal, 5*, 27–29.
Weisbord, M. R. (1987). *Productive workplaces: Organizing and managing for dignity, meaning and community*. San Francisco: Jossey Bass.
Weisbord, M. R. (2005). *Techniques to match our values. An address to the organization design forum*. San Francisco: MarvinWeisbord.com.
Weisbord, M. R. (2012). *Productive workplaces: Dignity, meaning and community in the 21st century* (3rd ed.). San Francisco: Jossey Bass.
Weisbord, M. R., & Janoff, S. (2007). *Don't just do something, stand there! Ten principles for leading meetings that matter*. San Francisco: Barrett-Koehler.
Weisbord, M. R., & Janoff, S. (2010). *Future search: Getting the whole system in the room for vision, commitment, and action* (3rd ed.). San Francisco: Barrett-Koehler.
Weisbord, M. R., & Janoff, S. (2015). *Lead more, control less: Eight advanced leadership skills that overturn convention*. San Francisco: Barrett-Koehler.

Further Reading

Beckhard, R. (1969). *Organization development: Strategies and models*. Reading: Addison-Wesley.
Bennis, W. G. (1969). *Organization development: Its nature, origins, and prospects*. Reading: Addison-Wesley.
Blake, R. R., & Mouton, J. S. (1969). *Building a dynamic corporation through grid organization development*. Reading: Addison-Wesley.
Lawrence, P. R., & Lorsch, J. W. (1969). *Developing organizations*. Reading: Addison-Wesley.
Schein, E. (1969). *Process consultation: Its role in organization development*. Reading: Addison-Wesley.
Walton, R. E. (1969). *Interpersonal peacemaking: Confrontations and third-party consultation*. Reading: Addison-Wesley.
Weisbord, M. R. (2004). *Productive workplaces revisited: Dignity, meaning and community in the 21st century* (2nd ed.). San Francisco: Jossey Bass.
Weisbord, M. R., Lamb, H., & Drexler, A. (1974). *Improving police department management through problem-solving task forces*. Reading: Addison-Wesley.
Weisbord, M. R., Lawrence, E. R., & Charns, M. E. (1978). Three dilemmas of academic medical centers. *The Journal of Applied Behavioral Science, 14*(3), 284–304.
Weisbord, M. R., et al. (1992). *Discovering common ground*. San Francisco: Barrett-Koehler.

Richard W. Woodman: Creativity and Change

85

Tomas G. Thundiyil and Michael R. Manning

Abstract

Richard (Dick) W. Woodman is a unique contemplative scholar who built his name in the field with his scholarship as well as his charming personality and satirical nature. The following chapter covers Dick's personal history starting with growing up in rural Oklahoma, followed by his service in the US Army, and then his extended contributions to the profession. We discuss his life experiences and some of his lasting influences on the field. Early in his career, Dick helped popularize the concept of creativity in the field of management and organizational behavior by publishing one of the most highly cited and still actively researched theories on organizational creativity (Woodman, Sawyer, & Griffin, Acad Manag Rev 18:293–321, 1993). This was followed with several other important streams of scholarship including an emphasis on bridging scholars and practitioners as well as a focus on strengthening methodologies in organizational change research. In addition to this scholarship, Dick has also directly shaped the direction of research and practice in organizational change and development over the last 30 years as editor of two of the most influential publications: *The Journal of Applied Behavioral Science* and *Research in Organizational Change and Development*. We end this essay with a discussion of his lasting legacy in the change arena. Although recently retiring from a 38-year career as an endowed professor at Texas A&M, Dick continues to write and contribute to change scholarship. He encourages us to strengthen change research methodology, and his legacy of scholarship on creativity and change provides the conceptual basis

T.G. Thundiyil (✉)
Management, Central Michigan University, Michigan, MI, USA
e-mail: thund1t@cmich.edu; tomasthundiyil@gmail.com

M.R. Manning
Center for Values-Driven Leadership, Goodwin College of Business, Benedictine University, Chicago, IL, USA
e-mail: mmanning@ben.edu

D.B. Szabla et al. (eds.), *The Palgrave Handbook of Organizational Change Thinkers*,
DOI 10.1007/978-3-319-52878-6_64

for ongoing research with the interactionist model of creativity. He also challenges the field with two fundamental issues/questions: (1) individual changeability – how does the organization affect, and how do individuals change during and following episodes where an organization attempts to change? and (2) a temporal model of change – how might the field better incorporate an understanding of temporality and change in order to extend beyond the Lewin model by creating a more dynamic process model of change?

Keywords
Organizational creativity • Creativity and change • Individual changeability • Change research methods • Temporality and change

Contents

Introduction

Richard (Dick) W. Woodman has been one of the most influential academics in the field of organization development and change over the last 35 years. He has held a faculty position at the Mays Business School at Texas A&M University since 1978 and just recently retired as the Lawrence E. Fouraker Professor of Business and Professor of Management. Woodman was editor of *The Journal of Applied Behavioral Science* from 2005 to 2010 at a very critical period in the life of this journal. Also, with his long-time colleague, Bill Pasmore, he created and edited the annual research series – *Research in Organizational Change and Development* (*ROCD*) – that has provided the space for many change scholars to explore and develop new emergent themes in change research. In addition, his scholarly contributions to the field have been highly influential.

Influences and Motivations: The Military and the World of Practice

Early Life Influences. Dick Woodman grew up in Elk City, Oklahoma as the oldest in a family with two boys. Dick's father was president of the local savings and loan, and both his parents were very influential instilling the value of education and service early in his life. During his formative school years, Dick was always very interested in math and science. He developed a value for "always doing a good job" and started working at the age of 12 picking cotton and caddying at the local golf course. Another influential aspect from his family was a commitment to service to our country. Woodman's grandfather served in WWI, and his father served in both WWII and the Korean War. In addition, an ancestor fought in the Revolutionary War and another in the War of 1812. When Dick started college at Oklahoma State University, he enrolled in ROTC and upon graduation was commissioned as a military intelligence officer in the US Army.

At Oklahoma State University, Dick studied engineering, in particular electrical and industrial engineering. These met his interests in science and math. Upon graduation with an engineering degree, reporting for active duty was delayed so that he might also complete an MBA at OSU, and he did this in a year's time. While in the MBA program, Woodman had his first introduction to the behavioral side of business. Right after graduation, at the height of the Vietnam War, Dick entered the Army in the role of military intelligence officer. He was assigned to the Army Security Agency Group Korea and became the commanding officer at Camp Alamo, a base camp on the DMZ which was the northernmost outpost of the American Army in the Republic of Korea. The troops at Camp Alamo operated a forward intelligence site located on top of a mountain a few miles north of their base camp. From this outpost Dick had a bird's eye view overlooking T-Bone Ridge – the same mountain range and valley in which his father over 18 years earlier had commanded troops in a highly contested and deadly aspect of the Korean War.

His military experience had a dramatic impact on Dick, and to this day he refers to this as a Hotel California experience ("You can check out, but you can never leave."). Dick never dwells much further on his Army experience, but it is clear from his reserved acknowledgment that it had a significant impact. One can get a glimpse of this impact from reading a New York Times article that was written by 25-year old First Lieutenant Richard W. Woodman and published on December 31, 1970 (Woodman 1970). From this reflective editorial, we can see the beginnings of a budding scholar, well aware of the moral dilemmas of war and the personal costs to individuals and society. The essay is also an early illustration of the talent Woodman has with the written word, something we all have benefited from in his scholarly writings over the years. To this day Dick stays connected with his Army experience via the network of an Army Security Agency website for veterans, personal communications, reunions, and working with veteran's support organizations. In recent years he has written several letters of support for men under his command who were exposed to Agent Orange, assisting them to receive disability claims.

Woodman served in the Army from 1969 to 1971. Both immediately before and after active duty, Dick held a series of positions (staff specialist in human resource planning and management development) in the oil industry from 1971 to 1972 with Sun Oil Company in both Tulsa (before) and Dallas (after). Shortly, however, he was lured back to hometown Elk City, Oklahoma, to join First Federal Savings and Loan Association as a vice-president of the firm where his father was president.

Although quite successful at an early age, he still felt there was a better fit for his talents. He enjoyed reading books in psychology, sociology, and anthropology and wondered how the behavioral sciences could be applied to business and management. After some introspection he decided that an academic life might be a better fit for him. He felt that research, writing, and teaching would fulfill his curiosity and be a rewarding occupation. So he contacted a former professor at OSU – Wayne Meinhart – who by that time was head of the Management Department. Dr. Meinhart invited him to campus to meet with several faculty to explore his interests. Among the faculty he met with that day was a newly minted assistant professor – Mike Hitt. Later, Dr. Hitt became a longtime colleague with Dick at Texas A&M. Dick then focused on graduate schools with doctoral programs of interest. He found Stanford, University of Washington, and Purdue University to his liking. Then, by surprise, a month or so after his visit to OSU, Wayne Meinhart called and offered a visiting faculty position for the Spring of 1975. Teaching 12 hours – two sections of principles of management and two sections of marketing – Dick embarked on his academic career. A major life transition was made as he pivoted away from his successful career in banking to an academic life.

Dick entered the doctoral program in the Department of Administrative Science, Krannert Graduate School of Industrial Administration, Purdue University, in the summer of 1975. His new wife and life companion Linda also joined him in West Lafayette. Dick fell in love with Purdue and the academic life right away. He was enthused that organizational behavior was a viable topic of study in business schools. The Administrative Science group at Purdue was a small tight-knit group of doctoral students and faculty. The faculty included Jack Sherwood and Don King, both leaders in organization development and the sociotechnical systems movement, as well as Howard Fromkin, a renowned social psychologist and research methodologist. Fellow doctoral students who have since developed their own prominence over the years included Bill Pasmore, Russ Lloyd, Jerome Adams, Dan Ganster, Paul Tolchinsky, Mike McCuddy, Conrad Jackson, Marci Fusilier, and Mike Manning. Dick jumped right in with both feet, not only with his coursework but also with research studies he initiated on his own and with other doctoral students. The Information Privacy Research Center provided some support. In addition, a state-of-the-art behavioral science laboratory existed within the Krannert School. This behavioral lab had an observation deck overlooking multiple rooms with one-way mirrors for observation. Video cameras, microphones, and recorders were in each room. There was a master control room, managed by a full-time engineer hired solely to assist researchers with any technical needs. All this made it possible to conduct very sophisticated experiments. It was a behavioral scientist's dream laboratory.

Woodman was particularly drawn to Jack Sherwood and his personable, easy-to-get-to-know style. Dick was impressed with Jack in many ways. Jack was a living "action figure" in that he was a scholar practitioner and one of the top organization development consultants at the time. Jack was also a member of the NTL Institute, a training institute founded in 1946 by Kurt Lewin and associates where the infamous T-Group was invented, and an APA Fellow. Along with his academic duties, Jack offered national workshops to train organization development consultants and teach sociotechnical systems principles. His writings and thoughts on high performance-high commitment (HP-HC) work systems were in Dick's words the "best articulated on this topic even today." In particular Jack's mentoring helped Dick gravitate to the field of organization development, and he attributes Jack's experience and knowledge of OD as being the foundational source to his research and writing.

By the time Woodman received his PhD (summer, 1978), he had four publications (Woodman and Sherwood 1977; Woodman and King 1978; Hanes et al. 1978; and in press Woodman 1979), and his dissertation research on team development shortly resulted in three major publications in highly desired journals, including *Psychological Bulletin* (Woodman and Sherwood 1980b), *The Journal of Applied Behavioral Science* (Woodman and Sherwood 1980a), and *Group & Organization Studies* (Woodman 1980). But it was one of Dick's beginning intellectual endeavors at Purdue that would become a major research interest throughout his career. During his second year at Purdue Woodman wrote a qualifying paper on creativity that coincidentally at the time was not well received (most felt then this was a topic out of bounds for a business school). Dick took great satisfaction in publishing this qualifying paper practically verbatim as originally written (Woodman 1981). More importantly, his subsequent work on creativity has had a major influence.

Early Career Influences. Woodman left Purdue with four academic job offers and he chose Texas A&M University, not only for the opportunities that existed there but because it was close to Oklahoma where he had significant family obligations. In 1978, Texas A&M was an aspiring institution. The oil boom of the 1960s and 1970s provided top salaries to faculty in the business school, and they accumulated a group of young faculty from the best universities. Dick joined the Department of Management led by Don Hellriegel. Hellriegel and John Slocum (then at SMU) quickly invited Dick to join in the authorship of the third edition of their highly acclaimed Organizational Behavior (West Publishing, later South-Western College Publishing) textbook that had many editions over some 20+ years and has been used in teaching thousands of undergraduate business students OB concepts. Also very early in his career at Texas A&M, Dick began teaching a doctoral seminar in research methods along with a graduate course on organizational change. He continued to faithfully teach these two courses until his retirement.

Major Contributions: Shaping the Field

Dick Woodman's influence on the field of organizational change and development spans far and wide. Not only has he published one of only two pieces of satire ever to appear in the *Academy of Management Review*, "The Devil's Dictionary" (Woodman 1979), but he also served as editor for two of the premier publications in the area of organizational change and development (i.e., *Research in Organizational Change and Development, The Journal of Applied Behavioral Science*) and developed several prominent streams of research.

Research in Organizational Change and Development. One of the grandest contributions Dick has made to the field of organizational change and development was the research series that Woodman and Pasmore cofounded with JAI Press in 1987, titled *Research in Organizational Change and Development (ROCD)*. Not only did this position Dick and Bill as leading scholars in the organizational change arena, but their efforts opened publication opportunities for many other scholars to publish in the field. *ROCD* has been on the cutting edge of change research, publishing a number of influential articles that address some of the most pressing questions in organizational change and development scholarship. For example, several original pieces of groundbreaking scholarship have first appeared in *ROCD*, including the first published article on appreciative inquiry (Cooperrider and Srivastva 1987), the dichotomy of organizational change theory (Porras and Robertson 1987), and the competing values model of organizational culture (Denison and Spreitzer 1991). Also, when the advancement of the discipline was predicated on particular questions, *ROCD* made it a priority to address these questions and advance the field. For example, when scholars began to call into question the efficacy of change interventions, *ROCD* published several meta-analyses in answer to the calls for research (e.g., Macy and Izumi 1993; Robertson et al. 1993).

However, it is not only the content of this publication that has been impressive but also its longevity. For 21 volumes, Woodman and Pasmore edited the series, and now the annual scholarly book series is on volume 24, and the editorship has been passed along to Debra Noumair (Columbia) and Rami Shani (Cal State Poly). Because of Dick and Bill's efforts of service and strong collaborative chemistry, the Organization Development and Change Division of the Academy of Management has established the Pasmore-Woodman Award given to honor research collaborators who, through their joint research endeavors and colleagueship, produce impactful research. The Emerald Group (current series publisher) provides a cash stipend for the annual winners. *ROCD* was established to be a forum for change scholars to share cutting edge conceptual and empirical scholarship without the constraints (e.g., on length) typically seen in journal publication. This has allowed researchers to share their latest thoughts and the emerging trends in both research and practice.

The Journal of Applied Behavioral Science. During Woodman's career as a change scholar, there has been considerable chatter about the impending death of organization development (c.f. Bartunek and Woodman 2012). Although many change scholars mock the idea of OD's demise, in the early 2000s, *The Journal of Applied Behavioral Science* was in serious trouble. It had missed publication dates due to an insufficient number of manuscripts and other complications and was promptly dropped from the Thompson Reuters Social Science Citation Index. To fall off this list is very problematic for a journal, since it means that tenure committees do not recognize publications in these journals as meeting quality standards, and subsequently potential authors are skeptical about submitting articles. To not be part of the Social Science Citation Index runs the risk that a journal can enter a death spiral toward irrelevance. Fortunately, Bob Marshak jumped in as acting editor for a year until a permanent editor could be identified. Dick Woodman was the choice to be the new editor of JABS, challenged to steer the journal back to academic standards. His service to the profession and dedication to JABS were unparalleled as he revived JABS. Woodman increased the number of manuscript submissions, met publication deadlines, bolstered the editorial board, and increased the number of citations of JABS articles. After Thompson Reuters conducted another review, JABS was reestablished as a journal listed in the Social Science Citation Index. Not only did this editorship influence Dick's scholarship, his commitment also had a great influence on the field of organization change and development. Without Woodman's influence, the flagship journal in our field most likely would not have continued, at least not with the reputation that it holds today.

Strengthening research methodology. Another area where Woodman has had considerable impact has been on strengthening the scientific rigor in our field by improving research methodology (e.g., Woodman 1989a, b, 2014b). For example, Woodman has argued for strengthening the "evaluation research" component of the field. In 1989, in the third volume of *ROCD*, Woodman issued a call. In this influential piece, during a discussion of statistical issues (i.e., evaluation biases, confounds, and statistical meaningfulness/significance), Woodman astutely noted that both quantitative and qualitative research lead to an emphasis on certain aspects of each statistical issue (e.g., Woodman and Wayne 1985) and therefore, studied independently, would be insufficient to effectively examine change. Dick suggested ways to combine qualitative and quantitative research with the hope for a greater use of "combined paradigm" studies (Woodman 1989a). In addition to advocating in his chapter of *ROCD*, Dick continued this type of advocacy for this increased rigor in numerous other publications (e.g., Pasmore et al. 2008; Woodman 2014b; Woodman et al. 2008).

Dick has also pushed for strengthening evaluation research through increased rigor in research design. For example, Woodman and Sherwood (1980a) utilized a true experimental design during a team development intervention with 67 groups in an engineering survey course. This study represents one of only a handful of "true" experiments conducted to evaluate an OD intervention. The intervention was designed to improve work group effectiveness by diagnosing problems of the work group. In 2008, Woodman and colleagues advocated for greater rigor in evaluation research suggesting the use of several different research designs, including, true experiments, quasi-experiments, nonexperimental survey research, longitudinal field research, and mixed method study design. Again, and more recently, in a response to a detailed examination of internal validity in organizational change research, Woodman (2014b) argued for the use of quasi-experimental designs because they have the advantage of being strong on internal validity plus are much more likely to be feasible than "true" experimental designs in most organizations. When you couple Woodman's scholarship on strengthening research methods with his teaching the doctoral research methods class at Texas A&M, it becomes clear that Woodman has made an enduring commitment to strengthening rigor in change research.

Organizational creativity. As mentioned previously, Dick has also had a strong interest in organizational creativity. He has long considered creativity in a complex social system to be a "special case" of organizational change (Woodman 2008b; Woodman et al. 1993). More specifically, Woodman argues that organizational creativity is "a subset of the broader domain of innovation. Innovation is then characterized to be a subset of an even broader construct of organizational change" (Woodman et al. 1993, p. 293). As such he has argued that linkages between the fields of organizational creativity and organizational change are both logical and valuable (e.g., Woodman et al. 1993; Woodman 2008a). To underscore the value of Woodman's work on this topic it is worth mentioning that out of the countless number of publications on his vitae, the interactionist theory of organizational creativity is his most cited journal article. Dick's theory of organizational creativity (Woodman et al. 1993) has been described in the literature, several times, as a prominent theory of creativity. For example, Shalley and Zhou (2008) note, "there are two main theoretical models that have guided the area of organizational creativity, that of Amabile (1988, 1996) and Woodman et al. (1993)" (p. 12). More recently, Zhou and Hoever (2014) structure their review of the workplace creativity literature using the basic interactionist premises of Woodman's conceptualization. They attest that "... Woodman et al.'s (1993) interactionist model of creativity constituted an important stimulus for the then nascent research on workplace creativity." (p. 350). They credit Woodman's novel approach to workplace creativity, codetermined through the interaction of actor and contextual factors, as the intellectual stimulus that moved the field forward.

Woodman's seminal theory grew out of earlier work by Woodman and Schoenfeldt (1989, 1990). In the 1989 chapter, the authors explored the interactionist perspective on individual creative behavior. In the 1990 paper, the authors advanced a theory of individual creativity grounded in an interactionist perspective, which, the authors argued, incorporated important elements of three historical perspectives used to explicate creativity – personality, cognitive, and social psychology explanations of creativity. Then finally, in 1993, Woodman brought this interactionist model of creativity into the organizational context, and he later traced out the development of the interactionist model of organizational creativity in a management encyclopedia (Woodman 2013). The 1993 paper is the most heavily cited paper from volume 18 of *The Academy of Management Review* (Corley and Gioia 2011). Further, as of May 19, 2016, the article has 3,308 citations according to Google Scholar. This major contribution is summarized in Fig. 1, a reprint of the original Interactionist Model of Organizational Creativity that appeared in this landmark publication.

Following this seminal piece, Woodman has made several additional contributions to creativity. He has further argued that organizational creativity is a special case of organizational change (Woodman 2008b) and has advocated for a deeper understanding of the intersection of these two literatures. He has conceptualized barriers to creativity (Kilbourne and Woodman 1999), suggested a model for managing creativity (Woodman 1995), and proposed a way to examine the role of relationships in creative action (Chakrabarty and Woodman 2009).

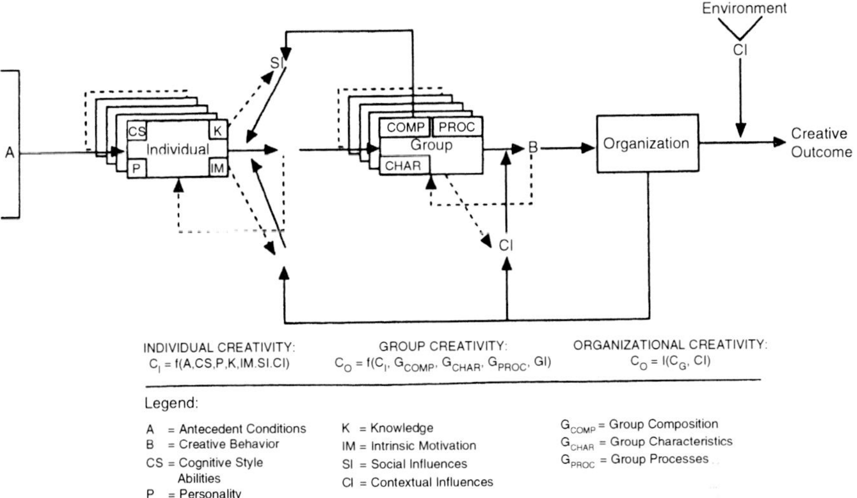

Fig. 1 An interactionist model of creativity from Woodman et al. (1993)

Scholar-practitioner application. As many scholars have written about the scholar-practitioner divide (e.g., Hay et al. 2008; Rynes et al. 2001), Woodman has made several attempts to bridge the divide. We suggest that one of the themes that occurs across Dick's research, that has spanned the length of his career, is that his work speaks to the "scholarly" practitioner and helps develop the practical application of OD and other change work (Hay et al. 2008). For example, in one of his early publications, Woodman (1980) differentiated between T-groups and team development to ensure each method of training could be "applied appropriately" and to facilitate "communication and intelligent decisions concerning their utility" (p. 141). Through this paper, he considered the idea of how practice and theory are related, which he also considers through several other articles (e.g., Woodman 2014b).

Another group of Woodman's practitioner-scholar research centers around what is happening in practice. For example, McMahan and Woodman (1992) surveyed Fortune 500 industrials to understand the actual practice of OD that occurred within the firms. This study uniquely ventured away from the traditional theory-heavy focus of academic research and shifted the attention to what organizations are actually utilizing. The authors explored several ideas, such as, how much of the outside experience base is generalizable, what are internal OD practitioners doing, and to gain an understanding of how OD is used within firms. Similarly, Woodman and Muse (1982) authored a chapter where they review techniques and methodologies that have been successful in improving work group or organizational effectiveness in the private sector.

Relatedly, Dick has several pieces that deal with the implementation of principles across spheres. For example, Lau et al. (1996) examined the applicability of OD theory across cultures. More specifically, the authors compared OD practices in

Hong Kong and the USA to better understand the applicability of OD principles in an Asian context with the intent to develop international theory and practice. In a similar vein, Woodman and several coauthors have examined the role of management during the implementation of technology (Thach and Woodman 1994), creativity (Woodman 1995), and work groups (Woodman and Pasmore 2002). In the last piece, the authors introduced a model to diagnose the needs of a work group prior to focusing on team building. Throughout the years and all through his work, Dick Woodman has focused on developing the application of scholarly research to OD practice.

New Insights: Seeing the Fundamental Essence in a Complex World

Although it is clear that Dick Woodman has made invaluable contributions to understanding organizational change and development, a deeper look at these contributions suggests a pattern in his writings. To understand Dick Woodman's contribution to organizational change, it is important to understand Dick Woodman. As noted above, he grew up in Elk City, Oklahoma, a small town in Oklahoma with a population of less than 10,000 people at the time. The small town upbringing has been a strong influence for Woodman. In fact, during classes and meetings, Dick often refers to "his small town country boy" way of understanding things to remind people to keep things simple and not to neglect the basic fundamental aspects of arguments. Some scholars have the ability to uncover complexities of human behavior. They complicate and reshape what we take for granted by illustrating how behavior is more complex than we thought, often leaving both scholars and practitioners frustrated searching for how one might manage all these complexities at the level of application. Only a few scholars, like Dick Woodman, can do the exact opposite. He has the uncanny skill to take the complex, stand above the fray, and help us understand human behavior in a more easily communicated manner, while still reflecting the complexity of the context. This straight talk also provides good potential for practical action, which in the end is the ultimate goal of research. Woodman eloquently explicates this talent throughout his research. And, as many know – budding organizational scholars in his doctoral seminars, students attending a conference doctoral consortium where Dick is a faculty member, scholars who are receiving Dick's reviews from a paper submitted for publication, etc. – Dick's talent of clarifying the complex, providing concrete actionable options, and conveying this in a caring and thoughtful way is unparalleled.

We can see this in his written work when Woodman (2008b) provides commentary for published articles. One example comes in 2008 when he was invited to provide comments on articles in a special issue of the British Journal of Management. When providing commentary for Marshak and Grant's (2008) piece in the journal, he cited Burrell and Morgan's advancement on the continua of ontology and epistemology. He highlighted this piece to provide readers (and possibly himself) a way to understand the paradigm of thought from which the authors made their contribution. By providing this pathway, his simplicity served as a bridge for scholars to gain better access to influential theory on organization development.

In another example, when Woodman commented on Palmer and Dunford's (2008) article in the same issue, Woodman brought the author's argument back to the basic assumptions underlying human action, which were raised in Rychlak's (1968) discussion of theorizing about human beings. By illuminating a path from which readers can view and appreciate the contribution of the authors, Woodman contributes to not only the reader and the author but to science itself.

Another example is the commentary Dick and Jean Bartunek provided for the book *The Psychology of Organizational Change: Viewing Change from the Employee's Perspective* (Oreg et al. 2013). At the end of this book, Woodman and Bartunek offered a context from which to understand the summation of contributions. More specifically, the authors made connections between all of the articles and in turn tied the contributions of the book to the interactionist perspective (Woodman and Bartunek 2013), with a reminder of the person-situation interactions that lie at the heart of organizational change and development. Through their writing, Woodman and Bartunek are able to connect the reader between the scholar's work and where it contributes to the larger picture of organization change and development.

Just as Woodman does with providing summaries of articles, he also brings this simplicity into developing an understanding of phenomena. For example, in his work on creativity, he does not get bogged down (or allow the readers to get bogged down) in the complexity of a theory that has provided a fundamental framework for research for more than 30 years. Rather, he uses the simplicity of a few sentences to introduce readers to the complex phenomenon he discusses, "the behavior of an organism at any point in time is a complex interaction of the situation and something else – this something else is the nature of the organism itself" (Woodman and Schoenfeldt 1990, p. 10). He further elicits in his interactionist theory for creativity, "group creativity is a function of the interaction of the individuals involved and group characteristics, group processes, and contextual influences" (Woodman et al. 1993, p. 296). Using his self-professed "country boy" mentality toward understanding phenomena, not surprisingly, the premise for his seminal theory on creativity (Woodman et al. 1993) was a comprehensive, yet simple to understand, interactionist model for organizational creativity. In this research, Woodman and colleagues examined individual creativity, group creativity, and organizational creativity by suggesting how the level of analysis (i.e., individual, group, or organization) interacts with the situational influences relevant to that level.

Similarly, this simplified and fundamental view of change continues through his comments on several other change phenomena. In his 2014 piece, Woodman (2014b) comments specifically on the art and science of several prominent features of change research. Similarly, in commenting on evaluation research, Woodman notes that it has two purposes "(1) to make valid inferences about effective and ineffective organizational change efforts and (2) to understand change phenomena and processes to contribute to theory development in the organizational sciences" (p. 469). Again, by breaking down evaluation research into two simple goals, Woodman gains facility with delineating how the science of organizational change may seem at conflict and that the art of organizational change can be used to pursue the two simultaneously. In his section on organization development, Woodman argues that all change research, with possibly the exception of appreciative inquiry, begins with a diagnosis. He argues that the process may be different for different types of change, but he also argues that an organization must be understood before it can be effectively changed. Thus, he suggests, a dialogic OD diagnosis occurs in the "meaning-making" process through the change endeavor. Woodman argues that although dialogic OD (e.g., Bushe and Marshak 2009) may not use diagnosis as a formal step, in order to know when to change something and when to keep things the same, it is imperative that a specific actor has some understanding of what needs to be changed or improved, which is a diagnosis. In a final example, Woodman's take on theory is that "theory articulates the organized common sense that represents the sum total of knowledge about organizational reality" (p. 467). Although this comment is not groundbreaking, Woodman astutely boils down what theory is to an academic into one simple sentence. Further, this point boils down Dick's take on the important, but fine line that OD plays as a bridge between academics and practitioners (e.g., Bartunek and Woodman 2012). Although each example that is highlighted above covers a different aspect of organizational change, the common theme that comes across is that, for Dick Woodman, no matter how complex the ideas, there is brilliance in its simplicity.

Legacies and Unfinished Business: Individual Changeability and a Temporal Model of Change

Dick Woodman has, without a doubt, left a lasting legacy on both the field of organizational change and development and the organizational sciences more broadly. Not only has his work as an editor of two highly regarded outlets for organizational change guided the field for decades, but much of his scholarship still receives attention today. As noted above, Woodman's interactionist model on organizational creativity (e.g., Woodman et al. 1993; Woodman and Schoenfeldt 1989, 1990) continues to shape creativity research, while his more recent research on innovative behavior (Yuan and Woodman 2010) has received a highly cited paper distinction through Web of Science. Also, Woodman's work on change schema (Lau et al. 2003; Lau and Woodman 1995; Woodman and King 1978) is continuing to receive considerable attention from change scholars and has continued into a viable research stream. Despite the forthright success with research (as an editor and scholar), there are at least two areas that remain unfinished for Woodman.

Individual change. The first stems from a book chapter he wrote with Todd Dewett in *The Handbook of Organizational Change and Innovation* (Woodman and Dewett 2004). Drawing on a theme of his research, bringing together multiple perspectives (e.g., Woodman 1989a, 2014a; Woodman et al. 1993), Woodman offers an interactionist perspective for organizational change. He and Dewett suggest that the role of the individual's effect on organizations has been examined voraciously, while the role of how organizations change individuals is barely examined. And, in order to understand organizational change, we must understand one fundamental premise to changing organizations, which is how people change. More specifically, in order for an organization to change, people must change – they must believe, think, and act differently. Further, Woodman and Dewett identify three dimensions in which people change: changeability, depth, and time.

The first dimension, changeability, refers to the extent to which an individual's characteristics vary through the change process. When an organization changes, it must determine what aspect of the individual it will attempt to change, and the effort needed will be dependent on the level of changeability. For example, in an organizational culture change, it will not suffice to focus on changing task-specific behavior, which is highly changeable. Instead, the organization must focus on changing norm-regulated behavior, which is harder to change and therefore has lower changeability. Similarly, when determining what type of cognitive change is needed, an organization may implement a change initiative that focuses on changing the highly changeable "task behavior" or the less changeable "knowledge about the organization." The authors suggest four types of individual change, behavioral, cognitive, affective, and conative, and suggest that organizations should consider these factors when deliberating the change endeavor.

The second dimension, depth of change, was drawn on Roger Harrison's (1970) term, which refers to the magnitude of individual change. For example, it is one thing to make a small procedural change to affect job behavior; it is something altogether different to completely alter all behaviors required to complete a task. Therefore, organizations ought to consider the magnitude of change that occurs for the individual when considering different change endeavors. The third dimension is time. The notion of time in organizational theory is sorely needed (Bartunek and Woodman 2015; Pettigrew et al. 2001; Woodman and Dewett 2004). Not only has time been neglected in theory but it has also been neglected in research. This is despite the fact that time has been shown to be extremely important for investigating change.

Although, since the initial publication of the book chapter, there have been many references to the chapter, little work that we are aware of has explicitly examined the premise of the chapter. However, in a dissertation that examines employee alignment with a strategic directive, Thundiyil (2015) uses social cognitive theory (e.g., Bandura 1989) and the theory of change momentum (Jansen 2004) to examine how changes in knowledge about the interventions can affect changes in knowledge of the behaviors needed to affect change and the actual behaviors. The results provide some preliminary support for Woodman and Dewett's model of individual changeability and encourage future research on the topic of changeability as a way to align employees with a change initiative. Overall, this area of research is mostly unexamined and will remain an area with fruitful opportunities for some time to come.

Moving beyond Lewin. Another legacy that Woodman leaves for scholars to develop as he enters the twilight of his career is a temporal model of change (Bartunek and Woodman 2015). In an early article that introduced the Special Research Forum on Change and Development's Journeys into a Pluralistic World in the *Academy of Management Journal*, Pettigrew et al. (2001) distinguished process as a major analytical challenge facing the field. Drawing on Van de Ven's (1992) explication of three ways to study processes, the authors proposed the most meaningful approach to studying change. The authors recommended exploring change processes as continuous rather than as movements between states. They then recommended exploring process in relation to time, history, linkage to action, and linkage to performance. This importance was later echoed in Woodman and Bartunek's summary chapter in *The Psychology of Organizational Change: Viewing Change from the Employee's Perspective* (Woodman and Bartunek 2013).

Once again, in a follow-up review of the field led by Jean Bartunek, Bartunek and Woodman (2015) considered in much greater detail models of organizational change. More specifically, they began with the most prevalent model of organizational change, the unfreeze, change, refreeze model (Lewin 1947) in the context of the shift from traditional organization development (OD), also termed diagnostic OD, to dialogic OD (Bushe and Marshak 2009, 2014). Through this review, the authors consider the change of OD through a Lewinian freezing lens and note the incompleteness as a tool to examine the dynamic nature of change. Instead the authors encourage the field to explore a new, more sophisticated model of change that examines several temporal dimensions of change, namely, sequence (e.g., stages, temporal order of events), timing (e.g., deadlines, presence of alternatives, environmental responsiveness), pacing (e.g., speed of change, momentum), rhythm of change (e.g., repetitive cycles of change, times of accelerated/slowed activity), and monophony/polyphony (e.g., types of entrainment, aligned or overlapping events, number of strands, sequencing, pacing, and rhythms).

Although Bartunek and Woodman brilliantly identified temporal dimensions related to change, their goal was not to conclusively theorize on the temporal dimensions of change, but instead, to approximate the temporal elements of planned change. The work that remains is manifold. To start, the temporal constructs noted above need to be developed more fully, and a deeper understanding of how the terms interrelate will be important. Also, empirical research that can carefully measure the temporal elements that were discussed can provide a gateway to better understand the underlying temporal structures of planned change. This research could assess the efficacy of different processes and their implications for change. A third area for future research would be to examine the individual's effects on the temporal dimensions. More specifically, for example, scholars can examine the role a leader plays on the temporal sequence of events within a change endeavor.

Conclusion

Dick Woodman's simplified view is not the elementary view that individuals have when they are trying to grasp a new topic. Rather, Dick's understanding of events is more than that. It is the simplicity that exists on the other side of complexity. It is the simplicity that can only exist when people have such a strong grasp of the content that they can see through the mess to what the complexity holds. And then at this point, they can rework the piece to boil it down to its fundamental essence. Dick Woodman is a master at boiling things down to their fundamental essence and being able to tie this essence into the greater contribution. It is this significant contribution that Woodman leaves the field of organizational change and development along with his legacy as being the editor of the two most influential publications in organization change.

References

Amabile, T. M. (1988). A model of creativity and innovation in organizations. *Research in Organizational Behavior, 10*(1), 123–167.

Amabile, T. (1996). *Creativity in context*. Boulder: Westview Press.

Bandura, A. (1989). Human agency in social cognitive theory. *American Psychologist, 44*(9), 1175–1184.

Bartunek, J. M., & Woodman, R. W. (2012). The spirits of organization development, or why OD lives despite its pronounced death. In K. Cameron & G. Spreitzer (Eds.), *Handbook of positive organizational scholarship* (pp. 727–736). Oxford: Oxford University Press.

Bartunek, J. M., & Woodman, R. W. (2015). Beyond Lewin: Towards a temporal approximation of organization development and change. In F. P. Morgeson, H. Aguinis, & S. J. Ashford (Eds.), *Annual review of organizational psychology and organizational behavior* (Vol. 2, pp. 157–182). Palo Alto: Annual Reviews.

Bushe, G. R., & Marshak, R. J. (2009). Revisioning organization development: Diagnostic and dialogic premises and patterns of practice. *The Journal of Applied Behavioral Science, 45*(3), 348–368.

Bushe, G. R., & Marshak, R. J. (2014). The dialogic mindset in organization development. In A. B. Shani & D. A. Noumair (Eds.), *Research in organizational change and development* (Vol. 22, pp. 55–97). Bingley: Emerald Group Publishing.

Chakrabarty, S., & Woodman, R. W. (2009). Relationship creativity in collectives at multiple levels. In T. Rickards, M. Runco, & S. Moger (Eds.), *The Routledge companion to creativity* (pp. 189–205). London: Routledge/Taylor & Francis Group.

Cooperrider, D. L., & Srivastava, S. (1987). Appreciative inquiry in organizational life. In R. W. Woodman & W. A. Pasmore (Eds.), *Research in organizational change and development* (Vol. 1, pp. 129–169). Greenwich: JAI Press.

Corley, K. G., & Gioia, D. A. (2011). Building theory about theory building: What constitutes a theoretical contribution? *Academy of Management Review, 36*(1), 12–32.

Denison, D. R., & Spreitzer, G. M. (1991). Organizational culture and organizational development: A competing values approach. In R. W. Woodman & W. A. Pasmore (Eds.), *Research in organizational change and development* (Vol. 7, pp. 1–39). Greenwich: JAI Press.

Hanes, P., Adams, J., Lloyd, R., & Woodman, R. (1978). Career planning: Who's ready for it? *Journal of College Placement, 38*(3), 47–50.

Harrison, R. (1970). Choosing the depth of organizational intervention. *The Journal of Applied Behavioral Science, 6*(2), 181–202.

Hay, G. W., Woodman, R. W., & Tenkasi, R. V. (2008). Closing the OD application gap by bringing theory closer to practice. *OD Practitioner, 20*, 55–60.

Jansen, K. J. (2004). From persistence to pursuit: A longitudinal examination of momentum during the early stages of strategic change. *Organization Science, 15*(3), 276–294.

Kilbourne, L. M., & Woodman, R. W. (1999). Barriers to organizational creativity. In R. Purser & A. Montuori (Eds.), *Social creativity in organizations* (pp. 125–150). Cresskill: Hampton Press.

Lau, C. M., & Woodman, R. W. (1995). Understanding organizational change: A schematic perspective. *Academy of Management Journal, 38*, 537–554.

Lau, C. M., McMahan, G. C., & Woodman, R. W. (1996). An international comparison of organization development practices the USA and Hong Kong. *Journal of Organizational Change Management, 9*(2), 4–19.

Lau, C. M., Kilbourne, L. M., & Woodman, R. W. (2003). A shared schema approach to understanding organizational culture change. In W. A. Pasmore & R. W. Woodman (Eds.), *Research in organizational change and development* (Vol. 14, pp. 225–256). Oxford: Elsevier Science.

Lewin, K. (1947). Frontiers in group dynamics: Concept, method and reality in social science; social equilibria. *Human Relations, 1*, 5–40.

Macy, B. A., & Izumi, H. (1993). Organizational change, design, and work innovation: A meta-analysis of 131 North American field studies – 1961–1991. In R. W. Woodman & W. A. Pasmore (Eds.), *Research in organizational change and development* (Vol. 7, pp. 235–313). Greenwich: JAI Press.

Marshak, R. J., & Grant, D. (2008). Organizational discourse and new organization development practices. *British Journal of Management, 19*(s1), S7–S19.

McMahan, G. C., & Woodman, R. W. (1992). The current practice of organization development within the firm: A survey of large industrial corporations. *Group & Organization Management, 17*, 117–134.

Oreg, S., Michel, A., & By, R. T. (Eds.). (2013). *The psychology of organizational change: Viewing change from the employee's perspective.* Cambridge: Cambridge University Press.

Palmer, I., & Dunford, R. (2008). Organizational change and the importance of embedded assumptions. *British Journal of Management, 19*(s1), S20–S32.

Pasmore, W. A., Woodman, R. W., & Simmons, A. L. (2008). Toward a more rigorous, reflective, and relevant science of collaborative management research. In A. B. Shani, N. Adler, S. A. Mohrman, W. A. Pasmore, & B. Stymne (Eds.), *Handbook of collaborative management research* (pp. 567–582). Thousand Oaks: Sage.

Pettigrew, A. M., Woodman, R. W., & Cameron, K. (2001). Studying organizational change and development: Challenges for future work. *Academy of Management Journal, 44*, 697–713.

Porras J. I., & Robertson P. J. (1987). Organizational development theory: A typology and evaluation. In R. W. Woodman & W. A. Pasmore (Eds.), *Research in organizational change and development* (Vol. 1, pp. 1–57). Greenwich: JAI Press.

Robertson, P. J., Roberts, D. R., & Porras, J. I. (1993). An evaluation of a model of planned organizational change: Evidence from a meta-analysis. In R. W. Woodman & W. A. Pasmore (Eds.), *Research in organizational change and development* (Vol. 7, pp. 1–39). Greenwich: JAI press.

Rychlak, J. F. (1968). *A philosophy of science for personality theory.* New York: Houghton Mifflin.

Rynes, S. L., Bartunek, J. M., & Daft, R. L. (2001). Across the great divide: Knowledge creation and transfer between practitioners and academics. *Academy of Management Journal, 44*(2), 340–355.

Shalley, C. E., & Zhou, J. (2008). Organizational creativity research: A historical overview. In C. E. Shalley & J. Zhou (Eds.), *Handbook of organizational creativity* (pp. 3–31). Hillsdale: Erlbaum.

Thach, L., & Woodman, R. W. (1994). Organizational change and information technology: Managing on the edge of cyberspace. *Organizational Dynamics, 23*(1), 30–46.

Thundiyil, T. (2015). *Employee alignment: A process for understanding individual changeability* (Doctoral dissertation). Texas A&M University.

Van de Ven, A. H. (1992). Suggestions for studying strategy process: A research note. *Strategic Management Journal, 13*(5), 169–188.

Woodman, R. W. (1970, December 31). Happy New Year! – From the DMZ. *The New York Times*, p. 18.

Woodman, R. W. (1979). A devil's dictionary of behavioral science research terms. *Academy of Management Review, 4*, 93–94.

Woodman, R. W. (1980). Team development versus T-group training. *Group & Organization Studies, 5*, 135–142.

Woodman, R. W. (1981). Creativity as a construct in personality theory. *Journal of Creative Behavior, 15*, 43–66.
Woodman, R. W. (1989a). Evaluation research on organizational change: Arguments for a 'combined paradigm' approach. In R. W. Woodman & W. A. Pasmore (Eds.), *Research in organizational change and development* (Vol. 3, pp. 161–180). Greenwich: JAI Press.
Woodman, R. W. (1989b). Organizational change and development: New arenas for inquiry and action. *Journal of Management, 15*, 205–228.
Woodman, R. W. (1995). Managing creativity. In C. M. Ford & D. A. Gioia (Eds.), *Creative action in organizations* (pp. 60–64). Newbury Park: Sage.
Woodman, R. W. (2008a). Creativity and organizational change: Linking ideas and extending theory. In J. Zhou & C. Shalley (Eds.), *Handbook of organizational creativity* (pp. 283–300). New York: Lawrence Earlbaum Associates.
Woodman, R. W. (2008b). Discourse, metaphor, and organizational change: The wine is new, but the bottle is old. *British Journal of Management, 19*(s1), 33–37.
Woodman, R. W. (2013). The interactionist model of organizational creativity. In E. H. Kessler (Ed.), *Encyclopedia of management theory*. Thousand Oaks: Sage.
Woodman, R. W. (2014a). The role of internal validity in evaluation research on organizational change interventions. *The Journal of Applied Behavioral Science, 50*, 40–49.
Woodman, R. W. (2014b). The science of organizational change and the art of changing organizations. *Journal of Applied Behavioral Science, 50*, 463–477.
Woodman, R. W., & Bartunek, J. M. (2013). Commentary: Change processes and action implications. In S. Oreg, A. Michel, & R. By (Eds.), *The psychology of organizational change: Viewing change from the employees' perspective* (pp. 301–323). Cambridge, UK: Cambridge University Press.
Woodman, R. W., & Dewett, T. (2004). Organizationally relevant journeys in individual change. In M. S. Poole & A. H. Van de Ven (Eds.), *Handbook of organizational change and innovation* (pp. 32–49). Oxford: Oxford University Press.
Woodman, R. W., & King, D. C. (1978). Organizational climate: Science or folklore? *Academy of Management Review, 3*, 816–826.
Woodman, R. W., & Muse, W. V. (1982). Organization development in the profit sector: Lessons learned. *New Directions for Community Colleges, 1982*(37), 23–44.
Woodman, R. W., & Pasmore, W. A. (2002). The heart of it all: Group- and team-based interventions in OD. In J. Waclawski & A. H. Church (Eds.), *Organization development: A data driven approach to organizational change* (pp. 164–176). San Francisco: Jossey-Bass.
Woodman, R. W., & Schoenfeldt, L. F. (1989). Individual differences in creativity: An interactionist perspective. In J. A. Glover, R. R. Ronning, & C. R. Reynolds (Eds.), *Handbook of creativity* (pp. 77–91). New York: Plenum.
Woodman, R. W., & Schoenfeldt, L. F. (1990). An interactionist model of creative behavior. *Journal of Creative Behavior, 24*, 279–290.
Woodman, R. W., & Sherwood, J. J. (1977). A comprehensive look at job design. *The Personnel Journal, 56*(384–390), 418.
Woodman, R. W., & Sherwood, J. J. (1980a). Effects of team development intervention: A field experiment. *Journal of Applied Behavioral Science, 16*, 211–227.
Woodman, R. W., & Sherwood, J. J. (1980b). The role of team development in organizational effectiveness: A critical review. *Psychological Bulletin, 88*, 166–186.
Woodman, R. W., & Wayne, S. J. (1985). An investigation of positive-findings bias in evaluation of organization development interventions. *Academy of Management Journal, 28*, 889–913.
Woodman, R. W., Sawyer, J. E., & Griffin, R. W. (1993). Toward a theory of organizational creativity. *Academy of Management Review, 18*, 293–321.
Woodman, R. W., Bingham, J. B., & Yuan, F. (2008). Assessing organization development and change interventions. In T. G. Cummings (Ed.), *Handbook of organization development* (pp. 187–215). Thousand Oaks: Sage.

Yuan, F., & Woodman, R. W. (2010). Innovative behavior in the workplace: The role of performance and image outcome expectations. *Academy of Management Journal, 53*, 323–342.
Zhou, J., & Hoever, I. J. (2014). Research on workplace creativity: A review and redirection. *Annual Review of Organizational Psychology and Organizational Behavior, 1*, 333–359.

Further Reading

Bartunek, J. M., & Woodman, R. W. (2012). The spirits of organization development, or why OD lives despite its pronounced death. In K. Cameron & G. Spreitzer (Eds.), *Handbook of positive organizational scholarship* (pp. 727–736). Oxford: Oxford University Press.
Bartunek, J. M., & Woodman, R. W. (2015). Beyond Lewin: Towards a temporal approximation of organization development and change. In F. P. Morgeson, H. Aguinis, & S. J. Ashford (Eds.), *Annual review of organizational psychology and organizational behavior* (Vol. 2, pp. 157–182). Palo Alto: Annual Reviews.
Chakrabarty, S., & Woodman, R. W. (2009). Relationship creativity in collectives at multiple levels. In T. Rickards, M. Runco, & S. Moger (Eds.), *The Routledge companion to creativity* (pp. 189–205). London: Routledge/Taylor & Francis Group.
Kilbourne, L. M., & Woodman, R. W. (1999). Barriers to organizational creativity. In R. Purser & A. Montuori (Eds.), *Social creativity in organizations* (pp. 125–150). Cresskill: Hampton Press.
Lau, C. M., & Woodman, R. W. (1995). Understanding organizational change: A schematic perspective. *Academy of Management Journal, 38*, 537–554.
Lau, C. M., Kilbourne, L. M., & Woodman, R. W. (2003). A shared schema approach to understanding organizational culture change. In W. A. Pasmore & R. W. Woodman (Eds.), *Research in organizational change and development* (Vol. 14, pp. 225–256). Oxford: Elsevier Science.
McMahan, G. C., & Woodman, R. W. (1992). The current practice of organization development within the firm: A survey of large industrial corporations. *Group & Organization Management, 17*, 117–134.
Pasmore, W. A., Woodman, R. W., & Simmons, A. L. (2008). Toward a more rigorous, reflective, and relevant science of collaborative management research. In A. B. Shani, N. Adler, S. A. Mohrman, W. A. Pasmore, & B. Stymne (Eds.), *Handbook of collaborative management research* (pp. 567–582). Thousand Oaks: Sage.
Pettigrew, A. M., Woodman, R. W., & Cameron, K. (2001). Studying organizational change and development: Challenges for future work. *Academy of Management Journal, 44*, 697–713.
Rubinstein, D., & Woodman, R. W. (1984). Spiderman and the Burma raiders: Collateral organization theory in action. *The Journal of Applied Behavioral Science, 20*, 1–16.
Sutton, C. D., & Woodman, R. W. (1989). Pygmalion goes to work: The effect of supervisor expectations in a retail setting. *Journal of Applied Psychology, 74*, 943–950.
Thach, L., & Woodman, R. W. (1994). Organizational change and information technology: Managing on the edge of cyberspace. *Organizational Dynamics, 23*(1), 30–46.
Woodman, R. W. (1979). A devil's dictionary of behavioral science research terms. *Academy of Management Review, 4*, 93–94.
Woodman, R. W. (1989a). Evaluation research on organizational change: Arguments for a 'combined paradigm' approach. In R. W. Woodman & W. A. Pasmore (Eds.), *Research in organizational change and development* (Vol. 3, pp. 161–180). Greenwich: JAI Press.
Woodman, R. W. (1989b). Organizational change and development: New arenas for inquiry and action. *Journal of Management, 15*, 205–228.
Woodman, R. W. (1995). Managing creativity. In C. M. Ford & D. A. Gioia (Eds.), *Creative action in organizations* (pp. 60–64). Newbury Park: Sage.
Woodman, R. W. (2008a). Creativity and organizational change: Linking ideas and extending theory. In J. Zhou & C. Shalley (Eds.), *Handbook of organizational creativity* (pp. 283–300). New York: Lawrence Earlbaum Associates.

Woodman, R. W. (2008b). Discourse, metaphor, and organizational change: The wine is new, but the bottle is old. *British Journal of Management, 19*, 33–37.
Woodman, R. W. (2013). The interactionist model of organizational creativity. In E. H. Kessler (Ed.), *Encyclopedia of management theory*. Thousand Oaks: Sage.
Woodman, R. W. (2014a). The role of internal validity in evaluation research on organizational change interventions. *The Journal of Applied Behavioral Science, 50*, 40–49.
Woodman, R. W. (2014b). The science of organizational change and the art of changing organizations. *Journal of Applied Behavioral Science, 50*, 463–477.
Woodman, R. W., & Bartunek, J. M. (2013). Commentary: Change processes and action implications. In S. Oreg, A. Michel, & R. By (Eds.), *The psychology of organizational change: Viewing change from the employees' perspective* (pp. 301–323). Cambridge, UK: Cambridge University Press.
Woodman, R. W., & Dewett, T. (2004). Organizationally relevant journeys in individual change. In M. S. Poole & A. H. Van de Ven (Eds.), *Handbook of organizational change and innovation* (pp. 32–49). Oxford: Oxford University Press.
Woodman, R. W., & King, D. C. (1978). Organizational climate: Science or folklore? *Academy of Management Review, 3*, 816–826.
Woodman, R. W., & Pasmore, W. A. (2002). The heart of it all: Group- and team-based interventions in OD. In J. Waclawski & A. H. Church (Eds.), *Organization development: A data driven approach to organizational change* (pp. 164–176). San Francisco: Jossey-Bass.
Woodman, R. W., & Schoenfeldt, L. F. (1989). Individual differences in creativity: An interactionist perspective. In J. A. Glover, R. R. Ronning, & C. R. Reynolds (Eds.), *Handbook of creativity* (pp. 77–91). New York: Plenum.
Woodman, R. W., & Schoenfeldt, L. F. (1990). An interactionist model of creative behavior. *Journal of Creative Behavior, 24*, 279–290.
Woodman, R. W., & Sherwood, J. J. (1980a). Effects of team development intervention: A field experiment. *Journal of Applied Behavioral Science, 16*, 211–227.
Woodman, R. W., & Sherwood, J. J. (1980b). The role of team development in organizational effectiveness: A critical review. *Psychological Bulletin, 88*, 166–186.
Woodman, R. W., & Tolchinsky, P. D. (1985). Expectation effects: Implications for organization development. In D. D. Warrick (Ed.), *Contemporary organization development: Current thinking and applications* (pp. 477–487). Glenview: Scott Foresman.
Woodman, R. W., Sawyer, J. E., & Griffin, R. W. (1993). Toward a theory of organizational creativity. *Academy of Management Review, 18*, 293–321.
Woodman, R. W., Bingham, J. B., & Yuan, F. (2008). Assessing organization development and change interventions. In T. G. Cummings (Ed.), *Handbook of organization development* (pp. 187–215). Thousand Oaks: Sage.
Woodman, R. W., & Wayne, S. J. (1985). An investigation of positive-findings bias in evaluation of organization development interventions. *Academy of Management Journal, 28*, 889–913.
Yuan, F., & Woodman, R. W. (2007). Formation of expectations regarding change outcomes: Integrating information and social effects. In W. A. Pasmore & R. W. Woodman (Eds.), *Research in organizational change and development* (Vol. 16, pp. 81–104). Oxford: Elsevier.
Yuan, F., & Woodman, R. W. (2010). Innovative behavior in the workplace: The role of performance and image outcome expectations. *Academy of Management Journal, 53*, 323–342.
Zhou, J., & Woodman, R. W. (2003). Manager's recognition of employees' creative ideas: A social-cognitive model. In L. V. Shavinina (Ed.), *International handbook on innovation* (pp. 631–640). Oxford: Elsevier Science.

Therese Yaeger: Lifting Up the Voices of the Field

86

Rachael L. Narel

Abstract

Therese Yaeger, Ph.D., has been a key contributor in the field of Organization Development for two decades. Beginning her career in the corporate world, Yaeger came to learn about the role of a scholar-practitioner through the MSMOB program at Benedictine University. She has since transitioned to academia focusing her research and publications on Appreciative Inquiry and Global OD. Therese is currently the Associate Director of Benedictine University's Ph.D. in OD program and was a key partner in its development and implementation. At the same time, she continued to consult to corporate and created executive development programs for some of the largest corporations in the Chicago area.

In addition to consulting and teaching, Yaeger has collaborated with colleagues and students on countless publications and presentations on a myriad of topics in the field. She has been involved in numerous roles in both professional and academic associations. Therese is a connector and has brought together scholarship and practice as well as people and organizations to continue to make key contributions. A humble yet prominent force in the field, many more years of exciting contributions are still ahead.

Keywords

Benedictine University • Therese Yaeger • Organization development • Appreciative inquiry • Global OD

R.L. Narel (✉)
Benedictine University, Chicago, IL, USA
e-mail: rlnarel@hotmail.com

D.B. Szabla et al. (eds.), *The Palgrave Handbook of Organizational Change Thinkers*,
DOI 10.1007/978-3-319-52878-6_99

Contents

Introduction

Therese Yaeger is an example of a true scholar-practitioner who is always thinking about change. Change in research, change in the field, change in the business environment, change in classroom techniques and technologies. While her key contributions and primary research interests have been in the areas of Appreciative Inquiry and Global OD, she has always kept a pulse on new topics and techniques. A lifelong learner, Therese is constantly searching for new knowledge through interactions with students in her classroom, by participating in conferences, and through her work in the field. Everyone who knows Therese marvels at her limitless energy and passion for her work.

This chapter illustrates the contributions that Therese has made in the field of OD, both individually and through her collaborations with colleagues and students. It is influenced by my personal experiences with her over the past 10 years as both a student in her classroom and as a coauthor and copresenter. It is informed by review of her work, discussions with her colleagues and students, and interviews with Therese about her background and perspectives. It is my pleasure to provide this chapter as part of this Change Thinkers Handbook to share how Therese has masterfully brought people and ideas together to the great benefit of our field. It will discuss her influences and motivations to enter the world of OD and contributions yet to come.

Influences and Motivations: A Winding Path to OD

Therese F. Yaeger was born on the south side of Chicago into a big Catholic family. Loving, smart parents, bright, supportive siblings, and the love of education made for a well-rounded childhood. As one of the oldest in a large family, time management, multitasking, and the ability to deal with unexpected disruptions were the requisite familial skills. Family mattered, and family values included the assumption that hard work paid off, that one must be goal-driven, and focus on the positive and potential in self and others.

At 16, Yaeger started traveling abroad and quickly fell in love with the world. Over the years, she would travel to various countries in Europe and Central America working part-time jobs to save for trips. During her travels, she was fascinated by other cultures and felt "out of her comfort zone" yet comfortable at the same time. Her interest in the global arena continues today, as it enriches her teaching of International OD in graduate and doctoral coursework.

All during her 20s, life was fast-paced. Fearless at 20, she married and started a small business with her husband, while working full time in downtown Chicago. Also in her 20s, she and her husband Paul started a family. She continued schoolwork and helped start other small businesses. Still, family mattered and life was full.

Long before she studied organizational behavior and organization development concepts in graduate school, in the 1970s and 1980s she experienced first-hand numerous challenges in corporate situations. These challenges included a lack of employee involvement, employee resistance to change, the need for improved teamwork, and the inappropriate use of consultants that often crippled organizational change efforts. Similarly, she realized that in order for successful change to happen, it required the buy-in of involved constituents. Yaeger explains, "Seeing a consultant or manager come in and say, 'we are going to do things differently now, we are going to do this, this and this.' Everybody in the room was nodding their head, and then those same workers would go out to the water cooler and say, 'That's not gonna happen.'" That kind of autocratic, top-down approach to change reinforced her belief in the importance of organizational change strategies that included job motivation and improved training. Additionally, she watched the struggles of technology implementations and thought, "there has got to be a better way to implement change." The reward for hard work and her ability to multitask enabled her to manage family, career, and her husband's small business. In her 30s, still pursuing her love of learning, she enrolled in the Masters of Science in Management and Organizational Behavior Program at Illinois Benedictine College (now Benedictine University) in the Chicago suburbs.

Early OD Influencers

While in the OB/OD program, Therese not only learned foundational OD concepts, but she also read the OD classics, such as the 1969 OD Six-Pack published by Addison-Wesley. Other impactful readings included Edgar Schein's work on culture, Richard Hackman and Greg Oldham's work on job motivation, and Douglas McGregor's Theory X and Theory Y.

For Yaeger, McGregor's *The Human Side of Enterprise* (1960) provided insight into management, leadership, and change that truly resonated with her. She found McGregor's Theory Y "fundamentally right," and his self-fulfilling prophecy merely confirmed her assumption that employees left their boss (not the organization). In *The Human Side of Enterprise,* McGregor stressed the importance of human potential, managerial assumptions, and motivation – concepts that intrigued her. McGregor, for Yaeger, was also a perfect model of the ideal scholar-practitioner having not only having worked as a consultant with leading organizations, but through publications, bringing his theories to the world of managers (McGregor 1957, 1960, 1967).

In graduate school, as part of Benedictine University's Contemporary Trends in Change Management Lecture Series, she was introduced to numerous OD/OB scholars such as Richard Hackman, Michael Beer, Thomas Head (Sorensen's primary coauthor), Susan Mohrman, and Victoria Marsick. Being able to engage with these scholars in person allowed her to deepen her knowledge and appreciation for their contributions and increased her excitement about the field, an early lesson that later influenced her teaching in bringing these same experiences to her students. There, she was also introduced to David Cooperrider's theory of Appreciative Inquiry. Similar to McGregor's work, Cooperrider's "appreciating the positive potential in others" (Cooperrider et al. 2005) had been her approach to people since her childhood, so it just made common sense to her. What surprised her was realizing that not everyone in the world approached human dynamics this way. Yaeger knew that she needed to find ways to share this knowledge with others so that they could understand the theoretical foundations of this research and how it could be applied in organizations.

In the mid-1990s, while working and writing with the MSMOB Program Director, Dr. Peter Sorensen, she was invited to assist in the start-up of the new Ph.D. Program in Organization Development at Benedictine University. With her past knowledge of business start-ups and her keen sense of maintaining a fledgling organization, she cautiously accepted.

While Yaeger thinks it was "mere coincidence" that she was offered the opportunity to help start-up Benedictine's Ph.D. program, it was Peter Sorensen who saw in her the passion, knowledge, and commitment to make the doctoral program a reality at the small liberal arts Catholic college. "Her core values of OD and her roots in the Catholic community were just what the program needed for the program's success at Benedictine," Sorensen explained. As a result, in 1996, the first doctoral program at Benedictine University began with 17 doctoral students from across the USA, which included consultants, executives, and HR experts. In the very first doctoral course, she worked with David Cooperrider, and heard first-hand his theory of Appreciative Inquiry.

Another opportunity arose as a result of meetings with David Cooperrider. As "Coop" was a former graduate student of Sorensen's at the former George Williams College, the three (Yaeger, Sorensen, and Cooperrider) discussed the need for a compendium of AI readings. In short order, Sorensen accepted the role of Guest Editor of OD Network's journal, the *OD Practitioner*, and Cooperrider along with Peter agreed to dedicate the special issue to Appreciative Inquiry. So, in 1996, with Sorensen and Cooperrider, Therese helped create the first *OD Practitioner* Special Issue on Appreciative Inquiry. To date, this 1996 issue of the *OD Practitioner* has been reprinted more than any other issue in OD Network's history.

Fast-forward 3 years, and in 1999, the idea of an "AI book" became reality. With David Cooperrider, Peter Sorensen, and Diana Whitney, Yaeger created the first book (a reader) of articles dedicated to Appreciative Inquiry entitled *Appreciative*

Inquiry: Rethinking Human Organization Toward a Positive Theory of Change (Stipes Publications).

Within 3 years, this book was incorporated into graduate curricula at more than two dozen schools including Stanford University, Harvard University, Case Western University, and countless organizations including healthcare and religious organizations. Her goal of promulgating AI to a broader audience had been met as through this work it was reaching both scholars and practitioners. As for the *OD Practitioner*, by 2000, the OD Network had invited Sorensen and Yaeger to publish yet another special issue dedicated to Appreciative Inquiry.

Mentors

Yaeger believes that mentoring has been a critical element to her learning – she has been fortunate to have strong mentors in her OD journey. Dr. Thomas Head was one such mentor. Tom and Therese met in the early 1990s, and over the next two decades, they researched, published, and presented on numerous management topics including Global OD, McGregor's legacy, and Appreciative Inquiry. Tom chaired Yaeger's dissertation, and even in his passing in 2015, they were still working on publications together. To honor Tom Head, at Benedictine University today there is a "Yaeger & Head OD Library" that houses classic works from the OD greats, along with the dissertations of Benedictine University Ph.D. in Organization Development program graduates.

Another mentor of hers was David Cooperrider. Not only was he a key influence in her early work, but Cooperrider was willing and excited to be a part of her dissertation committee which involved OD and global consulting. Similar to her early experiences in international travel, "Coop" pushed Therese out of her comfort zone and challenged her to take her research to a deeper level. He encouraged her to see the Global OD world through the not-for-profit and social responsibility sectors. David helped provide the positive vision for her research, made connections, and supported her every step of the way. A third mentor and role model is Dr. David Coghlan of Ireland. While Therese remembers this relationship in terms of mentoring, it was actually a 1997 interview by Therese of David Coghlan that appeared in the OD Journal that began their friendship. Therese emphasizes that David's writing discipline, his passion for teaching Organization Development, and his expertise in action research are elements that strengthen this life-long friendly mentorship. David has regularly visited her classroom at Benedictine as a visiting scholar, and they also continue to collaborate at Academy of Management.

It is not surprising, through understanding Yaeger's background, influences and shortly her key contributions, that one of her most influential colleagues was Peter Sorensen. Peter recognized early on that Therese would become an invaluable member of the field and worked to provide her as many opportunities as possible to grow and contribute through teaching, publishing, and collaborating with leading scholars. Sorensen and Yaeger have continued to partner over the years not only on the graduate programs at Benedictine University but on countless publications and presentations.

Key Contributions: A Scholar-Practitioner at Work

With books and publications, and a dissertation finished in 2001, the corporate arena again appeared inviting. In 2006, Yaeger took a sabbatical from Benedictine University to join Motorola Incorporated as the Director of Global Organization Development. She then returned to Benedictine University as a tenure-track faculty member in both the Ph.D. and MSMOB programs, where she continues today.

At Benedictine University, again with a track record of successful start-up efforts, she developed executive development programs for some of the largest corporations in the Chicago area including John Deere, Motorola, and McDonald's. With Sorensen, she created an OD certificate for the US Postal Service, wherein hundreds of US Postal managers completed graduate OD coursework in team building, organizational assessment, and Appreciative Inquiry. Committed to bringing knowledge of OD to organizations, Yaeger leveraged her skills as a practitioner to work directly with the people in organizations giving them the information and skills to help enact change. She knew not everyone would be able to come to Benedictine and so in living out the University's value of "community" she brought the education to them.

In the external consulting arena, Therese has consulted in government, healthcare, manufacturing, and education – she has even been called in to "consult to consultants" such as internal OD consultants within corporations. Leveraging her skills as both an educator and practitioner, she empowers them with the latest research and tools in the field to make them more effective in their work. Yaeger has indirectly assisted hundreds of companies by enhancing the skills of those actually doing the work through these programs. This has also enabled her to stay relevant in practice as well as scholarship as these consultants also present her with their current challenges and efforts. She has had many interesting and exciting opportunities presented to her and she finds it hard to decline interesting work even as busy as she is; especially when it will be enriching for both her and the organization. However, over the years she has learned the key components of a successful engagement is never a one-time fix. For that reason, she won't take work if she feels she cannot leave the organization better than how she found it.

Beyond teaching, Yaeger considers her key contributions to be her research and publications, and her professional roles to make meaningful contributions to OD (i.e., reviewing, Editorial Boards, officer roles, etc.), and collaboration. She has found volunteering in a variety of roles has provided her with broader exposure to research in the field and opportunities to connect with others which in turn leads to further collaborations and contributions.

Published Contributions

The importance of publications was something Yaeger realized early in her academic career. In reading a 1985 article entitled, "ODs Top Ten: Who they are, how they got there" by Hillman and Varney, she quickly understood that although each of the OD greats identified in the article came from various walks of life, publishing was an OD key to success. In her opinion, if you want to make an impact in OD, it is necessary to go beyond consulting to writing and publishing – consulting, education, and publishing are key.

The influence of David Cooperrider included his participation on her dissertation committee, as well as his influence on her various publications on Appreciative Inquiry. After the first AI reader, a second expanded edition appeared in 2001, and a third edition was published in 2005 (an arrangement with Stipes Publishing insists that no royalties were to be received by the authors).

"I believe that was the beginning of a powerful contribution to increase knowledge of the concept of AI to a more people – now just 15 years later, on Amazon's website, there are more than 1,500 books on the topic of Appreciative Inquiry," Yaeger contends.

Another Appreciative Inquiry work coauthored by Yaeger included "Assessment of the state of Appreciative Inquiry: Past, Present and Future," in Woodman and Pasmore's *Research in Organizational Change and Development,* Vol. 15, with Sorensen and Bengtsson (2005). Yaeger wanted to capture the increased use of AI in organizations to share its successes and continue to evangelize how appropriate it is to address positive change. "Feedback from the Positive Question – The integration of Appreciative Inquiry with survey feedback: from corporate to global cultures," with Sorensen, in Cooperrider and Avital's Advances *in Appreciative Inquiry* (2004) allowed Therese to leverage both her knowledge of AI with her knowledge of Global OD to illustrate its applicability throughout the world in all types of organizations.

Consistent with her readings in graduate school, the early influence of Douglas McGregor's work is reflected in a number of her writings. In 2006, while rereading McGregor's Human Side of Enterprise, she realized that Theory X and Y was approaching 50 years old, and 2007 would be the appropriate time to reflect on McGregor's theories at the National Academy of Management. The AOM session entitled "Doing well by doing good: The legacy of Douglas McGregor in today's corporate world" was presented with Ed Schein, Warner Burke, and corporate executives. As result of this session, in 2011, Yaeger was the Guest Editor of a special issue of the *Journal of Management History* entitled "Honoring Douglas McGregor and The Human Side of Enterprise." Through this work, she was able to collaborate with leading scholars including Edgar Schein, Warren Bennis, Marvin Weisbord, Peter Sorensen, Matt Minahan, and Warner Burke to revisit and honor McGregor's work. Her interest in McGregor currently continues – in 2015 with Sorensen she published "Theory X and Theory Y" in *Oxford Press Bibliography.* Finally, for this *Change Thinkers Handbook,* both Sorensen and Yaeger authored the Douglas McGregor biography.

Professional Roles

Yaeger considers her work in and with the national Academy of Management to be one of her major contributions. Since 1998, she has appeared in the Academy of Management annual programs more than 50 times. Her influence and contributions have included numerous showcase and all Academy panels, from historical panels that involved sessions dedicated to McGregor, Likert, and Jaques, and topics covering "meaningful research," the OD Six Pack, Global OD challenges, and Appreciative Inquiry. OD scholars who have participated on panels with Yaeger have included Edgar Schein, Warner Burke, Michael Beer, Jay Lorsch, David Cooperrider, Tom Cummings, and Chris Worley. Through these collaborations, Yaeger has continued to bring new perspectives on current and future trends in the field to both students and scholar-practitioners. Bringing diversity of thought together has provided new insights leading to innovative research.

An active member of many OD and management communities, she has presented both nationally and internationally at the Eastern Academy of Management, Southern Academy of Management, Southwest Academy of Management, and internationally with the MC Division of the Academy of Management in France, Switzerland, Denmark, and Austria. In these forums, she has continued to share leading research in AI and Global OD as well as other contemporary trends in the field. Through these organizations, she has also worked hard to raise up the voices of new doctoral students through collaborative work.

Her influence in the field is also reflected in her positions as Past Chair of the Management Consulting Division of the Academy of Management, the President of the Midwest Academy, and countless Track Chair roles for the Midwest and Southwest Academy of Management. Her contributions have been recognized by the Southwest Academy with the Outstanding Educator of the Year Award (2010); the Benedictine University Researcher of the Year Award (2011); Organization Consultant of the Year Award from the OD Institute (2010); and the Kathy Dannemiller Share the Wealth Award (with Sorensen) from the OD Network (2008), among others.

Yaeger admits the new learning she experiences when working in the background of conferences and journals. This includes her work as conference reviewer, journal reviewer, and the importance of staying current through the role of an Editorial Board member. "I prefer to be the guide on the side than the sage on the stage," she jokes as she references Alison King's 1993 work on education, "but it's the truth!" Joking aside, she maintains positions on Editorial Boards of the *Journal of Management Inquiry*, *Journal of Leadership and Organizational Studies*, *Revue Sciences de Gestion* (France), and the *OD Practitioner*, and has reviewed for numerous journals. Again, hard work pays off (in new learning). Even her volunteer work as judge on various committees for the OD Network, the ODN-Chicago Impact Award, and INC Magazine's "Top Small Company Workplaces" Award 2011 – even National Women's Associations – are opportunities for hard work but immeasurable payback. "The learnings from these committees and their discussions are enormous – you learn about and explore cutting-edge OD work that documents great change efforts that may positively impact future OD projects," says Yaeger.

Collaboration

Since the mid-1990s, for the Benedictine University OD Program, Therese has hosted the majority of the OD greats as part of the Benedictine Contemporary

Trends in Change Management Lecture Series, with such scholars as Edgar Schein, Robert Blake, Warner Burke, Billie Alban, Kathie Dannemiller, Edie and Charles Seashore, and Peter Vaill. For the doctoral coursework, she has also hosted OD scholar-practitioners such as Dick Woodman, Rami Shani, David Coghlan, Andy Van de Ven, Anthony Buono, David Jamieson, Chris Worley, and Robert Quinn. For Yaeger, being able to collaborate with so many OD scholars is like "being a kid in a candy store." Through the Ph.D. coursework, she has been able to sit with many notable thinkers featured in various chapters of this book and specifically mentions scholars like Hackman, Mohrman, Bartunek, and Cummings. She fondly remembers how excited both she and Robert Blake were when they first met and how Robert Blake gave her a stack of Managerial Grid books. As a result, in the 1990s, they began to collaborate on writing projects.

The influence of Head, Sorensen, and Cooperrider is reflected in her extensive teaching and publications in international OD including *Global and International Organization Development* (2011) now in its 5th edition, and *Global Organization Development: Managing Unprecedented Change* (2006). These works built upon her dissertation focused on the Global OD consultant. Through that research, Yaeger found these individuals were driven by the core OD values while at the same time possessed a unique ability to recognize and overcome cross-culture challenges they encountered. She has worked to bring emerging work in the field together in a way that contributes to the effective practice of OD. As OD has become more strategic and global, she has focused on topics such as Strategic OD, Global OD, and positive change. Her research has helped illustrate how we can sustain integrity and the core values of OD while addressing these issues, which are increasingly critical for the field. Here again, Yaeger partners with her students to continue to explore challenges in the application of OD on a global scale through scholar-practitioner collaborations in the field.

Yaeger has been a collegial influence on her colleagues over the years including her closest, Dr. Peter Sorensen. Yaeger and Sorensen have collaborated on more than 100 publications and presentations in the last 20 years. They were instrumental in developing and implementing the Ph.D. program in Organization Development at Benedictine University. They and their students have published and presented numerous books, articles, and papers in the areas of global, strategic and positive organization development. Together, with their faculty colleague Ram Tenkasi, the Ph.D. students have literally presented papers throughout the world, countries, and continents including Scandinavia, Europe, France, Africa, China, India, and Latin and South America. A number of their students have established doctoral programs modeled after the Benedictine program. They have mentored and been part of five generations of students in organization change.

In addition to her academic writing and collaborations, she has used her consulting engagements to help contribute additional case work to the field. One such publication with Homer Johnson (formerly of Loyola University) and Peter Sorensen is entitled *Critical Issues in Organization Development: Case Studies for Analysis and Discussion*, where they compiled 30 case studies into one book where both academics and practitioners address an OD challenge and value the differing responses from OD experts. Providing a diversity of research, these cases represent 90 OD consultants with expertise in the various areas of case topics including strategy, resources and the bottom line, power and ethics, conflict, and global and culture. Based on real situations, this work allows professionals and students to read and reflect but also allows the consultants to share their experiences. Yaeger was initially invited to be one of these case respondents and realizing the importance of this work became more involved with case writing and development.

In 2006, Sorensen and Yaeger created the book Series entitled Contemporary Trends in Organization Development through Information Age Publishing. Since then, more than six Benedictine Ph.D. graduates have contributed to the series, namely, Dalitso Sulamoyo on OD in Africa, Linda Sharkey with Paul Eccher on Optimizing Talent, Deb Colwill on OD in education, and Gina Hinrichs on Large Scale Change. The IAP OD book series will soon have ten books on innovative approaches to change.

New Insights: Collaboration Creates the Best Outcomes

A lesson learned early on in Therese's career was that it is not just enough to consult and teach – publishing is critical to being successful in OD. Knowing its importance, in working to reach the broadest audience to share research on Appreciative Inquiry and Global OD, Yaeger has focused not only on presenting at conferences but on partnering to publish readers and articles on these topics as well. She stays relevant on current trends in these topics through consulting work in the field and through the experiences of her students.

Yaeger embodies the spirit of a true scholar-practitioner with her work in both academia and business settings. However, it is also obvious that Therese is a true collaborator in the field as most every presentation or publication has been in conjunction with other scholars, practitioners, or her students. As Mirvis and Lawler (2011) remind us, cocreation with others truly creates useful research, and Yaeger is an exemplar in bringing people together to bring new insights into the field.

I will never forget sitting in the Vancouver Club at the 2015 MC Division AOM Annual Members and Friends Event and listening to Therese as the keynote speaker. In her speech, she humbly accepted the honor creatively tying her personal history to musical greats over the years. Notably, she paralleled how Frank Sinatra and Sammy Cahn worked together to create amazing (and award winning) music to how OD scholar-practitioners must do the same for the benefit of the field. I turned to a fellow student from my Ph.D. Cohort and said, "I really would love to accomplish a tenth of what she has done in her lifetime. Amazing." Yaeger has had a profound impact on so many in the field, especially the development of students into scholar-practitioners.

I consider myself fortunate that Yaeger took me under her wing and has always found time in her busy schedule to help me along my scholar-practitioner journey. We were introduced during my time in the MSMOB program at Benedictine during Research Methods. Therese always begins class the first evening discussing the leading experts in the field using Hillman and Varney's 1985 "ODs Top Ten" article. She makes explicit to hopeful future OD consultants that writing and publishing are necessary for one's OD consulting success. As someone with a passion for education who has worked in the corporate world, Yaeger opened up an entirely new world of knowledge for me as to how to become a larger part of the academic community.

Prior to her class, I had never heard of a scholar-practitioner before. From her first-hand experience, Yaeger discusses how organizations need people who have a blend of both research and practice that can speak the language of the business to the corporate audience while understanding theoretical foundations. Corporate executives want to know that OD isn't just theory but that it works in real situations. Alternatively, she reminds us of Lewin's quote "there is nothing so practical as a good theory." I was so excited to learn from her how I could take the knowledge I had been gaining in traditional and contemporary organizational theory and apply it to my work in the corporate arena; helping my company and others understand the change needed for optimal performance coupled with the knowledge and experience on how to implement that change.

A few years later, I came back to Benedictine for the Ph.D. program. We were able to work more closely together, and she agreed to be the chair for my dissertation. Seeing in me what I did not see in myself, I did not realize the full implications of the journey I had embarked upon. As she would always remind fellow students and myself we just needed to "trust the process" and I am glad that I did. She continually lives up to what she feels is her role to "lift it up, make the invisible visible."

The influence she has had on both my work and me personally over the past few years is immeasurable. First, I gained a broader and deeper exposure to Yaeger's work on Strategic OD, Global OD, and Appreciative Inquiry; the last, in particular was a strong influence on my dissertation research in the area of thriving in teams. I had always approached my work in organizations from the positive mindset. Her writing validated my thinking and opened me up to new possibilities in the application of AI at multiple levels in the workplace. The program continued to reinforce the concept of scholar-practitioner every step of the way, so the knowledge I gained could be immediately applied and I could bring back results from the world of business to discuss its implications to theory.

Change in organizations and the world of business is inevitable. Helping people adapt to it – often quickly – is of paramount importance. "Organizations are made up of people – if you address that first, everything else is a little more obvious to work with. Knowledge of change processes, knowledge of change theories, but above and beyond that you need the people skills that are important," she explains. Yaeger and I agree that change is happening at a more rapid pace than ever before and new approaches need to be brought to light to help organizations survive and thrive in the dynamic world of business today. We also agree that the people actually doing the work are critical to the organization and need to be viewed as a key element to the whole of the organizational system when thinking through any change effort.

For me, as chair of my dissertation, Therese helped shape my research as it evolved from general ideas along the same themes of change and people in organizations. What started as a broad topic of Organizational Agility transformed through insights gleaned in both the classroom and through readings she provided on AI, learning, dynamic change, strategy, structure, and the evolution of organizational theory. Through Benedictine University's Contemporary Trends in Change Management Lecture Series, my doctoral courses, and at Academy of Management, Yaeger took the time to introduce me to scholars in the field that could provide new and additional insights on my research. She is a connector – always seeming to know the right people at the right time to help with introductions for research projects, publications, and job opportunities.

Every time I needed to refine and move in a new direction, Yaeger knew exactly where to point me to go deeper into the topic. Similar to how Cooperrider influenced her, she encouraged me to look at my topic from multiple angles and submit papers to regional conferences for broader community feedback. Her questions made me step back and continually analyze my research and findings. The result of this work provided a new model of a Thriving and Agile Team that can be utilized by the academic world for further research and is immediately useful to organizations that are looking for ways to meet the needs of the new dynamic world of continual change. We are continuing to build on this model for the benefit of both scholarship and practice.

Yaeger has chaired or been on the committee of countless dissertations. Her work with students has led to new insights in a multitude of areas of OD including newer topics such as virtual teams, sustainability, and conscious capitalism. Similar to McGregor, Yaeger's work has not only influenced the development of others in the field but she has collaborated with many up and coming scholars and practitioners on writings to help give them their own voice and visibility. This has kept her close to new and exciting OD developments while supporting the growth and development of those newer to the discipline. Yaeger is a continual learner and a perpetual knowledge seeker; she feels that OD is about learning as much as change. She brings these connections to her students and colleagues as well.

Most importantly, however, I will forever be grateful to Therese for providing me with the means to more fully enter into the world of scholarship. Every time she would reach out with opportunities to publish or present, I would leap at the chance to grow and stretch myself in new ways. At times, this was not easy, but again Yaeger saw what I was unable to see. I recall one week during the holiday season where I was working on a qualifying paper for my Ph.D., research for a submission to International Academy in Lyon, and editing a book chapter. I have yet to comprehend how I was able to accomplish all of that, but through that exercise, I learned how to manage continual research and writing while working fulltime and still finding time for family and friends. Early in the Ph.D. program, that was a very important lesson to learn that still benefits me to this day as a scholar-practitioner.

I entered the Benedictine University doctoral program in OD with a blank CV and am leaving with one that is much more significant and includes publications in journals, a book chapter, paper presentations in the United States and internationally, and teaching as well. This was accomplished in two and a half short years. As someone who had successfully made a transition from corporate to academia, Therese shared with me her experience and knowledge as to how to enter this new phase of my life. While I had to put in the effort, she saw in me the potential and provided the opportunities. I have watched her do this countless times for other students as well. Not all students will take her up on her offers, but those that do benefit immensely. On a daily basis, she continues to build up our field with more scholarly practitioners who are refining existing theory, contributing new knowledge, and applying it directly to organizations through practice.

What is also notable for this biography is that Therese is a woman, and less than 20% of the biographies found in this book focus on females. While Yaeger has mentored and influenced countless women in the field, there were fewer leading females in the field of OD at the time of her studies and all of her mentors were male. She knows that at times she has been called in as the "token" female for a consulting project, but she has always used it positively to continue her learnings and gain knowledge. She realizes that with her husband of 40 years, she is a role model to her four daughters and to others in the field, and she strives to help create opportunities for even more women.

Yaeger has been an exceptional role model for me. Professionally, as a woman in the IT field, I have had similar experiences to Yaeger and being able to work with another woman who understands and relates to the same challenges was refreshing, especially as I was also entering a new field that was foreign to me. In my professional work, I continue to mentor women entering the IT field and hope that in the world of OD I can "pay forward" the support and mentoring Therese has provided me to encourage other women entering the field.

Legacy and Unfinished Business: The Journey on the Winding Road Continues

As the Guest Editor for the 2011 special issue of the *Journal of Management History* honoring Douglas McGregor, Yaeger quoted Blaise Pascal (1670) claiming, "Let no one say I have said nothing new: the arrangement of the material is new."

The contributors to this special JMH issue included Warren Bennis, Marvin Weisbord and Warner Burke, and some contributors wanted to republish their earlier writing on McGregor's theories. Hence, Yaeger needed to explain that not everything was new – Warren Bennis insisted on reprinting "Chairman Mac," and Marvin Weisbord wanted a portion of his *Productive Workplaces* reprinted. Hence, Yaeger still has an undeniable sense of nothing new about her.

With respect to this profile, it was a challenge at first collaborating with Yaeger on her for the foundation of this chapter as she truly feels she does not fit the list of change thinkers. Being published among such notable scholars triggers her latent imposter syndrome. In her perspective, she started much later in the field than others and states that she has contributed no new theory or innovative technique.

It is interesting to see how Yaeger's journey, as has been reviewed here, has already paralleled many ODs Top Ten. Her emergent career as an OD scholar-practitioner started in the world of business, working through years of focused education, and now strongly affiliated with the Ph.D. and MSMOB programs at

Benedictine University amid consulting and engaging in practice – all while reiterating that "family matters." She has published extensively and has been involved in numerous professional and academic associations. In fact, one could argue that Yaeger is one of the most influential integrators in our field, helping bring together not only theory and practice, but people as well.

It is easy to see why Yaeger is so influential. She embodies the core values of OD and enthusiastically approaches every effort continuing to stretch herself and challenging those around her to do the same. Similar to her earliest travels, she pushes out of her comfort zone while being comfortable in knowing herself at the same time. While Yaeger has contributed much to Organization Development already, she has many years of continued contribution ahead of her in both the areas of scholarship and practice. She feels we are actually just starting in the nascent field of OD and change.

Still today, she is a significant figure in the continued development of the Benedictine OD doctoral program, contributing to the establishment of one of the preeminent programs in the OD field and the success of over 200 Ph.D. alumni. The OD Program at Benedictine University has grown considerably over the past decades, and she is excited to get newer generations of OD scholar-practitioners and having them develop as change agents and practicing scholars. As the Benedictine program has evolved over the years, Yaeger delights to see the increase in publications and books from Benedictine students. These have been a result of high quality research in addition to practical application of the concepts of the Ph.D. in OD program brought back into the field.

From her earliest influences and motivations, to key contributions, to new insights, Yaeger continues to focus on OD's historical contributions such as the impact of McGregor, Likert, and Cooperrider. She believes that students should review and reflect on the work of organizational scholars that are still relevant today. For example, McGregor defined Theory Y in the 1950s and now, so many decades later, the contributions of his concepts are being questioned. "It is as if somebody gave us the recipe for organizational success and we still don't understand it," Yaeger stated. She hopes that we, as organizational members, will continue to progress and help organizations get a little closer to understanding Theory Y as McGregor intended his theory to be discussed.

Her advice to students who aspire to be ethical OD consultants reflects the key learnings and influences illustrated throughout her own journey. It includes (a) reading and rereading the works of the early scholars in the field; (b) traveling to understand other cultures unlike your home country; and (c) finding good mentors. OD is not learned in one course or 1 year, so in the meantime, enjoy learning about yourself and others.

Yaeger has been a humble yet prominent force in Organization Development for two decades now. A quote we discussed during her interview for this chapter is so appropriate to summarize her life thus far: "Well behaved women rarely make history." While this quote has been attributed to several women over the years including Marilyn Monroe and Eleanor Roosevelt, ironically its earliest origin is from an academic paper in the journal *American Quarterly* in 1976 by Laurel Thatcher Ulrich. As a student at the University of New Hampshire, where she earned her Ph.D., Ulrich wrote this paper to continue her goal of recovering the history of women who were not featured in history books of the past. It is exciting to see how far we have come in 30 years from the predominantly male dominated ODs Top Ten list, to Yaeger and other women now being featured in this Handbook on *Great Thinkers in Organizational Change*.

Yaeger contemplates her future contributions. Outside of her professional OD world, she focuses on family and close relationships with friends (the same people who provided the early interest in her OB/OD studies). More global research awaits as well. Professionally, however, she again reiterates her excitement about the nascent field of OD and how many research prospects lies ahead for doctoral research. Assuredly, she will continue to be a leading role model for her daughters and future women in the OD field. It will be exciting to see her continued contributions to the field in the years to come – opportunities abound.

References

Cooperrider, D., Sorensen, P., Whitney, D., & Yaeger, T. (1999). *Appreciative inquiry: Rethinking human organization toward a positive theory of change*. Champaign: Stipes Publishing.

Cooperrider, D., Sorensen, P., Yaeger, T., & Whitney, D. (2001). *Appreciative inquiry: An emerging direction for organization development*. Champaign: Stipes Publishing.

Cooperrider, D., Sorensen, P., Yaeger, T., & Whitney, D. (2005). *Appreciative inquiry: Foundations in positive organization development*. Champaign: Stipes Publishing.

Hillman, J., & Varney, G. (1985). OD's top 10: Who they are, how they got there. *Training and Development Journal, 39*(2), 54.

Johnson, H., Sorensen, P., & Yaeger, T. (2013). *Critical issues in organization development: Case studies for analysis and discussion*. Charlotte: Information Age Publishing.

McGregor, D. (1957). *An uneasy look at performance appraisal*. Boston: Soldiers Field.

McGregor, D. (1960). *The human side of enterprise*. New York 21.166.

McGregor, D. M. (1967). *The professional manager*. New York: McGraw-Hill.

Mirvis, P., & Lawler, E. (2011). Rigor and relevance in organizational research: experiences, reflections and a look ahead. *In Useful Research: Advancing Theory and Practice*, edited by Susan Albers Mohrman and Edward E. Lawler III. Berrett-Koehler Publishers, 113–136.

Schein, E. H. (2006). *Organizational culture and leadership* (Vol. 356). Chichester: John Wiley & Sons.

Sorensen, P., & Yaeger, T. (2004). Feedback from the positive question – The integration of appreciative inquiry with survey feedback: From corporate to global cultures. In D. Cooperrider & M. Avital (Eds.), *Advances in appreciative inquiry*. London: Elsevier Press.

Sorensen, P., Yaeger, T. (2015). Theory X and theory Y. *Oxford Press Bibliography*. doi:10.1093/obo/9780199846740-0078.

Sorensen, P., Head, T., Yaeger, T., & Cooperrider, D. (2011). *Global and international organization development* (5th ed.). Champaign: Stipes Publishing.

Yaeger, T. (as Guest Editor). (2011). Honoring Douglas McGregor and the 50th anniversary of 'The Human Side of Enterprise.' *Journal of Management History,* 17(2), 144–147.

Yaeger, T., Sorensen, P., & Bengtsson, U. (2005). Assessment of the state of appreciative inquiry: Past, present and future. In R. Woodman & W. Pasmore (Eds.), *Research in organizational change and development* (Vol. 15, pp. 297–319). London: Elsevier Ltd..

Yaeger, T., & Sorensen, P. (2009). *Strategic organization development: Managing change for success*. Charlotte: Information Age Publishing.

Yaeger, T., Head, T., & Sorensen, P. (2006). *Global organization development: Managing unprecedented change*. Charlotte: Information Age Publishing Inc.

Further Reading

Cooperrider, D., Sorensen, P., Whitney, D., & Yaeger, T. (1999). *Appreciative inquiry: Rethinking human organization toward a positive theory of change*. Champaign: Stipes Publishing.

Cooperrider, D., Sorensen, P., Yaeger, T., & Whitney, D. (2001). *Appreciative inquiry: An emerging direction for organization development*. Champaign: Stipes Publishing.

Johnson, H., Sorensen, P., & Yaeger, T. (2013). *Critical issues in organization development: Case studies for analysis and discussion*. Charlotte: Information Age Publishing.

Schein, E. H. (2006). Organizational culture and leadership (Vol. 356). Chichester: John Wiley & Sons.

Sorensen, P., Head, T., Yaeger, T., & Cooperrider, D. (2011). *Global and international organization development (5th ed.)*. Champaign: Stipes Publishing.

Sorensen, P., Yaeger, T. (2015). Theory X and theory Y. *Oxford Press Bibliography*. doi:10.1093/obo/9780199846740-0078.

Yaeger, T., Head, T., & Sorensen, P. (2006). *Global organization development: Managing unprecedented change*. Charlotte: Information Age Publishing Inc.

Yaeger, T., & Sorensen, P. (2009). *Strategic organization development: Managing change for success*. Charlotte: Information Age Publishing.

Index

D.B. Szabla et al. (eds.), *The Palgrave Handbook of Organizational Change Thinkers*,
DOI 10.1007/978-3-319-52878-6

C

M

Q

U